**Paul and Tracey
AAA Members,
Bargain Hunters**

At Days Inns our money gets the best mileage.

AAA Members: Save 10% - 30%* at 39 Days Inn® hotels in Michigan and Wisconsin.

Show Your Card & Save

AAA. Every Day.®

Just book and save at any of the AAA-approved Days Inn locations listed in this TourBook®. You'll get a free continental breakfast and a free *USA Today* newspaper. And your room comes with an AM/FM clock radio and hair dryer. Not to mention special bonus offers for AAA Members all year long! Pets are welcome at more than 900 Days Inn locations worldwide.

**For specific locations and reservations, call
1-800-432-9755 OR daysinn.com**

*Discount off published TourBook rate and may not be combined with any other discounts or special offers. Discounts and amenities vary by property. Some restrictions may apply. ©2004 Days Inns Worldwide, Inc.

Michigan & Wisconsin

Are we meeting your travel needs?

Send written comments to:

AAA Member Comments
1000 AAA Drive, Box 61
Heathrow, FL 32746-5063

Published by:
AAA Publishing
1000 AAA Drive
Heathrow, FL 32746-5063
Copyright AAA 2004

Advertising Rate and Circulation Information
Call: (407) 444-8280

Printed in the USA by
Quebecor World, Buffalo, NY

Photo Credit: (Cover & Title Page)
Pictured Rocks
National Lakeshore, MI
© Ric Ergenbright
Corbis

 Printed on recyclable paper.
Please recycle whenever possible.

Stock #4616

Michigan & Wisconsin

TourBook Navigator

Follow our simple guide to
make the most of this member benefit 9-25

Comprehensive City Index

■ Michigan

■ Wisconsin

Featured Information

When planning your next trip, check out the many time saving tools and member saving benefits on www.aaa.com to make your travels fun, easy and affordable. Highlights include:

Internet TripTik®/Traveler.
Ranked #1 by the *Wall Street Journal*, ITT provides sightseeing and dining recommendations, online hotel reservations at great rates and, of course, AAA's famous maps, driving directions and custom routes!

Online TourBook®. Reserve rooms at great rates PLUS get AAA Diamond ratings for lodgings and restaurants and insider tips on attractions and local events!

AAA Drive Trips. Over 50 driving tours nationwide with precise directions and candid area overviews*

Vacation Getaways. Take to the skies, hit the high seas or select a tour and receive exclusive benefits from AAA's Preferred Travel Partners.

Travel Accessories. Order luggage, car games for the kids, accessories, and more to make travel easy.

Travel Guides. Get a 5% discount on AAA's famed travel guides and learn your destination inside out.

Disney® Vacations. Get exclusive benefits and savings on AAA Vacations® Disney vacation packages.

Hertz Rental. Up to 20 % discount from AAA's Exclusive Car Rental Partner.

Show Your Card & Save. Search for savings on lodging, travel, entertainment, retail, and e-Merchants in the database.

AAA Travel Money. Get no-fee travelers cheques, foreign currency and prepaid cards.

AAA Map Gallery*. Know the best way to go wherever you travel.

Cash Back. Get a 5% rebate every time you use your AAA credit card to gas up.

AAA Approved Auto Repair. Enter your zip code to get your car road-trip ready at the nearest AAR shop.

Click on www.aaa.com for numerous products and services that will make your next trip easy to plan, more enjoyable and full of value. **Travel to www.aaa.com TODAY for all your vacation planning needs!**

www.aaa.com

Travel With Someone You Trust®

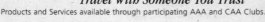

Trust

the AAA TourBook® guide for objective travel information. Follow the pages of the TourBook Navigator to thoroughly understand this unique member benefit.

Making Your Way Through the AAA Listings

Attractions, lodgings and restaurants are listed on the basis of merit alone after careful evaluation, approval and rating by one of our full-time, professionally trained Tourism Editors. Annual evaluations are unannounced to ensure that our Tourism Editors see an establishment just as our members would see it.

Those lodgings and restaurants listed with an fyi icon have not gone through the same evaluation process as other rated properties. Individual listings will typically denote the reason why this icon appears. Bulleted recreational activity listings are not inspected but are included for member information.

An establishment's decision to advertise in the TourBook guide has no bearing on its evaluation or rating. Advertising for services or products does not imply AAA endorsement.

How the TourBook is

Organized

Geographic listing is used for accuracy and consistency. This means attractions, lodgings and restaurants are listed under the city in which they physically are located—or in some cases under the nearest recognized city. The Comprehensive City Index located in the back of the book contains an A-to-Z list of cities. Most listings are alphabetically organized by state, province, region or island; city; and establishment name. A color is assigned to each state or province so that you can match the color bars at the top of the page to switch from ❶ Points of Interest to ❷ Lodgings and Restaurants.

Destination Cities and Destination Areas

The TourBook guide also groups information by destination city and destination area. If a city is grouped in a destination vicinity section, the city name will appear at its alphabetical location in the book, and a handy cross reference will give the exact page on which listings for that city begin. Maps are placed at the beginning of these sections to orient you to the destinations.

❸ Destination cities, established based on government models and local expertise, are comprised of metropolitan areas plus nearby vicinity cities.

Destination areas are regions with broad tourist appeal. Several cities will comprise the area.

All information in this TourBook guide was reviewed for accuracy before publication. However, since changes inevitably occur between annual editions, we suggest you contact establishments directly to confirm prices and schedules.

Points of Interest Section

Orientation maps

near the start of each Attractions section show only those places we call points of interest. Coordinates included with the city listings depict the locations of those cities on the map. A GEM symbol (⚡) accents towns with "must see" points of interest which offer a *Great Experience for Members®*. And the black ovals with white numerals (**22** for example) locate items listed in the nearby Recreation Areas chart.

Destination area maps

illustrate key travel areas defined by local travel experts. Communities shown have listings for AAA approved attractions.

National park maps

represent the area in and around the park. Some campground sites and lodges spotted on the maps do not meet AAA/CAA criteria, but are shown for members who nevertheless wish to stay close to the park area.

Walking or self-guiding tour maps

correspond to specific routes described in TourBook guide text.

City maps

show areas where numerous points of interest are concentrated and indicate their location in relation to major roads, parks, airports and other landmarks.

Lodgings & Restaurants Section

Destination area maps illustrate key travel areas defined by local travel experts. Communities shown have listings for AAA-RATED® lodgings and/or restaurants.

Spotting maps show the location of lodgings and restaurants. Lodgings are spotted with a black background (**22** for example); restaurants are spotted with a white background (**23** for example). Spotting map indexes have been placed immediately after each map to provide the user with a convenient method to identify what an area has to offer at a glance. The index references the map page number where the property is spotted, indicates if a property is an Official Appointment and contains an advertising reference if applicable. It also lists the property's diamond rating, high season rate range and listing page number.

Downtown/city spotting maps are provided when spotted facilities are very concentrated. GEM points of interest also appear on these maps.

Vicinity spotting maps spot those properties that are outside the downtown or city area. Major roads, landmarks, airports and GEM points of interest are shown on vicinity spotting maps as well. The names of suburban communities that have AAA-RATED® accommodations are shown in magenta type.

Featured Information Section

Driving distance maps are intended to be used only for trip-distance and driving-time planning.

Sample Attraction Listing

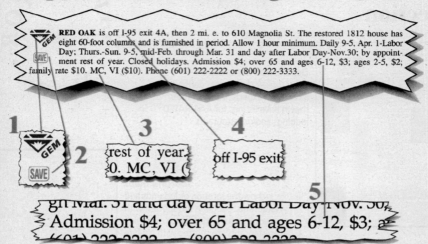

RED OAK is off I-95 exit 4A, then 2 mi. e. to 610 Magnolia St. The restored 1812 house has eight 60-foot columns and is furnished in period. Allow 1 hour minimum. Daily 9-5, Apr. 1-Labor Day; Thurs.-Sun. 9-5, mid-Feb. through Mar. 31 and day after Labor Day-Nov.30; by appointment rest of year. Closed holidays. Admission $4; over 65 and ages 6-12, $3; ages 2-5, $2; family rate $10. MC, VI ($10). Phone (601) 222-2222 or (800) 222-3333.

2 rest of year. 0. MC, VI (

4 off I-95 exit

5 Admission $4; over 65 and ages 6-12, $3;

1 ◈ This attraction is of exceptional interest and quality and therefore has been designated a AAA GEM—offering a *Great Experience for Members*®.

2 [SAVE] Participating attractions offer AAA/CAA, AAA MasterCard or AAA Visa cardholders a discount off the attraction's standard admission; members should inquire in advance concerning the validity of the discount for special rates. Present your card at the admission desk. A list of participating points of interest appears in the Indexes section of the book. The SAVE discount may not be used in conjunction with other discounts. Attractions that already provide a reduced senior or child rate may not honor the SAVE discount for those age groups. All offers are subject to change and may not apply during special events, particular days or seasons or for the entire validity period of the TourBook. Shopping establishments preceded by a SAVE icon also provide discounts and/or gift with purchase to AAA/CAA members; present your card at the mall's customer service center to receive your benefit.

3
AX=American Express	DS=Discover	MC=MasterCard
CB=Carte Blanche	JC=Japan Credit Bureau	VI=VISA
DC=Diners Club		

Minimum amounts that may be charged appear in parentheses when applicable.

4 Unless otherwise specified, directions are given from the center of town, using the following highway designations: I (interstate highway), US (federal highway), Hwy. (Canadian or Caribbean highway), SR (state route), CR (county road), FM (farm to market road), FR (forest road), MM (mile marker), Mex. (Mexican highway).

5 Admission prices are quoted without sales tax. Children under the lowest age specified are admitted free when accompanied by an adult. Days, months and age groups written with a hyphen are inclusive. Prices pertaining to points of interest in the United States are quoted in U.S. dollars; prices for Canadian province and territory points of interest are quoted in Canadian dollars; prices for points of interest in Mexico and the Caribbean are quoted as an approximate U.S. dollar equivalent.

Bulleted Listings: Casino gambling establishments are visited by AAA personnel to ensure safety; casinos within hotels are presented for member information regardless of whether the lodging is AAA approved. Recreational activities of a participatory nature (requiring physical exertion or special skills) are not inspected. Wineries are inspected by AAA Tourism Editors to ensure they meet listing requirements and offer tours. All are presented in a bulleted format for informational purposes.

AAA. Every Day.

These Show Your Card & Save® partners provide the listed member benefits. Admission tickets that offer greater discounts may be available for purchase at the local AAA/CAA club. A maximum of six tickets is available at the discount price.

Attraction Partners

SeaWorld/Busch Gardens

SAVE Save $4 at SeaWorld and Busch Gardens

SAVE Save $3 at Sesame Place, Water Country USA and Adventure Island

SAVE Save 10% on select up-close dining. Reservations are required; visit Guest Relations for details

Six Flags Theme Parks

SAVE Save $4 on general admission at the gate

SAVE Save $12 on general admission at the gate each Wednesday

SAVE Save 10% on selected souvenirs and dining (check at main gate for details)

Universal Orlando (www.aaa.com/Universal)

SAVE Save $4 on a 2-day/2-park pass or $5 on a 3-day/2-park pass at Universal Orlando's theme parks (savings apply to tickets purchased at the gate)

SAVE Save 10% on select dining and souvenirs at both Universal Orlando theme parks and at select Universal CityWalk Orlando restaurants (except Emeril's)

Universal Studios Hollywood

SAVE Save $3 on a 1-day Universal Hollywood pass (savings applies to tickets purchased at the gate)

SAVE Save 10% on select dining and souvenirs at Universal Studios Hollywood and Universal CityWalk

Gray Line

SAVE Save 10% on sightseeing tours of 1 day or less

Restaurant Partners

RESTAURANTS, INC.

Landry's Seafood House, The Crab House, Chart House, Muer Seafood Restaurants, Joe's Crab Shack

SAVE Save 10% on food and non-alcoholic beverages at Landry's Seafood House, The Crab House, Chart House, Muer Seafood Restaurants and Joe's Crab Shack and 10% on merchandise at Joe's Crab Shack. Savings applicable to AAA/CAA members and up to six people

Hard Rock Cafe

SAVE Save 10% on food, beverage, and merchandise at all U.S., Canada, and select international locations. Members also save 10% at The Hard Rock Vault.

Mexican Partners

Ahorra con AMA

SAVE An alliance between AAA/CAA and AMA (Mexican Automobile Association) provides members visting Mexico savings from Mexicana Airlines, Tony Roma restaurants and Six Flags of Mexico

---

Visit aaa.com to discover all the great Show Your Card & Save® discounts in your area.

Sample Lodging Listing

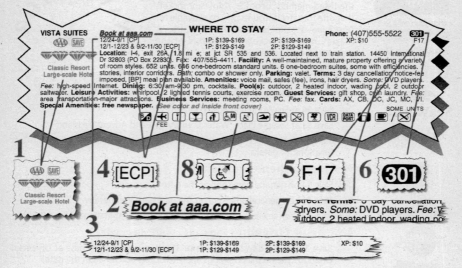

1

⬭⬭⬭ or ⬭⬭ indicates our Official Appointment (OA) lodgings. The OA program permits properties to display and advertise the ⬭⬭⬭ or ⬭⬭ emblem. We highlight these properties with red diamonds and classification. Some OA listings include special amenities such as free continental breakfast; expanded continental breakfast or full breakfast; early check-in/late check-out; free room upgrade or preferred room, such as ocean view or poolside (subject to availability); free local phone calls; and free daily newspaper. This does not imply that only these properties offer these amenities. The ⬭⬭⬭ or ⬭⬭ sign helps traveling members find accommodations that want member business.

🔷🔷🔷 🔷🔷 or 🔷🔷 🔷🔷 The number of diamonds—not the color—informs you of the overall level of quality in a lodging's amenities and service. More diamond details appear on page 16.

Classic Resort Large-scale Hotel or Classic Resort Large-scale Hotel: All diamond rated lodgings are classified using three key elements: style of operation, overall concept and service level. See pages 22-23 for details about our Lodging Classifications and Subclassifications.

Member Values

SAVE Official Appointment properties guarantee members a minimum 10% discount off the standard room rates published in TourBook guides or the lowest public rate available at the time of booking for the dates of stay, for standard rooms.

S$ Establishments offer a minimum senior discount of 10% off the listed rates. This discount is available to members 60 or older.

ASK Many properties offer discounts to members even though the lodgings do not participate in a formal discount program. The ASK is another reminder to inquire about available discounts when making your reservations or at check-in.

> Discounts normally offered at some lodgings may not apply during special events or holiday periods. Special rates and discounts may not apply to all room types. Some Member Values may not apply in Mexico or the Caribbean.

To obtain published rates or discounts, you must identify yourself as a AAA or CAA member, request AAA rates when making reservations and have written confirmation sent to you. The SAVE or senior discount may not be used in conjunction with other discounts. At registration, show your membership card and verify the room rate.

Discounts normally offered at some lodgings may not apply during special events or holiday periods. Special rates and discounts may not apply to all room types. Some Member Values may not apply in Mexico or the Caribbean.

The rates listed for approved properties are provided to AAA by each lodging and represent the regular (rack) rate for a standard room. Printed rates, based on rack rates and last room availability, are rounded to the nearest dollar. Rates do not include taxes and discounts. U.S., Mexican and Caribbean rates are in U.S. dollars; rates for Canadian lodgings are in Canadian dollars.

2 Book at aaa.com - Internet Reservations
Indicates AAA/CAA members can conveniently check room availability and make reservations in a secure online environment at aaa.com.

3 Rate Lines
Shown from left to right: dates the rates are effective; meal plan provided with rates (see Meal Plan Indicators-if no plan noted, rate includes room only); rates for 1 person or 2 persons; extra person charge (XP); and any applicable family plan indicator.

Rates Guaranteed
AAA/CAA members are guaranteed that they will not be charged more than the maximum regular rate printed in each rate range for a standard room. Rates may vary within the range depending on season and room type. Listed rates are based on last standard room availability. Rates for properties operating as concessionaires for the U.S. National Park Service are not guaranteed due to governing regulations. Rates in the Mexico TourBook are not guaranteed and may fluctuate based on the exchange rate of the peso.

Exceptions
Lodgings may temporarily increase room rates, not recognize discounts or modify pricing policies during special events. Examples of special events range from Mardi Gras and Kentucky Derby (including pre-Derby events) to college football games, holidays, holiday periods and state fairs. Although some special events are listed in AAA/CAA TourBook guides, it is always wise to check, in advance, with AAA travel professionals for specific dates.

Discounts
Member discounts will apply to rates quoted, within the rate range, applicable at the time of booking. Special rates used in advertising, and special short-term, promotional rates lower than the lowest listed rate in the range, are not subject to additional member discounts.

4 Meal Plan Indicators
The following types of meal plans may be available in the listed room rate:
AP = American Plan of three meals daily
BP = Breakfast Plan of full hot breakfast
CP = Continental Plan of pastry, juice and another beverage
ECP = Expanded Continental Plan, which offers a wider
variety of breakfast items
MAP = Modified American Plan of two meals daily
See individual listing "Terms" section for additional meal plans that are not included in the room rate.

> Check-in times are shown in the listing only if they are after 3 p.m.; check-out times are shown only if they are before 10 a.m.

5 Family Plan Indicators
F = Children stay free
D = Discounts for children
F17 = Children 17 and under stay free (age displayed will reflect property's policy)
D17 = Discount for children 17 and under

6 Lodging Locators
Black ovals with white numbers are used to locate, or "spot," lodgings on maps we provide for larger cities.

7 Unit Types
Unit types, amenities and room features preceded by the word "Some" indicate the item is available on a limited basis, potentially within only one unit.

8 Lodging Icons
A row of icons is included with each lodging listing. These icons represent the member values, member services, and facilities offered by that lodging. See page 19 for an explanation of each icon.

The Lodging Diamond Ratings

AAA Tourism Editors evaluate and rate each lodging based on the overall quality, the range of facilities and the level of services offered by a property. The size, age and overall appeal of an establishment are considered as well as regional architectural style and design.

While guest services are an important part of all diamond ratings, they are particularly critical at the four and five diamond levels. A property must provide a high level of service, on a consistent basis, to obtain and support the four and five diamond rating.

These establishments typically appeal to the budget-minded traveler. They provide essential, no-frills accommodations. They meet the basic requirements pertaining to comfort, cleanliness, and hospitality.

These establishments appeal to the traveler seeking more than the basic accommodations. There are modest enhancements to the overall physical attributes, design elements, and amenities of the facility typically at a modest price.

These establishments appeal to the traveler with comprehensive needs. Properties are multifaceted with a distinguished style, including marked upgrades in the quality of physical attributes, amenities and level of comfort provided.

These establishments are upscale in all areas. Accommodations are progressively more refined and stylish. The physical attributes reflect an obvious enhanced level of quality throughout. The fundamental hallmarks at this level include an extensive array of amenities combined with a high degree of hospitality, service, and attention to detail.

These establishments reflect the characteristics of the ultimate in luxury and sophistication. Accommodations are first-class. The physical attributes are extraordinary in every manner. The fundamental hallmarks at this level are to meticulously serve and exceed all guest expectations while maintaining an impeccable standard of excellence. Many personalized services and amenities enhance an unmatched level of comfort.

The lodging listings with **fyi** in place of diamonds are included as an "information only" service for members. The icon indicates that a property has not been rated for one or more of the following reasons: too new to rate; under construction; under major renovation; not evaluated; or may not meet all AAA requirements. Those properties not meeting all AAA requirements are included for either their member value or because it may be the only accommodation available in the area. Listing prose will give insight as to why the **fyi** designation was assigned.

Guest Safety

Room Security

In order to be approved for listing in AAA/CAA TourBook guides for the United States and Canada, all lodgings must comply with AAA's guest room security requirements.

In response to AAA/CAA members' concern about their safety at properties, AAA-RATED® accommodations must have dead-bolt locks on all guest room entry doors and connecting room doors.

If the area outside the guest room door is not visible from inside the room through a window or door panel, viewports must be installed on all guest room entry doors. Bed and breakfast properties and country inns are not required to have viewports. Ground floor and easily accessible sliding doors must be equipped with some other type of secondary security locks.

Tourism Editors view a percentage of rooms at each property since it is not feasible to evaluate every room in every lodging establishment. Therefore, AAA cannot guarantee that there are working locks on all doors and windows in all guest rooms.

Fire Safety

Because of the highly specialized skills needed to conduct professional fire safety inspections, AAA/CAA Tourism Editors cannot assess fire safety.

Properties must meet all federal, state and local fire codes. Each guest unit in all U.S. and Canadian lodging properties must be equipped with an operational, single-station smoke detector. A AAA/CAA Tourism Editor has evaluated a sampling of the rooms to verify this equipment is in place.

For additional fire safety information, read the page posted on the back of your guest room door, or write:
National Fire Protection Association
1 Batterymarch Park
P.O. Box 9101
Quincy, MA 02269-9101

Requirements for some features, such as door locks and smoke detectors/sprinkler systems, differ in Mexico and the Caribbean. If a property met AAA's security requirements at the time of the evaluation, the phrase "Meets AAA guest room security requirements" appears in the listing.

Access for Mature Travelers and Travelers with Disabilities

Qualified properties listed in this guide are shown with symbols indicating they meet the needs of the hearing-impaired or offer some accessible features for mature travelers or travelers with disabilities.

 ## *Hearing Impaired*

Indicates a property has the following equipment available for hearing-impaired travelers: TDD at front desk or switchboard; visual notification of fire alarm, incoming telephone calls, door knock or bell; closed caption decoder; text telephone or TDD for guest room use; telephone amplification device, with shelf or electric outlet next to guest room telephone.

 ## *Accessible Features*

Indicates a property has some accessible features meeting the needs of mature travelers and travelers with disabilities. Lodging establishments will provide at least one guest room meeting the designated criteria as well as accessible restrooms and parking facilities. Restaurants provide accessible parking, dining rooms and restrooms.

> **AAA/CAA strongly urges members to call the property directly to fully understand the property's exact accessibility features. Some properties do not fully comply with AAA/CAA's exacting accessibility standards but may offer some design standards that meet the needs of some guests with disabilities.**
>
> **AAA/CAA does not evaluate recreational facilities, banquet rooms, or convention or meeting facilities for accessibility.**

Service Animals

> **No fees or deposits, even those normally charged for pets, may be charged for service animals. Service animals fulfill a critical need for their owners—they are *not* pets.**

The Americans With Disabilities Act (ADA) prohibits U.S. businesses that serve the public from discriminating against persons with disabilities. Some businesses have mistakenly denied access to persons who use service animals. ADA, a federal mandate, has priority over all state and local laws, as well as a business owner's standard of business, which might bar animals from the premises. Businesses must permit entry to guests and their service animals, as well as allow service animals to accompany guests to all public areas of a property. A property is permitted to ask whether the animal is a service animal or a pet, and whether the guest has a disability. The property may not, however, ask questions about the nature of the disability, the service provided by the animal or require proof of a disability or certification that the animal is a service animal.

Note: These regulations may not apply in Canada, Mexico or the Caribbean.

What The Lodging Icons Mean

Member Values
(see p. 14)

(AAA) or (AA) Official Appointment

[SAVE] Offers minimum 10% discount or lowest public rate *(see p. 14)*

[ASK] May offer discount

[S𝐃] Offers senior discount

[fyi] Informational listing only

Member Services

✈ Airport transportation

🐾 Pets allowed

[🍴] Restaurant on premises

[🍴+] Restaurant off premises (walking distance)

[24🍴] 24-hour room service

[𝕐] Cocktail lounge

[🍼] Child care

Accessibility Feature
(see p. 18)

[&M] Accessible features

[&] Roll-in showers

[🕗] Hearing impaired

Safety Features
(Mexico and Caribbean only)

[S] Sprinklers

[D] Smoke detectors

Leisure Activities

🎲 Full service casino

🏊 Pool

[💪] Health club on premises

[💪+] Health club off premises

[✗] Recreational activities

In-Room Amenities

[✗] Designated non-smoking rooms

[𝐀𝐂] No air conditioning

[𝐓𝐕] No TV

[C𝐓𝐕] No cable TV

[VCR] VCR

[🎬] Movies

[DATA PORT] Data port/modem line

[☎] No telephones

🔌 Refrigerator

🔲 Microwave

🔳 Coffee maker

Availability and Additional Fees

If an in-room amenity is available only on a limited basis (in one or more rooms), the term "SOME UNITS" will appear above those icons. Fees may be charged for some of the services represented by the icons listed here. The word "FEE" will appear below each icon when an extra charge applies.

SOME UNITS

[&M] [🕗] [VCR] [🎬] [🔳] / [✗] [DATA PORT] [🔌] /
FEE   FEE   FEE

Preferred Lodging Partners

AAA. Every Day.

SAVINGS. SELECTION. SATISFACTION. — When contacting one of the partners listed, you will be given AAA's best rates for your dates of stay. Your valid membership card must be presented at check-in.

SATISFACTION GUARANTEE — If you are not satisfied with any part of your stay, you must provide the property the opportunity to correct the situation during your stay. If the matter cannot be resolved, you will be entitled to recompense for a portion of, or your entire, stay. Satisfaction guarantee varies by chain.

Select the chain you want and have your membership card available when making a reservation and checking in.

| **Visit** | Over 1,100 AAA Offices | **Click** | aaa.com | **Call** | 866-AAA-SAVE |

Special rates and discounts may not apply to all room types. All discounts are off full rates and vary by location and time of year. Special rates and discounts are not available to groups and cannot be combined with other discounts. Restrictions apply to satisfaction guarantees. Valid AAA/CAA membership card must be presented at check-in. Offers good at time of publication; chains and offers may change without notice. Lodging partners offering discounts to AAA/CAA members may vary in Mexico and the Caribbean.

Making Reservations

When making reservations, you must identify yourself as a AAA or CAA member. Give all pertinent information about your planned stay. Ask about the lodging's pet policy, or the availability of any other special feature that is important to your stay. Request written confirmation to guarantee: type of room, rate, dates of stay, and cancellation and refund policies. At registration, show your membership card. Note: Age restrictions may apply.

Confirm Deposit, Refund and Cancellation Policies

Most establishments give full deposit refunds if they have been notified at least 48 hours before the normal check-in time. Listing prose will note if more than 48 hours notice is required for cancellation. However, when making reservations, confirm the property's deposit, cancellation and refund policies. Some properties may charge a cancellation or handling fee.

When this applies, "cancellation fee imposed" will appear in the listing. If you cancel too late, you have little recourse if a refund is denied.

When an establishment requires a full or partial payment in advance, and your trip is cut short, a refund may not be given.

When canceling reservations, phone the lodging immediately. Make a note of the date and time you called, the cancellation number if there is one, and the name of the person who handled the cancellation. If your AAA/CAA club made your reservation, allow them to make the cancellation for you as well so you will have proof of cancellation.

Review Charges for Appropriate Rates

When you are charged more than the maximum rate listed in the TourBook guide for a standard room, question the additional charge. If management refuses to adhere to the published rate, pay for the room and submit your receipt and membership number to AAA/CAA within 30 days. Include all pertinent information: dates of stay, rate paid, itemized paid receipts, number of persons in your party, the room number you occupied, and list any extra room equipment used. A refund of the amount paid in excess of the stated maximum will be made if our investigation indicates that unjustified charging has occurred.

Get the Room You Reserved

When you find your room is not as specified, and you have written confirmation of reservations for a certain type of accommodation, you should be given the option of choosing a different room or finding one elsewhere. Should you choose to go elsewhere and a refund is refused or resisted, submit the matter to AAA/CAA within 30 days along with complete documentation, including your reasons for refusing the room and copies of your written confirmation and any receipts or canceled checks associated with this problem.

How to Get the Best Room Rates

You'll find the best room rate if you book your reservation in advance with the help of a travel professional or agent at your local AAA/CAA office.

If you're not yet ready to make firm vacation plans or if you prefer a more spontaneous trip, take advantage of the partnerships that preferred hotel chains have arranged with AAA. Phone the toll-free number 866-AAA-SAVE that has been set up exclusively for members for the purpose of reserving with these Show Your Card & Save® chain partners.

Even if you were unable to make a reservation, be sure to show your membership card at the desk and ask if you're being offered the lowest rate available for that time. Many lodgings offer reduced rates to members.

Lodging Classifications

To ensure that your lodging needs/preferences are met, we recommend that you consider an establishment's classification when making your travel choices.

While the quality and comfort at properties with the same diamond rating should be consistent (regardless of the classification), there are differences in typical décor/theme elements, range of facilities and service levels. Please see the descriptions below.

Large-scale Hotel

A multistory establishment with interior room entrances. A variety of guest unit styles is offered. Public areas are spacious and include a variety of facilities such as a restaurant, shops, fitness center, spa, business center, or meeting rooms.

Hotel Royal Plaza, Lake Buena Vista, FL

Small-scale Hotel

A multistory establishment typically with interior room entrances. A variety of guest unit styles is offered. Public areas are limited in size and/or the variety of facilities available.

Baymont Inn, Dallas/Ft. Worth-Airport North, TX

Motel

A one- to three-story establishment typically with exterior room entrances facilitating convenient access to parking. The standard guest units have one bedroom with a bathroom and are typically similar in décor and design throughout. Public areas are limited in size and/or the variety of facilities available.

Best Western Deltona Inn, Deltona, FL

Country Inn

Similar in definition to a bed and breakfast, but usually larger in scale with spacious public areas and offers a dining facility that serves at least breakfast and dinner.

Greenville Inn, Greenville, ME

Bed & Breakfast

Small-scale properties emphasizing a high degree of personal touches that provide guests an "at home" feeling. Guest units tend to be individually decorated. Rooms may not include some modern amenities such as televisions and telephones, and may have a shared bathroom. Usually owner-operated with a common room or parlor separate from the innkeeper's living quarters, where guests and operators can interact during evening and breakfast hours.

Harbour Town Inn, Boothbay Harbor, ME

Evening office closures are normal. A continental or full, hot breakfast is served and is included in the room rate.

Condominium

Vacation-oriented or extended-stay, apartment-style accommodations that are routinely available for rent through a management company. Units vary in design and décor and often contain one or more bedrooms, living room, full kitchen, and an eating area. Studio-type models combine the sleeping and living areas into one room. Typically, basic cleaning supplies, kitchen utensils and complete bed and bath linens are supplied. The guest registration area may be located off-site.

Sands of Kahana, Kahana, Maui, HI

Desert Rose Inn, Bluff, UT

Cabin/Cottage

Vacation-oriented, small-scale, freestanding houses or cabins. Units vary in design and décor and often contain one or more bedrooms, living room, kitchen, dining area, and bathroom. Studio-type models combine the sleeping and living areas into one room. Typically, basic cleaning supplies, kitchen utensils, and complete bed and bath linens are supplied. The guest registration area may be located off-site.

C Lazy U Ranch, Granby, CO

Ranch

Typically a working ranch with an obvious rustic, Western theme. In general, equestrian-related activities are featured, but ranches may include other animals and activities as well. A variety of guest unit styles is offered in a family-oriented atmosphere.

Vacation Home

Vacation-oriented or extended-stay, large-scale, freestanding houses that are routinely available for rent through a management company. Houses vary in design and décor and often contain two or more bedrooms, living room, full kitchen, dining room, and multiple bathrooms. Typically, basic cleaning supplies, kitchen utensils, and complete bed and bath linens are supplied. The guest registration area may be located off-site.

ResortQuest, Hilton Head Island, SC

Lodging Subclassifications

The following are subclassifications that may appear along with the classifications listed above to provide a more specific description of the lodging.

Casino

Extensive gambling facilities are available such as blackjack, craps, keno, and slot machines. **Note:** This subclassification will not appear beneath its diamond rating in the listing. It will be indicated by a dice icon and will be included in the row of icons immediately below the lodging listing.

Classic

Renowned and landmark properties, older than 50 years, well-known for their unique style and ambience.

Historic

These properties are typically over 75 years of age and exhibit many features of a historic nature with respect to architecture, design, furnishings, public record, or acclaim. Properties must meet one of the following criteria:

- Maintained the integrity of the historical nature
- Listed on the U.S. National Register of Historic Places
- Designated a U.S. National Historic Landmark
- Located in a U.S. National Register Historic District

Separate criteria designate historic properties in Canada, Mexico and the Caribbean.

Resort

Recreation-oriented, geared to vacation travelers seeking a specific destination experience. Travel packages, meal plans, theme entertainment, and social and recreational programs are typically available. Recreational facilities are extensive and may include spa treatments, golf, tennis, skiing, fishing, or water sports, etc. Larger resorts may offer a variety of guest accommodations.

Sample Restaurant Listing

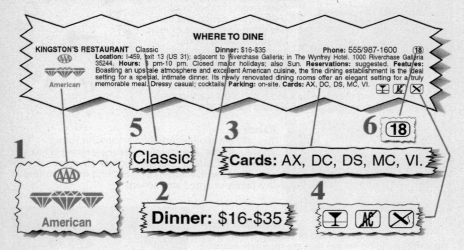

WHERE TO DINE

KINGSTON'S RESTAURANT Classic   **Dinner:** $16-$35   **Phone:** 555/987-1600   18
Location: I-459, exit 13 (US 31); adjacent to Riverchase Galleria; in The Wynfrey Hotel. 1000 Riverchase Galleria 35244. **Hours:** 5 pm-10 pm. Closed major holidays; also Sun. **Reservations:** suggested. **Features:** Boasting an upscale atmosphere and excellent American cuisine, the fine dining establishment is the ideal setting for a special, intimate dinner. Its newly renovated dining rooms offer an elegant setting for a truly memorable meal. Dressy casual; cocktails. **Parking:** on-site. **Cards:** AX, DC, DS, MC, VI.

1 **AAA** or **AAA** indicates our Official Appointment (OA) restaurants. The OA program permits properties to display and advertise the **AAA** or **AAA** emblem. We highlight these properties with red diamonds and cuisine type. The **AAA** or **AAA** sign helps traveling members find restaurants that want member business.

◆◆◆ or ◆◆◆◆ The number of diamonds—not the color—informs you of the overall level of quality for food and presentation, service and ambience. Menus for red Diamond restaurants can be viewed on aaa.com.

A cuisine type is assigned for each restaurant listing. AAA currently recognizes more than 90 different cuisine types.

2 Prices represent the minimum and maximum entree cost per person. Exceptions may include one-of-a-kind or special market priced items.

3 AX = American Express
CB = Carte Blanche   DS = Discover   MC = MasterCard
DC = Diners Club   JC = Japan Credit Bureau   VI = VISA

4 These three icons are used in restaurant listings. When present, they indicate: the presence of a cocktail lounge, the lack of air conditioning, and/or that the restaurant has a designated non-smoking section or is entirely smoke-free.

5 If applicable, restaurants may be further defined as:

Classic—renowned and landmark restaurant operations in business longer than 25 years, known for unique style and ambience.

Historic—properties must meet one of the following criteria:
- Listed on the U.S. National Register of Historic Places
- Designated a U.S. National Historic Landmark
- Located in a U.S. National Register Historic District

Separate criteria designate historic properties in Canada, Mexico and the Caribbean.

6 These white ovals with black numbers serve as restaurant locators and are used to locate, or "spot," restaurants on maps we provide for larger cities.

The Restaurant Diamond Ratings

AAA Tourism Editors are responsible for determining a restaurant's diamond rating based on established criteria.

These criteria were established with input from AAA trained professionals, members, and restaurant industry experts. They are purposely broad to capture what is typically seen throughout the restaurant industry at each diamond rating level.

These establishments appeal to a diner seeking good, wholesome, no-nonsense eating at an affordable price. They typically provide simple, familiar, and unadorned foods served in a sensible, casual or self-service style. Often quick service and family oriented.

Examples include coffee shops, diners, cafeterias, short order, and modest full service eateries.

These establishments provide for dining needs that are increasingly complex, but still reasonably priced. They typically exhibit noticeable efforts in rising above the ordinary in many aspects of food, service and decor. Service is typically functional yet ambitious, periodically combining informal style with limited self-service elements. Often well-suited to traditional, special occasion, and family dining.

Examples include a varied range of specific concept (theme) and multi-purpose establishments.

These establishments impart an increasingly refined and upscale, adult-oriented experience. This is the entry level into fine dining. Creative and complex menus offer a blend of traditional and trendy foods. The service level is typically semi-formal with knowledgeable and proficient staff. Routinely these restaurants appeal to the diner in search of an experience rather than just a meal.

Examples include high-caliber, chic, boutique, and conventional restaurants.

These establishments impart a luxurious and socially refined experience. This is consistent fine dining. Menus typically reflect a high degree of creativity and complexity, featuring elaborate presentations of market-driven or traditional dishes. A cultured, professional, and highly proficient staff consistently demonstrates a profound desire to meet or exceed guest expectations. Restaurants of this caliber are geared to individuals with an appetite for an elite, fine-dining experience.

Examples include dining rooms associated with luxury lodgings, or exclusive independent restaurants often found in metropolitan areas.

Often renowned, these establishments impart a world-class and opulent, adult-oriented experience. This is "haute cuisine" at its best. Menus are often cutting edge, with an obvious dedication to use of only the finest ingredients available. Even the classic dishes become extraordinary under the masterful direction of highly acclaimed chefs. Presentations are spectacular, reflecting impeccable artistry and awareness. An expert, formalized staff continuously anticipates and exceeds guest expectations. Staff members' unfailing attention to detail appears effortless, well-rehearsed and unobtrusive. Undoubtedly, these restaurants appeal to those in search of the ultimate dining experience.

Examples include renowned dining rooms associated with luxury lodgings, or exclusive independent restaurants often found in metropolitan areas.

The restaurants with 🔲fyi in place of diamonds are included as an "information only" service for members. These listings provide additional dining choices but have not yet been evaluated.

YOU'RE READY...

NOW YOU'RE READY FOR ANYTHING.

Travelers Cheques
Available in US Dollars, Canadian Dollars, Euros, and Pounds Sterling; AAA VISA® Travelers Cheques are accepted worldwide.

Cash Passport Card
With AAA Cash Passport you can withdraw cash in the local currency from any VISA® ATM in the world.

Credit Card
The AAA VISA® Credit Card is accepted in over 24 million locations around the world.

Foreign Currency
We supply over 100 different currencies and can advise which is the best for your destination.

AAA TRAVEL MONEY
Know Before You Go.

Visit Participating AAA offices   **Click** aaa.com and go to Travel Money   **Call** 866-339-3378

Savings for all Seasons

Hertz rents Fords and other fine cars. ® REG. U.S. PAT. OFF. © HERTZ SYSTEM INC., 1999/2000-99.

No matter the season, Hertz offers AAA members exclusive discounts and benefits.

Operating in 150 countries at over 7,000 locations, Hertz makes traveling more convenient and efficient wherever and whenever you go. Hertz offers AAA members discounts up to 20% on car rentals worldwide.

To receive your exclusive AAA member discounts and benefits, mention your AAA membership card at time of reservation and present it at time of rental. **In addition**, to receive a free one car class upgrade, in the United States mention PC# 929714, in Canada mention PC# 929725 and in Puerto Rico mention PC# 929736 at the time of reservation. Offer available through 12/31/04.

For reservations and program details, call your AAA Travel office or the Hertz/AAA Desk at **1-800-654-3080**.

USED   CERTIFIED PRE-OWNED

When you purchase a Ford Quality Checked Certified Pre-owned vehicle, Lincoln Premier Certified Pre-owned vehicle or a Mercury Certified Pre-owned vehicle, you'll get more than a great deal. You'll get up to 141 points of inspection by certified technicians, a vehicle history report, 24-hour roadside assistance and 6-year/75,000-mile limited warranty coverage.* All backed by Ford Motor Company. Why risk it? Visit your Ford or Lincoln-Mercury Dealer today for a Certified Pre-owned vehicle. It's really the safe choice.

For a Certified Pre-owned dealer and special financing options, visit www. fordcpo.com or call 866-222-6798.

IF IT'S NOT CERTIFIED, IT'S JUST USED.

*See dealer for warranty details.

Michigan

Touring at a Snail's Pace

Savor historic Mackinac Island on foot, on a bicycle or by carriage—it's the only way!

Museums, All in a Row

Buildings dedicated to science, surveying and transportation line Lansing's Museum Drive

Motors and Music

Explore Detroit's homes of the automobile barons and the birthplace of the Motown sound

The Unspoiled Upper

The Upper Peninsula preserves a national lakeshore, virgin forests, mountains and wildlife

Seeing the Soo

The Soo Locks can be observed from several vantage points in Sault Ste. Marie

Crisp Point,
Lake Superior
© G. Ahrens
Robertstock

all in the palm of its hand

Grand Traverse Bay, Northport / © SuperStock

Mitten-shaped Michigan greets visitors with a hearty wave hello.

When exploring the Wolverine State, start at the base of the thumb, where Henry Ford's jumpy Model-T turned Detroit into the world's best known assembly line.

Head to the pinkie, where Sleeping Bear Dunes National Lakeshore is lapped by Lake Michigan, only one of the truly "great" lakes bordering the state. Lining the lakes are more than 100 lighthouses that illuminate the way for American and Canadian ships.

Near the heel of the hand is Holland, a town proud of its Dutch heritage. On any given day you can see shopkeepers scrubbing the cobblestone sidewalks and crafting wooden shoes.

Between the thumb and forefinger is Frankenmuth, which has a decidedly German flavor. Melodies ring through the streets from the 35 bells of the Glockenspiel Tower.

And at the fingertip, Mackinac Bridge, one of the longest suspension bridges in the world, connects Colonial-style Mackinaw City to the Upper Peninsula, where more than 150 waterfalls, including cascading waterfalls, including spectacular Tahquamenon Falls, delight spectators. Here boats chug through Soo Locks and steep cliffs are dubbed Pictured Rocks.

Spend some time in Michigan; you'll find it carries a bit of everything in its hand.

Ever since Charles King drove the first "horseless carriage" down the streets of Detroit in 1896, Michigan has been synonymous with motoring. Henry Ford and Ransom E. Olds hopped on the wagon, so to speak, and before long, "merry Oldsmobiles" and "Tin Lizzies" came to represent a freedom not previously known to travelers—putting Michigan on the map and making millionaires of many.

Ford's assembly line concept made mass production of automobiles possible, bringing great wealth to auto barons. Visit Henry Ford's Fair Lane mansion in Dearborn to get a glimpse of how the Fords spent their earnings. If the house itself isn't enough to make your jaw drop, Clara Ford's formal rose garden should do it. It once was attended by 20 full-time gardeners.

Take a tour of Edsel and Eleanor Ford's sprawling estate in Grosse Pointe Shores. On its 87 acres is the Play House given to daughter Josephine on her seventh birthday. Constructed in mock-Tudor style and in three-fourths scale, the cottage is every little girl's dream—and is probably more expensive than most *real* houses.

Hit the Road, Jack

The automobile remains the most convenient form of travel, and there's no better means of visiting some of Michigan's smaller towns.

Take to the highway and explore Holland. Be sure to arrive in May, when millions of colorful tulips bloom during the spring festival. Slip into a pair of wooden shoes, clomp around the town's adorable restored downtown and check out the wee Dutch village surrounding De Zwaan windmill.

If you prefer sausage and sauerkraut, cruise to Frankenmuth, which sports a Bavarian architectural flair. You'll think you're smack in the middle of Munich when you hear the Glockenspiel Tower's twinkling bells. Sneak a smooch under the Holz-Brücke covered bridge before heading to giant Bronner's Christmas Wonderland, rumored to be the world's largest Christmas store. With a showroom bigger than a football field, the talk may be true.

Heading north, you'll reach Mackinaw City. Costumed guides at Fort Michilimackinac, built by the French in 1715, reenact life during Colonial days by launching cannons on Lake Huron's shore, cutting logs with

Father Jacques Marquette establishes the first settlement at Sault Ste. Marie.

1668

© Richard Cummins
Corbis

© Joseph Sohm/Corbis

Lansing becomes the new state capital, succeeding Detroit.

1847

The Soo Locks are completed, marking the first continuous shipping route between lakes Superior and Huron.

1855

© Lowell Georgia/Corbis

1783

The Treaty of Paris awards land that includes future Michigan territory to the United States.

1894

The Kellogg brothers create a breakfast food industry when they develop a flake cereal for use at their Battle Creek Sanitarium.

Michigan Historical Timeline

crosscut saws, peddling furs and singing French songs.

By Bridge or Ferry

With most of Michigan surrounded by those "great" lakes, bridges provide another handy way to get around. For starters, take the Mackinac Bridge from Michigan's Lower Peninsula to the rugged Upper Peninsula (U.P.). The bridge, affectionately termed "Big Mac," stretches across the Straits of Mackinac, where lakes Michigan and Huron meet.

How about lunch in Canada? Drive over the Detroit River on the Ambassador Bridge, which links Detroit and Windsor, Ontario. Impress friends back home with your fancy international itinerary.

To get to peaceful Mackinac Island, you'll have to take a ferry, catamaran or plane. Once you're there, ride in a horse-drawn carriage, bike or stroll—but leave your car behind, since no automobiles are allowed on this little island. Browse the boutiques in downtown's gingerbread-laced buildings, sampling homemade fudge at one of many candy shops. Even if locals call you a "fudgie" (tourist), the chocolatey goodness will make up for it! Next, take a tour of the 1887 Grand Hotel, a beautiful white Victorian building with a sweeping 600-foot-long veranda topped by a sky-blue ceiling.

Outdoorsy folks will love Isle Royale National Park, off the western tip of the U.P. in Lake Superior; a ferry or floatplane can escort you. This roadless island is home to historic lighthouses, shipwrecks, ancient copper mining sites and lots of spots to see moose and wolves.

A unique mode of transit exists on the U.P.—the Soo Locks, which allow ships to navigate the rapids between lakes Huron and Superior. You can take a boat tour through the locks to experience a 21-foot lift to the level of Lake Superior. Adjacent St. Marys Rapids are a frothy, delightful sight.

And there's more—from a space center in Jackson to a stop on the Underground Railroad in Kalamazoo to Greenfield Village in Dearborn, where the Wright brothers tinkered with the airplane. Michigan will encourage you to gas up the ol' Chevy and put the "pedal to the metal."

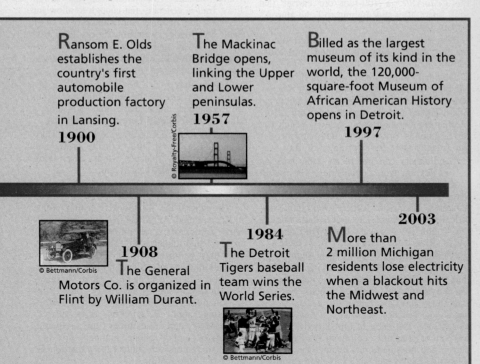

Ransom E. Olds establishes the country's first automobile production factory in Lansing.
1900

The Mackinac Bridge opens, linking the Upper and Lower peninsulas.
1957

© Royalty-Free/Corbis

Billed as the largest museum of its kind in the world, the 120,000-square-foot Museum of African American History opens in Detroit.
1997

© Bettmann/Corbis

1908
The General Motors Co. is organized in Flint by William Durant.

1984
The Detroit Tigers baseball team wins the World Series.

2003
More than 2 million Michigan residents lose electricity when a blackout hits the Midwest and Northeast.

© Bettmann/Corbis

Recreation

You've gotta hand it to Michigan. Complete with three national forests, one national park and two national lakeshores—not to mention four Great Lakes and nearly a hundred state parks from Bald Mountain to Sleepy Hollow—it's no wonder the state packs a punch when it comes to recreation options.

Water Watch

Perhaps the coolest outdoor activity here—literally—is donning wet suit and tanks to go **scuba diving** at one of more than 3,000 shipwrecks littering 38,000 square miles of Michigan's Great Lakes bottomlands. Largely dating to the last quarter of the 19th century, the wrecks are remarkably well-preserved due to the fresh and—here's the key—*extremely* cold waters of lakes Huron, Michigan and Superior. Depths range from 20 to 150 feet, and visibility varies from excellent to muddy.

Some ships worth looking for: the *Bermuda*, an 1880s schooner resting only 25 feet below the surface in Murray Bay, off Munising; and the skeletal *Michael Groh*, which met its fate on a Lake Superior sandbar in November 1895. Of more recent vintage is the *Cedarville*, a 700-foot ore carrier that sank intact after succumbing to Lake Huron's fury in 1966.

Non-diving adventurers aren't left out of the fun, though: **Glass-bottomed boat tours** can be chartered in Munising.

Downed ships aren't all you'll find in Michigan's many waterways; **fishing** is good, too. Along Lake Michigan's shoreline at South Haven and Saugatuck there are plenty of charters targeting coho salmon, which can top 25 pounds. For walleye, float your boat in the Tittabawassee River or Saginaw Bay.

Landlubbers can opt to try their luck on one of several fishing platforms. The 1,000-foot North Pier in St. Joseph and Grand Haven's South Pier are both renowned as perch hangouts. Near Rockford, a deck built specifically to accommodate wheelchairs borders the Rogue River's west bank. And at Lansing's Riverfront Park and Trail there's a water-level dock favored by local anglers.

Those who would rather swing a paddle than cast a line will find ideal conditions for **sea kayaking** off Pictured Rocks National Lakeshore on Lake Superior, whose waters lap sandy beaches and richly layered sandstone cliffs. But even in top-skirted kayaks a wet suit is standard equipment on frigid Superior, and all small-craft boaters are advised to avoid open water and stay well-informed of weather conditions. Popular put-in points include Sand Point, Miners Beach, the Munising Municipal Boat Ramp and Grand Island Landing. Twelvemile Beach Campground and Grand Marais Marina are at the park's east end.

Should you prefer rubbing shoulders with the big ships, board an authentic ferry steamer in Ludington for a Lake Michigan **cruise** with an "ocean liner" feel. Or head to Sault Ste. Marie, where 2-hour tours through the Soo Locks put you right alongside enormous freighters.

In addition to its border lakes, Michigan has many inviting interior waterways offering myriad **boating** options, from low-key **canoeing** on the Au Sable River, near Roscommon, to high-speed **water skiing** at Haughton Lake, the state's largest inland body of water.

Shore Leave

You can enjoy Michigan's wealth of water from a distance, too. **Climb** the dunes to a sweeping view of Lake Michigan at Sleeping Bear Dunes National Lakeshore. Or **hike** in sight of five waterfalls in the Ottawa National Forest's Black River Harbor area. Within Huron-Manistee National Forest, the Jewell Lake Trail is generally flat enough to allow for easy lakeside ambling. And **walkers** will enjoy Sault Ste. Marie's waterfront Locks Park Historic Walkway and Silver City's .5-mile elevated boardwalk, which follows the Presque Isle River and passes still more waterfalls.

Scenic drives do the job as well. Especially pretty are the lakeside highway north of Muskegon State Park and Bessemer's Black River National Forest Scenic Byway.

But to really get an overview of the landscape, visit Tower Hill, outside Bridgman, where perfectly placed winds lure **hang gliders** into the sky year-round.

Recreational Activities

Throughout the TourBook, you may notice a Recreational Activities heading with bulleted listings of recreation-oriented establishments listed underneath. Similar operations also may be mentioned in Destination City recreation sections. Since normal AAA inspection criteria cannot be applied, these establishments are presented only for information. Age, height and weight restrictions may apply. Reservations often are recommended and sometimes are required. Addresses and/or phone numbers are provided so visitors can contact the attraction for additional information.

Fast Facts

POPULATION: 9,938,444.

AREA: 56,804 square miles; ranks 23rd.

CAPITAL: Lansing.

HIGHEST POINT: 1,979 ft., Mount Arvon.

LOWEST POINT: 572 ft., Lake Erie.

TIME ZONE(S): Eastern/Central. DST.

MINIMUM AGE FOR DRIVERS: 17.

MINIMUM AGE FOR GAMBLING: 21.

SEAT BELT/CHILD RESTRAINT LAWS: Seat belts required for driver and front-seat passengers, and all rear-seat passengers ages 4-15; child restraints required for under 4.

HELMETS FOR MOTORCYCLISTS: Required.

RADAR DETECTORS: Permitted.

FIREARMS LAWS: Vary by state or county. Contact local law enforcement agencies or the Michigan Department of State Police, Central Records, Firearms Unit, 7150 Harris Dr., Lansing, MI 48913.

HOLIDAYS: Jan. 1; Martin Luther King Jr. Day, Jan. (3rd Mon.); Presidents Day, Feb. (3rd Mon.); Memorial Day, May (last Mon.); July 4; Labor Day, Sept. (1st Mon.); Veterans Day, Nov. 11; Thanksgiving; Dec. 25.

TAXES: Michigan's statewide sales tax is 6 percent. Local options allow taxes ranging from 1.5 to 6 percent on lodgings in convention hotels and lodging taxes of up to 5 percent at other facilities. An additional 2 percent tax is charged in metropolitan areas.

STATE INFORMATION CENTERS: Centers are maintained all year on I-94 at New Buffalo; on I-69 at Coldwater; on US 23 at Dundee; on US 2 at Ironwood; on US 2 in Iron Mountain; on US 41S in Marquette; on US 41 in Menominee; on I-75N in St. Ignace; on I-75 at the south end of the International Bridge at Sault Ste. Marie; on I-94 at Water Street in Port Huron; on US 127 at a rest area 1 mile north of Clare; on SR 108 in Mackinaw City; and on I-75 at Monroe.

FURTHER INFORMATION FOR VISITORS:

Travel Michigan
Michigan Economic
  Development Corporation
P.O. Box 30226
Lansing, MI 48909
(888) 784-7328

RECREATION, FISHING & HUNTING INFORMATION:

Department of Natural
  Resources
P.O. Box 30028
Lansing, MI 48909
(517) 373-0908 (fishing information)
(517) 373-9453 (hunting information)

NATIONAL FOREST INFORMATION:

U.S. Forest Service
310 W. Wisconsin Ave., Suite 500
Milwaukee, WI 53203
(414) 297-3693
(877) 444-6777 (reservations)

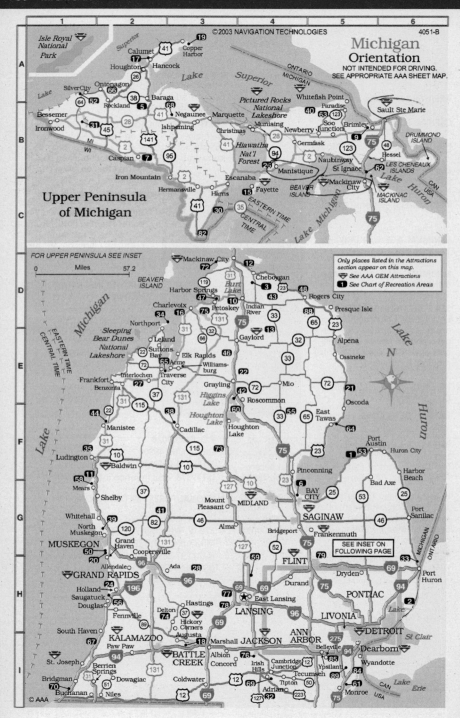

© 2003 NAVIGATION TECHNOLOGIES

4051-B

Michigan
Orientation
NOT INTENDED FOR DRIVING.
SEE APPROPRIATE AAA SHEET MAP.

Upper Peninsula of Michigan

FOR UPPER PENINSULA SEE INSET

0   Miles   57.2

Only places listed in the Attractions section appear on this map.

See AAA GEM Attractions

See Chart of Recreation Areas

SEE INSET ON FOLLOWING PAGE

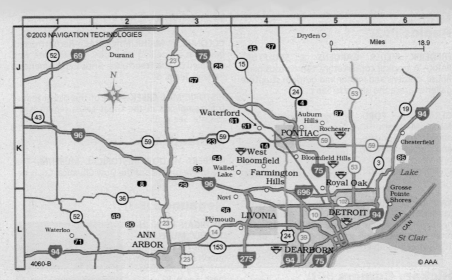

©2003 NAVIGATION TECHNOLOGIES

Miles 18.9

4060-B

© AAA

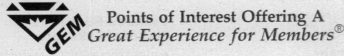

Points of Interest Offering A
Great Experience for Members®

Baldwin (F-2)

SHRINE OF THE PINES—The beauty and versatility of the white pine—the state tree—is seen in handmade furnishings and decorative pieces created by one man and fittingly displayed in a log cabin. See p. 45.

Battle Creek (I-3)

BINDER PARK ZOO—Exotic animals are displayed in natural settings. See p. 46.

Bloomfield Hills (K-5)

CRANBROOK INSTITUTE OF SCIENCE—Discover live bats, interactive science exhibits and a full-size Tyrannosaurus rex skeleton. See p. 63.

Dearborn (L-4)

HENRY FORD MUSEUM & GREENFIELD VILLAGE—American ingenuity is the theme that links collections of inventions, vehicles and buildings. See p. 63.

Detroit (H-5)

THE DETROIT INSTITUTE OF ARTS—Collections feature artwork spanning several centuries. See p. 55.

Fayette (C-4)

HISTORIC FAYETTE TOWNSITE—Fayette is a preserved 1867 town that thrived along with the iron industry for nearly 25 years. See p. 67.

Flint (H-4)

ALFRED P. SLOAN MUSEUM—Regional history topics ranging from archeology to automobiles are covered. See p. 68.

Frankenmuth (G-5)

BRONNER'S CHRISTMAS WONDERLAND—It's Christmas all year at this gigantic showroom of yuletide trappings. See p. 69.

Gaylord (E-4)

CALL OF THE WILD MUSEUM—Lifelike sounds of animals and birds permeate this specimen-filled museum. See p. 70.

Grand Rapids (H-2)

FREDERIK MEIJER GARDENS & SCULPTURE PARK—A tropical conservatory, carnivorous plant house, gardens and indoor and outdoor sculpture galleries grace the grounds. See p. 71.

GERALD R. FORD MUSEUM—Learn about the private and public sides of one of our nation's presidents. See p. 72.

VAN ANDEL MUSEUM CENTER OF THE PUBLIC MUSEUM OF GRAND RAPIDS—In addition to heritage and manufacturing exhibits, this museum features a full-scale reproduction of an 1890s street, complete with shops. See p. 72.

Hickory Corners (H-3)

GILMORE CAR MUSEUM—Antique barns stable a diverse collection of classic vehicles. See p. 74.

Isle Royale National Park (A-1)

ISLE ROYALE NATIONAL PARK—Truly a natural wilderness, this wooded island with wildlife is a U.S. Biosphere Reserve. See p. 77.

Jackson (I-4)

MICHIGAN SPACE & SCIENCE CENTER—Apollo, *Challenger* and Mercury are some of the space flight subjects explored at this center. See p. 78.

Kalamazoo (I-2)

KALAMAZOO AVIATION HISTORY MUSEUM (AIR ZOO)—Vintage flying aircraft, aviation equipment and a museum are highlights. See p. 79.

Mackinac Island (C-6)

FORT MACKINAC—Original buildings constructed in the 18th and 19th centuries still overlook the Straits of Mackinac. See p. 83.

Mackinaw City (D-3)

COLONIAL MICHILIMACKINAC—Reconstructed buildings are telling reminders that this site was occupied by the French, the British and American Indians. See p. 84.

HISTORIC MILL CREEK—One of the oldest industrial complexes in the Great Lakes region is on this site. See p. 85.

Midland (G-4)

HERBERT H. DOW HISTORICAL MUSEUM—The life of the founder of the Dow Chemical Co. is depicted. See p. 88.

Negaunee (B-3)

MICHIGAN IRON INDUSTRY MUSEUM—Exhibits focus on the importance of iron to area development. See p. 91.

Pictured Rocks National Lakeshore

PICTURED ROCKS NATIONAL LAKESHORE—Dunes and cliffs that tower above Lake Superior are the focal point of this park, where recreation opportunities abound. See p. 94.

Rochester (K-5)

OAKLAND UNIVERSITY'S MEADOW BROOK HALL—Built in the Tudor style, this 1920s mansion is the showpiece of the campus along with its counterpart, a miniature playhouse. See p. 64.

Royal Oak (K-5)

DETROIT ZOOLOGICAL PARK—A short drive outside the Detroit city limits will take you to the continents of the world and the animals that inhabit them. See p. 64.

Saginaw (G-5)

JOHNNY PANTHER QUESTS—Get a close-up view of the wildlife and habitats of the Saginaw Valley water system. See p. 97.

St. Joseph (I-1)

CURIOUS KIDS' MU-SEUM—A world of fantasy and fact awaits children here. See p. 98.

Sault Ste. Marie (B-6)

SOO LOCKS BOAT TOURS—The workings of the locks between lakes Superior and Huron are explained through narrated tours. See p. 100.

West Bloomfield (K-4)

HOLOCAUST MEMO-RIAL CENTER—This center is dedicated to perpetuating the memory of the Holocaust. See p. 65.

Whitefish Point (A-5)

GREAT LAKES SHIP-WRECK MUSEUM—Ship disasters—including the wreck of the *Edmund Fitzgerald*—are recalled with artifacts, photographs and film presentations. See p. 104.

RECREATION AREAS

	MAP LOCATION	CAMPING	PICNICKING	HIKING TRAILS	BOATING	BOAT RAMP	BOAT RENTAL	FISHING	SWIMMING	PETS ON LEASH	BICYCLE TRAILS	WINTER SPORTS	VISITOR CENTER	LODGE/CABINS	FOOD SERVICE
NATIONAL PARKS *(See place listings)*															
Isle Royale (A-1) 571,790 acres in Lake Superior.		•	•	•	•		•						•	•	•
NATIONAL FORESTS *(See place listings)*															
Hiawatha 893,348 acres in the Upper Peninsula.		•	•	•	•	•		•	•	•	•	•	•	•	•
Huron-Manistee 964,711 acres in the northern part of the Lower Peninsula.		•	•	•	•	•	•	•	•	•	•	•	•	•	•
Ottawa 986,518 acres in the Upper Peninsula.		•	•	•	•	•		•	•	•	•	•		•	
NATIONAL LAKESHORES *(See place listings)*															
Pictured Rocks (A-4) 70,822 acres along Lake Superior n.e. of Munising.		•	•	•	•	•		•	•	•			•	•	
Sleeping Bear Dunes (E-2) 71,105 acres along Lake Michigan n. of Frankfort.															
STATE															
Albert E. Sleeper (F-5) 723 acres 5 mi. n.e. of Caseville on SR 25.	**1**	•	•	•		•		•	•	•		•		•	
Algonac (H-6) 1,307 acres 2 mi. n. of Algonac on SR 29.	**2**	•	•	•	•			•		•		•		•	
Aloha (D-4) 106 acres 9 mi. s. of Cheboygan on SR 33.	**3**	•	•		•	•		•	•	•					
Bald Mountain (J-5) 4,637 acres 7 mi. n. of Pontiac off SR 24. Shooting range.	**4**		•	•	•	•	•	•	•	•	•	•	•		•	•
Baraga (B-2) 53 acres 1 mi. s. of Baraga on US 41.	**5**	•	•	•				•	•	•					
Bay City (G-4) 1,300 acres 5 mi. n. of Bay City on SR 247. Nature center.	**6**	•	•	•		•		•	•	•			•	•	•
Bewabic (B-2) 315 acres 4 mi. w. of Crystal Falls on US 2. Tennis.	**7**	•	•	•	•			•	•	•					
Brighton (K-2) 4,913 acres 3 mi. w. of Brighton on Main St. (Brighton Rd.), then s. on Chilson Rd. Horse rental.	**8**	•	•	•	•	•	•	•	•	•	•	•	•		•	
Brimley (B-5) 151 acres 1 mi. e. of Brimley on SR 221.	**9**	•	•		•	•		•	•	•					
Burt Lake (D-3) 405 acres .5 mi. s.w. of Indian River on SR 68.	**10**	•	•	•	•	•		•	•	•					
Charles Mears (F-1) 50 acres 1 mi. n. of Pentwater off US 31 Bus. Rte.	**11**	•	•	•				•	•	•					•
Cheboygan (D-4) 932 acres 4 mi. e. of Cheboygan on US 23.	**12**	•	•					•	•	•			•		•
Clear Lake (D-4) 290 acres 9 mi. n. of Atlanta off SR 33.	**13**	•	•	•	•	•		•	•	•		•		•	

RECREATION AREAS

	MAP LOCATION	CAMPING	PICNICKING	HIKING TRAILS	BOATING	BOAT RAMP	BOAT RENTAL	FISHING	SWIMMING	PETS ON LEASH	BICYCLE TRAILS	WINTER SPORTS	VISITOR CENTER	LODGE/CABINS	FOOD SERVICE
Dodge No. 4 (K-4) 136 acres 6 mi. w. of Pontiac off SR 59. Playground.	14		•	•	•			•	•	•					•
Fayette (C-4) 711 acres in Fayette off SR 183. Historic.	15	•	•	•	•			•	•	•	•	•			
Fisherman's Island (D-2) 2,942 acres 3 mi. s.w. of Charlevoix off US 31.	16	•	•	•				•	•	•					
F.J. McLain (A-2) 417 acres 8 mi. w. of Calumet on SR 203.	17	•	•	•				•	•	•				•	•
Fort Custer (I-3) 3,033 acres 8 mi. w. of Battle Creek on SR 96.	18	•	•	•	•	•		•	•	•	•	•	•		
Fort Wilkins (A-3) 700 acres 1 mi. e. of Copper Harbor on US 41. Historic. Cross-country skiing. *(See Copper Harbor p. 51)*	19	•	•	•	•	•	•	•	•	•		•	•		
Grand Haven (H-1) 48 acres 1 mi. w. of Grand Haven off US 31. *(See Grand Haven p. 70)*	20	•	•	•				•	•	•					•
Harrisville (E-5) 107 acres 1 mi. s. of Harrisville on US 23.	21	•	•	•				•	•	•					
Hartwick Pines (E-4) 9,672 acres 7 mi. n.e. of Grayling on SR 93. Historic. Cross-country skiing. *(See Grayling p. 72)*	22	•	•	•				•		•		•	•	•	
Highland (K-3) 5,524 acres 2 mi. e. of Highland off SR 59. Cross-country skiing; horse rental.	23	•	•	•	•			•	•	•		•		•	
Holland (H-2) 142 acres 7 mi. w. of Holland on US 31.	24	•	•	•	•	•		•	•	•					•
Holly (J-3) 7,670 acres 12 mi. n.w. of Pontiac off I-75.	25	•	•	•	•			•	•	•		•			
Indian Lake (B-4) 567 acres 5 mi. w. of Manistique on SR 442.	26	•	•	•	•	•		•	•	•				•	
Interlochen (E-2) 187 acres 1 mi. s. of Interlochen on SR 137.	27	•	•	•	•			•	•	•				•	
Ionia (H-3) 4,085 acres 2 mi. w. of Ionia on SR 66. Hunting, snowmobiling; playground.	28	•	•	•	•			•	•	•		•			
Island Lake (K-3) 3,466 acres 4 mi. s.e. of Brighton off US 23.	29		•	•	•	•		•	•	•		•			
J.W. Wells (C-3) 694 acres 2 mi. s. of Cedar River on SR 35. Cross-country skiing.	30	•	•	•				•	•	•		•		•	
Lake Gogebic (B-1) 361 acres 12 mi. n.e. of Marenisco on SR 64.	31	•	•	•	•	•		•	•	•					
Lake Hudson (I-4) 2,650 acres 6 mi. s.e. of Hudson on SR 156.	32	•	•		•	•		•		•					
Lakeport (H-6) 565 acres 10 mi. n. of Port Huron on SR 25.	33	•	•	•				•	•	•				•	•
Leelanau (D-2) 1,300 acres 7 mi. n. of Northport on SR 201. Hunting; playground.	34	•	•	•	•			•	•	•					
Ludington (F-1) 5,202 acres 8 mi. n. of Ludington on SR 116. Cross-country skiing; nature center. *(See Ludington p. 82)*	35	•	•	•	•	•		•	•	•		•	•		
Maybury (L-3) 944 acres w. of Detroit on I-96 to I-275N, then 5 mi. w. on Eight Mile Rd. Horse rental.	36		•	•				•		•	•	•	•		
Metamora-Hadley (J-4) 683 acres 10 mi. s. of Lapeer off SR 24.	37	•	•	•	•			•	•	•		•			
Mitchell (F-3) 334 acres 4 mi. w. of Cadillac on SR 115. Museum.	38	•	•	•	•	•	•	•	•	•			•		
Muskegon (G-2) 1,165 acres 4 mi. w. of North Muskegon on Memorial Dr.	39	•	•	•	•			•	•	•		•		•	
Muskellunge Lake (B-5) 217 acres 31 mi. w. of Whitefish Point on H-58 at Deer Park.	40	•	•	•	•			•	•	•					
Newaygo (G-2) 257 acres 8 mi. w. of Morley off US 131 following signs.	41	•			•			•		•					
North Higgins Lake (E-4) 429 acres 7 mi. w. of Roscommon via US 127 and Military Rd.	42	•	•	•	•			•	•	•		•	•	•	•
Onaway (D-4) 158 acres on Black Lake 7 mi. n.w. of Onaway on SR 211.	43	•	•	•	•			•	•	•					
Orchard Beach (F-1) 201 acres 2 mi. n. of Manistee on SR 110.	44	•	•	•					•	•				•	
Ortonville (J-5) 4,875 acres 4 mi. n.e. of Ortonville on SR 15. Shooting range.	45	•	•	•	•			•	•	•		•			
Otsego Lake (E-3) 62 acres 7 mi. s. of Gaylord off I-75.	46	•	•		•			•	•	•				•	•
Petoskey (D-3) 305 acres at Petoskey off SR 119. *(See Petoskey p. 94)*	47	•	•	•				•	•	•		•			
P.H. Hoeft (D-4) 301 acres 5 mi. n.w. of Rogers City on US 23. Cross-country skiing; Huron dunes. *(See Rogers City p. 96)*	48	•	•	•	•			•	•	•			•		

RECREATION AREAS

	MAP LOCATION	CAMPING	PICNICKING	HIKING TRAILS	BOATING	BOAT RAMP	BOAT RENTAL	FISHING	SWIMMING	PETS ON LEASH	BICYCLE TRAILS	WINTER SPORTS	VISITOR CENTER	LODGE/CABINS	FOOD SERVICE
Pinckney (L-2) 10,201 acres 4 mi. s.w. of Pinckney via SR 36. Cross-country skiing; horse rental.	49	•	•	•	•			•	•	•	•	•			•
P.J. Hoffmaster (G-1) 1,043 acres 10 mi. n.w. of Grand Haven off US 31. Cross-country skiing; nature center. *(See Grand Haven p. 70)*	50		•	•				•	•	•		•	•		•
Pontiac Lake (K-4) 3,700 acres 8 mi. w. of Pontiac on SR 59. Archery and rifle ranges, horse rental.	51	•	•	•	•	•	•	•	•	•		•			•
Porcupine Mountains Wilderness (A-1) 63,000 acres 3 mi. w. of Silver City on SR 107. Scenic. Cross-country skiing. *(See Silver City p. 100)*	52	•	•	•	•	•	•	•	•	•	•	•	•	•	•
Port Crescent (F-5) 569 acres 5 mi. s.w. of Port Austin on SR 25. Cross-country skiing.	53	•	•	•				•	•	•		•		•	
Proud Lake (K-3) 3,614 acres 4 mi. s.e. of Milford off I-96. Cross-country skiing.	54	•	•	•	•	•		•	•	•		•			
Rifle River (F-4) 4,329 acres 6 mi. s.e. of Rose City on Rose City Rd.	55	•	•	•	•	•		•	•	•		•		•	
Saugatuck Dunes (H-2) 889 acres 1 mi. n. of Saugatuck off US 31. Cross-country skiing.	56		•	•					•	•		•			
Seven Lakes (J-3) 1,730 acres 1 mi. w. of Holly off US 23. Cross-country skiing, hunting; playground.	57	•	•	•	•	•	•	•	•	•		•			•
Silver Lake (F-1) 3,400 acres on Silver Lake 7 mi. w. of Mears via US 31. Off-road vehicle area. *(See Mears p. 88)*	58	•	•		•	•	•	•	•	•		•			
Sleepy Hollow (H-4) 2,860 acres 15 mi. n.e. of Lansing off US 127. Cross-country skiing, hunting; playgrounds.	59	•	•	•	•	•		•	•	•		•			
South Higgins Lake (F-3) 962 acres 8 mi. s.w. of Roscommon off US 127. Cross-country skiing.	60	•	•	•	•	•		•	•	•		•			
Sterling (I-5) 1000 acres e. of I-75 on the n. edge of Monroe on State Park Rd. Cross-country skiing.	61	•	•	•	•			•	•	•		•			•
Straits (B-5) 181 acres 1 mi. s.w. of St. Ignace on US 2.	62	•	•					•		•				•	
Tahquamenon Falls (B-5) 40,000 acres 12 mi. w. of Paradise on SR 123. Scenic. Cross-country skiing. *(See Paradise p. 93)*	63	•	•	•	•	•		•	•	•		•			•
Tawas Point (F-5) 183 acres 3 mi. e. of East Tawas off US 23.	64	•	•					•	•	•				•	
Traverse City (E-2) 45 acres 2 mi. e. of Traverse City on US 31.	65	•	•					•	•	•				•	
Twin Lakes (A-2) 175 acres 25 mi. s. of Houghton on SR 26.	66	•	•	•	•	•		•	•	•		•		•	
Van Buren (I-1) 400 acres 4 mi. s. of South Haven off I-196.	67	•	•						•	•					•
Van Riper (B-3) 1,044 acres 3 mi. w. of Champion on US 41.	68	•	•	•	•	•		•	•	•		•		•	
Walter J. Hayes (I-4) 654 acres 9 mi. w. of Clinton off US 12.	69	•	•		•	•	•	•	•	•				•	
Warren Dunes (I-1) 1,950 acres on Lake Michigan 3 mi. s.w. of Bridgman via Red Arrow Hwy. Cross-country skiing. *(See Bridgman p. 49)*	70	•	•	•					•	•		•		•	
Waterloo (L-1) 19,962 acres 7 mi. w. of Chelsea off I-94. Cross-country skiing; horse rental, geology center.	71	•	•	•	•	•		•	•	•	•	•	•	•	
Wilderness (D-3) 8,500 acres 11 mi. w. of Mackinaw City on Wilderness Park Dr.	72	•	•	•	•	•		•	•	•		•		•	
Wilson (F-3) 36 acres 1 mi. n. of Harrison on US 127 Bus. Rte.	73	•	•		•	•	•	•	•	•				•	
Yankee Springs (H-2) 5,014 acres 8 mi. e. of Bradley off A-42 following signs.	74	•	•	•	•	•	•	•	•	•		•		•	
Young (D-3) 563 acres 2 mi. n.w. of Boyne City on SR 75.	75	•	•	•	•	•	•	•	•	•	•	•	•	•	
OTHER															
Ella Sharp (I-4) 562 acres 2 mi. s. of Jackson on 4th St. Golf (18 holes), tennis; driving range. *(See Jackson p. 78)*	76		•	•					•		•	•			
Fitzgerald (H-3) 78 acres 2 mi. w. of Grand Ledge on SR 43.	77		•	•	•		•	•		•			•	•	
Fox Memorial (H-3) 35 acres 1 mi. n. of Potterville off SR 100.	78		•	•			•	•	•			•			
Genesee (G-5) 4,540 acres 6 mi. n.e. of Flint off I-475 exit 13. *(See Flint p. 68)*	79	•	•	•	•	•	•	•	•	•	•	•	•		•

RECREATION AREAS

	MAP LOCATION	CAMPING	PICNICKING	HIKING TRAILS	BOATING	BOAT RAMP	BOAT RENTAL	FISHING	SWIMMING	PETS ON LEASH	BICYCLE TRAILS	WINTER SPORTS	VISITOR CENTER	LODGE/CABINS	FOOD SERVICE
Hudson Mills (L-2) 1,600 acres 12 mi. n.w. of Ann Arbor via US 23 and N. Territorial Rd. Cross-country skiing; nature trails.	80		•	•				•		•	•	•	•		•
Indian Springs (K-4) 2,300 acres 5 mi. s.w. of Clarkston on White Lake Rd. Golf (18 holes); nature trails.	81		•	•						•	•	•	•		•
John Henes (C-3) 45 acres 2.5 mi. n.e. of Menominee off SR 35.	82		•	•					•				•		
Kensington (K-3) 4,350 acres 35 mi. n.w. of Detroit via I-96. Cross-country skiing; farm, nature trails.	83		•	•	•	•	•	•	•	•	•	•	•		•
Lake Erie (I-5) 1,590 acres near Gibraltar on W. Jefferson. Golf (18 holes); marina, wave pool.	84		•		•	•	•	•	•	•		•	•		•
Lower Huron (I-5) 1,200 acres 5 mi. s. of Belleville via Huron River Dr. to Waltz Rd. Cross-country skiing; nature trails, pool.	85		•	•				•	•	•	•	•	•		•
Metro Beach (K-6) 770 acres 3 mi. e. of Mount Clemens via Metropolitan Pkwy. (Sixteen Mile Rd.). Cross-country skiing; nature trails.	86		•	•	•	•		•	•	•	•	•	•		•
Stony Creek (K-5) 4,460 acres near Utica on 26 Mile Rd. Cross-country skiing, golf (18 holes); nature trails.	87		•	•	•	•	•	•	•	•	•	•	•		•
Sunken Lake Campground (D-5) 160 acres 5 mi. s. of Posen on SR 65, 1 mi. w. on Maple Ln., then 2 mi. n. on Leer Rd.	88	•	•	•	•			•	•						•
Willow Metropark (I-5) 1,525 acres 4 mi. n.w. of Flat Rock on Willow Rd. Cross-country skiing, golf (18 holes), tobogganing; paddle boats, pool.	89		•	•	•			•	•	•	•	•	•		•

Michigan Temperature Averages
Maximum / Minimum
From the records of the National Weather Service

	JAN	FEB	MAR	APR	MAY	JUNE	JULY	AUG	SEPT	OCT	NOV	DEC
Detroit	32/19	34/20	43/28	58/39	68/48	79/59	83/63	82/62	74/55	63/45	48/34	35/24
Grand Rapids	30/16	33/16	42/24	57/36	69/45	79/56	83/60	82/58	74/51	63/41	46/31	34/21
Houghton Lake	26/9	28/8	37/16	53/30	65/40	75/50	79/54	77/53	68/46	58/37	42/27	30/15
Marquette	25/12	26/13	34/20	48/32	59/41	70/50	75/57	74/57	65/49	56/41	40/29	29/18
Sault Ste. Marie	22/6	24/7	32/15	47/29	59/38	70/47	75/52	73/53	64/46	55/38	39/26	27/13

Points of Interest

ACME (E-3) pop. 4,332, elev. 604′

[SAVE] **MUSIC HOUSE MUSEUM** is 1.5 mi. n. of SR 72 at 7377 US 31N. The late 19th-century farm complex includes re-creations of a general store, saloon, lyric theater and candy store. Music boxes, nickelodeons and organs are featured in period displays. Entrance is by guided tour only. Allow 2 hours minimum. Tours are offered Mon.-Sat. 10-4, Sun. noon-4, May-Oct.; phone for holiday hours. Admission $8; ages 6-15, $2.50. DS, MC, VI. Phone (231) 938-9300.

ADA (H-3) pop. 9,882, elev. 664′

ALTICOR CORPORATION VISITOR CENTER is 5 mi. e. of I-96 via SR 21 at 7575 Fulton St. E. Alticor is the parent company of Amway. The center offers interactive displays and audiovisual presentations about product manufacturing and the history of the company. Allow 1 hour minimum. Mon.-Fri. 8:30-noon and 1-5. Free. Under 16 must be with an adult. Phone (616) 787-6701.

ADRIAN (I-4) pop. 21,574, elev. 812′

An industrial city on the Raisin River, Adrian has an impressive historic district centered on Dennis and State streets. The 79 houses in the district exemplify the evolution of architectural styles in the area, from the Greek and Gothic revivals of the 1830s to Italianate to the Queen Anne-style houses that became popular after the Civil War. The houses are all privately owned.

The Croswell Opera House, 129 E. Maumee St., is an example of the utilitarian architecture prevalent after the Civil War. It has been offering musicals, plays, lectures and operas since 1866; phone (517) 264-7469.

Lenawee County Chamber of Commerce: 202 N. Main St., Suite A, Adrian, MI 49221; phone (517) 265-5141.

Shopping areas: Adrian Mall, at the junction of US 223 and SR 52, has Elder-Beerman, JCPenney and Sears.

ALBION (I-3) pop. 9,144, elev. 950′

Established at the forks of the Kalamazoo River, Albion retains its history in restored buildings along a brick-lined main street. The Historic Walkway winds around and across the river to notable landmarks, including Albion College.

The Greater Albion Chamber of Commerce: 416 S. Superior St., P.O. Box 238, Albion, MI 49224; phone (517) 629-5533.

WHITEHOUSE NATURE CENTER is e. on Erie St. and s. on Hannah St. to the Albion College campus. The 135-acre outdoor education facility offers five self-guiding nature trails through a variety of natural and man-made habitats. The interpretive building houses a small observation room with live exhibits; tour brochures are available.

Guided tours are available by appointment. Allow 1 hour minimum. Building open daily 10:30-4:30; closed major and college holidays. Trails open daily dawn-dusk. Free. Phone (517) 629-0582.

ALLENDALE (H-2) pop. 11,555, elev. 657′

In downtown Allendale, visitors will find the Engine House No. 5 Museum, 6610 Lake Michigan Dr., which displays firefighting equipment and memorabilia; phone (616) 895-4347.

VETERANS GARDEN OF HONOR is just off SR 45 (Lake Michigan Dr.) on 68th St. The memorial, dedicated to U.S. veterans, features eight life-size statues placed in a circle surrounding an 18-foot-tall obelisk. Seven soldiers represent the seven U.S. wars, and a female statue honors female veterans. Daily dawn-dusk. Free. Phone (616) 895-6295.

ALMA (G-3) pop. 9,275, elev. 730′

Alma is near the geographical center of the Lower Peninsula. It is the home of Alma College, a private liberal arts college.

Gratiot Area Chamber of Commerce: 110 W. Superior St., P.O. Box 516, Alma, MI 48801-0516; phone (989) 463-5525.

ALPENA (E-5) pop. 11,304, elev. 594′

Settled in 1840 at the head of Thunder Bay, Alpena served the booming lumber enterprises in the late 19th century. It is a center for industry and recreational boating, diving, fishing, snowmobiling, cross-country skiing and hunting. Diving and fishing charters are popular in nearby Lake Huron. The remains of approximately 80 shipwrecks are in the area of Thunder Bay, making Alpena an excellent diving location. The area also is home to a number of lighthouses.

Limestone quarries remain important in the region. North and west of the city is an area of natural sinkholes created by the settling of the limestone crust into caverns formed by subterranean streams. Some of the sinkholes are more than 150 feet deep.

Island Park and Alpena Wildlife Sanctuary, US 23N at the Thunder Bay River, offers nature trails, bird and wildlife viewing and fishing.

An 8-mile bicycling and hiking path winds through the city's parks and beaches.

Alpena Area Convention and Visitors Bureau: 235 W. Chisholm St., Alpena, MI 49707; phone (989) 354-4181 or (800) 425-7362.

JESSE BESSER MUSEUM is at 491 Johnson St. The museum is a regional center for the art, history and science of northeastern Michigan. Displays include a re-created 1890s street with period shops, Michigan wildlife paintings, sculpture, American Indian artifacts and lumbering, agricultural and industrial equipment. Historical structures are outside. Changing exhibits and a planetarium are featured.

Allow 1 hour minimum. Tues.-Sat. 10-5, Sun. noon-4; closed major holidays. Planetarium shows Sun. at 2. Museum $3; over 60 and ages 5-17, $2. Planetarium $1. Phone (989) 356-2202.

ANN ARBOR (L-2) pop. 114,024, elev. 766′

"Kaw-GOOSH-kaw-nick,   kaw-GOOSH-kaw-nick"—the chant of a gristmill resounding through the woods along Allen's Creek about 1824 allegedly furnished the local American Indians with the name for the hamlet that grew up around the mill. The less phonetically inclined settlers preferred Ann Arbor, referring to a grape arbor and the first pioneers' wives, Ann Allen and Ann Rumsey.

While only a mere upstart of 13 years and with fewer than 2,000 residents, Ann Arbor bid for and was granted the University of Michigan. Civic foresight paid off. Since its move from Detroit in 1837 the university has been the primary influence in the growth and life of the city. Research and development industries also contribute significantly to the economy.

Ann Arbor Area Convention and Visitors Bureau: 120 W. Huron St., Ann Arbor, MI 48104; phone (800) 888-9487.

Shopping areas: Kerrytown is a complex of specialty shops housed in three renovated historic buildings next to Farmer's Market on N. Fifth Avenue. Marshall Field's, Jacobson's, JCPenney and Sears can be found at Briarwood Mall, I-94 and State Street.

THE ANN ARBOR HANDS-ON MUSEUM is at 220 E. Ann St. The museum offers hundreds of opportunities to explore the worlds of science and technology. More than 250 interactive exhibits are featured, including an operating TV station where children assume roles of director, weatherperson or news anchor. The Measure Up exhibit tests heart rates, body mass index and flexibility. A pre-school gallery is designed for those under age 5.

Allow 2 hours minimum. Mon.-Sat. 10-5, Sun. noon-5; closed major holidays. Admission $7.50; over 65, students with ID and ages 2-17, $6. MC, VI. Phone (734) 995-5439.

UNIVERSITY OF MICHIGAN is e. on Huron St. to State St. The university, having outgrown the original 40 acres donated to form the campus, now covers more than 2,800 acres. Highlights include the Gothic buildings of the Law Quadrangle, Power Center for the Performing Arts, Natural Science

Museum and the school's two carillons: the 55-bell Baird Carillon at Burton Memorial Tower and the 60-bell carillon at Lurie Tower.

Burton Tower carillon bells play Mon.-Fri. noon-12:30. Lurie Tower carillon bells play Mon.-Fri. 1-1:30, Sun. 1:15-2. Weekly concerts are offered Mon. at 7 p.m., mid-June through July 31. Carillons are closed during exams and university vacations. Phone (734) 764-4636 for general campus information or (734) 764-2539 for Burton Memorial and Lurie towers.

Exhibit Museum of Natural History is at Geddes and Washtenaw aves. The museum has a planetarium and exhibits about dinosaurs, prehistoric life, fossils, minerals, anthropology, astronomy, biology and Michigan wildlife. Museum open Mon.-Sat. 9-5, Sun. noon-5. Planetarium shows Sat. every hour 11:30-3:30, Sun. 1:30-3:30. Museum accepts donations. Planetarium $3.50. Phone (734) 764-0478.

Kelsey Museum of Archaeology is at 434 S. State St. Displays feature pottery, glass, statues and other artifacts excavated at the university's Mediterranean and Near Eastern digs. Tues.-Fri. 9-4, Sat.-Sun. 1-4; closed holidays. Free. Phone (734) 764-9304.

Matthaei Botanical Gardens is e. of US 23 at 1800 N. Dixboro Rd. Exotic plants from around the world bloom in the conservatory all year. Along the outdoor nature trails are changing seasonal displays. Conservatory open daily 10-4:30. Grounds open daily 8-dusk. Conservatory admission $3; ages 5-18, $1; free to all Mon. until 1. Grounds free. Phone (734) 998-7061.

Museum of Art is at 525 S. State St. at S. University Ave. The collection includes Western art from the sixth century to the present, Near and Far Eastern art, African art and a collection of prints and drawings. The museum also offers changing exhibitions, concerts, family programs and other events. Tues.-Sat. 10-5 (also Thurs. 5-9), Sun. noon-5; closed major holidays. Donations. Phone (734) 764-0395.

Nichols Arboretum is next to the University of Michigan central campus at 1610 Washington Heights Rd. From the James D. Reader, Jr. Urban Environmental Education Center, visitors can follow nature trails through grounds containing more than 400 labeled tree species. A peony garden blooms in early June.

Self-guiding tour brochures are available. Guided tours are available by reservation. Grounds open daily dawn-dusk. Education center open Mon.-Fri. 8:30-4:30. Donations. Phone (734) 998-9540.

William L. Clements Library is at 909 S. University Ave. The library houses notable collections of Americana, including original manuscripts, maps, prints, photographs and rare books about the Revolution and Civil War. Exhibits open Mon.-Fri. 1-4:45. Reading room open Mon.-Fri. 9-11:45 and 1-4:45. Free. Phone (734) 764-2347.

AUBURN HILLS—*see Detroit p. 62.*

AUGUSTA (I-3) pop. 899, elev. 790′

The Barn Theatre, 1 mile west on SR 96, is the home of the oldest professional resident summer theater in Michigan, which presents Broadway plays and musicals. Numerous alumni of the theater company are now stars in theater, film and television. Housed in a renovated dairy barn, the theater presents shows mid-May to mid-September; phone (269) 731-4121.

FORT CUSTER NATIONAL CEMETERY is 1 mi. e. on SR 96 to 15501 Dickman Rd. The 770-acre portion of Fort Custer was dedicated as a national cemetery in 1981. Allow 30 minutes minimum. Daily dawn-dusk. Free. Phone (269) 731-4164.

BAD AXE (F-5) pop. 3,462, elev. 765′

SANILAC PETROGLYPHS HISTORIC STATE PARK is 13 mi. s. on SR 53, 3.5 mi. e. on Bay City/Forestville Rd., then .5 mi. s. on Germania Rd. The park contains the Sanilac Petroglyphs, a series of American Indian rock carvings on sandstone. The 300- to 1,000-year-old carvings consist of figures that resemble animals, birds and humans. A mile-long nature trail winds around the site. Allow 30 minutes minimum. Wed.-Sun. 11:30-4:30, Memorial Day-Labor Day. Free. Phone (989) 269-7186.

BALDWIN (F-2) pop. 1,107, elev. 841′

A railroad junction in earlier days, Baldwin offers access to the numerous lakes and streams of the surrounding Huron-Manistee National Forests *(see place listing p. 75).*

Lake County Chamber of Commerce: 911 Michigan Ave., P.O. Box 130, Baldwin, MI 49304; phone (231) 745-4331 or (800) 245-3240.

SHRINE OF THE PINES is 2 mi. s. on SR 37. The shrine was created by Raymond W. Oberholzer as a memorial to the white pine. He hand-chiseled furnishings from tree stumps and roots gleaned from virgin stands of white pine cut in the late 1800s.

Oberholzer scraped the roots with broken glass and wire brushes, then rubbed each piece with handmade sandpaper, natural resin and deer hide. From these pieces he fashioned beds, chairs, chandeliers and candlesticks; particularly impressive is a table with drawers, carved from a 700-pound stump. The furnishings are housed in a log hunting lodge in a wooded park on the banks of the Pere Marquette River. A nature trail meanders through the pines.

Allow 30 minutes minimum. Mon.-Sat. 10-6, Sun. 1:30-6, May 15-Oct. 15. Last tour begins 30 minutes before closing. Admission $3.75; over 54, $3; ages 13-18, $2; ages 6-12, $1; family rate (parents and children under 18) $10. Phone (231) 745-7892.

BARAGA (A-2) pop. 1,285, elev. 621′

HANKA HOMESTEAD MUSEUM is 7 mi. w. of US 41 on Arnheim Rd., following signs. The century-old Finnish farming homestead is restored to its 1920s appearance. Guided tours of the farm and its outbuildings are available. Allow 1 hour minimum. Tues., Thurs., Sat.-Sun. and holidays noon-4 and by appointment, Memorial Day-Aug. 31; by appointment Sept. 1 to mid-Oct. Donations. Phone (906) 353-6239.

THE SHRINE OF THE SNOWSHOE PRIEST is 3.5 mi. s. on US 41. The six-story structure includes a 35-foot-tall brass statue featuring Bishop Frederic Baraga, a Catholic priest who moved to the Great Lakes region in 1830 and devoted his life to American Indians. He earned his nickname because he traveled by snowshoe up to 700 miles to visit the tribes. The statue overlooks Keweenaw Bay. Allow 30 minutes minimum. Mon.-Sat. 9-8, Sun. 10-6. Free. Phone (906) 524-7021.

BATTLE CREEK (I-3) pop. 53,364, elev. 819′

In 1894 two brothers named Kellogg, experimenting in the kitchens of the Battle Creek Sanitarium, developed a flake cereal. From this modest beginning grew the Kellogg Co., the Post Division of Kraft-General Foods Corp. and the Ralston Purina Co., which have made Battle Creek the breakfast food center of the nation.

Battle Creek residents' progressive attitudes are manifested in other issues. In the decades before the Civil War the city was an abolitionist stronghold and an overt station on the Underground Railroad. Thus the names Kellogg and Post are no more important than that of Sojourner Truth. An ex-slave, this tall, persuasive woman carried her crusade for truth and freedom from tiny rooms to President Lincoln's office. She came to Battle Creek in 1858 and died in 1883; her grave is in Oak Hill Cemetery at South Avenue and Oak Hill Drive. Statues in Monument Park and Linear Park honor her work.

Residents find respite from industrial and commercial activities in city parks. Bailey Park and C.O. Brown Stadium, between Capital Avenue and the Battle Creek River, are the scenes of national amateur baseball tournaments. South of town on Goguac Lake, landscaped Willard Park offers water sports and picnicking. Linear Park extends across much of the city, offering 17 miles of landscaped walkways highlighted by gazebos, boardwalks and bridges, which provide opportunities for jogging, bicycling, walking and picnicking.

Guided tours are offered of the Historic Adventist Village, 480 N. Van Buren St. The religious community features restored and re-created 19th-century buildings; phone (269) 965-3000.

Greater Battle Creek/Calhoun County Visitor and Convention Bureau: 77 E. Michigan Ave., Suite 100, Battle Creek, MI 49017; phone (269) 962-2240 or (800) 397-2240.

Shopping areas: Lakeview Square, east on Beckley Road from I-94 and Capital Avenue, has almost 100 stores, including Marshall Field's, JCPenney and Sears. McCamly Place offers specialty stores and restaurants in a high-rise complex on W. Jackson Street.

ART CENTER OF BATTLE CREEK is at 265 E. Emmett St. Changing exhibits of works by regional and national artists as well as art of other cultures are on display. Works by 20th-century Michigan artists and craftspeople, classes and workshops also can be seen. Tours are available by reservation. Tues.-Sat. 10-5 (also Thurs. 5-7); closed holidays. Free. Phone (269) 962-9511.

 BINDER PARK ZOO is 3 mi. s. of I-94 exit 100, at 7400 Division Dr. The zoo has wooden boardwalks and a conservation adventure station with hands-on activities. Exotic animals live in a natural park setting. Visitors can board a train to tour the safari-style habitat of Wild Africa.

Food is available. Allow 2 hours minimum. Mon.-Fri. 9-5, Sat. and holidays 9-6, Sun. 11-6, late Apr. to mid-Oct. Last admission 30 minutes before closing. Admission (includes safari train) $8.50; over 65, $7.50; ages 2-10, $6.50. DS, MC, VI. Phone (269) 979-1351.

Miller Children's Zoo features a life-size dinosaur replica, a petting area, a miniature train and domestic animal exhibits. Miniature train $2.

SAVE **KELLOGG BIOLOGICAL STATION** is 8 mi. n.w. on SR 89 following signs to 12685 E. C Ave., between 40th St. and E. Gull Lake Dr. An experimental facility of Michigan State University, the area is inhabited by birds of prey, wild ducks, geese, swans, peacocks, pheasants and other upland species. The sanctuary has displays and an observation deck. Allow 1 hour, 30 minutes minimum. Daily 9-8, Apr.-Oct.; 9-5, rest of year. Admission $3; over 64, $2; ages 2-12, $1. Phone (269) 671-2510.

KELLOGG'S CEREAL CITY USA is off I-94 to exit 98B, n. to Michigan Ave., then w. to 171 Michigan Ave. The family attraction celebrates Will Kellogg's accidental creation of the cereal industry. Exhibits focus on the trivia, advertising, marketing and history of breakfast cereal. A simulated cereal production line, a historical time line, four theaters and an interactive Cereal City are included.

Food is available. Allow 2 hours minimum. Mon.-Fri. 9:30-5, Sat. 9:30-6, Sun. 11-5, early June-late Aug.; Tues.-Fri. 10-4, Sat. 10-5, Sun. noon-5, late Mar.-early June and late Aug.-early Nov.; Sat. 10-5, Sun. noon-5, rest of year. Closed Jan. 1, Thanksgiving and Dec. 24-25. Admission $7.95; over 64, $6.50; ages 3-12, $4.95. AX, DS, MC, VI. Phone (269) 962-6230.

LEILA ARBORETUM is on W. Michigan Ave. at 20th St. A 72-acre tract of ornamental trees and shrubs, the arboretum is known for its collection of mature conifers and perennial demonstration beds. Daily dawn-dusk. Free. Phone (269) 969-0270.

BAY CITY (G-5) pop. 36,817, elev. 594′

Bay City is a major distribution point for the industrial and agricultural wealth of east-central Michigan. Many domestic and foreign freighters pass through the city's busy port, and boat races are often held on the river. Shipping and commerce have been the foundation of Bay City's prosperity since the demise of its lumber industry around 1900. Mansions built by the lumber barons can be seen along the tree-shaded residential streets in the city's three historic districts.

The Saginaw River and Saginaw Bay provide ample recreational opportunities. Bay City State Recreation Area (see Recreation Chart) is 5 miles north on SR 247 on the Lake Huron shore.

Bay Area Convention and Visitors Bureau: 901 Saginaw St., Bay City, MI 48708; phone (888) 229-8696.

HISTORICAL MUSEUM OF BAY COUNTY is at 321 Washington Ave. Displays, which trace the development of Bay County, include period rooms and exhibits pertaining to agriculture, maritime history, American Indian culture, the fur trade and the lumber, shipbuilding and shipping industries. A research library also is included. Allow 1 hour minimum. Museum open Mon.-Fri. 10-5, Sat.-Sun. noon-4. Library open Tues.-Thurs. 1-5. Free. Phone (989) 893-5733.

SAGINAW BAY VISITORS CENTER is 3 mi. n. in Bay City State Recreation Area. Permanent and changing exhibits depict life in the wetlands. A 15-minute multimedia presentation about wetlands development is offered. The paved Frank N. Anderson Nature Trail leads to Tobico Marsh, a 1,700-acre refuge for more than 100 species of birds and migratory waterfowl. Nature trails, observation towers and a boardwalk are included.

Allow 30 minutes minimum. Tues.-Sun. noon-5. Admission $5 per private vehicle. Phone (989) 667-0717.

BEAVER ISLAND (B-4)

About 30 miles offshore in Lake Michigan, Beaver Island is the largest island of the Beaver Archipelago. The French established the island's first settlement but abandoned it in 1603. The arrival of the Mormons in 1847, led by tyrannical king and politician James Jesse Strang, aroused resentment on the mainland, leading to dissolution of the colony by force in 1856. The island was eventually settled by Irish fishermen.

The island is popular for fishing and hunting. A museum occupies an 1850 print shop built by the Mormons. St. James, the former Mormon capital and a pleasant vacation spot, is accessible from Charlevoix (see place listing p. 50) by boat or plane.

BELLEVILLE—see Detroit p. 62.

BENZONIA (E-2) pop. 519

BENZIE AREA HISTORICAL MUSEUM is 1 blk. w. of US 31 at 6941 Traverse Ave. (River Rd.). Housed in a century-old church, the museum contains a large display about the farmers, fishermen, lumberjacks and sailors who tamed the northern Michigan wilderness. Exhibits about local author Bruce Catton and artist Gwen Frostic also are included. Allow 1 hour minimum. Mon.-Sat. 10-4, May-Dec.; closed holidays. Admission $2; under 13, 50c. Phone (231) 882-5539.

GWEN FROSTIC PRINTS is 2 mi. w. of US 31 on Traverse Ave. (River Rd.). A small wooden building is within a 285-acre wildlife sanctuary on the Betsie River. Carvings of wild birds and animals are among the collection and works of Gwen Frostic, an artist and poet specializing in nature themes. A nature library is available. Guided tours are given by reservation. Allow 30 minutes minimum. Daily 9-5:30, May-Oct.; Mon.-Sat. 9-4:30, rest of year. Presses make prints from original blocks Mon.-Fri. 9-5:30, May-Oct. Free. Phone (231) 882-5505.

BERRIEN SPRINGS (I-2)
pop. 1,862, elev. 671′

1839 COURTHOUSE MUSEUM is at Old US 31 and Union St. An 1870 sheriff's residence, an 1830s log house, a re-created county jail and the 1860 county office building are included. The 1839 courthouse contains local history exhibits and a courtroom restored to its original appearance. Allow 1 hour minimum. Tues.-Fri. 9-4, Sat.-Sun. 1-5. Free. Phone (269) 471-1202.

WINERIES
• **Lemon Creek Fruit Farm and Winery** is off I-94 exit 16, n. 2.5 mi. to Lemon Creek Rd., then 6 mi. e. to 533 Lemon Creek Rd. Mon.-Sat. 9-6, Sun. noon-6, May-Nov. Phone (269) 471-1321.

BESSEMER (B-1) pop. 2,148, elev. 1,437′

BLACK RIVER NATIONAL FOREST SCENIC BYWAY (CR 513) follows the winding course of the Black River to Lake Superior. The scenic 11-mile drive passes five waterfalls, which range from 25 to 40 feet high and are accessible by well-marked trails. Black River Harbor, at the end of Black River Drive, has picnicking and camping areas and a playground. Phone the Bessemer Rangers District, (906) 932-1330, for more information.

BLOOMFIELD HILLS—see Detroit p. 62.

BRIDGEPORT (G-4) pop. 7,849, elev. 610′

JUNCTION VALLEY RAILROAD is 2 mi. s. on Dixie Hwy. Two-mile train rides are offered on a railroad built to one-quarter size. Trains wind past buildings and across bridges built to scale. Visitors may depart the train at a park equipped with picnic tables and a playground and return on a later train. Special excursions are scheduled during the Halloween season.

Food is available. Allow 1 hour minimum. Mon.-Sat. 10-6, Sun. 1-6, mid-May through Labor Day; Sat.-Sun. 1-5, day after Labor Day-early Oct. Phone for holiday schedules. Fare $5.25; over 65, $5; ages 2-12, $4.50. Additional charge for special excursions. Phone (989) 777-3480.

BRIDGMAN (I-1) pop. 2,428

Hang gliders are a familiar sight in the sky south of Bridgman. Prevailing winds from Lake Michigan and a 240-foot vertical drop afforded by Tower Hill have made nearby Warren Dunes State Park *(see Recreation Chart)* a popular all-year locale for the sport. Flights more than an hour long have been recorded.

BRIMLEY (B-5) elev. 655′

CASINOS

• **Bay Mills Casino** is at 11386 W. Lakeshore. Daily 24 hours. Phone (906) 248-3701 or (906) 248-3720.

BUCHANAN (I-1) pop. 4,681, elev. 732′

BEAR CAVE is 4 mi. n. on Red Bud Tr. to 4085 Bear Cave Rd. The 150-foot-long tufa rock cave is accessible by a 40-foot winding stairway. A taped narration guides visitors past unique geological formations, among them the 250,000-year-old Kansan Boulder. The cave maintains a constant temperature of 58 F; suitable clothing is advised. Walkways are narrow, and visitors also should be aware that the cave contains bats. Allow 30 minutes minimum. Daily 10-4, Memorial Day-Labor Day. Admission $3; ages 5-11, $1.50. Phone (269) 695-3050.

WINERIES

• **Tabor Hill Winery** is at 185 Mt. Tabor Rd. Tours are available noon-4:30; closed Jan. 1 and Dec. 25. Phone (800) 283-3363.

CADILLAC (F-3) pop. 10,000, elev. 1,292′

Begun as a lumber camp in 1871, Cadillac was named for the founder of Detroit, Antoine de la Mothe Cadillac. The rolling terrain of the Huron-Manistee National Forests *(see place listing p. 75)* and the proximity of Cadillac and Mitchell lakes have made the town a popular recreational center.

Cadillac Area Visitors Bureau: 222 Lake St., Cadillac, MI 49601; phone (231) 775-0657 or (800) 225-2537.

JOHNNY'S WILD GAME AND FISH PARK is w. on I-55, s. on CR 3, then e. on 46½ Mile Rd. The park houses a variety of wild and domestic game animals in a natural setting. Visitors can feed and pet deer, goats, birds and other animals. Trout fishing and fish cleaning also are available. Allow 30

minutes minimum. Daily 10-6, Memorial Day-Labor Day. Admission $4.50; over 55, $4.25; ages 3-14, $4. Phone (231) 775-3700.

CALUMET (A-2) pop. 879, elev. 1,202′

CALUMET THEATRE is at 340 Sixth St. A variety of scheduled theater events are offered. The building opened in 1900 for stage performances and for a time was used as a motion picture theater. The theater is now used for concerts and stage performances. Tours are offered. Allow 30 minutes minimum. Tues.-Sat. 11-2, late May to mid-Sept.; closed holidays. Admission $4; ages 6-12, $2. Self-guiding tours $2. Phone (906) 337-2610.

COPPERTOWN MINING MUSEUM is on Red Jacket Rd., 2 blks. w. of US 41. A co-operating site of Keweenaw National Historical Park, Coppertown traces the evolution of mines and mining through displays of mining equipment. A simulated mine at the entrance provides a glimpse of the miner's world. Allow 30 minutes minimum. Mon.-Sat. 10-5, late May-early Oct. (also Sun. 12:30-4, July-Aug.). Admission $3; national parks pass holders $2; ages 12-18, $1. Phone (906) 337-4354.

CAMBRIDGE JUNCTION (I-4)

A nostalgic Irishman who settled in the rolling region around Cambridge Junction dubbed it Irish Hills. The significance of the junction, however, predated the area's name: Two major turnpikes from Detroit and Monroe converge en route to Chicago.

North of US 12 and west of SR 50 is Michigan International Speedway, the site of NASCAR and Indy-car races during the summer.

WALKER TAVERN HISTORIC SITE is at jct. US 12 and SR 50. The history of Michigan's stagecoach era is presented through exhibits, audiovisual presentations and walking tours. The tavern is an 1840s clapboard house that was used as a stagecoach stop on the Detroit to Chicago path. Picnicking is permitted. Daily 10-4, Memorial Day-Labor Day. Free. Phone (517) 467-4414.

CASPIAN (B-2) pop. 997

IRON COUNTY MUSEUM is 1.5 mi. s. of US 2 on SR 189, then e. on CR 424 to Museum Rd. Several outdoor complexes depict life in the late 1800s. Exhibits examine the lumber industry, farming, mining, transportation, domestic life and homesteading. Among the 22 structures are an 1890 train depot, the Caspian Mine Headframe Mining Memorial, a logging camp and the home of Carrie Jacobs-Bond, composer of such tunes as "I Love You Truly" and "End of a Perfect Day."

Mon.-Sat. and holidays 9-5, Sun. 1-5, June-Aug.; Mon.-Sat. 10-4, Sun. 1-4 in May and Sept. Admission $5; ages 5-18, $2.50. Phone (906) 265-2617 or (906) 265-3942.

CHARLEVOIX (D-3) pop. 2,994, elev. 592'

Its early history linked to the stormy affairs of the Mormon monarchy on Beaver Island *(see place listing p. 48)*, Charlevoix is an enterprising resort center. Lakes Michigan and Charlevoix offer excellent beaches and opportunities for boating. Round Lake, lying between the two, provides the city with its fine yacht harbor. The city offers band shell musical entertainment during July and August.

Charlevoix is on US 31, a scenic route that follows the shore between Traverse City and Petoskey.

Beaver Island Boat Co., 103 Bridge Park Dr., offers ferry service to Beaver Island; phone (231) 547-2311 or (888) 446-4095.

Charlevoix Area Chamber of Commerce: 408 Bridge St., P.O. Box 358, Charlevoix, MI 49720; phone (231) 547-2101.

CHEBOYGAN (D-4) pop. 5,295, elev. 600'

The crew members of the Coast Guard icebreaker *Mackinaw* make Cheboygan their home port. Specialized construction fits the ship for rescue towing as well as icebreaking; it is credited with extending the shipping season on the Great Lakes by 6 weeks. When in port, the *Mackinaw* is docked on the Cheboygan River; visitors are welcome.

This industrial and resort city is surrounded by some of Michigan's largest lakes. Mullett and Burt lakes, both noted for bass and muskellunge, are part of the historic inland waterway. The waterway became a major transportation link in the late 19th century after a lock was built at Cheboygan. Traffic consists of pleasure boaters, who can still cruise as far as Conway.

One of the Great Lakes' largest cattail marshes, a nesting site for 54 bird species, can be viewed from a boardwalk in Gordon Turner Park at the north end of Huron Street. The Mackinac Bridge and Round and Bois Blanc islands also can be seen from the boardwalk and from the nearby fishermen's walkway.

Cheboygan Area Chamber of Commerce: 124 N. Main St., P.O. Box 69, Cheboygan, MI 49721; phone (231) 627-7183 or (800) 968-3302.

HISTORICAL SOCIETY MUSEUM OF CHEBOYGAN COUNTY is at 404 S. Huron St. at the corner of Court St. The 1882, two-story brick structure, which includes a county jail, served as the sheriff's home until 1969. The parlor, kitchen, schoolroom and bedrooms are re-created in period style. Logging, railroad, veterans' and marine displays are included.

A flower garden, country store, schoolroom and a 19th-century furnished log cabin are on the grounds. Allow 30 minutes minimum. Mon.-Fri. 1-4, May 1-Oct. 5; otherwise by appointment. Admission $2, under 18 free. Phone (231) 627-9597, or (231) 627-5448 for appointments.

THE OPERA HOUSE is at 403 N. Huron St. The Victorian theater was constructed in 1877, rebuilt

following a fire in 1888 and restored in 1984. Mary Pickford, Annie Oakley and Marie Dressler were among the theater's actors and entertainers; it now plays host to local and professional entertainment and arts events. Guided tours are given Tues.-Fri. 1-4, June-Sept. Admission $1. Phone (231) 627-5432 or (231) 627-5841 for the box office.

CHESTERFIELD—*see Detroit p. 63.*

CHRISTMAS (B-4) elev. 619'

CASINOS

• **Christmas Kewadin Casino** is on SR 28. Daily 8 a.m.-3 a.m. Phone (906) 387-5475.

COLDWATER (I-3) pop. 12,697

From cabin to inn to village was the early progression of Coldwater, on the Chicago Turnpike, a primary east-west transportation route. By the 1880s the city had assumed its present character as a trading and supply center.

Branch County Chamber of Commerce: 20 Division St., Coldwater, MI 49036; phone (517) 278-5985.

TIBBITS OPERA HOUSE is at 14 S. Hanchett St. The theater opened in 1882 to house the many performers and theater companies that played Coldwater en route between Chicago and Detroit. Its excellent acoustics and sophisticated backstage equipment were widely acclaimed. The renovated French-Victorian building presents a variety of concerts and art exhibitions. Theater tours are available by request. Mon.-Fri. 9-5. Free. Phone (517) 278-6029.

CONCORD (I-3) pop. 1,101, elev. 940'

MANN HOUSE MUSEUM is .2 mi. s. of SR 60 at 205 Hanover St. The 1884 house contains Mann family heirlooms dating from 1840 and depicts family life in the Midwest during the Victorian period. A carriage house and Victorian and herb gardens are on the grounds. Guided tours are available. Allow 30 minutes minimum. Daily 10-4, Memorial Day-Labor Day. Free. Phone (517) 524-8943.

COOPERSVILLE (G-2) pop. 3,910

COOPERSVILLE AREA HISTORICAL SOCIETY MUSEUM is at 363 Main St. This former depot contains such area artifacts as a railroad collection and re-creations of a local drugstore and the interior of a one-room schoolhouse. An exhibit is dedicated to Del Shannon, a member of the Rock and Roll Hall of Fame and a Coopersville native. An additional building contains a sawmill exhibit. Guided tours are available by request. Allow 30 minutes minimum. Tues. 2-8, Sat. 10-4 (also Sun. 2-5, Aug. 1 to mid-Dec.). Donations. Phone (616) 837-6978.

COPPER HARBOR (A-3) elev. 621′

Tales of copper lying on the lakeshore first drew explorers, then miners, to the remote Keweenaw Peninsula. The deposits proved scant, and Copper Harbor lost its vitality as its mines, timber and port activity successively dwindled.

Michigan's northernmost community is a popular summer vacation spot. Boat trips to Isle Royale National Park *(see place listing p. 77)* are available mid-May to late September. Lake Superior and the surrounding woodlands can be viewed along the 9.5-mile Brockway Mountain Drive, which runs west from Copper Harbor and rejoins SR 26 about 10 miles east of Eagle Harbor.

The Astor House Museum at US 41 and SR 26 contains antique dolls, American Indian relics and local historic artifacts. The Estivant Pines, a grove of 100-foot-tall white pines, some 500 years old, grow along the Montreal River. *See Upper Peninsula p. 103.*

DELAWARE COPPER MINE TOUR is 12 mi. s. on US 41. Visitors can take a 45-minute underground walking tour into a mid-1800s copper mine where veins of copper can be seen. On the grounds are deer, llamas, rabbits and a skunk. The mine temperature averages 45 F; warm clothing is recommended. Allow 1 hour minimum. Guided tours depart every 20 minutes daily 10-5:15, July-Aug. Self-guiding tours are available daily 10-5, mid-May through June 30 and Sept. 1 to mid-Oct. Admission $9; ages 6-12, $5. Phone (906) 289-4688.

FORT WILKINS STATE PARK is 1 mi. e. on US 41. The 700-acre park contains the restored buildings of Fort Wilkins, the Army post established in 1844 to protect copper miners. The fort had no hostilities and was finally abandoned in 1870. Refurbished officers' quarters and other buildings can be visited; wildflower and historical exhibits also are included. From late June to late August costumed staff members portray life at the fort in the 1800s.

Allow 1 hour minimum. Daily 8-dusk, Memorial Day to mid-Oct. Park admission $4 per private vehicle. Round-trip fare to Copper Harbor Lighthouse $13; under 12, $8. Phone (906) 289-4215. *See Recreation Chart and the AAA Great Lakes CampBook.*

Copper Harbor Lighthouse is reached by boat departing from the Copper Harbor Marina, .5 mi. w. on SR 26. Visitors can see the 1866 Copper Harbor Lighthouse, the 1848 lighthouse keeper's house and a 1933 steel light tower. Transportation to the lighthouse is by narrated cruise. Boats depart the harbor daily 10-5 on the hour, July-Aug.; at 10, noon, 2 and 4, May-June and in Sept. Fare $13; under 12, $8. AX, DS, MC, VI. Phone (906) 289-4966 for the marina, or (906) 289-4215 for Fort Wilkins.

DEARBORN—*see Detroit p. 63*

DELTON (H-2) elev. 935′

BERNARD HISTORICAL MUSEUM is at 7135 W. Delton Rd. Displays housed in a 1930s hospital include artifacts and items used in the hospital. An 1873 schoolhouse, a 1900 country store and a blacksmith shop are nearby. A re-created seamstress cottage with sewing machines is featured. Also on the grounds are a working windmill, a marked nature trail, a barn with farm equipment and handmade tools, and a house where visiting medical professionals resided. Allow 1 hour minimum. Daily 1-5, July-Aug.; Sun. 1-5 in June and Sept. Donations. Phone (269) 623-2077.

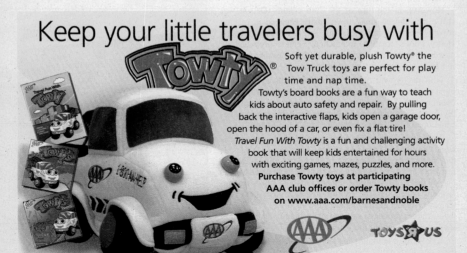

Detroit

One of the world's greatest automobile manufacturing cities, Detroit is an international symbol of America's productive might. The spirit of Detroit—the automobile and the assembly line—has spread around the globe, profoundly changing the lives of millions of people.

The French settled the city in 1701 and called it *d'etroit* or city "of straits," referring to the 27-mile Detroit River that connects lakes Erie and St. Clair. The Detroit River, a segment of the international border between the United States and Canada, marks the only point where Canada lies directly south of the United States. A remnant of the early settlement is Ste. Anne de Detroit Catholic Church. Its original log chapel was built in 1701. Another historic place of worship is the Old Mariners' Church at 170 E. Jefferson Ave. Built in 1849, it was moved to its present location in 1955 to make way for the construction of the civic center. Tours are available; phone (313) 259-2206.

Strategically located, Detroit was the objective of several major campaigns during the struggle for supremacy between the French and British. During the Revolutionary War the community served as Northwest headquarters for the British. The settlement took on new life following the War of 1812; the launching in 1818 of the first steam vessel on the Great Lakes and the subsequent expansion of shipbuilding and commerce helped to assure the future prosperity of the city.

However, at the turn of the 20th century Detroit was still a tree-shaded small town busily engaged in making stoves, beer and carriages. This serenity was broken by Henry Ford's creation, a practical vehicle propelled by power generated from within itself, the wheezing, sputtering Model T. Detroit was never the same.

With the growth of the automobile industry the town burst its river-hugging confines and absorbed surrounding communities. To augment local manpower for the assembly lines, Detroit turned to Europe for help and soon became one of the largest cities in the United States.

While still recovering from rapid growth and expansion, the city has recast its image. Although such tags as the Motor City are foremost in outsiders' minds, Detroit residents are eager to point out that the port of Detroit is one of the world's busiest inland ports and ranks high in customs collection. The Detroit area is a great steel center and a leader in the manufacture of office equipment, paint, rubber products, salt and more than half the garden seed used throughout the country.

A polyglot community pulled together by high aspirations and hard work, Detroit has many sports and cultural activities. The city boasts a civic center complex, the Renaissance Center, as well as varied sports facilities, an

Greenfield Village, Dearborn / © Detroit Metro CVB

Renaissance Center / © SuperStock

excellent park system and numerous theaters, museums and galleries.

The Detroit Civic Center covers 75 acres along the downtown riverfront. The center includes Cobo Conference/ Exhibition Center, phone (313) 877-8111; Cobo Arena, phone (313) 983-6616; Joe Louis Arena, phone (313) 983-6606; and Renaissance Center, phone (313) 568-5600.

Approaches

By Car

Interstate highway systems provide speedy access to Detroit from the north, south and west. I-75 enters Detroit from the south and the north; SR 10 also enters from the north. Approaching from the west and the northeast is I-94; also entering from the west is I-96. From the east, Canadian Hwy. 401 becomes SR 3 when entering Detroit from Windsor, Ontario, via the toll bridge, and SR 3B when entering via the toll tunnel.

Getting Around

Street System

City planners originally patterned Detroit after Washington, D.C., but abandoned this plan during its rapid growth. Instead, planners superimposed the basic grid system on Detroit's downtown streets. The result is confusing to drivers; since most of the downtown streets are one-way, a detailed map is necessary. Detroit's freeway system provides access to points within the city. Rush hours, 7-9 and 4-6:30, should be avoided.

Parking

Metered parking is minimal in downtown Detroit; most of the 8,000 meters are in the fringe areas. To compensate for this, Detroit has many municipal and privately operated parking lots and garages. Rates range from approximately $1 to $2.50 for the first hour and average 50c to 85c for each additional hour. Some offer flat daily rates of $3.50 to $8, with reduced fees for evenings and during events.

Public Transportation

Considering the confusing maze of downtown streets and the hectic pace of traffic, Detroit's Department of Transportation might be the answer to getting from one place to another with minimal frustration. Bus fare is generally $1.50, plus 25c for each transfer. For schedules and routes phone (313) 933-1300.

For those who would like to ride in a different style, antique red and brass trolleys run from Times Square to the Renaissance Center Mon.-Fri. 7-6, Sat.-Sun. 10-6, May-Nov. (weather permitting). An English double-decker trolley travels the same route Memorial Day to Labor Day. Hours are extended

(continued on p. 55)

The Informed Traveler

City Population: 951,270

Elevation: 635 ft.

WHOM TO CALL

Emergency: 911

Police (non-emergency): (313) 267-4600

Time: (313) 472-1111

Hospitals: Detroit Receiving Hospital, (313) 745-3600; Harper Hospital, (313) 745-8040; Henry Ford Hospital, (313) 916-2600.

WHERE TO LOOK

Newspapers

The two daily newspapers—*News* and *Free Press*—are supplemented with a variety of weekly papers.

Radio

Detroit radio station WWJ (950 AM) is an all-news/weather station; WDET (101.9 FM) is a member of National Public Radio.

Visitor Information

Maps, brochures, calendars of events, lists of sightseeing companies and hotel location maps are available from the visitors bureau. Write Detroit Metro Convention and Visitors Bureau, 211 W. Fort St., Suite 1000, Detroit, MI 48226; phone (313) 202-1800 or (800) 338-7648.

TRANSPORTATION

Air Travel

Major commercial airlines have regularly scheduled flights to the Detroit Metropolitan Airport, 21 miles west of downtown. Allow approximately 45 minutes travel time to the airport. Van service from downtown hotels to the airport is available daily by reservation. The one-way cost is $19. For information phone Commuter Express, (888) 854-6700.

Rental Cars

Car rental companies may be found at the airport. Hertz, (800) 654-3131, offers discounts to AAA members.

Rail Service

Amtrak Stations are at 11 W. Baltimore Ave. in the New Center area, in Dearborn at 16121 Michigan Ave. and at Greenfield Village. Train service to various parts of the country is provided; phone (800) 872-7245.

Buses

Greyhound Lines Inc. serves Detroit. The terminal is at 1001 Howard St.; for information about fares and schedules phone (800) 231-2222.

Taxis

Taxis operate on a meter system; the basic charge is $2.50, plus $1.60 per mile. There is no extra charge for additional riders. The two largest companies are Checker Cab, (313) 963-7000, and City Cab, (313) 833-7060.

Boats

Detroit, one of the world's busiest inland freight ports, is linked by 25 steamship companies to more than 40 countries worldwide. Vessels ranging from ocean-going freighters to private craft dock in Detroit's well-protected harbor.

during events and shortened during winter months. The fare is 50c each way; phone (313) 224-6449.

The automated People Mover, a 2.9-mile elevated light-rail system, operates through the central business district, including the Civic Center, Mon.-Thurs. 7 a.m.-11 p.m., Fri. 7 a.m.-midnight, Sat. 9 a.m.-midnight, Sun. noon-8. Hours are extended during events. The fare is 50c, under 5 free, and must be in exact change or tokens. For more information phone (313) 962-7245.

What To See

CHARLES H. WRIGHT MUSEUM OF AFRICAN AMERICAN HISTORY is at 315 E. Warren Ave. Exhibits include Mae Jemison's NASA flight suit, a replica of Dr. Martin Luther King's Birmingham jailhouse door and numerous other artifacts. Two galleries feature changing exhibits. A research library and archives contain materials relating to African and American history.

Allow 1 hour minimum. Wed.-Sat. 9:30-5, Sun. 1-5; closed major holidays. Admission $5; under 18, $3. Phone (313) 494-5800.

[SAVE] **DETROIT HISTORICAL MUSEUM** is at 5401 Woodward Ave. at Kirby Ave. The museum depicts lifestyle changes of the average American from 1701 to the 1900s. Reconstructions of early streets, historic model railroads and period automobiles trace Detroit's growth from American Indian settlement to the present. Films and educational programs are offered.

Allow 1 hour minimum. Tues.-Fri. 9:30-5, Sat.-Sun. 10-5; closed major holidays except Easter. Admission $5; senior citizens and ages 5-18, $3; $1 for all on Wed. Phone (313) 833-1805.

[GEM] **THE DETROIT INSTITUTE OF ARTS** is at 5200 Woodward Ave. at Farnsworth Ave. [SAVE] Exhibits trace the development of art from ancient to modern times. Notable are 17th-century Dutch and Flemish paintings, the William Hearst Collection of armor, the Tannahill Collection of impressionist paintings, the Pre-Columbian Native American Art exhibit, the G. Mennen Williams collection of African art and Diego Rivera's Detroit industry murals.

Films are shown Friday through Monday evenings; programs and concerts also are presented. Guided tours are available. Allow 1 hour, 30 minutes minimum. Galleries open Wed.-Fri. 10-4 (also Fri. 4-9), Sat.-Sun. 10-5; closed holidays. Tours are given Wed.-Sat. at 1, Sun. at 1 and 2:30. Admission $4, ages 6-17, $1. Phone (313) 833-7900.

DETROIT PUBLIC LIBRARY is at 5201 Woodward Ave. at Kirby Ave. The Italian Renaissance building features white Vermont marble. Murals by Edwin H. Blashfield and Gari Melchers, painted-glass windows designed by Frederick J. Wiley, mosaic panels depicting Shakespeare's "Seven Ages of Man" and Pewabic tiles adorn the interior. The Burton Historical Collection in the rare book room also is of interest. The National Automotive History Collection is open limited hours. Library open Tues.-Wed. noon-8, Thurs.-Sat. 10-6; closed holidays. Free. Phone (313) 833-1000.

[SAVE] **DETROIT SCIENCE CENTER** is at 5020 John R. St. at Warren Ave. in the midtown cultural center. The hands-on science center features an IMAX theater and a digital dome planetarium. Physics-related programs are presented on the Science Stage, and electrical demonstrations are the focus in the Sparks Theater. Exhibit laboratories explore matter and energy; waves and vibration; life sciences; and mechanics and motion. Classrooms offer hands-on activities about applied, earth, life, physical and space sciences.

Allow 2 hours minimum. Tues.-Fri. 9-3, Sat.-Sun. 10:30-6, June-Aug.; Tues.-Fri. 9-3, Sat. 10:30-6, Sun. noon-6, rest of year. Closed major holidays. Admission $7; over 60 and ages 2-12, $6. IMAX theater and planetarium $4 extra. Parking $5. AX, MC, VI. Phone (313) 577-8400.

GRAND CIRCUS PARK is at Adams and Woodward aves. This park has defined the northern limit of the downtown area since the 1860s. There are two notable statues and a fountain, illuminated in summer, that honor Thomas Edison. Trolley car rides to Grand Circus Park leave from the Renaissance Center, Cobo Conference/Exhibition Center and Cobo Arena *(see Getting Around, Public Transportation)*. Daily 24 hours. Free.

MOTOWN HISTORICAL MUSEUM is at 2648 W. Grand Blvd. The Motown sound of the early 1960s originated in this old brick house that now houses the museum. Such entertainers as Marvin Gaye, Smokey Robinson, Diana Ross and the Supremes, and Stevie Wonder got their starts here under the direction of Motown Records founder Berry Gordy Jr. The galleries contain a variety of musical instruments, photographs, artifacts and the original Studio A and control room.

Tues.-Sat. 10-6; otherwise by appointment. Closed major holidays. Admission $8; under 13, $5. Phone (313) 875-2264.

PEWABIC POTTERY is at 10125 E. Jefferson Ave. The ceramics museum, gallery, workshop and studio offers changing contemporary exhibits. A collection of historic work by Mary Chase Perry Stratton, Pewabic's founder, also is displayed. Mon.-Sat. 10-6; closed holidays. Free. Phone (313) 822-0954.

CASINOS

- **MGM Grand** is at 1300 John C. Lodge. Daily 24 hours. Phone (313) 393-7777.

- **Motor City Casino** is at 2901 Grand River Ave. Daily 24 hours. Phone (313) 237-7711 or (877) 777-0711. *See color ad p. 61.*

Destination Detroit

*I*t's the Motor City. Motown's hometown. And an inland port on par with some of the world's busiest.

*B*ut diverse Detroit is much more than an industrial hub. Also assembled here are cultural diversions, professional sports teams and a wealth of sites embracing wonders of progress and reminders of the past.

© Layne Kennedy / Corbis

Detroit Zoological Park, Royal Oak. Perched on a tall, nearly-natural cliff, resident lions scope out the happenings in the rest of the zoo. (See listing page 64)

The Detroit Institute of Arts

The Detroit Institute of Arts, Detroit. Vincent van Gogh's "Self-Portrait with Straw Hat" is one of many prestigious works of art on display at the museum. (See listing page 55)

See Vicinity map page 58

Waterford •

West Bloomfield

Walled Lake

96 Farmington Hills

Novi 102

Northville Livonia

14 Plymouth 96

275

23 94

Belleville 275

*P*laces included in this AAA Destination City:

Charles H. Wright Museum of African American History, Detroit. Outstanding African Americans are honored here, and archives preserve past lessons. (See listing page 55)

Henry Ford Museum & Greenfield Village, Dearborn. Is it 1920? Tunes from a banjo mingle with the swish of the paddlewheel on the *Suwanee,* which takes guests around a peaceful lagoon. (See listing page 63)

See Downtown Inset page 58

© Ralf-Finn Hestoft
Corbis-Saba

Automotive Hall of Fame, Dearborn. Walter P. Chrysler and Henry Ford were among the hall's first inductees; recent honorees include Joe Girard, who holds the world record for one-on-one retail automobile sales—18 in one day! (See listing page 63)

2174-B

What To Do

Sightseeing

Various tours encompassing the city and its environs are available; the most economical is by bus. [SAVE] Gray Line Bus Tours, based at 1301 E. Warren Ave., makes regularly scheduled visits to many of the city's points of interest. Phone (313) 870-5012.

Boat Tours

[SAVE] **DIAMOND JACK'S RIVER TOURS** departs from docks at both Hart Plaza and Bishop Park in Wyandotte *(see place listing p. 65)*. Passengers ride on a former Mackinac Island ferry for a 2-hour narrated cruise. The Detroit trip passes historic and modern buildings, shipyards and downtown Windsor, Ontario, as well as under the Ambassador Bridge and around Belle Isle. The Wyandotte trip focuses on nature and wildlife.

Allow 2 hours minimum. Cruises depart from Hart Plaza or Bishop Park Thurs.-Sun. at 1 and 3:30, mid-June through Sun. before Labor Day. Passengers should arrive 30 minutes before departure. Fare for either trip $14; senior citizens $12; ages 6-16, $10. Parking is available in nearby garages; fees vary. Phone (313) 843-9376, ext. 100. *See ad.*

Sports and Recreation

Sports enthusiasts can watch the Detroit Tigers **baseball** team at Comerica Park, (313) 962-4000, and the Lions **football** team at Ford Field, (313) 262-2000 or (313) 262-2003 for ticket information. The Palace of Auburn Hills is the home of the Detroit Pistons **basketball** team; phone (248) 377-0100. The 2001-02 Stanley Cup champion Red Wings **hockey** team challenges rivals in the Joe Louis Arena; phone (313) 983-6606. Since Detroit sports are popular, tickets should be ordered at least a month before the scheduled date of the event.

Harness racing can be enjoyed at Northville Downs, (248) 349-1000; Hazel Park Harness Raceway, (248) 398-1000; and Windsor Raceway in Windsor, Ontario, (313) 961-9545 or (519) 969-8311.

Note: Policies concerning admittance of children to pari-mutuel betting facilities vary. Phone ahead for information.

Several public courses offer **golf** in Detroit: Chandler Park, 12801 Chandler Park Dr., (313) 331-7755; Palmer Park, Woodward at Seven Mile Road, (313) 883-2525; Rackham, 10100 W. Ten Mile Rd. in Huntington Woods, (248) 543-4040; Rogell, 18601 Berg Rd., (313) 578-8006; and Rouge Park, 11701 Burt Rd., (313) 837-5900.

Swimming is permitted at Belle Isle and at the mile-long Metropolitan Beach Metropark; phone (586) 463-4581. Twelve other metro parks have playgrounds and facilities for swimming, golfing, **boating, ice skating, picnicking** and nature study. Many parks have courts for **tennis** and **shuffleboard** in addition to winter recreation facilities.

Shopping

From an automobile right off the assembly line to an ice cream cone from a vendor; from imported, pewter-topped, glazed beer steins to poodle shampoos—all these and much more can be purchased in Detroit. The Stores of Renaissance Center are popular with shoppers.

Suburban shopping centers contain many major department store chains and smaller specialty shops and theaters. Among the largest malls are Eastland, at SR 102 (Eight Mile Road) and Kelly Road; Fairlane Town Center, at SR 39 (Southfield) and US 12 (Michigan Avenue) in Dearborn; Lakeside, at SR 59 (Hall Road) and Schoenherr in Sterling Heights; Northland, north of SR 102 at SR 10 (Northwestern Highway); The Somerset Collection and Somerset North, at Big Beaver (Sixteen Mile Road) and Coolidge in Troy; Southland, at Eureka and Pardee roads in Taylor; Twelve Oaks Mall, off I-96 Novi Road exit in Novi; and Westland, at Wayne Road and Warren Avenue.

Bass Pro Shops Outdoor World, in Great Lakes Crossing Mall at 4500 Baldwin Rd. in Auburn Hills, features a waterfall, 30,000-gallon aquarium, wildlife exhibits and sporting demonstrations;

phone (248) 209-4200. The mall features more than
200 stores, restaurants and entertainment facilities.

Theater and Concerts

The industrial side of Detroit is tempered by the
city's notable cultural offerings. The Detroit Symphony plays a full season of concerts, including
children's concerts at Orchestra Hall; phone (313)
576-5111. Throughout the year the following theaters offer a variety of stage presentations, including concert artists, drama, opera and dance: Fox
Theatre, (313) 471-3200; the Masonic Temple,
(313) 832-2232; and the Music Hall Center for the
Performing Arts, (313) 963-7622.

Detroit ranks high in sales of theater tickets. Professional repertory, including first-run and off-
Broadway productions, can be enjoyed at the Fisher
Theater at 3001 W. Grand Blvd.; phone (313)
872-1000. Evening and matinee performances are
offered at the Detroit Repertory Theatre; phone
(313) 868-1347.

Other area theaters offer concerts and plays spon-
sored by the drama departments of the University
of Detroit-Mercy, (313) 993-1130, and Wayne State
University, (313) 577-2960 or (313) 577-2972.
Among the area's popular suburban theaters are the
Meadowbrook Music Festival, (248) 475-5668; the
DTE Energy Music Theatre, (248) 377-0100; the
Palace of Auburn Hills, (248) 377-0100; and the
Freedom Hill Amphitheatre, 14900 Metropolitan
Pkwy. in Freedom Hill County Park, Sterling
Heights, (586) 268-5100.

Several first-run multiple cinemas dot the suburbs. Local newspapers carry complete information
concerning concerts, theater, movies and other
events.

Special Events

Summers in Detroit, though at times hot and hu-
mid, are celebrated with a variety of events. Festivities begin with Flower Day at Eastern Market in
May.

In late June and early July, Detroit and Windsor,
Ontario, share the International Freedom Festival,
considered to be the largest transborder festival in
North America. The two holidays celebrated are
Canada Day, July 1, and Independence Day, July 4.
Sports events, concerts, fireworks, parades and cul-
tural arts and craft shows take place during the two-
week-long celebration.

The Michigan State Fair follows in late August.
For music lovers the Detroit International Jazz
Festival is presented over Labor Day weekend.
Initiating the holiday season is the Michigan
Thanksgiving Day Parade on Thanksgiving Day.

Up all night.

MotorCity
CASINO The pulse of Detroit.

Detroit, Michigan • 1-877-777-0711 • motorcitycasino.com

The Detroit Vicinity

AUBURN HILLS (K-5) pop. 19,837, elev. 975′

SAVE **WALTER P. CHRYSLER MUSEUM** is off I-75 exit 78, then 1.3 mi. e. to One Chrysler Dr. Interactive displays and vignettes relate the history of Walter P. Chrysler and the Chrysler Corporation. Seventy cars, including restored classics, muscle cars, trucks and race cars, are on display. Visitors may watch three 7-minute films in the theater. Allow 30 minutes minimum. Tues.-Sat. 10-6, Sun. noon-6; closed holidays. Admission $6; over 61 and ages 6-12, $3; Chrysler employees and retirees free. AX, MC, VI. Phone (888) 456-1924. *See ad.*

BELLEVILLE (I-5) pop. 3,997, elev. 670′

YANKEE AIR MUSEUM is off I-94 exit 190, 1 mi. n. to Tyler Rd., 1 mi. w. to Beck Rd., then .8 mi. n. to the Willow Run Airport gate. The museum features a number of displays describing the history of the Willow Run B-24 Liberator production facilities as well as rooms dedicated to the history of flight and women in flight. Nearly 25 aircraft can be seen, including a Boeing B-52D Stratofortress. Allow 30 minutes minimum. Mon.-Sat. 10-4, Sun. noon-4, Apr.-Dec.; closed holidays. Admission $7; over 62 and ages 13-19, $5. Phone (734) 483-4030.

BLOOMFIELD HILLS (K-5) pop. 3,940

In 1819 Judge Amasa Bagley cleared land for a tavern and a farm on what was to become known as Bagley's Corner. It remained an agricultural center until about 1900 when city dwellers from Detroit began to buy acreage for estates. In 1932 the name was changed to Bloomfield Hills.

Among the wealthy who were attracted to this quiet community during the first decade of the 20th century were the publisher of *The Detroit News*, George G. Booth, and his wife, Ellen Scripps Booth. Their estate, Cranbrook, has become a notable cultural and educational center.

CRANBROOK EDUCATIONAL COMMUNITY is on Woodward Ave. (SR 1). The 315-acre campus includes a graduate art school and lower, middle and upper schools. Architect Eliel Saarinen designed many of the buildings. The fountains and statuary include works by sculptor Carl Milles.

SAVE **Cranbrook Art Museum** is at 39221 Woodward Ave. (SR 1). Changing displays of contemporary art as well as faculty and student artwork are the focus of the museum's collection. Traveling exhibitions are featured throughout the year. Allow 1 hour minimum. Tues.-Sun. 11-5 (also fourth Fri. of the month 5-9); closed major holidays. Admission $6, over 65 and ages 13-19, $4. Phone (248) 645-3323.

SAVE **Cranbrook House and Gardens** is at 380 Lone Pine Rd. Designed by Albert Kahn, the Arts and Crafts-style house is situated on 40 acres that include formal plantings, woods, sculpture, fountains, pine walks and two lakes. Allow 1 hour minimum. House tours Thurs. at 11 and 1:15, Sun. at 3, June-Oct. Gardens daily 10-5, May-Aug.; daily 11-3 in Sept.; Sat.-Sun. 11-3 in Oct. House $10; over 65, $8. Gardens $6, over 65 and students with ID $5, under 5 free. Phone (248) 645-3147.

Cranbrook Institute of Science is at 39221 Woodward Ave. (SR 1). This museum of science and natural history boasts one of the country's largest mineral collections as well as a planetarium and the Bat Zone. Interactive and hands-on exhibits demonstrate such physical principles as the laws of gravity, motion and plate techtonics and the creation of minerals and the Earth's crust. Laser light shows also are offered.

Allow 2 hours minimum. Daily 10-5 (also Fri. 5-10); closed Jan. 1, July 4 and Dec. 24. Laser shows Fri. at 7 p.m. and 9 p.m., Sat.-Sun. at 2 and 4. Astronomy shows Fri. at 8 p.m., Sat.-Sun. at 11:30, 12:30 and 3. Admission $7; over 65 and ages 2-12, $5. Astronomy shows extra $3. Laser shows extra $3, under 2 free. DS, MC, VI. Phone (248) 645-3200 or (877) 462-7262.

CHESTERFIELD (K-6) pop. 37,405

LIONEL VISITORS CENTER is off I-94 exit 243, then 2 mi. w. on 23 Mile Rd. Tours are offered of the operating model train display in the visitor center. Following a 10-minute videotape presentation, visitors have access to the interactive exhibit, featuring up to 16 trains operating simultaneously on more than 1,000 feet of track. Other operating models also are shown.

Allow 1 hour minimum. Tours are given Wed.-Thurs. at 10, 3 and 4, Fri. at 10, 1:30 and 2:30, Sat. at 10, 11 and noon; closed major holidays and holiday weekends. Free. Reservations are required. Phone (586) 949-4100.

DEARBORN (L-4) pop. 97,775, elev. 604'

While its giant neighbor Detroit absorbed adjoining townships, Dearborn—itself created from the merger of Fordson and Dearborn—did not lose its identity. It had a giant of its own, Henry Ford, who put Dearborn on the map by putting the nation on wheels.

Dearborn Chamber of Commerce: 15544 Michigan Ave., Dearborn, MI 48126; phone (313) 584-6100.

AUTOMOTIVE HALL OF FAME is at 21400 Oakwood Blvd. adjacent to the Henry Ford Museum. Plaques and memorabilia are dedicated to the men and women of the automotive industry. Honorees include designers, educators, inventors, journalists, manufacturers, race car drivers and automotive association members. A transportation display, library and archives also are available.

Allow 1 hour, 30 minutes minimum. Daily 10-5, Memorial Day-Oct. 31; Tues.-Sun. 10-5, rest of year. Closed Jan. 1, Thanksgiving and Dec. 25. Admission $6; over 62, $5; ages 5-18, $3. Phone (313) 240-4000. *See color ad p. 60.*

DEARBORN HISTORICAL MUSEUM has collections at 21950 Michigan Ave. and 915 Brady St. The museum includes two buildings of the original United States Government Arsenal. An exhibit annex has farm equipment, wagons and buggies. The commandant's quarters and the McFadden-Ross House date from the early 1800s and contain period furnishings. The Richard Gardner House, built in 1831 and furnished in period, belonged to the family of Henry Ford's childhood friend Richard Gardner. Allow 30 minutes minimum. Mon.-Sat. 9-5, May-Oct.; 1-5, rest of year. Closed holidays. Free. Phone (313) 565-3000.

HENRY FORD ESTATE—FAIR LANE is on the campus of the University of Michigan-Dearborn at 4901 Evergreen Rd. Tours of the mansion and powerhouse are given. The Fords entertained such luminaries as Charles Lindbergh, the Duke of Windsor and President Herbert Hoover in their spacious mansion. The powerhouse, the combined creation of Ford and Thomas Edison, gave the estate the independence to produce its own power, heat and light. Gardens and trails are on the grounds.

Food is available. Allow 1 hour, 30 minutes minimum. Tours depart Mon.-Sat. at 10, 11, 1, 2 and 3, Sun. every 30 minutes 1-4:30, Apr.-Dec.; Mon.-Fri. at 1, Sun. every 30 minutes 1-4:30, rest of year. Closed Jan. 1, Easter, Thanksgiving and Dec. 24-25. Admission $8; over 62, $7; ages 5-12, $5. Phone (313) 593-5590.

HENRY FORD MUSEUM & GREENFIELD VILLAGE is at 20900 Oakwood Blvd. at Village Rd. The 93-acre complex serves as a monument to American innovation and enterprise. Collections explore nearly 3 centuries of communications, transportation, industry, agriculture and domestic life.

The museum includes the Rosa Parks bus; the chair in which Abraham Lincoln was assassinated; and a folding camp bed used by George Washington during the Revolutionary War. Fifteen historic aircraft are displayed.

Exhibits in Greenfield Village span more than 300 years. The 81-acre site includes steam locomotives, a steamboat and houses once owned by Noah Webster, the Wright brothers and Henry Ford. Harvey Firestone's boyhood farmstead now is a working 1880s farm.

An IMAX theater is housed in the visitor center, and the Ford Rouge Factory Tour highlights the history of automobile manufacturing.

Light clothing and comfortable shoes are recommended. Food is available. Allow a full day. Museum open daily 10-5. Village open daily 10-9, mid-June to late Aug.; 10-5, late Aug.-Dec. 31 and Apr. 1 to mid-June. Both closed Jan. 1, Thanksgiving and Dec. 25. Admission (includes museum and village) $24; over 60, $22; ages 5-12, $18. Factory tour and IMAX $10; over 60, $9; ages 5-12, $8.50. AX, DS, MC, VI. Phone (313) 982-6001 or (800) 835-5237 (outside 313 area code). *See color ad p. 60.*

FARMINGTON HILLS (K-4) pop. 82,111

MARVIN'S MARVELOUS MECHANICAL MUSEUM is at 31005 Orchard Lake Rd. Displays include antique slot and pinball machines and other mechanical memorabilia and video games, including nickelodeons, vintage neon signs and magic show posters. Mon.-Thurs. 10-10, Fri.-Sat. 10 a.m.-11 p.m., Sun. 11-9. Free. Phone (248) 626-5020.

GROSSE POINTE SHORES (L-6)
pop. 2,823, elev. 586'

EDSEL & ELEANOR FORD HOUSE is 1.5 mi. e. from I-94 Vernier/Eight Mile exit, then 1 mi. n. on Lake Shore Rd. The 60-room house, styled after houses in the Cotswold area of England, was built 1926-29 by the Ford Motor Co. executive and his wife. The estate and landscaped grounds were created to accommodate their family and an extensive collection of fine and decorative arts. Twenty of the rooms are shown on guided tours that begin with a 15-minute videotape presentation in the Activities Center.

Allow 2 hours minimum. Tours are given on the half-hour Tues.-Sat. 10-4, Sun. noon-4, Apr.-Dec.; Tues.-Sun. noon-4, rest of year. Admission $6; over 59, $5; ages 6-12, $4. Phone (313) 884-4222.

LIVONIA (L-4) pop. 100,545, elev. 638'

GREENMEAD HISTORICAL PARK is at jct. Eight Mile and Newburgh rds. at 20501 Newburgh Rd. Tours of up to nine historical buildings are offered. Picnic facilities are available on the 95-acre farm site. Allow 2 hours minimum. Grounds open daily dawn-dusk. Tours of historic buildings Sun. 1-4, May-Oct. and in Dec. Closed holiday weekends. Admission $3, students with ID $2; under 18, $1. Phone (248) 477-7375.

NOVI (L-4) pop. 47,386, elev. 909'

MOTORSPORTS MUSEUM AND HALL OF FAME is inside the Novi Expo Center at the s.w. corner of I-96 and Novi Rd. The museum contains motorized race vehicles, including stock cars, boats, trucks, motorcycles and Indy cars. Racing videotapes, uniforms and memorabilia also are on display. Visitors can try slot car racing. Allow 1 hour minimum. Daily 10-5, Memorial Day-Labor Day; Thurs.-Sun. 10-5, rest of year. Closed Easter and Dec. 25. Admission $4; over 60 and under 12, $2. Slot cars extra. MC, VI. Phone (248) 349-7223.

PLYMOUTH (L-3) pop. 9,022, elev. 741'

Plymouth was founded in 1867 by a group of settlers from Plymouth, Mass. Their Colonial influence can still be seen in the town's architecture.

Plymouth Community Chamber of Commerce: 386 S. Main St., Plymouth, MI 48170; phone (734) 453-1540.

[SAVE] **PLYMOUTH HISTORICAL MUSEUM** is 1 blk. n. of Kellogg Park at 155 S. Main St. The history of early Plymouth is explored. A gallery houses Main Street shops and offices and reflects many trades and professions of 19th-century

Plymouth. Highlights include the Abraham Lincoln and Victorian Rooms exhibits. The 15,000-square-foot museum has what is said to be the only Alter car, built in Plymouth 1916-17. A collection of Daisy air rifles also is displayed.

Allow 1 hour minimum. Wed.-Thurs. and Sat.-Sun. 1-4. Admission $3, students with ID $1; family rate $7. Phone (734) 455-8940.

PONTIAC (K-4) pop. 66,337, elev. 933'

Pontiac was established in 1818 where the Pontiac Trail crossed the Clinton River. Settlers began pouring in, and by the 1880s the city entertained a major wagon and carriage making industry. In a sense, it still does: What began as the Pontiac Spring Wagon Works is known as General Motors. The Pontiac Division of General Motors perpetuates the name of the great Ottawa Indian chief who reputedly spent his summers at nearby Orchard Lake.

A number of municipal parks and more than 400 nearby lakes that arc around the western side of the city offer outdoor recreation.

Greater Pontiac Area Chamber of Commerce: 30 N. Saginaw, Suite 404, Pontiac, MI 48342; phone (248) 335-9600.

ROCHESTER (K-5) pop. 10,467, elev. 745'

Although on the fringe of metropolitan Detroit, Rochester lies among wooded hills—an apt home for Oakland University.

Rochester Regional Chamber of Commerce: 71 Walnut Blvd., Suite 110, Rochester, MI 48307; phone (248) 651-6700.

[GEM] **OAKLAND UNIVERSITY'S MEADOW BROOK HALL** is 3 mi. e. via Walton Blvd., then .3 mi. s. on Adams Rd. on the eastern campus of Oakland University. This 1920s Tudor Revival-style mansion was once the residence of Matilda Dodge Wilson and lumber broker Alfred G. Wilson. The 80,000-square-foot, 100-room home boasts a two-story ballroom, 24 fireplaces, hand-carved paneling, sculptured ceilings and many original furnishings and works of art.

Knole Cottage, also on the premises, is a brick six-room playhouse built for the Wilson's daughter. It is furnished in the same style as Meadow Brook Hall.

Allow 1 hour, 30 minutes minimum. Guided tours are given daily every 45 minutes 10:30-3, Memorial Day-Labor Day; Mon.-Fri. at 1:30, Sat.-Sun. at 12:30, 1:30 and 2:30, rest of year. Admission $15; over 61, $10.50; ages 5-12, $8.50. Prices slightly higher during events. Phone (248) 370-3140.

ROYAL OAK (K-5) pop. 60,062, elev. 661'

DETROIT ZOOLOGICAL PARK is at 8450 W. Ten Mile Rd. at Woodward Ave. One of the most modern zoos in the country, it features spacious, open exhibits. Designed

to simulate natural environments, habitats are laid out over 125 acres of landscaped grounds. Highlights are a 4-acre great ape complex, a snow monkey area with a hot spring, a reptile house, a free-flight aviary and penguin and polar bear exhibits.

A miniature railroad carries passengers across the grounds. A hands-on learning center also is available. The Wildlife Interpretive Gallery features art and an indoor butterfly garden.

Picnicking is permitted. Food is available. Allow 4 hours minimum. Daily 10-5, Apr.-Oct.; 10-4, rest of year. Closed Jan. 1, Thanksgiving and Dec. 25. Admission $9; over 62 and ages 2-12, $6. Parking $5. AX, MC, VI. Phone (248) 398-0900.

NATIONAL SHRINE OF THE LITTLE FLOWER is at jct. SR 1 (Woodward Ave.) and Twelve Mile Rd. at 2123 Roseland Ave. The shrine became known through the radio broadcasts of its pastor, Father Charles E. Coughlin, now deceased. A striking feature is the 90-foot crucifixion tower, girded by four crosses; below the figure is a carving of the last words of Christ.

The church is built of granite and limestone interspersed with stone blocks from America's states and territories; on each is carved the state name and flower. Guided tours are available by appointment. Allow 30 minutes minimum. Mon.-Fri. 6 a.m.-7:30 p.m., Sat. 7:30-7:30, Sun. 6:30 a.m.-7:30 p.m. Free. Phone (248) 541-4122.

WALLED LAKE (K-3) pop. 6,713

COE RAIL SCENIC TRAIN is at the Railroad Depot at 840 N. Pontiac Tr. One-hour train rides in vintage cars are offered through scenic Walled Lake and West Bloomfield. Trips depart Sun. at 1 and 2:30, late Apr.-late Oct. Fare $9; over 65 and ages 2-10, $8. Phone (248) 960-9440.

WATERFORD (K-4) pop. 73,150

DRAYTON PLAINS NATURE CENTER is at jct. US 24 (Dixie) and Hatchery Rd., following signs to 2125 Denby Dr. An interpretive center displays mounted animals in re-creations of their natural habitats. The surrounding grounds encompass 137 acres along the Clinton River and feature 4 miles of marked trails. Allow 30 minutes minimum. Grounds open dawn-dusk. Interpretive center open Mon.-Fri. 11-5, Sat. 11-4, Sun. noon-4. Closed major holidays. Donations. Phone (248) 674-2119.

WEST BLOOMFIELD (K-4) pop. 64,862

HOLOCAUST MEMORIAL CENTER is on the Jewish Community Campus at 6602 W. Maple Rd., at the corner of Drake Rd. The center documents the history of the Holocaust with exhibits, videotape presentations, photographs, dioramas and a memorial flame. The Morris and Emma Schaver Library and Archives is dedicated to the study of the Holocaust and Jewish history, culture and genealogy. Outside the memorial center is the Bernard Maas Garden of the Righteous.

Sun.-Thurs. 10-3:30 (also Fri. 9-noon, Sept.-June); closed holidays. Guided tours are offered Sun. and Wed. at 1. Reservations are required for tours. Donations. Phone (248) 661-0840.

WYANDOTTE (I-6) pop. 28,006, elev. 590′

THE FORD-MacNICHOL HOME/WYANDOTTE MUSEUM is at 2630 Biddle Ave. The 1896 Victorian house includes original fixtures, furnishings, wallpaper and woodwork. The lower level houses a museum that chronicles the development of the town from an Indian village through the 19th century. A Christmas open house is held during the first two weekends in December. Allow 1 hour minimum. Mon.-Fri. noon-4, first Sun. of the month 2-5; closed holidays. Admission $1; over 60, 50c; under 12, 25c. Phone (734) 324-7297.

This ends listings for the Detroit Vicinity.
The following page resumes the alphabetical listings
of cities in Michigan.

DOUGLAS (H-1) pop. 1,214

Before a bridge linked the towns of Douglas and Saugatuck *(see place listing p. 99)*, the only way across the Kalamazoo River was by a hand-cranked, chain-powered ferry. Despite the presence of a bridge, the ferry continued until recently to operate as it had since the 1830s, carrying pedestrians and bicyclists between the two towns daily.

In keeping with the town's quaint atmosphere and charm, no fast food restaurants can be found. On area beaches, rockhounds can find septarian nodules. When halved and polished, these concretions display an endless array of designs.

SS *KEEWATIN* is moored off CR A2 (Blue Star Hwy.) at the Kalamazoo River s. of the Saugatuck-Douglas Bridge. One of the last of the classic steamships, it was built in Scotland in 1907 for the Canadian Pacific Railway's upper Great Lakes passenger route. Now a marine museum, the 350-foot coal-burning vessel is maintained and preserved as it was during its 57 years of service on the lakes. Daily 10:30-4:30, Memorial Day weekend-Labor Day. Admission $8; ages 6-12, $4. MC, VI. Phone (269) 857-2464.

DOWAGIAC (I-2) pop. 6,147, elev. 772′

MUSEUM AT SOUTHWESTERN MICHIGAN COLLEGE is e. on SR 62 from SR 51, then .2 mi. s. to 58900 Cherry Grove Rd., following signs. The museum explores science, technology and regional history through hands-on exhibits, artifacts and pictures. Allow 30 minutes minimum. Tues.-Sat. 10-5 (also Wed. 5-8); closed holidays. Free. Phone (269) 782-1374.

DRUMMOND ISLAND (B-6) pop. 500

Part of the rocky Manitoulin archipelago that separates Georgian Bay and the North Channel from the rest of Lake Huron, Drummond Island lies off the eastern tip of the Upper Peninsula at the mouth of the St. Marys River.

Anglers, boaters, hunters and vacationers are drawn to this cliff-bound, deeply indented wilderness isle. Its woodlands harbor deer, grouse and rabbits; duck hunting is particularly good. From the bays and inlets come bass, northern pike, yellow perch and walleye. Hiking in the summer and snowmobiling in the winter are favorite pastimes along the forest trails. Dolomite quarries augment the economy. The island is accessible by automobile ferry from De Tour Village on SR 134.

When the treaty ending the War of 1812 ousted the British from Mackinac Island, they re-established their garrison on the southwest promontory of Drummond Island, despite the fact that the boundary through the archipelago was still indefinite. British attempts to obtain the island failed, and in 1828 the Union Jack was lowered.

The Drummond Island Historical Society Museum, 10 miles from the ferry on the northwest end of the island, contains rocks and minerals, American Indian artifacts, furniture and written accounts of the island's history. Phone (906) 493-5746.

DRYDEN (H-5) pop. 815

SEVEN PONDS NATURE CENTER is e. on Dryden Rd., then 1 mi. s. on Havens Rd. to 3854 Crawford Rd. Various natural communities—Earl's Prairie, glacial lakes, an herb garden, wetlands, a wildflower garden and a butterfly garden—are accessible by 6 miles of trails contained within 323 acres. Maps are available at an interpretive center. Allow 1 hour minimum. Tues.-Sun. 9-5; closed Jan. 1, Thanksgiving, day after Thanksgiving and Dec. 25. Admission $3; under 12, $1. Phone (586) 796-3200.

DURAND (H-4) pop. 3,933, elev. 796′

MICHIGAN RAILROAD HISTORY MUSEUM AND DURAND UNION STATION is at 200 Railroad St. Railroad artifacts are on display, and a library houses abundant literature about railroads. Tues.-Fri. 11-4, Sat.-Sun. 1-5; closed holidays. Donations. Phone (989) 288-3561.

EAST LANSING (H-4) pop. 46,525

Primarily residential, East Lansing complements the governmental and industrial emphasis of Lansing *(see place listing p. 80)*, which it abuts. The creation of Michigan Agricultural College in 1855 spurred the town's growth; since then East Lansing's development has paralleled that of the school, which became Michigan State University.

MICHIGAN STATE UNIVERSITY is e. on Grand River Ave. (SR 43), following signs. The school is on a 5,320-acre educational campus; its housing complex lodges more than 20,000 students and student families.

On the main campus are the Kellogg Center for Continuing Education; the Munn Ice Arena; the Breslin Student Events Center; seasonal displays of the 1873 Beal Botanical Garden; and the Wharton Center for Performing Arts. Tours of the Wharton Center are offered Sun. at 2. Phone (517) 355-4458 for general campus information, (517) 432-9508 for campus tour information or (517) 432-2000 for the Wharton Center.

Abrams Planetarium is on the Michigan State University campus. The planetarium offers a variety of exhibits about astronomy and features a Digistar II projector. It is recommended that early elementary and preschool children attend the family show. Exhibit hall open Mon.-Fri. 8:30-noon and 1-4:30. Planetarium shows Fri.-Sat. at 8 p.m., Sun. at 4. Family show Sun. at 2:30. Exhibit hall and planetarium closed in Aug. Exhibit hall free. Planetarium shows $3; over 64 and students with ID $2.50; under 13, $2. Ticket sales begin 30 minutes prior to show times. Phone (517) 355-4676.

Beaumont Tower is on the Michigan State University campus. On the site of one of the Michigan Agricultural College's original buildings, the tower contains a 49-bell carillon.

Kresge Art Museum is on the Michigan State University campus. Noted for its comprehensive collections of art from many cultures; the museum contains exhibits spanning more than 5,000 years of art history. Changing exhibits are presented. Tours are available by appointment. Mon.-Fri. 10-5 (also Thurs. 5-8), Sat.-Sun. noon-5, Sept.-May; Tues.-Fri. 11-5, Sat.-Sun. noon-5, June-July. Closed major holidays. Free. Phone (517) 355-7631 or (517) 353-9834.

MSU Museum is on campus opposite the library. Three floors display permanent and changing natural and cultural history exhibits. The museum features full dinosaur skeletons and audiovisual presentations. Tours are available. Allow 30 minutes minimum. Mon.-Fri. 9-5, Sat. 10-5, Sun. 1-5; closed major holidays. Donations. Limited metered parking is available; parking permits are sold in the museum store and at the visitor counter. Phone (517) 355-2370, or (517) 432-1472 for tours.

Television Studio (WKAR-TV) is in the MSU Communication Arts and Sciences Building at Wilson and Red Cedar rds. The station contains three studios and complete facilities for live programming and student training. Tours are available by appointment. Mon.-Fri. 9-noon and 1-4. Free. Phone (517) 432-9527.

EAST TAWAS (F-5) pop. 2,951, elev. 588′

East Tawas, a resort community on Tawas Bay, offers opportunities for exploring the woodlands of nearby Huron-Manistee National Forests *(see place listing p. 75).* Fishing is good, particularly for perch, salmon, trout and walleye. Recreational opportunities also are available at Tawas Point State Park *(see Recreation Chart and the AAA Great Lakes CampBook).*

ELK RAPIDS (E-3) pop. 1,700, elev. 587′

GUNTZVILLER'S SPIRIT OF THE WOODS MUSEUM is 2 mi. s. on US 31. The museum houses collections of American Indian artifacts and dioramas displaying North American animals and fish. Arrowheads, pipes, ceremonial pieces, bows and moccasins are exhibited, while preserved beavers, otters, deer, bison, bears and minks are among the animals mounted in natural settings. Collections of early hunting and fishing gear also are displayed.

Allow 1 hour minimum. Mon.-Sat. 9-6, Sun. 11-4, June-Aug.; Mon.-Sat. 9-5, rest of year. Closed Dec. 25. Admission $3; over 64 and students with ID $2; ages 6-12, $1; two adults $5. DS, MC, VI. Phone (231) 264-5597.

ESCANABA (C-3) pop. 13,140, elev. 598′

The logging industry's hunger for the seemingly inexhaustible stands of Upper Peninsula pine spurred the establishment of Escanaba in the early 1800s. Its excellent deepwater harbor at the mouth of the Escanaba River on Little Bay de Noc also attracted the attention of the various iron enterprises; therefore the town continued to flourish once the virgin forests were depleted.

Second growth forests are the basis for paper and lumber industries. The only ore port on Lake Michigan, Escanaba still ships several million tons of iron ore every year. North of town lies Hiawatha National Forest *(see place listing p. 73).*

An especially scenic highway is the section of US 2 that extends 143 miles—about 50 of them along the Lake Michigan shore—between Escanaba and St. Ignace *(see place listing p. 98). Also see Upper Peninsula p. 103.*

Delta County Area Chamber of Commerce: 230 Ludington St., Escanaba, MI 49829; phone (906) 786-2192 or (888) 335-8264.

DELTA COUNTY HISTORICAL MUSEUM is in Ludington Park at the e. end of Ludington St. Displays chronicle the development of Delta County and the Upper Peninsula. Items include logging, railroad, shipping, military and household artifacts. A 1905 motor launch powered by a one-cylinder engine also is on display. Allow 30 minutes minimum. Daily 9-5, June-Aug.; 1-4 in Sept. Free. Phone (906) 786-3428.

Sand Point Lighthouse is next door to the Delta County Historical Museum. Restored to its original 1867 appearance, the tower adjoins the keeper's house, furnished in period. Winding stairs lead to the tower's observation deck. Allow 30 minutes minimum. Daily 9-5, June 1-Labor Day; 1-4, day after Labor Day-Sept. 30. Admission $1; under 14, 50c; family rate $3. Phone (906) 786-3763.

FARMINGTON HILLS—*see Detroit p. 63.*

FAYETTE (C-4)

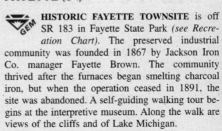 **HISTORIC FAYETTE TOWNSITE** is off SR 183 in Fayette State Park *(see Recreation Chart).* The preserved industrial community was founded in 1867 by Jackson Iron Co. manager Fayette Brown. The community thrived after the furnaces began smelting charcoal iron, but when the operation ceased in 1891, the site was abandoned. A self-guiding walking tour begins at the interpretive museum. Along the walk are views of the cliffs and of Lake Michigan.

Museum buildings open daily 9-dusk, mid-June through Labor Day; 9-5, mid-May to mid-June and day after Labor Day to mid-Oct. Park open daily 24 hours. Admission $6 per private vehicle. Phone (906) 644-2603.

FENNVILLE (H-2) pop. 1,459, elev. 664'

WINERIES

- **Fenn Valley Vineyards** is at 6130 122nd Ave. Mon.-Sat. noon-5, Sun. 1-5; closed Jan. 1, Easter, Thanksgiving and Dec. 25. Phone (269) 561-2396.

FLINT (H-4) pop. 124,943, elev. 800' .

From its inception Flint has been associated with transportation. In its early days the site was an important river crossing on the Pontiac Trail, one of the network of Indian routes that crisscrossed the wilderness. The logging boom created the need for katydids—two-wheeled log-hauling contrivances—in addition to road carts and wagons; Flint soon became a major center for their manufacture.

The city's subsequent carriage-making industry quickly gained international repute. Flint remains one of the world's largest manufacturers of carriages of the horseless variety and was where General Motors originated.

Flint Area Convention and Visitors Bureau: 519 S. Saginaw St., Flint, MI 48502; phone (810) 232-8900 or (800) 253-5468.

Shopping areas: Genesee Valley Center Mall, off I-75 at the junction of Miller and Linden roads, offers Marshall Field's, JCPenney and Sears as well as specialty stores and restaurants.

SAVE **THE CHILDREN'S MUSEUM** is at 1602 W. Third Ave. The hands-on learning center has exhibits related to science, technology and the arts. Children should be accompanied by an adult. Allow 2 hours minimum. Mon.-Sat. 10-5, Sun. noon-5; closed major holidays. Admission $3.50; over 60, $2.80; under 1 free. MC, VI. Phone (810) 767-5437.

DID YOU KNOW

Aviator Charles Lindbergh was born in Detroit.

CROSSROADS VILLAGE AND HUCKLEBERRY RAILROAD is off I-475 exit 13, n. on Saginaw St., e. on Stanley Rd., then s. on Bray Rd., following signs to 6140 Bray Rd. The restored 1800s Genesee County community features 34 historic structures, including an operating blacksmith shop, cider mill, sawmill, gristmill, general store, school and residences.

Huckleberry Railroad, a steam train with antique passenger cars pulled by a steam-powered Baldwin locomotive, departs from the Crossroads Depot for 35-minute trips through the recreation area.

Food is available. Allow 4 hours minimum. Tues.-Sun. 10-5, Memorial Day weekend-Labor Day; Mon.-Fri. 4-9, Sat.-Sun. noon-9, Oct. 2-31; Tues.-Sun. 4-9, day after Thanksgiving-Dec. 30. Closed Dec. 25. Admission (includes village, train and boat ride) $11; over 60, $10; ages 3-12, $8.50. Holiday rates vary; phone ahead. MC, VI. Phone (810) 736-7100 or (800) 648-7275.

Genesee Belle is docked inside Crossroads Village. Visitors can take 45-minute sightseeing cruises on Mott Lake. Dinner, lunch and evening cruises also are offered. Cruises are offered Tues.-Fri., May-Sept. Departure times vary; phone ahead. Admission (includes village and boat ride) $11; over 60, $10; ages 3-12, $8.50. AX, MC, VI. Phone (810) 736-7100 or (800) 648-7275.

FLINT CULTURAL CENTER is off I-475 exit 8A to 817 E. Kearsley St. The campus includes an art institute, gallery, planetarium, museum, auditorium, youth theater and music center.

GEM **Alfred P. Sloan Museum** is at 1221 E. Kearsley St. The museum has a variety of permanent and changing exhibits, highlighting fur trading and pioneer life to lumbering, carriage manufacturing and the General Motors automobile boom. The Buick Gallery displays vintage and experimental prototype automobiles. A Discovery Center features hands-on science displays. Mon.-Fri. 10-5, Sat.-Sun. noon-5; closed holidays. Admission $5; over 55, $4; ages 4-11, $3. MC, VI. Phone (810) 237-3450.

Flint Institute of Arts is at 1120 E. Kearsley St. African, American, Asian, European, impressionist and contemporary art is on display. Tues.-Sat. 10-5, Sun. 1-5; closed holidays. Free. Phone (810) 234-1695.

SAVE **Longway Planetarium** is at 1310 E. Kearsley St., across from Whiting Auditorium. The projector reproduces the night sky on a 60-foot dome. Family programs are offered throughout the year; phone for information. Traveling exhibits also are featured. Star shows Sat.-Sun. at 1 and 2:30. Laser light shows Fri.-Sat. evenings; phone ahead for schedule. Admission $5; over 55 and under 12, $4. MC, VI. Phone (810) 237-3400 or (877) 477-8277.

GENESEE RECREATION AREA is 6 mi. n.e. off I-475 exit 13. Covering 4,540 acres along the Flint River, the area contains beaches, bicycle paths, a boat launch, a campground, fishing sites, hiking and horse trails, picnic areas and a recreational vehicle area. After sunset from Memorial Day through Labor Day colored lights play upon Stepping Stone Falls, a spillway impounding 600-acre Mott Lake. Free. Phone (810) 736-7100. *See Recreation Chart.*

FRANKENMUTH (G-5) pop. 4,838

Pastors in Bavaria, concerned over the religious life of Lutheran immigrants and their American Indian neighbors, sent a colony to the United States to demonstrate their faith on a day-to-day basis. Fifteen Franconians from Bavaria arrived in the Saginaw Valley in 1845 and named their settlement Frankenmuth, meaning "courage of the Franconians."

The Indian tribe soon moved elsewhere, but the Bavarian heritage remained and was reinforced by other arrivals from Germany. For many years after 1900 German remained the principal language of the community. The Old World atmosphere is still evident in the architecture.

The 35-bell automatic carillon in the Bavarian Inn's Glockenspiel Tower plays selected melodies followed by a presentation of carved wooden figures depicting the legend of the Pied Piper of Hamelin. Nearby is a replica of the 19th-century Holz-Brücke—Frankenmuth's wooden covered bridge that spans the Cass River.

Frankenmuth Chamber of Commerce and Convention and Visitors Bureau: 635 S. Main St., Frankenmuth, MI 48734; phone (800) 386-8696.

Shopping areas: More than 100 gift shops can be found in the business district. River Place Shopping Area, 925 S. Main St., features 30 shops and a nightly laser light show.

BRONNER'S CHRISTMAS WONDERLAND is 1 mi. s. at 25 Christmas Ln.
More than 50,000 Christmas ornaments, lights and decorations—including nativity scenes ranging from tiny hand-carved figures to life-size scenes, animated figures and more than 260 artistically decorated Christmas trees—are displayed. A multi-image presentation offers historical information, and a spectacular outdoor light display is featured every evening. The Bronner's Silent Night Memorial Chapel is open daily.

Food is available. Allow 1 hour, 30 minutes minimum. Mon.-Sat. 9-9, Sun. noon-7, June-Dec.; Mon.-Sat. 9-5:30 (also Fri. 5:30-9), Sun. noon-5:30, rest of year. Closed Jan. 1, Easter, Thanksgiving and Dec. 25; shorter hours on Good Friday and Dec. 24 and 31. Free. Phone (989) 652-9931 or (800) 255-9327. *See color ad.*

FRANKENMUTH HISTORICAL MUSEUM is at 613 S. Main St. Permanent and changing exhibits depict the area's German ancestry and history from American Indian mission days. Mon.-Fri. 10:30-7 (also Fri. 7-8 p.m.), Sat. 10-8, Sun. 11-7, day after Labor Day-Dec. 31; Mon.-Fri. 10:30-5, Sat. 10-5, Sun. noon-5, June 1-Labor Day. Admission $1; under 13, 50c. Phone (989) 652-9701.

FRANKENMUTH RIVERBOAT TOURS is at 425 S. Main St. The tour company offers 45-minute sightseeing cruises on the Cass River. The captain of the *Riverview Queen* narrates Cass River folklore and history. Allow 1 hour minimum. Departures Mon.-Sat. at noon, 1:30, 3, 4:30 and 6, Sun. at 1, 2:30, 4 and 5:30, June 1-Labor Day. Fare $6; ages 4-12, $3. Phone (989) 652-6183.

MICHIGAN'S OWN INC.—MILITARY AND SPACE MUSEUM is at 1250 Weiss St. The museum honors Michigan's veterans. Included are displays

about the World War I Polar Bears, an army unit based in northern Russia. Visitors can see the uniforms of the state's Medal of Honor recipients as well as the uniforms and flight suits of Michigan's astronauts.

An exhibit is dedicated to POWs and MIAs from the Vietnam and Persian Gulf wars. Mon.-Sat. 10-5, Sun. 11-5, Mar.-Dec. Admission $3; over 64, $2; ages 6-18, $1. Phone (989) 652-8005.

FRANKFORT (E-1) pop. 1,513, elev. 585′

High bluffs surround the natural harbor of Frankfort, one of northwest Michigan's busiest ports. Beach lovers are drawn to the area's sandy shores, and the city's natural harbor, yacht facilities and launching ramp accommodate boating and fishing. North of the city off SR 22 is the Point Betsie Lighthouse, near the entrance to Sleeping Bear Dunes National Lakeshore *(see place listing p. 100)*.

Some think that Jesuit explorer and missionary Pere Jacques Marquette died at the mouth of Betsie Bay in 1675; a marker and wooden cross signify the supposed site. It is generally believed that he died near Ludington *(see place listing p. 81)*, about 50 miles south.

GAYLORD (E-4) pop. 3,681, elev. 1,348′

In the center of the northern end of the Lower Peninsula, Gaylord is one of the highest incorporated communities in Michigan. The Black, Manistee, Pigeon and Sturgeon rivers and the North Branch of the Au Sable River all rise nearby and flow in different directions.

A sister city to Pontresina, Switzerland, Gaylord maintains the atmosphere of an Alpine village. Buildings of Swiss-style architecture line Main and surrounding streets.. An average of nearly 150 inches of snow falls on the town and nearby ski slopes and cross-country trails each year. A Swiss essence also pervades community activities throughout the year.

Gaylord Area Convention and Tourism Bureau: 101 W. Main St., P.O. Box 3069, Gaylord, MI 49734; phone (989) 732-6333 or (800) 345-8621.

CALL OF THE WILD MUSEUM is e. on Main St., then .2 mi. s. to 850 S. Wisconsin Ave. More than 150 lifelike North American wild animals and game birds are displayed. Beavers, elk and polar bears appear in re-created natural settings, complete with sound effects. Allow 1 hour minimum. Daily 8:30 a.m.-9 p.m., mid-June through Labor Day; 9:30-6, rest of year. Closed Jan. 1, Thanksgiving and Dec. 25. Admission $6; over 62, $5.50; ages 5-13, $4. DS, MC, VI. Phone (989) 732-4336.

GERMFASK (B-4) pop. 491

During the lumberjack era Germfask was on the old tote road from Manistique to Seney, 8 miles north. Named by combining the initials of the town

founders, the settlement was referred to as the dump because logs were dropped into the Manistique River to be floated to the mill. *See Upper Peninsula p. 103.*

SENEY NATIONAL WILDLIFE REFUGE visitor center entrance is about 2 mi. n. on SR 77. More than 200 species of birds and other wildlife inhabit the 95,000-acre refuge. Large numbers of Canadian geese breed here; the refuge also has one of the state's highest concentrations of nesting loons and is home to bald eagles, ospreys, sandhill cranes and trumpeter swans. A 1.5-mile walking trail and unpaved 7-mile driving tour route are available. An orientation slide program is shown at the visitor center.

Visitor center open daily 9-5, May 15-Oct. 15. Refuge office open Mon.-Fri. 8-4. Walking trail open daily dawn dusk. Driving tour route open daily dawn-dusk, May 15-Oct. 15. Free. Phone (906) 586-9851, ext. 15.

GRAND HAVEN (G-2) pop. 11,168, elev. 603′

At the mouth of the Grand River, Grand Haven benefits equally from its busy port and from the tourists attracted to the beaches, bayous, rolling dunes and wooded hills along Lake Michigan, Spring Lake and Ferrysburg. According to geologists, this is one of the few areas where singing sand is found. When walked upon the tiny sand particles emit a peculiar musical whistle.

Popular beach areas include Grand Haven State Park *(see Recreation Chart and the AAA Great Lakes CampBook)*, 1 mile west, and P.J. Hoffmaster State Park, 10 miles northwest off US 31 *(see Recreation Chart)*. Grand Haven's waterfront features shopping and dining areas and a 2.5-mile boardwalk along the Grand River. The city also has an open-air Farmers Market and Harbourfront Place, a renovated historic piano factory building containing shops and restaurants.

A large musical fountain on Dewey Hill at the waterfront combines light, water and music in nightly concerts held at dusk, Memorial Day through Labor Day and weekends in May and September. During the holiday season it appears as a 40-foot nativity scene and offers evening performances during December.

Trolley car routes through Grand Haven, Spring Lake and Ferrysburg offer convenient access to area attractions and a pleasant way to tour the town. The trolleys operate from Memorial Day through Labor Day. For views from the water there are sailing charters on Lake Michigan and riverboat cruises on the Grand River and Spring Lake. Peak fall color is early to mid-October.

Grand Haven/Spring Lake Area Visitors Bureau: One S. Harbor Dr., Grand Haven, MI 49417; phone (616) 842-4499 or (800) 303-4096.

HARBOR STEAMER EXCURSION BOAT is docked at Chinook Pier, 301 N. Harbor Dr. The paddlewheel riverboat escorts visitors on narrated 1- and

1.5-hour scenic cruises of the Grand Haven harbor, Grand River and Spring Lake. Tours depart Tues.-Sat. at 1:30, 3, 5, 6:30 and 8:30, Sun. at 1:30, 3, 5 and 6:30, June 1-Labor Day. Fare for 1-hour trip $9; ages 5-17, $6. Fare for 1.5-hour trip $11; ages 5-17, $8. Phone (616) 842-8950.

TRI-CITIES HISTORICAL MUSEUM is at Harbor Dr. and Washington St. Displays about the railroad, shipping and lumber industries as well as exhibits about area pioneers and local history are in an original 1868-70 train depot. Allow 1 hour minimum. Tues.-Sat. 10-9:30, Sun. noon-9:30, Memorial Day weekend-Labor Day; Tues.-Fri. 10-5, Sat.-Sun. noon-4, rest of year. Donations. Phone (616) 842-0700.

GRAND RAPIDS (H-2)
pop. 197,800, elev. 610'

Grand Rapids is a vigorous manufacturing, cultural and convention center. It owes its development and its name to the rapids of the Grand River, a place of gathering and exchange since Louis Campau established a trading post in 1826. The water power and transportation afforded by the river and the abundance of wood from the forests made the growth of the furniture industry almost inevitable. By 1900 the city was renowned as a producer of quality office furniture, a reputation it still maintains.

DeVos Place on Monroe Avenue includes large convention and exhibit halls. Also downtown, the Calder sculpture "La Grande Vitesse" pays homage to the rapids (vitesse). In contrast are the stolid lines of a reconstructed covered bridge that spans the Thornapple River at Ada, east of Grand Rapids via SR 21.

In the Heritage Hill historic district is the three-story Voigt House Victorian Museum. Built in the late 19th century, the opulent house retains the original furnishings of the Voigt family; phone (616) 456-4600. In nearby Lowell the James C. Veen Observatory is open to the public the second and last Saturdays of each month, weather permitting, April through October; phone (616) 897-7065 after 7:30 p.m. for status.

Broadway shows and performances by the Grand Rapids Ballet, Opera Grand Rapids and the Grand Rapids Symphony are presented at DeVos Performance Hall, on Monroe Avenue N.W. The Grand Rapids Civic Theatre, 30 N. Division Ave., presents community theatrical performances. Concerts and sporting events are held at the Van Andel Arena, 130 W. Fulton St.

Grand Rapids/Kent County Convention and Visitors Bureau: 140 Monroe Center N.W., Suite 300, Grand Rapids, MI 49503; phone (616) 459-8287 or (800) 678-9859. See ad.

BLANDFORD NATURE CENTER is at 1715 Hillburn Ave. N.W. The center is surrounded by 143 acres of fields, forests, ponds and streams. On the grounds are several self-guiding trails. A visitor center has a wildlife care program. Allow 1 hour minimum. Mon.-Fri. 9-5, Sat.-Sun. 1-5; closed holidays. Free. Phone (616) 453-6192.

FISH LADDER SCULPTURE is n. on the Grand River at jct. Leonard and Front sts. The concrete, five-step environmental ladder was built by a local artist to assist salmon in jumping over a 6-foot dam to reach their spawning grounds. Although the leaping fish can be viewed at any time, the best time to see them scale the aquatic steps is late Sept.-late Oct. Daily 24 hours. Free. Phone (800) 678-9859.

FREDERIK MEIJER GARDENS & SCULPTURE PARK is n.e. of jct. I-96 exit 38 and E. Beltline at 1000 E. Beltline N.E. The 125-acre gardens and sculpture park contains perennial, American, Victorian, shade and arid gardens; nature trails; a carnivorous plant house; and tropical plants in the five-story, 15,000-square-foot Lena Meijer Conservatory, said to be the state's largest. A 30-acre outdoor sculpture park boasts more than 30 bronze sculptures by such artists as Henry Moore, Claes Oldenburg and Auguste Rodin. Most notable is a 24-foot-tall Leonardo da Vinci horse by Nina Akamu.

A children's garden also is featured, and a tropical butterfly exhibit takes place March through April. Narrated tram tours are available. Food is available. Allow 2 hours minimum. Mon.-Sat. 9-5

(also Thurs. 5-9, June-Aug.), Sun. noon-5; closed Jan. 1 and Dec. 25. Admission $10; over 64 and students with ID $8; ages 5-13, $6. Tram fee $2; ages 5-13, $1. Phone (616) 957-1580 or (888) 957-1580.

GEM **GERALD R. FORD MUSEUM** is off US 131 exit 85B at 303 Pearl St. N.W. The triangular building has a glass wall that mirrors downtown from the west bank of the Grand River. Displays portray both the private life and public career of President Ford. Exhibits include a re-creation of the Ford Paint & Varnish Company where the future president worked as a boy as well as information about the October 1973 vice-presidential confirmation hearings when Ford served as House Minority Leader.

Visitors can take a holographic tour of the White House, observe foreign policy procedures in the White House Situation Room and view the nomination of Ford at the Republican National Convention in 1976. Allow 1 hour minimum. Daily 9-5; closed Jan. 1, Thanksgiving and Dec. 25. Admission $4; over 62, $3; under 16 free. Phone (616) 254-0400.

SAVE **THE GRAND RAPIDS ART MUSEUM** is at 155 Division St. N. Housed in the renovated 1910 Federal Building that served as post office and courthouse, the museum features works from Alexander Calder, Richard Diebenkorn, Childe Hassam and Max Pechstein. Collections include 19th- and 20th-century prints, paintings, photographs, sculptures and decorative arts. A children's gallery features hands-on art and color displays. Tues.-Sun. 11-6 (also Fri. 6-9 p.m.); closed holidays. Admission $6; senior citizens and college students with ID $5; ages 6-17, $3; free to all Fri. after 5. Phone (616) 831-1000 or (616) 831-1001.

SAVE **GRAND RAPIDS CHILDREN'S MUSEUM** is at 11 Sheldon Ave. N.E. Colorful play areas are both recreational and educational. Children can make bubbles, create poems on a large magnetic wall or paint. Hands-on and seasonal exhibits also are presented. Allow 1 hour, 30 minutes minimum. Mon.-Sat. 9:30-5 (also Thurs. 5-8), Sun. noon-5, Memorial Day-Aug. 31. Closed Labor Day. Admission $4, under 2 free, $1 for all Thurs. 5-8. MC, VI. Phone (616) 235-4726.

SAVE **JOHN BALL ZOO** is at jct. I-196 and SR 45. One of the largest zoos in the state, it houses 1,000 animals from many parts of the world. Of particular interest are the nocturnal animals, snake house, aquarium and children's zoo. Allow 1 hour minimum. Daily 10-6, mid-May through Labor Day; 10-4, rest of year. Admission $4; over 62 and ages 5-13, $2.50; free to all Dec.-Feb. Phone (616) 336-4300 or (616) 336-4301.

GEM **VAN ANDEL MUSEUM CENTER OF THE PUBLIC MUSEUM OF GRAND RAPIDS** is **SAVE** at 272 Pearl St. N.W. Exhibits depict the heritage and manufacturing traditions of Grand Rapids and include a partially operational re-construction of an early 20th-century furniture factory. The museum also houses a 76-foot finback whale skeleton as well as an operational Spillman carousel. Visitors can walk through a re-creation of a downtown street in 1890s Grand Rapids. The street includes a theater, department store, nine other shops and the sounds and sights of the times.

Food is available. Allow 2 hours minimum. Tues.-Sat. 9-5; closed Jan. 1, Easter, Thanksgiving and Dec. 25. Admission $7; senior citizens $6; ages 3-17, $2.50. Carousel ride $1. Phone (616) 456-3977.

The Roger B. Chaffee Planetarium is within the Van Andel Museum Center. Equipped with technical sound, laser and videotape projection equipment, the dome sky theater features performances related to space technology. Phone (616) 456-3663.

GRAYLING (E-3) pop. 1,952, elev. 1,132'

Grayling is on the Au Sable River in one of the Lower Peninsula's leading recreation regions. Although the game fish for which it was named no longer inhabits nearby rivers, the town remains a starting point for trout fishing, canoeing, hunting, cross-country skiing and snowmobiling expeditions. Canoeing is especially popular; canoes, supplies and guides are available in the community.

In spring the rare Kirtland warbler nests in a re-stricted area east of Grayling. This tiny, elusive songbird winters in the Bahamas. Guided tours of the area are offered by the Department of Natural Resources from mid-May through July 4.

Grayling Visitors Bureau: P.O. Box 217, Grayling, MI 49738; phone (800) 937-8837.

HARTWICK PINES STATE PARK is 7 mi. n.e. on SR 93. The park contains stands of virgin pine and hemlock. The Michigan Forest Visitor Center, a chapel and reproductions of a kitchen, mess hall and workshop from an early logging camp and sawmill are on the grounds. A museum contains displays depicting the state's 19th-century logging industry.

Park open daily 8 a.m.-10 p.m. Visitor center and park buildings open daily 9-7, Labor Day to mid-Oct.; Sat.-Sun. 9-4, rest of year. Admission $6 per private vehicle. Phone (989) 348-7068. *See Recreation Chart and the AAA Great Lakes CampBook.*

GROSSE POINTE SHORES—
see Detroit p. 64.

HANCOCK (A-2) pop. 4,323, elev. 607'

Among the many groups of Europeans who settled the Upper Peninsula during the mid-1800s copper boom were Finnish farmers and Cornish miners. Traces of their influence remain. A pasty, the meat pie that often was the lunch of the tough Cornish miners, can still be found. Suomi College in Hancock is the only college in the country founded by Americans of Finnish descent.

Like its sister city Houghton *(see place listing p. 75)*, Hancock depends on tourism and commerce along the Keweenaw Waterway. Created by dredging Portage Lake and cutting a canal to Lake Superior, the waterway bypasses the dangerous waters off Keweenaw Point. Rockhounds can find agates along the beach at F.J. McLain State Park, north on SR 203 (see Recreation Chart and the AAA Great Lakes CampBook). Also north, on US 41, is the Lookout-Historic Monument, which provides fine views of the waterway. See Upper Peninsula p. 103.

[SAVE] **QUINCY MINE HOIST** is 1 mi. n. on US 41.

A guided tour takes visitors to the seventh level of the mine, about 400 feet underground. The mine houses what is believed to be the largest steam-powered hoist ever manufactured. Weighing 880 tons and occupying a four-story hoist house, it could lift 13 tons of ore in an ore car at 36.4 miles per hour. Structures reflect the site's appearance 1846-1945.

Mon.-Sat. 8:30-7, Sun. 12:30-7, mid-June through late Aug.; Mon.-Sat. 9:30-5, Sun. 12:30-5, late Apr. to mid-June and late Aug.-early Nov. Hours vary; phone ahead. Admission $12.50; senior citizens $11.50; ages 6-12, $7.50. Phone (906) 482-3101.

HARBOR BEACH (F-6) pop. 1,837, elev. 610′

FRANK MURPHY MEMORIAL MUSEUM is at 142 S. Huron Ave. A collection of historical items relating to the politician—who served as an associate justice of the Supreme Court, mayor of Detroit, governor-general of the Philippines, governor of Michigan and U.S. attorney general—are housed in the Murphy family home. Guided tours are given daily 10-4, Memorial Day-Labor Day. Admission $2; ages 5-12, $1. Phone (989) 479-3363.

HARBOR SPRINGS (D-3) pop. 1,567

On the north shore of Little Traverse Bay, Harbor Springs is both a center for winter recreation and a summer resort. SR 119, a scenic lakeshore drive through the tunnel of trees, passes through Harbor Springs as it travels north to Cross Village.

Harbor Springs Chamber of Commerce: 368 E. Main St., Harbor Springs, MI 49740; phone (231) 526-7999.

HARRIS (C-3) pop. 1,895, elev. 790′

CASINOS

- **Chip-in Island Resort and Casino** is at W399 US 2/41. Write P.O. Box 351, Harris, MI 49845. Daily 24 hours. Phone (906) 466-2941 or (800) 682-6040.

HASTINGS (H-3) pop. 7,095, elev. 790′

HISTORIC CHARLTON PARK VILLAGE MUSEUM AND RECREATION AREA is 2 mi. s. on SR 37, then 4 mi. e. on SR 79, following signs. The 300-acre complex includes a re-created turn-of-the-20th-century rural Midwestern village and a recreation area with nature trails, picnic areas,

playgrounds, a beach and boat launch. The village contains 16 buildings—shops, stores, a church, town hall and residences. The museum is furnished in period and contains Civil War artifacts. Farm implements are housed in a separate building.

Village and museums daily 8:30-4:30, Memorial Day-Labor Day. Recreation area daily 8 a.m.-9 p.m., Memorial Day-Labor Day. Free. Admission charged for special events. Phone (269) 945-3775.

HERMANSVILLE (C-3) elev. 887′

IXL HISTORICAL MUSEUM is s. from US 2 to First St., then 2.5 blks. w. to IXL Dr. and W. River St. The museum is housed in the offices of the Wisconsin Land & Lumber Company, once the largest hardwood flooring plant in the country. Begun in the 1880s, the brand name was derived from the phrase "I excel." Exhibits contain late 19th-century furnishings and office equipment, tools and equipment used in the early lumber era and the second-story living quarters of the owners and company executives.

Allow 1 hour minimum. Daily 12:30-4, Memorial Day-Labor Day. Admission $2, students with ID $1. Phone (906) 498-2181.

HESSEL (B-5) elev. 603′

CASINOS

- **Kewadin Hessel** is 13 mi. e. on SR 134, then 3 mi. n. on Three Mile Rd. Sun.-Thurs. 9 a.m.-midnight, Fri.-Sat. 9 a.m.-1 a.m. Phone (906) 484-2903.

HIAWATHA NATIONAL FOREST

Elevations in the forest range from 580 ft. at Lake Michigan to 960 ft. next to Lake Superior in Munising, Grand Island. Refer to AAA maps for additional elevation information.

With shorelines on lakes Huron, Michigan and Superior, the two portions of the Hiawatha National Forest embrace 893,348 acres of Upper Peninsula and feature the only Great Lakes lighthouses in the national forest system. The broad western unit extends southward from Munising to Rapid Rivers and includes Big Bay de Noc and Little Bay de Noc. The eastern unit reaches from St. Ignace (see place listing p. 98) north to Whitefish Bay.

The forest also manages Government Island, one of Les Cheneaux Islands (see place listing p. 81), which offers an unspoiled environment for boating and other outdoor activities. Grand Island National Recreation Area near Munising is adjacent to Pictured Rocks National Lakeshore.

Recreational opportunities in the forest include hunting for black bears, deer, grouse, turkeys and rabbits; fishing for bass, pike, trout and walleye; cross-country skiing and snowmobiling; camping; canoeing along canoe routes and boating on more than 400 lakes; and hiking or bicycling along miles of trails. Visitors may enjoy a drive along the Lake Superior shoreline on the Whitefish Bay scenic byway.

West of Munising near the town of Christmas are the Bay Furnace ruins, the remains of an 1870s iron furnace. Forest daily 24 hours. Furnace daily dawn-dusk. Free. For further information contact the Forest Supervisor, 2727 N. Lincoln Rd., Escanaba, MI 49829; phone (906) 786-4062. *See Upper Peninsula, Recreation Chart and the AAA Great Lakes CampBook.*

HICKORY CORNERS (H-3) elev. 967′

GILMORE CAR MUSEUM is at 6865 Hickory Rd. More than 175 antique, classic and high performance cars show the development of the automobile, from an 1899 Locomobile to 1960s muscle cars and 2002 models. American models include Cadillac, Checker, Duesenberg, Ford, Packard, Pierce-Arrow and Tucker, while Alfa-Romeo, Bentley, BMW, Ferrari, Jaguar, Porsche and Rolls Royce represent European models. Vehicles are exhibited in nine restored antique barns on 90 landscaped acres.

An interpretive center resembling a 1932 Shell filling station displays a 1950 Shell Ford pickup truck, nostalgic signs, tools, photographs and equipment. The Pierce-Arrow Museum features vehicles dating from the early 1900s. Allow 1 hour, 30 minutes minimum. Mon.-Fri. 9-5, Sat.-Sun. 9-6, May-Oct. Admission $7; over 62, $6; ages 7-15, $5. MC, VI. Phone (269) 671-5089.

HOLLAND (H-2) pop. 35,048, elev. 612′

Settled by Dutch immigrants in 1847, Holland retains the essence of a Dutch town. Millions of blooming tulips in the parks and neighborhoods provide a spectacular floral display during May.

Seven miles west on Lake Michigan is Holland State Park *(see Recreation Chart and the AAA Great Lakes CampBook)*.

Holland Area Convention and Visitors Bureau: 76 E. Eighth St., Holland, MI 49423; phone (800) 506-1299.

Shopping areas: Holland Outlet Center, at US 31 and James Street next to Dutch Village *(see attraction listing)*, offers more than 20 factory outlet stores. Westshore Mall, also next to Dutch Village on US 31, features specialty stores as well as JCPenney, Sears and Younker's department stores. More than 100 shops and galleries highlight the downtown area.

CAPPON HOUSE AND SETTLERS HOUSE MUSEUM are at 228 W. 9th St. The Cappon House, built in 1874 in the Italianate Victorian style, was the family residence of Isaac Cappon, a Dutch immigrant who was the city's first mayor. A nursery, kitchen, parlor and sitting room contain nearly all original woodwork and furnishings. Displays in the tiny Settlers House reflect the hardships early settlers faced. Both homes are on the National Register of Historic Places.

Allow 30 minutes minimum. Wed.-Sat. 1-4, June-Oct.; Fri.-Sat. 1-4, rest of year. Closed holidays. Admission to both houses $3, family rate $7. Phone (616) 392-6740.

DE KLOMP WOODEN SHOE AND DELFTWARE FACTORY is at 12755 Quincy St. at US 31 next to Veldheer Tulip Gardens. Self-guiding tours of the premises allow visitors to see craftspeople demonstrate wooden shoe carving and the making of blue and white Delftware. Allow 30 minutes minimum. Daily 8 a.m.-9 p.m. in May; Mon.-Fri. 8-6, Sat.-Sun. 9-5, rest of year. Phone ahead for demonstration schedule. Free. Phone (616) 399-1900.

DUTCH VILLAGE is 1 mi. n. of SR 21 on US 31. The village features canals, gardens, windmills, museums, a film, klompen dancers, carving exhibits, a Frisian farmhouse and children's rides. Food is available. Allow 2 hours minimum. Daily 9-5, mid-Apr. to mid-Oct. Admission $8; ages 3-11, $5. AX, DS, MC, VI. Phone (616) 396-1475.

THE HOLLAND MUSEUM is at 31 W. Tenth St. Exhibits focus on the early Dutch settlement and development of the city of Holland and include a room from a Dutch fisherman's cottage. Dutch decorative arts and historical collectibles also are featured. Allow 1 hour minimum. Mon. and Wed.-Sat. 10-5 (also Thurs. 5-8), Sun. 2-5. Closed major holidays. Admission $3; family rate $7. MC, VI. Phone (616) 392-9084 or (888) 200-9123.

VELDHEER TULIP GARDENS is 3 mi. n. on US 31 at Quincy St. On display are more than 275 varieties of tulips and daffodils in a setting of windmills, drawbridges and canals. The main flowering season, with 15 acres of blooms, is late April to early May. A wide selection of bulbs and flowering plants replaces the tulips for the remainder of the year. Daily 8-dusk in May; Mon.-Fri. 8-6, Sat.-Sun. 9-5 in Apr. and June-Dec.; Mon.-Fri. 9-5, rest of year. Admission $5; ages 3-13, $3. DS, MC, VI. Phone (616) 399-1900.

WINDMILL ISLAND is at Seventh St. and Lincoln Ave. The island is an unusual 30-acre park. Canals, a drawbridge, a miniature Dutch village and spring tulip gardens surround the park's main feature, a 1780s operating windmill brought from the Netherlands. Called De Zwaan, the mill produces a fine graham flour. The post house is a replica of a 14th-century Netherlands wayside inn. A slide presentation is presented all year.

Guided tours are offered. Allow 2 hours minimum. Mon.-Sat. 9-6, Sun. 11:30-6 in May and July-Aug.; Mon.-Sat. 10-5, Sun. 11:30-5 in June and Sept.-Oct. Admission $6.50; ages 5-12, $3.50. Phone (616) 355-1030.

HOUGHTON (A-2) pop. 7,010, elev. 637'

Houghton shares its multinational origins, copper mining heritage and guardianship of the Keweenaw Waterway with nearby Hancock *(see place listing p. 72)*. The Portage Lake Vertical Lift Bridge links the two cities. Mineralogical interests are served at Michigan Technological University.

The city is the mainland headquarters of Isle Royale National Park *(see place listing p. 77)*. Boat service is available between Houghton and the park June to mid-September. Float plane service is available mid-May through September. *Also see Upper Peninsula p. 103.*

Keweenaw Tourism Council: 56638 Calumet Ave., Calumet, MI 49913; phone (800) 338-7982.

A.E. SEAMAN MINERAL MUSEUM is on the fifth floor of the Electrical Energy Resources Center at Michigan Technological University; metered parking is available on Townsend Dr. (US 41). Displays include copper and silver specimens native to the Upper Peninsula, fluorescent minerals, natural copper crystals and a simulated iron-manganese cave. Guided tours are offered by appointment. Mon.-Fri. 9-4:30 (also Sat. noon-4, July-Sept.); closed university holidays. Schedule may vary; phone ahead. Donations. Phone (906) 487-2572.

HOUGHTON LAKE (F-3) pop. 3,749

Sportsmen and vacationers have replaced the loggers and commercial anglers who once were the vital elements of Houghton Lake. The village is the core of a year-round resort area that borders the lake of the same name. Michigan's largest inland lake, Houghton Lake is 10 miles long and 6 miles wide with a 32-mile shoreline.

Although summer brings boaters and water skiers and winter attracts snow skiers, fishing knows no season. Ice fishing for bluegill, crappie and walleye is popular, and snowmobile trails are prevalent.

Houghton Lake Chamber of Commerce: 1625 W. Houghton Lake Dr., Houghton Lake, MI 48629; phone (989) 366-5644 or (800) 248-5253.

HURON CITY (F-6)

In 1871 and 1881 catastrophic forest fires twice destroyed Huron City, dashing its hopes of becoming a prosperous lumber center. It was reconstructed after these disasters only to be abandoned a short time later when the wells dried up. Not quite a ghost town, Huron City is owned by the William Lyon Phelps Foundation, which operates the remaining buildings as a museum.

HURON CITY MUSEUMS are on SR 25. The area consists of several restored buildings—a general store, log cabin, church, carriage shed, inn, U.S. Life Saving Station, barns and an information center—containing a variety of artifacts. The House of Seven Gables is a restored 1881 Victorian mansion with original furnishings. Thurs.-Mon. 10-6, July

1-Labor Day; Sat.-Sun. 11-6, Memorial Day-June 30 and day after Labor Day-Sept. 30. Combination buildings and mansion admission $10; over 62, $8; ages 10-15, $5. Buildings or mansion admission $6; over 62, $5; ages 10-15, $3. Phone (989) 428-4123.

HURON-MANISTEE NATIONAL FORESTS

> Elevations in the forest range from 580 ft. around Lake Michigan to 1,407 ft. at Briar Hills north of Harrietta. Refer to AAA maps for additional elevation information.

In the northern part of the Lower Peninsula, Huron-Manistee National Forests extend over 964,711 acres. Through the Huron National Forest flows the Au Sable River, once heavily used to float logs to the sawmills at East Tawas and Oscoda. The river provides electricity generated by the dams along its course.

The forests offer a variety of outdoor recreational opportunities, including hunting for the morel mushroom in the spring, swimming in lakes Huron and Michigan in the summer and cross-country skiing in the winter. Trout fishing is excellent in many lakes and streams as well as in the Au Sable River. The Au Sable, Manistee, Pine and Pere Marquette rivers in the Manistee National Forest are favorites of canoeists; from mid-May to early September a permit is required to canoe on the Pine and Pere Marquette rivers.

The Nordhouse Dunes are spread across a mile of undeveloped shoreline along Lake Michigan in the Manistee National Forest. The dunes provide opportunities for solitude and seasonal deer hunting. The Loda Lake Wildflower Sanctuary offers a 1-mile trail through marsh, forest and orchard. A 11.5-mile trail offers hiking along the Manistee River and connects to the North Country Trail via a wooden suspension bridge across the river. Together the trails make a 22-mile loop.

The River Road Scenic Byway, in the Huron National Forest, runs 22 miles along the south bank of the Au Sable River. The byway provides vistas of tree-banked reservoirs and offers views of bald eagles, spawning salmon, the Canoeists Memorial and the Lumberman's Monument. Part of the Shore-to-Shore Hiking-Riding Trail also traverses the forest. The North Country Trail offers snowshoeing, camping, backpacking and hiking in the Manistee National Forest.

The Lumberman's Monument, a bronze statue depicting early loggers, overlooks the river valley 10 miles northwest of East Tawas. A visitor center at the monument houses interpretive displays that explore the rich logging legacy of the Au Sable River.

The forests are open daily 24 hours. Information and maps of the Huron National Forest can be obtained at district offices in Oscoda and Mio. Offices in Baldwin, Cadillac and Manistee provide information on the Manistee National Forest.

Some areas require a vehicle pass; contact the Huron-Manistee National Forests Headquarters, 1755 S. Mitchell St., Cadillac, MI 49601; phone (231) 775-2421 or (800) 821-6263. *See Recreation Chart and the AAA Great Lakes CampBook.*

INDIAN RIVER (D-4) pop. 2,008

Today's and yesterday's highways intersect at the heart of the inland waterway in Indian River: I-75 crosses the inland waterway that was once used by Indians to avoid the Straits of Mackinac. Nearby Burt Lake State Park offers recreational opportunities *(see Recreation Chart and the AAA Great Lakes CampBook).*

Indian River Chamber of Commerce: 3435 S. Straits Hwy., P.O. Box 57, Indian River, MI 49749; phone (231) 238-9325 or (800) 394-8310.

THE CROSS IN THE WOODS is 1 mi. w. of I-75. Said to be the world's largest crucifix, the 55-foot-high cross weighs 21 tons and is made from one California redwood tree. The 13-acre site has an outdoor church, flower gardens and several shrines. A museum features more than 500 nun and priest dolls dressed in the costumes of different religious orders. Allow 30 minutes minimum. Church open daily dawn-dusk. Museum open daily 9-6, Apr.-Oct. Donations. Phone (231) 238-8973 or (231) 238-8722.

INTERLOCHEN (E-2) elev. 849′

The northern Michigan village of Interlochen is headquarters for the Interlochen Center for the Arts, which includes Interlochen Arts Camp, Interlochen Arts Academy and Interlochen Public Radio. Founded in 1928, the camp enrolls students in music, art, dance and drama for 8 weeks each summer. During the winter students participate in academics and fine arts at the academy.

The 1,200-acre campus includes two large outdoor concert halls, a theater, an art gallery, an indoor auditorium, a chapel/recital hall and a complex of buildings that contains classrooms and studios. For further information contact the Interlochen Center for the Arts, P.O. Box 199, Interlochen, MI 49643; phone (231) 276-7200.

Interlochen Area Chamber of Commerce: P.O. Box 13, Interlochen, MI 49643; phone (231) 276-7141.

IRISH HILLS (I-4)

In the verdant, rolling region of the same name, Irish Hills has many lakes and is a popular vacation center. Recreational facilities are available at nearby Walter J. Hayes State Park *(see Recreation Chart and the AAA Great Lakes CampBook).*

MYSTERY HILL is on US 12 opposite Walter J. Hayes State Park. Twenty-minute guided tours are offered through exhibits that seem to defy the laws of gravity, such as water running uphill. A 19-hole miniature golf course and radio-controlled race cars

are also offered for an extra fee. Daily 11-7, Memorial Day-Labor Day; Sat.-Sun. 11-7, day after Labor Day-Sept. 30. Admission $6; ages 4-12, $5. Phone (517) 467-2517.

ST. JOSEPH'S SHRINE is 3 mi. e. of SR 50 on US 12. The shrine sits at the site of an early religious settlement visited by Father Gabriel Richard, minister to the Potawatomi Indians. The church is a combination of an original fieldstone chapel, erected by Irish settlers in the 1840s and '50s, and a 1929 addition. On the grounds are a life-size crucifixion group, a monument to early Irish settlers and an outdoor Stations of the Cross overlooking Iron Lake. Church open daily 8-dusk. Grounds open daily 24 hours. Free. Phone (517) 467-2183.

STAGECOACH STOP, U.S.A. is at 7203 US 12. The re-created 19th-century village contains a general store, trading post, saloons, print shop, ice cream parlor and a bank. More than 10,000 antiques are displayed. There are sawmill demonstrations as well as a wild country train ride, petting zoo, playground, picnic area and children's rides. Staged gunfights and magic shows take place daily.

Food is available. Tues.-Fri. noon-5:30, Sat.-Sun. 10:30-6:30, Memorial Day-Labor Day; closed Tues. following Mon. holidays. Admission $12; over 65 and ages 4-11, $8. AX, DS, MC, VI. Phone (517) 467-2300.

IRON MOUNTAIN (B-2) pop. 8,154

Iron Mountain was established in 1879 following the discovery of rich iron deposits. The mines continued to operate into the 1940s. *See Upper Peninsula p. 103.*

Tourism Association of the Dickinson County Area: 600 S. Stevenson St., Iron Mountain, MI 49801; phone (906) 774-2945 or (800) 236-2447.

CORNISH PUMPING ENGINE AND MINING MUSEUM is 2 blks. w. of US 2 on Kent St. The museum features one of the largest steam engines built in North America. Displays of mining equipment and artifacts relate the history of mining in the eastern Menominee Range. A World War II glider exhibit also is on display. Mon.-Sat. 9-5, Sun. noon-4, Memorial Day-Labor Day; otherwise varies. Admission $4; over 62, $3.50; ages 10-18, $2. Combination admission with the Menominee Range Historical Foundation Museum $7; over 62, $6; ages 10-18, $3. Phone (906) 774-1086.

IRON MOUNTAIN IRON MINE is 8 mi. e. on US 2. The mine, which operated 1877-1945, produced some 21,625,000 tons of ore. Guided tours by rail include demonstrations of mining machinery. Visitors should wear warm clothing. Daily 9-5, Memorial Day to mid-Oct. Admission $7.50; ages 6-12, $6.50. Phone (906) 563-8077.

MENOMINEE RANGE HISTORICAL FOUNDATION MUSEUM is at 300 E. Ludington St. The museum depicts local history from American Indian habitation to the present through chronological displays and re-created period rooms. Mon.-Sat. 10-4, May-Sept. Admission $4; over 62, $3.50; ages 10-18, $2. Combination admission with the Cornish Pumping Engine and Mining Museum $7; over 62, $6; ages 10-18, $3. Phone (906) 774-4276.

IRONWOOD (B-1) pop. 6,293, elev. 1,500′

Largest city in the Gogebic Range, Ironwood grew with the iron mining boom of the 1880s. It is the main trading, lumber and winter recreation center of the region. An imposing local landmark is the 52-foot colored fiberglass statue of Hiawatha, on Houk Street. *See Upper Peninsula p. 103.*

Western Upper Peninsula Convention and Visitors Bureau: 648 W. Cloverland Dr., P.O. Box 706, Ironwood, MI 49938; phone (906) 932-4850.

BLACK RIVER NATIONAL FOREST SCENIC BYWAY—*see Bessemer p. 48.*

RECREATIONAL ACTIVITIES
Skiing

• **Big Powderhorn** is off US 2 to 11375 Powderhorn Rd. N., Bessemer, MI 49911. Daily 9-4, mid-Nov. to early Apr. Phone (906) 932-4838.

• **Blackjack** is 6 mi. e. on US 2 to Blackjack Rd., Bessemer, MI 49911. Daily 9-4, early Dec.-late Mar. Phone (906) 229-5115 or (888) 906-9835.

• **Indianhead/Bear Creek** is 2 mi. w. on US 2. Write 500 Indianhead Rd., Wakefield, MI 49968. Daily 9-4, late Nov.-early Apr. Phone (800) 346-3426.

• **Mount Zion** is at 4946 Jackson Rd. Ironwood, MI 49938. Daily 9-4, Dec. 16-Mar. 1. Phone (906) 932-3718.

ISHPEMING (B-3) pop. 6,686, elev. 1,434′

In accordance with its name, which is thought to mean heaven, the Marquette iron range city of Ishpeming has become a well-known ski center. Organized skiing began in Ishpeming in 1887, when three Norwegians formed a ski club that eventually grew into a national ski association. *See Upper Peninsula p. 103.*

Ishpeming-Negaunee Chamber of Commerce: 661 Palms Ave., Ishpeming, MI 49849; phone (906) 486-4841.

SAVE **U.S. NATIONAL SKI HALL OF FAME AND MUSEUM** is on US 41 between Second and Third sts. at 610 Palms Ave. The greats of American skiing are honored here. The development of the sport is shown through photographs, antique grooming equipment, a cable car, trophies and other memorabilia. An 18-minute orientation videotape also is available.

Allow 1 hour minimum. Mon.-Sat. 10-5; closed Jan. 1, Easter, Thanksgiving and Dec. 25. Donations. DS, MC, VI. Phone (906) 485-6323.

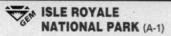

ISLE ROYALE NATIONAL PARK (A-1)

Elevations in the park range from 600 ft. at Lake Superior to 1,394 ft. at Mt. Desor. Refer to AAA maps for additional elevation information.

Northwest of the Upper Peninsula, Isle Royale is the largest island in Lake Superior. Dedicated as a national park in 1946, the main island is about 45 miles long and 8.5 miles across at the widest point. The park boundary extends 4.5 miles offshore. A rugged coastline and numerous crags and ridges add to the park's beauty; 99 percent of the island is wilderness.

Although the soil is only a few inches to a few feet deep, Isle Royale is covered with dense growths of spruce and balsam fir softened by carpets of wildflowers. Beavers, loons, wolves, moose, red foxes and snowshoe hares are abundant in the park. The island is an important research site and is designated as a U.S. Biosphere Reserve.

General Information and Activities

The park is open mid-April through October, with full services from mid-June through Labor Day. The park's 165 miles of trails are rocky and often wet and slippery; proper footwear should be worn when hiking. Visitors planning hiking trips should write for information. Camping is based on a first-come, first-served basis and is free. Permits are required and are available at ranger stations. Campfires are prohibited at most campgrounds, so visitors should bring self-contained fuel stoves; check with park headquarters or ranger stations.

All surface drinking water must be boiled for 2 minutes or filtered with a .4-micron filter before consumption. Chemical purification will not kill the tapeworm eggs that may exist in the water. No medical facilities are available on Isle Royale.

Swimming in the park is undesirable due to low water temperatures in Lake Superior (35-60 F). Swimming is allowed in the inland lakes; however, there are no lifeguards or beaches. Scuba diving should be attempted only by experienced divers; charters are available. Though a license is not necessary for fishing in the park's inland lakes and streams, Michigan state fishing regulations apply. Only artificial lures are permitted on inland waters. A Michigan state license is required for fishing in Lake Superior's waters. Guides are available for fishing trips.

Travel in the park is on foot or by boat. Boats and motors can be rented and gasoline purchased at Rock Harbor Lodge from late May to mid-September and at Windigo from early June to mid-September. The marina at Rock Harbor Lodge is open from mid-May to mid-September.

Transportation to the park is by boat or seaplane; reservations are recommended. Boat service to the island is available from Copper Harbor aboard the

Isle Royale Queen III mid-May through Sept. 29. Crossings take 4.5 hours one way. Boat service is available from Houghton aboard the park-owned *Ranger III* mid-May to mid-September. Crossings take 6 hours one-way. From Grand Portage, Minn., service is available from the *Wenonah* mid-June to early September; or *Voyageur II* mid-May through October. Crossings to Windigo take 1.5 hours one way, while the voyage to Rock Harbor takes 7 hours one way.

Float plane service also is available from Houghton mid-May to late September. Schedules and information for all vessels can be obtained from park headquarters. *See Upper Peninsula, the Recreation Chart and the AAA Great Lakes CampBook.*

WARNING— Crossing Lake Superior to the park in a craft less than 20 feet long is not advised. Private outboards, canoes, kayaks and boats up to 20 feet long may be transported on the *Ranger III* out of Houghton. Gasoline is available on the island but may not be carried on private boats.

ADMISSION is $4 per day, under 12 free. There are costs for transportation to the park.

PETS are not permitted in the park, including 4.5 miles offshore and on private or commercial vessels going to the park.

ADDRESS inquiries to park headquarters at Isle Royale National Park, 800 E. Lakeshore Dr., Houghton, MI 49931-1869; phone (906) 482-0984. Reservations for Rock Harbor Lodge or housekeeping cabins should be made with National Park Concessions Inc., Mammoth Cave, KY 42259-0027, (502) 773-2191, or from mid-May to mid-September with Rock Harbor Lodge, P.O. Box 605, Houghton, MI 49931-0605, (906) 337-4993.

Points of Interest

Beginning some 4,000 years ago, the park was mined for copper—evidence that the island might have been the source of much of the copper used by early American Indians. The metal has been found throughout the Ohio and Mississippi valleys. Mining activity also took place in the late 1800s on Isle Royale.

GREENSTONE RIDGE AND MINONG TRAILS generally follow the prominent ridges after which they are named. The Greenstone Ridge Trail permits access to points at either end of the island.

MOUNT FRANKLIN is reached by a scenic hike from the head of Tobin Harbor or by trail from Rock Harbor.

MOUNT OJIBWAY is reached by a 1.7-mile hike from Daisy Farm Campground. The peak affords a view of the surrounding countryside.

ROCK HARBOR LIGHTHOUSE is 6 mi. by launch from Rock Harbor Lodge. The restored 1855 lighthouse is reached by a .3-mile trail from the Edisen Fishery.

JACKSON (I-4) pop. 36,316, elev. 942′

Although the Republican Party itself was founded in Ripon, Wis., in 1854, Jackson played host to the party's first formal meeting. The city also was one of the key stops on the Underground Railroad. Some of the houses that served as way stations and sanctuaries still can be seen. Today diversified industry and transportation services anchor Jackson's economy. With 188 lakes, the area offers plenty of recreational opportunities.

Jackson County Convention and Visitors Bureau: 6007 Ann Arbor Rd., Jackson, MI 49201; phone (517) 764-4440 or (800) 245-5282.

Shopping areas: Jackson Crossing Mall, at the junction of US 127 and I-94, features Kohl's, Sears and Toys R Us; Westwood Mall, at Michigan Avenue and Brown Street, features Elder-Beerman and JCPenney.

CASCADES AT SPARKS FOUNDATION COUNTY PARK is s.w. of city limits at jct. Brown and Denton sts. The park occupies 465 acres and contains the Illuminated Cascades—a giant waterfall and six fountains over which water tumbles in continually changing patterns. There also is a small museum depicting the history of Cascades Falls, two golf courses, tennis courts, a picnic area, lagoons, paddleboats, batting cages and a miniature golf course.

Park open daily until 11 p.m. Illuminated Cascades can be seen 8:30-11 p.m., Memorial Day-Labor Day. Park free. Admission to Cascades $3, under 6 free. Phone (517) 788-4320.

ELLA SHARP PARK is 2 mi. s. on 4th St. The largest park in the city, it covers 562 partially wooded acres. On the grounds are athletic fields, bicycle and jogging paths, cross-country ski trails, an 18-hole golf course, a driving range, a miniature golf course, picnic areas, nature trails and a swimming pool. Food is available. Daily 24 hours. Free. Phone (517) 788-4343. *See Recreation Chart.*

[SAVE] **Ella Sharp Museum** is at 3225 4th St. The museum provides a look at 19th-century farmstead life. It includes tours of a Victorian house; a pioneer log house; a barn with 1800s carriages, sleighs and farm implements; a woodshop; an 1885 one-room schoolhouse; and a country store complex featuring a print shop and doctor's office. The museum also features art and history in three exhibition galleries.

Food is available. Tues.-Fri. 10-4, Sat.-Sun. 11-4; closed major holidays. Last tour begins 30 minutes before closing. Museum $4; over 55 and students with ID $3; ages 5-18, $2; family rate (2 adults and 2 children under 18) $10. Phone (517) 787-2320.

[GEM] **MICHIGAN SPACE & SCIENCE CENTER** is on the Jackson Community College campus at 2111 Emmons Rd. A striking gold geodesic dome houses the *Apollo 9* command module, a memorial to the space shuttle *Challenger*, space suits, satellites, a moon rock, the Astrotheatre, an infinity room, a model of the Hubble Space

Telescope and a Mars PathFinder exhibit. Other displays deal with past and future space voyages and black holes. Visitors may climb inside a space capsule. There are several interactive computer exhibits. Outside is an 85-foot Mercury Redstone rocket, rocket engines and missiles.

Picnic facilities are available. Allow 1 hour minimum. Tues.-Sat. 10-5, Sun. noon-5, May-Oct.; Tues.-Sat. 10-5, rest of year. Closed Jan. 1, Thanksgiving and Dec. 25. Last tour begins 1 hour before closing. Admission $5, over 60 and students with ID $3, under 5 with parent free. DS, MC, VI. Phone (517) 787-4425.

KALAMAZOO (I-2) pop. 77,145, elev. 792'

Springs bubbling up in the riverbed are said to have been the inspiration for Kalamazoo's catchy name, an American Indian word meaning "place where the water boils." Whatever its origin, Kalamazoo has enlivened many a poem and song.

Produce from the nearby vegetable-growing region and the diverse yields of many industries provide the basis of Kalamazoo's economy. Western Michigan University and other schools contribute to the city's cultural life. River Oaks Park and Bronson Park are sites for numerous festivals.

Kalamazoo County Convention and Visitors Bureau: 346 W. Michigan Ave., P.O. Box 1169, Kalamazoo, MI 49007; phone (269) 381-4003.

KALAMAZOO AVIATION HISTORY MUSEUM (AIR ZOO) is off I-94 exit 78, .7 mi. s. on Portage Rd., then .5 mi. e. to 3101 E. Milham Rd. Museum exhibits include rare planes dating from pre-World War II, most of which still fly, and several aircraft used in Korea and Vietnam. Among the collection of more than 70 vintage aircraft are a Curtiss P-40 and four Grumman Cats.

Among the displays are several functioning aircraft engines, a USMC jeep, memorabilia and more than 100 model aircraft. Highlights include the Guadalcanal Memorial Museum; Simulation Station, which features Hudson full-motion flight simulators and trainers; and the Michigan Aviation Hall of Fame. Videotape presentations are shown continuously. Guided tours of the restoration center are available.

Allow 1 hour, 30 minutes minimum. Mon.-Sat. 9-6, Sun. noon-6, June-Aug.; Mon.-Sat. 9-5; Sun. noon-5, rest of year. Closed Jan. 1, Easter, Thanksgiving and Dec. 24-25. Admission $10; over 60, $8; ages 6-15, $5. AX, DS, MC, VI. Phone (269) 382-6555.

KALAMAZOO INSTITUTE OF ARTS is at 314 S. Park St. The complex combines galleries, a school, a library and an auditorium in a contemporary structure. Displayed in the galleries are permanent and temporary exhibits of 20th-century American

art, European prints and works from Michigan artists. Tues.-Sat. 10-5, Sun. noon-5 in Sept.; Tues.-Sat. 10-5, rest of year. Closed major holidays. Donations. Phone (269) 349-7775.

KALAMAZOO NATURE CENTER is at 7000 N. Westnedge Ave. The area's natural history is illustrated through an interactive exhibit at the center, which is situated on a 1,000-acre preserve. Nature trails and an 11-acre arboretum with a hummingbird and butterfly garden are offered. A sun/rain room features tropical plants, geckos and tropical fish. A restored pioneer homestead is open during special events; a petting farm is operated May through September.

Tours are available by appointment. Nature center and grounds Mon.-Sat. 9-5, Sun. and holidays 1-5; closed Jan. 1, Thanksgiving and Dec. 24-25. Admission $5.50; over 54, $4; ages 4-13, $3.50. Phone (269) 381-1574.

KALAMAZOO VALLEY MUSEUM is at 230 N. Rose St. on the Arcadia Commons Campus of the Kalamazoo Valley Community College. Permanent exhibits include a 2,500-year-old mummy and science and history galleries that house interactive exhibits, photographs and artifacts. Mini-missions simulate a trip to Mars in the Challenger Learning Center. The Digistar II Planetarium and Theater also are available.

Mon.-Sat. 9-5 (also Wed. 5-8), Sun. 1-5; closed major holidays. Phone for program schedules. Challenger admission $3. Planetarium admission $3. Museum free. Under 12 must be accompanied by an adult in the Challenger center. Under 6 are not permitted. Phone (269) 373-7990.

WINERIES

• **Peterson & Sons Winery** is s. off I-94 exit 85, following signs to 9375 E. P Ave. Mon. and Fri.-Sat. 10-6, Sun. noon-6. Phone (269) 626-9755.

LANSING (H-3) pop. 119,128, elev. 843´

Lansing became the permanent state capital in 1847 more by default than design. Weary of wrangling and unable to suggest a better place, the legislature—amid laughter because the chosen site then consisted of one log cabin and a sawmill—gave the honor to Lansing. Because proponents of renaming the new capital Michigan or Michigamme reached a similar impasse, Lansing it remained.

Once the decision was made, the town began to grow. By the time it was incorporated in 1859, there were some 4,000 enterprising residents, an increasing number of small industries, a new brick Capitol and two newspapers that provided more political entertainment than news.

The real industrial flowering of the city is credited to R.E. Olds, whose buggy was one of the first practical motor vehicles. By the early 1900s Lansing was a leading maker of automobiles and gasoline engines. Although its economy is more diversified, Lansing is still a stronghold of the automotive industry. The atmosphere of manufacturing

and government is leavened with that of education by Michigan State University and its many points of interest *(see East Lansing p. 66).*

Greater Lansing Convention and Visitors Bureau: 1223 Turner St., Suite 200, Lansing, MI 48906; phone (888) 252-6746 or (800) 648-6630.

CARL G. FENNER NATURE CENTER is at 2020 E. Mount Hope Ave. The center has 4 miles of nature trails, an herb garden, a butterfly garden and a visitor center building with reptiles, amphibians, native birds and environmental displays.

Picnicking is permitted. Grounds open daily 8-dusk. Visitor center open Tues.-Fri. 9-4, Sat.-Sun. 11-5, mid-Mar. through Nov. 30; Sat.-Sun. 11-4, rest of year. Closed Jan. 1, Easter, Thanksgiving, day after Thanksgiving, and Dec. 22-25 and 29-31. Free. Phone (517) 483-4224.

[SAVE] **IMPRESSION 5 SCIENCE CENTER** is at 200 Museum Dr. Housed in a renovated century-old building with original wood floors and brick walls, the hands-on museum has a chemistry lab and displays about energy, water, chemistry, simple mechanics, medicine and physics. Allow 2 hours minimum. Mon.-Sat. 10-5; closed major holidays, first week in Sept. and Dec. 24. Admission $5; over 62 and ages 3-17, $3.50. AX, DS, MC, VI. Phone (517) 485-8116.

MICHIGAN LIBRARY AND HISTORICAL CENTER COMPLEX is at 702 W. Kalamazoo St. The museum has displays about state history from prehistoric times to the late 20th century. Twenty-six permanent galleries and a temporary exhibit area feature a three-story relief map; a re-created, walkthrough copper mine; a one-room schoolhouse; a 1920s street scene; and a large diorama. The center also houses the state library and archives. Museum open Mon.-Fri. 9-4:30, Sat. 10-4, Sun. 1-5; closed holidays. Free. Phone (517) 373-3559 for the museum, (517) 373-1300 for the library or (517) 373-1408 for the archives.

MICHIGAN WOMEN'S HISTORICAL CENTER & HALL OF FAME is at 213 W. Main St. Rotating exhibits call attention to the lives, history and achievements of Michigan women. An art gallery features the work of the state's outstanding female artists and photographers, while the Michigan Women's Hall of Fame honors those who have made significant contributions to the state. Allow 30 minutes minimum. Wed.-Fri. noon-5, Sat. noon-4, Sun. 2-4; closed major holidays. Admission $2.50; senior citizens $2; ages 5-18, $1. MC, VI. Phone (517) 484-1880.

MUSEUM OF SURVEYING is .2 mi. w. on Michigan Ave., then .2 mi. s. to 220 S. Museum Dr. The museum houses a collection of historical land surveying artifacts. Educational programs, archives and a videotape library also are available. Allow 30 minutes minimum. Mon.-Fri. 9-4; closed major holidays. Free. Phone (517) 484-6605.

POTTER PARK ZOO is at 1301 S. Pennsylvania Ave. Primates, lions, penguins, snow leopards, rhinoceroses, a camel, tiger, reptiles, farm animals and birds live at the zoo. Pony rides are offered in summer, and light shows are presented late November through December. Picnicking is permitted. Food is available. Allow 1 hour minimum. Park open daily 9-7. Buildings open daily 10-5. Admission $6; over 59 and ages 3-15, $2. Parking $2; oversized vehicles Sat.-Sun. $5. Phone (517) 483-4222.

R.E. OLDS TRANSPORTATION MUSEUM is .2 mi. w. on Michigan Ave., then .2 mi. s. to 240 Museum Dr. Artifacts and documents trace the history of area transportation from 1883 to the present. Antique vehicles and automotive memorabilia as well as aircraft, bicycles and carriages are displayed. Automobiles exhibited range from the first Oldsmobile, built in 1897 to contemporary vehicles.

Guided tours are available by request. Allow 30 minutes minimum. Tues.-Sat. 10-5, Sun. noon-5, May-Oct.; Tues.-Sat. 10-5, rest of year. Closed most holidays. Admission $4; over 60, ages 6-17 and students with ID $2; family rate $8. MC, VI. Phone (517) 372-0422 or (517) 372-0529.

STATE CAPITOL is at Capitol and Michigan aves. One of the first state capitols designed to resemble the U.S. Capitol, it was dedicated in 1879 and since has been restored to reflect that period. Tours lasting 45 minutes are offered every 30 minutes Mon.-Fri. 9-4. Free. Phone (517) 373-2353.

LELAND (E-2) pop. 2,033, elev. 656′

The village of Leland, bordered by Lake Michigan to the west and Lake Leelanau to the east, is a popular departure point for lake cruises and fishing charters. Settled in 1853, Leland was named by the many sailors who used the harbor. On the harbor is Fishtown, a collection of shops, galleries and art studios in a rustic fishing village setting.

Passenger ferry service is available to the North and South Manitou islands *(see Sleeping Bear Dunes National Lakeshore p. 100)* by Manitou Island Transit. Daily service is provided to South Manitou Island, while transportation to North Manitou Island is available daily July 1 to mid-Aug.; Wed., Fri. and Sun.,

June 1-15; Wed. and Fri.-Mon., June 16-30. Reservations are recommended. Tours of South Manitou Island also are available. Phone (231) 256-9061.

LEELANAU HISTORICAL MUSEUM is at 203 E. Cedar St. The museum, on the Leland River, offers permanent and changing historical displays documenting the settlement and development of the Leelanau peninsula. Traditional and folk arts exhibits also are included. Allow 30 minutes minimum. Mon.-Sat. 10-4, Sun. 1-4, mid-June through Labor Day; Fri.-Sat. 1-4 and by appointment, rest of year. Closed holidays. Admission $2; ages 5-11, $1; family rate $5. VI. Phone (231) 256-7475.

WINERIES

- **Good Harbor Vineyards** is 3 mi. s. on SR 22. Mon.-Sat. 11-6, Sun. noon-5, Apr. 1-day before Labor Day; Mon.-Sat. 11-5, Sun. noon-5, Labor Day-Oct. 30; Sat. 11-5, rest of year. Phone (231) 256-7165.

LES CHENEAUX ISLANDS (B-6)

The many bays and channels *(cheneaux)* created by the 36 wooded islands that dot Lake Huron off the south shore of the eastern Upper Peninsula account for the islands' name as well as their popularity. This is one of the most scenic snowmobiling, boating and fishing areas in the state. Government Island is maintained as an uninhabited isle by the Hiawatha National Forest *(see place listing p. 73)*.

The islands can be reached from both Hessel and Cedarville. An information center on SR 134 at Cedarville is open Mon.-Fri. 9-5.

Les Cheneaux Area Welcome Center: P.O. Box 10, Cedarville, MI 49719; phone (906) 484-3935 or (888) 364-7526.

LIVONIA— *see Detroit p. 64*

LUDINGTON (F-1) pop. 8,357, elev. 593′

Ludington is a popular fishing center and port on the eastern shore of Lake Michigan at the mouth of the Pere Marquette River. Freighters and pleasure

craft find safe deepwater harborage in Pere Marquette Lake. Chinook, coho and king salmon can be caught in Lake Michigan and in the Pere Marquette River.

The SS *Badger*, operated by the Lake Michigan Carferry Service, offers 4-hour cruises and automobile ferry service from Ludington to Manitowoc, Wis. For information and fares phone (800) 841-4243. *See color ad p. 81 & color ad p. 145.*

The huge illuminated cross that overlooks the harbor marks the spot where Pere Jacques Marquette is thought to have died in 1675. Eight miles north on SR 116, Ludington State Park *(see Recreation Chart and the AAA Great Lakes CampBook)* borders both Lake Michigan and Hamlin Lake and offers fine beaches, dunes and a visitor center.

Ludington Area Convention and Visitors Bureau: 5300 W. US 10, Ludington, MI 49431; phone (231) 845-5430 or (800) 542-4600.

HISTORIC WHITE PINE VILLAGE is 2 mi. s. via Pere Marquette Hwy. to Iris Rd., then w. 1.5 mi. to 1687 S. Lakeshore Dr. This reconstructed community of 22 buildings dating from 1850-1950 overlooks Lake Michigan. Included are a blacksmith shop, courthouse, hardware store, fire hall, chapel and schoolhouse along with music, logging and maritime museums.

Self-guiding tours are available. Picnicking is permitted. Allow 1 hour, 30 minutes minimum. Tues.-Sat. 11-5, Apr.-Oct. Admission $6; over 59, $4.50; ages 6-17, $4; family rate (parents or grandparents and children under 18) $18. Admission is slightly higher during events. MC, VI. Phone (231) 843-4808.

MACKINAC ISLAND (C-6) pop. 523

American Indians called it Michilimackinac, or "Great Turtle," but time and usage have shortened the island's name to Mackinac (MACK-i-naw). This limestone outcrop became a frontier outpost in 1780, when the English moved the old French garrison on the mainland to the more strategic island. It remained the stronghold of the Straits of Mackinac for 115 years.

The island is 3 miles long and 2 miles wide with high cliffs fronting the shore. Ravines, natural bridges, caves and strange rock formations can be found. Arch Rock and Sugar Loaf are scenic points. Mackinac Island State Park is particularly attractive in mid-June when the lilacs bloom.

The island can be reached by boat from St. Ignace or Mackinaw City *(see place listings p. 98 and p. 84)*. Summer sports facilities include a yacht

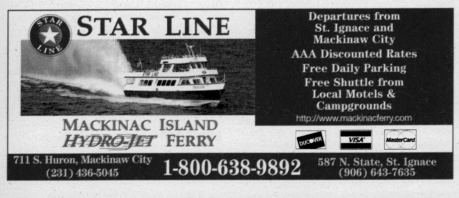

harbor and golf courses. Pets must be physically restrained at all times. Accommodations are available from mid-May to late October and mid-December to March.

Ferry service from St. Ignace to Mackinac Island operates from early May through October. For schedules and prices, contact Arnold Mackinac Island Ferry *(see color ad p. 82)*, (906) 847-3351 or (800) 542-8528; SAVE Shepler's Mackinac Island Ferry *(see color ad p. 85)*, (906) 643-9440, (231) 436-5023 or (800) 828-6157; or Star Line Mackinac Island Hydro-Jet Ferry *(see color ad p. 82)*, *(906) 643-7635 or (800) 638-9892.*

Once on the island, transportation is by horse-drawn carriage, bicycle or saddle horse; no motorized vehicles are permitted, except for a public utilities truck, a fire truck and an ambulance. For this reason, SR 185, which rims the island, is possibly the only state highway in the nation on which a motor vehicle accident has never occurred. Bicycles may be brought over on the ferry or rented on the island.

Mackinac Island Tourism Bureau: Main St., P.O. Box 451, Mackinac Island, MI 49757; phone (906) 847-3783 or (800) 454-5227.

CARRIAGE TOURS depart from the center of the shopping district on Main St. Narrated tours (lasting 1 hour, 45 minutes) visit Mackinac Island's scenic and historic points of interest, including Arch Rock, Fort Mackinac, Governor's Mansion, the Grand Hotel, Skull Cave and Surrey Hill. Daily 9-5,

mid-June through Labor Day; 9-3, mid-May to mid-June and day after Labor Day-Oct. 31. Fare $16.50; ages 5-12, $7.50. Phone (906) 847-3307.

EARLY MISSIONARY BARK CHAPEL is in Marquette Park. The church is a reconstruction patterned after chapels built on the island in the late 1600s. The original was erected by early Jesuit missionaries. Daily 9:30-4:30, mid-May to mid-Oct. Free. Phone (906) 847-3328.

FORT MACKINAC is on a bluff overlooking the harbor. The restored 18th- and 19th-century British and American military outpost is preserved as a museum. All the buildings are original; their history is interpreted through period settings, audiovisual presentations and the children's discovery room. Costumed guides offer reenactments, military music and cannon and rifle firings.

Food is available. Daily 9:30-6, mid-June to late Aug.; 9-4, early May to mid-June and late Aug.-early Oct. Admission $9; ages 6-17, $5.75 (admission mid-June to late Aug. includes Dr. Beaumont Museum, Benjamin Blacksmith Shop, Biddle House, Mission Church and McGulpin House). Combination admission with Colonial Michilimackinac and Historic Mill Creek $18.50; ages 6-17, $11. MC, VI. Phone (906) 847-3328 or (231) 436-4100.

Benjamin Blacksmith Shop is on Market St. Demonstrations using original 19th- and 20th-century blacksmith equipment are offered. Daily 11-6, mid-June to late Aug.

Biddle House is on Market St. The house contains early 19th-century furnishings. Domestic craft demonstrations are offered. Daily 11-6, mid-June to late Aug.

Dr. Beaumont Museum is on Fort St. Housed in the restored 1820 American Fur Company Store, the museum is dedicated to Dr. William Beaumont, who pioneered studies of the human digestive system. His medical instruments are on display and are explained by costumed interpreters. Daily 11-6, mid-June to late Aug.

McGulpin House is on Fort St. An example of French-Canadian architecture, the house may have been one of the buildings brought to Mackinac Island from Fort Michilimackinac, established in 1780. Daily 11-6, mid-June to late Aug.

Mission Church is 1 mi. e. on Huron St. The church is the first Protestant work of the American Indians at Fort Mackinac and is said to be the oldest surviving church in the state. It was built in 1829 by local residents in the New England Colonial style and contains an antique organ. Allow 30 minutes minimum. Daily noon-4, mid-June to late Aug.

MACKINAW CITY (D-3) pop. 859, elev. 591′

First a guardian of the Straits of Mackinac, now a destination for thousands of northbound vacationers, Mackinaw City was once a trading post established by early French settlers; the post became Fort Michilimackinac in 1715. During the ensuing decades the strategically situated garrison was held successively by the French, the British, the Indians, then the British again. The British moved the fort to Mackinac Island 1780-81.

The city is connected to the Upper Peninsula by way of the Mackinac Bridge. One of the longest suspension spans in the world, it stretches for 5 miles. Built in 1957, it provided a convenient means of transportation between the two peninsulas. The toll is $2.50.

Mackinaw Area Visitors Bureau: 10300 US 23, P.O. Box 160, Mackinaw City, MI 49701; phone (231) 436-5664 or (800) 666-0160. *See color ad p. 85.*

Shopping areas: Mackinaw Crossing, at 248 S. Huron Ave., is a shopping, dining and entertainment complex containing a five-screen movie theater, restaurants, stores and courtyards. More than 100 shops line Central Avenue (Main Street).

COLONIAL MICHILIMACKINAC is on the site of Fort Michilimackinac. The fort comprises 27 acres. Built by the French in 1715, it was occupied by British forces 1761-1781. Among the reconstructed buildings are a priest's house, a guardhouse, blockhouses, barracks, a storehouse, a blacksmith shop, a French church and a British trader's house.

Costumed reenactments, an audiovisual program and exhibits illustrate the history of the fort. Other programs include blacksmithing and cooking demonstrations, musket and cannon firings, a Colonial wedding and dance, an American Indian encampment, an archeological tunnel exhibit and the arrival of French voyageurs. Archeological excavations are conducted daily mid-June through Labor Day.

Allow 2 hours minimum. Daily 9-5:30, mid-June to late Aug.; 9-4, early May to mid-June and late Aug.-early Oct. Admission $9; ages 6-17, $5.75. Combination admission with Fort Mackinac and Historic Mill

Creek $18.50; ages 6-17, $11. DS, MC, VI. Phone (231) 436-4100.

HISTORIC MILL CREEK is 3 mi. s.e. on US 23. This is the site of an 18th-century industrial complex believed to be the oldest in the Great Lakes region. A water powered sawmill built about 1790 provided lumber for construction on Mackinac Island. Archeological evidence of the sawmill, a dam and several houses was discovered in 1972 by a Cheboygan high school history teacher.

Demonstrations of sawmill operations are given daily. Interpretive nature trails lead to scenic overlooks, including a view of the Mackinac Bridge and a beaver colony. There is a 12-minute audiovisual orientation.

Food is available. Daily 9-5, mid-June to late Aug.; 9-4, early May to mid-June and late Aug.-early Oct. Admission $7.50; ages 6-17, $4.50. Combination admission with Fort Mackinac and Colonial Michilimackinac $18.50; ages 6-17, $11. DS, MC, VI. Phone (231) 436-4100.

MACKINAC BRIDGE MUSEUM is at 231 E. Central Ave. Memorabilia and artifacts pertain to the history and construction of the Mackinac Bridge. A film about the bridge is presented continuously. Food is available. Allow 30 minutes minimum. Daily 8 a.m.-midnight, May-Oct. Free. Phone (231) 436-5534.

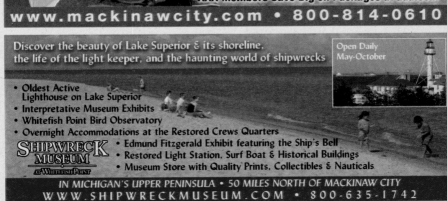

MANISTEE (F-2) pop. 6,586, elev. 598'

As early as 1790 French and English fur traders inhabited the area that the Chippewa called Manistee, "spirit of the woods." The 19th-century logging frenzy ensured that the name would outlive the woods, yet the people—mainly Swedes and Norwegians—who came to shear the timber stayed to develop the city.

The port handles the deluge of fruit grown in the area. Vast brine deposits make Manistee a primary producer of salt.

Manistee Area Chamber of Commerce: 11 Cypress St., Manistee, MI 49660; phone (800) 288-2286.

Self-guiding tours: Relics of the logging era, many ornate Victorian mansions line the residential streets, and refurbished buildings can be found in the commercial section. Walking tour brochures are available at the chamber of commerce and the Lyman Building.

MANISTEE COUNTY HISTORICAL MUSEUM is at 425 River St. Historical exhibits are housed in the old A. H. Lyman Company store. Displays include the fittings of an 1885 drugstore and general store, photographs and exhibits of Civil War and pioneer memorabilia. Allow 1 hour minimum.

Mon.-Sat. 10-5, June-Sept.; Tues.-Sat. 10-5, rest of year. Closed holidays except July 4. Admission (includes Water Works Building) $2, family rate $5. Phone (231) 723-5531.

Water Works Building is at 540 W. First St. Built in 1882, it houses marine and logging exhibits. Allow 30 minutes minimum. Tues.-Sat. 10:30-4:30, mid-June to late Aug. Admission is included with Manistee County Historical Museum. Phone (231) 723-5531.

CASINOS

- **Little River Casino** is at 2700 Orchard Hwy. Daily 24 hours. Phone (231) 723-1535. *See ad.*

MANISTIQUE (B-4) pop. 3,583, elev. 613'

Manistique provides access to the 300 lakes and numerous streams of the Lake Superior State Forest and 135 miles of maintained snowmobile trails. The bridge carrying SR 94 across the Manistique River is unusual in that its floor is below river level.

Palms Book State Park, 12 miles northwest, is best known for Kitch-iti-ki-pi, a clear, cold spring 200 feet wide and 40 feet deep. Seven miles southwest via US 2 and SR 149 is the state fish hatchery that introduced the coho salmon into Michigan waters to counteract the invasion of alewives that followed the opening of the St. Lawrence Seaway.

A scenic portion of US 2 passes through Manistique on its way from Escanaba *(see place listing p. 67)* to St. Ignace *(see place listing p. 98)*. About one-third of the distance follows the shore of Lake Michigan. *See Upper Peninsula p. 103.*

Schoolcraft County Chamber of Commerce: 1000 W. Lake Shore Dr., Manistique, MI 49854; phone (906) 341-5010.

CASINOS

- **Kewadin Casino** is 4.5 mi. e. on US 2. Fri.-Sat. 24 hours, Sun.-Thurs. 8 a.m.-3 a.m. Phone (906) 341-5510.

MARQUETTE (B-3) pop. 19,661, elev. 636′

First settled in 1849 as a shipping center, Marquette was named for the French missionary and explorer Father Jacques Marquette. Surrounded by the rugged Laurentian Uplands on the southern shore of Lake Superior, the city is heralded as the medical, shopping and political center of the Upper Peninsula. The wooden dome at Northern Michigan University's Great Lakes Sports Training Center offers football, soccer and an Olympic training facility.

Marquette is the western terminus of a scenic 42-mile drive that is US 41 for a few miles south, then SR 28 along the lakeshore to Munising *(see place listing p. 90)*. *Also see Upper Peninsula p. 103.*

Marquette Country Convention and Visitors Bureau: 2552 US 41W, Suite 300, Marquette, MI 49855; phone (906) 228-7749 or (800) 544-4321.

Self-guiding tours: Walking tour maps of historic Marquette can be purchased at the Marquette County History Museum.

MARQUETTE COUNTY HISTORY MUSEUM is at 213 N. Front St. Visitors can see pioneer artifacts and mining and lumber displays. Mon.-Fri. 10-5 (also third Thurs. of the month 5-9), Sat. 11-4, June-Aug.; closed holidays. Admission $3, students with ID $1, under 13 free. Phone (906) 226-3571.

MARQUETTE MARITIME MUSEUM is at 300 Lakeshore Blvd. Displays in an 1890s water works building describe the maritime heritage of Marquette and Lake Superior. A film is shown. Dockside offices of Marquette's first commercial fishing and passenger freight companies are re-created; a fishing shanty contains sport fishing gear. A Coast Guard lighthouse is adjacent to the museum; guided tours of the lighthouse and grounds are available.

Allow 30 minutes minimum. Daily 10-5, May-Oct. Admission $3; students K-12, $2. Lighthouse and grounds tour $3; students K-12, $2. Combination ticket $5; students K-12, $3. MC, VI. Phone (906) 226-2006.

PRESQUE ISLE PARK is n. of the city. This 328-acre wooded peninsula juts into Lake Superior. The park offers picnic facilities and rock hunting; facilities include an outdoor pool with a waterslide. Nature trails wind throughout the park and are used for bog walks in the summer and snowshoeing and cross-country skiing in winter. Allow 30 minutes minimum. Daily 7 a.m.-11 p.m. Free. Phone (906) 228-0460.

[SAVE] **THE UPPER PENINSULA CHILDREN'S MUSEUM** is at 123 W. Baraga Ave. Interactive exhibits were designed with input from local children and families. Subjects range from reptiles and forests to trains and planes. Allow 1 hour minimum. Mon.-Wed. and Sat. 10-6, Thurs. 10-7:30, Fri. 10-8, Sun. noon-5; closed Jan. 1, Thanksgiving and Dec. 25. Admission $4.50; ages 2-17, $3.50. Phone (906) 226-3911.

MARSHALL (I-3) pop. 7,459, elev. 898′

In 1846 near the site of Triangle Park, an event occurred that bore nationwide import. Adam Crosswhite, a Marshall resident, was seized by agents of the Kentucky slaveholder from whom he had escaped 2 years earlier. The townsfolk sprang to his defense, sending the slave hunters home without him and providing the Crosswhite family with passage to freedom in Canada.

Sued by the former slave owner, the Marshall abolitionists lost. The Crosswhite case was instrumental in the creation of the 1850 Fugitive Slave Act, which in turn contributed to tensions that became the Civil War.

A historic houses tour held the first weekend after Labor Day focuses on one of Marshall's hallmarks: an unusual number of excellent, well-preserved examples of Greek and Gothic revival, Italianate and Queen Anne architecture. Their survival resulted in part from the dashing of two 19th-century dreams: Marshall failed to become the capital, and the railroad boom collapsed. Foresight has since supplanted chance, and the structures are carefully protected.

Marshall Area Chamber of Commerce: 424 E. Michigan Ave., Marshall, MI 49068; phone (269) 781-5163 or (800) 877-5163.

Self-guiding tours: A map detailing a tour of Marshall is available at local shops and inns, the chamber of commerce and the Honolulu House Museum.

HONOLULU HOUSE MUSEUM is off Fountain Cir. to 107 N. Kalamazoo Ave. The home was built in 1860 by a chief justice of the Michigan Supreme Court who later became U.S. Consul to Hawaii. A blend of Victorian and island living styles, the house was influenced by his Hawaiian house. A raised veranda, pagoda-capped tower and rooms with elaborate 15-foot ceilings hand-painted in high Victorian style are highlights. Daily noon-5, May-Sept.; Thurs.-Sun. noon-5 in Oct. Admission $5; senior citizens and ages 12-18, $4; under 5 free. Phone (269) 781-8544.

MEARS (G-1)

MAC WOOD'S DUNE RIDES is 9 mi. w. of US 31 on Silver Lake. Guides take passengers on 40-minute scenic rides over 8 miles of shifting sand dunes. Daily 9:30-dusk, May 1-early Oct. Fare $13.50; under 12, $9. Phone (231) 873-2817.

SILVER LAKE STATE PARK is off US 31 to Hart or Shelby exit, then 7 mi. w. following signs. The park encompasses 3,400 acres, approximately 1,800 of which are covered in sweeping sand dunes. The dunes can be explored in off-road vehicles in the northern portion of the park or on foot in the center section. Silver Lake is a good place for swimming, fishing or boating. Little Sable Point Lighthouse, built in 1873, overlooks a scenic portion of Lake Michigan.

Daily 9 a.m.-10 p.m., Memorial Day-Labor Day; 9-8, Apr. 1-day before Memorial Day and day after Labor Day-Oct. 31. Day pass $8, Mich. residents $6; off-road permit (to drive on dunes) $16.25. Phone (231) 873-3083 or (800) 447-2757. *See Recreation Chart.*

RECREATIONAL ACTIVITIES
Jeep Tours (Self-driving)
- **Sandy Korners Jeep Tours** is off US 31 Hart exit, then 2 mi. w., following signs to 1762 N. 24th Ave. Daily 10-8:30, May-Oct. Phone (231) 873-5048.

MIDLAND (G-4) pop. 41,685, elev. 610′

The development of Midland from a lumber town into a handsome, well-planned and culturally active city is entwined with the growth of the Dow Chemical Co. Large brine deposits precipitated the establishment of the company in Midland.

The Alden B. Dow Home and Studio, 315 Post St., integrates organic textures, geometric angles and rich colors with the natural surroundings. The building was designed by Dow, who apprenticed with Frank Lloyd Wright. Tours are given by appointment; phone (989) 839-2744 or (866) 315-7678.

The Tridge, a three-legged pedestrian bridge, is at the confluence of the Tittabawasee and Chippewa rivers. The Pere Marquette Rail-Trail provides 22 miles of paved hiking trails between the Tridge and Coleman. The riverfront area also features picnic facilities, walking trails, an outdoor concert park and a farmers' market.

Midland County Convention and Visitors Bureau: 300 Rodd St., Suite 101, Midland, MI 48640; phone (989) 839-9522 or (888) 464-3526.

CHIPPEWA NATURE CENTER is 3.5 mi. s.w. at 400 S. Badour Rd. More than 1,000 acres of woods, fields, ponds, rivers and wetlands as well as hiking and cross-country skiing trails are featured. A museum has interactive exhibits, a library, a restored 1870s farm, an 1880s log school house, a sugarhouse and an arboretum with Michigan trees and shrubs.

Allow 2 hours minimum. Visitor center open Mon.-Fri. 8-5, Sat. 9-5, Sun. 1-5; holiday hours vary. Closed Thanksgiving and Dec. 25. Grounds open daily dawn-dusk. Donations. Phone (989) 631-0830.

DOW GARDENS is next to Midland Center for the Arts at 1809 Eastman Ave. On display are 600 species of flowers and shrubs on 100 landscaped acres. Allow 1 hour minimum. Daily 9 until 2 hours before dusk; closed Jan. 1, Thanksgiving and Dec. 25. Admission $5; ages 6-17, $2. Phone (989) 631-2677 or (800) 362-4874.

HERBERT H. DOW HISTORICAL MUSEUM is w. on W. Main St. to 3200 Cook Rd. Displays chronicle the life of the founder of Dow Chemical Co., Herbert H. Dow, who conducted his pioneering chemical experiments in a nearby shed. The museum is housed in a replica of a gristmill. Exhibits include Dow's first office and his father's workshop. A 12-minute videotape presentation features a miniature image of Dow explaining his contributions to chemistry.

Next to the mill is a replica of the 1890 Midland Chemical Co., Dow's first manufacturing plant. A laboratory, steam engine and chemical tank help convey the humble beginnings of the Dow Chemical Co. Allow 1 hour, 30 minutes minimum. Wed.-Sat. 10-4, Sun. 1-5; closed holidays. Admission $4; under 13, $2. Phone (989) 832-5319.

Bradley Home Museum & Carriage House is at 3200 Cook Rd. The 1874 Victorian house contains Victorian furnishings, fixtures and costumes. The Carriage House exhibits 15 horse-drawn vehicles, blacksmithing equipment and related items. Allow 30 minutes minimum. Wed.-Sat. 10-4, Sun. 1-5; closed holidays. Free with admission to Dow Historical Museum. Phone (989) 832-5319.

MIDLAND CENTER FOR THE ARTS is 2 mi. s. of US 10 at Eastman and W. St. Andrews rds. Concerts, plays and musicals are presented here. The center contains a museum with changing displays about science, technology, health, hands-on discovery, art and history. The Art Midland galleries and Midland Historical Society exhibits also can be seen. Guided tours are available. Allow 1 hour minimum. Tues.-Sat. 10-6, Sun. noon-6; closed major holidays. Admission $4; under 13, $2. Phone (989) 631-5930.

MIO (E-4) pop. 2,016

Surrounded by the Huron-Manistee National Forests *(see place listing p. 75)* and with the Au Sable River nearby, Mio is a popular departure point and equipment rental center for fishing and canoeing expeditions. In spring the rare Kirtland Warbler nests in protected areas south of Mio near Mack Lake. Guided tours of the nesting area leave from the U.S. Forest Service station; contact the chamber of commerce for information.

Chamber of Commerce for Oscoda County: P.O. Box 670 Mio, MI 48647; phone (989) 826-3331 or (800) 800-6133.

OUR LADY OF THE WOODS SHRINE is 1.5 blks. w. of SR 33 on SR 72. Visitors can see replicas of Roman Catholic shrines. Daily dawn-dusk, Memorial Day-Labor Day; by appointment rest of year. Free. Phone (989) 826-5509.

MONROE (I-5) pop. 22,076, elev. 590'

One of the oldest communities in the state, Monroe was founded in 1780 by the French at the site of an American Indian village where the River Raisin enters Lake Erie. The settlement, originally called Frenchtown, was the scene of the River Raisin Massacre in 1813 during the War of 1812. Gen. George Custer lived in Monroe for many years before his Army service. A 1920 bronze statue of Custer titled "Sighting the Enemy" is on the southwest corner of N. Monroe Street and W. Elm Avenue.

Shipping and industry support the city. The Vietnam War Memorial is off I-75 exit 15, then one-fourth mile west on SR 50 in Heck Park. The memorial is similar to the one in Washington, D.C., and lists the names of Monroe County soldiers.

Monroe County Convention and Tourism Bureau: 106 W. Front St., P.O. Box 1094, Monroe, MI 48161; phone (734) 457-1030 or (800) 252-3011.

Shopping areas: Frenchtown Square Mall, a half mile north on US 125 at 2121 N. Monroe St., includes Elder-Beerman, JCPenney and Sears among its stores. Horizon Outlet Center at I-75 exit 11 and LaPlaisance Road offers more than 70 factory outlet stores.

MONROE COUNTY HISTORICAL MUSEUM is at 126 S. Monroe St. Exhibits in the old post office building focus on the family of Gen. George A. Custer as well as on area history. The museum also contains local maps, Victorian furnishings and displays about American Indian and French pioneer history.

Allow 1 hour minimum. Daily 10-5, May-Sept.; Wed.-Sun. 10-5, rest of year. Closed Jan. 1, Easter, Thanksgiving and Dec. 25. Admission June-Aug. $2; ages 7-17, $1. Phone (734) 240-7780.

NAVARRE-ANDERSON TRADING POST AND MARTHA BARKER COUNTRY STORE MUSEUM are 5 mi. w. on Elm St. to 3775 and 3815 N. Custer Rd. Said to be the oldest wooden residence in the state, the trading post retains a bullet reputedly fired during the War of 1812. It is furnished as it appeared in 1797. The Martha Barker Country Store Museum, housed in a 1860s schoolhouse, contains items dating from 1900-10. Wed.-Sun. 1-5, Memorial Day-Labor Day. Free. Phone (734) 240-7780.

RIVER RAISIN BATTLEFIELD VISITOR CENTER is off I-75 exit 14 to 1403 E. Elm Ave. Displays depict the Battle of the River Raisin, one of the largest engagements of the War of 1812. Exhibits include dioramas, maps and mannequins. A 15-minute auditorium presentation explains the major turning points of that war. The center also provides information about Monroe County. Allow 30 minutes minimum. Daily 10-5, Memorial Day-Labor Day; Sat.-Sun. 10-5, rest of year. Closed major holidays. Donations. Phone (734) 243-7136 or (734) 240-7780.

MOUNT PLEASANT (G-3)
pop. 25,946, elev. 761'

Originally known as Ojibway Besse, Mount Pleasant was a hunting ground for the Chippewa Indians. Magnificent pine and hardwoods destined the town to become a major lumber center. Mount Pleasant is home to Central Michigan University, founded in 1892, and the Saginaw Chippewa Indian Tribe on the Isabella Indian Reservation.

Horse racing takes place at Mount Pleasant Meadows May through September; phone (989) 773-0012.

Note: Policies concerning admittance of children to pari-mutuel betting facilities vary. Phone ahead for information.

Mount Pleasant Area Convention and Visitors Bureau: 114 E. Broadway, Mount Pleasant, MI 48858; phone (800) 772-4433.

Shopping areas: Loafers Glory Village of Yesteryear, about 15 miles west at 431 Main St. in Blanchard, is an early 1800s building that comprises several shops featuring antiques, crafts and food.

THE MUSEUM OF CULTURAL AND NATURAL HISTORY is in Rowe Hall on Bellows St. on the Central Michigan University campus. Displays explore human and natural history through exhibits and dioramas; among the displays are lumber exhibits, Civil War artifacts and handmade tools and implements as well as American Indian art. Dioramas feature mammals, birds and fish native to Michigan. The skeletal remains of an American mastodon also can be seen. Allow 1 hour minimum. Mon.-Fri. 8-5. Free. Phone (989) 774-3829.

CASINOS

- **Soaring Eagle Casino** is at 6800 Soaring Eagle Blvd. Daily 24 hours. Phone (888) 732-4537. *See color ad p. 405.*

RECREATIONAL ACTIVITIES

Canoeing

- **Chippewa River Outfitters** is 2 mi. w. on Broomfield Rd., then .3 mi. n. to 3763 S. Lincoln Rd., Mount Pleasant, MI 48858. Other activities are offered. Daily 10-8, May-Sept.; by appointment rest of year. Phone (989) 772-5474 or (888) 775-6077.

MUNISING (B-4) pop. 2,539, elev. 626'

Munising's harbor is protected from the brunt of Lake Superior's gales by Grand Island; the town is guarded on the landward side by a ring of sharply rising hills. A number of waterfalls cascade down the slopes within the city limits. Grand Island is a national recreation area; Munising also provides access to Hiawatha National Forest *(see place listing p. 73)* and is the eastern gateway to Pictured Rocks National Lakeshore *(see place listing p. 94).*

The city is the eastern terminus of a scenic section of SR 28 that skirts the shore of Lake Superior to US 41 and Marquette *(see place listing p. 87). Also see Upper Peninsula p. 103.*

Alger County Chamber of Commerce: 501 SR 28E, P.O. Box 405, Munising, MI 49862; phone (906) 387-2138.

PICTURED ROCKS CRUISES depart from Municipal Pier. Cruises, which cover 37 miles and last 2 hours and 40 minutes, follow the colorful rock formations that rise sharply from Lake Superior to heights of 200 feet. Cruises depart daily on the

hour 9-5, July 1-late Aug.; at 9, 11, 1, 3 and 5, late Aug.-early Sept.; at 10 and 2, late May to mid-June and early Sept.-early Oct. (weather permitting). Fare $25; ages 6-12, $10. Phone (906) 387-2379.

SHIPWRECK TOURS is at 1204 Commercial St. Passengers ride in a glass-bottom boat for narrated tours of three Lake Superior shipwrecks. Additional highlights include views of the South Lighthouse and an original settlement on Grand Island. Two-hour cruises depart daily at 10 and 1, June 1-Oct. 7 (also at 4, July-Aug.). Fare $23; ages 6-12, $10. MC, VI. Phone (906) 387-4477. *See ad p. 90.*

MUSKEGON (G-1) pop. 40,105, elev. 599'

Formerly known as the Lumber Queen of the World, Muskegon produced 665 million board feet of lumber in 1888 alone. Although the languishing of the logging boom severely affected the town, the excellence of its harbor and success in attracting new enterprises prospered it. Muskegon is the largest city on the eastern shore of Lake Michigan, with a diversified mix of industry, tourism, culture and recreational activities comprising its economy.

More than 3,000 acres of recreational land balance Muskegon's industrial image. Pere Marquette Park occupies the southern flank of the channel; Muskegon State Park *(see Recreation Chart)* is to the north. The lakeside highway leading north from Muskegon State Park is an especially scenic drive.

The Muskegon River offers fishing for walleyed pike, boating and canoeing; numerous lakes and streams are restocked yearly. Hundreds of anglers line the channel and breakwater walls on Lake Michigan during the perch and salmon runs.

Muskegon County Convention and Visitors Bureau: 610 Western Ave., Muskegon, MI 49440; phone (231) 724-3100 or (800) 250-9283.

GILLETTE SAND DUNE VISITOR CENTER is in P.J. Hoffmaster State Park, 3 mi. w. off US 31 Pontaluna exit. Hands-on exhibits, displays and a multimedia presentation illustrate the history and ecology of sand dunes and plant and animal life. Nature trails lead from the center to observation decks.

Center open Tues.-Sat. 10-4:30, Sun. noon-4:30, Memorial Day-Labor Day; Tues.-Fri. and Sun. noon-4, Sat. 10-4, day after Labor Day-Oct. 31. Park open daily 8 a.m.-10 p.m., Apr. 1-early Nov.; 8-6:30, rest of year. Park admission (includes visitor center) $6 per private vehicle. Phone (231) 798-3573.

GREAT LAKES NAVAL MEMORIAL AND MUSEUM is on the south side of the channel at 1346 Bluff St. The focus of the memorial is the USS *Silversides*, a restored, much-decorated World War II submarine. Guided tours through the sub's compartments explain how sailors lived and worked despite cramped quarters. Allow 30 minutes minimum. Daily 10-5:30, June-Aug.; Mon.-Fri. 1-5:30, Sat.-Sun. 10-5:30 in May and Sept.; Sat.-Sun. 10-5:30 in Apr. and Oct. Admission $5.50; ages 12-18,

$4.50; over 62, $4; ages 5-11, $3.50. Phone (231) 755-1230.

MICHIGAN'S ADVENTURE AMUSEMENT PARK is 8 mi. n. via US 31 Russell Rd. exit. The park has 47 rides, including six roller coasters. A large water park has 20 slides, three wave pools and two play areas. Amusement park open daily at 11, mid-May through Labor Day. Water park open daily at noon. Closing times for both parks vary; phone ahead. Admission $23, under 3 free. Phone (231) 766-3377.

MUSKEGON COUNTY MUSEUM is at 430 W. Clay Ave. Displays describe Michigan's lumber industry and fur trade. Hands-on science and health displays as well as exhibits relating to American Indians also are offered. Mon.-Fri. 9:30-4:30, Sat.-Sun. 12:30-4:30; closed major holidays. Free. Phone (231) 722-0278 or (888) 843-5661.

MUSKEGON MUSEUM OF ART is at 296 W. Webster Ave. Works of such American artists as Ralph Albert Blakelock, Winslow Homer, Edward Hopper and James Abbot McNeill Whistler are displayed. John Steuart Curry's "Tornado Over Kansas" also can be seen. A European collection has objects ranging from ancient glass to contemporary art. Guided tours are available by appointment. Tues.-Sat. 10-4:30 (also Thurs. 4:30-8), Sun. noon-4:30; closed major holidays. Admission $3. Phone (231) 720-2570.

NAUBINWAY (B-5) elev. 595'

GARLYN ZOOLOGICAL PARK is 6 mi. e. on US 2. A variety of animals, including wolves, bears, camels, cougars, otters and wallabies, live in a wooded park setting. Daily 11-7, Apr.-Oct.; Sat.-Sun. 11-5, Nov. 1-Dec. 25. Admission $6.50; ages 3-16, $4.50; family rate (up to four people) $22. AX, DS, MC, VI. Phone (906) 477-1085.

NEGAUNEE (B-3) pop. 4,576, elev. 1,400'

Negaunee, the first mining city on the Marquette Range, was brought into being in 1844 by a group of explorers who were led to the ore beds by an Indian chief from the Keweenaw country. *See Upper Peninsula p. 103.*

MICHIGAN IRON INDUSTRY MUSEUM is 3 mi. e. off US 41E to Maas St., e. to Forge Rd. then w. to 73 Forge Rd. The museum overlooks the Carp River and the site of the first iron forge in the Lake Superior region. Through exhibits and audiovisual displays the museum presents the history of Michigan's iron ranges and the people who worked them. "The Yankee," an 1860s locomotive from the Jackson Mine, is on display. Allow 1 hour, 30 minutes minimum. Daily 9:30-4:30, May-Oct. Free. Phone (906) 475-7857.

NEWBERRY (B-5) pop. 2,686, elev. 788'

OSWALDS BEAR RANCH is 4 mi. n. on SR 123 to Four Mile Corner, then 4.5 mi. w. to 13814 CR 407. Twenty-six American black bears are raised and kept on the 80-acre ranch. Visitors may view them in re-created natural habitats. Allow 30 minutes minimum. Daily 10-6, Memorial Day weekend-Sept. 30. Admission $10 per private vehicle. Phone (906) 293-3147.

TAHQUAMENON LOGGING MUSEUM is 1.5 mi. n. on SR 123. The complex, situated on 29 acres, includes a museum with logging memorabilia, a one-room schoolhouse, a memorial to the Depression-era CCC program, a cook shack and a circa 1900 log cabin. A slide presentation also is offered. Allow 1 hour minimum. Daily 9-5, Memorial Day-Labor Day. Admission $3; ages 6-12, $1.50. Phone (906) 293-3700.

NILES (I-2) pop. 12,204, elev. 659'

Because the banners of France, England, Spain and the United States have flown successively over this region, Niles is called the City of Four Flags. Its position as a stop on the 1830s Detroit-to-Chicago stagecoach route encouraged industrial and commercial development. Among Niles' natives are Montgomery Ward, Ring Lardner and the Dodge brothers of automobile fame.

Four Flags Area Council on Tourism: 321 E. Main St., P.O. Box 1300, Niles, MI 49120; phone (269) 684-7444.

FERNWOOD BOTANICAL GARDEN AND NATURE PRESERVE is off US 31N (St. Joseph Valley Pkwy.) exit 7 to 13988 Range Line Rd. The 105-acre nature preserve offers gardens, woodland trails and prairie. A visitor center includes gallery shows, exhibits and a fern conservatory. Food is available. Allow 2 hours minimum. Tues.-Sat. 10-6, Sun. noon-6, May-Oct.; Tues.-Sat. 10-5, Sun. noon-5, rest of year. Admission $5; over 65, $4; ages 13-18, $3; ages 6-12, $2. Phone (269) 695-6491.

FORT ST. JOSEPH MUSEUM is at 508 E. Main St. The museum, located in the carriage house of the 1882 Chapin home, contains more than 10,000 historic items, including Sioux and Potawatomi Indian relics, artifacts from the site of Fort St. Joseph and Sitting Bull pictographs. Allow 30 minutes minimum. Wed.-Sat. 10-4. Free. Phone (269) 683-4702.

NORTH MUSKEGON (G-2)
pop. 4,031, elev. 621'

RECREATIONAL ACTIVITIES
Skiing (cross-country)
• **Muskegon Winter Sports Complex** is in Muskegon State Park. Write P.O. Box 5085, North Muskegon, MI 49445. Other activities are offered. Lodge open daily 10-10, Dec.-Mar. Phone (231) 744-9629.

NORTHPORT (D-2) pop. 648

The coastal community of Northport lies in the northern end of the Leelanau Peninsula. The town is noted for its sandy beaches and spectacular sunsets. Several area wineries offer tours and tastings. Leelanau State Park *(see Recreation Chart)* is 7 miles north on SR 201. The Grand Traverse Lighthouse and Museum offers tours.

Leelanau Peninsula Chamber of Commerce: 5046 S. West Bay Shore Dr., Suite G, Suttons Bay, MI 49682; phone (231) 271-9895.

NOVI — *see Detroit p. 64.*

ONTONAGON (A-2) pop. 1,769, elev. 605'

Named Place of the Bowl by American Indians due to the shape of the river's mouth, Ontonagon was visited frequently from the 1600s to the mid-1800s by voyageurs and Jesuits. All who came took note of a huge copper boulder that measured 50 inches by 41 inches. American Indians believed the boulder to be the mediator between them and the Great Spirit. Publication of the discovery of copper led to an influx of prospectors and settlers on Lake Superior. Within the county that shares Ontonagon's name are 45 waterfalls. *See Upper Peninsula p. 103.*

Ontonagon County Chamber of Commerce: P.O. Box 266, Ontonagon, MI 49953; phone (906) 884-4735.

ONTONAGON COUNTY HISTORICAL MUSEUM is at 422 River St. Artifacts reflect the history of the county. Exhibits include photographs, Finnish items, logging and mining equipment and a replica of the Ontonagon copper boulder, which was recorded in 1843 as weighing 3,708 pounds. Tours of an on-site lighthouse are given by appointment. Mon.-Fri. 10-5, Sat. 10-4. Admission $2, under 16 free. Phone (906) 884-6165.

OSCODA (E-5) pop. 992

Oscoda is a resort community, offering access to the Huron-Manistee National Forests *(see place listing p. 75).*

Fishing and canoeing on the Au Sable River are especially popular. The town also is a major sport fishing center for Lake Huron, with chinook salmon and lake and brown trout the main catches.

Oscoda-Au Sable Chamber of Commerce: 4440 N. US 23, Oscoda, MI 48750; phone (989) 739-7322 or (800) 235-4625.

[SAVE] **PADDLEWHEEL RIVER BOAT TRIPS** depart Foote Dam, 7 mi. w. on W. River Rd. on the Au Sable River. The 19-mile, round-trip cruise, which provides a narrative about historic and scenic points of interest, lasts approximately 2 hours.

The *Au Sable River Queen of Oscoda* features a cocktail bar and glass-enclosed decks. Trips depart daily at noon and 3, Memorial Day weekend, late June-late Aug. and Sept. 1-Labor Day; at 1, day after Memorial Day-late June and day after Labor Day-late Sept. Fall color tours Mon.-Fri. at noon and 2:30, Sat.-Sun. at 10:30, 1 and 3:30, fourth weekend in Sept.-third weekend in Oct.

Tour fare $10; over 60, $9; ages 5-12, $5. Fall color tour fare $13; over 60, $11.75 (Mon.-Thurs.); ages 5-12, $6. Reservations are required for fall color tours and recommended for regular tours. AX,

DC, DS, MC, VI. Phone (989) 739-7351, or (989) 728-3131 after 6 p.m.

OSSINEKE (E-5) pop. 1,059, elev. 604'

At the mouth of the Devil River and the site of an American Indian village in 1839, Ossineke was named for a native word, *wawsineke,* meaning "image stones," which referred to a prominent landmark. The pair of boulders were thought to encase the spirit of Chief Shinggabaw, who had promised to return there after death.

When a rival tribe removed the sacred stones during a raid, the waters of Thunder Bay are said to have destroyed the raiders and returned the stones to their original site at the village. An angler later used the boulders to anchor fishing nets; the stones now repose at the bottom of Lake Huron.

DINOSAUR GARDENS PREHISTORICAL ZOO is on US 23S. Nature trails, a miniature golf course and life-size reproductions of prehistoric creatures are in a 40-acre forest. Allow 1 hour minimum. Daily 9-6, Memorial Day-Labor Day. Admission $5; ages 6-11, $4; under 6, $3. Phone (989) 471-5477.

OTTAWA NATIONAL FOREST

Elevations in the forest range from 602 ft. at Lake Superior, Black River Harbor to 1,826 ft. at Wolfe Mountain. Refer to AAA maps for additional elevation information.

In the Upper Peninsula, the 986,518 acres of the Ottawa National Forest are intermingled with approximately 606,300 acres of state, county and privately owned land. Included are Lake Gogebic State Park *(see Recreation Chart and the AAA Great Lakes CampBook)* near Marenisco and Sylvania Wilderness and Sturgeon Gorge Wilderness.

In excess of 50,000 acres in the forest remain as a federally designated wilderness, with pristine lakes and old growth trees. More than 35 waterfalls within the forest are accessible by woodland trails. Those falls that can be reached by road include Potawatomi Conglomerate, Gorge, Sandstone and Rainbow on the Black River north of Ironwood and Bessemer; the Agate Falls observation deck west on SR 28 near Trout Creek; and Bond Falls via Bond Falls Road.

More than 500 named lakes and more than 2,700 miles of rivers and streams yield varieties of panfish and trout. Fishing for coho salmon and rainbow trout is good on Lake Superior. Hunting for deer, bears and small game is permitted. Snowmobiling, snowshoeing, cross-country skiing and ice fishing are popular winter sports.

The J.W. Toumey Forest Nursery in Watersmeet supplies seed and tree stock to Great Lakes state forests; guided and self-guiding tours are offered on request. The Ottawa National Forest Visitor Center, US 2 and US 45 in Watersmeet, has exhibits, an interpretive trail, audiovisual programs and scheduled naturalist-conducted activities; phone (906) 358-4724.

For further information contact the Forest Supervisor, Ottawa National Forest, E6248 US 2, Ironwood, MI 49938; phone (906) 932-1330. *See Recreation Chart and the AAA Great Lakes CampBook.*

PARADISE (B-5) pop. 4,191, elev. 615'

The town's name is derived from a conversation between two of Paradise's pioneer developers who were commenting about the area's natural beauty. "This is a regular paradise," one said, and the name stuck. Snowmobilers and cross-country skiers enjoy the recreational facilities provided by the state and national forests that surround the village. *See Upper Peninsula p. 103.*

TAHQUAMENON FALLS STATE PARK is 12 mi. w. on SR 123. The 40,000-acre park includes two waterfalls on the Tahquamenon River. The Upper Falls are nearly 50 feet high and 200 feet wide at the crest. The Lower Falls, divided by an island, are a series of rapids and cascades.

The park offers a variety of recreational opportunities. Allow 30 minutes minimum. Daily 8 a.m.-10 p.m. Admission $6 per private vehicle. Phone (906) 492-3415. *See Recreation Chart.*

PAW PAW (I-2) pop. 3,363, elev. 739'

WINERIES

- **St. Julian Winery** is off I-94 exit 60 at 716 S. Kalamazoo St. Mon.-Sat. 9-5:30, Sun. noon-5:30, July 1-Labor Day; Mon.-Sat. 9-5, Sun. noon-5, rest of year. Closed Jan. 1, Easter, Thanksgiving and Dec. 25. Phone (269) 657-5568.

- **Warner Vineyards** is off I-94 exit 60 at 706 S. Kalamazoo St. Mon.-Wed. 10-5, Thurs.-Sat. 10-6, Sun. noon-6. Phone (269) 657-3165 or (800) 756-5357.

DID YOU KNOW

The state capitol was modeled after the U.S. Capitol.

PETOSKEY (D-3) pop. 6,080, elev. 636'

Petoskey is a resort center on Little Traverse Bay. On the bottom of the bay at a depth of 34 feet, an 11-foot figure of Christ serves as the Skin Divers' Shrine. Rockhounds crowd the Petoskey State Park (see Recreation Chart) and Magnus Park in spring, sorting through winter's debris for Petoskey stones. The remains of an extinct coral that inhabited the shallow waters of 350 million years ago, the stones were designated Michigan's state stone in 1965.

Fishing in Little Traverse Bay and area rivers and lakes yields bass, blue gill, lake and rainbow trout, perch, salmon and walleye. A number of scenic drives can be enjoyed in the other seasons: The lakeshore routes along US 31 west through Charlevoix then south to Traverse City (see place listing p. 103) and SR 119 north through Harbor Springs (see place listing p. 73) to Cross Village are particularly enjoyable. Closer to town, US 131 and Walloon Lake Drive provide a pleasant loop.

Petoskey/Harbor Springs/Boyne Country Visitors Bureau: 401 E. Mitchell St., Petoskey, MI 49770; phone (231) 348-2755 or (800) 845-2828. See ad.

Shopping areas: The Gaslight Shopping District along Lake, Howard and Bay streets offers more than 60 shops. Some shops are closed in the winter.

Shopping also is available in the Bay Harbor Marina District.

LITTLE TRAVERSE HISTORY MUSEUM is on the waterfront at Bayfront Park. Housed in an 1892 railroad depot, the museum features exhibits from the area's Odawa Indian, pioneer and Victorian past as well as exhibits about Ernest Hemingway, Civil War author Bruce Catton and the area's lumber and resort industries. Allow 30 minutes minimum. Mon.-Sat. and holidays 10-4, Memorial Day-Labor Day; Tues.-Sat. and holidays 10-4, day after Labor Day-Dec. 24; Tues.-Sat. 10-4, May 1-day before Memorial Day. Admission $1, under 18 free. Phone (231) 347-2620.

▼GEM PICTURED ROCKS NATIONAL LAKESHORE (A-4)

Pictured Rocks National Lakeshore extends 40 miles along Lake Superior from Grand Marais to Munising (see place listing p. 90). The Pictured Rocks cliffs rise to 200 feet above the lake, a spectacular example of the erosive action of waves, wind and ice. The Grand Sable Dunes expose part of a glacial deposit up to 200 feet high. Five square miles of dunes that once edged an ancient predecessor of Lake Superior top the banks by another 100 feet.

Lake Superior and the many inland lakes and streams harbor a variety of fish. Fishing is excellent in spring and fall; a Michigan license is required. Summer months offer swimming, hiking, picnicking, backpacking and a scenic boat ride along the Pictured Rocks.

Twenty-one miles of cross-country ski trails, abundant off-trail skiing and a yearly snowfall approaching 200 inches accommodate winter sports enthusiasts. Snowshoeing and ice fishing are popular activities.

Park rangers conduct campfire programs and guided walks in summer. Drive-in camping areas are at Hurricane River, Little Beaver Lake and Twelvemile Beach; roads to these areas are closed by snow from November through April. Backcountry, hike-in permits are required. Advance reservations are accepted; the fee is $15. Upon arrival, the additional user fee is $5 per person, per night. The fee for drive-in camping is $10 per night and is on a first-come, first-served basis. Phone (906) 387-3700.

The Hiawatha National Forest/Pictured Rocks National Lakeshore Visitor Information Center, SR 28 and CR-H58 in Munising, is open daily 8-6, mid-June to mid-Sept.; Mon.-Sat. 9-4:30, rest of year; phone (906) 387-3700. The unstaffed Munising Falls Interpretive Center at the beginning of Sand Point Road is open daily, May-Oct. The Grand Sable Visitor Center, CR-H58 just west of Grand Marais, is open daily, late May-Labor Day; phone (906) 494-2660.

The Grand Marais Maritime Museum and Ranger Station on Coast Guard Point in Grand Marais usually is open July 1-Labor Day but hours vary. Park headquarters on Sand Point Road near Munising is open Mon.-Fri. 8-4:30. The park is open daily 24 hours. For more information contact Pictured Rocks National Lakeshore, P.O. Box 40, Munising, MI 49862; phone (906) 387-2607. *See Upper Peninsula p. 103 and the Recreation Chart.*

PICTURED ROCKS begin 5 mi. n.e. of Munising. These cliffs, from Longfellow's "The Song of Hiawatha," are notable for their rich color and interesting formations. Except for Miners Castle, they are accessible only by boat or on foot. Pictured Rocks Cruises offers 2.5-hour tours of the formations leaving from Munising *(see place listing p. 90).*

PINCONNING (F-4) pop. 1,386, elev. 596′

Once an important railhead during the lumber era, Pinconning serves the surrounding agricultural and dairy region and is known as the cheese capital of Michigan. It also is known for perch and walleye fishing on Saginaw Bay.

Pinconning Area Chamber of Commerce: P.O. Box 856, Pinconning, MI 48650; phone (989) 879-2816.

DEER ACRES STORYBOOK AMUSEMENT PARK is 3 mi. s. on SR 13. Sculptured, life-size Mother Goose characters are the focus of the park, which includes a playground. Deer and other animals may be fed by hand. Other amusements are train, antique car and safari rides, a moon walk, a Ferris wheel and a merry-go-round.

Picnicking is permitted. Food is available. Allow 1 hour minimum. Mon.-Fri. 10-6, Sat.-Sun. 10-7, mid-May through Labor Day; Sat.-Sun. 10-5, day after Labor Day to mid-Oct. Admission $9.50; over 62, $8.50; ages 3-12, $7.50. Fee $1.75 per ride, or 10 rides for $14. DS, MC, VI. Phone (989) 879-2849.

PLYMOUTH—*see Detroit p. 64.*

PONTIAC—*see Detroit p. 64.*

PORT AUSTIN (F-5) pop. 737, elev. 604′

Named for P.C. Austin in 1839, Port Austin is at the tip of Michigan's thumb. The town is known for its picturesque sunrises and sunsets on Lake Huron.

MISS PORT AUSTIN **PERCH PARTY BOAT** departs from the Port Austin State Dock, 8787 Lake St. Perch fishing trips lasting 4.5 hours are available on the 20-passenger *Miss Port Austin.* Bait is provided; fishing poles are available for $2. A valid state fishing license is required for those over 17; 1-day licenses are available at local bait and tackle shops. Soft-soled shoes are recommended. Sunset cruises also are available.

Trips depart Mon., Wed. and Sat.-Sun. at 7:30 and 2:30, Fri. at 7:30, July-Aug.; Sat. at 7:30 and 2:30, Wed. and Sun. at 7:30, May-June and in Sept. Sunset cruises are offered Fri.-Sat. Fare $30, over 55 and family rate (Mon.-Fri.) $25 per person. Sunset cruise $20. Phone (989) 738-5271.

PORT HURON (H-6) pop. 32,338, elev. 596′

Linked by the Blue Water International Bridge with Sarnia, Ontario, at the point where Lake Huron empties into the St. Clair River, Port Huron is the center of the St. Clair River manufacturing district. It is one of the oldest settlements in the state, dating from 1686 when the French built Fort St. Joseph to guard against possible British incursions into their fur trade. The first permanent colony, however, was not established until 1790.

The fact that Thomas Edison spent his youth in Port Huron seems to reflect the city's proclivity for electrical pioneering. One of the earliest electrical utilities was formed in 1844. The 1891 railway tunnel, built beneath the St. Clair River to accommodate double-decker trains, is considered to have been the first electrified underwater tunnel.

Some of Port Huron's popular parks are Lakeside Park, with opportunities for swimming and picnicking, and Lighthouse Park, which surrounds Fort Gratiot Lighthouse, one of the oldest working lighthouses on the Great Lakes. Tours are available by appointment in summer. Another popular spot is Pine Grove Park, where the Huron, the last commissioned lightship, is docked.

Blue Water Area Convention and Visitors Bureau: 520 Thomas Edison Pkwy., Port Huron, MI 48060; phone (810) 987-8687 or (800) 852-4242.

Shopping areas: Birchwood Mall, north on SR 25 at Keewahdin Road, features 90 specialty stores as well as Marshall Field's, JCPenney, Sears, Target and Younker's. Horizon Outlet Center, west on Range Road at I-94 exit 269, offers 33 factory outlet shops. Main Street Port Huron offers more than 70 specialty shops, restaurants and art galleries along an 11-block historic area concentrated on Huron Avenue between Quay Street and McMorran Boulevard.

HURON **LIGHTSHIP MUSEUM** is in Pine Grove Park. Built in 1920, the lightship was used until it was decommissioned in 1970. It is believed to be the only remaining lightship that served on the Great Lakes and has been certified a National Treasure. Allow 30 minutes minimum. Daily 1-4:30, Memorial Day-Labor Day; Wed.-Sun. 1-4:30, rest of year. Closed Jan. 1, Easter and Dec. 25. Admission $3, senior citizens and students with ID $2. Combination admission with Port Huron Museum and Thomas Edison Depot Museum $5; over 54 and ages 7-17, $3. Phone (810) 984-9768.

PORT HURON MUSEUM is at 1115 Sixth St. Displays—which include American Indian relics and marine items, a pioneer log house, Thomas Edison memorabilia and fine arts—trace 300 years of local history. Allow 30 minutes minimum. Wed.-Sun. 1-4:30; closed holidays. Admission $3; over 54 and ages 7-17, $2. Combination admission with *Huron* Lightship Museum and Thomas Edison Depot Museum $5; over 54 and ages 7-17, $3. AX, MC, VI. Phone (810) 982-0891.

Thomas Edison Depot Museum is at 1115 Sixth St. Housed in the Fort Gratiot Railroad Station where Thomas Edison worked, the museum features re-created period displays, hands-on activities that focus on his inventions and a vintage baggage car that contains a mock-up of Edison's first laboratory. A videotape presentation also is offered. Allow 30 minutes minimum. Daily 1-4:30, Memorial Day-Labor Day; Wed.-Sun. 1-4:30, rest of year. Closed major holidays. Admission $3; over 54 and ages 7-17, $2. Combination admission with Port Huron Museum and *Huron* Lightship Museum $5; over 54 and ages 7-17, $3. AX, MC, VI. Phone (810) 982-0891.

PORT SANILAC (G-6) pop. 658

Until 1857 when Port Sanilac was allegedly renamed for a well-known Wyandotte Indian chief, this locale was called Bark Shanty Point, a name stoutly defended in one issue of the village's newspaper, the *Bark Shanty Times.*

No editors, reporters, printers or editorial policies complicated the production of the paper, which was known throughout the region. Everyone who came through the general store/post office simply wrote news or commentary on a sheet of newsprint paper kept on the counter. Once thoroughly perused, the edition was bound and filed, and a new one was begun.

SANILAC COUNTY HISTORICAL MUSEUM AND VILLAGE is at 228 S. Ridge St. (SR 25). The Victorian 1875 Loop-Harrison House contains original furnishings. Displays include medical instruments, antique glassware and marine, military and American Indian artifacts.

On the grounds are a dairy museum; the late 19th-century Banner Cabin; Huckins School; and a general store. A carriage barn contains exhibits. Allow 1 hour minimum. Wed.-Fri. 11-4:30, Sat.-Sun. noon-4:30, mid-June through Labor Day. Admission $5; over 55, $4; ages 5-12, $2. Phone (810) 622-9946.

PRESQUE ISLE (D-5) pop. 1,691

Presque Isle, on the eastern shore of Grand Lake, is a supply center for the surrounding resort area. Three miles north is Presque Isle Harbor, an active lumber port in the mid-1800s, with a full marina facility.

OLD LIGHTHOUSE PARK AND MUSEUM stands on the northern arm of land enclosing the harbor. Built in 1840, the lighthouse was replaced in 1870 by the current lighthouse a mile north on the tip of the peninsula. The tower and 1905 keeper's house are restored. A 3,425-pound bronze bell, larger than the Liberty Bell, is on display. Allow 30 minutes minimum. Old and new lighthouses open daily 9-6, mid-May to mid-Oct. Keeper's House open daily 11-5. Fee to climb new lighthouse tower $2.50.

Admission for both lighthouses (includes museum) $2.50; ages 6-12, $1. Only old lighthouse $1. Phone (989) 595-9917 for new lighthouse, or (989) 595-6979 for old lighthouse.

ROCHESTER—*see Detroit p. 64.*

ROCKLAND (B-2) pop. 324, elev. 1,093′

OLD VICTORIA is 4 mi. s.w. on a paved road near the Victoria dam. This is a restored late 19th-century company town. The original settlement was established by miners from Cornwall, England. Mines opened 1847-49 and operated until 1921, when they suffered due to low copper prices and competition from open pit mines in the West.

Guided tours explain the history of the village and its decline. Three houses, a sauna and barn can be seen. Hiking trails and picnic facilities are available. Daily 11:30-5:30, Memorial Day-Sept. 30. Donations. Phone (906) 886-2617.

ROGERS CITY (D-5) pop. 3,322, elev. 655′

Rogers City's principal industry is readily apparent: Possibly the world's largest open limestone quarry—more than 3 miles long and nearly 2 miles across at its widest point—extends southeastward from the city limits. Worked continuously since 1912, the quarry is expected to produce into the 21st century. Operations can be seen from the rim of the pit at Quarry View; except in winter, the docking and loading of the huge freighters are visible from Harbor View.

Established during the 1870s lumber boom, Rogers City remains the largest community in Presque Isle County. P.H. Hoeft State Park *(see Recreation Chart and the AAA Great Lakes CampBook)* is 5 miles northwest on US 23 and includes a section of Huron dunes. Ocqueoc Falls, the largest falls in the Lower Peninsula, is 12 miles west of Rogers City off SR 68. A 7-mile self-guiding trail originates there.

Rogers City Chamber of Commerce: 292 S. Bradley Hwy., P.O. Box 55, Rogers City, MI 49779; phone (989) 734-2535 or (800) 622-4148.

PRESQUE ISLE COUNTY HISTORICAL MUSEUM is at 176 W. Michigan Ave. Exhibits about maritime and local history are in the restored Bradley House. Three floors are furnished in the style of the 1920s, while others re-create a general store and a Victorian sitting room. Displays include American Indian artifacts as well as carpentry, farming, household and lumber-related items. Tues.-Sat. noon-4, June-Oct. Donations. Phone (989) 734-4121.

ROSCOMMON (E-4) pop. 1,133, elev. 1,123′

A resort area and starting point for canoe trips down the Au Sable River, Roscommon is near both North Higgins Lake and South Higgins Lake state parks *(see Recreation Chart and the AAA Great Lakes CampBook).*

CIVILIAN CONSERVATION CORPS MUSEUM is at the entrance of North Higgins Lake State Park.

Housed in replica barracks, the museum showcases the accomplishments of the men who helped "put Americans back to work." Many photographs were donated by CCC alumni. Two original buildings used during the 1930s are on the grounds. Hiking trail maps are available for self-guiding tours.

Picnic areas are available. Allow 30 minutes minimum. Daily 11-4, Memorial Day-Labor Day. An interpreter is on site Thurs.-Mon. Admission $4 per private vehicle. Phone (989) 821-6125.

MICHIGAN FIREMEN'S MEMORIAL is 2.5 mi. s. on CR 18, then .5 mi. e. on Robinson Rd. The 12-foot bronze statue was created by Detroit's Edward Chesney. Daily 8-6, May-Nov. Free.

ROYAL OAK—*see Detroit p. 64.*

SAGINAW (G-5) pop. 61,799, elev. 592′

When the Saginaw Valley was shorn of its pine forests, the once busy lumber center of Saginaw turned to the processing and shipping of shorter crops such as beans and sugar beets. Tourism contributes heavily to the economy.

The city's Celebration Square is home to attractions and parks, including the Lucille E. Andersen Memorial Garden, Ezra Rust Drive, which adorns the top of the city's 20-million-gallon underground reservoir; phone (989) 759-1362.

Saginaw County Convention and Visitors Bureau: 1 Tuscola St., Suite 101, Saginaw, MI 48607; phone (989) 752-7164 or (800) 444-9979.

CHILDREN'S ZOO AT CELEBRATION SQUARE is at jct. SRs 13/46 at 1730 S. Washington Ave. The zoo features 14 exhibits, including a walk-through butterfly encounter, timber wolf and monkey exhibits and eight warm-water penguins. Pony rides and miniature train rides are offered. Food is available. Allow 1 hour, 30 minutes minimum. Mon.-Sat. 10-5 (also Wed. 5-8), Sun. 11-6, May 1-Labor Day; Sat. 10-5, Sun. 11-6, day after Labor Day-Sept. 30. Closed Feb. 14, Easter, Oct. 31 and Dec. 25. Admission $4.75; over 64 and ages 3-12, $3.75. Phone (989) 759-1408.

HISTORICAL SOCIETY OF SAGINAW COUNTY is at 500 Federal Ave. The renovated 1897 post office building was designed in French chateau style and sports a spiral staircase and corner towers. Permanent and changing exhibits trace the social and industrial development of the Saginaw Valley. Guided tours are available by appointment. Allow 1 hour minimum. Mon.-Sat. 10-4:30, Sun. 1-4:30; closed holidays. Admission $1; ages 5-18, 50c. Phone (989) 752-2861.

JAPANESE CULTURAL CENTER AND TEA HOUSE is at the corner of Ezra Rust Dr. and S. Washington Ave. The center offers insights into Japanese culture and the ritual and ceremony of the tea service. Saginaw's ties with Tokushima, its sister city in Japan, were the impetus for the establishment of the Friendship Garden; many of the trees, bridges and stones used in the garden came from Japan. Following a tour of the garden, tea and sweets are served. Every second Saturday at 2 a full tea ceremony is offered.

Allow 1 hour minimum. Gardens open Tues.-Sat. 9-8, June-Sept.; 9-4, Apr.-May and Oct.-Nov. Tea House open Tues.-Sat. noon-4, May 30-Dec. 1. Gardens free. Tea House tour $3. Full tea ceremony $6. Phone (989) 759-1648.

JOHNNY PANTHER QUESTS departs from various points in the Saginaw River valley. Personalized boat tours through the Shiawassee National Wildlife Refuge put visitors up close to bald eagles, beavers, deer and their natural habitats. Tours can be customized depending on size of party and preferred destination. A jacket is recommended for afternoon cruises. Daily dawn-dusk. Tours $40-$100 per person. Reservations are required. Phone (810) 653-3859.

MARSHALL M. FREDERICKS SCULPTURE MUSEUM is in the Arbury Fine Arts Center at 7400 Bay Rd. (SR 84) on the Saginaw Valley State University campus. The museum houses hundreds of original plaster models that span the career of the noted sculptor. Free-standing sculptures, reliefs, portraits and drawings by Fredericks are exhibited. Photographs show finished bronze and stone sculptures now exhibited around the world. An adjacent

sculpture garden and fountain also feature works by the sculptor. Allow 1 hour minimum. Tues.-Sun. noon-5, Memorial Day-Labor Day; Mon.-Sat. noon-5, rest of year. Closed holidays. Free. Phone (989) 964-7125.

SAGINAW ART MUSEUM is at 1126 N. Michigan Ave. Housed in the 1904 Georgian-revival Ring Mansion, the museum has a permanent collection of art by E. Irving Couse, an education wing and a children's hands-on gallery. Major collections include 19th- and 20th-century American art, Asian art, landscapes, contemporary prints, plaster sculpture by John Rogers and textiles. The garden is landscaped to its original design. Allow 1 hour minimum. Tues.-Sat. 10-5, Sun. 1-5; closed holidays. Admission $3, under 16 free. Phone (989) 754-2491.

ST. IGNACE (B-5) pop. 2,678, elev. 592′

St. Ignace's strategic location on the north shore of the Straits of Mackinac was quickly recognized by explorers. The town was founded in 1671 when Father Jacques Marquette established a mission; a fortress was built shortly thereafter. In 1701 the garrison moved to Detroit and St. Ignace's military importance became a thing of the past; by 1706 so was the mission.

St. Ignace, on the Upper Peninsula, is joined to the Lower Peninsula by the 5-mile-long Mackinac Bridge, which links the town with Mackinaw City. Each Labor Day morning thousands participate in the Mackinac Bridge Walk, from St. Ignace to Mackinaw City.

Ferry service to Mackinac Island is available at the harbor from early April until ice forms on the Straits of Mackinac, usually in October.

Scenic US 2, heading west from St. Ignace, winds down to the sand dunes and up into the wooded hills along Lake Michigan to Escanaba *(see place listing p. 67).* Castle Rock, 4 miles north, was an ancient lookout for the Algonquin Indians and offers a scenic view. *See Upper Peninsula p. 103.*

St. Ignace is home to what is reportedly the world's largest all-category auto show on the last Saturday in June.

St. Ignace Area Chamber of Commerce and Convention and Visitors Bureau: 560 N. State St., St. Ignace, MI 49781; phone (906) 643-8717 or (800) 338-6660. *See color ad p. 351.*

FATHER MARQUETTE NATIONAL MEMORIAL is .2 mi. n.w. of the bridge via US 2; exit in the Marquette unit of Straits State Park. The memorial honors Jacques Marquette, the French explorer who established the state's first European settlements at Sault Ste. Marie and St. Ignace. Interpretive trails through the 52-acre park provide panoramic views of the straits and Mackinac Bridge. Picnicking is permitted. Allow 1 hour minimum. Park open daily 9 a.m.-dusk, May-Oct. Admission to park $4 per private vehicle. Memorial free. Phone (906) 643-8620 for Straits State Park.

SAVE **FORT DE BAUDE INDIAN MUSEUM** is at 334 N. State St. Built on the site of the original fort, the museum houses displays and dioramas depicting the lives of the area's early inhabitants. Local beadwork, stonework and weapons are displayed. Daily 9-9, Memorial Day to mid-Sept. Admission $5; ages 6-17, $3. Phone (906) 643-6622.

MARQUETTE MISSION PARK AND MUSEUM OF OJIBWA CULTURE is at 500 N. State St. The park is the presumed site of Father Jacques Marquette's grave. A statue, interpretive kiosk about his life and a garden are on the grounds. The museum, in a restored 19th-century Jesuit church, is dedicated to the Ojibwa—the original inhabitants of the upper Great Lakes region. Displays include artifacts, some dating from 6000 B.C., and reproductions.

Allow 30 minutes minimum. Daily 10-8, July 1-Labor Day; Mon.-Sat. 11-5, Sun. 1-5, Memorial Day-June 30. Admission $2; ages 6-12, $1; family rate $5. Phone (906) 643-9161.

CASINOS

- **Kewadin Shores Casino** is at 3039 Mackinac Tr. Daily 24 hours. Phone (906) 643-7071 or (800) 539-2346.

ST. JOSEPH (I-1) pop. 8,789, elev. 591′

In 1833 Newberryport was renamed St. Joseph after the St. Joseph River bordering the peninsular city along with Lake Michigan. Originally St. Joseph grew as a stopping place for travelers between Chicago and Detroit. Today there are more than 75 specialty shops as well as a variety of beaches and parks.

Self-guiding tours: Historic walking tour information can be obtained from St. Joseph Today, 413 State St., St. Joseph, MI 49085; phone (269) 982-0032.

GEM **CURIOUS KIDS' MUSEUM** is at 415 Lake Blvd. Curiosity and learning is encouraged through hands-on exhibits. Each exhibit comes with its own costumes for young visitors to wear. Children can serve customers in their own diner; type their names in braille; and pick apples from simulated trees, follow the crop through processing and then sell apple-related products at a market stand. Allow 2 hours minimum. Mon.-Sat. 10-5, Sun. noon-5, June 1-Labor Day. Admission $5, under 1 free. Phone (269) 983-2543.

KRASL ART CENTER is at 707 Lake Blvd. Three galleries and an outdoor sculpture collection contain folk art, traditional art and works by regional artists. Traveling exhibitions from such major museums as the Smithsonian Institution and the Detroit Institute of Arts also are included. Allow 30 minutes minimum. Mon.-Sat. 10-4, Sun. 1-4, Memorial Day-Labor Day; Fri. 10-1, rest of year. Closed holidays. Free. Phone (269) 983-0271.

SAUGATUCK (H-1) pop. 1,065

The dunes along Lake Michigan and the pretty countryside around Lake Kalamazoo helped make Saugatuck a well-known art colony. Along with its sister city, Douglas *(see place listing p. 66)*, the town is a popular resort.

STAR OF SAUGATUCK **BOAT CRUISE** departs from 716 Water St. The 1.2- to 1.5-hour narrated tour aboard the 150-passenger stern-wheeler travels down the Kalamazoo River to Lake Michigan. Sunset cruises also are available. Cruises depart daily at 11, 1, 3 and 5, Memorial Day weekend and July 1-Labor Day; Mon.-Fri. and Sun. at 1 and 3, Sat. at 1, 3 and 5, early May-day before Memorial Day weekend; Mon.-Fri. at 1 and 3, Sat.-Sun. at 11, 1, 3 and 5, day after Memorial Day-June 30; Mon.-Fri. and Sun. at 1 and 3, Sat. at 11, 1, 3 and 5, day after Labor Day-Sept. 30; Mon. at 11 and 1, Fri.-Sun. at 1 and 3 in Oct. Fare $13; ages 3-12, $7. Phone (269) 857-4261.

SAULT STE. MARIE (B-6) pop. 16,542, elev. 617'

The oldest town in the state, Sault Ste. Marie was first visited by a European about 1620 when the French *voyageur* Étienne Brulé passed through the area on his way to the Lake Superior region. The first Jesuit missionaries, Isaac Jogues and Charles Raymbault, arrived about 1641; the first mission was established in 1668 by fathers Jacques Marquette and Claude Dablon, who named the town in honor of the Virgin Mary.

The French and British competed for the profitable fur trade in the upper Great Lakes. The Treaty of Paris established the Michigan Territory as part of America, and in 1820 a treaty with the Chippewa Indians brought the area and its inhabitants under government regulation. Fort Brady was built shortly thereafter and trade increased. The first American lock was built in 1855, and later sailors and travelers began referring to the town as the Soo. Railroad and highway bridges link the city with its Canadian twin, Sault Ste. Marie, Ontario.

The rapids of the St. Marys River, which drop some 21 feet from Lake Superior to Lake Huron, are the reason for the town's greatest attraction, the Soo Locks. Four locks on the U.S. side bypass this beautiful barrier. More than 95 million tons of freight pass through the Soo every year.

Parkland parallels the locks; in the upper park are three observation platforms and a Corps of Engineers information center. Originating at the information center, the Locks Park Historic Walkway follows the waterfront for about a mile. It links many historic attractions and four main points of interest: the Locks Overlook; Plank Alley, site of the original business district; Fort Brady, site of both French and American forts; and the Johnston

Homestead, a preserved neighborhood. *See Upper Peninsula p. 103.*

Sault Area Convention and Visitor's Bureau: 2650 I-75 Business Spur, Sault Ste. Marie, MI 49783; phone (906) 632-3366 or (800) 647-2858.

MUSEUM SHIP *VALLEY CAMP* is e. of the Soo Locks at 501 E. Water St. Walk-in tours of the retired Great Lakes freighter include the pilot house, captain's quarters, the Marine Museum and an aquarium. Also on board are two lifeboats recovered from the *Edmund Fitzgerald*, a freighter that sank with all hands during a storm on Lake Superior in 1975.

Daily 10-8, July-Aug.; 10-6, mid-May through June 30 and Sept. 1 to mid-Oct. Last admission 1 hour before closing. Admission $8; ages 6-16, $4. Phone (888) 744-7867.

SAVE **RIVER OF HISTORY MUSEUM** is at 209 E. Portage Ave. on the first floor of the restored Federal Building. Galleries chronicle more than 8,000 years of St. Marys River history. The valley's development is traced from the Anishnabeg (Chippewa) Indians—the area's first settlers—through the 18th-century French fur trade to modern industrial and environmental issues. An audio system re-creates sounds of history.

Allow 30 minutes minimum. Mon.-Sat. 10-5, Sun. noon-5, May 15-Oct. 15. Phone for holiday schedule. Admission $5; over 55, $3.50; ages 8-16, $2.50; family rate $15 (five or more members). Phone (906) 632-1999.

GEM **SOO LOCKS BOAT TOURS** depart from two locations, 515 and 1157 E. Portage Ave. Two-hour narrated tours take visitors through the Soo Locks and alongside giant ships. A guide explains the operation and the history of the locks, St. Marys Rapids, Algoma Steel Plant, waterfronts of twin Saults and other sights. A sunset dinner cruise along the St. Marys River (including a locks tour) is available. A lighthouse cruise passes U.S. and Canadian lighthouses in Whitefish Bay.

Locks tours depart daily 10-6:30, July-Aug.; 9-5:30, June 21-30; 9-4:30, mid-May through June 20 and Sept.-Oct. Fare for locks tour $18; ages 13-18, $16; ages 4-12, $8.50. Reservations are recommended for dinner and lighthouse cruises. DS, MC, VI. Phone (906) 632-6301 or (800) 432-6301. *See color ad p. 99.*

TOWER OF HISTORY is e. of Soo Locks at 326 E. Portage Ave. The 21-story structure offers a panoramic view of the locks, the St. Marys River and rapids, and the city's historical sites. The tower has artifacts and a videotape show depicting the history of the Great Lakes and Sault Ste. Marie. The ride to the top is by elevator. Allow 1 hour minimum. Daily 10-6, mid-May to mid-Oct. Last admission 1 hour before closing. Admission $4; ages 6-16, $2. Phone (906) 632-3658 or (888) 744-7867.

CASINOS

• **Kewadin Casino**, .7 mi. e. on Marquette St. to 2186 Shunk Rd. Daily 24 hours. Phone (906) 632-0530 or (800) 539-2346.

SHELBY (G-2) pop. 1,914

Orchards and asparagus farms form a backdrop for this small western Michigan town.

SHELBY MAN-MADE GEMSTONES is n. of Shelby Rd. at 1330 Industrial Dr. Visitors can see gem-producing equipment and gems that are made on the premises. An audiovisual presentation about artificial gem making is offered. Allow 30 minutes minimum. Mon.-Fri. 9-5:30, Sat. noon-4; closed holidays and Dec. 25-Jan. 1. Free. Phone (231) 861-2165.

SILVER CITY (A-1)

In 1872 hopeful miners fanned out across the Silver City countryside searching for the source of the silver nuggets sold to traders by local Indians. Little mining was done; by 1876 the few tunnels were abandoned. *See Upper Peninsula p. 103.*

PORCUPINE MOUNTAINS WILDERNESS STATE PARK is 3 mi. w. on SR 107. The 63,000-acre park is popular for camping, skiing and backpacking; natural history programs are offered. Lake of the Clouds Scenic Overlook, on an escarpment above the lake at the western end of SR 107, offers an excellent view. Panoramas also can be enjoyed from Summit Peak. A .75-mile boardwalk along Presque Isle River passes several waterfalls.

Park open daily 24 hours. Visitor center open daily 10-6 (EST), late May to mid-Oct. Admission $6 per private vehicle. Phone (906) 885-5275. *See Recreation Chart and the AAA Great Lakes CampBook.*

SLEEPING BEAR DUNES NATIONAL LAKESHORE (E-2)

Sleeping Bear Dunes National Lakeshore lies along 35 miles of the Lower Peninsula's northwestern shore and includes the Manitou Islands. The name is derived from a Ojibway Indian legend that tells of a bear and her two cubs forced to swim across Lake Michigan to escape a forest fire. The mother reached the shore safely and climbed to the top of a dune to await the cubs, who lagged behind and never arrived. She still maintains her vigil in the form of a dark hill of sand atop a plateau, while the errant cubs have become the North and South Manitou islands.

The dunes are the product of several glacial assaults that ended 11,000 years ago. The glaciers left a legacy of rock, sand and silt as they melted. Rugged bluffs rise as high as 480 feet above the lake. Among the dunes are ghost forests, the bleached remains of trees that were once covered by advancing dunes, then exposed as the sand moved on. The 7-mile Pierce Stocking Scenic Drive, open mid-May to mid-October, provides access to the high dunes of Sleeping Bear Plateau and affords views from the bluffs overlooking the lake.

Fishing and canoeing are popular on the Platte and Crystal rivers and adjoining lakes, as are hiking and cross-country skiing on the park's 55 miles of marked trails. On South Manitou Island is a lighthouse, the wreck of the Liberian freighter *Francisco Morazan* and the Valley of Giants—a virgin white-cedar forest. North Manitou Island, 15,000 acres of wilderness, attracts backpackers. The islands are accessible by passenger ferry from Leland (*see place listing p. 81*).

The Maritime Museum at the Sleeping Bear Point Coast Guard Station, 1 mile west of Glen Haven, has displays depicting the maritime history of the area; it is open daily, Memorial Day through Labor Day. The visitor center and park headquarters, on SR 72 in Empire, has exhibits about the region's natural history and a slide program about the park. The center is open daily, but is closed during off-season holidays.

Admission is $7 per week. For further information contact the Superintendent, Sleeping Bear Dunes National Lakeshore, 9922 Front St., Empire, MI 49630; phone (231) 326-5134. *See Recreation Chart and the AAA Great Lakes CampBook.*

SOO JUNCTION (B-5)

TOONERVILLE TROLLEY AND RIVERBOAT TOUR TO TAHQUAMENON FALLS is 2 mi. n. of SR 28 to CR 381. Tour 1 is a 6.5-hour narrow-gauge train trip and riverboat ride to the Tahquamenon River. A nature trail leads to the falls. Tour 2, offered in the summer, is a wilderness train ride to the river and back lasting approximately 1 hour, 45 minutes. Tour 1 departs Mon.-Thurs. at 10:30, mid- to late June; Mon.-Sat. at 10:30, July 1-Aug. 24; Wed.-Sat. at 10:30, Aug. 25-early Oct. Tour 2 departs Fri.-Sat. at noon, mid- to late June; Tues.-Sat. at noon, July 1-Aug. 24 and Labor Day weekend.

Tour 1 fare $29.50; ages 6-15, $14. Tour 2 fare $12; ages 6-15, $6. DS, MC, VI. Phone (906) 876-2311 or (888) 778-7246.

SOUTH HAVEN (H-1) pop. 5,021, elev. 589′

Greater South Haven Area Chamber of Commerce: 606 Phillips St., South Haven, MI 49090; phone (269) 637-5171.

SAVE **MICHIGAN MARITIME MUSEUM** is off I-196 exit 20, then w. to 260 Dyckman Ave. Exhibits tell about the people who built and used boats on the Great Lakes and about changes in fishing history. U.S. Coast Guard exhibits also are displayed. Daily 10-5, Sun. noon-5; closed major holidays. Admission $2.50; over 62 and ages 5-12, $1.50. Phone (269) 637-8078 or (800) 747-3810.

SUTTONS BAY (E-2) pop. 589

Suttons Bay is surrounded by fragrant orchards and vineyards; several nearby wineries offer tours and tastings. Farm markets and antique shops can be found along SR 22 between Suttons Bay and Northport.

Suttons Bay Chamber of Commerce: P.O. Box 46, Suttons Bay, MI 49682; phone (231) 271-5077.

CASINOS

- **Leelanau Sands Casino** is at 2521 N.W. Bayshore Dr. Fri.-Sat. 8 a.m.-3 a.m., Sun.-Thurs. 8 a.m.-2 a.m. Phone (231) 271-4104 or (800) 922-2946. *See color ad p. 102.*

TECUMSEH (I-4) pop. 8,574, elev. 795′

TECUMSEH AREA HISTORICAL MUSEUM is at 302 E. Chicago Blvd. The museum is housed in Tecumseh's first Catholic church, which was built in 1913 by local farmers with stones from their fields. Displays include 19th-century dresses, Civil War items, arrowheads, old quilts and the surveying equipment used to lay out the town in 1824. Changing exhibits also are featured. Allow 30 minutes minimum. Wed.-Sat. 11-3; closed holidays. Free. Phone (517) 423-2374.

TIPTON (I-4)

HIDDEN LAKE GARDENS is 8 mi. w. of SR 52 on SR 50. The 755-acre garden is part of Michigan State University and has a greenhouse complex displaying plants from arid, tropical and temperate climates. There also are gardens, natural and developed landscapes, an all-America display, a lake, a picnic area, several hiking trails and a 6-mile scenic drive. There are thousands of labeled trees, shrubs and flowers and a display of dwarf and unusual evergreens. Daily 8-dusk, Apr.-Oct.; 8-4, rest of year. Admission $3, Apr.-Oct.; $2, rest of year. Phone (517) 431-2060.

DID YOU KNOW

Sault Ste. Marie

is

the oldest town

in the state.

TRAVERSE CITY (E-2)
pop. 14,532, elev. 589′

Old orchards found when the lumber mill village of Traverse City was expanding during the late 1800s might have pointed the way for the future. By the time the timber was exhausted, the town was the center of a flourishing cherry-growing region. Several wineries contribute to the area's growing wine industry.

The city's setting at the base of Grand Traverse Bay makes it a busy resort in all seasons. Winter sports are widely available. In summer the bay provides good sailing and fishing. Traverse City State Park (see Recreation Chart and the AAA Great Lakes CampBook) is 2 miles east. The area has more than 30 golf courses, including courses designed by Jack Nicklaus, Arnold Palmer and Gary Player.

Particularly picturesque among the area's many scenic drives is the 36-mile trip on SR 37 through Old Mission Peninsula, which splits the bay into two long, narrow arms. It is especially lovely when the cherry trees bloom in mid-May and when leaves take on their fall colors, beginning in September. The tip of the peninsula, marked by a lighthouse, is equidistant from the Equator and the North Pole. At Old Mission is a reconstructed Indian mission originally built in 1836. Another scenic route along the lakeshore is US 31 between Traverse City and Petoskey, then SR 119 to Cross Village.

Traverse City Convention and Visitors Bureau: 101 W. Grandview Pkwy., Traverse City, MI 49684-2252; phone (800) 872-8377.

CLINCH PARK is at jct. Cass St. and Grandview Pkwy. The park contains a sandy beach and zoo with native wildlife. A steam train circles the park Memorial Day weekend through Labor Day. Daily 9:30-5:30, Memorial Day weekend-Labor Day; 10-4, mid-Apr. through day before Memorial Day weekend and day after Labor Day-Oct. 31. Admission $3; ages 5-12, $1.50. Train ride $1; ages 5-12, 50c. Phone (231) 922-4904.

Madeline is berthed at the Clinch Marina, jct. Cass St. and Grandview Pkwy. Tours are offered of this 92-foot replica of an 1845 schooner. Tours daily 8 a.m.-9 p.m. when docked, June-Sept. Donations. Reservations are required. Phone (231) 946-2647.

DENNOS MUSEUM CENTER is at 1701 E. Front St. on the campus of Northwestern Michigan College. Permanent and changing art exhibits in the galleries include the Discovery Gallery, offering hands-on art, science and technological exhibits; and the Inuit Art Gallery, featuring an extensive collection of Eskimo art. Allow 1 hour minimum. Mon.-Sat. 10-5, Sun. 1-5. Admission $4; under 13, $2; family rate $12. Phone (231) 995-1055.

WINERIES

- **Chateau Chantal Winery** is 12 mi. n. on SR 37 to 15900 Rue de Vin. Mon.-Sat. 11-8, Sun. noon-5, June 15-Labor Day; Mon.-Sat. 11-7, Sun. noon-5, day after Labor Day-Oct. 31; Mon.-Sat. 11-5, Sun. noon-5, rest of year. Tours daily at 1, 2 and 3, June 1-Labor Day. Phone (231) 223-4110 or (800) 969-4009.

- **Chateau Grand Traverse** is 8.5 mi. n. on SR 37 at 12239 Center Rd. Mon.-Sat. 10-7, Sun. noon-6, Memorial Day-Labor Day; Mon.-Sat. 10-6, Sun. noon-6, May 1-day before Memorial Day and day after Labor Day-Oct. 31; Mon.-Sat. 10-5, Sun. noon-5, rest of year. Phone (231) 223-7355.

UPPER PENINSULA

That the Upper Peninsula is part of Michigan at all was the result of the unpopular compromise that won Michigan its statehood. The crucial issue at stake was the sole proprietorship of a strip of territory along the Michigan-Ohio border that included the city of Toledo. The bitterly fought Toledo War (contested in Congress with blazing words, not in Toledo with bullets) resulted in Michigan's ceding that land to Ohio in exchange for statehood.

Michigan somewhat grudgingly accepted the Upper Peninsula—then considered a barren wasteland—as a consolation prize. Hardly a Michigander today would have it any other way. In terms of natural resources alone the raw deal turned out to be a steal. When Michigan became a state in 1837, the Upper Peninsula's fabulous deposits of pure copper were already being uncovered; the deposits were, however, not news to American Indians, who had mined the metal thousands of years before.

In 1957 the slender strand of the Mackinac Bridge anchored the Upper Peninsula to the Lower, making the U.P.—as locals call it—easily accessible from the south. Recreation and tourism have since helped alleviate some of the region's economic slack.

Known now for its unspoiled beauty rather than its industrial scars, the Upper Peninsula is a popular haven for outdoors enthusiasts. State and national forests cover much of the land; Isle Royale National Park (see place listing p. 77) and Pictured Rocks National Lakeshore (see place listing p. 94) preserve some of the rugged peninsula's most impressive terrain. Aspen, birch, fir, maple and spruce trees shelter such animals as black bears, Eastern timber wolves, white-tailed deer and moose.

The Porcupine Mountains in the west have a large stand of virgin hemlock and one of the largest relatively undisturbed northern hemlock hardwood forests west of New York's Adirondack Mountains. Recreational opportunities range from swimming to skiing, with almost legendary popularity in fishing.

The following places in the Upper Peninsula are listed separately under their individual names: Bessemer, Calumet, Caspian, Copper Harbor, Escanaba, Fayette, Germfask, Hancock, Hiawatha National Forest, Houghton, Iron Mountain, Ironwood, Ishpeming, Isle Royale National Park, Manistique, Marquette, Munising, Negaunee, Ontonagon, Paradise, Pictured Rocks National Lakeshore, Rockland, St. Ignace, Sault Ste. Marie, Silver City, Soo Junction and Whitefish Point.

WALLED LAKE—*see Detroit p. 65.*

WATERFORD—*see Detroit p. 65.*

WATERLOO (L-1) pop. 3,069

Plentiful game attracted many of the Great Lakes Indian tribes to Waterloo, an area of low hills and marshes that divides the headwaters of the westward-flowing Grand River from the eastbound Huron River. Waterloo is in the midst of Waterloo State Recreation Area *(see Recreation Chart and the AAA Great Lakes CampBook).*

GERALD E. EDDY DISCOVERY CENTER is at 17030 Bush Rd. in the Waterloo State Recreation Area, exit 157 off I-94, following signs. Hands-on exhibits and 17 miles of walking trails are featured. A slide presentation discusses the geology of Earth and of Michigan. Allow 1 hour minimum. Tues.-Sat. 10-5, Sun. noon-5. Park admission $6 per private vehicle. Discovery Center free. Phone (734) 475-3170.

WATERLOO AREA FARM MUSEUM AND DEWEY SCHOOL is 3 mi. n. to 9998 Waterloo-Munith Rd. Several restored buildings comprise the complex: two barns, a corn crib, schoolhouse, Victorian farmhouse, granary, workshop, icehouse, milk cellar, windmill and log house. Displays of tools, clothing, furnishings and decorations depict 19th-century farm life. Guides in period garb lead tours. Allow 1 hour minimum. Fri.-Sun. 1-5, June-Aug.; tours by appointment in Sept. Last tour departs 30 minutes before closing. Admission $3; over 62, $2.50; ages 5-18, $1. Phone (517) 596-2254, (517) 851-7539 or (517) 851-7890.

WEST BLOOMFIELD—*see Detroit p. 65.*

WHITEFISH POINT (A-5)

▼▼▼ **GREAT LAKES SHIPWRECK MUSEUM** GEM is at 18335 N. Whitefish Point Rd. Displays include artifacts, a memorial that features the bell from the *Edmund Fitzgerald* and pictures of shipping disasters. The Shipwreck Theater offers a short videotape presentation about the *Edmund Fitzgerald.* A boardwalk extends to Lake Superior. Allow 30 minutes minimum. Daily 10-6, May-Oct. Admission $8.50; ages 6-17, $5.50; family rate (two adults and two children under 17) $23. MC, VI. Phone (906) 635-1742. *See color ad p. 85.*

Whitefish Point Light Station is at jct. SR 123 and Whitefish Point Rd. The restored light station began operation in 1849 and is the oldest working lighthouse on Lake Superior. Overlooking the graveyard of the Great Lakes, it marks the critical turning point for all ships leaving and entering Lake Superior.

WHITEHALL (G-1) pop. 2,884, elev. 599'

WHITE RIVER LIGHT STATION MUSEUM is w. off US 31 to Lakewood Club exit, w. on White Lake Dr., s. on S. Shore Dr., following signs to 6199 Murray Rd. This 1875 lighthouse displays photographs, paintings and marine artifacts. Allow 30 minutes minimum. Tues.-Fri. 11-5, Sat.-Sun. noon-6, June-Sept.; Sat.-Sun. noon-6, Memorial Day weekend. Admission $2; ages 10-18, $1. Phone (231) 894-8265.

WILLIAMSBURG (E-3) elev. 732'

CASINOS

• **Turtle Creek Casino** is at 7741 E. SR 72, Williamsburg, MI 49690. Daily 24 hours. Phone (231) 267-9546 or (888) 777-8946. *See color ad p. 102.*

WYANDOTTE—*see Detroit p. 65.*

YPSILANTI (I-5) pop. 22,362, elev. 720'

When the youthful Greek revolutionary general Demetrios Ypsilanti held the entire Turkish Army at bay and escaped without losing even one of his 300 soldiers, he had no idea that his bravery would cause a muddy but energetic village in the wilds of southeastern Michigan to become his namesake in 1832. This city on the Huron River is an industrial center and the home of Eastern Michigan University, Riverside Park and the noted Water Tower.

The city's 40-block historic district, centered around Huron Street, contains some 700 restored buildings in the Greek Revival, Gothic Revival, Italianate, Second Empire, Queen Anne and Tudor Revival architectural styles.

Ypsilanti Area Convention and Visitors Bureau: 106 W. Michigan Ave., Ypsilanti, MI 48197; phone (734) 483-4444.

WIARD'S ORCHARDS & COUNTRY FAIR is s. of I-94 exit 183 (Huron St.) following signs to 5565 Merritt Rd. The property has been run by the Wiard family since 1853. Nearly 200 acres contain apple orchards, a pumpkin patch and a cider mill. Activities (which may vary due to the seasonal nature of farm operations) include picking apples and pumpkins, petting animals, riding ponies and exploring a hay barn. A recurring country fair features a haunted barn, monster maze and wagon rides.

Food is available. Tues.-Fri. 10-6, mid-Sept. through Oct. 31. Country fair Sat.-Sun. 10-6, day after Labor Day-Oct. 31. Closed holidays. Orchards free. Country fair (includes rides) $8.50. Phone (734) 482-7744.

YPSILANTI AUTOMOTIVE HERITAGE COLLECTION AND MILLER MOTORS HUDSON is at 100 E. Cross St. Housed in the last Hudson dealership, the museum contains more than 35 original and restored cars, from a copy of the Tucker Torpedo to an original Kaiser. Corvairs, Chevy IIs and Hudsons also are on display, along with Hudson memorabilia. Mon.-Fri. 1:30-5:30, Sat. 9-5, Sun. noon-5; closed holidays. Admission $2. Phone (734) 482-5200.

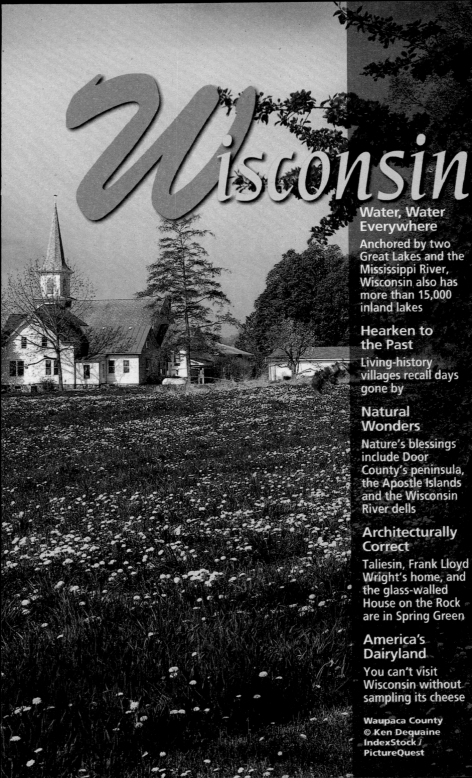

Wisconsin

Water, Water Everywhere

Anchored by two Great Lakes and the Mississippi River, Wisconsin also has more than 15,000 inland lakes

Hearken to the Past

Living-history villages recall days gone by

Natural Wonders

Nature's blessings include Door County's peninsula, the Apostle Islands and the Wisconsin River dells

Architecturally Correct

Taliesin, Frank Lloyd Wright's home, and the glass-walled House on the Rock are in Spring Green

America's Dairyland

You can't visit Wisconsin without sampling its cheese

Waupaca County
© Ken Dequaine
IndexStock /
PictureQuest

say "cheese"

Whitefish Dunes State Park / © Todd Phillips/IndexStock / PictureQuest

I n America's Dairyland, there are
lots of reasons to say "cheese."
Smiles, rest and relaxation are a
way of life in the communities along the
Door County peninsula. Although square
in the Midwest, you'll experience the
flavor of New England in a rugged
landscape peppered with fishing villages,
farms, lighthouses and sand beaches.

The state's biggest city, Milwaukee,
reflects a decidedly German heritage.
Key players in its development—such
sudsy names as Miller, Pabst and
Schlitz—are sure to elicit a grin or two.
Noted architect Frank Lloyd Wright
left his mark in the middle of the state.
The Richland Center native brought his
visions to life in such cities as Madison
and Spring Green.

Affectionately called "cheeseheads," fans of the Green Bay Packers (the oldest team in the NFL) cheer wildly and beam like Cheshire cats.

Stretching along the western border is the St. Croix River, a recreational hot spot with scenic gorges, rock formations and waterfalls.

And like sprinkled Parmesan, the intriguing Apostle Islands top the state.

The national lakeshore features more lighthouses than any other national park. Wisconsin. It's whey more than dairy.

Milk Wisconsin for all it's worth, and you end up with more than just cheese.

Sure, the state earned its nickname as America's Dairyland by being a leader in dairy production. However, it's also a big processor of snap beans, sweet corn, hay, oats and potatoes. It manufactures much of the nation's mining machinery, x-ray equipment and power cranes. And its economy thrives on a booming tourism business—which is no small wonder, given the seemingly endless number of things you can do.

Take steps into the past. A replica of the log cabin in which "Little House" books author Laura Ingalls Wilder was born is in Pepin. Historic lighthouses line the Door Peninsula. Costumed interpreters perform daily chores around the 360-acre grounds of the 1851 Wade House in Greenbush.

Explore another culture. A strong Norwegian influence embraces Blue Mounds. Scandinavian customs prevail on Washington Island, the country's oldest Icelandic settlement. New Glarus, often called "Little Switzerland," reflects a decidedly Swiss heritage. German, Danish, Polish and Finnish

homesteads are among the more than 65 preserved buildings at the 1870s rural village in Eagle.

Awakening the Senses

Admire great architecture. Massive fireplaces, waterfalls and a windowed room that juts out over Wyoming Valley are among the wonders of The House on the Rock, south of Spring Green. Richland Center native Frank Lloyd Wright designed buildings in Madison, Milwaukee, Racine and Spring Green. The State Capitol in Madison shows a Roman Renaissance flair. A 40-foot circular stairway winds among five floors of the 1854 Octagon House in Watertown.

Give your palate a treat. Sip apple, cherry and grape wines in Algoma, Barneveld, Cedarburg and Prairie du Sac. Taste brewery samples in the city made famous for beer: Milwaukee. Nibble on cheese in Monroe and Rudolph. Savor cranberry refreshments made from berries cultivated in marshes around Manitowish Waters and Warrens.

Play the slots and scream out "Bingo!" Casinos in Baraboo, Carter, Green Bay and Keshena invite you to test your luck. Gamble on the greyhounds at a park in Kenosha.

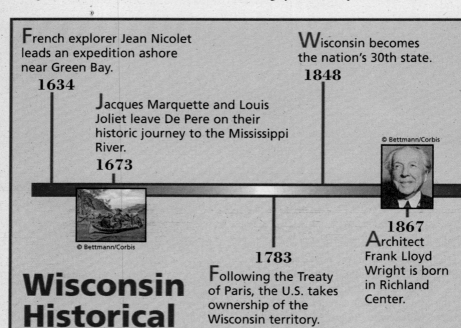

French explorer Jean Nicolet leads an expedition ashore near Green Bay.
1634

Jacques Marquette and Louis Joliet leave De Pere on their historic journey to the Mississippi River.
1673

© Bettmann/Corbis

Wisconsin becomes the nation's 30th state.
1848

© Bettmann/Corbis

1867
Architect Frank Lloyd Wright is born in Richland Center.

1783
Following the Treaty of Paris, the U.S. takes ownership of the Wisconsin territory.

Wisconsin Historical Timeline

Learn about locomotives. You can ride the rails through the St. Croix River Valley in Osceola and the lake country of Spooner, where a former train depot holds railroad memories. Iron horses from the steam and diesel eras also are preserved at museums in Green Bay and North Freedom.

Focus on other transportation. Aircraft are showcased at an Oshkosh museum. Classic automobiles beg to be admired in Hartford. Maritime vessels are centerpieces at museums in Gills Rock, Sturgeon Bay and Superior. Circus wagons have a big-top home in Baraboo.

Remember veterans. Museums and parks in Madison, Neillsville, Oshkosh and Waupaca pay tribute to those who served in conflicts.

Trees, Caves and Wildlife

Trace the papermaking trade. The "Lumberjack Special" steam-powered train carries visitors from the historic depot in Laona to Camp Five Museum Complex, where logging relics and an audiovisual presentation detail the history of an industry that feeds off 15 million acres of forestland. Tours of paper mills in Wisconsin Rapids guide you through to the finished product.

Get back to nature. Rose-colored cliffs punctuate the weathered caves and hollows at Apostle Islands National Lakeshore. The glacial phenomena of Devil's Lake State Park and Kettle Moraine State Forest are a sight to behold. River tours wander among unusual rock formations and caverns in Wisconsin Dells.

Confront a local legend. The folksy myth of the Hodag, a creature once said to have inhabited the forests around Rhinelander, is kept very much alive in the area.

Study native wildlife. Cruises departing from Hazelhurst and Horicon bring you face-to-face with all kinds of creatures. Birdwatchers gather on the shores of St. Croix National Scenic Riverway and in a Waupun refuge.

Catch a great view. On a clear day, you can see practically forever from the lofty vantage point atop Granddad Bluff, which towers 600 feet above La Crosse.

When it comes to family fun, America's Dairyland may just be the cream of the crop.

On the night the Great Chicago Fire kills 300 people, a forest fire in Peshtigo claims 1,200 lives.
1871

Earl "Curly" Lambeau founds the Green Bay Packers.
1919

Wisconsin senator Joseph McCarthy takes his anti-Communist stand on national television.
1954

Library of Congress

1932
Wisconsin becomes the first state to pass an unemployment compensation act.

© Vince Streano/Corbis

1884
The Ringling Brothers give their first circus performance in Baraboo.

2000
A dairy farm in Omro is the country's first to use robots to milk cows.

Recreation

With 15,000 inland lakes and 25,000 miles of waterways—plus borders touching lakes Michigan and Superior, the Brule, St. Croix and Menominee rivers and the mighty Mississippi—Wisconsin is an H_2O utopia.

Sailing enthusiasts float through the steely waters of Chequamegon and Sturgeon bays, while **windsurfers** unfurl sails of their own around the southern tip of Lake Winnebago and at Kohler-Andrae State Park, on the shores of Lake Michigan.

Break the surface during a **scuba diving** trip along Apostle Islands National Lakeshore, or explore the shipwrecks lining "death's door," the nautical passage between Door County and Washington Island.

Such lazy rivers as the Apple, Chippewa and Namekagon are prime territory for **tubing.** Moderate currents enhance the **canoeing** experience on the Baraboo, Crystal, La Crosse, Oconto, St. Croix, Upper Bois Brule and Wisconsin rivers. The winding Kickapoo—dubbed the "crookedest river in the world"—is navigable its entire length.

Challenging rapids result in irresistible **kayaking** on the Flambeau, Grant, Ontonagon and Tomahawk rivers. Stretches of class V rapids make the Montreal River a great spot for expert kayakers to put their skills to the test. Although the waters around the Apostle Islands are more placid, paddlers won't be disappointed. Rugged sea caves riddling the bases of sandstone cliffs beckon you to explore. For **white-water rafting,** take on the Menominee, Peshtigo or Wolf rivers.

Differing Vantage Points

If thoughts of lofty heights don't leave you quivering, Wisconsin delivers thrills. **Rock climbing** in Devil's Lake State Park, near Baraboo, leads you atop 500-foot bluffs around the lake for which the park is named. **Hang gliders** who launch from similar bluffs shouldering the Upper Mississippi River Valley enjoy a memorable perspective of the area.

Once you've taken advantage of a bird's-eye view of the land, check it out up close from **hiking** and **horseback riding** trails. You'll find facilities for both activities at Wildcat Mountain State Park, southeast of Ontario, and at several state forests, including Black River, near Black River Falls; Brule River, in Brule; Flambeau River, east of Draper; and Governor Knowles, west of Grantsburg.

On-road **bicycling** trails paint a fitting picture of the varied landscape. The 22-mile High Falls Tour, which weaves through Marinette County, passes the cascade of Veterans Falls and the glimmering waters of High Falls Reservoir. Take your bike over an original covered bridge on the 30-mile trail that begins at Cedar Creek Park in Cedarburg, or pedal through the stone railroad tunnels of the 32-mile Elroy-Sparta Trail.

For off-road excitement, **mountain biking** trails cater to cyclists of all abilities. The Boulder Junction Area Trail System, or B.A.T.S., covers 10 mostly easy miles around Boulder Junction. Skilled riders favor the tough Washburn Lake trails, near Rhinelander, or the wild and jarring experience afforded by the Swiss-cheeselike terrain of Kettle Moraine State Forest, much of which only extreme adventurists would like.

"Snow" Much Fun

During winter, the groomed trails at many state parks entice **cross-country skiers** and **snowshoers.** Some of the more extensive systems trek through Governor Dodge State Park, north of Dodgeville; Mirror Lake State Park, southwest of Lake Delton; and Newport State Park, northeast of Ellison Bay. Nearly 120 miles of snowmobiling trails traverse the northern and southern units of Kettle Moraine State Forest. Quadruple your fun on the 480-plus miles of trails in Northern Highland-American Legion State Forest.

Among the popular **downhill skiing** and **snowboarding** areas are Cascade Mountain, southwest of Portage; Devil's Head, near Merrimac; Trollhaugen, in Dresser; and Whitecap Mountain, west of Montreal.

Trout and salmon **fishing** is excellent in the Great Lakes. For northern pike, bass, muskellunge, perch and walleye, head to smaller lakes and streams. Many state parks have **camping** facilities.

Recreational Activities

Throughout the TourBook, you may notice a Recreational Activities heading with bulleted listings of recreation-oriented establishments listed underneath. Similar operations also may be mentioned in Destination City recreation sections. Since normal AAA inspection criteria cannot be applied, these establishments are presented only for information. Age, height and weight restrictions may apply. Reservations often are recommended and sometimes are required. Visitors should phone or write the attraction for additional information; the address and phone number are provided for this purpose.

Fast Facts

POPULATION: 5,363,675.

AREA: 56,154 square miles; ranks 26th.

CAPITAL: Madison.

HIGHEST POINT: 1,953 ft., Timm's Hill.

LOWEST POINT: 581 ft., Lake Michigan.

TIME ZONE(S): Central. DST.

MINIMUM AGE FOR DRIVERS: 18; 16 with drivers' education.

MINIMUM AGE FOR GAMBLING: 18; 21 if alcohol is served on the premises.

SEAT BELT/CHILD RESTRAINT LAWS: Seat belts required for driver and all passengers; child restraints required for under 4. Under 16 must ride in a rear seat.

HELMETS FOR MOTORCYCLISTS: Required for those under 18 or when operating with a learner's permit.

RADAR DETECTORS: Permitted.

FIREARMS LAWS: Vary by state and/or county. Contact Wisconsin State Police Headquarters, 4802 Sheboygan Ave., Madison, WI 53707; phone (608) 266-3212.

HOLIDAYS: Jan. 1; Martin Luther King Jr. Day, Jan. (3rd Mon.); Presidents' Day, Feb. (3rd Mon.); Memorial Day, May (last Mon.); July 4; Labor Day, Sept. (1st Mon.); Columbus Day, Oct. (2nd Mon.); Veterans Day, Nov. 11; Thanksgiving; Dec. 25.

TAXES: Wisconsin's statewide sales tax is 5 percent, with local options for an additional increment of 0.5 percent, plus a lodgings tax.

STATE INFORMATION CENTERS: Centers are in Madison at 201 W. Washington Ave., in Grant County on US 151/61, at La Crosse off I-90, at Hudson and Kenosha off I-94, near Genoa City on US 12, at Superior on US 2, at Hurley on US 51, in Prairie du Chien at 211 S. Main St. and in Marinette on US 41. Madison center open Mon.-Fri. 7:45-4:30. Other centers open daily 8-6, June 1-Labor Day; 8-4 (except Superior 9-5), day after Labor Day-Oct. 31. Hudson, Hurley, Kenosha and La Crosse open Tues.-Sat. 8-4, Nov.-Apr.

FURTHER INFORMATION FOR VISITORS:

Wisconsin Department of Tourism
P.O. Box 7976
Madison, WI 53707-7976
(608) 266-2161
(800) 432-8747

FISHING AND HUNTING REGULATIONS:

Wisconsin Department of Natural Resources
P.O. Box 7921
Madison, WI 53707
(608) 266-2621

NATIONAL FOREST INFORMATION:

U.S. Forest Service, Eastern Region
626 E. Wisconsin Ave., Suite 800
Milwaukee, WI 53203
(414) 297-3600
(877) 444-6777 (for reservations)

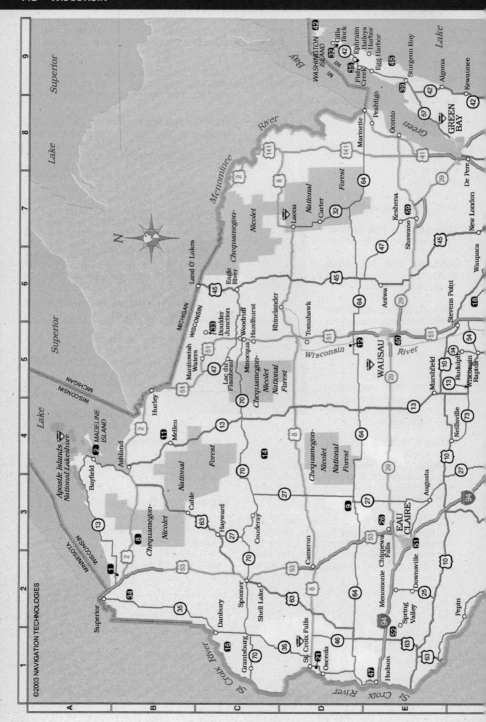

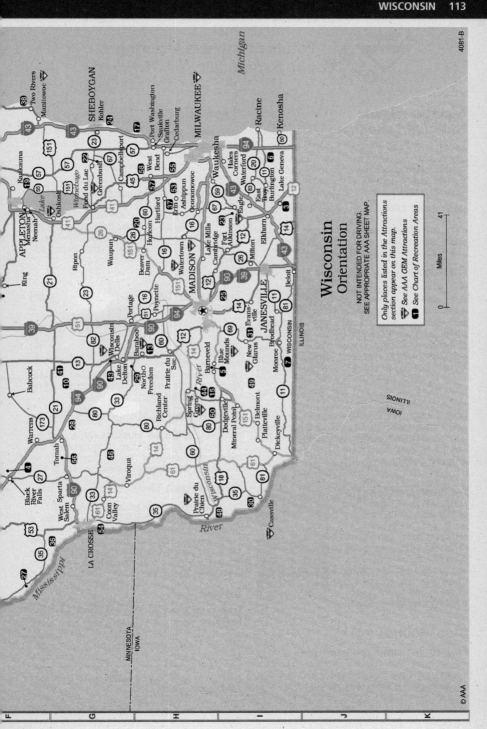

Wisconsin Orientation

NOT INTENDED FOR DRIVING.
SEE APPROPRIATE AAA SHEET MAP.

Only places listed in the Attractions section appear on this map.

▼ See AAA GEM Attractions

🔟 See Chart of Recreation Areas

0   Miles   41

4081-B

© AAA

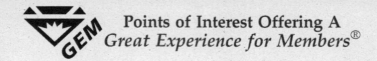

Points of Interest Offering A
Great Experience for Members®

Apostle Islands National Lakeshore (A-3)

APOSTLE ISLANDS NATIONAL LAKESHORE—Surrounded by the waters of Lake Superior, the Apostle Islands were early fur-trading outposts; the lakeshore is now visited for recreational pursuits. See p. 119.

SIGHTSEEING CRUISES—The Apostle Islands are explored by a variety of narrated cruises; area geology, history and legends are related, and stops might include nature hikes or visits to lighthouses or a restored fish camp. See p. 120.

Baraboo (G-5)

CIRCUS WORLD MUSEUM—Step right up, ladies and gentlemen, for big-top circus performances, parades, a circus museum and a collection of handcrafted circus wagons; don't forget the elephant rides! See p. 122.

DEVIL'S LAKE STATE PARK—Bordered on three sides by quartzite cliffs, Devil's Lake is part of the Ice Age National Scientific Reserve; the park is a favorite for camping, climbing, hiking and swimming. See p. 122.

THE INTERNATIONAL CRANE FOUNDATION—Guided tours of this world center for the study and preservation of cranes introduce visitors to a variety of crane species; an overlook, chick exercise yard, and nature trails through restored wetlands, prairies and savannas add to the understanding of these creatures. See p. 122.

Blue Mounds (I-5)

CAVE OF THE MOUNDS—Uncovered by a 1939 quarry blast, this National Natural Landmark boasts crystallized rock formations and shimmering underground pools. See p. 124.

Cassville (I-3)

GOVERNOR NELSON DEWEY HOMESITE—The home of Wisconsin's first governor has been reconstructed to reflect the lifestyle of the Dewey family; the agricultural estate is reminiscent of a Virginia plantation. See p. 126.

STONEFIELD STATE HISTORIC SITE—The site consists of Stonefield, the farm estate of Wisconsin's first governor; the State Agricultural Museum, where farm machinery helps trace the state's agricultural history; and a turn-of-the-20th-century village where everyday life of that period still goes on. See p. 126.

Eagle (I-7)

OLD WORLD WISCONSIN—This 576-acre state historic site depicts 19th-century Wisconsin through representations of a rural crossroads village, Yankee farmsteads and African-American settlements; costumed interpreters recreate pioneer life. See p. 159.

Green Bay (E-8)

NATIONAL RAILROAD MUSEUM—All aboard for a chance to see more than 70 locomotives and rolling stock, including "The Big Boy," said to be the world's largest steam locomotive. See p. 135.

Greenbush (G-7)

WADE HOUSE & WESLEY JUNG CARRIAGE MUSEUM—This restored stagecoach inn includes a smithy, a smokehouse and a residence typical of the 1850s, with costumed interpreters conducting tours and performing daily chores; the carriage museum contains a collection of horse-and-buggy era vehicles. See p. 136.

Laona (D-7)

LUMBERJACK SPECIAL AND CAMP FIVE MUSEUM COMPLEX TOUR—A steam-powered train takes visitors from the Laona depot to the museum complex, where they can visit a logging museum, an active blacksmith shop, an old country store and a nature center; other options include a forest tour by surrey and a wildlife tour on a pontoon boat. See p. 141.

Madison (H-6)

OLBRICH BOTANICAL GARDENS—On the shores of Lake Monona, this oasis includes 14 acres of specialty gardens and a 50-foot-high glass conservatory. See p. 143.

WISCONSIN STATE CAPITOL—The 1917 Roman Renaissance structure has a white granite dome topped by a bronze statue; guided tours cover the rotunda, the Supreme Court and the state's Senate and Assembly chambers. See p. 144.

WISCONSIN VETER-ANS MUSEUM—Dedicated to the Wisconsin residents who served their country in military service from the Civil War to the Persian Gulf War, the mu-  seum features lifelike dioramas utilizing actual military equipment in realistic settings. See p. 144.

Manitowoc (F-8)

RAHR-WEST ART MUSEUM—In a Victorian mansion, the museum contains period furnishings, dolls, and ivory and porcelain objects. See p. 145.

ISCONSIN MARITIME MU-SEUM—Shipping on the Great Lakes from the days of three-masted schooners to today's vessels is depicted through maps, nautical equipment and models; a highlight is an exhibit about the World War II submarines built in Manitowoc. See p. 145.

Milwaukee (H-8)

MILWAUKEE ART MUSEUM—More than 20,000 works of art ranging from Frank Lloyd Wright to German Expressionism are housed inside this lakefront museum. See p. 154.

MILWAUKEE COUNTY ZOO—The zoo's collections, grouped by continent in settings that resemble their natural habitats, can be seen close-up courtesy of a zoomobile tour; sea lion and raptor shows and a working dairy farm are highlights. See p. 154.

MILWAUKEE PUBLIC MUSEUM—The museum interprets the world's natural and cultural heritage through such displays as life-size dinosaurs, the streets of old Milwaukee and environmental exhibits about rain forests, Africa and Latin America. See p. 154.

MITCHELL PARK HORTICULTURAL CONSERVATORY—"THE DOMES"—The conservatory's three domes have individual motifs: One  features tropical plants; another, the world's deserts; and the third has five themed floral shows each year. See p. 154.

New Glarus (I-5)

SWISS HISTORICAL VILLAGE—The Swiss heritage of New Glarus is depicted here in 14 buildings, replicas of the first structures built by  the community's 19th-century Swiss settlers; a hall of history traces Swiss immigration to America. See p. 163.

Oshkosh (F-7)

EAA AIRVENTURE MUSEUM—More than 95 historic aircraft, a hangar and an airport typical of the early days of air travel are part of this complex; come during the summer for flights in a restored 1929 airplane or open-cockpit bi-plane. See p. 165.

Prairie du Chien (H-3)

VILLA LOUIS—This Victorian mansion and several outbuildings were built by a pioneering family prominent in the business of fur trading; the opulent furnishings include a fine collection of decorative arts. See p. 167.

St. Croix Falls (D-1)

INTERSTATE STATE PARK—Wisconsin's oldest state park is well-known for its scenic beauty and for the Old Man of the Dalles, a rock outcropping along the St. Croix River. See p. 169.

Spring Green (H-4)

THE HOUSE ON THE ROCK—This multi-level house perched on a precipice overlooking the Wyoming Valley has a glass-walled room extending out over the valley, waterfalls and an observation deck; other buildings house a variety of eclectic collections. See p. 172.

Watertown (H-6)

OCTAGON HOUSE—
The 1854 house has five antique-filled floors as well as a 40-foot circular stairway; a late 19th-century barn contains farm-related exhibits. See p. 174.

Wausau (E-5)

LEIGH YAWKEY WOODSON ART MUSEUM—In addition to its permanent collection, the Woodson, housed in an English Tudor-style building, presents changing exhibitions both inside the museum and outdoors in its landscaped, parklike gardens. See p. 175.

Wisconsin Dells (G-5)

DELLS BOAT TOURS—Boat tours through the Upper and Lower dells of the Wisconsin River cruise past sandstone cliffs, canyons, and erosion-carved islands and rock formations. See p. 177.

RECREATION AREAS

	MAP LOCATION	CAMPING	PICNICKING	HIKING TRAILS	BOATING	BOAT RAMP	BOAT RENTAL	FISHING	SWIMMING	PETS ON LEASH	BICYCLE TRAILS	WINTER SPORTS	VISITOR CENTER	LODGE/CABINS	FOOD SERVICE
NATIONAL FORESTS *(See place listings)*															
Chequamegon-Nicolet 1,518,138 acres. North-central and north-eastern Wisconsin. Horse rental.		•	•	•	•	•		•	•	•	•	•			•
NATIONAL LAKESHORES *(See place listings)*															
Apostle Islands (A-5) 69,372 acres off northern Wisconsin's Bayfield peninsula in Lake Superior.		•	•	•	•	•	•	•	•	•			•	•	
NATIONAL RIVERWAYS *(See place listings)*															
St. Croix (E-1, B-2) 252 mi. from Cable to Prescott.		•	•	•	•	•	•	•	•	•			•		
STATE															
Amnicon Falls (A-2) 825 acres 10 mi. s.e. of Superior on US 2. Scenic.	❶	•	•	•				•		•					
Big Bay (A-4) 2,358 acres e. of Bayfield on Madeline Island via ferry.	❷	•	•	•				•	•	•					
Big Foot Beach (I-7) 271 acres 2.5 mi. s. of Lake Geneva on SR 120.	❸	•	•	•				•	•	•			•		
Black River (F-4) 67,000 acres. *(See Black River Falls p. 124)*	❹	•	•	•	•	•		•	•	•		•			
Blue Mound (H-5) 1,124 acres off US 18/151 in Blue Mounds. Scenic. Cross-country skiing. *(See Blue Mounds p. 124)*	❺	•	•	•				•	•	•		•	•		•
Bong (I-8) 4,515 acres 4 mi. s. of Kansasville on SR 142. Horse rental.	❻	•	•	•	•	•		•	•	•	•	•	•		
Browntown-Cadiz Springs (I-5) 644 acres 1 mi. e. of Browntown off SR 11.	❼		•	•	•	•		•	•	•					
Brule River (B-3) 40,367 acres at Brule.	❽	•	•	•				•		•		•			
Brunet Island (D-3) 1,032 acres 1 mi. n. of Cornell off SR 27. Historic.	❾	•	•	•	•	•		•	•	•		•			
Buckhorn (G-5) 2,507 acres 13 mi. n. of Mauston on CRs Q and G.	❿	•	•	•	•	•		•	•	•					
Copper Falls (B-4) 2,483 acres 2 mi. n.e. of Mellen on SR 169. Nature programs.	⓫	•	•	•				•	•	•		•	•		•
Council Grounds (D-5) 462 acres 2 mi. n.w. of Merrill on SR 107.	⓬	•	•	•	•	•		•	•	•					•
Devil's Lake (H-5) 10,000 acres 3.5 mi. s. of Baraboo on SR 123. Scenic. *(See Baraboo p. 122)*	⓭	•	•	•	•	•	•	•	•	•		•	•		•

RECREATION AREAS

RECREATION AREAS	MAP LOCATION	CAMPING	PICNICKING	HIKING TRAILS	BOATING	BOAT RAMP	BOAT RENTAL	FISHING	SWIMMING	PETS ON LEASH	BICYCLE TRAILS	WINTER SPORTS	VISITOR CENTER	LODGE/CABINS	FOOD SERVICE
Flambeau River (C-4) 89,914 acres 5 mi. e. of Draper on SR 70.	14	•	•	•	•	•		•	•	•		•			
Governor Dodge (H-5) 5,029 acres 3 mi. n. of Dodgeville on SR 23. Nature programs. Scenic. Bridle trails. *(See Dodgeville p. 128)*	15	•	•	•	•	•	•	•	•	•	•		•		•
Governor Knowles (C-1) 19,185 acres 5 mi. w. of Grantsburg on SR 70. Bridle trails.	16		•	•	•	•	•	•	•	•			•		
Harrington Beach (G-8) 636 acres 2 mi. e. of Belgium on CR O. Nature trails.	17		•	•				•	•	•	•		•		•
Hartman Creek (F-6) 1,323 acres 6 mi. w. of Waupaca on SR 54. Nature programs.	18	•	•	•	•			•	•	•			•		
High Cliff (F-7) 1,145 acres 3 mi. s. of Sherwood off SR 55. Nature programs.	19	•	•	•	•	•		•	•	•					•
Horicon Marsh (G-7) 11,000 acres n. of Horicon. *(See Horicon p. 136)*	20		•	•	•	•	•	•			•	•	•		
Interstate (D-1) 1,377 acres .5 mi. s. of US 8 on US 35. Scenic. Nature programs. *(See St. Croix Falls p. 169)*	21	•	•	•	•	•		•	•	•		•	•		
Kettle Moraine North (G-8) 28,910 acres. Nature programs. Bridle trails, horse rental. *(See Campbellsport p. 125)*	22	•	•	•	•	•		•	•	•	•		•		
Kettle Moraine South (I-7) 18,391 acres at Eagle. Nature programs. Bridle trails.	23	•	•	•	•	•		•	•	•	•		•		
Kohler-Andrae (G-8) 879 acres 6 mi. s.e. of Sheboygan off US 141. Nature programs.	24	•	•	•				•	•	•			•		
Lake Kegonsa (H-6) 343 acres 10 mi. s. of Madison off CR N.	25	•	•	•	•	•		•	•	•			•		
Lake Wissota (E-3) 1,062 acres 5 mi. e. of Chippewa Falls on SR 29. Nature programs. Horse rental.	26	•	•	•	•	•		•	•	•	•		•		
Merrick (F-2) 322 acres 2 mi. n.w. of Fountain City off SR 35.	27	•	•	•	•	•		•	•	•			•		
Mill Bluff (G-4) 1,258 acres 4 mi. n.w. of Camp Douglas off I-90.	28	•	•	•					•	•					
Mirror Lake (G-5) 2,057 acres 4 mi. s.w. of Lake Delton on SR 23. Nature programs.	29	•	•	•	•	•	•	•	•	•			•		
Nelson Dewey (I-3) 756 acres 1.2 mi. n.w. of Cassville on CR VV. *(See Cassville p. 126)*	30	•	•	•						•					
New Glarus Woods (I-5) 350 acres 1.5 mi. s. of New Glarus via SR 69 on CR NN.	31	•	•	•						•	•				
Newport (D-9) 2,368 acres n.e. of Ellison Bay via SR 42. Cross-country skiing.	32		•	•				•	•	•		•	•		
Northern Highland-American Legion (C-5) 220,455 acres 3 mi. w. of Eagle River on SR 70. Nature programs.	33	•	•	•	•	•		•	•	•			•		
Pattison (B-2) 1,374 acres 10 mi. s. of Superior on SR 35. Nature programs.	34	•	•	•				•	•	•		•	•	•	
Peninsula (D-9) 3,763 acres .25 mi. n. of Fish Creek. Nature programs. Nature trails. Golf, tennis.	35	•	•	•	•	•		•	•	•	•	•	•		•
Perrot (F-3) 1,300 acres 1 mi. n. of Trempealeau off SR 35. Nature programs. Historic.	36	•	•	•	•	•		•		•			•	•	
Pike Lake (H-7) 678 acres 2 mi. e. of Hartford on SR 60.	37	•	•	•				•	•	•					
Point Beach (F-8) 2,903 acres 6 mi. n.e. of Two Rivers. Nature programs.	38	•	•	•				•	•	•		•	•	•	•
Potawatomi (E-9) 1,226 acres 2 mi. n.w. of Sturgeon Bay on CR M. Downhill and cross-country skiing, snowmobiling.	39	•	•	•	•	•		•		•		•	•		
Rib Mountain (E-5) 941 acres 4 mi. s.w. of Wausau on CR N. Nature trails. *(See Wausau p. 175)*	40	•	•	•						•		•			•
Roche A Cri (G-5) 411 acres 2 mi. n. of Friendship on SR 13.	41	•	•	•					•	•					
Rock Island (D-9) 912 acres on Rock Island via ferry. Historic.	42	•	•	•	•	•		•	•	•				•	
Rocky Arbor (G-5) 226 acres 2 mi. n.w. of Wisconsin Dells off I-90.	43	•	•	•						•					
Tower Hill (H-5) 77 acres 3 mi. s.e. of Spring Green on SR 23.	44	•	•	•	•	•		•		•					

RECREATION AREAS

	MAP LOCATION	CAMPING	PICNICKING	HIKING TRAILS	BOATING	BOAT RAMP	BOAT RENTAL	FISHING	SWIMMING	PETS ON LEASH	BICYCLE TRAILS	WINTER SPORTS	VISITOR CENTER	LODGE/CABINS	FOOD SERVICE
Whitefish Dunes (E-9) 863 acres 10 mi. n.e. of Sturgeon Bay via SR 57.	45		•	•				•	•	•			•		•
Wildcat Mountain (G-4) 3,526 acres 3 mi. s.e. of Ontario off SR 33. Bridle trails.	46	•	•	•	•	•		•		•		•	•		
Willow River (E-1) 2,843 acres 7 mi. n.e. of Hudson. Nature programs.	47	•	•	•	•			•	•	•		•	•	•	
Wyalusing (H-3) 2,596 acres 7 mi. s.e. of Prairie du Chien on US 18 and SR 35, then 5 mi. w. on CR C. Scenic. Nature programs. *(See Prairie du Chien p. 167)*	48	•	•	•	•	•		•		•		•	•		
Yellowstone (I-5) 771 acres 7 mi. n.w. of Argyle on CR N.	49	•	•	•	•	•	•	•	•	•		•			
OTHER															
Blackhawk Lake Recreation Area (H-4) 2,200 acres 3.5 mi. n. of Cobb via SR 80, then e. on CR BH. Cross-country skiing.	50	•	•	•	•	•		•	•	•		•			
Carson (E-3) 135 acres. Cross-country skiing. No motor vehicles. *(See Eau Claire p. 132)*	51		•							•	•	•	•		
Eau Galle Lake (E-1) n.w. of Spring Valley via CR CC (Van Buren Rd.). Ice fishing, snowmobiling; bridle trails.	52	•	•	•	•	•		•	•	•		•			
Glacier Hills (H-7) 140 acres 10 mi. w. of Richfield on Freiss Lake Rd. Nature programs. Cross-country skiing.	53	•	•	•				•	•	•		•			
Goose Island (G-3) 3 mi. s. of La Crosse on SR 35, then 2.5 mi. w. on CR GI. Cross-country skiing.	54	•	•	•	•	•		•		•		•			•
Homestead Hollow (H-8) 105 acres 20 mi. n. of Milwaukee on US 41.	55		•	•					•		•	•			
Pine View (G-4) 200 acres on the Fort McCoy Base, 6 mi. e. of Sparta. Miniature golf; canoe rental.	56	•	•	•	•	•	•	•	•	•		•	•		
Ridge Run (H-7) 140 acres on University Dr. in West Bend. Nature trails.	57		•	•					•	•		•			
Sandy Knoll (G-8) 267 acres 1 mi. n.w. on SR 28, then 1 mi. e. on Wallace Lake Rd. Cross-country skiing, snowmobiling.	58		•	•				•	•	•		•			
Shawano Lake (E-7) 6,062 acres 3 mi. n.e. of Shawano via SR 29 on CR H. Cross-country skiing, golf, snowmobiling, tennis; bridle trails.	59	•	•	•	•	•		•	•	•		•	•	•	•

Wisconsin Temperature Averages
Maximum / Minimum
From the records of the National Weather Service

	JAN	FEB	MAR	APR	MAY	JUNE	JULY	AUG	SEPT	OCT	NOV	DEC
Green Bay	24/7	27/9	37/20	54/33	66/43	76/53	81/58	79/56	70/48	60/39	42/26	29/13
La Crosse	25/7	30/10	40/22	58/37	69/49	78/58	83/62	82/61	72/52	62/42	43/28	30/14
Madison	25/8	29/11	39/21	56/34	67/45	77/55	81/59	80/57	71/48	61/39	43/26	30/14
Milwaukee	27/11	30/15	39/23	55/35	65/43	75/54	80/59	80/59	71/51	61/41	44/28	31/17

Points of Interest

ALGOMA (E-9) pop. 3,357, elev. 600'

Algoma began with a sawmill and store in the 1850s. The community, on the shore of Lake Michigan, is a popular recreation center, offering opportunities for anglers, boaters and hikers.

Algoma Area Chamber of Commerce: 1226 Lake St., Algoma, WI 54201; phone (920) 487-2041 or (800) 498-4888.

WINERIES

- **Von Stiehl Winery**, 115 Navarino St. Tastings daily 9-5:30, July-Aug.; 9-5, May-June and Sept.-Oct.; 11-5, Nov.-Dec.; 11-4, rest of year. Tours daily May-Oct. Phone (920) 487-5208 or (800) 955-5208.

ANIWA (E-6) pop. 272, elev. 1414'

DELLS OF THE EAU CLAIRE PARK is 14 mi. e. on CR Z, then 1.5 mi. n. on CR Y following signs. Trails crisscross the 192-acre park, noted for its unusual rock formations. Daily 7:30 a.m.-11 p.m., May-Oct. Free. Phone (715) 261-1550. *See the AAA Great Lakes CampBook.*

APOSTLE ISLANDS NATIONAL LAKESHORE (A-3)

The Apostle Islands lie offshore from Bayfield Peninsula in Lake Superior. The Apostle Islands total 22 and range in size from 3 acres to 14,000 acres. All but Madeline Island *(see place listing p. 141)* are within the national lakeshore, which also includes a 12-mile strip of shoreline on the peninsula.

The Apostles are the result of the ice age, when huge ice sheets gouged channels into the bedrock and then left piles of debris in their wake. As the glaciers retreated, the islands were exposed, revealing rose-colored cliffs that the lake's waters since have shaped into twisted formations, caves and hollows.

Fur trading began here as early as the 17th century, and commercial fishing and logging continue around the islands today. For the early traders the islands offered plentiful game and refuge from the lake's storms. Later developers harvested such resources as timber and sandstone. The latter became the brownstone used extensively in buildings in Chicago and other Midwestern cities in the late 19th century.

By the turn of the 20th century, wealthy city dwellers had transformed the remote islands into a

fashionable retreat, building summer cottages on Madeline Island. This idyllic period ended with the Depression.

Once again sugar maple, birch, balsam fir, red pine and an array of wildflowers blanket the islands, and with the new forest are renewed populations of deer, bears and a variety of birds.

Stockton Island, the largest island in the lakeshore, has the most extensive trail system and such facilities as docks, campgrounds and a regular camper shuttle service from the mainland. Recreational activities on the other islands vary and can include hiking, camping, sailing, kayaking and fishing. Lake Superior rarely is warm enough for swimming, and the area's treacherous weather can make canoeing and boating hazardous.

There are scheduled ranger programs on some of the islands, including Raspberry and Stockton. For additional information write the Superintendent, Apostle Islands National Lakeshore, Route 1, Box 4, Bayfield, WI 54814; phone (715) 779-3397. *See Recreation Chart and the AAA Great Lakes CampBook.*

HOKENSON FISHERY HISTORIC SITE is in the Apostle Islands at Little Sand Bay. This complex of buildings was used for more than 30 years by the Hokenson Brothers Fishery. During the summer, guided tours describe the tools and techniques of the rigorous family occupation. A visitor center displays historic artifacts and lakeshore exhibits. Picnicking is permitted. Allow 1 hour minimum. Grounds open year-round. Visitor center and tours daily 9:30-4, Memorial Day-Labor Day; Fri.-Sun. 9:30-4, day after Labor Day-Sept. 30. Free. Phone (715) 779-7007.

SIGHTSEEING CRUISES depart from Bayfield Dock. The Grand Tour is a narrated cruise past the 22 Apostle Islands as well as the historic Raspberry Island and Devils Island lighthouses and the Devils Island Sea Caves. Other cruises include stops at Manitou Island, Oak Island, Sand Island and Stockton Island, and several include stops to tour island lighthouses. A camper shuttle service to many of the islands also is available.

Inquire about weather policies. Allow 3 hours minimum. Grand Tour departs daily (weather permitting) at 10, mid-May to mid-Oct. Grand Tour $25.95; ages 6-12, $14.95. Reservations are recommended. MC, VI. Phone (715) 779-3925 or (800) 323-7619.

VISITOR CENTER is at 4th St. and Washington Ave. in Bayfield. The Apostle Islands are detailed in exhibits, a movie and publications. Maps, weather information and a schedule of naturalist programs also are available. Daily 8-6, Memorial Day weekend-Labor Day; 8-5, day after Labor Day-late Oct.; Mon.-Fri. 8-4:30, rest of year. Little Sand Bay Information Center, off SR 13, offers similar services to visitors early June-late Sept. Phone (715) 779-3397.

APPLETON (F-7) pop. 70,087, elev. 714′

The largest of the five cities along the Fox River, Appleton and its neighboring communities make up the third largest metropolitan area in Wisconsin. Early settlers and French explorers quickly learned the economic value of the "water highway" that tumbles from Lake Winnebago toward Green Bay.

As the lumber industry became established in the mid-19th century, many mills were built along the river's shores. Now known as "Paper Valley," the area supports numerous paper mills and related industries. With the construction of a hydroelectric station in 1882, Appleton became the first city in North America to generate its electricity with water power.

The city is home to Wisconsin's first co-educational institution of higher learning, Lawrence University, which is noteworthy for the Henry M. and Ruth B. Wriston Art Center at Alton and Law streets. "Metamorphosis," a sculpture in Houdini Plaza, is the city's tribute to magician and Appleton native Harry Houdini. Sen. Joe McCarthy, a fervent anti-communist during the 1950s, also hailed from Appleton; a bust of McCarthy is displayed at the county courthouse.

The diverse cultural population lends a distinct ethnic flavor to the area. Descendants of the original New England settlers mingle with Dutch, German, Polish and Vietnamese immigrants.

Fox Cities Convention & Visitors Bureau: 3433 W. College Ave., Appleton, WI 54914; phone (920) 734-3358 or (800) 236-6673. *See color ad p. 120.*

Shopping areas: Fox River Mall, 1 block off US 41 on Wisconsin Avenue, has more than 180 stores, including Dayton's, JCPenney, Sears and Younkers. Vande Walle's Candies, 400 Mall Dr., offers self-guiding tours through its candy-manufacturing areas.

FOX CITIES CHILDREN'S MUSEUM is at 100 W. College Ave. An art workshop and a fire engine are among 18 hands-on exhibits for children, infants and toddlers. Special programs teach children about science, art, safety and other cultures. Allow 1 hour minimum. Tues.-Fri. 9-5, Sat. 10-5, Sun. noon-5. Admission $4.50, under 1 free. MC, VI. Phone (920) 734-3226.

THE GORDON BUBOLZ NATURE PRESERVE is 1.5 mi. n. of US 41 on CR A. This privately maintained reserve covers 775 acres and provides 8 miles of trails for year-round outdoor activities. Six trails range from a half-mile to 4.5 miles in length and accommodate cross-country skiers in winter. Abundant wildlife, including more than 150 species of birds, can be seen at the refuge. Exhibits at the nature center describe the seasonal changes of indigenous plants and animals.

Picnicking is permitted. Allow 1 hour minimum. Preserve daily dawn-dusk; nature center Tues.-Fri. 8-4:30, Sat. 11-4:30, Sun. 12:30-4:30. Donations. Fee for cross-country skiing. Phone (920) 731-6041.

SAVE **HEARTHSTONE HISTORIC HOUSE MUSEUM** is at 625 W. Prospect Ave. Hearthstone is said to have been the first house in the world to be lit by a central hydroelectric station using the Edison System. Hands-on electrical exhibits and working models are featured. The restored 1882 structure contains period furniture, intricate woodwork and original light switches designed by the Edison Co. Five of the nine fireplaces are decorated with Minton tiles.

Allow 1 hour minimum. Tues.-Fri. 10-4, Sun. 1-4. Admission $4.50; ages 7-17, $2.50. An additional fee is charged during the Christmas season. Phone (920) 730-8204.

OUTAGAMIE MUSEUM is at 330 E. College Ave. Displays represent the region's social, technological and economic history. The Tools of Change exhibit includes a Model-T Ford, an 1896 wire weaving loom, a 1920s newspaper composing room, a 19th-century paper shop, a 1930s burglarproof bank and a 1940s physician's office. A World War II and an Edna Ferber exhibit also are included.

Allow 1 hour, 30 minutes minimum. Mon.-Sat. 10-4, Sun. noon-4, June-Aug.; Tues.-Sat. 10-4, Sun. noon-4, rest of year. Closed major holidays. Admission (includes Houdini Historical Center) $4; over 65, $3.50; ages 5-17, $2; family rate $10. MC, VI. Phone (920) 735-9370 or (920) 733-8445.

Houdini Historical Center displays items once owned by magician Harry Houdini. The collection includes videotape clips, photographs, posters, handcuffs, leg irons and lock picks. Allow 1 hour minimum. Phone(920) 733-8445.

ASHIPPUN (H-7) elev. 858'

HONEY ACRES MUSEUM is 2 mi. n. on SR 67. The history and techniques of beekeeping are preserved at Honey Acres, which has been owned by a family of beekeepers and honey packers since 1852. A 20-minute multimedia presentation and various displays highlight pollination and the enemies of the bee. Visitors can taste five varieties of honey and four varieties of mustard and view an active beehive.

Allow 30 minutes minimum. Mon.-Fri. 9-3:30, Sat.-Sun. noon-4, mid-May through Oct. 31; Mon.-Fri. 9-3:30, rest of year. Closed holidays. Free. Phone (920) 474-4411.

ASHLAND (B-4) pop. 8,620, elev. 660'

Whether Fourth of July festivities on Madeline Island inspired Asaph Whittlesey to establish a new town is uncertain, but on July 5, 1854, he arrived on the southeast shore of Chequamegon Bay of Lake Superior, built a cabin and founded Ashland. Once his cabin was complete, Whittlesey opened negotiations with the railroad in Chicago to provide an outlet for the area's timber, brownstone and iron ore.

The railroad, completed in 1877, combined with Ashland's natural harbor, soon made the community a thriving port; millions of tons of iron ore and timber were shipped annually. Legacies of this prosperous period are the distinctive facades of preserved, early 20th-century commercial buildings in the Main Street Historic District.

Although the area's commercial resources are important, its other resources—local parks, national forests and Lake Superior—have made Ashland an active recreation center. Trout, walleye, perch, salmon, northern pike and muskellunge thrive in Lake Superior and inland lakes and streams. Deep-water charter and sailboat excursions can be arranged in Ashland.

Prentice Park, 100 acres at the west edge of town, is a refuge for deer, ducks and swans; camping, hiking and picnicking are available. Band concerts take place at Memorial Park Thursday evenings in the summer.

Ashland is part of a statewide network of well-groomed snowmobile trails, which include the Tri-County Trail and the Mount Valhalla Recreational Area in Chequamegon-Nicolet National Forest (*see place listing p. 126*). A map outlining area snowmobile touring loops and cross-country ski trails is available from the chamber of commerce.

Ashland Area Chamber of Commerce: 805 W. Lakeshore Dr., P.O. Box 746, Ashland, WI 54806; phone (715) 682-2500 or (800) 284-9484.

NORTHERN GREAT LAKES VISITOR CENTER is 2.5 mi. w. on US 2 to CR G. A 30-minute multi-image, musical presentation chronicles area history, highlighting the cultural heritage of the region. Also at the center are exhibits, videotape presentations, nature trails and archives. Allow 1 hour minimum. Visitor center daily 9-7, June-Oct.; 9-5, rest of year. Archives Tues.-Fri. 1-4:30. Free. Phone (715) 685-9983.

AUGUSTA (E-3) pop. 1,186, elev. 972′

DELL'S MILL is 3 mi. n. on SR 27, then w. on CR V. The flour and feed mill served the community for 137 years. No major commercial milling has been done since the building was converted to a museum in 1968. The machinery still is in working order and a small amount of milling continues. Visitors can tour the five-story 1864 structure to observe how the water-powered parts—including 3,000 feet of belting and 175 pulleys—interact. Allow 1 hour minimum. Daily 10-5, May-Oct. Admission $7; ages 6-18, $3.50; ages 3-5, $1.50. Phone (715) 286-2714.

BABCOCK (F-5) elev. 975′

SANDHILL WILDLIFE AREA is on CR X. Automobile and hiking trails with observation towers permit visitors to view the woods and wide marshes of this 9,500-acre wildlife refuge, home to ferns, ducks, bison, deer, beavers and other native flora and fauna. Allow 2 hours minimum. Park open daily dawn-dusk. Automobile trails open daily, mid-Apr. through Oct. 31; also mid-Dec. to mid-Mar. for cross-country skiing. Free. Phone (715) 884-2437.

BAILEYS HARBOR—*see Door County p. 129.*

BARABOO (G-5) pop. 10,711, elev. 879′

The river, the nearby mountains of purplish quartzite and the trim little city of Baraboo all took their name from the French trader Baribault, whose post stood here in the early 19th century. Another name is almost synonymous with Baraboo—Ringling. Fond memories of a circus boat they had seen in Iowa spurred five sons of a German harness-maker to present their first "Classic and Comic Concert Company" show in 1882.

From 1884 to 1918 Baraboo was home of their enterprise, which ultimately became Ringling Bros. and Barnum & Bailey Circus. Many old circus buildings have been converted to industrial and commercial uses.

Baraboo Area Chamber of Commerce: 660 W. Chestnut St., P.O. Box 442, Baraboo, WI 53913; phone (608) 356-8333 or (800) 227-2266.

CIRCUS WORLD MUSEUM is at 550 Water St., following signs. Preserving the original winter quarters of the Ringling Brothers, the museum celebrates the history of the American circus. Throughout the summer season the museum offers big-top circus performances, hands-on programs and exhibits, including what is described as the world's largest collection of circus wagons.

Allow 4 hours minimum. Daily 9-6, mid-May through Labor Day; Mon.-Sat. 10-4, Sun. 11-4, rest of year. Closed Jan. 1, Easter, Thanksgiving, Dec. 24-25 and 31. Admission mid-May through Labor Day $14.95; over 64, $12.95; ages 5-11, $7.95. Admission day after Labor Day-late Oct. $7; over 64, $6; ages 5-11, $3.50. Admission rest of year $5; over 64, $4; ages 5-11, $2.50. AX, DS, MC, VI. Phone (608) 356-8341 or (866) 693-1500.

DEVIL'S LAKE STATE PARK is 3.5 mi. s. on SR 123. Devil's Lake, spring fed and having no visible outlet, is bounded on three sides by the quartzite cliffs of the Baraboo Range. Bear, Lynx and Eagle Indian mounds were created by ancient tribes. The 10,000-acre park is one of several units of the Ice Age National Scientific Reserve, which is under development. Naturalist programs and exhibits explain the glacial phenomena of the area.

Park open daily 6 a.m.-11 p.m. Admission per private vehicle $10, state residents $5. Annual permit $30, state residents $20. Phone (608) 356-8301. *See Recreation Chart and the AAA Great Lakes CampBook.*

THE INTERNATIONAL CRANE FOUNDATION is 5.2 mi. n. on US 12, then 1.2 mi. e. on Shady Lane Rd.; from I-90/94 exit 92, 1.5 mi. s. on US 12, then 1.2 mi. e. on Shady Lane Rd. This center is dedicated to the study, propagation and preservation of endangered species of cranes and the protection of their wetland and grassland habitats.

The foundation maintains a collection of cranes for breeding and reintroduction into the wild. Visitors can see rare whooping cranes, young crane chicks in their exercise yard and an art exhibit. Nature trails that wind through restored wetlands, prairies and savannas also are on the grounds. Self-guiding and guided tours are available. Open daily 9-5, Apr. 15-Oct. 31. Guided 90-minute tours are given daily at 10, 1 and 3, June-Aug.; Sat.-Sun. at 10, 1 and 3, Apr. 15-May 30 and Sept.-Oct. Admission $7; over 61, $6; ages 5-11, $3.50. DS, MC, VI. Phone (608) 356-9462.

MID-CONTINENT RAILWAY MUSEUM— *see North Freedom p. 163.*

SAUK COUNTY HISTORICAL MUSEUM is at 531 4th Ave. Housed in a 1903 mansion, the museum displays American Indian and pioneer relics, Civil War equipment, household furnishings, toys, textiles and genealogical records. Tues.-Sat. noon-5. Museum free. A $10 fee is charged to use genealogical records. Phone (608) 356-1001.

CASINOS

• **Ho-Chunk Casino and Bingo**, S3214A Hwy. 12. Daily 24 hours. Phone (800) 746-2486.

BARNEVELD (H-5) pop. 1,088

WINERIES

- **Botham Vineyards and Winery** is off US 18/151; take CR K 1.7 mi. s. to Langberry Rd., then .2 mi. w. to 8180 Langberry Rd. Wed.-Sun. 10-5, early Apr.-late Dec.; Sat.-Sun. 10-5 in Mar. Phone (608) 924-1412 or (888) 478-9463.

BAYFIELD (A-3) pop. 611, elev. 607′

Mansions grace the side streets of Bayfield, once the main shipping point for the popular building material. The town now relies on fishing, fruit crops and the annual throng of summer vacationers.

Sightseeing cruises among the Apostle Islands (see Apostle Islands National Lakeshore p. 119) and ferry service to Madeline Island (see place listing p. 141), both offshore in Lake Superior, depart from Bayfield. In the winter a motorized windsled offers transportation to the island until the lake freezes and cars can travel on an ice highway.

The area affords good hunting, fishing, skiing, snowmobiling, kayaking, boating and sailing. Deepwater fishing trips leave the pier daily; a fishing license is required.

Bayfield Chamber of Commerce: 42 S. Broad St., P.O. Box 138, Bayfield, WI 54814; phone (715) 779-3335 or (800) 447-4094.

LAKE SUPERIOR BIG TOP CHAUTAUQUA is 3.5 mi. s. on SR 13, then 1 mi. w. on Ski Hill Rd. at the foot of Mount Ashwabay. Concerts, plays and illuminated historical musicals are presented under a big-top canvas tent. Food is available. Allow 2 hours, 30 minutes minimum. Show times Tues.-Thurs. at 7:30 p.m., Fri.-Sat. at 8:15 p.m., early June-early Sept. Reserved seats $18; ages 1-12, $8. General admission $12; ages 1-12, $4. Some big-name acts cost more. MC, VI. Phone (715) 373-5552 or (888) 244-8368.

BEAVER DAM (H-6) pop. 15,169, elev. 872′

A trading and manufacturing center, Beaver Dam serves the surrounding dairy region. The Dodge County Historical Society, in an 1890 Romanesque library at 105 Park Ave., houses more than 4,000 items relating to city and county history; phone (920) 887-1266. Nearby Beaver Dam Lake is noted for good fishing.

Beaver Dam Area Chamber of Commerce: 127 S. Spring St., Beaver Dam, WI 53916; phone (920) 887-8879.

BELMONT (I-4) pop. 871, elev. 1,063′

Belmont held high hopes for growth and prominence when it served as the first capital of the Wisconsin Territory in 1836. But representatives who convened there objected so vehemently to the site that the governor agreed to move the capital to a location upon which the majority could agree. After a long dispute Madison was selected, although at the time it existed only on paper.

With little other reason to thrive, Belmont declined. The coup de grace was the removal of the railroad to a point 3 miles distant; most of the town moved with it, leaving Old Belmont and its vacant capitol complex to molder. Contemporary Belmont is an agricultural village.

FIRST CAPITOL STATE HISTORIC SITE is 3 mi. n.w. on CR G. Two restored buildings stand on the site where the first territorial legislature met in 1836. In the Council House the legislature drafted many laws and fixed the permanent government seat in Madison. The lodging house contains displays about Wisconsin's early territorial government and history. Daily 10-4, mid-June through Labor Day. Schedule may vary; phone ahead. Free. Phone (608) 987-2122.

BELOIT (I-6) pop. 35,775, elev. 745′

The agent for New England Emigrating Co. must be credited with having a silver tongue, for nearly the entire town of Colebrook, N.H., moved to this site on the Rock River in 1837. Determined to sustain "science and religion and all the adjuncts that contribute to the elevation of society," the cultured arrivals promptly established a church and chartered Beloit College in 1846.

The college and light industry are the lifeblood of the city. The Beloit College campus also is the site of more than two dozen American Indian mounds. Wright Museum of Art on the Beloit College campus, exhibits Oriental art, graphics and sculpture.

Other points of interest in town include the Near East Side and Bluff Street historic districts, which contain rare 19th-century cobblestone houses, and Neese Performing Arts Theatre, on Bushnell Street, which presents theater, dance and other performing arts events. Pohlman Field is the site of all home games for Beloit's minor-league baseball team.

Beloit Convention and Visitors Bureau: 1003 Pleasant St., Beloit, WI 53511; phone (608) 365-4838 or (800) 423-5648.

Self-guiding tours: Walking tour brochures about local historic districts are available from the convention and visitors bureau.

SAVE **THE ANGEL MUSEUM** is at 656 Pleasant St. (US 51). Housed in a renovated historic church built by Italian immigrants, the museum features more than 6,000 angels from the Berg Angel Collection as well as nearly 500 black angels donated by Oprah Winfrey. Allow 1 hour minimum. Tues.-Sat. 10-4, Sun. 1-4, June-Aug.; Tues.-Sat. 10-4, Feb.-May and Sept.-Dec. Closed holidays. Admission $5; over 62 and ages 12-17, $4; ages 5-11, $3. Phone (608) 362-9099.

LOGAN MUSEUM OF ANTHROPOLOGY is at 700 College St. in Memorial Hall on the Beloit College campus. The 1869 building houses a highly regarded collection of more than 225,000 artifacts, including Paleolithic art, jewelry from ancient civilizations, pre-Columbian ceramics and American Indian beadwork, baskets and clothing. A two-story glass cube allows visitors to see the pieces as well as watch the ongoing conservation and cataloging of objects. Allow 30 minutes minimum. Tues.-Sun. 11-4; closed Thanksgiving and college holidays. Free. Phone (608) 363-2677.

BLACK RIVER FALLS (F-3)
pop. 3,618, elev. 809'

Canoeing on the Black River, hunting, fishing and winter sports are among the attractions offered by Black River Falls. However, the cascade for which the town is named is now tamed by an upstream power dam. One of the first sawmills in Wisconsin was built here in 1819; the city was a busy logging center throughout the 19th century.

Black River Falls Area Chamber of Commerce: 120 N. Water St., Black River Falls, WI 54615; phone (715) 284-4658 or (800) 404-4008.

BLACK RIVER STATE FOREST is e. on US 12. Comprising 67,000 acres primarily in Jackson County, the forest lies in the former bed of a glacial lake. Hunting is permitted in season. Daily 6 a.m.-11 p.m. Admission per private vehicle $10, state residents $5. Annual permit $30, state residents $20. Fees are charged for camping, bicycling and cross-country skiing. Phone (715) 284-1406. *See Recreation Chart and the AAA Great Lakes CampBook.*

BLUE MOUNDS (I-5) pop. 708, elev. 1,296'

Serving as landmarks for Winnebago Indians and lead miners following the ore veins from Galena, Ill., two blue hills, the highest in southern Wisconsin, attracted Ebenezer Brigham in 1828. Using nothing more than a windlass, rope and tub, Brigham extracted more than 4 million pounds of lead from the ground. With his establishment of a smelting furnace, the town of Blue Mounds took shape.

When the Black Hawk War threatened, settlers built Fort Blue Mounds, which successfully defended the town during an ambush by Sac Indians. The fort later helped supply the troops who drove Black Hawk out of the state. A bronze plaque now commemorates the site.

Mt. Horeb Area Chamber of Commerce: 100 S. First St., P.O. Box 84, Mt. Horeb, WI 53572; phone (608) 437-5914 or (888) 765-5929.

BLUE MOUND STATE PARK is off US 18/151. The 1,124-acre park's centerpiece is 1,716-foot Blue Mound, the highest point in southern Wisconsin. According to legend, Winnebago treasure is buried in the mound. The summit offers views of the Baraboo Range and Wisconsin River Valley. Park open daily 6 a.m.-11 p.m. Office open daily 8-4:30. Admission per private vehicle $10, state residents $5. Annual permit $30, state residents $20. MC, VI. Phone (608) 437-5711. *See Recreation Chart and the AAA Great Lakes CampBook.*

CAVE OF THE MOUNDS is off US 18/151 on Cave of the Mounds Rd. This National Natural Landmark has theatrical lighting enhancing a variety of brilliantly colored stalactites, stalagmites and underground pools. A short film explains the history of the cave and its formation. Guided 1-hour tours follow concrete walkways through the cave, which maintains a uniform temperature of 50 F. The grounds also offer rock gardens and picnic areas.

Food is available in summer. Tours depart every 15 min. daily 9-7, Memorial Day weekend-Labor Day; on the hour Mon.-Fri. 10-4, every 30 min. Sat.-Sun. 9-5, day after Labor Day-Nov. 15 and Mar. 15-day before Memorial Day weekend; on the hour Sat.-Sun. 10-4 and by appointment, rest of year. Admission $12; over 65, $11; ages 5-12, $6. DS, MC, VI. Phone (608) 437-3038.

LITTLE NORWAY is off US 18/151 between Mount Horeb and Blue Mounds; exit Cave of the Mounds Rd. and follow signs to CR JG. This farmstead, known as Nissedahle ("Valley of the Elves"), was built by Norwegian settlers in the mid-1800s and houses pioneer furnishings, arts and crafts. On the grounds is a replica of a stave church built in Norway for the 1893 World's Columbian Exposition. Costumed guides conduct 45-minute tours.

Daily 9-7, July-Aug.; 9-5, May-June and Sept.-Oct. Admission $10; over 62, $8; ages 5-12, $4. MC, VI. Phone (608) 437-8211.

BOULDER JUNCTION (C-5) elev. 1,648'

Boulder Junction offers access to the woodlands and lakes of the surrounding Northern Highland-American Legion State Forest *(see Recreation Chart and the AAA Great Lakes CampBook).* Recreational activities include hiking, boating, cross-country skiing and bicycling. Fishing for muskellunge is particularly rewarding in the area, which bills itself as the "Musky Capital of the World." There are nearly 200 lakes within a 9-mile radius of Boulder Junction. The forest is a major producer of seedling pines for state reforestation programs.

Boulder Junction Chamber of Commerce: 5352 Park St., P.O. Box 286 W, Boulder Junction, WI 54512; phone (715) 385-2400 or (800) 466-8759.

BRODHEAD (I-5) pop. 3,180, elev. 792'

Edward Brodhead, chief engineer of the Milwaukee and Minnesota Railroad, is credited with having brought the railroad into the treeless sand prairie where the town began in 1856. Ancient trails already crossed the area, known to American Indians as the halfway point between the Mississippi and Lake Michigan. Both American Indians and European settlers once collected sap from the hard maples lining the Sugar River to make maple syrup and sugar.

The First Brigade Band, organized in 1857, achieved considerable popularity. Enlisted in the Civil War, the six-horse bandwagon followed Union general William T. Sherman on his Atlanta campaign and marched in the grand review in Washington, D.C., at the war's end.

The 23-mile Sugar River Trail, built on an abandoned railroad bed, follows the meandering river from Brodhead to New Glarus *(see place listing p. 163)*.

Brodhead Chamber of Commerce: 602 E. 2nd Ave., P.O. Box 16, Brodhead, WI 53520; phone (608) 897-8411.

Self-guiding tours: Brodhead's Exchange Square and North Residential historic districts can be explored on a self-guiding walking tour. Maps are available from Brodhead Historical Museum in the old railroad depot on SR 11; phone (608) 897-2639 or (608) 897-2549.

BURLINGTON (I-7) pop. 9,936, elev. 790′

Burlington is most noted for being the home of the Burlington Liars' Club. This organization encourages the telling of tall tales in the classic country manner. Contributors from all over the world have promoted the tradition since 1929, when the first competition gained national attention. The tradition continues as scores of tall-tale tellers vie for first place each January 1. Visitors can explore the "Tall Tale Trail," a trail through town where tall tales can be heard at several locations.

St. Francis Retreat Center, 2 miles northeast on CR W between SRs 11 and 36, contains gardens and picturesque grottoes open to visitors year-round. Another popular Burlington attraction is the dramatic offerings of the Haylofters from May through October at Malt House Theatre, the oldest community theater group in Wisconsin. Free water-skiing performances by the Aquaducks are offered at Fischer Park on Browns Lake Saturday at 6:30, Memorial Day through Labor Day. Burlington, home to the Nestle Co., has been designated by the state legislature as "Chocolate City USA."

Burlington Area Chamber of Commerce: 112 E. Chestnut St., P.O. Box 156, Burlington, WI 53105; phone (262) 763-6044.

CABLE (B-3) elev. 1,370′

The Cable vicinity is a popular year-round vacation area in northwest Wisconsin set in the heart of Chequamegon-Nicolet National Forest. Fine hunting and fishing are available along more than 150 lakes. More than 300 miles of mapped and marked trails, stretching from Hayward to Delta, are available for mountain bicyclists. Hiking trails surround the area.

Cable Area Chamber of Commerce: P.O. Box 217, Cable, WI 54821; phone (715) 798-3833 or (800) 533-7454.

CABLE NATURAL HISTORY MUSEUM is .2 mi. e. on CR M. Exhibits about northern Wisconsin wildlife include displays of native animals and birds mounted in natural settings. A summer lecture series is offered the first Wednesday evening in July through the last Wednesday in August at the community center on CR M.

Tues.-Sat. 10-4, Sun. 10-2, June-Aug.; Tues.-Sat. 10-4, rest of year. Junior naturalist programs are offered Tues.-Wed. 10-noon, mid-June to mid-August. Closed holidays. Free. Phone (715) 798-3890.

RECREATIONAL ACTIVITIES

Skiing

• **Telemark Ski Area** is n. on US 63, e. on CR M, then 2 mi. s. on Telemark Rd. Write 42225 Telemark Rd., Cable, WI 54821. Other activities are offered. Daily Nov.-Apr. Phone (715) 798-3999 or (877) 798-4718.

CAMBRIDGE (H-6) pop. 1,101, elev. 855′

Founded in the mid-1800s, Cambridge has long been a popular vacation spot for Chicagoans and other city dwellers lured to the spring-fed waters of nearby Lake Ripley. Ripley Park, on the lake's western shore, encompasses sandy beaches and a swimming area. The Cambridge area also is popular with cross-country skiers and hikers. The Glacial Drumlin Bike Trail, which follows the path of the 19th-century Chicago & Northwestern Railway, provides a winding, 47-mile-long scenic trail for bicyclists. Hiking and mountain biking trails, canoeing and picnicking are available.

Cambridge is noted for its salt-glazed pottery, antiques and artwork displayed in historic buildings along its Victorian-style Main Street.

Cambridge Chamber of Commerce: 102 W. Main St., P.O. Box 572, Cambridge, WI 53523; phone (608) 423-7559 or (608) 423-3780.

CAMERON (D-2) pop. 1,546, elev. 998′

PIONEER VILLAGE MUSEUM is 1.5 mi. w. on CR W (Museum Rd.). The pioneer street setting features 32 old buildings, including a train depot, church, general store, town hall, smithy, farmstead and late 19th-century house. Most buildings are furnished in period. Five display buildings house additional items relating to the county's settlement. An exhibit hall contains 40 display cases with historic artifacts. Thurs.-Sun. 1-5, June 1-Labor Day. Admission $5; under 13, $3. Phone (715) 458-2841 or (715) 458-2080.

CAMPBELLSPORT (G-8)
pop. 1,913, elev. 1,062′

KETTLE MORAINE STATE FOREST is 7 mi. e. on SR 67. Geological formations in the area were created by glaciers more than 20,000 years ago. Visitors can take a self-guiding automobile tour that features glacial eskers, kames and kettles. Recreational activities include boating, camping, fishing, hiking, horseback riding, mountain biking, swimming, cross-country skiing and snowmobiling.

Picnicking is permitted. Allow 3 hours minimum. Park and Mauthe Lake Recreation Area open daily 6 a.m.-11 p.m. Long Lake Recreation Area open daily 6 a.m.-11 p.m., May 1-second week in Oct. Admission per private vehicle $10, state residents $5. Annual permit $30, state residents $20. Phone (262) 626-2116 Mon.-Fri. or (920) 533-8322. *See Recreation Chart.*

CARTER (D-7) elev. 1,525′

CASINOS

- **Potawatomi Bingo and Northern Lights Casino** is on SR 32. Casino opens daily at 9; closing hours vary. Closed major holidays. Phone (715) 473-2021 or (800) 487-9522.

CASSVILLE (I-3) pop. 1,085, elev. 622′

In the 1830s the Mississippi River community of Cassville was among several towns that vied for the status of territorial capital. It lost, but continued its existence as grain port and trading center for the surrounding farms.

Cassville Car Ferry, which departs from the Prime Street landing, makes trips across the Mississippi River to Turkey River Landing, near Millville, Iowa. The ferry operates Friday through Sunday, May through October, with Wednesday and Thursday trips added from Memorial Day through Labor Day. Phone (608) 725-5180.

▼ **STONEFIELD STATE HISTORIC SITE** is 1.2 mi. n.w. on CR VV, next to Nelson Dewey State Park *(see Recreation Chart and the AAA Great Lakes CampBook).* The first of the site's three parts is Stonefield, the reconstructed home of Nelson Dewey, Wisconsin's first governor. The second part, the State Agricultural Museum, exhibits farm tools and machinery, manufacturers' models and domestic items tracing the evolution of agriculture and rural life from frontier days.

A covered bridge leads to the third section, a turn-of-the-20th-century village. More than 30 reconstructed buildings are furnished in period and include a bank, saloon, newspaper office, smithy and general store; shopkeepers and craftsmen are stationed throughout the site.

Allow 2 hours minimum. Daily 10-4, Memorial Day weekend-Labor Day; Sat.-Sun. 10-4, day after Labor Day-early Oct. Last admission 2 hours before closing. Admission $8; over 64, $7.20; ages 5-12, $4. MC, VI. Phone (608) 725-5210.

▼ **Governor Nelson Dewey Homesite** is at 12195 CR VV. The Gothic Revival home of Wisconsin's first governor has been reconstructed on the site. The original red brick house burned in 1873, but the doors, walls and millwork that remained intact were used in the reconstruction. Books and personal belongings of the Dewey family are displayed. The 2,000-acre estate was one of the few Midwestern farms planned in the manner of a Virginia plantation. Tours are given daily at 11 and 2, Memorial Day weekend-Labor Day; Sat.-Sun., weekend after Labor Day to mid-Oct. Last tour begins 1 hour before closing.

CEDARBURG—*see Milwaukee p. 159.*

CHEQUAMEGON-NICOLET NATIONAL FOREST

Elevations in the forest range from 600 ft. at Lake Superior to 1,860 ft. near Twin Lake. Refer to AAA maps for additional elevation information.

In north-central and northeastern Wisconsin, the Chequamegon-Nicolet National Forest comprises 1.5 million acres in four separate regions. The Chequamegon (she-Wa-ma-gon) area covers 856,938 acres east, south and northwest of Park Falls on SRs 182 and 13; the Nicolet (nik-oh-LAY) area totals 661,200 acres east of Rhinelander and is accessible via several major highways.

More than 800 lakes dot the Chequamegon forest, where tree species include maple, aspen, pine, spruce, balsam, oak and birch. Licensed hunting and fishing are available in season. The Chippewa, Flambeau, Jump, St. Croix and Yellow rivers provide good canoeing in the spring and early summer. Muskellunge fishing is excellent.

An extensive 200-mile trail system threads through the Chequamegon, where a 40-mile segment of the Ice Age National Scenic Trail follows the terminal moraines of the last glaciers. Providing a system of loops used for cross-country skiing as well as hiking, the Rock Lake National Recreation Trail passes near Cable. Maps of snowmobile and cross-country ski trails are available at the forest supervisor headquarters.

The North Country National Scenic Trail traverses 60 miles of the northern part of the forest, roughly between Mellen and Iron River. Part of this route crosses the Rainbow Lake and Porcupine Lake wildernesses. Together covering about 11,000 acres of glaciated, lake-dotted woodlands, the wilderness areas offer an opportunity to experience a Northern hardwood forest free of development.

Primitive trails thread through the Nicolet region's three wilderness areas: Whisker Lake Wilderness Area, 8 miles west of Florence on SR 70, containing Riley and Whisker lakes; Blackjack Springs Wilderness Area, 8 miles east of Eagle River on SR 70, containing spring ponds; and the 22,000-acre Headwaters Wilderness Area, 8 miles east of Three Lakes on SR 32 and FR 2183.

With 1,200 lakes, 1,100 miles of trout streams and more than 400 spring ponds, the Nicolet forest also offers good fishing; there is hunting for deer, bears and upland game in season. Canoeing on the Wolf and Peshtigo rivers provides white-water excitement, while the Oconto, Pine, Popple and Wisconsin rivers are gentler.

The Great Divide Scenic Byway (SR 77) provides visitors with some of the most picturesque scenery in Wisconsin. The portion of this route between Hayward and Glidden is punctuated by several highlands known as the Penokee Range. The byway takes its name from the ridges that form the Great Divide, which separates waters flowing north to Lake Superior from waters flowing south to the Mississippi River.

There are more than 45 developed campgrounds in the combined forests; campsites are available on a first-come, first-served basis, but a limited number may be reserved in advance. For reservations phone, (877) 444-6777 daily 10-8.

For information about Chequamegon campgrounds and facilities, contact the forest headquarters at 1170 4th Ave. S., Park Falls, WI 54552; phone (715) 762-2461, or TTY (715) 762-5701, Mon.-Fri. 8-4:30. For information about facilities in the Nicolet forest, contact the forest office at 68 S. Stevens St., Rhinelander, WI 54501; phone (715) 362-1300, or TTY (715) 362-1383, Mon.-Fri. 8-4:30. Information also is available from district ranger offices in Eagle River, Florence, Glidden, Hayward, Lakewood, Laona, Medford, Park Falls and Washburn. *See Recreation Chart and the AAA Great Lakes CampBook.*

CHIPPEWA FALLS (E-2)
pop. 12,925, elev. 848′

That several locally made beverages have attained critical acclaim is credited to the purity of Chippewa Falls' ground water. It was not the clear water, however, that first attracted settlement to the banks of the Chippewa in 1837, but the vast white-pine forests and the river's potential for producing power.

With the passing of the logging era, attention turned to serving the local farmers, generating electricity for use throughout the region and developing diversified industry—including brewing and spring water bottling. Chippewa Water Co., which still operates today, was founded in 1880 by Thaddeus Pound—former Wisconsin lieutenant governor and grandfather of poet Ezra Pound.

Impounded by the Chippewa Falls dam, Lake Wissota provides fishing and other recreational activities. Lake Wissota State Park *(see Recreation Chart and the AAA Great Lakes CampBook)* is on the east shore. The Chippewa Rose Society Garden, Jefferson Avenue and Bridgewater, is among Wisconsin's largest.

Chippewa Falls Area Chamber of Commerce: 10 S. Bridge St., Chippewa Falls, WI 54729; phone (715) 723-0331 or (888) 723-0024.

IRVINE PARK is .5 mi. n. on SR 124. The 364-acre park contains a zoo with native animals that are best viewed mid-April through September, though the park is open all year. Cross-country skiing trails, hiking trails and picnic facilities are on the grounds. The park also includes Glen Loch Dam

and Overlook, an old log house and an old schoolhouse.

Park open daily 7 a.m.-dusk. Christmas Village open Thanksgiving through Jan. 1. Free. A fee is charged for use of the swimming pool. Phone (715) 723-3890 or (715) 723-0051.

LEINENKUGEL BREWERY TOURS is on SR 124 at 124 E. Elm St. Guided 30-minute tours detail the brewing process. Displays depict the history of brewing in the area. Tastings are available. Guided tours are given Mon.-Sat. 9:30-4, Sun. 11:30-3; closed holidays. Free. Reservations are recommended. Phone (715) 723-5557.

COON VALLEY (G-3) pop. 714, elev. 735′

In a valley laced with numerous springs and surrounded by high bluffs, Coon Valley lies in a landscape forever captured in the books of Hamlin Garland, who grew up on a farm in nearby West Salem *(see place listing p. 175).* Reminiscent of the valleys of Norway, the ravines in the Coon Valley area attracted Norwegian and Bohemian immigrants beginning in 1849.

The hills around the village are among the highest along US 14/61. Between the bluffs are tobacco and dairy farms run by descendants of the village's original settlers.

[SAVE] **NORSKEDALEN NATURE & HERITAGE CENTER** is 3 mi. n.e. via CRs P and PI. The 400-acre educational, nature and heritage area offers trails, a museum, an arboretum, a visitor center and a restored 1890s pioneer homestead. Skumsrud Heritage Farm, south of Norskedalen off US 14/61, offers self-guiding tours through 12 historic buildings. Programs are offered Sundays at 2. Special events are featured throughout the year.

Guided tours are available. Pets are not allowed. Picnicking is permitted. Allow 1 hour minimum. Mon.-Fri. 9-4, Sat. 10-4, Sun. noon-4, Apr. 15-Oct. 31; Mon.-Fri. 10-4, Sun. noon-4, rest of year. Homestead open daily 10-4, May-Oct. Last tour begins 30 minutes before closing. Skumsrud open Mon.-Fri. 11-4, Sat. 10-4, Sun. noon-4, June-Aug. Admission (including Skumsrud) $5; ages 5-17, $2; family rate $12. MC, VI. Phone (608) 452-3424.

COUDERAY (C-3) pop. 96, elev. 1,265′

THE HIDEOUT is 6 mi. n. on CR CC. The stone lodge, Al Capone's northwoods hideout in the 1920s, includes a massive fireplace, spiral staircases, a machine-gun tower, a blockhouse and furnishings. Food is available. Guided tours are offered daily on the hour noon-6, Memorial Day weekend-Labor Day; Fri.-Sun. noon-5, May 1-day before Memorial Day weekend and day after Labor Day-last weekend in Sept. Admission $9.75; ages 7-12, $4.75. MC, VI. Phone (715) 945-2746.

DANBURY (C-2) elev. 947'

FORTS FOLLE AVOINE HISTORICAL PARK is 2.5 mi. w. on CR U from jct. SR 35. This 80-acre living history site includes reconstructions of an Ojibwe Indian village and fur trading posts that flourished along the Yellow River 1802-04. Costumed interpreters provide guided tours of the park, which includes museum displays, archeological exhibits and a research library. Allow 1 hour minimum. Tours depart on the hour Wed.-Sun. 9-5, Memorial Day weekend-Labor Day. Admission $5; ages 6-11, $4; family rate $12. MC, VI. Phone (715) 866-8890.

DE PERE (F-7) pop. 20,559, elev. 595'

De Pere originally was called "Rapides des Pères" for the Jesuits who established the first mission in the state in 1669. From this point explorers Jacques Marquette and Louis Joliet departed on their voyage of discovery. Tours of the St. Joseph National Shrine are free and can be arranged at St. Norbert Abbey, 1016 N. Broadway; phone (920) 337-4300.

WHITE PILLARS is at 403 N. Broadway. Built in 1836 and remodeled in 1912, this building once housed the first bank offices in Wisconsin. It is now home to the De Pere Historical Society and its Historical Museum. An extensive collection includes rare documents, photographs and archives. Allow 30 minutes minimum. Mon.-Fri. noon-4; closed holidays. Donations. Phone (920) 336-3877.

DICKEYVILLE (I-4) pop. 1,043, elev. 955'

DICKEYVILLE GROTTO is on US 61 and SR 35. Made of colorful bits of stone, glass and shell from around the world, the grotto was built 1925-30 by Father Mathias Wernerus as an expression of unity between religion and patriotism. Allow 30 minutes minimum. Grotto open daily 24 hours. Guided tours daily 11-4, June-Aug.; Sat.-Sun. 11-4 in May and Sept.-Oct. Donations. Phone (608) 568-3119.

DODGEVILLE (I-4) pop. 4,220, elev. 1,249'

Along with Mineral Point *(see place listing p. 162)*, Dodgeville was a metropolis of the lead-mining region during the 1820s and 1830s. The town bears the name of Henry Dodge, a colorful frontiersman who pioneered the mining industry, figured prominently in the defeat of Black Hawk and served as the first territorial governor of Wisconsin and later as a U.S. senator.

Dodgeville Chamber of Commerce: 338 N. Iowa St., Dodgeville, WI 53533; phone (608) 935-5993.

GOVERNOR DODGE STATE PARK is 3 mi. n. on SR 23. This unglaciated area contains scenic rock formations, which can be seen from the network of hiking and riding trails. During the summer park

naturalists conduct nature hikes and evening programs. Daily 6 a.m.-11 p.m. Admission per private vehicle $10, state residents $5. Annual permit $30, state residents $20. Phone (608) 935-2315. *See Recreation Chart and the AAA Great Lakes CampBook.*

SAVE **MUSEUM OF MINERALS AND CRYSTALS** is 4 mi. n. on SR 23. More than 3,000 rock, mineral and crystal specimens were collected mostly from Africa, Australia, Brazil, England and Mexico. Pieces include materials from the mines of southwestern Wisconsin and other parts of the United States. A 90-pound quartz crystal from Arkansas, a 315-pound Brazilian agate and a 215-pound amethyst geode are highlights. Horseback riding is available.

Allow 1 hour minimum. Daily 9-5, June-Aug.; 9-4, Apr.-May and Sept.-Oct. Admission $5; over 64, $4.50; ages 6-18, $4. Two-hour horseback rides $35; 1-hour rides $17; 45-minute rides $13. Trail pass $3. DS, MC, VI. Phone (608) 935-5205.

DOOR COUNTY (E-9)

Door County stretches northeast from Sturgeon Bay to the tip of the Door Peninsula. Wisconsin's most conspicuous feature extends like the spout of a teapot into Green Bay and Lake Michigan. The waters on either side of the 75-mile-long peninsula have carved much of its rocky shoreline into caves, arches and cliffs. The overall effect is that this rugged landscape—dotted with fishing villages, farms and orchards—resembles New England more than the Midwest.

Despite its scenic allure, the treacherously narrow channel between the peninsula's end and its outlying rocky islands was feared by American Indians and trappers. They named the channel *porte des morts,* or death's door, from which the peninsula and county take their names.

According to legend 17th-century French fur traders first ran afoul of the strait when Robert La Salle's ship *Griffin* sank. To circumvent the straits and the tedious trip around the peninsula, traders followed the American Indians' portage at Sturgeon Bay, which allowed easier passage to the important trade route at the head of Green Bay.

Fur trading dominated the area for 200 years, and it was not until the 19th century that Moravians, Scandinavians and other immigrants settled the peninsula. Around the turn of the 20th century wealthy city dwellers discovered the region's charms, transforming rustic villages into resorts.

Much of the peninsula caters to vacationers. Sailing on the surrounding waters, hiking and golf in one of the nearby state parks, as well as such cultural activities as summer theater and concerts, are area draws. Historic lighthouses, cherry blossoms and the sand beaches along Lake Michigan further accentuate the allure.

Door County Chamber of Commerce: 1015 Green Bay Rd., P.O. Box 406, Sturgeon Bay, WI 54235; phone (920) 743-4456 or (800) 527-3529 for a vacation planning guide.

Baileys Harbor (D-9) elev. 595′

During a fierce storm in 1848, Captain Justice Bailey found a safe port for his schooner on the Lake Michigan coast. Baileys Harbor, as the place came to be known, is the oldest village in Door County. The scenic harbor, notched into the Door Peninsula, is a popular vacation center. A half-mile north, the Ridges Sanctuary offers hiking trails in a natural wildlife area where wildflowers and species of native orchids can be seen from May to September. Tours are conducted during the summer and early fall.

Nearby recreational activities include salmon and trout fishing, bicycling, sea kayaking, windsurfing, snowmobiling and cross-country skiing. The Cana Island Lighthouse, about 4 miles northeast of Baileys Harbor via CR Q, was built in 1851; phone (920) 743-5958 Memorial Day-late Oct.

Egg Harbor (E-9) pop. 250, elev. 635′

Although some sources credit Increase Claflin, the first settler of Door County, with naming the town for a nest of duck eggs, one legend claims the "Battle of the Eggs" gave Egg Harbor its name. A group of Green Bay men supposedly sailed into the harbor in 1825 and engaged in an egg-throwing fight when they reached the townsite.

From mid-June to mid-August, Birch Creek Music Performance Center, a performing arts school and concert venue 3 miles east via CR E, presents symphony, percussion/steel band and big band performances in an early 1900s barn adapted as a concert hall; phone (920) 868-3763.

Ephraim (D-9) pop. 353, elev. 710′

Founded in 1853 by Moravians from Norway, Ephraim is a resort village. A monument to the Moravian founders overlooks the town. South of town is Peninsula State Park. *See Recreation Chart and Door County as well as Fish Creek in the AAA Great Lakes CampBook.*

The 1848 Goodletson Cabin, on Moravia St., offers a glimpse into how families lived during the era. Guided walking tours of Ephraim's historic district are offered Monday, Wednesday and Friday at 10:30, mid-June through Labor Day, departing from Anderson Barn Museum, 3060 Anderson Lane. For further information contact the Ephraim Foundation, Box 165, Ephraim, WI 54211; phone (920) 854-9688.

THE ANDERSON STORE is .5 mi. n. on SR 42. The restored 1858 general store displays typical retail items of the period as well as antiques, tools and possessions of Ephraim's settlers. Allow 30 minutes minimum. Mon.-Sat. 10:30-4, mid-June through Labor Day; Fri.-Sat. 10:30-4, day after Labor Day to mid-Oct. Admission (includes Anderson Barn Museum, Goodletson Cabin and Pioneer Schoolhouse) $3; ages 6-18, $2. Phone (920) 854-9688.

PIONEER SCHOOLHOUSE is 1.5 mi. e. of SR 42 on Moravia St. Built in 1880, the school was in operation until 1949. Exhibits include artifacts, photographs and costumes of local origin. Mon.-Sat. 10:30-4, mid-June through Labor Day; Fri.-Sat. 10:30-4, day after Labor Day-second weekend in Oct. Admission (includes Anderson Barn Museum, Anderson Store and Goodletson Cabin) $3; ages 6-18, $2. Phone (920) 854-9688.

Fish Creek (D-9) elev. 583′

A huge castellated cliff rising above Green Bay dominates Fish Creek's western waterfront. Sheltered coves provide the finest natural harbors on this side of the peninsula, augmented by the town's marina.

North of the village in Peninsula State Park *(see Recreation Chart and the AAA Great Lakes CampBook)* is the restored Eagle Bluff Lighthouse. From mid-June through November the American Folklore Theatre, (920) 854-6117, presents original musical productions at Peninsula State Park Amphitheatre; performances are at various Door County town halls through October.

The Peninsula Players, (920) 868-3287, the oldest resident professional summer stock company in the country, performs a variety of comedy, music and drama at Theatre in a Garden Tuesday through Sunday evenings, late June to mid-October.

Gills Rock (D-9) elev. 594′

SAVE **DOOR COUNTY MARITIME MUSEUM AT GILLS ROCK** is just n. of jct. SR 42 and Wisconsin Bay Rd. This museum on the tip of the Door Peninsula chronicles the area's fishing heritage with exhibits including shipwreck artifacts, navigational instruments, antique motors and models. *The Hope,* a restored commercial tugboat, is featured. Guided tours are offered. Allow 30 minutes minimum. Daily 10-4, Memorial Day weekend to mid-Oct. Admission (includes guided tour) $4; ages 5-17, $1; family rate $9 (two adults and children under 18). MC, VI. Phone (920) 854-1844.

Sturgeon Bay (E-9) pop. 9,437, elev. 922′

Where once a tedious portage was necessary to avoid the 100-mile voyage around the tip of the Door Peninsula, boats and giant freighters easily ply the ship canal between Green Bay and Lake Michigan. Sturgeon Bay, named for its fine natural harbor, is one of the largest shipbuilding ports on the Great Lakes. Boat tours leading south through the canal to Lake Michigan and north into Green Bay are available daily, July and August, at the municipal dock.

Sturgeon Bay also processes the ruby yield of Door County's cherry orchards, the most extensive in the state. Some 3,000 acres of cherry trees produce from 8 to 20 million pounds of fruit annually.

The trees bloom in late May, carpeting the peninsula in blossoms; harvest occurs from mid-July to early August.

During the annual chinook salmon spawning run each fall, as many as 500 anglers attack the waters daily in Sturgeon Bay Harbor in search of the 20- to 40-pound fish. Abundant winter recreation opportunities are available, including cross-country skiing and snowmobiling. The slopes at Potawatomi State Park *(see Recreation Chart and the AAA Great Lakes CampBook)* are lighted for nighttime skiing.

DOOR COUNTY HISTORICAL MUSEUM is at 18 N. Fourth Ave. A wildlife diorama, pioneer items, an early firehouse and items pertinent to Door County are among the exhibits. Allow 1 hour minimum. Daily 10-4:30, May-Oct. Donations. Phone (920) 743-5809.

DOOR COUNTY MARITIME MUSEUM is on the waterfront at 120 N. Madison Ave. Exhibits span the nautical history of Door County from early American Indian canoes to post-World War II bulk carriers. The museum features a model ship gallery, a small craft workshop, a lighthouse exhibit, an art gallery and vintage outboard motors and marine engines. The pilot house from a Great Lakes ore carrier is displayed, and a nuclear ballistic submarine periscope offers a bay area view. Allow 1 hour, 30 minutes minimum. Daily 9-6, Memorial Day-Labor Day; 10-5, rest of year. Admission $6.50; ages 5-17, $3; family rate $16. MC, VI. Phone (920) 743-5958.

SAVE **THE FARM** is 4 mi. n. on SR 57. The 40-acre rural environment includes various farm buildings, a pioneer homestead and farm animals, including young animals that can be held and fed. Particularly noteworthy are the nature cabin, with displays about the natural attractions of Door County, and the woodshed, with farm tools and utensils. There also are milking demonstrations, nature trails and vegetable, flower and herb gardens.

Picnicking is permitted. Allow 1 hour minimum. Daily 9-5, Memorial Day weekend to mid-Oct. Admission $7; over 62, $5.60; ages 4-13, $3.50. MC, VI. Phone (920) 743-6666.

MILLER ART MUSEUM is in the Door County Public Library at 107 S. Fourth Ave. Permanent and changing exhibits include paintings and graphics by Door County and other Midwestern artists. The main gallery also serves as a community center for musical programs and a winter lecture series about the arts. Allow 30 minutes minimum. Mon.-Thurs. 10-8, Fri.-Sat. 10-5; closed holidays. Donations. Phone (920) 746-0707.

SCENIC AIRPLANE RIDES depart from the Door County Cherryland Airport, 1 mi. s. on SR 42/57, then 1.5 mi. n. on Park Dr. Air tours of the Door Peninsula are offered by Orion Flight Services, Inc. A 172 Cessna high-wing aircraft cruises at 1,000 feet and provides excellent views of beaches, state parks, fruit orchards, resorts, Green Bay and Lake

Michigan. Four different [...] utes to 1 hour. Up to thre[...] commodated.

Mon.-Sat. 8-5 (also Fri.-Sat. [...] morial Day-late Oct. Fare $40-$1[...] length of flight; under 2 free. Reser[...] ommended and there is a two-person [...] or the 15-minute flight. AX, DS, MC, VI. [...]e (920) 743-6952.

WINERIES

- **Door Peninsula Winery** is 6 mi. n. on SR 42. Daily 9-6. Tours depart daily every 45 minutes 9:30-4:45. Phone (920) 743-7431 or (800) 551-5049.

Washington Island (D-9)

Six miles off the tip of the Door Peninsula, Washington Island is surrounded by the waters of Lake Michigan and Green Bay. More than 200 years ago Potawatomi Indians inhabited the island. The tribe later almost was destroyed by a sudden, severe squall that swamped the canoes of a war party as they crossed what is now known as Death's Door Strait, en route to the mainland.

The island's population is predominantly Scandinavian and constitutes the oldest Icelandic settlement in the United States. It is reached by daily ferry service from the Northport Pier, 2 miles east of Gills Rock on SR 42; phone (920) 847-2546. Narrated sightseeing tram trips of the island are offered; tours depart the Washington Island dock. Passenger excursion service to Rock Island State Park *(see Recreation Chart)* also is offered late May to mid-October.

Washington Island Chamber of Commerce: R.R. 1, Box 222, Washington Island, WI 54246; phone (920) 847-2179.

JACOBSEN'S MUSEUM is 6 mi. n. of the ferry dock on Little Lake. A cedar log building houses American Indian artifacts, antiques, rocks and fossils gathered on the island. Allow 30 minutes minimum. Daily 10-4, Memorial Day weekend to mid-Oct. Donation. Phone (920) 847-2213.

WASHINGTON ISLAND FARM MUSEUM is 5.4 mi. n. of the ferry dock on Jackson Harbor Rd. The museum provides a detailed look at Washington Island's farming history. Items displayed include horse-drawn farm equipment, log buildings, tools, a weaving loom and historic photographs. A blacksmith shop also is on the property. Daily 10-6, late June to mid-Oct. Donations. Phone (920) 847-2577.

EAGLE—*see Milwaukee p. 159.*

EAGLE RIVER (C-6) pop. 1,443, elev. 1,628'

Eagle River is in an all-year resort area. The Eagle chain of lakes, consisting of 28 navigable lakes, is one of the best known boating and fishing areas in northern Wisconsin. At 611 Sheridan Street

...ees for Tomorrow Environmental Education ...ter, which has a self-guiding demonstration forest trail; phone (715) 479-6456.

The U.S. Forest Service maintains about 40 miles of cross-country ski trails in nearby Chequamegon-Nicolet National Forest *(see place listing p. 126)*; there also are 600 miles of groomed trails in the area.

Eagle River Area Chamber and Visitors Center: 201 N. Railroad St., P.O. Box 1917, Eagle River, WI 54521; phone (715) 479-6400 or (800) 359-6315.

Shopping areas: Antiques and arts and crafts can be found on Wall Street and in the surrounding area.

EAST TROY (I-7) pop. 3,564, elev. 860′

EAST TROY ELECTRIC RAILROAD MUSEUM is at 2002 Church St. Historical exhibits chronicle the role the electric railroad played in the advancement of transportation. Visitors may take an 11-mile round-trip ride from East Troy to a farmer's market in Mukwonago aboard a restored trolley car. Guided tours are available. Allow 1 hour, 30 minutes minimum. Daily 11:30-4, Memorial Day-last weekend in Oct. Train departs every 45 min. Admission $9; ages 3-11, $5. MC, VI. Phone (262) 642-3263.

EAU CLAIRE (E-3) pop. 61,704, elev. 796′

Relations with Eau Claire's upstream neighbor, Chippewa Falls *(see place listing p. 127)*, were not always amicable in the days when rival logging companies from both towns drove their cuts down the *eau claire* ("clear water") of the Chippewa River. A number of midnight log drives and battles took place before cooperation supplanted warfare. When the timber was exhausted, Eau Claire, like Chippewa Falls, turned to diversified manufacturing.

Eau Claire's position at the confluence of the Chippewa and Eau Claire rivers enhances its status as a gateway to the resort areas of northwestern Wisconsin. Outdoor activities, such as bicycling, hiking, fishing and skiing, abound throughout the year.

Chippewa Valley Convention & Visitors Bureau: 3625 Gateway Dr., Suite F, Eau Claire, WI 54701; phone (715) 831-2345 or (888) 523-3866.

Shopping areas: Oakwood Mall, at US 53 and Golf Road, has more than 100 stores, including Dayton's, JCPenney and Sears.

CARSON PARK is a 135-acre peninsula on Half Moon Lake. A quarter-scale railroad is among the park's highlights. Hank Aaron started his professional baseball career at the park with the Eau Claire Bears; a sculpture of Aaron is in front of Carson Park Stadium. Many sports events and recreational activities are held at the park. Daily 4

a.m.-11 p.m. Free. Phone (715) 839-5032. *See Recreation Chart.*

SAVE **Chippewa Valley Museum** is in Carson Park. Regional history exhibits range from prehistoric times to the early 1900s. Displayed are Ojibwe Indian artifacts, agricultural and early industrial exhibits, a working early 20th-century ice cream parlor and a 21-room doll house. An 18-minute multimedia production is offered.

The 1880 Sunnyview School and 1860s Lars Anderson log house on the museum grounds are furnished in period. Mon.-Sat. 10-5 (also Tues. 5-8), Sun. 1-5, Memorial Day weekend-Labor Day; Tues.-Fri. 1-5 (also Tues. 5-8), Sat. 10-5, rest of year. Closed Jan. 1, Thanksgiving and Dec. 24-25. Admission $4; ages 3-18, $1.50; free to all Tues. 5-8. Phone (715) 834-7871.

Paul Bunyan Logging Camp and Interpretive Center is in Carson Park. It features a re-created 1890s logging camp. Artifacts are displayed in the cook shanty, bunkhouse, barn, smithy and shed. The Interpretive Center introduces visitors to the logging industry by means of a movie, an exhibit room, a tall tales room and a forest history exhibit. Daily 10-4:30, first Mon. in Apr.-first Mon. in Oct. Admission $4; ages 5-17, $1.50. MC, VI. Phone (715) 835-6200.

EGG HARBOR — *see Door County p. 129.*

ELKHORN (I-7) pop. 7,305, elev. 996′

A busy industrial community, Elkhorn traditionally has been associated with the manufacture of band instruments. Joseph Philbrick Webster, a popular composer during the Civil War era, wrote "Lorena" and "The Sweet Bye and Bye" while living in Elkhorn.

Elkhorn Area Chamber of Commerce: 114 W. Court St., P.O. Box 41, Elkhorn, WI 53121; phone (262) 723-5788.

WEBSTER HOUSE MUSEUM is at 9 E. Rockwell St. Built in 1836 as the local land office during Wisconsin's territorial years, the house was moved from the public square to its present site in 1840. It was home of composer Joseph Webster until his death in 1875 and contains some of his memorabilia, as well as American Indian, Civil War and Victorian items and a 400-piece mounted bird collection. Costumed interpreters depict the Civil War era.

Guided tours are available by appointment. Allow 1 hour minimum. Wed.-Sat. 1-5, mid-May to mid-Oct. Admission $5; ages 6-12, $2; family rate $15. Phone (262) 723-4248.

EPHRAIM — *see Door County p. 129.*

ERIN — *see Milwaukee p. 159.*

EVANSVILLE (I-6) pop. 4,039, elev. 893′

Reports of prime agricultural land drew New Englanders from New York and Vermont during the

1840s to "The Grove," so named for the abundant forest edging part of the prairie belt settlement. The early economy of Evansville rested on wheat but was replaced by tobacco during the Civil War era. The need to market agricultural produce gave rise to a host of processing plants, including a sawmill and gristmill on Allen's Creek.

With the arrival of the railroad in 1864, tobacco warehouses and other commercial enterprises clustered around the tracks. On the main line of the North Western Railroad, the city became Wisconsin's largest shipping point for wool and a major distribution center for livestock during the mid-19th century.

Evansville's development is reflected in its wide range of architecture, spanning more than 125 years. The 22-block historic district has many unaltered structures in such diverse styles as Greek Revival, Italianate, Late Picturesque, Neoclassic and Prairie. Along the shores of Lake Leota are park and recreational facilities. An 18-hole golf course is nearby.

Evansville Chamber of Commerce: 30 W. Main St. P.O. Box 51, Evansville, WI 53536; phone (608) 882-5131.

Self-guiding tours: A brochure describing residential and commercial structures in Evansville's historic district can be obtained at the library, 39 W. Main St., and the City Hall, 31 S. Madison St.; phone (608) 882-2260.

FISH CREEK—*see Door County p. 129.*

FOND DU LAC (G-7) pop. 42,203, elev. 765′

The French traders who first visited this region referred to it as the *fond,* or "far end," of Lake Winnebago, Wisconsin's largest freshwater lake;

hence the name Fond du Lac. In 1835 Wisconsin's first judge and later territorial governor, James D. Doty laid out the town in hopes of it becoming the state capital; it lost to Madison in 1848.

Today mansions of industrial barons line Division Street. Fond du Lac offers a diversity of industry and business, including the world headquarters for Mercury Marine, and Giddings and Lewis/Thyssen, a supplier of industrial automation products and machine tools.

Fond du Lac Area Convention & Visitors Bureau: 171 S. Pioneer Rd., Fond du Lac, WI 54935-2342; phone (920) 923-3010 or (800) 937-9123.

Self-guiding tours: Fond du Lac County's Talking Country Roads CD-guided tour spans the history of the area from the ice age to a front porch view of Horicon National Wildlife Refuge. A "Talking House" tour gives information on 24 historic homes and architectural structures. The tour has 14 stops on the route which are heard by tuning into an AM radio frequency. Contact the convention and visitors bureau for information.

Shopping areas: Downtown Main Street offers specialty shops including antiques, gourmet coffee, stained glass and quilting shops. Kristmas Kringle Shoppe, at 1330 S. Main Street at the entrance to the city, features a large assortment of glass ornaments, trees, animated figures and collectibles displayed in a Bavarian village setting.

A variety of shops can be found in Fond du Lac Plaza, at the entrance to Lakeside Park *(see attraction listing).* Forest Mall, off US 41 at Johnson Street, has more than 60 stores, including JCPenney, Kohls, Sears and Younkers department stores.

GALLOWAY HOUSE AND VILLAGE AND BLAKELY MUSEUM is on the s. city limits at 336 Old Pioneer Rd.; from US 41 take exit 96A to Pioneer Rd., following signs. Made up of more than 30

buildings from the turn of the 20th century, the village includes a church, courtroom, general store, law office, one-room schoolhouse, operating gristmill, photo studio, post office, printshop, railroad depot, smithy, toy shop and vet office.

Allow 1 hour, 30 minutes minimum. Daily 10-4, Memorial Day weekend-Sept. 15; Sat.-Sun. 10-4 in Oct. Admission $8; under 13, $4; preschoolers free; family rate $20; half-price to all Memorial Day weekend. Under 12 must be with an adult. Phone (920) 922-6390.

LAKESIDE PARK is on the n. end of Main St. The 400-acre park on Lake Winnebago contains a white-tailed deer enclosure, a children's playground, miniature train rides, a carousel, gardens, covered wooden bridges, a lighthouse and a scenic drive. Aqua bikes and canoes can be rented. Boats can launch from a number of launch ramps. Park open daily 7 a.m.-11 p.m. Lighthouse open daily 8-dusk (weather permitting), Apr. 15-Oct. 15. Free. Phone (800) 937-9123.

ST. PAUL'S EPISCOPAL CATHEDRAL is at 51 W. Division St. The interior features American and German woodcarvings and stained-glass windows from European and American studios. A 1-hour guided tour is available by reservation. Office open Tues.-Fri. 9-4 during the school year; Mon.-Thurs. 9-1, rest of year. Donations. Guided tour $2. Phone (920) 921-3363.

FORT ATKINSON (I-7)
pop. 11,621, elev. 790'

American Indian effigy mounds are numerous in the Fort Atkinson area. Panther Intaglio, west on SR 106 at 1236 Riverside Dr., is of interest: Rather than forming a mound on the site, Indians dug an effigy into the earth. The Fireside Restaurant and Playhouse is an entertainment complex offering theatrical and musical productions.

Fort Atkinson Area Chamber of Commerce: 244 N. Main St., Fort Atkinson, WI 53538; phone (920) 563-3210 or (888) 733-3678.

HOARD HISTORICAL MUSEUM AND NATIONAL DAIRY SHRINE'S VISITORS CENTER is at 407 Merchants Ave. (US 12). The Hoard House contains exhibits about the Black Hawk War and collections of American Indian artifacts, mounted birds, historic clothing and textiles, 19th-century tools, Civil War exhibit room and library and decorative arts.

Allow 1 hour minimum. Tues.-Sat. 9:30-4:30, Sun. 11-3, June 1-Labor Day; Tues.-Sat. 9:30-3:30, day after Labor Day-Dec. 31 and Jan. 18-May 31. Free. Phone (920) 563-7769.

GILLS ROCK—see Door County p. 129.
see Door County p. 129.

GRAFTON—see Milwaukee p. 159
see Milwaukee p. 159

GRANTSBURG (C-1) pop. 1,369, elev. 940'

Named after General Ulysses S. Grant's victory at Vicksburg, the village of Grantsburg was incorporated in 1886. One resident of notable stature was Gust Anderson, local marshal and lamplighter, who stood 7 1/2 feet tall. A wooden statue of "Big Gust" is in front of the community center on Pine Street.

CREX MEADOWS WILDLIFE AREA is .5 mi. n. on CR D, following signs. This state wildlife management area includes more than 30,000 acres of wetlands, brush prairie and forests. Some 270 species of birds have been observed in the area, including blue herons, bald eagles, Canada geese, ospreys, sandhill cranes and migrating waterfowl. Spring and fall are peak migration times. A visitor center offers maps, brochures, a herbarium and wildlife exhibits.

Picnicking is permitted. Allow 1 hour, 30 minutes minimum. Daily 24 hours. Visitor center open Mon.-Fri. 8-4:30, Sat.-Sun. 10-4, Apr. 1-Nov. 1; Mon.-Fri. 8-4:30, rest of year. Donations. Phone (715) 463-2739 or (715) 463-2896.

GREEN BAY (E-8) pop. 102,313, elev. 604'

Green Bay, at the head of its namesake bay, has two claims to fame that no other town in the state can match: its longevity and the Green Bay Packers. Permanent settlement began in 1669 when Father Allouez established a mission. By the time the United States assumed dominance in 1816, the town—a major fur trading and military post—had changed hands three times.

In 1850 Norwegian Otto Tank came to Green Bay to serve as a Moravian missionary to about 50 families of farmers. Bringing with him a large amount of development capital, Tank bought 800 acres of land along the west bank of the Fox River and parceled them out to members of his religious colony. The Moravians built a lumber mill and steel foundry—the first industrial stirrings in Green Bay.

Christ Church (Episcopal), at Cherry and Madison streets, was established in 1829. It is the oldest permanent church site in the state. Phone (920) 432-0042 for information.

In addition to its success as a paper- and cheese-producing and shipping center, the enthusiasm generated by the Green Bay Packers, the oldest professional football team in the National Football League, helps keep the old town young. The team was founded in 1919.

Green Bay Area Visitor & Convention Bureau: 1901 S. Oneida St., P.O. Box 10596, Green Bay, WI 54307; phone (920) 494-9507 or (888) 867-3342.

Shopping areas: Bay Park Square, south of Lambeau Field on Oneida Street, houses more than 60 stores, including Elder-Beerman, Kohl's, Old Navy, ShopKo and Younkers. Port Plaza Mall, in downtown's City Centre, features more than 100 stores, including Boston Store, JCPenney and Younkers.

BAY BEACH AMUSEMENT PARK AND WILDLIFE SANCTUARY is at the n. end of Irwin St. A small amusement park is combined with a 700-acre urban wildlife sanctuary featuring nature programs, wildlife exhibits and cross-country ski trails. A nature center has interactive exhibits, including a two-story forest with native habitats. Nocturnal animals, a family of timber wolves and a deer habitat also can be seen.

Picnicking is permitted. Amusement park open daily 10-9, June 5-Aug. 22 and May 29-31; daily 10-6, Aug. 23-Sept. 3 and June 1-4; daily 8-3, May 25-28; Sat.-Sun. 10-6, May 1-23 and Sept. 4-26. Sanctuary open daily 8-7:30, mid-Apr. to mid-Sept.; 8-4:30, rest of year. Free; individual ride tickets 20c (some rides require more than one ticket). Phone (920) 391-3671.

GREEN BAY BOTANICAL GARDEN is at 2600 Larsen Rd. Forty-seven acres of landscaped grounds include a four seasons garden with magnolias, crab apples, lilacs and perennials; a contemporary rose garden with shrub and English varieties; an American perennial garden; a cottage garden; a children's garden; a woodland garden featuring plants and wildflowers native to Wisconsin; a color and foliage garden and the memorial grove. Daily 9-5, May-Oct.; Mon.-Fri. 9-4, rest of year. Admission $5; ages 5-12, $2. Phone (920) 490-9457.

GREEN BAY PACKER HALL OF FAME is located in the Lambeau Field atrium at 1265 Lombardi Ave. The hall of fame features a wide variety of Packers memorabilia, including mementos chronicling the team's history through NFL championships and Super Bowl victories, as well as interactive and historical displays. Game highlights are available for viewing. Allow 2 hours minimum. Daily 9-5; closed home game days, Easter, Thanksgiving and Dec. 25. Admission $10; over 62, $8; ages 6-11, $5. MC, VI. Phone (920) 496-5700 or (888) 442-7225.

HAZELWOOD HISTORIC HOUSE is at 1008 S. Monroe Ave. Overlooking the Fox River, the 10-room Greek Revival home was the residence of Morgan L. Martin, a prominent politician, businessman, attorney and judge for 60 years. The home, which contains many items belonging to the family, depicts the 1890s period. Guided tours are given Mon. and Wed.-Fri. 10-2, Sat.-Sun. 1-4, June-Aug.; Sat.-Sun. 1-4 in May. Admission $4; senior citizens $3.50; ages 6-12, $2.50. Phone (920) 437-1840.

HERITAGE HILL STATE PARK is e. of the Fox River at jct. Webster Ave. and SR 172. A 40-acre complex of furnished historical buildings is grouped into four themed areas including the La Baye, Fort Howard, A Growing Community and Belgian Farm.

A schedule of events is available from the park. A visitor's center is also on the grounds. Living-history presentations take place at the museum buildings daily. Allow 2 hours minimum. Tues.-Sat. 10-4:30, Sun. noon-4:30, Memorial Day weekend-Labor Day. Guided tours are given at 1:30 (also Sat. at 11), Sept. 20-Oct. 29. Admission $7; over

62, $6; ages 5-17, $5. MC, VI. Phone (920) 448-5150 or (800) 721-5150.

NATIONAL RAILROAD MUSEUM is at 2285 S. Broadway, .2 mi. e. of Ashland Ave. via Cormier on the Fox River. The museum houses more than 70 locomotives and rolling stock from the steam and diesel eras. Highlights include Eisenhower's World War II command train and "The Big Boy," said to be the world's largest steam locomotive. A reception center has an exhibit hall and theater featuring an audiovisual presentation. A 1.5-mile ride on a standard-gauge train is included in admission. On the grounds, a 65-foot tower overlooks the Fox River.

Picnic facilities are available. Guided tours are available. Allow 2 hours minimum. Mon.-Sat. 9-5, Sun. 11-5 (house closes at 2 on Dec. 31). Train rides depart Mon.-Sat. at 10, 11:30, 1, 2:30 and 4, Sun. at 11:30, 1, 2:30 and 4, May-Sept.; closed Jan. 1, Thanksgiving and Dec. 24-25. Admission May-Sept. $7; over 62, $6; ages 4-12, $5. Admission rest of year $6; over 62, $5; ages 4-12, $4. DS, MC, VI. Phone (920) 437-7623.

NEVILLE PUBLIC MUSEUM OF BROWN COUNTY is at 210 Museum Pl. Galleries on two floors are devoted to art, history and science. Major traveling exhibits complement art, natural science, history and technology exhibits and changing displays of local art and artifacts. Particularly noteworthy is the exhibit "On the Edge of the Inland Sea," which traces 12,000 years of northeast Wisconsin's development.

Allow 2 hours minimum. Tues.-Sat. 9-4 (also Wed. 4-9), Sun. noon-4. Closed Jan. 1, Thanksgiving and Dec. 25; closes at 12:30 Good Friday, Dec. 24 and Dec. 31. Donations. Phone (920) 448-4460.

NEW ZOO AND REFORESTATION CAMP is off US 41 exit 176, 2.5 mi. w. on CR B, then 1 mi. n. on CR IR to 4418 Reforestation Rd. The zoo features 1,600 acres of trails, trout ponds and animal exhibits. The Wisconsin Trails exhibit features bears, wolves, lynxes, foxes and game birds. The Prairie Grasslands Area is home to prairie dogs, buffaloes, elk, cranes and swans; lions, baboons, snow monkeys and penguins live in the International Trail section. A children's area offers the opportunity to feed goats and reindeer.

Food is available. Allow 1 hour, 30 minutes minimum. Daily 9-6, Apr.-Oct.; 9-4 in Mar. and Nov.-Dec. Admission $4; senior citizens and ages 3-15, $2; family rate $12. Phone (920) 434-7841.

ONEIDA NATION MUSEUM is 5 mi. w. on SR 54 from US 41 exit 168, then 5 mi. s. on CR E and just w. on CR EE. This museum has displays and hands-on exhibits tracing the history and culture of the Oneida Indian Nation as it moved from New York to Wisconsin. Two nature trails are on the grounds. Guided tours are available by appointment. Picnicking is permitted. Allow 1 hour minimum. Tues.-Sat. 9-5, June-Aug.; Tues.-Fri. 9-5, Feb.-May and Sept.-Dec. Admission $2; senior citizens and under 18, $1. MC, VI. Phone (920) 869-2768.

CASINOS

- **Oneida Bingo & Casino** is at 2020/2100 Airport Dr. Daily 24 hours. Phone (920) 497-8118 or (800) 238-4263.

GREENBUSH (G-8)

WADE HOUSE & WESLEY JUNG CARRIAGE MUSEUM is off SR 23 at Plank Rd. The Wade House stagecoach inn, built in 1850 along the plank road that linked Sheboygan and Fond du Lac, has been restored. Settings include the taproom, ballroom, dining room, bedrooms and kitchens. Other restored buildings on the 360-acre state historic site include a smokehouse, smithy and a water-powered Herrling sawmill. Costumed interpreters conduct tours and can be seen performing such daily chores as cooking, weaving, spinning and blacksmithing.

Wesley Jung Carriage Museum has about 120 carriages, wagons and sleighs dating 1870-1915. Horse-drawn carriage rides are included with admission. Site daily 9-5, mid-May through mid-Oct. Last admission is 1 hour before closing. Admission $10; over 64, $9; ages 5-12, $5; family rate (2 adults and children under 18) $27. MC, VI. Phone (920) 526-3271.

HARTFORD—*see Milwaukee p. 160.*

HAYWARD (C-3) pop. 2,129, elev. 1,192′

NATIONAL FRESH WATER FISHING HALL OF FAME is at jct. SR 27/CR B. Housed in a building designed to resemble a muskellunge, the museum includes an observation deck in the mouth of the giant fish. Five other buildings on 6 acres of landscaped grounds display more than 400 specimens of fish from around the world, as well as angling equipment, trophies and other items.

Allow 1 hour minimum. Daily 10-5, June-Sept.; 10-4:30, Apr. 15-May 30 and in Oct. Last admission 30 minutes before closing. Admission $5; over 65, $4.50; ages 10-17, $3.50; under 10, $2.50. MC, VI. Phone (715) 634-4440.

WILDERNESS WALK is 3 mi. s. on SR 27. The 35-acre park features live animals in natural habitats, an animal nursery and the Old West Town. Picnicking is permitted. Food is available. Allow 1 hour minimum. Daily 10-5:30, mid-May through Labor Day. Last admission is 1 hour before closing. Admission $7; over 65 and ages 2-11, $5.50. MC, VI. Phone (715) 634-2893.

HAZELHURST (C-5) elev. 1,595′

WILDERNESS CRUISES depart 7 mi. w. off US 51 on CR Y, then 3 mi. w. on Willow Dam Rd. Two-hour and 2.5-hour narrated boat tours through the scenic Willow Flowage area are offered. Sights include wildlife, islands, coves and nearly 100 miles of undeveloped shoreline. Lunch and dinner cruises also are available. Sightseeing cruises depart Memorial Day weekend-early Oct. Fare $9.95; ages 3-10, $5.95. Reservations are required. Phone to verify fares. DS, MC, VI. Phone (715) 453-3310 or (800) 472-1516.

HORICON (H-7) pop. 3,775, elev. 886′

The Horicon area presents visitors with many sightseeing opportunities. Tours of John Deere Horicon Works, 300 N. Vine St., are offered by appointment; phone (920) 485-4411.

Horicon Chamber of Commerce: 407 E. Lake St., P.O. Box 23, Horicon, WI 53032; phone (920) 485-3200.

BLUE HERON TOURS, INC. departs from the bridge at SR 33. Narrated 1-hour pontoon boat tours explore Horicon Marsh, a wetland inhabited by more than 260 species of birds. A 2-hour birding tour also is available May through September. Canoe and kayak rentals are available April through September.

Marsh tour departs daily at 1, May-Sept; Mon.-Fri. at 1, Sat.-Sun. departures vary, Oct.1-third weekend in Oct.; phone ahead. Marsh tour $9; ages 12-15, $5.50; ages 4-11, $4.50. Birding tour $17; ages 12-15, $10; ages 4-11, $8. Reservations are required for birding tour. MC, VI. Phone (920) 485-4663.

HORICON MARSH WILDLIFE AREA is at N7725 SR 28. The southernmost third of the Horicon Marsh, an 11,000-acre state-owned area, is primarily used for recreation. Activities include nature study, fishing, hunting, canoeing, hiking, birdwatching and photography. Naturalist programs on the weekends in the spring and fall also are offered. Allow 1 hour minimum. Marsh open daily dawn-dusk. Office daily 8-4:30. Free. Phone (920) 387-7860. *See Recreation Chart.*

HUDSON (E-1) pop. 8,775, elev. 669′

Founded by fur traders on the St. Croix River in the 1840s, Hudson developed into a prosperous steamboat and lumbering center within 20 years. Evoking the Victorian era are renovated historic buildings in Hudson's downtown and residential areas. The stately houses along Third and Vine streets formerly were the showplaces of wealthy merchants and lumber barons.

Phipps Center for the Arts, First and Locust streets, presents theatrical productions, concerts, art exhibitions and other cultural programs. Lakefront Park along the St. Croix River offers fishing, boating and swimming. Just outside of town is Willow River State Park *(see Recreation Chart and the AAA Great Lakes CampBook).*

Hudson Area Chamber of Commerce & Tourism Bureau: 502 Second St., Hudson, WI 54016; phone (715) 386-8411 or (800) 657-6775.

Self-guiding tours: Maps outlining walking, bicycling and driving tours of historic Hudson are available at the chamber of commerce and tourism bureau.

SAVE **OCTAGON HOUSE,** 1004 Third St., represents architectural styles of the 1850s. It contains dolls and period furnishings. The garden house displays a general store, a blacksmith shop and a woodworking area.

Guided tours are available. Allow 30 minutes minimum. Tues.-Sat. 11-4, Sun. 2-4:30, May-Oct. and the 3 weeks after Thanksgiving; closed holidays. Last tour departs 30 minutes before closing. Admission $5; ages 13-19, $2; ages 5-12, $1. Phone (715) 386-2654.

HURLEY (B-4) pop. 1,818, elev. 1,502'

Begun as an iron-mining and logging town around 1884, Hurley enjoyed more than 30 years of prosperity and high living—its main street once was studded with 76 saloons and taverns along a five-block stretch.

The town's colorful past is celebrated in several books, including Pulitzer Prize-winner Edna Ferber's "Come and Get It." The movie version of Ernest Hemingway's novel "Adventures of a Young Man" was filmed in Hurley. A museum in the old county courthouse, Iron Street and 3rd Avenue, contains relics recalling Hurley's mining and logging heritage; phone (715) 561-2244.

Summer adventurers can try out miles of hiking, mountain bicycling and all-terrain vehicle trails. During winter, skiers can visit Whitecap Mountain in nearby Ironbelt. Hurley also is a convenient base for exploring Iron County's 450 miles of snowmobile trails.

Hurley Area Chamber of Commerce: 316 Silver St., Hurley, WI 54534; phone (715) 561-4334, or (715) 561-3866 for recorded information.

JANESVILLE (I-6) pop. 59,498, elev. 804'

Soldiers returning home from the Black Hawk War were the first to promote Janesville's fertile valley on the Rock River. One who heard their praise was pioneer and visionary Henry F. Janes, who arrived in 1836, became the town's first postmaster and started a ferry and tavern. In 1892 George Parker opened Parker Pen Co., and 1919 brought the arrival of General Motors Corp., which became the town's largest employer. Guided tours of the GM plant at 1000 Industrial Ave. are offered by appointment; phone (608) 756-7681.

Several accomplished women hail from Janesville. Carrie Jacobs Bond, one of the first female songwriters to become published, wrote "A Perfect Day," which sold more than 5 million copies in 10 years. During the 19th century, Frances Willard became the national president of the Women's Christian Temperance Union and a relentless suffragist. A resident of nearby Johnstown, poet Ella Wheeler

Wilcox sent the public stampeding to the bookstores after her "Poems of Passion" was printed by a progressive publisher.

Free water-skiing shows are performed at Traxler Park on Wednesday and Sunday evenings in summer.

Janesville Area Convention & Visitors Bureau: 51 S. Jackson St., Janesville, WI 53545; phone (608) 757-3171 or (800) 487-2757.

Self-guiding tours: The Janesville Historic Commission has identified six residential and four downtown commercial historic districts. Brochures describing each district and the Janesville Heritage self-guiding tour map are available from the Janesville Historic Commission, 200 W. Milwaukee, P.O. Box 5005; phone (608) 755-3107.

HELEN JEFFRIS WOOD MUSEUM CENTER is at 426 N. Jackson St. Housed in the 1912 Prairie-style home of Stanley Dexter Tallman, the Rock County Historical Society museum offers temporary and traveling exhibits and educational programs. Facilities include the Lincoln-Tallman Restorations visitor and ticketing center *(see attraction listing)* and a children's interactive area. Daily 9-4 during exhibitions; phone for schedule. Closed major holidays. Exhibit admission $3.50; over 61, $3; grades K-12, $2.50. Admission to center is free. Phone (608) 756-4509 or (800) 577-1859.

SAVE **THE LINCOLN-TALLMAN RESTORATIONS** is at 440 N. Jackson St., on US 14 Bus. Rte., 2 blks. n.e. of jct. US 51. The 26-room Italian Villa-style house was built by William Morrison Tallman, a wealthy attorney and abolitionist from New York. When the house was built 1855-57, it had such conveniences as running water, a communication system, central heating, plumbing and gas lighting. Abraham Lincoln was a weekend guest in 1859.

DID YOU KNOW

Famous Wisconsinites include actor Spencer Tracy, author Thornton Wilder, magician Harry Houdini and architect Frank Lloyd Wright.

Tours are given daily on the hour 9-4, June-Sept.; Sat.-Sun. 9-4, rest of year. Closed major holidays. Christmas tours are offered daily Nov. 20-Dec. 31. Admission $8; over 61, $7.50; grades K-12, $4; under 6, free. MC, VI. Phone (608) 756-4509.

ROTARY GARDENS is .7 mi. w. of I-90 via SR 11, then .7 mi. s. at 1455 Palmer Dr. Fifteen acres of internationally-themed botanical gardens surround a 2-acre pond. A footpath, boardwalk and Japanese bridge connect the 16 gardens. The Rath Environmental Center houses the administrative office. Special events, classes and programs take place at Parker Educational Center throughout the year. Allow 1 hour minimum. Gardens open daily dawn-dusk. Parker Center open Mon.-Fri. 8:30-4:30, Sat.-Sun. and holidays 10-6, May-Oct.; Sat.-Sun. Nov. 1-second weekend in Dec. Donations. Phone (608) 752-3885.

KAUKAUNA (F-8) pop. 12,983, elev. 712'

Five gallons of rum was the price paid for the parcel of land that created Kaukauna in 1793, in the first deeded transaction executed in Wisconsin. On the portage that bypassed the long rapids of the Fox River, the community developed into a busy trading and milling center. The same cascade that once hampered travel long since has been tamed for industrial use.

Fox Cities Convention and Visitors Bureau: 3433 W. College Ave., Appleton, WI 54914; phone (920) 734-3358 or (800) 236-6673.

1000 ISLANDS ENVIRONMENTAL CENTER is at 1000 Beaulieu Ct. The 350-acre center features an indoor exhibition of mounted animals from Africa, Asia and North America. The collection includes antelopes, lions, polar bears, rhinoceroses, tigers and zebras. Bald eagles, deer, ducks, herons and owls can be seen on the grounds. Nature trails follow the Fox River and go through the woods. Snowshoes can be rented. Picnicking is permitted. Allow 2 hours minimum. Mon.-Fri. 8-4, Sat.-Sun. 10-3:30; closed holidays. Free. Phone (920) 766-4733.

KENOSHA (I-8) pop. 90,352, elev. 611'

Wisconsin's southernmost Lake Michigan port, Kenosha is an important manufacturing city. Residential streets shaded by elms and oaks hint of the town's settlement by New Englanders in 1835. Municipal parks line much of the lakefront. The area is headquarters to such firms as Snap-on Tools, G. Leblanc Corp. and Jockey International, Inc.

Self-guiding tours are available at the international headquarters of the Society for the Preservation and Encouragement of Barber Shop Quartet Singing in America in Harmony Hall, overlooking the lake at 6315 3rd Ave.; phone (262) 653-8440. Guided tours of the Civil War Museum on the Carthage College campus are offered by appointment; phone (262) 551-5801.

Greyhound racing is available year-round at Dairyland Greyhound Park, I-94 and SR 158; phone (262) 657-8200 or (800) 233-3357.

Note: Policies concerning admittance of children to pari-mutuel betting facilities vary. Phone for information.

Kenosha Area Convention & Visitors Bureau: 812 56th St., Kenosha, WI 53140; phone (262) 654-7307 or (800) 654-7309.

Shopping areas: The Original Outlet Mall, I-94 and SR 50 exit 344, has some 80 stores, including such brand-name outlets as Eddie Bauer, Pfaltzgraff and Sony. Nike, Oshkosh B'Gosh, Polo/Ralph Lauren and Timberland are just four of the nearly 70 stores that can be found at Prime Outlets at Pleasant Prairie, I-94 and SR 165 exit 347.

(SAVE) **BRISTOL RENAISSANCE FAIRE** is at 12550 120th Ave.; take I-94 s. to exit 347, w. to Frontage Rd., then 2 mi. w., following signs. This site depicts a 16th-century English village; costumed performers provide entertainment on 16 stages and in the streets. Visitors experience the food, games and crafts of Elizabethan England. Highlights include Queen Elizabeth I and her court, jousting, falconry demonstrations, sword fighting, juggling and the Kids Kingdom.

Allow a full day. Sat.-Sun. and Labor Day 10-7, July 10-Sept. 6, 2004. Admission $17.50; over 54 and students with ID $16.50; ages 5-12, $8.50. MC, VI. Phone (847) 395-7773.

KENOSHA PUBLIC MUSEUM is at 5500 First Ave. in HarborPark. A two-story atrium cuts through the center of this museum, an architectural representation of the glacier that sculpted Wisconsin during the Ice Age. Natural history exhibits include pottery, fossils, dioramas and the Schaefer mammoth, excavated in Kenosha County. An art gallery features works by Marc Chagall, Salvador Dali, Joan Miró, Pablo Picasso and Auguste Renoir. Allow 1 hour minimum. Tues.-Sat. 9-5, Sun.-Mon. noon-5; closed major holidays. Free. Phone (262) 653-4140.

KESHENA (E-7) pop. 1,394, elev. 825'

CASINOS

- **Menominee Casino Bingo Hotel**, 1.5 mi. s. on SR 47/55. Daily 24 hours; closed noon Dec. 24-noon Dec. 25. Phone (715) 799-3600 or (800) 343-7778.

KEWAUNEE (F-9) pop. 2,806, elev. 672'

Although the growth of Chicago and the development of the railroads foiled Kewaunee's plan to become a major Lake Michigan shipping center, the town still is a busy port. Both commercial and sport fishing boats depart from its harbor.

Kewaunee Chamber of Commerce: 308 N. Main St., P.O. Box 243, Kewaunee, WI 54216; phone (920) 388-4822 or (800) 666-8214.

Self-guiding tours: A booklet detailing a walking tour of 43 homes and a school in Kewaunee's Marquette Historic District is available from the Kewaunee County Historical Museum and Old Jail in Court House Square.

KEWAUNEE COUNTY HISTORICAL MUSEUM AND OLD JAIL is in Court House Sq. at 613 Dodge St. Housed in the 1876 former sheriff's house and jail wing, the museum displays area relics and antiques. Notable are a large basswood carving, "Custer's Last Stand," and four life-size carvings of Father Marquette and American Indians, depicting his landing in 1674. Allow 30 minutes minimum. Daily noon-4, Memorial Day weekend-Labor Day. Admission $2; ages 14-17, $1. Phone (920) 388-7176 or (920) 388-3858.

KING (F-6) pop. 898

WISCONSIN VETERANS MUSEUM is at N2665 CRQQ in Marden Memorial Center of the Wisconsin Veterans Home. Dedicated to veterans of all wars, this museum displays memorabilia and weapons from nations involved in those wars. Allow 30 minutes minimum. Daily 8-4; closed holidays. Free. Phone (715) 258-5586.

KOHLER (G-8) pop. 1,926, elev. 680'

Kohler is a planned, landscaped, incorporated village surrounding the factories of Kohler Co., manufacturers of plumbing and leisure products, engines and generators. The model village has won national recognition for its architecture.

KOHLER DESIGN CENTER is at 101 Upper Rd. The center includes a ceramic art gallery, archives, relics from its early factory and village and a theater. A multi-level product showroom features designer bathrooms and kitchens. A 2.5-hour factory tour is available. Allow 1 hour minimum. Design center open Mon.-Fri. 8-5, Sat.-Sun. and holidays 10-4; closed Thanksgiving and Dec. 25. Factory tour offered Mon.-Fri. at 8:30. Free. Under 14 are not permitted on factory tours, and reservations are required. Phone (920) 457-3699.

WAELDERHAUS is reached from I-43 exit 126 (Kohler Memorial Dr.), w. on SR 23 to Highland Dr., then 1.25 mi. s. This house employs a style of architecture found in Bregenzerwald, Austria. Waelderhaus is a replica of the John M. Kohler house. Allow 1 hour minimum. Guided tours are given daily at 2, 3 and 4; closed major holidays. Free. Phone (920) 452-4079.

LAC DU FLAMBEAU (C-5)
pop. 1,646, elev. 1,609'

The village of Lac du Flambeau lies in the center of the 144-square-mile Lac du Flambeau Chippewa Indian Reservation. Said to be the world's most concentrated lake region, the Lac du Flambeau country was named "the Lake of the Flaming Torch" after an old American Indian custom of catching fish by the light of flares.

Lac du Flambeau Chamber of Commerce: 14075 Gauthier Ln., Lac du Flambeau, WI 54538; phone (715) 588-3346 or (877) 588-3346.

GEORGE W. BROWN, JR. OJIBWE MUSEUM & CULTURAL CENTER is 2 blks. s. of SR 47 on Peace Pipe Rd., just s. of the Indian Bowl. A collection of American Indian artifacts dates to the mid-18th century. A four-seasons display demonstrates Indian activities, clothing and living arrangements. Of interest is a 24-foot dugout canoe discovered off the shores of Strawberry Island and thought to be 200 years old.

Guided tours are available. Allow 1 hour minimum. Mon.-Sat. 10-4 or by appointment, May-Oct.; Tues.-Thurs. 10-2, rest of year. Admission $3; over 55 and ages 5-15, $2. MC, VI. Phone (715) 588-3333.

RECREATIONAL ACTIVITIES
Fishing
- **Lac Du Flambeau Tribal Fish Hatchery** is at the lower end of Pokegama Lake. Daily May-Aug. Phone (715) 588-3303.

LA CROSSE (G-2) pop. 51,818, elev. 640'

On the Mississippi River where the Black and La Crosse rivers meet, La Crosse was founded in 1842 as an American Indian trading post. Serious development began a decade later, when settlers from New York, Ohio and Vermont established sawmills and gristmills and spurred the arrival of the railroad. The Easterners were joined by German and Norwegian immigrants attracted by the extensive pine groves.

La Crosse was faced with a crippling depression when the La Crosse and Milwaukee Railroad Co. went bankrupt in 1857. However, when the Civil War closed river traffic on the Mississippi below the Ohio River, La Crosse provided a major link with the East, thus ensuring the town's economic recovery. A railroad bridge erected over the Mississippi in 1876 precipitated a dramatic increase in trade and manufacturing, as the network of railroads radiating from La Crosse found new markets.

The city lies on a scenic route that follows the Mississippi. The route consists of SR 35, which heads southeast to Prairie du Chien, and US 53, which runs northwest to its junction with SR 54/35. Overseeing all river traffic is a 25-foot carved wooden American Indian in Riverside Park at the base of State Street near the downtown area. The park is the docking site for the steamboats *The American Queen* and *The Mississippi Queen*. Lock and Dam No. 7, a U.S. Army Corps of Engineers project 5 miles north of La Crosse, has an observation deck.

Goose Island County Park *(see Recreation Chart and the AAA Great Lakes CampBook)* offers developed recreational facilities and a wildlife refuge. During the winter downhill and cross-country skiing are available in the area.

Tours of the University of Wisconsin-La Crosse campus are available; phone (608) 785-8067. The university's art gallery exhibits works by prominent artists September through May. Cultural events also take place at Viterbo College.

La Crosse Area Convention & Visitors Bureau: Riverside Park, 410 Veterans Memorial Dr., La Crosse, WI 54601; phone (608) 782-2366 or (800) 658-9424.

Shopping areas: Valley View Mall, I-90 exit 4 on US 16, has more than 85 stores, including Dayton's, JCPenney and Sears.

GRANDAD BLUFF is 2 mi. e. on Main St. Towering about 600 feet above the city, the summit offers a panoramic view. On clear days you can see three states—Iowa, Wisconsin and Minnesota. The bluff can be visited daily 6 a.m.-11 p.m.

THE HIXON HOUSE AND MUSEUM is at 429 N. 7th St. The mid-19th-century Italianate house reflects an affluent lifestyle. Original contents include Oriental rugs, ceramics from Europe and the Orient and furniture of the Victorian period. Guided museum tours are available. Daily 1-5, Memorial Day-Labor Day; closed July 4. Admission $5; under 12, $3; family rate $12. Phone (608) 782-1980.

LA CROSSE QUEEN departs at the n. end of Riverside Park, 3 blks. w. of US 53 off State St. An authentic paddlewheeler offers 90-minute narrated sightseeing cruises on the Mississippi River. Weekend brunch, dinner and lunch cruises and some 3-hour cruises also are available. Sightseeing cruises depart daily May-Oct.; phone for schedule. Sightseeing fare varies; phone ahead. Reservations are required for meal cruises. MC, VI. Phone (608) 784-2893 or (608) 784-8523.

MYRICK PARK ZOO is at 2000 La Crosse St. (SR 16). The park contains a small collection of domestic and wild animals and birds, as well as picnic areas, children's amusement rides, a wading pool and nature trails. Daily 8-7:45, May-Aug.; 8-3, Sept.-Oct. Park free. Fee charged for rides. Phone (608) 789-7190.

PUMP HOUSE REGIONAL ARTS CENTER is 1 blk. w. of US 53 at 119 King St. Built in the Romanesque Revival style, the 1880 waterworks building now houses a performing arts theater and fine-arts galleries with changing exhibits by local and regional artists. Allow 30 minutes minimum. Tues.-Sat. noon-5. Donations. Phone (608) 785-1434.

RIVERSIDE MUSEUM is at the base of State St. in Riverside Park. The history of La Crosse is chronicled through historic photographs and a videotape presentation. The museum displays an extensive collection of American Indian artifacts. Riverboat history is emphasized. Allow 30 minutes minimum. Daily 10-5, Memorial Day weekend-Labor Day. Donations. Phone (608) 782-1980.

SWARTHOUT MUSEUM is in the Main Library at 9th and Main sts. Changing exhibits relate to local

history, including such topics as early social customs, American Indians, transportation, river life, agriculture, industry and commerce. Allow 30 minutes minimum. Tues.-Fri. 10-5, Sat.-Sun. 1-5; closed major holidays. Donations. Phone (608) 782-1980.

LAKE GENEVA (I-7) pop. 7,148, elev. 864'

This noted year-round resort is on spring-fed Geneva Lake. At the western end of the lake is Fontana, occupied in the late 1800s by the Potawatomi village of Chief Big Foot. Recreational facilities include beaches, boat ramps, golf courses, excursion boats, a greyhound racing facility, hanggliding, hot-air balloon rides, parasailing and horseback riding.

Note: Policies concerning admittance of children to pari-mutuel betting facilities vary. Phone for information.

Lake Geneva also has hiking, snowmobile and cross-country ski trails. In winter Lake Geneva is host to legions of downhill skiers and ice skaters. Big Foot Beach State Park is 2.5 miles south of Lake Geneva *(see Recreation Chart and the AAA Great Lakes CampBook).*

Lake Geneva Area Convention & Visitors Bureau: 201 Wrigley Dr., Lake Geneva, WI 53147-2004; phone (262) 248-4416 or (800) 345-1020.

[SAVE] **LAKE GENEVA CRUISE LINE** departs from the Riviera Docks. Sightseeing trips on Geneva Lake are offered aboard restorations or replicas of historic yachts. Mail boat, luncheon, dinner, ice cream social and Sunday brunch cruises also are available. One-hour Geneva Bay Mansion tours depart daily at 10, 11:15, 12:30, 1:45, 3 and 4:15, mid-June to late Aug.; at 11 and 3, late Aug.-late Oct.; at 11, 1 and 3:45, May 1 to mid-June. Two-hour full lake tours depart daily at 12:35 and 2:50, mid-June to late Aug.; at 12:45, late Aug.-late Oct.

Geneva Bay Mansion tour $14.50; over 65, $13.50; ages 13-17, $11.25; ages 4-12, $7.95. Full lake tour $18; over 65, $16.95; ages 13-17, $13.75; ages 4-12, $9.95. Reservations are recommended for all cruises, and are required for food cruises and those lasting longer than 1 hour. Phone (262) 248-6206 or (800) 558-5911.

LAKE MILLS (H-7) pop. 4,843, elev. 857'

Archeologists theorize that Aztalan, 3 miles east of Lake Mills on CR B, then right on CR Q, was the northernmost city of the Middle Mississippian Phase Indians, a culture influenced by the Aztecs in Mexico. Established 1075-1175, a 21-acre stockaded village once was occupied by about 500 Aztalan Indians. The Aztalans had a settled farming culture characterized by pyramidal mounds, complex pottery and crafts, and cannibalism.

After the Black Hawk War ended in 1836, settlers flooding into the area founded the second village of Aztalan at the junction of two stagecoach roads just northwest of the stockade. By 1842, the pioneer town had evolved into an industrial center, with Jefferson County's first post office, two hotels, a brickyard and five small factories. Aztalan's demise came in 1859, after the railroad bypassed the town.

Truncated mounds and stockade sections of the ancient Indian village are identified with markers in Aztalan State Park, quarter-mile south of the Aztalan Museum *(see attraction listing).*

Lake Mills Area Chamber of Commerce: 200C Water St., P.O. Box 125, Lake Mills, WI 53551-0125; phone (920) 648-3585.

AZTALAN MUSEUM is 3 mi. e. on CR B at jct. CR Q, next to Aztalan State Park. The only remaining building from the 1830s pioneer village of Aztalan, this former Baptist church houses a collection of Aztalan and Woodland Indian artifacts, as well as exhibits, maps and documents relating to Aztalan and early Lake Mills. Four log cabins on the 4-acre site date from the mid- to late 1800s.

Allow 1 hour minimum. Thurs.-Sun. noon-4, mid-May to late Sept.; other times by appointment. Admission $3; ages 7-18, $1. Phone (920) 648-4632.

LAND O'LAKES (B-6) elev. 1,709′

Heart of the region of the same name, the attractive village of Land O'Lakes is surrounded by some 135 lakes. To the west, the Cisco chain of 17 lakes forms the second longest chain in Wisconsin. Lac Vieux Desert, east of town, is the source of the Wisconsin River. A popular resort center, the region offers summer and winter sports.

Land O'Lakes Chamber of Commerce: CR B at US 45, P.O. Box 599, Land O'Lakes, WI 54540; phone (715) 547-3432 or (800) 236-3432.

LAONA (D-7) elev. 1,580′

Laona is a lumbering and vacation center providing access to the varied recreational opportunities available in Chequamegon-Nicolet National Forest *(see place listing p. 126).*

Laona Chamber of Commerce: P.O. Box 229, Laona, WI 54541; phone (715) 674-3007.

LUMBERJACK SPECIAL AND CAMP FIVE MUSEUM COMPLEX TOUR is on US 8 jct. SR 32. Steam-powered train rides aboard the Laona and Northern Railway's "Lumberjack Special" travel from the historic depot in Laona to the Camp Five Museum Complex. At the complex a logging museum contains logging relics from the river and railroad eras through the gasoline era, an active blacksmith and harness shop, transportation and agricultural displays, a lumber company money collection and an audiovisual presentation about logging history.

A 30-minute forest tour by surrey and a hayrack/pontoon boat ride along banks of wild rice and through a bird refuge are available.

Allow 2 hours minimum. Museum open Mon.-Sat. 11-4, mid-June to late Aug. Trains depart at 11, noon, 1 and 2. Fall color tours are offered Sept. 25, Oct. 2 and 9, 2004. Museum, surrey ride and train $15; ages 13-17, $10; ages 4-12, $5; family rate $40. Hayrack/pontoon ride $2.50; ages 4-12, $1.25. DS, MC, VI. Phone (715) 674-3414 or (800) 774-3414.

MADELINE ISLAND (A-4)

Madeline Island is east of the Bayfield Peninsula in Lake Superior. The largest of the Apostle Islands group *(see Apostle Islands National Lakeshore p. 119),* Madeline has a permanent population of fewer than 200 residents. The island was the focus of some of the earliest trading, missionary activity and commercial fishing in the interior of North America. It is possible that Etienne Brule visited the region as early as 1622 in his attempt to find the mythical Northwest Passage to China and the East Indies.

The French explorers Radisson and Groseilliers explored Madeline in 1659. Trading posts were established by the French in 1693 and by the British in 1793. La Pointe became headquarters for a post of the American Fur Co. in 1816. It currently serves the thousands of summer visitors to the island. Big Bay State Park *(see Recreation Chart)* is on the east shore of the island. Just across the lagoon is Big Bay Town Park.

Ferries operate between Bayfield *(see place listing p. 123)* and the island town of La Pointe daily from April to early December (weather permitting). They run about every 30 minutes during the peak season, mid-June to early October. Fares vary according to season; phone (715) 747-2051. In the winter a motorized windsled offers transportation to the island until the lake freezes and cars can travel on an ice highway.

Tours of the island, offered by Madeline Island Bus Tours, depart several times daily, mid-June through Labor Day, from the Madeline Island Ferry Lines office near the ferry landing; phone (715) 747-2051 or (715) 747-6801.

Madeline Island Chamber of Commerce: 274 Middle Rd., P.O. Box 274, La Pointe, WI 54850; phone (715) 747-2801 or (888) 475-3386.

Shopping area: During the summer Woods Hall Craft Shop, 3 blocks south of the ferry landing, features craftspersons displaying their wares.

MADELINE ISLAND HISTORICAL MUSEUM is 1 blk. from the ferry landing in La Pointe. Surrounded by a log stockade, this state historic site consists of an American Fur Co. warehouse, the island jail, a barn and the old Sailors' Home. Exhibits depict American Indian life, the expeditions of French *voyageurs,* the arrival of the fur traders and the development of the fishing and logging industries in the Chequamegon Bay region. A 23-minute film also is available.

Daily 10-5, Memorial Day weekend-first Sat. in Oct. Last admission 30 minutes before closing. Admission $5.50; over 64, $4.95; ages 5-12, $2.75; family rate $15. MC, VI. Phone (715) 747-2415.

MADISON (H-6) pop. 208,054, elev. 845′

Madison existed only as a plan when it was selected as the territorial capital in 1836. By 1838 there was one inn and a general store, and construction had just begun on the Capitol. The going was slow, and the legislature, weary of cold, crowded and bedless accommodations, repeatedly threatened to move the capital elsewhere.

With the completion of the statehouse, Wisconsin's attainment of statehood and the establishment of the University of Wisconsin in 1848, the city began to assume some of its present character. Madison is a thriving center for business, government, education and recreation.

Much of the recreation is available on more than 18,000 acres of lake surface within or just outside the city limits. The "Four Lakes of Madison" are Mendota, Monona, Wingra and Waubesa. Mendota, about 8 miles long, is the largest. From Picnic Point, a narrow spit jutting into Lake Mendota, there is a spectacular view of the city.

The city center is on an eight-block-wide isthmus between lakes Mendota and Monona. By ordinance, the city's skyline is dominated by the 2,500-ton dome of the state Capitol. Capitol Square is connected to the university campus by State Street Mall, a tree-lined shopping district with import shops, ethnic restaurants and crafts studios. The Madison Civic Center, housing three performing arts theaters and Madison Art Center, is in the middle of the mall at 211 State St.

The Unitarian Church at 900 University Bay Dr. is an especially noteworthy example of Frank Lloyd Wright's architectural style. Wright intended its ascending triangular forms to symbolize unity and prayer. The Madison Mallards play minor-league baseball at Warner Park.

Greater Madison Convention & Visitors Bureau: 615 E. Washington Ave., Madison, WI 53703; phone (608) 255-2537 or (800) 373-6376.

Shopping areas: Madison has two major malls: East Towne at I-90/94 and US 151, which has 100 stores, and West Towne at Gammon and Mineral Point roads, which has more than 100 stores. Anchor stores are Boston Store, JCPenney, Sears and Younkers.

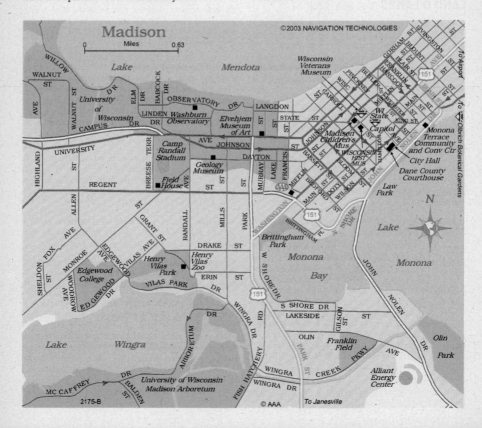

 **CAVE OF THE MOUNDS—**
see Blue Mounds p. 124.

HENRY VILAS ZOO is on Lake Wingra via W. Washington Ave., then .5 mi. w. on Drake St. Founded in 1911, the park contains 150 species of animals, including 17 that are endangered. Prairie dogs and miniature horses are among the residents of a children's zoo, which includes interactive exhibits and feeding stations.

Picnicking is permitted. Grounds open daily 9:30-5; closed afternoons Jan. 1, Martin Luther King Jr. Day, Thanksgiving, day after Thanksgiving and Dec. 24-25 and 31. Children's zoo open daily 10-4, Memorial Day weekend-Labor Day. Free. Phone (608) 266-4732.

MADISON CHILDREN'S MUSEUM is at 100 State St. across from the State Capitol. This educational and cultural museum is designed for children up to age 8. Exhibits include Dig Into Dinosaurs, the Shadow Room, First Feats: Celebrating the Early Years and Let's Grow. Additional hands-on exhibits change periodically. Allow 1 hour minimum. Mon.-Fri. 9-4, Sat. 9-5, Sun. noon-5, June-Aug.; Tues.-Fri. 9-4, Sat. 9-5, Sun. noon-5 (also last Mon. of the month 1-5), rest of year. Closed holidays. Admission $4, under 1 free; free to all first Sun. of the month. MC, VI. Phone (608) 256-6445.

MONONA TERRACE COMMUNITY AND CONVENTION CENTER is 2 blks. e. of Capitol Sq. at 1 John Nolen Dr. Frank Lloyd Wright proposed this civic center on the shore of Lake Monona in 1938.

The 250,000-square-foot complex bears Wright's signature style of dramatic open spaces, circular forms and expansive views of the outdoors.

A photograph exhibition of Wright's work and the Madison Sports Hall of Fame are included.

Food is available. Center open daily 8-5. Guided tours are offered daily at 1. Center free. Tours $3; under 18, $2. MC, VI. Phone (608) 261-4000.

OLBRICH BOTANICAL GARDENS is at 3330 Atwood Ave. This oasis on the shores of Lake Monona includes 14 acres of specialty gardens, a 50-foot-high glass conservatory and what is said to be the only Thai pavilion and garden in the United States. The rose garden has more than 125 varieties and 700 individual rose bushes, while the rock garden features hardier flora. Other gardens display herbs, hostas, perennials, wildflowers and annuals.

Guided tours are available by appointment. Allow 2 hours minimum. Gardens open daily 8-8, Apr.-Sept.; 9-4, rest of year. Conservatory open Mon.-Sat. 10-4, Sun. 10-5. Closed Jan. 1, Thanksgiving and Dec. 25. Gardens and Thai pavilion admission free. Conservatory $1, under 6 free; free to all Wed. and Sat. 10-noon except during special exhibits. Phone (608) 246-4550.

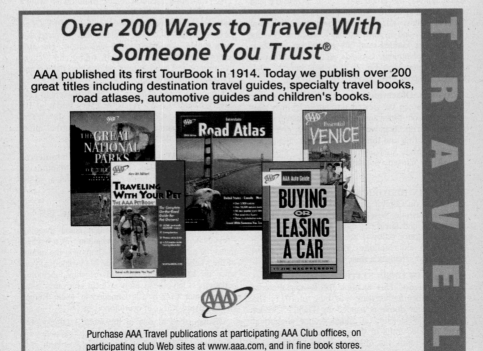

THE UNIVERSITY OF WISCONSIN is w. of downtown. Opened in 1848 with 20 students, the university now occupies a 1,000-acre campus. The Kohl Center Arena, on campus, is home to the university's basketball and hockey teams. A campus assistance and visitor center is in the "Old Red Gym" at 716 Langdon St. The center is open Mon.-Fri. 8-6, Sat. 10-3, Sun. 11-3; hours vary during university breaks and holidays. Phone (608) 263-2400.

Elvehjem Museum of Art is at 800 University Ave. The permanent collection includes more than 16,000 artworks dating from 2300 B.C. to the present. American and western European paintings, sculpture, prints and drawings as well as ancient and Asian art are featured. Other highlights are changing exhibits and the Kohler Art Library, with more than 100,000 volumes. Tues.-Fri. 9-5, Sat.-Sun. 11-5; closed Jan. 1, Thanksgiving and Dec. 24-25. Free. Phone (608) 263-2246.

Geology Museum is in Weeks Hall at Charter and W. Dayton sts. Mineral, rock and fossil exhibits include the skeletons of a 33-foot-long duck-billed dinosaur and a Wisconsin mastodon. Additional highlights include a 6-foot rotating globe and a walk-through model of a limestone cave. Mon.-Fri. 8:30-4:30, Sat. 9-1; closed holidays. Free. Phone (608) 262-1412 or (608) 262-2399.

University of Wisconsin Madison Arboretum is at 1207 Seminole Hwy. Covering 1,260 acres along Lake Wingra, the arboretum acts as a research and study area and features natural plant and animal communities native to Wisconsin, including flowering trees, shrubs and a renowned lilac collection. Pets are not allowed. Guided tours are offered on weekends and by appointment. Grounds daily 7 a.m.-10 p.m. Visitor center Mon.-Fri. 9:30-4, Sat.-Sun. 12:30-4. Closed holidays. Free. Phone (608) 263-7888.

Washburn Observatory is at 1401 Observatory Dr. Objects can be viewed through a 15-inch telescope. Astronomers are available to answer questions. Open in clear weather every Wed. at 9 p.m., June-Aug.; first and third Wed. at 9 p.m., Sept.-Oct. and April-May; first and third Wed. at 7:30 p.m., Nov.-Mar. Closed holidays. Free. Phone (608) 262-9274.

WISCONSIN HISTORICAL MUSEUM is at 30 N. Carroll St. on Capitol Sq. Permanent and changing exhibits illustrate Wisconsin's history from prehistoric times and territorial days to social issues and the 20th century. Allow 1 hour minimum. Tues.-Sat. 9-4; closed major holidays. Donations. Phone (608) 264-6557 to schedule a tour.

 WISCONSIN STATE CAPITOL is on Capitol Sq. This example of Roman Renaissance architecture was built in 1917. The white granite dome is topped by Daniel Chester French's "Wisconsin," a gilded bronze allegorical statue. Guided tours of the rotunda, the governor's conference room, the Supreme Court of Wisconsin and the Senate and Assembly chambers include commentary about the building's history and the artworks in the various rooms.

Allow 1 hour minimum. Building open Mon.-Fri. 8-6, Sat.-Sun. and holidays 8-4. Tours are given on the hour Mon.-Fri. 9-11 and 1-4, Sat. 9-11 and 1-3, Sun. 1-3. Free. Phone (608) 266-0382.

WISCONSIN VETERANS MUSEUM is downtown at 30 W. Mifflin St. The site is dedicated to the men and women of Wisconsin who served in America's conflicts from the Civil War to the Persian Gulf War.

The 19th Century Gallery houses exhibits recounting events of the Civil War and Spanish American War; it features a diorama dramatizing the Battle of Antietam. Visitors can view displays illustrating the Mexican Border Campaign, World War I, World War II, the Korean War, the Vietnam War and the Persian Gulf War in the 20th Century Gallery.

Three aircraft are suspended from the gallery ceiling: a Sopwith "Camel" biplane from World War I, a P-51 "Mustang" from World War II and a "Huey" helicopter from the Vietnam War.

Allow 1 hour minimum. Mon.-Sat. 9-4:30, Sun. noon-4, Apr.-Sept.; Mon.-Sat. 9-4:30, rest of year. Closed holidays. Free. Phone (608) 267-1799.

MANITOWISH WATERS (B-5) elev. 1,640′

A year-round vacation center, Manitowish Waters is in the Northern Highland-American Legion State Forest *(see Recreation Chart and the AAA Great Lakes CampBook)*. The waters that inspired the town's name consist of a 10-lake chain. The area offers water sports, tennis, golf, riding and archery in summer and cross-country skiing, ice fishing and snowmobiling in winter.

Cranberry tours depart from North Lakeland Discovery Center, US 51 to CR W, every Friday at 10, mid-July to mid-October. A videotape is shown and cranberry refreshments are served. For further information contact the chamber of commerce.

Manitowish Waters Chamber of Commerce: US 51 and Airport Rd., P.O. Box 251, Manitowish Waters, WI 54545; phone (715) 543-8488 or (888) 626-9877.

MANITOWOC (F-8) pop. 34,053, elev. 595′

Manitowoc, an American Indian name meaning "the abode of the Great Spirit Manitou," is a leading industrial and shipping center. Its harbor at the mouth of the Manitowoc River has made it an important port since the early 1830s. Hundreds of ships, including submarines, have been built at local shipyards since the schooner *Citizen* was launched in 1848; Burger Boat shipyard still is in operation.

Distinguished as one of the world's largest producers of aluminum ware, the city balances its commercial enterprises with refuges for both animals and nature lovers. Collins Marsh Wildlife

Refuge, 16 miles west of Manitowoc on CR JJ, is a natural haven for wildfowl; it is open May through October on a limited basis.

The SS *Badger*, operated by the Lake Michigan Carferry Service, offers 4-hour cruises and car-ferry service from Manitowoc to Ludington, Mich. For information and fares phone (888) 643-3779. Several charter fishing associations also operate out of the town. *See color ad p. 81 & color ad below.*

Manitowoc Visitor & Convention Bureau & Visitor Information Center: junction I-43 and US 151, P.O. Box 966, Manitowoc, WI 54221-0966; phone (920) 683-4388 or (800) 627-4896.

Shopping areas: In nearby Mishicot, 7 miles north via CR B at 315 Elizabeth St., is the Old School House, which contains 12 shops. Particularly noteworthy are the Frances Hook Room, which displays paintings and figurines, and the Rockwell Center. The latter contains one of the country's largest collections of Norman Rockwell paintings, plates and artwork and offers slide presentations; phone (920) 755-4560.

[SAVE] **PINECREST HISTORICAL VILLAGE** is 3 mi. w. of I-43 via CR JJ to Pine Crest Ln. The village, which depicts rural life in Manitowoc County from the 1850s to the early 1900s, contains a collection of restored buildings relocated to this 60-acre site. Structures include three log houses, a smokehouse, cheese factory, church, school, blacksmith shop, harness shop, saloon, general store, firehouse, town hall and train depot with a caboose and an 1887 engine.

Allow 1 hour minimum. Daily 9-5, July 1-Labor Day; 9-4, May-June; 10-4, day after Labor Day-third Sun. in Oct. Admission $6; ages 6-17, $4; family rate $15. Phone (920) 684-5110 or (920) 684-4445.

[GEM] **RAHR-WEST ART MUSEUM** is at 610 N. 8th St. Housed in a Victorian mansion, the museum contains period furnishings, Chinese ivory, dolls and porcelain objects. An art gallery presents changing exhibits. Mon.-Fri. 10-4 (also Wed. 4-8), Sat.-Sun. 11-4; closed holidays. Free. Phone (920) 683-4501.

[GEM] **WISCONSIN MARITIME MUSEUM** is off I-43 exit 152, 4 mi. e. on US 10, then 1 mi. s. to 75 Maritime Dr. Exhibit galleries [SAVE] depict the history of shipping on the Great Lakes. Model ships range from an 1847 three-masted schooner to present-day vessels. Maps, charts and nautical equipment also are displayed. Of note is an exhibit about submarine building during World War II. Special events take place during the year.

Allow 2 hours minimum. Daily 9-6, Memorial Day weekend-Labor Day; Mon.-Fri. 9-5, Sat.-Sun. 9-6, day after Labor Day-Oct. 31 and Apr.1-day before Memorial Day weekend; Mon.-Fri. 9-5, rest of year. Closed Jan. 1, Easter, Thanksgiving and Dec. 25. Admission $7; over 59, $6.75; ages 6-12, $6. Combination ticket with submarine tour $9; over 59, $8.50; ages 6-12, $7; family rate $28 (two adults and two children under 18). DS, MC, VI. Phone (920) 684-0218.

The Submariners Memorial USS *Cobia* is docked in the Manitowoc River next to the museum. The *Cobia* is a World War II submarine of the same class as those built at the Manitowoc shipyards during the war. Allow 1 hour minimum. Guided tours are given daily; phone ahead for schedule information. Admission is only with a combination ticket from the Wisconsin Maritime Museum. Phone (920) 684-0218.

MARINETTE (D-8) pop. 11,749, elev. 597′

Wisconsin's "Queen City" was named after Queen Marinette, a woman of French and Chippewa Indian extraction. With her husband, William Farnsworth, she operated a fur-trading post during Marinette's early years. From 1830 to 1930 the city was regarded as the white pine producing center of the world. In all, more than 10 billion board feet of logs were floated down the Menominee River when the sawmills were in operation.

Wood products still figure in the economy of Marinette, but diversified industry and retail merchandising are now the principal support of this port at the mouth of the Menominee River. The city also serves as a trade center for the surrounding

area in Marinette County, which encompasses 250 lakes, 50 trout streams and numerous waterfalls.

Marinette Area Chamber of Commerce: 601 Marinette Ave., P.O. Box 512, Marinette, WI 54143; phone (715) 735-6681 or (800) 236-6681.

MARINETTE COUNTY HISTORICAL MUSEUM is downtown on US 41 in Stephenson Island Park. The museum houses early farming and logging tools and hand-carved miniatures of logging operations. American Indian items as well as furniture and other household items also are displayed. Stephenson Island Park offers picnic facilities, a playground and a boat ramp. Allow 1 hour minimum. Tues.-Sat. 10-4:30, Sun. noon-4, Memorial Day weekend-Labor Day; otherwise by appointment. Admission $2; ages 13-18, $1. Phone (715) 732-0831.

MARSHFIELD (E-5) pop. 18,800, elev. 1,276'

Marshfield once was a railroad hub with 50 trains stopping daily as hotels were crowded with passengers awaiting connections to go "out West" or "back East." In the early days of the Marshfield Clinic, one of the country's largest medical clinics, physicians rode the trains to serve patients in smaller outlying communities.

Hiking, bicycling, camping and swimming are popular during summer. In winter Marshfield provides ample opportunity for cross-country skiing, snowmobiling and hunting. Marshfield Super Speedway is host to stock car races; phone (715) 384-8325.

Marshfield Convention & Visitors Bureau: 700 S. Central Ave., P.O. Box 868, Marshfield, WI 54449; phone (715) 384-4016 or (800) 422-4541.

NEW VISIONS GALLERY is 8 blks. n. of SR 13 in the Marshfield Clinic at 1000 N. Oak Ave. Permanent displays include posters by Marc Chagall, West African sculpture, Japanese prints, Haitian paintings, Australian aboriginal art and original prints by modern artists. Temporary exhibits change every 6 to 8 weeks. Allow 1 hour minimum. Mon.-Fri. 9-5:30, Sat. 11-3; closed holidays. Free. Phone (715) 387-5562.

WILDWOOD PARK & ZOO is at 1800 S. Central Ave., 1 blk. w. of SR 13. Home to more than 200 animals and birds, the 60-acre park offers picnic facilities, tennis courts, a swimming pool, nature trails, a nine-hole Frisbee golf course and cross-country skiing areas. Allow 1 hour minimum. Park open daily 6 a.m.-10:30 p.m. Zoo open daily 8-7:30, early May to late Sept.; 8-6, late Sept. to mid-Oct.; Mon.-Sat. 8-3, rest of year. Closed Jan. 1, Thanksgiving, Dec. 24-25 and 31. Free. Phone (715) 384-4642.

MELLEN (B-4) pop. 835, elev. 1,240'

South of Copper Falls State Park *(see attraction listing)* and surrounded by the wooded hills of the Penokee Mountain Range, Mellen is a lumbering town

as well as an eastern gateway to Chequamegon-Nicolet National Forest *(see place listing p. 126)*. The red and black granite quarried in the area is used widely for monuments and buildings.

Mellen Area Chamber of Commerce: 125 E. Bennett Ave., P.O. Box 193, Mellen, WI 54546; phone (715) 274-2330.

COPPER FALLS STATE PARK is 2 mi. n.e. on SR 169. The 2,483-acre park is named for falls where the Bad and Tyler Forks rivers flow over the edge of the Keeweenawan traprock into a canyon. A self-guiding nature trail leads to several observation points. Loon Lake has a sand beach for swimming as well as a canoe launch and access to hiking trails with waterfalls.

Daily 6 a.m.-11 p.m. Admission per private vehicle $10, state residents $5. Annual permit $30, state residents $20. Phone (715) 274-5123. *See Recreation Chart and the AAA Great Lakes CampBook.*

MENOMONIE (E-2) pop. 14,937, elev. 794′

Menomonie began as a lumber mill settlement on the Red Cedar River in 1830. Almost 50 years later the town's lumber corporation had become one of the largest in the world. Dairying later replaced lumbering as the city's economic mainstay.

Several 19th-century attractions downtown recall the days of the early lumber barons. Near Lake Menomin stand the 1868 John Holly Knapp House and the 1846 Wilson Place, stately Victorian mansions of the founders of Knapp Stout & Co. At Wilson Circle, Wilson Place, now a museum depicting the early settlement era, was the estate of Sen. James H. Stout, founder of the University of Wisconsin-Stout in Menomonie.

Of humbler origin is the home of Caddie Woodlawn, the subject of the award-winning children's book "Caddie Woodlawn" by Carol Ryrie Brink. A memorial park, 8 miles south on SR 25, contains the pioneer girl's home and provides picnic facilities.

Bordering the Red Cedar River along the western city limits is the 14-mile limestone-surfaced Red Cedar State Park Trail for bicyclists, hikers and cross-country skiers. Lake Menomin offers boating, and the Red Cedar River provides good fishing. Hoffman Hills State Recreation Area, 9 miles northeast, has 8 miles of trails. During the summer the Ludington Guard Band performs every Tuesday evening at 8 in the Wilson Park band shell.

Menomonie Area Chamber of Commerce: 342 E. Main St., Suite 200, Menomonie, WI 54751; phone (715) 235-9087 or (800) 283-1862.

SAVE **THE MABEL TAINTER MEMORIAL BUILD-ING** is at 205 Main St. Built in 1889, the Moorish-style building contains a public reading room, meeting rooms and an ornate Victorian theater. Decorated with mahogany, oak, Italian marble and polished brass, the theater features an unusual organ with 1,597 pipes and 25 stops. Performing arts programs, an exhibit gallery and daily historic guided tours also are featured.

Allow 1 hour minimum. Tours are given daily on the hour 1-4, except when theater is in use; a 15-minute peek tour also is available; closed Easter and Dec. 25. Admission $5; over 61, $4; ages 6-12, $3. Peek tour $3. AX, DS, MC, VI. Phone (715) 235-0001.

SAVE **RUSSELL J. RASSBACH HERITAGE MU-SEUM** is at 1820 Wakanda St. in Wakanda Park. The museum features Victorian rooms, an interactive bank robbery exhibit, a children's discovery area, American Indian artifacts and historical displays including Civil War memorabilia. Wed.-Sun. 10-5, Memorial Day-Labor Day; Wed.-Sun. noon-4, rest of year. Closed July 4 and Dec. 25. Admission $4; over 65, $3; ages 12-17, $2; ages 6-11, $1; family rate $12. Phone (715) 232-8685.

MILTON (I-7) pop. 5,132, elev. 875′

Joseph Goodrich, an abolitionist from New York, fostered the growth of Milton when he established a stagecoach inn in 1844 on the site of three well-traveled trails. That same year marked the founding of Milton College, which closed in 1982. The former campus now accommodates a museum and visitor center as well as antique and craft shops. Milton is a leading manufacturer of electronic medical instruments. Agribusiness also supports the community.

Milton Area Chamber of Commerce: 508 Campus St., P.O. Box 222, Milton, WI 53563; phone (608) 868-6222.

MILTON HOUSE MUSEUM is at 18 S. Janesville St. Built by Joseph Goodrich in 1844, the six-sided house was the first poured-concrete home in the United States. A guided tour includes the house, a 20-room former stagecoach inn, an Underground Railroad tunnel, an 1837 log cabin and a country store. Also featured is a miniature replica of the original inn. Allow 1 hour minimum. Daily 10-5, Memorial Day-Labor Day; Sat.-Sun. 10-5, May 1-day before Memorial Day. Admission $5; over 61, $4; ages 5-12, $2. Phone (608) 868-7772.

DID YOU KNOW

The Green Bay Packers are the only NFL team to have won three championships in a row; they accomplished that feat twice.

Milwaukee

During the 19th century immigrants from more than 30 European countries flocked to Milwaukee, bringing with them their skills, arts and cuisines. Germans were the largest group; as the decades passed their *gemütlichkeit* (hospitality) assumed Italian, Polish, Scandinavian, Irish and other national overtones.

Milwaukee's watery surroundings, while a boon to its eventual development as a river port, posed a few problems during its early years. A fierce rivalry developed over the question of payment for the Milwaukee River bridges that connected the two villages of Juneautown and Kilbourntown. The Great Bridge War was settled by the legislature in 1845, but not before both factions angrily had torn down every bridge and the residents of Juneautown had trained a loaded cannon on Kilbourntown.

The new city of Milwaukee witnessed the arrival of the Forty-eighters, refugees from unsuccessful revolutionary movements against German monarchies in 1848. This intellectual minority launched the city into new cultural and political directions, endowing the city with theaters, music societies, athletic clubs and Freethinker groups. They also established a reform tradition that later gave rise to Milwaukee's distinctive brand of socialism.

During the last half of the 19th century, the reference to Milwaukee as the German Athens was hardly an exaggeration. Only the Polish and Irish populations came close in number. English was almost never heard in some neighborhoods, especially on the northwest side. By the late 1870s Milwaukee had six daily newspapers published in German.

Public schools zealously enforced their requirement that German be taught from kindergarten on. Ever-popular were family picnics at such open-air beer gardens as the Schlitz Palm Garden. By the end of the century, however, German cultural allegiances had begun to fade. The decision of the Stadt Theater, pride of Milwaukee's German culture, to alternate plays in German and English was an indisputable sign of changing times.

In reality Milwaukee's northern European heritage never disappeared. Its influence survived, despite such setbacks as World War I's repressive effect on the German community and Prohibition's nearly fatal blow to the city's brewing industry. The period following World War II brought massive development.

Milwaukee is the state's largest city, its primary commercial and manufacturing center and one of its busiest ports, as well as a major grain market. Called the "machine shop of America," Milwaukee ranks among the nation's principal industrial cities and is a leader in the production of equipment for the generation and distribution of electrical power. Factories also manufacture motorcycles, mining machinery and combustion engines.

Saukville / Donald S. Abrams / Wisconsin Dept of Tourism

Wisconsin Avenue Bridge / © Richard Cummins / SuperStock

But what really has made Milwaukee famous is beer. Though other industries have dethroned the king since 1889, the brewing industry remains synonymous with the city. Besides the ubiquitous smell of malt in the air, associations with brewing are everywhere. Wealthy brewers and other industrialists built lavish houses, some of which have been converted to public museums. One of the nation's largest breweries has its headquarters in Milwaukee.

Although modern steel and glass high rises occupy much of the downtown area, Milwaukee's European heritage is evident in the design of some of the city's noteworthy buildings and residences. The blue-domed Annunciation Greek Orthodox Church, a magnificent example of Byzantine architecture, came from the drawing board of Frank Lloyd Wright.

City Hall and Pabst Theater, both built in the 1890s in the Flemish Renaissance style, have been preserved carefully. Residents also embrace the return of a few old German cafes and beer gardens, where zither music is played and sauerbraten is served with the suds.

Approaches

By Car

From the north I-43 provides controlled access into downtown Milwaukee. I-94 affords direct access to the downtown area from Chicago and other southern points. From the west I-94 is the controlled-access highway into the city. Bypassing the metropolitan area to the south and west, I-894 provides the best connection for the I-94 through corridor.

Getting Around

Street System

Lake Michigan flanks the city on the east, and Wisconsin Avenue is the main downtown east-west thoroughfare. The Milwaukee River divides the downtown area into approximately equal east and west sections; I-94 is the approximate dividing line between north and south street addresses. Streets are numbered in ascending order west of the Milwaukee River and continue well into the suburbs to the Milwaukee County line.

The official unposted speed limit is 25 mph; other limits are posted. Rush hours are 7-9 a.m. and 3:30-6 p.m. Right turns are permitted on red unless otherwise posted.

Parking

Private commercial lots are scattered throughout the downtown area and near the airport. Lot rates are $3-$4 per hour and $7-$13 for all-day parking. Private lots within four blocks of the Midwest

(continued on p. 152)

The Informed Traveler

City Population: 596,974

Elevation: 740 ft.

Sales Tax: The sales tax in Milwaukee is 5.6 percent. There also is a 9 percent tax on hotel rooms, a 3 percent tax on car rentals and a .25 percent tax on food and beverage purchases.

WHOM TO CALL

Emergency: 911

Police (non-emergency): (414) 765-2323

Time: (414) 844-1414

Weather: (414) 936-1212

Hospitals: Aurora Sinai Medical Center, (414) 219-2000, Columbia Hospital, (414) 961-3300; Froedtert Memorial Lutheran Hospital, (414) 805-3000; St. Francis Hospital, (414) 647-5000; St. Luke's Medical Center, (414) 649-6000 and St. Mary's Hospital, (414) 291-1000.

WHERE TO LOOK

Newspapers

The morning daily *Milwaukee Journal/Sentinel* is Milwaukee's major newspaper.

Radio

Milwaukee radio station WTMJ (620 AM) is an all-news/weather/sports station; WUWM (89.7 FM) is a member of National Public Radio.

Visitor Information

Information is available at the Greater Milwaukee Convention and Visitors Bureau inside the Midwest Airlines Center, 400 W. Wisconsin Ave., Milwaukee, WI 53203, Mon.-Fri. 8-5. Phone (414) 908-6205 or (800) 554-1448.

TRANSPORTATION

Air Travel

General Mitchell International Airport, 8 miles south via I-94 East, is served by several major domestic and international passenger carriers. Transportation to and from the airport by taxi takes about 20 minutes. One-way fares range from $15 to $20. The Milwaukee County Transit System operates buses to and from the airport from all points on its system via transfers from 5 a.m. to 12:30 a.m.; the fare is $1.75. Phone (414) 344-6711.

Rental Cars

Hertz, at the airport, (414) 747-5200 or (800) 654-3080, offers discounts to AAA members.

Rail Service

Amtrak, 433 W. St. Paul Ave., provides railroad passenger service to the city; phone (414) 271-9037, or (800) 872-7245 for reservations.

Buses

The Greyhound Lines Inc. terminal is at 606 N. James Lovell St.; phone (414) 272-2156 or (800) 231-2222.

Taxis

All taxis in Milwaukee use the meter system. The fare is $3.75 for the first mile, $2 for each additional mile and 75c for each additional person. Taxis can be ordered by phone or hired at taxi stands at most major hotels. Yellow Cab is the city's major taxi service; phone (414) 271-1800.

Public Transport

The Milwaukee County Transit System, 1942 N. 17th St., operates 22-hour service throughout Milwaukee County and eastern Waukesha County. The fare is $1.75; ages 6-11, 90c. Exact fare is required. For schedule and route information daily 6 a.m.-10 p.m. phone (414) 344-6711.

Destination Milwaukee

Milwaukee has a lot to offer visitors-from art museums to a variety of parks, gardens and nature centers.

Sightseeing is at its best here; horse-and-carriage tours, cruises and scenic drives are offered. The young and young-at-heart can enjoy an impressive zoo, an enormous ice-skating facility and a clown hall of fame.

© Gibson Stock Photography

Milwaukee Public Museum. Ocean exhibits give visitors a fish-eyed view of underwater life. (See listing page 154)

Greater Milwaukee CVB

Pabst Mansion, Milwaukee. Stained-glass windows and ornamental ironwork adorn this 37- room mansion built for beer baron Capt. Frederick Pabst. (See listing page 152)

West Bend

Saukville • Port Washington

Cedarburg • Grafton

Hartford

Erin

Milwaukee

Oconomowoc

Waukesha

Eagle

See Downtown map page 152

© Richard Cummins Lonely Planet Images

Old World Wisconsin, Eagle. See what life in 19th-century Wisconsin entailed at this 576-acre state historic site, which includes Yankee farmsteads. (See listing page 159)

Places included in this AAA Destination City:

Airlines Center and Bradley Center provide parking for functions at the centers.

What To See

AMERICA'S BLACK HOLOCAUST MUSEUM is at 2233 N. 4th St. Historical exhibits, a video presentation and a live commentary follow the struggle of African-Americans through slavery and the battle for civil rights. Guided tours are available. Allow 1 hour minimum. Mon.-Sat. 9-5; closed major holidays. Admission $5; senior citizens, $4; ages 5-17, $3. MC, VI. Phone (414) 264-2500.

BASILICA OF ST. JOSAPHAT is at 569 W. Lincoln Ave. Built in 1901 by Polish immigrants, this Romanesque basilica was designed after St. Peter's in Rome and features one of the largest domes in the world. The interior is noted for its hand-carved marble pulpit, ornate stained glass, murals and gilded plasterwork.

Guided tours are available by appointment. Allow 30 minutes minimum. Mon.-Fri. 9-4; closed holidays. Masses are open to the public Sat. at 4:30, Sun. at 8, 10 and noon. Donations. Phone (414) 645-5623.

BETTY BRINN CHILDREN'S MUSEUM is at 929 E. Wisconsin Ave. in the Miller Pavilion at O'Donnell Park. Designed specifically for children under 11, the museum offers hands-on exhibits, interactive programs, activities and workshops. Exhibits include A Trading Place; WBB-TV; Toys by Us; Sound All Around; My Body Works; Let's Play Railway; and Betty's Busy Backyard, a play area for children under 3.

Allow 1 hour minimum. Mon.-Sat. 9-5, Sun. noon-5, June-Aug.; Tues.-Sat. 9-5, Sun. noon-5, rest of year. Closed major holidays. Admission $4; under 1 free. DS, MC, VI. Phone (414) 390-5437.

THE CAPTAIN FREDERICK PABST MANSION is at 2000 W. Wisconsin Ave. This 37-room Flemish Renaissance mansion was built in 1892 for beer baron Capt. Frederick Pabst. The building is highlighted by carved wood, stained-glass windows, nine bedrooms, 14 fireplaces and ornamental ironwork.

Allow 1 hour, 30 minutes minimum. Guided tours depart on the hour Mon.-Sat. 10-3:30, Sun. noon-3:30, Mar. 1 to mid Nov.; Mon.-Sat. 10-4, Sun. noon-4, mid-Nov. to mid-Jan.; Tues.-Sat. 10:30-3:30, Sun. noon-3:30, rest of year. Closed

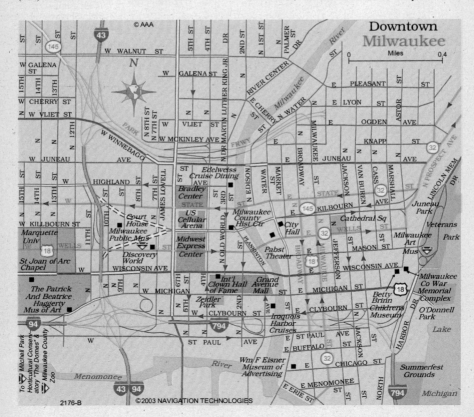

major holidays. Admission $7; over 62 and students with ID $6; ages 6-17, $3. Prices may vary during special events. MC, VI. Phone (414) 931-0808.

CENTRAL UNITED METHODIST CHURCH is on Wisconsin Ave. at 639 N. 25th St. Noted for its revolutionary architecture based on energy efficiency, the church building is partially underground with an earth-covered roof. Prairielike landscaping is incorporated in the overall design; a large bell tower collects solar energy. Mon.-Fri. 9-3:30. Free. Phone (414) 344-1600.

DISCOVERY WORLD:—THE JAMES LOVELL MUSEUM OF SCIENCE, ECONOMICS AND TECHNOLOGY is at 815 N. James Lovell St. More than 150 hands-on exhibits explore science, technology and economics. Shows demonstrating scientific principles are offered on weekends. Allow 1 hour minimum. Daily 9-5; closed July 4, Thanksgiving and Dec. 25. Admission $6; over 61, $5; ages 3-15, $4.25. DS, MC, VI. Phone (414) 765-9966.

[SAVE] **THE INTERNATIONAL CLOWN HALL OF FAME** is at 161 W. Wisconsin Ave., Suite LL700, in Grand Avenue Mall. Dedicated to the preservation and advancement of clown art, the museum displays clown clothing, shoes, props and memorabilia. Paintings and videotaped presentations of clowns can be seen. Clown shows are scheduled periodically; phone ahead.

Guided tours are available. Allow 1 hour, 30 minutes minimum. Mon.-Fri. 10-4; closed Jan. 1, Memorial Day, Labor Day, Thanksgiving and Dec. 25. Admission $2, under 6 free. Additional fee for clown shows. MC, VI. Phone (414) 319-0848.

MILWAUKEE CITY HALL is at 200 E. Wells St. Built in 1895 in the Flemish Renaissance style, the building is noted for its stained-glass windows, ornately carved woodwork and stenciled ceilings in the Common Council Chamber and anteroom. Guided tours are available by appointment when council is not in session. Open Mon.-Fri. 8-4; closed major holidays. Free. Phone (414) 286-2266.

MILWAUKEE COUNTY HISTORICAL CENTER is at 910 N. Old World 3rd St. The city's past is preserved through permanent and changing exhibits. Displays chronicle Milwaukee's early settlers; the Milwaukee socialist era; military history, including the Civil War and World War I; and panorama painters. There also is a slide presentation about the history of Milwaukee. Allow 1 hour minimum. Mon.-Fri. 9:30-5, Sat. 10-5, Sun. 1-5; closed holidays. Donation. Phone (414) 273-8288.

MILWAUKEE COUNTY WAR MEMORIAL COMPLEX includes five sites throughout the city. This living memorial consists of a performing arts center, three museums and a war memorial center. The Marcus Center for Performing Arts, 929 N. Water St., is the setting for concerts, plays and other cultural productions of the Milwaukee Symphony Orchestra, the Florentine Opera, the Milwaukee Ballet Company and First Stage Milwaukee Theater for Children. Tours of the complex are available by appointment. Phone (414) 273-7121 or (414) 273-7206 for the box office and tour reservations.

The Charles Allis Art Museum is at 1801 N. Prospect Ave. at the corner of E. Royall Pl. The museum occupies a Tudor-style mansion built in 1909 by Charles Allis, the first president of Allis-Chalmers Co. Spanning 2,000 years, the collection includes Chinese, Greek, Japanese, Korean, Persian and Roman art objects; fine American, English and French period furniture; Renaissance bronze objects; and landscapes by major 19th- and 20th-century French and American painters.

Allow 30 minutes minimum. Wed.-Sun. 1-5; closed holidays. Docent-guided tours are available Sun. 2-4. Admission $5, over 62 and students $3, under 13 free. Phone (414) 278-8295.

Milwaukee Art Museum is at 700 N. Art Museum Dr. Visitors enter the lakefront museum through Quadracci Pavilion, a 90-foot-high reception hall designed by Spanish architect Santiago Calatrava. Soaring above the white marble and glass pavilion is the Burke Brise Soleil, a winglike sunscreen that serves as a moving sculpture.

The museum was established in 1888 and houses more than 20,000 works dating from antiquity to the 20th century. Highlights include collections of the old masters; 19th- and 20th-century European and American art, including products of German Expressionism and the American Ash Can School; and modern art. Also featured are collections of Haitian art, American decorative arts and folk art and the Prairie School archives of Frank Lloyd Wright.

Allow 2 hours minimum. Daily 10-5 (also Thurs. 5-8); closed Jan. 1, Thanksgiving and Dec. 25. Admission $8; over 64, $6; students with ID $4; under 12 free with adult. Prices vary for special exhibitions. AX, MC, VI. Phone (414) 224-3200.

Villa Terrace Decorative Arts Museum is at 2220 N. Terrace Ave. Of 16th-century Italian Renaissance style, this 1923 villa was designed by architect David Adler. From the house, terraces cascade down a bluff to a formal garden at beach level. Exhibits of 15th- through 20th-century decorative arts include Spanish, Dutch and Italian paintings, English porcelains and wrought-iron works by Milwaukee blacksmith Cyril Colnik. Allow 30 minutes minimum. Wed.-Sun. 1-5. Admission $5, over 62 and students $3, under 13 free. Phone (414) 271-3656.

MILWAUKEE COUNTY ZOO is 6 mi. w. on US 18 between US 45 and SR 100 at 10001 W. Bluemound Rd. The zoo represents one of the country's largest, most comprehensive collections. More than 2,000 animals are displayed in five continental groupings giving the illusion that predator and prey are together. Among the exhibits are Humboldt penguins, African elephants and Guam Micronesian kingfishers.

The Apes of Africa features lowland gorillas and bonobos. The Wolf Woods exhibit is home to young timber wolves. Koalas can be seen in the Australian Building. The Aquatic and Reptile Center features endangered Chinese alligators, Caribbean iguanas and a 23,000-gallon Pacific Coast aquarium.

Other highlights include a close-up educational tour in open-air zoomobiles, rubber-tired trackless trains and 20 minute "Animals in Action" programs.

Stroller and wheelchair rentals and food are available. Allow 3 hours minimum. Zoo open Mon.-Sat. 9-5, Sun. and holidays 9-6, May-Sept.; daily 9-4:30, rest of year. Zoomobiles, petting zoo and miniature train daily Memorial Day weekend-Labor Day; Sat.-Sun. in spring and fall. Animals in Action shows daily 10:30-3 (weather permitting). Admission Apr.-Oct. $9; over 59, $8; ages 3-12, $6. Admission rest of year $7.50; over 59, $6; ages 3-12, $4.50. Zoomobile $1.50; ages 3-12, $1. Miniature train $2; ages 3-12, $1. Parking $7. DS, MC, VI. Phone (414) 771-3040. *See ad p. 153.*

MILWAUKEE PUBLIC MUSEUM is at 800 W. Wells St. Natural and cultural history are the focus of such walk-through exhibits as Temples, Tells and Tombs, a display of artifacts from ancient Mediterranean civilizations. The Tribute to Survival exhibit provides an overview of North American Indian history and culture.

Visitors to the museum can walk through a Costa Rican rain forest and the turn-of-the-20th-century streets of Old Milwaukee. A glass-enclosed tropical garden showcases butterflies and a live insect display features bugs from around the world. Cultural celebrations and changing exhibits are offered throughout the year at the museum, which houses the Humphrey IMAX Dome Theater.

Guided tours and food are available. Daily 9-5; closed July 4, Thanksgiving and Dec. 25. Admission $7; over 61, $6; ages 3-15, $4.75. IMAX movies are additional. Combination tickets are available. MC, VI. Phone (414) 278-2702, or (414) 319-4629 for IMAX information.

MITCHELL PARK HORTICULTURAL CONSERVATORY—"THE DOMES" is off I-94 exit 309B, just w. on St. Paul Ave., then .7 mi. s. on 27th St. to 524 S. Layton Blvd. Three glass domes, each seven stories high and 140 feet in diameter, house a variety of exotic gardens.

The Arid Dome features plants from the world's deserts, such as cactuses, succulents, palms and grasses. More than 750 species of plants, including orchids, thrive in the Tropical Dome; birds, lizards and frogs also inhabit this rain forest-like environment. Five themed floral displays each year are presented in the Show Dome; the displays of lilies and poinsettias are spectacular at Easter and Christmas. Picnicking is allowed with a permit.

Allow 1 hour, 30 minutes minimum. Daily 9-5. Admission $4.50; ages 6-17 and the physically impaired $3. Free to Milwaukee County residents with ID Mon. 9-11:30. Phone (414) 649-9800, or (414) 649-4954 for a picnic permit.

THE PATRICK AND BEATRICE HAGGERTY MUSEUM OF ART is on the e. mall of the Marquette University campus at 13th and Clybourn sts. More than 4,000 works of art include Renaissance, Baroque and modern paintings; sculpture, prints and photographs; and Asian, tribal and decorative arts. Traveling exhibits also are featured. Allow 1 hour minimum. Mon.-Sat. 10-4:30 (also Thurs. 4:30-8), Sun. noon-5; closed Jan. 1, Easter, Thanksgiving and Dec. 25. Free. Phone (414) 288-1669.

PETTIT NATIONAL ICE CENTER is s. of I-94 exit 306 at 500 S. 84th St. The 200,000-square-foot U.S. Olympic training facility houses one of three 400-meter speed skating ovals in North America, and two full-internationally-sized rinks for hockey, figure skating and short-track speed skating. The center hosts local, regional, national and international competitions in skating sports, and the ice is open to the public several times daily. Warm clothing is recommended.

Guided tours are available by appointment only. Allow 30 minutes minimum. Daily 8 a.m.-9 p.m. Phone for public skating times. Spectators free except during special events. Guided tours $3; over 61 and under 12, $2. Skating $6; over 61 and under 13, $5. Skate rentals $2.50. MC, VI. Phone (414) 266-0100.

ST. JOAN OF ARC CHAPEL is at 601 N. 14th St. on Central Mall on the campus of Marquette University. This 15th-century French chapel stood in the Rhone River Valley for more than 500 years. After the French Revolution, the chapel was moved in 1927 to a Long Island estate and reconstructed stone by stone by architect John Russell Pope.

In 1965 it again was reconstructed at Marquette University. Incorporated within the structure is the Joan of Arc Stone, before which the saint supposedly prayed.

Mon.-Sat. 10-4, Sun. noon-4; closed major holidays. Free. Phone (414) 288-6873.

SCHLITZ AUDUBON NATURE CENTER is 1 mi. e. of I-43 exit 82A at 1111 E. Brown Deer Rd. This 185-acre nature center and sanctuary on the shores of Lake Michigan, once the home of wagon horses, has about 6 miles of trails. Clump planting has provided habitats for native animals and birds, and a 60-foot observation tower offers views of Lake Michigan and the surrounding countryside.

The Dorothy K. Vallier Environmental Learning Center is a 30,000-square-foot facility housing an auditorium, classrooms, exhibits and a nature preschool.

Center and trails open daily 9-5; closed Jan. 1, Thanksgiving and Dec. 25. Admission $4; over 61 and ages 2-12, $2. MC, VI. Phone (414) 352-2880.

UNIVERSITY OF WISCONSIN-MILWAUKEE encompasses 90 acres on Downer Ave. Founded in 1885 as the Milwaukee Normal School, UWM now has an enrollment of more than 22,000 students. The university's programs in architecture and urban planning are considered among the best in the country. The Institute of Visual Arts offers contemporary exhibitions at several sites on campus; for information phone (414) 229-5070.

American Geographical Society Library is at 2311 E. Hartford Ave. in the Golda Meir Library. An exceptional collection of material relates to geography, exploration, map making, earth science and history. Highlights include maps, globes and geography-related books, including many rare items. Mon.-Fri. 8-4:30; closed major holidays. Free. Phone (414) 229-6282.

WHITNALL PARK is at 5879 S. 92nd St. One of the largest municipal parks in the nation, the 660-acre grounds encompass an 18-hole golf course, an archery range, a variety of all-year recreational facilities, picnic areas, nature trails, an environmental education center and botanical gardens. In winter the park is popular for cross-country skiing and sledding. Park open daily dawn-dusk. Free. Phone (414) 425-7303.

Boerner Botanical Gardens is at 9400 Boerner Dr. The rose garden has more than 3,000 rose plants of 500 varieties; each year more than 11,000 annuals are planted for seasonal floral exhibitions. Also included are the perennial and herb gardens, as well as the tulip display and the crab apple collection, which is one of the largest in North America. The Garden House contains art exhibits.

Allow 1 hour minimum. Formal gardens and Garden House open daily 8 a.m.-dusk, mid-Apr. through Sept. 30; otherwise varies. Admission $4; over 59, $3; ages 6-17, $2. Phone (414) 525-5610.

Wehr Nature Center is in the center of the park at 9701 W. College Ave. Natural history displays are featured at the center, which includes a 30-acre prairie restoration site and more than 5 miles of nature trails in its surrounding woodlands and wetlands. Seasonal hikes and lectures are conducted by naturalists. Daily 8-4:30; closed Thanksgiving and Dec. 24-26. Donations; fee for special events. Parking (May-Sept.) $2.50. Phone (414) 425-8550.

WILLIAM F. EISNER MUSEUM OF ADVERTISING is at 208 N. Water St. The museum is a component of the Milwaukee Institute of Art & Design. The development of graphic design and its relationship to advertising is explained with an interactive video and exhibits, an educational center and a simulated radio station. Allow 30 minutes minimum. Wed.-Fri. 11-5 (also Thurs. 5-8), Sat. noon-5, Sun. 1-5; closed major holidays. Admission $4.50; over 55, $2.50; under 12 free with adult. AX, DS, MC, VI. Phone (414) 847-3290.

What To Do

Sightseeing

Boat Tours

EDELWEISS CRUISE DINING departs from Riverfront Plaza; take the I-794 Plankinton Ave. exit, 6 blks. n. to Kilbourne Ave., then 1 blk. to 1110 Old World 3rd St. Visitors can enjoy lunch, dinner, brunch and hors d'oeuvre cruises through downtown Milwaukee via the river and the harbors of Lake Michigan. The 2-hour cruises depart at various times Thurs.-Sun. between noon and 7:30, Apr.-Oct., rain or shine. Fare $15-$59. Reservations and full payment are required; no refunds within 72 hours of departure. AX, DS, MC, VI. Phone (414) 272-3625.

IROQUOIS HARBOR CRUISES departs between the Michigan and Clybourn St. bridges on the w. bank of the Milwaukee River at 505 N. Riverwalk Way. Narrated 75-minute cruises include such sights as the international shipping docks, breakwater, lighthouse and harbor entrance. Food is available. Trips depart daily at 1 (also Sat.-Sun. at 3), June 1-Labor Day. Fare $11.50; over 59, $11; ages 12-17, $9; one child under 12 free with adult (each additional child $8). MC, VI. Phone (414) 294-9450.

Bus and Limousine Tours

Several public and private charter transportation companies offer sightseeing tours that explore the city. Customized tours devoted to Milwaukee's industrial, cultural, civic and residential sights are available, often complemented by lunch or dinner.

Carriage Tours

Horse-drawn carriages offer a memorable means of transportation through downtown and along the shores of Lake Michigan. Shamrock Coach & Carriage, (414) 272-6873, provides nightly service (weather permitting).

Driving Tours

A scenic drive extends from the downtown area at Lincoln Memorial Drive, north to SR 32 through beautiful parks and past the lakeside mansions of the early brewers to Brown Deer Road. North Lake Drive along the bluffs is particularly attractive.

Industrial Tours

MILLER BREWING CO. is at 4251 W. State St. A guided tour of the facility includes a theater presentation, visits to the packaging and shipping centers, the brew house and the historic caves where beer barrels were cooled in the 1800s. Miller products can be sampled by guests over 21 with ID following the 1-hour guided tour that includes stairs and 4 blocks of walking. Strollers are not permitted on the tour. Tours depart the visitor center Mon.-Sat. Tour times and holiday schedules vary; phone ahead. Free. Phone (414) 931-2337 or (414) 931-2467.

Walking Tours

Brochures outlining historic walking tours of Milwaukee's east, west and south sides are available at the Greater Milwaukee Convention and Visitors Bureau as well as at visitor centers throughout the city *(see The Informed Traveler box)*. Campus tours are available at the University of Wisconsin-Milwaukee, (414) 229-2222, and at Marquette University, (414) 288-7302.

Historic Milwaukee Inc. offers guided walking tours that concentrate on the city's historical and architectural heritage. Ninety-minute tour options include Milwaukee's skywalk system, the Riverwalk, the city's historic German and Polish neighborhoods, mansions along Lake Drive, and historic districts such as Walker's Point, the Third Ward and Yankee Hill; phone (414) 277-7795.

Sports and Recreation

Milwaukee sports fans enthusiastically support their professional teams. **Baseball** fans make their pilgrimage to Miller Park, where the beloved Brewers play from April through September; phone (414) 902-4000. Almost before the last baseball game's hot dog can be digested, the NBA's Milwaukee Bucks begin **basketball** exhibition games. Regular season games are played until April at Bradley Center, 1001 N. 4th St.; phone (414) 227-0400 or (414) 227-0500. The Marquette University Golden Eagles also play at Bradley Center; phone (414) 227-0400 or (414) 288-7127.

Three indoor sports fill the calendar at Bradley Center. The Milwaukee Wave play indoor **soccer** October through April; phone (414) 224-9283. The Milwaukee Admirals compete with other teams of the American **Hockey** League October through April; phone (414) 227-0550 or (414) 227-0400.

Spectators are outdoors again in the spring and the fall to watch fierce **rugby** matches at Veterans Park. National championship **automobile races** are held at the Milwaukee Mile, (414) 453-8277, from May through September. **Sailboat races** skirt Lake Michigan's shoreline, off N. Lincoln Memorial Drive, weekends during the summer.

The lakefront also is the playground of anglers, sailors and swimmers during the warm months. **Swimming** is possible at five beaches with dressing facilities: Bradford Beach, 2400 N. Lincoln Memorial Dr.; Doctor's Park Beach, 1870 E. Fox Ln.; Grant Beach, 100 Hawthorne Ave.; McKinley Beach, 1750 N. Lincoln Memorial Dr.; and South Shore Beach, 2900 S. Superior St. For those who cannot adjust to Lake Michigan's chilly waters, there are 20 more tepid public pools. Sailors with their own **boating** craft may use the launch ramps at Grant Park, Riverfront, McKinley Marina and South Shore Yacht Club for a fee.

Fishing in Lake Michigan can reward anglers with prize catches of salmon and trout as big as 30 pounds. Full- and half-day charters are offered by numerous companies; check the telephone directory.

Tennis is available at 30 county parks; many courts are lighted. Court use is free, though a $4 fee is charged for reservations; phone (414) 257-8030. North Shore Elite Fitness and Racquet Club, (414) 351-2900, at 5750 N. Glen Park Rd., is one of several clubs that offers indoor tennis courts. Lawn bowling is popular at Lake and Dineen parks; instruction and equipment are available during the summer.

About two-thirds of the **golf** courses in the Milwaukee vicinity are 18-hole courses. Brown Deer Golf Course, (414) 352-8080, 7835 N. Green Bay Rd., is home to the PGA Greater Milwaukee Open and is open to the public. The county also maintains par-three and regulation 18-hole courses and an 18-hole pitch-and-putt course. In the winter, the Currie Park Golf Dome, 3535 N. Mayfair Rd., offers an indoor driving range; phone (414) 453-1742.

The Milwaukee County Park System offers a variety of public facilities among its 140 parks, including beaches, swimming pools, golf courses, tennis courts, soccer fields, **hiking** trails and the 90-mile Oak Leaf Trail, a paved path for **bicycling,** inline skating and jogging that encircles the city. Many county parks also are equipped for winter sports. For information about county park facilities phone (414) 257-4575.

Although Milwaukee's winters are somewhat formidable, the lure of various winter sports entices even the frostbite-prone outdoors. The park department floods more than 17 sites for **ice skating.** The premier site, however, is Pettit National Ice Center *(see attraction listing p. 155).* Wilson Park Center and Red Arrow Park also offer skating.

Brown Deer, Currie, Dretzka and Grant parks have trails for **cross-country skiing.** Old World Wisconsin *(see Eagle p. 159)* and Schlitz Audubon Nature Center *(see attraction listing p. 155)* also provide cross-country ski trails. Favorite weekend destinations for Milwaukee residents include Kettle Moraine State Forest *(see Recreation Chart and Campbellsport p. 125)* and any of the 60 inland lakes in the metropolitan area.

Greyhound tracks attract locals as well as visitors and include Dairyland Greyhound Park in Kenosha; phone (262) 657-8200 or (800) 233-3357 and Geneva Lakes Greyhound Track in Delavan; phone (262) 728-8000 or (800) 477-4552.

Note: Policies concerning admittance of children to pari-mutuel betting facilities vary. Phone for information.

Shopping

In the heart of Milwaukee, a legacy of cobblestone streets and ethnic specialty shops blend gracefully with the skywalks and covered malls that characterize the modern emporiums. The city's centerpiece are The Shops of Grand Avenue, a three-block multilevel marketplace on Wisconsin Avenue between N. 4th Street and the Milwaukee River that incorporates the historic Plankinton Arcade. It is anchored by Boston Store and encloses more than 115 shops and eateries.

Such marketplaces as The Shops of Grand Avenue have not displaced Milwaukee's traditional shopping areas. Just below one of the mall's skywalks is Old World 3rd Street, between Wells and Juneau avenues, where late 19th-century buildings house specialty stores along a cobblestone street. Some shops include Usinger's famous sausage, the Wisconsin Cheese Mart, Spice House and others offering Hummel figurines, furniture and crafts.

Across the Milwaukee River in East Town, the elegant shops along Jefferson Street include George Watts' china and crystal and those offering antiques, furnishings and other items. Two other colorful east-side neighborhoods are Brady Street, between Farwell Avenue and Marshall Street, steeped in Old World tradition, and Downer Avenue, between E. Webster and E. Park.

An archway welcomes shoppers to Milwaukee's Historic Third Ward, the city's original commercial district. Renovated warehouses and factories now house art galleries, antique stores, restaurants, specialty shops and performing arts centers along streets lined with old-fashioned street lights. Antiques enthusiasts can browse along three floors of antiques and collectibles at Milwaukee Antique Center, 341 N. Milwaukee St. Downtown, the Milwaukee River and Lake Michigan form the boundaries for the Ward's 17-block shopping area.

Cedar Creek Settlement *(see Cedarburg p. 159)* offers a delightful step back in time. Stonewood Village, 17700 W. Capitol Dr. in Brookfield, markets Colonial wares.

Shopping centers in the metropolitan area are Bayshore, 5900 N. Port Washington Rd.; Brookfield Square, 95 N. Moorland Rd.; Mayfair Mall, 2500 N. Mayfair Rd. and Southridge, 5300 S. 76th St. The stores generally are open Mon.-Fri. 10-9, Sat. 10-6, Sun. 11-6.

Theater and Concerts

Milwaukee boasts several nationally acclaimed performing arts companies. The Marcus Center for the Performing Arts, 929 N. Water St., is home to many of these, including the Florentine Opera Company, Milwaukee Ballet Company and the Milwaukee Symphony Orchestra. The Milwaukee Symphony Orchestra's regular season is early September through July; phone (414) 291-7605 or (888) 612-3500.

Free Rainbow Summer concerts and other cultural offerings are presented at the Marcus Center for the Performing Arts' riverfront tent stage on summer afternoons. The park department also sponsors less well-known groups in free concerts at various parks during the summer.

The Milwaukee Repertory Theater performs a variety of dramatic productions at 108 E. Wells St. from early September to mid-May; phone (414) 224-9490. Since the restoration of the late 19th-century European Pabst Theater at 144 E. Wells St., the grand old theater presents musical and theatrical productions ranging from Broadway shows to chamber music and other concerts. Tours of the theater are offered Saturday at 11:30; phone (414) 286-3663. The Ko-Thi Dance Co. is among the groups performing at the Pabst Theater.

The Helfaer Theater, (414) 288-7504, at 13th and Clybourn on the Marquette University campus, presents quality theater and concert offerings. The Milwaukee Riverside Theater, (414) 224-3000, at 116 W. Wisconsin Ave., presents touring Broadway shows and musical artists. Marcus Amphitheater on the Summerfest Grounds at 200 N. Harbor Dr. features concerts; phone (414) 273-2600.

Musicals and operettas are staged by the Skylight Opera Theater, which performs at the Broadway Theatre Center, 158 N. Broadway in the Historic Third World; phone (414) 291-7800. The Broadway Theatre Center also is home to the Milwaukee

Chamber Theatre, which stages both classical and contemporary works, phone (414) 291-7800, and Theater X, an experimental theater group.

The events sections of the city's newspaper carries current information about local cultural activities. Visitors also can contact the Milwaukee Convention and Visitors Bureau for an update; phone (800) 554-1448.

Special Events

Annual events begin in January with the U.S. International Snow Sculpting Competition. The regular sports calendar includes the *Milwaukee Journal/Sentinel* Sports Show, which draws crowds to the Wisconsin State Fair Park in mid-March.

State Fair Park in the suburb of West Allis plays host to several automobile races throughout the year, including the PPG CART FedEx Championship Miller Lite 250 the weekend after Memorial Day and the NASCAR/Busch Series Diehard 250 in late June. The Greater Milwaukee Open Golf Tournament takes place in mid-July and the 250-Mile IRL Indy Car Series is held in late July.

Supreme among Milwaukee's cultural events are the Lakefront Festival of the Arts in June and Summerfest, held from late June to early July. RiverSplash!, in late May-early June, offers 10 city blocks of music, food and fireworks along the river. Ethnic festivals include the Polish Fest and the Asian Moon Festival in June and the Fiesta Italiana, Bastille Days and German Fest in July.

The Great Circus Parade, considered the only one of its kind in the country, offers bands, costumed units, animals and the Ringling Bros. circus wagons, also in July. Rainbow Summer at the Performing Arts Center includes noon and evening musical performances on the riverfront June through August. The same months offer sailboat races, held every weekend off North Lincoln Memorial Drive.

Big-name entertainment is prominent in August among the festivities that surround the Wisconsin State Fair. Also in August are the African World Festival, the Irish Fest and Mexican Fiesta. Indian Summer and Oktoberfest take place in September. More than 50 ethnic groups gather in mid-November for the Holiday Folk Fair, which salutes Old World culture.

Colorful floats and other displays launch yuletide festivities at the Christmas Parade, traditionally held in November.

Each season of the year is celebrated with a spectacular flower show at Mitchell Park Horticultural Conservatory—"The Domes." Waves of color and fragrance treat the senses during the Spring Flower Show, late March to mid-May, and the Summer Flower Show, held from June to mid-September. The Fall Flower Show takes place from late September to mid-November. The Christmas Flower Show is held from Thanksgiving to early January, and the Winter Flower Show, held mid-January to mid-March, closes the season.

The Milwaukee Vicinity

CEDARBURG (H-8) pop. 10,908, elev. 778′

Thanks to the water power provided by Cedar Creek and an abundant supply of limestone, Cedarburg had become a busy milling, textile, quarrying and industrial center by the 1850s. The original center of activity was New Dublin, later renamed Hamilton, southeast of the present downtown section. Now designated a historic district, Hamilton includes the 1853 Concordia Mill and several other historic stone buildings.

The 1855 Cedarburg Mill, used as a refuge for families during the Great Indian Scare of 1862, still stands near the Columbia Road bridge over Cedar Creek. One of the last two surviving covered bridges in the state crosses Cedar Creek about 3 miles north via CR NN and Covered Bridge Road. The other spans the Crystal River in Waupaca *(see place listing p. 174).*

Lime Kiln Park, on Green Bay Road in nearby Grafton, features restored lime kiln chimneys and a picturesque dam. The park, on the Milwaukee River, offers a picnic area and a canoe launch. Landmark Tours provides guided tours of Cedarburg and Ozaukee County; phone (262) 375-1426.

Cedarburg Chamber of Commerce: Washington Ave. and Spring St., P.O. Box 104, Cedarburg, WI 53012; phone (262) 377-9620 or (262) 377-5856.

Self-guiding tours: Several brochures describing Cedarburg's historic district and outlining a walking tour are available from the chamber of commerce.

Shopping areas: Hidden treasures can be found in the numerous antiques shops lining Washington Avenue in the historic district. Cedar Creek Settlement, Washington Avenue and Bridge Road, offers some 30 shops and cafes surrounding the five-story Cedarburg Mill.

CEDAR CREEK SETTLEMENT is downtown at jct. Bridge Rd. and Washington Ave. at N70 W6340 Bridge Rd. Built in 1864 and in operation until 1969, the old Wittenberg Woolen Mill was restored in the early 1970s to house nearly 30 retail establishments, including Cedar Creek Winery. Mon.-Sat. 10-5, Sun. 11-5. Free. Phone (800) 827-8020.

THE OZAUKEE ART CENTER/BREWERY WORKS ARTS COMPLEX is at W62 N718 Riveredge Dr. An 1843 brewery has been converted into the art studios of sculptor Paul J. Yank and the Ozaukee County Art Center. Working artisans sometimes can be seen. Allow 1 hour minimum. Wed.-Sun. 1-4; closed Jan. 1, Thanksgiving and Dec. 25. Donations. Phone (262) 377-8230 or (262) 377-7220.

WINERIES

- **Cedar Creek Winery** is at jct. Bridge Rd. and Washington Ave. at N70 W6340 Bridge Rd. Mon.-Sat. 10-5, Sun. 11-5; closed Jan. 1, Easter, Thanksgiving and Dec. 25. Phone (262) 377-8020 or (800) 827-8020.

EAGLE (I-7) pop. 1,707, elev. 947′

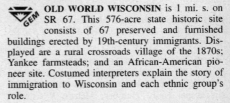 **OLD WORLD WISCONSIN** is 1 mi. s. on SR 67. This 576-acre state historic site consists of 67 preserved and furnished buildings erected by 19th-century immigrants. Displayed are a rural crossroads village of the 1870s; Yankee farmsteads; and an African-American pioneer site. Costumed interpreters explain the story of immigration to Wisconsin and each ethnic group's role.

A 15-minute orientation film about 19th-century Wisconsin is offered on the lower level of Ramsey Barn Visitor Center. If walking, allow 4 to 6 hours and wear comfortable shoes. Tram service is available. Seasonal events take place some weekends. The 5-mile Aldo Leopold Environmental History Trail includes interpretive signs about the area's heritage and habitats.

Food is available. Daily 10-5, May-Oct. Last admission is 1 hour before closing; tickets purchased after 3 p.m. also are good for an additional day. Open selected dates in December for holiday programs; phone for hours and prices. Admission (includes all-day tram pass and audio guide) $14; over 64, $12.80; ages 5-12, $8.50; family rate (2 adults and children under 17) $39. MC, VI. Phone (262) 594-6300.

ERIN (H-7)

HOLY HILL is 6 mi. w. of US 41/45 on SR 167 to 1525 Carmel Rd. This national shrine to Mary, Help of Christians, is staffed by Discalced Carmelites. Settlers erected a 15-foot oak cross and chapel on the summit in the early 19th century. The log chapel evolved into a Romanesque church, a national shrine to the Virgin Mary and a monastery for the 17 friars who staff the shrine. A tower affords picturesque views.

Allow 1 hour minimum. Daily 6 a.m.-5 p.m. Scenic tower Mon.-Sat. 9-4:45, Sun. 1:30-4:45. Donations. Phone (262) 628-1838.

GRAFTON (H-8) pop. 10,312, elev. 757′

THE FAMILY FARM is at 328 W. Port Washington Rd. A 46-acre restored turn-of-the-20th-century farmstead comprises five historic buildings and livestock including goats, chickens, donkeys, horses, rabbits, pigs, cows and a llama. Antique farm implements are displayed. A nature walk, horse-drawn rides and food are available. Allow 1 hour minimum. Wed.-Sat. 9-4, Sun. 11-4, mid-May through Sept. 30; Tues.-Fri. 9-4, Sat. 9-5, Sun. 11-5 in Oct. Admission $6.25; over 61, $5.25; ages 2-12, $3.75. Horse-drawn rides $1. Phone ahead to verify schedule and prices. MC, VI. Phone (262) 377-6161.

HARTFORD (H-7) pop. 10,905, elev. 988'

Pike Lake State Park, 2 miles east on SR 60, offers a variety of recreational activities year-round, including camping, picnicking, hiking, fishing, swimming and cross-country skiing. *See Recreation Chart and the AAA Great Lakes CampBook.*

Hartford Area Chamber of Commerce: 225 N. Main St., P.O. Box 270305, Hartford, WI 53027; phone (262) 673-7002.

WISCONSIN AUTOMOTIVE MUSEUM is at 147 N. Rural St. More than 100 antique and classic automobiles are exhibited, including Austin-Americans, Fords, Hudsons, Metzes, Wisconsin-built Nashes and the locally manufactured Kissel. Also displayed are single-cylinder farm engines, automotive relics, outboard motors, gas pumps and a 250-ton steam locomotive.

Allow 1 hour minimum. Mon.-Sat. and holidays 10-5, Sun. noon-5, May-Sept.; Mon.-Sat. 10-5, Sun. noon-5, rest of year. Closed Jan. 1, Easter, Thanksgiving and Dec. 24-25 and 31. Admission $7; over 62 and students with ID $6; ages 8-13, $3. Phone (262) 673-7999.

OCONOMOWOC (H-7) pop. 12,382, elev. 869'

Surrounded by lakes and easily accessible from Milwaukee, Chicago and other cities, Oconomowoc was a wealthy resort in the late 19th century. The most fashionable people of the period built their elaborate summer cottages on the nearby lakes. Many of these houses remain and lend their charm to this popular vacation community.

Oconomowoc Convention & Visitors Bureau: 174 E. Wisconsin Ave., Oconomowoc, WI 53066; phone (800) 524-3744.

Self-guiding tours: The historic houses around Fowler Lake can be viewed on a self-guiding 2-mile-long walking tour. Maps are available from the chamber of commerce.

OCONOMOWOC AND LAKE COUNTRY MUSEUM is at 103 W. Jefferson St. The history of Oconomowoc and the Lake Country area is depicted in permanent and temporary exhibits and special events. Displays include a model train, railroad memorabilia, a marine railroad exhibit and a vintage outboard motors display. Representations of local architecture include a Victorian home, dentist's office, barbershop, print shop, general store, bank and a medical clinic.

Fri.-Sun. 1-5, early May-Dec. 31; other times by appointment. Donations. Phone (262) 569-0740.

PORT WASHINGTON (G-8)
pop. 10,467, elev. 668'

Patriotic fervor was hardly the reaction of Ozaukee County farmers when the governor ordered all able-bodied citizens to enroll for service during the Civil War. On Nov. 10, 1862, an angry mob stampeded Port Washington's courthouse and destroyed the draft rolls.

Lest their point of view go unacknowledged, they later seized the small cannon ordinarily used for Fourth of July celebrations and positioned it on the south bluff overlooking the harbor. The rebels were no match for government troops, however, who sailed into the harbor by night and easily subdued the small army.

Port Washington is a fishing and yachting center on Lake Michigan distinguished by many pre-Civil War houses, including the 19th-century Eghart House, 316 Grand Ave. On a hill overlooking the downtown area is St. Mary's Church, a much-photographed Gothic church built in 1882. Upper Lake Park offers a fine vantage point for viewing the harbor, where coal carriers regularly deposit huge supplies to fuel the waterfront power plant.

Numerous charter boats operate from the marina during the summer and fall; fishing for trout as well as coho and chinook salmon is popular all year.

Port Washington Chamber of Commerce: 126 E. Grand Ave., P.O. Box 514, Port Washington, WI 53074; phone (262) 284-0900 or (800) 719-4881.

SAUKVILLE (H-8) pop. 4,068, elev. 771'

[SAVE] **OZAUKEE COUNTY PIONEER VILLAGE** is at 4880 CR I. A collection of 1800s Wisconsin buildings is preserved. Ranging from a log hay barn, smokehouse and residence to a trading post, smithy and railroad station, the structures represent a cross section of frontier architecture. All are furnished in period. Costumed guided tours are available.

Allow 1 hour minimum. Sat.-Sun. noon-5, Memorial Day weekend to mid-Oct. Admission $6; over 55 and ages 11-18, $4; ages 5-10, $2. Special events $8; over 55 and ages 11-18, $6; ages 5-10, $3. Phone (262) 377-4510.

WAUKESHA (H-8) pop. 64,825, elev. 867'

Waukesha takes its name from an American Indian word meaning "by the Little Fox." Although the Fox River has been important in the city's steady industrial growth, it was the many mineral springs and their purported curative powers that brought Waukesha its fame as the elegant "Saratoga of the West" during the late 19th century. Plants bottling carbonated beverages are the only vestiges of those halcyon days.

Another small reminder of past notoriety is a marker in Cutler Park honoring a local citizen who safely transported the first slave through Wisconsin to Canada. Waukesha was an important station on the Underground Railroad and an abolitionist stronghold; the *American Freeman* was published in the town 1844-48.

Waukesha is an industrial and college town serving the surrounding dairying and farming area. Colleges include Carroll College, University of Wisconsin-Waukesha and Waukesha County Technical College. Frame Park, the largest of seven municipal parks, is noted for its formal garden.

Waukesha Area Convention & Visitors Bureau: 2240 N. Grandview Blvd., Suite 2, Waukesha, WI 53188; phone (262) 542-0330 or (800) 366-8474.

WAUKESHA COUNTY HISTORICAL SOCIETY AND MUSEUM is at 101 W. Main St. at East Ave. Exhibits, tours, events, camps and a research center focus on the history of Waukesha County and its people. The research center, which specializes in family and local history, is open to the public. Guided tours are available for a fee. Allow 30 minutes minimum. Museum open Tues.-Sat. 10-4:30. Research center Tues. and Fri-Sat. 10-noon and 12:30-4:30, Thurs. 12:30-4:30. Closed holidays. Museum admission by donation. Phone (262) 521-2859.

WEST BEND (G-8) pop. 28,152, elev. 906'

West Bend, a busy industrial community on the Milwaukee River, has its name appearing in homes worldwide on small appliances and kitchenware. Outdoor recreation abounds throughout the more than 650 acres of city park land. Challenging terrain makes the area popular with cyclists and hikers. Sledding and skiing keep adventure seekers busy in winter.

Riverfront Parkway, a trail that winds along the Milwaukee River through West Bend, can be enjoyed by joggers, walkers or those on bicycles. In addition to the scenic beauty of the trail is a series of sculptures at the river's edge.

West Bend Area Chamber of Commerce: 735 S. Main St., P.O. Box 522, West Bend, WI 53095; phone (262) 338-2666 or (888) 338-8666.

LIZARD MOUND COUNTY PARK is 4 mi. n. on SR 144, then .2 mi. e. on CR A. The archeological site is named after its most prominent effigy mound. Between A.D. 400 and 1200, the American Indians built the mounds to cover their burial and ceremonial sites. Designed in animal, bird and geometric shapes, the 31-acre park's 25 mounds and earthworks are among the best preserved in Wisconsin.

A nature trail and picnic facilities are available. Allow 1 hour minimum. Daily dawn-dusk, April-Nov. Free. Phone (262) 335-4445.

OLD COURTHOUSE SQUARE MUSEUM is at 320 S. 5th Ave. This restoration of the 1889 Romanesque-revival courthouse contains a variety of permanent and temporary exhibits centering on local history. Adjacent to the museum is the restored 1886 jailhouse and home of the county sheriff. Wed.-Fri. 11-5, Sat. 9-1, Sun. noon-4. Free. Phone (262) 335-4678.

WEST BEND ART MUSEUM is at 300 S. 6th Ave. Permanent and changing displays showcase the work of locally, regionally and nationally known artists. The museum features hundreds of works by Carl von Marr, an internationally recognized painter from the area. Also featured is a collection of early Wisconsin art dating 1800-1950. An elaborate doll house also is exhibited. Allow 1 hour minimum. Wed.-Sat. 10-4:30, Sun. 1-4:30; closed holidays. Free. Phone (262) 334-9638.

This ends listings for the Milwaukee Vicinity.
The following page resumes the alphabetical listings
of cities in Wisconsin.

MINERAL POINT (I-4)
pop. 2,617, elev. 1,041'

Some of the early surface miners who came to Mineral Point in search of "mineral," or lead, were so obsessed that they lived in the holes they were digging—and provided the source for Wisconsin's nickname, "The Badger State." Beginning in 1830 they were joined by Cornish miners skilled in hard-rock mining.

Their English heritage survives in the town's stone houses, colorful stories and traditional pasties (PAST-ees), saffron cakes and tea biscuits. The name of Shake Rag Street stems from the Cornish wives' custom of waving rags to summon their men working on the opposite hillside.

Lately Mineral Point has become a center for arts and handicrafts, with some of the buildings in the restored areas devoted to studio space.

Mineral Point Chamber of Commerce: 225 High St., Mineral Point, WI 53565; phone (608) 987-3201 or (888) 764-6894.

Self-guiding tours: Maps outlining a driving tour and a walking tour of Mineral Point's historical and architectural attractions can be obtained at the chamber of commerce.

PENDARVIS STATE HISTORIC SITE is at 114 Shake Rag St. On the site are 10 carefully restored stone and log houses built by Cornish lead miners in the 1840s; six of the structures are open to the public and furnished in period. The Pendarvis site offers information about a self-guiding tour of nearby Merry Christmas Mine Hill, where visitors can see mining history by viewing abandoned mine shafts and "badger holes."

Open daily 10-5, mid-May through Oct. 31. Hours may vary; phone ahead. Last tour begins 1 hour before closing. Fee $8; over 65, $7.20; ages 5-12, $4. MC, VI. Phone (608) 987-2122.

MINOCQUA (C-5) elev. 1,603'

Calling itself the "Island City," Minocqua is in the Lakeland area, which has more than 3,200 lakes. The region is known for fishing and boating in summer and cross-country skiing and snowmobiling in winter. Minocqua Winter Park, 6 miles west on SR 70 and 6 miles south on Squirrel Lake Road, offers 75 miles of groomed cross-country trails.

Northern Lights Playhouse in Minocqua presents Broadway musicals and comedies nightly from Memorial Day weekend to mid-September; phone (715) 356-7173.

Minocqua-Arbor Vitae-Woodruff Area Chamber of Commerce: 8216 US 51S, P.O. Box 1006, Minocqua, WI 54548; phone (715) 356-5266 or (800) 446-6784.

CIRCLE M CORRAL is 2.5 mi. w. of US 51 on SR 70. This amusement park offers children's rides, water games and a waterslide, go-carts, bumper boats, train rides, pony rides, miniature golf, horseback riding, batting cages and video games. Food is available. Daily 10-5, mid-May to late Sept. Admission free; prices for activity packages start at $5. MC, VI. Phone (715) 356-4441.

PECK'S WILDWOOD WILDLIFE PARK AND NATURE CENTER is 2 mi. w. of US 51 on SR 70. More than 600 birds and other animals live in the 25-acre park. Visitors can walk among deer and pet baby animals. Nature programs are offered daily, and a nature walk, "Explore and Learn" area and a timber wolf and bald eagle presentation also are featured. Boat rides and food are available. Picnicking is permitted. Daily 9-5:30, June 1-Labor Day; 9-4:30 in May and day after Labor Day to mid-Oct. Admission $8; ages 2 months-11 years, $6. MC, VI. Phone (715) 356-5588.

MONROE (I-5) pop. 10,843, elev. 1,050'

Monroe and its environs are known as the Swiss cheese capital of the United States. Many inhabitants are of Swiss descent, and old customs prevail at certain festivals. Some of the shops on the business square that surrounds the red brick courthouse have ornate Swiss-style facades. Of note is the Old Methodist Church, designed by Milwaukee architect E. Townsend Mix in 1869.

The Alp and Dell Cheese Factory, north on SR 69, offers free tours of its factory; phone (608) 328-3355.

Monroe Chamber of Commerce: 1505 9th St., Monroe, WI 53566; phone (608) 325-7648.

NEENAH-MENASHA (F-7)
pop. 40,838, elev. 753'

The twin cities of Neenah and Menasha meet at the junction of Nicolet Boulevard and Abbey Avenue, on the island separating the two channels through which Lake Winnebago empties into the Fox River. Although they have separate governments, the cities share many civic and industrial enterprises, including their reputation as Wisconsin's papermaking center.

It was the possibility of water power that spurred the birth of the two villages in the 1840s. Neenah was incorporated in 1873. A year later Menasha was established and awarded the charter to develop the water power for the area.

Fox Cities Convention and Visitors Bureau: 3433 W. College Ave., Appleton, WI 54914; phone (920) 734-3358 or (800) 236-6673. *See color ad p. 120.*

BERGSTROM-MAHLER MUSEUM is at 165 N. Park Ave. on Lake Winnebago. Displays include antique and modern glass paperweights, German glass and changing exhibitions. Allow 1 hour minimum. Tues.-Fri. 10-4:30, Sat. 9-4:30, Sun. 1-4:30; closed holidays except Easter. Donations. Phone (920) 751-4658.

DOTY GRAND LOGGERY is at Lincoln and Fifth sts. in Doty Park. This replica of the home of James Doty, second territorial governor, contains American Indian artifacts, belongings of the Doty family and other historical items. Allow 30 minutes minimum. Daily noon-4, June to mid-Aug. Donations. Phone (920) 886-6060.

NEILLSVILLE (F-4) pop. 2,731, elev. 977'

The Wisconsin Pavilion from the 1964-65 New York World's Fair is at 1200 E. Division St. It contains the radio station WCCN and a cheesehouse. Visitors can observe the radio station through windows. A replica of the world's largest cheese, weighing 34,500 pounds, and Chatty Belle, an enormous mechanical talking cow, are on the grounds.

Neillsville Area Chamber of Commerce: 118 W. Sixth St., P.O. Box 52, Neillsville, WI 54456; phone (715) 743-6444.

THE HIGHGROUND is 4 mi. w. on US 10. A 140-acre veterans memorial park features monuments to soldiers of World War I, World War II and the Wisconsin veterans of the Vietnam War. Also on the grounds are a replica of the Liberty Bell and memorials dedicated to female veterans, and American Indian veterans also are on the premises.

A half-million acres of woodland and glacial moraine are visible from the memorial's plaza. Picnicking is permitted. Allow 1 hour minimum. Daily 24 hours. Donations. Phone (715) 743-4224.

NEW GLARUS (I-5) pop. 2,111, elev. 859'

Impelled by economic adversity in Switzerland, 118 emigrants from the canton of Glarus settled New Glarus in 1845. "Little Switzerland," as the community often is called, remains essentially Swiss in character. Emblems of the Swiss cantons adorn buildings and street signs. Dairying and cheesemaking brought New Glarus its prosperity.

New Glarus also is a popular departure point for the Sugar River State Trail, a 23-mile hiking, bicycling and snowmobiling route leading to Brodhead.

New Glarus Chamber of Commerce: P.O. Box 713, New Glarus, WI 53574-0713; phone (608) 527-2095 or (800) 527-6838.

CHALET OF THE GOLDEN FLEECE is at 618 2nd St. Modeled after a Swiss Bernese mountain chalet, the 1937 house museum is furnished with many items from Switzerland and other parts of the world. The interior woodwork is particularly impressive. Guided tours are available. Allow 1 hour minimum. Thurs.-Mon. 10-4, Memorial Day weekend-Oct. 31. Admission $5; ages 6-17, $2. Phone (608) 527-2614.

SWISS HISTORICAL VILLAGE is at 612 7th Ave. Fourteen buildings on the landscaped grounds include a firehouse, smithy, log church, butcher shop, tool shed, general store, print shop, Swiss bee house and cheese factory. A log cabin and schoolhouse are original. The Hall of History contains displays tracing Swiss immigration to America and the settlement of the New Glarus area. Allow 1 hour, 30 minutes minimum. Daily 10-4, May-Oct. Last tour begins 30 minutes before closing. Admission $7; ages 6-13, $3. Phone (608) 527-2317.

NEW LONDON (F-7) pop. 7,085, elev. 758'

New London, on the Wolf River near its junction with the Embarrass River, witnessed the booming days when great log drives traveled down both streams. Agribusiness and timber-related industries employ much of the area's population. The area offers numerous recreational opportunities, including cross-country skiing, snowmobiling, white water rafting and fishing.

The New London Heritage Historical Village, just east of Mill Street at 900 Montgomery St., consists of five historical buildings—a log cabin, an octagon-shaped house, a chapel, a school and a railroad depot—all moved to the site. The village is open limited weekends June through August and by appointment; phone (920) 982-5186 or (920) 982-8557.

New London Area Chamber of Commerce: 301 E. Beacon Ave., New London, WI 54961; phone (920) 982-5822.

MOSQUITO HILL NATURE CENTER is 2 mi. s. of CR S from jct. SR 54 at N3880 Rogers Rd. Several miles of nature trails wind through the center's 430 acres along the Wolf River, and an interpretive building has natural history displays and an outdoors observation deck. A butterfly house also is available. Snowshoeing along marked trails can be enjoyed during the winter months; phone ahead for trail conditions. Tues.-Fri. 8-4:30, Sat.-Sun. 10-3. Butterfly house Wed. and Sat.-Sun. 11-3, July-Aug. Closed holidays. Donations. Phone (920) 779-6433.

NEW LONDON PUBLIC MUSEUM is on US 45 at 406 S. Pearl St. The museum contains American Indian and African artifacts, minerals, fossils, shells, an exhibit about Thomas Edison in New London, displays about the extinct passenger pigeon and regional historical items. Regular changing exhibits are featured. Allow 1 hour minimum. Tues.-Fri. 10-5 (also Tues. 5-8), Sat. 9-2, Labor Day-Memorial Day; Tues.-Fri. 10-5 (also Tues. 5-8), rest of year. Closed holidays. Free. Phone (920) 982-8520.

NICOLET NATIONAL FOREST—
see Chequamegon-Nicolet National Forest p. 126.

NORTH FREEDOM (H-5) pop. 649, elev. 867'

[SAVE] **MID-CONTINENT RAILWAY MUSEUM** is w. on W. Walnut St. Vintage trains take passengers on a 50-minute ride. The museum includes an 1894 depot, a wooden water tower, restored locomotives and railroad cars and equipment displays. A winter ride runs the third weekend in February; an autumn color train ride takes place the first two weekends in October; and Santa Claus Express is offered Thanksgiving weekend. A dinner train ride also is available.

Picnicking is permitted. Museum open daily 9:30-5, mid-May through Labor Day; Sat.-Sun. 9:30-5, day after Labor Day to mid-Oct. Trains depart at 10:30, 12:30, 2 and 3:30, mid-May to Labor Day. Passengers should arrive at least 15 minutes prior to departure. Museum free. Train fare $11; over 62, $10; ages 3-12, $6. Caboose rides $13; ages 3-12, $7. AX, DS, MC, VI. Phone (608) 522-4261.

OCONOMOWOC—*see Milwaukee p. 160.*

OCONTO (E-8) pop. 4,708, elev. 590′

The Oconto that attracts duck hunters and anglers to its favorable Green Bay location once was the burial site of an ancient Copper Culture people. The discovery of the burial site, now a park on Mill Street, revealed that they had populated the area more than 4,000 years ago.

Modern by comparison is the West Main Street Historic District, a three-block area lined with elegant houses marking the period when lumber was supreme in Oconto. Among the houses dating 1860-1928 is one that belonged to Edward Scofield, the last of Wisconsin's lumberman governors. The first church built by the Christian Science denomination is at Chicago and Main streets.

Oconto Area Chamber of Commerce: 110 Brazeau Ave., P.O. Box 174, Oconto, WI 54153; phone (920) 834-6254.

SAVE **BEYER HOME MUSEUM** is at 917 Park Ave. The 1868 Victorian house is furnished to reflect the 1890s. A museum annex on the grounds contains Old Main Street and its shops, a log cabin,

Copper Culture artifacts, a veterans exhibit and displays of Oconto County history. A barn/carriage house houses tools and historic vehicles, including two antique electric cars. Allow 1 hour minimum. Tours are given Mon.-Sat. 10-4, Sun. noon-4, June 1-Labor Day. Admission $3; ages 6-18, $1. Phone (920) 834-6206.

OSCEOLA (D-1) pop. 2,421, elev. 809′

On the bluffs of the St. Croix River, Osceola was a popular stop for late 19th-century excursion steamboats. Passengers disembarked to follow a boardwalk to scenic Cascade Falls. Visitors today can duplicate that hike along a path leading to the waterfall. Interstate State Park, known for its cliffs, potholes and hiking trails, is a short drive north (*see St. Croix Falls p. 169*).

Osceola Chamber of Commerce: 114 Depot Rd., P.O. Box 251, Osceola, WI 54020; phone (715) 755-3300 or (800) 947-0581.

SAVE **OSCEOLA & ST. CROIX VALLEY RAILWAY** departs from 114 Depot Rd. Scenic 50- and 90-minute narrated excursions aboard restored diesel-powered trains take passengers along the St. Croix River Valley separating Wisconsin from Minnesota. Brunch and dinner trips also are offered. Trips depart Sat.-Sun. at 11, 1 and 2:30, Memorial Day weekend-late Oct. Fare $10-$14; over 62, $9-$12; ages 5-15, $5-$7; family rate $25-$38. AX, DS, MC, VI. Phone (715) 755-3570.

OSHKOSH (F-7) pop. 62,916, elev. 755′

Oshkosh is an important manufacturing center on the west shore of Lake Winnebago at the mouth of the upper Fox River. Because the Fox and its tributaries could transport logs from far to the north and because nearby lakes Poygan and Butte des Morts provided natural storage facilities, the lumbering

boom lasted longer in Oshkosh than in other central Wisconsin sawmill towns.

Streets inches deep in sawdust elicited the nickname "Sawdust City" and probably contributed to the fact that the downtown area was destroyed by fire five times 1859-75. After the last conflagration, rebuilding was done with brick.

A noted Oshkosh resident, Helen Farnsworth Mears, won national acclaim for her sculpture "Genius of Wisconsin," now at the Capitol in Madison. More than 240 acres of municipal parks and the University of Wisconsin-Oshkosh enhance the community. Campus tours are offered; phone (920) 424-1234.

A swimming beach, marina and children's zoo are among the recreational facilities available at Menominee Park, open daily May through October. Also featured is Little Oshkosh, a playground complete with castles, mazes, tunnels and a fire truck.

A collection of nativity scenes, including one made by German POWs in World War II, is displayed at the United Methodist Church on Algoma Boulevard. Viewing is available during church office hours; phone (920) 231-2800.

Oshkosh Convention & Visitors Bureau: 2 N. Main St., Oshkosh, WI 54901; phone (920) 303-9200 or (877) 303-9200.

Shopping areas: The Aviation Plaza, 2185 S. Koeller, has the Miles Kimball Warehouse. The CCA Candle Outlet is at 1122 S. Koeller. Prime Outlets, US 41 and SR 44, offers more than 60 outlet stores.

EAA AIRVENTURE MUSEUM is at 3000 Poberezny Rd., .25 mi. s.e. of jct. US 41/SR 44. A collection of more than 95 full-size aircraft includes home-built sport planes, gliders, barnstormers, helicopters, racers and aerobatic planes as well as antique, military, solar-powered and ultralight aircraft. Hangar X! is a hands-on exhibit for children.

The museum also has a multimedia exhibit as well as models, engines, propellers, components and cutaways to show structural design. Allow 1 hour, 30 minutes minimum. Mon.-Sat. 8:30-5, Sun. 10-5; closed Jan. 1, Easter, Thanksgiving and Dec. 25. Airplane rides are available May-Oct. (weather permitting). Admission Memorial Day weekend-Labor Day $10; over 61, $9; ages 8-17, $8; family rate $26. Admission rest of year $8; over 61, $7; ages 8-17, $6.50; family rate $21. Aircraft rides $25-$50. AX, DS, MC, VI. Phone (920) 426-4818. *See color ad p. 164.*

GRAND OPERA HOUSE is at 100 High Ave. The restored 1883 660-seat Victorian theater offers concerts, plays and community events. Public performances by national and international touring artists are held here. Guided tours are available by appointment. Allow 30 minutes minimum. Box office hours Mon.-Fri. 11-6, Sat. 10-3. Admission $2. MC,

VI. Phone (920) 424-2355 for tours and information, or (920) 424-2350 for tickets.

MENOMINEE PARK ZOO is in Menominee Park at the corner of Hazel St. and Merritt Ave. This small zoo displays a variety of animals in cages. Recreational activities are available in the vicinity. Allow 1 hour minimum. Daily 9-7:30, May-Sept. Admission $1; ages 4-17, 50c. Phone (920) 236-5082.

MILITARY VETERANS MUSEUM is in the City Center Complex on Pearl Ave. Memorabilia represents all branches of U.S. military service—and all major wars from the American Revolution to the Persian Gulf. Exhibits include Jeeps from Korea and Vietnam; ships logs from the USS *California* dated Dec. 7, 1941; weapons; women's service uniforms; and an original *New York Herald* newspaper article announcing President Lincoln's assassination.

Allow 1 hour minimum. Mon.-Sat. and holidays noon-5, Sun. noon-3. Free. Phone (920) 426-8615.

OSHKOSH PUBLIC MUSEUM is at 1331 Algoma Blvd. A collection of exhibits represents the people and history of the Lake Winnebago Region. The 8-foot-tall Apostles Clock, created by German immigrant Mathias Kitz in 1895, is a prized example of Wisconsin folk art. Allow 1 hour minimum. Tues.-Sat. 9-5, Sun. 1-5; closed holidays. Donations. Phone (920) 424-4730 or (920) 424-4731.

PAINE ART CENTER AND GARDENS is at 1410 Algoma Blvd. The center features period rooms, decorative arts, sculpture and American and French 19th-century paintings. Changing exhibitions supplement the permanent collections. Four acres surround the art center and include 19 themed areas and what is said to be the only public walled garden in the state.

Allow 1 hour, 30 minutes minimum. Tues.-Sun. 11-4; closed holidays. Admission $6; over 65, $5; students with ID $4; ages 5-12, $3. MC, VI. Phone (920) 235-6903.

PEPIN (F-2) pop. 878, elev. 688'

Charles Ingalls acquired a small tract of land near Pepin in 1863, where he built his "Little House in the Big Woods." His daughter, author Laura Ingalls Wilder, was born there in 1867. A replica of the log cabin is on the site at Little House Wayside—north of town off CR CC. The "beautiful lake" about which she wrote is scenic Lake Pepin, which still attracts nature lovers.

Pepin Visitor Information Center: P.O. Box 277, Pepin, WI 54759; phone (715) 442-3011.

PEPIN HISTORICAL MUSEUM is at 306 Third St. Items pertain to the history of Pepin County as well as memorabilia of Laura Ingalls Wilder, author of the "Little House" books. A kitchen and bedroom are furnished in period. Allow 1 hour minimum. Daily 10-5, May 15-Oct. 15; noon-4, rest of year. Closed Jan. 1, Easter, Thanksgiving and Dec. 25. Donations. Phone (715) 442-3011.

PESHTIGO (E-8) pop. 3,357, elev. 600'

On Oct. 8, 1871, Chicago was not the only community in flames. About 270 miles to the north was a forest area that had been plagued for days with small fires in the dry woodlands. On that October day winds whipped the small blazes into great ones; towns were leveled and more than 1,200 people perished. In Peshtigo alone 800 residents died.

A monument to the dead is in the Peshtigo Fire Cemetery. The Peshtigo Fire Museum, containing local items relating to the tragedy, is on Oconto Avenue; phone (715) 582-3244. The Peshtigo Wildlife Area, about 6 miles southeast on CR BB, is primarily a waterfowl habitat and refuge.

Peshtigo Chamber of Commerce: P.O. Box 36, Peshtigo, WI 54157; phone (715) 582-0327.

PLATTEVILLE (I-4) pop. 9,989, elev. 968'

On hillsides where dairy cattle now graze, miners once burrowed for lead. Platteville was settled in 1827, following John Rountree's discovery of "mineral" nearby. Rountree had the small mining town designed in the 1820s by an English architect who incorporated features of his native village of Yorkshire into the town plan.

Although some lead and zinc still are mined, cheese production is a more common industry. The town is a trading center for the surrounding agricultural and dairying region. Platteville also has the University of Wisconsin-Platteville.

Platteville Chamber of Commerce: 275 US 151W, P.O. Box 16, Platteville, WI 53818; phone (608) 348-8888.

SAVE **THE MINING MUSEUM** is at 385 E. Main St. The development of lead and zinc mining in the area is traced through dioramas, models, relics and photographs. A guided tour includes a walk into the Bevans Lead, an 1845 lead mine 50 feet underground; a visit to the hoist house; and a train ride around the museum grounds in ore cars pulled by a 1931 mine locomotive. Changing exhibits are offered in the Rountree Gallery.

Allow 1 hour, 30 minutes minimum. Guided tours daily 9-5, May-Oct. Rountree Gallery Tues.-Sun. 11-4, May 1-Labor Day; otherwise varies. Closed holidays. Museum admission (including the Rollo Jamison Museum) $7; over 64, $6.30; ages 5-15, $3. Rountree Gallery free. Phone (608) 348-3301.

Rollo Jamison Museum is next to the Mining Museum at 405 E. Main St. Exhibits include carriages, farm implements, tools, a tavern/general store, a kitchen and parlor, musical instruments and mechanical music boxes. Daily 9-5, May-Oct.; otherwise varies. Phone (608) 348-3301.

PORTAGE (G-6) pop. 9,728, elev. 798'

In 1673 Jacques Marquette and Louis Joliet were probably the first Europeans to make the portage between the Fox and Wisconsin rivers, thus linking the Great Lakes with the Mississippi River. This junction rapidly developed into an important trade route. By 1835 the portage had become a plank road, which was replaced by a canal in the 1870s.

The town of Portage grew up around Fort Winnebago, which was built to protect the stream of commerce. Jefferson Davis, a young West Point lieutenant, was assigned in 1829 to cut logs for the barracks. He later became president of the Confederacy.

Modern and attractive, Portage acknowledges its origins with several restorations and the Marquette Trail, a hiking trail that follows the Fox River from the Governor's Bend Locks to the Fort Winnebago Surgeon's Quarters. The city attends to the present by serving the surrounding farming and dairying area.

Portage Area Chamber of Commerce: 139 W. Cook St., Portage, WI 53901; phone (608) 742-6242 or (800) 474-2525.

FORT WINNEBAGO SURGEON'S QUARTERS RESTORATION is 2 mi. e. on SR 33. The 1819-24 log building was built by Francis LeRoi, a fur trader and portaging businessman. It was the home of Fort Winnebago Army surgeons from 1834-45. Exhibits include period furnishings, original fort pieces, medical equipment and drafting plans for the fort. Allow 1 hour minimum. Daily 10-4, May 15-Oct. 15. Admission $4; over 64, $3.50; ages 4-12, $2; family rate $10. Phone (608) 742-2949.

SAVE **HISTORIC INDIAN AGENCY HOUSE** is .2 mi. e. on SR 33, then .5 mi. n. along the canal. The house was built in 1832 by the U.S. government for John Kinzie, agent to the Ho-Chunk (Winnebago) Indians, and his wife, Juliette. The structure has been restored and furnished in period and has a visitor center. Guided tours are available. Allow 1 hour minimum. Mon.-Sat. 10-4, Sun. 11-4, May 15-Oct. 15; by appointment rest of year. Admission $4; over 63, $3; ages 4-14, $2. Phone (608) 742-6362.

PORT WASHINGTON—see Milwaukee p. 160.

POYNETTE (H-6) pop. 2,266, elev. 852'

Poynette is the southeastern terminus of a scenic stretch of I-94, which follows the Wisconsin River and ends at the junction with I-90.

Poynette Chamber of Commerce: P.O. Box 625, Poynette, WI 53955; phone (608) 635-2425.

MACKENZIE ENVIRONMENTAL EDUCATION CENTER is 2 mi. e. on CRs CS and Q off US 51. This Department of Natural Resources facility includes a wildlife exhibit with live animals native to Wisconsin, a model forest nursery, a fire tower and an arboretum. The center also has logging and conservation museums, hiking trails and picnic facilities. Allow 2 hours minimum. Grounds open daily dawn-dusk. Exhibits open daily 8-4, May 1 to mid-Oct.; Mon.-Fri. 8-4, rest of year. Free. Phone (608) 635-8110.

PRAIRIE DU CHIEN (H-3)
pop. 6,018, elev. 635'

Dating from 1673, when Jacques Marquette and Louis Joliet reached this site at the confluence of the Mississippi and Wisconsin rivers, Prairie du Chien is pre-dated only by Green Bay. Its name, French for "prairie of the dog," refers to the American Indian chief Alim, whose name meant "dog." The oldest part of the town is on St. Feriole Island in the Mississippi.

Prairie du Chien became a flourishing fur market soon after the French explorers' visit, attracting American Indians from the remote upper reaches of the Mississippi and Wisconsin rivers, as well as traders and settlers. From 1685 to 1831 four forts were built and occupied at various times by French, British and American forces. It was at Fort Crawford that Jefferson Davis and Zachary Taylor were stationed.

Prairie du Chien is the southeastern terminus of an especially scenic route that follows the Mississippi River. The route consists of SR 35 running north to La Crosse, then northwest along the Mississippi River to Prescott.

Prairie du Chien Chamber of Commerce: 211 S. Main St., P.O. Box 326, Prairie du Chien, WI 53821; phone (608) 326-8555 or (800) 732-1673.

FORT CRAWFORD MUSEUM is at 717 S. Beaumont Rd. Located in the hospital of the second Fort Crawford built 1829-33, the museum chronicles area history, including the American Indian treaties, the first and second Fort Crawford and the Blackhawk War and the Civil War. Local collections and exhibits related to Prairie du Chien history also are displayed.

Allow 1 hour minimum. Daily 10-5, June-Aug.; 10-4 in May and Sept.-Oct. Admission $4; over 55, $3.25; ages 5-12, $2.25. Phone (608) 326-6960.

VILLA LOUIS is 1 mi. n.w. at 521 N. Villa Louis Rd. on St. Feriole Island. This state historic site was the estate of Col. H.L. Dousman, fur trader and agent of John Jacob Astor's American Fur Co., and his son Louis Dousman, an art collector and horse breeder. The present mansion, named for the younger Dousman, was built in 1870 on an ancient American Indian mound. This Victorian-style mansion replaced a house called House on the Mound, built in 1843 by the elder Dousman.

The house contains one of the finest collections of Victorian decorative arts in the country. Almost all the furnishings, artworks, china, glass, silver and books belonged to the Dousman family and were used 1843-1913. Next to the mansion are the icehouse, preserve house and office.

Tours are conducted by costumed guides. Allow 1 hour, 30 minutes minimum. Daily 9:30-5, early

May-Oct. 31. Tours are given on the hour 10-4. Tour $8.50; over 65, $7.50; ages 5-12, $4.50; family rate (2 adults and children under 18) $23. MC, VI. Phone (608) 326-2721.

WYALUSING STATE PARK is 7 mi. s.e. on US 18 and SR 35, then 5 mi. w. on CR C. The 2,596-acre park encompasses the spot where Father Jacques Marquette and Louis Joliet discovered the Mississippi River. On Sentinel Ridge, 520 feet above the Mississippi, are prehistoric mounds said to be the most valuable undepleted group in existence. Interesting rock formations, bluffs and lookouts are found throughout the park. Camping, picnicking and hiking are popular.

Daily 6 a.m.-11 p.m. Admission per private vehicle $10, state residents $5. Annual permit $30, state residents $20. Phone (608) 996-2261. *See Recreation Chart and the AAA Great Lakes CampBook.*

PRAIRIE DU SAC (H-5)
pop. 3,231, elev. 767'

Prairie du Sac and its neighbor Sauk City, on the high-bluffed west bank of the Wisconsin River, share a colorful historical character, Aguston Haraszthy. Arriving in 1841 with flamboyant attire, an international perspective and high ideals, the Hungarian nobleman fostered free thought in the Wisconsin wilderness. He also established some of the first vineyards in this fertile area before moving on to California, where his vineyards became the foundation of the wine industry.

The towns constitute the eastern terminus of a scenic route that follows SR 60 along the Wisconsin River and ends in Prairie du Chien. The river provides fishing and canoeing opportunities; bald eagles roost along the banks of the river during the winter.

Sauk-Prairie Area Chamber of Commerce: 207 Water St., Suite D, Sauk City, WI 53583; phone (608) 643-4168 or (800) 683-2453.

Self-guiding tours: Brochures describing a walking tour of Prairie du Sac's historic homes and businesses are available from the chamber of commerce.

WINERIES

- **Wollersheim Winery** is .2 mi e. on SR 60, then .7 mi. s. on SR 188. Guided tours are given daily at 10:15, 11:15, 12:15, 1:15, 2:15, 3:15 and 4:15; closed Jan. 1, Easter, Thanksgiving and Dec. 25. Tastings are available daily 10-5. Phone (608) 643-6515 or (800) 847-9463.

RACINE (I-8) pop. 81,855, elev. 626'

Heavily industrialized Racine occupies a promontory jutting into Lake Michigan. Bisected by the winding Root River, it has many residential areas and about 900 acres of parkland. Like many Wisconsin cities, it is multinational in makeup, but the emphasis is Danish. West Racine is often dubbed "Kringleville" for its bakeries specializing in Danish kringle.

A powerful orator promoting women's suffrage, Olympia Brown came to Racine in 1880 to take over the ministry of a Universalist church. Later she devoted herself completely to the suffrage issue, becoming president of the Wisconsin Suffrage Association. When the 19th Amendment was passed in 1920, Olympia, at the age of 85, was the only suffragist to have participated in the movement from beginning to end.

Racine's architectural legacy includes five buildings designed by Frank Lloyd Wright, among them the landmark SC Johnson Administration Building at 1525 Howe St. The great workroom with its lilypad columns is still in use today. Guided tours of the facility are offered on Fridays at 11 and 1:15, departing from the Golden Rondelle Theater. Reservations are required; phone (262) 260-2154.

Downtown Racine is the sight of Reefpoint Marina, with some 1,000 boat slips and Racine Civic Centre Festival Park.

Racine County Convention & Visitors Bureau: 14015 Washington Ave., Sturtevant, WI 53177. Phone (262) 884-6400 or (800) 272-2463.

Shopping areas: The Regency Mall, I-94 exit 335 on US 11, includes Boston Store, JCPenney, Sears and Younkers among its 115 stores. The shops in Market Square, I-94 at 7 Mile Road, feature antiques and collectibles.

CHARLES A. WUSTUM MUSEUM OF FINE ARTS is at 2519 Northwestern Ave. (SR 38). The museum contains a permanent collection and offers several annual exhibitions of national, regional and local artists. The 13-acre grounds also accommodate the Racine Theater Guild; phone (262) 633-4218. Museum open Tues.-Sat. 10-5 (also Thurs. 5-9), Sun. noon-5; closed holidays and during exhibition changes. Donations. Phone (262) 636-9177.

RACINE HERITAGE MUSEUM is at 7th and Main sts. Exhibits detail Racine's manufacturing innovations, inventions and cultural heritage. Allow 30 minutes minimum. Museum open Tues.-Fri. 9-5 (also Thurs. 5-8), Sat.10-3, Sun. noon-4. Archives open Tues. 1-4:30, Wed. 3-4:30, Thurs. 5-7:30 and by appointment. Closed holidays. Donations. Phone (262) 636-3926.

RACINE ZOOLOGICAL GARDEN is at 2131 N. Main St. (park in lot off Walton Ave. using Main St. entrance). This 32-acre park on the shore of Lake Michigan is home to 250 animals, including the endangered orangutan, African penguin, red wolf, black rhinoceros and Masai giraffe. Animal Crackers Jazz Series concerts are offered selected Wednesday evenings during the summer. Allow 1 hour minimum. Park open daily 9-8, Memorial Day-Labor Day; 9-4, rest of year. Closed Dec. 25. Donations. Phone (262) 636-9189.

RHINELANDER (C-5) pop. 7,735, elev. 1,553'

Rhinelander had its beginning in the 1880s during the days of the pioneer lumber industry. Besides lumber, the area's forests yielded the Hodag, a creature that became the town's most popular legend. Finally exposed as a hoax composed of wood and oxhides, the Hodag myth is kept alive in local symbols and also can be seen at the Rhinelander Logging Museum (see attraction listing).

Within a radius of 12 miles are 232 lakes, 11 trout streams and two rivers offering nearly every type of water sport. More than 1,000 miles of snowmobile trails near Rhinelander are open to the public. The region also is noted for its scenic hiking, mountain bicycling and Nordic ski trails.

The Consolidated Industrial Forest, 12 miles east of the city near US 8 and US 45, offers an 11-mile driving tour that demonstrates forest management techniques; it is open daily, June through September. Booklets can be obtained at the forest entrance, .2 mile west of US 8 and US 45 at the Consolidated Monico Timberlands' office and at the Rhinelander Chamber of Commerce.

Nicolet College, on CR G and Oneida Avenue, is noted for its architecture, which blends into the surrounding woods. Free tours are given Mon.-Fri. 8-3 by appointment; phone (715) 365-4410.

Rhinelander Area Chamber of Commerce: 450 Kemp Ave., P.O. Box 795, Rhinelander, WI 54501; phone (715) 365-7464 or (800) 236-4386.

THE RHINELANDER HISTORICAL SOCIETY MUSEUM is at 9 S. Pelham St. Housed in a restored 1894 boarding house, the museum portrays area history from the turn of the 20th century to the present. Tues.-Fri. 10-4 or by appointment, June-Aug.; Tues. 10-4, rest of year. Donations. Phone (715) 369-3833.

RHINELANDER LOGGING MUSEUM is in Pioneer Park at jct. US Bus. Rte. 8/CR G. This reproduction of an 1870s logging camp features the Sioux Line Depot, built in 1892, loggers' living quarters, a cook's shack, schoolhouse, smithy and all the tools of their respective trades. Displays include a narrow-gauge engine built in 1879 and a replica of the Hodag. Allow 1 hour minimum. Daily 10-5, Memorial Day-Labor Day; Sat.-Sun. 10-5, day after Labor Day-second weekend in Oct. Donations. Phone (715) 369-5004.

RICHLAND CENTER (H-4)
pop. 5,114, elev. 736'

Richland Center was settled in 1849. It is the birthplace of Frank Lloyd Wright, whose fine early work is represented by the A.D. German Warehouse. Another noted resident was Ada James, an avid suffragette. Upon learning of Wisconsin's ratification of the 19th Amendment, James quickly put her 76-year-old father on the first train to Washington to present the ratification papers before any other state could secure the honor.

In an unglaciated corner of Wisconsin, Richland Center is surrounded by countryside characterized by fruit orchards, hardwood trees, steep hills, deep valleys and unusual rock formations. A natural bridge is in a county park 9 miles north on SR 80 near Rockbridge. Scenic SR 60 follows the Wisconsin River south from Richland Center.

Richland Area Chamber of Commerce: 397 W. Seminary St., P.O. Box 128, Richland Center, WI 53581-0128; phone (608) 647-6205 or (800) 422-1318.

Self-guiding tours: A map outlining a historical and architectural tour of Richland Center is available at the chamber of commerce.

Shopping areas: Richland Center offers numerous antique shops including Treasures in the Bakery, 155 E. Seminary St.

RIPON (G-7) pop. 6,828, elev. 932′

Ripon began as an experiment in communal living called Ceresco, established in 1849 by 200 followers of the 19th-century socialist philosopher Charles Fourier. On the west edge of town stands one of the longhouses of the commune, which disbanded in 1851.

The Republican Party was founded in Ripon in 1854 at a local political meeting, which originally was called in order to organize against the extension of slavery. Alvan E. Bovay, a local lawyer and prominent Whig, proposed the party name. Four months later the name "Republican" formally was adopted at a state party convention in Jackson, Mich.

Ripon College, established in 1851, occupies a 250-acre campus on the highest hill in the city. A highlight of the college is C.J. Rodman Center for the Arts, with two Anthony Van Dyck portraits and changing exhibits. Free guided tours of the campus can be arranged; phone (920) 748-8364.

Ripon Area Chamber of Commerce: 214 Jefferson St., P.O. Box 305, Ripon, WI 54971; phone (920) 748-6764.

Self-guiding tours: Brochures outlining walking tours of the city are available from the chamber of commerce.

[SAVE] **LARSON'S FAMOUS CLYDESDALES** is 4 mi. s. on SR 44/49, then 1.6 mi. e. on Reeds Corner Rd. A 90-minute behind-the-scenes guided tour and show about Clydesdales includes performances by the horses, explanations of their history and how they are prepared for show and judged. The barn, where Clydesdale colts can be seen and petted, is open after the program. Video cameras are prohibited. Shows are scheduled Mon.-Sat. at 1, May-Oct. Admission $10; under 12, $5. Reservations are recommended. Phone (920) 748-5466.

LITTLE WHITE SCHOOL HOUSE is on Blackburn St. This mid-19th-century schoolhouse was the birthplace of the Republican Party. Allow 30 minutes minimum. Daily 10-4, June-Aug.; Sat.-Sun. 10-4, in May and Sept.-Oct. or by appointment. Donations. Phone (920) 748-6764.

RUDOLPH (F-5) pop. 423, elev. 1,139′

DAIRY STATE CHEESE CO. is at SR 34 and CR C. An observation area and a multimedia presentation about cheesemaking are offered. Mon.-Fri. 8-5:15, Sat. 8-5, Sun. 9-noon. Free. Phone (715) 435-3144.

GROTTO GARDENS AND WONDER CAVE is on SR 34. The site includes the Shrine of Peace and Our Lady of Lourdes Shrine and Museum, which contains pictures, plans and tools depicting the history of the grounds. The lush gardens of St. Phillips Church contain several other shrines and St. Jude's Chapel, constructed entirely of hand-cut logs. The .2-mile-long Wonder Cave contains 26 shrines depicting the life and teachings of Jesus.

Daily 10-5, Memorial Day weekend-Labor Day; by appointment rest of year. Wonder Cave $2.50; ages 12-17, $1.25; ages 6-11, 25c. Grotto Gardens by donation. Phone (715) 435-3120.

ST. CROIX FALLS (D-1)
pop. 2,033, elev. 884′

St. Croix Falls is a center for outdoor recreation in the scenic valley of the St. Croix River. Long noted for excellent lake and stream fishing, the area is gaining popularity as a winter playground.

Two state fish hatcheries are easily accessible from St. Croix Falls. On River Street downtown, the St. Croix Falls Fish Hatchery stocks brook and brown trout. Osceola Fish Hatchery, 7 miles south on CR S, breeds all of the state's rainbow trout.

Polk County Information Center: 710 US 35S, St. Croix Falls, WI 54024; phone (715) 483-1410 or (800) 222-7655.

[GEM] **INTERSTATE STATE PARK** is .5 mi. s. of US 8 on US 35. The oldest of Wisconsin's state parks, it lies along the east side of the Dalles of the St. Croix River, a scenic gorge carved by glacial meltwater out of ancient bedrock. The canyon walls rise to a height of 200 feet above the river.

The Old Man of the Dalles, a strange rock formation, and potholes formed by the swirling current of glacial meltwaters are located in the park.

The area is one of nine units that make up the Ice Age National Scientific Reserve. A 20-minute film about the reserve is shown in the Ice Age Interpretive Center, near the park entrance off SR 35.

Naturalist programs are offered Memorial Day weekend-Labor Day. The park has several hiking trails, and the lake offers a beach and bathhouse.

Boat trips through the Dalles of the St. Croix River leave Taylors Falls, Minn., daily May 1 to mid-Oct. Park open daily 6 a.m.-11 p.m. Interpretive center open daily 8:30-4:30, Memorial Day-Labor Day; hours vary, rest of year. Admission per private vehicle $10, state residents $5. Annual permit $30, state residents $20. Phone (715) 483-3747. *See Recreation Chart and the AAA Great Lakes CampBook.*

ST. CROIX NATIONAL SCENIC RIVERWAY (E-1, B-2)

Reaching from northern Wisconsin to the St. Croix's juncture with the Mississippi River just s.e. of Minneapolis-St. Paul, the St. Croix National Scenic Riverway is a 252-mile river reserve. The Upper St. Croix River and its tributary, the Namekagon River, were among the original eight rivers designated as National Wild and Scenic Rivers in 1968. Four years later the Lower St. Croix River from St. Croix Falls to Prescott was added to the system by the National Park Service.

For hundreds of years the St. Croix was an important link between the Mississippi and Lake Superior. Besides being a major waterway, the St. Croix possessed marshes, pools and rapids that provided a wealth of food and fur for the Chippewa who once lived in this area. Beaver, otter and other pelts became the currency of a profitable trade with the French.

During the 17th and 18th centuries the river rang with the raucous songs of *voyageurs* as they paddled their loaded canoes up the St. Croix and down the Brule River to Lake Superior and eventually to Fort William. By the mid-19th century a new sound was heard, as logs thundered down the St. Croix from the sawmills strung along its banks.

Other than the development along its lower portion and the legacy of dams, the river retains much of its pristine nature. Both the Namekagon and St. Croix begin as narrow streams winding through forests, marshes and wide valleys. When the two rivers join, the riverway becomes wider, deeper and slower, making the area popular for small powerboats and canoes. The last segment below St. Croix Falls becomes wider and more civilized yet, marked by towns and pleasure craft.

General Information and Activities

The upper reaches of the St. Croix Riverway are canoe waters, with only a few rapids and none classified as white water. The canoeing season generally begins in May and ends in September; outfitters can be found in Trego, Webb Lake and other towns on the riverway.

Canoe-access primitive camping predominates. Along the Wisconsin-Minnesota border several state forests and parks offer developed campsites, hiking and cross-country skiing.

Bass and muskellunge can be found along the entire riverway; trout are found in the headwaters. Anglers favor the upper reaches. Otters and such

birds as osprey compete with the anglers for fish. The presence of these and other animals and waterfowl draw both birdwatchers and hunters. Fishing and hunting licenses are required within the riverway.

The proximity to urban areas and the river's width and placidity make the lower reaches below St. Croix Falls a popular area for boaters, water skiers and sailors. Highlights in this area include the scenic gorge in Interstate State Park *(see St. Croix Falls p. 169)* and the Apple River, which joins the St. Croix and is one of the most popular rivers in the state for tubing.

ADDRESS inquiries to the Superintendent, St. Croix National Scenic Riverway, 401 Hamilton St., P.O. Box 708, St. Croix Falls, WI 54024; phone (715) 483-3284.

Points of Interest

NAMEKAGON VISITOR CENTER is in Trego on US 63. Animal tracks and a handmade birch bark canoe are among the exhibits, which focus on logging, the riverway, fur trade and wildlife. Thurs.-Mon. 9-4:30, Memorial Day weekend-Labor Day. Hours may vary; phone ahead. Phone (715) 635-8346.

ST. CROIX VISITOR CENTER is in St. Croix Falls at Hamilton and Massachusetts aves. The center has exhibits about logging, the area's Scandinavian immigrants and regional geology, as well as a slide program, movie and information about the riverway. Fri.-Mon. 9:30-4:30, May 1 to mid-Oct.; Mon.-Fri. 8:30-4:30, rest of year. Phone (715) 483-3284, ext. 638.

SAUKVILLE—*see Milwaukee p. 160.*

SHAWANO (E-7) pop. 8,298, elev. 822′

Shawano has grown from a lumber boom town to a retail trade center for the region's small farms. Shawano is among Wisconsin's leading dairy counties.

With its rolling hills beckoning cross-country skiers and its miles of snowmobile trails, Shawano is popular for winter recreation. Ice fishing as well as summer water sports are available on the Wolf River and Shawano Lake *(see Recreation Chart).* The Navarino Nature Center, 15 miles south on CR K, offers bicycling and nature trails and cross-country skiing in winter.

Two former railroad corridors, now serving as recreational trails, pass through Shawano. The Mountain Bay and the Wiouwash state trails are open to hikers all year and to other recreational users seasonally; a fee is charged. Phone (715) 526-9150 for information.

Shawano Area Chamber of Commerce: 213 E. Green Bay St., P.O. Box 38, Shawano, WI 54166; phone (715) 524-2139 or (800) 235-8528.

SHEBOYGAN (G-8) pop. 50,792, elev. 625'

Although the audible thunder of the falls 3 miles up the Sheboygan River may have inspired the American Indian term (Shawb-wa-way-going—"rumbling underground") for this location, the town means sausage and cheese to many people because of its industries. Sheboygan also is an active Lake Michigan port; in addition to its savories, it produces and distributes steel, furniture, clothing and leather goods. It also is a major retail trade center for the surrounding dairying region.

Scenic drives along the lakeshore include Broughton Drive, and Lakeshore Drive and North 3rd Street. Lake Michigan offers good boating and fishing; other recreational pastimes are available at nearby Kohler-Andrae State Park *(see Recreation Chart and the AAA Great Lakes CampBook).*

Sheboygan County Convention and Visitors Bureau: 712 Riverfront Dr., Suite 101, Sheboygan, WI 53081-4665; phone (920) 457-9495 or (800) 457-9497.

JOHN MICHAEL KOHLER ARTS CENTER is at 608 New York Ave. Visual and performing arts are presented in a restored house and gallery. Folk art exhibitions are displayed and a theater presents stage, dance and concert productions. An interactive exhibit offers a chance for children to explore various aspects of art; phone for schedule to the interactive exhibit. Center open Mon.-Fri. 10-5 (also Tues. and Thurs. 5-8), Sat.-Sun. 10-4; closed major holidays. Free. Phone (920) 458-6144.

SHEBOYGAN COUNTY HISTORICAL SOCIETY MUSEUM is at 3110 Erie Ave. The museum includes an 1850s Victorian mansion, an 1860s log house furnished with pioneer items, an early 20th-century barn that houses farm tools and machinery used by early settlers, and an 1867 cheese factory.

Other exhibits highlight American Indian history, ice harvesting, immigration, the circus, sports, maritime history and early agriculture. Allow 1 hour minimum. Tues.-Sat. 10-5, Apr.-Oct.; Wed.-Sun. noon-5, Thanksgiving to mid-Dec. Admission $3; ages 7-12, $1. Phone (920) 458-1103.

SHEBOYGAN INDIAN MOUND PARK is just s. of Panther Ave. at 5000 S. 9th St. American Indian burial mounds in the park are shaped like panthers and deer. Dating from A.D. 500 to 1000, this is one of the few mound groups still intact. A nature trail leads to the lush valley of Hartman Creek, where both upland and lowland plant communities are identified. Self-guiding tours daily 10-10. Free. Phone (920) 459-3444.

SHELL LAKE (C-2) pop. 1,309, elev. 1,241'

[SAVE] **MUSEUM OF WOODCARVING** is at jct. SR 63/CR B. The collection of Joseph Barta's hand-carved wood figurines depicts such Biblical events as The Last Supper. Barta created the 400 miniature and 100 life-size figures over a span of 30 years, using oak, poplar, walnut and basswood.

Allow 30 minutes minimum. Daily 9-6, May-Oct. Admission $4.50; under 12, $2.50. Phone (715) 468-7100.

SPARTA (G-4) pop. 8,648, elev. 793'

Sparta calls itself "the bicycling capital of the world" and is home to the western end of the Elroy-Sparta State Trail. Running through Kendall, the 32-mile bicycling trail was the nation's first to be converted from an abandoned railroad bed. For maps and information, phone (608) 463-7109 May through Oct.

The [SAVE] Deke Slayton Memorial Space & Bicycle Museum displays artifacts, documents and photographs related to the Sparta native's career as an aviator and astronaut, as well as exhibits related to the history of the bicycle. The exhibits are on the second floor of the Monroe County Museum at 200 W. Main St.; phone (608) 269-0033.

Six miles east of Sparta is Fort McCoy, the state's only U.S. Army installation. Two recreation areas on the base are open to the public: Pine View offers camping, hiking, boating, swimming, fishing and hunting. For information, phone (608) 388-3517. Whitetail Ridge is a winter facility for downhill and cross-country skiing, snow-tubing and snowmobiling. For information, phone (608) 388-4498.

SPOONER (C-2) pop. 2,653, elev. 1,065'

A railroad junction during the lumbering era, Spooner was named after John Coit Spooner, a railroad attorney elected to the U.S. Senate in 1885 and 1897. Spooner is now a popular resort in the wooded lake country of northwestern Wisconsin. More than 900 lakes attract tourists to Washburn County. A float trip down the Namekagon River is a popular pastime; landings are in Trego, 5 miles north of Spooner at the junction of US 53 and US 63, and on CR K, 10 miles north of Spooner.

Washburn County Tourist Information Center: 122 N. River St., Spooner, WI 54801; phone (715) 635-9696 or (800) 367-3306.

Self-guiding tours: The Spooner Heritage Walking Tour showcases some of the city's oldest homes and businesses. Also on the tour are the sites of Spooner's first school and church services. The tour guidebook can be obtained from the tourist information center.

GOVERNOR TOMMY G. THOMPSON STATE FISH HATCHERY is .5 mi. w. of US 63 on SR 70 to 951 W. Maple St. Said to be the world's largest muskellunge-rearing facility, the hatchery also produces Northern pike and walleye. The best viewing opportunities are available in May. A visitor center is on the premises. Guided tours are given Mon.-Fri. at 10 and 2, May 1-Labor Day. Free. Phone (715) 635-4147.

RAILROAD MEMORIES MUSEUM is at 424 Front St. behind the post office parking lot. This museum in the former Chicago and Northwestern Depot displays 12 rooms of railroad memorabilia including tools used by track workers, firemen and brakemen; headlights; lanterns; uniforms; railroad logos; office equipment; and promotional materials from various railroads.

A library, an art room featuring railroad prints and originals, and a video room are offered. Allow 30 minutes minimum. Daily 10-5, Memorial Day-Labor Day. Admission $3; ages 6-12, 50c. Phone (715) 635-3325 or (715) 635-2752.

WISCONSIN GREAT NORTHERN RAILROAD is at 426 N. Front St. Round-trip sightseeing excursions travel from Spooner to Trego and Springbrook. The historic train features a 1940 locomotive with restored cars from 1912 and 1918. Dinner trains, hobo specialty train tours and special events are offered.

Allow 3 hours minimum. Sightseeing trips depart from the Spooner depot daily at 1 and 4 (also Tues.-Sat. at 10 a.m.), June 30-Oct. 7; Sat.-Sun. at 1 and 4, May 5-June 24; Sat.-Sun. at 10, 12:30 and 3, Oct. 13-28. Schedule may vary; phone ahead. Reservations are recommended. Fare $10-$18, ages 3-12, $10-$12. Phone (715) 635-3200.

SPRING GREEN (H-4) pop. 1,444, elev. 729′

Frank Lloyd Wright chose this farming community on the Wisconsin River as the site for his home, Taliesin, and for his architectural school. As a result, Spring Green has a great concentration of Wright-influenced structures. In contrast to Wright's break with tradition, Spring Green's American Players Theatre bases its reputation on its adherence to the classics.

Across the river is Tower Hill State Park (see Recreation Chart and the AAA Great Lakes CampBook). The restored Civil War shot tower is the last vestige of the town of Helena, a busy river port and railhead that once contended for the status of territorial capital.

Spring Green Area Chamber of Commerce/ Visitors Council: 150 Jefferson St., P.O. Box 3, Spring Green, WI 53588; phone (608) 588-2054 or (800) 588-2042.

FRANK LLOYD WRIGHT'S TALIESIN is 3 mi. s. on SR 23. The noted architect's primary home and studio was designed in 1902 out of sandstone and native oak. Wright continued to enhance the site throughout his life. Included on the grounds are a school, small theater, living and dining rooms, drafting studios, a gallery containing furniture Wright designed, artwork from his Asian collection and photograph murals and models of buildings he designed.

Food is available. Allow 1 hour minimum. Visitor center open daily 9-6, May-Oct. Hours may vary; phone ahead. Hillside tours depart daily on the hour 10-4. Tour fees $15-$75. Reservations are recommended for tours of the Wright home. Phone (608) 588-7900.

THE HOUSE ON THE ROCK is 9 mi. s. on SR 23. Designed and built by Alex Jordan Jr. beginning in the early 1940s, this once architecturally-innovative 14-room house is now a complex of interconnecting buildings with themed rooms, streets and gardens on 200 acres. The house contains pools of running water, waterfalls, massive fireplaces and a room of windows jutting out over the valley. Exhibits cover a broad range of themes including antique guns, a carousel, crown jewelry replicas, cannons, bisque dolls and Oriental art, among others.

The view from the observation deck stretches 30 miles; the Infinity Room, extending 218 feet out over the Wyoming Valley below, also offers an excellent view through some 3,264 panes of glass. A 350-foot-long overhead walkway connects the gatehouse to the house.

Self-guiding tours take 2 to 4 hours. Strollers are not permitted. The entire complex is open daily 9-7, mid-Mar. through the last full weekend in Oct.; closed Thanksgiving and Dec. 24-25. Christmas tours are conducted Tues.-Sun. 9-6, early Nov.-early Jan. Last admission 1 hour before closing. Fee to the complex is $19.50; ages 7-12, $11.50; ages 4-6, $5.50. Fee for holiday tours $12.50; ages 7-12, $7.50; ages 4-6, $3.50. DS, MC, VI. Phone (608) 935-3639, ext. 123.

SPRING VALLEY (E-2)
pop. 1,189, elev. 1,100′

CRYSTAL CAVE is 1 mi. w. on SR 29. Passageways carved by an underground river and thousands of cave formations can be seen. Allow 1 hour minimum. Guided 1-hour tours depart daily 9:30-5:30, every 30 minutes, May 15-Labor Day; daily 9:30-4:30, day after Labor Day-Oct. 31; Sat.-Sun. 9:30-4:30, Apr. 1-May 14. Fee $8.75; ages 13-17, $6.75; ages 4-12, $4.75. DS, MC, VI. Phone (715) 778-4414 or (800) 236-2283.

STEVENS POINT (E-6)
pop. 24,551, elev. 1,084′

Stevens Point was founded by George Stevens as a trading post on the Wisconsin River in 1838. Since its incorporation as a city in 1859, Stevens Point has fostered many industries including Worzalla Publishing; Herrschners, a needlecraft distribution center; Sentry Insurance; and the Stevens Point Brewery.

For recreation there are 11 swimming lakes and 19 public parks in or around Stevens Point; lakes DuBay and Emily and Sunset Lake are particularly popular. Rainbow Falls Family Park in Plover features five waterslides and a wave pool. In winter cross-country skiers glide along more than 36 miles of trails that lace the surrounding countryside, and downhill skiers enjoy the two nearby slopes.

The University of Wisconsin-Stevens Point campus offers a wealth of activities at minimal or no cost. "E Pluribus Unum," a mosaic mural on the wall of the College of Natural Resources, depicts the university and its environs using 25 tons of tiled panels.

Stevens Point Area Convention & Visitors Bureau: 340 Division St. N., Stevens Point, WI 54481; phone (715) 344-2556, or (800) 236-4636 in Iowa, Wis., upper Mich. and Minneapolis.

MUSEUM OF NATURAL HISTORY is in the Albertson Learning Resources Center of the University of Wisconsin-Stevens Point. Exhibits include a large collection of preserved birds and bird eggs as well as other wildlife displays. The museum features minerals, dinosaur fossils, exhibits about ecosystems and two African savanna dioramas. Allow 1 hour minimum. Mon.-Fri. 9-4 (also Mon. 4-7), Sat. 10-3, Sun. 1-4, Sept. 4 to mid-May; Mon.-Fri. 9-4, rest of year. Hours may vary during semester breaks and in summer. Free. Phone (715) 346-2858.

SCHMEECKLE RESERVE is on Northpoint Dr. The 275-acre wildlife preservation area offers natural history programs. Bicycling and hiking trails are available. A visitor center and the Wisconsin Conservation Hall of Fame are on the grounds. Picnicking is permitted. Daily 8-5. Free. Phone (715) 346-4992.

STURGEON BAY—

see Door County p. 129.

SUPERIOR (A-2) pop. 27,368, elev. 638′

By the millions of tons, ore, grain and coal pour through the great port at Superior-Duluth. This excellent deepwater harbor at the head of Lake Superior ranks among the nation's leading ports in tonnage. Along the 28 miles of shoreline in Superior are shipyards, grain elevators, many heavy industries and some of the world's largest docks.

The campus of the University of Wisconsin-Superior and a number of parks are part of the municipal geography. Billings Park, at the west end of 21st Street, includes many lagoons and gardens.

Scenic Amnicon Falls highlights nearby Amnicon Falls State Park. Pattison State Park, south of the city, offers varied summer and winter recreation and has the highest waterfall in the state. *See Recreation Chart and the AAA Great Lakes CampBook.*

Superior also boasts one of the largest municipal forests in the country. The 4,500-acre Superior Municipal Forest offers 17 miles of trails for cross-country skiing and hiking. The Tri-County Corridor provides a snowmobile and all-terrain vehicle trail through the city of Superior. The trail allows travel through Wisconsin from Canada, Minnesota and Michigan.

Superior/Douglas County Chamber of Commerce and Convention & Visitors Bureau: 205 Belknap St., Superior, WI 54880; phone (715) 392-2773 or (800) 942-5313.

BARKER'S ISLAND is at US 2/53. Accessible from the mainland, the island combines a 420-slip marina with a shopping village, an 18-hole miniature golf course, playground, picnic area, beach and the SS *Meteor* Maritime Museum *(see attraction listing).* Charters are available for fishing, sailing and harbor cruises. Phone (715) 392-2773.

FAIRLAWN MANSION is off US 2/53 to 906 E. 2nd St. The 42-room Victorian mansion is styled after a French chateau. Overlooking Lake Superior and Barker's Island, Fairlawn was built in 1890 for the family of Martin Pattison, a late 19th-century lumber and mining baron and the second mayor of Superior. The first-floor rooms are restored, showing the lavish use of carved wood, marble, silver trim, brass and English tile and Victorian paintings.

Allow 1 hour minimum. Guided tours on the hour daily 9-4, Memorial Day-Labor Day; otherwise varies. Closed Jan. 1, Easter, Thanksgiving and Dec. 25. Fee $7; over 62 and students with ID, $5.50. Phone (715) 394-5712.

SS *METEOR* MARITIME MUSEUM is on US 2/53 on Barker's Island. Now a museum, this Great Lakes vessel, the last remaining whaleback ship, carried a cargoes of iron ore, oil, grain and automobiles 1896-1962. Guided tours are offered. Daily 9-5, mid-May to mid-Oct. Admission $5, over 62 and students with ID $3.50; ages 6-12, $3.50. Phone (715) 394-5712.

VISTA FLEET/SUPERIOR-DULUTH HARBOR CRUISES depart from the Barker's Island Dock, jct. US 2/SR 13. Passengers can enjoy a narrated sightseeing tour of the Superior-Duluth Harbor aboard the *Vista King.* The tour passes by some of the world's largest grain elevators, Great Lakes freighters, ore docks and the open span of the Aerial Lift Bridge. Lunch, dinner and moonlight cruises are available aboard the *Vista Star* and depart from the D.E.C.C. Dock in Duluth, Minn. *(see attraction listing in AAA North Central TourBook).*

Cruises depart daily, mid-May to mid-Oct. Sightseeing fare $10; ages 3-12, $5. AX, DS, MC, VI. Phone (715) 394-6846 or (218) 722-6218.

TOMAHAWK (D-5) pop. 3,770, elev. 1,450′

The joining of the Somo, Spirit and Tomahawk rivers with the Wisconsin abetted Tomahawk's early growth as a lumber town and continues to enhance its popularity as an all-year North Woods resort area. Game fish, deer and small game are abundant. Eleven local parks provide opportunities for picnicking and other outdoor activities. The Hiawatha Trail, a 6.6-mile bicycle, hiking and snowmobile trail, begins in Tomahawk and extends northward to Lake Nokomis.

Water ski shows are held 3 nights a week mid-June through August at Kwahamot Bay. Winter sports activities include snowmobiling, cross-country skiing and ice fishing.

Tomahawk Regional Chamber of Commerce: 208 N. 4th St., P.O. Box 412, Tomahawk, WI 54487; phone (715) 453-5334 or (800) 569-2160.

TWO RIVERS (F-9) pop. 12,639, elev. 587'

As it has been since the 1830s, the harbor at Two Rivers is the home of an important commercial fishing fleet. Light, diversified industry augments the economy. Point Beach State Forest *(see Recreation Chart and the AAA Great Lakes CampBook)* lies along Lake Michigan north of town.

Woodland Dunes Nature Center, west off SR 310, is a bird-banding station, wildlife research area and wildflower sanctuary in a woodland and meadow habitat with hiking trails and nature displays; phone (920) 793-4007.

HAMILTON WOOD TYPE AND PRINTING MUSEUM is at 1619 Jefferson St. Housed in a 1926 Hamilton factory, this museum preserves an extensive collection of 19th- and 20th-century wood type and printing equipment, much of it in working condition and used in visitor demonstrations. Exhibits include hand-operated printing presses, artisan tools, cutting patterns, rare type specimen catalogs and printing memorabilia. Allow 30 minutes minimum. Daily 1-5; closed Dec. 25. Free. Phone (920) 794-6272.

VIROQUA (G-4) pop. 4,335, elev. 1,280'

Following the initial wave of Eastern settlers, Norwegian immigrants successfully introduced tobacco farming and dairying into the region around Viroqua. Arriving by covered wagon in 1853 was Jeremiah McLain Rusk, who served in Congress for 6 years and as governor for three successive terms.

VERNON COUNTY HISTORICAL MUSEUM is at 410 S. Center Ave. County history is depicted through displays about pioneer farming, Civil War items and genealogical material. Tours are available by appointment. Tues.-Sat. noon-4, May 15-Sept. 15; Tues.-Thurs. noon-4 or by appointment, rest of year. Closed major holidays. Donations. Phone (608) 637-7396.

WASHINGTON ISLAND—

see Door County p. 129.

WATERFORD (I-8) pop. 4,048, elev. 949'

GREEN MEADOWS FARM is 3 mi. w. on SR 20. This working farm has more than 200 farm animals. A 2-hour guided tour includes tractor-drawn hay rides, pony rides, a petting farm, milking demonstrations followed by hands-on experience, and, in October, pumpkin picking. Tours Tues.-Sat. 10-noon, mid-June to late Aug.; Mon.-Fri. 10-noon, Sat.-Sun. 10-2 in Oct. Admission $9.50, under 2 free. Phone (262) 534-2891.

WATERTOWN (H-6) pop. 21,598, elev. 825'

Watertown has been essentially industrial since its founding in the 1830s, when New Englanders harnessed the rapids of the Rock River to produce power for their sawmills, wagonworks and other factories. Many of the first arrivals were German intellectuals fleeing political conditions in the fatherland after the 1848 revolution.

One of these was Carl Schurz, who entered local politics on the new Republican ticket and ultimately became minister to Spain under President Abraham Lincoln. It is his wife, however, who is remembered: While living in Watertown in 1856, Margarethe Meyer established what is considered to be the nation's first kindergarten. She was a student of Fredrich Froebel, the renowned German pioneer of infant education.

Watertown Area Chamber of Commerce: 519 E. Main St., Watertown, WI 53094; phone (920) 261-6320.

OCTAGON HOUSE is at 919 Charles St. This 1854 dwelling includes five floors furnished with antiques. The house contains a central 40-foot circular stairway. What is considered to have been the nation's first kindergarten, furnished in period, also is on the grounds. A late 1800s barn, moved from the old Watertown-Milwaukee Plank Road, houses farm implements and exhibits.

Allow 1 hour, 30 minutes minimum. Daily 10-4, Memorial Day-Labor Day; 11-3, May 1-day before Memorial Day and day after Labor Day-Oct. 31. Admission $5.50; over 65, $5; ages 6-17, $3; family rate (2 adults and children under 18) $15. Phone (920) 261-2796.

WAUKESHA—*see Milwaukee p. 160.*

WAUPACA (F-6) pop. 5,676, elev. 868'

The resort community of Waupaca, near a chain of 22 lakes to the southwest, supposedly was named after Sam Waupaca, a Potawatomi chief credited with persuading his braves not to massacre the white settlers in the area. The chief collapsed and died at the conclusion of the speech.

Waupaca is a popular departure point for canoe and launch trips through the spring-fed lakes and along Crystal River; canoe rentals are available locally. The area's well-stocked trout streams, also filled with pickerel, bass and small pan fish, are extremely popular with anglers.

Nearby Hartman Creek State Park *(see Recreation Chart and the AAA Great Lakes CampBook)* has developed recreational facilities, including snowmobile trails that connect with 288 miles of groomed trails and 150 miles of club trails throughout Waupaca County.

Near the property of The Red Mill, 3 miles south on CR K, are the quaint Chapel in the Woods and one of the two surviving covered bridges in Wisconsin *(see Cedarburg p. 159).* The old mill, built in 1855, has a 24-foot waterwheel, one of the largest in America. Friday night band concerts are performed in the summer in the Gay '90s bandstand in City Square.

Waupaca Area Chamber of Commerce: 221 S. Main St., Waupaca, WI 54981; phone (715) 258-7343 or (888) 417-4040.

CHIEF WAUPACA STERNWHEELER CRUISE is at Clear Water Harbor, 3.7 mi. s.w. of US 10 on CR QQ. Narrated 90-minute cruises travel the Waupaca Chain o' Lakes. Brunch cruises also are available. Cruises depart daily at 11:30, 1, 2:30 and 4, Memorial Day weekend-Labor Day; Sat.-Sun. at 1, weekend after Labor Day-last weekend in Oct. Sightseeing fare $6.95; ages 3-12, $4.95. Phone (715) 258-2866.

WAUPUN (G-7) pop. 10,718, elev. 894′

Waupun sometimes is called the "City of Sculpture." Statues, presented to the city by the late industrialist Clarence Shaler, include the first bronze casting of James Earl Fraser's "End of the Trail." "The Recording Angel," by Lorado Taft, stands in the Forest Mound Cemetery.

Shaler himself was a sculptor; some of his works include "Dawn of Day" on the City Hall terrace, "The Pioneers" in Wilcox Park and "Doe and Fawn" at Rock River Country Club. Others include "Pioneer Woman" and "The Citadel" as well as two of his other sculptures found on the campus of Ripon College in Ripon *(see place listing p. 169)*.

Waupun Chamber of Commerce: 121 E. Main St., Suite A, Waupun, WI 53963; phone (920) 324-3491.

HORICON MARSH is entered e. on SR 49. The marsh occupies 32,000 acres of wetlands and uplands.

During the mid-April migration as many as 20,000 Canada geese use the marsh as a stopover point. Fall migration from mid-September to mid-November brings more than 1 million birds through the marsh. Mallards, redheads, ruddy ducks and blue-wing teals nest during the summer; egrets, herons, muskrats, coots and deer also are common. Write Superintendent, W4279 Headquarters Rd., Mayville, WI 53050.

Hiking trails open dawn-dusk. Free. Phone (920) 387-2658 or (920) 387-7860.

MARSH HAVEN NATURE CENTER is adjacent to the Horicon Marsh on SR 49. A 30-foot-tall observation tower, theater, wildlife dioramas, art exhibits and a display of live birds are housed at the center, which offers information about American Indian history, glaciers, trees and tools. Picnicking is permitted. Mon.-Fri. noon-4, Sat.-Sun. and holidays 9-5, mid-May to mid-Nov. Admission $1; under 13, 50c. Phone (920) 324-5818.

WAUSAU (E-5) pop. 38,426, elev. 1,204′

No longer considered far away (Wausau means "far away place"), Wausau ranks among the state's major industrial centers. This busy Wisconsin Valley city began as a sawmill settlement called Big Bull Falls. After the timber supply was depleted, farming and diversified manufacturing sustained the economy. Marathon County continues to be one of the nation's leading producers of cheddar cheese and ginseng.

Glimpses of the town's past can be seen in the Andrew Warren Historic District, a 10-block area of Wausau that preserves more than 60 historic buildings.

Wausau/Central Wisconsin Convention & Visitors Bureau: 10204 Park Plaza, Suite B, Mosinee, WI 54455; phone (715) 355-8788 or (888) 948-4748.

Shopping areas: Cedar Creek Factory Stores, US 51 exit 185, offer outlet shopping. Dealers display antiques at Rib Mountain Antique Mall, 3300 Eagle Ave. Wausau Center, 3rd and Washington streets, features more than 60 stores, including JCPenney, Sears and Younkers.

LEIGH YAWKEY WOODSON ART MUSEUM is at 700 N. 12th St. Housed in a Tudor-style building, the museum presents changing exhibitions by national and international artists. Highlights include wildlife paintings and sculptures, decorative arts and a large outdoor sculpture garden. Birds in Art, presented each fall, is recognized as one of the finest exhibitions of bird paintings and sculpture, in the world. Allow 1 hour minimum. Tues.-Fri. 9-4, Sat.-Sun. noon-5; closed holidays. Free. Phone (715) 845-7010.

MARATHON COUNTY HISTORICAL MUSEUM is at 403 and 410 McIndoe St. The first floor preserves the 1900 neoclassical house of Cyrus Yawkey, a wealthy lumberman. Ionic columns and elaborate door and window frames mark the entrance. The living room, music room, dining room and den are furnished in period. The basement contains a model railroad display. A library and exhibit area are located across the street in the Woodson House. Tues.-Thurs. 9-4:30, Sat.-Sun. 1-4:30; closed holidays. Admission for Yawkey house $3, ages 12-12, $2. Phone (715) 842-5750.

RIB MOUNTAIN STATE PARK is near the jct. US 51 and CR N. Rising to 1,940 feet, Rib Mountain is one of the highest points in Wisconsin. The park has hiking trails, an observation tower with two observation decks offering a view of the scenic Wisconsin River valley, camping sites, a 170-seat amphitheater and one of the Midwest's finest ski areas. Daily 6 a.m.-11 p.m. Admission per private vehicle $10, state residents $5. Annual permit $30, state residents $20. Phone (715) 842-2522. *See Recreation Chart and the AAA Great Lakes CampBook.*

WEST BEND—*see Milwaukee p. 161.*

WEST SALEM (G-3) pop. 4,540, elev. 746′

When the railroad was laid a mile south of Neshonoc in 1858, the village's population of Easterners and Norwegians packed up and moved to West Salem near the tracks. Thomas Leonard, West Salem's founder, had offered the railroad free land if it would build a station in West Salem rather than in one of the neighboring towns. The railroad accepted Leonard's offer, ensuring the town's growth. Historic Salem, 99 Jefferson St., is Leonard's 1859 home.

This farm trade center became best known for its creamery, capable of producing a million pounds of butter annually. Emerging from this rural environment was one of Wisconsin's foremost authors, Hamlin Garland. Deeply influenced by his childhood on the frontier, Garland set his autobiographical "Middle Border" books and some dozen short stories in the coulee area around La Crosse.

HAMLIN GARLAND HOMESTEAD is at 357 W. Garland St. The house has been restored as a memorial to the winner of 1921 Pulitzer Prize. Of particular note is the upstairs study where Garland did much of his writing. Allow 30 minutes minimum. Guided tours Mon.-Sat. 10-4:30, Sun. 1-4:30, Memorial Day weekend-Labor Day; by appointment rest of year. Admission $1; ages 6-18, 50c; family rate $2.50. Phone (608) 786-1399 or (608) 786-1675.

PALMER-GULLICKSON OCTAGON HOUSE is at 360 N. Leonard St. Built in 1856, the eight-sided house displays original Victorian furnishings. Allow 30 minutes minimum. Guided tours Mon.-Sat. 10-4:30, Sun. 1-4:30, Memorial Day weekend-Labor Day; by appointment rest of year. Admission $1; ages 6-18, 50c; family rate $2.50. Phone (608) 786-1675 or (608) 786-1399.

WISCONSIN DELLS (G-5)
pop. 2,418, elev. 899'

Believed by the early Winnebago Indians to be the path of a giant serpent, considered a bane by 19th-century log drivers, and a fascination to geologists and photographers—the scenic dells of the Wisconsin River are the state's foremost natural attraction. The river has cut a channel through soft sandstone to a depth of 150 feet and, for a distance of 15 miles, has carved the rock into fantastic forms. A dam separates the river into the Upper and Lower dells.

In 1856 the center of population and business of the region was the flourishing town of Newport. Then the railroad decided to build its bridge 2 miles north, and Newport ceased to exist almost overnight. Several buildings were moved to the new site, called Kilbourn City. To publicize the geologic novelty of the dells, Kilbourn City was renamed Wisconsin Dells in 1931.

In addition to countless summer recreational opportunities, Wisconsin Dells offers varied winter diversions, including 610 miles of snowmobile trails. Devil's Lake and Mirror Lake state parks *(see Recreation Chart and Baraboo and Lake Delton in the AAA Great Lakes CampBook)* offer cross-country ski trails, and four downhill ski areas are within a 20-mile radius.

Wisconsin Dells Visitor & Convention Bureau: 701 Superior St., Wisconsin Dells, WI 53965; phone (608) 254-8088 or (800) 223-3557.

DELLS ARMY DUCKS is off I-90 exit 92, then n. on US 12 to 1550 Wisconsin Dells Pkwy. Passengers board amphibious vehicles for 1-hour land and water tours through the Lower Dells glacial area of the Wisconsin River region. Among the formations seen are the Sugar Bowl & Grotto Island, Twin Ink Stand and Lone Rock. A tour of the Upper Dells aboard the *Mark Twain* features such sites as Black Hawk Island, Chapel Gorge and Chimney Rock. Daily 9-6, May-Oct. Fare $17.50; ages 6-11, $9. DS, MC, VI. Phone (608) 254-6080.

[SAVE] **DELLS AUTO MUSEUM** is at 591 Wisconsin Dells Pkwy. Displays include antique automobiles, Indianapolis pace cars, license plates, a doll collection, toys and antique clothing. The museum specializes in antique convertibles. Allow 30 minutes minimum. Daily 9-9, mid-April through Labor Day; Sat.-Sun. 10-5, day after Labor Day-Oct. 31. Admission $4.50; senior citizens $3.25; ages 6-12, $2.25. Phone (608) 254-2008 or (608) 221-1964.

[GEM] **DELLS BOAT TOURS** depart from the center of town at the Upper Dells Landing on SR 13/16/23, and from the Lower Dells Landing at jct. US 12 and SR 13/16/23. The trips offer tours through the Upper and Lower dells of the Wisconsin River. The 2-hour Upper Dells tour includes sandstone cliffs, rock formations and stops at Witches Gulch and Stand Rock to walk along nature trails. The 1-hour, non-stop Lower Dells cruise goes past unusual rock formations, caverns and the Rocky Islands. Tickets are available at booths throughout the Dells area.

Boats depart daily every 30-45 minutes 9-6, June-Aug.; less frequently in Apr.-May and Sept.-Oct. Fare for 2-hour Upper Dells tour $17.75; ages 6-11, $9. Fare for 1-hour Lower Dells tour $14.75; ages 6-11, $7.50. Combination Upper and Lower Dells tour $24.75; ages 6-11, $13. AX, DS, MC, VI. Phone (608) 254-8555.

[SAVE] **FAMILY LAND** is 1 mi. s. on US 12. This 35-acre water park offers 29 waterslides, a wave pool, double speedslide, flume slides, inner tube ride, water playground, bumper boats, miniature golf, the Huck's Lagoon interactive water-play site and the Demon's Drop and Dragon's Tail rides. Allow 4 hours minimum. Daily 9-7, Memorial Day weekend-Labor Day. Admission (includes Bay of Dreams) $23.95, under 3 free. AX, DS, MC, VI. Phone (608) 254-7766.

Bay of Dreams is adjacent to Family Land. Open year-round, this indoor water park features a Mayan-themed adventure river, a children's pirate ship and one of the longest and tallest waterslides in the nation. Daily 10-10, Memorial Day weekend-Labor Day. Park opens at 10:30 a.m. rest of year; closing times vary. Admission Memorial Day weekend-Labor Day (includes Family Land)

$23.95, under 3 free. Admission rest of year Mon.-Thurs. $14.95; Fri.-Sun., holidays and spring break $19.95. AX, DS, MC, VI. Phone (608) 254-7766.

[SAVE] **H.H. BENNETT STUDIO & HISTORY CENTER** is at 215 Broadway. Personal photographs, equipment and an interactive exhibit area explain the life and contributions of Henry Hamilton Bennett to the photography industry. Guided tours are available. Allow 1 hour, 30 minutes minimum. Daily 10-5, May-Oct. Admission $5; over 64 and students with ID $4.50; ages 5-12, $2.50; family rate $13.50. MC, VI. Phone (608) 253-3523 or (866) 944-7483.

LOST CANYON is 3.5 mi. s. on US 12, then .5 mi. e. on Canyon Rd. Horse-drawn wagons leaving every 15 minutes tour the sandstone formations in the canyon. The walls of the canyon reach 80 feet in height. Picnic facilities are available. Allow 30 minutes minimum. Daily 8:30-dusk, mid-May through Labor Day; 10-6, day after Labor Day-Oct. 31. Admission $6.75; ages 4-11, $3.75. MC, VI. Phone (608) 254-8757.

[SAVE] **NOAH'S ARK WATERPARK** is 1.5 mi. s. on US 12 and SR 23. The park, located on 70 acres, features 36 water slides, two wave pools, two floating rivers, a paradise lagoon activity area, four play areas for children, an 18-hole miniature golf course and the thrill ride Noah's Incredible Adventure. Picnicking is permitted. Food is available. Allow 5 hours minimum. Daily 9-8, Memorial Day weekend-Labor Day. Hours may vary; phone ahead. All-day pass $27.99; over 55 and under 47" tall, $22.89; under 3 free. DS, MC, VI. Phone (608) 254-6351.

ORIGINAL WISCONSIN DUCKS INC. is 1 mi. s. on US 12 and SR 23. One-hour land and water tours aboard green and white vehicles cover 8.5 miles of the Wisconsin River, Lake Delton and scenic wilderness trails. Daily 8-7, June-Aug.; 9-5 in May; 9-4, Sept.-Oct.; 10-4 in Apr. Fare $17.75; ages 6-11, $9. AX, DS, MC, VI. Phone (608) 254-8751.

[SAVE] **RIPLEY'S BELIEVE IT OR NOT!** is downtown at 115 Broadway. The museum displays bizarre and unusual items and relates events of the type featured in the well-known comic strip. Videotape displays throughout the two-story building describe other strange items discovered by Ripley. Allow 1 hour minimum. Daily 9 a.m.-midnight, June-Aug.; 10-6, mid-Apr. through May 31 and Sept. 1 to mid-Oct.; otherwise varies. Admission $8.95; ages 5-12, $5.95. DS, MC, VI. Phone (608) 253-7556.

RIVERVIEW PARK AND WATERWORLD is .2 mi. s. on US 12. The park offers amusement rides and racing vehicles, including Grand Prix cars and high-speed go-carts. Waterworld has two speed slides, three curved waterslides, a rapids tube ride, a children's pool and a wave pool. Allow 4 hours minimum. Opens daily at 10 a.m., Memorial Day weekend-Labor Day. Closing times for park and water rides vary from 5 to 11 p.m. Individual rides $3-$4. All-day pass for water activities $14. All-day pass for "you-drive" rides and other activities $21; under 5, $10.75. DS, MC, VI. Phone (608) 254-2608.

STORYBOOK GARDENS is at 1500 Wisconsin Dells Pkwy. The gardens contain a petting zoo and life-size statues that depict nursery rhyme characters. Miniature train rides also are featured. Daily 9:30-5, late May-Labor Day (weather permitting). Admission $7.95, under 2 free. MC, VI. Phone (608) 253-2391.

SAVE **TOMMY BARTLETT'S ROBOT WORLD AND EXPLORATORY** is 3 mi. s. on US 12 at 560 Wisconsin Dells Pkwy. This playground for the imagination includes virtual-reality exhibits, simulators, mirrors, puzzles, holograms and hands-on activities. The original Russian space station MIR also is displayed. Daily 8 a.m.-10 p.m., Memorial Day weekend-Labor Day; 10-4, rest of year. Admission $9.43, over 64, $7.55, under 6 free. DS, MC, VI. Phone (608) 254-2525.

SAVE **TOMMY BARTLETT SHOW** is 3 mi. s. on US 12 at 560 Wisconsin Dells Pkwy. A live outdoor entertainment show features professional water skiers, daredevil performers, a comedy juggler and an evening laser show fireworks finale. Shows daily at 1, 4:30 and 8:30, June 26-Labor Day; at 4:30 and 8:30, Memorial Day weekend-June 25. Admission $13.16-$20.24; over 64,

$10.75-$17.64; under 6 on lap free. Upgraded seating is available. DS, MC, VI. Phone (608) 254-2525.

WISCONSIN DEER PARK is 1 mi. s. on US 12. This 28-acre wildlife area is home to more than 100 deer of many varieties. Visitors may feed and pet the deer. Allow 1 hour minimum. Daily 9-7, Memorial Day-Labor Day; 10-4, day after Labor Day to mid-Oct. Admission $7.50; ages 3-11, $5.50. MC, VI. Phone (608) 253-2041.

WISCONSIN OPRY is .2 mi. s. of I-90/94 exit 92 on US 12. Country music by local and national professionals is showcased. Allow 2 hours minimum. Mon.-Sat. at 8 p.m. (dinner at 6 p.m.), some Sun. at 3 and 8 p.m., Memorial Day weekend-late Sept. Admission Mon.-Sat. $28.50, including meal; $15.50, without meal. Admission Sun. $30, including meal; $18, without meal. Phone (608) 254-7951 for schedule information.

RECREATIONAL ACTIVITIES
Fishing

- **B & H Trout Fishing** is 7 mi. n. to 3640 SR 13. Daily 6 a.m.-9 p.m. Phone (608) 254-7280.

- **Beaver Springs Fishing Park** is at 600 Trout Rd. Daily 9-8. Phone (608) 254-2735.

WISCONSIN RAPIDS (F-5)
pop. 18,435, elev. 1,028'

Wisconsin Rapids, on the Wisconsin River, is in the center of the world's largest inland cranberry-producing area. Cranberry harvests take place from early September through October.

Some of the nation's largest manufacturers of business papers came after the river's rapids were harnessed to provide water power. Stora Enso North America, formerly Consolidated Papers, offers guided tours of its papermaking facilities; phone (715) 422-3789 for reservations.

Wisconsin Rapids Municipal Zoo at 1911 Gaynor Ave. is open from Memorial Day-Labor Day; a petting zoo, playground and picnic facilities are available. The area's historical background is described at South Wood County Historical Society Museum, 540 3rd St. S.; phone (715) 423-1580.

Wisconsin Rapids Area Convention & Visitors Bureau: 2507 Eighth St. S., Wisconsin Rapids, WI 54494-5229; phone (715) 423-1830 or (800) 554-4484.

Self-guiding tours: Three historic walking tours in Wisconsin Rapids all have the Wisconsin River as their focal point. Brochures can be obtained from the convention and visitors bureau.

WOODRUFF (C-5) elev. 1,618'

Once a roistering settlement whose establishments provided for the pleasures of loggers in from the woods, Woodruff now caters to outdoors enthusiasts and vacationers enjoying the nearby forest and lake country. The area boasts one of the largest concentrations of freshwater lakes in the world. Old logging trails are groomed in the winter for cross-country skiing and snowmobiling, while bicyclists and hikers use them in the summer.

A unit of the Chequamegon-Nicolet National Forest *(see place listing p. 126)* and the Northern Highland-American Legion State Forest *(see Recreation Chart and the AAA Great Lakes CampBook)* flank the community.

Minocqua-Arbor Vitae-Woodruff Area Chamber of Commerce: 8216 US 51S, P.O. Box 1006, Minocqua, WI 54548; phone (715) 356-5266 or (800) 446-6784.

ART OEHMCKE STATE FISH HATCHERY is .7 mi. s.e. on SR 47, then 1.5 mi. e. on CR J. Muskellunge, northern pike, walleye and suckers are produced at the facility; more than 100 million fish can be hatched annually. Hatchery operations are best viewed May through June. Aquarium displays are featured. Allow 1 hour minimum. Mon.-Fri. 8-4. Guided tours are offered Mon.-Fri. at 11 and 2, day after Memorial Day-day before Labor Day. Free. Phone (715) 358-9213.

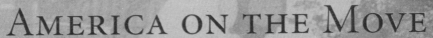

AMERICA ON THE MOVE

A NEW EXHIBITION ON TRANSPORTATION IN AMERICAN HISTORY

Smithsonian
National Museum of American History
Behring Center

National Museum of American History

14th and Constitution Ave. NW
Washington, D.C.

Open Daily: 10 a.m. - 5:30 p.m.
(Except December 25)

americanhistory.si.edu/onthemove
Free Admission

Made possible by generous
support from:

General Motors Corporation

AAA

State Farm Companies Foundation
The History Channel
United States Congress
U.S. Department of Transportation

ExxonMobil

American Public Transportation
Association
American Road & Transportation
Builders Association
Association of American Railroads
National Asphalt Pavement
Association
The UPS Foundation

AMERICA
ON THE MOVE

$\mathcal{B}$ecause it's an enchanting time for a fairytale vacation.

Trust AAA Travel to take you there.

Storybook lands. Magical worlds. Fantastic voyages to paradise. Whatever your dream, there's a Disney vacation for you. And when you book select vacation packages through AAA Travel, you can enjoy exclusive AAA benefits and great values. Your fairytale is just a phone call away. Call or visit your AAA Travel office today.

Walt Disney World®

Disneyland® RESORT IN CALIFORNIA

Disney Cruise Line®

Shop the Travel Store You Can Trust

In addition to over 200 great travel books, AAA offers top quality luggage, coolers, umbrellas, children's products, and much more. Visit your local AAA Travel Store to take advantage of significant AAA member discounts on a wide variety of travel items and gifts.

TRAVEL STORE

AAA Travel Stores are available at participating AAA club offices.

TRAVEL STORE

Michigan

Crisp Point,
Lake Superior
© G. Ahrens
Robertstock

ACME pop. 4,332

——— WHERE TO STAY ———

GRAND TRAVERSE RESORT & SPA   *Book at aaa.com*   Phone: (231)938-2100

▼▼▼	6/11-8/14	1P: $211-$256	2P: $211-$256	XP: $15 F17
	8/15-3/31	1P: $103-$211	2P: $103-$211	XP: $15 F17
Resort	4/23-6/10	1P: $134-$179	2P: $134-$179	XP: $15 F17
Large-scale Hotel	4/1-4/22	1P: $103-$152	2P: $103-$152	XP: $15 F17

Location: On US 31, 0.5 mi n of jct SR 72. 100 Grand Traverse Village Blvd 49610. Fax: 231/938-5494. **Facility:** Extensive recreational facilities are featured at this resort, which is on spacious, manicured grounds. 658 units. 460 one-bedroom standard units, some with efficiencies and/or whirlpools. 122 one-, 56 two- and 20 three-bedroom suites, some with kitchens and/or whirlpools. 3-17 stories, interior/exterior corridors. **Parking:** on-site. **Terms:** check-in 4 pm, 3 day cancellation notice-fee imposed, package plans - seasonal & weekends, $9 service charge. **Amenities:** video games, voice mail, irons, hair dryers. *Some:* dual phone lines, honor bars. **Dining:** Trillium, see separate listing. **Pool(s):** 2 heated outdoor, 2 heated indoor. **Leisure Activities:** saunas, whirlpools, paddleboats, fishing, cross country skiing, snowmobiling, ice skating, recreation programs, bicycles, hiking trails, jogging, basketball, volleyball. *Fee:* charter fishing, golf-54 holes, 9 tennis courts (5 indoor, 9 lighted), massage, game room. **Guest Services:** gift shop, valet laundry, area transportation. **Business Services:** conference facilities, business center. **Cards:** AX, DC, DS, MC, VI.

SOME UNITS
(ASK) (SD) ✈ ⊩ ⊻ 🛗 ⚓ ⟲ ✕ 🎬 DATA PORT ▤ / ✕ 🗄 🖥 ▦ /

HOLIDAY INN EXPRESS HOTEL & SUITES   *Book at aaa.com*   Phone: (231)938-2600

▼▼▼	6/27-9/4 [ECP]	1P: $139-$219	2P: $139-$219	XP: $6 F19
	10/17-3/31 [ECP]	1P: $89-$199	2P: $89-$199	XP: $6 F19
Small-scale Hotel	9/5-10/16 [ECP]	1P: $99-$179	2P: $99-$179	XP: $6 F19
	4/1-6/26 [ECP]	1P: $79-$149	2P: $79-$149	XP: $6 F19

Location: Jct US 31 and SR 72, 0.5 mi sw. Located in a commercial area. 3536 Mount Hope Rd 49610 (PO Box 177). Fax: 231/938-0945. **Facility:** 81 one-bedroom standard units, some with whirlpools. 3 stories, interior corridors. **Parking:** on-site. **Amenities:** dual phone lines, voice mail, irons, hair dryers. **Pool(s):** heated indoor. **Leisure Activities:** whirlpool. *Fee:* game room. **Guest Services:** valet laundry. **Business Services:** meeting rooms. **Cards:** AX, DC, DS, MC, VI. *(See color ad card insert & p 457)*

SOME UNITS
(ASK) (SD) ⊩ ⊾M ⟲ 🎬 DATA PORT / ✕ 🗄 🖥 ▤ /

SLEEP INN AND SUITES   *Book at aaa.com*   Phone: (231)938-7000

▼▼ ▼▼	6/27-9/1	1P: $99-$189	2P: $99-$189	XP: $5 F17
	9/2-3/31	1P: $59-$139	2P: $59-$139	XP: $5 F17
Small-scale Hotel	6/1-6/26	1P: $69-$109	2P: $69-$109	XP: $5 F17
	4/1-5/31	1P: $59-$99	2P: $59-$99	XP: $5 F17

Location: Jct US 31 and SR 72, 0.5 mi sw. Located in a commercial area. 5520 US 31 N 49610. Fax: 231/938-7001. **Facility:** 74 units. 73 one-bedroom standard units. 1 one-bedroom suite. 3 stories, interior corridors. *Bath:* combo or shower only. **Parking:** on-site. **Terms:** check-in 4 pm, 2 night minimum stay - weekends 6/1-10/31, cancellation fee imposed, [ECP] meal plan available. **Amenities:** safes (fee). *Some:* irons, hair dryers. **Pool(s):** heated indoor. **Leisure Activities:** whirlpool, exercise room. **Guest Services:** coin laundry. **Business Services:** meeting rooms. **Cards:** AX, DC, DS, MC, VI. *(See color ad p 468)*

SOME UNITS
(ASK) (SD) ⊩ ⊾M 🍴 ⟲ 🎬 DATA PORT / ✕ 🗄 🖥 ▤ /

——— WHERE TO DINE ———

TRILLIUM   **Dinner:** $19-$34   Phone: 231/938-2100

AAA
▼▼▼
American

Location: On US 31, 0.5 mi n of jct SR 72; in Grand Traverse Resort & Spa. 100 Grand Traverse Village Blvd 49610. **Hours:** 6 pm-10 pm; hours vary in season. Closed: Sun. **Reservations:** suggested. **Features:** The busy restaurant is popular for its fantastic, 16th-floor view of the bay and its surroundings. Such dishes as rack of lamb are well-presented and tasty. Utilizing fresh ingredients, the menu represents regional specialties. Dressy casual; cocktails. **Parking:** on-site. **Cards:** AX, DC, DS, JC, MC, VI.

⊾M ⊻ ✕

ADA pop. 9,882

WHERE TO DINE

THORNAPPLE/THE BISTRO
American

Lunch: $7-$10   **Dinner:** $15-$26   **Phone:** 616/676-1233
Location: Corner of Fulton St and Ada Dr SE. 445 Thornapple Village Dr 49301. **Hours:** 11:30 am-10 pm, Fri-11 pm, Sat 5 pm-11 pm. **Closed:** Sun. **Reservations:** suggested. **Features:** A family friendly restaurant with unique menu items. Start your meal with crispy portabella fries, complete with banana catsup, and then choose from specialty pizza or a variety of fish, meat and vegetarian entrees. Casual dress; cocktails.
Parking: on-site. **Cards:** AX, DC, DS, MC, VI.

ADRIAN pop. 21,574

WHERE TO STAY

CARLTON LODGE   *Book at aaa.com*
Small-scale Hotel

Phone: 517-263-7000
All Year [ECP]   1P: $89-$199   2P: $89-$199   XP: $8   F18
Location: Jct US 223 and SR 52, 3 mi w on US 223. 1629 W Maumee St 49221. **Fax:** 517-263-7000. **Facility:** 98 units. 96 one-bedroom standard units, some with whirlpools. 2 one-bedroom suites. 2 stories, interior corridors. **Parking:** on-site. **Amenities:** high-speed Internet (fee), voice mail, irons, hair dryers. **Pool(s):** heated indoor/outdoor. **Leisure Activities:** exercise room. **Guest Services:** valet laundry. **Business Services:** meeting rooms. **Cards:** AX, CB, DC, DS, JC, MC, VI.

SOME UNITS

HOLIDAY INN EXPRESS   *Book at aaa.com*
Small-scale Hotel

Phone: 517-265-5700
All Year [ECP]   1P: $99-$199   2P: $99-$199   XP: $8   F18
Location: Just w of jct US 223 and SR 52. 1077 W US 223 49221. **Fax:** 517-265-5700. **Facility:** 60 one-bedroom standard units. 3 stories, interior corridors. *Bath:* combo or shower only. **Parking:** on-site. **Amenities:** voice mail, irons, hair dryers. *Some:* CD players. **Pool(s):** small heated indoor. **Leisure Activities:** exercise room. **Guest Services:** valet laundry. **Cards:** AX, CB, DC, DS, JC, MC, VI.

SOME UNITS

SUPER 8 MOTEL   *Book at aaa.com*
Small-scale Hotel

Phone: 517-265-8888
Property failed to provide current rates
Location: Just w of jct US 223 and SR 52. 1091 W US 223 49221. **Fax:** 517-265-8888. **Facility:** 51 one-bedroom standard units. 2 stories, interior corridors. *Bath:* combo or shower only. **Parking:** on-site. **Guest Services:** valet laundry.

SOME UNITS

ALANSON pop. 700

WHERE TO STAY

CROOKED RIVER LODGE
Small-scale Hotel

Phone: (231)548-5000
All Year   1P: $105-$200   2P: $105-$200   XP: $10   F17
Location: On US 31, just n. 6845 US 31 N 49706. **Fax:** 231/548-1105. **Facility:** 40 units. 25 one-bedroom standard units, some with whirlpools. 12 one- and 3 two-bedroom suites ($136-$220). 3 stories, interior corridors. *Bath:* combo or shower only. **Parking:** on-site, winter plug-ins. **Terms:** cancellation fee imposed, small pets only ($15 extra charge, with prior approval). **Amenities:** voice mail, irons, hair dryers. **Pool(s):** heated indoor. **Leisure Activities:** whirlpools, snowmobiling. *Fee:* game room. **Guest Services:** gift shop. **Cards:** AX, MC, VI. **Special Amenities:** free continental breakfast and free local telephone calls. *(See color ad p 419)*

SOME UNITS
FEE

ALGONAC pop. 4,613

WHERE TO STAY

LINDA'S LIGHTHOUSE INN
Bed & Breakfast

Phone: (810)794-2992
5/1-10/31   1P: $95-$135   2P: $95-$135
Location: I-94, exit 243, 14 mi e. 5965 Pointe Tremble Rd (SR 29) 48001. **Fax:** 810/794-2992. **Facility:** Smoke free premises. 4 one-bedroom standard units, some with whirlpools. 2 stories (no elevator), interior corridors. *Bath:* combo or shower only. **Terms:** open 5/1-10/31, check-in 4 pm, 7 day cancellation notice, [BP] meal plan available, small pets only ($15 extra charge). **Amenities:** video library. **Leisure Activities:** whirlpool, boat dock, fishing, bicycles, horseshoes. **Guest Services:** TV in common area. **Cards:** MC, VI.

SOME UNITS
FEE

ALLEGAN pop. 4,050

WHERE TO STAY

CASTLE IN THE COUNTRY B & B
Historic Bed & Breakfast

Phone: 269-673-8054
All Year [BP]   1P: $85-$205   2P: $95-$205   XP: $10
Location: M-40 S, 6 mi s. Located in a quiet, rural area. 340 M-40 S 49010. **Fax:** 269/686-0058. **Facility:** Some guest rooms at this 1906 Queen Anne-style home on five acres of farmland have Italian-tile fireplaces and whirlpool tubs. Designated smoking area. 5 units. 4 one-bedroom standard units, some with whirlpools. 1 one-bedroom suite with whirlpool. 3 stories (no elevator), interior corridors. *Bath:* combo or shower only. **Parking:** on-site. **Terms:** check-in 4 pm, 2 night minimum stay - 5/1-10/31, 7 day cancellation notice, weekly rates available. **Amenities:** video library. *Some:* CD players. **Leisure Activities:** recreation programs, hiking trails, basketball. **Guest Services:** gift shop, complimentary evening beverages. **Cards:** AX, MC, VI.

ALLENDALE pop. 11,555

——— WHERE TO STAY ———

SLEEP INN & SUITES   *Book at aaa.com*   Phone: (616)892-8000
▽▽▽ ▽▽▽   All Year [ECP]   1P: $80-$150   2P: $80-$150   XP: $5   F18
◆◆◆   **Location:** I-96, exit 16, 6 mi s, then 2.5 mi e on SR 45. Located opposite Grand Valley State University. 4869 Becker Dr
Small-scale Hotel   49401. Fax: 616/892-8020. **Facility:** 60 one-bedroom standard units, some with whirlpools. 3 stories, interior
corridors. *Bath:* combo or shower only. **Parking:** on-site, winter plug-ins. **Terms:** 3 day cancellation notice-fee
imposed, small pets only ($10 extra charge). **Amenities:** dual phone lines, voice mail, safes (fee); irons, hair dryers. *Some:* high-
speed Internet. **Pool(s):** small heated indoor. **Guest Services:** valet and coin laundry. **Business Services:** meeting rooms.
Cards: AX, CB, DC, DS, MC, VI.

SOME UNITS
(ASK) (S̄ᴅ) (🛏) (🖥️) (🏊) (DATA PORT) (🖥️) / (✕) (📶) (🖼️)
FEE

——— WHERE TO DINE ———

——— *The following restaurants have not been evaluated by AAA* ———
but are listed for your information only.

COUNTRY CUPBOARD   Phone: 616/895-5155
[fyi]   Not evaluated. **Location:** 1 mi e on SR 45. 6031 Lake Michigan Dr 49401. **Features:** This popular family
restaurant still serves old-fashioned comfort foods; breakfast is served all day and you can create your
own omelette.

THE MEADOWS   Phone: 616/895-1010
[fyi]   Not evaluated. **Location:** At Grand Valley State University. One W Campus Dr 49401. **Features:** The restaurant
overlooks the golf course and serves pork chops, steaks, salmon, chicken and, of course, BBQ ribs.

ALLEN PARK —*See Detroit p. 245.*

ALMA pop. 9,275

——— WHERE TO STAY ———

DAYS INN   *Book at aaa.com*   Phone: (989)463-6131
▽▽▽ ▽▽▽   4/1-10/31 [CP]   1P: $59-$99   2P: $59-$99   XP: $6   F12
11/1-3/31 [CP]   1P: $49-$99   2P: $49-$99   XP: $6   F12
Motel   **Location:** Jct SR 27 and 46. 7996 Alger Rd 48801. Fax: 989/463-2456. **Facility:** 49 one-bedroom standard units.
2 stories (no elevator), exterior corridors. **Parking:** on-site. **Terms:** cancellation fee imposed. **Amenities:** hair
dryers. **Pool(s):** heated indoor. **Leisure Activities:** sauna. **Cards:** AX, CB, DC, DS, MC, VI.

SOME UNITS
(ASK) (S̄ᴅ) (🍴) (🏊) (🎥) (DATA PORT) / (✕) /

ALPENA pop. 11,304

——— WHERE TO STAY ———

40 WINKS MOTEL   Phone: 989/354-5622
▽   All Year   1P: $45-$49   2P: $47-$52   XP: $5   F12
Motel   **Location:** 1 mi s on US 23. Located opposite the Lake Huron public bleach. 1021 State St 49707. Fax: 989/358-8839.
Facility: 15 one-bedroom standard units. 1 story, exterior corridors. **Parking:** on-site. **Cards:** AX, DS,
MC, VI.

SOME UNITS
(ASK) (S̄ᴅ) (🍴) (🖥️) / (✕) /

DAYS INN   *Book at aaa.com*   Phone: (989)356-6118
(AAA) [SAVE]   All Year [ECP]   1P: $79-$125   2P: $79-$125   XP: $5   F17
▽▽▽   **Location:** 2.5 mi w of jct US 23. 1496 Hwy 32 W 49707. Fax: 989/356-4208. **Facility:** 77 units. 76 one- and 1 two-
bedroom standard units, some with efficiencies and/or whirlpools. 1-2 stories (no elevator), interior corridors.
Small-scale Hotel   *Bath:* combo or shower only. **Parking:** on-site, winter plug-ins. **Amenities:** safes (fee), irons, hair dryers.
Pool(s): heated indoor. **Leisure Activities:** sauna, whirlpool, exercise room. **Guest Services:** coin laundry.
Business Services: meeting rooms. **Cards:** AX, CB, DC, DS, JC, MC, VI. **Special Amenities:** free ex-
panded continental breakfast and preferred room (subject to availability with advanced reservations).
(See color ad card insert)

SOME UNITS
(S̄ᴅ) (🖥️) (🏊) (✕) (🎥) (DATA PORT) (🖥️) (🖼️) / (✕) (🖼️) /

DEW DROP INN   Phone: (989)356-4414
(AAA) [SAVE]   5/1-10/31   1P: $42-$46   2P: $42-$52   XP: $5   F12
▽   4/1-4/30 & 11/1-3/31   1P: $38-$42   2P: $38-$48   XP: $5   F12
Motel   **Location:** 1 mi n of hospital on US 23. 2469 French Rd 49707. **Facility:** 14 one-bedroom standard units. 1 story,
exterior corridors. *Bath:* shower only. **Parking:** on-site, winter plug-ins. **Cards:** AX, DS, MC, VI.

SOME UNITS
(S̄ᴅ) (🍴) (🎥) (🖥️) / (✕) (📶) (🖼️) /

HOLIDAY INN   *Book at aaa.com*   Phone: (989)356-2151
▽▽▽   All Year   1P: $79-$99   2P: $79-$99
Small-scale Hotel   **Location:** On US 23, 1 mi n. 1000 Hwy 23 N 49707. Fax: 989/356-2151. **Facility:** 148 one-bedroom standard
units. 2 stories, interior corridors. **Parking:** on-site, winter plug-ins. **Amenities:** voice mail, irons, hair dryers.
Fee: video games, high-speed Internet. **Pool(s):** heated indoor. **Leisure Activities:** sauna, whirlpool, putting
green, exercise room. *Fee:* game room. **Guest Services:** valet and coin laundry. **Business Services:** conference facilities.
Cards: AX, CB, DC, DS, JC, MC, VI.

SOME UNITS
(ASK) (S̄ᴅ) (🛏) (🍴) (🍸) (🏊) (✕) (🎥) (DATA PORT) (🖥️) / (✕) (📶)
FEE

——— WHERE TO DINE ———

JOHN A LAU SALOON & STEAKHOUSE   Lunch: $5-$9   Dinner: $12-$18   Phone: 989/354-6898

American

Location: Located in the old town section. 414 N 2nd Ave 49707. **Hours:** 11:30 am-11 pm, Sun 4 pm-9 pm. Closed major holidays. **Features:** Housed in the oldest historic salon in Alpena, this microbrewery offers a varied menu of standard bar favorites such as hamburgers as well as a number of daily specials. Casual dress; cocktails. **Parking:** on-site and street. **Cards:** AX, DS, MC, VI.

SPINNAKERS   Lunch: $5-$9   Dinner: $10-$17   Phone: 989/354-8900

American

Location: 1 mi s on US 23. 1100 State Ave 49707. **Hours:** 11 am-8 pm; hours may vary seasonally. Closed major holidays; also Sun. **Reservations:** suggested, in season. **Features:** Overlooking the beach, this nautically themed restaurant specializes in locally caught seafood such as perch and whitefish as well as offering a variety of steaks. Casual dress; cocktails. **Parking:** on-site. **Cards:** AX, DC, DS, MC, VI.

ANN ARBOR pop. 114,024

——— WHERE TO STAY ———

BELL TOWER HOTEL   Phone: (734)769-3010

Small-scale Hotel

4/1-12/17 & 1/3-3/31 [ECP]   1P: $149-$263   2P: $169-$283   XP: $20   F4
Location: Located on the University of Michigan campus. 300 S Thayer St 48104. Fax: 734/769-4339. **Facility:** 66 units. 58 one-bedroom standard units. 8 two-bedroom suites ($186-$263). 3-4 stories, interior corridors. *Bath:* combo or shower only. **Parking:** on-site (fee) and valet. **Terms:** check-in 4 pm.
Amenities: dual phone lines, voice mail, irons, hair dryers. *Some:* safes, honor bars. **Guest Services:** valet laundry. **Business Services:** meeting rooms. **Cards:** AX, DC, DS, MC, VI.

SOME UNITS

BEST WESTERN EXECUTIVE PLAZA   *Book at aaa.com*   Phone: (734)665-4444

Small-scale Hotel

All Year [CP]   1P: $89-$129   2P: $89-$129   XP: $10   F17
Location: I-94, exit 172, just e. 2900 Jackson Rd 48103. Fax: 734/665-5558. **Facility:** 163 units. 161 one-bedroom standard units, some with whirlpools. 2 one-bedroom suites, some with efficiencies and/or whirlpools. 2-4 stories, interior/exterior corridors. **Parking:** on-site. **Terms:** 7 day cancellation notice, weekly rates available. **Dining:** 6-11 am, Thurs-Sat 4 pm-midnight, Sun 7-11 am, cocktails. **Pool(s):** heated indoor/outdoor. **Leisure Activities:** sauna, whirlpool, exercise room. *Fee:* game room.
Guest Services: valet and coin laundry. **Business Services:** conference facilities. **Cards:** AX, CB, DC, DS, JC, MC, VI.
Special Amenities: free continental breakfast and free newspaper.

SOME UNITS

CANDLEWOOD SUITES   *Book at aaa.com*   Phone: (734)663-2818

Small-scale Hotel

All Year   1P: $45-$169   2P: $45-$169
Location: I-94, exit 175 (Ann Arbor/Saline Rd), just e on Eisenhower Rd. 701 Waymarket Way 48103. Fax: 734/663-6750. **Facility:** 124 units. 96 one-bedroom standard units with efficiencies. 28 one-bedroom suites with efficiencies. 3 stories, interior corridors. *Bath:* combo or shower only. **Parking:** on-site. **Terms:** office hours 7 am-11 pm, small pets only. **Amenities:** video library, CD players, dual phone lines, voice mail, irons, hair dryers. **Guest Services:** sundries. **Cards:** AX, CB, DC, DS, JC, MC, VI.

SOME UNITS

Look For Savings

When you pick up a AAA TourBook® guide, look for establishments that display a bright red AAA logo, SAVE icon, and Diamond rating in their listing. These AAA Official Appointment establishments place a high value on the patronage they receive from AAA members. And, by offering members great room rates*, they are willing to go the extra mile to get your business.

So, when you turn to the AAA TourBook guide to make your travel plans, look for the establishments that will give you the special treatment you deserve.

* See TourBook Navigator section, page 14, for complete details.

COMFORT INN — *Book at aaa.com* — Phone: (734)761-8838

4/1-10/31 & 2/1-3/31 [ECP]	1P: $89-$139	2P: $89-$139	XP: $5	F15
11/1-1/31 [ECP]	1P: $79-$129	2P: $79-$129	XP: $5	F15

Small-scale Hotel **Location:** I-94, exit 177 (State St), just ne. 3501 S State St 48108. **Fax:** 734/761-8834. **Facility:** 83 units. 68 one-bedroom standard units. 15 one-bedroom suites, some with whirlpools. 3 stories, interior corridors. *Bath:* combo or shower only. **Parking:** on-site. **Amenities:** high-speed Internet, voice mail, irons, hair dryers. **Pool(s):** heated indoor. **Leisure Activities:** whirlpool, exercise room. **Guest Services:** valet laundry. **Cards:** AX, DC, DS, MC, VI.

SOME UNITS
(ASK) (SD) (T+) (GM) (&) (≈) (♥) (DATA PORT) (▭) / (✕) (🔒) (☐) /

COURTYARD BY MARRIOTT — *Book at aaa.com* — Phone: (734)995-5900

7/1-10/31	1P: $129	2P: $129
4/1-6/30	1P: $124	2P: $124
11/1-3/31	1P: $109-$119	2P: $109-$119

Small-scale Hotel **Location:** I-94, exit 177 (State St), just n, then just e on Victor's Way. 3205 Boardwalk St 48108. **Fax:** 734/995-2937. **Facility:** 160 units. 120 one-bedroom standard units. 40 one-bedroom suites. 4 stories, interior corridors. **Parking:** on-site. **Terms:** cancellation fee imposed, [BP] meal plan available. **Amenities:** video games (fee), voice mail, irons, hair dryers. *Some:* dual phone lines. **Pool(s):** heated indoor. **Leisure Activities:** whirlpool, exercise room. **Guest Services:** valet and coin laundry. **Business Services:** conference facilities. **Cards:** AX, DC, DS, JC, MC, VI. **Special Amenities:** free newspaper. *(See color ad below)*

SOME UNITS
(SD) (Y) (≈) (♥) (DATA PORT) (▭) / (✕) (🔒) /

THE DAHLMANN CAMPUS INN — *Book at aaa.com* — Phone: (734)769-2200

All Year	1P: $190-$250	2P: $210-$270	XP: $20

Large-scale Hotel **Location:** At E Huron and State sts. Located adjacent to the University of Michigan campus. 615 E Huron St 48104. **Fax:** 734/769-6222. **Facility:** 208 units. 198 one-bedroom standard units. 10 one-bedroom suites ($275-$500). 15 stories, interior corridors. **Parking:** on-site. **Terms:** check-in 4 pm, 60 day cancellation notice. **Amenities:** voice mail, irons, hair dryers. *Some:* DVD players, high-speed Internet, safes, honor bars. **Pool(s):** outdoor. **Leisure Activities:** saunas, exercise room. **Guest Services:** gift shop, valet laundry. **Business Services:** meeting rooms. **Cards:** AX, DC, DS, MC, VI.

SOME UNITS
(T+) (Y) (🖥) (≈) (♥) (DATA PORT) / (✕) (VCR) (🔒) /

EXTENDED STAY AMERICA — *Book at aaa.com* — Phone: (734)332-1980

All Year	1P: $39-$64	2P: $42-$68

Small-scale Hotel **Location:** I-94, exit 177 (State St), just nw. 1501 Briarwood Circle Dr 48108. **Fax:** 734/332-1998. **Facility:** 112 one-bedroom standard units with efficiencies. 3 stories, interior corridors. *Bath:* combo or shower only. **Parking:** on-site. **Terms:** office hours 7 am-11 pm, weekly rates available, package plans. **Amenities:** voice mail. **Guest Services:** coin laundry. **Cards:** AX, CB, DC, DS, MC, VI.

SOME UNITS
(T+) (GM) (&) (🖥) (📷) (DATA PORT) (🔒) (☐) (▭) / (✕) /

FAIRFIELD INN BY MARRIOTT *Book at aaa.com* Phone: (734)995-5200

AAA SAVE

11/1-3/31   1P: $89-$99   2P: $89-$99
4/1-10/31   1P: $94   2P: $94

Location: I-94, exit 177 (State St), just n, then e on Victor's Way. 3285 Boardwalk St 48108. Fax: 734/995-5394. **Facility:** 110 one-bedroom standard units. 4 stories, interior corridors. **Parking:** on-site. **Terms:** [ECP] meal

Small-scale Hotel   plan available. **Amenities:** video games (fee), irons. **Pool(s):** heated indoor. **Leisure Activities:** whirlpool. **Guest Services:** valet laundry. **Cards:** AX, DC, DS, JC, MC, VI. **Special Amenities: free continental breakfast and free newspaper.** *(See color ad p 190)*

SOME UNITS

FOUR POINTS BY SHERATON-ANN ARBOR *Book at aaa.com* Phone: (734)996-0600

All Year   1P: $89-$119   2P: $89-$119

Location: I-94, exit 177 (State St), just ne. 3200 Boardwalk 48108. Fax: 734/996-8136. **Facility:** 197 one-bedroom

Small-scale Hotel   standard units, some with whirlpools. 6 stories, interior corridors. *Bath:* combo or shower only. **Parking:** on-site. **Terms:** age restrictions may apply. **Amenities:** video games (fee), high-speed Internet, dual phone lines, voice mail, irons, hair dryers. **Pool(s):** heated indoor/outdoor. **Leisure Activities:** sauna, whirlpool, exercise room. **Guest Services:** sundries, valet laundry, area transportation. **Business Services:** conference facilities, business center. **Cards:** AX, CB, DC, DS, JC, MC, VI. *(See color ad below)*

SOME UNITS

HAMPTON INN-NORTH *Book at aaa.com* Phone: (734)996-4444

4/1-11/1 [ECP]   1P: $71-$80   2P: $71-$80
1/1-3/31 [ECP]   1P: $69-$78   2P: $69-$78
11/2-12/31 [ECP]   1P: $67-$76   2P: $67-$76

Small-scale Hotel   **Location:** US 23, exit 41 (Plymouth Rd), just nw. 2300 Green Rd 48105. Fax: 734/996-0196. **Facility:** 130 one-bedroom standard units. 4 stories, interior corridors. **Parking:** on-site. **Terms:** small pets only ($25 fee). **Amenities:** voice mail, irons, hair dryers. **Pool(s):** heated indoor. **Leisure Activities:** whirlpool, exercise room. **Guest Services:** valet and coin laundry. **Business Services:** meeting rooms. **Cards:** AX, DC, DS, MC, VI.

SOME UNITS

FEE

HAMPTON INN-SOUTH   *Book at aaa.com*   **Phone:** 734/665-5000

(AAA) (SAVE)   All Year [ECP]   1P: $89-$189   2P: $89-$189   XP: $5   F18
▽▽▽▽   **Location:** I-94, exit 177 (State St), just ne. 925 Victor's Way 48108. Fax: 734/665-8452. **Facility:** 149 one-bedroom
            standard units. 4 stories, interior corridors. **Parking:** on-site. **Amenities:** voice mail, irons. **Pool(s):** heated
Small-scale Hotel   indoor. **Leisure Activities:** whirlpool, exercise room. **Guest Services:** valet and coin laundry. **Business
            Services:** meeting rooms. **Cards:** AX, DC, DS, MC, VI. **Special Amenities:** free expanded continental
            breakfast and free local telephone calls. *(See ad below)*   SOME UNITS

HAWTHORN SUITES   *Book at aaa.com*   **Phone:** (734)327-0011

▽▽▽▽   All Year   1P: $125-$225   2P: $125-$225
            Location: US 23, exit 41 (Plymouth Rd), just sw. 3535 Green Rd 48105. Fax: 734/327-6109. **Facility:** 82 units. 21
            one-bedroom standard units with efficiencies. 40 one- and 21 two-bedroom suites ($125-$225), some with
Small-scale Hotel   efficiencies or kitchens. 3 stories, interior corridors. *Bath:* combo or shower only. **Parking:** on-site.
Terms: [BP] meal plan available, small pets only ($150 fee). **Amenities:** video library (fee), dual phone lines, voice mail, irons,
hair dryers. **Pool(s):** heated indoor. **Leisure Activities:** whirlpool, exercise room, sports court. **Guest Services:** sundries, valet
and coin laundry, area transportation. **Business Services:** meeting rooms. **Cards:** AX, CB, DC, DS, JC, MC, VI.

HOLIDAY INN EXPRESS HOTEL & SUITES   *Book at aaa.com*   **Phone:** (734)761-2929

▽▽▽▽   All Year   1P: $99-$149   2P: $99-$149
            Location: I-94, exit 177 (State St), just n, then w. 600 Hilton Blvd 48108. Fax: 734/761-2997. **Facility:** 107 one-
            bedroom standard units. 4 stories, interior corridors. *Bath:* combo or shower only. **Parking:** on-site.
Small-scale Hotel   **Terms:** cancellation fee imposed, [ECP] meal plan available. **Amenities:** video games (fee), dual phone
lines, voice mail, irons, hair dryers. **Pool(s):** heated indoor. **Guest Services:** valet and coin
laundry. **Business Services:** meeting rooms. **Cards:** AX, CB, DC, DS, JC, MC, VI.   SOME UNITS

HOLIDAY INN NORTH CAMPUS   *Book at aaa.com*   Phone: (734)769-9800
All Year   1P: $115
Location: US 23, exit 41 (Plymouth Rd), just sw. 3600 Plymouth Rd 48105. Fax: 734/761-1290. **Facility:** 223 one-bedroom standard units. 2-5 stories, interior corridors. **Parking:** on-site. **Amenities:** high-speed Internet (fee), dual phone lines, voice mail, irons, hair dryers. **Pool(s):** heated indoor/outdoor. **Leisure Activities:** whirlpool, 2 tennis courts, exercise room, basketball, volleyball. *Fee:* game room. **Guest Services:** valet and coin laundry, area transportation. **Business Services:** conference facilities. **Cards:** AX, CB, DC, DS, JC, MC, VI. *(See color ad p 192)*
Small-scale Hotel

SOME UNITS

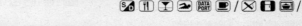

MICROTEL INN & SUITES   *Book at aaa.com*   Phone: 734/997-9100
All Year   1P: $55-$85   2P: $65-$95
Location: US 23, exit 41 (Plymouth Rd), just sw. 3610 Plymouth Rd 48105. Fax: 734/997-9012. **Facility:** 83 one-bedroom standard units. 3 stories, interior corridors. *Bath:* combo or shower only. **Parking:** on-site. **Amenities:** voice mail, hair dryers. **Leisure Activities:** 2 tennis courts, basketball. **Cards:** AX, DC, DS, MC, VI.
Small-scale Hotel

SOME UNITS

QUALITY INN & SUITES   *Book at aaa.com*   Phone: (734)971-2000
All Year [CP]   1P: $69-$139   2P: $69-$139
Location: US 23, exit 37B, just w. 3750 Washtenaw Ave 48104. Fax: 734/971-1149. **Facility:** 103 units. 93 one-bedroom standard units, some with whirlpools. 10 one-bedroom suites ($129-$139). 3 stories, interior corridors. **Parking:** on-site. **Terms:** cancellation fee imposed, package plans - seasonal. **Amenities:** irons, hair dryers. **Dining:** 11 am-10 pm. **Pool(s):** outdoor. **Business Services:** meeting rooms. **Cards:** AX, DC, DS, MC, VI. **Special Amenities:** free continental breakfast and free newspaper.
Small-scale Hotel

SOME UNITS

RED ROOF INN   *Book at aaa.com*   Phone: (734)996-5800

△△△ SAVE

5/23-9/11	1P: $57-$70	2P: $62-$75	XP: $5	F18
9/12-12/31	1P: $53-$70	2P: $58-$75	XP: $5	F18
4/1-5/22 & 1/1-3/31	1P: $52-$70	2P: $57-$75	XP: $5	F18

Motel   **Location:** US 23, exit 41 (Plymouth Rd), just nw. 3621 Plymouth Rd 48105. Fax: 734/996-5707. **Facility:** 108 one-bedroom standard units. 2 stories, exterior corridors. *Bath:* combo or shower only. **Parking:** on-site. **Terms:** small pets only. **Amenities:** video games, voice mail. **Cards:** AX, CB, DC, DS, MC, VI. **Special Amenities: free local telephone calls and free newspaper.**

SOME UNITS

RESIDENCE INN BY MARRIOTT   *Book at aaa.com*   Phone: 734/996-5666

Property failed to provide current rates

Location: I-94, exit 177 (State St), just ne. 800 Victor's Way 48108. Fax: 734/996-1919. **Facility:** 114 units. 78 one-and 36 two-bedroom standard units with kitchens. 2-3 stories, interior/exterior corridors. *Bath:* combo or shower only. **Parking:** on-site. **Terms:** pets ($125 fee). **Amenities:** dual phone lines, voice mail, irons, hair dryers. **Pool(s):** heated outdoor. **Leisure Activities:** whirlpool, exercise room, sports court. **Guest Services:** valet and coin laundry. **Business Services:** meeting rooms.

Small-scale Hotel

SOME UNITS
FEE

SUPER 8 MOTEL   *Book at aaa.com*   Phone: 734/741-8888

△△△ SAVE

All Year [CP]   1P: $54-$99   2P: $54-$99   XP: $10   F17

Location: I-94, exit 172, just e. 2910 Jackson Ave 48103. Fax: 734/741-4288. **Facility:** 55 one-bedroom standard units. 2 stories (no elevator), interior/exterior corridors. *Bath:* combo or shower only. **Parking:** on-site. **Terms:** weekly rates available, small pets only (with prior approval). **Amenities:** voice mail, irons, hair dryers. Small-scale Hotel **Guest Services:** valet laundry. **Cards:** AX, CB, DC, DS, JC, MC, VI.

SOME UNITS

WEBER'S INN   *Book at aaa.com*   Phone: (734)769-2500

△△△ SAVE

All Year [CP]   1P: $125-$140   2P: $125-$140   XP: $10   F17

Location: I-94, exit 172, just n. 3050 Jackson Rd 48103. Fax: 734/769-4743. **Facility:** 158 one-bedroom standard units, some with whirlpools. 4 stories, interior corridors. *Bath:* combo or shower only. **Parking:** on-site. Small-scale Hotel **Terms:** check-in 4 pm, 7 day cancellation notice, package plans - weekends. **Amenities:** video games (fee), voice mail, safes, irons, hair dryers. *Some:* CD players. **Dining:** restaurant, see separate listing. **Pool(s):** heated indoor. **Leisure Activities:** sauna, whirlpool, sun deck, indoor recreation area, adjacent hiking & jogging trails, exercise room. *Fee:* game room. **Guest Services:** valet laundry. **Business Services:** meeting rooms. **Cards:** AX, CB, DC, DS, MC, VI. **Special Amenities: free continental breakfast and free newspaper.** *(See ad p 193)*

SOME UNITS

--------- **WHERE TO DINE** ---------

AMADEUS RESTAURANT & CAFE   Lunch: $6-$10   Dinner: $10-$18   Phone: 734/665-8767

Hungarian   **Location:** Between Main St and Fourth Ave; downtown. 122 E Washington 48104. **Hours:** 11:30 am-3 & 5-10 pm, Fri-11 pm, Sat 11:30 am-11 pm, Sun 11 am-3 pm. Closed major holidays; also Mon. **Reservations:** accepted. **Features:** This cozy, European style restaurant features Polish and Central European cuisine, and fabulous pastry creations. The Hungarian combination plate is a fine example of a distinctive recipe prepared with care and fresh ingredients. Casual dress; cocktails; entertainment. **Parking:** street. **Cards:** AX, DS, MC, VI.

CHINA GATE   Lunch: $5-$6   Dinner: $7-$11   Phone: 734/668-2445

Chinese   **Location:** Downtown. 1201 S University 48104. **Hours:** 11 am-10 pm. Closed major holidays. **Features:** Nestled in the downtown area near the University of Michigan Campus, this Chinese restaurant offers a predictable menu including Szechuan, Hunan, Mandarin and Taiwanese dishes. Casual dress. **Parking:** street. **Cards:** MC, VI.

THE CHOP HOUSE   Dinner: $25-$40   Phone: 734/669-9977

Steak House   **Location:** Downtown. 322 S Main St 48104. **Hours:** 5 pm-10 pm, Fri & Sat-11 pm, Sun 4 pm-9 pm. Closed major holidays. **Reservations:** accepted. **Features:** The perfect place for that special dinner; trendy, yet refined. The restaurant serves an excellent selection of steak, seafood and poultry, and features an extensive wine list. This is a venue to be seen in. Dressy casual; cocktails. **Parking:** on-site and street. **Cards:** AX, DC, DS, MC, VI.

DON CARLOS MEXICAN RESTAURANTE   Lunch: $6-$8   Dinner: $8-$14   Phone: 734/572-0050

Mexican   **Location:** US 23, exit 37A (Washtenaw Ave), 0.3 mi e. 4890 Washtenaw Ave 48108. **Hours:** 11:30 am-10 pm, Mon-9 pm, Fri & Sat-11 pm, Sun noon-9 pm. Closed major holidays. **Reservations:** accepted. **Features:** Colorful paintings add to the upbeat, festive look of this casual restaurant. Fajitas, chiles rellenos and lots of burrito creations are among the Mexican dishes on the menu. Try the luncheon buffet, and sample it all. Casual dress; cocktails. **Parking:** on-site. **Cards:** AX, DC, DS, MC, VI.

THE EARLE   Dinner: $12-$18   Phone: 734/994-0211

Provincial French   **Location:** Just w of Main St; downtown. 121 W Washington St 48104. **Hours:** 5:30 pm-10 pm, Fri-midnight, Sat 6 pm-midnight. Closed major holidays; also Sun. **Reservations:** accepted. **Features:** Provincial French and Italian cuisine are the specialties of this cellar level restaurant. Candlelight and live jazz music fill this space with warmth and energy, serving as a popular escape from the hustle and bustle of the outside world. Dressy casual; cocktails. **Parking:** street. **Cards:** AX, DS, MC, VI.

GANDY DANCER   **Lunch:** $8-$14   **Dinner:** $16-$26   **Phone:** 734/769-0592

American
Location: Jct State and Fuller sts. 401 Depot St 48104. **Hours:** 11:30 am-3:30 & 4:30-10 pm, Fri-11 pm, Sat 4:30 pm-11 pm, Sun 10 am-1:30 & 3:30-9 pm. Closed: 12/25. **Reservations:** suggested. **Features:** Located near the University of Michigan, this restored 1886 railroad depot with its beautifully appointed dining room features stained glass windows and red oak ceilings. The menu offers a tempting selection of fresh seafood specialties including shrimp fettuccine verde, potato encrusted whitefish, and crab stuffed rainbow trout. Casual dress; cocktails. **Parking:** valet and street. **Cards:** AX, DC, DS, MC, VI.

GRATZI   **Lunch:** $8-$12   **Dinner:** $15-$20   **Phone:** 734/663-6387

Italian
Location: Downtown. 326 S Main St 48104. **Hours:** 11:30 am-10 pm, Fri & Sat-11:30 pm, Sun 4 pm-9 pm. Closed major holidays. **Reservations:** accepted. **Features:** Housed in a former theater space, this dramatic restaurant comes complete with bold trompe l'oeil affects and larger than life framed mirrors. Regional Itailian cuisine such as veal, seafood and pastas are presented with flair. Dressy casual; cocktails. **Parking:** street. **Cards:** AX, CB, DC, DS, MC, VI.

GRIZZLY PEAK BREWING COMPANY   **Lunch:** $8-$10   **Dinner:** $9-$20   **Phone:** 734/741-7325

American
Location: Downtown. 120 W Washington St 48104. **Hours:** 11 am-11 pm, Fri & Sat-midnight, Sun noon-11 pm. Closed: 11/25, 12/24, 12/25. **Features:** Copper kettles dominate the front windows of this local microbrewery that specializes in handcrafted beers, and as much attention has been placed into the continental menu that serves both daily specials and bar favorites. Cocktails. **Parking:** on-site and street. **Cards:** AX, DC, DS, MC, VI.

JONATHON B PUB   **Lunch:** $5-$10   **Dinner:** $5-$20   **Phone:** 734/668-7500

American
Location: I-94, exit 177 (State St), just n; in Briarwood Mall near JC Penney. 468 Briarwood Cir 48108. **Hours:** 11 am-11 pm, Fri & Sat-midnight, Sun noon-6 pm. Closed major holidays. **Features:** This small chain location features an English pub menu and decor. They serve gigantic portions of fish & chips and their shepherd's pie is also terrific. Casual dress; cocktails. **Parking:** on-site. **Cards:** AX, DS, MC, VI.

KAI GARDEN   **Lunch:** $8-$10   **Dinner:** $8-$10   **Phone:** 734/995-1786

Chinese
Location: Just s of jct W Huron and S Main sts; downtown. 116 S Main St 48104. **Hours:** 11 am-10 pm, Fri & Sat-11 pm, Sun noon-10 pm. Closed major holidays. **Features:** Underneath the surface of this quiet and unassuming restaurant, which serves a menu of contemporary Chinese-American favorites, is the second menu. Focusing on authentic Cantonese and Taiwanese food, the "little menu," as regulars call it, offers adventurous diners such choices as fried taro with duck, shang -tun fired chicken and pig's ear. Casual dress; cocktails. **Parking:** street. **Cards:** DC, DS, MC, VI.

LA DOLCE VITA   **Dinner:** $6-$8   **Phone:** 734/669-9977

Bakery/Desserts
Location: Downtown. 322 S Main St 48104. **Hours:** 5 pm-midnight, Fri & Sat-1 am, Sun 4 pm-10 pm. Closed major holidays. **Features:** Squeezed between Gratzi and The Chop House, this after-dinner restaurant is reminiscent of a beautifully appointed living room. Overstuffed chairs, coffee tables, intimate lighting and a fireplace make for the perfect place to relax and enjoy house-made desserts and an extensive designer drink menu. A well-ventilated downstairs cigar bar is a popular hang out for aficionados. Dressy casual; cocktails. **Parking:** street. **Cards:** AX, DS, MC, VI.

MEDITERRANO   **Lunch:** $8-$14   **Dinner:** $10-$21   **Phone:** 734/332-9700

Mediterranean
Location: I-94, exit 177 (State St), just n; corner of State St and Eisenhower. 2900 S State St 48104. **Hours:** 11 am-10 pm, Fri-11 pm, Sat noon-11 pm, Sun noon-10 pm. Closed major holidays. **Features:** The theme is decidedly Greek in the cozy dining room, which is decorated with colorful landscapes and statues of mythological figures. The summer patio resembles a gazebo. Such dishes as Moroccan sea bass are colorful and tasty. Casual dress; cocktails. **Parking:** on-site. **Cards:** AX, MC, VI.

METZGER'S GERMAN RESTAURANT   **Lunch:** $6-$9   **Dinner:** $12-$18   **Phone:** 734/668-8987

German
Location: I-94, exit 169; in Baxter's Plaza. 305 N Zeeb Rd 48103. **Hours:** 11 am-10 pm, Sun-8 pm. Closed major holidays. **Reservations:** accepted. **Features:** After enjoying a brief retirement, the owners have returned to a new location at the request of their many friends and fans. The comfortable dining room features brief glimpses of local and personal history culled over the years that this restaurant has been serving fine German cuisine. Dressy casual; cocktails. **Parking:** on-site. **Cards:** AX, MC, VI.

PACIFIC RIM BY KANA   **Dinner:** $15-$22   **Phone:** 734/662-9303

Pacific Rim
Location: Between S Ashley and S Main sts; downtown. 114 W Liberty St 48104. **Hours:** 5:30 pm-9:30 pm, Fri & Sat-10:30 pm. Closed major holidays. **Reservations:** accepted. **Features:** Rather than traveling to California to experience the fusion of Asian and American ingredients with French culinary techniques, the chef/owner brings the latest trends to this warm, inviting restaurant. Among selections are firecracker prawns, Pacific Rim salmon and Malaysian barbecue ribs. Casual dress; cocktails. **Parking:** street. **Cards:** DS, MC, VI.

PAESANO'S RESTAURANT   **Lunch:** $7-$10   **Dinner:** $12-$22   **Phone:** 734/971-0484

Italian
Location: US 23, exit 37B (Washtenaw Ave), 0.3 mi w. 3411 Washtenaw Ave 48104. **Hours:** 11 am-11 pm, Fri-midnight, Sat noon-midnight, Sun noon-10 pm. Closed major holidays. **Reservations:** accepted. **Features:** This contemporary restaurant bustles with festive action. The menu runs the gamut of Italian specialties, sampling preparations of veal, seafood and chicken. Pasta is made in many varieties, such as lasagna and fettuccine. Salads are innovative and tasty. Casual dress; cocktails. **Parking:** on-site. **Cards:** AX, DC, DS, MC, VI.

WEBER'S RESTAURANT   **Lunch:** $7-$10   **Dinner:** $13-$27   **Phone:** 734/665-3636

Location: I-94, exit 172, just n; in Weber's Inn. 3050 Jackson Rd 48103. **Hours:** 6:30 am-10:30 pm, Fri-11 pm, Sat 8 am-11 pm, Sun 8 am-9:30 pm. Closed: 12/25. **Reservations:** suggested. **Features:** Prime rib, fresh fish, pasta and lobster are among dishes on the menu of this established restaurant, an area fixture since the late 1930s. You will find a well-illuminated, comfortable dining room, and pleasing cuisine. Dressy casual; cocktails; entertainment. **Parking:** on-site. **Cards:** AX, DC, DS, MC, VI. *(See ad p 193)*

American

ZINGERMAN'S DELI   **Lunch:** $6-$12   **Dinner:** $6-$12   **Phone:** 734/663-3354

Location: Jct Detroit and Kingsley sts; downtown. 422 Detroit St 48104. **Hours:** 7 am-10 pm. Closed: 11/25, 12/25. **Features:** It's not unusual to see long line ups outside of this widely popular deli/gourmet grocery. A wide selection of made-to-order sandwiches are prepared using house-made bread and imported meats and cheeses. A wide variety of gourmet groceries are also available. Casual dress. **Parking:** street. **Cards:** AX, MC, VI.

Deli/Subs
Sandwiches

ZYDECO LOUISIANA KITCHEN   **Lunch:** $10-$15   **Dinner:** $12-$18   **Phone:** 734/995-3600

Location: Downtown; beside Arc Theatre. 314 S Main St 48104. **Hours:** 11:30 am-11 pm, Fri & Sat-1 am, Sun noon-11 pm. Closed major holidays. **Features:** Only the lack of marching bands might tip patrons off that they are not in the heart of the French Quarter at the Cajun-themed restaurant. French doors open onto the patio. Diners can enjoy a host of traditional dishes, including seafood gumbo, gumbo ya ya, poorboys, jambalaya and shrimp and crawfish etouffee. Casual dress; cocktails. **Parking:** street. **Cards:** AX, MC, VI.

Cajun

AUBURN pop. 2,011

——— WHERE TO STAY ———

SUPER 8 MOTEL   *Book at aaa.com*   **Phone:** 989/662-7888

All Year   1P: $52-$109   2P: $52-$109   XP: $10   F16
Location: US 10, exit Garfield Rd. Located in a commercial area. 4955 S Garfield Rd 48611. Fax: 989/662-7607. **Facility:** 75 units. 63 one-bedroom standard units, some with whirlpools. 12 one-bedroom suites, some with whirlpools. 3 stories (no elevator), interior corridors. *Bath:* combo or shower only. **Parking:** on-site, winter plug-ins. **Terms:** [CP] meal plan available. **Amenities:** *Some:* irons, hair dryers. **Pool(s):** heated indoor. **Leisure Activities:** sauna, whirlpool, exercise room. **Guest Services:** coin laundry, airport transportation (fee)-MBS Airport. **Cards:** AX, DS, MC, VI. **Special Amenities:** free continental breakfast.

Small-scale Hotel

SOME UNITS

AUBURN HILLS —*See Detroit p. 245.*

AU GRES pop. 1,028

——— WHERE TO STAY ———

BEST WESTERN PINEWOOD LODGE   *Book at aaa.com*   **Phone:** (989)876-4060

All Year   1P: $69-$79   2P: $69-$79
Location: Just w on US 23. Located in a semi-commercial area. 510 W US 23 48703. Fax: 989/876-4290. **Facility:** 30 one-bedroom standard units, some with whirlpools. 1 story, interior corridors. **Parking:** on-site, winter plug-ins. **Terms:** pets ($10 fee). **Amenities:** irons, hair dryers. **Pool(s):** heated indoor. **Leisure Activities:** whirlpool, exercise room. *Fee:* game room. **Guest Services:** coin laundry. **Cards:** AX, DC, MC, VI.

Small-scale Hotel

SOME UNITS

AUGUSTA pop. 899

——— WHERE TO STAY ———

——— *The following lodgings were either not evaluated or did not* ———
meet AAA rating requirements but are listed for your information only.

BROOK LODGE HOTEL AND CONFERENCE RESORT   **Phone:** 269/731-2200

Did not meet all AAA rating requirements for some guest rooms at time of last evaluation on 05/01/2003. **Location:** Jct SR 89 (W Michigan Ave), 1.5 mi n. Located in a rural area. 6535 N 42nd St 49012. Facilities, services, and decor characterize a mid-range property.

Resort Cottage

YARROW GOLF & CONFERENCE CENTER   **Phone:** 269/731-2090

Did not meet all AAA rating requirements for some guest rooms at time of last evaluation on 05/01/2003. **Location:** Jct SR 89 (W Michigan Ave), 3.3 mi n. Located in a rural area. 10499 N 48th St 49012. Facilities, services, and decor characterize a mid-range property.

Resort
Small-scale Hotel

BAD AXE pop. 3,462

——— WHERE TO STAY ———

ECONO LODGE INNS & SUITES Phone: 989/269-3200
♦♦♦ ♦♦♦
Small-scale Hotel
heated indoor.
All Year 1P: $59-$79 2P: $59-$79
Location: Just s of jct SR 142 and SR 53 (Van Dyke Rd). 898 N Van Dyke Rd 48413. Fax: 989/269-8366. **Facility:** 38 one-bedroom standard units, some with whirlpools. 2 stories, interior corridors. **Parking:** on-site. **Terms:** weekly rates available, [ECP] meal plan available, $6 service charge, small pets only. **Pool(s):** heated indoor. **Leisure Activities:** whirlpool, exercise room. **Business Services:** meeting rooms. **Cards:** AX, DS, MC, VI.

SOME UNITS
(ASK) [🐕] [🏊] [📹] [DATA PORT] / [✕] /

HOLIDAY INN EXPRESS HOTEL & SUITES *Book at aaa.com* Phone: 989/269-5293
(AAA) (SAVE)
♦♦♦ ♦♦♦♦
Small-scale Hotel
All Year 1P: $70-$150 2P: $77-$150 XP: $8 F18
Location: 1 mi n of jct SR 142 and SR 53 (Van Dyke Rd). 55 Rapson Ln W 48413. Fax: 989/269-5294. **Facility:** 65 units. 48 one-bedroom standard units. 17 one-bedroom suites, some with whirlpools. 2 stories, interior corridors. *Bath:* combo or shower only. **Parking:** on-site. **Amenities:** dual phone lines, voice mail, irons, hair dryers. **Pool(s):** heated indoor. **Leisure Activities:** whirlpool, exercise room. **Business Services:** meeting rooms. **Cards:** AX, DC, DS, MC, VI.

SOME UNITS
[S/D] [🍴] [🏊] [📹] [DATA PORT] [💻] / [✕] [🛏] [🖨] /

BARAGA pop. 1,285

——— WHERE TO STAY ———

BEST WESTERN BARAGA LAKESIDE INN *Book at aaa.com* Phone: (906)353-7123
♦♦♦ ♦♦♦
Large-scale Hotel
6/1-10/14 & 12/16-3/31 1P: $75-$84 2P: $79-$115 XP: $5 F16
4/1-5/31 & 10/15-12/15 1P: $65-$74 2P: $69-$105 XP: $5 F16
Location: On US 41, 0.8 mi s of SR 38. Located on the shores of Keweenaw Bay. 900 US 41 S 49908 (PO Box 873). Fax: 906/353-7799. **Facility:** 36 one-bedroom standard units, some with whirlpools. 3 stories, interior corridors. **Parking:** on-site, winter plug-ins. **Terms:** 7 day cancellation notice. **Amenities:** irons, hair dryers. **Dining:** restaurant, see separate listing. **Pool(s):** heated indoor. **Leisure Activities:** sauna, whirlpool, marina, fishing, snowmobiling. **Guest Services:** gift shop. **Business Services:** meeting rooms. **Cards:** AX, CB, DC, DS, MC, VI.

SOME UNITS
(ASK) [S/D] [🍴] [🍸] [🏊] [✕] [DATA PORT] [💻] / [✕] [🛏] /

CARLA'S LAKE SHORE MOTEL & RESTAURANT Phone: 906/353-6256
♦♦♦
Motel
All Year 1P: $45 2P: $45-$52 XP: $4 F12
Location: 6 mi n on US 41. Located opposite the Keweenaw Bay. (Rt 1, Box 233). **Facility:** 10 one-bedroom standard units. 1 story, exterior corridors. *Bath:* combo or shower only. **Parking:** on-site. **Terms:** pets ($5 extra charge). **Leisure Activities:** sauna, snowmobiling. **Cards:** DS, MC, VI.

SOME UNITS
(ASK) [S/D] [🐕] [🍴] [✕] / [✕] [🛏] /
FEE

SUPER 8 MOTEL *Book at aaa.com* Phone: (906)353-6680
♦♦♦
Small-scale Hotel
7/1-8/31 1P: $54 2P: $59 XP: $5 F12
9/1-3/31 1P: $53 2P: $58 XP: $5 F12
4/1-6/30 1P: $49 2P: $54 XP: $5 F12
Location: 1 mi w on SR 38. Located opposite a casino. 790 Michigan Ave 49908. Fax: 906/353-7246. **Facility:** 40 one-bedroom standard units. 2 stories (no elevator), interior corridors. **Parking:** on-site, winter plug-ins. **Terms:** [ECP] meal plan available, pets ($5 extra charge). **Leisure Activities:** snowmobiling. **Cards:** AX, CB, DC, DS, MC, VI.

SOME UNITS
(ASK) [S/D] [🐕] [🍴] [DATA PORT] / [✕] /
FEE

——— WHERE TO DINE ———

BEST WESTERN BARAGA LAKESIDE INN **Lunch:** $5-$12 **Dinner:** $7-$22 Phone: 906/353-7123
♦♦
American
Location: On US 41, 0.8 mi s of SR 36; in Best Western Baraga Lakeside Inn. 900 US 41 S 49908. **Hours:** 7 am-9 pm; hours may vary. **Reservations:** accepted. **Features:** During breakfast, lunch or dinner, patrons can enjoy the beautiful Keweenaw Bay while they eat. Casual dress; cocktails. **Parking:** on-site. **Cards:** AX, CB, DC, DS, MC, VI.

[🍸] [✕]

BATTLE CREEK pop. 53,364

——— WHERE TO STAY ———

AMERIHOST INN & SUITES *Book at aaa.com* Phone: (269)565-0500
(AAA) (SAVE)
♦♦♦ ♦♦♦
Small-scale Hotel
6/1-9/1 1P: $75-$85 2P: $79-$85 XP: $6 F16
4/1-5/31 & 9/2-3/31 1P: $65-$79 2P: $69-$79 XP: $6 F16
Location: I-94, exit 98B, 4 mi n, then 0.5 mi w. 182 W Van Buren 49017. Fax: 269/565-0501. **Facility:** 62 one-bedroom standard units, some with whirlpools. 2 stories (no elevator), interior corridors. *Bath:* combo or shower only. **Parking:** on-site. **Terms:** cancellation fee imposed, [CP] meal plan available. **Amenities:** voice mail, safes (fee), irons, hair dryers. **Pool(s):** heated indoor. **Leisure Activities:** whirlpool, exercise room. **Guest Services:** valet laundry. **Business Services:** meeting rooms. **Cards:** AX, CB, DC, DS, JC, MC, VI. **Special Amenities:** free expanded continental breakfast and free local telephone calls.

SOME UNITS
[S/D] [♿] [📋] [🏊] [📹] [DATA PORT] [🛏] [🖨] [💻] / [✕] /

BATTLE CREEK QUALITY INN *Book at aaa.com* Phone: (269)964-3000

5/28-9/5 [ECP]	1P: $55-$129	2P: $55-$129	XP: $7 F18
9/6-3/31 [ECP]	1P: $55-$119	2P: $55-$119	XP: $7 F18
4/1-5/27 [ECP]	1P: $49-$119	2P: $55-$119	XP: $7 F18

Small-scale Hotel **Location:** I-94, exit 104, just se. 11081 E Michigan Ave 49014. Fax: 269/963-9915. **Facility:** 93 units. 89 one-bedroom standard units. 4 one-bedroom suites ($79-$219). 2 stories (no elevator), interior corridors. **Parking:** on-site. **Terms:** package plans. **Amenities:** safes. *Some:* irons, hair dryers. **Pool(s):** heated indoor. **Leisure Activities:** whirlpool, exercise room. *Fee:* game room. **Guest Services:** valet and coin laundry. **Business Services:** meeting rooms. **Cards:** AX, CB, DC, DS, JC, MC, VI. **Special Amenities: free expanded continental breakfast and free local telephone calls.**

SOME UNITS

BAYMONT INN & SUITES-BATTLE CREEK *Book at aaa.com* Phone: (269)979-5400

All Year [ECP] 1P: $60-$100 XP: $7 F18

Small-scale Hotel **Location:** I-94, exit 97, just sw. 4725 Beckley Rd 49015. Fax: 269/979-3390. **Facility:** 87 units. 86 one-bedroom standard units, some with whirlpools. 1 one-bedroom suite ($75-$200) with kitchen. 3 stories, interior corridors. *Bath:* combo or shower only. **Parking:** on-site. **Terms:** 2-3 night minimum stay - seasonal, 3 day cancellation notice, package plans - seasonal, pets (1st floor, in smoking units). **Amenities:** video games, voice mail, irons, hair dryers. **Pool(s):** heated indoor. **Leisure Activities:** whirlpool. **Guest Services:** valet and coin laundry. **Cards:** AX, DC, DS, MC, VI.

SOME UNITS

COMFORT INN *Book at aaa.com* Phone: (269)965-3201

All Year [ECP] 1P: $59-$79 2P: $59-$79 XP: $10 F18

Small-scale Hotel **Location:** I-94, exit 97, just n. 2590 Capital Ave SW 49015. Fax: 269/965-0740. **Facility:** 99 one-bedroom standard units, some with whirlpools. 2 stories, interior corridors. *Bath:* combo or shower only. **Parking:** on-site. **Terms:** check-in 4 pm. **Amenities:** dual phone lines, voice mail, irons, high-speed Internet. **Pool(s):** heated indoor. **Leisure Activities:** exercise room. *Fee:* game room. **Guest Services:** valet laundry. **Business Services:** meeting rooms, business center. **Cards:** AX, CB, DC, DS, JC, MC, VI.

SOME UNITS

DAYS INN *Book at aaa.com* Phone: (269)979-3561

All Year 1P: $35-$60 2P: $40-$85 XP: $5 F

Motel **Location:** I-94, exit 97. 4786 Beckley Rd 49017. Fax: 269/979-1400. **Facility:** 84 units. 83 one-bedroom standard units, some with whirlpools. 1 one-bedroom suite. 1 story, exterior corridors. **Parking:** on-site. **Terms:** check-in 4 pm, [CP] meal plan available, small pets only ($25 extra charge). **Guest Services:** valet laundry. **Business Services:** meeting rooms. **Cards:** AX, CB, DC, DS, MC, VI. *(See color ad card insert)*

SOME UNITS
FEE

FAIRFIELD INN BY MARRIOTT *Book at aaa.com* Phone: 269/979-8000

Property failed to provide current rates

Small-scale Hotel **Location:** I-94, exit 97, 0.3 mi sw. Located in a quiet area. 4665 Beckley Rd 49015. Fax: 269/979-3341. **Facility:** 74 one-bedroom standard units, some with whirlpools. 3 stories, interior corridors. *Bath:* combo or shower only. **Parking:** on-site. **Terms:** check-in 4 pm. **Amenities:** dual phone lines, voice mail, irons, hair dryers. **Pool(s):** small heated indoor. **Leisure Activities:** whirlpool, exercise room. **Guest Services:** valet and coin laundry. **Business Services:** meeting rooms. *(See ad below)*

SOME UNITS

HAMPTON INN *Book at aaa.com* Phone: (269)979-5577

All Year 1P: $65-$85 2P: $65-$85 XP: $6 F18

Small-scale Hotel **Location:** I-94, exit 97, 0.3 mi e. 1150 Riverside Dr 49015. Fax: 269/979-1041. **Facility:** 64 one-bedroom standard units. 3 stories, interior corridors. *Bath:* combo or shower only. **Parking:** on-site. **Terms:** [ECP] meal plan available. **Amenities:** voice mail, irons, hair dryers. **Pool(s):** small heated indoor. **Leisure Activities:** whirlpool. **Guest Services:** valet laundry. **Cards:** AX, CB, DC, DS, MC, VI.

SOME UNITS
FEE

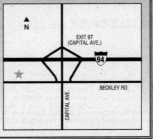

MCCAMLY PLAZA HOTEL   *Book at aaa.com*   **Phone:** (269)963-7050
All Year   1P: $149   2P: $159   XP: $10   F18
Large-scale Hotel   **Location:** Downtown. 50 Capital Ave SW 49017. **Fax:** 269/963-4335. **Facility:** 239 units. 236 one-bedroom standard units. 3 one-bedroom suites. 16 stories, interior corridors. *Bath:* combo or shower only. **Parking:** on-site (fee) and valet. **Terms:** small pets only. **Amenities:** video games (fee), voice mail, honor bars, irons, hair dryers. **Dining:** Porter's Steak House, see separate listing. **Pool(s):** heated indoor. **Leisure Activities:** saunas, whirlpool, exercise room. **Guest Services:** valet laundry, area transportation. **Business Services:** conference facilities, business center. **Cards:** AX, CB, DC, DS, JC, MC, VI.

SOME UNITS

WHERE TO DINE

BIRCH   **Lunch:** $7-$8   **Phone:** 269/966-8767
American   **Location:** Downtown. 17 W Michigan Ave 49017. **Hours:** 11 am-2 pm. Closed major holidays; also Sun & Mon. **Reservations:** suggested. **Features:** Diners can watch the chefs prepare meals in the copper-clad open kitchen. Attractive but somewhat minimalist in decor, the downtown restaurant prepares a range of selections that includes prime rib, pork chops and seafood. Dressy casual; cocktails. **Parking:** on-site. **Cards:** AX, DC, DS, MC, VI.

CLARA'S ON THE RIVER   **Lunch:** $7-$16   **Dinner:** $7-$18   **Phone:** 269/963-0966
American   **Location:** Near McCamly Pl; downtown. 44 McCamly St N 49017. **Hours:** 11 am-10 pm, Fri & Sat-midnight, Sun 10 am-10 pm. Closed: 11/25, 12/25. **Reservations:** suggested, weekends. **Features:** This refurbished train depot is appointed with stained glass, old wood and antiques. The lengthy menu includes a little bit of everything—from burgers and steak to seafood and enchiladas. The emphasis is on fun, rather than fine, family dining. Cocktails. **Parking:** on-site. **Cards:** AX, DC, DS, MC, VI.

FINLEY'S AMERICAN RESTAURANT   **Lunch:** $4-$8   **Dinner:** $9-$20   **Phone:** 269/968-3938
American   **Location:** I-94, exit 97, 2 mi n on Capital Ave, 0.3 mi e. 140 E Columbia Ave 49015. **Hours:** 11 am-10 pm, Fri & Sat-11 pm. Closed: 11/25, 12/25. **Features:** A busy restaurant that is packed most evenings, so expect a short wait when you arrive. Famous for their award-winning baby back ribs that are so tender, the meat falls off the bone. Casual dress; cocktails. **Parking:** on-site. **Cards:** AX, DC, DS, MC, VI.

PORTER'S STEAK HOUSE   **Dinner:** $15-$30   **Phone:** 269/963-9686
American   **Location:** Downtown; in McCamly Plaza Hotel. 50 Capital Ave SW 49017. **Hours:** 5:30 pm-10 pm, Fri & Sat-11 pm. **Reservations:** suggested, weekends. **Features:** A full service dining room situated on the 16th floor of the hotel. The specialty is real beef for hearty appetites. Both the beef and dessert selections are presented tableside on rolling carts. Casual dress; cocktails. **Parking:** on-site (fee) and valet. **Cards:** AX, CB, DC, DS, JC, MC, VI.

WATERFRONT RESTAURANT   **Lunch:** $5-$10   **Dinner:** $7-$30   **Phone:** 269/962-7622
American   **Location:** I-94, exit 97, 2 mi n on Capital Ave, 0.3 mi w. 315 W Columbia Ave 49015. **Hours:** 11 am-9 pm, Sat from 4 pm. Closed major holidays; also Sun. **Reservations:** suggested, weekends. **Features:** A casual dining retreat with floor to ceiling windows for panoramic views of the adjacent lake. Lunch buffet is popular with the retired circle and the dinner menu featuring steaks and seafood always packs in the locals. Cocktails. **Parking:** on-site. **Cards:** AX, DS, MC, VI.

BAY CITY pop. 36,817

WHERE TO STAY

AMERICINN OF BAY CITY   *Book at aaa.com*   **Phone:** 989/671-0071
All Year [ECP]   1P: $66-$76
Small-scale Hotel   **Location:** I-75, exit 164. Located in a semi-commerical area. 3915 3 Mile Rd 48706. **Fax:** 989/671-0311. **Facility:** 65 one-bedroom standard units, some with whirlpools. 2 stories (no elevator), interior corridors. *Bath:* combo or shower only. **Parking:** on-site. **Amenities:** voice mail, irons. **Pool(s):** heated indoor. **Leisure Activities:** sauna, whirlpool. **Guest Services:** coin laundry. **Business Services:** meeting rooms. **Cards:** AX, DS, MC, VI.
(See color ad p 311, below & p 299)

SOME UNITS

BAY MOTEL

AAA **SAVE**
◆◆◆

Motel

Phone: (989)684-4100

All Year   1P: $33-$47   2P: $39-$54   XP: $6   F9
Location: Jct I-75 and US 10, 1.8 mi e on SR 25, then 0.5 mi s on SR 13. Located in a commercial area. 910 S Euclid Ave 48706. **Facility:** 18 one-bedroom standard units. 1 story, exterior corridors. *Bath:* combo or shower only. **Parking:** on-site. **Terms:** weekly rates available, package plans - seasonal. **Cards:** AX, DC, MC, VI. **Special Amenities:** free local telephone calls and preferred room (subject to availability with advanced reservations).

SOME UNITS
🅢🅓 🍴 🎥 🔒 / ☒ /

BEST VALUE INN & SUITES   *Book at aaa.com*

AAA **SAVE**
◆◆◆ ◆◆◆

Small-scale Hotel

Phone: (989)686-0840

6/2-11/1   1P: $56-$60   2P: $65-$70
4/1-6/1 & 11/2-1/1   1P: $40-$45   2P: $50-$60
1/2-3/31   1P: $40-$55   2P: $45-$55
Location: Jct I-75 and SR 84, exit 160 (Saginaw Rd). Located in a commerical area. 6285 W Side Saginaw Rd 48706. Fax: 989/686-0840. **Facility:** 70 one-bedroom standard units, some with whirlpools. 2 stories (no elevator), interior corridors. **Parking:** on-site, winter plug-ins. **Terms:** weekly rates available. **Pool(s):** heated outdoor. **Leisure Activities:** sauna, whirlpool, exercise room. **Guest Services:** valet laundry. **Business Services:** meeting rooms. **Cards:** AX, DS, MC, VI. **Special Amenities:** free local telephone calls and early check-in/late check-out.

SOME UNITS
🅢🅓 🍴 🏊 ☒ 🎥 💻 / ☒ 🅳🅰🆃🅰 🔒 /

CLEMENTS INN

◆◆◆ ◆◆◆

Bed & Breakfast

Phone: (989)894-4600

All Year   1P: $75-$190   2P: $75-$190   XP: $25
Location: 1 mi e on SR 25. 1712 Center Ave 48708. Fax: 989/891-9442. **Facility:** Smoke free premises. 6 one-bedroom standard units, some with kitchens. 3 stories (no elevator), interior corridors. *Bath:* combo or shower only. **Parking:** on-site. **Terms:** check-in 4 pm, 7 day cancellation notice-fee imposed, [ECP] meal plan available, no pets allowed (owner's pet on premises). **Amenities:** video library, voice mail, hair dryers. **Cards:** AX, DS, MC, VI.

SOME UNITS
☒ 🆅🅲🆁 🅳🅰🆃🅰 / 🔒 📺 💻 /

EUCLID MOTEL

AAA **SAVE**
◆◆◆

Motel

Phone: (989)684-9455

All Year   1P: $31-$51   2P: $41-$61   XP: $6   F17
Location: Jct I-75 and US 10, 1.8 mi e on SR 25, 0.8 mi n on SR 13. Located in a commercial area. 809 N Euclid Ave 48706. Fax: 989/686-6440. **Facility:** 36 one-bedroom standard units. 1 story, exterior corridors. **Parking:** on-site, winter plug-ins. **Terms:** weekly rates available, [ECP] meal plan available. **Amenities:** high-speed Internet, irons, hair dryers. **Pool(s):** heated outdoor. **Leisure Activities:** playground, basketball. **Cards:** AX, CB, DC, DS, JC, MC, VI. **Special Amenities:** free continental breakfast and early check-in/late check-out. *(See ad below)*

SOME UNITS
🅢🅓 🍴 🏊 🎥 🔒 📺 💻 / ☒ /

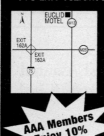

FAIRFIELD INN *Book at aaa.com*

♦♦♦ ♦♦♦

Small-scale Hotel

Phone: (989)667-7050

All Year   1P: $65-$85   2P: $65-$85   XP: $6   F18

Location: 1 mi e of SR 13. Located at the Bay City Mall. 4015 E Wilder Rd 48706. **Fax:** 989/667-7050. **Facility:** 64 one-bedroom standard units. 3 stories, interior corridors. *Bath:* combo or shower only. **Parking:** on-site. **Terms:** [ECP] meal plan available. **Amenities:** irons. **Pool(s):** small heated indoor. **Leisure Activities:** whirlpool. **Guest Services:** valet laundry. **Business Services:** meeting rooms. **Cards:** AX, CB, DC, DS, MC, VI.

SOME UNITS

HOLIDAY INN *Book at aaa.com*

♦♦♦ ♦♦♦

Large-scale Hotel

Phone: (989)892-3501

All Year   1P: $93   2P: $93   XP: $7   F

Location: Center line on I-75 business loop, SR 15 and 25; downtown. 501 Saginaw St 48708. **Fax:** 989/892-9342. **Facility:** 100 one-bedroom standard units. 4 stories, interior corridors. *Bath:* combo or shower only. **Parking:** on-site. **Terms:** check-in 4 pm, [AP] meal plan available. **Amenities:** irons, hair dryers. **Pool(s):** heated indoor. **Leisure Activities:** sauna, whirlpool. **Guest Services:** complimentary laundry. **Business Services:** meeting rooms. **Cards:** AX, CB, DC, DS, JC, MC, VI.

SOME UNITS

——— WHERE TO DINE ———

BERGER'S FAMILY RESTAURANT   **Lunch:** $4-$6   **Dinner:** $8-$11   **Phone:** 989/686-0224

♦♦♦

American

Location: Jct I-75 and SR 84, 0.5 mi s. 6519 W Side Saginaw Rd 48706. **Hours:** 10 am-11 pm, Sun noon-8 pm; to 7:30 pm in winter. **Features:** Owned and operated through four generations of the same family, this established restaurant is a local favorite for fish, steak, sandwiches and delicious homemade pie. Attractive painted mirrors are among decor touches that enhance the dining room. Casual dress; cocktails. **Parking:** on-site. **Cards:** DS, MC, VI.

CHAR HOUSE   **Lunch:** $4-$9   **Dinner:** $9-$25   **Phone:** 989/893-5881

(AAA)

♦♦♦

American

Location: On SR 15, 1.5 mi s of SR 25. 432 Tuscola Rd 48708. **Hours:** 8 am-9 pm, Fri & Sat-10 pm. Closed: 11/25, 12/24, 12/25. **Reservations:** suggested. **Features:** Tried-and-true American staples—steak, seafood, chops and chicken—are at the heart of the family-oriented restaurant's menu. A nautical theme is prevalent in the comfortable dining room, which is decorated with some shipwreck memorabilia. Breakfast anytime. Casual dress; cocktails. **Parking:** on-site. **Cards:** AX, DS, MC, VI.

HEREFORD & HOPS   **Lunch:** $8-$18   **Dinner:** $8-$18   **Phone:** 989/891-4677

♦♦♦ ♦♦♦

American

Location: Center. 804 E Midland St 48708. **Hours:** 11 am-11 pm, Fri & Sat-1 am, Sun noon-8 pm. Closed: 12/25. **Reservations:** accepted. **Features:** Patrons of the brew pub and restaurant can grill their own steaks, kebabs or catch-of-the day on the charcoal grill. The Friday night fish fry is also popular. Casual dress; cocktails. **Parking:** on-site. **Cards:** AX, DS, MC, VI.

KRZYSIAK'S HOUSE RESTAURANT   **Lunch:** $3-$5   **Dinner:** $7-$15   **Phone:** 989/894-5531

(AAA)

♦♦♦

Polish

Location: 2.3 mi s on SR 13, 0.5 mi e on Cass Ave. 1605 S Michigan Ave 48708. **Hours:** 6:30 am-9 pm, Fri & Sat-10 pm, Sun-8 pm. Closed: 5/31, 12/25. **Reservations:** suggested, weekends. **Features:** Lively and upbeat, the friendly restaurant is a favorite for family dining. The menu meshes the cuisines of Poland and America. The seafood buffet on Friday and Saturday evenings draws a good crowd. Colorful hand-painted murals decorate the walls. Casual dress; cocktails. **Parking:** on-site. **Cards:** AX, DC, MC, VI.

THE LANTERN   **Lunch:** $4-$8   **Dinner:** $10-$19   **Phone:** 989/894-0772

♦♦♦

American

DC, DS, MC, VI.

Location: 3 blks n; on the river. 1019 N Water St 48706. **Hours:** 11 am-9 pm, Fri-10 pm, Sat noon-10 pm, Sun 10 am-8 pm. Closed: 1/1, 12/25. **Features:** Overlooking the Saginaw River. Serving beef and seafood dishes, and a handful of surprises, such as Jamaican jerk-style ribs. Popular buffet and outdoor dining in season. The atmosphere is livliest on weekends. Casual dress; cocktails. **Parking:** on-site. **Cards:** AX, CB,

---

——— *The following restaurant has not been evaluated by AAA but is listed for your information only.* ———

LINDEN HOF

[fyi]

Phone: 989/686-2209

Not evaluated. **Location:** Jct I-75/US 10, 1.8 mi e on SR 25, then just s on SR 13. 201 N Euclid Ave 48706. **Features:** This well-established restaurant has been popular with families in the area for many years.

BAY HARBOR

——— WHERE TO STAY ———

THE INN AT BAY HARBOR-A RENAISSANCE RESORT *Book at aaa.com*   Phone: (231)439-4000

AAA SAVE	6/12-9/6 [BP]	1P: $220-$265	2P: $220-$265	XP: $15 F17
◆◆◆	9/7-10/31 [BP]	1P: $185-$240	2P: $185-$240	XP: $15 F17
◆◆◆◆	5/1-6/11 & 12/15-3/31 [BP]	1P: $99-$129	2P: $99-$129	XP: $15 F17

Resort
Large-scale Hotel

Location: On US 31; center. Located on Little Traverse Bay. 3600 Village Harbor Dr 49770. Fax: 231/439-4904. **Facility:** The resort is along a five-mile stretch which includes village shops, a marina and a yacht club. Designated smoking area. 136 units. 89 one-bedroom standard units, some with efficiencies and/or whirlpools. 40 one- and 7 two-bedroom suites with whirlpools, some with efficiencies. 6 stories, interior corridors. *Bath:* combo or shower only. **Parking:** on-site and valet. **Terms:** open 5/1-10/31 & 12/15-3/31, check-in 4 pm, 10 day cancellation notice-fee imposed. **Amenities:** video games (fee), CD players, dual phone lines, voice mail, irons, hair dryers. **Dining:** 2 restaurants, 8 am-10 pm; to 9 pm off season, cocktails, also, Sagamore's, see separate listing. **Pool(s):** heated outdoor. **Leisure Activities:** whirlpool, snowmobiling, recreation programs in season, jogging, exercise room, spa. *Fee:* charter fishing, golf-45 holes, bicycles, game room. **Guest Services:** gift shop, valet and coin laundry, airport transportation-Pellston Airport, area transportation. **Business Services:** conference facilities, business center. **Cards:** AX, DS, MC, VI. **Special Amenities:** free local telephone calls and free newspaper. *(See color ad below)*

SOME UNITS

✈ 🍴 🍸 🛗 🕸 🏊 ✂ ✕ 📷 DATA PORT 🔌 🖥 / 🖥 /

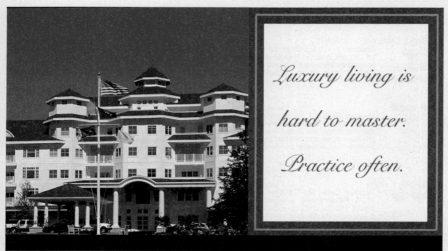

——— **WHERE TO DINE** ———

SAGAMORE'S
▼▼▼▼
American
Dinner: $18-$22   **Phone:** 231/439-4059
Location: On US 31; center; in The Inn at Bay Harbor-A Renaissance Resort. 3600 Village Harbor Dr 49770. **Hours:** 5:30 pm-10 pm. **Reservations:** suggested. **Features:** Elegant French doors in the dining room open out over the bay and receding sailboats. Specializing in regional cuisine, the chef pairs such classics as whitefish with an international palette of flavors. Dressy casual; cocktails. **Parking:** on-site and valet.
Cards: AX, DC, DS, MC, VI.

BAY VIEW pop. 1,000

——— **WHERE TO STAY** ———

COACHHOUSE INN LLC
ⒶⒶⒶ ⓈⒶⓋⒺ
▼▼
Motel
Phone: 231/347-8281
All Year   1P: $70-$110   2P: $70-$110
Location: Center. Located in a commercial area. 1011 US 31 N 49770. Fax: 231/347-1828. **Facility:** 21 one-bedroom standard units. 1 story, exterior corridors. *Bath:* combo or shower only. **Parking:** on-site. **Terms:** cancellation fee imposed, [CP] & [ECP] meal plans available, pets ($10 extra charge). **Cards:** AX, DS, MC, VI. **Special Amenities:** free continental breakfast and free local telephone calls.

SOME UNITS

COMFORT INN   *Book at aaa.com*
ⒶⒶⒶ ⓈⒶⓋⒺ
▼▼ ▼▼
Small-scale Hotel
Phone: (231)347-3220
All Year   1P: $50-$190   2P: $60-$200   XP: $10   F18
Location: Jct US 31 and SR 119. Located in a quiet area. 1314 US 31 N 49770 (1314 US 31 N, PETOSKEY). Fax: 231/347-9191. **Facility:** 65 units. 64 one-bedroom standard units, some with whirlpools. 1 one-bedroom suite ($125-$300) with kitchen and whirlpool. 2 stories (no elevator), interior corridors. **Parking:** on-site, winter plug-ins. **Terms:** check-in 4 pm, [ECP] meal plan available. **Amenities:** voice mail, irons, hair dryers. **Cards:** AX, DC, DS, MC, VI. **Special Amenities:** free expanded continental breakfast and free newspaper. *(See color ad p 418)*

SOME UNITS

STAFFORD'S BAY VIEW INN
▼▼▼▼
Small-scale Hotel
Phone: (231)347-2771
5/28-10/24   2P: $118-$175   XP: $20   F6
10/25-12/23   2P: $89-$175   XP: $20   F6
4/1-5/27 & 12/24-3/31   2P: $89-$138   XP: $20   F6
Location: 0.5 mi n on US 31. 2011 Woodland Ave 49770. Fax: 231/347-3413. **Facility:** Smoke free premises. 31 units. 18 one-bedroom standard units. 13 one-bedroom suites ($109-$260), some with whirlpools. 3 stories, interior corridors. *Bath:* combo or shower only. **Parking:** on-site. **Terms:** 2 night minimum stay - seasonal weekends, 7 day cancellation notice, [BP] meal plan available, package plans. **Amenities:** *Some:* irons, hair dryers. **Leisure Activities:** bicycles. **Guest Services:** TV in common area, gift shop. **Business Services:** meeting rooms. **Cards:** AX, DS, MC, VI.

TERRACE INN
▼▼▼ ▼▼▼
Small-scale Hotel
Phone: (231)347-2410
6/1-10/31 [ECP]   1P: $79-$109   2P: $79-$109
4/1-5/31 & 11/1-3/31 [ECP]   1P: $49-$109   2P: $49-$109
Location: Center; follow signs off US 31. 1549 Glendale 49770 (PO Box 266, PETOSKEY). Fax: 231/347-2407. **Facility:** Smoke free premises. 43 units. 42 one-bedroom standard units. 1 one-bedroom suite ($99-$159) with whirlpool. 3 stories (no elevator), interior corridors. *Bath:* combo or shower only. **Parking:** street. **Terms:** check-in 4 pm, cancellation fee imposed, package plans. **Leisure Activities:** cross country skiing, bicycles, limited exercise equipment. **Guest Services:** TV in common area. **Cards:** MC, VI.

SOME UNITS

——— **WHERE TO DINE** ———

LA SENORITA
▼▼
Mexican
Lunch: $5-$7   **Dinner:** $7-$12   **Phone:** 231/347-7750
Location: Jct US 31 and SR 119. 1285 US 31 N 49770. **Hours:** 11 am-10 pm, Fri & Sat-11 pm, Sun noon-10 pm; Fri & Sat-midnight 5/29-9/4. **Closed:** 11/25, 12/25 & Easter. **Features:** Casual dining. Warm atmosphere with Mexican knickknacks throughout. Good variety of reasonably priced Mexican dishes, snacks and salad. Mesquite cooked items. Smoking permitted in the lounge only. Casual dress; cocktails. **Parking:** on-site. **Cards:** AX, DC, DS, MC, VI.

SCHELDE'S
▼▼
American
Lunch: $5-$10   **Dinner:** $10-$17   **Phone:** 231/347-7747
Location: Just n of jct US 31 and SR 119. 1315 US 31 N 49770. **Closed:** 11/25, 12/24, 12/25. **Features:** The menu comprises traditional, wholesome preparations of chicken, steak, fish, ribs and pasta. The family-oriented restaurant, decorated with knickknacks from the past, is homey and relaxed. Portion sizes are ample and food is reasonably priced. Casual dress; cocktails. **Parking:** on-site. **Cards:** AX, DS, MC, VI.

BELLEVILLE —See Detroit p. 248.

BENTON HARBOR pop. 11,182

——— **WHERE TO STAY** ———

BEST WESTERN T.C. INN & SUITES   *Book at aaa.com*
ⒶⒶⒶ ⓈⒶⓋⒺ
▼▼▼ ▼▼
Small-scale Hotel
Phone: (269)925-1880
All Year   1P: $59-$119   2P: $69-$119
Location: I-94, exit 29 (Pipestone Rd), just n to Mall Dr, then just w. 1598 Mall Dr 49022. Fax: 269/925-0164. **Facility:** 52 one-bedroom standard units. 2 stories, interior corridors. **Parking:** on-site. **Terms:** [ECP] meal plan available, pets (in limited units). **Pool(s):** heated indoor. **Leisure Activities:** whirlpool. **Cards:** AX, DC, DS, MC, VI. **Special Amenities:** free newspaper and early check-in/late check-out.

SOME UNITS

COMFORT SUITES   *Book at aaa.com*   Phone: (269)925-8800
All Year [ECP]   1P: $99-$229   2P: $99-$229   XP: $10   F17
Small-scale Hotel   **Location:** I-94, exit 29 (Pipestone Rd), just s. 1825 Meadowbrook Rd 49022. Fax: 269/925-8700. **Facility:** 62 one-
bedroom standard units, some with whirlpools. 3 stories, interior corridors. *Bath:* combo or shower only.
Parking: on-site. **Amenities:** high-speed Internet (fee), dual phone lines, voice mail, irons, hair dryers.
Pool(s): heated indoor. **Leisure Activities:** sauna, whirlpool, exercise room. **Guest Services:** valet and coin laundry. **Business
Services:** meeting rooms, business center. **Cards:** AX, DC, DS, MC, VI.

SOME UNITS

COURTYARD BY MARRIOTT   *Book at aaa.com*   Phone: (269)925-3000
6/1-9/2   1P: $99-$159   2P: $99-$159
4/1-5/31   1P: $79-$129   2P: $79-$129
9/3-3/31   1P: $59-$129   2P: $59-$129
Small-scale Hotel   **Location:** I-94, exit 29 (Pipestone Rd), just n to Mall Dr, then just w. 1592 Mall Dr 49022. Fax: 269/925-8796.
Facility: 98 one-bedroom standard units, some with whirlpools. 2 stories (no elevator), interior corridors. **Parking:** on-site.
Terms: [BP] meal plan available. **Amenities:** video games (fee), voice mail, irons, hair dryers. **Pool(s):** heated indoor/outdoor.
Leisure Activities: whirlpool, exercise room. **Guest Services:** valet and coin laundry. **Business Services:** meeting rooms, busi-
ness center. **Cards:** AX, DC, DS, JC, MC, VI.

SOME UNITS

HOLIDAY INN EXPRESS   *Book at aaa.com*   Phone: (269)927-4599
All Year   1P: $62-$199   2P: $62-$199   XP: $10   F17
Small-scale Hotel   **Location:** I-94, exit 29 (Pipestone Rd), just s. 2276 Pipestone Rd 49022. Fax: 269/927-4699. **Facility:** 79 one-
bedroom standard units, some with whirlpools. 3 stories, interior corridors. *Bath:* combo or shower only.
Parking: on-site. **Terms:** cancellation fee imposed, weekly rates available, [CP] & [ECP] meal plans available. **Amenities:** dual phone lines, voice mail, irons, hair dryers. **Pool(s):** heated indoor. **Leisure Activities:** whirlpool, exercise
room. **Guest Services:** valet laundry. **Business Services:** meeting rooms. **Cards:** AX, CB, DC, DS, JC, MC, VI.

SOME UNITS

MOTEL 6 - 1141   *Book at aaa.com*   Phone: 269/925-5100
5/27-9/5   1P: $37-$49   2P: $43-$55   XP: $3   F17
9/6-10/30   1P: $36-$46   2P: $42-$52   XP: $3   F17
10/31-3/31   1P: $34-$44   2P: $40-$50   XP: $3   F17
Motel   4/1-5/26   1P: $29-$39   2P: $35-$45   XP: $3   F17
Location: I-94, exit 29 (Pipestone Rd), just nw. 2063 Pipestone Rd 49022. Fax: 269/934-8404. **Facility:** 88 one-bedroom standard units.
1 story, exterior corridors. **Parking:** on-site. **Terms:** small pets only. **Pool(s):** small outdoor. **Guest Services:** coin laundry.
Cards: AX, CB, DC, DS, MC, VI.

SOME UNITS

RAMADA INN   *Book at aaa.com*   Phone: (269)927-1172
4/1-9/3 [BP]   1P: $79-$89   2P: $89-$99   XP: $10   F18
9/4-3/31 [BP]   1P: $69-$79   2P: $79-$89   XP: $10   F18
Small-scale Hotel   **Location:** I-94, exit 28, just sw. 798 Ferguson Dr 49022. Fax: 269/927-1198. **Facility:** 118 one-bedroom standard
units, some with whirlpools. 5 stories, interior corridors. **Parking:** on-site. **Terms:** weekly rates available, pets
($25 deposit, $5 extra charge). **Amenities:** voice mail, irons, hair dryers. **Pool(s):** heated indoor. **Leisure Activities:** whirlpool,
exercise room. *Fee:* game room. **Guest Services:** valet laundry. **Business Services:** meeting rooms. **Cards:** AX, CB, DC, DS,
MC, VI.

SOME UNITS

FEE

RED ROOF INN   *Book at aaa.com*   Phone: (269)927-2484
5/23-9/11   1P: $42-$74   2P: $42-$79   XP: $5   F18
4/1-5/22   1P: $38-$59   2P: $43-$64   XP: $5   F18
9/12-3/31   1P: $39-$52   2P: $44-$57   XP: $5   F18
Motel   **Location:** I-94, exit 29 (Pipestone Rd), just n, then just w. 1630 Mall Dr 49022. Fax: 269/927-1805. **Facility:** 108
one-bedroom standard units. 2 stories, exterior corridors. **Parking:** on-site. **Terms:** small pets only.
Amenities: video games (fee), voice mail. **Cards:** AX, CB, DC, DS, MC, VI. **Special Amenities:** free local
telephone calls and free newspaper.

SOME UNITS

———— **WHERE TO DINE** ————

BENTON'S FAMILY RESTAURANT   Lunch: $7-$12   Dinner: $7-$12   Phone: 616/926-2286
American   **Location:** I-94, exit 29 (Pipestone Rd), just n, then just w. 1650 Mall Dr 49022. **Hours:** 24 hours. **Closed:** 12/25.
Features: Within walking distance of many local hotels, the 24-hour family restaurant offers diners an
extensive selection of menu items. Casual dress. **Parking:** on-site. **Cards:** DS, MC, VI.

HACIENDA MEXICAN RESTAURANT   Lunch: $6-$12   Dinner: $6-$12   Phone: 616/927-4593
Mexican   **Location:** I-94, exit 29 (Pipestone Rd), just n, then 0.4 mi w; in strip mall. 1599B Mall Dr 49022. **Hours:** 11 am-10
pm, Fri & Sat-11 pm. **Closed:** 11/25, 12/25. **Features:** Delicious dishes—such as sizzling steak and shrimp
fajitas—are served in generous portions. Cheerful colors of stucco, pottery and sombreros brighten the
decor. Casual dress; cocktails. **Parking:** on-site. **Cards:** AX, DC, DS, MC, VI.

BIG RAPIDS pop. 10,849

——— WHERE TO STAY ———

BEST WESTERN BIG RAPIDS   *Book at aaa.com*   Phone: (231)592-5150
▼▼▼ ▼▼▼   All Year   1P: $69-$79   2P: $69-$79   XP: $10   F17
      Location: US 131, exit 139, 2.1 mi e on SR 20, then 1 mi s. Located close to Ferris State University. 1705 S State St
Motel   49307. Fax: 231/592-5157. **Facility:** 96 units. 80 one-bedroom standard units. 16 one-bedroom suites. 2-3
      stories, interior/exterior corridors. **Parking:** on-site. **Terms:** check-in 4 pm, weekly rates available, [CP] meal
plan available. **Amenities:** voice mail, irons, hair dryers. **Pool(s):** small heated outdoor. **Cards:** AX, DC, DS, JC, MC, VI.
SOME UNITS
〔ASK〕 〔S🐕〕 〔🍴➕〕 〔🍽〕 〔🏊〕 〔📷〕 〔DATA PORT〕 〔💻〕 / 〔✕〕 /

COUNTRY INN & SUITES BY CARLSON   *Book at aaa.com*   Phone: (231)527-9000
▼▼▼ ▼▼▼   All Year   1P: $80-$100   2P: $80-$100   XP: $10   F12
      Location: US 131, exit 139, just e. Located next to Meijer Shopping Center. 15344 Waldron Way 49307.
Small-scale Hotel   Fax: 231/527-9030. **Facility:** 63 units. 48 one-bedroom standard units, some with whirlpools. 15 one-
      bedroom suites ($120-$160). 3 stories, interior corridors. *Bath:* combo or shower only. **Parking:** on-site,
winter plug-ins. **Terms:** check-in 4 pm, cancellation fee imposed, [ECP] meal plan available. **Amenities:** voice mail, safes, irons,
hair dryers. **Pool(s):** small heated indoor. **Leisure Activities:** whirlpool, exercise room. *Fee:* game room. **Guest Services:** coin
laundry. **Business Services:** meeting rooms. **Cards:** AX, CB, DC, DS, MC, VI.
SOME UNITS
〔ASK〕 〔S🐕〕 〔🔊M〕 〔🗝〕 〔🏊〕 〔✕〕 〔📷〕 〔DATA PORT〕 〔💻〕 / 〔✕〕 〔🛏〕 〔🍴〕 /

HOLIDAY INN HOTEL & CONFERENCE CENTER   *Book at aaa.com*   Phone: (231)796-4400
▼▼▼ ▼▼▼   All Year   1P: $85-$105   2P: $85-$105   XP: $10   F18
      Location: US 131, exit 139, 1.3 mi e on SR 20. Located at Ferris State University. 1005 Perry St 49307.
Large-scale Hotel   Fax: 231/796-0220. **Facility:** 118 one-bedroom standard units. 4 stories, interior corri-
      dors. *Bath:* combo or shower only. **Parking:** on-site. **Terms:** check-in 4 pm, pets ($10 fee). **Amenities:** dual
phone lines, voice mail, irons, hair dryers. *Some:* high-speed Internet. **Pool(s):** heated indoor. **Leisure Activities:** whirlpool, ex-
ercise room. *Fee:* golf-18 holes, game room. **Guest Services:** valet and coin laundry. **Business Services:** conference facilities.
Cards: AX, CB, DC, DS, MC, VI. *(See ad below)*
SOME UNITS
〔ASK〕 〔S🐕〕 〔🐕〕 〔🍴〕 〔🍷〕 〔🔊M〕 〔🗝〕 〔🏊〕 〔✕〕 〔📷〕 〔DATA PORT〕 〔💻〕 / 〔✕〕 〔🛏〕 〔🍴〕 /
FEE

SUPER 8 MOTEL   *Book at aaa.com*   Phone: (231)796-1588
▼▼▼ ▼▼▼   All Year   1P: $60-$70   2P: $65-$75   XP: $10   F12
      Location: US 131, exit 139, 1.4 mi e on SR 20. Located opposite Ferris State University. 845 Water Tower Rd 49307.
Small-scale Hotel   Fax: 231/796-1588. **Facility:** 52 one-bedroom standard units, some with whirlpools. 2 stories (no elevator),
      interior corridors. *Bath:* combo or shower only. **Parking:** on-site. **Terms:** check-in 4 pm, cancellation fee im-
posed, [ECP] meal plan available. **Amenities:** hair dryers. *Some:* irons. **Pool(s):** heated indoor. **Leisure Activities:** whirlpool.
Guest Services: coin laundry. **Business Services:** meeting rooms. **Cards:** AX, CB, DC, DS, MC, VI.
SOME UNITS
〔ASK〕 〔S🐕〕 〔🍴➕〕 〔🗝〕 〔🏊〕 〔📷〕 〔DATA PORT〕 / 〔✕〕 〔🛏〕 〔💻〕 〔💻〕 /

SAVE Yourself From Paying Full Room Rates

When selecting a AAA Approved lodging, look for the 〔SAVE〕 in TourBook® guide listings, and save money on your travel expenses. These properties actively solicit AAA business and offer members great room rates. See the TourBook Navigator section, pages 14 and 20, for details.

BIRCH RUN pop. 1,653

―――――― WHERE TO STAY ――――――

COMFORT INN
Book at aaa.com
▽▼▲▽▼   All Year [ECP]   1P: $69-$169   2P: $69-$169   XP: $10   F18
Small-scale Hotel   **Location:** I-75, exit 136, just e. 11911 Dixie Hwy 48415. Fax: 989/624-7273. **Facility:** 99 units. 93 one-bedroom standard units, some with whirlpools. 6 one-bedroom suites with whirlpools. 3 stories, interior corridors. *Bath:* combo or shower only. **Parking:** on-site. **Amenities:** voice mail, hair dryers. *Some:* irons. **Pool(s):** small heated indoor. **Leisure Activities:** whirlpool, exercise room. *Fee:* game room. **Guest Services:** valet and coin laundry. **Business Services:** meeting rooms, business center. **Cards:** AX, CB, DC, DS, JC, MC, VI.

SOME UNITS
ASK SD TI+ E ▲ X ♥ DATA/PORT / X VCR ▯ ▭ ▯ /

COUNTRY INN & SUITES BY CARLSON   *Book at aaa.com*   Phone: (989)624-8000
(AAA) SAVE   6/1-3/31 [ECP]   1P: $69-$129   2P: $69-$129
▽▼▲▽▼   4/1-5/31 [ECP]   1P: $69-$109   2P: $69-$109
Small-scale Hotel   **Location:** I-75, exit 136, just w; at entrance to outlets at Birch Run. 12112 S Beyer Rd 48415. Fax: 989/624-8080. **Facility:** 71 units. 61 one-bedroom standard units, some with whirlpools. 10 one-bedroom suites ($89-$160). 3 stories, interior corridors. *Bath:* combo or shower only. **Parking:** on-site. **Amenities:** irons, hair dryers. **Pool(s):** small heated indoor. **Leisure Activities:** whirlpool. **Business Services:** meeting rooms. **Cards:** AX, DC, DS, MC, VI. **Special Amenities:** free expanded continental breakfast and free newspaper. *(See color ad p 313)*

SOME UNITS
SD TI+ E ⊘ ▲ X ♥ DATA/PORT ▯ / X ▯ ▭ /

HAMPTON INN
Book at aaa.com
▽▼▲▽▼   All Year [ECP]   1P: $59-$175   2P: $59-$175
Small-scale Hotel   **Location:** I-75, exit 136, just e. 12130 Tiffany Blvd 48415. Fax: 989/624-2501. **Facility:** 89 one-bedroom standard units, some with whirlpools. 3 stories, interior corridors. *Bath:* combo or shower only. **Parking:** on-site. **Terms:** check-in 4 pm, cancellation fee imposed. **Amenities:** voice mail, irons, hair dryers. **Pool(s):** heated indoor. **Leisure Activities:** whirlpool, exercise room. *Fee:* game room. **Guest Services:** valet and coin laundry. **Business Services:** meeting rooms. **Cards:** AX, DC, DS, JC, MC, VI.

SOME UNITS
ASK SD TI+ E ▲ X ♥ DATA/PORT ▯ / X ▯ ▭ /
FEE FEE

HOLIDAY INN EXPRESS   *Book at aaa.com*   Phone: (989)624-9300
(AAA) SAVE   All Year [ECP]   1P: $79-$129
▽▼▲▽▼   **Location:** I-75, exit 136, just e. 12150 Dixie Hwy 48415. Fax: 989/624-2053. **Facility:** 95 units. 91 one-bedroom standard units, some with whirlpools. 4 one-bedroom suites ($130-$160) with whirlpools. 3 stories, interior corridors. *Bath:* combo or shower only. **Parking:** on-site. **Terms:** check-in 4 pm, cancellation fee imposed. **Amenities:** irons, hair dryers. **Pool(s):** heated indoor. **Leisure Activities:** whirlpool, exercise room. *Fee:* game room. **Guest Services:** coin laundry. **Business Services:** meeting rooms. **Cards:** AX, DC, DS, MC, VI. **Special Amenities:** free expanded continental breakfast and free local telephone calls.

SOME UNITS
SD TI+ E ⊘ ▲ X ♥ DATA/PORT ▯ / X ▯ ▭ /

SUPER 8 MOTEL   Phone: (989)624-4440
(AAA) SAVE   6/1-12/31   1P: $55-$70   2P: $55-$70   XP: $5   F12
▽▼▲▽▼   4/1-5/31 & 1/1-3/31   1P: $42-$65   2P: $42-$65   XP: $5   F12
Small-scale Hotel   **Location:** I-75, exit 136, just w. 9235 E Birch Run Rd 48415. Fax: 989/624-9439. **Facility:** 109 one-bedroom standard units, some with whirlpools. 2 stories, interior corridors. **Parking:** on-site, winter plug-ins. **Terms:** [CP] meal plan available. **Amenities:** *Some:* irons. **Leisure Activities:** sauna, whirlpool. *Fee:* game room. **Guest Services:** valet laundry. **Business Services:** meeting rooms. **Cards:** AX, DC, DS, JC, MC, VI. **Special Amenities:** free continental breakfast and free local telephone calls.

SOME UNITS
SD ▭ TI+ X ♥ / X ▯ ▭ /

BIRMINGHAM —See Detroit p. 249.

BLANCHARD

―――――― WHERE TO STAY ――――――

MAXFIELD'S INN   *Book at aaa.com*   Phone: 989/427-8888
(AAA) SAVE   4/1-9/30 [ECP]   1P: $70-$80   2P: $70-$80   XP: $5   F16
▽▼▲▽▼   10/1-3/31 [ECP]   1P: $60-$70   2P: $60-$70   XP: $5   F16
Small-scale Hotel   **Location:** On SR 46; center. 1106 E Main St 48829 (1106 E Main St, EDMORE). Fax: 989/427-8411. **Facility:** 50 units. 45 one-bedroom standard units. 5 one-bedroom suites ($80-$120), some with whirlpools. 2 stories, interior corridors. *Bath:* combo or shower only. **Parking:** on-site. **Terms:** weekly rates available, 8% service charge. **Amenities:** hair dryers. **Pool(s):** heated indoor. **Leisure Activities:** whirlpool, steamrooms, exercise room. *Fee:* game room. **Guest Services:** coin laundry. **Business Services:** meeting rooms. **Cards:** AX, CB, DC, DS, MC, VI.

SOME UNITS
SD ▭M E ▲ X ♥ DATA/PORT ▯ / X ▯ ▭ /

―――――― WHERE TO DINE ――――――

MAXFIELD'S   Lunch: $6-$8   Dinner: $12-$20   Phone: 989/427-5630
(AAA)   **Location:** 3 mi n of SR 46 and blinker light. 11228 Wyman Rd 49310. **Hours:** 11 am-9 pm, Fri & Sat-10 pm, Sun noon-7 pm. Closed: 12/24, 12/25; also Mon. **Features:** An area institution since 1959, the family-oriented restaurant is decorated with paintings and tapestries created by the owner's mother. More than 100 homemade items line the tempting salad bar—the cornerstone of guests' dining experience. Casual dress; cocktails. **Parking:** on-site. **Cards:** AX, DS, MC, VI.
American

Y X

BLISSFIELD pop. 3,223

———— WHERE TO STAY ————

H. D. ELLIS INN
♦♦ ♦♦
Bed & Breakfast

All Year [BP]   1P: $75-$120   2P: $90-$120   XP: $20
Location: Just w of town on US 223. 415 W Adrian St 49228. Fax: 517/486-5002. **Facility:** Smoke free premises. 4 one-bedroom standard units. 2 stories, interior corridors. *Bath:* combo or shower only. **Parking:** on-site. **Terms:** check-in 4 pm, 7 day cancellation notice. **Cards:** AX, MC, VI.

Phone: (517)486-3155
D18

SOME UNITS

(ASK) [SD] [Y↑] [✕] [🎥] / [🖥] /

———— WHERE TO DINE ————

HATHAWAY HOUSE   Historic   **Lunch:** $6-$14   **Dinner:** $16-$26   Phone: 517/486-2141
ⒶⒶⒶ
♦♦♦ ♦♦♦
American

Location: 0.3 mi w of town on US 223. 424 W Adrian St 49228. **Hours:** 11:30 am-9 pm, Fri & Sat-10 pm, Sun noon-8 pm. Closed: 1/1, 12/24, 12/25; also Mon. **Reservations:** suggested. **Features:** You'll find several inviting period dining rooms in this 1851 Greek revival mansion. The menu lists imaginatively prepared soups, salads, seafood, beef, and poultry. Try the broiled whitefish, its delicate flavors will please you. Dressy casual; cocktails. **Parking:** on-site. **Cards:** DS, MC, VI.

[Y] [✕]

MAIN STREET STABLE & TAVERN   Historic   **Lunch:** $6-$20   **Dinner:** $6-$20   Phone: 517/486-2144
♦♦♦ ♦♦♦
American

Location: 0.3 mi w of town on US 223; adjacent to Hathaway House. 116 N Main St 49228. **Hours:** 11:30 am-10 pm, Fri & Sat-midnight, Sun 11 am-9 pm. Closed: 1/1, 12/25. **Features:** This rustic restored carriage house is a fitting spot for meal and a drink. The menu offers light fare—snacks, soup, sandwiches and salad as well as entrees from salmon to steak. The banana cream pie is to die for. Casual dress; cocktails.
Parking: on-site. **Cards:** DS, MC, VI.

[✕]

BLOOMFIELD HILLS —See Detroit p. 251.

BOYNE CITY pop. 3,500

———— WHERE TO STAY ————

WATER STREET INN
ⒶⒶⒶ (SAVE)
♦♦♦ ♦♦♦
Condominium

1/1-3/31	1P: $85-$235	2P: $85-$235	XP: $10	F12
5/28-12/31	1P: $85-$200	2P: $85-$200	XP: $10	F12
4/1-5/27	1P: $85-$95	2P: $85-$95	XP: $10	F12

Phone: 231/582-3000

Location: Center. Located on the lake. 240 Front St 49712. Fax: 231/582-3001. **Facility:** Rooms at this lakefront inn are all individually decorated and feature fireplaces. Smoke free premises. 27 one-bedroom suites with whirlpools, some with efficiencies or kitchens. 3 stories, exterior corridors. **Parking:** on-site. **Terms:** cancellation fee imposed. **Amenities:** video library (fee), irons. **Leisure Activities:** rental paddleboats, snowmobiling, rental bicycles. *Fee:* kayaks. **Guest Services:** coin laundry. **Cards:** AX, MC, VI.

[SD] [Y↑] [✕] [✕] [VCR] [🎥] [🖥] [🖥] [🖥]

———— WHERE TO DINE ————

———— The following restaurant has not been evaluated by AAA ———— but is listed for your information only.

RED MESA GRILL   Phone: 231/582-0049
[fyi]

Not evaluated. **Location:** Downtown. 117 Water St 49712. **Features:** The menu displays a mix of Cajun, Creole and Mexican dishes.

BOYNE FALLS pop. 370

———— WHERE TO STAY ————

DEER LAKE BED & BREAKFAST   Phone: (231)582-9039
♦♦♦ ♦♦♦

All Year [BP]   1P: $85-$105   2P: $95-$115   XP: $15
Bed & Breakfast

Location: Jct US 131 and CR C48, 0.8 mi w, then 2.2 mi s. Located in a quiet, rural area. 00631 E Deer Lake Rd 49712 (00631 E Deer Lake Rd, BOYNE CITY). Fax: 231/582-5385. **Facility:** This B&B offers lake views and tastefully furnished accommodations; two rooms have private balconies. Smoke free premises. 5 one-bedroom standard units. 2 stories (no elevator), interior corridors. *Bath:* shower only. **Parking:** on-site. **Terms:** 2 night minimum stay - weekends, 10 day cancellation notice. **Amenities:** irons, hair dryers. **Leisure Activities:** paddleboats, sailboats, horseshoes, volleyball. **Guest Services:** TV in common area. **Cards:** DS, MC, VI.

[SD] [✕] [✕] [W]

BREVORT

———— WHERE TO STAY ————

CHAPEL HILL MOTEL   Phone: 906/292-5521
♦♦♦
Motel

6/16-9/14	1P: $44-$49	2P: $44-$54	XP: $5
11/15-3/31	1P: $44-$49	2P: $44-$49	XP: $5
4/1-6/15 & 9/15-11/14	1P: $37-$39	2P: $37-$39	XP: $5

Location: Center. Located in a semi-commercial area. 4422 W US 2 49760. **Facility:** 26 units. 25 one- and 1 two-bedroom standard units. 1 story, interior/exterior corridors. *Bath:* combo or shower only. **Parking:** on-site, winter plug-ins. **Terms:** 3 day cancellation notice-fee imposed, small pets only ($5 extra charge). **Pool(s):** heated outdoor. **Leisure Activities:** snowmobiling, playground. **Cards:** DC, MC, VI.

SOME UNITS

[🐾] [🛥] [🎬] [🖥] / [✕] [✕] [🖥] [🖥] /
FEE

BRIDGEPORT pop. 7,849

------ WHERE TO STAY ------

BAYMONT INN & SUITES-FRANKENMUTH/BRIDGEPORT   *Book at aaa.com*   **Phone:** (989)777-3000
(AAA) (SAVE)   All Year [ECP]   1P: $69-$99   2P: $69-$99
     Location: I-75, exit 144A. Located in a commercial area. 6460 Dixie Hwy 48722. Fax: 989/777-2070. **Facility:** 100
units. 98 one-bedroom standard units, some with whirlpools. 2 one-bedroom suites. 3 stories, interior corri-
dors. *Bath:* combo or shower only. **Parking:** on-site. **Terms:** 3 day cancellation notice, pets ($10 extra
Small-scale Hotel   charge, in limited units). **Amenities:** video games, voice mail, irons, hair dryers. **Pool(s):** heated indoor.
Leisure Activities: whirlpool, exercise room. **Guest Services:** coin laundry. **Cards:** AX, DC, DS, MC, VI.
Special Amenities: free local telephone calls and free newspaper.

SOME UNITS
[icons] FEE

HEIDELBERG INN MOTEL   **Phone:** (989)777-2195
(AAA) (SAVE)   12/1-3/31   1P: $120-$140   2P: $150-$170   XP: $10   F16
            4/1-11/30 [ECP]   1P: $40-$55   2P: $45-$70   XP: $5   F16
     Location: I-75, exit 144A, 1 mi s. Located in a semi-rural area, next to a bowling alley. 6815 Dixie Hwy 48722.
Fax: 989/777-8324. **Facility:** 14 one-bedroom standard units. 1 story, exterior corridors. *Bath:* shower only.
Motel   **Parking:** on-site. **Terms:** weekly rates available. **Cards:** AX, DC, MC, VI. **Special Amenities:** free local
telephone calls and early check-in/late check-out.

SOME UNITS
[icons]

------ WHERE TO DINE ------

------ *The following restaurant has not been evaluated by AAA*
but is listed for your information only. ------

FREEWAY FRITZ   **Phone:** 989/777-8730
(fyi)   Not evaluated. **Location:** I-75, exit 144, just s. 6560 Dixie Hwy 48722. **Features:** This fast-food restaurant
serves Frankenmuth-style chicken dinner and snacks. Also at this location are several other food outlets
and a gift shop.

BRIDGMAN pop. 2,428

------ WHERE TO DINE ------

HYERDALL'S CAFE   **Lunch:** $5-$7   **Dinner:** $8-$12   **Phone:** 269/465-5546
[icon]   **Location:** I-94, exit 16, 1 mi n. 9673 Red Arrow Hwy 49106. **Hours:** 7 am-9 pm. Closed major holidays; also
Mon. **Reservations:** accepted. **Features:** This is a small town, main street cafe that has been operating
American   since 1927. Caters to the families and couples looking for fresh home cooking with items like chicken, fish,
chops and steak. **Parking:** on-site.

[icons]

BRIGHTON pop. 6,701

------ WHERE TO STAY ------

COURTYARD BY MARRIOTT   *Book at aaa.com*   **Phone:** (810)225-9200
[icon]   All Year   1P: $79-$96   2P: $79-$96   XP: $10   F17
     Location: I-96, exit 145 (Grand River S), just ne. 7799 Conference Center Dr 48114. Fax: 810/225-2028. **Facility:** 90
Small-scale Hotel   units. 88 one-bedroom standard units, some with whirlpools. 2 one-bedroom suites. 3 stories, interior corridors. *Bath:* combo or shower only. **Parking:** on-site. **Terms:** weekly rates available, [BP] & [ECP] meal plans
available, package plans - seasonal. **Amenities:** video games (fee), dual phone lines, voice mail, irons, hair dryers. **Pool(s):**
heated indoor. **Leisure Activities:** whirlpool, exercise room. **Guest Services:** valet and coin laundry. **Business Services:**
meeting rooms. **Cards:** AX, DC, DS, MC, VI.

SOME UNITS
[icons]

HOLIDAY INN EXPRESS HOTEL & SUITES   *Book at aaa.com*   **Phone:** (810)225-4300
[icon]   All Year [ECP]   1P: $99
     Location: I-96, exit 145 (Grand River S). Located in Towne Square Shopping Plaza. 8079 Challis Dr 48116.
Small-scale Hotel   Fax: 810/225-0250. **Facility:** 107 units. 72 one-bedroom standard units, some with efficiencies. 35 one-
bedroom suites ($109-$169), some with whirlpools. 2 stories, interior corridors. *Bath:* combo or shower only.
Parking: on-site. **Amenities:** video games (fee), dual phone lines, voice mail, irons, hair dryers. **Pool(s):** heated indoor. **Leisure
Activities:** whirlpool, exercise room. **Fee:** game room. **Guest Services:** valet and coin laundry. **Business Services:** meeting
rooms, business center. **Cards:** AX, CB, DC, DS, JC, MC, VI.

SOME UNITS
[icons]

------ WHERE TO DINE ------

CIAO AMICI'S   **Lunch:** $8-$12   **Dinner:** $12-$25   **Phone:** 810/227-9000
[icon]   **Location:** I-96, exit 145 (Grand River S), downtown. 217 W Main St 48116. **Hours:** 11 am-10 pm, Fri & Sat-11
pm, Sun 3 pm-9 pm. Closed major holidays. **Reservations:** accepted. **Features:** With the soft strains of
Italian   Frank Sinatra playing in the background and gold-framed pictures of the rat pack decorating the elegant
walls, it would be hard not to guess this is an Italian restaurant. Classic recipes employ fresh pasta,
homemade sauces and seasonal produce. Dressy casual; cocktails. **Parking:** on-site and street. **Cards:** AX, DC, DS, MC, VI.

LU & CARL'S
AAA
▼▼ ▼▼
American

Lunch: $8-$12   **Dinner:** $10-$15   **Phone:** 810/229-9660
Location: I-96, exit 145 (Grand River S), downtown. 100 W Main St 48116. **Hours:** 11 am-midnight, Thurs-Sat to 2 am. Closed major holidays. **Features:** Dog lovers will particularly enjoy this bright and airy restaurant that pays homage to man's best friend. A varied menu offers both daily specials and traditional favorites. Casual dress; cocktails. **Parking:** street. **Cards:** AX, DC, MC, VI.

BRIMLEY

———— **WHERE TO STAY** ————

BAY MILLS RESORT & CASINO
▼▼▼ ▼▼▼
Resort
Large-scale Hotel

	2P: $79-$89	XP: $15	F17
6/1-10/14			
4/1-5/31 & 10/15-3/31	2P: $59-$69	XP: $15	F17

Phone: (906)248-3701

Location: From the end of SR 221, 2 mi w. Located on Waishkey Bay. 11386 W Lakeshore Dr 49715. **Fax:** 906/248-3720. **Facility:** 142 units. 137 one-bedroom standard units, some with whirlpools. 5 one-bedroom suites ($140-$190) with whirlpools. 2 stories, interior corridors. *Bath:* combo or shower only. **Parking:** on-site. **Terms:** cancellation fee imposed, [AP] meal plan available, package plans. **Amenities:** hair dryers. **Leisure Activities:** cross country skiing, snowmobiling. *Fee:* golf-18 holes. **Guest Services:** gift shop. **Business Services:** conference facilities. **Cards:** AX, MC, VI. *(See color ad p 441)*

SOME UNITS

WILLABEE'S MOTEL
▼▼ ▼▼
Motel

	1P: $66-$72	2P: $66-$72	XP: $8	F18
10/16-3/31				
6/16-10/15	1P: $64-$72	2P: $64-$72	XP: $8	F18
4/1-6/15	1P: $55-$62	2P: $55-$62	XP: $8	F18

Phone: 906/248-3090

Location: At the end of SR 221. Located on the river. 9903 W 6 Mile Rd 49715 (PO Box 386). **Fax:** 906/248-3169. **Facility:** 36 units. 35 one- and 1 two-bedroom standard units. 2 stories (no elevator), exterior corridors. *Bath:* combo or shower only. **Parking:** on-site. **Terms:** 3 day cancellation notice. **Leisure Activities:** boat dock, fishing, snowmobiling. **Cards:** AX, DS, MC, VI.

SOME UNITS

BROOKLYN pop. 1,176

———— **WHERE TO STAY** ————

CHICAGO STREET INN
▼▼▼ ▼▼▼
Historic Bed
& Breakfast

| All Year | 2P: $60-$155 | XP: $20 | D |

Phone: (517)592-3888

Location: Jct Chicago and Main sts (SR 50), just w; downtown. 219 Chicago St 49230. **Fax:** 517/592-9025. **Facility:** The inn boasts a wealth of architectural details from handcrafted moldings to stained-glass windows. Smoke free premises. 6 one-bedroom standard units, some with whirlpools. 3 stories (no elevator), interior corridors. *Bath:* combo or shower only. **Parking:** on-site. **Terms:** check-in 4 pm, cancellation fee imposed, [BP] meal plan available, package plans. **Cards:** DS, MC, VI.

SOME UNITS

SUPER 8 MOTEL
▼▼▼ ▼▼▼
Small-scale Hotel

	1P: $66-$130	2P: $66-$130	XP: $5	F
5/1-9/30				
4/1-4/30 & 10/1-3/31	1P: $58-$120	2P: $58-$120	XP: $5	F

Phone: 517/592-0888

Location: Jct SR 50 and SR 124; downtown. 155 Wamplers Rd 49250 (PO Box 687). **Fax:** 517/592-0880. **Facility:** 52 units. 48 one-bedroom standard units, some with kitchens and/or whirlpools. 4 one-bedroom suites with whirlpools. 2 stories (no elevator), interior corridors. *Bath:* combo or shower only. **Parking:** on-site. **Terms:** [CP] meal plan available, small pets only ($5 extra charge). **Amenities:** *Some:* irons, hair dryers. **Guest Services:** coin laundry. **Business Services:** conference facilities. **Cards:** AX, DC, DS, MC, VI.

SOME UNITS
FEE

BYRON pop. 595

———— **WHERE TO STAY** ————

———— *The following lodging was either not evaluated or did not* ————
meet AAA rating requirements but is listed for your information only.

HOLIDAY INN EXPRESS INN & SUITES
fyi
Small-scale Hotel

Property failed to provide current rates
Too new to rate. **Location:** I-131, exit 68th St. 6565 Clay Ave. **Amenities:** 79 units, coffeemakers, microwaves, refrigerators, pool.

BYRON CENTER pop. 3,777

———— **WHERE TO STAY** ————

AMERIHOST INN-GRAND RAPIDS SOUTH   *Book at aaa.com*   **Phone:** (616)827-9900
AAA SAVE
▼▼▼ ▼▼▼
Small-scale Hotel

| All Year | 1P: $82-$91 | 2P: $82-$91 | XP: $6 | F |

Location: US 131, exit 76. Located in a business park. 7625 Caterpillar Ct SW 49548. **Fax:** 616/827-9998. **Facility:** 61 one-bedroom standard units, some with whirlpools. 2 stories (no elevator), exterior corridors. *Bath:* combo or shower only. **Parking:** on-site. **Terms:** [ECP] meal plan available. **Amenities:** voice mail, safes (fee), irons, hair dryers. **Pool(s):** heated indoor. **Leisure Activities:** sauna, whirlpool, exercise room. **Guest Services:** valet laundry. **Business Services:** meeting rooms. **Cards:** AX, CB, DC, DS, JC, MC, VI. **Special Amenities:** free expanded continental breakfast and free newspaper.

SOME UNITS

BAYMONT INN & SUITES GRAND RAPIDS SOUTHWEST/BYRON CENTER *Book at aaa.com*   **Phone:** (616)583-9535

⬡⬡⬡ SAVE All Year   1P: $89-$129   2P: $89-$129

▽▽▽▽ **Location:** US 131, exit 74, just w. 8282 Pfeiffer Farms Dr SW 49315. **Fax:** 616/583-9544. **Facility:** 88 units. 84 one-bedroom standard units, some with whirlpools. 4 one-bedroom suites ($99-$129). 4 stories, interior corridors. *Bath:* combo or shower only. **Parking:** on-site, winter plug-ins. **Terms:** [CP] meal plan available.

Small-scale Hotel **Amenities:** high-speed Internet, dual phone lines, voice mail, irons, hair dryers. **Dining:** 24 hours. **Pool(s):** heated indoor. **Leisure Activities:** whirlpool, sun deck, snowmobiling, exercise room. **Guest Services:** valet and coin laundry, airport transportation-Gerald R Ford International Airport. **Business Services:** meeting rooms, business center. **Cards:** AX, CB, DC, DS, MC, VI. **Special Amenities:** free continental breakfast and free room upgrade (subject to availability with advanced reservations).

SOME UNITS

🛅 ✈ 🍽 📶 🅼 🍳 🛢 🏊 ⊠ 📷 DATA PORT 🖥 / ⊠ 🖪 🧳 /

─── *The following lodging was either not evaluated or did not meet AAA rating requirements but is listed for your information only.* ───

COMFORT SUITES-GRAND RAPIDS SOUTH

fyi   Property failed to provide current rates
                    Too new to rate. **Location:** US 131, exit 76. Located in a business park. Caterpillar Ct SW 49548. **Amenities:** 66
Small-scale Hotel units.

CADILLAC pop. 10,000

─── **WHERE TO STAY** ───

BEST VALUE INN OF CADILLAC   **Phone:** (231)775-2458

⬡⬡⬡ SAVE 12/24-2/28   1P: $69-$109   2P: $79-$109   XP: $10   F12
          7/1-12/23   1P: $69-$89   2P: $69-$89   XP: $10   F12
▽▽▽ ◈◈◈ 4/1-6/30 & 3/1-3/31   1P: $49-$69   2P: $59-$69   XP: $10   F12

Small-scale Hotel **Location:** On SR 55, 0.5 mi w of jct SR 115. Located in a semi-commercial area. 5676 E M55 49601 (PO Box 668). **Fax:** 231/775-8383. **Facility:** 66 one-bedroom standard units. 1 story, exterior corridors. **Parking:** on-site, winter plug-ins. **Terms:** weekly rates available, package plans, pets ($10 extra charge). **Amenities:** irons, hair dryers. **Dining:** 7 am-10 pm, Sun 8 am-6 pm; breakfast hours vary off season, cocktails. **Pool(s):** heated indoor. **Leisure Activities:** sauna, whirlpool, 2 tennis courts, snowmobiling. *Fee:* golf privileges, bowling. **Guest Services:** valet laundry. **Business Services:** conference facilities. **Cards:** AX, DC, DS, MC, VI. **Special Amenities:** free continental breakfast and early check-in/late check-out.

SOME UNITS

🛅 🐎 🍽 🍸 🛢 ⊠ 📷 🖥 / ⊠ 🖪 /
   FEE

DAYS INN *Book at aaa.com*   **Phone:** (231)775-4414

▽▽▽ ◈◈◈ 6/8-10/14 & 12/14-3/31   1P: $79-$140   2P: $79-$140   XP: $5   F17
          4/1-6/7 & 10/15-12/13   1P: $69-$119   2P: $69-$119   XP: $5   F17

Small-scale Hotel **Location:** On SR 115, 0.5 mi n of SR 55. Located next to an amusement park. 6001 M-115 49601. **Fax:** 231/799-0370. **Facility:** 60 one-bedroom standard units. 2 stories (no elevator), interior corridors. **Parking:** on-site, winter plug-ins. **Amenities:** safes (fee), irons, hair dryers. **Pool(s):** heated indoor. **Leisure Activities:** whirlpool, snowmobiling. **Guest Services:** valet laundry. **Business Services:** meeting rooms. **Cards:** AX, CB, DC, DS, MC, VI. *(See color ad card insert)*

SOME UNITS

ASK 🛅 🛢 📷 🖥 / ⊠ DATA PORT 🖪 🧳 /

ECONO LODGE *Book at aaa.com*   **Phone:** (231)775-6700

⬡⬡⬡ SAVE 6/27-9/5   1P: $70-$95   2P: $70-$95   XP: $8   F18
          12/26-3/31   1P: $50-$85   2P: $50-$85   XP: $8   F18
▽▽▽   4/1-6/26 & 9/6-12/25 1P: $50-$75   2P: $50-$75   XP: $8   F18

Small-scale Hotel **Location:** Jct SR 55 and 115. Located on the main highway. 2501 Sunnyside Dr 49601. **Fax:** 231/775-8828. **Facility:** 30 one-bedroom standard units. 2 stories (no elevator), interior/exterior corridors. **Parking:** on-site, winter plug-ins. **Terms:** office hours 7 am-midnight, pets ($10 extra charge). **Leisure Activities:** snowmobiling. **Cards:** AX, CB, DC, DS, JC, MC, VI. **Special Amenities:** free continental breakfast and free local telephone calls.

SOME UNITS

🛅 🐎 🛢 📷 / ⊠ 🖪 🛢 🖥 /
   FEE

HAMPTON INN

Book at aaa.com

Phone: (231)779-2900

All Year 1P: $79-$99 2P: $79-$99

Small-scale Hotel

Location: US 131, exit 177, 1 mi n. 1650 S Mitchell St 49601. Fax: 231/779-0846. **Facility:** 120 one-bedroom standard units. 4 stories, interior corridors. **Parking:** on-site. **Terms:** [ECP] meal plan available. **Amenities:** video games, dual phone lines, voice mail, irons, hair dryers. **Pool(s):** heated indoor. **Leisure Activities:** whirlpool, snowmobiling. **Guest Services:** valet laundry. **Business Services:** meeting rooms. **Cards:** AX, CB, DC, DS, MC, VI.

HOLIDAY INN EXPRESS

Phone: 231/779-4656

12/25-3/31	1P: $99-$139	2P: $99-$139	XP: $10 F
9/7-12/24	1P: $79-$139	2P: $79-$139	XP: $10 F
7/1-9/6	1P: $89-$119	2P: $89-$119	XP: $10 F
4/1-6/30	1P: $79-$119	2P: $79-$119	XP: $10 F

Small-scale Hotel

Location: US 131, exit 177, 0.7 mi n. 7642 S Business Rt US 131 49601. Fax: 231/779-4642. **Facility:** 70 one-bedroom standard units. 3 stories, interior corridors. **Bath:** combo or shower only. **Parking:** on-site. **Terms:** cancellation fee imposed, [ECP] meal plan available. **Amenities:** dual phone lines, voice mail, irons, hair dryers. **Pool(s):** heated indoor. **Leisure Activities:** whirlpool, snowmobiling, exercise room. **Guest Services:** valet and coin laundry. **Business Services:** meeting rooms. **Cards:** AX, DC, DS, MC, VI.

MCGUIRES RESORT

Book at aaa.com

Phone: (231)775-9947

10/10-2/28	1P: $69-$124	2P: $79-$124	XP: $20 F18
8/15-10/9	1P: $79-$109	2P: $89-$109	XP: $20 F18
4/1-8/14	1P: $69-$109	2P: $79-$109	XP: $20 F18
3/1-3/31	1P: $69-$89	2P: $79-$89	XP: $20 F18

Resort
Large-scale Hotel

Location: US 131, exit 177, 0.7 mi n, then 0.5 mi w. Located in a semi-rural area. 7880 Mackinaw Tr 49601. Fax: 231/775-9621. **Facility:** A variety of rooms, some with patios, is offered at this resort set on spacious grounds. 122 units. 119 one-bedroom standard units, some with whirlpools. 3 one-bedroom suites ($99-$204), some with whirlpools. 2-3 stories, interior corridors. **Parking:** on-site. **Terms:** check-in 4 pm, 7 day cancellation notice-fee imposed, [BP], [CP], [ECP] & [MAP] meal plans available, package plans, pets ($15 extra charge, in smoking units). **Amenities:** irons, hair dryers. **Dining:** 7 am-10 pm, cocktails, also, Terrace Room, see separate listing. **Pool(s):** heated indoor. **Leisure Activities:** sauna, whirlpool, driving range, snowmobiling, tobogganing, exercise trail, basketball, horseshoes, shuffleboard, volleyball. **Fee:** golf-27 holes, 2 lighted tennis courts, cross country skiing, cross country skis & snowshoes, game room. **Guest Services:** gift shop, valet laundry, airport transportation-Cadillac Airport. **Business Services:** conference facilities. **Cards:** AX, DC, DS, MC, VI. *(See color ad p 210)*

SUNSET SHORES RESORT

Book at aaa.com

Phone: (231)876-3700

All Year 1P: $229-$259 2P: $229-$259

Condominium

Location: US 131, exit 176, 2.3 mi nw on SR 115, then 1.1 mi ne. Located on Lake Cadillac. 1246 Sunnyside Dr 49601. Fax: 231/876-9255. **Facility:** On Lake Cadillac, the resort features many rooms with a view and a lakeside entrance or patio. Smoke free premises. 22 units. 12 two- and 10 three-bedroom suites with kitchens. 3 stories (no elevator), interior corridors. **Parking:** on-site, winter plug-ins. **Terms:** 7 day cancellation notice-fee imposed. **Amenities:** voice mail, irons. **Leisure Activities:** boat dock, fishing, snowmobiling. **Guest Services:** complimentary laundry. **Cards:** MC, VI.

——— WHERE TO DINE ———

HERMANN'S EUROPEAN CAFE & INN

Lunch: $7-$11 **Dinner:** $17-$22 **Phone:** 231/775-9563

American

Location: Center. 214 N Mitchell St 49601. **Hours:** 11 am-9:30 pm, Fri & Sat-10 pm. Closed: 1/1, 11/25, 12/25; also Sun & 12/24 for dinner. **Features:** The Austrian chef-owner prepares an interesting array of European dishes, such as schnitzel, wild boar, pork loin and apple strudel. Couples favor the quiet restaurant for moderately upscale fine dining. Attentive servers provide good follow-up. Casual dress; cocktails. **Parking:** street. **Cards:** DS, MC, VI.

LAKESIDE CHARLIES

Lunch: $5-$7 **Dinner:** $10-$17 **Phone:** 231/775-5332

American

Location: Jct SR 55 and 115. 301 S Lake Mitchell 49601. **Hours:** 11:30 am-9 pm, Fri & Sat-10 pm, Sun-8 pm; to 10 pm, Fri & Sat-11 pm 6/1-9/6. Closed: 11/25, 12/25. **Reservations:** suggested. **Features:** Overlooking Lake Mitchell, the restaurant has three dining rooms decorated with hunting and fishing memorabilia and various antiques. The focus of the menu is on beef and seafood. The basic ice cream fudge sundae is hard to beat. Casual dress; cocktails. **Parking:** on-site. **Cards:** AX, DS, MC, VI.

TERRACE ROOM

Lunch: $5-$10 **Dinner:** $10-$20 **Phone:** 231/775-9947

American

Location: US 131, exit 177, 0.7 mi n, then 0.5 mi w; in McGuires Resort. 7880 Mackinaw Tr 49601. **Hours:** 7 am-10 pm. **Reservations:** accepted. **Features:** Overlooking the golf course, this somewhat upscale dining room has a popular salad bar; you'll find more casual dining in their Curly's Up North Bar and Grill. Casual dress. **Parking:** on-site. **Cards:** AX, DC, DS, MC, VI.

——— The following restaurant has not been evaluated by AAA but is listed for your information only. ———

THE TIMBERS

Phone: 231/775-6751

[fyi]

Not evaluated. **Location:** Located between Division and 13th. 5535 E M-115 49601. **Features:** The prime rib is seasoned and slow roasted, the steaks are delicious and the walleye fillet can be potato encrusted or beer battered.

CALUMET pop. 879

——— WHERE TO STAY ———

AMERICINN OF CALUMET *Book at aaa.com* **Phone:** (906)337-6463

▽▽▽ 1/1-3/31 [ECP] 1P: $81-$126 2P: $86-$131 XP: $5 F12
7/1-10/31 [ECP] 1P: $78-$123 2P: $83-$128 XP: $5 F12
Small-scale Hotel 4/1-6/30 & 11/1-12/31 [ECP] 1P: $73-$118 2P: $78-$123 XP: $5 F12
Location: US 41; just w of Visitors Center. Located next to Mine St Station Complex. 56925 S 6th St 49913.
Fax: 906/337-4990. **Facility:** 68 units. 66 one-bedroom standard units, some with whirlpools. 2 one-bedroom suites, some with
whirlpools. 2 stories (no elevator), interior corridors. *Bath:* combo or shower only. **Parking:** on-site, winter plug-ins. **Terms:** 3 day
cancellation notice. **Amenities:** hair dryers. *Some:* irons. **Pool(s):** heated indoor. **Leisure Activities:** sauna, whirlpool, snowmobiling. *Fee:* game room. **Guest Services:** coin laundry. **Business Services:** meeting rooms. **Cards:** AX, DC, DS, MC, VI.
(See color ad p 311)

SOME UNITS
ASK ⊤⊩ 🛠 ⊇ ⊠ 🎦 [DATA PORT] ▣ / ⊠ 🖪 🖾 /

CANTON —See Detroit p. 252.

CARP LAKE

——— WHERE TO DINE ———

*The following restaurant has not been evaluated by AAA
but is listed for your information only.*

GOLDIES CAFE **Phone:** 231/537-4089
[fyi] Not evaluated. **Location:** Just e of US 31; center. 6492 Paradise Tr 49718. **Features:** On Paradise Lake, the
restaurant presents a menu of home-style specialties. Diners can request inside or deck seating.

CASCADE —See also GRAND RAPIDS.

——— WHERE TO STAY ———

AMERISUITES GRAND RAPIDS/AIRPORT *Book at aaa.com* **Phone:** (616)940-8100
🅰🅰🅰 SAVE All Year [ECP] 1P: $71-$129 2P: $71-$129 XP: $10 F
▽▽▽ **Location:** I-96, exit 43B, just e on SR 11. Located next to Meijer's Shopping Center. 5401 28th St Ct SE 49546 (5401
28th St Ct SE, GRAND RAPIDS). Fax: 616/940-0914. **Facility:** 121 one-bedroom standard units, some with
Small-scale Hotel whirlpools. 3 stories, interior corridors. **Parking:** on-site. **Terms:** small pets only. **Amenities:** voice mail,
safes, irons, hair dryers. **Pool(s):** heated indoor. **Leisure Activities:** whirlpool, golf-1 holes, exercise room,
basketball, volleyball. **Guest Services:** meeting rooms. **Cards:** AX, DC, DS, JC, MC, VI. *(See color ad p 311)*
Airport transportation-Gerald R Ford International Air-
port. **Business Services:** meeting rooms. **Cards:** AX, DC, DS, JC, MC, VI. *(See color ad p 311)*

SOME UNITS
🆂🅳 ✈ 🛏 ⊤⊩ ⊇ ⊠ 🎦 [DATA PORT] 🖪 🖾 ▣ / ⊠ /

BAYMONT INN-GRAND RAPIDS AIRPORT *Book at aaa.com* **Phone:** (616)956-3300
▽▽▽ ▽▽▽ All Year 1P: $59-$99 2P: $59-$99 XP: $7 F18
Location: I-96, exit 43B, just e. Located in a commercial area. 2873 Kraft Ave SE 49512. Fax: 616/956-5561.
Small-scale Hotel **Facility:** 102 one-bedroom standard units. 3 stories, interior corridors. **Parking:** on-site. **Terms:** weekly rates
available, [ECP] meal plan available, small pets only (in designated units). **Amenities:** video games, voice
mail, irons, hair dryers. **Guest Services:** valet and coin laundry. **Business Services:** meeting rooms. **Cards:** AX, DC, DS,
MC, VI.

SOME UNITS
ASK 🆂🅳 🛏 ⊤⊩ 🎦 [DATA PORT] ▣ / 🖪 🖾 /

COUNTRY INN & SUITES BY CARLSON OF GRAND RAPIDS *Book at aaa.com* **Phone:** (616)977-0909
▽▽▽ All Year 1P: $65-$85 2P: $65-$85 XP: $6 F18
Location: I-96, exit 43B, just e on SR 11. Located next to a shopping center. 5399 28th St SE 49512. Fax: 616/977-0909.
Small-scale Hotel **Facility:** 61 units. 51 one-bedroom standard units. 10 one-bedroom suites. 3 stories, interior corridors. *Bath:*
combo or shower only. **Parking:** on-site. **Terms:** [ECP] meal plan available, small pets only (in smoking
units). **Amenities:** voice mail, irons, hair dryers. **Pool(s):** heated indoor. **Leisure Activities:** whirlpool. **Guest Services:** valet
laundry. **Cards:** AX, CB, DC, DS, MC, VI. *(See color ad p 313)*

SOME UNITS
ASK 🆂🅳 🛏 ⊤⊩ &M 🛠 ⊘ ⊇ 🎦 [DATA PORT] ▣ / ⊠ 🖪 🖾 /
FEE

CROWNE PLAZA HOTEL-GRAND RAPIDS *Book at aaa.com* **Phone:** (616)957-1770
▽▽▽▽ All Year 1P: $79-$159 2P: $79-$159 XP: $15 F12
Location: I-96, exit 43B, 0.3 mi e on SR 11. Located in a commercial area. 5700 28th St SE 49546 (5700 28th St SE,
Large-scale Hotel GRAND RAPIDS). Fax: 616/957-0629. **Facility:** 320 units. 316 one-bedroom standard units. 4 one-bedroom
suites. 5 stories, interior corridors. *Bath:* combo or shower only. **Parking:** on-site. **Terms:** check-in 4 pm,
cancellation fee imposed, [AP] meal plan available, $3 service charge. **Amenities:** video games, voice mail, irons, hair dryers.
Some: high-speed Internet. **Pool(s):** heated indoor/outdoor. **Leisure Activities:** sauna, whirlpool, exercise room. **Guest Services:** gift shop, valet and coin laundry, area transportation. **Business Services:** conference facilities, business center.
Cards: AX, CB, DC, DS, JC, MC, VI. *(See color ad p 312)*

SOME UNITS
ASK 🆂🅳 ✈ ⊤⊩ 🍸 🛠 ⊘ ⊇ ⊠ 🎦 [DATA PORT] ▣ / ⊠ 🖪 🖾 /

DAYS INN AIRPORT *Book at aaa.com* **Phone:** (616)949-8400
▽▽▽ All Year 1P: $53-$89 **Phone:** (616)949-8400
Location: I-96, exit 43B, just e on SR 11. Located opposite Meijer's Shopping Center. 5500 28th St SE 49512.
Small-scale Hotel Fax: 616/949-9021. **Facility:** 140 one-bedroom standard units, some with whirlpools. 3 stories, interior corri-
dors. **Parking:** on-site. **Terms:** [ECP] meal plan available. **Amenities:** voice mail, hair dryers. *Some:* irons.
Pool(s): heated indoor. **Leisure Activities:** sauna, whirlpool, exercise room. **Guest Services:** coin laundry. **Business Services:**
meeting rooms. **Cards:** AX, DC, DS, MC, VI.

SOME UNITS
ASK 🆂🅳 ✈ ⊤⊩ ⊇ ⊠ 🎦 ▣ / ⊠ [DATA PORT] 🖪 🖾 /

EXEL INN OF GRAND RAPIDS   *Book at aaa.com*   Phone: (616)957-3000

(AAA) [SAVE]   All Year [CP]   1P: $40-$60   2P: $46-$66   XP: $6   F18
▼▼▼ ▼▼   Location: I-96, exit 43A, 0.5 mi w on SR 11. Located in a commercial area. 4855 28th St SE 49512 (4855 28th St SE,
Small-scale Hotel   GRAND RAPIDS). Fax: 616/957-0194. Facility: 109 one-bedroom standard units, some with whirlpools. 2 sto-
ries (no elevator), interior corridors. Parking: on-site. Terms: weekly rates available, small pets only.
Amenities: irons, hair dryers. Leisure Activities: exercise room. Guest Services: coin laundry. Cards: AX,
CB, DC, DS, MC, VI. Special Amenities: free continental breakfast and early check-in/late check-out.

SOME UNITS

HAMPTON INN   *Book at aaa.com*   Phone: (616)956-9304

▼▼▼ ▼▼   All Year   1P: $77-$90   2P: $82-$97
Small-scale Hotel   Location: I-96, exit 43A, 0.5 mi w on SR 11. Located in a commercial area. 4981 28th St SE 49512 (4981 28th St SE,
GRAND RAPIDS). Facility: 119 one-bedroom standard units. 2 stories, interior corridors.
Parking: on-site. Terms: [ECP] meal plan available. Amenities: video games, voice mail, irons. Pool(s):
heated outdoor. Leisure Activities: exercise room. Guest Services: valet laundry. Business Services: meeting rooms.
Cards: AX, DC, DS, MC, VI. (See color ad p 312)

SOME UNITS

HOWARD JOHNSON EXPRESS INN & SUITES   *Book at aaa.com*   Phone: (616)940-1777

(AAA) [SAVE]   All Year [ECP]   1P: $59-$109   2P: $59-$109
▼▼▼ ▼▼   Location: I-96, exit 43B, just e. Located in a commercial area. 2985 Kraft Ave SE 49512. Fax: 616/940-9809.
Facility: 40 one-bedroom standard units. 2 stories, interior corridors. Parking: on-site. Terms: pets ($10 fee,
$20 deposit, in designated units). Amenities: irons, hair dryers. Guest Services: valet and coin laundry.
Small-scale Hotel   Cards: AX, DC, DS, MC, VI.

FEE   FEE

RED ROOF INN   *Book at aaa.com*   Phone: (616)942-0800

(AAA) [SAVE]   5/2-8/28   1P: $50-$62   2P: $56-$68   XP: $6   F18
▼▼▼ ▼▼   4/1-5/1 & 8/29-3/31   1P: $49-$62   2P: $55-$68   XP: $6   F18
Motel   Location: I-96, exit 43A, 0.3 mi w on SR 11. Located in a busy, commercial area. 5131 28th St 49512 (5131 28th St,
GRAND RAPIDS). Fax: 616/942-8341. Facility: 107 one-bedroom standard units. 2 stories (no elevator), ex-
terior corridors. Bath: combo or shower only. Parking: on-site. Amenities: video games, voice mail.
Cards: AX, CB, DC, DS, MC, VI. Special Amenities: free local telephone calls and free newspaper.

SOME UNITS

——— WHERE TO DINE ———

——— *The following restaurant has not been evaluated by AAA* ———
but is listed for your information only.

NOTO'S   Phone: 616/493-6686
[fyi]   Not evaluated. Location: I-96, exit 43B, 1.5 mi e on SR 11. 6600 28th St SE 49546. Features: The upscale
restaurant serves steak, chops and seafood with fine Italian wines and homemade-style desserts.

CASEVILLE pop. 888

——— WHERE TO DINE ———

BAY CAFE   Lunch: $4-$6   Dinner: $6-$16   Phone: 989/856-2676
▼▼   Location: Center. 6750 Main St 48725. Hours: 6 am-7:30 pm; to 9 pm 5/31-9/6. Closed: 11/25, 12/25; also
American   Sun in winter. Features: Burgers, steak, seafood and pasta make up the bulk of the family restaurant's
classic menu. An outdoorsy decor, with fish and wildlife, punctuates the relaxed dining room. The summer
patio is popular in season. For dessert, have a slice of homemade pie. Casual dress. Parking: street.
Cards: AX, DS, MC, VI.

SHAKERS   Lunch: $4-$7   Dinner: $4-$7   Phone: 989/856-2663
▼▼   Location: Center. 6685 Main St 48725. Hours: 8 am-8 pm, Fri & Sat-10 pm. Closed major holidays.
Features: A bright red and white roadside diner that along with an ice cream bar serves such favorites as
American   hamburgers and sandwiches. Casual dress. Parking: on-site.

CEDARVILLE

——— WHERE TO STAY ———

CEDARVILLE INN   Phone: 906/484-2266

(AAA) [SAVE]   6/27-8/10 [ECP]   1P: $99-$139   2P: $99-$139   XP: $10
▼▼▼ ▼▼   8/11-3/31 [ECP]   1P: $99   2P: $119   XP: $10
Motel   4/1-6/26 [ECP]   1P: $79-$99   2P: $79-$99   XP: $10
Location: On SR 134, just w of SR 129. 106 W M-134 49719 (PO Box 189). Fax: 906/484-3066. Facility: 50 one-
bedroom standard units, some with whirlpools. 2 stories (no elevator), interior corridors. Parking: on-site,
winter plug-ins. Terms: pets (in limited units). Amenities: video library (fee). Some: irons, hair dryers.
Pool(s): heated indoor. Leisure Activities: whirlpool, snowmobiling, exercise room. Fee: game room. Guest Services: coin
laundry. Business Services: meeting rooms. Cards: AX, CB, DC, DS, JC, MC, VI.

SOME UNITS

FEE

CENTRAL LAKE pop. 990

—— WHERE TO DINE ——

MURPHY'S LAMPLIGHT INN
♦♦♦ ♦♦♦
Steak & Seafood

Dinner: $9-$19   **Phone:** 231/544-6443

Location: On SR 88; center. 2535 N Main St 49622. **Hours:** 5 pm-9 pm; hours may vary seasonally. Closed: Mon-Wed 11/1-5/31. **Reservations:** suggested. **Features:** Hand-cut steaks and fresh local seafood are the menu's focus. Fireplaces, artwork and pottery lend to the turn-of-the-20th-century atmosphere of the dining room. Finish off your meal with a slice of delicious Kentucky Derby pie or a hot fudge sundae. Cocktails. **Parking:** on-site. **Cards:** AX, DS, MC, VI.   🍸 ✕

CHARLEVOIX pop. 2,994

—— WHERE TO STAY ——

SLEEP INN   **Book at aaa.com**   **Phone:** (231)547-0300
♦♦ ♦♦
Small-scale Hotel

6/25-8/31 [ECP]	1P: $100-$145	2P: $100-$145	XP: $10	F18
6/11-6/24 [ECP]	1P: $80-$125	2P: $80-$125	XP: $10	F18
9/1-3/31 [ECP]	1P: $60-$125	2P: $60-$125	XP: $10	F18
4/1-6/10 [ECP]	1P: $60-$105	2P: $60-$105	XP: $10	F18

Location: 1 mi n on US 31. Located in a commercial area. 800 Petoskey Ave 49720. **Fax:** 231/547-3995. **Facility:** 55 one-bedroom standard units. 3 stories, interior corridors. *Bath:* combo or shower only. **Parking:** on-site. **Terms:** 3 day cancellation notice-fee imposed, package plans - seasonal & weekends, pets ($25 deposit). **Amenities:** *Some:* irons. **Pool(s):** heated indoor. **Leisure Activities:** whirlpool. **Business Services:** meeting rooms. **Cards:** AX, DC, DS, MC, VI.

SOME UNITS

(ASK) (S🐕) (🐎) (🍴✦) (👤) (🏊) (🎥) (DATA PORT) / (✕) (💻) /
FEE

WEATHERVANE TERRACE INN & SUITES   **Phone:** (231)547-9955
(AAA) (SAVE)   All Year   1P: $55-$249   XP: $5   F18
♦♦♦ ♦♦♦
Motel

Location: Just off US 31; at Harbor Bridge. Located in a commercial area. 111 Pine River Ln 49720. **Fax:** 231/547-0070. **Facility:** 68 units. 41 one-bedroom standard units, some with efficiencies and/or whirlpools. 27 one-bedroom suites ($79-$249), some with efficiencies, kitchens and/or whirlpools. 2-3 stories, exterior corridors. *Bath:* combo or shower only. **Parking:** on-site, winter plug-ins. **Terms:** check-in 4 pm, 7 day cancellation notice, [ECP] meal plan available. **Amenities:** video library (fee), irons, hair dryers. **Pool(s):** heated outdoor. **Leisure Activities:** whirlpool. **Business Services:** meeting rooms. **Cards:** AX, DS, MC, VI. **Special Amenities:** free expanded continental breakfast and free local telephone calls. *(See color ad below)*

SOME UNITS

(🍴✦) (🏊) (VCR) (🎥) (DATA PORT) (📠) (🖨) / (✕) (💻) /

WHERE TO DINE

GREY GABLES INN
American
Dinner: $13-$20 **Phone:** 231/547-9261
Location: Just e of US 31. 308 Belvedere Ave 49720. **Hours:** 5 pm-10 pm, Fri & Sat-11 pm. Closed major holidays. **Reservations:** suggested. **Features:** Pork chops, veal, lobster, prime-graded meat and pasta are among the dishes on the restaurant's varied menu. Well-prepared whitefish is a house specialty. Seating is offered in four rooms of the Victorian house. In-house desserts are tempting. Casual dress; cocktails. **Parking:** street. **Cards:** AX, MC, VI.

STAFFORD'S WEATHERVANE RESTAURANT
American
Lunch: $7-$12 **Dinner:** $15-$39 **Phone:** 231/547-4311
Location: US 31 at Pine River Bridge; downtown. 106 Pine River Ln 49720. **Hours:** 11 am-3 & 4:30-10 pm; hours vary off season. Closed: 12/25. **Reservations:** accepted. **Features:** Weathervane scallops and planked whitefish stand out on a menu of mostly steak and seafood selections. The nautical theme is evident in the dining room decor, as well as in the seagull-shaped roof of the building itself. Families are welcomed. Casual dress; cocktails. **Parking:** on-site. **Cards:** AX, DS, MC, VI.

CHARLOTTE pop. 8,389

WHERE TO STAY

COMFORT INN — *Book at aaa.com* **Phone:** (517)543-7307

5/1-10/31 [ECP]	1P: $79-$99	2P: $84-$99	XP: $5	F12
4/1-4/30 & 11/1-3/31 [ECP]	1P: $69-$89	2P: $69-$89	XP: $5	F12

Small-scale Hotel **Location:** I-69, exit 61 (Lansing Rd), 0.5 mi e. 1302 E Packard Hwy 48813. Fax: 517/543-7311. **Facility:** 61 one-bedroom standard units, some with whirlpools. 3 stories, interior corridors. *Bath:* combo or shower only. **Parking:** on-site. **Amenities:** voice mail, irons, hair dryers. **Pool(s):** heated indoor. **Leisure Activities:** exercise room. **Guest Services:** coin laundry. **Cards:** AX, CB, DC, DS, MC, VI. **Special Amenities:** free expanded continental breakfast and free local telephone calls.

HOLIDAY INN EXPRESS & SUITES — *Book at aaa.com* **Phone:** (517)541-5000
All Year [CP] 1P: $72-$89 2P: $72-$89 XP: $7 F18
Small-scale Hotel **Location:** I-69, exit 60, just e on SR 50. Located adjacent to Meijer Shopping Mall. 500 Meijer St 48813. Fax: 517/541-0000. **Facility:** 67 one-bedroom standard units, some with whirlpools. 3 stories, interior corridors. *Bath:* combo or shower only. **Parking:** on-site. **Amenities:** dual phone lines, voice mail, irons, hair dryers. **Pool(s):** heated indoor. **Leisure Activities:** whirlpool, exercise room. **Guest Services:** coin laundry. **Business Services:** meeting rooms. **Cards:** AX, CB, DC, DS, JC, MC, VI. **Special Amenities:** free continental breakfast and free local telephone calls.

SUPER 8 MOTEL — *Book at aaa.com* **Phone:** (517)543-8288
4/1-11/1	1P: $55-$62	2P: $65-$72	XP: $10	F12
11/2-3/31	1P: $50-$57	2P: $62-$67	XP: $10	F12

Small-scale Hotel **Location:** I-69, exit 60, just w on SR 50. 828 E Shepherd St 48813. Fax: 517/543-8481. **Facility:** 50 one-bedroom standard units, some with whirlpools. 2 stories, interior corridors. **Parking:** on-site. **Terms:** [CP] meal plan available, small pets only. **Business Services:** meeting rooms. **Cards:** AX, DC, DS, MC, VI. **Special Amenities:** free continental breakfast and free local telephone calls.

WHERE TO DINE

THE GAVEL
American
Lunch: $4-$6 **Dinner:** $8-$10 **Phone:** 517/543-1620
Location: I-69, exit 61 (Lansing Rd), jct Lansing Rd and Cochran St; downtown. 112 S Cochran St 48813. **Hours:** 7 am-9:30 pm, Fri-11 pm. Closed major holidays; also Sun. **Features:** Wide storefront windows are a good spot for people watching at this neighborhood eatery. Casual dress; cocktails. **Parking:** street. **Cards:** AX, MC, VI.

LOOK FOR THE RED

*N*ext time you pore over a AAA TourBook® guide in search of a lodging establishment, take note of the vibrant red AAA logo, icon, and SAVE Diamond rating just under a select group of property names! These Official Appointment properties place a high value on the business they receive from dedicated AAA travelers and offer members great room rates*.

* See TourBook Navigator section, page 14, for complete details.

CHEBOYGAN pop. 5,295

------ WHERE TO STAY ------

BEST WESTERN RIVER TERRACE MOTEL   *Book at aaa.com*   **Phone:** (231)627-5688

AAA [SAVE]   6/18-9/5   1P: $68-$137   2P: $88-$147   XP: $10   F12
▽▽▽▽   4/1-6/17 & 9/6-3/31   1P: $48-$98   2P: $58-$137   XP: $10   F12
Motel   **Location:** 1 mi s on SR 27. Located on the Cheboygan River. 847 S Main St 49721. Fax: 231/627-2472. **Facility:** 53 one-bedroom standard units, some with whirlpools. 2 stories (no elevator), interior/exterior corridors. **Parking:** on-site. **Terms:** office hours 7 am-11 pm. **Amenities:** voice mail, irons, hair dryers. **Pool(s):** heated indoor. **Leisure Activities:** whirlpool, boat dock, exercise room. **Cards:** AX, CB, DC, DS, MC, VI.
Special Amenities: early check-in/late check-out. *(See color ad below)*

SOME UNITS
🍽️ 🛶 ⊠ 🎿 [DATA PORT] ☕ / ⊠ /

BIRCH HAUS MOTEL   **Phone:** (231)627-5862

AAA [SAVE]   All Year [CP]   1P: $35-$45   2P: $40-$60
▽   **Location:** On US 23, 0.8 mi nw. Located in a semi-commercial area. 1301 Mackinaw Ave 49721. **Facility:** 13 units. 12 one- and 1 two-bedroom standard units. 1 story, exterior corridors. **Parking:** on-site, winter plug-ins.
Motel   **Terms:** cancellation fee imposed, small pets only ($5 extra charge). **Leisure Activities:** snowmobiling. **Cards:** AX, DS, MC, VI. **Special Amenities:** free continental breakfast and free local telephone calls.

SOME UNITS
🐾 🎿 📞 / ⊠ /
FEE

CONTINENTAL INN   **Phone:** 231/627-7164

▽▽ ▽▽   6/16-9/6   1P: $62-$110   2P: $68-$120
Motel   4/1-6/15 & 9/7-3/21   1P: $39-$78   2P: $49-$88
  Location: At jct US 23 and SR 27. Located in a commercial area. 613 N Main St 49721. Fax: 231/627-8753. **Facility:** 42 units. 22 one- and 20 two-bedroom standard units. 2 stories, exterior corridors. *Bath:* combo or shower only. **Parking:** on-site. **Amenities:** hair dryers. **Pool(s):** heated outdoor. **Cards:** AX, DS, MC, VI.

SOME UNITS
[ASK] [S/D] 🍽️ ⛓️ 🏊 [DATA PORT] / ⊠ 📞 🖥️ /
FEE FEE

DAYS INN   *Book at aaa.com*   **Phone:** (231)627-3126

▽▽ ▽▽   6/25-8/29 [CP]   1P: $49-$179   2P: $49-$179   XP: $5   F18
Small-scale Hotel   4/1-6/24 & 8/30-3/31 [CP]   1P: $42-$98   2P: $42-$98   XP: $5   F18
  Location: On SR 27, 1.3 mi s. Located on the river. 889 S Main St 49721. Fax: 231/627-2889. **Facility:** 42 one-bedroom standard units, some with whirlpools. 2 stories (no elevator), interior corridors. **Parking:** on-site, winter plug-ins. **Terms:** 7 day cancellation notice. **Amenities:** voice mail, hair dryers. **Leisure Activities:** boat dock, fishing. **Cards:** AX, CB, DC, DS, MC, VI. *(See color ad card insert)*

SOME UNITS
[ASK] [S/D] 🍽️ ⛓️M [DATA PORT] / ⊠ 📞 🖥️ ☕ /

PINE RIVER MOTEL
Phone: 231/627-5119

9/4-3/31	1P: $40-$80	2P: $40-$80	XP: $5 F11
4/1-6/14	1P: $30-$80	2P: $40-$80	XP: $5 F11
6/15-9/3		2P: $40-$80	XP: $5 F11

AAA SAVE

Motel

Location: 0.5 mi e on US 23. Located in a semi-commercial area. 102 Lafayette 49721. **Fax:** 231/627-2779. **Facility:** 15 one-bedroom standard units. 1 story, exterior corridors. *Bath:* combo or shower only. **Parking:** on-site, winter plug-ins. **Terms:** 3 day cancellation notice, weekly rates available, package plans, pets ($10 extra charge). **Leisure Activities:** snowmobiling. **Cards:** DS, MC, VI. **Special Amenities:** free local telephone calls and preferred room (subject to availability with advanced reservations).

SOME UNITS

🛏 🍽 🎥 / ✕ 📷 🖥 /
FEE

──────── **WHERE TO DINE** ────────

THE BOATHOUSE
Lunch: $6-$9 Dinner: $14-$19 Phone: 231/627-4316

American

Location: Center. 106 Pine St 49721. **Hours:** 11 am-10 pm, Sat from 4 pm, Sun 11 am-8 pm. Closed: 12/25; also Mon-Wed in winter. **Reservations:** suggested. **Features:** Representative of menu selections is the flavorful honey-pecan walleye, which is sauteed in honey and sprinkled with pecans. The converted former boathouse was built by a Purple Gang member in the 1930s to run whiskey from Canada during Prohibition. Casual dress; cocktails. **Parking:** on-site. **Cards:** AX, DC, DS, MC, VI.

🍷 ✕

HACK-MA-TACK INN Historic
Dinner: $19-$29 Phone: 231/625-2919

AAA

American

Location: 3.3 mi s on SR 27, 0.3 mi e on US 33, then 2 mi sw, follow signs. 8131 Beebe Rd 49721. **Hours:** Open 5/1-10/15; 5 pm-10 pm. **Features:** This historic 1894 log lodge overlooks the Cheboygan River, sitting amid a mature cedar, pine and birch setting. Rustic appointments, a moosehead mounted on a stone fireplace, a canoe and racing boat hanging from the log rafters all add to the ambience. Prime rib and whitefish are house specialties. Casual dress; cocktails. **Parking:** on-site. **Cards:** AX, DC, DS, MC, VI.

🍷 🎖 ✕

CHELSEA pop. 4,398

──────── **WHERE TO STAY** ────────

CHELSEA COMFORT INN & CONFERENCE CENTER *Book at aaa.com*
Phone: 734/433-8000

All Year	1P: $94-$189	2P: $94-$189	XP: $10 F

Small-scale Hotel

Location: I-94, exit 159, just n. 1645 Commerce Park Dr 48118. **Fax:** 734/433-9565. **Facility:** 84 units. 82 one- and 2 two-bedroom standard units, some with whirlpools. 3 stories, interior corridors. *Bath:* combo or shower only. **Parking:** on-site. **Terms:** [ECP] meal plan available. **Amenities:** dual phone lines, voice mail, irons, hair dryers. **Pool(s):** heated indoor. **Leisure Activities:** whirlpool, exercise room. **Guest Services:** valet laundry. **Business Services:** conference facilities, business center. **Cards:** AX, DC, MC, VI.

SOME UNITS

(ASK) 🅢🅓 🛏 🄼 🈯 🏊 🎥 DATA PORT 🖥 / ✕ 📷 /

HOLIDAY INN EXPRESS *Book at aaa.com*
Phone: 734/433-1600

All Year [ECP]	1P: $99-$199	2P: $99-$199	XP: $8 F18

Small-scale Hotel

Location: I-94, exit 159, 0.3 mi n. 1540 Commerce Park Dr 48118. **Fax:** 734/433-1600. **Facility:** 65 one-bedroom standard units. 3 stories, interior corridors. *Bath:* combo or shower only. **Parking:** on-site. **Amenities:** dual phone lines, voice mail, irons, hair dryers. *Some:* CD players. **Pool(s):** heated indoor. **Leisure Activities:** exercise room. **Guest Services:** valet laundry. **Cards:** AX, CB, DC, DS, JC, MC, VI.

SOME UNITS

(ASK) 🍽 🄼 🈯 🏊 🎥 DATA PORT 🖥 / ✕ VCR 📷 /

──────── **WHERE TO DINE** ────────

THE COMMON GRILL
Lunch: $8-$14 Dinner: $17-$24 Phone: 734/475-0470

American

Location: I-94, exit 159, 2 mi n. 112 S Main St 48118. **Hours:** 11 am-10 pm, Fri & Sat-11 pm, Sun-9 pm. Closed major holidays; also Mon. **Features:** This busy eatery has a trendy look and an imaginative menu. They serve American food, and use exotic spices to give it a new twist. The owner constantly searches the markets of such cities as Los Angeles and San Francisco, to bring back fresh new recipes. Casual dress; cocktails. **Parking:** on-site. **Cards:** AX, MC, VI.

✕

CHESANING pop. 2,548

──────── **WHERE TO STAY** ────────

COLONIAL MOTEL
Phone: (989)845-3292

All Year	1P: $65-$85	2P: $75-$90	XP: $10 F5

AAA SAVE

Motel

Location: 0.5 mi e on SR 57. 9475 E M-57 48616. **Fax:** 989/845-3230. **Facility:** 14 one-bedroom standard units, some with whirlpools. 1 story, exterior corridors. **Parking:** on-site. **Terms:** [ECP] meal plan available. **Cards:** DS, MC, VI.

SOME UNITS

🅢🅓 🎥 🖥 / ✕ /

──────── **WHERE TO DINE** ────────

CHESANING HERITAGE HOUSE Historic
Lunch: $7-$14 Dinner: $11-$21 Phone: 989/845-7700

American

DS, MC, VI.

Location: Center. 605 W Broad St 48616. **Hours:** 11 am-9 pm, Fri & Sat-10 pm, Sun noon-9 pm. Closed: 12/24, 12/25. **Features:** In the historic district, the 1908 Southern-style home boasts three glassed-in porches and loads of cozy charm. Menu selections include ample portions of seafood, tenderloin, prime rib and pork specialties. Service is friendly and efficient. Casual dress; cocktails. **Parking:** on-site. **Cards:** AX,

🍷 ✕

CHRISTMAS

―――――― WHERE TO STAY ――――――

PAIR-A-DICE INN　　*Book at aaa.com*　　　　　　　　　　　　　**Phone:** (906)387-3500

(AAA) (SAVE)　　6/24-9/5 & 12/16-3/31　　1P: $69-$85　　2P: $79-$95　　XP: $12　　F10
▽▽▽ ▽▽▽　　4/1-6/23 & 9/6-12/15　　1P: $59-$69　　2P: $69-$79　　XP: $12　　F10

Small-scale Hotel　　**Location:** On SR 28; center. Located next to Kewadin Casino. E7889 W M-28 49862. Fax: 906/387-2774. **Facility:** 48 one-bedroom standard units. 2 stories, interior corridors. **Parking:** on-site, winter plug-ins. **Terms:** 3 day cancellation notice, weekly rates available, [CP] meal plan available, pets (with prior approval, in designated units). **Amenities:** irons, hair dryers. **Leisure Activities:** whirlpool, snowmobiling. **Guest Services:** gift shop. **Business Services:** meeting rooms. **Cards:** AX, DS, MC, VI. **Special Amenities:** free continental breakfast and free local telephone calls.

SOME UNITS

$\boxed{S/D}$ $\boxed{\text{🐾}}$ $\boxed{\text{🍴+}}$ $\boxed{\text{DATA PORT}}$ $\boxed{\square}$ / $\boxed{\times}$ $\boxed{\blacksquare}$ $\boxed{\square}$ /

―――――― WHERE TO DINE ――――――

FOGGY'S STEAK HOUSE　　　　**Lunch:** $5-$8　　　　**Dinner:** $8-$17　　　　**Phone:** 906/387-3357

▽▽▽ ▽▽▽　　**Location:** On SR 28; center. E7876 W M-28 49862. **Hours:** 11 am-11 pm; hours may vary. Closed: 12/25. **Features:** Along the main highway and the snowmobile trails, the steak house offers cuts of beef and other traditional dishes. Guests can sip a drink in the active sports bar before dinner, then grill their own steak. Casual dress; cocktails. **Parking:** on-site. **Cards:** DS, MC, VI.

American

$\boxed{\text{🍸}}$ $\boxed{\times}$

CLARE pop. 3,000

―――――― WHERE TO STAY ――――――

DAYS INN　　*Book at aaa.com*　　　　　　　　　　　　　　**Phone:** 989/802-0144

▽▽▽ ▽▽▽　　6/1-9/30　　　　　　1P: $89-$109　　2P: $89-$109　　XP: $7　　F
Small-scale Hotel　　4/1-5/31 & 10/1-3/31　　1P: $57-$89　　2P: $57-$89　　XP: $7　　F

Location: On Business Rt US 10 and 127, just w of jct 127 and Old 27. Located in a commercial area. 10100 S Clare Ave 48617. Fax: 989/802-0148. **Facility:** 60 one-bedroom standard units, some with whirlpools. 2 stories (no elevator), interior corridors. *Bath:* combo or shower only. **Parking:** on-site, winter plug-ins. **Terms:** cancellation fee imposed, [ECP] meal plan available, package plans. **Amenities:** irons, hair dryers. **Leisure Activities:** whirlpool, snowmobiling. **Guest Services:** valet and coin laundry. **Business Services:** meeting rooms. **Cards:** AX, CB, DC, DS, JC, MC, VI.

SOME UNITS

$\boxed{\text{🍴+}}$ $\boxed{\text{♿M}}$ $\boxed{\text{♿}}$ $\boxed{\text{👶+}}$ $\boxed{\text{🎥}}$ $\boxed{\text{DATA PORT}}$ $\boxed{\square}$ / $\boxed{\times}$ $\boxed{\blacksquare}$ $\boxed{\square}$ /

HOLIDAY INN EXPRESS CLARE　　*Book at aaa.com*　　　　　　　**Phone:** 989/386-1111

▽▽▽ ▽▽▽　　6/1-9/30　　　　　　1P: $59-$109　　2P: $59-$109　　XP: $7　　F
Small-scale Hotel　　4/1-5/31 & 10/1-3/31　　1P: $59-$99　　2P: $59-$99　　XP: $7　　F

Location: On Business Rt US 10 and 127; just w of jct US 127 and US 27. Loated in a commercial area. 10318 S Clare Ave 48617. Fax: 989/386-2211. **Facility:** 96 one-bedroom standard units, some with whirlpools. 2 stories (no elevator), interior corridors. *Bath:* combo or shower only. **Parking:** on-site, winter plug-ins. **Terms:** cancellation fee imposed, [ECP] meal plan available, package plans. **Amenities:** video games, dual phone lines, voice mail, irons, hair dryers. **Pool(s):** heated indoor. **Leisure Activities:** whirlpool, snowmobiling. **Guest Services:** coin laundry. **Business Services:** meeting rooms. **Cards:** AX, CB, DC, DS, JC, MC, VI.

SOME UNITS

$\boxed{\text{🍴+}}$ $\boxed{\text{♿}}$ $\boxed{\text{📷}}$ $\boxed{\text{🏊}}$ $\boxed{\text{👶+}}$ $\boxed{\text{🎥}}$ $\boxed{\text{DATA PORT}}$ $\boxed{\square}$ / $\boxed{\times}$ $\boxed{\blacksquare}$ $\boxed{\square}$ /

FEE

―――――― WHERE TO DINE ――――――

The following restaurant has not been evaluated by AAA but is listed for your information only.

DOHERTY HOTEL DINING ROOM　　　　　　　　　　　　　　**Phone:** 989/386-3441

(fyi)　　Not evaluated. **Location:** Center; in the Doherty Hotel. 604 N McEwan St 48617. **Features:** In the historic section of the landmark hotel, the dining room prepares house specialties of prime rib, chargrilled steaks and fresh seafood.

CLARKSTON —*See Detroit p. 253.*

CLAWSON —*See Detroit p. 253.*

COLDWATER pop. 12,697

―――――― WHERE TO STAY ――――――

CHICAGO PIKE INN　　　　　　　　　　　　　　　　　　**Phone:** 517/279-8744

▽▽▽ ▽▽▽　　All Year　　　　　　1P: $100-$195　　2P: $100-$195　　XP: $20
Historic Bed & Breakfast　　**Location:** I-69, exit 13, 0.8 mi w. 215 E Chicago St 49036. Fax: 517/278-8597. **Facility:** Stained-glass windows are among the vintage details at this 1903 Victorian inn, which also boasts latter-day conveniences. Designated smoking area. 8 units. 7 one-bedroom standard units, some with whirlpools. 1 one-bedroom suite. 2 stories (no elevator), interior corridors. *Bath:* combo or shower only. **Parking:** on-site. **Terms:** age restrictions may apply, 7 day cancellation notice-fee imposed, [BP] meal plan available. **Leisure Activities:** bicycles. **Guest Services:** gift shop. **Cards:** AX, DS, MC, VI.

SOME UNITS

$\boxed{\times}$ / $\boxed{\text{AC}}$ $\boxed{\text{VCR}}$ $\boxed{\blacksquare}$ $\boxed{\square}$ /

HOLIDAY INN EXPRESS   *Book at aaa.com*   **Phone:** (517)279-0900
All Year [ECP]   1P: $79-$129   2P: $79-$129   XP: $6   F19
Location: I-69, exit 13, just sw. 630 E Chicago St 49036. Fax: 517/278-3775. **Facility:** 80 units. 76 one-bedroom
Small-scale Hotel standard units, some with whirlpools. 4 one-bedroom suites. 3 stories, interior corridors. *Bath:* combo or
shower only. **Parking:** on-site. **Amenities:** dual phone lines, voice mail, irons, hair dryers. **Pool(s):** heated
indoor. **Leisure Activities:** whirlpool, exercise room. **Guest Services:** valet and coin laundry. **Business Services:** meeting
rooms. **Cards:** AX, DC, DS, MC, VI. *(See color ad below & card insert)*

SOME UNITS
(ASK) (SD) (&M) (icons) / (X) (fridge) (microwave) / FEE

RAMADA INN   *Book at aaa.com*   **Phone:** (517)278-2017
5/31-9/15 [ECP]   1P: $79-$129   2P: $84-$129   XP: $5
4/1-5/30 & 9/16-3/31 [ECP]   1P: $69-$119   2P: $74-$119   XP: $5
Location: I-69, exit 13, 0.3 mi w on E Chicago St, just n on N Michigan Ave, then just e. 1000 Orleans Blvd 49036.
Fax: 517/279-7214. **Facility:** 128 units. 90 one-bedroom standard units, some with whirlpools. 38 one-
Small-scale Hotel bedroom suites, some with kitchens and/or whirlpools. 2 stories, interior corridors. **Parking:** on-site.
Terms: small pets only. **Amenities:** voice mail, safes, irons, hair dryers. **Dining:** 6:30 am-11 & 5-9 pm, Sun-
noon, cocktails. **Pool(s):** heated indoor. **Leisure Activities:** whirlpool, exercise room. *Fee:* game room. **Guest Services:** coin
laundry. **Business Services:** meeting rooms. **Cards:** AX, DC, DS, MC, VI.

SOME UNITS
(SD) (icons) (X) (fridge) (microwave) / FEE FEE

RED ROOF INN   *Book at aaa.com*   **Phone:** (517)279-1199
All Year [CP]   1P: $49-$89   2P: $49-$89   XP: $6   F18
Location: I-69, exit 13, just e. 348 S Willowbrook Rd 49036. Fax: 517/279-0869. **Facility:** 65 one-bedroom stan-
Small-scale Hotel dard units. 3 stories, interior corridors. *Bath:* combo or shower only. **Parking:** on-site, winter plug-ins.
Terms: small pets only ($25 deposit). **Amenities:** voice mail. **Guest Services:** valet laundry. **Cards:** AX, DC,
DS, MC, VI. *(See color ad below)*

SOME UNITS
(ASK) (SD) (icons) (&M) (icons) / (X) /

SUPER 8 MOTEL   *Book at aaa.com*   **Phone:** (517)278-8833
All Year [CP]   1P: $47-$62   2P: $54-$73   XP: $7   F18
Location: I-69, exit 13, 0.3 mi w on E Chicago St, just n on N Michigan Ave, then just e. 600 Orleans Blvd 49036.
Fax: 517/278-2347. **Facility:** 58 one-bedroom standard units, some with whirlpools. 2 stories, interior corri-
Small-scale Hotel dors. *Bath:* combo or shower only. **Parking:** on-site. **Terms:** small pets only. **Cards:** AX, DC, DS, MC, VI.
Special Amenities: free continental breakfast and free local telephone calls.

SOME UNITS
(SD) (icons) (&M) (icons) / (X) (fridge) (microwave) / FEE FEE

—— WHERE TO DINE ——

CARNEGIE'S

American

Lunch: $5-$8   **Dinner:** $10-$20   **Phone:** 517/278-9775
Location: I-69, exit 13, 1.5 mi w on E Chicago St, 0.4 mi s on Divison St; 32 Railroad St 49036. **Hours:** 11 am-9:30 pm, Fri & Sat-10 pm. Closed major holidays; also Sun & Mon. **Features:** Railroad memorabilia is housed along the walls and in the ceiling rafters of this converted train station. The continental menu offers a wide range of food from burgers to daily specials. Casual dress; cocktails. **Parking:** on-site. **Cards:** MC, VI.

COMSTOCK PARK pop. 10,674—See also GRAND RAPIDS.

—— WHERE TO STAY ——

SWAN INN

Small-scale Hotel

Phone: 616/784-1224
All Year   1P: $45-$65   2P: $50-$80   XP: $3   F12
Location: Jct I-96 and Alpine Ave, 3 mi n on SR 37. Located in a semi-commercial area. 5182 Alpine Ave 49321. Fax: 616/784-6565. **Facility:** 38 one-bedroom standard units, some with efficiencies or kitchens (no utensils). 1-2 stories (no elevator), exterior corridors. *Bath:* combo or shower only. **Parking:** on-site, winter plug-ins. **Terms:** [AP] meal plan available, small pets only. **Pool(s):** heated outdoor. **Guest Services:** coin laundry. **Business Services:** meeting rooms. **Cards:** AX, DC, DS, MC, VI.

SOME UNITS

COOPERSVILLE pop. 3,910

—— WHERE TO STAY ——

AMERIHOST INN-COOPERSVILLE   Book at aaa.com

Small-scale Hotel

Phone: (616)837-8100
All Year [ECP]   1P: $59-$79   2P: $65-$85   XP: $6   F18
Location: I-96, exit 16, just n. Located in a semi-commercial area. 1040 O'Malley Dr 49404. Fax: 616/837-5179. **Facility:** 60 one-bedroom standard units, some with whirlpools. 2 stories (no elevator), interior corridors. *Bath:* combo or shower only. **Parking:** on-site. **Amenities:** safes, irons, hair dryers. **Pool(s):** heated indoor. **Leisure Activities:** sauna, whirlpool, exercise room. **Business Services:** meeting rooms. **Cards:** AX, DC, DS, MC, VI. **Special Amenities:** free expanded continental breakfast and free newspaper.

SOME UNITS

—— WHERE TO DINE ——

—— *The following restaurant has not been evaluated by AAA* ——
but is listed for your information only.

SAM'S JOINT
[fyi]

Phone: 616/837-8558
Not evaluated. **Location:** I-96, exit 19, just s. 15520 48th Ave 49404. **Features:** Memorabilia spills over from the lounge into the dining areas at this fun spot.

COPPER HARBOR

—— WHERE TO STAY ——

LAKE FANNY HOOE RESORT & CAMPGROUND

Motel

Phone: 906/289-4451
All Year   1P: $69-$84   2P: $69-$84   XP: $7   F12
Location: Just s on Manganese Rd. Located on the lake. 505 2nd St 49918 (PO Box 31). Fax: 906/289-4450. **Facility:** 17 units. 14 one-bedroom standard units with efficiencies. 3 cabins. 2 stories (no elevator), exterior corridors. *Bath:* combo or shower only. **Parking:** on-site. **Terms:** 7 day cancellation notice-fee imposed, pets ($5 extra charge). **Leisure Activities:** rental boats, rental canoes, rental paddleboats, boat dock, fishing, cross country skiing, snowmobiling, hiking trails. *Fee:* game room. **Guest Services:** gift shop, coin laundry. **Cards:** AX, DS, MC, VI.

SOME UNITS

FEE

—— WHERE TO DINE ——

TAMARACK INN

American

Lunch: $4-$7   **Dinner:** $8-$16   **Phone:** 906/289-4522
Location: Jct US 41 and SR 26. 512 Gratiot 49918. **Hours:** Open 6/10-10/10; 8 am-9 pm. **Features:** In the heart of the small, remote town, the casual restaurant is a nice spot for a relaxed meal. Menu offerings include broasted chicken, prime rib and fresh whitefish and trout from Lake Superior. Wait times are typically short, even during summer. Casual dress. **Parking:** on-site. **Cards:** MC, VI.

CROSS VILLAGE pop. 100

———— WHERE TO DINE ————

LEGS INN

Polish

Lunch: $4-$9   **Dinner:** $8-$18   **Phone:** 231/526-2281
Location: At end of SR 119; center. 6425 Lake Shore Dr 49723. **Hours:** Open 5/21-10/16; noon-10 pm; closing hours vary 5/21-6/30 & 9/1-10/16. **Features:** More than 100 varieties of beer and wine complement authentic entrees of Polish and American cuisine. The historic stone and timber landmark is decorated with distinctive driftwood furniture. The outdoor patio and gardens overlook the lake. Casual dress; cocktails. **Parking:** on-site. **Cards:** DS, MC, VI.

DAVISON pop. 5,536

———— WHERE TO STAY ————

COMFORT INN OF DAVISON   *Book at aaa.com*
Small-scale Hotel

All Year   1P: $64-$125   2P: $69-$125   XP: $10   F18   **Phone:** (810)658-2700
Location: I-69, exit 145, just n on SR 15, then e. Located in a quiet area. 10082 Lapeer Rd 48423. Fax: 810/658-2640. **Facility:** 67 one-bedroom standard units, some with whirlpools. 2 stories (no elevator), interior corridors. *Bath:* combo or shower only. **Parking:** on-site. **Terms:** age restrictions may apply, [CP] & [ECP] meal plans available. **Amenities:** video library (fee), irons, hair dryers. **Pool(s):** heated outdoor. **Guest Services:** valet laundry. **Business Services:** meeting rooms. **Cards:** AX, CB, DC, DS, JC, MC, VI.

SOME UNITS

———— WHERE TO DINE ————

ITALIA GARDENS
Italian

Lunch: $7-$10   **Dinner:** $8-$11   **Phone:** 810/653-6899
Location: I-69, exit 145, 1 mi n on SR 15. 1141 S State Rd 48423. **Hours:** 11 am-9 pm, Fri & Sat-11 pm, Sun noon-8 pm. Closed major holidays. **Features:** The small restaurant serves up many favorite entrees such as spaghetti, ribs, manicotti and pizza. The casually upscale dining room features a modern Italian theme, which is evident in the stone columns and candle-topped pedestal tables. Casual dress; beer & wine only. **Parking:** on-site. **Cards:** AX, DC, DS, MC, VI.

DEARBORN —*See Detroit p. 254.*

Destination Detroit
pop. 951,270

*M*otor in. Sail out. And shop till you drop. Detroit offers it all.

*D*epending on the season, you could root for the home team with some of hockey's proudest fans. Catch a concert. Or just enjoy one of the many amenities that make this symbol of America's might a mighty fine place to play.

© M. Gibson / Robertstock

Detroit skyline.
Commerce and culture mingle in this vibrant riverside metropolis.

Hydroplane Races, Detroit River.
Sleek boats scream across the river, attracting thousands to this summer event.

© Gibson Stock Photography

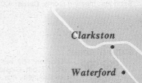

See Vicinity map page 226

*P*laces included in this AAA Destination City:

Greektown District, Detroit.
Opa! Centered on Monroe Street, the historic area boasts Victorian-era commercial buildings housing boutiques, small groceries, restaurants and excellent pastry shops.

© Gibson Stock Photography

Detroit Metro CVB

Comerica Park, Detroit.
Tigers resting on the scoreboard roar to celebrate home runs at the home of Detroit's major league baseball team.
(See mention page 59)

See Downtown
map page 224

Eastern Market, Detroit.
Any local knows that this outdoor farmer's market is the place to shop on Saturday mornings. (See mention page 60)

© Gibson Stock Photography

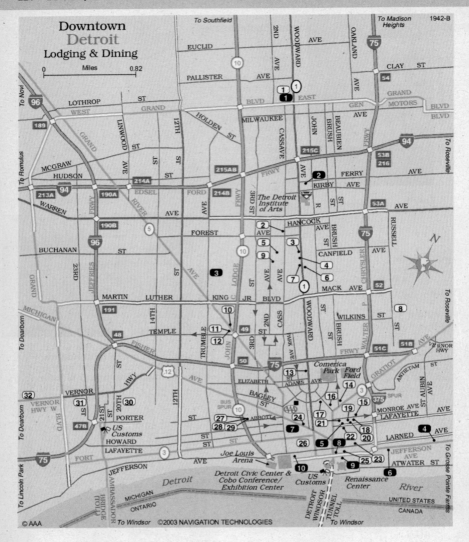

Downtown
Detroit
Lodging & Dining

0   Miles   0.82

1942-B

© AAA   To Windsor   ©2003 NAVIGATION TECHNOLOGIES   To Windsor

Downtown Detroit

This index helps you "spot" where approved accommodations and restaurants are located on the corresponding detailed maps. Lodging rate ranges are for comparison only and show the property's high season; rates are per night, unless only weekly (W) rates are available. Restaurant rate range is for dinner, unless only lunch (L) is served. Turn to the listing page for more detailed rate information and consult display ads for special promotions.

Spotter/Map Page Number	OA	**DOWNTOWN DETROIT - Lodgings**	Diamond Rating	Rate Range High Season	Listing Page
1 / below		Hotel St. Regis - see ad p 237	◈◈◈	$119-$129	238
2 / below		The Inn on Ferry Street	◈◈◈	$109-$219	238
3 / below		Woodbridge Star Bed & Breakfast	◈◈	$100-$150	238
4 / below	AAA	**Comfort Inn-Downtown Detroit**	◈◈	$79-$199 SAVE	236

Spotter/Map Page Number	OA	**DOWNTOWN DETROIT -** Lodgings (continued)	Diamond Rating	Rate Range High Season	Listing Page
5 / p. 224	AAA	**The Atheneum Suite Hotel & Conference Center**	◈◈◈◈	$189-$1000 SAVE	236
6 / p. 224	AAA	**The Shorecrest Motor Inn**	◈◈	$69-$99 SAVE	238
7 / p. 224		Holiday Inn Express	◈◈◈	$119-$159	237
8 / p. 224		Detroit Downtown Courtyard by Marriott	◈◈◈	$109-$169	237
9 / p. 224		Detroit Marriott Renaissance Center	◈◈◈	$199	237
10 / p. 224		Hotel Pontchartrain	◈◈◈	$125-$650	238
		DOWNTOWN DETROIT - Restaurants			
1 / p. 224		Cuisine	◈◈◈	$20-$30	239
2 / p. 224		Twingo's	◈◈	$10-$16	241
3 / p. 224		Whitney Restaurant	◈◈◈	$19-$35	242
4 / p. 224		Agave	◈◈	$12-$18	238
5 / p. 224		Traffic Jam & Snug	◈◈	$10-$18	241
6 / p. 224		Majestic Cafe	◈◈	$7-$18	240
7 / p. 224		Union Street	◈◈	$8-$16	242
8 / p. 224		Roma Cafe	◈◈	$13-$18	241
9 / p. 224		Mario's	◈◈	$12-$35	240
10 / p. 224		Carl's Chop House	◈◈	$14-$26	239
11 / p. 224	AAA	**Iridescence Restaurant**	◈◈◈◈	$32-$42	240
12 / p. 224		Classics Buffet	◈◈	$30	239
13 / p. 224		Johnny Rockets	◈	$3-$6	240
14 / p. 224		Courthouse Brasserie	◈◈	$25-$35	239
15 / p. 224		Cyprus Taverna	◈◈	$6-$18	239
16 / p. 224		Intermezzo	◈◈	$16-$35	240
17 / p. 224		Small Plates	◈◈	$10-$15	241
18 / p. 224		Pegasus Taverna Restaurant	◈	$7-$24	241
19 / p. 224		Grapevine Cafe'	◈◈	$5-$10	239
20 / p. 224		The Alley Grille Steakhouse	◈◈	$20-$35	238
21 / p. 224		Fishbone's Rhythm Kitchen Cafe	◈◈	$5-$25	239
22 / p. 224		Loco Bar & Grill	◈	$5-$17	240
23 / p. 224		Opus One	◈◈◈	$20-$39	240
24 / p. 224		American Coney Island	◈	$3-$10	239
25 / p. 224		Tom's Oyster Bar	◈◈	$13-$24	241
26 / p. 224		Caucus Club	◈◈	$11-$22	239
27 / p. 224	AAA	**Hollywood Brown Derby**	◈◈◈	$20-$40	240
28 / p. 224		Venti Uno	◈◈	$15-$25	242
29 / p. 224		MGM Grand Buffet	◈	$20	240
30 / p. 224	AAA	**Mexican Village Restaurant**	◈	$6-$16	240
31 / p. 224		Evie's Tamales	◈	$6-$7	239
32 / p. 224		Armando's	◈	$6-$26	239

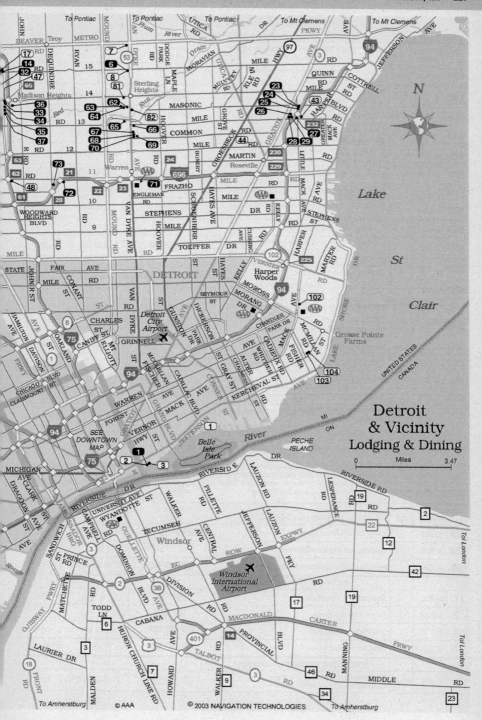

Detroit
& Vicinity
Lodging & Dining

Lake

St

Clair

© 2003 NAVIGATION TECHNOLOGIES

✈ Airport Accommodations

Spotter/Map Page Number	OA	DETROIT METROPOLITAN WAYNE COUNTY	Diamond Rating	Rate Range High Season	Listing Page
152 / p. 226	AAA	Baymont Inn & Suites Detroit-Airport, opposite airport	▽▽	$79-$89 SAVE	271
154 / p. 226	AAA	Best Western Gateway International Hotel, opposite airport	▽▽▽	$89-$99 SAVE	272
147 / p. 226	AAA	Clarion Barcelo' Hotel, opposite airport	▽▽▽	$79-$149 SAVE	272
146 / p. 226	AAA	Courtyard by Marriott-Metro Airport, opposite airport	▽▽▽	$79-$129 SAVE	272
141 / p. 226		Crowne Plaza Hotel and Resort Detroit Metro Airport, opposite airport	▽▽▽	Failed to provide	272
156 / p. 226	AAA	Days Inn, opposite airport	▽▽	$69-$79 SAVE	272
148 / p. 226		Detroit Metro Airport Marriott, opposite airport	▽▽▽	$69-$139	272
155 / p. 226		DoubleTree Hotel Detroit Airport, opposite airport	▽▽▽	$149-$249	272
149 / p. 226		Extended Stay America, opposite airport	▽▽	$55-$74	273
145 / p. 226		Fairfield Inn by Marriott-Metro Airport, opposite the terminal	▽▽	$79-$84	273
151 / p. 226	AAA	Four Points by Sheraton Detroit Metro Airport, opposite airport	▽▽▽	$89-$99 SAVE	273
144 / p. 226		Hampton Inn-Detroit Metro Airport, opposite airport	▽▽	$68-$125	273
150 / p. 226	AAA	Hilton Suites-Detroit Metro Airport, opposite airport	▽▽▽	$139-$159 SAVE	273
157 / p. 226	AAA	Howard Johnson Inn, opposite airport	▽▽	$69-$79 SAVE	274
153 / p. 226	AAA	Northwest Inn, opposite airport	▽	$44-$69 SAVE	274
143 / p. 226		Park Inn-Detroit Metro Airport, opposite airport	▽▽	$63	274
140 / p. 226	AAA	Quality Inn Metro Airport, opposite airport	▽▽	$59-$125 SAVE	274
158 / p. 226		Super 8 Motel-Romulus, opposite airport	▽▽	$60	274
159 / p. 226	AAA	The Westin Detroit Metropolitan Airport, at terminal	▽▽▽▽	$99-$269 SAVE	274

Detroit and Vicinity

This index helps you "spot" where approved accommodations and restaurants are located on the corresponding detailed maps. Lodging rate ranges are for comparison only and show the property's high season; rates are per night, unless only weekly (W) rates are available. Restaurant rate range is for dinner, unless only lunch (L) is served. Turn to the listing page for more detailed rate information and consult display ads for special promotions.

Spotter/Map Page Number	OA	DETROIT - Lodgings	Diamond Rating	Rate Range High Season	Listing Page
1 / p. 226		Omni Detroit River Place	▽▽▽▽	$119-$429	243
2 / p. 226	AAA	Holiday Inn Fairlane/Dearborn	▽▽▽	$79-$129 SAVE	242
3 / p. 226		Residence Inn By Marriott-Dearborn	▽▽▽	$69-$199	243
		DETROIT - Restaurants			
1 / p. 226		Sindbad's At The River	▽▽	$9-$18	244
2 / p. 226		Baron's on the River	▽▽	$16-$26	244
3 / p. 226		The Rattlesnake Club	▽▽▽	$17-$31	244
4 / p. 226		Giovanni's Ristorante	▽▽▽	$12-$18	244
		STERLING HEIGHTS - Lodgings			
6 / p. 226	AAA	Best Western Sterling Inn Banquet & Conference Ctr - see ad p 282	▽▽▽	$109-$209 SAVE	282

Spotter/Map Page Number	OA	**STERLING HEIGHTS** - Restaurants	Diamond Rating	Rate Range High Season	Listing Page
7 / p. 226		Mezzaluna	◆◆	$12-$22	283
8 / p. 226		Loon River Cafe - see ad p 282	◆◆	$6-$15	283
		TROY - Lodgings			
9 / p. 226		Troy Marriott	◆◆◆	$104-$279	285
10 / p. 226		Drury Inn	◆◆◆	$103-$123	284
11 / p. 226		Residence Inn by Marriott	◆◆◆	$99-$159	285
12 / p. 226		Holiday Inn-Troy	◆◆◆	$69-$125	284
13 / p. 226	AAA	**Red Roof Inn-Troy**	◆◆	$56-$76 SAVE	285
14 / p. 226		Courtyard by Marriott	◆◆◆	$89-$169	284
15 / p. 226	AAA	**Homewood Suites by Hilton**	◆◆◆	$143-$154 SAVE	285
		TROY - Restaurants			
11 / p. 226		Shula's Steak House	◆◆◆	$22-$30	286
12 / p. 226		The Capital Grille	◆◆◆	$20-$30	285
13 / p. 226		Ruth's Chris Steak House	◆◆◆	$18-$30	286
14 / p. 226		McCormick & Schmick's Seafood Restaurant	◆◆◆	$15-$20	286
15 / p. 226		Portabella	◆◆	$11-$20	286
16 / p. 226		P.F. Chang's China Bistro	◆◆	$10-$15	286
17 / p. 226	AAA	**Mon Jin Lau**	◆◆◆	$12-$22	286
18 / p. 226		Priya	◆◆	$10-$20	286
19 / p. 226		Anita's Kitchen	◆	$7-$10	285
20 / p. 226		Shield's of Troy	◆	$5-$10	286
21 / p. 226		Cafe' Sushi	◆◆	$12-$20	285
		BIRMINGHAM - Lodgings			
18 / p. 226	AAA	**Hamilton Hotel** - see color ad p 249	◆◆◆	$119-$159 SAVE	249
19 / p. 226		Holiday Inn Express Birmingham - see color ad p 250	◆◆◆	$160	250
20 / p. 226	AAA	**The Townsend Hotel**	◆◆◆◆	$279 SAVE	250
		BIRMINGHAM - Restaurants			
28 / p. 226		Mitchell's Fish Market	◆◆	$15-$30	251
29 / p. 226	AAA	**Big Rock Chop House**	◆◆	$9-$35	251
30 / p. 226		Peabody's	◆◆	$8-$16	251
31 / p. 226		Forte'	◆◆	$15-$32	251
32 / p. 226		220	◆◆	$15-$25	251
33 / p. 226		Rugby Grille	◆◆◆◆	$25-$40	251
34 / p. 226		The Original Pancake House	◆◆	$6-$10	251
		ROSEVILLE - Lodgings			
23 / p. 226	AAA	**Comfort Inn**	◆◆◆	$82-$118 SAVE	275
24 / p. 226		Holiday Inn Express & Suites	◆◆◆	$99-$109	275
25 / p. 226	AAA	**Red Roof Inn**	◆◆	$47-$72 SAVE	275
26 / p. 226	AAA	**Best Western Georgian Inn**	◆◆◆	$69-$179 SAVE	275
27 / p. 226	AAA	**Baymont Inn & Suites Detroit-Roseville** - see color ad p 287	◆◆◆	$79-$89 SAVE	275

Spotter/Map Page Number	OA	ROSEVILLE - Lodgings (continued)	Diamond Rating	Rate Range High Season	Listing Page
28 / p. 226		Microtel Inn & Suites	◈◈	$44-$69	275
29 / p. 226		Extended StayAmerica	◈◈	Failed to provide	275
		ROSEVILLE - Restaurants			
43 / p. 226		Pearl City	◈	$7-$10	276
44 / p. 226	AAA	**Mr. Paul's Chophouse**	◈◈◈	$10-$23	276
		MADISON HEIGHTS - Lodgings			
32 / p. 226	AAA	**Best Western Troy-Madison Inn**	◈◈	$70-$154 [SAVE]	264
33 / p. 226		Fairfield Inn by Marriott	◈◈	$59-$109	265
34 / p. 226	AAA	**Econo Lodge**	◈	$47-$56 [SAVE]	265
35 / p. 226		Residence Inn by Marriott-Madison Heights	◈◈◈	$239-$339	265
36 / p. 226	AAA	**Red Roof Inn**	◈◈	$53-$72 [SAVE]	265
37 / p. 226	AAA	**Hampton Inn -** see color ad p 264	◈◈◈	$69-$109 [SAVE]	265
		MADISON HEIGHTS - Restaurants			
47 / p. 226		Big Fish Seafood Bistro	◈◈	$7-$24	265
48 / p. 226		Boodle's Restaurant	◈◈	$9-$28	265
		ROYAL OAK - Lodgings			
40 / p. 226	AAA	**Travelodge**	◈	$51-$67 [SAVE]	276
		ROYAL OAK - Restaurants			
51 / p. 226		Boocoo	◈◈◈	$16-$28	276
52 / p. 226		WOW Pan-Asian Cuisine	◈◈	$10-$24	277
53 / p. 226		Red Coat Tavern	◈◈	$8-$16	277
54 / p. 226		Rexy's Bangkok Cuisine	◈◈◈	$10-$15	277
55 / p. 226		Memphis Smoke	◈	$7-$15	277
56 / p. 226		Andiamo Osteria	◈◈◈	$10-$15	276
57 / p. 226		Comet Burger	◈	$3-$5	276
58 / p. 226		Tom's Oyster Bar	◈◈	$11-$20	277
59 / p. 226		D'Amato's Neighborhood Restaurant	◈◈	$10-$20	276
60 / p. 226		Royal Oak Brewery	◈◈	$8-$12	277
61 / p. 226		Lepanto	◈◈◈	$13-$25	276
62 / p. 226		Goombah's Pizzeria	◈	$7-$14	276
63 / p. 226		Lily's Seafood	◈◈	$16-$25	277
64 / p. 226		Wood-Ruff's Supper Club	◈◈◈	$14-$27	277
65 / p. 226		Pronto! 608	◈◈	$4-$8	277
		SOUTHFIELD - Lodgings			
43 / p. 226		Homestead Studio Suites Hotel-Detroit/Southfield	◈◈◈	$69-$89	279
44 / p. 226		SpringHill Suites by Marriott Detroit/Southfield	◈◈◈	$114-$175	280
45 / p. 226	AAA	**Red Roof Inn-Southfield**	◈◈	$60-$71 [SAVE]	279
46 / p. 226		Hilton Inn-Southfield	◈◈◈	$69-$169	278
47 / p. 226		Extended StayAmerica	◈◈	Failed to provide	278
48 / p. 226		Hampton Inn-Southfield	◈◈◈	$79-$159	278

Spotter/Map Page Number	OA	SOUTHFIELD - Lodgings (continued)	Diamond Rating	Rate Range High Season	Listing Page
49 / p. 226		Candlewood Suites	◈◈	$175	278
50 / p. 226		Residence Inn by Marriott	◈◈	$109-$149	279
51 / p. 226		Courtyard by Marriott-Southfield	◈◈◈	$79-$129	278
52 / p. 226		Southfield Marriott Hotel	◈◈◈	$169	279
53 / p. 226		Holiday Inn-Southfield	◈◈	$121-$145	278
54 / p. 226	AAA	Best Western Southfield Inn	◈◈◈	$79-$99 SAVE	277
55 / p. 226	AAA	Westin Hotel Southfield-Detroit - see color ad p 279	◈◈◈◈	$89-$270 SAVE	280
56 / p. 226		Hawthorn Suites Ltd	◈◈◈	$89-$134	278
57 / p. 226		Comfort Suites	◈◈◈	$79-$229	278
58 / p. 226		Ramada Inn-Southfield	◈◈	$79-$109	279
59 / p. 226	AAA	Motor City Howard Johnson Plaza Hotel	◈◈	$59-$169 SAVE	279
		SOUTHFIELD - Restaurants			
68 / p. 226		Beverly Hills Grill	◈◈	$12-$23	280
69 / p. 226		Joe Muer's Grill	◈◈	$19-$27	281
70 / p. 226		Morels-A Michigan Bistro	◈◈◈	$15-$27	281
71 / p. 226		Beans & Cornbread: A Soulful Bistro	◈◈	$12-$16	280
72 / p. 226		Bacco Ristorante	◈◈◈	$20-$30	280
73 / p. 226		Tom's Oyster Bar	◈◈	$13-$24	281
74 / p. 226	AAA	Il Posto Ristorante	◈◈◈◈	$18-$28	280
75 / p. 226		New Seoul Restaurant	◈◈	$9-$20	281
76 / p. 226		Morton's of Chicago	◈◈◈	$25-$40	281
77 / p. 226		C A Muer's Merriwether	◈◈	$14-$30	280
78 / p. 226		The Original Pancake House	◈◈	$6-$8(L)	281
		WARREN - Lodgings			
62 / p. 226	AAA	Hampton Inn-Warren/Sterling Heights	◈◈◈	$99-$179 SAVE	289
63 / p. 226		Candlewood Suites-Detroit Warren	◈◈◈	$109-$149	289
64 / p. 226		Fairfield Inn by Marriott	◈◈	$64-$79	289
65 / p. 226		Hawthorn Suites Ltd	◈◈◈	$89-$169	289
66 / p. 226	AAA	Baymont Inn & Suites Detroit-Warren Tech Center - see color ad p 287	◈◈◈	$67 SAVE	288
67 / p. 226		Courtyard by Marriott-Warren	◈◈◈	$69-$109	289
68 / p. 226		Homewood Suites by Hilton	◈◈◈	$79-$159	290
69 / p. 226	AAA	Residence Inn by Marriott	◈◈◈	$94 SAVE	290
70 / p. 226		Four Points by Sheraton Hotel & Suites Detroit North - see color ad p 5	◈◈◈	$79-$229	289
71 / p. 226		Holiday Inn Express	◈◈◈	$114-$124	289
72 / p. 226	AAA	Comfort Suites	◈◈◈	$69-$259 SAVE	289
73 / p. 226	AAA	Red Roof Inn-Warren	◈◈	$55-$75 SAVE	290
		WARREN - Restaurants			
81 / p. 226		Andiamo Italia Ristorante	◈◈◈	$12-$24	290
82 / p. 226		Michelle's Restaurant & Sweetheart Bakery	◈◈	$7-$10	290

Spotter/Map Page Number	OA		Diamond Rating	Rate Range High Season	Listing Page
76 / p. 226		**FARMINGTON HILLS - Lodgings**	◆◆◆	Failed to provide	259
77 / p. 226		Fairfield Inn by Marriott	◆◆◆	Failed to provide	259
77 / p. 226		Courtyard by Marriott	◆◆◆	$104	259
78 / p. 226		Candlewood Suites	◆◆◆	$99-$144	259
79 / p. 226	AAA	**Red Roof Inn-Farmington Hills**	◆◆	$52-$71 SAVE	259
80 / p. 226		Holiday Inn Farmington Hills	◆◆◆	$89-$129	259
81 / p. 226	AAA	**Radisson Suite Hotel Farmington Hills - see color ad p 313**	◆◆◆	$85-$119 SAVE	259
		FARMINGTON HILLS - Restaurants			
91 / p. 226		Family Buggy Restaurant	◆◆	$9-$15	260
92 / p. 226		Hong Hua	◆◆◆	$10-$25	260
93 / p. 226		Tribute	◆◆◆◆	$30-$37	260
94 / p. 226		Loving Spoonful	◆◆	$11-$24	260
95 / p. 226		Cafe' Cortina	◆◆◆◆	$24-$35	260
96 / p. 226		Everest Express Nepali Cuisine	◆	$8-$12	260
		NOVI - Lodgings			
84 / p. 226		Country Inn & Suites By Carlson - see color ad p 313	◆◆◆	$105-$115	267
85 / p. 226		Sheraton-Detroit-Novi - see color ad p 267	◆◆◆	$59-$169	268
86 / p. 226		Studio Plus Deluxe Studios	◆◆	Failed to provide	268
		NOVI - Restaurant			
99 / p. 226		New Ah Wok	◆◆	$8-$12	269
		NORTHVILLE - Lodgings			
89 / p. 226		Ramada Limited of Novi	◆◆	$59-$69	266
90 / p. 226		Hampton Inn	◆◆◆	$104	266
		NORTHVILLE - Restaurant			
107 / p. 226		Bonfire Bistro & Brewery	◆◆◆	$9-$18	266
		LIVONIA - Lodgings			
93 / p. 226		Embassy Suites Hotel	◆◆◆	$109-$189	262
94 / p. 226	AAA	**AmeriSuites (Detroit/Livonia) - see color ad p 236**	◆◆◆	$89-$129 SAVE	262
95 / p. 226	AAA	**Courtyard by Marriott**	◆◆◆	$69-$124 SAVE	262
96 / p. 226	AAA	**Fairfield Inn Detroit/Livonia**	◆◆◆	$64-$89 SAVE	262
97 / p. 226		TownePlace Suites	◆◆◆	$59-$109	264
98 / p. 226		Holiday Inn Livonia-West - see color ad p 263	◆◆◆	$89-$159	263
99 / p. 226		Residence Inn Detroit-Livonia	◆◆◆	$99-$144	263
100 / p. 226		Livonia Marriott	◆◆◆	$179-$209	263
101 / p. 226		Best Western Laurel Park Suites	◆◆	$79-$109	262
102 / p. 226	AAA	**Comfort Inn**	◆◆◆	$89-$109 SAVE	262
103 / p. 226	AAA	**Super 8 Motel**	◆	$49-$125 SAVE	263
104 / p. 226		Quality Inn & Suites - see color ad p 243	◆◆	Failed to provide	263
		LIVONIA - Restaurants			
110 / p. 226		J. ALexander's Restaurant	◆◆	$7-$23	264
111 / p. 226		Sweet Lorraine's Cafe & Bar	◆◆	$8-$12	264

Spotter/Map Page Number	OA	**LIVONIA - Restaurants (continued)**	Diamond Rating	Rate Range High Season	Listing Page
(112) / p. 226		Fonte D'Amore	◈◈◈	$16-$25	264
(113) / p. 226		Family Buggy Restaurant	◈◈	$9-$15	264
		PLYMOUTH - Lodgings			
107 / p. 226	ⒶⒶⒶ	**Red Roof Inn-Plymouth**	◈◈	$52-$74 SAVE	269
108 / p. 226	ⒶⒶⒶ	**Comfort Inn Plymouth Clocktower**	◈◈	$79-$125 SAVE	269
		PLYMOUTH - Restaurants			
(116) / p. 226		Ernesto's-An Italian Country Inn	◈◈	$15-$24	270
(117) / p. 226		La Bistecca Italian Grille	◈◈◈	$20-$30	270
		DEARBORN - Lodgings			
111 / p. 226		TownePlace Suites	◈◈◈	$109	257
112 / p. 226		Courtyard by Marriott-Dearborn	◈◈◈	$69-$169	254
113 / p. 226	ⒶⒶⒶ	**The Ritz-Carlton, Dearborn**	◈◈◈◈	$135-$295 SAVE	257
114 / p. 226		Extended StayAmerica	◈◈	Failed to provide	256
115 / p. 226	ⒶⒶⒶ	**Hyatt Regency Dearborn -** see color ad p 256	◈◈◈	$99-$199 SAVE	256
116 / p. 226		Hampton Inn Dearborn	◈◈◈	$98-$160	256
117 / p. 226	ⒶⒶⒶ	**Red Roof Inn-Dearborn**	◈◈	$69-$97 SAVE	257
118 / p. 226	ⒶⒶⒶ	**The Dearborn Inn, A Marriott Hotel**	◈◈◈◈	$79-$189 SAVE	255
		DEARBORN - Restaurants			
(120) / p. 226		Benihana	◈◈	$14-$30	257
(121) / p. 226		Kabob Village	◈◈	$6-$10	258
(122) / p. 226		The Grill at The Ritz-Carlton, Dearborn	◈◈◈◈	$25-$45	258
(123) / p. 226		Big Fish Seafood Bistro	◈◈	$7-$24	257
(124) / p. 226		Bistro on 2	◈◈	$10-$15	258
(125) / p. 226		Castaldi's Market & Grill	◈◈	$7-$12	258
(126) / p. 226		George & Harry's Blue's Cafe	◈◈	$14-$22	258
(127) / p. 226		Kiernan's Steak House	◈◈	$12-$20	258
(128) / p. 226		Ristorante Ciao	◈◈	$11-$20	259
(129) / p. 226		Buddy's Restaurant Pizzeria	◈◈	$6-$17	258
(130) / p. 226		La Shish	◈◈	$8-$14	258
(131) / p. 226	ⒶⒶⒶ	**Annam Restaurant Vietnamien**	◈◈◈	$10-$18	257
(132) / p. 226		BD's Mongolian Barbeque	◈	$13	257
(133) / p. 226		LaPita	◈◈	$10-$14	258
(134) / p. 226	ⒶⒶⒶ	**Richter's Chalet**	◈◈	$7-$17	259
(135) / p. 226		The Grill at the Early American Room	◈◈◈	$18-$26	258
		CANTON - Lodgings			
121 / p. 226		Fairfield Inn by Marriott	◈◈	$61-$109	253
122 / p. 226		Motel 6 - 1070	◈	$46-$62	253
123 / p. 226	ⒶⒶⒶ	**Baymont Inn & Suites Detroit-Canton -** see color ad p 287	◈◈◈	$75 SAVE	252
124 / p. 226		Extended StayAmerica-Canton	◈◈	$49-$60	252
125 / p. 226		Days Inn - see color ad card insert	◈◈	$49-$75	252

Spotter/Map Page Number	OA	CANTON - Lodgings (continued)	Diamond Rating	Rate Range High Season	Listing Page
126 / p. 226		Super 8 Motel-Canton	◈◈	$55-$60	253
127 / p. 226		Holiday Inn Express Hotel & Suites - see color ad card insert	◈◈◈	$109-$199	253
		CANTON - Restaurant			
138 / p. 226		Carrabba's Italian Grill	◈◈	$12-$18	253
		ALLEN PARK - Lodgings			
130 / p. 226	AAA	**Best Western Greenfield Inn** - see color ad p 254	◈◈	$79-$149 SAVE	245
131 / p. 226	AAA	**Holiday Inn Express & Suites** - see color ad card insert, p 255	◈◈◈	$110-$130 SAVE	245
		LINCOLN PARK - Lodgings			
134 / p. 226	AAA	**Sleep Inn & Suites** - see color ad p 256	◈◈◈	$99-$199 SAVE	262
		TAYLOR - Lodgings			
137 / p. 226	AAA	**Quality Inn & Suites**	◈◈◈	$79-$89 SAVE	283
		ROMULUS - Lodgings			
140 / p. 226	AAA	**Quality Inn Metro Airport**	◈◈	$59-$125 SAVE	274
141 / p. 226		Crowne Plaza Hotel and Resort Detroit Metro Airport	◈◈◈	Failed to provide	272
142 / p. 226		Hilton Garden Inn-Detroit Metro Airport	◈◈◈	$69-$189	273
143 / p. 226		Park Inn-Detroit Metro Airport	◈◈	$63	274
144 / p. 226		Hampton Inn-Detroit Metro Airport	◈◈	$68-$125	273
145 / p. 226		Fairfield Inn by Marriott-Metro Airport	◈◈◈	$79-$84	273
146 / p. 226	AAA	**Courtyard by Marriott-Metro Airport**	◈◈◈	$79-$129 SAVE	272
147 / p. 226	AAA	**Clarion Barcelo' Hotel**	◈◈◈	$79-$149 SAVE	272
148 / p. 226		Detroit Metro Airport Marriott	◈◈◈	$69-$139	272
149 / p. 226		Extended Stay America	◈◈	$55-$74	273
150 / p. 226	AAA	**Hilton Suites-Detroit Metro Airport** - see ad p 273	◈◈◈	$139-$159 SAVE	273
151 / p. 226	AAA	**Four Points by Sheraton Detroit Metro Airport** - see color ad p 5	◈◈◈	$89-$99 SAVE	273
152 / p. 226	AAA	**Baymont Inn & Suites Detroit-Airport** - see color ad p 287	◈◈	$79-$89 SAVE	271
153 / p. 226	AAA	**Northwest Inn**	◈	$44-$69 SAVE	274
154 / p. 226	AAA	**Best Western Gateway International Hotel** - see color ad p 242	◈◈	$89-$99 SAVE	272
155 / p. 226		DoubleTree Hotel Detroit Airport	◈◈◈	$79-$169	272
156 / p. 226	AAA	**Days Inn**	◈◈	$69-$79 SAVE	272
157 / p. 226	AAA	**Howard Johnson Inn**	◈◈	$69-$79 SAVE	274
158 / p. 226		Super 8 Motel-Romulus	◈◈	$60	274
159 / p. 226	AAA	**The Westin Detroit Metropolitan Airport** - see color ad p 243	◈◈◈◈	$99-$269 SAVE	274
		ROMULUS - Restaurants			
141 / p. 226		Leonardo's Pizzeria & Ristorante	◈◈	$6-$10	274
142 / p. 226		Merriman Street Grill	◈◈	$6-$10	274
		SOUTHGATE - Lodgings			
162 / p. 226	AAA	**Comfort Suites**	◈◈◈	$79-$199 SAVE	282
163 / p. 226	AAA	**Baymont Inn & Suites Detroit-Southgate** - see color ad p 287	◈◈◈	$79-$89 SAVE	281

Spotter/Map Page Number	OA	SOUTHGATE - Lodgings (continued)	Diamond Rating	Rate Range High Season	Listing Page
164 / p. 226		Holiday Inn Southgate Heritage Center	▽▽▽	$99-$215	282
165 / p. 226	⊕⊕⊕	**Best Value Inn & Suites**	▽▽	$249-$299(W) ⓈⒶⓋⒺ	281
		BLOOMFIELD HILLS - Restaurants			
㉔ / p. 226		Beau Jack's Food & Spirits	▽▽	$7-$17	252
㉕ / p. 226		Andiamo Italia West	▽▽▽	$16-$25	252
		CLAWSON - Restaurant			
㊲ / p. 226		Clawson Steak House	▽▽	$15-$25	253
		WEST BLOOMFIELD - Restaurant			
㊵ / p. 226		The Lark	▽▽▽▽	$60-$70	291
		FERNDALE - Restaurants			
㊅ / p. 226		Toast	▽▽	$5-$10(L)	261
㊆ / p. 226		Assaggi Mediterranean Bistro	▽▽▽	$18-$26	260
㊇ / p. 226		The Fern	▽	$7-$8	260
㊈ / p. 226		Maria's Front Room	▽▽	$14-$17	261
		GROSSE POINTE FARMS - Restaurants			
⑩² / p. 226		Mack Avenue Diner	▽	$5-$10	261
⑩³ / p. 226		Lucy's Tavern On The Hill	▽▽	$5-$23	261
⑩⁴ / p. 226		The Hill Seafood and Chop House	▽▽▽	$15-$25	261

DOWNTOWN DETROIT   (See map and index starting on p. 224)

──────── WHERE TO STAY ────────

THE ATHENEUM SUITE HOTEL & CONFERENCE CENTER   *Book at aaa.com*   Phone: (313)962-2323
⑤
F17
F17

(AAA) (SAVE)
♦♦♦ ♦♦♦♦

Large-scale Hotel

1/1-3/31	1P: $189-$1000	2P: $189-$1000	XP: $20
4/1-12/31	1P: $185-$950	2P: $185-$950	XP: $20

Location: Jct of Brush Ave and Lafayette Blvd. Located in the heart of Greektown and opposite MGM Grand Casino. 1000 Brush Ave 48226. Fax: 313/962-2424. **Facility:** In the middle of Greektown and across from the casino, this luxury hotel features a lobby dominated by murals of Trojan warriors. 174 units. 21 one-bedroom standard units. 153 one-bedroom suites, some with whirlpools. 10 stories, interior corridors. **Parking:** on-site (fee) and valet. **Amenities:** CD players, high-speed Internet (fee), dual phone lines, voice mail, safes, honor bars, irons, hair dryers. **Dining:** Fishbone's Rhythm Kitchen Cafe, see separate listing. **Leisure Activities:** exercise room. **Guest Services:** gift shop, valet laundry, area transportation-downtown area. **Business Services:** conference facilities, business center. **Cards:** AX, CB, DC, DS, JC, MC, VI.

SOME UNITS

FEE

COMFORT INN-DOWNTOWN DETROIT   *Book at aaa.com*   Phone: (313)567-8888   ④

(AAA) (SAVE)
♦♦ ♦♦

Small-scale Hotel

All Year [ECP]   1P: $79-$199   2P: $79-$199
Location: I-375, exit E Jefferson Ave, 0.5 mi e. 1999 E Jefferson Ave 48207. Fax: 313/567-5842. **Facility:** 78 one-bedroom standard units, some with whirlpools. 3 stories, interior corridors. *Bath:* combo or shower only. **Parking:** on-site. **Terms:** 14 day cancellation notice-fee imposed, pets ($200 deposit). **Amenities:** voice mail, hair dryers. *Fee:* video games, safes. *Some:* irons. **Leisure Activities:** exercise room. **Guest Services:** valet and coin laundry. **Cards:** AX, DC, DS, MC, VI. **Special Amenities:** free expanded continental breakfast and free newspaper.

SOME UNITS

FEE

(See map and index starting on p. 224)

DETROIT DOWNTOWN COURTYARD BY MARRIOTT *Book at aaa.com* Phone: (313)222-7700 **⑧**
All Year 1P: $109-$169 2P: $109-$169
Location: In the Millender Center. Located opposite Renaissance Center. 333 E Jefferson Ave 48226.
Large-scale Hotel Fax: 313/222-6509. **Facility:** 260 units. 255 one-bedroom standard units. 5 one-bedroom suites. 21 stories, interior corridors. *Bath:* combo or shower only. **Parking:** on-site (fee) and valet. **Amenities:** dual phone lines, voice mail, irons, hair dryers. *Fee:* video games, high-speed Internet. **Pool(s):** heated indoor. **Leisure Activities:** sauna, whirlpool, jogging. *Fee:* 2 tennis courts, massage. **Guest Services:** gift shop, valet laundry, tanning facility. **Business Services:** conference facilities, PC. **Cards:** AX, CB, DC, DS, JC, MC, VI.
SOME UNITS

DETROIT MARRIOTT RENAISSANCE CENTER *Book at aaa.com* Phone: 313/568-8000 **⑨**
9/12-3/31 1P: $199 2P: $199
4/1-9/11 1P: $189 2P: $189
Location: Renaissance Center 48243. Fax: 313/568-8146. **Facility:** 1298 units. 1246 one-bedroom standard
Large-scale Hotel units. 52 one-bedroom suites. 73 stories, interior corridors. *Bath:* combo or shower only. **Parking:** on-site (fee) and valet. **Terms:** cancellation fee imposed, [AP] meal plan available. **Amenities:** dual phone lines, voice mail, safes, irons, hair dryers. *Fee:* video games, high-speed Internet. **Leisure Activities:** Fee: massage. **Guest Services:** gift shop, valet laundry. **Business Services:** conference facilities, business center. **Cards:** AX, CB, DC, DS, JC, MC, VI.
SOME UNITS

HOLIDAY INN EXPRESS *Book at aaa.com* Phone: (313)887-7000 **⑦**
All Year [ECP] 1P: $119-$159 2P: $119-$159
Location: At corner of Washington Blvd and Michigan Ave. 1020 Washington Blvd 48226. Fax: 313/965-4307.
Large-scale Hotel **Facility:** 241 one-bedroom standard units, some with efficiencies. 17 stories, interior corridors. *Bath:* combo or shower only. **Parking:** valet. **Terms:** cancellation fee imposed, weekly rates available, small pets only ($25 fee). **Amenities:** voice mail, irons, hair dryers. *Fee:* video games, high-speed Internet. **Pool(s):** heated indoor. **Leisure Activities:** exercise room. **Guest Services:** sundries, valet and coin laundry. **Business Services:** meeting rooms, business center. **Cards:** AX, CB, DC, DS, MC, VI.
SOME UNITS

(See map and index starting on p. 224)

HOTEL PONTCHARTRAIN   *Book at aaa.com*   **Phone:** (313)965-0200   **10**
▼▼▼▼▼   All Year   1P: $125-$650   2P: $125-$650   XP: $20   F17
Location: Opposite Cobo Hall. 2 Washington Blvd 48226. Fax: 313/965-9464. **Facility:** 413 units. 401 one-
Large-scale Hotel bedroom standard units, some with whirlpools. 12 one-bedroom suites ($450-$650). 25 stories, interior cor-
ridors. *Bath:* combo or shower only. **Parking:** valet. **Terms:** [AP], [BP], [CP], [ECP] & [MAP] meal plans
available. **Amenities:** voice mail, irons, hair dryers. *Fee:* video games, high-speed Internet. **Pool(s):** heated outdoor. **Leisure
Activities:** saunas, steamroom, exercise room. **Guest Services:** gift shop, valet and coin laundry. **Business Services:** conference facilities, business center. **Cards:** AX, DC, DS, MC, VI.
                                                                SOME UNITS
(ASK) (S/D) 🏊 ➔ ✕ 🏃 (DATA PORT) 🖥 / ✕ 🛢 /
                                                                    FEE

HOTEL ST. REGIS   *Book at aaa.com*   **Phone:** (313)873-3000   **1**
▼▼▼▼   All Year   1P: $119-129   2P: $119-$219
Location: Jct W Grand Blvd and Cass Ave. 3071 W Grand Blvd 48202. Fax: 313/873-2574. **Facility:** 221 units. 204
Small-scale Hotel one-bedroom standard units, some with whirlpools. 17 one-bedroom suites, some with efficiencies (no uten-
sils) and/or whirlpools. 6 stories, interior corridors. *Bath:* combo or shower only. **Parking:** on-site (fee) and
valet. **Amenities:** dual phone lines, voice mail, irons, hair dryers. **Leisure Activities:** exercise room. **Guest Services:** gift shop,
valet laundry. **Business Services:** conference facilities. **Cards:** AX, CB, DC, DS, JC, MC, VI. *(See ad p 237)*
                                                                SOME UNITS
(ASK) (S/D) 🍴 🍷 (&M) 🏃 (DATA PORT) 🖥 / ✕ 🛢 📷 /

THE INN ON FERRY STREET   *Book at aaa.com*   **Phone:** (313)871-6000   **2**
▼▼▼▼   All Year [ECP]   1P: $109-$219   2P: $109-$219
Location: Jct Woodward Ave and Ferry St, just e. 84 E Ferry St 48202. Fax: 313/871-1473. **Facility:** Walking dis-
Historic   tance from The Detroit Institute of Arts, these four restored Victorian mansions and two carriage houses offer
Small-scale Hotel elegant rooms. 42 units. 36 one-bedroom standard units, some with whirlpools. 5 one- and 1 two-bedroom
suites, some with whirlpools. 2-3 stories (no elevator), interior corridors. *Bath:* combo or shower only.
Parking: on-site. **Terms:** check-in 4 pm. **Amenities:** CD players, dual phone lines, voice mail, irons, hair dryers. **Guest Serv-
ices:** valet laundry, area transportation. **Business Services:** meeting rooms. **Cards:** AX, DC, DS, MC, VI.
                                                                SOME UNITS
(ASK) (S/D) 🍴 (&M) 🏃 (DATA PORT) 🖥 / ✕ /

THE SHORECREST MOTOR INN   **Phone:** (313)568-3000   **6**
(AAA) (SAVE)   All Year   1P: $69-$89   2P: $89-$99
▼▼▼ ▼▼▼   **Location:** Just e of Renaissance Center. 1316 E Jefferson Ave 48207. Fax: 313/568-3002. **Facility:** 54 one-
bedroom standard units. 2 stories, exterior corridors. *Bath:* combo or shower only. **Parking:** on-site.
Motel   **Terms:** weekly rates available, package plans. **Amenities:** *Some:* irons, hair dryers. **Dining:** 6 am-3 pm, Sat
& Sun from 7 am. **Guest Services:** valet laundry. **Business Services:** PC, fax (fee). **Cards:** AX, CB, DC,
DS, MC, VI. **Special Amenities:** early check-in/late check-out and preferred room (subject to avail-
ability with advanced reservations).
                                            🍴 🏃 (DATA PORT) 🛢 🖥

WOODBRIDGE STAR BED & BREAKFAST   **Phone:** 313/831-9668   **3**
▼▼▼   All Year   1P: $100-$150
Location: Jct Alexandrine St. 3985 Trumbull St 48208. **Facility:** Built as a residence for the Northwood family, this
Historic Bed restored 1891 Victorian house features ornate plasterwork, stained glass and parquet wood floors. Smoke
& Breakfast   free premises. 6 units. 3 one-bedroom standard units. 3 one-bedroom suites ($150), some with whirlpools. 3
stories (no elevator), interior corridors. *Bath:* combo or shower only. **Parking:** street. **Terms:** 10 day cancel-
lation notice-fee imposed, [BP] meal plan available, package plans, no pets allowed (owner's dogs on premises).
Amenities: video library. *Some:* DVD players, irons, hair dryers. **Guest Services:** TV in common area. **Cards:** AX, MC, VI.
                                                                SOME UNITS
(ASK) (S/D) ✕ 🅦 🆉 / (VCR) /

──────── *The following lodging was either not evaluated or did not* ────────
meet AAA rating requirements but is listed for your information only.

HILTON GARDEN INN DETROIT/DOWNTOWN   **Phone:** 313/967-0900
(fyi)   Under construction, scheduled to open May 2004. **Location:** Jct Randolph St and Gratiot Ave, just e. 351 Gratiot
Ave 48226. **Planned Amenities:** 198 units, coffeemakers, microwaves, refrigerators, pool. *(See ad p 237)*
Small-scale Hotel

──────── **WHERE TO DINE** ────────

AGAVE   Lunch: $8-$14   Dinner: $12-$18   **Phone:** 313/833-1120   **4**
▼▼▼ ▼▼▼   **Location:** Jct Canfield Ave. 4265 Woodward Ave 48201. **Hours:** 11 am-3 & 5-11 pm, Sun 5
pm-11 pm. Closed major holidays. **Reservations:** accepted. **Features:** It may not be surprising that a
Mexican   restaurant named after the agave plant would have an extensive selection of tequilas, but this singular
restaurant outside of the MexicanTown strip serves little in the way of tacos and burritos. Instead, it strives
to add creative touches, such as homemade mole, to typical Mexican regional dishes. Dressy casual; cocktails. **Parking:**
on-site and valet. **Cards:** MC, VI.
                                                            (&M) ✕

THE ALLEY GRILLE STEAKHOUSE   Dinner: $20-$35   **Phone:** 313/223-2999   **20**
▼▼▼ ▼▼▼   **Location:** Jct E Lafayette and Beaubien aves; in Greektown Casino. 555 E Lafayette Ave 48226. **Hours:** 5 pm-11
pm. **Reservations:** accepted. **Features:** Patrons may need to ask for directions to find the quiet, elegant,
Steak House hidden-away oasis, which feels a world away from the hustle and bustle of the casino floor. The a la carte
menu lists steaks, seafood and accompaniments large enough to share. Dressy casual; cocktails. **Parking:**
on-site and street. **Cards:** AX, DC, DS, MC, VI.
                                                            (&M) 🍷 ✕

Dale,
Accountant, Dad,
Outdoorsman

"Days Inns floated us an offer we couldn't refuse."

It's hard to pass up 20% off at 35 participating Days Inn® hotels all over Michigan and Wisconsin.* And don't forget the free continental breakfast and the free *USA Today*.** When you find a vacation value like Days Inns, it pays to go with the flow.

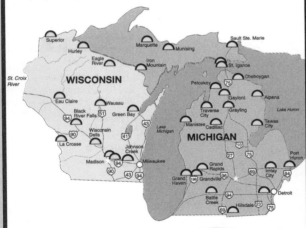

1-800-DAYS-INN® OR
DAYSINN.COM/TRAVELPLANNER
PARA ESPAÑOL 1-888-709-4024

**Amenities not available at all locations. All Days Inn hotels are independently owned and operated.
©2004 Days Inns Worldwide, Inc.

Participating Days Inn® Hotels

Michigan

Alpena 🖴
(989) 356-6118

Battle Creek
(269) 979-3561

Cadillac 🖴
(231) 775-4414

Cheboygan
(231) 627-3126

Detroit Canton
(734) 721-5200

Gaylord
(989) 732-2200

Grand Haven
(616) 842-1999

Grand Rapids - Downtown 🖴
(616) 235-7611

Grandville
(616) 531-5263

Grayling
(989) 344-0204

Hillsdale
(517) 439-3297

Imlay City
(810) 724-8005

Iron Mountain
(906) 774-2181

Manistee
(231) 723-8385

Marquette
(906) 225-1393

Munising
(906) 387-2493

Petoskey
(231) 348-3900

Port Huron - Marysville
(810) 364-8400

Sault Ste. Marie
(906) 635-5200

St. Ignace
(906) 643-7777

St. Ignace - Lakefront
(906) 643-8008

Tawas City
(989) 362-0088

Traverse City 🖴
(231) 941-0208

Wisconsin

Black River Falls
(715) 284-4333

Eagle River
(715) 479-5151

Eau Claire - West
(715) 874-5550

Green Bay - Lambeau Field
(920) 498-8088

Hurley
(715) 561-3500

Johnson Creek
(920) 699-8000

La Crosse - Conference Center 🖴
(608) 783-1000

Madison - Monona/Stoughton 🖴
(608) 223-1800

Madison - NE Windsor/ DeForest/Sun Prairie
(608) 846-7473

Superior
(715) 392-4783

Wausau 🖴
(715) 355-5501

Wisconsin Dells
(608) 254-6444

🖴 Days Business Place® hotels which feature rooms that include a microwave, refrigerator, large work desk, in-room coffee, iron/ironing boards, and dataports.

Dale,
Accountant, Dad,
Outdoorsman

"Days Inns floated us an offer we couldn't refuse."

It's hard to pass up 20% off at 35 participating Days Inn® hotels all over Michigan and Wisconsin.* And don't forget the free continental breakfast and the free *USA Today*.** When you find a vacation value like Days Inns, it pays to go with the flow.

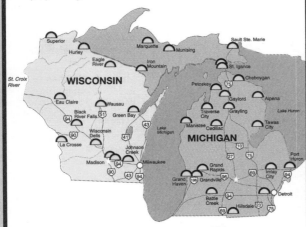

1-800-DAYS-INN® OR
DAYSINN.COM/TRAVELPLANNER
PARA ESPAÑOL 1-888-709-4024

**Amenities not available at all locations. All Days Inn hotels are independently owned and operated.
©2004 Days Inns Worldwide, Inc.

Participating Days Inn® Hotels

Michigan

Alpena 📧
(989) 356-6118

Battle Creek
(269) 979-3561

Cadillac 📧
(231) 775-4414

Cheboygan
(231) 627-3126

Detroit Canton
(734) 721-5200

Gaylord
(989) 732-2200

Grand Haven
(616) 842-1999

Grand Rapids - Downtown 📧
(616) 235-7611

Grandville
(616) 531-5263

Grayling
(989) 344-0204

Hillsdale
(517) 439-3297

Imlay City
(810) 724-8005

Iron Mountain
(906) 774-2181

Manistee
(231) 723-8385

Marquette
(906) 225-1393

Munising
(906) 387-2493

Petoskey
(231) 348-3900

Port Huron - Marysville
(810) 364-8400

Sault Ste. Marie
(906) 635-5200

St. Ignace
(906) 643-7777

St. Ignace - Lakefront
(906) 643-8008

Tawas City
(989) 362-0088

Traverse City 📧
(231) 941-0208

Wisconsin

Black River Falls
(715) 284-4333

Eagle River
(715) 479-5151

Eau Claire - West
(715) 874-5550

Green Bay - Lambeau Field
(920) 498-8088

Hurley
(715) 561-3500

Johnson Creek
(920) 699-8000

La Crosse - Conference Center 📧
(608) 783-1000

Madison - Monona/Stoughton 📧
(608) 223-1800

Madison - NE Windsor/ DeForest/Sun Prairie
(608) 846-7473

Superior
(715) 392-4783

Wausau 📧
(715) 355-5501

Wisconsin Dells
(608) 254-6444

📧 Days Business Place® hotels which feature rooms that include a microwave, refrigerator, large work desk, in-room coffee, iron/ironing boards, and dataports.

(See map and index starting on p. 224)

AMERICAN CONEY ISLAND   Lunch: $3-$10   Dinner: $3-$10   Phone: 313/961-7758   24
American
Location: Corner of Griswold St. 114 W Lafayette Blvd 48226. **Hours:** 24 hours. **Features:** Stretch limousines still idle at 3 am in front of the famous hot dog and chili compound. The restaurant does a fine job with its steamed buns, spicy chili, onions, mustard and natural casings that snap when bitten. The decor is red, white and blue. Casual dress; beer only. **Parking:** street.

ARMANDO'S   Lunch: $5-$12   Dinner: $6-$26   Phone: 313/554-0666   32
Mexican
Location: Between Clark and Scotten sts. 4242 W Vernor Hwy 48209. **Hours:** 10:30 am-2 am, Fri & Sat-4 am. Closed: 11/25, 12/25. **Reservations:** accepted. **Features:** This local favorite offers a menu largely of Mexican dishes with specialty cuisine from Cuba, Guatemala and other Latin American countries. Casual dress; cocktails. **Parking:** on-site. **Cards:** AX, MC, VI.

CARL'S CHOP HOUSE   Lunch: $6-$15   Dinner: $14-$26   Phone: 313/833-0700   10
American
Location: 1 mi nw. 3020 Grand River Ave 48201. **Hours:** 11:30 am-11 pm, Fri & Sat-midnight, Sun 10:30 am-10 pm. Closed: 12/25. **Reservations:** suggested. **Features:** Reputed to have the best relish tray in Detroit, this local favorite made its reputation on serving quality meat and a secret zip sauce. Casual dress; cocktails. **Parking:** on-site and valet. **Cards:** AX, CB, DC, DS, MC, VI.

CAUCUS CLUB   Lunch: $9-$18   Dinner: $11-$22   Phone: 313/965-4970   26
American
Location: In Penobscot Building. 150 W Congress 48226. **Hours:** 11:30 am-8 pm, Fri-10 pm, Sat 5 pm-9 pm. Closed major holidays; also Sun. **Reservations:** suggested. **Features:** Low lighting and attractive settings give the clublike dining room a sophisticated ambience. Standard favorites—such as seafood, barbecue pork ribs, Dover sole and fresh perch—are well-prepared, consistent and appropriately seasoned. Dressy casual; cocktails. **Parking:** on-site (fee). **Cards:** AX, DC, DS, MC, VI.

CLASSICS BUFFET   Lunch: $16   Dinner: $30   Phone: 313/237-7711   12
American
Location: In Motor City Casino. 2901 Grand River Ave 48201. **Hours:** 10:30 am-4:30 & 5-4 am, Fri 10:30 am-4 & 5-1:30 am, Sat & Sun 11 am-4 & 5-2 am. **Features:** With such a large and varied selection it will be hard to know where to start. The all-you-can-eat seafood buffet on Friday is quickly becoming legendary for its seemingly endless supply of crab legs. Casual dress; beer only. **Parking:** on-site and valet. **Cards:** AX, CB, DC, DS, JC, MC, VI.

COURTHOUSE BRASSERIE   Lunch: $15-$19   Dinner: $25-$35   Phone: 313/963-8887   14
American
Location: At Brush St and Gratiot Ave. 1436 Brush St 48226. **Hours:** 11:30 am-2:30 & 5-10 pm, Sat from 5 pm, Sun 4:30 pm-8 pm. Closed: 11/25, 12/25. **Reservations:** accepted. **Features:** Ring the doorbell to enter the eatery, which serves classic cuisine in a 10-table serene, elegant room. Dishes are distinctively presented works of art. Try the sauteed chicken breast with a mushroom white sauce or the perfectly poached salmon. Dressy casual; cocktails. **Parking:** on-site. **Cards:** AX, DC, DS, MC, VI.

CUISINE   Dinner: $20-$30   Phone: 313/872-5110   1
French
Location: Jct 2nd St and Lothrop Rd. 670 Lothrop Rd 48202. **Hours:** 4 pm-10 pm, Sun-7 pm. Closed major holidays; also Mon. **Reservations:** accepted. **Features:** Hidden from view behind the Fisher Theatre, the chef/owner of this upscale converted house has turned French-American cuisine completely on its head. Using premium ingredients and boundless creativity, even classically prepared dishes such as beef Rossini find a new and exciting life when paired with seared foie gras, a potato-daikon cake and topped with black truffle demi glace. Dressy casual; cocktails. **Parking:** valet and street. **Cards:** AX, DC, MC, VI.

CYPRUS TAVERNA   Lunch: $5-$7   Dinner: $6-$18   Phone: 313/961-1550   15
Greek
Location: Corner of Monroe St and St. Antoine; in Greektown. 579 Monroe St 48226. **Hours:** 11 am-2 am, Fri & Sat-4 am. Closed: 11/25, 12/25. **Reservations:** accepted. **Features:** The restaurant, tastefully decorated with Greek murals and art. A local favorite for great spinach pie and lamb; mouthwatering Cypriot specialties, such as koupes; minced meat in bulgar casing; and a coriander-fragrant braised pork dish called afelia. Casual dress; cocktails. **Parking:** street. **Cards:** AX, DS, MC, VI.

EVIE'S TAMALES   Lunch: $6-$7   Dinner: $6-$7   Phone: 313/843-5056   31
Mexican
Location: Corner of Bagley and 24th sts; in Mexicantown. 3454 Bagley St 48216. **Hours:** 8 am-6 pm, Sun-3 pm. Closed major holidays. **Features:** Dine in at the tiny, cozy restaurant, or pick up the perfectly seasoned and nearly grease-free steamed corn-husk-wrapped pork and cornmeal delights by the bag for carryout. Another flavorful Mexican selection is the chicken enchilada suiza. Casual dress. **Parking:** street.

FISHBONE'S RHYTHM KITCHEN CAFE   Lunch: $6-$13   Dinner: $5-$25   Phone: 313/965-4600   21
Cajun
Location: Jct Brush Ave and Lafayette Blvd; in The Atheneum Suite Hotel & Conference Center. 400 Monroe St 48226. **Hours:** 6:30 am-midnight, Fri & Sat-2 am, Sun 10:30 am-midnight. Closed: 11/25, 12/25. **Features:** The restaurant lures a loud and lively crowd eager to dine on New Orleans Cajun specialties, such as whiskey barbecue ribs, chicken and seafood gumbo. Casual dress; cocktails. **Parking:** on-site (fee). **Cards:** AX, DC, DS, MC, VI.

GRAPEVINE CAFE'   Lunch: $5-$10   Dinner: $5-$10   Phone: 313/961-8888   19
American
Location: Jct Beaubien Ave; in Greektown Casino. 500 Monroe St 48226. **Hours:** 10 am-11 pm, Fri & Sat-1 am. **Features:** On the ground floor of the Greektown casino, the comfortable cafe has exposed brick walls and wall-mounted televisions. Casino patrons often drop in for generously sized sandwiches, including the signature 16-ounce burger, and the constantly changing menu of comfort foods. Casual dress; cocktails. **Parking:** on-site and street. **Cards:** AX, DC, DS, MC, VI.

(See map and index starting on p. 224)

HOLLYWOOD BROWN DERBY　　　　Dinner: $20-$40　　　　Phone: 877/847-8471　　㉗
Steak & Seafood
Location: On SR 10; in MGM Grand Casino. 1300 John C Lodge 48226. **Hours:** 6 pm-11 pm, Fri & Sat-midnight, Sun 11 am-3 & 6-11 pm. **Reservations:** required. **Features:** Set just off the bustling casino floor, this fine eatery presents a sophisticated clubby atmosphere with cherrywood walls, fine chandeliers, velvety red high back chairs and white linen tabletops. The faces of Hollywood are skillfully etched into the glass throughout the dining room. The menu features well-prepared prime steak, chops and fresh seafood that are beautifully presented on fine china. Tableside preparations are also featured and are skillfully done by the talented service staff. Dressy casual; cocktails; entertainment. **Parking:** on-site (fee) and valet. **Cards:** AX, CB, DC, DS, JC, MC, VI.

INTERMEZZO　　　Lunch: $13-$20　　　Dinner: $16-$35　　　Phone: 313/961-0707　　⑯
Italian
Location: Between Gratiot Ave and Madison St near Music Hall and the new opera house; in Harmonie Park. 1435 Randolph St 48226. **Hours:** 11 am-4 & 5-10 pm, Fri-11 pm, Sat 5 pm-11 pm, Mon-11 am-2:30 pm. Closed major holidays; also Sun except for seasonal theater events. **Reservations:** suggested. **Features:** The restaurant's seasonal menu outlines dishes prepared with care and presented with style. Much of the pasta is made on the premises, and the tasty biscotti is baked fresh twice a week. The atmosphere is eclectic, yet casually sophisticated. Casual dress; cocktails. **Parking:** valet and street. **Cards:** AX, DC, DS, MC, VI.

IRIDESCENCE RESTAURANT　　　　Dinner: $32-$42　　　　Phone: 313/237-7711　　⑪
American
Location: In Motor City Casino. 2901 Grand River Ave 48201. **Hours:** 5 pm-midnight. **Reservations:** suggested. **Features:** Located in the former site of a Wonder Bread factory, this upscale and richly appointed restaurant will make everyone feel like a high roller. While specializing in steak and seafood such as lobster tail, Dover sole and a Delmonico with wild mushrooms and au gratin potatoes, the signature Kaboom dessert is not to be missed. Dressy casual; cocktails. **Parking:** on-site and valet. **Cards:** AX, CB, DC, DS, JC, MC, VI.

JOHNNY ROCKETS　　　Lunch: $3-$6　　　Dinner: $3-$6　　　Phone: 313/471-3446　　⑬
American
Location: Fox Theater Office Center; located across from Commerce Park. 2239 Woodward Ave 48201. **Hours:** 11 am-9 pm, Fri & Sat-midnight. Closed major holidays. **Features:** This 1950s retro diner serves hamburgers, hot dogs and other comfort foods in a loud dining room that evokes a nostalgic feel. Casual dress. **Parking:** street. **Cards:** MC, VI.

LOCO BAR & GRILL　　　Lunch: $5-$17　　　Dinner: $5-$17　　　Phone: 313/965-3737　　㉒
Tex-Mex
Location: At Lafayette Blvd and Beaubien St. 454 E Lafayette Blvd 48226. **Hours:** 11 am-midnight, Fri-2 am, Sat & Sun noon-2 am. Closed major holidays. **Reservations:** accepted. **Features:** The rough-and-tumble cowboy bar serves up tasty renditions of Tex-Mex cuisine, with a large selection of hot sauces and beer. Sink your teeth into zippy enchiladas, quesadillas, tacos, chunky salsa and spicy Mexican sausage with rice and beans. Casual dress; cocktails. **Parking:** on-site (fee) and street. **Cards:** AX, DC, DS, MC, VI.

MAJESTIC CAFE　　　Lunch: $5-$11　　　Dinner: $7-$18　　　Phone: 313/833-0120　　⑥
American
Location: Between Alexandrine and Canfield sts. 4140 Woodward Ave 48202. **Hours:** 11 am-2 am, Sat & Mon from 4:30 pm, Sun from 11:30 am. Closed major holidays. **Reservations:** suggested, weekends. **Features:** Big, bright windows and cool, faux-Miro murals lend to the casually upscale feel of the dining room. The spicy menu falls somewhere between Midwest and Middle Eastern. Symphony and cultural crowds frequent the reserved restaurant before shows. Casual dress; cocktails. **Parking:** on-site. **Cards:** AX, DC, MC, VI.

MARIO'S　　　Lunch: $7-$15　　　Dinner: $12-$35　　　Phone: 313/832-1616　　⑨
Italian
Location: 1.5 mi n of civic center. 4222 2nd Ave 48201. **Hours:** 11:30 am-11 pm, Fri-midnight, Sat 4 pm-midnight, Sun 2 pm-11 pm. Closed: 12/25. **Reservations:** suggested. **Features:** Dark and romantic, you will almost expect to see Old Blue Eyes himself at this local institution, famous for its 1960s style Italian dishes and ambience. Casual dress; cocktails. **Parking:** valet and street. **Cards:** AX, DC, DS, MC, VI.

MEXICAN VILLAGE RESTAURANT　　　Lunch: $6-$16　　　Dinner: $6-$16　　　Phone: 313/237-0333　　㉚
Mexican
Location: At jct Bagley and 18th sts. 2600 Bagley St 48216. **Hours:** 11 am-11 pm, Fri & Sat-2 am. Closed major holidays. **Features:** In business since 1943, the restaurant is an established favorite for fajitas, burritos, nachos and combination plates. White stucco arches, paintings depicting Mexican history and colorful decorations add to the lively ambience of the dining room. Casual dress; cocktails. **Parking:** on-site. **Cards:** AX, DC, MC, VI.

MGM GRAND BUFFET　　　Lunch: $16　　　Dinner: $20　　　Phone: 313/393-7777　　㉙
International
Location: On US 10 (Lodge Frwy); in MGM Grand Casino. 1300 John C Lodge 48226. **Hours:** 11 am-1 am, Fri & Sat-4 am. **Features:** On the second floor of the MGM Grand Casino, the popular buffet offers diners a wide range of international choices. Among the 10 stations are The American Grille, The Bayou, The Wok, Mexican Fiesta and Local Favorites, as well as the bountiful dessert station, which is sure to please diners with a sweet tooth. Casual dress; cocktails. **Parking:** on-site and valet. **Cards:** AX, CB, DC, DS, JC, MC, VI.

OPUS ONE　　　Lunch: $10-$19　　　Dinner: $20-$39　　　Phone: 313/961-7766　　㉓
American
Location: Corner of E Larned St and St. Antoine. 565 E Larned St 48226. **Hours:** 11:30 am-10 pm, Fri-11 pm, Sat 5 pm-11 pm. Closed major holidays; also Sun. **Reservations:** suggested. **Features:** Much like the wine of the same name, this restaurant is quietly opulent and meticulous in detail. An extensive wine list which includes its namesake, fresh preparations of seafood, fowl and beef and a renown dessert tray make this an enjoyable experience. Dressy casual; cocktails; entertainment. **Parking:** on-site and valet. **Cards:** AX, DC, DS, MC, VI.

(See map and index starting on p. 224)

PEGASUS TAVERNA RESTAURANT   Lunch: $6-$20   Dinner: $7-$24   Phone: 313/964-6800   ⑱
Greek
Location: In Greektown area. 558 Monroe St 48226. **Hours:** 11 am-midnight, Fri & Sat-2 am. **Features:** Located in Greektown, this restaurant offers couples intimate booth seating and a wide selection of authentic Greek dishes and dessert to choose from. Casual dress; cocktails. **Parking:** on-site. **Cards:** AX, DC, DS, JC, MC, VI.

ROMA CAFE   Lunch: $8-$12   Dinner: $13-$18   Phone: 313/831-5940   ⑧
Italian
Location: Jct Riopelle and Erskine sts; near Eastern Market area. 3401 Riopelle St 48207. **Hours:** 11 am-10:30 pm, Sat-midnight. Closed major holidays; also Sun. **Reservations:** suggested. **Features:** Homemade pasta and a flavorful house meat sauce add to the great taste of such dishes as spaghetti and lasagna. Attractive prints and a hand-carved bar decorate the appealingly unpretentious dining room. Tuxedoed servers are friendly and efficient. Casual dress; cocktails. **Parking:** on-site and valet. **Cards:** AX, DC, MC, VI.

SMALL PLATES   Lunch: $10-$15   Dinner: $10-$15   Phone: 313/963-0497   ⑰
American
Location: Jct Park St; across from Detroit Opera House. 1521 Broadway St 48226. **Hours:** 11 am-10 pm, Fri-2 am, Sat noon-2 am, Sun noon-10 pm. Closed major holidays. **Reservations:** accepted. **Features:** Within walking distance of downtown's major entertainment venues, the casually upscale restaurant takes its cue from Spanish tapas and adds a creative American twist. Portion sizes are large enough to be comfortably shared. Dressy casual; cocktails. **Parking:** street. **Cards:** AX, MC, VI.

TOM'S OYSTER BAR   Lunch: $11-$20   Dinner: $13-$24   Phone: 313/964-4010   ㉕
Seafood
Location: Jct Beaubien St; across from GM World Headquarters at the Renaissance Center. 519 E Jefferson Ave 48226. **Hours:** 11 am-11 pm, Fri-midnight, Sat 4 pm-midnight. Closed major holidays; also Sun. **Reservations:** accepted. **Features:** From tin ceilings to checkered tablecloths, the local chain of raw bars bears more than a slight resemblance to New England fish houses. Fresh oysters are the signature item on a menu of diverse seafood selections, including panko fried shrimp and grilled yellowfin tuna. Among other choices are burgers and pasta. Casual dress; cocktails. **Parking:** on-site and valet. **Cards:** AX, DS, MC, VI.

TRAFFIC JAM & SNUG   Lunch: $8-$12   Dinner: $10-$18   Phone: 313/831-9470   ⑤
American
Location: W Canfield St at 2nd Ave; 2 blks w of Woodward Ave, then 2 blks s of Forest. 511 W Canfield St 48201. **Hours:** 11 am-10:30 pm, Fri-midnight, Sat noon-midnight. Closed major holidays; also Sun. **Features:** On the end of a cobblestone street of restored turn-of-the-20th-century Victorian mansions, the restaurant serves complex and creative preparations, such as the smoked turkey Reuben with sauerkraut and melted Swiss cheese on a potato roll. Casual dress; cocktails. **Parking:** no self-parking. **Cards:** MC, VI.

TWINGO'S   Lunch: $6-$10   Dinner: $10-$16   Phone: 313/832-3832   ②
American
Location: Jct Cass Ave and Prentis St. 4710 Cass Ave 48201. **Hours:** 11 am-10 pm, Thurs-11 pm, Fri-midnight, Sat 5 pm-midnight, Sun 11 am-8 pm. Closed major holidays; also Mon. **Reservations:** suggested. **Features:** Reminiscent of a Paris cafe, this two story eclectic space offers a small menu of French influenced entrees and a wide variety of soups and sandwiches. Casual dress; wine only. **Parking:** on-site (fee) and street. **Cards:** AX, DC, DS, MC, VI.

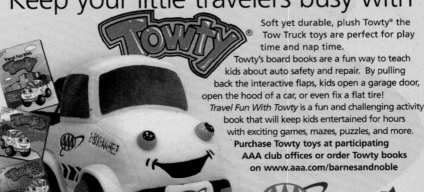

(See map and index starting on p. 224)

UNION STREET   **Lunch:** $8-$14   **Dinner:** $8-$16   **Phone:** 313/831-3965   ⑦
▼▼ ▼▼
American   **Location:** Between Alexandrine and Canfield sts. 4145 Woodward Ave 48201. **Hours:** 11 am-10 pm, Sat 4 pm-2 am. Closed major holidays; also Sun. **Features:** Loud, noisy and fun, the energetic restaurant is a hangout for students and professionals. Seafood bisque, pasta with flavorful sauces and fiery foods, such as ribs slathered with hot sauce, are representative of menu choices. Servers are upbeat. Casual dress; cocktails.
Parking: on-site (fee) and street. **Cards:** AX, DC, MC, VI.   &M ⊠

VENTI UNO   **Dinner:** $15-$25   **Phone:** 877/847-8471   ㉘
▼▼ ▼▼
Italian   **Location:** On US 10 (Lodge Frwy); in MGM Grand Casino. 1300 John C Lodge 48226. **Hours:** 5 pm-11:30 pm, Fri & Sat 5:30 pm-midnight. **Reservations:** suggested. **Features:** Set behind slot machines on the second floor of the MGM Grand Casino, the quiet oasis of Mediterranean charm prepares both Northern and Southern Italian dishes. Among choices are veal Marsala, linguine marinara, pollo alla parmigiana and thin-crust pizzas. Dressy casual; cocktails. **Parking:** on-site and valet. **Cards:** AX, CB, DC, DS, JC, MC, VI.   &M ⊤ ⊠

WHITNEY RESTAURANT   Historic   **Lunch:** $12-$30   **Dinner:** $19-$35   **Phone:** 313/832-5700   ③
▼▼ ▼▼
American   **Location:** Between Mack and Warren aves. 4421 Woodward Ave 48201. **Hours:** Mon 6 pm-9 pm, Tues 11 am-2 & 6-9 pm, Wed & Thurs 11 am-2 & 5-9 pm, Fri-10 pm, Sat 5 pm-10 pm, Sun-8 pm. Closed major holidays. **Reservations:** suggested. **Features:** The chef uses fresh ingredients in creative preparations of contemporary cuisine. In a restored 1894 Victorian mansion, the restaurant exudes elegant charm. Stained glass windows, lovely woodwork and a hand-laid mosaic tile floor enhance the decor. Dressy casual; cocktails. **Parking:** valet and street. **Cards:** AX, CB, DC, DS, MC, VI.   &M ⊤ ⊠

DETROIT pop. 951,270   (See map and index starting on p. 226)

———— **WHERE TO STAY** ————

HOLIDAY INN FAIRLANE/DEARBORN   *Book at aaa.com*   **Phone:** (313)336-3340   ❷
 [SAVE]   All Year   1P: $79-$129   2P: $79-$129
▼▼ ▼▼   **Location:** Just w of Southfield Frwy at jct Ford Rd. 5801 Southfield Service Dr 48228. Fax: 313/336-7037.
Small-scale Hotel   **Facility:** 347 units. 342 one-bedroom standard units, some with whirlpools. 5 one-bedroom suites. 2-6 stories, interior corridors. **Parking:** on-site. **Terms:** package plans - seasonal. **Amenities:** dual phone lines, voice mail, irons, hair dryers. *Some:* high-speed Internet. **Dining:** 6 am-2 & 5-10 pm, Sat & Sun from 7 am, cocktails. **Pool(s):** heated outdoor, heated indoor. **Leisure Activities:** whirlpools, exercise room, sports court. **Guest Services:** gift shop, valet laundry. **Business Services:** conference facilities, business center. **Cards:** AX, CB, DC, DS, JC, MC, VI. **Special Amenities:** free newspaper.

SOME UNITS
⑤❒ ⊪ ⊘ ⊷ ⊠ ⊡ ⊞ ⊑ / ⊠ ⊟ /

(See map and index starting on p. 226)

OMNI DETROIT RIVER PLACE
Phone: (313)259-9500 **1**
All Year · 1P: $119-$429 2P: $119-$429 XP: $10 F18
Small-scale Hotel
Location: 1.5 mi on E Jefferson Ave, 4 blks s on McDougall. 1000 River Place 48207. Fax: 313/259-3744. **Facility:** Many rooms in this quiet and refined hotel have spectacular views of the Detroit River, which is just steps away. 108 units. 99 one-bedroom standard units. 9 one-bedroom suites, some with whirlpools. 5 stories, interior corridors. **Parking:** valet. **Terms:** [AP], [BP] & [CP] meal plans available. **Amenities:** high-speed Internet (fee), dual phone lines, voice mail, safes, honor bars, irons, hair dryers. **Dining:** Baron's on the River, see separate listing. **Pool(s):** heated indoor. **Leisure Activities:** saunas, whirlpool. Fee: 2 tennis courts, massage. **Guest Services:** valet laundry, area transportation (fee), tanning facility. **Business Services:** meeting rooms. **Cards:** AX, DC, DS, MC, VI.

(ASK) (SD) (TI) (Y) (≈) (hw) (X) (K) (DATA PORT) (□) / (X) (VCR) /
SOME UNITS
FEE

RESIDENCE INN BY MARRIOTT-DEARBORN
Book at aaa.com
Phone: 313/441-1700 **3**
4/1-12/23 & 12/26-3/31 [BP] 1P: $69-$199 2P: $69-$199
Small-scale Hotel
Location: Just w of Southfield Frwy at jct Ford Rd. 5777 Southfield Service Dr 48228. Fax: 313/441-4144. **Facility:** 128 one-bedroom standard units with kitchens, some with whirlpools. 2 stories, exterior corridors. Bath: combo or shower only. **Parking:** on-site. **Terms:** open 4/1-12/23 & 12/26-3/31, cancellation fee imposed, pets ($100 fee, $7 extra charge). **Amenities:** dual phone lines, voice mail, irons, hair dryers. **Pool(s):** heated outdoor. **Leisure Activities:** whirlpool, exercise room, sports court. **Guest Services:** valet and coin laundry. **Cards:** AX, CB, DC, DS, JC, MC, VI.

SOME UNITS
(♨) (⊘) (≈) (X) (K) (DATA PORT) (▤) (▦) (□) / (X) (VCR) /
FEE

(See map and index starting on p. 226)

──── WHERE TO DINE ────

BARON'S ON THE RIVER **Lunch:** $6-$14   **Dinner:** $16-$26   **Phone:** 313/259-9500   ②
Location: 1.5 mi on E Jefferson Ave, 4 blks s on McDougall; in Omni Detroit River Place. 1000 River Place Dr 48207.
Hours: 7 am-2 & 5-10 pm, Fri-Sun to 10:30 pm. **Reservations:** accepted. **Features:** Enormous portions of
American   aged prime Angus beef—as well as chops, seafood and pasta dishes—make up the dinner menu, while
scaled-down lunch selections include meatloaf, pot pie and sandwiches. The atmosphere is casual and
clublike. Patio views are great. Dressy casual; cocktails. **Parking:** valet. **Cards:** AX, CB, DC, DS, MC, VI.

GIOVANNI'S RISTORANTE **Lunch:** $8-$13   **Dinner:** $12-$18   **Phone:** 313/841-0122   ④
Location: Between Schaefer and Fort St. 330 S Oakwood Blvd 48217. **Hours:** 11 am-9 pm, Fri-10 pm, Sat 4
pm-10 pm. Closed major holidays; also Sun & Mon. **Reservations:** suggested. **Features:** A favorite haunt
Italian   of Frank Sinatra when he came to town, the completely remodeled restaurant exudes refinement. It
continues to delight diners with its food and polished service. Dressy casual; cocktails. **Parking:** on-site.
Cards: AX, DC, MC, VI.

THE RATTLESNAKE CLUB **Lunch:** $9-$16   **Dinner:** $17-$31   **Phone:** 313/567-4400   ③
Location: 1.5 mi on E Jefferson Ave, 4 blks s on McDougall. 300 River Pl 48207. **Hours:** 11:30 am-10 pm, Fri-11
pm, Sat 5:30 pm-11 pm. Closed major holidays; also Sun. **Reservations:** accepted. **Features:** Trendy and
American   cutting edge, this riverside restaurant located in Detroit's river place area, offers sophisticated American
cuisine geared toward the hip and lively. Dressy casual; cocktails. **Parking:** valet and street. **Cards:** AX,
DC, DS, JC, MC, VI.

SINDBAD'S AT THE RIVER **Lunch:** $5-$8   **Dinner:** $9-$18   **Phone:** 313/822-7817   ①
Location: From jct E Jefferson Ave and Marquette, follow Marquette e to St. Clair. 100 St. Clair 48214. **Hours:** 11
am-11 pm, Fri & Sat-1 am. Closed major holidays. **Features:** On the banks of the Detroit River, the
Steak & Seafood   restaurant has been an area institution for casual dining and great waterfront views since 1949. The menu
centers on a good selection of seafood and steaks. Outdoor dining is popular during pleasant weather.
Casual dress; cocktails. **Parking:** valet. **Cards:** AX, DC, DS, MC, VI.

The Detroit Vicinity

ALLEN PARK pop. 29,376   (See map and index starting on p. 226)

──────── WHERE TO STAY ────────

BEST WESTERN GREENFIELD INN   *Book at aaa.com*   **Phone:** (313)271-1600   **130**
(AAA) (SAVE)   All Year   1P: $79-$139   2P: $89-$149   XP: $10   F
Location: I-94, exit 206 (Oakwood Blvd), just s. 3000 Enterprise Dr 48101. Fax: 313/271-1600. **Facility:** 209 one-bedroom standard units. 3 stories, interior corridors. **Parking:** on-site. **Terms:** [AP] & [BP] meal plans available, package plans - seasonal & weekends, pets ($100 deposit, small dogs only). **Amenities:** video library
Small-scale Hotel (fee), dual phone lines, voice mail, safes, irons, hair dryers. **Dining:** 6 am-10 pm, Fri & Sat-11 pm 6/1-8/31, cocktails. **Leisure Activities:** sauna, whirlpool, exercise room. **Guest Services:** valet and coin laundry, area transportation-within 5 mi. **Business Services:** meeting rooms, PC, fax. **Cards:** AX, DC, DS, MC, VI. **Special Amenities:** early check-in/late check-out and free room upgrade (subject to availability with advanced reservations).
(See color ad p 254)

SOME UNITS

HOLIDAY INN EXPRESS & SUITES   *Book at aaa.com*   **Phone:** (313)323-3500   **131**
(AAA) (SAVE)   All Year [ECP]   1P: $110-$130   2P: $110-$130
Location: I-94, exit 206 (Oakwood Blvd), just s. 3600 Enterprise Dr 48101. Fax: 313/323-3553. **Facility:** 121 units. 92 one-bedroom standard units, some with whirlpools. 29 one-bedroom suites, some with whirlpools. 3 stories, interior corridors. *Bath:* combo or shower only. **Parking:** on-site. **Terms:** package plans, pets (dogs
Small-scale Hotel only). **Amenities:** high-speed Internet, dual phone lines, voice mail, safes, irons, hair dryers. **Pool(s):** heated indoor. **Leisure Activities:** whirlpool, exercise room. **Guest Services:** valet and coin laundry. **Business Services:** meeting rooms. **Cards:** AX, CB, DC, DS, MC, VI. **Special Amenities:** free local telephone calls and free newspaper.** *(See color ad card insert & p 255)*

SOME UNITS

AUBURN HILLS pop. 19,837

──────── WHERE TO STAY ────────

AMERISUITES (DETROIT/AUBURN HILLS)   *Book at aaa.com*   **Phone:** (248)475-9393
(AAA) (SAVE)   All Year [ECP]   1P: $109   2P: $109   XP: $10   F17
Location: I-75, exit 79 (University Dr), just w, then just n. 1545 Opdyke Rd 48326. Fax: 248/475-9399. **Facility:** 128 one-bedroom standard units. 6 stories, interior corridors. *Bath:* combo or shower only. **Parking:** on-site. **Terms:** small pets only. **Amenities:** voice mail, irons, hair dryers. *Some:* dual phone lines. **Pool(s):** heated
Small-scale Hotel indoor. **Leisure Activities:** exercise room. **Guest Services:** valet and coin laundry. **Business Services:** meeting rooms. **Cards:** AX, CB, DC, DS, JC, MC, VI. **Special Amenities:** free expanded continental breakfast and free newspaper.** *(See color ad p 236)*

SOME UNITS

CANDLEWOOD SUITES   *Book at aaa.com*   **Phone:** 248/373-3342
Property failed to provide current rates
Location: I-75, exit 79 (University Dr), just w, then 0.4 mi n. 1650 N Opdyke Rd 48326. Fax: 248/373-4523. **Facility:** 110 units. 96 one-bedroom standard units with efficiencies. 14 one-bedroom suites with kitchens. 3 stories, interior corridors. **Parking:** on-site. **Amenities:** video library, CD players, dual phone lines, voice **Small-scale Hotel** mail, irons, hair dryers. **Leisure Activities:** exercise room. **Guest Services:** sundries.

SOME UNITS

COMFORT SUITES OF AUBURN HILLS   *Book at aaa.com*   **Phone:** (248)370-0200
(AAA) (SAVE)   All Year [CP]   1P: $109-$189   2P: $109-$189   XP: $10   F18
Location: I-75, exit 79 (University Dr), just w, then just n. 1565 N Opdyke Rd 48326. Fax: 248/370-0980. **Facility:** 63 units. 53 one-bedroom standard units, some with whirlpools. 10 one-bedroom suites, some with whirlpools. 3 stories, interior corridors. *Bath:* combo or shower only. **Parking:** on-site. **Terms:** cancellation fee imposed, **Small-scale Hotel** weekly rates available. **Amenities:** voice mail, irons, hair dryers. *Some:* dual phone lines. **Pool(s):** heated indoor. **Leisure Activities:** whirlpool. **Guest Services:** valet and coin laundry. **Business Services:** meeting rooms, business center. **Cards:** AX, DC, DS, MC, VI.

SOME UNITS

COURTYARD BY MARRIOTT-AUBURN HILLS   *Book at aaa.com*   **Phone:** 248/373-4100
All Year   1P: $89-$149
Location: I-75, exit 79 (University Dr), just w, then just n. 1296 Opdyke Rd 48326. Fax: 248/373-1885. **Facility:** 148 units. 138 one-bedroom standard units. 10 one-bedroom suites ($129-$169). 2-3 stories, interior corridors. **Small-scale Hotel** *Bath:* combo or shower only. **Parking:** on-site. **Terms:** [BP] meal plan available, package plans - weekends. **Amenities:** high-speed Internet, voice mail, irons, hair dryers. **Pool(s):** heated indoor. **Leisure Activities:** whirlpool, exercise room. **Guest Services:** valet and coin laundry. **Business Services:** meeting rooms. **Cards:** AX, CB, DC, DS, MC, VI.

SOME UNITS

EXTENDED STAYAMERICA-AUBURN HILLS   *Book at aaa.com*   **Phone:** 248/373-1335
Property failed to provide current rates
Location: I-75, exit 79 (University Dr), just w, just s on Opdyke Rd, then just e. 1180 Doris Rd 48326. Fax: 248/373-1354. **Facility:** 113 one-bedroom standard units with efficiencies. 3 stories, interior corridors. **Small-scale Hotel** *Bath:* combo or shower only. **Parking:** on-site. **Amenities:** voice mail, hair dryers. **Guest Services:** sundries, valet and coin laundry.

SOME UNITS

FAIRFIELD INN BY MARRIOTT-AUBURN HILLS
Book at aaa.com
Phone: (248)373-2228
6/1-10/31 [CP]   1P: $79-$89
4/1-5/31 [CP]   1P: $69-$79
11/1-3/31 [CP]   1P: $64-$74
Small-scale Hotel   **Location:** I-75, exit 79 (University Dr), just w, then s. 1294 Opdyke Rd 48326. Fax: 248/373-2228. **Facility:** 134 one-bedroom standard units. 3 stories, interior/exterior corridors. *Bath:* combo or shower only. **Parking:** on-site, winter plug-ins. **Amenities:** irons. *Some:* hair dryers. **Pool(s):** heated outdoor. **Guest Services:** valet laundry. **Cards:** AX, CB, DC, DS, JC, MC, VI.

SOME UNITS

HAMPTON INN
Book at aaa.com
Phone: (248)370-0044
All Year [CP]   1P: $79-$114
Location: I-75, exit 79 (University Dr), just w, then just n. 1461 N Opdyke Rd 48326. Fax: 248/370-9590.
Small-scale Hotel   **Facility:** 124 one-bedroom standard units. 3 stories, interior corridors. **Parking:** on-site. **Amenities:** high-speed Internet, dual phone lines, voice mail, irons, hair dryers. **Pool(s):** heated outdoor. **Leisure Activities:** exercise room. **Guest Services:** valet laundry. **Business Services:** meeting rooms, business center. **Cards:** AX, DC, DS, MC, VI.

SOME UNITS

HILTON SUITES AUBURN HILLS
Book at aaa.com
Phone: (248)334-2222
All Year   1P: $89-$199   2P: $89-$199   XP: $15   F18
Location: I-75, exit 79 (University Dr), just w, 0.5 mi s on Opdyke Rd, then just e. 2300 Featherstone Rd 48326.
Small-scale Hotel   Fax: 248/322-2300. **Facility:** 224 one-bedroom suites. 5 stories, interior corridors. *Bath:* combo or shower only. **Parking:** on-site, winter plug-ins. **Terms:** cancellation fee imposed, [AP] meal plan available. **Amenities:** video games (fee), dual phone lines, voice mail, irons, hair dryers. *Some:* high-speed Internet. **Pool(s):** heated indoor. **Leisure Activities:** sauna, whirlpool, exercise room. **Guest Services:** gift shop, area transportation. **Business Services:** conference facilities, business center. **Cards:** AX, CB, DC, DS, JC, MC, VI.

SOME UNITS

HOLIDAY INN SELECT-AUBURN HILLS
Book at aaa.com
Phone: (248)373-4550
All Year   1P: $85-$126   2P: $85-$126   XP: $10   F16
Location: I-75, exit 79 (University Dr). 1500 Opdyke Rd 48326. Fax: 248/373-8220. **Facility:** 190 units. 188 one-bedroom standard units, some with whirlpools. 2 one-bedroom suites. 8 stories, interior corridors. *Bath:* combo or shower only. **Parking:** on-site. **Terms:** check-in 4 pm. **Amenities:** high-speed Internet, voice mail, Small-scale Hotel   irons, hair dryers. **Dining:** 6 am-11 pm, Fri & Sat-midnight. **Pool(s):** heated indoor. **Leisure Activities:** sauna, whirlpool, exercise room. **Guest Services:** valet and coin laundry, area transportation-Auburn Hills. **Business Services:** conference facilities, business center. **Cards:** AX, DS, MC, VI. **Special Amenities:** free local telephone calls.

SOME UNITS

HOMESTEAD STUDIO
SUITES HOTEL-DETROIT/AUBURN HILLS *Book at aaa.com* Phone: (248)340-8888
▼▼ ▼▼ All Year 1P: $64-$79 2P: $69-$84 XP: $5 F17
Location: I-75, exit 79 (University Dr), 0.9 mi e. 3315 University Dr 48326. **Fax:** 248/340-8622. **Facility:** 134 one-
Small-scale Hotel bedroom standard units with efficiencies. 3 stories, interior corridors. *Bath:* combo or shower only. **Parking:**
on-site, winter plug-ins. **Terms:** pets ($75 deposit). **Amenities:** voice mail, irons. **Guest Services:** sundries,
valet and coin laundry. **Cards:** AX, CB, DC, DS, MC, VI.
SOME UNITS
(ASK) (S🔊) 🐶 (†↓) (♨) (📷) (DATA PORT) 🖥 🖨 🖵 / ✕ (VCR) /
FEE FEE

STAYBRIDGE SUITES *Book at aaa.com* Phone: (248)322-4600
▼▼▼ ▼▼ All Year 1P: $109-$169 2P: $109-$169
Location: I-75, exit 79 (University Dr), just w, 0.5 mi s on Opdyke Rd, just e. 2050 Featherstone Rd 48326.
Small-scale Hotel **Fax:** 248/322-4700. **Facility:** 118 units. 58 one-bedroom standard units with efficiencies. 38 one- and 22 two-
bedroom suites with efficiencies. 3 stories, interior corridors. *Bath:* combo or shower only. **Parking:** on-site.
Terms: cancellation fee imposed, [ECP] meal plan available, pets ($75 fee). **Amenities:** high-speed Internet (fee), dual phone
lines, voice mail, irons, hair dryers. **Pool(s):** heated outdoor. **Leisure Activities:** exercise room, sports court. **Guest Services:**
sundries. **Business Services:** meeting rooms, business center. **Cards:** AX, CB, DC, DS, JC, MC, VI.
SOME UNITS
(ASK) (S🔊) 🐶 (†↓) (🖑) (🏊) (📷) (DATA PORT) 🖥 🖨 🖵 / ✕ /
FEE

WELLESLEY INN &
SUITES (DETROIT/AUBURN HILLS) *Book at aaa.com* Phone: (248)335-5200
(AAA) (SAVE) All Year [ECP] 1P: $69-$89 2P: $69-$99 XP: $10 F16
Location: I-75, exit 79 (University Dr), just w, 0.5 mi s on Opdyke Rd, then just e. 2100 Featherstone Rd 48326.
▼▼ ▼▼ **Fax:** 248/335-5800. **Facility:** 139 units. 68 one-bedroom standard units with efficiencies. 71 one-bedroom
Small-scale Hotel suites with efficiencies. 3 stories, interior corridors. *Bath:* combo or shower only. **Parking:** on-site.
Terms: pets ($50 deposit). **Amenities:** video games (fee), dual phone lines, voice mail, irons, hair dryers.
Pool(s): heated outdoor. **Leisure Activities:** exercise room. **Guest Services:** valet and coin laundry. **Busi-
ness Services:** meeting rooms. **Cards:** AX, DC, DS, MC, VI. **Special Amenities:** free expanded continental breakfast and
free newspaper. *(See color ad p 236)*
SOME UNITS
🐶 (🏊) (📷) (DATA PORT) 🖥 🖨 🖵 / ✕ /
FEE

WINGATE INN *Book at aaa.com* Phone: (248)334-3324
▼▼ ▼▼ 4/1-10/31 & 3/1-3/31 1P: $129-$139 2P: $139-$149 XP: $10 F17
11/1-2/28 1P: $109-$129 2P: $129-$139 XP: $10 F17
Small-scale Hotel **Location:** I-75, exit 79 (University Dr), just w, 0.5 mi s on Opdyke Rd, just e. 2200 Featherstone Rd 48326.
Fax: 248/334-2057. **Facility:** 102 one-bedroom standard units, some with whirlpools. 4 stories, interior corri-
dors. **Parking:** on-site. **Terms:** [ECP] meal plan available. **Amenities:** video games, high-speed Internet, voice mail, safes, irons,
hair dryers. **Pool(s):** heated indoor. **Leisure Activities:** whirlpool, exercise room. **Guest Services:** valet laundry. **Business
Services:** meeting rooms, business center. **Cards:** AX, CB, DC, DS, MC, VI.
SOME UNITS
(ASK) (S🔊) (†↓) (🏊) (📷) (DATA PORT) 🖥 🖨 🖵 / ✕ /

——— **WHERE TO DINE** ———

BIG BUCK BREWERY & STEAKHOUSE Lunch: $7-$29 Dinner: $7-$29 Phone: 248-276-2337
▼▼ ▼▼ **Location:** I-75, exit 79 (University Dr), just w, then just s. 2550 Takata Dr 48326. **Hours:** 11 am-11 pm,
Steak House Fri-midnight, Sat noon-midnight, Sun noon-10 pm. Closed major holidays. **Features:** The Big Buck
Brewery and Steakhouse produces fine brews, bound to please the beer connoisseur, and features the
finest "Sterling Silver" certified premium USDA choice beef, for steak that is guaranteed to be tender, juicy
and flavorful or your money back. Casual dress; beer only. **Parking:** on-site. **Cards:** AX, DC, DS, MC, VI.
(🍸) ✕

BISTRO BOURDEAU Lunch: $10-$15 Dinner: $15-$20 Phone: 248/852-3410
▼▼▼ ▼▼ **Location:** Jct Squirrel Rd. 3315 Auburn Rd 48321. **Hours:** 11 am-9 pm, Fri-10 pm, Sat 4 pm-10 pm. Closed
American major holidays. **Reservations:** suggested. **Features:** A bit off the beaten path, the casually upscale
restaurant's circle-in-a-square dining room creates a number of intimate seating areas. Candlelit tables, live
music on weekends and a creative touch to plate presentations further enhance a menu that features
whitefish, gulf shrimp, a variety of steaks, roast chicken and jambalaya. Dressy casual; cocktails. **Parking:** on-site. **Cards:** AX,
CB, DC, DS, MC, VI.
(♿M) (🍸) ✕

FRAN O'BRIEN'S MARYLAND CRAB HOUSE Lunch: $7-$15 Dinner: $9-$25 Phone: 248/332-7744
▼▼ ▼▼ **Location:** I-75, exit 79 (University Dr), just w, 1 mi s. 621 S Opdyke Rd 48342. **Hours:** 11 am-10 pm, Sat 3 pm-11
American pm, Sun 3 pm-9 pm. Closed major holidays. **Features:** Located in a shopping plaza, a short distance from
the Pontiac Silverdome, this modest nautically themed restaurant is popular with the post and pre game
crowd. Casual dress; cocktails. **Parking:** on-site. **Cards:** AX, DC, MC, VI.
✕

LELLI'S INN OF AUBURN HILLS Lunch: $8-$15 Dinner: $10-$25 Phone: 248/373-4440
▼▼ ▼▼ **Location:** I-75, exit 79 (University Dr), just w, then 0.5 mi s. 885 N Opdyke Rd 48326. **Hours:** 11 am-10 pm, Fri &
Sat-11 pm, Sun noon-9 pm. Closed major holidays. **Reservations:** suggested. **Features:** A Detroit legend
Northern in a new location overlooking the Pontiac Silverdome. Still serving the filet mignon and shrimp Lelli that
Italian made the original restaurant famous, Lelli's Inn is perfect for special occasions. Dressy casual; cocktails.
Parking: on-site and valet. **Cards:** AX, DC, MC, VI.
(🍸) ✕

RANGOLI INDIAN CUISINE Lunch: $5-$8 Dinner: $7-$12 Phone: 248/377-3800
▼▼ ▼▼ **Location:** I-75, exit 79 (University Dr), just w on Opdyke Rd, then 0.5 mi e. 3055 E Walton Blvd 48326. **Hours:** 11
Indian am-2:30 & 5-9:30 pm, Fri-10:30 pm, Sat 11:30 am-3 & 5-10 pm, Sun 11:30 am-3 & 5-9 pm. Closed major
holidays. **Reservations:** accepted. **Features:** Named for a type of traditional Indian Folk painting, this
attractive restaurant showcases India's widely varied regional cuisines. Expert waiters will help guide you
through the extensive menu. Casual dress. **Parking:** on-site. **Cards:** AX, DS, MC, VI.
✕

BELLEVILLE pop. 3,997

--------- WHERE TO STAY ---------

COMFORT INN
Book at aaa.com

Small-scale Hotel

4/1-8/31	1P: $74-$129	2P: $74-$129	XP: $5	F17
9/1-3/31	1P: $69-$119	2P: $69-$129	XP: $5	F17

Phone: (734)697-8556

Location: I-94, exit 190 (Belleville Rd), just s. 45945 S I-94 Service Dr 48111. Fax: 734/697-8513. **Facility:** 64 one-bedroom standard units, some with whirlpools. 2 stories, interior corridors. *Bath:* combo or shower only. **Parking:** on-site. **Terms:** cancellation fee imposed, [ECP] meal plan available, pets (with prior approval). **Amenities:** voice mail, safes, irons, hair dryers. **Pool(s):** small heated indoor. **Leisure Activities:** whirlpool. **Guest Services:** coin laundry. **Business Services:** meeting rooms. **Cards:** AX, CB, DC, DS, JC, MC, VI.

HAMPTON INN
Book at aaa.com

Small-scale Hotel

All Year   1P: $89-$119   2P: $89-$119   XP: $10   F18

Phone: (734)699-2424

Location: I-94, exit 190 (Belleville Rd), just w. 46280 N I-94 Service Dr 48111. Fax: 734/699-7340. **Facility:** 90 one-bedroom standard units. 3 stories, interior corridors. *Bath:* combo or shower only. **Parking:** on-site. **Terms:** [ECP] meal plan available. **Amenities:** dual phone lines, voice mail, irons, hair dryers. **Pool(s):** heated indoor. **Leisure Activities:** whirlpool, exercise room. **Guest Services:** valet and coin laundry, airport transportation-Detroit Metro Willow Run Airport. **Cards:** AX, DC, DS, MC, VI. **Special Amenities:** free expanded continental breakfast and free newspaper.

HOLIDAY INN EXPRESS HOTEL & SUITES

Small-scale Hotel

All Year   1P: $99-$109   2P: $99-$109

Phone: (734)857-6200

Location: I-94, exit 190 (Belleville Rd), just w. 46194 N I-94 Service Dr 48111. Fax: 734/857-6229. **Facility:** 108 one-bedroom standard units, some with whirlpools. 3 stories, interior corridors. *Bath:* combo or shower only. **Parking:** on-site. **Terms:** [ECP] meal plan available. **Amenities:** dual phone lines, voice mail, irons, hair dryers. **Pool(s):** heated indoor. **Leisure Activities:** saunas, whirlpool, steamrooms, exercise room. **Guest Services:** valet and coin laundry, airport transportation-Willow Run Airport. **Business Services:** meeting rooms, business center. **Cards:** AX, DC, DS, MC, VI. **Special Amenities:** free local telephone calls and free newspaper.
(See color ad below)

RED ROOF INN METRO AIRPORT
Book at aaa.com

Motel

4/28-9/28	1P: $52-$58	2P: $58-$64	XP: $6	F18
9/29-3/31	1P: $50-$55	2P: $56-$61	XP: $6	F18
4/1-4/27	1P: $50-$54	2P: $56-$60	XP: $6	F18

Phone: (734)697-2244

Location: I-94, exit 190 (Belleville Rd). 45501 N I-94 Service Dr 48111. Fax: 734/697-4384. **Facility:** 112 one-bedroom standard units. 2 stories, exterior corridors. *Bath:* combo or shower only. **Parking:** on-site. **Terms:** small pets only. **Amenities:** video games. **Cards:** AX, CB, DC, DS, MC, VI. **Special Amenities:** free local telephone calls and free newspaper.

SUPER 8 MOTEL
Book at aaa.com

Small-scale Hotel

6/1-8/31 [ECP]	1P: $54-$62	2P: $59-$71
4/1-5/31 & 9/1-3/31 [ECP]	1P: $45-$62	2P: $50-$71

Phone: (734)699-1888

Location: I-94, exit 190 (Belleville Rd), just s. 45707 S I-94 Service Dr 48111. Fax: 734/699-3596. **Facility:** 63 one-bedroom standard units, some with whirlpools. 3 stories, interior corridors. **Parking:** on-site. **Terms:** pets ($20 extra charge). **Amenities:** safes. **Business Services:** fax (fee). **Cards:** AX, CB, DC, DS, MC, VI.

――――― **WHERE TO DINE** ―――――

BAYOU GRILL

Cajun
cocktails. **Parking:** on-site. **Cards:** AX, MC, VI.

Lunch: $8-$12 **Dinner:** $12-$16 **Phone:** 734/697-2300
Location: I-94, exit 190 (Belleville Rd), jct Main St and 4th Ave; downtown. 404 Main St 48111. **Hours:** 11 am-11 pm, Sat from 2 pm, Sun noon-9 pm. Closed major holidays. **Features:** Using a wide range of Cajun and Creole ingredients such as crawfish, andouille sauage and shrimp, this Mardi Gras-themed restaurant can be loud and boisterous at times but does faithfully recreate authentic Cajun dishes. Casual dress;

BELLEVILLE GRILLE
American
porterhouse steaks. Casual dress; cocktails. **Parking:** on-site. **Cards:** AX, DC, DS, MC, VI.

Lunch: $7-$12 **Dinner:** $11-$20 **Phone:** 734/699-1777
Location: I-94, exit 190 (Belleville Rd), jct Main St; downtown. 146 High St 48111. **Hours:** 11 am-10 pm, Fri & Sat-11 pm. Closed major holidays. **Reservations:** accepted. **Features:** With a lakefront vista, a patio and a number of boat slips, the local fixture is a popular gathering spot for boaters and locals alike. Contemporary American selections range from coconut shrimp and mesquite-braised spareribs to

DOS PESOS RESTAURANT
Mexican

Lunch: $5-$7 **Dinner:** $7-$11 **Phone:** 734/697-5777
Location: I-94, exit 190 (Belleville Rd), just s; in shopping plaza. 11800 Belleville Rd 48111. **Hours:** 11 am-9:30 pm, Fri & Sat-10:30 pm. Closed major holidays; also Sun. **Features:** Nestled in a small shopping plaza, this casual Mexican eatery serves modestly prepared Mexican fare including unique renditions of flautas, quesadillas and enchiladas. Casual dress; cocktails. **Parking:** on-site. **Cards:** AX, MC, VI.

BIRMINGHAM pop. 19,291 (See map and index starting on p. 226)

――――― **WHERE TO STAY** ―――――

HAMILTON HOTEL *Book at aaa.com* **Phone:** (248)642-6200 **18**
Small-scale Hotel
rooms. **Cards:** AX, DC, DS, MC, VI. **Special Amenities:** free full breakfast and free newspaper. *(See color ad below)*

4/1-10/31 [BP]	1P: $119-$159	2P: $119-$159	XP: $10	F18
11/1-3/31 [BP]	1P: $99-$139	2P: $99-$139	XP: $10	F18

Location: Jct Woodward Ave and Maple Rd; center. 35270 Woodward Ave 48009. Fax: 248/642-6567. **Facility:** 64 one-bedroom standard units. 5 stories, interior corridors. **Parking:** on-site. **Terms:** small pets only ($25 deposit). **Amenities:** dual phone lines, voice mail, irons, hair dryers. **Fee:** video games, high-speed Internet, safes. **Leisure Activities:** exercise room. **Guest Services:** valet laundry. **Business Services:** meeting

SOME UNITS

(See map and index starting on p. 226)

HOLIDAY INN EXPRESS BIRMINGHAM   *Book at aaa.com*   **Phone:** (248)646-7300   🔟
All Year [ECP]   1P: $160   2P: $160   XP: $10   F18
Location: On SR 1, jct Woodward Ave and Maple Rd; center. 34952 Woodward Ave 48009. Fax: 248/646-4501.
Small-scale Hotel   **Facility:** 124 units. 123 one-bedroom standard units. 1 one-bedroom suite with kitchen. 2-5 stories,
interior/exterior corridors. *Bath:* combo or shower only. *Parking:* on-site. **Terms:** small pets only.
Amenities: dual phone lines, voice mail, irons, hair dryers. *Fee:* video games, safes. *Some:* high-speed Internet. **Leisure Activities:** exercise room. **Guest Services:** valet laundry. **Business Services:** meeting rooms. **Cards:** AX, CB, DC, DS, MC, VI.
(See color ad below)

SOME UNITS

(ASK) (S🌐) (🐾) (🍴➕) (&M) (🖐️) (🏊) (DATA PORT) (🅱️) (📖) / (⊗) (📷) /

THE TOWNSEND HOTEL   *Book at aaa.com*   **Phone:** (248)642-7900   🔟
   11/2-3/31   1P: $279   2P: $279
   6/2-11/1   1P: $275   2P: $275
   4/1-6/1   1P: $269   2P: $269
Location: Center. 100 Townsend St 48009. Fax: 248/645-9061. **Facility:** Exuding style and class, this elegant
Small-scale Hotel   European-type hotel is within walking distance of the trendy boutiques of downtown Birmingham. 151 units.
145 one-bedroom standard units. 4 one- and 2 two-bedroom suites ($362-$1500), some with kitchens. 6 stories, interior corridors. *Bath:* combo or shower only. *Parking:* valet and street. **Terms:** check-in 4 pm, cancellation fee imposed.
Amenities: video games, CD players, high-speed Internet, dual phone lines, voice mail, safes, honor bars, irons, hair dryers.
Dining: Rugby Grille, see separate listing. **Leisure Activities:** *Fee:* massage. **Guest Services:** valet laundry, area transportation (fee). **Business Services:** meeting rooms, business center. **Cards:** AX, CB, DC, DS, JC, MC, VI. Affiliated with A Preferred Hotel.

SOME UNITS

(S🌐) (➕) (🍴) (24) (🍸) (&M) (🖐️) (🏊) (💦) (📺) (DATA PORT) / (⊗) (🅱️) (📖) /
FEE   FEE

Savings at Your Fingertips

When you have a AAA TourBook® guide in your hand, you have a world of savings right at your fingertips. AAA Official Appointment lodgings that display the bright-red AAA logo, (SAVE) icon and Diamond rating in their listing want business from AAA Members, and many offer discounts and special amenities to them*.

So, when planning your next vacation, be sure to consult your AAA TourBook for the familiar red (SAVE) icon.

See TourBook Navigator, page 14, for details.

(See map and index starting on p. 226)

──────── WHERE TO DINE ────────

220
♥♥ ♥♥
American
Dressy casual; cocktails.
Lunch: $10-$15　　Dinner: $15-$25　　Phone: 248/645-2150　32
Location: Center. 220 Merrill St 48009. **Hours:** 11 am-11 pm, Thurs-midnight, Fri & Sat-1 am. Closed major holidays; also Sun. **Features:** Paying homage to the inventor of the light bulb, this comfortable "see and be seen" restaurant offers a creative Italian-Continental menu featuring risotto, pasta, veal chops and a variety of fish dishes. A walk-down martini-cigar bar is popular with the often boisterous cell phone set. **Parking:** street. **Cards:** AX, DC, MC, VI.

BIG ROCK CHOP HOUSE
ⓐ
♥♥ ♥♥ ♥♥
Steak & Seafood
Cards: AX, DC, DS, MC, VI.
Lunch: $8-$19　　Dinner: $9-$35　　Phone: 248-647-7774　29
Location: 1 mi e of SR 1 (Woodard Ave), s on Maple Rd. 245 S Eton St 48009. **Hours:** 11 am-midnight. Closed major holidays; also Sun. **Reservations:** required. **Features:** A sophisticated interpretation of the microbrewery-steakhouse concept, the Big Rock serves some very fine beef cooked the way meat lovers like it. There is award winning beer to sample, and even a cigar and martini lounge upstairs for the connoisseurs of those particular pleasures. All the above, combined with a whimsical flying buffalo, make for an above average dining experience. Semi-formal attire; cocktails. **Parking:** on-site and valet.

FORTE'
♥♥ ♥♥
American
brick-oven roasted rosemary
MC, VI.
Lunch: $8-$20　　Dinner: $15-$32　　Phone: 248/594-7300　31
Location: Center. 201 S Old Woodward Ave 48009. **Hours:** 11:30 am-2 & 5-10 pm, Thurs & Fri-11 pm, Sat 5 pm-11 pm. Closed major holidays; also Sun. **Reservations:** accepted. **Features:** A loud and trendy "see and be seen" bar overlooks the elegant and somewhat eclectic dining room. A mix of styles ranging through French, Mediterranean and California fuse into a menu that offers everything from tapas to rubbed chicken breast. Dressy casual; cocktails. **Parking:** valet and street. **Cards:** AX, DC, DS,

MITCHELL'S FISH MARKET
♥♥♥ ♥♥♥
Seafood
focus, the menu also lists
street. Cards: AX, DC, DS, MC, VI.
Lunch: $15-$30　　Dinner: $15-$30　　Phone: 248/646-3663　28
Location: 0.3 mi n of jct Maple Rd and Old Woodward Ave; center. 117 Willits St 48009. **Hours:** 11:30 am-10 pm, Fri & Sat-11 pm, Sun-9 pm. Closed: 5/31. **Reservations:** suggested. **Features:** Part of a small but growing chain, the whimsical, nautically themed restaurant changes its menu daily to reflect more than a dozen daily specials flown in from around the world. While the fresh fish and accompanying raw bar are the main a number of steak, pasta and chicken selections. Dressy casual; cocktails. **Parking:** valet and

THE ORIGINAL PANCAKE HOUSE
♥♥ ♥♥
American
Casual dress. Parking: on-site.
Lunch: $6-$8　　Dinner: $6-$10　　Phone: 248/642-5775　34
Location: 0.8 mi s of jct Maple Rd. 33703 Woodward Ave 48009. **Hours:** 6:30 am-9 pm. Closed major holidays. **Features:** Although the menu lists many varied options, long morning lines at the front entrance testify to the popularity of the freshly made breakfasts. Part of a nationwide chain, the restaurant focuses on using quality ingredients, such as freshly squeezed orange juice and fresh creamery butter. Portions are large.

PEABODY'S
♥♥ ♥♥
American
MC, VI.
Lunch: $6-$10　　Dinner: $8-$16　　Phone: 248/644-5222　30
Location: Jct Woodward Ave and Maple Rd. 34965 Woodward Ave 48009. **Hours:** 11 am-10:30 pm. Closed major holidays; also Sun. **Features:** At this well known local eating and drinking establishment you will find a friendly, yet dressy tavern atmosphere. Great food, is served up in generous portions, by a congenial staff that delivers what you order quickly. Casual dress; cocktails. **Parking:** on-site. **Cards:** AX, CB, DC, DS,

RUGBY GRILLE
♥♥♥ ♥♥♥
American
Parking: valet and street.
Lunch: $10-$20　　Dinner: $25-$40　　Phone: 248/642-7900　33
Location: Center; in The Townsend Hotel. 100 Townsend St 48009. **Hours:** 6:30 am-midnight, Fri & Sat-1 am. Closed: 12/25. **Reservations:** suggested. **Features:** Evocative of an English Country Club, the waiters avoid the snootiness and, with a little panache, concentrate on preparing such traditional favorites such as Steak Tartar, Chateau-Briand for two and Cherries Jubilee at your table side. Dressy casual; cocktails. **Cards:** AX, CB, DC, DS, JC, MC, VI.

BLOOMFIELD HILLS pop. 3,940　(See map and index starting on p. 226)

──────── WHERE TO STAY ────────

RADISSON KINGSLEY HOTEL　*Book at aaa.com*　　Phone: (248)644-1400
ⓐ SAVE　All Year　　　　1P: $109-$179
♥♥ ♥♥ ♥♥
Small-scale Hotel
Location: On SR 1 (Woodward Ave), just s of jct Long Lake Rd. 39475 Woodward Ave 48304. Fax: 248/644-5449. **Facility:** 150 units. 141 one-bedroom standard units. 9 one-bedroom suites, some with whirlpools. 2-4 stories, interior corridors. **Parking:** on-site. **Terms:** cancellation fee imposed, small pets only ($15 fee). **Amenities:** video games (fee), high-speed Internet, dual phone lines, voice mail, safes, irons, hair dryers. **Dining:** 2 restaurants, 6 am-midnight, cocktails, also, Northern Lakes Seafood Company, see separate listing. **Pool(s):** heated indoor. **Leisure Activities:** whirlpool, exercise room. **Guest Services:** gift shop, valet laundry, area transportation-within 5 mi. **Business Services:** conference facilities. **Cards:** AX, CB, DC, DS, JC, MC, VI. **Special Amenities:** free room upgrade (subject to availability with advanced reservations). *(See color ad p 313 & p 246)*

SOME UNITS

(See map and index starting on p. 226)

——— WHERE TO DINE ———

ANDIAMO ITALIA WEST   Lunch: $13-$17   Dinner: $16-$25   Phone: 248/865-9300   (25)
◆◆◆ ◆◆◆   **Location:** W Maple Rd and US 24 (Telegraph Rd). 6676 Telegraph Rd 48301. **Hours:** 11 am-11 pm, Fri-midnight, Sat 4 pm-midnight, Sun 3 pm-9 pm. Closed major holidays. **Reservations:** suggested.
Italian   **Features:** Featuring traditional Italian dishes such as ravioli and lasagna, prepared using authentic recipes, high quality ingredients, and accented with an exquisite Parmesan cheese. The spacious dining room, with its upscale artwork, and comfortable furnishings is an ideal setting for an intimate dinner. Dressy casual; cocktails. **Parking:** on-site and valet. **Cards:** AX, MC, VI.

BEAU JACK'S FOOD & SPIRITS   Lunch: $5-$9   Dinner: $7-$17   Phone: 248/626-2630   (24)
◆◆◆ ◆◆◆   **Location:** Just w of jct US 24 (Telegraph Rd). 4108 W Maple Rd 48301. **Hours:** 11:30 am-10:30 pm, Fri & Sat-11:30 pm, Sun 4 pm-9 pm. Closed major holidays. **Features:** The rustic restaurant, relaxed in its sports tavern decor, encourages laid-back dining. Menu choices range from burgers and steaks to seafood and stir-fry. A pianist further adds to the boisterous and noisy atmosphere Thursdays through Saturdays.
American
Casual dress; cocktails; entertainment. **Parking:** on-site. **Cards:** AX, MC, VI.

FOX & HOUNDS RESTAURANT   Lunch: $7-$18   Dinner: $14-$30   Phone: 248/644-4800
◆◆◆ ◆◆◆   **Location:** On SR 1 (Woodward Ave), just s of jct Long Lake Rd. 39560 N Woodward Ave 48304. **Hours:** 11 am-3 & 5-10 pm, Sat 5 pm-11 pm, Sun 4 pm-9 pm. Closed major holidays. **Reservations:** suggested.
Steak & Seafood   **Features:** Tudor-style architecture and an Olde English atmosphere set the stage for traditional fish and fowl dishes as well as as desserts made at the on-site bakery. Casual dress; cocktails; entertainment.
Parking: on-site and valet. **Cards:** AX, DS, MC, VI.

THE MOOSE PRESERVE BAR & GRILL   Lunch: $8-$12   Dinner: $10-$15   Phone: 248/858-7688
◆◆◆ ◆◆◆   **Location:** Jct Square Lake Rd. 43034 Woodward Ave 48302. **Hours:** 11 am-2 am, Sun from noon. Closed major holidays. **Features:** As the name might suggest, the boisterous, northwoods-inspired sports bar and lodge features plenty of duck prints and mounted trophy heads. Farmed game—such as elk, emu, venison, buffalo and duck—highlight a menu that also lists beef steaks, chicken and burgers. Casual dress; cocktails. **Parking:** on-site. **Cards:** AX, DC, DS, MC, VI.

NORTHERN LAKES SEAFOOD COMPANY   Lunch: $8-$15   Dinner: $19-$30   Phone: 248/646-7900
◆◆◆ ◆◆◆   **Location:** On SR 1 (Woodward Ave), just s of jct Long Lake Rd; in Radisson Kingsley Hotel. 39495 Woodward Ave 48304. **Hours:** 11 am-2:30 & 5-10 pm, Fri-11 pm, Sat 5 pm-11 pm, Sun 5 pm-9 pm. Closed major holidays.
Seafood   **Reservations:** suggested, weekends. **Features:** This popular restaurant features a comfortable dining room decorated with marine accents, like light globes that include a glass octopus. They serve generous portions of deliciously prepared fish, shrimp and lobster. Their special "martini menu" includes a spectacular selection of variations on the basic drink that you can enjoy, like olives stuffed with blue cheese or anchovies. It is a great place for that special family dinner. Casual dress; cocktails. **Parking:** on-site and valet. **Cards:** AX, DC, DS, MC, VI.

CANTON pop. 76,366   (See map and index starting on p. 226)

——— WHERE TO STAY ———

BAYMONT INN & SUITES DETROIT-CANTON   *Book at aaa.com*   Phone: (734)981-1808   123
(AAA) (SAVE)   All Year   1P: $75   2P: $75
◆◆◆ ◆◆◆   **Location:** I-275, exit 25 (Ford Rd), just w on SR 153. Located behind White Castle. 41211 Ford Rd 48187. Fax: 734/981-7150. **Facility:** 98 one-bedroom standard units. 3 stories, interior corridors. **Parking:** on-site.
Small-scale Hotel   **Terms:** [ECP] meal plan available, small pets only. **Amenities:** video games, voice mail, irons, hair dryers. **Guest Services:** valet and coin laundry. **Business Services:** fax (fee). **Cards:** AX, CB, DC, DS, MC, VI. **Special Amenities:** free local telephone calls and free newspaper. *(See color ad p 287)*
SOME UNITS

DAYS INN   *Book at aaa.com*   Phone: (734)721-5200   125
◆◆ ◆◆   All Year   1P: $49-$75   2P: $49-$75   XP: $5   F15
Motel   **Location:** I-275, exit 22, just e on US 12; entry at Wendy's. 40500 Michigan Ave 48188. Fax: 734/721-8814. **Facility:** 84 one-bedroom standard units, some with whirlpools. 2 stories, exterior corridors. **Parking:** on-site.
Terms: 4 day cancellation notice-fee imposed, weekly rates available, [CP] meal plan available.
Amenities: video games (fee), hair dryers. **Pool(s):** outdoor. **Guest Services:** valet laundry. **Cards:** AX, DC, DS, MC, VI.
(See color ad card insert)
SOME UNITS

EXTENDED STAYAMERICA-CANTON   *Book at aaa.com*   Phone: (734)844-6725   124
◆◆ ◆◆   All Year   1P: $49-$59   2P: $54-$60
Small-scale Hotel   **Location:** I-275, exit 25, just w on SR 153 (Ford Rd), then just s. 2000 Haggerty N 48187. Fax: 734/844-6726. **Facility:** 104 one-bedroom standard units with efficiencies. 3 stories, interior corridors. *Bath:* combo or shower only. **Parking:** on-site. **Terms:** weekly rates available. **Amenities:** dual phone lines, voice mail.
Guest Services: coin laundry. **Business Services:** meeting rooms. **Cards:** AX, DC, DS, MC, VI.
SOME UNITS

(See map and index starting on p. 226)

FAIRFIELD INN BY MARRIOTT ___Book at aaa.com___ **Phone:** (734)981-2440 [121]
All Year 1P: $61-$99 2P: $79-$109
Location: I-275, exit 25 (Ford Rd), just w on SR 153. 5700 Haggerty Rd 48187. **Fax:** 734/981-2440. **Facility:** 133
one-bedroom standard units. 3 stories, interior/exterior corridors. *Bath:* combo or shower only. **Parking:** on-
Small-scale Hotel site. **Terms:** [CP] meal plan available. **Amenities:** irons. **Pool(s):** outdoor. **Guest Services:** valet laundry.
Cards: AX, DC, DS, MC, VI.

SOME UNITS

HOLIDAY INN EXPRESS HOTEL & SUITES ___Book at aaa.com___ **Phone:** (734)721-5500 [127]
All Year [ECP] 1P: $109-$199 2P: $109-$199 XP: $10 F
Location: I-275, exit 22, just e. 3950 Lotz Rd 48188. **Fax:** 734/721-1300. **Facility:** 81 one-bedroom standard
units, some with whirlpools. 3 stories, interior corridors. *Bath:* combo or shower only. **Parking:** on-site.
Small-scale Hotel **Amenities:** video games (fee), dual phone lines, voice mail, irons, hair dryers. **Pool(s):** small heated indoor.
Leisure Activities: whirlpool, exercise room. **Guest Services:** valet laundry. **Business Services:** meeting rooms, business
center. **Cards:** AX, DC, DS, MC, VI. *(See color ad card insert)*

SOME UNITS

MOTEL 6 - 1070 ___Book at aaa.com___ **Phone:** 734/981-5000 [122]
5/27-9/5 1P: $46-$56 2P: $52-$62 XP: $3 F17
9/6-3/31 1P: $41-$51 2P: $47-$57 XP: $3 F17
4/1-5/26 1P: $39-$49 2P: $45-$55 XP: $3 F17
Motel **Location:** I-275, exit 25, just w on SR 153 (Ford Rd). 41216 Ford Rd 48187. **Fax:** 734/981-5432. **Facility:** 107 one-
bedroom standard units. 1 story, exterior corridors. *Bath:* combo or shower only. **Parking:** on-site. **Terms:** small pets only.
Pool(s): outdoor. **Business Services:** fax (fee). **Cards:** AX, CB, DC, DS, MC, VI.

SOME UNITS

SUPER 8 MOTEL-CANTON ___Book at aaa,com___ **Phone:** (734)722-8880 [126]
5/1-9/30 1P: $55 2P: $60 XP: $6 F17
4/1-4/30 & 10/1-3/31 1P: $49 2P: $54 XP: $6 F17
Location: I-275, exit 22, just e on US 12, then just s. 3933 Lotz Rd 48188. **Fax:** 734/722-8880. **Facility:** 70 one-
Small-scale Hotel bedroom standard units, some with whirlpools. 3 stories, interior corridors. **Parking:** on-site. **Terms:** 7 day
cancellation notice, weekly rates available, [CP] meal plan available. **Amenities:** safes (fee). **Business Services:** fax (fee).
Cards: AX, CB, DC, DS, JC, MC, VI.

SOME UNITS

——— WHERE TO DINE ———

CARRABBA'S ITALIAN GRILL **Dinner:** $12-$18 **Phone:** 734/844-7400 [138]
Location: I-275, exit 25 (Ford Rd), just w, then just s. 1900 N Haggerty Rd 48187. **Hours:** 4 pm-10 pm, Fri-11 pm,
Sat 3 pm-11 pm, Sun 1 pm-9 pm. Closed major holidays. **Reservations:** accepted. **Features:** Tuscan
Italian influences run deep in the surprisingly cozy, intimate space. A large open kitchen lets diners watch such
dishes as calamari, eggplant parmigiana and pizza being prepared. Dressy casual; cocktails. **Parking:**
on-site. **Cards:** AX, DC, MC, VI.

THAI BISTRO **Lunch:** $6-$12 **Dinner:** $6-$12 **Phone:** 734/416-2122
Location: I-275, exit 25 (Ford Rd), 2 mi w, jct Canton Center Rd. 45620 Ford Rd 48187. **Hours:** 11:30 am-2:30 &
5-9 pm, Fri-10 pm, Sat 5 pm-9 pm. Closed major holidays; also Sun. **Features:** Tucked away in a strip
Thai mall, this modest but pleasant dining serves up a strong menu of Thai specialties. Using fresh ingredients
and stellar sauces, the chef/owner faithfully recreates the flavors of Thailand. Casual dress; beer only.
Parking: on-site. **Cards:** AX, DC, DS, MC, VI.

CLARKSTON pop. 1,000

——— WHERE TO DINE ———

THE CLARKSTON UNION **Lunch:** $6-$8 **Dinner:** $13-$23 **Phone:** 248/620-6100
Location: Downtown. 54 S Main St 48346. **Hours:** 11 am-10 pm, Fri & Sat-11 pm, Sun-9 pm. Closed major
holidays. **Features:** Savor hearty, homemade comfort foods in a resurrected 1840s church. An extensive
American selection of European and American microbrewed beer complements a limited offering of pub-type food. A
nice variety of tea and gourmet coffee are also available. Casual dress; cocktails. **Parking:** on-site.
Cards: AX, DS, MC, VI.

CLAWSON pop. 12,732 (See map and index starting on p. 226)

——— WHERE TO DINE ———

CLAWSON STEAK HOUSE **Lunch:** $10-$15 **Dinner:** $15-$25 **Phone:** 248/588-5788 [37]
Location: I-75, exit 65, 1 mi w, jct 14 Mile and Rochester rds. 56 S Rochester Rd 48017. **Hours:** 11 am-11 pm, Fri
& Sat-midnight. Closed major holidays; also Sun. **Reservations:** accepted. **Features:** Reminiscent of a
1950s supper club, the mauve dining room has been popular with locals of all ages for over 40 years.
Steak House Wednesday through Saturday live music is featured after 8 pm while diners enjoy traditional steak house
favorites. Dressy casual; cocktails. **Parking:** on-site and valet. **Cards:** AX, CB, DC, DS, MC, VI.

DEARBORN pop. 97,775 (See map and index starting on p. 226)

──────── WHERE TO STAY ────────

COURTYARD BY MARRIOTT-DEARBORN *Book at aaa.com* Phone: 313/271-1400 **112**

▼▼▼ 4/1-12/23 & 12/26-3/31 1P: $69-$169 2P: $69-$169

Small-scale Hotel **Location:** SR 39 (Southfield Frwy), exit 25 (Ford Rd), just e, then s. 5200 Mercury Dr 48126. Fax: 313/271-1184. **Facility:** 147 units. 137 one-bedroom standard units. 10 one-bedroom suites. 1-3 stories, interior corridors. *Bath:* combo or shower only. **Parking:** on-site. **Terms:** open 4/1-12/23 & 12/26-3/31, cancellation fee imposed. **Amenities:** high-speed Internet, dual phone lines, voice mail, irons, hair dryers. **Pool(s):** small heated indoor. **Leisure Activities:** whirlpool, exercise room. **Guest Services:** coin laundry. **Business Services:** meeting rooms, fax (fee). **Cards:** AX, CB, DC, DS, JC, MC, VI.

SOME UNITS

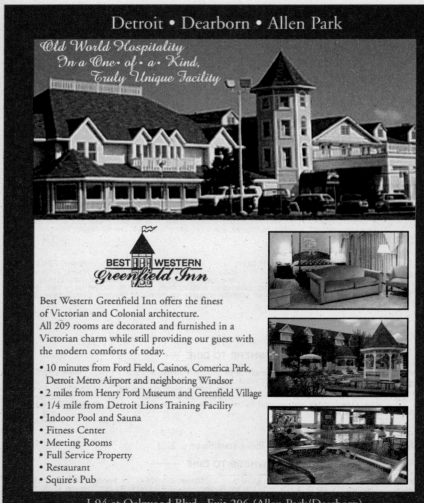

Detroit • Dearborn • Allen Park

Old World Hospitality In a One-of-a-Kind, Truly Unique Facility

BEST WESTERN
Greenfield Inn

Best Western Greenfield Inn offers the finest of Victorian and Colonial architecture.
All 209 rooms are decorated and furnished in a Victorian charm while still providing our guest with the modern comforts of today.

• 10 minutes from Ford Field, Casinos, Comerica Park, Detroit Metro Airport and neighboring Windsor
• 2 miles from Henry Ford Museum and Greenfield Village
• 1/4 mile from Detroit Lions Training Facility
• Indoor Pool and Sauna
• Fitness Center
• Meeting Rooms
• Full Service Property
• Restaurant
• Squire's Pub

I-94 at Oakwood Blvd., Exit 206 (Allen Park/Dearborn)
3000 Enterprise Drive, Allen Park, MI • 313.271.1600

(See map and index starting on p. 226)

THE DEARBORN INN, A MARRIOTT HOTEL   *Book at aaa.com*   **Phone:** (313)271-2700   **118**

All Year   1P: $79-$189   2P: $79-$189

Location: SR 39 (Southfield Frwy), exit Oakwood Blvd, 1 mi w. 20301 Oakwood Blvd 48124. Fax: 313/271-7464. **Facility:** Built in 1931 by Henry Ford, this modern hotel's stunning historic lobby is a great example of Georgian-style architecture and opulence. 222 units. 215 one-bedroom standard units. 3 one- and 4 three-bedroom suites ($150-$300). 2-4 stories, interior/exterior corridors. *Bath:* combo or shower only. **Parking:** on-site and valet. **Terms:** check-in 4 pm, cancellation fee imposed, package plans - weekends. **Amenities:** high-speed Internet (fee), dual phone lines, voice mail, irons, hair dryers. **Dining:** 2 restaurants, 6:30 am-11 pm, cocktails, also, The Grill at the Early American Room, see separate listing. **Pool(s):** heated outdoor. **Leisure Activities:** 2 tennis courts, exercise room. **Guest Services:** gift shop, valet laundry, area transportation-within 3 mi. **Business Services:** meeting rooms, business center. **Cards:** AX, CB, DC, DS, JC, MC, VI. **Special Amenities:** free newspaper and preferred room (subject to availability with advanced reservations).

SOME UNITS

Historic Small-scale Hotel

FEE

(See map and index starting on p. 226)

EXTENDED STAYAMERICA *Book at aaa.com* Phone: 313/336-0021 **114**

Property failed to provide current rates

◇◇◇

Small-scale Hotel

Location: SR 39 (Southfield Frwy) between exits Ford Rd and Michigan Ave, just w of jct Service and Hubbard drs. Located adjacent to shopping mall. 260 Towne Center Dr 48126. Fax: 313/336-0052. **Facility:** 93 one-bedroom standard units with efficiencies. 4 stories, interior corridors. *Bath:* combo or shower only. **Parking:** on-site. **Terms:** office hours 7 am-11 pm. **Amenities:** dual phone lines, voice mail. **Guest Services:** coin laundry.

SOME UNITS

HAMPTON INN DEARBORN *Book at aaa.com* Phone: (313)436-9600 **116**

◇◇◇

Small-scale Hotel

All Year [ECP] 1P: $98-$150 2P: $108-$160
Location: Off SR 39 (Southfield Frwy), exit Michigan Ave, just w. 20061 Michigan Ave 48124. Fax: 313/436-8345. **Facility:** 119 one-bedroom standard units. 4 stories, interior corridors. **Parking:** on-site. **Amenities:** video games, voice mail, irons, hair dryers. **Leisure Activities:** exercise room. **Guest Services:** valet and coin laundry. **Business Services:** meeting rooms. **Cards:** AX, CB, DC, DS, MC, VI.

SOME UNITS

HYATT REGENCY DEARBORN *Book at aaa.com* Phone: (313)593-1234 **115**

ⒶⒶⒶ (SAVE)

◇◇◇ ◇◇◇

Large-scale Hotel

All Year 1P: $99-$199 2P: $99-$199 XP: $25 F18
Location: Jct SR 39 (Southfield Frwy), 0.3 mi w on Michigan Ave, 0.3 mi n on Evergreen Rd, then e on Fairlane Rd. Located opposite Ford Motor Company World Headquarters. Fairlane Town Center 48126. Fax: 313/593-3366. **Facility:** A spectacular 16-story atrium and a chic lobby of stainless steel, polished wood and dramatic lighting give this hotel a modern, sophisticated feel. 772 units. 741 one-bedroom standard units. 31 one-bedroom suites, some with whirlpools. 13 stories, interior corridors. *Bath:* combo or shower only. **Parking:** on-site and valet. **Terms:** cancellation fee imposed. **Amenities:** voice mail, irons, hair dryers. *Some:* fax. **Dining:** 3 restaurants, 6:30 am-10 pm, Fri-Sun to midnight, cocktails, also, Bistro on 2, see separate listing, nightclub. **Pool(s):** heated indoor. **Leisure Activities:** sauna, whirlpool, exercise room. **Guest Services:** gift shop, valet laundry, airport transportation (fee)-Detroit Metro Airport. **Business Services:** conference facilities, business center. **Cards:** AX, CB, DC, DS, JC, MC, VI.
(See color ad below)

FEE SOME UNITS FEE FEE

(See map and index starting on p. 226)

RED ROOF INN-DEARBORN   *Book at aaa.com*   Phone: (313)278-9732   **117**

AAA SAVE

6/13-9/11	1P: $69-$90	2P: $76-$97	XP: $7	F18
4/1-6/12	1P: $62-$83	2P: $69-$90	XP: $7	F18
9/12-12/31	1P: $59-$80	2P: $66-$87	XP: $7	F18
1/1-3/31	1P: $57-$65	2P: $64-$72	XP: $7	F18

Motel   **Location:** Jct US 12 (Michigan Ave) and SR 24 (Telegraph Rd). 24130 Michigan Ave 48124. Fax: 313/278-9741. **Facility:** 111 one-bedroom standard units. 2 stories, exterior corridors. *Bath:* combo or shower only. **Parking:** on-site. **Terms:** small pets only. **Amenities:** video games (fee), voice mail. **Cards:** AX, CB, DC, DS, MC, VI. **Special Amenities:** free local telephone calls and free newspaper.

SOME UNITS

🛏 🛗 🖥 🗝 📷 🐾 📠 / ⨉ 🔲 🖥 /

THE RITZ-CARLTON, DEARBORN   *Book at aaa.com*   Phone: (313)441-2000   **113**

AAA SAVE

All Year   1P: $135-$295   2P: $135-$295

Large-scale Hotel   **Location:** SR 39 (Southfield Frwy), between Ford Rd and Michigan Ave exits, on Service Dr. 300 Town Center Dr 48126. Fax: 313/441-2051. **Facility:** Elegance and a refined atmosphere are the hallmarks of this luxurious in-town hotel. 308 units. 295 one-bedroom standard units. 13 one-bedroom suites ($339-$1500). 11 stories, interior corridors. *Bath:* combo or shower only. **Parking:** on-site and valet. **Terms:** [AP], [BP] & [CP] meal plans available, package plans - weekends, pets ($200 deposit). **Amenities:** video games (fee), CD players, dual phone lines, voice mail, safes, honor bars, irons, hair dryers. **Dining:** The Grill at The Ritz-Carlton, Dearborn, see separate listing, entertainment. **Pool(s):** heated indoor. **Leisure Activities:** saunas, whirlpool, tennis & racquetball privileges, exercise room. *Fee:* massage. **Guest Services:** gift shop, valet laundry, area transportation-within 5 mi. **Business Services:** conference facilities, business center. **Cards:** AX, DC, DS, JC, MC, VI. **Special Amenities:** free newspaper.

SOME UNITS

[S D] 🔌 🛏 🍽 24 🖥 🗝 📷 🐾 ⨉ 📠 / ⨉ VCR 🖥 🖥 /
FEE FEE   FEE

TOWNEPLACE SUITES   *Book at aaa.com*   Phone: (313)271-0200   **111**

6/1-10/31	1P: $109
4/1-5/31	1P: $104
11/1-3/31	1P: $99

Small-scale Hotel   **Location:** SR 39 (Southfield Frwy), exit 7 (Ford Rd), just e, then 0.8 mi n. 6141 Mercury Dr 48126. Fax: 313/271-3177. **Facility:** Smoke free premises. 148 units. 120 one-bedroom standard units with kitchens. 6 one- and 22 two-bedroom suites with kitchens. 3 stories, interior corridors. *Bath:* combo or shower only. **Parking:** on-site. **Terms:** pets ($100 deposit, $5 extra charge). **Amenities:** dual phone lines, voice mail, irons, hair dryers. *Some:* high-speed Internet (fee). **Pool(s):** heated outdoor. **Leisure Activities:** exercise room. **Guest Services:** sundries, valet and coin laundry. **Business Services:** business center. **Cards:** AX, DC, DS, JC, MC, VI.

SOME UNITS

🛏 🖥 🗝 🐾 📷 📠 🔲 🖥 🖥 / ⨉ VCR
FEE   FEE

─────── **WHERE TO DINE** ───────

ANNAM RESTAURANT VIETNAMIEN   Lunch: $10-$15   Dinner: $10-$18   Phone: 313/565-8744   **131**

AAA

Nouvelle Vietnamese   **Location:** Jct US 24 (Telegraph Rd) and 12 (Michigan Ave). 22053 Michigan Ave 48124. **Hours:** 11 am-2:30 & 5-9 pm, Fri-11 pm, Sat 5 pm-11 pm. Closed major holidays; also Sun. **Reservations:** accepted. **Features:** Named for ancient Vietnam, this small, tastefully decorated and designed space offers a representative menu of authentic dishes such as Pho. Extraordinary flavors and colourful presentations are emphasized through subtle use of seasonings and mini bouquets of fresh herbs. Dressy casual; wine only. **Parking:** street. **Cards:** AX, MC, VI.

🖥 ⨉

BD'S MONGOLIAN BARBEQUE   Lunch: $7-$11   Dinner: $13   Phone: 313/792-9660   **132**

Mongolian   **Location:** Jct US 24 (Telegraph Rd) and 12 (Michigan Ave), 0.3 mi e. 22115 Michigan Ave 48124. **Hours:** 10:30 am-10:30 pm, Fri-11:30 pm, Sat 11 am-11:30 pm, Sun 11 am-10 pm. Closed major holidays. **Features:** A busy, popular, sometimes loud, and always informal dining spot that features a do-it-yourself stir-fry. Make up your own combination, and they cook it for you. There is also a varied salad bar. Casual dress; cocktails. **Parking:** on-site. **Cards:** AX, DS, MC, VI.

🖥 ⨉

BENIHANA   Lunch: $7-$12   Dinner: $14-$30   Phone: 313/593-3200   **120**

Japanese   **Location:** 18601 Hubbard Dr 48126. **Hours:** 11 am-2:30 & 5:30-10 pm, Sat 4:30 pm-10:30 pm, Sun 3 pm-9 pm. Closed major holidays. **Reservations:** accepted. **Features:** For those who have never tried Japanese cuisine, this restaurant—with its trademarked tableside preparations, including flashing knifes and a great deal of showmanship and fun—is a good place to start. The menu reflects a wide range of Japanese specialties, including teriyaki, tempura and sushi bar creations. Dressy casual; cocktails. **Parking:** on-site. **Cards:** AX, MC, VI.

🍸 ⨉

BIG FISH SEAFOOD BISTRO   Lunch: $6-$13   Dinner: $7-$24   Phone: 313/336-6350   **123**

Seafood   **Location:** At Fairlane Town Center near Evergreen Rd. 700 Town Center Dr 48126. **Hours:** 11 am-10 pm, Fri & Sat-11 pm, Sun 3 pm-9 pm. Closed major holidays. **Features:** Popular with the local corporate types, the eclectic restaurant is dotted with stylized fish and nautical memorabilia. Specializing in fresh seafood flown in daily, the daily catch menu changes constantly, but the varied steak, chicken and pasta dishes are reliable choices. Casual dress; cocktails. **Parking:** on-site and valet. **Cards:** AX, DC, DS, MC, VI.

🖥 🍸 ⨉

(See map and index starting on p. 226)

BISTRO ON 2 Lunch: $10-$15 Dinner: $10-$15 Phone: 313/593-1234 124
American
Location: Jct SR 39 (Southfield Frwy), 0.3 mi w on Michigan Ave, 0.3 mi n on Evergreen Rd, then e on Fairlane Rd; in Hyatt Regency Dearborn. Fairlane Town Center 48126. **Hours:** 6:30 am-10 pm, Fri & Sat-midnight. **Reservations:** accepted. **Features:** On the second floor of the hotel, the quiet restaurant overlooks the lobby. Locals frequent this place for the creative twists on its luncheon buffet. Casual dress; cocktails. **Parking:** on-site and valet. **Cards:** AX, DC, DS, MC, VI.

BUDDY'S RESTAURANT PIZZERIA Lunch: $6-$17 Dinner: $6-$17 Phone: 313/562-5900 129
Pizza
Location: Jct US 24 (Telegraph Rd) and US 12 (Michigan Ave), 0.3 mi e. 22148 Michigan Ave 48124. **Hours:** 11 am-10 pm, Sat 11:30 am-11 pm, Sun noon-10 pm. Closed: 11/25, 12/25 & Easter. **Features:** In business since 1946, the pizzeria is known for its square, deep-dish pizza with crispy, buttery crust and a blend of four cheeses. Diners might want to save room for the huge brownie sundae, which could probably serve a family of four. The decor is styled after an old-time diner and soda fountain, making this a great place for a casual dinner with friends or family. Nine locations are in the greater Detroit area, so finding a convenient one shouldn't be difficult. Casual dress; cocktails. **Parking:** on-site. **Cards:** AX, DC, DS, MC, VI.

CASTALDI'S MARKET & GRILL Lunch: $6-$8 Dinner: $7-$12 Phone: 313/441-6600 125
Italian
Location: At Fairlane Town Center; next to Star Theatres. 18900 Michigan Ave 48126. **Hours:** 11 am-9 pm, Fri & Sat-10 pm, Sun 3 pm-9 pm. Closed: 11/25, 12/25. **Reservations:** accepted. **Features:** Designed with an Italian marketplace in mind, the restaurant has tentlike swags and bunches of garlic, sausages and peppers hanging from the pillars. Accompanied by live musicians, strolling servers serenade diners with an impressive repertoire of songs. Among classic dishes are a good array of pasta dishes and a number of homemade desserts. Casual dress; cocktails. **Parking:** on-site and valet. **Cards:** AX, DC, DS, MC, VI.

GEORGE & HARRY'S BLUE'S CAFE Lunch: $6-$12 Dinner: $14-$22 Phone: 313/359-2799 126
American
Location: Jct US 24 (Telegraph Rd) and US 12 (Michigan Ave), 0.4 mi e. 22048 Michigan Ave 48124. **Hours:** 10:30 am-2 am, Sat 4 pm-2 am, Sun noon-8 pm. Closed major holidays. **Features:** Slightly reminiscent of the art deco style, the dining room doubles as a large, open listening room most Wednesdays through Saturdays as local and national jazz and blues musicians play live after 9 p.m. Representative of the extensive offerings are prime rib, barbecue ribs, red snapper Key West, jambalaya and chicken Marsala. Casual dress; cocktails. **Parking:** valet and street. **Cards:** AX, MC, VI.

THE GRILL AT THE EARLY AMERICAN ROOM Dinner: $18-$26 Phone: 313/271-2700 135
American
Location: SR 39 (Southfield Frwy), exit Oakwood Blvd, 1 mi w; in The Dearborn Inn, A Marriott Hotel. 20301 Oakwood Blvd 48124. **Hours:** 5:30 pm-10 pm, Sun 10 am-2 pm. Closed: Mon & Tues. **Reservations:** accepted. **Features:** Located in the first airport hotel in the country, this traditional and elegant dining room features attentive service and a creative menu that changes seasonally. Dressy casual; cocktails. **Parking:** on-site and valet. **Cards:** AX, CB, DC, DS, MC, VI.

THE GRILL AT THE RITZ-CARLTON, DEARBORN Lunch: $18-$25 Dinner: $25-$45 Phone: 313/441-2000 122
Continental
Location: SR 39 (Southfield Frwy), between Ford Rd and Michigan Ave exits, on Service Dr; in The Ritz-Carlton, Dearborn. 300 Town Center Dr 48126. **Hours:** 6 am-2:30 & 6-10 pm, Fri & Sat-11 pm. **Reservations:** suggested. **Features:** This elegant restaurant, reminiscent of an English country club, offers impeccable service and creative takes on a continental menu that features classics such as Steak Tartare, Muscovy Duck Breast and Dover Sole. Dressy casual; cocktails. **Parking:** on-site and valet. **Cards:** AX, CB, DC, DS, JC, MC, VI.

KABOB VILLAGE Lunch: $6-$10 Dinner: $6-$10 Phone: 313/581-0055 121
Lebanese
Location: Downtown. 13823 Michigan Ave 48126. **Hours:** 11 am-11 pm. Closed major holidays. **Features:** All your Middle Eastern favorites such as chicken and lamb kabobs, tabbouleh and humus are found at this bright and comfortable eatery. Casual dress. **Parking:** on-site. **Cards:** AX, MC, VI.

KIERNAN'S STEAK HOUSE Lunch: $8-$15 Dinner: $12-$20 Phone: 313/565-4260 127
American
Location: 1.3 mi w of jct SR 39 on US 12. 21931 Michigan Ave 48124. **Hours:** 11 am-11 pm, Sat from 5 pm, Sun 4 pm-9 pm. Closed major holidays. **Reservations:** suggested. **Features:** As its name suggests, the restaurant focuses on steakhouse fare: veal, pork, chicken, seafood and, of course, beef. Silk lampshades and subtle illumination add to the romantic ambience of the tavern-like dining room. Servers are friendly and attentive. Casual dress; cocktails. **Parking:** on-site and valet. **Cards:** AX, DS, MC, VI.

LAPITA Lunch: $6-$7 Dinner: $10-$14 Phone: 313/565-7482 133
Ethnic
Location: On US 12 (Michigan Ave), between Outer Dr and Military Rd; 1 mi e of jct US 24 (Telegraph Rd). 22435 Michigan Ave 48124. **Hours:** 10 am-11 pm, Sun 11 am-10 pm. Closed: 11/25, 12/25. **Features:** The comfortable restaurant specializes in Middle Eastern cuisine, such as chicken and lamb kabobs, tabbouleh and hummus. Wall murals depict such scenes as people riding horses, a woman carrying a basket of bread, towering palm trees and a mosque. Casual dress. **Parking:** on-site. **Cards:** AX, DC, DS, MC, VI.

LA SHISH Lunch: $7-$9 Dinner: $8-$14 Phone: 313/562-7200 130
Lebanese
Location: Jct SR 39 (Southfield Frwy), 1.3 mi w. 22039 Michigan Ave 48124. **Hours:** 10 am-11 pm, Fri & Sat-midnight. Closed: 11/25, 12/25. **Features:** If you haven't tried Lebanese cuisine, here's your opportunity. Among the authentic Middle Eastern selections are seafood entrees and such delicious kabobs as the lamb. The flat bread is fresh and flavorful. Service is friendly and attentive. Casual dress; cocktails. **Parking:** on-site. **Cards:** AX, DC, DS, MC, VI.

(See map and index starting on p. 226)

RICHTER'S CHALET   Lunch: $4-$8   Dinner: $7-$17   Phone: 313/565-0484   134
   Location: Jct US 24 (Telegraph Rd) and 12 (Michigan Ave), just e. 23920 Michigan Ave 48124. **Hours:** 11 am-8:30
   pm, Fri-9 pm, Sat 3 pm-9 pm, Sun noon-7 pm. Closed: 7/4, 11/25, 12/24, 12/25; also Mon. **Features:** The
   cozy restaurant offers a menu of authentic German dishes—such as potato pancakes, Wiener schnitzel
   and sauerbraten—with a handful of American dishes also described. Light background music and Bavarian

German   appointments set the tone in the dining room. Casual dress. **Parking:** on-site. **Cards:** MC, VI.

RISTORANTE CIAO   Lunch: $11-$20   Dinner: $11-$20   Phone: 313/274-2426   128
   Location: 1.3 mi w of jct SR 39 (Southfield Frwy) and US 12 (Michigan Ave), just s. 1024 Monroe St 48124.
   Hours: 11 am-2:30 & 5-11 pm, Sat from 5 pm. Closed major holidays; also Sun.
   Reservations: suggested. **Features:** Evoking images of the Tuscan countryside, this cozy and candlelit

Italian   restaurant is well known for its creative preparations of Italian favorites. Dressy casual; wine only. **Parking:**
street. **Cards:** AX, DS, MC, VI.

FARMINGTON HILLS pop. 82,111   (See map and index starting on p. 226)

──────── WHERE TO STAY ────────

CANDLEWOOD SUITES   *Book at aaa.com*   Phone: (248)324-0540   78
   All Year   1P: $99-$144   2P: $99-$144
   Location: I-696, exit I-96E/I-275S/SR 5, just s to SR 5 N, then 2 mi n to 12 Mile Rd, 1.3 mi e on 12 Mile Rd, then 0.3
Small-scale Hotel   mi s on Halsted Rd. 37555 Hills Tech Dr 48331. Fax: 248/324-0541. **Facility:** 127 units. 94 one-bedroom standard units with efficiencies. 33 one-bedroom suites with efficiencies. 4 stories, interior corridors. **Parking:** on-
site. **Terms:** weekly rates available, small pets only ($150 deposit). **Amenities:** video library, CD players, voice mail, irons, hair
dryers. **Leisure Activities:** exercise room. **Cards:** AX, DC, DS, MC, VI.

SOME UNITS

COURTYARD BY MARRIOTT   *Book at aaa.com*   Phone: 248/553-0000   77
   All Year   1P: $104   2P: $104
   Location: I-696, exit 5 (Orchard Lake Rd), just w. 31525 12 Mile Rd 48334. Fax: 248/553-7630. **Facility:** 202 units.
   158 one-bedroom standard units, some with whirlpools. 44 one-bedroom suites ($129), some with whirlpools.
Small-scale Hotel   3 stories, interior corridors. **Parking:** on-site. **Terms:** [BP] meal plan available. **Amenities:** voice mail, irons,
hair dryers. *Fee:* video games, high-speed Internet. **Pool(s):** heated indoor. **Leisure Activities:** saunas, whirlpool, exercise
room. **Guest Services:** sundries, valet and coin laundry, area transportation. **Business Services:** conference facilities, business
center. **Cards:** AX, CB, DC, DS, JC, MC, VI.

SOME UNITS

FAIRFIELD INN BY MARRIOTT   *Book at aaa.com*   Phone: 248/442-9800   76
   Property failed to provide current rates
   Location: I-696, exit 5 (Orchard Lake Rd), just n, then just e on 12 Mile Rd, then just s. 27777 Stansbury Blvd 48334.
   Fax: 248/442-9563. **Facility:** 91 one-bedroom standard units, some with whirlpools. 3 stories, interior corri-
Motel   dors. *Bath:* combo or shower only. **Parking:** on-site. **Amenities:** video games, voice mail, irons, hair dryers.
Pool(s): heated indoor. **Leisure Activities:** whirlpool, exercise room. **Guest Services:** valet and coin laundry.

SOME UNITS

HOLIDAY INN FARMINGTON HILLS   *Book at aaa.com*   Phone: (248)477-4000   80
   All Year   1P: $89-$129   2P: $89-$129
   Location: I-275, exit 165 (SR 5/Grand River Ave), 1 mi e, then just s. 38123 W 10 Mile Rd 48335. Fax: 248/476-4570.
Small-scale Hotel   **Facility:** 262 one-bedroom standard units, some with whirlpools. 3-5 stories, interior corridors. **Parking:** on-
site. **Terms:** [AP] meal plan available. **Amenities:** video games, voice mail, irons, hair dryers. **Pool(s):**
heated outdoor, heated indoor. **Leisure Activities:** sauna, whirlpool, putting green, exercise room. *Fee:* game room. **Guest Services:** gift shop, valet and coin laundry. **Cards:** AX, CB, DC, DS, JC, MC, VI.

SOME UNITS
FEE   FEE

RADISSON SUITE HOTEL FARMINGTON HILLS   *Book at aaa.com*   Phone: (248)477-7800   81
   All Year [BP]   1P: $85-$119   2P: $85-$119   XP: $10   F
   Location: I-96/275 and SR 102, exit 165 (Grand River Ave), just s to Halsted Rd. 37529 Grand River Ave 48335.
   Fax: 248/478-3799. **Facility:** 137 one-bedroom suites, some with whirlpools. 4 stories, interior corridors.
   Bath: combo or shower only. **Amenities:** video games, voice mail, irons, hair dryers.
Small-scale Hotel   **Dining:** 6:30-9:30 am, 11-2 & 5-10 pm, Sat & Sun 8 am-11 & 5-10 pm, cocktails. **Pool(s):** heated indoor.
   Leisure Activities: sauna, whirlpool, exercise room. *Fee:* game room. **Guest Services:** valet laundry. **Busi-
ness Services:** meeting rooms. **Cards:** AX, CB, DC, DS, JC, MC, VI. **Special Amenities:** free full breakfast and free news-
paper.** *(See color ad p 313)*

SOME UNITS
FEE

RED ROOF INN-FARMINGTON HILLS   *Book at aaa.com*   Phone: (248)478-8640   79
   All Year   1P: $52-$66   2P: $57-$71   XP: $5   F18
   Location: I-96/275 and SR 5, exit 165 (Grand River Ave), just w. 24300 Sinacola Ct 48335. Fax: 248/478-4842.
   Facility: 108 one-bedroom standard units. 2 stories, exterior corridors. *Bath:* combo or shower only. **Parking:**
   on-site. **Amenities:** video games (fee), voice mail. **Cards:** AX, CB, DC, DS, MC, VI. **Special Amenities:** free
Motel   local telephone calls and free newspaper.

SOME UNITS
FEE   FEE

(See map and index starting on p. 226)

──────── WHERE TO DINE ────────

CAFE' CORTINA Classic   **Lunch:** $12-$18   **Dinner:** $24-$35   **Phone:** 248/474-3033   ⑨⑤
▼▼▼▼▼ ▼▼▼▼▼ **Location:** 0.3 mi e of jct Orchard Lake Rd. 30715 W 10 Mile Rd 48336. **Hours:** 11 am-10:30 pm, Sat from 5 pm.
          Closed major holidays; also Sun. **Reservations:** required. **Features:** While the area by the fireplace is the
Traditional Italian most requested, there isn't a bad seat in the dimly lit, demurely elegant dining room. Northern Italian
          cuisine reflects a few Southern accents and employs fresh herbs and vegetables grown in the kitchen's
own garden. Both homemade and luxurious imported ingredients abound. While attentive and professional, service lends to a
relaxed and unobtrusive experience. Dressy casual; cocktails. **Parking:** on-site and valet. **Cards:** AX, DC, DS, MC, VI.
                                                                              Ⓜ ☒

EVEREST EXPRESS NEPALI CUISINE   **Lunch:** $6-$10   **Dinner:** $8-$12   **Phone:** 248/474-8024   ⑨⑥
▼▼▼▼ **Location:** I-696, exit 5 (Orchard Lake Rd), 2.4 mi s. 23331 Orchard Lake Rd 48336. **Hours:** 11 am-3 & 5-10 pm.
          Closed major holidays; also Mon. **Features:** The distinct cuisine of the Himalayas merges influences of
Nepali   both Indian and Tibetan cultures. The rare cuisine, prepared in only a handful of Nepali restaurants in
          America, is simple and subtle in flavor. In addition to vegetarian preparations are several dishes that
incorporate meat, excluding beef. Nepali cuisine makes extensive use of common ingredients and a variety of spices. Casual
dress. **Parking:** on-site. **Cards:** AX, DS, MC, VI.
                                                                              ☒

FAMILY BUGGY RESTAURANT   **Lunch:** $7-$9   **Dinner:** $9-$15   **Phone:** 248/553-9090   ⑨①
▼▼▼▼ ▼▼▼▼ **Location:** I-696, exit 5 (Orchard Lake Rd), 1 mi n. 29335 Orchard Lake Rd 48334. **Hours:** 11 am-9 pm, Fri &
          Sat-10 pm. Closed: 1/1, 11/25, 12/25. **Features:** Antique furnishings and decorations give you the feeling
American   that you've slipped into yesteryear. The homey, family-oriented restaurant is a comfortable place in which
          to enjoy such reliable favorites as smothered chicken breast and barbecue ribs. Casual dress. **Parking:**
on-site. **Cards:** MC, VI.
                                                                              Ⓜ ☒

HONG HUA   **Lunch:** $7-$9   **Dinner:** $10-$25   **Phone:** 248/489-2280   ⑨②
▼▼▼▼▼ **Location:** I-696, exit 5, just n. 27925 Orchard Lake Rd 48334. **Hours:** 11 am-10:30 pm, Fri & Sat-midnight, Sun
          noon-midnight. **Reservations:** accepted. **Features:** An exacting eye for detail is evident in this upscale,
Cantonese   white table-clothed Cantonese restaurant. Everything from the "floral" arrangements of carved vegetables
          to the fresh fish kept in aerated freshwater tanks in the kitchen speak volumes about the 120-item menu.
Offering such specialties such as shark's fin and bird's nest soups as well as fresh abalone, the menu also pays a brief nod to
hot and spicy Szechuan style and does offers more traditional Chinese-American fare. Dressy casual; cocktails. **Parking:**
on-site. **Cards:** AX, DC, DS, MC, VI.
                                                                              Ⓜ ☒

LOVING SPOONFUL   **Lunch:** $11-$24   **Dinner:** $11-$24   **Phone:** 248/489-9400   ⑨④
▼▼▼▼ ▼▼▼▼ **Location:** 12 Mile Rd between Halsted and Haggerty rds; adjacent to Copper Creek Golf Course. 27925 Golf Pointe
          Blvd 48331. **Hours:** 11 am-3 & 5-10 pm, Sat 11 am-11 pm, Sun 4 pm-9 pm. Closed major holidays.
American   **Reservations:** accepted. **Features:** Large French doors open out over the ninth hole of the Copper Creek
          golf course in the casually elegant dining room. Although creative offerings range from fried red tomatoes
and smoked grouper to slow-smoked country ribs, the sophisticated comfort food never loses sight of clean, precise flavors.
Dressy casual; cocktails. **Parking:** on-site. **Cards:** AX, DS, MC, VI.
                                                                              Ⓜ ⍫ ☒

TRIBUTE   **Dinner:** $30-$37   **Phone:** 248/848-9393   ⑨③
▼▼▼▼▼ ▼▼▼▼▼ **Location:** I-696, exit 5 (Orchard Lake Rd), just n, then just w. 31425 W 12 Mile Rd 48334. **Hours:** 5:30 pm-9:30
          pm. Closed major holidays; also Sun & Mon. **Reservations:** required. **Features:** This restaurant will get
Nouvelle French your attention as you enter and are greeted by a pleasant and charming hostess. The extensive wine racks
          on the way to your table will tempt your patience. The dining room ambience is surrounded with high
banquette booths and an elegant open drape between the two main dining rooms. A nightly seven-course vegetable or the
special degustation menu is a popular item that may be your choice among the several entree offerings. An exceptional dining
experience. Semi-formal attire; cocktails. **Parking:** valet. **Cards:** AX, DC, DS, MC, VI.
                                                                              Ⓜ ⍫ ☒

FERNDALE pop. 22,105 (See map and index starting on p. 226)

──────── WHERE TO DINE ────────

ASSAGGI MEDITERRANEAN BISTRO   **Lunch:** $12-$15   **Dinner:** $18-$26   **Phone:** 248/584-3499   ⑧⑥
▼▼▼▼ **Location:** Jct Woodward Ave and 9 Mile Rd, just w. 330 W 9 Mile Rd 48220. **Hours:** 11 am-2 & 5-10 pm, Fri &
          Sat-11 pm, Sun 11 am-3 & 4-9 pm; Sunday brunch. Closed major holidays; also Mon.
Mediterranean **Reservations:** accepted. **Features:** Using fresh herbs and vegetables grown in its own kitchen garden,
          this storefront restaurant highlights an innovative menu that mixes and matches Mediterranean styles such
as French, Spanish, Greek and Lebanese dishes, regardless of national borders. Dressy casual; wine only. **Parking:** valet and
street. **Cards:** AX, DC, DS, MC, VI.
                                                                              Ⓜ ☒

THE FERN   **Lunch:** $7-$8   **Dinner:** $7-$8   **Phone:** 248/542-6180   ⑧⑦
▼▼▼ **Location:** Jct Woodward Ave and 9 Mile Rd, just w. 205 W 9 Mile Rd 48220. **Hours:** 11:30 am-3 & 4:30-9 pm, Sat
          noon-7 pm. Closed major holidays. **Features:** Ordering sandwiches by street name could be confusing for
Deli/Subs   an out-of-towner, but a little local geography never hurt anyone. Customers can mix and match to create
Sandwiches their own combinations of delicatessen sandwiches, soups and salads. Casual dress. **Parking:** street.
          Cards: MC, VI.
                                                                              ☒

(See map and index starting on p. 226)

MARIA'S FRONT ROOM | **Dinner: $14-$17** | **Phone:** 248/542-7379 | 88
♦♦ ♦♦
Italian
Location: Jct Woodward Ave and 9 Mile Rd, just w. 215 W 9 Mile Rd 48220. **Hours:** 5 pm-10 pm, Mon-9 pm. Closed major holidays; also Sun. **Reservations:** accepted. **Features:** A long, narrow storefront location, this unassuming restaurant comes complete with red and white table cloths and candles stuck in chianti bottles. Focusing on simple Italian dishes such as spaghetti alla puttanesca and pizzas, this restaurant also features the only house-made wine in Michigan. Casual dress; wine only. **Parking:** street. **Cards:** AX, DS, MC, VI.

TOAST | **Lunch: $5-$10** | **Phone:** 248/398-0444 | 85
♦♦♦♦ ♦♦♦♦
American
Location: Just n of 9 Mile Rd. 23144 Woodward Ave 48220. **Hours:** 7 am-3 pm, Sat & Sun from 8 am. Closed major holidays; also Mon. **Features:** True to its namesake, the cheerful restaurant displays a collection of toasters on one wall as a gentle reminder that breakfast is indeed the most important meal of the day. In addition to traditional breakfast items, the menu lists such creative takes as Grand Marnier or bananas Foster French toast and breakfast burritos. Casual dress. **Parking:** on-site and street. **Cards:** AX, MC, VI.

FLAT ROCK pop. 8,488

——— **WHERE TO STAY** ———

SLEEP INN | *Book at aaa.com* | **Phone:** (734)782-9898
♦♦♦♦ ♦♦♦♦
Small-scale Hotel
All Year   1P: $59-$89   2P: $59-$89
Location: I-75, exit 29 (Gibraltar Rd), just e. 29101 Commerce Dr 48134. Fax: 734/783-5029. **Facility:** 62 one-bedroom standard units. 3 stories, interior corridors. **Terms:** [ECP] meal plan available. **Amenities:** hair dryers. *Some:* irons. Pool(s): heated indoor. **Leisure Activities:** whirlpool, exercise room. **Guest Services:** valet laundry, area transportation (fee). **Cards:** AX, DC, DS, MC, VI.

SOME UNITS

GROSSE POINTE FARMS pop. 9,764   (See map and index starting on p. 226)

——— **WHERE TO DINE** ———

THE HILL SEAFOOD AND CHOP HOUSE | **Lunch: $15-$25** | **Dinner: $15-$25** | **Phone:** 313/886-8101 | 104
♦♦ ♦♦ ♦♦
Steak & Seafood
Location: Downtown. 123 E Kercheval Ave 48236. **Hours:** 11 am-3 & 5-10 pm, Fri-11 pm, Sat 5 pm-11 pm, Sun 5 pm-9 pm. Closed major holidays. **Reservations:** accepted. **Features:** A country club atmosphere exudes through this comfortable and subtly upscale space. Simple and classic dishes such as Dover sole meuniere are prepared from the freshest fish while the 20 ounce rib chop is prepared with a light bourbon-butter sauce. Dressy casual; cocktails. **Parking:** valet and street. **Cards:** AX, DC, DS, MC, VI.

LUCY'S TAVERN ON THE HILL | **Lunch: $5-$23** | **Dinner: $5-$23** | **Phone:** 313/640-2020 | 103
♦♦ ♦♦
American
Location: Downtown. 115 Kercheval Ave 48236. **Hours:** 11 am-10 pm, Fri & Sat-midnight, Sun 2 pm-11 pm. Closed: 11/25, 12/25. **Features:** A popular local drinking and dining establishment, featuring a cozy, friendly pub-like atmosphere and sophisticated tavern-style meals. Try one of their scrumptious steaks complemented with tasty waffle fries and your favorite beer or wine. Casual dress; cocktails. **Parking:** street. **Cards:** AX, DS, MC, VI.

MACK AVENUE DINER | **Lunch: $5-$10** | **Dinner: $5-$10** | **Phone:** 313/886-0680 | 102
♦♦
American
Location: Just e of Moross Ave. 19841 Mack Ave 48236. **Hours:** 7 am-9 pm, Sun 8 am-3 pm. Closed major holidays. **Features:** The occasional wait for one of the limited number of tables may be an indication of the popularity of this spot. While the decor is straightforward, it's the homemade daily specials and desserts that bring regulars back. Casual dress. **Parking:** street. **Cards:** AX, DS, MC, VI.

GROSSE POINTE WOODS pop. 17,080

——— **WHERE TO DINE** ———

——— *The following restaurant has not been evaluated by AAA* ———
but is listed for your information only.

ALINOSI'S | **Phone:** 313/884-1993
[fyi]
Not evaluated. **Location:** Jct Vernier Rd. 20737 Mack Ave 48236. **Features:** The city's oldest confectioner has been handed down through several generations since its 1921 inception. Crowds flock here for hand-dipped chocolates and old-fashioned soda fountain three-layered spumoni: a top layer of pistachio ice cream, a middle layer of rum ice cream with chopped fruits and nuts and a bottom layer of chocolate ice cream.

LAKE ORION pop. 2,715

——— **WHERE TO STAY** ———

BEST WESTERN PALACE INN | *Book at aaa.com* | **Phone:** (248)391-2755
AAA [SAVE]
♦♦♦♦ ♦♦♦♦
Small-scale Hotel
All Year   1P: $100
Location: I-75, exit 81 (Lapeer Rd), 3.3 mi n. 2755 N Lapeer Rd 48360. Fax: 248/391-9722. **Facility:** 76 one-bedroom standard units, some with whirlpools. 2 stories, interior/exterior corridors. *Bath:* combo or shower only. **Parking:** on-site. **Terms:** [CP] meal plan available, small pets only ($25 fee). **Amenities:** voice mail, irons, hair dryers. Pool(s): heated indoor. **Leisure Activities:** whirlpool, exercise room. *Fee:* game room. **Guest Services:** valet and coin laundry. **Business Services:** meeting rooms, business center. **Cards:** AX, DC, DS, MC, VI. **Special Amenities:** free expanded continental breakfast and free local telephone calls.

SOME UNITS

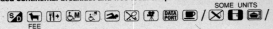

LINCOLN PARK pop. 40,008 (See map and index starting on p. 226)

------ WHERE TO STAY ------

SLEEP INN & SUITES　　　　　　　　　　　　　　　　　　　　　Phone: (313)381-5600　[134]
ⒶⒶⒶ [SAVE]　4/1-8/31 [ECP]　　　　1P: $99-$199　　　2P: $99-$199　　　XP: $10　　　F18
ⓋⓋⓋ　9/1-3/31 [ECP]　　　　1P: $89-$189　　　2P: $89-$189　　　XP: $10　　　F18
　　　　Location: I-75, exit 41 (Southfield Hwy). Located in front of the railway tracks. 1805 John A Papalas Dr 48146.
Small-scale Hotel　Fax: 313/381-5900. **Facility:** 82 one-bedroom standard units, some with whirlpools. 3 stories, interior corridors. *Bath:* combo or shower only. **Parking:** on-site. **Amenities:** dual phone lines, voice mail, safes (fee),
irons, hair dryers. **Pool(s):** heated indoor. **Leisure Activities:** sauna, exercise room. **Guest Services:** valet
and coin laundry. **Business Services:** meeting rooms. **Cards:** AX, CB, DC, DS, MC, VI. **Special Amenities:** free expanded
continental breakfast and free local telephone calls. *(See color ad p 256)*

SOME UNITS
🅂Ⓓ 🅛Ⓜ ⚿ ➰ 🎥 [DATA PORT] 🖵 / ✕ 🗄 🖼 /
FEE

LIVONIA pop. 100,545 (See map and index starting on p. 226)

------ WHERE TO STAY ------

AMERISUITES (DETROIT/LIVONIA)　*Book at aaa.com*　　　　　Phone: (734)953-9224　[94]
ⒶⒶⒶ [SAVE]　All Year [ECP]　　　1P: $89-$129　　　2P: $89-$129　　　XP: $10　　　F17
ⓋⓋⓋ　**Location:** I-275, exit 169A, just w on 7 Mile Rd. 19300 Haggerty Rd 48152. Fax: 734/953-9225. **Facility:** 128 one-
bedroom standard units. 6 stories, interior corridors. *Bath:* combo or shower only. **Parking:** on-site.
Terms: small pets only. **Amenities:** video games, voice mail, irons, hair dryers. *Some:* dual phone lines.
Small-scale Hotel　**Pool(s):** heated indoor. **Leisure Activities:** exercise room. **Guest Services:** coin laundry. **Business Services:** meeting rooms, business center. **Cards:** AX, CB, DC, DS, JC, MC, VI. **Special Amenities: free expanded continental breakfast and free newspaper.** *(See color ad p 236)*

SOME UNITS
🅂Ⓓ 🛏 🍽 ⚿ ➰ VCR 🎥 [DATA PORT] 🗄 🖼 🖵 / ✕ /

BEST WESTERN LAUREL PARK SUITES　*Book at aaa.com*　　Phone: (734)464-0050　[101]
ⓋⓋⓋ　All Year [ECP]　　　1P: $79-$109　　　2P: $79-$109
　　　　Location: I-275, exit 170, just e, then just s. Located across from the Laurel Park Mall. 16999 S Laurel Park Dr 48154.
Small-scale Hotel　Fax: 734/464-5869. **Facility:** 124 one-bedroom standard units, some with whirlpools. 2 stories (no elevator),
interior corridors. **Parking:** on-site. **Terms:** cancellation fee imposed. **Amenities:** video games, voice mail,
irons, hair dryers. **Pool(s):** heated outdoor. **Leisure Activities:** exercise room. **Guest Services:** valet laundry. **Business Services:** meeting rooms. **Cards:** AX, DC, DS, MC, VI.

SOME UNITS
[ASK] 🅂Ⓓ 🍽 📺 🍴 ➰ 🎥 [DATA PORT] 🗄 🖵 / ✕ /

COMFORT INN　*Book at aaa.com*　　　　　　　　　　　　　Phone: (734)458-7111　[102]
ⒶⒶⒶ [SAVE]　All Year [CP]　　　1P: $89-$99　　　2P: $89-$109　　　XP: $10　　　F18
ⓋⓋⓋ　**Location:** I-96, exit 176, just n on Middlebelt Rd. 29235 Buckingham Ave 48154. Fax: 734/458-1530. **Facility:** 112
one-bedroom standard units, some with whirlpools. 3 stories, interior corridors. **Parking:** on-site.
Amenities: video games, irons, hair dryers. *Some:* safes. **Leisure Activities:** exercise room. **Guest Serv-
ices:** valet and coin laundry. **Business Services:** meeting rooms. **Cards:** AX, CB, DC, DS, JC, MC, VI.
Small-scale Hotel　**Special Amenities: free continental breakfast and free local telephone calls.**

SOME UNITS
🅂Ⓓ 🍽 🍴 ➰ VCR 🎥 [DATA PORT] 🖵 / ✕ 🗄 🖼 /

COURTYARD BY MARRIOTT　*Book at aaa.com*　　　　　　　Phone: (734)462-2000　[95]
ⒶⒶⒶ [SAVE]　All Year　　　1P: $69-$124　　　2P: $69-$124
ⓋⓋⓋ　**Location:** I-275, exit 170, just e. 17200 N Laurel Park Dr 48152. Fax: 734/462-5907. **Facility:** 149 units. 137 one-
bedroom standard units. 12 one-bedroom suites. 2-3 stories, interior corridors. *Bath:* combo or shower only.
Parking: on-site. **Terms:** [BP] meal plan available. **Amenities:** high-speed Internet, voice mail, irons, hair
dryers. **Dining:** 6:30-10 am, Sat & Sun 7-11 am. **Pool(s):** heated indoor. **Leisure Activities:** whirlpool, ex-
Small-scale Hotel　ercise room. **Guest Services:** valet and coin laundry. **Business Services:** meeting rooms. **Cards:** AX, CB,
DC, DS, JC, MC, VI. **Special Amenities: early check-in/late check-out and preferred room (subject to availability with ad-
vanced reservations).**

SOME UNITS
🅂Ⓓ 🍽 📺 ➰ 🎥 [DATA PORT] 🖵 / ✕ 🖼 /

EMBASSY SUITES HOTEL　*Book at aaa.com*　　　　　　　Phone: (734)462-6000　[93]
ⓋⓋⓋ　All Year [BP]　　　1P: $109-$179　　　2P: $119-$189　　　XP: $10　　　F17
　　　　Location: I-275, exit 169B (7 Mile Rd), just e, then 0.5 mi n. Located in Victor Corporate Park. 19525 Victor Pkwy 48152.
Small-scale Hotel　Fax: 734/462-6003. **Facility:** 239 units. 236 one- and 3 two-bedroom suites, some with whirlpools. 5 stories,
interior corridors. **Parking:** on-site. **Terms:** cancellation fee imposed. **Amenities:** dual phone lines, voice
mail, irons, hair dryers. *Fee:* video games, high-speed Internet. **Pool(s):** heated indoor. **Leisure Activities:** sauna, whirlpool, exercise room. **Guest Services:** gift shop, complimentary evening beverages, valet and coin laundry. **Business Services:** conference facilities. **Cards:** AX, CB, DC, DS, JC, MC, VI.

SOME UNITS
[ASK] 🅂Ⓓ 🍽 ➰ ✕ 🎥 [DATA PORT] 🗄 🖼 🖵 / ✕ VCR /
FEE

FAIRFIELD INN DETROIT/LIVONIA　*Book at aaa.com*　　　Phone: (734)953-8888　[96]
ⒶⒶⒶ [SAVE]　All Year　　　1P: $64-$89
ⓋⓋⓋ　**Location:** I-275, exit 170 (6 Mile Rd), just nw. 17350 Fox Dr 48152. Fax: 734/953-0732. **Facility:** 103 one-bedroom
standard units, some with whirlpools. 4 stories, interior corridors. *Bath:* combo or shower only. **Parking:** on-
site. **Terms:** [CP] meal plan available. **Amenities:** video mail, irons, hair dryers. **Pool(s):** heated indoor.
Small-scale Hotel　**Leisure Activities:** whirlpool, exercise room. **Guest Services:** valet and coin laundry. **Business Services:**
meeting rooms. **Cards:** AX, DC, DS, MC, VI. **Special Amenities: free expanded continental breakfast and
free local telephone calls.**

SOME UNITS
🅂Ⓓ 🍴 🍽 ➰ 🎥 [DATA PORT] 🗄 🖼 🖵 / ✕ 🗄 🖼 /

(See map and index starting on p. 226)

HOLIDAY INN LIVONIA-WEST *Book at aaa.com*   **Phone:** (734)464-1300 98
All Year   1P: $89-$149   2P: $99-$159   XP: $10   F16
Location: I-275, exit 170 (6 Mile Rd), just e. Located across from the Laurel Park Mall. 17123 Laurel Park Dr N 48152.
Small-scale Hotel Fax: 734/464-1596. **Facility:** 226 one-bedroom standard units, some with whirlpools. 3 stories, interior corridors. **Parking:** on-site. **Terms:** check-in 4 pm, cancellation fee imposed, [AP] meal plan available.
Amenities: video games (fee), dual phone lines, voice mail, irons, hair dryers. **Pool(s):** heated indoor. **Leisure Activities:** sauna, whirlpool, putting green, exercise room. **Guest Services:** valet and coin laundry. **Business Services:** conference facilities. **Cards:** AX, DC, DS, MC, VI. *(See color ad below)*

SOME UNITS

LIVONIA MARRIOTT *Book at aaa.com*   **Phone:** (734)462-3100 100
12/31-3/31   1P: $179-$209
4/1-12/30   1P: $169-$199
Small-scale Hotel **Location:** I-275, exit 170 (6 Mile Rd), just w. Located in the Laurel Park Mall. 17100 Laurel Park Dr N 48152.
6 stories, interior corridors. **Parking:** on-site. **Terms:** check-in 4 pm, cancellation fee imposed. **Amenities:** video games (fee), high-speed Internet, voice mail, irons, hair dryers. **Dining:** Sweet Lorraine's Cafe & Bar, see separate listing. **Pool(s):** heated indoor. **Leisure Activities:** saunas, whirlpool, exercise room. **Guest Services:** gift shop, valet laundry. **Business Services:** conference facilities. **Cards:** AX, CB, DC, DS, MC, VI.

SOME UNITS

FEE

QUALITY INN & SUITES *Book at aaa.com*   **Phone:** 734/261-6800 104
Property failed to provide current rates
Location: I-96, exit 176 (Middlebelt Rd), 1 mi s, then 0.5 mi w on SR 14 (Plymouth Rd). 30375 Plymouth Rd 48150.
Small-scale Hotel Fax: 734/261-9478. **Facility:** 127 units. 121 one-bedroom standard units. 6 one-bedroom suites with whirlpools. 2 stories (no elevator), interior corridors. **Parking:** on-site. **Amenities:** voice mail, irons, hair dryers.
Pool(s): outdoor. **Leisure Activities:** exercise room. **Fee:** game room. **Guest Services:** valet and coin laundry. **Business Services:** meeting rooms. *(See color ad p 243)*

SOME UNITS

RESIDENCE INN DETROIT-LIVONIA *Book at aaa.com*   **Phone:** (734)462-4201 99
5/1-10/31   1P: $99-$144
4/1-4/30 & 11/1-3/31   1P: $89-$129
Location: I-275, exit 170 (6 Mile Rd), just nw. 17250 Fox Dr 48152. Fax: 734/462-4203. **Facility:** 112 units. 56 one-bedroom standard units with efficiencies. 38 one- and 18 two-bedroom suites, some with efficiencies or kitchens. 4 stories, interior corridors. *Bath:* combo or shower only. **Parking:** on-site. **Terms:** check-in 4 pm, cancellation fee imposed, [BP] meal plan available, pets ($200 fee). **Amenities:** video games, dual phone lines, voice mail, irons, hair dryers. **Pool(s):** heated outdoor. **Leisure Activities:** whirlpool, exercise room, sports court. **Guest Services:** complimentary evening beverages: Mon-Thurs, valet and coin laundry. **Business Services:** meeting rooms. **Cards:** AX, CB, DC, DS, JC, MC, VI.

SOME UNITS

FEE

SUPER 8 MOTEL *Book at aaa.com*   **Phone:** (734)425-5150 103
All Year [CP]   1P: $49-$125   2P: $49-$125
Location: I-96, exit 176 (Middlebelt Rd), just e; exit 177 (Inkster Rd) westbound. 28512 Schoolcraft Rd 48150.
Motel Fax: 734/524-9646. **Facility:** 83 one-bedroom standard units, some with kitchens (no utensils). 2 stories (no elevator), exterior corridors. **Parking:** on-site. **Terms:** cancellation fee imposed. **Amenities:** *Some:* irons.
Guest Services: coin laundry. **Cards:** AX, DC, DS, MC, VI. **Special Amenities:** free continental breakfast and free local telephone calls.

SOME UNITS

(See map and index starting on p. 226)

TOWNEPLACE SUITES *Book at aaa.com* Phone: 734/542-7400 **97**

	6/1-9/2	1P: $59-$109	2P: $59-$109
	4/1-5/31 & 9/3-11/17	1P: $59-$99	2P: $59-$99
	11/18-3/31	1P: $54-$89	2P: $54-$89

Small-scale Hotel **Location:** I-275, exit 170 (6 Mile Rd), just nw. 17450 Fox Dr 48152. **Fax:** 734/542-7401. **Facility:** 95 units. 69 one-bedroom standard units with kitchens. 4 one- and 22 two-bedroom suites with kitchens. 3 stories, interior corridors. *Bath:* combo or shower only. **Parking:** on-site. **Amenities:** dual phone lines, voice mail, irons, hair dryers. **Pool(s):** heated outdoor. **Leisure Activities:** exercise room. **Guest Services:** sundries, valet and coin laundry. **Business Services:** business center. **Cards:** AX, CB, DC, DS, MC, VI.

SOME UNITS

ASK SD TI+ &M ▭ ≈ ♥ DATA PORT ▤ ▥ ▯ / ✕ /

──────── **WHERE TO DINE** ────────

FAMILY BUGGY RESTAURANT **Lunch:** $7-$9 **Dinner:** $9-$15 **Phone:** 734/427-8360 **113**

American **Location:** I-96, exit 176 (Middlebelt Rd), 1 mi s. 11502 Middlebelt Rd 48150. **Hours:** 11 am-9 pm, Fri & Sat-10 pm. Closed: 1/1, 11/25, 12/25. **Reservations:** accepted. **Features:** Antique furnishings and decorations give you the feeling that you've slipped into yesteryear. The homey, family-oriented restaurant is a comfortable place in which to enjoy such reliable favorites as smothered chicken breast and pot roast. Casual dress. **Parking:** on-site. **Cards:** MC, VI.

✕

FONTE D'AMORE **Lunch:** $8-$16 **Dinner:** $16-$25 **Phone:** 734/422-0770 **112**

Italian **Location:** I-96, exit 176 (Middlebelt Rd), 1 mi s, then 1.6 mi w. 32030 Plymouth Rd 48150. **Hours:** 11:30 am-4 & 5-10 pm, Fri-11 pm, Sat 5 pm-11 pm. Closed major holidays; also Sun. **Reservations:** suggested. **Features:** Named after the Italian village "Fountain of Love," the charming and romantic restaurant lives up to its name. Closely mirroring current trends in regional Italian cuisine, rustica cooking takes a lighter approach. Dishes seasoned with fresh herbs have clear, distinct flavors. Dressy casual; cocktails. **Parking:** on-site and valet. **Cards:** DS, MC, VI.

&M Y ✕

J. ALEXANDER'S RESTAURANT **Lunch:** $7-$23 **Dinner:** $7-$23 **Phone:** 734/464-9220 **110**

American **Location:** I-275, exit 169A (7 Mile Rd), 0.5 mi w. then just n. 19200 Haggerty Dr 48152. **Hours:** 11 am-11 pm, Fri & Sat-midnight, Sun-10 pm. Closed major holidays. **Features:** Part of a small but growing national chain, the informal dining room features exposed brick walls, carriage lights and a large, open kitchen as the focal point. Focusing on in-house-made items, the contemporary menu lists varied hardwood-grilled steaks, daily fresh seafood specials and prime rib. Casual dress; cocktails. **Parking:** on-site. **Cards:** AX, DC, DS, MC, VI.

&M Y ✕

SWEET LORRAINE'S CAFE & BAR **Lunch:** $6-$10 **Dinner:** $8-$12 **Phone:** 734/953-7480 **111**

American **Location:** I-275, exit 170 (6 Mile Rd), just w; in Livonia Marriott. 17100 N Laurel Park Dr 48152. **Hours:** 6:30 am-11 pm, Fri-midnight, Sat 7 am-midnight, Sun 7 am-11 pm. **Reservations:** suggested. **Features:** A step above the typical hotel restaurant, this bright and cheerful space serves an eclectic menu of continental standards such as steak and seafood as well as globally influenced items such as French pot pie or Spanish paella. Casual dress; cocktails. **Parking:** on-site. **Cards:** AX, CB, DC, DS, MC, VI.

Y ✕

MADISON HEIGHTS pop. 31,101 (See map and index starting on p. 226)

──────── **WHERE TO STAY** ────────

BEST WESTERN TROY-MADISON INN *Book at aaa.com* Phone: (248)583-7000 **32**

AAA SAVE All Year [ECP] 1P: $70-$149 2P: $75-$154 XP: $5 F16

Location: I-75, exit 65B (14 Mile Rd), just w. 1331 W 14 Mile Rd 48071. **Fax:** 248/583-1455. **Facility:** 81 one-bedroom standard units, some with whirlpools. 2 stories, interior corridors. **Parking:** on-site. **Amenities:** high-speed Internet, safes, irons, hair dryers. **Pool(s):** small heated indoor. **Leisure Activi-**

Small-scale Hotel **ties:** exercise room. **Fee:** game room. **Guest Services:** valet laundry. **Business Services:** meeting rooms, business center. **Cards:** AX, CB, DC, DS, MC, VI. **Special Amenities:** free expanded continental break-fast and free newspaper.

SOME UNITS

SD TI+ ≈ ♥ DATA PORT ▤ ▥ ▯ / ✕ /

(See map and index starting on p. 226)

ECONO LODGE *Book at aaa.com*

AAA SAVE
Motel

			Phone: (248)583-7700	34
6/1-9/30 [CP]	1P: $47-$56	2P: $47-$56	XP: $4	F18
4/1-5/31 & 10/1-3/31 [CP]	1P: $43-$52	2P: $43-$52	XP: $4	F18

Location: I-75, exit 65B, just w, then just s. 32703 Stephenson Hwy 48071. Fax: 248/583-0516. **Facility:** 149 one-bedroom standard units, some with kitchens (no utensils) and/or whirlpools. 1 story, exterior corridors. **Parking:** on-site. **Terms:** weekly rates available. **Pool(s):** outdoor. **Cards:** AX, DC, DS, MC, VI. **Special Amenities:** free continental breakfast and free local telephone calls.

SOME UNITS

FAIRFIELD INN BY MARRIOTT *Book at aaa.com*

Small-scale Hotel

		Phone: (248)588-3388	33
6/2-9/30	1P: $59-$109		
10/1-3/31	1P: $59-$89		
4/1-6/1	1P: $59-$79		

Location: I-75, exit 65B, just w, then just s. 32800 Stephenson Hwy 48071. Fax: 248/588-3388. **Facility:** 134 one-bedroom standard units. 3 stories, interior/exterior corridors. *Bath:* combo or shower only. **Parking:** on-site. **Terms:** cancellation fee imposed, weekly rates available. **Amenities:** irons, hair dryers. **Pool(s):** heated outdoor. **Guest Services:** valet laundry. **Cards:** AX, DC, DS, MC, VI.

SOME UNITS

HAMPTON INN *Book at aaa.com*

AAA SAVE
Small-scale Hotel

			Phone: (248)585-8881	37
All Year [ECP]	1P: $69-$109	2P: $69-$109		

Location: I-75, exit 65B, just w, then just s. 32420 Stephenson Hwy 48071. Fax: 248/585-9446. **Facility:** 124 one-bedroom standard units. 4 stories, interior corridors. **Parking:** on-site. **Terms:** [ECP] meal plan available. **Amenities:** voice mail, irons, hair dryers. **Leisure Activities:** sauna, exercise room. **Guest Services:** valet laundry. **Business Services:** meeting rooms. **Cards:** AX, CB, DC, DS, JC, MC, VI. **Special Amenities:** free expanded continental breakfast and free local telephone calls. *(See color ad p 264)*

SOME UNITS

RED ROOF INN *Book at aaa.com*

AAA SAVE
Motel

			Phone: (248)583-4700	36
5/23-10/30	1P: $53-$67	2P: $58-$72	XP: $5	F18
10/31-3/31	1P: $48-$65	2P: $53-$70	XP: $5	F18
4/1-5/22	1P: $47-$59	2P: $52-$64	XP: $5	F18

Location: I-75, exit 65A, just e, then just s. Located opposite the shopping mall. 32511 Concord Dr 48071. Fax: 248/583-2982. **Facility:** 108 one-bedroom standard units. 2 stories, exterior corridors. *Bath:* combo or shower only. **Parking:** on-site. **Terms:** small pets only. **Amenities:** video games (fee), voice mail. **Cards:** AX, CB, DC, DS, MC, VI. **Special Amenities:** free local telephone calls and free newspaper.

SOME UNITS
FEE FEE

RESIDENCE INN BY MARRIOTT-MADISON HEIGHTS *Book at aaa.com*

Condominium

			Phone: (248)583-4322	35
9/1-10/1	1P: $239	2P: $339		
1/1-3/31	1P: $134-$144	2P: $161-$181		
4/1-8/31 & 10/2-12/31	1P: $134	2P: $161		

Location: I-75, exit 65B, just w, then just s. 32650 Stephenson Hwy 48071. Fax: 248/583-9092. **Facility:** Designed for the extended-stay traveler or families, many of these apartment-style units feature fireplaces. 96 units. 72 one-bedroom standard units with kitchens. 24 one-bedroom suites with kitchens. 2 stories, exterior corridors. *Bath:* combo or shower only. **Parking:** on-site. **Terms:** cancellation fee imposed, [ECP] meal plan available, pets ($300 fee, $6 extra charge). **Amenities:** voice mail, irons, hair dryers. **Pool(s):** heated outdoor. **Leisure Activities:** whirlpool, exercise room, sports court. **Guest Services:** valet and coin laundry. **Cards:** AX, CB, DC, DS, JC, MC, VI.

SOME UNITS
FEE

───────── **WHERE TO DINE** ─────────

BIG FISH SEAFOOD BISTRO

Seafood

Lunch: $6-$13   **Dinner:** $7-$24   **Phone:** 248/585-9533   47

Location: I-75, exit 65, just w. 1111 W 14 Mile Rd 48071. **Hours:** 11 am-10 pm, Fri & Sat-11 pm, Sun 3 pm-9 pm. **Closed:** 12/25. **Reservations:** suggested. **Features:** Hot and cold soups, varied appetizers and creative desserts complement such innovatively prepared seafood entrees as whitefish Oscar. The festive, nautical atmosphere is inviting to families. The wait staff provides attentive service from start to finish. Casual dress; cocktails. **Parking:** on-site. **Cards:** AX, DC, DS, MC, VI.

BOODLE'S RESTAURANT

American

Lunch: $8-$13   **Dinner:** $9-$28   **Phone:** 248/399-5960   48

Location: I-75, exit 62, just e. 935 W 11 Mile Rd 48071. **Hours:** 11 am-11 pm, Fri-midnight, Sat 4 pm-midnight, Sun 10 am-10 pm. **Closed:** major holidays. **Reservations:** suggested, weekends. **Features:** A wide selection of well-prepared entrees—from steak Diane to Alaskan crab legs to seafood pasta—is listed on the restaurant's menu. The dark-stained walls give the dining room a warm, comfortable feel. Dessert choices are tempting and tasty. Casual dress; cocktails; entertainment. **Parking:** on-site. **Cards:** AX, DC, DS, MC, VI.

MILFORD pop. 6,272

——— WHERE TO DINE ———

APPLETEASER
American
Lunch: $8-$15   **Dinner:** $12-$20   **Phone:** 248/685-0989
Location: Downtown. 355 Main St 48381. **Hours:** 11 am-midnight, Sun 10:30 am-2:30 & 3-midnight. Closed major holidays. **Features:** In business for more than 20 years, this three story restaurant and bar offers something for every taste and whim. Burgers and pizza are offered beside grilled herb salmon and chocolate souffles. Dressy casual; cocktails. **Parking:** street. **Cards:** AX, DC, MC, VI.

FIVE LAKES GRILL
Regional American
Dinner: $14-$20   **Phone:** 248/684-7455
Location: At Main St and Commerce Rd. 424 N Main 48381. **Hours:** 4 pm-10 pm, Fri & Sat-11 pm. Closed major holidays; also Sun. **Reservations:** suggested. **Features:** Stylishly avant-garde and SoHo chic, the inviting dining room is deliberately stark. Imaginative creations include potato-crusted Lake Superior whitefish with lobster mousseline, pastaless Mediterranean vegetable lasagna and grilled portobello sandwich. Dressy casual; cocktails. **Parking:** on-site and street. **Cards:** AX, MC, VI.

MOUNT CLEMENS pop. 17,312

——— WHERE TO STAY ———

BEST WESTERN CONCORDE INN
Small-scale Hotel
Book at aaa.com

5/21-9/6	1P: $109	2P: $109	XP: $10	F18
4/1-5/20 & 9/7-3/31	1P: $99	2P: $99	XP: $10	F18

Phone: (586)493-7300
Location: I-94, exit 240B, 1 mi w, 0.5 mi s. 44315 Gratiot Ave 48036. Fax: 586/493-7330. **Facility:** 160 units. 141 one-bedroom standard units, some with kitchens and/or whirlpools. 19 one-bedroom suites ($139-$189) with whirlpools. 4 stories, interior corridors. *Bath:* combo or shower only. **Parking:** on-site. **Terms:** [CP] meal plan available. **Amenities:** video games, dual phone lines, voice mail, irons, hair dryers. **Leisure Activities:** sauna, racquetball court. *Fee:* massage, game room. **Guest Services:** sundries, valet and coin laundry, area transportation. **Business Services:** conference facilities, business center. **Cards:** AX, CB, DC, DS, MC, VI.

SOME UNITS

——— WHERE TO DINE ———

PAUL'S RIVERHOUSE
American
Lunch: $5-$13   **Dinner:** $9-$23   **Phone:** 586/465-5111
Location: I-94, exit 237, just w. 24240 N River Rd 48043. **Hours:** 11:30 am-11 pm, Fri & Sat noon-midnight, Sun noon-10 pm. Closed: 1/1, 12/25. **Reservations:** suggested, weekends. **Features:** Hearty portions of creative preparations of seafood, chicken and veal characterize the restaurant's menu. From the cozy lakefront patio, diners enjoy great views of the river and its resident wildlife. Black bean chili is among interesting soup choices. Casual dress; cocktails. **Parking:** on-site. **Cards:** AX, DC, DS, MC, VI.

NORTHVILLE pop. 6,459   (See map and index starting on p. 226)

——— WHERE TO STAY ———

HAMPTON INN
Small-scale Hotel
Book at aaa.com
All Year   1P: $104   **Phone:** 734/462-1119   90
Location: I-275, exit 167, just w, then just s. 20600 Haggerty Rd 48167. Fax: 734/462-6270. **Facility:** 125 one-bedroom standard units. 4 stories, interior corridors. *Bath:* some combo or shower only. **Parking:** on-site. **Terms:** [ECP] meal plan available, package plans - weekends & seasonal. **Amenities:** voice mail, irons, hair dryers. **Pool(s):** heated outdoor. **Leisure Activities:** sauna, exercise room. **Guest Services:** valet laundry. **Business Services:** meeting rooms. **Cards:** AX, DC, DS, MC, VI.

SOME UNITS

RAMADA LIMITED OF NOVI
Motel
All Year [ECP]   1P: $59-$69   2P: $59-$69   XP: $5   F17
Phone: (248)349-7400   89
Location: I-275, exit 167 (8 Mile Rd), just w, then 0.4 mi n. 21100 Haggerty Rd 48167. Fax: 248/349-7454. **Facility:** 125 one-bedroom standard units. 2 stories, interior/exterior corridors. **Parking:** on-site. **Terms:** weekly rates available. **Amenities:** voice mail, safes (fee), irons, hair dryers. **Leisure Activities:** exercise room. **Guest Services:** valet and coin laundry. **Business Services:** meeting rooms. **Cards:** AX, DC, DS, MC, VI.

SOME UNITS

——— WHERE TO DINE ———

BONFIRE BISTRO & BREWERY
American
Lunch: $6-$10   **Dinner:** $9-$18   **Phone:** 248/735-4570   107
Location: I-96, exit 169 (7 Mile Rd), 1 mi w of jct Haggerty Rd. 39550 7 Mile Rd 48167. **Hours:** 11 am-11 pm, Fri & Sat-midnight, Sun noon-10 pm. Closed major holidays. **Reservations:** accepted. **Features:** Decidedly upscale, the restaurant securely encloses gleaming brewing equipment behind windows as a tip-off of its secondary role as a brewpub. The open kitchen—with its wood-burning oven—is responsible for a creative menu with offerings that range from maple-glazed pork chops to four-herb-grilled lamp chops, as well as steaks, chops, seafood and pizzas. Dressy casual; cocktails. **Parking:** on-site. **Cards:** AX, DS, MC, VI.

(See map and index starting on p. 226)

EMILY'S

▼▼▼

American

cocktails. **Parking:** on-site. **Cards:** AX, DC, DS, MC, VI.

Dinner: $22-$39   **Phone:** 248/349-0505

Location: Just n of jct Main and Center sts; downtown. 505 N Center St 48167. **Hours:** 5:30 pm-10 pm. Closed major holidays; also Sun, Mon. **Reservations:** accepted. **Features:** Be prepared for an enjoyable evening at this attractive converted house, as the chef/owner is an advocate of slow-cooked food. Seasonal and fresh ingredients are used to create a Mediterranean menu that changes regularly. Dressy casual;

LITTLE ITALY RISTORANTE

▼▼▼

Italian

is individually decorated and romantic nooks are available. Casual dress; cocktails. **Parking:** on-site. **Cards:** AX, DC, DS, MC, VI.

Lunch: $12-$15   **Dinner:** $19-$25   **Phone:** 248/348-0575

Location: Jct Main and Sutton sts, just w; downtown. 227 Hutton St 48167. **Hours:** 11 am-11:30 pm, Fri & Sat-midnight, Sun 4 pm-11:30 pm. Closed: 11/25, 12/25. **Reservations:** suggested. **Features:** An upscale lounge just off the main dining room is perfect for meeting friends or relaxing before enjoying an extensive menu of Italian specialties including handmade pasta in this converted Victorian house, where every room

MACKINNON'S RESTAURANT

▼▼▼

Steak & Seafood

Cards: AX, DC, DS, MC, VI.

Lunch: $9-$12   **Dinner:** $19-$34   **Phone:** 248/348-1991

Location: Downtown. 126 E Main St 48167. **Hours:** 11:30 am-3 & 5-10 pm, Fri & Sat 5 pm-11 pm. Closed: Sun. **Reservations:** suggested. **Features:** Innovative steak, chops, seafood and live lobster served in charming country inn ambience; all food is fresh and all sauces, entrees and desserts are homemade. Very popular are the blown-up duck and the chicken strudel. Dressy casual; cocktails. **Parking:** on-site.

NOVI pop. 47,386 (See map and index starting on p. 226)

——— WHERE TO STAY ———

COUNTRY INN & SUITES BY CARLSON *Book at aaa.com*

▼▼▼

Small-scale Hotel

posed, [ECP] meal plan available. **Amenities:** high-speed Internet, voice mail, irons, hair dryers. **Pool(s):** heated indoor. **Leisure Activities:** whirlpool, exercise room. **Guest Services:** valet and coin laundry. **Business Services:** meeting rooms. **Cards:** AX, CB, DC, DS, MC, VI. *(See color ad p 313)*

All Year   1P: $105-$115   2P: $105-$115   **Phone:** (248)596-9800   84   XP: $10   F18

Location: I-275, exit 167, just w, then 0.5 mi n. 21625 Haggerty Rd 48375. Fax: 248/596-9875. **Facility:** Smoke free premises. 100 units. 73 one-bedroom standard units, some with whirlpools. 27 one-bedroom suites ($99-$115). 4 stories, interior corridors. *Bath:* combo or shower only. **Parking:** on-site. **Terms:** cancellation fee im-

SOME UNITS

COURTYARD BY MARRIOTT *Book at aaa.com*

▼▼▼

Small-scale Hotel

Terms: [BP] meal plan available. **Amenities:** high-speed Internet, dual phone lines, voice mail, irons, hair dryers. **Pool(s):** heated indoor. **Leisure Activities:** whirlpool, exercise room. **Guest Services:** valet and coin laundry. **Business Services:** meeting rooms. **Cards:** AX, CB, DC, DS, JC, MC, VI.

All Year   1P: $69-$124   2P: $69-$124   **Phone:** (248)380-1234

Location: I-96, exit 162, just s, 0.5 mi e on Crescent Dr, then just s on Town Center Dr. Located beside Novi Town Center. 42700 11 Mile Rd 48375. Fax: 248/380-5699. **Facility:** 122 units. 118 one-bedroom standard units, some with whirlpools. 4 one-bedroom suites. 4 stories, interior corridors. *Bath:* combo or shower only. **Parking:** on-site.

SOME UNITS

DOUBLETREE HOTEL NOVI/DETROIT *Book at aaa.com*

ⒶⒶⒶ SAVE

▼▼▼

Small-scale Hotel

meeting rooms, business center. **Cards:** AX, CB, DC, DS. **Special Amenities:** free newspaper and early check-in/late check-out.

All Year   1P: $69-$170   2P: $79-$180   **Phone:** (248)348-5000   XP: $10   F18

Location: I-96, exit 162, just n, then just w. 27000 Sheraton Dr 48377. Fax: 248/348-2315. **Facility:** 217 units. 209 one-bedroom standard units. 8 one-bedroom suites ($195-$375), some with whirlpools. 3 stories, interior corridors. **Parking:** on-site. **Amenities:** voice mail, irons, hair dryers. **Dining:** 6:30 am-10 pm, Fri & Sat-11 pm, cocktails. **Pool(s):** heated outdoor, heated indoor. **Leisure Activities:** sauna, whirlpool, exercise room. *Fee:* game room. **Guest Services:** gift shop, valet laundry, area transportation-within 5 mi. **Business Services:**

SOME UNITS

(See map and index starting on p. 226)

HOTEL BARONETTE *Book at aaa.com*   Phone: (248)349-7800

(AAA) (SAVE)   All Year [BP]   1P: $139-$165   2P: $149-$175   XP: $10   F18

▼▼▼   **Location:** I-96, exit 162, just n. Located in 12 Oaks Mall. 27790 Novi Rd 48377. Fax: 248/349-7467. **Facility:** 153

Small-scale Hotel   units. 145 one-bedroom standard units, some with kitchens. 8 one-bedroom suites ($199-$425), some with kitchens and/or whirlpools. 3 stories, interior corridors. **Parking:** on-site. **Terms:** check-in 4 pm, cancellation fee imposed. **Amenities:** video games (fee), high-speed Internet, voice mail, honor bars, irons, hair dryers. **Dining:** No. VI Chop House & Lobster Bar, see separate listing. **Pool(s):** heated indoor. **Leisure Activities:** sauna, whirlpool, putting green, exercise room. **Guest Services:** gift shop, complimentary evening beverages, valet and coin laundry. **Business Services:** conference facilities, business center. **Cards:** AX, CB, DC, DS, JC, MC, VI. **Special Amenities:** free full breakfast and free newspaper.

SOME UNITS

(S D) (⬚) (Y) (▱) (📷) (⊠) (VCR) (✦) (DATA PORT) (🖥) / (⊠) (📠) /

SHERATON-DETROIT-NOVI *Book at aaa.com*   Phone: (248)349-4502   85

▼▼▼▼   All Year   1P: $59-$169   2P: $59-$169   XP: $10   F17

   Location: I-275, exit 167 (8 Mile Rd), just w, then just n. 21111 Haggerty Rd 48375. Fax: 248/349-4302. **Facility:** 238

Large-scale Hotel   units. 236 one-bedroom standard units. 2 one-bedroom suites. 7 stories, interior corridors. *Bath:* combo or shower only. **Parking:** on-site. **Terms:** cancellation fee imposed. **Amenities:** dual phone lines, voice mail, irons, hair dryers. **Pool(s):** heated indoor. **Leisure Activities:** sauna, whirlpool, exercise room. **Guest Services:** valet laundry, area transportation. **Business Services:** conference facilities. **Cards:** AX, CB, DC, DS, MC, VI. *(See color ad p 267)*

SOME UNITS

(ASK) (S D) (⬚) (Y) (& M) (&) (▱) (📷) (⊠) (📷) (DATA PORT) (🖥) / (⊠) (VCR) (📠) (📠) /

STUDIO PLUS DELUXE STUDIOS *Book at aaa.com*   Phone: 248/344-4555   86

▼▼ ▼▼   Property failed to provide current rates

   Location: I-275, exit 167 (8 Mile Rd), 0.4 mi w, then just w. Located behind shopping plaza. 39640 Orchard Hill Pl 48375.

Small-scale Hotel   Fax: 248/344-1991. **Facility:** 86 one-bedroom standard units with kitchens. 3 stories, interior corridors. *Bath:* combo or shower only. **Parking:** on-site. **Terms:** office hours 7 am-11 pm. **Amenities:** voice mail, irons. **Leisure Activities:** exercise room. **Guest Services:** sundries, valet and coin laundry.

SOME UNITS

(⬚➜) (& M) (&) (📷) (DATA PORT) (🖥) (📠) (🖥) / (⊠) /

TOWNEPLACE SUITES *Book at aaa.com*   Phone: (248)305-5533

▼▼ ▼▼   All Year   1P: $69-$119   2P: $69-$119

   Location: I-96, exit 162, just s, 0.5 mi e on Crescent Dr, then just s on Town Center Dr. Located beside Novi Town Center.

Small-scale Hotel   42600 11 Mile Rd 48375. Fax: 248/305-5566. **Facility:** 95 units. 54 one-bedroom standard units with kitchens. 4 one- and 37 two-bedroom suites with kitchens. 3 stories, interior corridors. **Parking:** on-site. **Terms:** [CP] meal plan available, small pets only ($100 fee). **Amenities:** dual phone lines, voice mail, irons, hair dryers. **Pool(s):** small heated outdoor. **Leisure Activities:** exercise room. **Guest Services:** valet and coin laundry. **Business Services:** business center. **Cards:** AX, DC, DS, JC, MC, VI.

SOME UNITS

(S D) (🐾) (⬚➜) (&) (▱) (📷) (DATA PORT) (🖥) (📠) (🖥) / (⊠) /
FEE

WYNDHAM GARDEN HOTEL-NOVI *Book at aaa.com*   Phone: (248)344-8800

(AAA) (SAVE)   All Year   1P: $59-$109   2P: $59-$119   XP: $10   F17

▼▼ ▼▼   **Location:** I-96, exit 162, just s, then 0.5 mi e. Located behind the Novi Town Center. 42100 Crescent Blvd 48375.

   Fax: 248/344-8535. **Facility:** 148 one-bedroom standard units. 2 stories (no elevator), interior corridors.

Small-scale Hotel   **Parking:** on-site. **Terms:** cancellation fee imposed. **Amenities:** dual phone lines, voice mail, irons, hair dryers. *Fee:* video games, high-speed Internet. **Dining:** 6:30 am-1 & 5-10 pm, Sat & Sun from 7 am, cocktails. **Pool(s):** heated indoor. **Leisure Activities:** sauna, whirlpool. **Guest Services:** valet laundry. **Business Services:** meeting rooms. **Cards:** AX, CB, DC, DS, MC, VI.

SOME UNITS

(S D) (⬚) (Y) (▱) (📷) (⬚➜) (📷) (DATA PORT) (🖥) / (⊠) /

───── *The following lodging was either not evaluated or did not* ─────
meet AAA rating requirements but is listed for your information only.

RESIDENCE INN BY MARRIOTT DETROIT/NOVI   Phone: 248/735-7400

(fyi)   All Year [ECP]   1P: $159-$299   2P: $159-$299

   Too new to rate. **Location:** I-275 N to I-96 W, exit 162, 0.5 mi n on Novi Rd, left on 12 Mile Rd. 27477 Caberet Dr

Small-scale Hotel   48376. Fax: 248/735-3765. **Amenities:** 107 units, coffeemakers, microwaves, refrigerators, pool. **Cards:** AX, CB, DC, DS, JC, MC, VI.

───── **WHERE TO DINE** ─────

CHERRY BLOSSOM   **Lunch:** $11-$20   **Dinner:** $15-$25   Phone: 248/380-9160

▼▼ ▼▼   **Location:** I-96, exit 162, just n; at west end of West Oaks II Shopping Plaza. 43588 W Oaks Dr 48377. **Hours:** 11:30 am-2 & 5:30-10:30 pm, Sun 4 pm-10 pm. Closed major holidays. **Reservations:** accepted.

Japanese   **Features:** Squeezed between two big box stores in the West Oaks II shopping center, the restaurant draws many Japanese business travelers, who bear witness to the authenticity of the food. While standard dishes of yakitori, tempura and teriyaki are prominently displayed on the menu, it's the incredibly fresh sushi, prepared by a chef reputed to have cooked for the emperor of Japan, that stands out. Dressy casual; cocktails. **Parking:** on-site. **Cards:** AX, DC, DS, MC, VI.

(& M) (⊠)

DIAMOND JIM BRADY'S BISTRO   **Lunch:** $10-$15   **Dinner:** $15-$20   Phone: 248/380-8460

(AAA)   **Location:** 26053 Town Center Dr 48375. **Hours:** 11:30 am-10 pm, Fri & Sat-11 pm, Sun 4 pm-9 pm. Closed major holidays. **Features:** Somewhat difficult to find, the restaurant is behind the Novi shopping center

▼▼ ▼▼   beside the movie theater. Those willing to search for this gem can expect to be rewarded for their efforts.

American   Most items are homemade, and the diverse menu lists everything from standard bar food, such as buffalo wings, to British Isle fish and chips and shepherd's pie. Casual dress; cocktails. **Parking:** on-site. **Cards:** AX, DC, DS, MC, VI.

(& M) (⊠)

(See map and index starting on p. 226)

LOCAL COLOR BREWING COMPANY | **Lunch:** $10-$18 | **Dinner:** $10-$18 | **Phone:** 248/349-2600
Location: I-96, exit 162, 1 mi s, then just e; in east end of Main Street Shopping Mall. 42705 Grand River Ave 48375. **Hours:** 11 am-midnight, Fri & Sat-1 am, Sun 3 pm-10 pm. Closed major holidays. **Features:** An open, two-story dining room—with a gleaming industrial design and a multitude of colors—leads toward the gleaming brewing tanks of the local hangout. While the menu offers a number of bar standards, it also features such items as barbecue chicken, pizza and cedar-planked salmon. Casual dress; cocktails. **Parking:** on-site.
American
Cards: AX, MC, VI.

NEW AH WOK | **Lunch:** $6-$10 | **Dinner:** $8-$12 | **Phone:** 248/349-9260 | 99
Location: I-275 N, exit 1 (Grand River), just e, then just s on Grand River Ave, 2 mi w. 41563 W 10 Mile Rd 48375. **Hours:** 11 am-9:30 pm, Fri-11:30 pm, Sat 4 pm-11:30 pm, Sun noon-9:30 pm. Closed major holidays.
Chinese
Reservations: accepted. **Features:** For the adventuresome and others alike offering plenty of favorites but also serves up plenty of new and interesting choices such as Winter Melon Soup and Eight Treasures Taro Nest. Casual dress; cocktails. **Parking:** on-site. **Cards:** AX, DC, DS, MC, VI.

NO. VI CHOP HOUSE & LOBSTER BAR | **Dinner:** $25-$40 | **Phone:** 248/305-5210
Location: I-96, exit 162, just n; in Hotel Baronette. 27790 Novi Rd 48377. **Hours:** 5 pm-10 pm, Fri & Sat-11 pm, Sun 5 pm-9 pm. Closed major holidays. **Reservations:** suggested. **Features:** The dramatic and somewhat
Steak & Seafood
seductive interior mirrors the creativity and drama generated in the food. Using high-quality ingredients, such as USDA prime cuts of beef, and a global palette of influences, the kitchen not only prepares varied steaks, which range in size from 7-ounce filets to massive 20-ounce porterhouses, but also hoisin-glazed beef short ribs, steak au poivre, coriander- and lime-grilled ahi tuna and fresh lobster. Dressy casual; cocktails. **Parking:** on-site and valet.
Cards: AX, DS, MC, VI.

STEVE & ROCKY'S | **Lunch:** $6-$16 | **Dinner:** $14-$29 | **Phone:** 248/374-0688
Location: I-96, exit 162, 1 mi s, then just e. 3150 Grand River 48375. **Hours:** 11 am-10 pm, Fri-11 pm, Sat noon-11 pm, Sun 1 pm-9 pm. Closed major holidays. **Features:** Vibrant contrasting colours and an eclectic
American
decor set the tone for this restaurant known for its fresh fish and seafood. Emphasizing fresh food, the kitchen shows its creative side in both food presentation and creation. Daily specials such as the "Just Today" or "Just Tonight" highlight an ever-changing menu. Dressy casual; cocktails; entertainment. **Parking:** on-site.
Cards: AX, DC, DS, MC, VI.

W F BIBIMBAB | **Lunch:** $6-$9 | **Dinner:** $10-$18 | **Phone:** 248/348-6800
Location: I-96, exit 162, 1.6 mi n, then just e; rear and inside Main St Development Mall. 43155 Main St, Suite 300 48375. **Hours:** 11:30 am-10:30 pm, Fri & Sat-11 pm, Sun noon-10 pm. Closed major holidays.
Korean
Features: It's easy to overlook this bright and lively space. Specializing in Korean barbeque, where diners grill their own meat and seafood from barbeque tops set into most tables, the restaurant also offers sushi and it's namesake dish which has been described as "offering a different taste with every bite". Casual dress; cocktails.
Parking: on-site. **Cards:** AX, DC, MC, VI.

PLYMOUTH pop. 9,022   (See map and index starting on p. 226)

———— WHERE TO STAY ————

COMFORT INN PLYMOUTH CLOCKTOWER | *Book at aaa.com* | | | **Phone:** (734)455-8100 | 108

| | 5/28-3/31 [ECP] | 1P: $79-$125 | 2P: $79-$125 | XP: $10 | F17 |
| | 4/1-5/27 [ECP] | 1P: $79-$119 | 2P: $79-$119 | XP: $10 | F17 |

Location: I-275, exit 28, just w; entry on Massey Dr. 40455 Ann Arbor Rd 48170. Fax: 734/455-5711. **Facility:** 123 one-bedroom standard units. 2 stories, interior corridors. **Parking:** on-site. **Amenities:** voice mail, irons, hair
Small-scale Hotel
dryers. **Pool(s):** outdoor. **Leisure Activities:** exercise room. **Guest Services:** valet laundry. **Business Services:** meeting rooms. **Cards:** AX, CB, DC, DS, JC, MC, VI. **Special Amenities:** free expanded continental breakfast.

SOME UNITS

HILTON GARDEN INN - PLYMOUTH | *Book at aaa.com* | | | **Phone:** (734)354-0001

| | All Year | 1P: $89-$199 | 2P: $99-$209 | XP: $10 | F |

Location: SR 14, exit 20, just n. 14600 Sheldon Rd 48170. Fax: 734/354-5121. **Facility:** 157 units. 155 one-bedroom standard units, some with whirlpools. 2 one-bedroom suites. 6 stories, interior corridors. **Bath:**
Small-scale Hotel
combo or shower only. **Amenities:** dual phone lines, voice mail, irons, hair dryers. **Fee:** video games, high-speed Internet. **Pool(s):** small heated indoor. **Leisure Activities:** whirlpool, exercise room. **Guest Services:** sundries, valet and coin laundry, area transportation. **Business Services:** meeting rooms, business center. **Cards:** AX, CB, DC, DS, JC, MC, VI.

SOME UNITS

RED ROOF INN-PLYMOUTH | *Book at aaa.com* | | | **Phone:** (734)459-3300 | 107

| | 5/30-10/16 | 1P: $52-$67 | 2P: $59-$74 | XP: $7 | F18 |
| | 4/1-5/29 & 10/17-3/31 | 1P: $50-$64 | 2P: $57-$71 | XP: $7 | F18 |

Location: I-275, exit 28, just e. 39700 Ann Arbor Rd 48170. Fax: 734/459-3072. **Facility:** 109 one-bedroom standard units. 2 stories, exterior corridors. **Bath:** combo or shower only. **Parking:** on-site. **Terms:** small pets only.
Motel
Amenities: video games, voice mail. **Cards:** AX, CB, DC, DS, MC, VI. **Special Amenities:** free local telephone calls and free newspaper.

SOME UNITS

(See map and index starting on p. 226)

———— WHERE TO DINE ————

CAFE BON HOMME   **Lunch:** $7-$13   **Dinner:** $29-$33   **Phone:** 734/453-6260
▼▼▼▼▼
American
Location: Between Main and Harvey sts; downtown. 844 Penniman Ave 48170. **Hours:** 11:30 am-3 & 5-9 pm, Fri-10 pm, Sat noon-3 & 5-10 pm. Closed major holidays; also Sun. **Reservations:** suggested, dinner. **Features:** In a quaint area of downtown, the small, romantic cafe has the feel of a European bistro. Innovative French-American cuisine shows an unusual fusion of Asian influences in some preparations. The wine list is well-rounded. Desserts are homemade. Dressy casual; cocktails. **Parking:** on-site and street. **Cards:** AX, DC, MC, VI.
🍸✕

COMPARI'S ON THE PARK   **Lunch:** $8-$10   **Dinner:** $12-$16   **Phone:** 734/416-0100
▼▼▼▼
Italian
Location: Downtown. 350 S Main St 48170. **Hours:** 11 am-10 pm, Thurs-11 pm, Fri & Sat-midnight, Sun 3 pm-9 pm. Closed major holidays. **Reservations:** accepted. **Features:** Exposed brick walls, murals and large picture windows that overlook the city park give this upscale restaurant a comfortable feel. Focusing on well-prepared Italian specialities and pizza, this restaurant is popular with the local crowd. Casual dress; cocktails. **Parking:** street. **Cards:** AX, MC, VI.
🍸✕

ERNESTO'S-AN ITALIAN COUNTRY INN   **Dinner:** $15-$24   **Phone:** 734/453-2002   116
◆▼ ▼▼▼
Italian
Location: Just w of jct Haggerty Rd. 41661 Plymouth Rd 48170. **Hours:** 4 pm-10 pm, Fri & Sat-11 pm, Sun noon-9 pm. Closed: 12/25. **Reservations:** accepted. **Features:** Whether accommodating an intimate family gathering or a large, boisterous group, the charming restaurant reflects a country decor, with fireplaces and wood crossbeams. Representative of the extensive list of classic and original dishes are risotto e pollo, pollo rosamarina, lasagna and spaghetti with meatballs. Dressy casual; cocktails. **Parking:** on-site and valet. **Cards:** AX, MC, VI.
🍸✕

LA BISTECCA ITALIAN GRILLE   **Lunch:** $8-$15   **Dinner:** $20-$30   **Phone:** 734/254-0400   117
▼▼▼
Steak House
Location: Jct Eckles Rd; between Haggerty and Newburgh rds. 39405 Plymouth Rd 48170. **Hours:** 4 pm-10 pm, Wed 11:30 am-10 pm, Sat 5 pm-10 pm. Closed major holidays; also Sun. **Reservations:** suggested. **Features:** An open ceiling, dark woods, fine art, attentive service and soft background music combine to give the Italian chophouse a warm, intimate feeling. Featuring certified Piedmontese beef exclusively, the menu also lists creative daily specials and a number of fresh fish, lamb and chicken selections. Dressy casual; cocktails. **Parking:** on-site and valet. **Cards:** AX, DC, MC, VI.
♿M 🍸✕

PONTIAC pop. 66,337

———— WHERE TO STAY ————

COURTYARD BY MARRIOTT   *Book at aaa.com*   **Phone:** 248/858-9595
▼▼▼▼
Small-scale Hotel
Property failed to provide current rates
Location: I-75, exit 75 (Square Lake Rd), w via Opdyke Rd. 3555 Centerpoint Pkwy 48341. **Fax:** 248/858-9696. **Facility:** 110 units. 106 one-bedroom standard units. 4 one-bedroom suites. 4 stories, interior corridors. **Bath:** combo or shower only. **Parking:** on-site, winter plug-ins. **Amenities:** dual phone lines, voice mail, irons, hair dryers. **Fee:** video games, high-speed Internet. **Pool(s):** heated indoor. **Leisure Activities:** whirlpool, exercise room. **Guest Services:** valet and coin laundry. **Business Services:** meeting rooms, business center.
SOME UNITS
🎮 🍸 🈂 ✒ 🏊 🎦 DATAPORT 💻 /✕ 🔌 🖥 /

DETROIT MARRIOTT PONTIAC AT CENTERPOINT   *Book at aaa.com*   **Phone:** (248)253-9800
ⒶⒶⒶ SAVE
▼▼▼▼▼
Large-scale Hotel

1/1-3/31	1P: $199-$235	2P: $199-$245	XP: $10 F18
4/1-12/31	1P: $189-$225	2P: $189-$235	XP: $10 F18

Location: I-75, exit 75 (Square Lake Rd), w via Opdyke Rd. 3600 Centerpoint Pkwy 48341. **Fax:** 248/253-9682. **Facility:** 290 units. 285 one-bedroom standard units. 5 one-bedroom suites ($425). 11 stories, interior corridors. **Bath:** combo or shower only. **Parking:** on-site and valet. **Terms:** cancellation fee imposed. **Amenities:** dual phone lines, voice mail, safes, irons, hair dryers. **Fee:** video games, high-speed Internet. **Some:** CD players. **Dining:** Parkway Grille, see separate listing. **Pool(s):** heated indoor, heated indoor. **Leisure Activities:** whirlpool, exercise room. **Fee:** massage. **Guest Services:** sundries, valet and coin laundry, area transportation (fee)-within 5 mi. **Business Services:** conference facilities, business center. **Cards:** AX, CB, DC, DS, JC, MC, VI.
SOME UNITS
🅂🄳 🍽 🍸 ♿ 🏊 ✕ 🎦 DATAPORT 🔌 💻 /✕/

RESIDENCE INN BY MARRIOTT DETROIT/PONTIAC   *Book at aaa.com*   **Phone:** (248)858-8664
▼▼▼▼
Small-scale Hotel
All Year   1P: $159-$189   2P: $159-$189
Location: I-75, exit 75 (Square Lake Rd), w via Opdyke Rd. 3333 Centerpoint Pkwy 48341. **Fax:** 248/858-8665. **Facility:** 114 units. 47 one-bedroom standard units, some with efficiencies or kitchens. 43 one- and 24 two-bedroom suites, some with efficiencies or kitchens. 3 stories, interior corridors. **Bath:** combo or shower only. **Parking:** on-site. **Terms:** check-in 4 pm, [BP] meal plan available, pets ($50 deposit, $5 extra charge). **Amenities:** video games (fee), dual phone lines, voice mail, irons, hair dryers. **Some:** high-speed Internet (fee). **Pool(s):** heated indoor. **Leisure Activities:** whirlpool, playground, exercise room, sports court. **Guest Services:** valet and coin laundry. **Business Services:** meeting rooms, business center. **Cards:** AX, DS, MC, VI.
SOME UNITS
Ⓐ🅂🄺 🅂🄳 🐾 🍽 ♿ 🍸 🏊 ✕ 🎦 DATAPORT 🔌 🖥 💻 /✕/
FEE

———— WHERE TO DINE ————

PARKWAY GRILLE   **Lunch:** $13-$25   **Dinner:** $13-$25   **Phone:** 248/648-6034
▼▼▼▼
American
Location: I-75, exit 75 (Square Lake Rd), w via Opdyke Rd; in Detroit Marriott Pontiac at Centerpoint. 3600 Centerpoint Pkwy 48341. **Hours:** 6:30 am-10:30 pm. **Features:** This upscale and lively space is a definite step above the typical hotel restaurant. The gently trendy and daring menu offers a "Napoleon" of tri-colored tomatoes, rack of lamb with a mustard, mint and rosemary crust, and sinful and creative desserts such as white-chocolate cherry bread pudding. Dressy casual; cocktails. **Parking:** on-site and valet. **Cards:** AX, DC, DS, MC, VI.
♿M 🍸✕

ROCHESTER pop. 10,467

———— WHERE TO DINE ————

ANDIAMO OSTERIA RISTORANTE
Italian
Lunch: $8-$12   **Dinner:** $12-$18   **Phone:** 248/582-9300
Location: Just s of jct Walton Blvd; downtown. 401 W Main St 48307. **Hours:** 11 am-11 pm, Fri-midnight, Sat 4 pm-midnight, Sun 4 pm-9 pm. Closed major holidays. **Reservations:** accepted. **Features:** Part of a local restaurant chain, the restaurant serves traditional dishes, such as ravioli and lasagna, which are prepared using authentic recipes and high-quality ingredients and accented with an exquisite Parmesan cheese. The spacious dining room, with its upscale artwork and comfortable furnishings, is an ideal setting for an intimate dinner. Dressy casual; cocktails. **Parking:** street. **Cards:** AX, MC, VI.

FAMILY BUGGY RESTAURANT
American
Lunch: $5-$7   **Dinner:** $8-$13   **Phone:** 248/656-0850
Location: SR 59, 2.5 mi n on Rochester Rd; in South Hills Shopping Plaza. 870 S Rochester Rd 48307. **Hours:** 11 am-9 pm, Fri & Sat-10 pm. Closed: 1/1, 11/25, 12/25. **Features:** Located in the South Hills Shopping Plaza, the restaurant is a popular local eatery 20th-century artifacts reminiscent of rural America. Their menu is full of heartland American dishes that will please everyone in the family. Casual dress. **Parking:** on-site. **Cards:** MC, VI.

SALSA'S MEXICAN CANTINA
Mexican
Lunch: $5-$8   **Dinner:** $9-$14   **Phone:** 248/853-6800
Location: 1 mi n of SR 59. 2601 S Rochester Rd 48307. **Hours:** 11 am-11 pm, Fri & Sat-midnight, Sun 11:30 am-10 pm. Closed: 11/25, 12/25. **Features:** A lively Mexican restaurant serving traditional Mexican dishes like enchiladas, tacos and fajitas. Mexican beers, and tequilas are also available. You can expect quick, friendly service at the bar or in the dining room. Casual dress; cocktails. **Parking:** on-site. **Cards:** AX, DC, DS, MC, VI.

ROCHESTER HILLS pop. 68,825

———— WHERE TO STAY ————

BEST WESTERN CONCORDE INN   *Book at aaa.com*
Small-scale Hotel
All Year [ECP]   1P: $95-$185   2P: $95-$185   **Phone:** (248)299-1210
XP: $10   F17
Location: Jct Hall (SR 59) and Crooks rds. 1919 Star-Batt Dr 48309. Fax: 248/852-4678. **Facility:** 124 units. 115 one-bedroom standard units, some with whirlpools. 9 one-bedroom suites with whirlpools. 2 stories, interior corridors. **Parking:** on-site. **Amenities:** video games (fee), voice mail, irons, hair dryers. **Pool(s):** heated indoor. **Leisure Activities:** sauna, whirlpool. **Guest Services:** valet and coin laundry, tanning facility. **Business Services:** meeting rooms. **Cards:** AX, CB, DC, DS, MC, VI.

SOME UNITS

RED ROOF INN   *Book at aaa.com*
Motel
5/2-10/9   1P: $60-$72   2P: $66-$78   XP: $6   F18
10/10-3/31   1P: $52-$72   2P: $58-$78   XP: $6   F18
4/1-5/1   1P: $52-$67   2P: $58-$73   XP: $6   F18
Phone: (248)853-6400
Location: Jct Hall (SR 59) and Crooks rds. 2580 Crooks Rd 48309. Fax: 248/853-6391. **Facility:** 111 one-bedroom standard units. 2 stories, exterior corridors. *Bath:* combo or shower only. **Parking:** on-site. **Terms:** small pets only. **Amenities:** video games, voice mail. **Cards:** AX, CB, DC, DS, MC, VI. **Special Amenities:** free local telephone calls and free newspaper.

SOME UNITS

ROMEO pop. 3,721

———— WHERE TO STAY ————

THE BRABB HOUSE   *Book at aaa.com*
Historic Bed & Breakfast
All Year [CP]   1P: $89-$109   **Phone:** (586)752-4726
Location: Just s, then just w; downtown. 185 S Main St 48065. Fax: 586/752-6060. **Facility:** In the heart of a charming town, this grand Victorian home offers tastefully decorated rooms with private baths. Smoke free premises. 5 one-bedroom standard units. 2 stories (no elevator), interior corridors. *Bath:* shower only. **Parking:** on-site. **Terms:** check-in 4 pm, age restrictions may apply, 14 day cancellation notice-fee imposed. **Business Services:** meeting rooms. **Cards:** AX, MC, VI.

ROMULUS pop. 22,979   (See map and index starting on p. 226)

———— WHERE TO STAY ————

BAYMONT INN & SUITES DETROIT-AIRPORT   *Book at aaa.com*   **Phone:** (734)722-6000   152
Small-scale Hotel
All Year   1P: $79-$89   2P: $79-$89
Location: I-94, exit 198 (Merriman Rd), just w. 9000 Wickham Rd 48174. Fax: 734/722-4737. **Facility:** 100 units. 97 one-bedroom standard units. 3 one-bedroom suites ($89-$99), some with kitchens. 3 stories, interior corridors. **Parking:** on-site. **Terms:** [ECP] meal plan available, small pets only. **Amenities:** video games (fee), dual phone lines, voice mail, irons, hair dryers. **Guest Services:** valet and coin laundry. **Cards:** AX, CB, DC, DS, MC, VI. **Special Amenities:** free local telephone calls and free newspaper. *(See color ad p 287)*

SOME UNITS

(See map and index starting on p. 226)

BEST WESTERN GATEWAY INTERNATIONAL HOTEL
Book at aaa.com   Phone: (734)728-2800   154

(AAA) (SAVE)
All Year [CP]   1P: $89-$99   2P: $89-$99
Location: I-94, exit 198 (Merriman Rd), just n, then just w. 9191 Wickham 48174, Fax: 734/728-2260. Facility: 233
units. 220 one-bedroom standard units, some with whirlpools. 13 one-bedroom suites, some with whirlpools.
2 stories (no elevator), interior corridors. Parking: on-site. Terms: 7 day cancellation notice, [AP] & [BP] meal
Small-scale Hotel   plans available. Amenities: voice mail, irons, hair dryers. Dining: 6 am-1 & 5-11 pm; closed Sun, cocktails.
Pool(s): heated outdoor, heated indoor. Leisure Activities: sauna, whirlpool, atrium recreation room, pool
table, exercise room. Fee: game room. Guest Services: valet and coin laundry, tanning facility. Business Services: conference
facilities. Cards: AX, DC, DS, MC, VI. Special Amenities: free continental breakfast. (See color ad p 242)

SOME UNITS

CLARION BARCELO' HOTEL
Book at aaa.com   Phone: (734)728-7900   147

(AAA) (SAVE)
All Year   1P: $79-$129   2P: $89-$149
Location: I-94, exit 198 (Merriman Rd), just n. 8600 Merriman Rd 48174. Fax: 734/728-6518. Facility: 153 one-
bedroom standard units. 2 stories, interior corridors. Parking: on-site. Terms: [AP] meal plan available.
Amenities: dual phone lines, voice mail, irons, hair dryers. Dining: 6:30 am-2 & 5-10 pm, cocktails. Pool(s):
Small-scale Hotel   heated indoor. Leisure Activities: exercise room. Guest Services: valet laundry. Business Services:
meeting rooms. Cards: AX, CB, DC, DS, JC, MC, VI. Special Amenities: free newspaper and early check-
in/late check-out.

SOME UNITS

FEE

COURTYARD BY MARRIOTT-METRO AIRPORT
Book at aaa.com   Phone: (734)721-3200   146

(AAA) (SAVE)
All Year   1P: $79-$129
Location: I-94, exit 198 (Merriman Rd), just e. 30653 Flynn Dr 48174. Fax: 734/721-1304. Facility: 146 units. 134
one-bedroom standard units. 12 one-bedroom suites. 3 stories, interior corridors. Bath: combo or shower
only. Parking: on-site. Terms: [BP] & [CP] meal plans available. Amenities: voice mail, irons, hair dryers.
Small-scale Hotel   Dining: 6-10:30 am, Sat & Sun 7 am-noon. Pool(s): heated indoor. Leisure Activities: whirlpool, exercise
room. Guest Services: valet and coin laundry. Business Services: meeting rooms. Cards: AX, CB, DC, DS,
JC, MC, VI.

SOME UNITS

CROWNE PLAZA HOTEL AND RESORT DETROIT METRO AIRPORT
Book at aaa.com   Phone: 734/729-2600   141
Property failed to provide current rates

Location: I-94, exit 198 (Merriman Rd), just n. 8000 Merriman Rd 48174. Fax: 734/729-9414. Facility: 364 one-
bedroom standard units. 11 stories, interior corridors. Parking: on-site. Amenities: voice mail, irons, hair
Large-scale Hotel   dryers. Leisure Activities: whirlpool, exercise room. Fee: game room. Guest Services: gift shop, valet
laundry. Business Services: conference facilities, business center.

SOME UNITS

DAYS INN
Book at aaa.com   Phone: (734)946-4300   156
F14
(AAA) (SAVE)
All Year   1P: $69-$79   2P: $69-$79   XP: $10
Location: I-94, exit 199 (Middlebelt Rd), 0.4 mi s. 9501 Middlebelt Rd 48174. Fax: 734/946-7787. Facility: 127 one-
bedroom standard units, some with whirlpools. 3 stories, interior corridors. Parking: on-site. Terms: [CP]
meal plan available. Amenities: voice mail, irons, hair dryers. Dining: 11 am-11 pm, cocktails. Leisure Ac-
Small-scale Hotel   tivities: exercise room. Business Services: meeting rooms. Cards: AX, DC, DS, MC, VI.
Special Amenities: free continental breakfast and free newspaper.

SOME UNITS

DETROIT METRO AIRPORT MARRIOTT
Book at aaa.com   Phone: 734/729-7555   148

All Year   1P: $69-$139   2P: $69-$139
Location: I-94, exit 198 (Merriman Rd). 30559 Flynn Dr 48174. Fax: 734/729-4888. Facility: 245 units. 244 one-
bedroom standard units. 1 one-bedroom suite. 4 stories, interior corridors. Parking: on-site. Terms: cancel-
Small-scale Hotel   lation fee imposed, [AP] meal plan available, pets ($75 extra charge). Amenities: voice mail, irons, hair
dryers. Fee: video games, high-speed Internet. Pool(s): heated indoor. Leisure Activities: whirlpool, exercise room. Guest
Services: gift shop, valet laundry, area transportation. Business Services: conference facilities, business center. Cards: AX,
CB, DC, DS, JC, MC, VI.

SOME UNITS

FEE

DOUBLETREE HOTEL DETROIT AIRPORT
Book at aaa.com   Phone: (734)467-8000   155
1/1-3/31	1P: $79-$159	2P: $79-$169	XP: $10	F18
9/20-12/31	1P: $79-$149	2P: $79-$149	XP: $10	F18
4/1-9/19	1P: $79-$139	2P: $79-$139	XP: $10	F18

Small-scale Hotel   Location: I-94, exit 198 (Merriman Rd), 0.6 mi w. 31500 Wick Rd 48174. Fax: 734/721-8870. Facility: 263 units.
260 one-bedroom standard units. 3 one-bedroom suites ($119-$209). 4 stories, interior corridors. Bath: combo or shower only.
Parking: on-site. Terms: [AP], [BP] & [ECP] meal plans available. Amenities: video games, dual phone lines, voice mail, irons,
hair dryers. Pool(s): heated indoor/outdoor. Leisure Activities: sauna, whirlpool, exercise room. Guest Services: gift shop,
valet laundry, area transportation. Business Services: conference facilities, business center. Cards: AX, CB, DC, DS, JC,
MC, VI.

SOME UNITS

(See map and index starting on p. 226)

EXTENDED STAY AMERICA *Book at aaa.com* Phone: (734)722-7780 149
▼▼▼ ▼▼▼ All Year 1P: $55-$69 2P: $60-$74 XP: $5 F
Small-scale Hotel **Location:** I-94, exit 198 (Merriman Rd), 0.6 mi e. 30325 Flynn Dr 48174. **Facility:** 110 one-bedroom standard units with efficiencies. 3 stories, interior corridors. *Bath:* combo or shower only. **Parking:** on-site. **Terms:** weekly rates available. **Amenities:** dual phone lines, voice mail. **Guest Services:** coin laundry. **Cards:** AX, DC, DS, MC, VI.

SOME UNITS 📹 📶 🛢 ⬚ / 🗙 /

FAIRFIELD INN BY MARRIOTT-METRO AIRPORT *Book at aaa.com* Phone: (734)728-2322 145
▼▼▼▼▼ 4/1-10/31 1P: $79-$84 2P: $79-$84
11/1-3/31 1P: $69-$79 2P: $69-$79
Small-scale Hotel **Location:** I-94, exit 198 (Merriman Rd). Located opposite Detroit Metro Airport. 31119 Flynn Dr 48174. Fax: 734/641-8726. **Facility:** 133 one-bedroom standard units. 3 stories, interior/exterior corridors. *Bath:* combo or shower only. **Parking:** on-site. **Terms:** [ECP] meal plan available. **Amenities:** irons, hair dryers. **Pool(s):** heated outdoor. **Guest Services:** valet laundry. **Cards:** AX, CB, DC, DS, JC, MC, VI.

SOME UNITS 🅂🄳 ➔ 🍴 ♿ 👤 🐾 🏊 🦟 📹 📶 / 🗙 /

FOUR POINTS BY SHERATON
DETROIT METRO AIRPORT *Book at aaa.com* Phone: 734/729-9000 151
🅰🅰🅰 SAVE All Year [CP] 1P: $89-$99 2P: $89-$99
▼▼▼ ▼▼▼ **Location:** I-94, exit 198 (Merriman Rd). 8800 Wickham Rd 48174. Fax: 734/728-5580. **Facility:** 175 one-bedroom standard units, some with whirlpools. 7 stories, interior corridors. **Parking:** on-site. **Terms:** cancellation fee imposed, small pets only. **Amenities:** video games (fee), dual phone lines, voice mail, irons, hair dryers.
Small-scale Hotel **Dining:** 5 am-1 am, cocktails. **Pool(s):** small heated indoor. **Leisure Activities:** whirlpool, exercise room. **Guest Services:** valet laundry, area transportation-within 2 mi. **Business Services:** meeting rooms, business center. **Cards:** AX, CB, DC, DS, MC, VI. **Special Amenities: free continental breakfast and free local telephone calls.** *(See color ad p 5)*

SOME UNITS ➔ 🛏 🍴 🍸 🦟 🐾 🦌 📶 ⬚ / 🗙 🛢 🖼 /

HAMPTON INN-DETROIT METRO AIRPORT *Book at aaa.com* Phone: (734)721-1100 144
▼▼▼ ▼▼▼ All Year [ECP] 1P: $68-$115 2P: $78-$125 F18
Location: I-94, exit 198 (Merriman Rd), just e. 30847 Flynn Dr 48174. Fax: 734/721-9915. **Facility:** 136 one-
Small-scale Hotel bedroom standard units. 3 stories, interior corridors. **Parking:** on-site. **Terms:** package plans. **Amenities:** dual phone lines, voice mail, irons, hair dryers. **Pool(s):** heated outdoor. **Leisure Activities:** exercise room. **Guest Services:** valet laundry. **Business Services:** meeting rooms. **Cards:** AX, DC, DS, MC, VI.

SOME UNITS 🄰🅂🄺 🅂🄳 ➔ 🍴 ♿ 🐾 🏊 🦌 📶 ⬚ / 🗙 /

HILTON GARDEN INN-DETROIT METRO AIRPORT *Book at aaa.com* Phone: (734)727-6000 142
▼▼▼▼▼ All Year 1P: $69-$179 2P: $79-$189 XP: $10 F18
Small-scale Hotel **Location:** I-94, exit 198 (Merriman Rd), 0.4 mi w. 31800 Smith Rd 48174. Fax: 734/727-6006. **Facility:** 165 one-bedroom standard units. 6 stories, interior corridors. *Bath:* combo or shower only. **Parking:** on-site. **Terms:** [MAP] meal plan available. **Amenities:** video games (fee), high-speed Internet, dual phone lines, voice mail, irons, hair dryers. **Pool(s):** heated indoor. **Leisure Activities:** whirlpool, exercise room. **Guest Services:** sundries, valet and coin laundry. **Business Services:** meeting rooms, business center. **Cards:** AX, CB, DC, DS, JC, MC, VI.

SOME UNITS 🄰🅂🄺 🅂🄳 ➔ 🍴 ♿ 🐾 🏊 🦌 📶 🛢 🖼 ⬚ / 🗙 /

HILTON SUITES-DETROIT METRO AIRPORT *Book at aaa.com* Phone: (734)728-9200 150
🅰🅰🅰 SAVE 4/1-6/30 [BP] 1P: $139-$149 2P: $149-$159 XP: $10 F18
▼▼▼▼▼ 7/1-9/30 [BP] 1P: $139-$149 2P: $139-$149 XP: $10 F18
10/1-3/31 [BP] 1P: $109-$119 2P: $109-$119 XP: $10 F18
Small-scale Hotel **Location:** I-94, exit 198 (Merriman Rd), just n. 8600 Wickham Rd 48174. Fax: 734/728-9278. **Facility:** 151 one-bedroom suites. 3 stories, interior corridors. *Bath:* combo or shower only. **Parking:** on-site. **Terms:** cancellation fee imposed, [CP] meal plan available, package plans - seasonal & weekends. **Amenities:** video library (fee), high-speed Internet, dual phone lines, voice mail, irons, hair dryers. **Dining:** 6 am-10 pm, Sat & Sun from 7 am. **Leisure Activities:** whirlpool, exercise room. *Fee:* game room. **Guest Services:** complimentary evening beverages, valet and coin laundry, area transportation. **Business Services:** meeting rooms, business center. **Cards:** AX, CB, DC, MC. **Special Amenities: free full breakfast.** *(See ad below)*

SOME UNITS 🅂🄳 ➔ 🍴 🕐 🍸 ♿ 🐾 🗙 📼 🦌 📶 🛢 🖼 ⬚ / 🗙 /

(See map and index starting on p. 226)

HOWARD JOHNSON INN   *Book at aaa.com*   Phone: (734)946-1400   157
(AAA) (SAVE)   All Year   1P: $69-$79   2P: $69-$79   XP: $10   F14
Location: I-94, exit 199 (Middlebelt Rd), just s. 9555 Middlebelt Rd 48174. Fax: 734/946-7480. **Facility:** 124 one-
bedroom standard units, some with whirlpools. 3 stories, interior corridors. **Parking:** on-site. **Terms:** [CP]
meal plan available. **Amenities:** voice mail, irons, hair dryers. **Leisure Activities:** exercise room. **Guest**
Small-scale Hotel **Services:** valet and coin laundry. **Business Services:** meeting rooms. **Cards:** AX, DC, DS, MC, VI.
Special Amenities: free continental breakfast and free newspaper.   SOME UNITS

NORTHWEST INN   Phone: (734)595-7400   153
(AAA) (SAVE)   All Year [CP]   1P: $44-$69   2P: $52-$69
Location: I-94, exit 198 (Merriman Rd), just n, then just w. 9095 Wickham Rd 48174. Fax: 734/595-8591. **Facility:** 78
one-bedroom standard units. 3 stories, interior corridors. *Bath:* combo or shower only. **Parking:** on-site.
Terms: cancellation fee imposed. **Amenities:** hair dryers. **Cards:** AX, C, DS, MC, VI.
Small-scale Hotel *(See color ad p 242)*   SOME UNITS

PARK INN-DETROIT METRO AIRPORT   Phone: (734)729-6300   143
    All Year [CP]   1P: $63   2P: $63
Location: I-94, exit 198 (Merriman Rd), just n. 8270 Wickham Rd 48174. Fax: 734/722-8740. **Facility:** 232 units.
Small-scale Hotel 226 one-bedroom standard units, some with whirlpools. 6 one-bedroom suites ($129), some with whirlpools.
4 stories, interior corridors. *Bath:* combo or shower only. **Parking:** on-site. **Terms:** package plans.
Amenities: dual phone lines, voice mail, safes, irons, hair dryers. **Pool(s):** heated indoor. **Leisure Activities:** exercise room.
Fee: game room. **Guest Services:** valet laundry. **Business Services:** meeting rooms. **Cards:** AX, DC, DS, MC, VI.
        SOME UNITS

QUALITY INN METRO AIRPORT   *Book at aaa.com*   Phone: (734)728-2430   140
(AAA) (SAVE)   All Year   1P: $59-$119   2P: $64-$125   XP: $5   F18
Location: I-94, exit 198 (Merriman Rd). 7600 Merriman Rd 48174. Fax: 734/728-3756. **Facility:** 140 one-bedroom
standard units, some with whirlpools. 1 story, exterior corridors. **Parking:** on-site. **Terms:** [CP] meal plan
available. **Amenities:** video games, voice mail, irons, hair dryers. **Dining:** 11 am-1:30 & 4-midnight. **Leisure**
Motel   **Activities:** exercise room. **Guest Services:** valet and coin laundry. **Business Services:** meeting rooms.
Cards: AX, CB, DC, DS, MC, VI. **Special Amenities:** free continental breakfast and free local telephone
calls.   SOME UNITS

SUPER 8 MOTEL-ROMULUS   *Book at aaa.com*   Phone: (734)946-8808   158
    All Year   1P: $60   2P: $60   XP: $6   F16
Location: I-94, exit 199 (Middlebelt Rd), just s. 9863 Middlebelt Rd 48174. Fax: 734/946-8808. **Facility:** 63 one-
Small-scale Hotel bedroom standard units, some with whirlpools. 3 stories, interior corridors. **Parking:** on-site. **Terms:** 7 day
cancellation notice, weekly rates available, package plans, small pets only. **Amenities:** safes. *Some:* hair
dryers. **Cards:** AX, CB, DC, MC, VI.   SOME UNITS

**THE WESTIN DETROIT
    METROPOLITAN AIRPORT**   *Book at aaa.com*   Phone: (734)942-6500   159
(AAA) (SAVE)   All Year   1P: $99-$269   2P: $99-$269
Location: I-94, exit 198 (Merriman Rd). 2501 Worldgateway Pl 48242. Fax: 734/942-6600. **Facility:** Located in the
new Midfield terminal, this Asian-inspired hotel features a large serenity pool, and a bamboo forest in the
lobby. 404 units. 394 one-bedroom standard units. 10 one-bedroom suites ($329-$450). 11 stories, interior
Large-scale Hotel corridors. *Bath:* combo or shower only. **Parking:** on-site (fee) and valet. **Terms:** cancellation fee imposed.
Amenities: high-speed Internet (fee), dual phone lines, voice mail, safes, honor bars, irons, hair dryers.
Some: CD players. **Dining:** 6 am-10 pm, cocktails. **Pool(s):** small heated indoor. **Leisure Activities:** exercise room. **Guest Serv-**
ices: sundries, valet laundry. **Business Services:** conference facilities, business center. **Cards:** AX, CB, DC, DS, JC, MC, VI.
Special Amenities: free newspaper. *(See color ad p 243)*   SOME UNITS

──────── **WHERE TO DINE** ────────

LEONARDO'S PIZZERIA & RISTORANTE   Lunch: $6-$10   Dinner: $6-$10   Phone: 734/326-2560   141
    Location: I-94, exit 198 (Merriman Rd), just n. 7575 Merriman Rd 48174. **Hours:** 11 am-10 pm, Fri-midnight, Sat
    4 pm-midnight, Sun 4 pm-10 pm. Closed major holidays. **Features:** Located near a number of the airport
American   hotels, this family oriented restaurant specializes in home style Italian food such as fettucine alfredo,
    lasagna and pizzas. Casual dress; cocktails. **Parking:** on-site. **Cards:** AX, DC, MC, VI.

MERRIMAN STREET GRILL   Lunch: $6-$10   Dinner: $6-$10   Phone: 734/595-6166   142
    Location: I-94, exit 198 (Merriman Rd), just n. 7660 Merriman Rd 48174. **Hours:** 11 am-midnight, Sun 4 pm-10
    pm. Closed major holidays. **Reservations:** accepted. **Features:** Located a short distance from a number
American   of the airport hotels, this restaurant is a nice change from the deluge of fast food places and airport food.
    Casual dress; cocktails. **Parking:** on-site. **Cards:** AX, DS, MC, VI.

ROSEVILLE pop. 48,129 (See map and index starting on p. 226)

──────── WHERE TO STAY ────────

BAYMONT INN & SUITES DETROIT-ROSEVILLE
Book at aaa.com

Phone: (586)296-6910 [27]

AAA SAVE

Small-scale Hotel

4/1-8/31	1P: $79-$89
9/1-3/31	1P: $69-$79

Location: I-94, exit 232 (Little Mack Ave). 20675 13 Mile Rd 48066. Fax: 586/296-6073. **Facility:** 100 units. 99 one-bedroom standard units. 1 one-bedroom suite ($84-$104) with kitchen. 3 stories, interior corridors. **Parking:** on-site, winter plug-ins. **Terms:** [ECP] meal plan available, pets ($50 deposit). **Amenities:** video games (fee), voice mail, irons, hair dryers. **Guest Services:** valet and coin laundry. **Cards:** AX, CB, DC, DS, MC, VI. **Special Amenities:** free local telephone calls and free newspaper. *(See color ad p 287)*

SOME UNITS

[SD] [🛏] [📶] [🍽] [📷] [DATA PORT] [💻] / [✕] [🔌] [🖨] / FEE

BEST WESTERN GEORGIAN INN
Book at aaa.com

Phone: (586)294-0400 [26]

AAA SAVE

Motel

5/1-10/31	1P: $69-$179	2P: $69-$179	XP: $5 F12
4/1-4/30 & 11/1-3/31	1P: $59-$169	2P: $59-$169	XP: $5 F12

Location: I-94, exit 232 (Little Mack Ave), just s, then 0.5 mi n on 13 Mile Rd, just n. 31327 Gratiot Ave 48066. Fax: 586/294-1020. **Facility:** 111 units. 109 one-bedroom standard units, some with efficiencies and/or whirlpools. 2 one-bedroom suites ($150-$200) with whirlpools. 2 stories, exterior corridors. **Parking:** on-site. **Terms:** cancellation fee imposed. **Amenities:** irons, hair dryers. **Dining:** 6 am-10 pm, Fri & Sat-11 pm, Sun from 7 am, cocktails. **Pool(s):** heated outdoor. **Leisure Activities:** exercise room. **Guest Services:** valet and coin laundry. **Business Services:** meeting rooms. **Cards:** AX, CB, DC, DS, MC, VI. **Special Amenities: free continental breakfast and preferred room (subject to availability with advanced reservations).**

SOME UNITS

[SD] [🛏] [🍽] [🏊] [DATA PORT] [💻] / [✕] [🔌] [🖨] /

COMFORT INN
Book at aaa.com

Phone: (586)296-6700 [23]

AAA SAVE

Small-scale Hotel

All Year [CP]	1P: $82-$118	2P: $82-$118	XP: $10 F18

Location: I-94, exit 232 (Little Mack Ave), just s. 31960 Little Mack Ave 48066. Fax: 586/296-7412. **Facility:** 118 units. 104 one-bedroom standard units. 14 one-bedroom suites ($250) with kitchens. 3 stories, interior corridors. **Parking:** on-site, winter plug-ins. **Terms:** 3 day cancellation notice-fee imposed. **Amenities:** voice mail, hair dryers. **Dining:** 5 pm-11 pm, Fri & Sat-midnight. **Pool(s):** heated indoor. **Leisure Activities:** whirlpool, billiards. *Fee:* racquetball courts, massage, game room. **Guest Services:** valet and coin laundry. **Business Services:** meeting rooms. **Cards:** AX, DC, DS, MC, VI. **Special Amenities: free continental breakfast and free local telephone calls.**

SOME UNITS

[SD] [🍽] [📷] [🏊] [♨] [✕] [📷] [DATA PORT] / [✕] [VCR] [🖨] [💻] / FEE   FEE

EXTENDED STAYAMERICA
Book at aaa.com

Phone: 586/294-0141 [29]

Small-scale Hotel

Property failed to provide current rates

Location: I-94, exit 232 (Little Mack Ave), 0.3 mi n, then just w. 20200 13 Mile Rd 48066. Fax: 586/294-0141. **Facility:** 110 one-bedroom standard units with efficiencies. 3 stories, interior corridors. *Bath:* combo or shower only. **Parking:** on-site. **Amenities:** dual phone lines, voice mail, hair dryers. **Guest Services:** coin laundry.

SOME UNITS

[&M] [🔌] [📷] [DATA PORT] [🔌] [🖨] [💻] / [✕]

HOLIDAY INN EXPRESS & SUITES
Book at aaa.com

Phone: (586)285-5800 [24]

Small-scale Hotel

All Year	1P: $99-$109	2P: $99-$109	XP: $10 F20

Location: I-94, exit 232 (Little Mack Ave), just n. 31900 Little Mack Ave 48066. Fax: 586/285-5811. **Facility:** 90 one-bedroom standard units, some with whirlpools. 3 stories, interior corridors. *Bath:* combo or shower only. **Parking:** on-site. **Amenities:** video games (fee), dual phone lines, voice mail, irons, hair dryers. **Pool(s):** heated indoor. **Leisure Activities:** whirlpool, exercise room. **Guest Services:** valet and coin laundry. **Business Services:** meeting rooms, business center. **Cards:** AX, DC, DS, MC, VI.

SOME UNITS

[ASK] [SD] [📶] [&M] [🏊] [📷] [DATA PORT] [💻] / [✕] [🔌] [🖨] /

MICROTEL INN & SUITES
Book at aaa.com

Phone: (586)415-1000 [28]

Small-scale Hotel

All Year	1P: $44-$64	2P: $49-$69	XP: $5 F

Location: I-94, exit 232 (Little Mack Ave), just s, then 0.4 mi w. 20313 13 Mile Rd 48066. Fax: 586/415-1414. **Facility:** 98 one-bedroom standard units. 3 stories, interior corridors. *Bath:* combo or shower only. **Parking:** on-site. **Terms:** weekly rates available, [CP] & [ECP] meal plans available. **Amenities:** video games, voice mail. *Some:* irons, hair dryers. **Pool(s):** heated indoor. **Leisure Activities:** exercise room. **Guest Services:** complimentary laundry. **Business Services:** meeting rooms. **Cards:** AX, DC, DS, MC, VI.

SOME UNITS

[ASK] [SD] [📶] [&M] [🏊] [📷] [DATA PORT] / [✕] [🔌] [🖨] [💻] /

RED ROOF INN
Book at aaa.com

Phone: (586)296-0310 [25]

AAA SAVE

Motel

5/16-10/16	1P: $47-$67	2P: $52-$72	XP: $5 F18
10/17-3/31	1P: $42-$63	2P: $47-$68	XP: $5 F18
4/1-5/15	1P: $40-$62	2P: $45-$62	XP: $5 F18

Location: I-94, exit 232 (Little Mack Ave), just n. 31800 Little Mack Ave 48066. Fax: 586/296-0316. **Facility:** 109 one-bedroom standard units. 2 stories (no elevator), exterior corridors. *Bath:* combo or shower only. **Parking:** on-site. **Terms:** small pets only. **Amenities:** video games (fee), voice mail. **Cards:** AX, CB, DC, DS, MC, VI. **Special Amenities: free local telephone calls and free newspaper.**

SOME UNITS

[🛏] [📶] [&] [📷] [DATA PORT] / [✕] [🔌] [🖨] /

(See map and index starting on p. 226)

———— WHERE TO DINE ————

MR. PAUL'S CHOPHOUSE **Lunch:** $8-$15 **Dinner:** $10-$23 **Phone:** 586/777-7770 44
American
Location: I-94, exit 232 (Little Mack Ave), 0.3 mi n, 1.5 mi w on 13 Mile Rd, then 1 mi n. 29850 Groesbeck Hwy 48066. **Hours:** 11 am-11 pm, Sat from 4:30 pm. Closed major holidays; also Sun. **Reservations:** suggested. **Features:** Don't let the industrial corridor location fool you. Inside you will find wonderful tableside preparations of Chateau-Briand for two and Cherries Jubilee that make this restaurant perfect for special occasions. Dressy casual; cocktails. **Parking:** on-site and valet. **Cards:** AX, DC, DS, MC, VI.

PEARL CITY **Lunch:** $6-$9 **Dinner:** $7-$10 **Phone:** 586/293-4640 43
Chinese
Location: I-94, exit 232 (Little Mack Ave), just e. 20749 13 Mile Rd 48066. **Hours:** 11 am-10 pm, Fri & Sat-11 pm, Sun from noon. Closed: 7/4, 11/25. **Features:** Traditional preparations of chicken, beef and seafood show Cantonese, Mandarin, Szechuan and Hunan influences. The menu also lists a handful of American dishes. The large, open dining room is inviting to families. Service is attentive and cordial. Casual dress; cocktails. **Parking:** on-site. **Cards:** AX, DC, DS, MC, VI.

ROYAL OAK pop. 60,062   (See map and index starting on p. 226)

———— WHERE TO STAY ————

TRAVELODGE *Book at aaa.com* **Phone:** (248)549-1600 40
Motel
All Year 1P: $51-$65 2P: $53-$67 XP: $5 F16
Location: At jct 13 Mile Rd and Woodward Ave. 30776 Woodward Ave 48073. Fax: 248/549-2870. **Facility:** 78 one-bedroom standard units. 2 stories, exterior corridors. *Bath:* combo or shower only. **Parking:** on-site. **Terms:** weekly rates available, [ECP] meal plan available. **Amenities:** hair dryers. **Cards:** AX, CB, DC, DS, MC, VI. **Special Amenities:** free continental breakfast and free local telephone calls.

SOME UNITS

———— WHERE TO DINE ————

ANDIAMO OSTERIA **Lunch:** $8-$12 **Dinner:** $10-$15 **Phone:** 248/582-9300 56
Italian
Location: Just s of 11 Mile Rd; downtown. 129 S Main St 48067. **Hours:** 11 am-11 pm, Fri-midnight, Sat 4 pm-midnight, Sun 4 pm-9 pm. Closed major holidays. **Reservations:** accepted. **Features:** Perfect for people-watching, the stylish restaurant, part of a local chain, has quickly become the spot to enjoy a leisurely meal of classic fare. Homemade pasta, such as gnocchi and ravioli, stands out among diverse selections of fresh seafood, steak and chicken. Cocktails. **Parking:** valet and street. **Cards:** AX, DS, MC, VI.

BOOCOO **Lunch:** $6-$14 **Dinner:** $16-$28 **Phone:** 248/655-5000 51
French
Location: Just e of jct Crooks Rd. 1824 W 14 Mile Rd 48072. **Hours:** 11 am-2:30 & 5-10:30 pm, Thurs-Sat to 11 pm, Sun 4 pm-9 pm. Closed major holidays. **Reservations:** accepted. **Features:** In the best traditions of European bistros, the exposed brick walls are hung with large, gold-framed circus murals that lend to a casually sophisticated, yet none too serious, atmosphere. Focusing on European country cuisine, the kitchen produces a large range of French-Italian dishes as diverse as flat-iron steaks, cassoulets, braised osso buco and pan-seared duck breasts. Casual dress; cocktails. **Parking:** on-site. **Cards:** AX, DS, MC, VI.

COMET BURGER **Lunch:** $3-$5 **Dinner:** $3-$5 **Phone:** 248/414-4567 57
American
Location: Just s of 11 Mile Rd; downtown. 207 S Main St 48307. **Hours:** 11 am-midnight, Thurs-Sat 11 am-3 am. Closed: 12/25, 12/26. **Features:** The claims to fame for this stereotypical hole-in-the-wall restaurant aren't the homages to Elvis, Buddy or Marilyn that adorn the walls but rather the quintessential sliders, a perfect match to satisfy late-night cravings. Casual dress. **Parking:** street. **Cards:** DS, MC, VI.

D'AMATO'S NEIGHBORHOOD RESTAURANT **Dinner:** $10-$20 **Phone:** 248/584-7400 59
Italian
Location: At corner of S Washington Ave and Sherman Dr; downtown. 222 S Sherman Dr 48067. **Hours:** 5 pm-10 pm, Fri & Sat-11 pm, Sun 4 pm-9 pm. Closed major holidays. **Features:** The friendly restaurant delivers large portions of simple favorites: light bites, salad, pizza, pasta, chicken, fish and sausage. The atmosphere is warm and inviting. Diners can watch cooking through a partial wall and enjoy delectable desserts. Casual dress; cocktails. **Parking:** street. **Cards:** AX, DC, DS, MC, VI.

GOOMBAH'S PIZZERIA **Lunch:** $7-$14 **Dinner:** $7-$14 **Phone:** 248/398-9500 62
Pizza
Location: Jct 4th and Washington sts; downtown. 316 W 4th St 48063. **Hours:** 11 am-9 pm, Fri & Sat-10 pm, Mon-4 pm. Closed major holidays. **Features:** Next to Royal Oak Theatre, the tiny restaurant has limited seating inside. Everything is made from scratch, including such pizzas as roasted veggie, roasted garlic and meat mania. The menu offers a refreshing change from the ordinary. Casual dress. **Parking:** street. **Cards:** AX, MC, VI.

LEPANTO **Dinner:** $13-$25 **Phone:** 248/541-2228 61
Italian
Location: Jct Main and 4th sts, just w; downtown. 116 W 4th St 48067. **Hours:** 5:30 pm-10 pm, Fri & Sat-11 pm. Closed major holidays; also Sun & Mon. **Reservations:** accepted. **Features:** Soft background music and low level lighting foster a true sense of intimacy in this sophisticated and trendy dining room. Homemade pastas like the tortui "candy wrapper" pasta show what levels fresh ingredients and creativity can achieve. Dressy casual; cocktails. **Parking:** street. **Cards:** AX, MC, VI.

(See map and index starting on p. 226)

LILY'S SEAFOOD
◆◆ ◆◆

Seafood

Lunch: $8-$20   **Dinner:** $16-$25   **Phone:** 248/591-5459   63
Location: Jct W 4th and S Washington sts; downtown. 410 S Washington St 48067. **Hours:** 11 am-midnight, Fri & Sat-2 am. Closed major holidays. **Features:** Besides brewing its own beers and sodas on site, the casual yet chic restaurant with exposed brick walls and aquariums offers a diverse menu of fresh seafood. Also on the menu is a limited selection of pasta and steaks. Among choices are Creole soup with homemade seafood sausage, Prince Edward Island mussels, seafood boil and Mom's Key lime cheesecake, all of which are reminiscent of the East Coast. Casual dress; cocktails. **Parking:** street. **Cards:** AX, DC, DS, MC, VI.

MEMPHIS SMOKE
◆◆

Regional American

Lunch: $6-$9   **Dinner:** $7-$15   **Phone:** 248/543-4300   55
Location: At the corner of 11 Mile Rd and Main St; downtown. 100 S Main 48073. **Hours:** 11 am-12:30 am, Fri & Sat-1:15 am, Sun noon-12:30 am. Closed major holidays. **Features:** Southern-style pork ribs, beef brisket, smoked turkey and meat slow-cooked over wood coals are examples of tasty, home-style dishes. The large, open dining room is loud, bustling and fun. Blues bands perform late in the evening most nights. Casual dress; cocktails; entertainment. **Parking:** on-site. **Cards:** AX, MC, VI.

PRONTO! 608
◆◆ ◆◆

Deli/Subs
Sandwiches

Lunch: $4-$8   **Dinner:** $4-$8   **Phone:** 248/544-7900   65
Location: Jct 6th and Washington sts; center. 608 S Washington St 48067. **Hours:** 11 am-10 pm, Fri-midnight, Sat 9 am-midnight, Sun 9 am-2 pm. Closed major holidays. **Features:** Much of the produce that goes into the sandwiches and limited selection of entrees is specially grown for this fun and informal restaurant. While known for the enormous choices of sandwiches, the restaurant also offers a good selection of house-made desserts. Casual dress; cocktails. **Parking:** street. **Cards:** AX, DS, MC, VI.

RED COAT TAVERN
◆◆ ◆◆

American

Lunch: $8-$16   **Dinner:** $8-$16   **Phone:** 248/549-0300   53
Location: 1 mi n from jct W 13 Mile Rd and SR 1. 31542 Woodward Ave 48073. **Hours:** 11 am-2 pm. Closed major holidays; also Sun. **Features:** Patrons can watch for the red-coated soldier at the entrance to the British-style tavern. Deep red lights, dark woods and brick walls give the restaurant a charming atmosphere. While there are plenty of other items on the menu, burgers with a slightly spicy secret sauce are the main draw. Casual dress; cocktails. **Parking:** on-site. **Cards:** AX, DC, DS, MC, VI.

REXY'S BANGKOK CUISINE
◆◆ ◆◆

Thai

Lunch: $8-$10   **Dinner:** $10-$15   **Phone:** 248/288-0002   54
Location: Jct 13 Mile Rd; southside of shopping plaza. 30923 Woodward Ave 48073. **Hours:** 11 am-10 pm, Fri-11 pm, Sat noon-11 pm, Sun noon-10 pm. Closed major holidays. **Features:** Next to an office supply store, the surprisingly spacious and eclectic restaurant—with gold and red murals, smiling Buddha figures and stylized flame-like arches—is a visual feast. Representative of the surprisingly complex and flavorful food are such national dishes as satays, tom yum soups and pad thai. Casual dress; cocktails. **Parking:** on-site. **Cards:** AX, DC, MC, VI.

ROYAL OAK BREWERY
◆◆ ◆◆

American

Lunch: $6-$10   **Dinner:** $8-$12   **Phone:** 248/544-1141   60
Location: Just e of jct Main and 4th sts; downtown. 215 E 4th St 48067. **Hours:** 11:30 am-10 pm, Fri & Sat-11 pm. Closed major holidays. **Features:** A dozen rotating microbrewed ales complement selections of lighter fare: soup, salad, sandwiches, appetizers, pasta dishes and gourmet pizza. Try the delicious, freshly baked pita bread. The cozy patio is a great place to unwind after a long day. Casual dress; cocktails. **Parking:** on-site (fee). **Cards:** AX, DC, DS, MC, VI.

TOM'S OYSTER BAR
◆◆ ◆◆

Seafood

Lunch: $11-$20   **Dinner:** $11-$20   **Phone:** 248/541-1186   58
Location: 0.3 mi s of jct 11 Mile Rd; downtown. 318 S Main St 48067. **Hours:** 11 am-11 pm, Fri & Sat-midnight. Closed major holidays. **Features:** From tin ceilings to checkered tablecloths, the local chain of raw bars bears more than a slight resemblance to New England fish houses. Fresh oysters are the signature item on a menu of diverse seafood selections, including panko-fried shrimp and grilled yellowfin tuna. Among other choices are burgers and pasta. Casual dress; cocktails. **Parking:** street. **Cards:** AX, DS, MC, VI.

WOOD-RUFF'S SUPPER CLUB
◆◆ ◆◆

American

Dinner: $14-$27   **Phone:** 248/586-1519   64
Location: Just w of jct of Main St; downtown. 212 W 6th St 48067. **Hours:** 5 pm-10 pm, Thurs-Sat to 11 pm, Sun 4 pm-9 pm. Closed major holidays; also Mon. **Reservations:** suggested. **Features:** This upscale supper club features live music performed just above and behind the Flamingo bar several nights a week. A unique and creative continental menu offers such dishes as grilled jumbo shrimp, marinated pork chops and seafood specials. Dressy casual; cocktails. **Parking:** valet and street. **Cards:** AX, CB, DC, MC, VI.

WOW PAN-ASIAN CUISINE
◆◆ ◆◆

Pacific Rim

Lunch: $10-$12   **Dinner:** $10-$24   **Phone:** 248/554-8600   52
Location: Just s of jct 14 Mile Rd. 32832 Woodward Ave 48073. **Hours:** 11 am-11 pm, Fri-midnight, Sat 4 pm-midnight, Sun 4 pm-10 pm. Closed major holidays. **Reservations:** accepted. **Features:** While the metallic boxy exterior does not resemble that of a typical Chinese restaurant, the sushi bar in the main dining room should be reassuring. The extensive menu covers most every Asian cuisine type and more. Casual dress; cocktails. **Parking:** on-site. **Cards:** AX, MC, VI.

SOUTHFIELD pop. 78,296   (See map and index starting on p. 226)

——— **WHERE TO STAY** ———

BEST WESTERN SOUTHFIELD INN
AAA [SAVE]
◆◆ ◆◆

Small-scale Hotel

Phone: (248)368-6130   54
All Year   **1P:** $79-$99   **2P:** $79-$99   **XP:** $6   F18
Location: I-696, exit 10, just s. 26111 Telegraph Rd 48034. Fax: 248/368-6143. **Facility:** 105 one-bedroom standard units, some with whirlpools. 3 stories, interior corridors. *Bath:* combo or shower only. **Parking:** on-site. **Terms:** weekly rates available, [ECP] meal plan available. **Amenities:** voice mail, irons, hair dryers. **Leisure Activities:** exercise room. **Guest Services:** valet laundry. **Business Services:** meeting rooms. **Cards:** AX, CB, DC, DS, MC, VI. **Special Amenities:** free expanded continental breakfast and free newspaper.

SOME UNITS

(See map and index starting on p. 226)

CANDLEWOOD SUITES   *Book at aaa.com*   Phone: (248)945-0010   **49**
▼▼▼ ▼▼▼   All Year   1P: $175
Small-scale Hotel   **Location:** SR 10 (Northwestern Hwy), exit Lasher Rd, just e. 1 Corporate Dr 48076. Fax: 248/945-0115. **Facility:** 121 units. 83 one-bedroom standard units with efficiencies. 38 one-bedroom suites with efficiencies. 3 stories, interior corridors. *Bath:* combo or shower only. **Parking:** on-site. **Terms:** office hours 7 am-11 pm, small pets only ($5 extra charge). **Amenities:** video library, CD players, dual phone lines, voice mail, irons, hair dryers. **Leisure Activities:** exercise room. **Guest Services:** sundries. **Cards:** AX, DC, DS, MC, VI.
SOME UNITS
[ASK] [S/D] [🐾] [🍴] [&M] [&] [VCR] [📷] [DATA PORT] [📶] [📠] [💻] /[✕]/
FEE

COMFORT SUITES   *Book at aaa.com*   Phone: (248)357-9990   **57**
▼▼▼ ▼▼▼   All Year   1P: $79-$229   XP: $5   F
Small-scale Hotel   **Location:** SR 10 (Northwestern Hwy), exit 10 Mile Rd. 24977 Northwestern Hwy 48076. Fax: 248/358-0140. **Facility:** 81 one-bedroom standard units, some with whirlpools. 3 stories, interior corridors. *Bath:* combo or shower only. **Parking:** on-site. **Terms:** [CP] meal plan available. **Amenities:** high-speed Internet, dual phone lines, voice mail, irons, hair dryers. **Pool(s):** heated indoor. **Leisure Activities:** exercise room. **Guest Services:** valet and coin laundry. **Business Services:** meeting rooms. **Cards:** AX, DC, DS, JC, MC, VI.
SOME UNITS
[ASK] [S/D] [🍴] [&M] [&] [🏊] [📷] [DATA PORT] [📶] [📠] [💻] /[✕]/

COURTYARD BY MARRIOTT-SOUTHFIELD   *Book at aaa.com*   Phone: (248)358-1222   **51**
▼▼▼ ▼   5/23-9/11   1P: $79-$129   2P: $79-$129
          9/12-3/31   1P: $69-$129   2P: $69-$129
          4/1-5/22   1P: $59-$119   2P: $59-$119
Small-scale Hotel   **Location:** SR 10 (Northwestern Hwy), exit Lasher Rd, just nw. 27027 Northwestern Hwy 48034. Fax: 248/354-3820. **Facility:** 147 units. 133 one-bedroom standard units. 14 one-bedroom suites ($124-$144). 2-3 stories, interior corridors. *Bath:* combo or shower only. **Parking:** on-site. **Amenities:** high-speed Internet (fee), dual phone lines, voice mail, irons, hair dryers. **Pool(s):** heated indoor. **Leisure Activities:** whirlpool, exercise room. **Guest Services:** valet and coin laundry. **Business Services:** meeting rooms. **Cards:** AX, CB, DC, DS, JC, MC, VI.
SOME UNITS
[S/D] [🍴] [&] [🗂] [🏊] [📷] [DATA PORT] [💻] /[✕] [📶]/

EXTENDED STAYAMERICA   Phone: 248/355-2115   **47**
▼▼ ▼▼   Property failed to provide current rates
Small-scale Hotel   **Location:** SR 10 (Northwestern Hwy), exit Beck Rd, just w to Franklin Rd, 0.3 mi s, then just w. 2650 American Dr 48034. Fax: 248/355-1044. **Facility:** 122 one-bedroom standard units with efficiencies. 3 stories, interior corridors. *Bath:* combo or shower only. **Parking:** on-site. **Terms:** office hours 7 am-11 pm. **Amenities:** dual phone lines, voice mail.
SOME UNITS
[&M] [&] [📷] [DATA PORT] [📶] [📠] [💻] /[✕]/

HAMPTON INN-SOUTHFIELD   *Book at aaa.com*   Phone: 248/356-5500   **48**
▼▼▼ ▼   All Year   1P: $79-$159   2P: $79-$159
Small-scale Hotel   **Location:** I-696, exit 10 (Telegraph Rd N), just n to 11 Mile Rd, then 0.5 mi e on Northwestern Service Dr. 27500 Northwestern Hwy 48034. Fax: 248/356-2083. **Facility:** 154 one-bedroom standard units. 2 stories, interior corridors. **Parking:** on-site. **Terms:** [ECP] meal plan available. **Amenities:** voice mail, irons, hair dryers. **Pool(s):** heated indoor. **Leisure Activities:** whirlpool, exercise room. **Guest Services:** valet and coin laundry. **Business Services:** meeting rooms. **Cards:** AX, CB, DC, DS, MC, VI.
SOME UNITS
[ASK] [S/D] [🍴] [🗂] [🏊] [📷] [DATA PORT] [💻] /[✕] [VCR] [📶]/

HAWTHORN SUITES LTD   *Book at aaa.com*   Phone: (248)350-2400   **56**
▼▼▼ ▼   All Year [BP]   1P: $89-$134
Small-scale Hotel   **Location:** SR 10 (Northwestern Hwy), exit 10 Mile Rd. 25100 Northwestern Hwy 48075. Fax: 248/350-8771. **Facility:** 91 units. 82 one- and 9 two-bedroom suites, some with efficiencies and/or whirlpools. 3 stories, interior corridors. *Bath:* combo or shower only. **Parking:** on-site. **Terms:** small pets only ($150 fee). **Amenities:** dual phone lines, voice mail, irons, hair dryers. **Pool(s):** heated indoor. **Leisure Activities:** whirlpool, exercise room. **Guest Services:** complimentary evening beverages: Wed, valet and coin laundry. **Business Services:** meeting rooms. **Cards:** AX, DC, DS, JC, MC, VI.
SOME UNITS
[ASK] [S/D] [🐾] [🍴] [&M] [&] [🏊] [📷] [DATA PORT] [📶] [📠] [💻] /[✕] [VCR]/
FEE

HILTON INN-SOUTHFIELD   *Book at aaa.com*   Phone: (248)357-1100   **46**
▼▼▼ ▼   All Year   1P: $69-$169   2P: $69-$169   XP: $15   F17
Small-scale Hotel   **Location:** US 10 (Northwestern Hwy), just w on Beck Rd, then 0.3 mi s on Franklin Rd. 26000 American Dr 48034. Fax: 248/372-2323. **Facility:** 198 units. 196 one-bedroom standard units. 2 one-bedroom suites. 7 stories, interior corridors. **Parking:** on-site. **Terms:** [AP] meal plan available, package plans, pets ($50 deposit). **Amenities:** video games (fee), dual phone lines, voice mail, irons, hair dryers. **Pool(s):** heated indoor. **Leisure Activities:** sauna, whirlpool, exercise room. **Guest Services:** valet laundry, area transportation. **Business Services:** meeting rooms, business center. **Cards:** AX, DC, DS, MC, VI.
SOME UNITS
[ASK] [🐾] [🍴] [🍷] [🗂] [🏊] [✕] [📷] [DATA PORT] [💻] /[✕] [📶] [📠]/
FEE

HOLIDAY INN-SOUTHFIELD   *Book at aaa.com*   Phone: (248)353-7700   **53**
▼▼▼ ▼▼   All Year   1P: $121-$145
Large-scale Hotel   **Location:** I-696, exit 9, just s on US 24 (Telegraph Rd). 26555 Telegraph Rd 48034. Fax: 248/353-8377. **Facility:** 415 one-bedroom standard units. 2-15 stories, interior corridors. *Bath:* combo or shower only. **Parking:** on-site. **Terms:** package plans - seasonal & weekends, pets ($50 deposit, in smoking units). **Amenities:** voice mail, irons, hair dryers. **Pool(s):** heated indoor. **Leisure Activities:** whirlpool, exercise room. *Fee:* game room. **Guest Services:** gift shop, valet and coin laundry. **Business Services:** conference facilities. **Cards:** AX, DC, DS, MC, VI.
SOME UNITS
[ASK] [S/D] [🐾] [🍴] [🍷] [&M] [&] [🗂] [🏊] [✕] [📷] [DATA PORT] [💻] /[✕] [📶]/
FEE

(See map and index starting on p. 226)

HOMESTEAD STUDIO SUITES HOTEL-DETROIT/SOUTHFIELD · *Book at aaa.com* · Phone: (248)213-4500 · 43
▼▼▼▼ All Year · 1P: $69-$84 · 2P: $74-$89 · XP: $5 · F17
Small-scale Hotel · **Location:** I-696, exit 9, just nw of jct US 24 (Telegraph Rd). 28500 Northwestern Hwy 48034. Fax: 248/213-4600. **Facility:** 134 one-bedroom standard units with efficiencies. 3 stories, interior corridors. *Bath:* combo or shower only. **Parking:** on-site. **Terms:** pets ($75 extra charge). **Amenities:** voice mail, irons. **Guest Services:** valet and coin laundry. **Cards:** AX, CB, DC, DS, MC, VI.
SOME UNITS
(ASK) (S▣) (FEE) (▥↑) (▧M) (▧) (◢) (◆◆) (◆) (DATA PORT) (▤) (▭) (▤) / (✕) (VCR)

MOTOR CITY HOWARD JOHNSON PLAZA HOTEL · *Book at aaa.com* · Phone: (248)552-8833 · 59
(AAA) (SAVE) · All Year · 1P: $59-$159 · 2P: $69-$169
▼▼ ▼▼ · **Location:** SR 10 (Lodge Frwy), exit 8 Mile Rd, then 0.5 mi n. Located across from the shopping mall. 16400 JL Hudson Dr 48075. Fax: 248/559-3675. **Facility:** 264 units. 262 one-bedroom standard units. 2 one-bedroom suites with whirlpools. 14 stories, interior corridors. **Parking:** on-site. **Amenities:** voice mail, irons, hair dryers.
Large-scale Hotel · **Dining:** 7 am-10 pm. **Pool(s):** heated indoor/outdoor. **Leisure Activities:** saunas, tennis court, exercise room, volleyball. **Guest Services:** sundries, valet laundry. **Business Services:** conference facilities.
Cards: AX, DC, DS, MC, VI.
SOME UNITS
(S▣) (▥) (◢) (✕) (◆) (DATA PORT) (▭) / (✕) (▤) (▤) /

RAMADA INN-SOUTHFIELD · *Book at aaa.com* · Phone: (248)552-7777 · 58
▼▼ ▼▼ · All Year · 1P: $79-$109
Small-scale Hotel · **Location:** SR 10 (Lodge Frwy), exit 8 Mile Rd, 0.5 mi n on Northwestern Hwy access road, then 0.3 mi e. 17017 W 9 Mile Rd 48075-4566. Fax: 248/552-7778. **Facility:** 216 units. 199 one-bedroom standard units, some with whirlpools. 17 one-bedroom suites ($158). 17 stories, interior corridors. **Parking:** on-site. **Terms:** weekly rates available, [AP], [BP], [CP] meal plans available, 7% service charge. **Amenities:** video games (fee), voice mail, irons, hair dryers. **Pool(s):** heated outdoor. **Guest Services:** gift shop, valet laundry, area transportation. **Business Services:** conference facilities. **Cards:** AX, CB, DC, DS, MC, VI.
SOME UNITS
(ASK) (S▣) (▥) (Y) (◢) (◢) (◆) (DATA PORT) (▭) / (✕) (VCR) (▤) (▤) /
FEE FEE FEE

RED ROOF INN-SOUTHFIELD · *Book at aaa.com* · Phone: (248)353-7200 · 45
(AAA) (SAVE) · 4/27-8/30 · 1P: $60-$65 · 2P: $66-$71 · XP: $6 · F18
▼▼ ▼▼ · 8/31-12/31 · 1P: $57-$65 · 2P: $63-$71 · XP: $6 · F18
· 1/1-3/31 · 1P: $51-$65 · 2P: $57-$71 · XP: $6 · F18
Motel · 4/1-4/26 · 1P: $50-$65 · 2P: $56-$71 · XP: $6 · F18
Location: I-696, exit 9, just nw of Telegraph Rd. 27660 Northwestern Hwy 48034. Fax: 248/353-1580. **Facility:** 114 one-bedroom standard units. 3 stories, exterior corridors. *Bath:* combo or shower only. **Parking:** on-site.
Terms: small pets only. **Amenities:** video games (fee), voice mail. **Guest Services:** valet laundry. **Business Services:** meeting rooms. **Cards:** AX, CB, DC, DS, MC, VI. **Special Amenities:** free local telephone calls and free newspaper.
SOME UNITS
(◆◆) (▧M) (▧) (◢) (DATA PORT) / (✕) (▤) (▤) /
FEE FEE

RESIDENCE INN BY MARRIOTT · *Book at aaa.com* · Phone: (248)352-8900 · 50
▼▼ ▼▼ · All Year · 1P: $109-$149
Location: I-696, exit 11 (Evergreen Rd), just sw of jct 11 Mile and Evergreen rds. 26700 Central Park Blvd 48076.
Small-scale Hotel · Fax: 248/352-2579. **Facility:** 144 units. 108 one- and 36 two-bedroom standard units with kitchens. 2 stories (no elevator), exterior corridors. *Bath:* combo or shower only. **Parking:** on-site. **Terms:** [BP] meal plan available, package plans - weekends. **Amenities:** voice mail, irons, hair dryers. **Pool(s):** heated outdoor. **Leisure Activities:** exercise room, sports court. **Guest Services:** valet and coin laundry. **Business Services:** meeting rooms. **Cards:** AX, CB, DC, DS, JC, MC, VI.
SOME UNITS
(ASK) (S▣) (▥↑) (▧M) (▧) (◢) (◆) (DATA PORT) (▤) (▭) (▤) / (✕) /

SOUTHFIELD MARRIOTT HOTEL · *Book at aaa.com* · Phone: (248)356-7400 · 52
▼▼▼ ▼▼ · All Year · 1P: $169
Location: SR 10 (Northwestern Hwy), exit Lasher Rd, just nw. 27033 Northwestern Hwy 48034. Fax: 248/356-5501.
Small-scale Hotel · **Facility:** 226 one-bedroom standard units. 6 stories, interior corridors. **Parking:** on-site. **Terms:** check-in 4 pm, package plans - weekends. **Amenities:** dual phone lines, voice mail, irons, hair dryers. *Fee:* video games, high-speed Internet. **Pool(s):** heated indoor. **Leisure Activities:** saunas, whirlpool, exercise room. **Guest Services:** gift shop, valet laundry. **Business Services:** meeting rooms, business center. **Cards:** AX, CB, DC, DS, JC, MC, VI.
SOME UNITS
(ASK) (S▣) (▥) (Y) (◢) (◢) (✕) (◆) (DATA PORT) (▭) / (✕) (▤) (▤) /

(See map and index starting on p. 226)

SPRINGHILL SUITES BY MARRIOTT DETROIT/SOUTHFIELD   *Book at aaa.com*   Phone: 248/352-6100   44

4/1-9/20	1P: $114-$149	2P: $114-$175
9/21-10/31 & 1/1-3/31	1P: $114-$119	2P: $114-$119
11/1-12/31	1P: $109-$114	2P: $109-$114

Small-scale Hotel   **Location:** I-696, exit 8 (Northwestern Hwy), 0.5 mi nw on SR 10. 28555 Northwestern Hwy 48034. Fax: 248/352-6116. **Facility:** 84 one-bedroom standard units. 3 stories, interior corridors. *Bath:* combo or shower only. **Parking:** on-site. **Terms:** cancellation fee imposed. **Amenities:** video games (fee), high-speed Internet, voice mail, irons, hair dryers. **Pool(s):** small heated indoor. **Leisure Activities:** whirlpool, exercise room. **Guest Services:** sundries, valet and coin laundry. **Business Services:** meeting rooms. **Cards:** AX, DC, DS, MC, VI.

SOME UNITS

WESTIN HOTEL SOUTHFIELD-DETROIT   *Book at aaa.com*   Phone: (248)827-4000   55

All Year	1P: $89-$270	2P: $89-$270	XP: $10 F

Location: SR 10 (Northwestern Hwy), exit 10 Mile/Evergreen rds, 0.3 mi n. 1500 Town Center 48075. Fax: 248/827-4002. **Facility:** This distinctive hotel in the Southfield Town Center complex offers easy access to the Detroit-area business community. 387 one-bedroom standard units, some with whirlpools. 12 stories, Large-scale Hotel   interior corridors. *Bath:* combo or shower only. **Parking:** on-site and valet. **Amenities:** dual phone lines, voice mail, safes, honor bars, irons, hair dryers. *Some:* high-speed Internet. **Dining:** 6 am-10 pm, cocktails. **Pool(s):** heated indoor. **Leisure Activities:** saunas, whirlpool, exercise room. **Guest Services:** gift shop, valet laundry, area transportation-within 3 mi. **Business Services:** conference facilities, PC. **Cards:** AX, CB, DC, DS, JC, MC, VI. *(See color ad p 279)*

SOME UNITS

FEE   FEE   FEE

WHERE TO DINE

BACCO RISTORANTE   **Lunch:** $9-$17   **Dinner:** $20-$30   Phone: 248/356-6600   72

Italian   **Location:** Just n of jct 12 Mile Rd. 29410 Northwestern Hwy 48034. **Hours:** 11:30 am-2 & 5:30-10 pm, Sat 5:30 pm-11 pm. Closed major holidays; also Sun. **Reservations:** required. **Features:** "Modern" and "progressive" might be among words used to describe the restaurant, whose owners regularly travel to Italy to keep abreast of the ongoing evolution in Italian cuisine. An attractive yet comfortable dining room—brought to life with a large stylized mural and folds of fabric over the floor-to-ceiling windows—is the perfect venue in which diners can savor simple, lighter, modern fare with an expansive wine list. Dressy casual; cocktails. **Parking:** on-site and valet. **Cards:** MC, VI.

BEANS & CORNBREAD: A SOULFUL BISTRO   **Lunch:** $7-$9   **Dinner:** $12-$16   Phone: 248/208-1680   71

Soul Food   **Location:** Jct US 10 (Lodge Frwy/Northwestern Hwy) and I-94, 1 mi n; in Sunset Strip Plaza. 29508 Northwestern Hwy 48034. **Hours:** 11 am-3 & 5-9 pm, Fri-10 pm, Sat noon-10 pm, Sun noon-9 pm. Closed major holidays. **Features:** Cozy like a family room, the dining area has purple walls that display a collection of vintage magazine covers of prominent black Americans. Lines can be long, but lovers of Southern home cooking will find the wait well worth the effort. Items such as barbecue ribs, filet mignon and fried pork chops are served with traditional soul food accompaniments—from collard greens, black-eyed peas and grits to macaroni and cheese and candied sweet potatoes. Casual dress. **Parking:** on-site. **Cards:** DC, DS, MC, VI.

BEVERLY HILLS GRILL   **Lunch:** $8-$14   **Dinner:** $12-$23   Phone: 248/642-2355   68

American   **Location:** Just n of jct 13 Mile and Southfield rds. 31471 N Southfield Rd 48075. **Hours:** 7 am-11 pm, Fri-midnight, Sat 8 am-midnight, Sun 8 am-10 pm. Closed major holidays. **Reservations:** suggested. **Features:** Well known for their breakfast specials such as Banana Foster french toast and eggs benedict, this somewhat trendy diner also offers a California influenced lunch and dinner menu that has developed an ardent following, with specials such spicy rock shrimp on angel hair pasta. Casual dress; cocktails. **Parking:** on-site. **Cards:** AX, DC, MC, VI.

C A MUER'S MERRIWETHER   **Lunch:** $7-$15   **Dinner:** $14-$30   Phone: 248/358-1310   77

American   **Location:** I-696, exit US 24 (Telegraph Rd), 0.3 mi s. 25485 Telegraph Rd 48034. **Hours:** 11 am-10 pm, Sat from noon, Sun noon-9 pm. Closed major holidays. **Reservations:** suggested. **Features:** The surroundings are festive and upbeat in the English-style restaurant. Preparations of fowl, pork, beef and seafood are as eye-popping as they are palate-pleasing. Tantalizing desserts show the same artistic flair. Service is friendly and prompt. Casual dress; cocktails. **Parking:** valet. **Cards:** AX, DC, DS, MC, VI.

IL POSTO RISTORANTE   **Lunch:** $12-$18   **Dinner:** $18-$28   Phone: 248/827-8070   74

Italian   **Location:** I-696 W, exit 10, 0.6 mi w to SR 10 (Northwestern Hwy), then 1.1 mi n on SR 10/Northwestern Hwy. 29110 Franklin Rd 48034. **Hours:** 11:30 am-2:30 & 5:30-10 pm, Fri-10:30 pm, Sat 5:30 pm-10:30 pm. Closed major holidays; also Sun. **Reservations:** suggested, weekends. **Features:** An elegantly appointed restaurant that serves authentic regional Italian cuisine at its best. Highly recommended is the Carpaccio alla Mantovana and the desserts that are imported directly from Italy. Dressy casual; cocktails. **Parking:** on-site and valet. **Cards:** AX, CB, DC, MC, VI.

(See map and index starting on p. 226)

JOE MUER'S GRILL   Lunch: $8-$15   Dinner: $19-$27   Phone: 248/644-5330   69
Seafood
Location: Just s of jct Southfield (SR 39) and 13 Mile rds. 30855 Southfield Rd 48076. **Hours:** 11 am-10 pm, Fri-11 pm, Sat 5 pm-11 pm. Closed major holidays; also Sun. **Reservations:** suggested, weekends. **Features:** Experience casual, delightful dining in a formal atmosphere. The menu highlights innovative preparations of steak, seafood and signature side dishes. Seasonal choices, such as soft shell crab, also are listed. The attentive staff shows great follow-up. Casual dress; cocktails. **Parking:** on-site. **Cards:** AX, CB, DC, DS, MC, VI.

MORELS-A MICHIGAN BISTRO   Lunch: $9-$14   Dinner: $15-$27   Phone: 248/646-0370   70
Continental
Location: Between W 12 Mile and W 13 Mile rds; in Bingham Forms Office Complex. 30100 Telegraph Rd 48025. **Hours:** 11 am-10 pm, Fri-11 pm, Sat 5 pm-10 pm. Closed major holidays; also Sun. **Reservations:** suggested. **Features:** Named after a variety of mushroom grown in Michigan, the restaurant, not surprisingly, incorporates mushrooms into many of its menu items. A small herb and flower atrium is in the center of the place, which is illuminated with accent lighting. The ambience is decidedly romantic. Among creative interpretations of Michigan classics are sun-dried tomato and basil whitefish, sauteed Provini veal and hoisin-lacquered Peking duck. Dressy casual; cocktails. **Parking:** on-site and valet. **Cards:** AX, DS, MC, VI.

MORTON'S OF CHICAGO   Dinner: $25-$40   Phone: 248/354-6006   76
Steak House
Location: US 10 (Lodge Frwy), exit Evergreen Rd, 0.4 mi n on N Service Rd; on ground floor of Sterling Bank and Trust Building. One Town Square 48076. **Hours:** 5:30 pm-11 pm, Sun 5 pm-10 pm. Closed major holidays. **Reservations:** suggested. **Features:** In Southfield's Town Square, the upscale chain steakhouse exudes class and sophistication, with white table linens and dim lighting. Enormous cuts of marbled porterhouses, filets and strip steaks, as well as monster lobsters and fresh seafood, are presented on carts by personable servers. Dressy casual; cocktails. **Parking:** on-site and valet. **Cards:** AX, MC, VI.

NEW SEOUL RESTAURANT   Lunch: $9-$20   Dinner: $9-$20   Phone: 248/827-1600   75
Ethnic
Location: I-696, exit 9, jct US 24. 27566 Northwestern Hwy 48034. **Hours:** 11:30 am-10:30 pm, Sun noon-10 pm. Closed major holidays. **Reservations:** required. **Features:** A sushi bar and tempura choices are features that distinguish the restaurant, which delivers Korean and Japanese cuisine. Potted plants, natural lighting and attractive, solid-wood grill tables decorate the dining areas. Service is professional. Casual dress; cocktails. **Parking:** on-site. **Cards:** AX, DC, DS, MC, VI.

THE ORIGINAL PANCAKE HOUSE   Lunch: $6-$8   Phone: 248/357-3399   78
American
Location: SR 10 (Lodge Frwy), exit 10 Mile/Evergreen Rd, just e, then 1 mi s. 19355 W 10 Mile Rd 48075. **Hours:** 7 am-4 pm, Sat & Sun-5 pm. Closed major holidays. **Features:** Although the menu lists many varied options, long morning lines at the front entrance testify to the popularity of the freshly made breakfasts. Part of a nationwide chain, the restaurant focuses on using quality ingredients, such as freshly squeezed orange juice and fresh creamery butter. Portions are large. Casual dress. **Parking:** on-site.

TOM'S OYSTER BAR   Lunch: $11-$20   Dinner: $13-$24   Phone: 248/356-8881   73
Seafood
Location: Jct Northwestern Hwy, just n of 12 Mile Rd. 29106 Franklin Rd 48034. **Hours:** 11 am-11 pm, Fri-midnight, Sat 4 pm-midnight, Sun 5 pm-11 pm. Closed major holidays. **Reservations:** accepted. **Features:** From tin ceilings to checkered tablecloths, the local chain of raw bars bears more than a slight resemblance to New England fish houses. Fresh oysters are the signature item on a menu of diverse seafood selections, including panko fried shrimp and grilled yellowfin tuna. Among other choices are burgers and pasta. Casual dress; cocktails. **Parking:** on-site and valet. **Cards:** AX, DS, MC, VI.

SOUTHGATE pop. 30,136   (See map and index starting on p. 226)

-------- **WHERE TO STAY** --------

BAYMONT INN & SUITES DETROIT-SOUTHGATE   *Book at aaa.com*   Phone: (734)374-3000   163
All Year   1P: $79-$89   2P: $79-$89
Small-scale Hotel
Location: I-75, exit 37 (Northline Rd), just w. 12888 Reeck Rd 48195. Fax: 734/374-3010. **Facility:** 100 units. 97 one-bedroom standard units. 3 one-bedroom suites ($89-$109), some with kitchens. 3 stories, interior corridors. **Parking:** on-site. **Terms:** [ECP] meal plan available, small pets only. **Amenities:** video games, voice mail, irons, hair dryers. **Guest Services:** valet and coin laundry. **Business Services:** fax (fee). **Cards:** AX, CB, DC, DS, MC, VI. **Special Amenities:** free local telephone calls and free newspaper.
(See color ad p 287)

BEST VALUE INN & SUITES   *Book at aaa.com*   Phone: (734)287-8340   165
All Year Wkly [CP]   2P: $249-$299
Motel
Location: I-75, exit 37 (Northline Rd), just w. 18777 Northline Rd 48195. Fax: 734/287-4380. **Facility:** 134 units. 127 one-bedroom standard units, some with whirlpools. 7 one-bedroom suites ($119-$149) with whirlpools. 2 stories, exterior corridors. *Bath:* combo or shower only. **Parking:** on-site. **Terms:** cancellation fee imposed, daily rates available, 10% service charge. **Amenities:** video games (fee), voice mail. **Pool(s):** heated outdoor. **Business Services:** meeting rooms. **Cards:** AX, DS, JC, MC, VI. **Special Amenities:** free continental breakfast and early check-in/late check-out.

(See map and index starting on p. 226)

COMFORT SUITES *Book at aaa.com* Phone: (734)287-9200 162
All Year 1P: $79-$199 2P: $84-$199 XP: $5 F18
Location: I-75, exit 37 (Northline Rd), just w. 18950 Northline Rd 48195. Fax: 734/287-8373. **Facility:** 78 one-bedroom standard units, some with whirlpools. 3 stories, interior corridors. *Bath:* combo or shower only.
Parking: on-site. **Terms:** [ECP] meal plan available. **Amenities:** dual phone lines, voice mail, irons, hair dryers. *Fee:* video games, high-speed Internet, safes. **Pool(s):** heated indoor. **Leisure Activities:** sauna, steamroom, exercise room. **Guest Services:** valet and coin laundry. **Business Services:** meeting rooms, business center. **Cards:** AX, CB, DC, DS, JC, MC, VI. **Special Amenities: free expanded continental breakfast and free local telephone calls.**

SOME UNITS

HOLIDAY INN SOUTHGATE HERITAGE CENTER *Book at aaa.com* Phone: (734)283-4400 164
All Year 1P: $99-$215
Location: I-75, exit 37 (Northline Rd). 17201 Northline Rd 48195. Fax: 734/283-6855. **Facility:** 160 units. 157 one-bedroom standard units. 3 one-bedroom suites ($129-$215) with whirlpools. 2 stories, interior corridors. *Bath:* combo or shower only. **Parking:** on-site. **Terms:** check-in 4 pm. **Amenities:** video games, dual phone lines, voice mail, irons, hair dryers. **Pool(s):** heated indoor. **Leisure Activities:** whirlpool, exercise room. *Fee:* game room. **Guest Services:** valet and coin laundry, area transportation. **Business Services:** conference facilities. **Cards:** AX, CB, DC, DS, JC, MC, VI.

SOME UNITS

STERLING HEIGHTS pop. 124,471 (See map and index starting on p. 226)

—— **WHERE TO STAY** ——

BEST WESTERN STERLING INN BANQUET & CONFERENCE CTR *Book at aaa.com* Phone: (586)979-1400 6
All Year 1P: $109-$199 2P: $119-$209 XP: $25 F17
Location: I-696, exit 23, 4 mi n on SR 53, at jct 15 Mile Rd. 34911 Van Dyke Ave 48312. Fax: 586/979-7962. **Facility:** 246 units. 229 one-bedroom standard units, some with whirlpools. 17 one-bedroom suites, some with whirlpools. 2-5 stories, interior/exterior corridors. *Bath:* combo or shower only. **Parking:** on-site. **Terms:** cancellation fee imposed. **Amenities:** voice mail, safes, honor bars, irons, hair dryers. *Fee:* video games, high-speed Internet. **Dining:** 6 am-11 pm, Fri-midnight, Sat 7 am-midnight, Sun 7 am-10 pm, cocktails, also, Loon River Cafe, see separate listing. **Leisure Activities:** saunas, whirlpools, waterslide, indoor water park, jogging, exercise room, basketball. *Fee:* game room. **Guest Services:** gift shop. **Business Services:** conference facilities, business center. **Cards:** AX, CB, DC, DS, JC, MC, VI. **Special Amenities: free local telephone calls.** *(See ad below)*

SOME UNITS

TOWNEPLACE SUITES Phone: (586)566-0900
6/1-9/5 1P: $99-$129
4/1-5/31 & 9/6-11/18 1P: $89-$119
11/19-3/31 1P: $79-$109
Location: 1 mi e of jct SR 53 (Van Dyke Ave) and SR 59 (Hall Rd). Located across from the Lakeside Mall. 14800 Lakeside Cir 48313. Fax: 586/566-8901. **Facility:** 95 units. 73 one-bedroom standard units with kitchens. 22 one-bedroom suites with kitchens. 3 stories, interior corridors. *Bath:* combo or shower only. **Parking:** on-site. **Terms:** age restrictions may apply, small pets only ($100 fee, $5 extra charge). **Amenities:** dual phone lines, voice mail, irons, hair dryers. *Some:* high-speed Internet (fee). **Pool(s):** outdoor. **Leisure Activities:** exercise room. **Guest Services:** valet and coin laundry. **Cards:** AX, CB, DC, DS, JC, MC, VI.

SOME UNITS
FEE

(See map and index starting on p. 226)

------- WHERE TO DINE -------

LOON RIVER CAFE   Lunch: $6-$15   Dinner: $6-$15   Phone: 586/979-1420   8
▼▼▼   **Location:** I-696, exit 23, 4 mi n on SR 53, at jct 15 Mile Rd; in Best Western Sterling Inn Banquet & Conference Ctr.
American   34911 Van Dyke Ave 48312. **Hours:** 6 am-11 pm, Fri-midnight, Sat 7 am-midnight, Sun 7 am-10 pm.
Features: The rustic 1930s hunting lodge is a quaint setting in which to enjoy specialties of local wild
game and other creative dishes, such as lasagna soup and snake cakes. The master chef whips up all of
the tantalizing desserts on the premises. Casual dress; cocktails. **Parking:** on-site. **Cards:** AX, DC, DS, MC, VI.
(See ad p 282)   M Y X

MEZZALUNA   Lunch: $8-$20   Dinner: $12-$22   Phone: 586/268-7100   7
▼▼▼   **Location:** Just w of jct SR 53 (Van Dyke Rd). 7750 E Metro Pkwy 48310. **Hours:** 11 am-10 pm, Fri & Sat-11 pm,
Italian   Sun noon-9 pm. Closed major holidays. **Reservations:** accepted. **Features:** Vines, trellises and a large
trompe l'oeil Italian village scene give the restaurant a countryside feel. Daily specials, such as rabbit or
duck-filled ravioli, stand out among offerings of traditional cuisine. Dressy casual; cocktails. **Parking:**
on-site. **Cards:** AX, DC, DS, MC, VI.
                                                                                                                M Y X

TAYLOR pop. 65,868   (See map and index starting on p. 226)

------- WHERE TO STAY -------

QUALITY INN & SUITES   _Book at aaa.com_   Phone: (313)292-6730   137
AAA SAVE   All Year [ECP]   1P: $79-$89   2P: $79-$89   XP: $10   F18
▼▼▼▼   **Location:** I-94, exit 202B (Telegraph Rd), just s. 6778 S Telegraph Rd 48180. Fax: 313/292-5994. **Facility:** 78 units.
Small-scale Hotel   56 one-bedroom standard units, some with whirlpools. 22 one-bedroom suites, some with whirlpools. 3 stories, interior corridors. _Bath:_ combo or shower only. **Parking:** on-site. **Amenities:** high-speed Internet, dual
phone lines, voice mail, safes (fee), irons, hair dryers. **Pool(s):** heated indoor. **Leisure Activities:** sauna,
whirlpool, exercise room. **Guest Services:** valet and coin laundry. **Business Services:** meeting rooms.
Cards: AX, CB, DC, DS, MC, VI. **Special Amenities: free expanded continental breakfast and free room upgrade (subject
to availability with advanced reservations).**
                                                                                                    SOME UNITS
                                          S/D TI+ ⊃ X 📷 DATA PORT 📶 💻 / X 📠

RED ROOF INN-TAYLOR   _Book at aaa.com_   Phone: (734)374-1150
AAA SAVE   6/6-11/20   1P: $60-$75   2P: $65-$80   XP: $5   F18
4/25-6/5   1P: $55-$70   2P: $60-$75   XP: $5   F18
▼▼▼   11/21-3/31   1P: $54-$69   2P: $59-$74   XP: $5   F18
Motel   4/1-4/24   1P: $50-$65   2P: $55-$70   XP: $5   F18
Location: I-75, exit 36 (Eureka Rd), just w. 21230 Eureka Rd 48180. Fax: 734/374-1159. **Facility:** 111 one-bedroom
standard units. 2 stories, exterior corridors. _Bath:_ combo or shower only. **Parking:** on-site. **Amenities:** video
games, voice mail. **Cards:** AX, CB, DC, DS, MC, VI. **Special Amenities: free local telephone calls and free newspaper.**
                                                                                                    SOME UNITS
                                                              🐕 TI+ 📷 DATA PORT / X /

SUPER 8 MOTEL-TAYLOR   _Book at aaa.com_   Phone: (734)283-8830
▼▼▼   4/1-9/30 & 12/31-3/31   1P: $64   2P: $64   XP: $6   F17
10/1-12/30   1P: $54   2P: $54   XP: $6   F17
Small-scale Hotel   **Location:** I-75, exit 36 (Eureka Rd). 15101 Huron St 48180. Fax: 734/283-8830. **Facility:** 63 one-bedroom stan-
notice. **Amenities:** safes. **Cards:** AX, CB, DC, DS, JC, MC, VI.   dard units, some with whirlpools. 3 stories, interior corridors. **Parking:** on-site. **Terms:** 14 day cancellation
                                                                                                    SOME UNITS
                                          ASK S/D TI+ 📷 / X 📶 📠 /

TRENTON pop. 19,584

------- WHERE TO DINE -------

EIGHTEEN '97 SMOKEHOUSE RESTAURANT Historic   Lunch: $7-$11   Dinner: $11-$22   Phone: 734/671-3772
▼▼▼   **Location:** Just n of downtown. 2156 W Jefferson 48183. **Hours:** 11 am-10 pm, Fri & Sat-11 pm, Sun noon-9
Steak & Seafood   pm. Closed major holidays. **Reservations:** accepted. **Features:** In the older downtown area, the cozy,
historical home is known for its tempting selection of steak and seafood offerings, such as delicious
pan-fried perch, as well as veal, lamb, pasta and chicken. The service is upbeat and casual, and the host
sets the tone for a wonderful dining experience. Casual dress; cocktails. **Parking:** on-site. **Cards:** AX, DC, DS, MC, VI.
                                                                                                                Y X

FRATELLO'S   Lunch: $8-$14   Dinner: $12-$23   Phone: 734/692-1730
▼▼▼   **Location:** Jct of SR 85 (Fort St) and Van Horn Rd. 4501 Fort St 48183. **Hours:** 11 am-10 pm, Fri & Sat-11 pm,
Italian   Sun 11 am-8 pm. Closed: 12/25. **Reservations:** suggested. **Features:** Specializing in steak and fresh
seafood, with popular Italian items to choose from. Comfortable dining room with contemporary decor and
warm, cozy foyer fireplace. Cheerful and friendly waitstaff. Casual dress; cocktails. **Parking:** on-site.
Cards: AX, DC, MC, VI.
                                                                                                                Y X

SIBLEY GARDENS   Lunch: $8-$15   Dinner: $11-$22   Phone: 734/285-1707
▼▼▼   **Location:** 1 mi n of downtown. 916 W Jefferson 48183. **Hours:** 11 am-10 pm, Fri & Sat-11 pm. Closed major
Italian   holidays; also Sun. **Reservations:** accepted. **Features:** Just north of downtown Trenton, this local favorite
serves up traditional Italian fare such as veal piccata, fettuccine alfredo in a dark and romantic atmosphere.
Dressy casual; cocktails. **Parking:** on-site. **Cards:** AX, DC, DS, MC, VI.
                                                                                                                Y X

TROY pop. 72,900 (See map and index starting on p. 226)

———— **WHERE TO STAY** ————

COURTYARD BY MARRIOTT *Book at aaa.com* Phone: 248/528-2800 ⑭
All Year 1P: $89-$159 2P: $99-$169
Small-scale Hotel **Location:** I-75, exit 67, 1 mi s on Stephenson Hwy, then just e. 1525 E Maple 48083. Fax: 248/528-0963. **Facility:** 147 units. 133 one-bedroom standard units. 14 one-bedroom suites ($134-$164). 3 stories, interior corridors. *Bath:* combo or shower only. **Parking:** on-site. **Terms:** weekly rates available, package plans - weekends. **Amenities:** high-speed Internet, dual phone lines, voice mail, irons, hair dryers. **Pool(s):** heated indoor. **Leisure Activities:** whirlpool, exercise room. **Guest Services:** valet and coin laundry. **Business Services:** meeting rooms. **Cards:** AX, DC, DS, JC, MC, VI.
SOME UNITS

DRURY INN *Book at aaa.com* Phone: (248)528-3330 ⑩
All Year [BP] 1P: $103-$113 2P: $113-$123 XP: $10 F18
Small-scale Hotel **Location:** I-75, exit 69 (Big Beaver Rd), 0.3 mi e. 575 W Big Beaver Rd 48084. Fax: 248/528-3330. **Facility:** 217 units. 184 one-bedroom standard units, some with whirlpools. 33 one-bedroom suites ($123-$143), some with whirlpools. 4 stories, interior corridors. *Bath:* combo or shower only. **Parking:** on-site. **Terms:** small pets only. **Amenities:** voice mail, irons, hair dryers. **Pool(s):** heated indoor. **Leisure Activities:** whirlpool, exercise room. **Guest Services:** valet and coin laundry. **Business Services:** meeting rooms. **Cards:** AX, CB, DC, DS, MC, VI.
SOME UNITS

EMBASSY SUITES *Book at aaa.com* Phone: (248)879-7500
All Year [BP] 1P: $129-$169 2P: $129-$169 XP: $20 F16
Small-scale Hotel **Location:** I-75, exit 72 (Crooks Rd). 850 Tower Dr 48098. Fax: 248/879-9139. **Facility:** 251 units. 250 one- and 1 two-bedroom suites, some with whirlpools. 8 stories, interior corridors. **Parking:** on-site. **Terms:** cancellation fee imposed. **Amenities:** dual phone lines, voice mail, irons, hair dryers. **Dining:** 6:30 am-2 & 5:30-10 pm, Sun 7 am-10 & 5:30-10 pm, cocktails. **Pool(s):** heated indoor. **Leisure Activities:** saunas, whirlpool, sun deck, exercise room. **Guest Services:** gift shop, valet and coin laundry. **Business Services:** conference facilities, business center. **Cards:** AX, CB, DC, DS, JC, MC, VI. **Special Amenities:** free full breakfast and free newspaper.
(See color ad below)
SOME UNITS / VCR FEE

HILTON NORTHFIELD *Book at aaa.com* Phone: (248)879-2100
All Year 1P: $139 2P: $139 XP: $15 F18
Small-scale Hotel **Location:** I-75, exit 72 (Crooks Rd), just n. 5500 Crooks Rd 48098. Fax: 248/879-6054. **Facility:** 185 one-bedroom standard units. 3 stories, interior corridors. *Bath:* combo or shower only. **Parking:** on-site. **Terms:** small pets only ($25 deposit). **Amenities:** dual phone lines, voice mail, irons, hair dryers. **Dining:** 6:30 am-2 & 5-10 pm, Fri & Sat-11 pm, cocktails. **Pool(s):** indoor. **Leisure Activities:** saunas, exercise equipment on pool deck. **Guest Services:** sundries, valet and coin laundry, area transportation-within 5 mi. **Business Services:** meeting rooms, business center. **Cards:** AX, CB, DC, DS, MC, VI.
SOME UNITS / FEE

HOLIDAY INN-TROY *Book at aaa.com* Phone: (248)689-7500 ⑫
All Year 1P: $69-$125 2P: $69-$125
Small-scale Hotel **Location:** I-75, exit 67, 0.3 mi sw on Rochester Rd, just w. Located in a secluded area. 2537 Rochester Ct 48083. Fax: 248/689-9015. **Facility:** 150 units. 147 one-bedroom standard units, some with whirlpools. 3 one-bedroom suites ($169-$225) with whirlpools. 4 stories, interior corridors. **Parking:** on-site. **Terms:** weekly rates available. **Amenities:** video games, voice mail, irons, hair dryers. **Pool(s):** heated outdoor. **Leisure Activities:** exercise room. **Fee:** game room. **Guest Services:** valet and coin laundry. **Business Services:** meeting rooms. **Cards:** AX, CB, DC, DS, JC, MC, VI.
SOME UNITS

(See map and index starting on p. 226)

HOMEWOOD SUITES BY HILTON *Book at aaa.com*   Phone: (248)816-6500 **15**

| AAA SAVE | 5/1-3/31 | 1P: $143-$154 | 2P: $143-$154 |
| | 4/1-4/30 | 1P: $139-$149 | 2P: $139-$149 |

Location: Just s of Maple Rd, between Crooks Rd and Coolidge Hwy. Located adjacent to Cambridge Commons Shopping Plaza. 1495 Equity Dr 48084. Fax: 248/816-6530. **Facility:** 150 units. 24 one-bedroom standard units with

Small-scale Hotel efficiencies. 121 one- and 5 two-bedroom suites with efficiencies. 4 stories, interior corridors. *Bath:* combo or shower only. **Parking:** on-site. **Terms:** package plans. **Amenities:** video games (fee), high-speed Internet, dual phone lines, voice mail, irons, hair dryers. *Some:* DVD players (fee), CD players. **Pool(s):** heated indoor. **Leisure Activities:** exercise room. **Guest Services:** sundries, complimentary evening beverages: Mon-Thurs, valet and coin laundry. **Business Services:** meeting rooms, business center. **Cards:** AX, CB, DC, DS, JC, MC, VI. **Special Amenities:** free full breakfast and free newspaper.

SOME UNITS
FEE

RED ROOF INN-TROY *Book at aaa.com*   Phone: (248)689-4391 **13**

AAA SAVE	5/2-9/4	1P: $56-$70	2P: $62-$76	XP: $6	F18
	9/5-12/31	1P: $55-$68	2P: $61-$74	XP: $6	F18
	1/1-3/31	1P: $51-$68	2P: $57-$74	XP: $6	F18
Motel	4/1-5/1	1P: $50-$67	2P: $56-$73	XP: $6	F18

Location: I-75, exit 67, 0.3 mi sw. 2350 Rochester Ct 48083. Fax: 248/689-4397. **Facility:** 109 one-bedroom standard units. 2 stories, exterior corridors. **Parking:** on-site. **Terms:** small pets only. **Amenities:** voice mail. **Cards:** AX, CB, DC, DS, MC, VI. **Special Amenities:** free local telephone calls and free newspaper.

SOME UNITS

RESIDENCE INN BY MARRIOTT *Book at aaa.com*   Phone: (248)689-6856 **11**

| | All Year | 1P: $99-$159 | 2P: $99-$159 |

Location: I-75, exit 69 (Big Beaver Rd), 0.5 mi e, then 0.5 mi s. 2600 Livernois Rd 48083. Fax: 248/689-3788. **Facility:** 152 units. 114 one- and 28 two-bedroom standard units with kitchens. 10 two-bedroom suites with

Small-scale Hotel kitchens. 2 stories, exterior corridors. **Parking:** on-site. **Terms:** weekly rates available, [BP] meal plan available, small pets only ($75 deposit). **Amenities:** voice mail, irons, hair dryers. **Pool(s):** heated outdoor. **Leisure Activities:** whirlpool, exercise room, sports court. **Guest Services:** valet and coin laundry. **Business Services:** meeting rooms. **Cards:** AX, DC, DS, MC, VI.

SOME UNITS
FEE

TROY MARRIOTT *Book at aaa.com*   Phone: (248)680-9797 **9**

| | All Year | 1P: $104-$279 | 2P: $104-$279 | XP: $25 | F18 |

Location: I-75, exit 69 (Big Beaver Rd), just e. 200 W Big Beaver Rd 48084. Fax: 248/680-9724. **Facility:** 350 units. 346 one-bedroom standard units. 4 one-bedroom suites. 17 stories, interior corridors. *Bath:* combo or shower

Small-scale Hotel only. **Parking:** on-site. **Terms:** [AP] meal plan available, package plans - weekends. **Amenities:** high-speed Internet, dual phone lines, voice mail, irons, hair dryers. **Dining:** Shula's Steak House, see separate listing. **Pool(s):** heated indoor. **Leisure Activities:** sauna, whirlpool, steamroom, exercise room. **Guest Services:** gift shop, valet and coin laundry, area transportation. **Business Services:** conference facilities, business center. **Cards:** AX, CB, DC, DS, JC, MC, VI.

SOME UNITS
FEE

------- **WHERE TO DINE** -------

ANITA'S KITCHEN   **Lunch:** $6-$8   **Dinner:** $7-$10   **Phone:** 248/362-0680 **19**

Ethnic   **Location:** Just w of jct Livernois and W Maple Rd. 110 W Maple Rd 48084. **Hours:** 6 am-9 pm, Fri & Sat-10 pm, Sun 7 am-9 pm. Closed: 12/25. **Features:** In this modest diner, adventurous palates will enjoy an exceptional variety of Lebanese and Vegetarian dishes as humus, hashweh and falafel. Casual dress. **Parking:** on-site. **Cards:** AX, DC, DS, MC, VI.

CAFE' SUSHI   **Lunch:** $6-$12   **Dinner:** $12-$20   **Phone:** 248/280-1831 **21**

Japanese   **Location:** Between Crooks Rd and Coolidge Hwy; in Cambridge Crossings Shopping Plaza. 1933 W Maple Rd 48084. **Hours:** 11:30 am-2 & 5:30-10:30 pm, Fri & Sat-11 pm, Sun 4 pm-10 pm. Closed major holidays. **Reservations:** suggested. **Features:** In a small mall across from several automobile dealerships, the restaurant draws patrons primarily for its incredibly fresh sushi. Also offered are tempura, noodles and teriyaki. Dark and pale green striped wallpaper and Impressionist paintings belie the fact that this is first and foremost a Japanese restaurant, complete with two tatami rooms and a sushi bar. Casual dress; cocktails. **Parking:** on-site. **Cards:** AX, DC, MC, VI.

THE CAPITAL GRILLE   **Lunch:** $15-$20   **Dinner:** $20-$30   **Phone:** 248/649-5300 **12**

Steak & Seafood   **Location:** Somerset Collection-North; between Hudson's and Nordstrom. 2800 W Big Beaver Rd 48084. **Hours:** 11:30 am-3 & 5-10 pm, Fri & Sat-11 pm, Sun 5 pm-9 pm; holiday hours may vary. **Reservations:** accepted. **Features:** Everything from the presidential seal looming over the elegant dining room to the glass-fronted dry, aging lockers speaks volumes of this Washington-inspired steakhouse. Part of a national chain, this restaurant features outstanding cuts of aged beef and numerous seafood specials. Dressy casual; cocktails. **Parking:** on-site and valet. **Cards:** AX, DC, DS, MC, VI.

CHARLEY'S CRAB   **Lunch:** $7-$15   **Dinner:** $10-$33   **Phone:** 248/879-2060

Steak & Seafood   **Location:** I-75, exit 72 (Crooks Rd). 5498 Crooks Rd 48098. **Hours:** 11 am-10 pm, Fri-11 pm, Sat 5 pm-11 pm, Sun 11 am-2 & 4-9 pm. Closed major holidays. **Reservations:** suggested, weekends. **Features:** The comfortable restaurant is known for creative preparations of fresh seafood, such as tuna schimini, crab-stuffed trout and the signature Charley's chowder. A good variety of wine is available. Service is attentive, friendly and fittingly inquisitive. Dressy casual; cocktails. **Parking:** on-site and valet. **Cards:** AX, DC, DS, MC, VI.

(See map and index starting on p. 226)

CHINESE KENO   Lunch: $4-$6   Dinner: $5-$9   Phone: 248/879-3232
Chinese
DC, MC, VI.
Location: I-75, exit 72 (Crooks Rd), 1.4 mi n; jct W South Blvd and Crooks Rd. 2081 W South Blvd 48098. **Hours:** 11 am-9:30 pm, Fri-10:30 pm, Sat noon-10:30 pm, Sun noon-9:30 pm. Closed major holidays. **Reservations:** accepted. **Features:** This attractively decorated restaurant features a wide range of Cantonese, Hong Kong and Szechuan cuisine on its menu. Casual dress. **Parking:** on-site. **Cards:** AX,

MCCORMICK & SCHMICK'S SEAFOOD RESTAURANT   Lunch: $8-$12 Dinner: $15-$20 Phone: 248/637-6400   ⑭
Seafood
Location: Jct Big Beaver Rd; behind Sak's at the Somerset Collection Mall. 2850 Coolidge Hwy 48084. **Hours:** 11 am-11 pm. Closed major holidays. **Reservations:** accepted. **Features:** Although part of a Pacific Northwest chain, the elegant restaurant has seafood flown in from all over the world. Lending to the intimate club atmosphere are dark mahogany woods, leaded glass accents and dark green carpets. With more than three dozen seafood selections, the menu is reprinted twice a day to highlight the point of origin of its latest selections. Cocktails. **Parking:** on-site. **Cards:** AX, DS, MC, VI.

MON JIN LAU   Lunch: $7-$12   Dinner: $12-$22   Phone: 248/689-2332   ⑰
Chinese
Location: I-75, exit 67, 1 mi s on Stephenson Hwy. 1515 E Maple Rd 48083. **Hours:** 11 am-1 am, Fri-2 am, Sat 4 pm-2 am, Sun 3 pm-1 am. Closed: 11/25, 12/25. **Reservations:** suggested, weekends. **Features:** Food that is so original, that the term "Nu-Asian" was coined just to describe the endless influences that exert themselves in Mon Jin Lau's palate. Casual dress; cocktails. **Parking:** on-site. **Cards:** AX, DC, MC, VI.

PASTA TO GO   Lunch: $4-$7   Dinner: $9-$11   Phone: 248/828-3200
Italian
Cards: AX, DS, MC, VI.
Location: Jct of Rochester and Square Lake rds; in Venus Plaza Shopping Center. 6026 Rochester Rd 48098. **Hours:** 9 am-9 pm, Sat from 11 am. Closed major holidays; also Sun. **Features:** Pasta to Go says it all; for a quick, but very tasty Italian meal, this popular lunch spot in Troy, serves traditional fare such as pizza, lasagna, and meatball subs that are prepared from scratch daily. Casual dress. **Parking:** on-site.

P.F. CHANG'S CHINA BISTRO   Lunch: $10-$15   Dinner: $10-$15   Phone: 248/816-8000   ⑯
Chinese
Cards: AX, DC, DS, MC, VI.
Location: Somerset Collection South. 2801 W Big Beaver Rd 48084. **Hours:** 11 am-11 pm, Fri & Sat-midnight, Sun 11 am-10 pm. **Reservations:** accepted. **Features:** Faux Ming Dynasty steeds flank the entrance to this elegant but casual restaurant which is part of a small chain of more than a dozen restaurants nationwide featuring creative Szechuan-style dishes. Dressy casual; cocktails. **Parking:** on-site and valet.

PORTABELLA   Lunch: $9-$14   Dinner: $11-$20   Phone: 248/649-6635   ⑮
Italian
Cards: AX, DC, DS, MC, VI.
Location: 2nd floor of Somerset Collection South. 2745 W Big Beaver Rd 48084. **Hours:** 11 am-9 pm, Fri & Sat-10 pm, Sun noon-5 pm. Closed major holidays. **Reservations:** accepted. **Features:** On the second floor of South Somerset Collection Mall, this tribute to the mushroom features, among other things, gigantic blue mosaic mushrooms that sprout from the floors and a patio that overlooks a mall dotted with mushroom-colored umbrellas. As the name might imply, the restaurant's menu lines up many foods containing portobello mushrooms, but it also lists other daily specials and sandwiches. Dressy casual; cocktails. **Parking:** on-site and valet.

PRIYA   Lunch: $8-$15   Dinner: $10-$20   Phone: 248/269-0100   ⑱
Ethnic
Location: Just w of jct Livernois an W Maple Rd. 72 W Maple Rd 48084. **Hours:** 11 am-2:30 & 5-10 pm, Fri-Sun 11 am-9 pm. Closed major holidays. **Reservations:** accepted. **Features:** Intriguing South Indian dishes are delightful in fragrance, appearance and taste. The menu lists seven kinds of dosas served with sambar and little bowls of tomato, coconut and mint sauces. The dining room is pretty, stylish and quietly serene. Casual dress; cocktails. **Parking:** on-site. **Cards:** AX, DS, MC, VI.

RUTH'S CHRIS STEAK HOUSE   Lunch: $9-$17   Dinner: $18-$30   Phone: 248/269-8424   ⑬
Steak House
Location: I-75, exit 69 (Big Beaver Rd), just w. 755 W Big Beaver Rd, Suite 151 48084. **Hours:** 11 am-10 pm, Fri 3 pm-11 pm, Sat 4:30 pm-11 pm, Sun 4:30 pm-9 pm. Closed major holidays. **Reservations:** accepted. **Features:** Just a short drive from many area hotels, the country club-themed restaurant, part of an international chain, has built its reputation on large cuts of steak served on sizzling platters. All menu items are served a la carte and large enough to share. Dressy casual; cocktails. **Parking:** on-site and valet. **Cards:** AX, DC, DS, MC, VI.

SHIELD'S OF TROY   Lunch: $5-$10   Dinner: $5-$10   Phone: 248/637-3131   ⑳
Pizza
Parking: on-site. **Cards:** AX, DC, DS, MC, VI.
Location: I-75, exit 69, 0.7 mi w on Big Beaver Rd, 1 mi s on Crooks Rd, then w. 1476 W Maple Rd 48084. **Hours:** 11 am-11 pm, Fri & Sat-midnight, Sun noon-10 pm. Closed major holidays. **Features:** Part of metro Detroit since 1937, the family-oriented restaurant specializes in mouthwatering deep-dish square pizza and specialty salads. Other notable menu items include pasta and barbecue pork ribs. Casual dress; cocktails.

SHULA'S STEAK HOUSE   Lunch: $22-$30   Dinner: $22-$30   Phone: 248/680-9616   ⑪
Steak House
Location: I-75, exit 69 (Big Beaver Rd), just w; in Troy Marriott. 200 W Big Beaver Rd 48084. **Hours:** 5:30 am-10:30 pm, Fri & Sat-11 pm, Sun-10 pm. **Reservations:** required. **Features:** The surprisingly elegant dining room pays homage to Don Shula's coaching career and perfect season. Handwritten on a pigskin football, the menu lists a variety of steaks, including a massive 48-ounce porterhouse and several slightly smaller cuts, as well as a selection of seafood and pasta dishes. Dressy casual; cocktails. **Parking:** on-site and valet. **Cards:** AX, DC, DS, MC, VI.

UTICA pop. 4,577

──── WHERE TO STAY ────

AMERISUITES (DETROIT/UTICA)
(AAA) (SAVE)
▼▼▼▼
Small-scale Hotel

Book at aaa.com

Phone: (586)803-0100

All Year [ECP]　　　1P: $98-$107　　　2P: $98-$107　　　XP: $10　　　F17
Location: Jct Van Dyke Ave (SR 53) and Hall Rd (SR 59). 45400 Park Ave 48315. Fax: 586/803-0102. **Facility:** 124 one-bedroom standard units. 6 stories, interior corridors. *Bath:* combo or shower only. **Parking:** on-site. **Amenities:** video games (fee), voice mail, irons, hair dryers. *Some:* dual phone lines. **Pool(s):** heated indoor. **Leisure Activities:** exercise room. **Guest Services:** valet and coin laundry. **Business Services:** meeting rooms. **Cards:** AX, CB, DC, DS, JC, MC, VI. **Special Amenities:** free expanded continental breakfast and free newspaper. *(See color ad p 236)*

SOME UNITS

🔾 🐾 🍴 ᴴ🅼 📶 ⊷ 🍴 📠 🔌 🖥 ▤ / ⊠ /

BAYMONT INN & SUITES DETROIT-UTICA
(AAA) (SAVE)
▼▼▼▼
Small-scale Hotel

Book at aaa.com

Phone: (586)731-4700

4/1-9/14　　　1P: $99-$159　　　2P: $99-$159
9/15-3/31　　　1P: $89-$139　　　2P: $89-$139
Location: Jct of Van Dyke Ave (SR 53) and Hall Rd (SR 59), just n. 45311 Park Ave 48315. Fax: 586/731-9870. **Facility:** 102 units. 98 one-bedroom standard units, some with whirlpools. 4 one-bedroom suites ($79-$139). 4 stories, interior corridors. *Bath:* combo or shower only. **Parking:** on-site. **Terms:** [ECP] meal plan available, pets ($50 deposit). **Amenities:** video games (fee), voice mail, irons, hair dryers. **Pool(s):** heated indoor. **Leisure Activities:** whirlpool. **Guest Services:** valet and coin laundry. **Business Services:** meeting rooms. **Cards:** AX, CB, DC, DS, MC, VI. **Special Amenities:** free local telephone calls and free newspaper. *(See color ad below)*

SOME UNITS

🔾 🐾 🍴 📶 ⊘ ⊷ 🍴 📠 ▤ / ⊠ 🔌 🖥 /
　　　FEE

COMFORT INN
(AAA) (SAVE)
▼▼▼▼
Small-scale Hotel

Book at aaa.com

Phone: (586)739-7111

All Year [ECP]　　　1P: $89-$129　　　2P: $89-$129
Location: Jct Van Dyke Ave (SR 53) and Hall Rd (SR 59). 11401 Hall Rd 48317. Fax: 586/739-1041. **Facility:** 104 one-bedroom standard units, some with whirlpools. 3 stories, interior corridors. **Parking:** on-site. **Terms:** cancellation fee imposed. **Amenities:** video games (fee), irons, hair dryers. *Some:* safes. **Guest Services:** valet and coin laundry. **Business Services:** meeting rooms. **Cards:** AX, CB, DC, DS, JC, MC, VI. **Special Amenities:** free expanded continental breakfast and free local telephone calls.

SOME UNITS

🔾 ⊘ 🍴 🅅🅲🆁 🍴 📠 ▤ / ⊠ 🔌 /

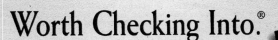

COURTYARD BY MARRIOTT *Book at aaa.com* **Phone:** (586)997-6100
▼▼▼▼ All Year   1P: $114-$129   2P: $114-$129
Small-scale Hotel **Location:** Jct of Van Dyke Ave (SR 53) and Hall Rd (SR 59), just n. 46000 Utica Park Blvd 48315. Fax: 586/997-9880.
Facility: 90 units. 87 one-bedroom standard units, some with whirlpools. 3 one-bedroom suites ($129-$184), some with whirlpools. 3 stories, interior corridors. *Bath:* combo or shower only. **Parking:** on-site. **Terms:** [BP] meal plan available. **Amenities:** video games (fee), voice mail, irons, hair dryers. **Pool(s):** heated indoor. **Leisure Activities:** whirlpool, exercise room. **Guest Services:** valet and coin laundry. **Business Services:** meeting rooms. **Cards:** AX, DC, DS, JC, MC, VI.

SOME UNITS
(ASK) (S⊘) (†↑+) (⊆M) (⚬✆) (⊘) (⊸) (☂) (DATA PORT) (▣) / (✕) (▤) (☷) /

STAYBRIDGE SUITES-UTICA *Book at aaa.com* **Phone:** (586)323-0101
▼▼▼▼ All Year [ECP]   1P: $129-$139   2P: $149-$169
Small-scale Hotel **Location:** Jct Van Dyke Ave (SR 53) and Hall Rd (SR 59), just n. 46155 Utica Park Blvd 48315. Fax: 586/323-0011.
Facility: 91 units. 46 one-bedroom standard units with efficiencies. 27 one- and 18 two-bedroom suites. 3 stories, interior corridors. *Bath:* combo or shower only. **Parking:** on-site. **Terms:** pets ($150 fee). **Amenities:** dual phone lines, irons, hair dryers. *Fee:* video library, video games, high-speed Internet. **Pool(s):** heated outdoor. **Leisure Activities:** whirlpool, exercise room. **Business Services:** meeting rooms, business center. **Cards:** AX, CB, DC, DS, JC, MC, VI.

SOME UNITS
(ASK) (S⊘) (🛏) (⊸) (VCR) (☂) (DATA PORT) (☷) (▣) (▣) / (✕) /
FEE

------- **WHERE TO DINE** -------

FILIPPA'S WINE BARREL **Lunch:** $6-$12   **Dinner:** $10-$15   **Phone:** 586/254-1311
▼▼▼ ▼▼▼ **Location:** At jct Mound Rd and SR 59 (Hall Rd). 45125 Mound Rd 48317. **Hours:** 11 am-10 pm, Fri & Sat-11 pm, Sun noon-9 pm. Closed: 7/4, 12/25; also Super Bowl Sun. **Features:** The warm, vintage surroundings invite diners to unwind while enjoying a wide array of choices from fowl to beef. The cool, delicious gazpacho is an excellent contrast to the well-seasoned encrusted, stuffed salmon. Service is attentive and adaptable. Casual dress; cocktails. **Parking:** on-site. **Cards:** AX, DS, MC, VI.
American
(Ⓨ) (✕)

RISTORANTE PICCIRILLI **Dinner:** $9-$21   **Phone:** 586/731-0610
▼▼▼ ▼▼▼ **Location:** Jct Van Dyke Ave and 24 Mile Rd, just s. 52830 Van Dyke Rd 48316. **Hours:** 4:30 pm-10 pm, Sun 2 pm-8:30 pm. Closed major holidays; also Mon. **Reservations:** suggested, weekends. **Features:** The intimate dining room is a cozy setting in which to savor homemade Italian fare. Strolling musicians enhance the romantic ambience on Saturday evenings. In addition to a nice list of wines, the restaurant rolls out a tempting assortment of dessert. Casual dress; cocktails. **Parking:** on-site. **Cards:** AX, DC, MC, VI.
Italian
(Ⓨ) (✕)

WALLED LAKE pop. 6,713

------- **WHERE TO DINE** -------

MICHIGAN STAR CLIPPER DINNER TRAIN **Lunch:** $39   **Dinner:** $70   **Phone:** 248/960-9440
ⒶⒶⒶ **Location:** I-96, exit 159 (Wixom Rd), 1 mi n, then 4 mi e. 840 N Pontiac Trail 48390. **Hours:** departures noon & 7 pm, Sun departures 5 pm. Closed: 11/25, 12/24, 12/25; also Mon. **Reservations:** required. **Features:** Take a relaxing and memorable three-hour, linear ride through the woods, meadows and lake country in vintage 1950s dining cars. The prix fixe menu includes a choice of fish, poultry or beef entree. Formal attire; cocktails; entertainment. **Parking:** on-site. **Cards:** AX, DC, DS, MC, VI.
American
(✕)

WALTZ

------- **WHERE TO DINE** -------

WALTZ INN Historic   **Lunch:** $6-$10   **Dinner:** $8-$15   **Phone:** 734/654-9040
▼▼▼ ▼▼▼ **Location:** I-275, exit 8, 0.5 mi w; in the village. 28080 Waltz Rd 48164. **Hours:** 11 am-9 pm, Fri & Sat-10 pm, Sun noon-8:30 pm. Closed major holidays; also Mon & Tues. **Features:** Built in 1900, the small country tavern is quaint and homey, with historical pictures decorating the walls. Reliable home-cooked food includes such choices as fish and chips, prime rib and porterhouse steak. Servers are personable and warm. Casual dress; cocktails. **Parking:** on-site. **Cards:** MC, VI.
American
(Ⓨ) (✕)

WARREN pop. 138,247 (See map and index starting on p. 226)

------- **WHERE TO STAY** -------

BAYMONT INN & SUITES DETROIT-WARREN TECH CENTER *Book at aaa.com* **Phone:** (586)574-0550 ⑥⑥
ⒶⒶⒶ (SAVE) All Year   1P: $67   2P: $67
▼▼▼▼ **Location:** I-696, exit 23 (Van Dyke Ave), 2 mi n on SR 53. 30900 Van Dyke Ave 48093. Fax: 586/574-0750.
Small-scale Hotel **Facility:** 98 units. 95 one-bedroom standard units. 3 one-bedroom suites, some with kitchens. 3 stories, interior corridors. **Parking:** on-site. **Terms:** [ECP] meal plan available, small pets only. **Amenities:** video games (fee), voice mail, irons, hair dryers. **Guest Services:** valet and coin laundry. **Business Services:** meeting rooms. **Cards:** AX, CB, DC, DS, MC, VI. **Special Amenities:** free local telephone calls and free newspaper. *(See color ad p 287)*

SOME UNITS
(S⊘) (🛏) (†↑+) (⊘) (↟↟↟) (☂) (DATA PORT) (▣) / (✕) (▤) (☷) /

(See map and index starting on p. 226)

CANDLEWOOD SUITES-DETROIT WARREN *Book at aaa.com*   Phone: (586)978-1261   63
All Year   1P: $109-$149   2P: $109-$149
Small-scale Hotel   **Location:** I-696, exit 23 (Van Dyke Ave), 2.8 mi n. 7010 Convention Blvd 48092. **Fax:** 586/978-1701. **Facility:** 122 units. 98 one-bedroom standard units with efficiencies. 24 one-bedroom suites with efficiencies. 3 stories, interior corridors. *Bath:* combo or shower only. **Parking:** on-site. **Terms:** weekly rates available. **Amenities:** video library, CD players, dual phone lines, voice mail, irons, hair dryers. **Guest Services:** complimentary laundry. **Cards:** AX, CB, DC, DS, JC, MC, VI.

SOME UNITS

COMFORT SUITES *Book at aaa.com*   Phone: (586)427-7000   72
All Year   1P: $69-$259   2P: $74-$259   XP: $5   F18
Small-scale Hotel   **Location:** I-696, exit 20 (Dequindre Rd). 2020 Walter Ruether Service Dr 48091. **Fax:** 586/427-6000. **Facility:** 65 one-bedroom standard units, some with whirlpools. 2 stories, interior corridors. *Bath:* combo or shower only. **Parking:** on-site. **Terms:** [CP] meal plan available. **Amenities:** dual phone lines, voice mail, irons, hair dryers. **Pool(s):** small heated indoor. **Guest Services:** valet laundry. **Business Services:** meeting rooms. **Cards:** AX, DC, DS, JC, MC, VI. **Special Amenities:** free continental breakfast and free local telephone calls.

SOME UNITS

COURTYARD BY MARRIOTT-WARREN *Book at aaa.com*   Phone: 586/751-5777   67
All Year   1P: $69-$109
Small-scale Hotel   **Location:** I-696, exit 23, 1.6 mi n. 30190 Van Dyke Ave 48093. **Fax:** 586/751-4463. **Facility:** 147 units. 133 one-bedroom standard units. 14 one-bedroom suites ($129). 2-3 stories, interior corridors. *Bath:* combo or shower only. **Parking:** on-site. **Terms:** [BP] meal plan available. **Amenities:** dual phone lines, voice mail, irons, hair dryers. **Pool(s):** small heated indoor. **Leisure Activities:** whirlpool, exercise room. **Guest Services:** valet and coin laundry. **Business Services:** meeting rooms. **Cards:** AX, DC, DS, MC, VI.

SOME UNITS

FAIRFIELD INN BY MARRIOTT *Book at aaa.com*   Phone: 586/939-1700   64
4/1-10/1   1P: $64-$79   2P: $64-$79
10/2-3/31   1P: $59-$64   2P: $59-$64
Motel   **Location:** I-696, exit 23 (Van Dyke Ave), 2.8 mi n on Van Dyke Ave. 7454 Convention Blvd 48092. **Fax:** 586/939-1700. **Facility:** 132 one-bedroom standard units. 3 stories, interior/exterior corridors. *Bath:* combo or shower only. **Parking:** on-site. **Terms:** [CP] meal plan available. **Amenities:** irons. **Pool(s):** heated outdoor. **Guest Services:** valet laundry. **Cards:** AX, CB, DC, DS, MC, VI.

SOME UNITS

FOUR POINTS BY SHERATON HOTEL & SUITES DETROIT NORTH *Book at aaa.com*   Phone: (586)573-7600   70
All Year   1P: $79-$229   2P: $79-$229   XP: $10   F12
Small-scale Hotel   **Location:** I-696, exit 23 (Van Dyke Ave), 1.5 mi n. 30000 Van Dyke Ave 48093. **Fax:** 586/573-7356. **Facility:** 127 units. 104 one-bedroom standard units, some with whirlpools. 23 one-bedroom suites ($109-$229), some with whirlpools. 6 stories, interior corridors. **Parking:** on-site. **Terms:** [AP] meal plan available. **Amenities:** dual phone lines, voice mail, irons, hair dryers. **Pool(s):** heated indoor. **Leisure Activities:** whirlpool, exercise room. **Guest Services:** valet laundry. **Business Services:** meeting rooms. **Cards:** AX, CB, DC, DS, JC, MC, VI. *(See color ad p 5)*

SOME UNITS
FEE. FEE

HAMPTON INN-WARREN/STERLING HEIGHTS *Book at aaa.com*   Phone: (586)977-7270   62
All Year [ECP]   1P: $99-$179   2P: $99-$179   XP: $10   F18
Small-scale Hotel   **Location:** I-696, exit 23 (Van Dyke Ave), 2.8 mi n. 7447 Convention Blvd 48092. **Fax:** 586/977-3889. **Facility:** 124 units. 120 one-bedroom standard units, some with whirlpools. 4 one-bedroom suites, some with whirlpools. 3 stories, interior corridors. **Parking:** on-site. **Amenities:** voice mail, irons, hair dryers. **Guest Services:** valet laundry. **Business Services:** meeting rooms. **Cards:** AX, CB, DC, DS, MC, VI. **Special Amenities:** free expanded continental breakfast and free newspaper.

SOME UNITS

HAWTHORN SUITES LTD *Book at aaa.com*   Phone: (586)264-8800   65
All Year [BP]   1P: $89-$169
Small-scale Hotel   **Location:** I-696, exit 23, 1.8 mi n on SR 53. 7601 Chicago Rd 48092. **Fax:** 586/264-8189. **Facility:** 79 units. 49 one-bedroom standard units, some with whirlpools. 30 one-bedroom suites with efficiencies, some with whirlpools. 3 stories, interior corridors. *Bath:* combo or shower only. **Parking:** on-site. **Terms:** small pets only ($75 fee). **Amenities:** video games (fee), high-speed Internet, dual phone lines, voice mail, irons, hair dryers. *Some:* safes. **Pool(s):** heated indoor. **Leisure Activities:** exercise room. **Guest Services:** sundries, valet and coin laundry. **Business Services:** meeting rooms, business center. **Cards:** AX, CB, DC, DS, MC, VI.

SOME UNITS
FEE

HOLIDAY INN EXPRESS *Book at aaa.com*   Phone: (586)754-9700   71
All Year   1P: $114-$124
Small-scale Hotel   **Location:** I-696, exit 24 (Hoover Rd), just s. 11500 11 Mile Rd 48089. **Fax:** 586/754-0376. **Facility:** 124 one-bedroom standard units, some with whirlpools. 2 stories, interior corridors. **Parking:** on-site. **Terms:** [ECP] meal plan available. **Amenities:** video games (fee), voice mail, irons, hair dryers. **Pool(s):** outdoor. **Leisure Activities:** exercise room. **Guest Services:** valet laundry. **Business Services:** meeting rooms. **Cards:** AX, CB, DC, DS, MC, VI.

SOME UNITS

(See map and index starting on p. 226)

HOMEWOOD SUITES BY HILTON   *Book at aaa.com*   Phone: (586)558-7870   68
▼▼▼
All Year   1P: $79-$159
Small-scale Hotel   **Location:** I-696, exit 23 (Van Dyke Rd), 2 mi n. 30180 N Civic Center Blvd 48093. Fax: 586/558-8072. **Facility:** 76 one-bedroom suites with efficiencies. 2-3 stories, interior/exterior corridors. *Bath:* combo or shower only. **Parking:** on-site. **Terms:** [ECP] meal plan available, small pets only ($100 fee). **Amenities:** dual phone lines, voice mail, irons, hair dryers. **Pool(s):** heated outdoor. **Leisure Activities:** exercise room, sports court. **Guest Services:** sundries, complimentary evening beverages: Mon-Thurs, valet and coin laundry. **Business Services:** meeting rooms, business center. **Cards:** AX, CB, DC, DS, JC, MC, VI.

SOME UNITS
ASK SO ⛺ 📶 ㋖ 🛋 🐖 📺 DATAPORT 🔲 🔳 🔲 / ✕ /
FEE

RED ROOF INN-WARREN   *Book at aaa.com*   Phone: (586)573-4300   73
AAA SAVE
5/30-10/16	1P: $55-$71	2P: $59-$75	XP: $4	F18
4/1-5/29 & 10/17-12/31	1P: $53-$69	2P: $57-$73	XP: $4	F18
1/1-3/31	1P: $51-$67	2P: $55-$71	XP: $4	F18

▼▼ ▼▼
Motel   **Location:** I-696, exit 20 (Dequindre Rd), just ne. 26300 Dequindre Rd 48091. Fax: 586/573-6157. **Facility:** 136 one-bedroom standard units. 2 stories, exterior corridors. *Bath:* combo or shower only. **Parking:** on-site. **Amenities:** video games (fee), voice mail. **Cards:** AX, CB, DC, DS, MC, VI. **Special Amenities:** free local telephone calls and free newspaper.

SOME UNITS
🛏 📶 📵 📺 DATAPORT / ✕ 🔲 🔳 /

──────── WHERE TO DINE ────────

ANDIAMO ITALIA RISTORANTE   **Lunch:** $9-$15   **Dinner:** $12-$24   Phone: 586/268-3200   81
▼▼▼
Italian   **Location:** Jct Van Dyke Ave and 14 Mile Rd, just w. 7096 E 14 Mile Rd 48092. **Hours:** 11 am-11 pm, Sat 4 pm-midnight, Sun 4 pm-9 pm. Closed major holidays. **Reservations:** suggested. **Features:** Andiamo is an Italian ristorante that combines a sophisticated atmosphere and skilled use of traditional Mediterranean ingredients to produce unique creations that will satisfy your craving for Italian-style fare. Dressy casual; cocktails. **Parking:** on-site and valet. **Cards:** AX, MC, VI.

🍽 ✕

MICHELLE'S RESTAURANT & SWEETHEART BAKERY   **Lunch:** $6-$7   **Dinner:** $7-$10   Phone: 586/795-1665   82
▼▼ ▼▼
American   **Location:** I-696, exit 23 (Van Dyke Ave), 2.7 mi n. 31920 Van Dyke Ave 48093. **Hours:** 7 am-9 pm, Fri & Sat-10 pm. Closed: 9/6, 12/25. **Features:** Business executives sit side by side with moms and their toddlers in this popular local eatery. The menu may be basic and straightforward but having an attached bakery might complicate the decision process. Casual dress; cocktails. **Parking:** on-site. **Cards:** AX, DS, MC, VI.

✕

WATERFORD pop. 73,150

──────── WHERE TO STAY ────────

BEST WESTERN CONCORDE INN OF WATERFORD   *Book at aaa.com*   Phone: (248)666-8555
▼▼▼
All Year [ECP]   1P: $89-$199   2P: $89-$199
Small-scale Hotel   **Location:** Jct SR 59 (Highland Rd) and Airport Rd, 1 mi w. Located adjacent to the shopping plaza. 7076 Highland Rd 48327. Fax: 248/666-8573. **Facility:** 111 units. 101 one-bedroom standard units, some with whirlpools. 10 one-bedroom suites ($109-$199) with whirlpools. 3 stories, interior corridors. *Bath:* combo or shower only. **Parking:** on-site. **Terms:** package plans - seasonal & weekends. **Amenities:** video games (fee), dual phone lines, voice mail, irons, hair dryers. *Some:* honor bars. **Pool(s):** heated indoor, wading. **Leisure Activities:** sauna, exercise room. *Fee:* game room. **Guest Services:** valet and coin laundry, area transportation. **Business Services:** meeting rooms. **Cards:** AX, CB, DC, DS, MC, VI.

SOME UNITS
ASK SO 📶 ㋖ 📵 🐖 ✕ 📺 DATAPORT 🔲 / ✕ 🔲 🔳 /

HOLIDAY INN EXPRESS & SUITES   *Book at aaa.com*   Phone: (248)674-3434
▼▼▼
All Year   1P: $77   2P: $77   XP: $10   F16
Small-scale Hotel   **Location:** Jct SR 59 (Highland Rd) and Pontiac Lake Rd. 4350 Pontiac Lake Rd 48328. Fax: 248/674-3446. **Facility:** 83 one-bedroom standard units, some with whirlpools. 3 stories, interior corridors. *Bath:* combo or shower only. **Parking:** on-site. **Amenities:** video games (fee), high-speed Internet, dual phone lines, voice mail, irons, hair dryers. **Pool(s):** indoor. **Leisure Activities:** exercise room. *Fee:* game room. **Guest Services:** valet laundry. **Business Services:** meeting rooms, business center. **Cards:** AX, DC, DS, MC.

SOME UNITS
ASK SO 📶 ㋖ 🛋 📵 🐖 📺 DATAPORT 🔲 / ✕ 🔲 🔳 /

WEST BLOOMFIELD pop. 64,862   (See map and index starting on p. 226)

———— WHERE TO DINE ————

THE LARK
♦♦♦♦ ♦♦♦♦
Continental

Dinner: $60-$70

Phone: 248/661-4466   [40]

Location: Just n of jct Maple and Farmington rds. 6430 Farmington Rd 48322. **Hours:** 6 pm-11 pm, Fri & Sat-midnight. Closed major holidays; also Sun & Mon. **Reservations:** required. **Features:** The dining room has the ambience of an intimate Portuguese country inn. The menu of classic European selections, which changes bimonthly, might include such selections as rack of lamb. The pre-appetizer and dessert carts are loaded with temptations. Formal attire; cocktails. **Parking:** on-site. **Cards:** AX, CB, DC, MC, VI.   [⟨M] [Y] [✕]

WIXOM pop. 13,263

———— WHERE TO STAY ————

BAYMONT INN & SUITES   *Book at aaa.com*
♦♦♦♦
Small-scale Hotel

Phone: (248)735-2781

All Year   1P: $99   2P: $99

Location: I-96, exit 159, just n. Located in a business park. 48953 Alpha Dr 48393. Fax: 248/735-3905. **Facility:** 109 one-bedroom standard units, some with whirlpools. 4 stories, interior corridors. *Bath:* combo or shower only. **Parking:** on-site. **Terms:** [ECP] meal plan available. **Amenities:** video games (fee), voice mail, irons, hair dryers. **Pool(s):** heated indoor. **Leisure Activities:** whirlpool, exercise room. **Guest Services:** valet and coin laundry. **Business Services:** meeting rooms. **Cards:** AX, CB, DC, DS, JC, MC, VI.

SOME UNITS
[ASK] [S⟨] [⟨M] [⟨] [≈] [♥] [DATA PORT] [▭] / [✕] [🛏] [▱] /

WOODHAVEN pop. 12,530

———— WHERE TO STAY ————

BEST WESTERN WOODHAVEN INN   *Book at aaa.com*
♦♦♦♦
Small-scale Hotel

Phone: (734)676-8000

All Year   1P: $72   2P: $79-$89   XP: $5   F18

Location: I-75, exit 32 (West Rd), just w. 21700 West Rd 48183. Fax: 734/676-7062. **Facility:** 126 one-bedroom standard units, some with whirlpools. 2 stories, interior corridors. **Parking:** on-site. **Terms:** 30 day cancellation notice. **Amenities:** video games, voice mail, safes, irons, hair dryers. **Pool(s):** heated indoor. **Leisure Activities:** sauna, exercise room. **Fee:** game room. **Guest Services:** valet laundry. **Business Services:** conference facilities, fax (fee). **Cards:** AX, CB, DC, DS, JC, MC, VI.

SOME UNITS
[ASK] [S⟨] [¶] [⟨] [≈] [✕] [♥] [DATA PORT] [▭] / [✕] [🛏] /

HOLIDAY INN EXPRESS & SUITES   *Book at aaa.com*
♦♦♦♦
Small-scale Hotel

Phone: (734)362-0933

All Year   1P: $99   2P: $99

Location: I-75, exit 32 (West Rd), just w. 21500 West Rd 48183. Fax: 734/362-0937. **Facility:** 77 one-bedroom standard units, some with whirlpools. 3 stories, interior corridors. *Bath:* combo or shower only. **Parking:** on-site. **Terms:** check-in 4 pm, cancellation fee imposed. **Amenities:** video games (fee), dual phone lines, voice mail, irons, hair dryers. **Pool(s):** heated indoor. **Leisure Activities:** whirlpool, exercise room. **Guest Services:** valet and coin laundry. **Business Services:** meeting rooms, business center. **Cards:** AX, CB, DC, DS, JC, MC, VI.

SOME UNITS
[ASK] [S⟨] [¶⁺] [⟨M] [⟨] [≈] [♥] [DATA PORT] [🛏] [▭] / [✕] [▱] /

This ends listings for the Detroit Vicinity.
The following page resumes the alphabetical listings of
cities in Michigan.

DE WITT pop. 4,702

——— WHERE TO STAY ———

AMERIHOST INN & SUITES-LANSING NORTH *Book at aaa.com*   **Phone:** (517)374-0000

[AAA] [SAVE]
▼▼▼ ▼▼▼
Small-scale Hotel

All Year [ECP]   1P: $74-$84   2P: $80-$90
Location: I-69, exit 87 (Business Rt 127), just s. Located across from outlet mall. 1055 Aaron Dr 48820. Fax: 517/316-0688. **Facility:** 75 one-bedroom standard units, some with whirlpools. 3 stories, interior corridors. *Bath:* combo or shower only. **Parking:** on-site, winter plug-ins. **Amenities:** voice mail, safes (fee), irons, hair dryers. **Pool(s):** heated indoor. **Leisure Activities:** whirlpool, exercise room. **Guest Services:** valet laundry. **Cards:** AX, DC, DS, MC, VI. **Special Amenities:** free expanded continental breakfast and free newspaper.

SOME UNITS

[S/D] [&M] [✆] [⊇] [🐕] [DATA PORT] [▭] / [✕] [VCR] [█] [📷] /

SLEEP INN *Book at aaa.com*   **Phone:** (517)669-8823

▼▼▼ ▼▼▼
Small-scale Hotel

All Year   1P: $70-$110   2P: $80-$120   XP: $10   F18
Location: I-69, exit 87 (Business Rt 127), 0.8 mi n. 1101 Commerce Park Dr 48820. Fax: 517/669-7816. **Facility:** 61 one-bedroom standard units. 2 stories, interior corridors. *Bath:* combo or shower only. **Parking:** on-site, winter plug-ins. **Terms:** [ECP] meal plan available. **Amenities:** safes (fee), irons, hair dryers. **Pool(s):** outdoor. **Guest Services:** coin laundry. **Cards:** AX, CB, DC, DS, JC, MC, VI.

SOME UNITS

[ASK] [S/D] [🍴] [✆] [⊇] [↔] [🐕] [DATA PORT] [▭] / [✕] [VCR] [█] [📷] /
FEE

DIXBORO

——— WHERE TO DINE ———

THE LORD FOX   Historic   **Lunch:** $9-$16   **Dinner:** $16-$25   **Phone:** 734/662-1647

▼▼▼ ▼▼▼
American

Location: US 23, exit 41 (Plymouth Rd), 2 mi e. 5400 Plymouth Rd 48105. **Hours:** 11:30 am-2 & 5-10 pm, Sat from 5 pm, Sun 3 pm-9 pm. Closed major holidays. **Reservations:** suggested. **Features:** Built in 1880, the rural family home is a sophisticated setting for classy dining. The menu blends classical preparations, such as beef Wellington and duck a l'orange, with innovative regional entrees, such as hazelnut whitefish and Amish chicken. Dressy casual; cocktails. **Parking:** on-site. **Cards:** AX, DC, MC, VI.

[✕]

DOUGLAS pop. 1,214—See also SAUGATUCK.

——— WHERE TO STAY ———

AMERICINN OF SAUGATUCK/DOUGLAS *Book at aaa.com*   **Phone:** 269/857-8581

▼▼▼ ▼▼▼
Small-scale Hotel

6/1-9/30   1P: $134-$254   2P: $134-$254   XP: $10   F16
4/1-5/31 & 1/1-3/31   1P: $74-$224   2P: $74-$224   XP: $10   F16
10/1-12/31   1P: $84-$134   2P: $84-$134   XP: $10   F16
Location: I-196, exit 36, 1 mi n. Located in a semi-commercial area. 2905 Blue Star Hwy 49406 (PO Box 2729). Fax: 269/857-3591. **Facility:** 46 units. 45 one-bedroom standard units, some with whirlpools. 1 one-bedroom suite with whirlpool. 2 stories (no elevator), interior corridors. *Bath:* combo or shower only. **Parking:** on-site. **Terms:** 2-3 night minimum stay - weekends 7/1-8/31, 7 day cancellation notice-fee imposed, [ECP] meal plan available, small pets only (in smoking units). **Amenities:** safes (fee), hair dryers. *Some:* irons. **Pool(s):** heated indoor. **Leisure Activities:** sauna, whirlpool. **Guest Services:** coin laundry. **Business Services:** meeting rooms. **Cards:** AX, DC, DS, MC, VI. *(See color ad p 311)*

SOME UNITS

[🐾] [&M] [✆] [⊿] [⊇] [DATA PORT] [▭] / [✕] [VCR] [█] [📷] /

THE KIRBY HOUSE   **Phone:** 269/857-2904

[AAA] [SAVE]
▼▼▼ ▼▼▼
Bed & Breakfast

5/1-10/31   1P: $115-$175   2P: $115-$175   XP: $25
4/1-4/30 & 11/1-3/31   1P: $85-$145   2P: $85-$145   XP: $25
Location: Center. 294 W Center St 49406 (PO Box 1174, SAUGATUCK, 49453). Fax: 269/857-6156. **Facility:** Three rooms of this Victorian manor have fireplaces. Smoke free premises. 6 one-bedroom standard units. 2 stories (no elevator), interior corridors. *Bath:* combo or shower only. **Parking:** on-site, winter plug-ins. **Terms:** 2-3 night minimum stay - weekends, age restrictions may apply, 14 day cancellation notice-fee imposed, [BP] meal plan available. **Amenities:** irons. **Pool(s):** heated outdoor. **Leisure Activities:** whirlpool, bicycles, horseshoes. **Guest Services:** TV in common area. **Business Services:** meeting rooms. **Cards:** MC, VI.

[🍴] [⊇] [✕] [✕] [W] [✆]

LAKE SHORE RESORT   **Phone:** 269/857-7121

▼▼▼ ▼▼
Motel

6/18-9/5 [CP]   2P: $150-$190   XP: $30
5/15-6/17 & 9/6-10/18 [CP]   2P: $75-$250   XP: $30
Location: CR A2, 1 mi w on Wiley Rd, then 1 mi s. Located opposite Lake Michigan. 2885 Lakeshore Dr 49406 (PO Box 121, SAUGATUCK, 49453). **Facility:** 30 one-bedroom standard units. 1 story, exterior corridors. **Parking:** on-site. **Terms:** open 5/15-10/18, 2-3 night minimum stay - weekends, 30 day cancellation notice-fee imposed. **Pool(s):** heated outdoor. **Leisure Activities:** putting green, bicycles, hiking trails, volleyball. **Business Services:** meeting rooms. **Cards:** MC, VI.

SOME UNITS

[⊇] [✕] [█] / [✕] /

ROSEMONT INN RESORT   **Phone:** (269)857-2637

▼▼▼ ▼▼▼
Bed & Breakfast

6/4-9/7 [BP]   1P: $215-$305   2P: $215-$305   XP: $15
4/1-6/3 & 9/8-11/15 [BP]   1P: $135-$255   2P: $135-$255   XP: $15
11/16-3/31 [BP]   1P: $115-$235   2P: $115-$235   XP: $15
Location: CR A2, 1 mi w on Center St, just n. Located opposite Lake Michigan. 83 Lakeshore Dr 49453 (PO Box 857, 49406-0857). Fax: 269/857-3968. **Facility:** An English garden and cozy accommodations with fireplaces are featured at this historic house. Smoke free premises. 14 one-bedroom standard units, some with whirlpools. 2 stories (no elevator), interior corridors. *Bath:* combo or shower only. **Parking:** on-site. **Terms:** 2-3 night minimum stay - weekends, age restrictions may apply, 14 day cancellation notice-fee imposed. **Amenities:** hair dryers. **Pool(s):** heated outdoor. **Leisure Activities:** sauna, whirlpool, bicycles. **Guest Services:** complimentary evening beverages. **Business Services:** meeting rooms. **Cards:** AX, DS, MC, VI.

SHERWOOD FOREST BED & BREAKFAST

Phone: (269)857-1246

7/1-8/31 [BP]	1P: $115-$185	2P: $115-$185	XP: $25
4/1-6/30 & 9/1-10/31 [BP]	1P: $105-$175	2P: $105-$175	XP: $25
11/1-3/31 [BP]	1P: $95-$165	2P: $95-$165	XP: $25

Bed & Breakfast **Location:** CR A2, 1 mi w. Located in a residential setting. 938 Center St 49406 (PO Box 315, SAUGATUCK, 49453). **Fax:** 269/857-1996. **Facility:** The property is in the Victorian style. Smoke free premises. 6 units. 5 one-bedroom standard units, some with whirlpools. 1 cottage ($125-$1000). 2 stories (no elevator), interior corridors. **Bath:** combo or shower only. **Parking:** on-site. **Terms:** 2 night minimum stay - weekends, age restrictions may apply, 10 day cancellation notice, package plans. **Amenities:** CD players, hair dryers. *Some:* irons. **Pool(s):** heated outdoor. **Leisure Activities:** bicycles. **Guest Services:** TV in common area. **Cards:** DS, MC, VI.

DOWAGIAC pop. 6,147

———— WHERE TO STAY ————

AMERIHOST INN & SUITES-DOWAGIAC   *Book at aaa.com*

Phone: (269)782-4270

All Year   1P: $82-$88   2P: $82-$88

Small-scale Hotel **Location:** 0.4 mi s of jct US 51 and 62. Located behind Parmide Shopping Plaza. 29291 Amerihost Dr 49047. **Fax:** 269/782-3219. **Facility:** 64 one-bedroom standard units, some with whirlpools. 2 stories (no elevator), interior corridors. **Bath:** combo or shower only. **Parking:** on-site. **Amenities:** dual phone lines, voice mail, safes (fee), irons, hair dryers. **Pool(s):** heated indoor. **Leisure Activities:** exercise room. **Business Services:** meeting rooms. **Cards:** AX, CB, DC, DS, MC, VI. **Special Amenities:** free expanded continental breakfast and free newspaper.

DUNDEE pop. 3,522

———— WHERE TO STAY ————

AMERIHOST INN-DUNDEE   *Book at aaa.com*

Phone: 734/529-5240

All Year   1P: $68-$72   2P: $72-$75   XP: $5   F17

Small-scale Hotel **Location:** US 23, exit 17, just w. 111 Waterstradt Commerce Dr 48131. **Fax:** 734/529-7435. **Facility:** 60 one-bedroom standard units, some with whirlpools. 2 stories, interior corridors. **Bath:** combo or shower only. **Parking:** on-site. **Terms:** 10 day cancellation notice, [ECP] meal plan available. **Amenities:** voice mail, safes (fee), irons, hair dryers. **Pool(s):** heated indoor/outdoor. **Leisure Activities:** whirlpool, exercise room. **Business Services:** meeting rooms. **Cards:** AX, DC, DS, MC, VI. **Special Amenities:** free expanded continental breakfast.

COUNTRY INN & SUITES BY CARLSON (CABELA'S LOCATION)   *Book at aaa.com*

Phone: (734)529-8822

All Year [ECP]   1P: $65-$169   2P: $65-$169   XP: $10   F18

Small-scale Hotel **Location:** US 23, exit 17. 665 Tecumseh St 48131. **Fax:** 734/529-5975. **Facility:** 70 units. 60 one-bedroom standard units, some with whirlpools. 10 one-bedroom suites ($99-$169). 3 stories, interior corridors. **Bath:** combo or shower only. **Parking:** on-site. **Amenities:** dual phone lines, voice mail, irons, hair dryers. **Pool(s):** heated indoor. **Leisure Activities:** whirlpool, exercise room. **Guest Services:** coin laundry. **Business Services:** meeting rooms. **Cards:** AX, CB, DC, DS, JC, MC, VI. *(See color ad p 313)*

HOLIDAY INN EXPRESS   *Book at aaa.com*

Phone: 734/529-5100

All Year [ECP]   1P: $89-$199   2P: $89-$199   XP: $8   F18

Small-scale Hotel **Location:** Jct US 23 and SR 50. 100 White Tail Dr 48131. **Fax:** 734/529-5100. **Facility:** 77 units. 74 one-bedroom standard units, some with whirlpools. 3 one-bedroom suites, some with whirlpools. 2 stories, interior corridors. **Bath:** combo or shower only. **Parking:** on-site. **Amenities:** high-speed Internet, dual phone lines, voice mail, irons, hair dryers. *Some:* DVD players. **Pool(s):** heated indoor. **Leisure Activities:** exercise room. **Guest Services:** valet and coin laundry. **Cards:** AX, CB, DC, DS, JC, MC, VI.

———— WHERE TO DINE ————

WILDERNESS SPORTS BAR & GRILLE

Lunch: $4-$12   **Dinner:** $6-$12   **Phone:** 734/529-7220

American **Location:** US 23, exit 17, just w. 103 Cabela Blvd E 48131. **Hours:** 11 am-2 am. Closed major holidays. **Features:** A hunting and fishing themed restaurant, the menu offers a modest selection of regional seafood and traditional bar foods. Casual dress; cocktails. **Parking:** on-site. **Cards:** AX, DS, MC, VI.

EAGLE HARBOR

———— WHERE TO STAY ————

SHORELINE RESORT

Phone: (906)289-4441

6/15-10/15 & 1/1-3/31   1P: $66-$77   2P: $66-$77   XP: $4   F13

Motel **Location:** On SR 26. Located along the water's edge of the harbor. 201 Front St, F #2015 49950 (HYC 1, Box 262). **Facility:** 8 one-bedroom standard units. 1 story, exterior corridors. **Bath:** shower only. **Parking:** on-site. **Terms:** open 6/15-10/15 & 1/1-3/31, weekly rates available, pets ($10 deposit). **Dining:** 8 am-8 pm. **Leisure Activities:** canoeing, paddleboats, kayaks. **Cards:** MC, VI.

EAST GRAND RAPIDS pop. 10,764

——— WHERE TO DINE ———

ROSE'S
American

| | Lunch: $7-$12 | Dinner: $8-$19 | Phone: 616/458-1122 |

Location: 1.4 mi w of E Belt Line, then just nw. 550 Lakeside Dr 49506. **Hours:** 11 am-11 pm. **Features:** The noisy, bustling bistro and its breezy outdoor deck, overlook Reed's Lake. Pizzas cooked in a brick oven and homemade pasta dishes are at the center of a menu that features daily fish specials. Tiramisu and creme brulee are delicious dessert choices. Casual dress; cocktails. **Parking:** on-site. **Cards:** AX, DS, MC, VI.

EAST LANSING pop. 46,525—See also LANSING.

——— WHERE TO STAY ———

CANDLEWOOD SUITES
Small-scale Hotel

Book at aaa.com
All Year
Phone: (517)351-8181

| | 1P: $99-$149 | 2P: $99-$149 |

Location: 1 mi e of I-496 and US 127, exit 11 (Jolly Rd). 3545 Forest Rd 48910. Fax: 517/351-8101. **Facility:** 128 units. 96 one-bedroom standard units with efficiencies. 32 one-bedroom suites with efficiencies. 3 stories, interior corridors. **Parking:** on-site. **Terms:** weekly rates available, [MAP] meal plan available. **Amenities:** video library, CD players, high-speed Internet, dual phone lines, voice mail, irons, hair dryers. **Leisure Activities:** exercise room. **Guest Services:** sundries. **Cards:** AX, CB, DC, DS, JC, MC, VI.

SOME UNITS

EAST LANSING MARRIOTT AT UNIVERSITY PLACE *Book at aaa.com* **Phone: (517)337-4440**
▼▼▼▼ All Year 1P: $199-$209 2P: $199-$209
Location: Just n of Grand River Ave; downtown. 300 Michigan Agricultural College Ave 48823. Fax: 517/337-5001.
Large-scale Hotel **Facility:** 180 one-bedroom standard units. 7 stories, interior corridors. *Bath:* combo or shower only. **Parking:** on-site. **Amenities:** voice mail, irons, hair dryers. **Pool(s):** heated indoor. **Leisure Activities:** sauna, whirlpool, exercise room. **Guest Services:** sundries, valet and coin laundry. **Business Services:** conference facilities, business center. **Cards:** AX, CB, DC, DS, JC, MC, VI.

SOME UNITS
(A$K) (S₀) (✈) (¶¶) (▼) (&M) (⌀) (➔) (✕) (🎥) (DATA PORT) (🖥) / (✕) (🔋) /

HAMPTON INN *Book at aaa.com* **Phone: 517/324-2072**
▼▼▼ All Year [ECP] 1P: $80-$90 2P: $90-$100
Location: US 127, exit Lake Lansing Rd, just e. 2500 Coolidge Rd 48823. Fax: 517/324-2073. **Facility:** 86 units. 84
Small-scale Hotel one-bedroom standard units, some with whirlpools. 2 one-bedroom suites ($129-$169). 4 stories, interior corridors. *Bath:* combo or shower only. **Parking:** on-site. **Amenities:** video games (fee), dual phone lines, voice mail, irons, hair dryers. **Pool(s):** heated indoor. **Leisure Activities:** whirlpool, exercise room. **Guest Services:** valet laundry, area transportation. **Business Services:** meeting rooms. **Cards:** AX, CB, DC, DS, MC, VI.

SOME UNITS
(A$K) (S₀) (✈) (¶¶+) (▼) (&M) (⌀) (➔) (🎥) (DATA PORT) (🖥) / (✕) (🔋) (🔋) /

KELLOGG HOTEL AND CONFERENCE CENTER *Book at aaa.com* **Phone: (517)432-4000**
(AAA) (SAVE) All Year 1P: $95-$179 2P: $95-$179 XP: $10 F18
Location: I-496, exit 9 (Trowbridge), just e, then 0.5 mi n. Located on Michigan State University Campus. 55 S Harrison
▼▼▼ Rd 48824. Fax: 517/353-1872. **Facility:** 165 one-bedroom standard units. 7 stories, interior corridors. *Bath:*
Large-scale Hotel combo or shower only. **Parking:** on-site. **Terms:** 3 day cancellation notice-fee imposed. **Amenities:** voice mail, irons, hair dryers. **Fee:** video games, high-speed Internet. **Dining:** 2 restaurants, 6:30 am-10 pm, cocktails, also, The State Room, see separate listing. **Leisure Activities:** exercise room. **Fee:** recreational priviliges. **Guest Services:** gift shop, valet laundry, airport transportation-Capital City Airport, area transportation-within 5 mi. **Business Services:** conference facilities. **Cards:** AX, CB, DC, DS, MC, VI. **Special Amenities:** free newspaper and free room upgrade (subject to availability with advanced reservations). *(See color ad p 294)*

SOME UNITS
(S₀) (✈) (¶¶) (▼) (&M) (&) (🎥) (DATA PORT) / (✕) (🔋) /

RESIDENCE INN BY MARRIOTT *Book at aaa.com* **Phone: 517/332-7711**
▼▼▼ All Year 1P: $79-$259 2P: $79-$259
Location: US 127, exit Grand River Ave, 2.6 mi se on SR 43. 1600 E Grand River Ave 48823. Fax: 517/332-7711.
Small-scale Hotel **Facility:** 60 units. 44 one- and 16 two-bedroom standard units with kitchens. 2 stories, exterior corridors. **Parking:** on-site. **Terms:** pets ($25-$150 fee). **Amenities:** voice mail, irons, hair dryers. **Pool(s):** heated outdoor. **Leisure Activities:** whirlpool, exercise room, sports court. **Guest Services:** valet and coin laundry. **Cards:** AX, DC, DS, MC, VI.

SOME UNITS
(A$K) (S₀) (🐾) (¶¶+) (⌀) (➔) (✕) (🎥) (DATA PORT) (🔋) (🛏) (🖥) / (✕) (VCR) /
FEE FEE

TOWNEPLACE SUITES *Book at aaa.com* **Phone: (517)203-1000**
▼▼▼ All Year 1P: $79-$94 2P: $79-$94
Location: I-96, exit 110 (Okemos Rd), 0.8 mi n, then 0.5 mi w, just n on Hagadorn Rd. 2855 Hannah Blvd 48823.
Small-scale Hotel Fax: 517/203-1234. **Facility:** 84 units. 63 one-bedroom standard units with kitchens. 21 two-bedroom suites with kitchens. 3 stories, interior corridors. *Bath:* combo or shower only. **Parking:** on-site. **Terms:** pets ($100 deposit, $5 extra charge). **Amenities:** video games (fee), dual phone lines, voice mail, irons, hair dryers. **Pool(s):** heated outdoor. **Leisure Activities:** exercise room. **Guest Services:** valet and coin laundry. **Business Services:** meeting rooms, business center. **Cards:** AX, CB, DC, DS, JC, MC, VI.

SOME UNITS
(A$K) (S₀) (🐾) (¶¶+) (&) (➔) (🎥) (DATA PORT) (🔋) (🛏) (🖥) / (✕) /
FEE

——— **WHERE TO DINE** ———

ALL SEASONS BISTRO **Dinner:** $9-$25 **Phone:** 517/336-9890
▼▼▼ **Location:** US 127, exit Lake Lansing Rd, just e. 1500 W Lake Lansing Rd 48823. **Hours:** 5 pm-10 pm. Closed major holidays; also Sun & Mon. **Reservations:** suggested. **Features:** French influenced design has
Regional French created a cozy and intimate dining room that speaks volumes with its seasonal menu. Traditional bistro inspired items such as pate du jour, coq au vin and cassoulet are featured along with classic dishes such as grilled tenderloin of beef. Dressy casual; cocktails. **Parking:** on-site. **Cards:** AX, DC, DS, MC, VI.

(&M) (▼) (✕)

BEGGAR'S BANQUET **Lunch:** $6-$26 **Dinner:** $6-$26 **Phone:** 517/351-4573
▼▼▼ **Location:** Just n of Grand River Ave; center. 218 Abbott Rd 48823. **Hours:** 11 am-11:30 pm, Fri-midnight, Sat 10 am-midnight, Sun 10 am-10:30 pm. Closed: 12/25. **Reservations:** suggested, weekends. **Features:** In
American business since the mid-1970s, the casual restaurant has two dining rooms: one classy and one rustic. Such dishes as baked chili and chicken Kiev make up the traditional menu. Artwork created and donated by local students decorates the walls. Casual dress; cocktails. **Parking:** street. **Cards:** AX, DS, MC, VI.

(&M) (▼) (✕)

EVERGREEN GRILL **Lunch:** $8-$10 **Dinner:** $17-$30 **Phone:** 517/337-1200
▼▼▼ **Location:** Just n of jct Grand River Ave; downtown. 327 Abbott Rd 48823. **Hours:** 11 am-10 pm, Fri & Sat-midnight, Sun 9 am-10 pm. Closed major holidays. **Features:** Based in a converted post office, this attractive dining
American room features stark walls showcasing the works of local artists and plenty of green plants. A fairly creative menu features regional ingredients such as Indiana Duck and Michigan Cherries used in conjunction with fresh imported seafoods and global seasonings. Dressy casual; cocktails. **Parking:** on-site and valet. **Cards:** AX, CB, DC, DS, MC, VI.

(&M) (▼) (✕)

THE STATE ROOM   **Lunch: $8-$12**   **Dinner: $12-$20**   **Phone:** 517/432-5049
▽▽△▽△▽ **Location:** I-496, exit 9 (Trowbridge), just e, then 0.5 mi n; in Kellogg Hotel and Conference Center. 55 S Harrison Rd
48824. **Hours:** 6:30 am-10 pm, Sun 10 am-2 pm. Closed major holidays. **Reservations:** accepted.
American **Features:** This quietly upscale restaurant offers relaxed dining for all three meals. Focusing on seasonal
Michigan products, the menu is further supplemented by a visiting chef series which has brought some of
the most exciting and innovative chefs to the restaurant. Dressy casual; cocktails. **Parking:** on-site (fee). **Cards:** AX, DC, DS,
MC, VI.

TROPPO   **Lunch: $6-$10**   **Dinner: $12-$20**   **Phone:** 517/336-7768
▽▽△▽△▽ **Location:** Just n of jct N Grand River and Michigan Agricultural College aves; downtown. 213 Ann St E 48823.
Hours: 11 am-2 am, Sun from noon. Closed major holidays. **Reservations:** accepted. **Features:** Half
American restaurant and half bar, this dark, eclectic upscale space offers a unique dining experience. Drawing from
Pacific Rim influenes, the contemporary menu offers such items as orange glazed salmon and sea bass
Papillote, as well as interesting takes on steaks and pastas. Dressy casual; cocktails. **Parking:** street. **Cards:** AX, DC, DS,
MC, VI.

EAST TAWAS pop. 2,951

------ WHERE TO STAY ------

BAMBI MOTEL   **Phone:** 989/362-4582
▽▽△▽
| | 5/1-10/31 | 1P: $50-$80 | 2P: $65-$85 | XP: $5 | F12 |
| Motel | 4/1-4/30 & 11/1-3/31 | 1P: $39-$59 | 2P: $45-$65 | XP: $5 | F12 |

Location: 0.5 mi on US 23. Located in a commercial area. 1100 E Bay St 48730. **Facility:** 15 one-bedroom standard units. 1 story, exterior corridors. **Parking:** on-site. **Terms:** 2 night minimum stay - seasonal & weekends,
cancellation fee imposed. **Cards:** DS, MC, VI.

SOME UNITS
⊠ 🛏 / FEE

HOLIDAY INN-TAWAS BAY RESORT   *Book at aaa.com*   **Phone:** 989/362-8601
(AAA) (SAVE)
| | 6/15-3/31 | 1P: $144-$180 | 2P: $144-$180 | XP: $8 | F |
| ▽▽△▽△▽ | 4/1-6/14 | 1P: $76-$90 | 2P: $76-$90 | XP: $8 | F |

Large-scale Hotel **Location:** On US 23 N. Located on Lake Huron, next to the state park marina. 300 E Bay St 48730. Fax: 989/362-5111.
Facility: 103 one-bedroom standard units, some with whirlpools. 2 stories (no elevator), interior corridors.
Parking: on-site. **Terms:** check-in 4 pm, 2-3 night minimum stay - weekends, 3 day cancellation notice,
weekly rates available, [AP] meal plan available, package plans. **Amenities:** irons, hair dryers. **Dining:** 6:30
am-10 pm, cocktails. **Pool(s):** heated indoor. **Leisure Activities:** sauna, whirlpool, rental paddleboats, boat dock, playground,
exercise room, shuffleboard. *Fee:* jet skis, game room. **Guest Services:** gift shop, coin laundry. **Business Services:** conference
facilities, business center. **Cards:** AX, CB, DC, DS, MC, VI. **Special Amenities:** free local telephone calls and preferred room
(subject to availability with advanced reservations).

SOME UNITS
🅢 🐕 🛏 🍴 🍸 🛶 ⊠ 🎿 DATA PORT 💻 / ⊠ 🛏 /

------ WHERE TO DINE ------

------ The following restaurant has not been evaluated by AAA ------
but is listed for your information only.

FALCO ROSSO RESTAURANT   **Phone:** 989/362-0800
[fyi] Not evaluated. **Location:** 1 mi w on SR 55, then 5 mi n. 350 W Davison Rd 48730. **Features:** Located at the Red
Hawk Golf Club, the restaurant is recommended by the locals for its food and friendly service.

ELK RAPIDS pop. 1,700

------ WHERE TO DINE ------

PEARL'S   **Lunch: $4-$8**   **Dinner: $8-$20**   **Phone:** 231/264-0530
▽▽△▽ ▽▽△▽ **Location:** From US 31, 0.5 mi e of stoplight. 617 Ames St 49629. **Hours:** 11 am-midnight, Sun-10 pm. Closed:
11/25, 12/24, 12/25. **Features:** Voodoo dolls, Mardi Gras beads, papier-mache doodads and the music all
English add to a taste of the Big Easy. On the menu is a variety of Cajun and Creole selections. Turn up the heat
with gumbo ya ya or pasta jambalaya, or turn it back down with beef brisket or a muffuletta sandwich.
Save room for one of the homemade desserts. Casual dress; cocktails. **Parking:** on-site. **Cards:** AX, MC, VI.

ELLSWORTH pop. 483

------ WHERE TO DINE ------

TAPAWINGO   **Dinner: $29-$44**   **Phone:** 231/588-7971
▽▽△▽△▽ **Location:** Center. 9502 Lake St 49729. **Hours:** Open 4/1-11/8 & 12/4-3/31; 5:30 pm-9 pm. Closed: Mon &
Tues 10/19-4/30. **Reservations:** required. **Features:** The changing menu revolves around the seasons,
American centering on creative modern American cooking in such entrees as rack of lamb and regional fish. The
atmosphere is upbeat and jovial, making the restaurant a favorite for comfortable, relaxed dining. Dressy
casual; cocktails. **Parking:** on-site. **Cards:** AX, MC, VI.

ESCANABA pop. 13,140

———— WHERE TO STAY ————

BAY VIEW MOTEL　　　　　　　　　　　　　　　　　　　　　　**Phone:** 906/786-2843

6/1-9/15	1P: $47-$61	2P: $51-$61	XP: $5	F12
4/1-5/31 & 9/16-3/31	1P: $37-$51	2P: $41-$51	XP: $5	F12

Motel　**Location:** 4.5 mi n on US 2/41 and SR 35. Located in a commercial area. (7110 Hwy 2, 41 & SR 35, GLADSTONE, 49837). Fax: 906/786-6218. **Facility:** 22 one-bedroom standard units, some with whirlpools. 1-2 stories (no elevator), interior/exterior corridors. *Bath:* combo or shower only. **Parking:** on-site, winter plug-ins. **Pool(s):** heated indoor. **Leisure Activities:** sauna, playground, basketball. **Cards:** AX, DS, MC, VI.

SOME UNITS

ECONO LODGE　　*Book at aaa.com*　　　　　　　　　　　**Phone:** (906)789-1066

6/1-9/30 [CP]	1P: $58-$71	2P: $63-$88	XP: $6	F18
10/1-3/31 [CP]	1P: $49-$59	2P: $54-$64	XP: $6	F18
4/1-5/31 [CP]	1P: $48-$58	2P: $53-$63	XP: $5	F18

Small-scale Hotel　**Location:** 0.5 mi n on US 2/41 and SR 35. Located next to the U.P. State Fairgrounds. 921 N Lincoln Rd 49829. Fax: 906/789-9202. **Facility:** 50 one-bedroom standard units. 2 stories (no elevator), interior corridors. **Parking:** on-site. **Terms:** 30 day cancellation notice. **Amenities:** irons, hair dryers. **Leisure Activities:** sauna, whirlpool. **Business Services:** meeting rooms. **Cards:** AX, DC, DS, MC, VI. **Special Amenities:** free continental breakfast and free local telephone calls.

SOME UNITS

HIAWATHA MOTEL　　　　　　　　　　　　　　　　　　　　　**Phone:** (906)786-1341

5/1-9/30 [CP]	1P: $35-$40	2P: $50-$65	XP: $5	D
4/1-4/30 & 10/1-3/31 [CP]	1P: $35-$40	2P: $45-$60	XP: $5	D

Motel　**Location:** 0.5 mi w on US 2/41. Located in a commercial area. 2400 Ludington St 49829. Fax: 906/786-0828. **Facility:** 20 one-bedroom standard units, some with whirlpools. 1 story, exterior corridors. **Parking:** on-site. **Terms:** pets ($2 extra charge, in designated units). **Amenities:** video library (fee). **Cards:** AX, DC, DS, MC, VI. **Special Amenities:** free continental breakfast and free local telephone calls.

SOME UNITS
FEE　　　　　　　　FEE

TERRACE BAY INN BUDGET HOST　　　　　　　　　　　　**Phone:** 906/786-7554

5/11-9/30	1P: $52-$58	2P: $63-$99	XP: $5	F16
4/1-5/10	1P: $36-$52	2P: $56-$69	XP: $5	F16
10/1-3/31	1P: $36-$50	2P: $50-$65	XP: $5	F16

Large-scale Hotel　**Location:** 4.6 mi n on US 2/41 and SR 35. Located on Bay de Noc of Lake Michigan. 7146 P Rd 49829 (PO Box 453). Fax: 906/786-7597. **Facility:** 71 one-bedroom standard units. 1-2 stories (no elevator), interior/exterior corridors. *Bath:* combo or shower only. **Parking:** on-site, winter plug-ins. **Terms:** [ECP] meal plan available. **Dining:** 5 pm-9 pm; also 7-11 am 6/1-9/30, cocktails. **Pool(s):** heated indoor. **Leisure Activities:** sauna, whirlpool, boat ramp, fishing, snowmobiling. *Fee:* golf privileges, game room. **Business Services:** meeting rooms. **Cards:** AX, DS, MC, VI. **Special Amenities:** free local telephone calls and early check-in/late check-out.

SOME UNITS

———— WHERE TO DINE ————

HEREFORD AND HOPS　　**Lunch:** $4-$10　　**Dinner:** $10-$18　　**Phone:** 906/789-1945

American　**Location:** Downtown. 624 Ludington St 49829. **Hours:** 11 am-10 pm, Sun 4 pm-9 pm. **Reservations:** accepted. **Features:** Patrons of the brew pub and restaurant can grill their own steaks, kebabs or catch of the day on the charcoal grill. Casual dress; cocktails. **Parking:** on-site. **Cards:** AX, DC, DS, MC, VI.

HONG KONG BUFFET　　**Lunch:** $5-$7　　**Dinner:** $7-$8　　**Phone:** 906/233-9999

International　**Location:** Just e of jct US 2/41 and SR 35. 2100 Ludington St 49829. **Hours:** 11 am-10 pm. **Features:** The casual restaurant overlooks the golf course at this western Michigan resort. Casual dress; cocktails. **Parking:** on-site. **Cards:** MC, VI.

LOG CABIN SUPPER CLUB　　**Lunch:** $5-$10　　**Dinner:** $10-$20　　**Phone:** 906/786-5621

Steak & Seafood　**Location:** 5.3 mi n on US 2/41. 7531 US 2 & 41 49837. **Hours:** 11 am-2 & 5-10 pm, Sun 4 pm-9 pm; to 9 pm in winter. Closed: 7/4, 9/6, 12/25. **Features:** Perched on a bluff overlooking the bay, the charming log cabin restaurant presents a menu of fresh fish, steak, pasta and ribs. Patrons should save room for such eye-catching treats as chocolate decadence, cheesecake and Key lime pie. Casual dress; cocktails. **Parking:** on-site. **Cards:** MC, VI.

STONEHOUSE RESTAURANT　　**Lunch:** $3-$9　　**Dinner:** $6-$19　　**Phone:** 906/786-5003

Steak & Seafood　**Location:** 0.3 mi n at jct US 2/41 and SR 35. 2223 Ludington St 49829. **Hours:** 10 am-2 & 5-9:30 pm, Fri & Sat 5 pm-10 pm. Closed major holidays; also Sun. **Reservations:** accepted. **Features:** The cozy dining room is a casual, informal spot for enjoying thoughtful preparations of chicken, seafood and steak. The house specialty is succulent prime rib. Take time to check out the artwork and appreciate the attentive, efficient service. Casual dress; cocktails. **Parking:** on-site. **Cards:** AX, DC, DS, MC, VI.

SWEDISH PANTRY　　**Lunch:** $5-$8　　**Dinner:** $8-$13　　**Phone:** 906/786-9606

Swedish　**Location:** Downtown. 819 Ludington St 49829. **Hours:** 8 am-7:30 pm, Sat-3 pm; hours may vary seasonally. Closed: 11/25, 12/25 & Easter. **Reservations:** accepted. **Features:** The cozy dining room is filled with unusual gifts and clocks, as well as apples for good luck. On the menu are some of the area's best homemade dishes and bakery items. Casual dress. **Parking:** on-site. **Cards:** MC, VI.

———— *The following restaurants have not been evaluated by AAA* ————
but are listed for your information only.

FERDINAND'S
Phone: 906/786-8484
[fyi]
Not evaluated. **Location:** Downtown. 1318 Ludington St 49829. **Features:** In the downtown area, the restaurant prepares not only Mexican fare but also American dishes.

GREAT NORTHERN BUFFETT
Phone: 906/789-0630
[fyi]
Not evaluated. **Location:** 0.4 mi n on US 2/41 and SR 35. 521 N Lincoln Rd 49829. **Features:** The popular family restaurant offers travelers a chance to make a quick stop for reasonably priced eats.

FAIR HAVEN pop. 1,500

———— **WHERE TO DINE** ————

TIN FISH RESORT
Lunch: $8-$15   Dinner: $15-$24   Phone: 586/725-7888

Seafood
Location: Just e of jct Church Rd and SR 29 (Dixie Hwy). 10069 Dixie Hwy 48023. **Fax:** 269/561-2593. **Hours:** 11 am-11 pm, Fri & Sat-midnight, Sun 4 pm-10 pm. Closed major holidays. **Reservations:** suggested. **Features:** Patrons should never get lost in the nautical restaurant, as the circular dining room has compass points around the border and nautical charts on the wall. Views of the lake are spectacular. True to the theme, fresh fish prepared in varied manners is the house specialty, but a number of steaks and pasta dishes also share space on the menu. Casual dress; cocktails. **Parking:** on-site. **Cards:** AX, DS, MC, VI.

FARMINGTON HILLS —*See Detroit p. 259.*

FENNVILLE pop. 1,459

———— **WHERE TO STAY** ————

THE KINGSLEY HOUSE
Phone: 269/561-6425

Property failed to provide current rates

Bed & Breakfast
Location: I-196, exit 34, 5 mi e on SR 89. 626 W Main St 49408. **Facility:** This Victorian home was built in 1886 by the prominent Kingsley family; a Michigan historic site, it features a three-story turret. Smoke free premises. 8 one-bedroom standard units, some with whirlpools. 3 stories (no elevator), interior corridors. **Bath:** combo or shower only. **Parking:** on-site. **Terms:** check-in 4 pm. **Amenities:** video library, hair dryers. **Some:** CD players. **Leisure Activities:** bicycles.

SOME UNITS

———— **WHERE TO DINE** ————

CRANE'S PIE PANTRY RESTAURANT
Lunch: $6-$10   Dinner: $8-$12   Phone: 269/561-2297

American
Location: I-196, exit 34 (SR 89), 4 mi e. 6054 124th Ave (SR 89) 49408. **Hours:** 9 am-7 pm, Sun from 11 am; 10 am-5 pm, Sun from 11 am, closed Mon 11/1-12/31; Sat & Sun only 11 am-5 pm 1/1-4/30. Closed major holidays. **Features:** Tucked at the back of the big "red barn," this popular restaurant serves freshly baked breads, seasonal fruit pies, fresh cider and hearty soups along with a section of hot or cold sandwiches. Casual dress. **Parking:** on-site. **Cards:** DS, MC, VI.

FENTON pop. 10,582

———— **WHERE TO STAY** ————

BEST WESTERN OF FENTON
Book at aaa.com
Phone: (810)750-1711

10/1-3/31	1P: $85-$139	2P: $85-$139	XP: $6	F12
4/1-9/30	1P: $73-$139	2P: $73-$139	XP: $6	F12

Motel
Location: US 23, exit 78 (Owen Rd). 3255 Owen Rd 48430. **Fax:** 810/750-9462. **Facility:** 82 units. 80 one-bedroom standard units, some with whirlpools. 2 one-bedroom suites ($130-$150), some with whirlpools. 2 stories, exterior corridors. **Parking:** on-site. **Terms:** [ECP] meal plan available. **Amenities:** video library, irons, hair dryers. **Pool(s):** heated indoor. **Guest Services:** coin laundry. **Business Services:** meeting rooms. **Cards:** AX, DC, DS, MC, VI. **Special Amenities:** free continental breakfast and free local telephone calls.

SOME UNITS
FEE

HOLIDAY INN EXPRESS HOTEL & SUITES
Book at aaa.com
Phone: (810)714-7171

5/1-9/30 [ECP]	1P: $89-$159	2P: $89-$159
4/1-4/30 & 10/1-3/31 [ECP]	1P: $79-$139	2P: $79-$139

Small-scale Hotel
Location: US 23, exit 78 (Owen Rd), just w, then 1 mi n. Located across from a shopping mall. 17800 Silver Pkwy 48430. **Fax:** 810/714-3402. **Facility:** 69 one-bedroom standard units, some with whirlpools. 2 stories, interior corridors. **Bath:** combo or shower only. **Parking:** on-site. **Terms:** small pets only. **Amenities:** dual phone lines, voice mail, irons, hair dryers. **Pool(s):** heated indoor. **Leisure Activities:** whirlpool, exercise room. **Guest Services:** valet and coin laundry. **Business Services:** meeting rooms. **Cards:** AX, CB, DC, DS, JC, MC, VI.

SOME UNITS

———— **WHERE TO DINE** ————

THE FENTON HOTEL
Lunch: $8-$12   Dinner: $10-$15   Phone: 810/750-9463

American
Location: US 23, exit 78 (Owen Rd), 1.1 mi e on Silver Lake Rd, just n. 302 N Leroy St 48430. **Hours:** 11:30 am-10 pm, Fri-11 pm, Sat 4 pm-11 pm. Closed major holidays; also Sun. **Reservations:** accepted. **Features:** Allegedly haunted by two ghosts, one of which occasionally orders a drink at the bar, the hotel is a charming Victorian-style restaurant with a hint of intrigue. Casual dress; cocktails. **Parking:** on-site. **Cards:** AX, CB, DC, DS, MC, VI.

THE FRENCH LAUNDRY

Deli/Subs
Sandwiches

Lunch: $7-$9 **Phone:** 810/629-8852

Location: US 23, exit 78 (Owen Rd), 1 mi e. 125 W Shiawassee Ave 48430. **Hours:** 7 am-4 pm. Closed major holidays. **Features:** Not far from the center of town, the loud, crowded, fun and trendy delicatessen serves a good variety of made-to-order sandwiches, salads and daily specials. Also offered are several Zingerman's products. Casual dress. **Parking:** on-site and street. **Cards:** AX, MC, VI.

FERNDALE —See Detroit p. 260.

FERRYSBURG pop. 3,040

——— **WHERE TO DINE** ———

ARBOREAL INN

Steak & Seafood

Dinner: $15-$53 **Phone:** 616/842-3800

Location: 1 mi n from US 31, exit Van Wagoner Rd W, 0.3 mi n on 174th Ave. 18191 Old Grand Haven Rd 49456. **Hours:** 5 pm-10 pm. Closed major holidays; also Sun. **Reservations:** suggested, weekends. **Features:** Established in 1981, the cozy, moderately upscale restaurant is a favorite of the local crowd. There are several dining areas, including one with a warm, intimate fireplace. An extensive selection of wine accompanies choices on the diverse menu. Cocktails. **Parking:** on-site. **Cards:** AX, DS, MC, VI. ⊠

FLAT ROCK —See Detroit p. 261.

FLINT pop. 124,943

——— **WHERE TO STAY** ———

AMERICINN FLINT *Book at aaa.com* **Phone:** (810)233-9000

Small-scale Hotel

All Year [ECP] 1P: $66-$80 XP: $6 F

Location: US 23, exit 90 (Hill Rd); I-75 N, exit 475 to Hill Rd exit, then 1.5 mi w. 6075 Hill 23 Dr 48507 (2100 W Wackerly St, MIDLAND, 48640). Fax: 810/233-5286. **Facility:** 72 one-bedroom standard units, some with whirlpools. 3 stories, interior corridors. *Bath:* combo or shower only. **Parking:** on-site. **Terms:** 7 day cancellation notice-fee imposed, small pets only ($50 deposit). **Amenities:** voice mail, irons, hair dryers. **Pool(s):** heated indoor. **Leisure Activities:** sauna, whirlpool. *Fee:* game room. **Guest Services:** coin laundry. **Business Services:** meeting rooms. **Cards:** AX, DC, DS, MC, VI. *(See color ad p 311, p 199 & below)*

SOME UNITS

(ASK) (SD) 🛏 🏊 ⊠ 🐾 (DATA PORT) 🖥 / ⊠ 📳 🖨 /
FEE

BAYMONT INN & SUITES-FLINT *Book at aaa.com* **Phone:** (810)732-2300

Small-scale Hotel

4/1-10/1 1P: $59-$159
10/2-3/31 1P: $49-$129

Location: I-75, exit 122, just w on Pierson Rd. 4160 Pier North Blvd 48504. Fax: 810/732-9777. **Facility:** 88 units. 85 one-bedroom standard units, some with kitchens and/or whirlpools. 3 one-bedroom suites. 4 stories, interior corridors. *Bath:* combo or shower only. **Parking:** on-site. **Terms:** weekly rates available, [ECP] meal plan available, small pets only ($10 extra charge). **Amenities:** video games (fee), voice mail, irons, hair dryers. **Guest Services:** valet and coin laundry. **Cards:** AX, DC, DS, MC, VI. **Special Amenities:** free local telephone calls and free newspaper.

SOME UNITS

(SD) 🛏 🍴 ♿ 🐾 (DATA PORT) 🖥 / ⊠ 📳 🖨 /
FEE

COURTYARD BY MARRIOTT *Book at aaa.com* **Phone:** 810/232-3500

Small-scale Hotel

All Year 1P: $79-$109

Location: US 23, exit 90, just e on Hill Rd; adjacent to Holiday Inn. 5205 Gateway Center 48507. Fax: 810/232-7373. **Facility:** 102 units. 99 one-bedroom standard units, some with whirlpools. 3 one-bedroom suites. 3 stories, interior corridors. *Bath:* combo or shower only. **Parking:** on-site. **Terms:** cancellation fee imposed, [BP] meal plan available. **Amenities:** dual phone lines, voice mail, irons, hair dryers. **Dining:** 6-9:30 am, Sat & Sun 7-10 am. **Pool(s):** small heated indoor. **Leisure Activities:** whirlpool, exercise room. **Guest Services:** valet and coin laundry. **Business Services:** meeting rooms, fax. **Cards:** AX, DC, DS, MC, VI. **Special Amenities:** free newspaper.

SOME UNITS

(SD) 🍴 🍸 🎱 ♿ 🐾 🏊 🐾 (DATA PORT) 🖥 / ⊠ 📳 🖨 /

HOLIDAY INN EXPRESS
Book at aaa.com

Phone: (810)238-7744

(AAA) (SAVE)

	6/17-8/1	1P: $113-$209	2P: $113-$209
	8/2-8/20	1P: $63-$209	2P: $63-$209
	4/1-6/16	1P: $63-$189	2P: $63-$189
	8/21-3/31	1P: $59-$189	2P: $63-$189

Small-scale Hotel **Location:** I-475, exit 8A. 1150 Robert T Longway Blvd 48503. **Fax:** 810/233-7444. **Facility:** 124 one-bedroom standard units, some with whirlpools. 5 stories, interior corridors. **Parking:** on-site. **Terms:** [ECP] meal plan available, small pets only ($25 extra charge). **Amenities:** dual phone lines, voice mail, safes, irons, hair dryers. **Guest Services:** valet and coin laundry, airport transportation-Bishop Airport, area transportation-within 5 mi. **Business Services:** meeting rooms. **Cards:** AX, CB, DC, DS, MC, VI. **Special Amenities:** free expanded continental breakfast.

SOME UNITS

HOLIDAY INN GATEWAY CENTRE
Book at aaa.com

Phone: (810)232-5300

(AAA) (SAVE)

All Year — 1P: $119-$189

Location: US 23, exit 90, just e on Hill Rd. 5353 Gateway Centre 48507. **Fax:** 810/232-9806. **Facility:** 171 one-bedroom standard units, some with whirlpools. 4 stories, interior corridors. **Bath:** combo or shower only. **Parking:** on-site. **Amenities:** video games (fee), dual phone lines, voice mail, irons, hair dryers. **Dining:** 6 am-10 pm, Fri-11 pm, Sat 7 am-11 pm, Sun from 7 am, cocktails. **Pool(s):** heated indoor. **Leisure Activities:** sauna, whirlpool, exercise room. **Fee:** game room. **Guest Services:** valet and coin laundry, area transportation. **Business Services:** conference facilities, business center. **Cards:** AX, CB, DC, DS, JC, MC, VI. **Special Amenities:** free newspaper and free room upgrade (subject to availability with advanced reservations).

Small-scale Hotel

SOME UNITS

HOWARD JOHNSON LODGE
Book at aaa.com

Phone: (810)733-5910

Motel

All Year — 1P: $49 — 2P: $49

Location: I-75, exit 117 southbound; exit 117B northbound, just w. G-3277 Miller Rd 48507. **Fax:** 810/733-2713. **Facility:** 138 one-bedroom standard units, some with kitchens (no utensils) and/or whirlpools. 1 story, exterior corridors. **Parking:** on-site. **Terms:** 1-3 night minimum stay - seasonal, [CP] & [ECP] meal plans available, small pets only ($10 extra charge). **Amenities:** video library (fee). **Pool(s):** outdoor. **Guest Services:** coin laundry. **Cards:** AX, DS, MC, VI. **(See color ad p 584)**

SOME UNITS

RAMADA INN & CONFERENCE CENTER
Book at aaa.com

Phone: (810)732-0400

(AAA) (SAVE)

| All Year [CP] | 1P: $59-$99 | 2P: $59-$99 | XP: $6 | F18 |

Location: I-75, exit 122, just w. 4300 W Pierson Rd 48504. **Fax:** 810/732-2811. **Facility:** 190 one-bedroom standard units, some with whirlpools. 5 stories, interior corridors. **Parking:** on-site. **Terms:** check-in 4 pm. **Amenities:** voice mail, safes, irons, hair dryers. **Dining:** 6:30 am-2 & 5-10 pm, Sun-1 pm, cocktails. **Pool(s):** heated indoor. **Leisure Activities:** whirlpool, exercise room. **Fee:** game room. **Guest Services:** valet and coin laundry, airport transportation-Bishop Airport. **Business Services:** conference facilities. **Cards:** AX, DC, DS, MC, VI. **Special Amenities:** free continental breakfast and early check-in/late check-out.

Small-scale Hotel

SOME UNITS

RED ROOF INN-FLINT
Book at aaa.com

Phone: (810)733-1660

(AAA) (SAVE)

| 6/6-9/25 | 1P: $50-$76 | 2P: $56-$82 | XP: $6 | F18 |
| 4/1-6/5 & 9/26-3/31 | 1P: $44-$76 | 2P: $50-$82 | XP: $6 | F18 |

Motel

Location: I-75, exit 117B (Miller Rd), just w. G-3219 Miller Rd 48507. **Fax:** 810/733-6310. **Facility:** 107 one-bedroom standard units. 2 stories, exterior corridors. **Bath:** combo or shower only. **Parking:** on-site. **Terms:** small pets only. **Guest Services:** valet laundry. **Cards:** AX, CB, DC, DS, MC, VI. **Special Amenities:** free local telephone calls and free newspaper.

SOME UNITS

RESIDENCE INN
Book at aaa.com

Phone: (810)424-7000

All Year — 1P: $89-$149 — 2P: $89-$149

Location: US 23, exit 90 (Hill Rd), just e. 2202 W Hill Rd 48507. **Fax:** 810/424-9850. **Facility:** Smoke free premises. 87 units. 36 one-bedroom standard units, some with efficiencies or kitchens. 36 one- and 15 two-bedroom suites, some with efficiencies or kitchens. 3 stories, interior corridors. **Bath:** combo or shower only. **Parking:** on-site. **Terms:** 14 day cancellation notice, [BP] meal plan available, small pets only ($50 deposit, $10 extra charge). **Amenities:** dual phone lines, voice mail, irons, hair dryers. **Pool(s):** heated indoor. **Leisure Activities:** whirlpool, exercise room. **Guest Services:** valet and coin laundry. **Business Services:** meeting rooms. **Cards:** AX, DC, DS, MC, VI.

Small-scale Hotel

SOME UNITS

SLEEP INN
Book at aaa.com

Phone: (810)232-7777

All Year [CP] — 1P: $59-$99 — 2P: $59-$99 — XP: $10 — F18

Location: I-75, exit 117B northbound; exit 117 southbound (Miller Rd). 2325 Austin Pkwy 48507. **Fax:** 810/232-9671. **Facility:** 60 one-bedroom standard units. 3 stories, interior corridors. **Bath:** combo or shower only. **Parking:** on-site. **Amenities:** voice mail, safes. Some: irons, hair dryers. **Pool(s):** heated indoor. **Leisure Activities:** whirlpool, exercise room. **Guest Services:** valet and coin laundry. **Business Services:** meeting rooms. **Cards:** AX, CB, DC, DS, JC, MC, VI.

Small-scale Hotel

SOME UNITS

——— **WHERE TO DINE** ———

ITALIA GARDENS

Lunch: $8-$12 — **Dinner:** $9-$16 — **Phone:** 810/720-4112

Italian

Location: Just w of jct I-75, exit 117 southbound; exit 117B northbound and Miller Rd. G-3273 Miller Rd 48507. **Hours:** 11 am-9 pm, Fri & Sat-10 pm, Sun noon-8 pm. Closed major holidays. **Features:** The small restaurant serves up many favorite entrees, such as spaghetti, ribs, manicotti and pizza. A modern Italian theme is evident in the casually upscale dining room, which is decorated with stone columns and candle-topped pedestal tables. Casual dress; beer & wine only. **Parking:** on-site. **Cards:** AX, DC, DS, MC, VI.

MAKUCH RED ROOSTER
Lunch: $5-$6   Dinner: $18-$30   Phone: 810/742-9310
▼▼ ▼▼
American
Location: 3.5 mi e at jct Davison Rd and Averill St; between Dort and Center rds. 3302 Davison Rd 48506. **Hours:** 11 am-9 pm, Sat from 5 pm. Closed major holidays; also Sun. **Reservations:** suggested, weekends. **Features:** The building may be small and unassuming, but the flavors are big and bold in innovative specialties prepared by the creative chef. Such dishes as the fruit, vegetable and salmon platter are colorful, fresh and tasty. Service is friendly and efficient. Casual dress; cocktails. **Parking:** on-site. **Cards:** MC, VI.

REDWOOD LODGE MESQUITE GRILL & BREW PUB
Lunch: $9-$14   Dinner: $13-$38   Phone: 810/233-8000
▼▼ ▼▼
Steak & Seafood
Location: US 23, exit 90 (Hill Rd), just e; jct I-75 N and 475, 1 mi n on I-475, 2 mi w on Hill Rd. 5304 Gateway Center Dr 48507. **Hours:** 11 am-midnight, Fri & Sat-1 am, Sun noon-10 pm. Closed: 1/1, 11/25, 12/25. **Features:** The warm hunting lodge theme of this micro-brewery sets the stage for a menu dedicated to mesquite grilled specialties including wild game, steak, seafood, and wood-fired pizza. Hand crafted beer and a relaxing cigar lounge add to your dining experience. Casual dress; cocktails. **Parking:** on-site. **Cards:** AX, DS, MC, VI.

SALVATORE SCALLOPINI
Lunch: $7-$8   Dinner: $9-$14   Phone: 810/732-1070
▼▼ ▼▼
Italian
Location: I-75, exit 117 southbound; exit 117B northbound, just w. G-3227 Miller Rd 48507. **Hours:** 11 am-10 pm, Fri & Sat-11 pm, Sun noon-10 pm. Closed major holidays. **Features:** Popular and informal, the family-oriented restaurant delivers fresh and authentic entrees from a lengthy menu of traditional specialties. Seafood linguine is served piping hot with fresh mussels and squid. The wait staff is professional and friendly. Casual dress; cocktails. **Parking:** on-site. **Cards:** AX, DS, MC, VI.

SHAP'S FAMILY RESTAURANT
Lunch: $4-$8   Dinner: $4-$8   Phone: 810/232-8677
▼
American
Location: I-75, exit 90 (Hill Rd), 1 mi w. G-2520 W Hill Rd 48507. **Hours:** 24 hours. Closed major holidays. **Features:** You won't find anything fancy at this family-oriented dinner; what you will find is fast friendly service, good food and a smile on everyone's face. Casual dress. **Parking:** on-site. **Cards:** AX, DC, DS, MC, VI.

Hungry? Look for the
RED AAA Logo

*N*ext time you look through a AAA TourBook® guide in search of a place to dine, take note of the bright red AAA logo just under a select group of restaurant names! These Official Appointment restaurants place a high value on the business they receive from dedicated AAA travelers.

As a member, you already turn to TourBooks for quality travel information. Now look for restaurants that display the bright red AAA logo in their listing for dining experiences you'll long remember!

FOWLERVILLE pop. 2,972

——— WHERE TO STAY ———

BEST WESTERN FOWLERVILLE   *Book at aaa.com*   **Phone:** (517)223-9165
♦♦♦ ◊
| | 4/1-9/30 | 1P: $85-$125 | 2P: $95-$145 | XP: $10 | F12 |
| | 10/1-3/31 | 1P: $80-$110 | 2P: $85-$125 | XP: $10 | F12 |

Motel   **Location:** I-96, exit 129, just n. 950 S Grand Ave 48836. Fax: 517/223-0497. **Facility:** 60 one-bedroom standard units. 2 stories (no elevator), exterior corridors. **Parking:** on-site. **Terms:** [BP] meal plan available. **Amenities:** voice mail, irons, hair dryers. **Pool(s):** heated indoor. **Guest Services:** coin laundry. **Business Services:** fax (fee). **Cards:** AX, DC, DS, MC, VI.

SOME UNITS
[ASK] [S/D] [↑↓] [⊠] [✷] [DATA PORT] [☐] [☐] / [✕] /

FRANKENMUTH pop. 4,838

——— WHERE TO STAY ———

BAVARIAN INN LODGE   *Book at aaa.com*   **Phone:** 989/652-7200
(AAA) [SAVE]
| | 6/25-10/2 | 1P: $128-$173 | 2P: $133-$178 |
♦♦♦
	10/3-12/31	1P: $115-$173	2P: $120-$178
	1/1-3/31	1P: $94-$173	2P: $99-$178
	4/1-6/24	1P: $105-$170	2P: $110-$175

Resort   **Location:** Just e across covered bridge. Located along the river, within walking distance of downtown area. 1 Covered
Large-scale Hotel   Bridge Ln 48734. Fax: 989/652-6711. **Facility:** This riverfront resort offers extensive recreational facilities. 355 units. 344 one-bedroom standard units, some with whirlpools. 11 one-bedroom suites ($143-$270). 5 stories, interior corridors. *Bath:* combo or shower only. **Parking:** on-site, winter plug-ins. **Terms:** cancellation fee imposed. **Amenities:** dual phone lines, voice mail, irons, hair dryers. **Dining:** 2 restaurants, 7 am-11 pm; to midnight in season, cocktails, entertainment. **Pool(s):** 5 heated indoor. **Leisure Activities:** whirlpools, 4 tennis courts (2 lighted), exercise room, basketball. *Fee:* expanded family fun center includes 18-hole indoor mini-golf course, game room. **Guest Services:** gift shop, airport transportation (fee)-Maitland Bay Saginaw and Bishop airports, area transportation-within 0.3 mi. **Business Services:** conference facilities. **Cards:** AX, DS, MC, VI. *(See color ad p 303)*

SOME UNITS
[S/D] [✈] [↑↓] [Y] [⌖M] [⚬] [✕] [DATA PORT] [☐] [☐] / [✕] [VCR]
       FEE   FEE

DRURY INN & SUITES   *Book at aaa.com*   **Phone:** (989)652-2800
♦♦♦
| | All Year [BP] | 1P: $83-$120 | 2P: $93-$130 | XP: $10 | F18 |

Small-scale Hotel   **Location:** On SR 83; center of downtown. Located in a commercial area. 260 S Main St 48734. Fax: 989/652-2800. **Facility:** 78 one-bedroom standard units. 5 stories, interior corridors. *Bath:* combo or shower only. **Parking:** on-site, winter plug-ins. **Terms:** check-in 4 pm, small pets only. **Amenities:** irons, hair dryers. **Pool(s):** heated indoor. **Leisure Activities:** whirlpool. **Guest Services:** complimentary evening beverages: Mon-Thurs. **Business Services:** meeting rooms. **Cards:** AX, CB, DC, DS, MC, VI.

SOME UNITS
[ASK] [🛏] [↑↓] [⌖M] [⚬] [⚬] [↑↑] [✷] [DATA PORT] [☐] / [✕] [☐] [☐] /
                                    FEE

FAIRFIELD INN   *Book at aaa.com*   **Phone:** 989/652-5000
                 5/31-10/31   1P: $69-$104   2P: $69-$104
                 11/1-12/31   1P: $59-$104   2P: $59-$104
Small-scale Hotel 4/1-5/30   1P: $59-$89   2P: $59-$89
                 1/1-3/31   1P: $54-$79   2P: $54-$79

Location: On SR 83; center of downtown. Located in a commercial area. 430 S Main St 48734. **Fax:** 989/652-0327. **Facility:** 63 one-bedroom standard units, some with whirlpools. 3 stories, interior corridors. *Bath:* combo or shower only. **Parking:** on-site. **Terms:** cancellation fee imposed, [CP] meal plan available. **Amenities:** video games, irons, hair dryers. **Pool(s):** heated indoor. **Leisure Activities:** whirlpool, exercise room. **Guest Services:** valet laundry. **Cards:** AX, CB, DC, DS, MC, VI.

SOME UNITS

5 Indoor Pools!
3 Whirlpools & Family Fun Center!

Now Taking Online Reservations!

♦ 360 Guestrooms including Family Suites
♦ 18-Hole Indoor Mini Golf
♦ Nightly Entertainment
♦ Conference Center for up to 450 People
♦ Walking Distance to 100 Main Street Shops
♦ Call for Seasonal Rates

Join our Perks Club and Save! Call 877-737-5707

Frankenmuth® Bavarian Inn Lodge

For reservations: 888-775-6343   www.bavarianinn.com

Frankenmuth is located just off I-75 between Flint and Saginaw, Michigan

SPRINGHILL SUITES BY MARRIOTT

Book at aaa.com

Phone: 989/652-7500

	6/1-10/31	1P: $89-$129	2P: $89-$129
	4/1-5/31	1P: $74-$104	2P: $74-$104
Small-scale Hotel	11/1-12/31	1P: $74-$99	2P: $74-$99
	1/1-3/31	1P: $69-$99	2P: $69-$99

Location: On SR 83; center. Located in a commercial area. 530 S Main St 48734. Fax: 989/652-3683. **Facility:** 64 one-bedroom standard units, some with whirlpools. 3 stories, interior corridors. *Bath:* combo or shower only. **Parking:** on-site. **Terms:** cancellation fee imposed. **Amenities:** video games, dual phone lines, voice mail, irons, hair dryers. **Pool(s):** heated indoor. **Leisure Activities:** whirlpool, exercise room. *Fee:* game room. **Guest Services:** coin laundry. **Business Services:** meeting rooms. **Cards:** AX, CB, DC, DS, JC, MC, VI.

SOME UNITS

In All the World, There's Only One...

Zehnder's Bavarian Haus
Features: 137 Deluxe
Accommodations
Indoor & Outdoor
Pools Sauna, Jacuzzi
& Exercise Room

Zehnders
OF FRANKENMUTH

Enjoy Family Style Chicken Dinners
Steaks, Seafood and more!
Visit Zehnder's Bakery, Gift Shops,
Z Chef's Café and
The Fortress Golf Course

For Reservations Call 800-863-7999
730 S. Main St. Frankenmuth, MI 48734 - www.zehnders.com

Family Fun In Frankenmuth!
"Michigan's Little Bavaria"

Famous Chicken Dinners!

30 Shops & Attractions!

River Place

800-228-2742
bavarianinn.com
713 South Main Street

800-600-0105
frankenmuth-riverplace.com
925 South Main Street

ZEHNDER'S BAVARIAN HAUS

Phone: (989)652-0470

AAA SAVE
Small-scale Hotel

6/1-12/31	1P: $59-$129	2P: $59-$129
1/1-3/31	1P: $49-$129	2P: $49-$129
4/1-5/31	1P: $49-$119	2P: $49-$119

Location: 0.5 mi s on SR 83. Located beside Bronner's Christmas Wonderland. 1365 S Main St 48734 (PO Box 263). Fax: 989/652-9777. **Facility:** 137 units. 133 one-bedroom standard units. 4 one-bedroom suites ($119-$209) with whirlpools. 2 stories, interior/exterior corridors. **Parking:** on-site. **Terms:** check-in 4 pm, [BP] meal plan available, package plans. **Amenities:** irons, hair dryers. **Dining:** 7-10:30 am. **Pool(s):** heated outdoor, heated indoor. **Leisure Activities:** sauna, whirlpools, exercise room. *Fee:* golf-18 holes, game room. **Guest Services:** valet laundry. **Business Services:** meeting rooms. **Cards:** AX, DS, MC, VI. **Special Amenities:** free local telephone calls and early check-in/late check-out. *(See color ad p 304)*

SOME UNITS

The following lodging was either not evaluated or did not meet AAA rating requirements but is listed for your information only.

FRANKENMUTH MOTEL

Phone: (989)652-6171

AAA SAVE
fyi
Motel

6/1-10/16	1P: $65-$69	2P: $70-$90
10/17-12/31	1P: $59-$69	2P: $65-$90
1/1-3/31	1P: $49-$69	2P: $55-$90
4/1-5/31	1P: $59-$69	2P: $59-$69

Under major renovation, scheduled to be completed June 2004. Last rated: ▼ **Location:** E on SR 83. Located close to the downtown area. 1218 Weiss St 48734. Fax: 989/652-4538. **Facility:** 54 one-bedroom standard units. 1 story, exterior corridors. *Bath:* combo or shower only. **Parking:** on-site, winter plug-ins. **Leisure Activities:** horseshoes. **Guest Services:** gift shop. **Cards:** AX, DS, MC, VI. **Special Amenities:** free local telephone calls and free room upgrade (subject to availability with advanced reservations). *(See ad p 302)*

SOME UNITS

WHERE TO DINE

BAVARIAN INN RESTAURANT

Lunch: $6-$9   Dinner: $12-$20   Phone: 989/652-9941

AAA
German

Location: On SR 83. 713 S Main St 48734. **Hours:** 11 am-9:30 pm. **Reservations:** suggested. **Features:** A dozen German-themed dining rooms are decorated with hand-painted murals, steins and other Bavarian decor. The menu lists a good selection of American comfort foods—such as chicken, mashed potatoes and applesauce—as well as German entrees. Casual dress; cocktails. **Parking:** on-site. **Cards:** AX, DS, MC, VI. *(See color ad p 304)*

FRANKEN ECK

Lunch: $8-$12   Dinner: $12-$16   Phone: 989/652-4586

German

Location: Jct Genesee St; just n of downtown. 100 S Main St 48734. **Hours:** 11 am-2 & 5:30-9:30 pm, Fri & Sat 11 am-10 pm, Sun-8 pm. Closed major holidays. **Features:** Enjoy home-style German specialties at the pub-style eatery. Casual dress; cocktails. **Parking:** on-site. **Cards:** AX, DS, MC, VI.

ZEHNDER'S

Lunch: $6-$10   Dinner: $14-$19   Phone: 989/652-9925

AAA
American

Location: On SR 83. 730 S Main St 48734. **Hours:** 11 am-9:30 pm. Closed: 12/24 for dinner. **Features:** One of America's largest family restaurants. This popular, well-established restaurant has a very good selection of main dishes. Specializing in all-you-can-eat family-style chicken dinners. Zehnder's Marketplace and Z Chef's Cafe is open 8 am-9 pm daily. Casual dress; cocktails. **Parking:** on-site. **Cards:** DS, MC, VI. *(See color ad p 304)*

The following restaurant has not been evaluated by AAA but is listed for your information only.

PEDALER'S EATERY

Phone: 989/652-3070

fyi

Not evaluated. **Location:** Center; at River Place. 925 S Main St 48734. **Features:** Located in Frankenmuth River Place, serving a number of light meals, sandwiches, salads & pizza.

FREELAND pop. 5,147

WHERE TO DINE

RIVERSIDE FAMILY RESTAURANT

Lunch: $2-$5   Dinner: $5-$9   Phone: 989/695-5563

American

Location: 0.5 mi nw on SR 47. 8295 Midland Rd 48623. **Hours:** 6 am-9 pm. **Features:** Beside the Tittabawassee River, this casual restaurant offers up-close views of the water, woods and wildlife. Country-style decorations complement country-style cooking in such daily specials as meatloaf and pot roast. Save room for homemade pie. Casual dress. **Parking:** on-site. **Cards:** DS, MC, VI.

FREMONT pop. 4,224

WHERE TO STAY

THE HARRINGTON INN

Phone: (231)924-3083

Small-scale Hotel

All Year   1P: $74-$139   2P: $74-$139   XP: $6   F12

Location: 1 mi w on SR 82. 1117 W Main St 49412. Fax: 231/924-3772. **Facility:** 38 one-bedroom standard units, some with whirlpools. 1 story, interior corridors. **Parking:** on-site. **Terms:** cancellation fee imposed, [ECP] meal plan available. **Amenities:** *Some:* hair dryers. **Pool(s):** heated outdoor. **Leisure Activities:** exercise room. **Guest Services:** valet laundry. **Business Services:** meeting rooms. **Cards:** AX, DS, MC, VI.

SOME UNITS

GAYLORD pop. 3,681

―――― WHERE TO STAY ――――

BEST VALUE ROYAL CREST INN
(AAA) (SAVE)
▼▼▼▼
Small-scale Hotel

Book at aaa.com
All Year   1P: $89-$99   2P: $89-$99   XP: $5   F18
Phone: (989)732-6451
Location: I-75, exit 279, 2.3 mi ne on I-75 business loop. Located in a semi-commercial area. 803 S Otsego Ave 49735. **Fax:** 989/732-7634. **Facility:** 44 one-bedroom standard units. 2 stories (no elevator), interior corridors. **Parking:** on-site, winter plug-ins. **Terms:** cancellation fee imposed, [ECP] meal plan available, package plans. **Amenities:** irons, hair dryers. **Pool(s):** heated indoor. **Leisure Activities:** sauna, whirlpool, snowmobiling, exercise room. **Fee:** game room. **Business Services:** meeting rooms, fax. **Cards:** AX, CB, DC, DS, JC, MC, VI. **Special Amenities:** free continental breakfast and preferred room (subject to availability with advanced reservations).** (See color ad below)

SOME UNITS
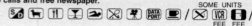

BEST WESTERN ALPINE LODGE
(AAA) (SAVE)
▼▼ ▼▼
Small-scale Hotel

Book at aaa.com
All Year   1P: $59-$99   2P: $69-$109
Phone: (989)732-2431
Location: I-75, exit 282, 0.3 mi e on SR 32. Located in a commercial area. 833 W Main St 49735. Fax: 989/732-9640. **Facility:** 138 one-bedroom standard units. 2 stories (no elevator), interior/exterior corridors. **Parking:** on-site. **Terms:** 7 day cancellation notice, [AP] meal plan available, package plans - seasonal, pets (in designated units). **Amenities:** voice mail, safes (fee), irons, hair dryers. **Dining:** 7 am-10 pm, cocktails. **Pool(s):** heated indoor. **Leisure Activities:** sauna, whirlpool, snowmobiling, exercise room, indoor recreational area, pool table, shuffleboard. **Fee:** game room. **Guest Services:** coin laundry. **Business Services:** meeting rooms. **Cards:** AX, CB, DC, DS, MC, VI. **Special Amenities:** free local telephone calls and free newspaper.

SOME UNITS
FEE FEE

DAYS INN
(AAA) (SAVE)
▼▼▼▼
Small-scale Hotel

Book at aaa.com
6/1-7/7 [ECP]   1P: $69-$89   2P: $89-$99   XP: $5   F17
7/8-3/31 [ECP]   1P: $59-$79   2P: $79-$99   XP: $5   F17
4/1-5/31 [ECP]   1P: $59-$69   2P: $69-$79   XP: $5   F17
Phone: (989)732-2200
Location: I-75, exit 282, just w on SR 32. Located in a commercial area. 1201 W Main St 49735 (PO Box 1370, 49734). Fax: 989/732-0300. **Facility:** 95 units. 94 one- and 1 two-bedroom standard units, some with whirlpools. 2 stories, interior corridors. **Parking:** on-site, winter plug-ins. **Terms:** package plans. **Amenities:** hair dryers. **Pool(s):** heated indoor. **Leisure Activities:** sauna, whirlpool, snowmobiling, exercise room. **Fee:** game room. **Guest Services:** coin laundry. **Business Services:** meeting rooms. **Cards:** AX, DC, DS, MC, VI. **Special Amenities:** free expanded continental breakfast and free local telephone calls. (See color ad card insert)

SOME UNITS

DOWNTOWN MOTEL
(AAA) (SAVE)
▼▼
Motel

All Year   1P: $36-$60   2P: $46-$75   XP: $5   F16
Phone: (989)732-5010
Location: I-75, exit 282, 0.5 mi e and 0.3 mi s on I-75 business loop. Located in a commercial area. 208 S Otsego Ave 49735. Fax: 989/732-5194. **Facility:** 22 one-bedroom standard units. 2 stories (no elevator), interior/exterior corridors. **Parking:** on-site. **Terms:** [CP] meal plan available. **Leisure Activities:** snowmobiling. **Cards:** AX, DS, MC, VI.

SOME UNITS

HAMPTON INN
△△△ SAVE
▽▽▽▽
Small-scale Hotel

Book at aaa.com

				Phone: (989)731-4000
6/1-3/31 [ECP]		1P: $69-$149	2P: $69-$149	
4/1-5/31 [ECP]		1P: $69-$89	2P: $69-$89	

Location: I-75, exit 282, just w. Located in a commercial area. 230 Dickerson Rd 49735. Fax: 989/731-4710. **Facility:** 83 one-bedroom standard units, some with whirlpools. 3 stories, interior corridors. *Bath:* combo or shower only. **Parking:** on-site. **Terms:** package plans - seasonal. **Amenities:** dual phone lines, voice mail, irons, hair dryers. **Pool(s):** heated indoor. **Leisure Activities:** whirlpool, snowmobiling, exercise room. *Fee:* game room. **Guest Services:** valet and coin laundry. **Business Services:** meeting rooms. **Cards:** AX, CB, DC, DS, MC, VI. **Special Amenities:** free expanded continental breakfast and free local telephone calls.

SOME UNITS
FEE FEE

QUALITY INN
△△△ SAVE
▽▽▽▽
Small-scale Hotel

Book at aaa.com

| | | | | Phone: (989)732-7541 |
| All Year [BP] | | 1P: $59-$139 | 2P: $69-$149 | XP: $5 F |

Location: I-75, exit 282, 0.3 mi e on SR 32. Located in a commercial area. 137 West St 49735. Fax: 989/732-0930. **Facility:** 117 one-bedroom standard units. 2 stories (no elevator), interior corridors. **Parking:** on-site, winter plug-ins. **Terms:** cancellation fee imposed, package plans - seasonal & weekends. **Amenities:** safes (fee), irons, hair dryers. **Dining:** 7 am-10 pm, cocktails. **Pool(s):** heated indoor. **Leisure Activities:** whirlpool, snowmobiling, exercise room. **Business Services:** meeting rooms. **Cards:** AX, CB, DC, DS, MC, VI. **Special Amenities:** free full breakfast and free local telephone calls.

SOME UNITS
FEE

RED ROOF INN
▽▽▽▽ ▽▽▽▽
Small-scale Hotel

Book at aaa.com

| | | | | Phone: 989/731-6331 |
| All Year | | 1P: $45-$99 | 2P: $45-$109 | XP: $5 F18 |

Location: I-75, exit 282, just e on SR 32, then 0.4 mi s. Located in a commercial area. 510 S Wisconsin 49735. Fax: 989/731-0190. **Facility:** 100 one-bedroom standard units. 2 stories (no elevator), interior corridors. *Bath:* combo or shower only. **Parking:** on-site. **Terms:** [CP] meal plan available. **Amenities:** video games, voice mail. **Pool(s):** heated indoor. **Leisure Activities:** snowmobiling. **Business Services:** meeting rooms. **Cards:** AX, CB, DC, DS, MC, VI.

SOME UNITS

TIMBERLY MOTEL
△△△ SAVE
▽▽▽
Motel

| | | | | Phone: 989/732-5166 |
| All Year [CP] | | 1P: $38-$68 | 2P: $48-$84 | XP: $4 F10 |

Location: I-75, exit 279, 2.5 mi n on I-75 business loop (Old US 27). Located in a commercial area. 881 S Otsego Ave 49735. Fax: 989/732-9189. **Facility:** 30 units. 28 one- and 2 two-bedroom standard units. 1-2 stories (no elevator), exterior corridors. **Parking:** on-site, winter plug-ins. **Terms:** 5 day cancellation notice-fee imposed, pets ($6 extra charge, in smoking units). **Leisure Activities:** snowmobiling. **Cards:** AX, CB, DC, DS, MC, VI. **Special Amenities:** free continental breakfast and early check-in/late check-out.

SOME UNITS
FEE

—— WHERE TO DINE ——

LA SENORITA
▽▽
Mexican

| | | Phone: 989/732-1771 |
| **Lunch:** $5-$7 | **Dinner:** $7-$12 | |

Location: I-75, exit 282, just e on SR 32. 737 W Main 49735. **Hours:** 11 am-10 pm, Fri & Sat-11 pm, Sun noon-10 pm; to 11 pm, Fri & Sat-midnight 5/29-9/4. **Closed:** 11/25, 12/25 & Easter. **Features:** This family-friendly restaurant offers such traditional favorites as burritos, enchiladas and fajitas, as well as mesquite-grilled entrees served in a festive, lively atmosphere. Casual dress; cocktails. **Parking:** on-site. **Cards:** AX, CB, DC, DS, MC, VI.

SUGAR BOWL
△△△
▽▽▽ ▽▽▽
American

| | | Phone: 989/732-5524 |
| **Lunch:** $3-$6 | **Dinner:** $8-$19 | |

Location: I-75, exit 282, 0.5 mi e on SR 32. 216 W Main St 49735. **Hours:** 7 am-11 pm, Sun-10 pm. **Closed:** 11/25, 12/25. **Features:** Established in 1919, the casual spot is one of Michigan's oldest family-owned restaurants. The menu includes Greek and American selections, with such popular choices as ribs, whitefish, perch and prime rib. Sink your teeth into homemade raspberry pie. Casual dress; cocktails. **Parking:** on-site. **Cards:** AX, DS, MC, VI.

GLADSTONE pop. 5,032

—— WHERE TO STAY ——

SHOREWOOD MOTEL
▽▽▽
Motel

				Phone: 906/428-9624
5/15-10/31		1P: $37-$40	2P: $48-$52	XP: $4
4/1-5/14 & 11/1-3/31		1P: $27-$30	2P: $38-$45	XP: $4

Location: US 41 N, exit Kipling; US 41 S, exit business district, 1 mi n. Located opposite Little Bay de Loc. 1226 N Lakeshore Dr 49837. **Facility:** 12 one-bedroom standard units. 1 story, exterior corridors. *Bath:* combo or shower only. **Parking:** on-site. **Terms:** 3 day cancellation notice. **Cards:** AX, DS, MC, VI.

SOME UNITS

GOULD CITY

—— WHERE TO DINE ——

THE FARMHOUSE
▽▽
American

| | | Phone: 906/477-6287 |
| **Lunch:** $5-$8 | **Dinner:** $9-$19 | |

Location: US 2, 1.3 mi w of CR H33. HCR Box 20 49838. **Hours:** 7 am-9 pm. **Closed:** 12/25. **Features:** The casual restaurant is a good place to stop for food along a long stretch of highway. Casual dress; cocktails. **Parking:** on-site. **Cards:** DS, MC, VI.

GRAND BLANC

———— WHERE TO STAY ————

AMERIHOST INN-GRAND BLANC   *Book at aaa.com*
Phone: (810)694-0000
All Year   1P: $69-$159   2P: $69-$159   XP: $6   F18
Small-scale Hotel   **Location:** I-75, exit 108 (Holly Rd), just e. 9040 Holly Rd 48439. Fax: 810/694-0155. **Facility:** 60 one-bedroom standard units, some with whirlpools. 2 stories (no elevator), interior corridors. *Bath:* combo or shower only. **Parking:** on-site. **Terms:** cancellation fee imposed, package plans - seasonal. **Amenities:** dual phone lines, voice mail, safes (fee), irons, hair dryers. **Pool(s):** heated indoor. **Leisure Activities:** sauna, whirlpool, exercise room. **Guest Services:** valet laundry. **Business Services:** meeting rooms. **Cards:** AX, DC, DS, JC, MC, VI.

SOME UNITS
(ASK) (SÐ) (点) (⌾) (⇌) (✕) (📺) (DATA PORT) (🖥) / (✕) (🖬) (🖨) /
FEE FEE

WINGATE INN   *Book at aaa.com*
Phone: (810)694-9900
All Year [ECP]   1P: $105   2P: $105   XP: $10   F17
Small-scale Hotel   **Location:** I-475, exit 2, just e. 1359 Grand Pointe Ct 48439. Fax: 810/694-9902. **Facility:** 82 one-bedroom standard units, some with whirlpools. 3 stories, interior corridors. *Bath:* combo or shower only. **Parking:** on-site. **Amenities:** dual phone lines, voice mail, safes, irons, hair dryers. *Fee:* video games, high-speed Internet. **Pool(s):** heated indoor. **Leisure Activities:** whirlpool, exercise room. **Guest Services:** valet and coin laundry, area transportation. **Business Services:** meeting rooms, business center. **Cards:** AX, CB, DC, DS, JC, MC, VI.

SOME UNITS
(ASK) (SÐ) (✈) (¶†) (⌾) (点) (⇌) (📺) (DATA PORT) (🖬) (🖥) (🖨) / (✕) /

———— WHERE TO DINE ————

DA EDOARDO   **Lunch:** $6-$10   **Dinner:** $15-$25   **Phone:** 810/694-1300
Italian   **Location:** I-75, exit 108 (Holly Rd), just e. 8185 Holly Rd, Suite 7 48439. **Hours:** 11:30 am-10 pm, Fri-11 pm, Sat 2 pm-11 pm, Sun 2 pm-8 pm. Closed major holidays. **Reservations:** accepted. **Features:** With large picture windows overlooking a large reeded pond, it might be hard to remember that you are inside a tastefully upscale Italian restaurant rather than outside. Gnocchi with Bolognese sauce or chicken saltimbocca highlight a menu that features a wide selection of Italian favorites. Dressy casual; cocktails. **Parking:** on-site. **Cards:** AX, DC, MC, VI.

(点M) (Y) (✕)

KRUSE AND MUER   **Lunch:** $6-$10   **Dinner:** $8-$15   **Phone:** 810/603-2711
American   **Location:** I-75, exit 108 (Holly Rd), 2 mi e. just s; in Tile Grand Mall. 12793 S Saginaw 48439. **Hours:** 11 am-9 pm, Fri-10 pm, Sat noon-10 pm, Sun 12:30 pm-8:30 pm. Closed major holidays. **Reservations:** accepted. **Features:** A slightly upscale atmosphere sets the stage for a good variety of seafood specialities such as lobster and shrimp in saffron sauce or mahi mahi and other daily specials. Dressy casual; cocktails. **Parking:** on-site. **Cards:** AX, DC, MC, VI.

(✕)

GRAND HAVEN pop. 11,168

———— WHERE TO STAY ————

BEST WESTERN BEACON INN   *Book at aaa.com*
Phone: 616/842-4720
6/18-9/6   1P: $100   2P: $150   XP: $4   F12
5/1-6/17 & 9/7-3/31   1P: $72   2P: $110   XP: $4   F12
4/1-4/30   1P: $64   2P: $110   XP: $4   F12
Small-scale Hotel   **Location:** 1.5 mi s on US 31. Located in a commercial area. 1525 S Beacon Blvd 49417. Fax: 616/847-7821. **Facility:** 107 one-bedroom standard units, some with whirlpools. 1-3 stories, interior/exterior corridors. *Bath:* combo or shower only. **Parking:** on-site. **Terms:** [CP] meal plan available. **Amenities:** voice mail, irons, hair dryers. **Pool(s):** heated indoor. **Leisure Activities:** whirlpool. **Guest Services:** valet laundry. **Business Services:** meeting rooms. **Cards:** AX, CB, DC, DS, MC, VI.

SOME UNITS
(ASK) (SÐ) (¶†) (⇌) (📺) (DATA PORT) (🖥) / (✕) (VCR) (🖬) (🖨) /

DAYS INN   *Book at aaa.com*
Phone: (616)842-1999
6/2-9/10   1P: $90-$125   2P: $90-$125   XP: $10   F18
4/1-6/1 & 9/11-12/30   1P: $75-$105   2P: $75-$105   XP: $10   F18
12/31-3/31   1P: $75-$95   2P: $75-$95   XP: $10   F18
Small-scale Hotel   **Location:** 1.5 mi s on US 31. Located in a commercial area. 1500 S Beacon Blvd 49417. Fax: 616/842-3892. **Facility:** 100 one-bedroom standard units. 2 stories (no elevator), interior corridors. **Parking:** on-site. **Terms:** check-in 4 pm, [CP] meal plan available. **Amenities:** voice mail, hair dryers. *Some:* irons. **Pool(s):** heated indoor. **Leisure Activities:** whirlpool. *Fee:* game room. **Guest Services:** valet and coin laundry. **Business Services:** meeting rooms. **Cards:** AX, DC, DS, MC, VI. *(See color ad card insert)*

SOME UNITS
(ASK) (SÐ) (¶†) (Y) (⌾) (⇌) (📺) (DATA PORT) (🖥) / (✕) /

HARBOR HOUSE INN
Phone: 616/846-0610
5/28-9/6 [ECP]   1P: $150-$190   2P: $150-$190   XP: $25
4/1-5/27 & 9/7-10/31 [ECP]   1P: $95-$170   2P: $95-$170   XP: $25
11/1-3/31 [ECP]   1P: $95-$155   2P: $95-$155   XP: $25
Bed & Breakfast   **Location:** Corner of Harbor Dr and Clinton. Located opposite Lake Michigan. 114 S Harbor Dr 49417. Fax: 616/846-0530. **Facility:** This attractive, modern Victorian style house is located across from the water, and is just steps from downtown stores. Smoke free premises. 17 units. 16 one-bedroom standard units, some with whirlpools. 1 cottage ($145-$210) with whirlpool. 3 stories (no elevator), interior corridors. **Parking:** on-site. **Terms:** 2 night minimum stay - weekends in summer & fall, age restrictions may apply, 7 day cancellation notice, package plans - seasonal. **Amenities:** video library, voice mail. **Cards:** AX, MC, VI.

SOME UNITS
(¶†) (✕) (VCR) (DATA PORT) / (🖬) (🖨) (🖥) /

———— WHERE TO DINE ————

KIRBY GRILL

American
Parking: street. **Cards:** AX, MC, VI.

Lunch: $6-$11   **Dinner:** $8-$20   Phone: 616/846-3299
Location: 0.7 mi w of US 31. 2 Washington St 49417. **Hours:** 11:30 am-10 pm, Fri & Sat-11 pm, Sun-9 pm. **Reservations:** accepted. **Features:** Old pictures and advertisements hang on the walls of the 1873 building, in the heart of downtown. Such specialties as white chili and fresh fish and lobster are favorites. Homemade cheesecakes, such as raspberry chocolate black bottom, are sinful. Casual dress; cocktails.

THE STABLE INN
Steak & Seafood
MC, VI.

Lunch: $4-$6   **Dinner:** $10-$16   Phone: 616/846-8581
Location: 5 mi s on US 31. 11880 US 31 49417. **Hours:** 11 am-10 pm. Closed major holidays; also Sun. **Features:** Chicken Monterey, beer-battered shrimp and the 10-ounce ribeye are representative of menu selections. The decor is Western, with plenty of American Indian accents. The large, open dining room is inviting to families. Service is friendly and prompt. Casual dress; cocktails. **Parking:** on-site. **Cards:** DS,

GRAND MARAIS

———— WHERE TO STAY ————

ARBORGATE INN
AAA (SAVE)
Motel

Phone: 906/494-2681

6/16-9/15 & 12/25-3/31	1P: $60
4/1-6/15 & 9/16-12/24	1P: $50

Location: Just e of SR 77. Located opposite Grand Marais Harbor. Randolph Rd 49839 (PO Box 188). **Fax:** 906/494-2283. **Facility:** 14 one-bedroom standard units. 2 stories (no elevator), exterior corridors. **Parking:** on-site. **Terms:** weekly rates available, pets (with prior approval). **Leisure Activities:** snowmobiling. **Fee:** ATV. **Cards:** DS, MC, VI.

SOME UNITS

VOYAGEUR'S MOTEL
Motel

Phone: 906/494-2389

All Year	1P: $73	2P: $73	XP: $20

Location: 0.5 mi e of SR 77. Located high on a ridge overlooking harbor. E Wilson St 49839 (PO Box 239). **Fax:** 906/494-2598. **Facility:** 10 one-bedroom standard units. 2 stories (no elevator), exterior corridors. **Parking:** on-site. **Terms:** cancellation fee imposed, small pets only. **Leisure Activities:** sauna, whirlpool, snowmobiling. **Cards:** MC, VI.

SOME UNITS

———— WHERE TO DINE ————

——— *The following restaurant has not been evaluated by AAA* ———
but is listed for your information only.

LAKE SUPERIOR BREWING COMPANY
(fyi)

Phone: 906/494-2337

Not evaluated. **Location:** Center. Lake Ave 49839. **Features:** Popular with families visiting the area, the downtown brew pub offers a number of American dishes and snacks.

GRAND RAPIDS pop. 197,800—
See also CASCADE, COMSTOCK PARK, GRANDVILLE, KENTWOOD, WALKER & WYOMING.

─────── **WHERE TO STAY** ───────

AMWAY GRAND PLAZA HOTEL   *Book at aaa.com*   **Phone:** (616)774-2000
(AAA) (SAVE)   All Year   1P: $175-$285   2P: $175-$285   XP: $15   F16
▼▼▼ ▼▼▼   **Location:** Pearl St at Monroe Ave; from US 131, exit Pearl St; center. 187 Monroe Ave NW 49503. Fax: 616/776-6489.
Large-scale Hotel   **Facility:** On the Grand River, the tower section of this service-oriented hotel features a number of rooms with a view of the waterway. 682 units. 650 one-bedroom standard units. 25 one- and 7 two-bedroom suites, some with whirlpools. 12-29 stories, interior corridors. *Bath:* combo or shower only. **Parking:** on-site and valet.
Terms: check-in 4 pm, [AP] meal plan available. **Amenities:** video games, voice mail, irons, hair dryers. *Some:* high-speed Internet, dual phone lines. **Dining:** 6 restaurants, 6:30 am-11 pm, cocktails, also, The 1913 Room, Cygnus, see separate listings. **Pool(s):** heated indoor. **Leisure Activities:** sauna, whirlpools, steamroom, 2 lighted tennis courts, racquetball courts, 1 squash court. **Guest Services:** gift shop, valet laundry, airport transportation (fee)-Gerald R Ford International Airport. *Fee:* tanning facility. **Business Services:** conference facilities, business center. **Cards:** AX, DC, DS, MC, VI.
(See color ad below)

SOME UNITS

[icons] FEE   FEE FEE

COURTYARD BY MARRIOTT-DOWNTOWN   *Book at aaa.com*   **Phone:** (616)242-6000

        12/31-3/31   1P: $89-$139   2P: $89-$139
4/1-12/30   1P: $89-$129   2P: $89-$129

Large-scale Hotel **Location:** Corner of Fulton St and Monroe Ave; center of downtown. 11 Monroe Ave NW 49503. Fax: 616/242-6605. **Facility:** 214 units. 209 one-bedroom standard units. 5 one-bedroom suites ($149-$199). 7 stories, interior corridors. *Bath:* combo or shower only. **Parking:** on-site. **Amenities:** dual phone lines, voice mail, irons, hair dryers. *Some:* high-speed Internet. **Pool(s):** heated indoor. **Leisure Activities:** sauna, whirlpool, steamroom, 2 lighted tennis courts, exercise room, basketball. **Guest Services:** gift shop, valet and coin laundry. **Business Services:** meeting rooms. **Cards:** AX, CB, DC, DS, JC, MC, VI.

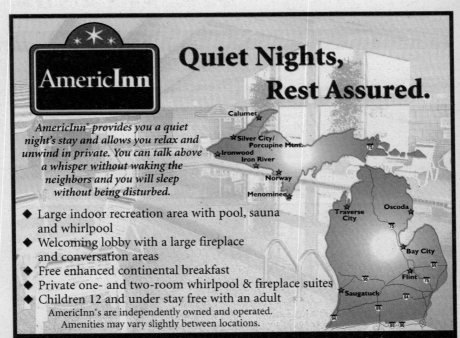

DAYS INN-DOWNTOWN   *Book at aaa.com*

All Year   1P: $72-$82   2P: $79-$86   XP: $7   **Phone:** (616)235-7611
                                                                                                                          F18
Large-scale Hotel   **Location:** US 131, exit Pearl St; downtown. 310 Pearl St NW 49504. Fax: 616/235-1995. **Facility:** 175 one-
bedroom standard units. 8 stories, interior corridors. **Parking:** on-site. **Terms:** [AP] meal plan available, small
pets only ($10 extra charge). **Amenities:** dual phone lines, voice mail, irons, hair dryers. **Pool(s):** heated in-
door. **Leisure Activities:** whirlpool, limited exercise equipment. **Guest Services:** valet and coin laundry. **Cards:** AX, CB, DC,
DS, MC, VI. *(See color ad card insert)*

SOME UNITS

FAIRFIELD INN   *Book at aaa.com*

All Year   1P: $65-$85   2P: $65-$85   XP: $6   **Phone:** (616)940-2700
                                                                                                                          F18
Small-scale Hotel   **Location:** I-96, exit 43A (28th St SW), 1.5 mi w on SR 11, just n on E Paris, then just w. Located in an upscale office
park. 3930 Stahl Dr SE 49546. Fax: 616/940-2700. **Facility:** 82 one-bedroom standard units. 3 stories, interior
corridors. *Bath:* combo or shower only. **Parking:** on-site. **Terms:** [ECP] meal plan available.
Amenities: voice mail, irons, hair dryers. **Pool(s):** heated indoor. **Leisure Activities:** whirlpool. **Guest Services:** valet laundry.
Cards: AX, CB, DC, DS, MC, VI.

SOME UNITS

HOMEWOOD SUITES BY HILTON *Book at aaa.com* **Phone:** (616)285-7100

All Year   1P: $80-$116   2P: $80-$116

Small-scale Hotel **Location:** I-96, exit 43A (28th St SW), 1.5 mi w to E Paris Ave, then just n. Located in an upscale office park. 3920 Stahl Dr SE 49546. Fax: 616/285-1505. **Facility:** 78 units. 71 one- and 7 two-bedroom suites with efficiencies. 3 stories, interior corridors. **Parking:** on-site. **Terms:** 14 day cancellation notice, [BP] meal plan available, pets ($80 fee, $5 extra charge). **Amenities:** voice mail, irons, hair dryers. **Pool(s):** heated indoor. **Leisure Activities:** whirlpool, exercise room. **Guest Services:** valet and coin laundry. **Business Services:** meeting rooms, business center. **Cards:** AX, DC, DS, MC, VI.

SOME UNITS

RADISSON HOTEL GRAND RAPIDS NORTH   *Book at aaa.com*   **Phone:** (616)363-9001

(AAA) (SAVE)   All Year   1P: $89-$129   2P: $89-$129
▼▼▼▼   **Location:** US 131, exit 88, 1.8 mi n. 270 Ann St NW 49504. **Fax:** 616/363-0670. **Facility:** 164 one-bedroom stan-
Large-scale Hotel   dard units. 7 stories, interior corridors. **Parking:** on-site. **Amenities:** dual phone lines, voice mail, irons, hair
dryers. **Dining:** 6:30 am-10 pm, Sat & Sun from 7 am, cocktails. **Pool(s):** heated indoor. **Leisure Activities:** sauna, whirlpool, exercise room. *Fee:* game room. **Guest Services:** valet and coin laundry. **Business
Services:** meeting rooms. **Cards:** AX, CB, DC, DS, JC, MC, VI. **Special Amenities:** free newspaper and
free room upgrade (subject to availability with advanced reservations).** *(See color ad p 313)*

SOME UNITS

─── WHERE TO DINE ───

THE 1913 ROOM   **Lunch: $9-$22**   **Dinner: $25-$65**   **Phone:** 616/774-2000

American
Location: Pearl St at Monroe Ave; from US 131, exit Pearl St; center; in Amway Grand Plaza Hotel. 187 Monroe Ave NW 49503. **Hours:** 11:30 am-2 & 5:30-10:30 pm, Fri & Sat from 5 pm. Closed: Sun. **Reservations:** suggested. **Features:** Business professionals and couples frequent the elegant restaurant, appointed in early 1900s decor. A number of exquisite dishes are offered, as are intriguing selections from the chef's tasting menu. For dessert, savor the forbidden apple or rich Viennese chocolate cake. Semi-formal attire; cocktails. **Parking:** on-site and valet. **Cards:** AX, CB, DC, DS, MC, VI.
(See color ad p 310)

THE B.O.B. RESTAURANTS   **Lunch: $5-$11**   **Dinner: $7-$30**   **Phone:** 616/356-2000
American
Location: Across from Van Andel Arena; downtown. 20 Monroe Ave NW 49503. **Hours:** 11:30 am-11 pm, Sat from 4 pm. Closed: 1/1, 11/25, 12/25; also Sun. **Reservations:** accepted. **Features:** B.O.B. stands for "big old building," in which several restaurants offering a cornucopia of food selections are housed. The location is a hotbed for multifaceted entertainment. Casual dress; cocktails. **Parking:** street. **Cards:** AX, DS, MC, VI.

CHARLEY'S CRAB   **Lunch: $7-$15**   **Dinner: $14-$25**   **Phone:** 616/459-2500
American
Location: Jct US 131 and SR 45, exit 85. 63 Market St SW 49503. **Hours:** 11:30 am-10 pm, Fri-11 pm, Sat 4:30 pm-11 pm, Sun 10 am-2 & 4:30-9 pm. Closed major holidays. **Reservations:** suggested. **Features:** The comfortable restaurant is known for creative preparations of fresh seafood, such as Maryland crab cakes and Charley's bucket, which samples lobster, crab, mussels and clams. The eclectic decor includes items from a mansion that was torn down. Casual dress; cocktails. **Parking:** on-site. **Cards:** AX, DC, DS, MC, VI.

CYGNUS   **Dinner: $21-$31**   **Phone:** 616/776-6425
American
Location: Pearl St at Monroe Ave; US 131, exit Pearl St; center; in Amway Grand Plaza Hotel. Pearl St at Monroe Ave 49503. **Hours:** 5:30 pm-10:30 pm, Sun 10:30 am-2 pm. Closed: Mon & Sun 4/16-9/9. **Reservations:** suggested. **Features:** Guests enjoy great views under the stars from the 27th- and 28th-floor rooftop setting. Beautiful furnishings and fine tableware add to the sophistication. Such specialties as Beefeater gin tomato soup are tasty and innovative. Dressy casual; cocktails. **Parking:** on-site and valet. **Cards:** AX, CB, DC, DS, MC, VI. *(See color ad p 310)*

DUBA'S   **Lunch: $8-$12**   **Dinner: $16-$23**   **Phone:** 616/949-1011
American
Location: Jct I-96 and SR 37; E Beltline, exit 38. 420 E Beltline NE 49506. **Hours:** 11 am-10 pm, Fri & Sat-11 pm. Closed major holidays; also Sun. **Reservations:** suggested, weekends. **Features:** Since the late 1950s, the restaurant has been a local fixture for fine dining. Elegant table settings, with flowers and candles, contribute to the sophistication. The menu centers on well-prepared prime rib and seafood, as well as decadent desserts. Casual dress; cocktails. **Parking:** on-site. **Cards:** AX, MC, VI.

GRAND RAPIDS BREWING CO.   **Lunch: $6-$8**   **Dinner: $6-$19**   **Phone:** 616/285-5970
American
Location: I-96, exit 43A, 2 mi w on SR 11; at Centerpointe Mall. 3689 28th St SE 49512. **Hours:** 11 am-10 pm, Fri & Sat-11 pm. Closed: 11/25, 12/24, 12/25. **Reservations:** accepted. **Features:** The brew pub is decorated with photographs and pictures of the original Grand Rapids Brewing Co., which prospered in the early 1900s. Menu choices range from typical starters to sandwiches, steaks, perch and the popular rotisserie chicken dishes. Casual dress; cocktails. **Parking:** on-site. **Cards:** AX, DC, DS, MC, VI.

THE GREAT LAKES SHIPPING COMPANY   **Lunch: $6-$8**   **Dinner: $10-$20**   **Phone:** 616/949-9440
Steak & Seafood
Location: At Breton Ave and Burton St; 3.8 mi e of US 131, exit 82A. 2455 Burton St SE 49546. **Hours:** 11:30 am-2 & 5-10 pm, Fri-11 pm, Sat from 5 pm. Closed major holidays; also Sun. **Reservations:** suggested, weekends. **Features:** Five fireplaces and nautical decorations give the restaurant a cozy, rustic flavor. Menu specialties include prime rib, pan-fried walleye and filet tenderloin. Casual dress; cocktails. **Parking:** on-site. **Cards:** AX, DS, MC, VI.

PIETRO'S ITALIAN RESTAURANT   **Lunch: $4-$6**   **Dinner: $9-$16**   **Phone:** 616/365-3550
Italian
Location: I-96, exit 33, 4.2 mi ne. 5301 Northland Dr NE 49525. **Hours:** 11:30 am-10 pm, Fri & Sat-11 pm. Closed: 11/25, 12/25. **Features:** The restaurant is popular with families and couples looking for specialties such as veal Marsala, oven-baked pasta, and the wood-fired pizza bubbles with flavor. Casual dress; cocktails. **Parking:** on-site. **Cards:** AX, DS, MC, VI.

PIETRO'S ITALIAN RESTAURANT   **Lunch: $4-$6**   **Dinner: $9-$16**   **Phone:** 616/452-3228
Italian
Location: I-96, exit 43A, 3.8 mi w on SR 11. 2780 Birchcrest Dr 49506. **Hours:** 11:30 am-10 pm, Fri & Sat-11 pm. Closed: 11/25, 12/25. **Features:** The restaurant is popular with families and couples looking for specialties such as veal Marsala and oven-baked pasta. The atmosphere is relaxed. Casual dress; cocktails. **Parking:** on-site. **Cards:** AX, DS, MC, VI.

SAN CHEZ, A TAPAS BISTRO   Lunch: $6-$12   Dinner: $6-$29   Phone: 616/774-8272

AAA
♦♦♦
Spanish

Location: Just e of Van Andel Arena; downtown. 38 W Fulton 49503. **Hours:** 11 am-10 pm, Fri-midnight, Sat noon-midnight, Sun from 4 pm. Closed major holidays. **Features:** So many tapas, so little time. Guests can prepare their taste buds for an explosion of flavorful options in the lively, energetic bistro. The specialty is tapas, available either hot or cold. Casual dress; cocktails. **Parking:** on-site (fee). **Cards:** AX, DC, DS, MC, VI.

SAYFEE'S   Lunch: $5-$10   Dinner: $16-$29   Phone: 616/949-5750

♦♦♦
American

Location: I-96, exit 43A, 2.5 mi w on SR 11, 0.3 mi n on SR 37, then 0.3 mi e; behind Eastbrook Shopping Mall. 3555 Lake Eastbrook Blvd 49546. **Hours:** 11 am-10 pm, Fri & Sat-11 pm. Closed: 12/25; also Sun. **Reservations:** suggested. **Features:** A professional clientele frequents the elegant, upscale restaurant, a local favorite for such entrees as steak Diane and Dover sole. Diners also may dance in the evenings from Wednesday through Saturday. A large deck overlooks the sparkling water. Dressy casual; cocktails; entertainment. **Parking:** on-site. **Cards:** AX, CB, DC, DS, MC, VI.

SCHNITZELBANK   Lunch: $5-$8   Dinner: $9-$18   Phone: 616/459-9527

AAA
♦♦♦
German

Location: Corner of Weathly SE and Jefferson Ave SE; downtown. 342 Jefferson Ave SE 49503. **Hours:** 11 am-8 pm, Fri-9 pm, Sat 4 pm-9 pm. Closed major holidays; also Sun. **Reservations:** suggested. **Features:** German music and mills painted in 1938 by the owner infuse the casual restaurant with Old World ambience. In addition to such specialties as schnitzels, red cabbage and potatoes, the menu lists American dishes. Save room for the wonderful apple strudel. Casual dress; cocktails. **Parking:** on-site. **Cards:** AX, DS, MC, VI.

——— *The following restaurants have not been evaluated by AAA* ———
but are listed for your information only.

ARNIE'S   Phone: 616/956-7901

[fyi]   Not evaluated. **Location:** At Centerpointe Mall. 3561 28th St SE 49512. **Features:** This popular family restaurant features wholesome food with tasty, fresh baked goods from their bakery.

GIBSON'S   Phone: 616/774-8535

[fyi]   Not evaluated. **Location:** Just w of jct Fuller Ave and Lake Dr. 1033 Lake Dr SE 49506. **Features:** In the restored Wurzurg/Clark mansion, the restaurant treats guests to a fine-dining experience.

GRANDVILLE pop. 16,263—*See also GRAND RAPIDS.*

——— **WHERE TO STAY** ———

BEST WESTERN GRANDVILLAGE INN   *Book at aaa.com*   Phone: (616)532-3222

All Year	1P: $69-$129	2P: $69-$129	XP: $10 F18

♦♦♦
Small-scale Hotel

Location: I-196, exit 69A, just e to Fairlanes Ave, then just s. Located in a commercial area. 3425 Fairlanes Ave 49418. Fax: 616/532-4959. **Facility:** 82 units. 75 one-bedroom standard units, some with whirlpools. 7 one-bedroom suites ($99-$149). 2 stories (no elevator), interior corridors. **Parking:** on-site. **Terms:** [CP] meal plan available. **Amenities:** dual phone lines, voice mail, irons, hair dryers. **Pool(s):** heated indoor. **Leisure Activities:** whirlpool. *Fee:* game room. **Guest Services:** valet and coin laundry. **Business Services:** meeting rooms. **Cards:** AX, DC, MC, VI. *(See ad p 312)*

SOME UNITS

COMFORT SUITES   *Book at aaa.com*   Phone: (616)667-0733

5/1-5/17 [ECP]	1P: $149-$169	2P: $149-$169
5/18-9/2 [ECP]	1P: $129-$169	2P: $129-$169
4/1-4/30 & 9/3-3/31 [ECP]	1P: $99-$129	2P: $99-$129

AAA [SAVE]
♦♦♦
Small-scale Hotel

Location: I-196, exit 67, just sw. Located next to the Wal-Mart Shopping Center. 4520 Kenowa Ave SW 49418. Fax: 616/667-9375. **Facility:** 66 units. 64 one-bedroom standard units, some with whirlpools. 2 one-bedroom suites with whirlpools. 3 stories, interior corridors. *Bath:* combo or shower only. **Parking:** on-site. **Terms:** 30 day cancellation notice-fee imposed, package plans - seasonal & weekends. **Amenities:** video games, voice mail, irons, hair dryers. **Pool(s):** heated indoor. **Leisure Activities:** whirlpool, exercise room. **Guest Services:** valet and coin laundry. **Business Services:** meeting rooms, business center. **Cards:** AX, DC, DS, JC, MC, VI. **Special Amenities:** free expanded continental breakfast. *(See color ad p 321)*

SOME UNITS

DAYS INN & SUITES   *Book at aaa.com*   Phone: (616)531-5263

5/1-8/31	1P: $69-$159	2P: $69-$159	XP: $10 F17
4/1-4/30 & 9/1-11/30	1P: $59-$119	2P: $59-$119	XP: $10 F17
12/1-3/31	1P: $49-$109	2P: $49-$109	XP: $10 F17

♦♦♦
Small-scale Hotel

Location: I-196, exit 70, 0.5 mi e. 3825 28th St SW 49418. Fax: 616/531-5213. **Facility:** 89 units. 30 one- and 59 two-bedroom standard units, some with whirlpools. 3 stories, interior corridors. **Parking:** on-site. **Terms:** weekly rates available, [ECP] meal plan available. **Amenities:** hair dryers. *Some:* irons. **Leisure Activities:** exercise room. **Guest Services:** coin laundry. **Business Services:** meeting rooms. **Cards:** AX, CB, DC, DS, MC, VI. *(See color ad card insert)*

SOME UNITS

HOLIDAY INN EXPRESS *Book at aaa.com* Phone: (616)532-0202

▼▼▼ 5/1-9/1 [ECP] 1P: $99-$149
4/1-4/30 & 9/2-3/31 [ECP] 1P: $99-$109
Small-scale Hotel **Location:** I-196, exit 69A, just e to Fairlanes Ave, then 0.4 mi s. Located in a semi-commercial area. 4651 36th St 49418. Fax: 616/257-3121. **Facility:** Smoke free premises. 78 units. 76 one-bedroom standard units, some with whirlpools. 2 one-bedroom suites. 3 stories, interior corridors. *Bath:* combo or shower only. **Parking:** on-site. **Terms:** cancellation fee imposed. **Amenities:** dual phone lines, voice mail, irons, hair dryers. **Pool(s):** heated indoor. **Leisure Activities:** whirlpool, exercise room. **Guest Services:** valet and coin laundry. **Business Services:** meeting rooms. **Cards:** AX, DC, DS, MC, VI.

SOME UNITS

(ASK) (S☐) (T┃┃) (☾M) (☐) (≈) (✕) (📷) (DATA PORT) (☐) / (☐) (☐) /

RESIDENCE INN BY MARRIOTT GRAND RAPIDS WEST *Book at aaa.com* Phone: (616)538-1100

▼▼▼ All Year 1P: $104-$174
Location: I-196, exit 67, 1.7 mi e. 3451 Rivertown Point Ct SW 49418. Fax: 616/538-6390. **Facility:** 90 units. 37
Small-scale Hotel one-bedroom standard units, some with efficiencies or kitchens. 40 one- and 13 two-bedroom suites, some with efficiencies or kitchens. 3 stories, interior corridors. *Bath:* combo or shower only. **Parking:** on-site. **Terms:** cancellation fee imposed, [ECP] meal plan available, pets ($125-$150 fee, $6 extra charge). **Amenities:** voice mail, irons, hair dryers. **Pool(s):** heated outdoor. **Leisure Activities:** whirlpool, exercise room, sports court, basketball, volleyball. **Guest Services:** valet and coin laundry. **Business Services:** meeting rooms. **Cards:** AX, CB, DC, DS, JC, MC, VI.

SOME UNITS

(S☐) (🛏) (T┃┃) (≈) (✕) (🐾) (DATA PORT) (☐) (☐) (☐) / (✕) (VCR) /
FEE

GRAYLING pop. 1,952

―――――――― **WHERE TO STAY** ――――――――

DAYS INN OF GRAYLING *Book at aaa.com* Phone: (989)344-0204

▼▼▼ 6/18-9/26 [ECP] 1P: $64-$85 2P: $69-$90 XP: $5 F
9/27-3/31 [ECP] 1P: $54-$59 2P: $64-$69 XP: $5 F
Small-scale Hotel 4/1-6/17 [ECP] 1P: $54-$64 2P: $59-$69 XP: $5 F
Location: I-75 business loop, 0.8 mi s. Located in a commercial area. 2556 I-75 Business Loop 49738.
Fax: 989/344-9076. **Facility:** 65 one-bedroom standard units, some with whirlpools. 2 stories, interior corridors. **Parking:** on-site. **Terms:** weekly rates available. **Amenities:** hair dryers. **Leisure Activities:** cross country skiing, snowmobiling. **Guest Services:** coin laundry. **Business Services:** meeting rooms. **Cards:** AX, CB, DC, DS, MC, VI. *(See color ad card insert)*

SOME UNITS

(ASK) (S☐) (T┃┃) (🐾) (☐) / (✕) (DATA PORT) /

HOLIDAY INN *Book at aaa.com* Phone: (989)348-7611

(AAA) (SAVE) 5/28-8/31 & 1/1-3/31 1P: $79-$129 2P: $79-$129 XP: $6 F19
9/1-12/31 1P: $79-$119 2P: $79-$119 XP: $6 F19
▼▼▼ 4/1-5/27 1P: $79-$94 2P: $79-$94 XP: $6 F19
Small-scale Hotel **Location:** I-75 business loop, 0.8 mi s. 2650 S Business Loop 49738 (PO Box 473). Fax: 989/348-7984. **Facility:** 151 one-bedroom standard units, some with whirlpools. 2 stories (no elevator), interior/exterior corridors. *Bath:* combo or shower only. **Parking:** on-site, winter plug-ins. **Terms:** weekly rates available, [BP] meal plan available, package plans. **Amenities:** voice mail, irons, hair dryers. **Dining:** 6 am-2 & 5-10 pm, cocktails, entertainment. **Pool(s):** heated indoor, wading. **Leisure Activities:** sauna, whirlpool, snowmobiling, ski shop, lighted cross country ski trails, domed recreation area, playground, exercise room, basketball, horseshoes, shuffleboard, volleyball, game room. *Fee:* ski equipment. **Guest Services:** valet laundry. **Business Services:** conference facilities. **Cards:** AX, CB, DC, DS, MC, VI. **Special Amenities:** free local telephone calls and early check-in/late check-out.

SOME UNITS

(S☐) (🛏) (T┃┃) (🍸) (☾M) (☾) (≈) (✕) (🐾) (DATA PORT) (☐) / (✕) (VCR) (☐) (☐) /
FEE

NORTH COUNTRY LODGE Phone: (989)348-8471

(AAA) (SAVE) All Year 1P: $53-$90 2P: $56-$160 XP: $5 F12
▼ **Location:** 1 mi n. Located in a semi-commercial area. 617 N I-75 Business Loop 49738 (PO Box 290).
Motel Fax: 989/348-6114. **Facility:** 24 units. 23 one- and 1 two-bedroom suites, some with efficiencies or kitchens (no utensils). 1-2 stories (no elevator), exterior corridors. *Bath:* combo or shower only. **Parking:** on-site. **Terms:** pets (in designated units). **Amenities:** *Some:* hair dryers. **Leisure Activities:** snowmobiling, horseshoes. **Cards:** AX, CB, DC, MC, VI. **Special Amenities:** free local telephone calls and early check-in/late check-out.

SOME UNITS

(🛏) (🍸) / (✕) (VCR) (☐) (☐) /

SUPER 8 MOTEL Phone: 989/348-8888

▼▼ 5/28-9/7 1P: $65-$95 2P: $69-$99 XP: $4 F17
4/1-5/27 & 9/8-3/31 1P: $53-$76 2P: $57-$80 XP: $4 F17
Small-scale Hotel **Location:** I-75, exit 251. Located in a semi-commercial area. 5828 Nelson A Miles Pkwy 49738. Fax: 989/348-2030. **Facility:** 60 one-bedroom standard units, some with whirlpools. 2 stories (no elevator), interior corridors. *Bath:* combo or shower only. **Parking:** on-site, winter plug-ins. **Terms:** [CP] meal plan available, pets ($50 deposit). **Pool(s):** heated indoor. **Leisure Activities:** whirlpool, snowmobiling, hiking trails. *Fee:* game room. **Guest Services:** coin laundry. **Cards:** AX, DC, DS, MC, VI.

SOME UNITS

(ASK) (🛏) (☾) (≈) (✕) (🐾) (DATA PORT) / (✕) (☐) /
FEE

GREENBUSH

―――――――― **WHERE TO DINE** ――――――――

RED ROOSTER Lunch: $4-$6 Dinner: $8-$10 Phone: 989/739-7659

▼ **Location:** On US 23, 1.8 mi s. 3228 S US 23 48738. **Hours:** 8 am-9 pm. **Features:** The dining room is homey and offers a view of Lake Huron. Selections of wholesome Italian cuisine are prepared with homemade
Italian pasta and sauces. Delicious cream pies melt in your mouth. Casual dress; cocktails. **Parking:** on-site. **Cards:** MC, VI.

(✕)

GROSSE POINTE FARMS —*See Detroit p. 261.*

GROSSE POINTE WOODS —*See Detroit p. 261.*

HANCOCK pop. 4,323

─────────── WHERE TO STAY ───────────

BEST WESTERN COPPER CROWN MOTEL   *Book at aaa.com*   Phone: (906)482-6111
▽▽▽▽   All Year   1P: $52-$55   2P: $55-$57   XP: $3   F12
Small-scale Hotel   **Location:** On US 41 S; downtown. 235 Hancock Ave 49930. Fax: 906/482-0185. **Facility:** 46 one-bedroom stan-
dard units. 2 stories (no elevator), interior/exterior corridors. **Parking:** on-site, winter plug-ins. **Terms:** can-
cellation fee imposed, small pets only (in limited units). **Amenities:** irons, hair dryers. **Pool(s):** heated indoor.
Leisure Activities: saunas, whirlpool, snowmobiling. **Business Services:** meeting rooms. **Cards:** AX, DC, DS, MC, VI.

SOME UNITS
[A$K] [S✆] [🐾] [🍴+] [🏊] [🚫] [🎥] [DATA PORT] [💻] / [🚫] /

RAMADA INN WATERFRONT   *Book at aaa.com*   Phone: (906)482-8400
(AAA) [SAVE]   6/1-10/31 & 12/10-3/31 [ECP]   1P: $80-$85   2P: $80-$85   XP: $5   F18
▽▽▽▽   4/1-5/31 & 11/1-12/9 [ECP]   1P: $70-$75   2P: $70-$75   XP: $5   F18
Small-scale Hotel   **Location:** Off US 41, just nw of bridge. Located along the canal. 99 Navy St 49930. Fax: 906/482-8403. **Facility:** 51
one-bedroom standard units, some with whirlpools. 2 stories (no elevator), interior corridors. *Bath:* combo or
shower only. **Parking:** on-site. **Amenities:** voice mail, irons, hair dryers. **Dining:** The Upper Deck, see separate listing. **Pool(s):** heated indoor. **Leisure Activities:** sauna, whirlpool, boat dock, fishing, snowmobiling.
Guest Services: coin laundry. **Business Services:** meeting rooms. **Cards:** AX, CB, DC, DS, JC, MC, VI. **Special Amenities:**
free expanded continental breakfast and early check-in/late check-out.

SOME UNITS
[S✆] [🍴] [Y] [🎥] [🏊] [🚫] [🎥] [DATA PORT] [💻] / [🚫] [🔒] /

─────────── WHERE TO DINE ───────────

THE UPPER DECK   Lunch: $5-$8   Dinner: $10-$18   Phone: 906/482-8494
▽▽▽▽   **Location:** Off US 41, just nw of bridge; in Ramada Inn Waterfront. 99 Navy St 49930. **Hours:** 11 am-10 pm; hours
American   may vary. **Features:** The restaurant and lounge offers a view of the water, particularly from the seasonal
patio. Dishes include steaks, seafood, sandwiches and daily specials. Casual dress; cocktails. **Parking:**
on-site. **Cards:** AX, DC, DS, MC, VI.   [Y] [🚫]

HARBOR SPRINGS pop. 1,567

——— WHERE TO STAY ———

BEST WESTERN OF HARBOR SPRINGS   *Book at aaa.com*   **Phone:** (231)347-9050
AAA SAVE   All Year   1P: $68-$119   2P: $68-$119   XP: $10   F12
Location: 3 mi se on SR 119. 8514 M119 49740. **Fax:** 231/347-0837. **Facility:** 46 units. 42 one-bedroom standard units, some with whirlpools. 4 one-bedroom suites ($120-$200) with kitchens. 1 story, exterior corridors.
Motel   **Parking:** on-site, winter plug-ins. **Terms:** 3 day cancellation notice-fee imposed. **Amenities:** voice mail, irons, hair dryers. **Pool(s):** heated indoor. **Leisure Activities:** whirlpool, snowmobiling, playground.
Cards: AX, DC, MC, VI. **Special Amenities:** free continental breakfast and free local telephone calls.
(See color ad below)   SOME UNITS

——— WHERE TO DINE ———

THE NEW YORK RESTAURANT   **Dinner:** $16-$30   **Phone:** 231/526-1904
Location: Just s of jct SR 119 and State St; center. 101 State St 49740. **Hours:** Open 5/1-3/31; 5 pm-10 pm.
Closed: 11/25, 12/25. **Features:** Menu selections, such as Colorado lamb shank, Great Lakes whitefish,
American   wolverine pork loin and petite filet of beef, are full in flavor and attractively presented. An antique bar and tin ceiling are charming characteristics of the 1904 building. Casual dress; cocktails. **Parking:** street.
Cards: AX, MC, VI.

STAFFORD'S PIER RESTAURANT   **Lunch:** $7-$15   **Dinner:** $18-$30   **Phone:** 231/526-6201
Location: Just s of jct SR 119 and State St; center. 102 Bay St 49740. **Hours:** 11:30 am-10 pm, Fri & Sat-11 pm.
Closed: 12/25. **Reservations:** suggested. **Features:** Casual upscale dining overlooking marina; two
American   favorites are the white fish and rack of lamb. Homemade style pie for dessert—don't forget the scoop of ice cream! Casual dress; cocktails. **Parking:** on-site. **Cards:** AX, DS, MC, VI.

Best Western of Harbor Springs

New in 2003
- Guest laundry
- Exercise room
- Suites with fireplaces
- Indoor heated pool / hot tub
- Inroom Spas
- 5 minutes from Boyne Highlands & Nubs Nob
- Continental breakfast
- Refrigerators

8514 M-119 • Harbor Springs, Michigan 49740
- Non-smoking rooms
- Color cable TVs w/remote
- Standard rooms w/queen beds
- Major credit cards accepted
- No bikes in rooms
- 10 championship golf courses nearby
- No pets on premises

231-347-9050 • 800-528-1234 • Fax: 231-347-0837

HARRISON (CLARE COUNTY)

———— WHERE TO STAY ————

THE CARRIAGE HOUSE INN
Phone: (989)539-1300
All Year   1P: $60-$140   2P: $60-$140   XP: $15   F3
Location: US 127, exit US 127 business route/SR 61, 2 mi w, follow signs. Located in a quiet area. 1515 Grant Ave 48625 (PO Box 757, HARRISON). Fax: 989/539-5661. **Facility:** On spacious grounds near Budd Lake, the inn offers rooms decorated with upscale antique furnishings. Smoke free premises. 10 one-bedroom standard
Bed & Breakfast   units, some with whirlpools. 2 stories (no elevator), interior corridors. *Bath:* combo or shower only. **Parking:** on-site, winter plug-ins. **Terms:** age restrictions may apply, cancellation fee imposed, weekly rates available, [AP], [BP], [CP] & [ECP] meal plans available. **Amenities:** video library. **Leisure Activities:** sun deck, hiking trails. **Guest Services:** gift shop. **Business Services:** meeting rooms. **Cards:** AX, DS, MC, VI.

SOME UNITS

SERENDIPITY BED & BREAKFAST INN   *Book at aaa.com*
Phone: 989/539-6602
All Year   1P: $75-$175   2P: $75-$175
Location: On SR 61, 2.2 mi w of US 127 business route. Located in a quiet area. 270 W M 61 48625 (PO Box 377, HARRISON). **Facility:** Smoke free premises. 4 one-bedroom standard units. 2 stories (no elevator), interior
Bed & Breakfast   corridors. *Bath:* combo or shower only. **Parking:** on-site. **Terms:** age restrictions may apply, 7 day cancellation notice-fee imposed, [BP] & [ECP] meal plans available. **Amenities:** video library. **Leisure Activities:** whirlpool, cross country skiing, snowmobiling, hiking trails. **Cards:** AX, DS, MC, VI.

SOME UNITS

HART pop. 1,950

———— WHERE TO STAY ————

BUDGET HOST HART MOTEL
Phone: (231)873-1855
6/20-9/15   1P: $65-$105   2P: $75-$119   XP: $10   F
4/1-6/19   1P: $45-$99   2P: $55-$99   XP: $10   F
9/16-12/1   1P: $69-$89   2P: $79-$89   XP: $10   F
Small-scale Hotel   12/2-3/31   1P: $39-$89   2P: $49-$89   XP: $10   F
Location: US 31, exit Mears/Hart, just e on US 31 business route. 4143 Polk Rd 49420. Fax: 231/873-1477. **Facility:** 21 units. 20 one-bedroom standard units. 1 one-bedroom suite ($75-$200). 2 stories (no elevator), interior corridors. **Parking:** on-site. **Terms:** small pets only ($20 deposit). **Leisure Activities:** rental bicycles. **Cards:** DC, MC, VI.

SOME UNITS
FEE

COMFORT INN   *Book at aaa.com*
Phone: (231)873-3456
6/18-9/5   1P: $79-$169   2P: $89-$179   XP: $10   F18
5/28-6/17   1P: $69-$109   2P: $79-$119   XP: $10   F18
4/1-5/27   1P: $55-$99   2P: $69-$109   XP: $10   F18
9/6-3/31   1P: $55-$95   2P: $65-$109   XP: $10   F18
Small-scale Hotel   **Location:** US 31, exit Mears/Hart, just e on US 31 business route. Located on a hill, back from the road. 2248 N Comfort Dr 49420. Fax: 231/873-2343. **Facility:** 61 one-bedroom standard units, some with whirlpools. 2 stories (no elevator), interior corridors. *Bath:* combo or shower only. **Parking:** on-site. **Terms:** [CP] meal plan available, pets ($10 extra charge). **Amenities:** video library (fee). *Some:* irons, hair dryers. **Pool(s):** heated indoor. **Leisure Activities:** sauna, whirlpool, snowmobiling. *Fee:* bicycles. **Guest Services:** tanning facility. **Business Services:** meeting rooms. **Cards:** AX, DC, DS, MC, VI. **Special Amenities:** free continental breakfast and free local telephone calls.

SOME UNITS
FEE   FEE

HARTLAND

———— WHERE TO STAY ————

BEST WESTERN HARTLAND   *Book at aaa.com*
Phone: (810)632-7177
All Year [ECP]   1P: $80-$84   2P: $90-$100   XP: $6   F12
Location: On SR 59, jct US 23, exit 67. 10087 M-59 48353. Fax: 810/632-6480. **Facility:** 60 one-bedroom standard units. 2 stories, exterior corridors. **Parking:** on-site. **Terms:** check-in 4 pm. **Amenities:** irons, hair
Motel   dryers. **Pool(s):** heated indoor. **Guest Services:** coin laundry. **Cards:** AX, DC, DS, MC, VI. **Special Amenities:** free expanded continental breakfast and free local telephone calls.

SOME UNITS
FEE

HASTINGS pop. 7,095

———— WHERE TO STAY ————

PARKVIEW MOTEL
Phone: 269/945-9511
All Year   1P: $47   2P: $54-$59   XP: $5   F10
Location: 0.3 mi n on SR 43. 429 N Broadway 49058. Fax: 269/945-4433. **Facility:** 18 units. 16 one- and 2 two-bedroom standard units. 1-2 stories, exterior corridors. **Parking:** on-site. **Terms:** cancellation fee imposed.
Motel   **Cards:** AX, DC, MC, VI.

SOME UNITS

HILLMAN pop. 685

——— WHERE TO STAY ———

THUNDER BAY GOLF RESORT
Phone: (989)742-4502

Resort Motel

All Year 1P: $59-$69 2P: $59-$69 XP: $10 F13
Location: Just e on SR 32. 27800 M-32 E 49746. Fax: 989/742-3380. **Facility:** Condominium-type units. 34 units. 18 one-bedroom standard units with kitchens. 12 two- and 4 three-bedroom suites ($115-$145), some with kitchens and/or whirlpools. 2 stories (no elevator), exterior corridors. **Parking:** on-site. **Terms:** 2 night minimum stay - weekends, 14 day cancellation notice, [AP] & [MAP] meal plans available. **Amenities:** irons, hair dryers. **Leisure Activities:** whirlpool, 2 tennis courts, cross country skiing, snowmobiling, ice skating, hiking trails. *Fee:* golf-18 holes. **Business Services:** meeting rooms. **Cards:** AX, DS, MC, VI.

SOME UNITS

ASK ⊷ ⊷ ⊷ ⊷ DATA PORT ⊷ ⊷ ⊷ / ⊗ /

HILLSDALE pop. 8,233

——— WHERE TO STAY ———

DAYS INN HILLSDALE *Book at aaa.com*
Phone: 517/439-3297

Small-scale Hotel

All Year 1P: $65-$125 2P: $73-$145 XP: $5 F17
Location: 2 mi n of town. 3241 Carleton Rd 49242. Fax: 517/439-1286. **Facility:** 47 units. 41 one-bedroom standard units, some with whirlpools. 6 one-bedroom suites ($75-$150). 1-2 stories (no elevator), interior corridors. *Bath:* combo or shower only. **Parking:** on-site. **Pool(s):** heated indoor. **Leisure Activities:** whirlpool, exercise room. **Guest Services:** valet laundry. **Business Services:** meeting rooms. **Cards:** AX, DC, DS, MC, VI.
(See color ad card insert)

SOME UNITS

ASK ⊷ ⊷ ⊷ ⊷ ⊷ ⊷ DATA PORT ⊷ ⊷ ⊷ / ⊗ /

HOLLAND pop. 35,048

——— WHERE TO STAY ———

BEST WESTERN KELLY INN & SUITES *Book at aaa.com*
Phone: (616)994-0400

AAA SAVE

Small-scale Hotel

5/1-5/16 1P: $129-$200
5/17-9/4 1P: $89-$149
9/5-3/31 1P: $85-$135
4/1-4/30 1P: $85-$90
Location: US 31, exit Felch St E, just n. 2888 W Shore Dr 49424. Fax: 616/994-9955. **Facility:** 80 one-bedroom standard units, some with whirlpools. 3 stories, interior/exterior corridors. **Parking:** on-site. **Terms:** weekly rates available, [ECP] meal plan available, package plans - seasonal. **Amenities:** video games, voice mail, irons, hair dryers. **Pool(s):** heated indoor. **Leisure Activities:** whirlpool, exercise room. *Fee:* game room. **Guest Services:** valet and coin laundry. **Business Services:** meeting rooms, business center. **Cards:** AX, CB, DC, DS, JC, MC, VI. **Special Amenities:** free expanded continental breakfast and free newspaper. *(See color ad below)*

SOME UNITS

⊷ ⊷ ⊷ ⊷ ⊷ ⊷ ⊷ ⊷ ⊷ ⊷ / ⊷ ⊷ /

BONNIE'S (THE) PARSONAGE 1908 B&B

AAA **SAVE**

▽▽ ▽▽

Historic Bed
& Breakfast

Phone: (616)396-1316

5/1-10/31	1P: $70-$100	2P: $100-$130
4/1-4/30 & 11/1-3/31	1P: $70-$80	2P: $100-$110

Location: US 31, 1 mi w on 24th St. Located in a quiet, residential area. 6 E 24th St and Central Ave 49423. **Facility:** This property is a former parsonage built in 1908. Smoke free premises. 3 one-bedroom standard units. 2 stories (no elevator), interior corridors. *Bath:* shared or private, combo, shower or tub only. **Parking:** on-site. **Terms:** check-in 4 pm, 2 night minimum stay - weekends 7/1-8/31, age restrictions may apply, weekly rates available, [BP] meal plan available. **Guest Services:** TV in common area.

[⊠] [📺] [☎]

COMFORT INN

AAA **SAVE**

▽▽▽ ▽▽▽

Small-scale Hotel

Book at aaa.com

Phone: (616)392-1000

5/1-9/30	1P: $90-$140	2P: $90-$140	XP: $10 F
4/1-4/30 & 10/1-3/31	1P: $70-$90	2P: $70-$90	XP: $10 F

Location: Just w of US 31. Located in a commercial area. 422 E 32nd St 49423. Fax: 616/392-1421. **Facility:** 71 one-bedroom standard units, some with whirlpools. 2 stories (no elevator), interior corridors. **Parking:** on-site. **Terms:** check-in 4 pm. **Amenities:** irons, hair dryers. **Pool(s):** heated outdoor. **Leisure Activities:** whirlpool. **Guest Services:** valet laundry. **Cards:** AX, DC, DS, MC, VI. **Special Amenities:** free continental breakfast and free newspaper.

SOME UNITS

[S/D] [🍽+] [🏊] [📹] [DATA PORT] [🖥] [📼] / [⊠] /

COUNTRY INN BY CARLSON

▽▽▽ ▽▽▽

Small-scale Hotel

Book at aaa.com

Phone: (616)396-6677

All Year [ECP]	1P: $79-$99	XP: $10 F18

Location: Jct US 31 N and James St, just e. Located at the Horizon Outlet Mall. 12260 James St 49424. Fax: 616/396-1197. **Facility:** 116 one-bedroom standard units, some with whirlpools. 2 stories (no elevator), interior corridors. **Parking:** on-site. **Terms:** cancellation fee imposed. **Amenities:** dual phone lines, voice mail, irons, hair dryers. **Pool(s):** heated indoor. **Guest Services:** valet laundry. **Business Services:** meeting rooms. **Cards:** AX, DC, DS, MC, VI. *(See color ad p 313)*

SOME UNITS

[ASK] [S/D] [🍽+] [🏊] [📹] [DATA PORT] [🖥] / [⊠] [VCR] [🖥] /
FEE

DUTCH COLONIAL INN

▽▽▽▽ ▽▽▽▽

Bed & Breakfast

Phone: 616/396-3664

All Year	1P: $100-$160	2P: $100-$160	XP: $20

Location: US 31, 1 mi w on 24th St, then just n. Located in a quiet, residential area. 560 Central Ave 49423. Fax: 616/396-0461. **Facility:** Built in 1928, the inn is outfitted with classic decor from the 1930s and '40s. Smoke free premises. 4 one-bedroom standard units, some with whirlpools. 3 stories (no elevator), interior corridors. *Bath:* combo or shower only. **Parking:** on-site. **Terms:** 10 day cancellation notice-fee imposed, [BP] meal plan available. **Amenities:** *Some:* DVD players, CD players. **Business Services:** meeting rooms. **Cards:** AX, DC, MC, VI.

[⊠] [DATA PORT]

FAIRFIELD INN BY MARRIOTT

▽▽ ▽▽▽

Small-scale Hotel

Book at aaa.com

Phone: (616)786-9700

5/1-9/30	1P: $85-$105	2P: $85-$105	XP: $6 F18
4/1-4/30 & 10/1-3/31	1P: $69-$89	2P: $69-$89	XP: $6 F18

Location: Jct US 31 and Felch St. Located in a commercial area. 2854 W Shore Dr 49424. Fax: 616/786-9700. **Facility:** 64 one-bedroom standard units. 3 stories, interior corridors. *Bath:* combo or shower only. **Parking:** on-site, winter plug-ins. **Terms:** [ECP] meal plan available. **Amenities:** irons. **Pool(s):** small heated indoor. **Leisure Activities:** whirlpool. **Guest Services:** valet laundry. **Cards:** AX, CB, DC, DS, MC, VI.

SOME UNITS

[S/D] [🍽+] [🖥] [🖥] [🏊] [📹] [DATA PORT] [🖥] / [⊠] [🖥] [🖥] /

HAMPTON INN OF HOLLAND

AAA **SAVE**

▽▽▽ ▽▽▽

Small-scale Hotel

Book at aaa.com

Phone: (616)399-8500

6/15-9/6 [ECP]	1P: $129-$189	2P: $139-$199
4/7-6/14 [ECP]	1P: $99-$149	2P: $109-$159
9/7-3/31 [ECP]	1P: $99-$139	2P: $109-$149

Location: Jct US 31 and Felch St. 12427 Felch St 49424. Fax: 616/399-9540. **Facility:** 178 one-bedroom standard units, some with whirlpools. 4 stories, interior corridors. *Bath:* combo or shower only. **Parking:** on-site. **Terms:** cancellation fee imposed. **Amenities:** dual phone lines, voice mail, irons, hair dryers. **Pool(s):** heated indoor. **Leisure Activities:** whirlpools, pool table, exercise room. *Fee:* game room. **Guest Services:** valet and coin laundry. **Business Services:** meeting rooms. **Cards:** AX, DC, DS, MC, VI. **Special Amenities:** free expanded continental breakfast and free local telephone calls.

SOME UNITS

[S/D] [Y] [🖥M] [🖥] [🏊] [⊠] [📹] [DATA PORT] [🖥] / [⊠] [🖥] [🖥] /

HAWORTH INN & CONFERENCE CENTER

▽▽ ▽▽▽

Small-scale Hotel

Phone: (616)395-7200

5/1-3/31 [ECP]	1P: $99-$159	2P: $99-$159
4/1-4/30 [ECP]	1P: $95-$119	2P: $95-$119

Location: Corner of 9th St and College Ave; center. Located on Hope College Campus. 225 College Ave 49423. Fax: 616/395-7151. **Facility:** 50 one-bedroom standard units. 3 stories, interior corridors. *Bath:* combo or shower only. **Parking:** on-site. **Amenities:** irons, hair dryers. **Leisure Activities:** exercise room. **Guest Services:** gift shop, valet laundry. **Business Services:** conference facilities. **Cards:** AX, DS, MC, VI.

SOME UNITS

[ASK] [S/D] [✈] [🍽+] [🖥] [DATA PORT] / [⊠] [🖥] /
FEE   FEE

HOLIDAY INN EXPRESS

AAA **SAVE**

▽▽▽ ▽▽▽

Small-scale Hotel

Book at aaa.com

Phone: (616)738-2800

6/16-9/10	1P: $89-$229
4/1-5/9	1P: $89-$189
9/11-3/31	1P: $79-$179
5/10-6/15	1P: $79-$159

Location: Jct US 31 and Felch St. Located in a commercial area. 12381 Felch St 49424. Fax: 616/738-3790. **Facility:** 118 one-bedroom standard units, some with whirlpools. 4 stories, interior corridors. *Bath:* combo or shower only. **Parking:** on-site. **Terms:** [CP] & [ECP] meal plans available. **Amenities:** high-speed Internet, dual phone lines, voice mail, irons, hair dryers. **Pool(s):** heated indoor. **Leisure Activities:** sauna, whirlpool, lighted tennis court, exercise room. *Fee:* game room. **Guest Services:** valet and coin laundry. **Business Services:** meeting rooms, business center. **Cards:** AX, CB, DC, DS, MC, VI. **Special Amenities:** free expanded continental breakfast and free newspaper.

SOME UNITS

[S/D] [🍽+] [🖥M] [🖥] [🏊] [⊠] [📹] [DATA PORT] [🖥] [🖥] [🖥] / [⊠] /

--------- *The following lodging was either not evaluated or did not* ---------
meet AAA rating requirements but is listed for your information only.

RESIDENCE INN BY MARRIOTT   **Phone:** 616/393-6900
  [fyi]   4/16-9/15 [BP]   1P: $119-$199   2P: $119-$199
            1/1-3/31 [BP]   1P: $129-$179   2P: $129-$179
Small-scale Hotel 4/1-4/15 & 9/16-12/31 [BP]   1P: $119-$169   2P: $119-$169
            Too new to rate. **Location:** I-196, exit 49 (SR 40), just n to Southpointe Ridge Rd. 631 Southpoint Ridge Rd 49423.
Fax: 616/393-6901. **Amenities:** 78 units, pets, coffeemakers, microwaves, refrigerators, pool. **Terms:** cancellation fee imposed.
Cards: AX, DC, DS, MC, VI.

--------- **WHERE TO DINE** ---------

PIETROS ITALIAN RESTAURANT   **Lunch:** $4-$6   **Dinner:** $9-$16   **Phone:** 616/396-1000
  ▽▽ ▽▽ **Location:** On I-196 business route, 1.3 mi w of US 31. 175 E 8th St 49423. **Hours:** 11:30 am-11 pm, Fri & Sat-11
          pm. Closed: 11/25, 12/25. **Features:** The menu fuses Italian and Mediterranean cuisine in such dishes as
  Italian   fettuccine Michael—spinach and egg noodles with chicken and mushrooms in a cream sauce. Wood-fired
          pizza bubbles with flavor. If you're craving something sweet, try the tiramisu. Casual dress; cocktails.
Parking: on-site. **Cards:** AX, DS, MC, VI.   ✕

RIO GRAND STEAKHOUSE   **Lunch:** $6-$13   **Dinner:** $11-$18   **Phone:** 616/392-9900
  ▽▽ ▽▽ **Location:** US 31 and Felch St. 12420 Felch St 49424. **Hours:** 11 am-11 pm, Fri & Sat-midnight, Sun-10 pm.
          Closed: 11/25, 12/25. **Features:** Casual dining offering large cut, charbroiled, mesquite steak, barbecue
  American ribs, rotisserie chicken and a variety of seafood entrees. Casual dress; cocktails. **Parking:** on-site.
          Cards: AX, DC, DS, MC, VI.   Ⓨ ✕

TILL MIDNIGHT   **Lunch:** $4-$8   **Dinner:** $16-$23   **Phone:** 616/392-6883
  ▽▽▽▽ **Location:** Between 8th and 9th sts; downtown. 208 College Ave 49423. **Hours:** 11 am-2:30 & 5-10 pm, Fri &
          Sat-midnight. Closed major holidays; also Sun. **Reservations:** suggested. **Features:** Close to the college
  American and downtown shopping areas, the small restaurant is often crowded. The use of fresh ingredients brings
the weather's nice. Casual dress; cocktails. **Parking:** street. **Cards:** AX, DS, MC, VI.
           to life the flavors in the contemporary American-style cooking. Sidewalk dining is hard to come by when
                                                           ✕

--------- *The following restaurant has not been evaluated by AAA* ---------
but is listed for your information only.

CHINA INN   **Phone:** 616/786-9230
  [fyi]   Not evaluated. **Location:** Located in the West Shore Shopping Center. 2863 West Shore Dr 49423. **Features:** The
          casual restaurant's menu incorporates Mandarin, Szechuan, Hunan and Cantonese dishes.

HOUGHTON pop. 7,010

--------- **WHERE TO STAY** ---------

BEST WESTERN-FRANKLIN SQUARE INN   *Book at aaa.com*   **Phone:** (906)487-1700
  Ⓐ Ⓢ   6/17-10/15 & 1/1-3/31   1P: $99-$189   2P: $99-$189   XP: $8   F15
            4/1-6/16 & 10/16-12/31   1P: $91-$179   2P: $91-$179   XP: $8   F15
  ▽▽ ▽▽ **Location:** Center of downtown. 820 Shelden Ave 49931. **Fax:** 906/487-9432. **Facility:** 103 units. 98 one-bedroom
          standard units, some with whirlpools. 5 one-bedroom suites, some with whirlpools. 7 stories, interior corri-
Large-scale Hotel dors. **Parking:** on-site, winter plug-ins. **Terms:** [BP] meal plan available, pets ($9 extra charge).
          Amenities: voice mail, irons, hair dryers. *Some:* dual phone lines. **Dining:** 7 am-2 & 5-10 pm, Sun 5 pm-9
pm, cocktails. **Pool(s):** heated indoor. **Leisure Activities:** sauna, whirlpool, snowmobiling. **Guest Services:** valet laundry. **Business Services:** conference facilities. **Cards:** AX, CB, DC, DS, MC, VI. **Special Amenities:** free full breakfast and free local
telephone calls.

SOME UNITS

BEST VALUE KING'S INN   **Phone:** (906)482-5000
  ▽▽ ▽▽ All Year [ECP]   1P: $67-$107   2P: $67-$107   XP: $6   F17
          Location: On US 41; downtown. 215 Shelden Ave 49931. **Fax:** 906/482-9795. **Facility:** 69 one-bedroom standard
          units. 3 stories, interior corridors. **Parking:** on-site, winter plug-ins. **Terms:** pets ($8 extra charge).
Small-scale Hotel **Amenities:** irons, hair dryers. **Pool(s):** heated indoor. **Leisure Activities:** sauna, whirlpool, snowmobiling.
Business Services: meeting rooms, business center. **Cards:** AX, DC, DS, MC, VI.

SOME UNITS

BUDGET HOST INN   **Phone:** (906)482-5351
  Ⓐ Ⓢ   6/25-10/23 [CP]   1P: $40-$70   2P: $45-$70   XP: $5   D11
            4/1-6/24 & 10/24-3/31 [CP] 1P: $35-$60   2P: $40-$60   XP: $5   D11
  ◇   **Location:** On US 41, 3.3 mi se. 46995 Hwy US 41 49931. **Facility:** 24 units. 22 one- and 2 two-bedroom standard
  Motel   units. 1-2 stories (no elevator), exterior corridors. *Bath:* combo or shower only. **Parking:** on-site. **Pool(s):**
          heated outdoor. **Leisure Activities:** snowmobiling, bike trails, hiking trails, basketball. **Cards:** AX, CB, DC,
          DS, MC, VI. **Special Amenities:** free continental breakfast and free room upgrade (subject to avail-
ability with advanced reservations).

SOME UNITS

CHARLESTON HOUSE HISTORIC INN

Phone: (906)482-7790

▼▼◇◇▼
Bed & Breakfast

All Year [ECP]   1P: $118-$168   2P: $118-$168   XP: $25   F5
Location: 1.1 mi se on US 41. 918 College Ave 49931. Fax: 906/482-7068. **Facility:** This inn is in a house dating from the turn of the 20th century. Smoke free premises. 4 one-bedroom standard units. 2 stories (no elevator), interior corridors. *Bath:* shower only. **Parking:** on-site. **Terms:** 14 day cancellation notice-fee imposed. **Amenities:** irons, hair dryers. **Business Services:** meeting rooms. **Cards:** AX, MC, VI.

(ASK) (SD) (✕) (▭)

THE DOWNTOWNER MOTEL

Phone: (906)482-4421

(AAA) (SAVE)
▼◇▼
Motel

All Year   1P: $48-$68   2P: $48-$78   XP: $4
Location: On US 41; downtown. 110 Shelden Ave 49931. Fax: 906/482-3189. **Facility:** 27 units. 26 one- and 1 two-bedroom standard units. 2 stories (no elevator), exterior corridors. **Parking:** on-site, winter plug-ins. **Leisure Activities:** snowmobiling, access to riverwalk. **Cards:** AX, CB, DC, DS, MC, VI. **Special Amenities:** free local telephone calls and early check-in/late check-out.

SOME UNITS

(⫴→) (📹) / (✕⃠)

SUPER 8 MOTEL   *Book at aaa.com*

Phone: 906/482-2240

▼▼▼
Small-scale Hotel

All Year   1P: $60-$65   2P: $65-$70   XP: $3   F12
Location: 0.3 mi e, follow signs. Located on the banks of the canal. 1200 E Lakeshore Dr 49931. Fax: 906/482-0686. **Facility:** 86 one-bedroom standard units, some with whirlpools. 2 stories (no elevator), interior corridors. *Bath:* combo or shower only. **Parking:** on-site. **Terms:** [ECP] meal plan available. **Amenities:** *Some:* dual phone lines. **Pool(s):** heated indoor. **Leisure Activities:** sauna, whirlpool, boat dock, fishing, snowmobiling, hiking trails. **Guest Services:** coin laundry. **Business Services:** meeting rooms. **Cards:** AX, DC, DS, MC, VI.

SOME UNITS

(ASK) (SD) (⬇🔒) (🛥) (✕⃠) (📹) / (✕⃠) (🔓) (🖥)

——— **WHERE TO DINE** ———

MING GARDEN WOK & GRILL   Lunch: $4-$10   Dinner: $10-$24   Phone: (906)482-8000

▼▼▼
Chinese

Location: 1.5 mi sw on SR 26. 1301 Ridge Rd 49931. **Hours:** 11:30 am-9 pm, Fri & Sat-10 pm, Sun-8 pm. Closed: 11/25, 12/25. **Reservations:** accepted. **Features:** On the outskirts of town, the modern Chinese restaurant serves wok and grill dishes. Casual dress; cocktails. **Parking:** on-site. **Cards:** AX, DS, MC, VI.

(🅐🅒) (✕⃠)

——— *The following restaurants have not been evaluated by AAA but are listed for your information only.* ———

AMBASSADOR

Phone: 906/482-5054

(fyi)

Not evaluated. **Location:** In the downtown area. 126 Shelden Ave 49931. **Features:** The popular downtown restaurant, with its antique bar and view of the canal, serves a number of snacks, salads and pizzas, as well as daily pasta specials.

THE LIBRARY

Phone: 906/487-5882

(fyi)

Not evaluated. **Location:** In the downtown area. 62 N Isle Royale 49931. **Features:** Pizza, steak, seafood and Mexican dishes—as well as on-site microbrews—are served.

HOUGHTON LAKE pop. 3,749

——— **WHERE TO STAY** ———

BEST WESTERN BEACHFRONT   *Book at aaa.com*

Phone: (989)366-9126

▼▼◇▼
Small-scale Hotel

5/23-9/27	1P: $129-$179	2P: $129-$179	XP: $10 F18
12/30-3/31	1P: $99-$159	2P: $99-$159	XP: $10 F18
4/1-5/22 & 9/28-12/29	1P: $79-$99	2P: $79-$99	XP: $10 F18

Location: On SR 55, 4.5 mi e of US 27; 11.5 mi w of I-75. Located in a commercial area. 4990 W Houghton Lake Dr 48629. Fax: 989/366-1547. **Facility:** 60 one-bedroom standard units, some with whirlpools. 4 stories, interior corridors. *Bath:* combo or shower only. **Parking:** on-site. **Terms:** [ECP] meal plan available. **Amenities:** irons, hair dryers. **Pool(s):** heated indoor. **Leisure Activities:** whirlpool, boat dock, fishing, snowmobiling, exercise room. *Fee:* game room. **Guest Services:** coin laundry. **Business Services:** meeting rooms. **Cards:** AX, CB, DC, DS, JC, MC, VI.

SOME UNITS

(ASK) (SD) (⬇🔒) (🛥) (✕⃠) (DATA PORT) (▭) / (✕⃠) (VCR) /
FEE

COMFORT SUITES LAKESIDE   *Book at aaa.com*   Phone: 989/422-4000

| | 1/1-3/31 | 1P: $129-$509 | 2P: $129-$509 | XP: $10 | F18 |
| | 4/1-12/31 | 1P: $119-$499 | 2P: $119-$499 | XP: $10 | F18 |

Small-scale Hotel **Location:** On Old US 27, 0.5 mi n of SR 55. Located on Houghton Lake. 100 Clearview Dr 48629. **Fax:** 989/422-4600. **Facility:** 69 units. 64 one- and 2 two-bedroom standard units, some with whirlpools. 3 one-bedroom suites with whirlpools. 4 stories, interior corridors. *Bath:* combo or shower only. **Parking:** on-site, winter plug-ins. **Terms:** cancellation fee imposed. **Amenities:** high-speed Internet, voice mail, irons, hair dryers. *Some:* video games. **Dining:** 11 am-11 pm, Sun from 10 am, cocktails. **Pool(s):** heated indoor, wading. **Leisure Activities:** waterslide, boat dock, indoor water park, lazy river, putting green, snowmobiling, exercise room. **Guest Services:** gift shop, coin laundry. **Business Services:** conference facilities. **Cards:** AX, DC, DS, MC, VI.

SOME UNITS

HILLSIDE MOTEL   Phone: (989)366-5711

| | 4/1-9/15 | 1P: $56-$64 | 2P: $64-$74 | XP: $6 | F12 |
| | 9/16-3/31 | 1P: $52 | 2P: $64 | XP: $6 | F12 |

Motel **Location:** On SR 55, 6 mi e of US 27; 10 mi w of I-75. Located next to Village Square Mall. 3419 W Houghton Lake Dr 48629. **Facility:** 12 one-bedroom standard units. 1 story, exterior corridors. **Parking:** on-site. **Terms:** 3 day cancellation notice. **Leisure Activities:** snowmobiling. **Cards:** AX, DC, DS, MC, VI.

SOME UNITS

HOLIDAY INN EXPRESS   *Book at aaa.com*   Phone: (989)422-7829

	5/23-9/25 [ECP]	1P: $99-$129	2P: $99-$129	XP: $6	F19
	12/25-3/31 [ECP]	1P: $89-$119	2P: $89-$119	XP: $6	F19
	4/1-5/22 & 9/26-12/24 [ECP]	1P: $69-$89	2P: $69-$89	XP: $6	F19

Small-scale Hotel **Location:** Jct US 27 and SR 55, just e. Located in a commerical area. 200 Cloverleaf Ln 48629. **Fax:** 989/422-2625. **Facility:** 68 units. 66 one-bedroom standard units, some with whirlpools. 2 one-bedroom suites. 2 stories (no elevator), interior corridors. *Bath:* combo or shower only. **Parking:** on-site, winter plug-ins. **Terms:** pets ($25 fee). **Amenities:** dual phone lines, voice mail, irons, hair dryers. **Pool(s):** heated indoor. **Leisure Activities:** whirlpool, snowmobiling. **Guest Services:** coin laundry. **Business Services:** meeting rooms. **Cards:** AX, CB, DC, DS, MC, VI. *(See color ad p 324 & card insert)*

SOME UNITS

SUPER 8 MOTEL *Book at aaa.com* Phone: (989)422-3119
6/1-10/31 [ECP]   1P: $65-$95   2P: $75-$105   XP: $10   F18
4/1-5/31 & 11/1-3/31 [ECP]   1P: $55-$85   2P: $65-$95   XP: $10   F18
Location: Jct US 27 and SR 55. Located in a commercial area. 9580 W Lake City Rd 48629. Fax: 989/422-5561. **Facility:** 70 one-bedroom standard units, some with whirlpools. 2 stories (no elevator), interior corridors.
Small-scale Hotel **Parking:** on-site, winter plug-ins. **Pool(s):** heated indoor. **Leisure Activities:** sauna, whirlpool, snowmobiling, playground. **Guest Services:** coin laundry. **Cards:** AX, CB, DC, DS, JC, MC, VI. **Special Amenities:** free continental breakfast and free local telephone calls. *(See ad p 325)*

SOME UNITS

─────── WHERE TO DINE ───────

COYLES RESTAURANT   Lunch: $3-$5   Dinner: $6-$11   Phone: 989/422-3812
Location: Just n of jct SR 55. 9074 Old US 27 48629. **Hours:** 8 am-10 pm, Fri & Sat-11 pm; hours may vary seasonally. Closed: 12/25. **Features:** Pick and choose from the wide assortment of tempting options on the
American lunch and dinner buffets, or order from a menu that includes Alaskan king crab, frog legs and steak dinners. Meals are reasonably priced and please every member of the family. Casual dress; cocktails.
Parking: on-site. **Cards:** DS, MC, VI.

HOWELL pop. 9,232

─────── WHERE TO STAY ───────

AMERIHOST INN & SUITES-HOWELL *Book at aaa.com* Phone: (517)546-0712
All Year   1P: $83-$89   2P: $83-$89   XP: $5   F18
Location: I-96, exit 133, just n on US 59 (Grand River Ave); then 0.5 mi e. 4120 Lambert Dr 48843. Fax: 517/546-0752. **Facility:** 75 one-bedroom standard units, some with whirlpools. 3 stories, interior corridors. *Bath:* combo or shower only. **Parking:** on-site. **Terms:** 7 day cancellation notice, [ECP] meal plan available.
Small-scale Hotel **Amenities:** voice mail, safes (fee), irons, hair dryers. **Pool(s):** heated indoor. **Leisure Activities:** whirlpool, exercise room. **Cards:** AX, CB, DC, DS, JC, MC, VI. **Special Amenities:** free expanded continental breakfast and free newspaper.

SOME UNITS

BEST WESTERN HOWELL *Book at aaa.com* Phone: (517)548-2900
4/1-9/30   1P: $120-$145   2P: $145-$155   XP: $10   F10
10/1-3/31   1P: $99-$135   2P: $135-$145   XP: $10   F10
Location: I-96, exit 137 (Pinkney Rd), just s on CR D19. Located in a semi-rural area. 1500 Pinckney Rd 48843. Fax: 517/548-2163. **Facility:** 60 one-bedroom standard units, some with whirlpools. 2 stories (no elevator), exterior corridors. **Terms:** [BP] meal plan available, package plans - seasonal & weekends,
Motel small pets only ($10 extra charge). **Amenities:** voice mail, irons, hair dryers. **Dining:** 6-11 am, Sun 7 am-noon. **Pool(s):** heated outdoor. **Guest Services:** coin laundry. **Business Services:** meeting rooms. **Cards:** AX, CB, DC, DS, MC, VI. **Special Amenities:** free local telephone calls and free newspaper.

SOME UNITS
FEE

KENSINGTON INN
All Year   1P: $44-$59   2P: $44-$59
Location: I-96, exit 137 (Pickney Rd), just n. 124 Holiday Ln 48843. Fax: 517/548-1022. **Facility:** 107 one-bedroom standard units, some with kitchens and/or whirlpools. 1 story, exterior corridors. **Parking:** on-site.
Motel **Terms:** weekly rates available, small pets only ($10 extra charge). **Pool(s):** outdoor. **Guest Services:** coin laundry. **Business Services:** meeting rooms. **Cards:** AX, DC, DS, MC, VI.

SOME UNITS
FEE

QUALITY INN BANQUET & CONFERENCE CENTER *Book at aaa.com* Phone: (517)546-6800
All Year   1P: $59-$89   2P: $59-$89   XP: $10   F18
Location: I-96, exit 137 (Pickney Rd), just n. 125 Holiday Ln 48843. Fax: 517/546-1820. **Facility:** 150 units. 146 one-bedroom standard units, some with whirlpools. 4 one-bedroom suites ($99-$139). 2 stories (no elevator),
Motel interior corridors. **Parking:** on-site. **Terms:** small pets only ($10 extra charge). **Amenities:** voice mail, irons, hair dryers. **Dining:** 5 pm-11 pm. **Pool(s):** outdoor. **Guest Services:** valet and coin laundry. **Business Services:** conference facilities. **Cards:** AX, CB, DC, DS, JC, MC, VI. **Special Amenities:** free expanded continental breakfast and early check-in/late check-out.

SOME UNITS
FEE

─────── WHERE TO DINE ───────

CHINESE DELIGHT   Lunch: $8-$12   Dinner: $8-$12   Phone: 517/545-9988
Location: Downtown. 111 W Grand River 48843. **Hours:** 11 am-9:30 pm, Fri & Sat-10:30 pm, Sun noon-9:30
Chinese pm. Closed major holidays. **Features:** Rustic brick walls and hardwood floors give this space a bright and cheerful feeling. Locally popular, the Cantonese - American based menu offers a wide selection of traditional dishes. Casual dress. **Parking:** street. **Cards:** AX, DC, MC, VI.

HUDSONVILLE pop. 7,160

------ **WHERE TO STAY** ------

AMERIHOST INN-HUDSONVILLE   *Book at aaa.com*
Phone: (616)662-4000

(AAA) (SAVE)   All Year   1P: $75-$149   2P: $85-$159   XP: $6   F18
◆◆◆   **Location:** I-196, exit 62 (32nd Ave), just nw. Located in a quiet area. 3301 Highland Dr 49426. Fax: 616/662-5000.
Small-scale Hotel   **Facility:** 61 one-bedroom standard units, some with whirlpools. 2 stories (no elevator), interior corridors. *Bath:* combo or shower only. **Parking:** on-site. **Amenities:** safes (fee), irons, hair dryers. **Pool(s):** heated indoor. **Leisure Activities:** sauna, whirlpool, exercise room. **Guest Services:** valet laundry. **Business Services:** meeting rooms. **Cards:** AX, DC, DS, MC, VI. **Special Amenities:** free expanded continental breakfast and free newspaper.

SOME UNITS

SUPER 8 MOTEL   *Book at aaa.com*
Phone: (616)896-6710

(AAA) (SAVE)   All Year [CP]   1P: $54-$64   2P: $54-$69
◆◆◆   **Location:** I-196, exit 62 (32nd Ave), just se. Located in a business park. 3005 Corporate Grove Dr 49426.
Small-scale Hotel   Fax: 616/896-9958. **Facility:** 60 units. 54 one-bedroom standard units. 6 one-bedroom suites ($89-$129), some with whirlpools. 2 stories (no elevator), interior corridors. *Bath:* combo or shower only. **Parking:** on-site, winter plug-ins. **Terms:** weekly rates available. **Amenities:** *Some:* irons, hair dryers. **Pool(s):** heated indoor. **Leisure Activities:** sauna, whirlpool. **Guest Services:** coin laundry. **Cards:** AX, DS, MC, VI. **Special Amenities:** free continental breakfast and free local telephone calls.

SOME UNITS

------ **WHERE TO DINE** ------

------ *The following restaurant has not been evaluated by AAA* ------
but is listed for your information only.

JERRY'S COUNTRY INN
Phone: 616/669-1140

(fyi)   Not evaluated. **Location:** Center. 3700 Chicago Dr 49426. **Features:** This popular family restaurant serves breakfast, lunch and classics such as lake perch, meatloaf or Swiss steak for dinner.

IMLAY CITY pop. 3,869

------ **WHERE TO STAY** ------

DAYS INN   *Book at aaa.com*
Phone: (810)724-8005

(AAA) (SAVE)   4/1-10/31 [ECP]   2P: $69-$79
◆◆◆   11/1-3/31 [ECP]   2P: $59-$69
Small-scale Hotel   **Location:** I-69, exit 168, 0.3 mi n, then w. 6692 Newark Rd 48444. Fax: 810/724-0251. **Facility:** 60 one-bedroom standard units, some with whirlpools. 2 stories (no elevator), interior corridors. **Parking:** on-site. **Terms:** age restrictions may apply, 14 day cancellation notice, pets ($50 deposit, $8 extra charge). **Amenities:** hair dryers. **Pool(s):** heated indoor. **Guest Services:** coin laundry. **Business Services:** meeting rooms. **Cards:** AX, DC, DS, MC, VI. **Special Amenities:** free expanded continental breakfast and free local telephone calls.
(See color ad card insert)

SOME UNITS
FEE

SUPER 8 MOTEL-IMLAY CITY   *Book at aaa.com*
Phone: 810/724-8700

◆◆◆   All Year   1P: $49-$59   2P: $59-$69   XP: $6   F12
Small-scale Hotel   **Location:** I-69, exit 168 (Van Dyke Rd), just n to Newark Rd, just e. 6951 Newark Rd 48444. Fax: 810/724-4013. **Facility:** 60 units. 59 one-bedroom standard units, some with whirlpools. 1 one-bedroom suite with efficiency (no utensils). 2 stories (no elevator), interior corridors. **Parking:** on-site. **Terms:** check-in 4 pm, small pets only ($50 deposit, $10 extra charge). **Amenities:** *Some:* hair dryers. **Leisure Activities:** whirlpool, playground. **Guest Services:** coin laundry. **Business Services:** meeting rooms, fax (fee). **Cards:** AX, DC, DS, MC, VI.

SOME UNITS
FEE

------ **WHERE TO DINE** ------

LUCKY'S STEAKHOUSE
Lunch: $10-$14   Dinner: $10-$14   Phone: 810/724-4100

◆◆◆   **Location:** I-69, exit 168 (Van Dyke Rd), just n. 2000 S Cedar 48444. **Hours:** 11 am-10 pm, Fri & Sat-11 pm, Sun noon-9 pm. Closed major holidays. **Features:** Big portions are the trademark for this local family oriented American   favorite where service is quick and attentive. Casual dress; cocktails. **Parking:** on-site. **Cards:** AX, DS, MC, VI.

INDIAN RIVER pop. 2,008

------ **WHERE TO STAY** ------

HOLIDAY INN EXPRESS   *Book at aaa.com*
Phone: (231)238-3000

◆◆◆   5/23-9/30 [ECP]   1P: $120-$150   2P: $120-$150   XP: $6   F19
   11/21-3/31 [ECP]   1P: $80-$130   2P: $80-$130   XP: $6   F19
Small-scale Hotel   10/1-11/20 [ECP]   1P: $100-$120   2P: $100-$120   XP: $6   F19
   4/1-5/22 [ECP]   1P: $80-$120   2P: $80-$120   XP: $6   F19
Location: I-75, exit 310, just e on SR 68. Located in a semi-rural area. 4375 Brudy Rd 49749 (PO Box 417). Fax: 231/238-8992. **Facility:** 50 one-bedroom standard units, some with whirlpools. 2 stories (no elevator), interior corridors. **Parking:** on-site, winter plug-ins. **Terms:** cancellation fee imposed. **Amenities:** irons, hair dryers. **Pool(s):** heated indoor. **Leisure Activities:** whirlpool, snowmobiling. *Fee:* game room. **Guest Services:** coin laundry. **Business Services:** meeting rooms. **Cards:** AX, CB, DC, DS, JC, MC, VI. *(See color ad card insert)*

SOME UNITS

NOR GATE MOTEL

AAA SAVE
▽▽▽
Motel

Phone: 231/238-7788

All Year   1P: $36-$40   2P: $42-$48   XP: $3   D5
Location: I-75, exit 310, 0.3 mi w, then 2 mi s on Old US 27. Located in a semi-rural area. 4846 S Straits Hwy 49749. **Facility:** 14 units. 6 one- and 6 two-bedroom standard units, some with efficiencies. 1 vacation home and 1 cabin ($60-$72). 1 story, exterior corridors. *Bath:* combo or shower only. **Parking:** on-site, winter plug-ins. **Terms:** 3 day cancellation notice, small pets only (with prior approval). **Leisure Activities:** snowmobiling, picnic area, children's basketball, hiking trails, playground. **Cards:** AX, DS, MC, VI.

SOME UNITS
🐾 ⁅↕⁆ ⊠ 🎦 / ⊠ 🕿 🅱 🖃 ▣ /

STAR GATE MOTEL

AAA SAVE
▽▽▽
Motel

Phone: 231/238-7371

All Year   1P: $42-$48   2P: $44-$52   XP: $6   D5
Location: I-75, exit 310, 0.3 mi w, then 1.8 mi s on Old US 27. Located in a semi-rural area. 4646 S Straits Hwy 49749. **Facility:** 16 units. 10 one- and 4 two-bedroom standard units. 1 vacation home ($75-$100) and 1 cabin ($65-$85). 1 story, exterior corridors. *Bath:* combo or shower only. **Parking:** on-site, winter plug-ins. **Terms:** 3 day cancellation notice-fee imposed, pets (with prior approval). **Leisure Activities:** snowmobiling, picnic area, hiking trails, playground, basketball, horseshoes. **Cards:** AX, DS, MC, VI. **Special Amenities:** free local telephone calls and preferred room (subject to availability with advanced reservations).

SOME UNITS
🐑 ⁅↕⁆ ⊠ 🎦 / ⊠ 🅱 🖃 /

──────── **WHERE TO DINE** ────────

VIVIO'S NORTHWOOD INN

AAA
▽▽ ▽▽
American

Dinner: $8-$19   **Phone: 231/238-9471**

Location: I-75, exit 310, 0.3 mi w, then 1 mi s. 4531 S Straits Hwy 49749. **Hours:** 5 pm-11 pm. Closed: Mon-Wed 11/1-4/30. **Features:** The rustic log cabin is decorated with wall-mounted wildlife, including deer heads and a black bear cub. Shaded lamps throw adequate, yet modest, light. American and Italian cuisine, such as the specialty pizza, make up the restaurant's menu. Casual dress; cocktails. **Parking:** on-site. **Cards:** MC, VI.

🍴 ⊠

──────── *The following restaurant has not been evaluated by AAA* ────────
but is listed for your information only.

THE BROWN TROUT

[fyi]

Phone: 231/238-9441

Not evaluated. **Location:** I-75, exit 310, 0.3 mi w, then 1.8 mi s on Old US 27. 4653 S Straits Hwy 49749. **Features:** Just south of town, the restaurant serves steaks, fresh seafood and prime rib in an up-north atmosphere.

IONIA

──────── **WHERE TO STAY** ────────

SUPER 8 MOTEL

AAA SAVE
▽▽ ▽▽
Small-scale Hotel

Book at aaa.com

Phone: (616)527-2828

All Year   1P: $55-$65   2P: $62-$75   XP: $7   F18
Location: I-96, exit 67 (SR 66). 7245 S State Rd 48846. Fax: 616/527-0729. **Facility:** 73 one-bedroom standard units, some with whirlpools. 2 stories (no elevator), interior corridors. **Parking:** on-site. **Terms:** [CP] meal plan available, small pets only. **Amenities:** *Some:* irons, hair dryers. **Business Services:** meeting rooms. **Cards:** AX, DC, DS, MC, VI. **Special Amenities:** free continental breakfast and free local telephone calls.

SOME UNITS
🐾 ⁅↕⁆ ♿M ⊘ 🎦 [DATA PORT] / ⊠ 🅱 ▣ /

IRON MOUNTAIN pop. 8,154

──────── **WHERE TO STAY** ────────

BUDGET HOST INN

AAA SAVE
▽▽
Motel

Phone: (906)774-6797

All Year   1P: $39-$43   2P: $49-$55   XP: $5   F10
Location: 1.5 mi nw on US 2 and 141. Located in a recreational area. 1663 N Stephenson Ave 49801. Fax: 906/774-6910. **Facility:** 19 one-bedroom standard units, some with kitchens. 1 story, exterior corridors. **Parking:** on-site, winter plug-ins. **Terms:** cancellation fee imposed, [CP] meal plan available, small pets only ($5 extra charge, in designated units). **Leisure Activities:** snowmobiling. **Cards:** AX, DS, MC, VI. **Special Amenities:** free continental breakfast and free local telephone calls.

SOME UNITS
[S/D] 🐾 ⁅↕⁆ [DATA PORT] / ⊠ 🅱 🖃 /
FEE

COMFORT INN

AAA SAVE
▽▽ ▽▽
Small-scale Hotel

Book at aaa.com

Phone: (906)774-5505

All Year [ECP]   1P: $49-$69   2P: $59-$79   XP: $7   F18
Location: 1.3 mi nw on US 2. Located next to a bowling alley/lounge. 1555 N Stephenson Ave 49801 (PO Box 807). Fax: 906/774-2631. **Facility:** 48 one-bedroom standard units. 2 stories (no elevator), interior corridors. **Parking:** on-site, winter plug-ins. **Amenities:** high-speed Internet (fee), irons, hair dryers. **Leisure Activities:** whirlpool, snowmobiling. **Guest Services:** coin laundry. **Business Services:** meeting rooms. **Cards:** AX, CB, DC, DS, JC, MC, VI. **Special Amenities:** free expanded continental breakfast and free local telephone calls.

SOME UNITS
[S/D] ⁅↕⁆ [DATA PORT] ▣ / ⊠ 🅱 🖃 /

DAYS INN *Book at aaa.com*
Phone: (906)774-2181

Small-scale Hotel

All Year 1P: $50-$120 2P: $55-$125 XP: $5 F17
Location: 1.8 mi e on US 2. Located in a commercial area. W8176 S US 2 49801. Fax: 906/774-8252. **Facility:** 43 one-bedroom standard units, some with whirlpools. 1-2 stories (no elevator), interior/exterior corridors. **Parking:** on-site, winter plug-ins. **Terms:** weekly rates available, [ECP] meal plan available, pets ($6 extra charge). **Amenities:** hair dryers. **Pool(s):** heated indoor. **Leisure Activities:** whirlpool, snowmobiling. **Guest Services:** valet laundry. **Business Services:** meeting rooms. **Cards:** AX, CB, DC, DS, MC, VI. *(See color ad card insert)*

SOME UNITS
ASK SD 🐾 🍴 🛏 📷 DATA PORT / ✕ 🔌 🖥 /
FEE

GUESTHOUSE INN
Phone: (906)774-6220

Small-scale Hotel

All Year 1P: $50 2P: $50 XP: $5 F12
Location: 1 mi e on US 2. Located in a commercial area. 1609 S Stephenson Ave 49801. Fax: 906/776-1236. **Facility:** 63 one-bedroom standard units. 2 stories (no elevator), interior/exterior corridors. *Bath:* combo or shower only. **Parking:** on-site. **Terms:** cancellation fee imposed, package plans, pets (in designated units). **Amenities:** safes (fee). **Leisure Activities:** snowmobiling. *Fee:* game room. **Business Services:** meeting rooms. **Cards:** AX, CB, DC, DS, MC, VI.

SOME UNITS
ASK SD 🐾 🍴 🖥 / ✕ 🔌 🖥 /

SUPER 8 MOTEL *Book at aaa.com*
Phone: 906/774-3400

Small-scale Hotel

All Year 1P: $54-$70 2P: $60-$70 XP: $7 F17
Location: 2 mi nw on US 2 and 141. 2702 N Stephenson Ave 49801. Fax: 906/744-9903. **Facility:** 91 units. 82 one-bedroom standard units, some with whirlpools. 9 one-bedroom suites ($76-$105). 2 stories (no elevator), interior corridors. **Parking:** on-site, winter plug-ins. **Terms:** [CP] meal plan available, pets (in designated units). **Amenities:** *Some:* hair dryers. **Pool(s):** heated indoor. **Leisure Activities:** sauna, whirlpool, snowmobiling. *Fee:* game room. **Guest Services:** coin laundry. **Business Services:** meeting rooms. **Cards:** AX, DC, DS, MC, VI.

SOME UNITS
ASK SD 🐾 🛏 ✕ 📷 DATA PORT / ✕ 🔌 🖥 🖥 /

———— WHERE TO DINE ————

FONTANA'S SUPPER CLUB
Dinner: $9-$23 Phone: 906/774-0044

Italian

MC, VI.

Location: On US 2; center. 115 S Stephenson Ave 49801. **Hours:** 5 pm-10 pm, Mon-9 pm. Closed: 11/25, 12/25; also Sun. **Features:** Noted for charbroiled steaks and homemade Italian dishes, the restaurant is a favorite spot for casual, intimate dining. Attractive paintings and soft background music set a romantic tone in the casually upscale dining room. Casual dress; cocktails. **Parking:** on-site. **Cards:** AX, DC, DS,

🍸 ✕

———— *The following restaurants have not been evaluated by AAA* ————
but are listed for your information only.

GREAT NORTHERN BUFFET
Phone: 906/779-1575

[fyi] Not evaluated. **Location:** On US 2; center. 1052 S Stephenson Ave 49801. **Features:** The popular family restaurant offers travelers a chance to make a quick stop for reasonably priced eats.

HIRSCH'S WEST
Phone: 906/776-2407

[fyi] Not evaluated. **Location:** Just s on US 141 from jct US 2. 7820 W Breitaing Catoss Rd 49801. **Features:** Just west of town you'll find this pub-type steakhouse that also serves pizzas and sandwiches; an Italian buffet is available on Wednesday nights.

IRON RIVER pop. 1,929

———— WHERE TO STAY ————

AMERICINN OF IRON RIVER *Book at aaa.com*
Phone: (906)265-9100

Small-scale Hotel

12/15-3/31 1P: $95-$130 2P: $100-$138 XP: $6 F12
4/1-12/14 1P: $74-$130 2P: $80-$134 XP: $6 F12
Location: On US 2; downtown. Located on the banks of Iron River. 40 E Adams St 49935 (PO Box 308). Fax: 906/265-4244. **Facility:** 66 units. 63 one-bedroom standard units, some with whirlpools. 3 one-bedroom suites ($100-$120), some with whirlpools. 3 stories, interior corridors. *Bath:* combo or shower only. **Parking:** on-site, winter plug-ins. **Terms:** cancellation fee imposed, [ECP] meal plan available. **Amenities:** hair dryers. *Some:* irons. **Pool(s):** heated indoor. **Leisure Activities:** sauna, whirlpool, snowmobiling, exercise room. **Guest Services:** coin laundry. **Business Services:** meeting rooms. **Cards:** AX, DC, DS, MC, VI. *(See color ad p 311)*

SOME UNITS
🍴 ♿ 🛏 ✕ DATA PORT 🖥 / ✕ 🔌 🖥 /

———— WHERE TO DINE ————

———— *The following restaurant has not been evaluated by AAA* ————
but is listed for your information only.

THE DEPOT
Phone: 906/265-6341

[fyi] Not evaluated. **Location:** Just s on SR 189; center. 50 4th Ave 49935. **Features:** Just south of town you'll find this restaurant that is popular with couples and families.

IRONWOOD pop. 6,293

——— WHERE TO STAY ———

AMERICINN OF IRONWOOD   Book at aaa.com   Phone: (906)932-7200
AAA SAVE

	12/15-3/31 [ECP]	1P: $99-$129	2P: $99-$129	XP: $6	F17
	6/11-9/5 [ECP]	1P: $89-$109	2P: $89-$109	XP: $6	F17
	9/6-12/14 [ECP]	1P: $79-$99	2P: $79-$99	XP: $6	F17
	4/1-6/10 [ECP]	1P: $69-$79	2P: $69-$79	XP: $6	F17

Small-scale Hotel **Location:** 0.8 mi e on US 2. Located in a commercial area. 1117 E Cloverland Dr 49938. Fax: 906/932-7222. **Facility:** 49 one-bedroom standard units, some with whirlpools. 2 stories (no elevator), interior corridors. *Bath:* combo or shower only. **Parking:** on-site, winter plug-ins. **Terms:** cancellation fee imposed. **Amenities:** hair dryers. *Some:* irons. **Pool(s):** heated indoor. **Leisure Activities:** sauna, whirlpool, snowmobiling, limited exercise equipment. **Business Services:** meeting rooms. **Cards:** AX, DS, MC, VI. **Special Amenities:** free expanded continental breakfast and free local telephone calls. *(See color ad p 311)*

SOME UNITS

COMFORT INN   Book at aaa.com   Phone: (906)932-2224

| | All Year [ECP] | 1P: $66-$200 | 2P: $72-$200 | XP: $6 | F18 |

Small-scale Hotel **Location:** Jct US 2 and US 2 business route. Located in a commercial area. 210 E Cloverland Dr 49938. Fax: 906/932-9929. **Facility:** 63 one-bedroom standard units, some with whirlpools. 2 stories (no elevator), interior corridors. **Parking:** on-site, winter plug-ins. **Amenities:** irons, hair dryers. **Pool(s):** heated indoor. **Leisure Activities:** whirlpool, snowmobiling. **Guest Services:** valet laundry. **Business Services:** meeting rooms. **Cards:** AX, DC, DS, MC, VI.

SOME UNITS

CRESTVIEW MOTEL   Phone: (906)932-4845
AAA SAVE

| | All Year | 1P: $35-$65 | 2P: $45-$75 | XP: $5 | F12 |

Motel **Location:** West edge. Located in a commercial area. US 2 49938. Fax: 906/932-4845. **Facility:** 12 one-bedroom standard units. 1 story, exterior corridors. **Parking:** on-site, winter plug-ins. **Terms:** pets ($10 extra charge). **Leisure Activities:** sauna, snowmobiling. **Guest Services:** coin laundry. **Cards:** MC, VI. **Special Amenities:** free local telephone calls and early check-in/late check-out.

SOME UNITS
FEE   FEE

ROYAL MOTEL   Phone: (906)932-4230
AAA SAVE

| | 12/1-3/31 | 1P: $36-$41 | 2P: $41-$46 | XP: $5 | |
| | 4/1-11/30 | 1P: $36 | 2P: $41 | XP: $5 | |

Motel **Location:** 1 mi w on US 2. Located in a semi-commercial area. 715 W Cloverland Dr 49938. **Facility:** 16 one-bedroom standard units. 1 story, exterior corridors. **Parking:** on-site, winter plug-ins. **Terms:** 2 night minimum stay - weekends in winter, 7 day cancellation notice-fee imposed, small pets only (in smoking units). **Leisure Activities:** snowmobiling. **Cards:** DS, MC, VI.

SOME UNITS

SUPER 8 MOTEL   Book at aaa.com   Phone: 906/932-3395

| | 12/18-3/31 [ECP] | 1P: $78-$98 | 2P: $88-$108 | XP: $10 | F14 |
| | 4/1-12/17 [ECP] | 1P: $58-$68 | 2P: $65-$88 | XP: $10 | F14 |

Motel **Location:** Jct US 2 and US 2 business route. Located in a commercial area. 160 E Cloverland Dr 49938. Fax: 906/932-2507. **Facility:** 42 one-bedroom standard units, some with whirlpools. 2 stories (no elevator), interior corridors. **Parking:** on-site, winter plug-ins. **Terms:** pets ($25 deposit, in designated units). **Amenities:** *Some:* irons, hair dryers. **Leisure Activities:** sauna, whirlpool, snowmobiling. **Cards:** AX, CB, DC, DS, MC, VI.

SOME UNITS
FEE

——— WHERE TO DINE ———

——— *The following restaurants have not been evaluated by AAA* ———
but are listed for your information only.

DON & GG'S   Phone: 906/932-2312
[fyi]   Not evaluated. **Location:** 0.9 mi e on US 2. 1300 Cloverland Dr 49938. **Features:** This friendly neighborhood restaurant and bar is right off the main highway, and a great place to stop for their salads and nightly specials.

THE ELK & HOUND   Phone: 906/932-3742
[fyi]   Not evaluated. **Location:** 2.5 mi e on US 2, 0.3 mi s. Country Club Rd 49938. **Features:** You have to go east of town for this restaruant which has a number of lunch and dinner specials. Pizza available nightly.

TACCONELLI'S   Phone: 906/932-2101
[fyi]   Not evaluated. **Location:** Center. 215 S Suffolk St 49938. **Features:** Located downtown this casual family restaurant has a number of mouth watering items on their menu from handcut steaks, to seafood, to a wide array of pasta.

ISHPEMING pop. 6,686

―――――― WHERE TO STAY ――――――

BEST WESTERN COUNTRY INN   *Book at aaa.com*   Phone: (906)485-6345

(AAA) (SAVE)
6/2-9/1	1P: $77-$95	2P: $82-$100	XP: $5	F17
1/1-3/31	1P: $72-$90	2P: $82-$100	XP: $5	F17
4/1-6/1	1P: $67-$85	2P: $72-$90	XP: $5	F17
9/2-12/31	1P: $70-$79	2P: $75-$84	XP: $5	F17

Small-scale Hotel **Location:** On US 41, just n of town. Located next to outdoor mall. 850 US 41 W 49849 (1035 Country Ln, # 281). Fax: 906/485-6348. **Facility:** 60 one-bedroom standard units, some with whirlpools. 2 stories (no elevator), interior corridors. **Parking:** on-site, winter plug-ins. **Terms:** [BP] meal plan available, small pets only (in smoking units). **Amenities:** irons, hair dryers. **Dining:** 6 am-10 pm, Fri & Sat-11 pm, cocktails. **Pool(s):** heated indoor. **Leisure Activities:** whirlpool, snowmobiling. *Fee:* game room. **Cards:** CB, DC, DS, MC, VI. **Special Amenities: free newspaper and early check-in/late check-out.**

SOME UNITS
(icons)

BEST WESTERN JASPER RIDGE INN   *Book at aaa.com*   Phone: (906)485-2378

(AAA) (SAVE)
1/1-3/31	1P: $93-$115	2P: $98-$120	XP: $5	F17
9/2-12/31	1P: $88-$110	2P: $93-$115	XP: $5	F17
6/2-9/1	1P: $81-$103	2P: $86-$108	XP: $5	F17
4/1-6/1	1P: $73-$91	2P: $78-$96	XP: $5	F17

Small-scale Hotel **Location:** Off US 41, just n of town. Located behind an outdoor mall. 1000 River Pkwy 49849 (1035 Country Ln, # 316). Fax: 906/485-5176. **Facility:** 26 one-bedroom standard units, some with whirlpools. 2 stories (no elevator), interior corridors. **Parking:** on-site. **Terms:** [CP] meal plan available. **Amenities:** irons, hair dryers. *Some:* dual phone lines. **Leisure Activities:** snowmobiling. **Business Services:** meeting rooms. **Cards:** CB, DC, DS, MC, VI. **Special Amenities: free continental breakfast and free newspaper.**

SOME UNITS
(icons)

―――――― WHERE TO DINE ――――――

JASPER RIDGE BREWERY   **Lunch:** $4-$8   **Dinner:** $8-$18   **Phone:** 906/485-6017

(AAA)   **Location:** Off US 41, just n of town. 1035 Country Ln 49849. **Hours:** 11 am-11 pm; hours may vary. Closed: 12/25. **Features:** Within walking distance of several area lodgings, the new brew pub pairs a number of traditional dishes with freshly brewed beer. Casual dress; cocktails. **Parking:** on-site. **Cards:** DS, MC, VI.

American
(icons)

ISLE ROYALE NATIONAL PARK

―――――― WHERE TO STAY ――――――

ROCK HARBOR LODGE   Phone: (906)337-4993

(AAA) (SAVE)
5/28-9/10	1P: $158-$173	2P: $178-$276	XP: $92 D12

Location: Northeast end of island; accessible by boat only. Located on Lake Superior. (PO Box 605, HOUGHTON). Fax: 906/337-4993. **Facility:** An exceptionally scenic wilderness island is the setting for this lodge. 80 one-bedroom standard units, some with efficiencies (no utensils). 2 stories, exterior corridors. *Bath:* combo or shower only. **Parking:** on-site. **Terms:** open 5/28-9/10, check-in 4 pm, 5 day cancellation notice. **Dining:** 2 restaurants, 7 am-8:30, noon-1:30 & 5:30-7:30 pm, wine/beer only. **Leisure Activities:** rental boats, rental canoes, marina, fishing, hiking trails. *Fee:* guides & boat tours of island. **Guest Services:** gift shop, coin laundry. **Business Services:** meeting rooms. **Cards:** AX, DS, MC, VI.

Resort Motel
SOME UNITS
(icons)

JACKSON pop. 36,316

―――――― WHERE TO STAY ――――――

BAYMONT INN-JACKSON   *Book at aaa.com*   Phone: 517/789-6000

                                     Property failed to provide current rates
Location: I-94, exit 138, just nw. 2035 Service Dr 49202. Fax: 517/782-6836. **Facility:** 67 one-bedroom standard units. 2 stories (no elevator), interior corridors. **Parking:** on-site. **Amenities:** video games (fee), voice mail, irons, hair dryers. **Guest Services:** valet laundry.

Small-scale Hotel
SOME UNITS
(icons)

COMFORT INN & SUITES   *Book at aaa.com*   Phone: (517)768-0088

All Year	1P: $80-$150	2P: $90-$150	XP: $5	F18

Location: I-94, exit 138, just n. 2435 Shirley Dr 49202. Fax: 517/768-4188. **Facility:** 70 one-bedroom standard units, some with whirlpools. 3 stories, interior corridors. *Bath:* combo or shower only. **Parking:** on-site. **Terms:** cancellation fee imposed, [ECP] meal plan available, package plans. **Amenities:** dual phone lines, voice mail, safes, irons, hair dryers. **Pool(s):** heated indoor. **Leisure Activities:** whirlpool, exercise room. **Guest Services:** valet and coin laundry. **Business Services:** meeting rooms. **Cards:** AX, CB, DC, DS, JC, MC, VI.

Small-scale Hotel
SOME UNITS
(icons)

COUNTRY HEARTH INN   *Book at aaa.com*   Phone: (517)783-6404

All Year [ECP]	1P: $68	2P: $68

Location: I-94, exit 138, just sw. Located adjacent to a shopping mall. 111 Boardman Rd 49202. Fax: 517/783-6529. **Facility:** 73 one-bedroom standard units. 2 stories (no elevator), exterior corridors. **Parking:** on-site. **Guest Services:** valet laundry. **Cards:** AX, CB, DC, DS, JC, MC, VI.

Motel
SOME UNITS
(icons)

FAIRFIELD INN

Book at aaa.com

Phone: (517)784-7877

All Year   1P: $69-$89   2P: $69-$89   XP: $6   F18

Small-scale Hotel

Location: I-94, exit 138, just ne. 2395 Shirley Dr 49202. Fax: 517/784-7877. **Facility:** 57 one-bedroom standard units. 3 stories, interior corridors. **Parking:** on-site. **Terms:** [ECP] meal plan available. **Amenities:** irons. **Pool(s):** heated outdoor. **Leisure Activities:** whirlpool. **Guest Services:** valet laundry. **Cards:** AX, CB, DC, DS, MC, VI.

SOME UNITS

HAMPTON INN-JACKSON

Book at aaa.com

Phone: (517)789-5151

All Year   1P: $69-$89   2P: $69-$89   XP: $6   F18

Small-scale Hotel

Location: I-94, exit 138, just ne. 2225 Shirley Dr 49202. Fax: 517/783-8696. **Facility:** 64 one-bedroom standard units. 3 stories, interior corridors. *Bath:* combo or shower only. **Parking:** on-site. **Terms:** [ECP] meal plan available. **Amenities:** dual phone lines, voice mail, irons, hair dryers. **Pool(s):** heated indoor. **Leisure Activities:** whirlpool. **Guest Services:** valet laundry. **Cards:** AX, CB, DC, DS, MC, VI.

SOME UNITS

HOLIDAY INN

Book at aaa.com

Phone: (517)783-2681

All Year   1P: $76-$121   2P: $76-$121

Small-scale Hotel

Location: I-94, exit 138, just nw. 2000 Holiday Inn Dr 49202. Fax: 517/783-5744. **Facility:** 184 one-bedroom standard units. 2 stories (no elevator), interior/exterior corridors. *Bath:* combo or shower only. **Parking:** on-site. **Terms:** check-in 4 pm, [AP] meal plan available, pets ($15 extra charge). **Amenities:** dual phone lines, voice mail, irons, hair dryers. **Pool(s):** heated indoor. **Leisure Activities:** whirlpool, putting green, miniature golf, playground, exercise room. **Fee:** game room. **Guest Services:** valet and coin laundry. **Business Services:** meeting rooms. **Cards:** AX, CB, DC, DS, JC, MC, VI.

SOME UNITS

FEE   FEE FEE

MOTEL 6 - 1088

Book at aaa.com

Phone: 517 789-7186

5/27-3/31   1P: $41-$51   2P: $47-$57   XP: $3   F17

4/1-5/26   1P: $39-$49   2P: $45-$55   XP: $3   F17

Motel

Location: I-94, exit 138, just se. 830 Royal Dr 49202. Fax: 517/789-5490. **Facility:** 96 one-bedroom standard units. 1 story, exterior corridors. *Bath:* combo or shower only. **Parking:** on-site. **Terms:** small pets only. **Guest Services:** coin laundry. **Cards:** AX, CB, DC, DS, MC, VI.

SOME UNITS

———— WHERE TO DINE ————

BELLA NOTTE RISTORANTE   Lunch: $7-$9   Dinner: $8-$15   Phone: 517/782-5727

Italian

Location: Downtown. 137 W Michigan Ave 49201. **Hours:** 11 am-10 pm, Fri-11 pm, Sat 4 pm-11 pm. Closed major holidays; also Sun. **Reservations:** accepted. **Features:** The soft glow of carriage lights illuminates hand-painted murals and creates a romantic courtyard setting in which guests dine on varied Italian-American dishes. Sauteed Michigan whitefish with pistachio risotto and fettuccine Alfredo grace a menu that also lists pizza and panini. Dressy casual; cocktails. **Parking:** street. **Cards:** AX, DC, MC, VI.

DARYL'S DOWNTOWN   Lunch: $8-$12   Dinner: $12-$23   Phone: 517/782-1895

American

Location: Downtown. 151 W Michigan 49201. **Hours:** 11 am-11 pm, Fri & Sat-midnight. Closed major holidays; also Sun. **Features:** A downtown storefront location, this large open space is warmed with the use of hardwood floors, soft wood accents, Tiffany lamps and a large fish tank near the kitchen. A good size menu of favorites from steak to seafood are well prepared and creatively presented. Dressy casual; cocktails. **Parking:** on-site and street. **Cards:** AX, MC, VI.

FINLEY'S AMERICAN RESTAURANT   Lunch: $6-$9   Dinner: $7-$15   Phone: 517/787-7440

American

Location: On I-94 business route; corner Michigan Ave and Brown St. 1602 W Michigan Ave 49201. **Hours:** 11 am-10 pm, Fri & Sat-11 pm; to 7 pm 12/24. **Closed:** 12/25. **Features:** Residing near Westwood Mall, this restaurant offers a wide variety of predictable menu items including char grilled steak, baby back ribs and seafood combinations. Casual dress; cocktails. **Parking:** on-site. **Cards:** AX, DC, DS, MC, VI.

GILBERT'S STEAK HOUSE   Lunch: $7-$9   Dinner: $10-$18   Phone: 517/782-7135

Steak & Seafood

Location: Jct I-94 and US 127, exit 138 N, 0.3 mi to Springport exit off US 127. 2323 Shirley Dr 49202. **Hours:** 11 am-10 pm, Fri & Sat-11 pm, Sun noon-7 pm. Closed major holidays. **Features:** Since 1946, this once quaint log cabin, serves a wide selection of steak and seafood items including USDA choice steaks, extra thick lamb chops, fried frog legs and stuffed flounder. The dining room boasts a collection of over 80 antique stained glass lamps and other memorabilia. Casual dress; cocktails. **Parking:** on-site. **Cards:** AX, DC, DS, MC, VI.

KALAMAZOO pop. 77,145

———— WHERE TO STAY ————

BAYMONT INN & SUITES-KALAMAZOO

Book at aaa.com

Phone: (269)372-7999

All Year   1P: $99-$129   2P: $109-$149   XP: $10   F

Small-scale Hotel

Location: US 131, exit 36B (Stadium Dr), just w. 2203 S 11th St 49009. Fax: 269/372-6095. **Facility:** 86 units. 83 one-bedroom standard units, some with whirlpools. 3 one-bedroom suites. 4 stories, interior corridors. **Parking:** on-site. **Terms:** [ECP] meal plan available. **Amenities:** video games (fee), voice mail, irons, hair dryers. **Guest Services:** valet and coin laundry. **Cards:** AX, DC, DS, MC, VI.

SOME UNITS

FEE FEE

BEST WESTERN HOSPITALITY INN

Book at aaa.com

Phone: (269)381-1900

AAA SAVE

10/1-3/31 [ECP]	1P: $69-$99	2P: $79-$109	XP: $10 F18
4/1-9/30 [ECP]	1P: $59-$89	2P: $69-$99	XP: $10 F18

Location: I-94, exit 80, just nw. 3640 E Cork St 49001. **Fax:** 269/373-6136. **Facility:** 124 one-bedroom standard units. 3 stories, interior corridors. **Parking:** on-site. **Amenities:** irons, hair dryers. *Fee:* video games, high-speed Internet. **Pool(s):** heated indoor. **Leisure Activities:** sauna, whirlpool, exercise room. **Guest Services:** valet and coin laundry. **Business Services:** meeting rooms. **Cards:** AX, DC, DS, MC, VI.
Special Amenities: free expanded continental breakfast and early check-in/late check-out.

Small-scale Hotel

SOME UNITS

CLARION HOTEL

Book at aaa.com

Phone: (269)385-3922

AAA SAVE

All Year 1P: $59-$169 2P: $69-$179 XP: $7 F12

Location: I-94, exit 80, just n. 3600 E Cork St 49001. **Fax:** 269/385-2747. **Facility:** 156 one-bedroom standard units, some with whirlpools. 6 stories, interior corridors. **Parking:** on-site. **Terms:** [BP] & [MAP] meal plans available, small pets only. **Amenities:** voice mail, irons, hair dryers. **Dining:** 6 am-midnight. **Pool(s):** heated indoor. **Leisure Activities:** sauna, whirlpool, exercise room. *Fee:* game room. **Guest Services:** valet laundry. **Business Services:** conference facilities, business center. **Cards:** AX, DC, DS, MC, VI.

Small-scale Hotel

SOME UNITS

COMFORT INN

Book at aaa.com

Phone: (269)381-7000

AAA SAVE

All Year 1P: $80-$150 2P: $80-$150 XP: $10 F17

Location: I-94, exit 80, 0.3 mi s. 3820 Sprinkle Rd 49001. **Fax:** 269/381-5334. **Facility:** 52 one-bedroom standard units, some with whirlpools. 3 stories, interior corridors. *Bath:* combo or shower only. **Parking:** on-site. **Amenities:** dual phone lines, voice mail, irons, hair dryers. **Pool(s):** small heated indoor. **Guest Services:** valet laundry. **Business Services:** meeting rooms. **Cards:** AX, DC, DS, MC, VI.

Small-scale Hotel

SOME UNITS

COUNTRY INN & SUITES BY CARLSON

Book at aaa.com

Phone: (269)382-2303

AAA SAVE

All Year [ECP] 1P: $77-$89 2P: $77-$89 XP: $10 F12

Location: I-94, exit 78, just se. 1912 E Kilgore Rd 49002. **Fax:** 269/381-0032. **Facility:** 81 units. 46 one-bedroom standard units, some with whirlpools. 35 one-bedroom suites ($89-$139). 2 stories, interior corridors. *Bath:* combo or shower only. **Parking:** on-site. **Amenities:** voice mail, irons, hair dryers. **Pool(s):** heated indoor. **Leisure Activities:** whirlpool, exercise room. **Guest Services:** valet and coin laundry. **Business Services:** meeting rooms. **Cards:** AX, DC, DS, MC, VI. **Special Amenities:** free local telephone calls and free newspaper. *(See color ad p 313)*

Small-scale Hotel

SOME UNITS

FAIRFIELD INN BY MARRIOTT

Book at aaa.com

Phone: (269)344-8300

All Year [ECP] 1P: $49-$89 2P: $49-$89

Location: I-94, exit 80, just nw. 3800 E Cork St 49001. **Fax:** 269/344-8300. **Facility:** 133 one-bedroom standard units. 3 stories, interior/exterior corridors. *Bath:* combo or shower only. **Parking:** on-site. **Amenities:** irons. **Pool(s):** heated outdoor. **Guest Services:** valet laundry. **Cards:** AX, DC, DS, MC, VI.

Small-scale Hotel

SOME UNITS

FAIRFIELD INN-WEST

Phone: (269)353-6400

All Year [ECP] 1P: $79-$89 2P: $79-$89

Location: I-94, exit 72, just e. 6420 Cracker Barrel Dr 49009. **Fax:** 269/353-0680. **Facility:** 62 one-bedroom standard units, some with whirlpools. 3 stories, interior corridors. *Bath:* combo or shower only. **Parking:** on-site. **Terms:** cancellation fee imposed. **Amenities:** irons. **Pool(s):** heated indoor. **Leisure Activities:** whirlpool, exercise room. **Guest Services:** valet laundry. **Cards:** AX, DC, DS, MC, VI.

Small-scale Hotel

SOME UNITS

HALL HOUSE BED & BREAKFAST

Phone: (269)343-2500

All Year [CP] 2P: $79-$155 XP: $15

Location: US 131, exit 38A, 2.9 mi e on W Main St, then just s. 106 Thompson St 49006. **Fax:** 269/343-1374. **Facility:** Set on a wooded hillside near downtown, this 1923 Georgian Revival inn offers themed rooms. Smoke free premises. 6 units. 4 one-bedroom standard units, some with whirlpools. 2 one-bedroom suites. 3 stories (no elevator), interior corridors. *Bath:* combo or shower only. **Parking:** on-site. **Terms:** check-in 4:30 pm, age restrictions may apply, 5 day cancellation notice-fee imposed, [BP] meal plan available. **Amenities:** video library. *Some:* CD players. **Cards:** AX, MC, VI.

Historic Bed & Breakfast

SOME UNITS

HAMPTON INN

Book at aaa.com

Phone: (269)344-7774

All Year 1P: $75-$95 2P: $75-$95 XP: $6 F18

Location: I-94, exit 78, just w. 1550 E Kilgore Rd 49001. **Fax:** 269/344-9447. **Facility:** 64 one-bedroom standard units. 3 stories, interior corridors. *Bath:* combo or shower only. **Parking:** on-site. **Terms:** [ECP] meal plan available. **Amenities:** voice mail, irons. **Pool(s):** small heated indoor. **Leisure Activities:** whirlpool. **Guest Services:** valet laundry. **Cards:** AX, CB, DC, DS, MC, VI.

Small-scale Hotel

SOME UNITS
FEE FEE FEE

HAMPTON INN & SUITES

Phone: (269)372-1010

All Year 1P: $89-$159

Location: I-94, exit 72, 0.5 mi n. 5059 S 9th St 49009. **Fax:** 269/372-1475. **Facility:** 78 one-bedroom standard units, some with whirlpools. 3 stories, interior corridors. *Bath:* combo or shower only. **Parking:** on-site. **Terms:** [ECP] meal plan available. **Amenities:** video games (fee), voice mail, irons, hair dryers. *Some:* dual phone lines. **Pool(s):** heated indoor. **Leisure Activities:** whirlpool, exercise room. **Guest Services:** sundries, valet and coin laundry. **Business Services:** meeting rooms, business center. **Cards:** AX, CB, DC, DS, MC, VI.

Small-scale Hotel

SOME UNITS

HAWTHORN SUITES   *Book at aaa.com*   Phone: (269)353-2547

▼▼▼▼

Small-scale Hotel

All Year   1P: $109-$169   2P: $109-$169
Location: US 131, exit 36B, just w. 2575 S 11th St 49009. Fax: 269/353-2548. **Facility:** 64 one-bedroom standard units, some with whirlpools. 4 stories, interior corridors. *Bath:* combo or shower only. **Parking:** on-site. **Terms:** weekly rates available, [BP] meal plan available. **Amenities:** video library (fee), high-speed Internet, dual phone lines, voice mail; irons, hair dryers. **Pool(s):** heated indoor. **Leisure Activities:** whirlpool, exercise room. **Guest Services:** sundries. **Business Services:** meeting rooms, business center. **Cards:** AX, CB, DC, MC, VI.

SOME UNITS

(ASK) (S🄳) (T⥮+) (⛊M) (⬩) (⚤) (VCR) (🎥) (DATA PORT) (🛏) (📺) (📷) / (⊠) /

HOLIDAY INN EXPRESS HOTEL & SUITES   *Book at aaa.com*   Phone: (269)373-0770

▼▼▼▼

Small-scale Hotel

All Year [ECP]   1P: $65-$130   2P: $75-$140
Location: I-94, exit 80, just n. 3630 E Cork St 49001. Fax: 269/373-0773. **Facility:** 64 units. 49 one-bedroom standard units, some with efficiencies and/or whirlpools. 15 one-bedroom suites, some with efficiencies. 3 stories, interior corridors. *Bath:* combo or shower only. **Parking:** on-site. **Amenities:** dual phone lines, voice mail, irons, hair dryers. **Pool(s):** heated indoor. **Leisure Activities:** exercise room. **Guest Services:** valet laundry. **Business Services:** meeting rooms, business center. **Cards:** AX, DC, DS, MC, VI.

SOME UNITS

(ASK) (S🄳) (✈) (T⥮+) (⬩) (⚤) (🎥) (DATA PORT) (📺) / (⊠) (🛏) (📷) /

HOLIDAY INN-WEST   *Book at aaa.com*   Phone: (269)375-6000

▼▼▼▼

Small-scale Hotel

All Year   1P: $119-$129
Location: US 131, exit 36B, just w. 2747 S 11th St 49009. Fax: 269/375-1220. **Facility:** 186 one-bedroom standard units. 4 stories, interior corridors. *Bath:* combo or shower only. **Parking:** on-site. **Terms:** check-in 4 pm, [AP] meal plan available. **Amenities:** voice mail, irons, hair dryers. **Pool(s):** heated indoor. **Leisure Activities:** sauna, whirlpool, putting green, exercise room. *Fee:* game room. **Guest Services:** valet and coin laundry, area transportation. **Business Services:** meeting rooms, fax. **Cards:** AX, DC, DS, MC, VI.

SOME UNITS

(ASK) (S🄳) (✈) (T⥮) (⛊M) (♿) (⊘) (⚤) (✗) (🎥) (DATA PORT) (📺) / (⊠) (VCR) (🛏) /
FEE FEE

KNIGHTS INN   *Book at aaa.com*   Phone: (269)381-5000

(AAA) (SAVE)
▼▼▼
Motel

All Year   1P: $40-$70   2P: $50-$80
Location: I-94, exit 76B, 3 mi n, w on Park Place, then just s. 1211 S Westnedge Ave 49008. Fax: 269/344-2061. **Facility:** 55 one-bedroom standard units. 2 stories, interior/exterior corridors. *Bath:* shower only. **Parking:** on-site. **Terms:** pets ($25 deposit). **Guest Services:** valet laundry. **Cards:** AX, CB, DC, DS, JC, MC, VI. **Special Amenities:** free continental breakfast and free local telephone calls.
(See color ad below)

SOME UNITS

(S🄳) (🐾) (🎥) / (⊠) (🛏) (📷) /
FEE

RADISSON PLAZA HOTEL   *Book at aaa.com*   Phone: 269/343-3333

(AAA) (SAVE)
▼▼▼▼

Large-scale Hotel

1/1-3/31   1P: $179-$189   2P: $189-$199   XP: $10
4/1-12/31   1P: $169-$179   2P: $179-$189   XP: $10
Location: Jct Michigan Ave and Rose St; downtown. Located in a historic area. 100 W Michigan Ave 49007. Fax: 269/381-1560. **Facility:** Currently under renovation, this stylish hotel is in town and within walking distance of the shops of the Kalamazoo Mall. 276 units. 265 one-bedroom standard units. 11 one-bedroom suites ($199-$1200), some with kitchens and/or whirlpools. 9 stories, interior corridors. *Bath:* combo or shower only. **Parking:** on-site (fee) and valet. **Terms:** check-in 4 pm, [AP] meal plan available. **Amenities:** video games (fee), voice mail, irons, hair dryers. *Some:* CD players. **Dining:** 3 restaurants, 6:30 am-12:30 am, cocktails, also, Webster's, see separate listing, entertainment. **Pool(s):** heated indoor. **Leisure Activities:** saunas, whirlpool. **Guest Services:** gift shop, valet laundry, tanning facility. **Business Services:** conference facilities, business center. **Cards:** AX, CB, DC, DS, JC, MC, VI. **Special Amenities:** free local telephone calls and free newspaper. *(See color ad p 313 & ad p 335)*

SOME UNITS

(✈) (T⥮) (⬩) (⊘) (⚤) (🕳) (🎥) (DATA PORT) (📺) / (⊠) (VCR) (🛏) (📷) /
FEE FEE

RED ROOF INN-EAST   *Book at aaa.com*   Phone: (269)382-6350

(AAA) (SAVE)

	5/24-10/2	1P: $52-$69	2P: $58-$69	XP: $6	F18
	10/3-3/31	1P: $43-$54	2P: $49-$54	XP: $6	F18
	4/1-5/23	1P: $42-$53	2P: $48-$53	XP: $6	F18

Motel

Location: I-94, exit 80, just nw. 3701 E Cork St 49001. Fax: 269/382-6354. **Facility:** 79 one-bedroom standard units. 2 stories (no elevator), exterior corridors. *Bath:* combo or shower only. **Parking:** on-site. **Amenities:** video games, voice mail. **Cards:** AX, CB, DC, DS, MC, VI. **Special Amenities:** free local telephone calls and free newspaper.

SOME UNITS

🛏️ 🍴 ⛑️ 📺 📡 / ✖️ /

RED ROOF INN-WEST   *Book at aaa.com*   Phone: (269)375-7400

(AAA) (SAVE)

	5/23-10/23	1P: $50-$67	2P: $55-$67	XP: $5	F18
	10/24-3/31	1P: $47-$67	2P: $52-$67	XP: $5	F18
	4/1-5/22	1P: $46-$67	2P: $51-$67	XP: $5	F18

Small-scale Hotel

Location: US 131, exit 36B, just nw. 5425 W Michigan Ave 49009. Fax: 269/375-7533. **Facility:** 108 one-bedroom standard units. 2 stories (no elevator), exterior corridors. *Bath:* combo or shower only. **Parking:** on-site. **Terms:** small pets only. **Amenities:** video games (fee), voice mail. **Cards:** AX, CB, DC, DS, MC, VI. **Special Amenities:** free local telephone calls and free newspaper.

SOME UNITS

🛏️ ⛑️ 📺 📡 / ✖️ 🖥️ 📠 /

RESIDENCE INN BY MARRIOTT   *Book at aaa.com*   Phone: (269)349-0855

| | 6/2-3/31 | 1P: $114-$119 | 2P: $134-$139 | |
| | 4/1-6/1 | 1P: $109-$114 | 2P: $129-$134 | |

Small-scale Hotel

Location: I-94, exit 78, just w. 1500 E Kilgore Rd 49001. Fax: 269/349-0862. **Facility:** 83 units. 59 one-bedroom standard units with kitchens. 24 one-bedroom suites ($109-$134) with kitchens. 2 stories (no elevator), interior corridors. *Bath:* combo or shower only. **Parking:** on-site. **Terms:** weekly rates available, package plans - weekends. **Amenities:** voice mail, irons, hair dryers. *Fee:* video games, high-speed Internet. **Pool(s):** heated outdoor. **Leisure Activities:** whirlpool, exercise room, sports court. **Guest Services:** valet and coin laundry, area transportation. **Business Services:** PC. **Cards:** AX, CB, DC, DS, JC, MC, VI.

SOME UNITS

(ASK) ✈️ ⛑️ 📺 🏊 ✖️ 📺 📡 🖥️ 📠 💻 / ✖️ /

STUART AVENUE INN BED AND BREAKFAST   Phone: (269)342-0230

(AAA) (SAVE)

| | All Year | 1P: $75-$95 | 2P: $85-$105 | XP: $10 | F12 |

Historic Bed & Breakfast

Location: US 131, exit 38A, 3 mi e on W Main St. Located in a historic district. 229 Stuart Ave 49007. Fax: 269/385-3442. **Facility:** Elegantly restored, the Victorian house is decorated with hand-painted wallpapers, Belgian lace curtains and many period antiques. Smoke free premises. 7 one-bedroom standard units. 3 stories (no elevator), interior corridors. **Parking:** on-site. **Terms:** cancellation fee imposed, [BP] meal plan available, no pets allowed (owner's dogs on premises). **Amenities:** *Some:* CD players. **Business Services:** meeting rooms. **Cards:** AX, DC, DS, MC, VI. **Special Amenities:** free expanded continental breakfast and free local telephone calls.

SOME UNITS

(S/D) ✖️ 🖥️ / (VCR) /

——— WHERE TO DINE ———

BLACK SWAN
American

Lunch: $6-$14   Dinner: $16-$26   Phone: 269/375-2105

Location: I-94, exit 75, 1.5 mi n on Oakland Dr, 1 mi w on Parkview Dr, then just s; in Parkview Hills Development. 3501 Greenleaf Blvd 49008. **Hours:** 11:30 am-2 & 5-9 pm, Fri & Sat-10 pm, Sun 5 pm-8 pm. Closed major holidays. **Reservations:** suggested, weekends. **Features:** Nestled alongside Willow Lake and surrounded by a canopy of mature sycamore trees, this restaurant offers a park-like setting. The lake is viewed through paranomic floor to ceiling windows in the handsome and stylish main dining room. Picture perfect views of beautiful black and white swans gracefully swimming across the water delight patrons as they dine comfortably on classic Continental gourmet cuisine. Dressy casual; cocktails. **Parking:** on-site and valet. **Cards:** AX, DC, DS, MC, VI.

BLUE DOLPHIN
Greek

Lunch: $5-$12   Dinner: $9-$15   Phone: 269/343-4993

Location: Jct of Westnedge Ave or Park St, just e on Cedar St; downtown. 502 S Burdick St 49009. **Hours:** 7 am-10 pm, Sun 8 am-3 pm. **Closed:** 5/31, 9/6, 12/25. **Reservations:** accepted. **Features:** The downtown restaurant serves Greek dishes—such as moussaka, pastitsio and spanakopita—and American fare. Casual dress; cocktails. **Parking:** on-site. **Cards:** AX, DC, DS, MC, VI.

BRAVO RESTAURANT & CAFE
American

Lunch: $10-$15   Dinner: $20-$25   Phone: 269/344-7700

Location: I-94, exit 78, just s of freeway. 5402 Portage Rd 49002. **Hours:** 11:30 am-10 pm, Sat 5 pm-11 pm, Sun 10:30 am-2 & 4-9 pm. Closed major holidays. **Reservations:** suggested. **Features:** This delightful Italian/American eatery makes good use of its wood-burning ovens in preparing a cuisine that is at once, attractive, well-prepared, and delicious. The atmosphere is casually chick and blends restrained traditional touches and attentive service in an entirely non-smoking environment. Casual dress; cocktails. **Parking:** on-site. **Cards:** AX, DS, MC, VI.

COSMO'S CUCINA
American

Lunch: $5-$8   Dinner: $11-$16   Phone: 269/344-5666

Location: From S Westnedge Ave, just w; center. 804 W Vine St 49007. **Hours:** 11 am-10 pm, Sat 8:30 am-1 & 5-10 pm, Sun 8:30 am-3 pm. Closed major holidays; also Mon. **Reservations:** accepted. **Features:** Above a pub, the comfortable, second-floor dining room offers a large patio and a creative menu that features such diverse items as lamb tenderloin, fresh fish specials and penne with meatballs. Casual dress; cocktails. **Parking:** street. **Cards:** DS, MC, VI.

DISTRICT TWO ELEVEN
American

Lunch: $8-$12   Dinner: $20-$25   Phone: 269/226-9000

Location: Jct Water and Edwards sts; downtown. 211 E Water St 49007. **Hours:** 11:30 am-2 & 5-10 pm, Fri-11 pm, Sat 5:30 pm-11 pm, Sun 4 pm-8 pm. Closed major holidays. **Reservations:** suggested. **Features:** Located in the historic Globe building, this two-level restaurant features century old exposed brick walls, rustic wood pillars and warm hardwood floors, and floor-to-ceiling windows offer a great view of the city skyline. A wood fired grill in the small open kitchen focuses on such specialties such as shrimp and scallops, gnocchi and veggie pasta and New York strip steaks. Dressy casual; cocktails. **Parking:** on-site. **Cards:** AX, CB, DC, DS, MC, VI.

EPIC BISTRO & BIN 359
American

Dinner: $18-$21   Phone: 269/342-1300

Location: In the Epic Center. 359 S Kalamazoo Mall, Suite 103 49007. **Hours:** 5 pm-10 pm, Fri & Sat-11 pm, Sun 4 pm-8 pm. Closed major holidays. **Reservations:** accepted. **Features:** Inside The Epic Centre, the stylish and contemporary restaurant is popular with theatergoers. With a menu that changes seasonally, the kitchen uses regional ingredients and global influences to create such dramatic items as braised lamb shank, cornmeal-dusted rainbow trout and grilled ancho chile barbecue pork rib-eye. Dressy casual; cocktails. **Parking:** street. **Cards:** AX, DC, DS, MC, VI.

FOOD DANCE CAFE
American

Lunch: $8-$10   Dinner: $10-$17   Phone: 269/382-1888

Location: Just e of Westnedge Ave; downtown. 161 E Michigan Ave 49007. **Hours:** 7 am-10 pm, Sun 8 am-3 pm. Closed major holidays; also Mon. **Reservations:** accepted. **Features:** You'll note this as a "food haven," from the herb garden at the entry to the 10-foot tall asparagus painted as a mural inside. Besides the eclectic interior, you'll enjoy interesting grilled and cold sandwich combinations such as white cheddar and tomatoes or smoked ham with horseradish and red onion. For dinner, choose from pasta dishes, entree salads or a fresh fish such as grilled, sesame ginger salmon. Casual dress; cocktails. **Parking:** on-site. **Cards:** DS, MC, VI.

FRANCOIS' MACARONI FACTORY
AAA
Italian

Lunch: $6-$12   Dinner: $12-$20   Phone: 269/381-4958

Location: Jct Michigan Ave and Portage Rd; downtown. 116 Portage Rd 49009. **Hours:** 11 am-11 pm, Sun 4 pm-10 pm. Closed major holidays. **Reservations:** accepted. **Features:** In the heart of downtown, the popular restaurant prepares an extensive selection of pasta dishes, including lobster ravioli and Alfredo carbonara, as well as fresh seafood and meat dishes, including veal piccata. Dressy casual; cocktails. **Parking:** street. **Cards:** AX, CB, DC, DS, MC, VI.

THE GREAT LAKES SHIPPING COMPANY
Steak & Seafood

Dinner: $13-$23   Phone: 269/375-3650

Location: US 131, exit 36A, 0.3 mi e on Stadium Dr, 0.5 mi n on Drake Ave, then e. 4525 W KL Ave 49006. **Hours:** 5 pm-10 pm, Fri & Sat-11 pm. Closed major holidays. **Reservations:** accepted. **Features:** Serving a variety of fresh fish, slow roasted prime rib, choice aged steaks, and creatively prepared chicken and pasta, this nautically themed restaurant has something to suit everyone's taste. The large salad bar offers fresh items and lets you pick out how much you want of it. Dressy casual; cocktails. **Parking:** on-site. **Cards:** AX, DS, MC, VI.

LONDON GRILL-SINGAPORE
Provincial British

Lunch: $6-$10   Dinner: $10-$20   Phone: 269/381-9212

Location: Just e of Westnedge Ave; downtown. 214 E Michigan Ave 49007. **Hours:** 11 am-2 & 4-10 pm, Fri & Sat 4 pm-11 pm. Closed major holidays; also Sun. **Features:** The weekend Celtic music in this bistro makes for happy times, but the pleasantly presented dishes featuring curries and fresh seafood will delight you any day of the week. Casual dress; cocktails; entertainment. **Parking:** street. **Cards:** AX, DS, MC, VI.

OLDE PENINSULA BREW PUB & RESTAURANT   Lunch: $6-$10   Dinner: $7-$14   Phone: 269/343-2739
American
Location: Just e of Westnedge Ave; downtown. 200 E Michigan Ave 49009. **Hours:** 11 am-10:30 pm, Wed-Sat to 1 am, Sun noon-10 pm. Closed major holidays. **Features:** Pub foods, fresh seafood, great pasta and over two dozen beers as well as seasonal, hand-crafted beers are served in one of the city's oldest buildings. Casual dress; cocktails. **Parking:** street. **Cards:** AX, CB, DS, MC, VI.

RYKSE'S RESTAURANT & BAKERY   Lunch: $6-$9   Dinner: $7-$12   Phone: 269/372-3838
American
Location: US 131, exit 36B, 0.5 mi w. 5924 Stadium Dr 49009. **Hours:** 6:30 am-8 pm. Closed major holidays; also Sun. **Features:** This family style restaurant offers home-style soup, a variety of vegetarian dishes, "crunchy" baked chicken and you may top it all off with a selection from the many fresh-baked goods, including giant cinnamon rolls. Casual dress. **Parking:** on-site. **Cards:** MC, VI.

THE UNION   Lunch: $6-$8   Dinner: $8-$16   Phone: 269/384-6756
American
MC, VI.
Location: Jct E Michigan Ave; downtown. 125 S Kalamazoo Mall 49007. **Hours:** 11 am-10 pm, Fri-11 pm, Sat 5 pm-11 pm. Closed major holidays; also Sun. **Features:** Specializing in grilled and roasted meats, the menu also features locally caught fish and freshly picked produce.Located at Pacific Bell Ball Park, it's a great place to hobnob before or after the game. Dressy casual; cocktails. **Parking:** street. **Cards:** AX, DS,

WEBSTER'S   Dinner: $17-$30   Phone: 269/343-4444
American
DC, DS, MC, VI.
Location: Jct Michigan Ave and Rose St; downtown; in Radisson Plaza Hotel. 100 W Michigan Ave 49007. **Hours:** 5:30 pm-10 pm, Sat-11 pm. **Reservations:** suggested. **Features:** The open display kitchen with its embossed copper front and Old World ambience set the stage for an exceptional dining experience. White tablecloths, monogrammed china, and subdued lighting combine to create a thoroughly gracious dining environment. Attentive, friendly service by the knowledgeable wait staff enhances the well-prepared and beautifully presented continental cuisine. Dressy casual; cocktails. **Parking:** on-site and valet. **Cards:** AX,

KALKASKA pop. 2,226

—— WHERE TO STAY ——

ALL SEASONS RESORT   Phone: (231)258-0000
Small-scale Hotel

	1P: $79-$129	2P: $89-$139	XP: $10	F13
6/16-9/2 [ECP]				
4/1-6/15 & 9/3-3/31 [ECP]	1P: $69-$109	2P: $79-$119	XP: $10	F13

Location: On US 131 and SR 72, 0.8 mi e. Located in a semi-commercial area. 760 S Cedar St 49646 (PO Box 1018). Fax: 231/258-7917. **Facility:** 61 one-bedroom standard units, some with whirlpools. 2 stories (no elevator), interior corridors. *Bath:* combo or shower only. **Parking:** on-site, winter plug-ins. **Pool(s):** heated indoor. **Leisure Activities:** whirlpool, snowmobiling, exercise room. **Business Services:** meeting rooms. **Cards:** AX, DC, DS, MC, VI.

SOME UNITS

KENTWOOD pop. 45,255—See also *GRAND RAPIDS.*

—— WHERE TO STAY ——

BEST WESTERN MIDWAY HOTEL   *Book at aaa.com*   Phone: (616)942-2550
Large-scale Hotel

| All Year | 1P: $79-$99 | 2P: $89-$109 | XP: $10 | F18 |

Location: I-96, exit 43A, 1.5 mi w on SR 11. 4101 28th St SE 49512. Fax: 616/942-2446. **Facility:** 147 one-bedroom standard units, some with whirlpools. 3 stories, interior corridors. **Parking:** on-site. **Terms:** [CP] meal plan available, pets ($25 deposit, in designated units). **Amenities:** voice mail, irons, hair dryers. **Dining:** The Hoffman House, see separate listing. **Pool(s):** heated indoor. **Leisure Activities:** saunas, whirlpool, indoor recreation area, exercise room. **Guest Services:** valet laundry, airport transportation-Gerald R Ford International Airport. **Business Services:** conference facilities, business center. **Cards:** AX, CB, DC, DS, MC, VI. **Special Amenities:** free continental breakfast and preferred room (subject to availability with advanced reservations).

SOME UNITS
FEE

COMFORT INN   *Book at aaa.com*   Phone: (616)957-2080
Small-scale Hotel

| All Year [ECP] | 1P: $65-$99 | | | |

Location: I-96, exit 43A, 1.5 mi w on SR 11. 4155 28th St SE 49512 (4155 28th St SE, GRAND RAPIDS). Fax: 616/957-9712. **Facility:** 107 one-bedroom standard units, some with whirlpools. 3 stories, interior corridors. *Bath:* combo or shower only. **Parking:** on-site. **Terms:** small pets only. **Amenities:** dual phone lines, voice mail, safes, irons, hair dryers. **Leisure Activities:** exercise room. **Guest Services:** valet laundry, airport transportation-Gerald R Ford International Airport. **Business Services:** meeting rooms. **Cards:** AX, CB, DC, DS, JC, MC, VI. **Special Amenities:** free expanded continental breakfast and preferred room (subject to availability with advanced reservations).

SOME UNITS

COURTYARD BY MARRIOTT   *Book at aaa.com*   Phone: 616/954-0500
Small-scale Hotel
Property failed to provide current rates
Location: I-96, exit 43A, 0.8 mi w on SR 11. Located in a commercial area. 4741 28th St SE 49512. Fax: 616/954-2299. **Facility:** 84 units. 81 one-bedroom standard units, some with whirlpools. 3 one-bedroom suites. 3 stories, interior corridors. *Bath:* combo or shower only. **Parking:** on-site. **Amenities:** voice mail, irons, hair dryers. **Pool(s):** heated indoor. **Leisure Activities:** whirlpool, exercise room. **Guest Services:** valet and coin laundry. **Business Services:** meeting rooms.

SOME UNITS

HILTON GRAND RAPIDS AIRPORT
Book at aaa.com   Phone: 616/957-0100

(AAA) (SAVE)

Large-scale Hotel

All Year   1P: $85-$159   2P: $85-$159   XP: $10   F18
Location: I-96, exit 43A, 0.5 mi w on SR 11. Located in a commercial area. 4747 28th St SE 49512. Fax: 616/957-2977. **Facility:** 224 one-bedroom standard units. 4 stories, interior corridors. *Bath:* combo or shower only. **Amenities:** video games, high-speed Internet, dual phone lines, voice mail, irons, hair dryers. **Dining:** 6:30 am-11 pm, Sat & Sun from 7 am, cocktails, entertainment. **Pool(s):** heated indoor. **Leisure Activities:** sauna, whirlpool, exercise room. **Guest Services:** valet laundry, airport transportation-Gerald R Ford International Airport, area transportation-within 2 mi. **Business Services:** conference facilities. **Cards:** AX, DC, DS, MC, VI. *(See ad p 314)*

SOME UNITS

HOLIDAY INN SELECT
Book at aaa.com   Phone: (616)285-7600

Large-scale Hotel

All Year   1P: $79-$109   2P: $79-$109
Location: I-96, exit 43A, 2 mi w on SR 11, then just s. Located in a commercial area. 3031 Lake Eastbrook Blvd SE 49512. Fax: 616/285-7601. **Facility:** 148 units. 145 one-bedroom standard units. 3 one-bedroom suites. 3 stories, interior corridors. *Bath:* combo or shower only. **Parking:** on-site, winter plug-ins. **Terms:** [AP] meal plan available. **Amenities:** video games, high-speed Internet, dual phone lines, voice mail, irons, hair dryers. **Pool(s):** small heated indoor. **Leisure Activities:** whirlpool, exercise room. **Guest Services:** sundries, valet and coin laundry. **Business Services:** meeting rooms, business center. **Cards:** AX, DC, DS, MC, VI.

SOME UNITS

QUALITY INN TERRACE CLUB
Book at aaa.com   Phone: 616/956-8080

Small-scale Hotel

Property failed to provide current rates
Location: I-96, exit 43A, 1 mi w on SR 11. Located in a commercial area. 4495 28th St SE 49512. Fax: 616/956-0619. **Facility:** 126 units. 125 one-bedroom standard units, some with whirlpools. 1 two-bedroom suite with efficiency. 3 stories, interior corridors. **Parking:** on-site. **Amenities:** voice mail, irons, hair dryers. **Pool(s):** heated indoor. **Leisure Activities:** whirlpool. **Guest Services:** complimentary evening beverages, valet and coin laundry. **Business Services:** meeting rooms. *(See color ad p 314)*

SOME UNITS

RADISSON HOTEL GRAND RAPIDS EAST
Book at aaa.com   Phone: (616)949-9222

(AAA) (SAVE)

Large-scale Hotel

All Year   1P: $89-$139   2P: $89-$139
Location: Jct SR 11 and E Beltline Ave (SR 37). Located at the Woodland Shopping Mall. 3333 28th St SE 49512. Fax: 616/949-3841. **Facility:** 195 one-bedroom standard units. 5 stories, interior corridors. *Bath:* combo or shower only. **Parking:** on-site. **Terms:** check-in 4 pm, [AP] meal plan available. **Amenities:** dual phone lines, voice mail, irons, hair dryers. **Dining:** 6:30 am-2 & 5-10 pm, Sat & Sun from 7 am, cocktails. **Pool(s):** heated indoor. **Leisure Activities:** sauna, whirlpool, indoor recreation area, exercise room. *Fee:* game room. **Guest Services:** valet and coin laundry, airport transportation-Gerald R Ford International Airport. **Business Services:** meeting rooms. **Cards:** AX, CB, DC, DS, JC, MC, VI. **Special Amenities:** free newspaper and early check-in/late check-out.
(See color ad p 313)

SOME UNITS
FEE

RESIDENCE INN BY MARRIOTT EAST
     Phone: 616/957-8111

Condominium

All Year   1P: $109-$145   2P: $109-$145
Location: Jct SR 11 and E Beltline Ave (SR 37). Located in a commercial area. 2701 E Beltline Ave 49546 (2701 E Beltline Ave, GRAND RAPIDS). Fax: 616/957-3699. **Facility:** The hotel offers studios and one-bedroom apartments, some with fireplaces. 96 one-bedroom standard units with kitchens. 2 stories (no elevator), exterior corridors. **Parking:** on-site. **Terms:** pets ($125-$150 fee). **Amenities:** video games, voice mail, irons, hair dryers. **Pool(s):** heated outdoor. **Leisure Activities:** whirlpool, exercise room, sports court, basketball, volleyball. **Guest Services:** complimentary evening beverages, valet and coin laundry. **Cards:** AX, DC, DS, JC, MC, VI.

SOME UNITS
FEE

SLEEP INN
Book at aaa.com   Phone: 616/975-9000

Small-scale Hotel

Property failed to provide current rates
Location: I-96, exit 43A, 1 mi w on SR 11, then just s on Acquest. Located in a commercial area. 4284 29th St 49512. Fax: 616/954-6767. **Facility:** 80 one-bedroom standard units. 3 stories, interior corridors. *Bath:* combo or shower only. **Parking:** on-site. **Amenities:** *Some:* irons, hair dryers. **Pool(s):** heated indoor. **Leisure Activities:** whirlpool, exercise room. *Fee:* game room. **Guest Services:** valet and coin laundry. **Business Services:** meeting rooms. *(See color ad p 314)*

SOME UNITS

STAYBRIDGE SUITES BY HOLIDAY INN
Book at aaa.com   Phone: 616/464-3200

Small-scale Hotel

All Year [ECP]   1P: $79-$159   2P: $79-$159
Location: I-96, exit 43A, 2 mi w on SR 11, then just s. Located in a commercial area. 3000 Lake Eastbrook Blvd SE 49512. Fax: 616/464-3600. **Facility:** 94 units. 49 one-bedroom standard units with kitchens. 27 one- and 18 two-bedroom suites with kitchens. 3 stories, interior corridors. *Bath:* combo or shower only. **Parking:** on-site. **Terms:** cancellation fee imposed, weekly rates available, pets ($75 fee). **Amenities:** video library (fee), high-speed Internet, dual phone lines, voice mail, irons, hair dryers. **Pool(s):** heated outdoor. **Leisure Activities:** whirlpool, exercise room. **Guest Services:** sundries, valet and coin laundry. **Business Services:** meeting rooms, business center. **Cards:** AX, DC, DS, JC, MC, VI.

SOME UNITS
FEE

————— **WHERE TO DINE** —————

THE HOFFMAN HOUSE
Lunch: $6-$8   Dinner: $12-$18   Phone: 616/949-3880

American

Location: I-96, exit 43A, 1.5 mi w on SR 11; in Best Western Midway Hotel. 4101 28th St SE 49512. **Hours:** 6:30 am-2 & 5-10 pm, Sat from 7 am, Sun 7 am-2 & 5-9 pm. **Features:** The menu centers on traditional offerings, such as prime rib, roasted turkey, lasagna and orange roughy. The Friday seafood buffet and Saturday prime rib and pasta buffet are popular, as are such tempting desserts as apple cobbler and fudge brownie. Casual dress; cocktails. **Parking:** on-site. **Cards:** AX, DC, DS, MC, VI.

SEOUL GARDEN

Ethnic

Lunch: $5-$6   **Dinner:** $8-$12   **Phone:** 616/956-1522
Location: Just w of jct SR 11 and E Beltline (SR 37); at Woodland Mall. 3321 28th St 49546. **Hours:** 11 am-10 pm, Fri & Sat-11 pm. Closed: 12/25; also Sun. **Features:** Mongolian beef and pepper steak are representative of Korean and Chinese dishes on the extensive menu. The contemporary dining room is simple and elegant. Cocktails. **Parking:** on-site. **Cards:** AX, DS, MC, VI.

The following restaurants have not been evaluated by AAA but are listed for your information only.

44TH STREET BISTRO

[fyi]

Phone: 616/455-9640
Not evaluated. **Location:** Corner of Stauffer Ave and 44th St. 1950 44th St SE 49508. **Features:** Away from the hustle of 28th Street, this restaurant is popular with couples and families.

YEN CHING

[fyi]

Phone: 616/940-4111
Not evaluated. **Location:** On SR 11; in Roaring 20s Mall. 4605 28th St SE 49508. **Features:** Mandarin and Szechuan dishes are served in a casual atmosphere.

LAKE CITY pop. 923

---- **WHERE TO STAY** ----

NORTHCREST MOTEL

[AAA] [SAVE]

Motel

Phone: 231/839-2075
All Year   1P: $53-$72   2P: $53-$72   XP: $5
Location: 1 mi s on SR 55 and 66. 1341 S Lakeshore 49651 (PO Box M). **Facility:** 22 one-bedroom standard units. 1-2 stories (no elevator), exterior corridors. *Bath:* combo or shower only. **Parking:** on-site. **Terms:** small pets only ($5 extra charge). **Pool(s):** heated indoor. **Leisure Activities:** whirlpool, snowmobiling. **Cards:** DC, MC, VI. **Special Amenities:** free local telephone calls and preferred room (subject to availability with advanced reservations).

LAKE ORION —See Detroit p. 261.

LAKESIDE

---- **WHERE TO STAY** ----

WHITE RABBIT INN

Bed & Breakfast

Phone: 269/469-4620
4/1-11/29 & 12/26-3/31 [CP]   1P: $95-$155   2P: $95-$155   XP: $15
Location: I-94, exit 6 (Union Pier Rd), 1 mi w, then 2 mi n. 14634 Red Arrow Hwy 49116 (PO Box 725, 49116-0725). Fax: 269/469-5843. **Facility:** Set back from the historic Red Arrow Highway, this adult-oriented property offers cozy rooms and a tranquil, retreatlike setting. 8 units. 6 one-bedroom standard units with whirlpools. 2 cabins ($175-$225) with whirlpools. 1 story, exterior corridors. **Parking:** on-site. **Terms:** open 4/1-11/29 & 12/26-3/31, 2-4 night minimum stay - weekends & in season 7/1-7/31, age restrictions may apply, 7 day cancellation notice, pets (with prior approval). **Amenities:** video library. **Cards:** AX, DC, MC, VI.

LANSING pop. 119,128—See also EAST LANSING.

---- **WHERE TO STAY** ----

BEST WESTERN MIDWAY HOTEL   *Book at aaa.com*

[AAA] [SAVE]

Small-scale Hotel

Phone: 517/627-8471
All Year   1P: $86-$155   2P: $86-$155   XP: $10   F18
Location: I-96/SR 43, exit 93B, just e. 7711 W Saginaw Hwy 48917. Fax: 517/627-8597. **Facility:** 149 one-bedroom standard units. 3 stories, interior corridors. **Parking:** on-site. **Terms:** age restrictions may apply, cancellation fee imposed, weekly rates available, small pets only ($15 extra charge). **Amenities:** voice mail, hair dryers. **Dining:** 6:30 am-2 & 5-10 pm, Fri & Sat-10:30 pm, Sun 8 am-2:30 & 4:30-8 pm, cocktails. **Pool(s):** heated indoor. **Leisure Activities:** sauna, whirlpool, exercise room. **Guest Services:** valet laundry. **Business Services:** meeting rooms. **Cards:** AX, DS, MC, VI. **Special Amenities:** free continental breakfast and free room upgrade (subject to availability with advanced reservations).

COUNTRY INN & SUITES BY CARLSON   *Book at aaa.com*

Small-scale Hotel

Phone: 517/827-7000
1/1-3/31   1P: $74-$94   2P: $74-$94
4/1-12/31   1P: $69-$89   2P: $69-$89
Location: I-496, exit 1 (Creyts Rd), just se. 6511 Centurion Dr 48917. Fax: 517/827-7001. **Facility:** 88 units. 83 one- and 5 two-bedroom standard units, some with whirlpools. 3 stories, interior corridors. *Bath:* combo or shower only. **Parking:** on-site. **Terms:** age restrictions may apply. **Amenities:** dual phone lines, voice mail, irons, hair dryers. **Pool(s):** heated indoor. **Leisure Activities:** whirlpool, exercise room. **Guest Services:** valet and coin laundry. **Business Services:** meeting rooms. **Cards:** AX, CB, DC, DS, JC, MC, VI. **(See color ad p 313)**

COURTYARD BY MARRIOTT   *Book at aaa.com*

Small-scale Hotel

Phone: 517/482-0500
All Year   1P: $109-$119   2P: $109-$119
Location: Jct US 127. 2710 Lake Lansing Rd 48912. Fax: 517/482-0557. **Facility:** 129 one-bedroom standard units, some with whirlpools. 2 stories (no elevator), interior corridors. *Bath:* combo or shower only. **Parking:** on-site. **Terms:** 7 day cancellation notice. **Amenities:** video games (fee), dual phone lines, voice mail, irons, hair dryers. **Pool(s):** heated indoor. **Leisure Activities:** whirlpool, exercise room. **Guest Services:** complimentary evening beverages, valet and coin laundry. **Business Services:** meeting rooms. **Cards:** AX, DC, DS, MC, VI.

FAIRFIELD INN BY MARRIOTT-WEST LANSING
Book at aaa.com

Phone: (517)886-1066

ᐁᐁᐁᐁ
Small-scale Hotel

All Year 1P: $65-$85 2P: $65-$85 XP: $6 F18
Location: I-96/SR 43, exit 93B, 0.8 mi e on Saginaw Hwy. 810 Delta Commerce Dr 48917. Fax: 517/886-1066. **Facility:** 64 one-bedroom standard units. 3 stories, interior corridors. *Bath:* combo or shower only. **Parking:** on-site. **Terms:** [ECP] meal plan available. **Amenities:** irons. **Pool(s):** heated indoor. **Leisure Activities:** whirlpool. **Guest Services:** valet laundry. **Cards:** AX, CB, DC, DS, MC, VI.

SOME UNITS

HAMPTON INN OF LANSING
Book at aaa.com

Phone: (517)627-8381

(AAA) (SAVE)
ᐁᐁᐁᐁ
Small-scale Hotel

All Year 1P: $59-$79 2P: $59-$79 XP: $8 F18
Location: I-96/SR 43, exit 93B, just e on Saginaw Hwy. 525 N Canal Rd 48917. Fax: 517/627-5502. **Facility:** 107 units. 101 one-bedroom standard units. 6 one-bedroom suites ($99-$159), some with whirlpools. 3 stories, interior corridors. **Parking:** on-site. **Terms:** [CP] meal plan available, small pets only ($100 deposit). **Amenities:** dual phone lines, voice mail, safes, irons, hair dryers. **Leisure Activities:** exercise room. **Guest Services:** valet laundry. **Business Services:** meeting rooms. **Cards:** AX, CB, DC, DS, MC, VI. **Special Amenities:** free expanded continental breakfast and free local telephone calls.

SOME UNITS

FEE

HOLIDAY INN LANSING WEST CONFERENCE CENTER
Book at aaa.com

Phone: (517)627-3211

(AAA) (SAVE)
ᐁᐁᐁᐁ
Small-scale Hotel

All Year 1P: $109-$129 2P: $109-$129
Location: I-96/SR 43, exit 93B, just e. 7501 W Saginaw Hwy 48917. Fax: 517/627-5240. **Facility:** 244 one-bedroom standard units. 3 stories, interior corridors. **Parking:** on-site. **Terms:** check-in 4 pm, age restrictions may apply. **Amenities:** video games (fee), dual phone lines, voice mail, irons, hair dryers. **Dining:** 7:30 am-11 pm, Fri & Sat-1 am, cocktails. **Pool(s):** heated indoor. **Leisure Activities:** sauna, whirlpool, indoor recreation area, exercise room. **Guest Services:** valet laundry, area transportation-within 5 mi. **Business Services:** conference facilities. **Cards:** AX, CB, DC, DS, MC, VI.

SOME UNITS

HOLIDAY INN-SOUTH/CONVENTION CENTER
Book at aaa.com

Phone: 517/694-8123

ᐁᐁᐁᐁ
Small-scale Hotel

All Year 1P: $95-$105 2P: $95-$105
Location: I-96, exit 104 (Cedar St/Holt), just s. 6820 S Cedar St 48911. Fax: 517/699-3753. **Facility:** 300 one-bedroom standard units, some with whirlpools. 5 stories, interior corridors. *Bath:* combo or shower only. **Parking:** on-site. **Amenities:** video games (fee), dual phone lines, voice mail, irons, hair dryers. **Pool(s):** heated indoor. **Leisure Activities:** sauna, whirlpool, exercise room. **Guest Services:** valet and coin laundry. **Business Services:** conference facilities. **Cards:** AX, CB, DC, MC, VI.

SOME UNITS

LANSING'S QUALITY SUITES HOTEL
Book at aaa.com

Phone: (517)886-0600

(AAA) (SAVE)
ᐁᐁᐁᐁ
Small-scale Hotel

All Year [BP] 1P: $99 2P: $99
Location: I-96/SR 43, exit 93B, 0.8 mi e on Saginaw St. 901 Delta Commerce Dr 48917. Fax: 517/886-0103. **Facility:** 117 one-bedroom suites. 4 stories, interior corridors. **Parking:** on-site. **Terms:** weekly rates available, pets ($125 fee). **Amenities:** dual phone lines, voice mail, irons, hair dryers. **Leisure Activities:** sauna, whirlpool, exercise room, game room. **Guest Services:** gift shop, complimentary evening beverages, valet laundry, area transportation-within 3 mi. **Business Services:** meeting rooms. **Cards:** AX, CB, DC, DS, JC, MC, VI. **Special Amenities:** free full breakfast.

SOME UNITS

FEE

QUALITY INN UNIVERSITY PLACE
Book at aaa.com

Phone: (517)351-1440

(AAA) (SAVE)
ᐁᐁᐁᐁ
Small-scale Hotel

All Year [BP] 1P: $65-$135 2P: $65-$135 XP: $10 F18
Location: On I-69 business route and SR 43, just e of US 127. 3121 E Grand River Ave 48912. Fax: 517/351-6220. **Facility:** 105 units. 103 one-bedroom standard units, some with whirlpools. 2 one-bedroom suites ($109-$199) with whirlpools. 2 stories, interior corridors. **Parking:** on-site. **Terms:** cancellation fee imposed, weekly rates available. **Amenities:** voice mail, safes, irons, hair dryers. **Pool(s):** heated indoor. **Leisure Activities:** whirlpool, domed recreation center, exercise room. **Guest Services:** coin laundry. **Business Services:** meeting rooms. **Cards:** AX, CB, DC, DS, MC, VI. *(See color ad p 341)*

SOME UNITS

RADISSON HOTEL LANSING — *Book at aaa.com* — **Phone:** (517)482-0188

 (AAA) (SAVE)
All Year   1P: $130   2P: $130
Location: Corner of Michigan and Grand Ave; center of downtown. 111 N Grand Ave 48933. Fax: 517/487-6646. **Facility:** 257 one-bedroom standard units, some with whirlpools. 11 stories, interior corridors. **Parking:** valet and street. **Terms:** check-in 4 pm, age restrictions may apply. **Amenities:** voice mail, irons, hair dryers. Large-scale Hotel *Some:* dual phone lines. **Dining:** 6 am-11 pm, Sat & Sun from 7 am, cocktails. **Pool(s):** heated indoor. **Leisure Activities:** sauna, whirlpool, exercise room. **Guest Services:** gift shop, valet laundry, airport transportation-Capital City Airport. **Business Services:** conference facilities, business center. **Cards:** AX, CB, DC, DS, JC, MC, VI. **Special Amenities:** free newspaper. *(See color ad p 313)*

SOME UNITS

RED ROOF INN-EAST — *Book at aaa.com* — **Phone:** (517)332-2575

(AAA) (SAVE)

4/1-10/23	1P: $55-$72	2P: $61-$72	XP: $6	F18
10/24-12/31	1P: $52-$63	2P: $58-$63	XP: $6	F18
1/1-3/31	1P: $48-$63	2P: $54-$63	XP: $6	F18

Motel
Location: Just e of I-496 and US 127, exit 11 (Jolly Rd). 3615 Dunckel Rd 48910. Fax: 517/332-1459. **Facility:** 80 one-bedroom standard units. 2 stories, exterior corridors. **Parking:** on-site. **Terms:** small pets only. **Amenities:** video games (fee), voice mail. **Cards:** AX, CB, DC, DS, MC, VI. **Special Amenities:** free local telephone calls and free newspaper.

SOME UNITS

RED ROOF INN-WEST — *Book at aaa.com* — **Phone:** (517)321-7246

(AAA) (SAVE)

4/1-10/30	1P: $50-$67	2P: $56-$67	XP: $6	F18
1/1-3/31	1P: $46-$61	2P: $52-$61	XP: $6	F18
10/31-12/31	1P: $50-$60	2P: $56-$60	XP: $6	F18

Small-scale Hotel
Location: I-96, exit 93B. 7412 W Saginaw Hwy 48917. Fax: 517/321-2831. **Facility:** 81 one-bedroom standard units. 2 stories, exterior corridors. **Parking:** on-site. **Terms:** age restrictions may apply, small pets only. **Amenities:** video games (fee), voice mail. **Cards:** AX, CB, DC, DS, MC, VI. **Special Amenities:** free local telephone calls and free newspaper.

SOME UNITS

RESIDENCE INN-LANSING WEST — *Book at aaa.com* — **Phone:** (517)886-5030

All Year   1P: $89-$110   2P: $89-$110
Location: I-96/SR 43, exit 93B, 0.8 mi e on Saginaw Hwy. 922 Delta Commerce Dr 48917. Fax: 517/886-5030. Small-scale Hotel **Facility:** 78 units. 66 one-bedroom standard units with efficiencies. 12 one-bedroom suites with kitchens. 3 stories, interior corridors. **Bath:** combo or shower only. **Parking:** on-site. **Terms:** age restrictions may apply, 7 day cancellation notice, [BP] meal plan available, pets ($100 fee). **Amenities:** dual phone lines, voice mail, irons, hair dryers. **Pool(s):** heated indoor. **Leisure Activities:** whirlpool, exercise room, sports court. **Guest Services:** valet and coin laundry. **Business Services:** meeting rooms. **Cards:** AX, DC, DS, MC, VI.

SOME UNITS

FEE

SHERATON LANSING HOTEL — *Book at aaa.com* — **Phone:** (517)323-7100

All Year   1P: $79-$184   2P: $79-$184   XP: $12   F17
Location: I-496, exit Creyts Rd, just n. Located in an office park. 925 S Creyts Rd 48917. Fax: 517/323-2180. Small-scale Hotel **Facility:** 219 one-bedroom standard units. 5 stories, interior corridors. **Parking:** on-site. **Terms:** age restrictions may apply. **Amenities:** video games (fee), dual phone lines, voice mail, irons, hair dryers. **Pool(s):** heated indoor. **Leisure Activities:** sauna, whirlpool, racquetball court, exercise room. **Guest Services:** gift shop, valet laundry, area transportation. **Business Services:** conference facilities. **Cards:** AX, CB, DC, DS, JC, MC, VI.

SOME UNITS

--------- **WHERE TO DINE** ---------

BRAVO! CUCINA ITALIANA   **Lunch:** $8-$20   **Dinner:** $8-$20   **Phone:** 517/485-3779
▼▼ ▼▼   **Location:** Jct US 127 and Lake Lansing Rd, just w; in the Eastwood Towne Center. 2970 Towne Center Blvd 48912.
              Hours: 11 am-11 pm, Thurs-Sat to midnight, Sun 5 pm-10 pm. Closed major holidays.
Italian   **Reservations:** accepted. **Features:** With fractured columns, arches and exposed brick walls, the dining
              area evokes the feel of the courtyard of an Italian ruin. The atmosphere is lively and casual. In the open
kitchen, chefs put together such specials as Parmesan-crusted Chilean sea bass and shrimp with angel hair pasta, as well as
varied traditional dishes and pizzas. Casual dress; cocktails. **Parking:** on-site. **Cards:** AX, DC, MC, VI.

CARRABBA'S ITALIAN GRILLE   **Dinner:** $8-$18   **Phone:** 517/323-8055
▼▼ ▼▼   **Location:** I-96/SR 43, exit 93B, 1 mi e. 6540 W Saginaw Hwy 48917. **Hours:** 4 pm-10 pm, Fri-11 pm, Sat 3
              pm-11 pm, Sun 1 pm-9 pm. Closed: 11/25, 12/25. **Reservations:** accepted. **Features:** Tuscan influences
Italian   run deep in this surprising cozy and intimate space. A large open kitchen allows diners to watch the Italian
              based dishes such as calamari, eggplant parmesan and pizza being prepared. Casual dress; cocktails.
Parking: on-site. **Cards:** AX, DC, DS, MC, VI.

THE CLADDAGH IRISH PUB   **Lunch:** $8-$12   **Dinner:** $12-$20   **Phone:** 517/484-2523
▼▼ ▼▼   **Location:** Jct US 127 and Lake Lansing Rd, just w; in west end of Eastwood Towne Center. 2900 Towne Center
              48912. **Hours:** 11 am-11 pm, Fri & Sat-midnight, Sun-10 pm. Closed major holidays. **Features:** Nooks and
Irish   crannies dotted throughout lend to the Irish pub's authentic character. A large section of imported beers
              complements typical pub food, including fish and chips and Celtic corned beef and cheese. Dressy casual;
cocktails. **Parking:** on-site. **Cards:** AX, DC, DS, MC, VI.

CLARA'S LANSING STATION   **Lunch:** $6-$16   **Dinner:** $6-$16   **Phone:** 517/372-7120
▼▼ ▼▼   **Location:** Just e of Capitol Building Complex; downtown. 637 E Michigan Ave 48912. **Hours:** 11 am-11 pm, Fri &
              Sat-midnight, Sun 10 am-10 pm. Closed: 11/25, 12/25. **Reservations:** accepted. **Features:** Clara's is a
American   railroad station built in 1905, that is now a restaurant with a long menu that has something to please
              everyone. Try the delicious chicken Hawaiian. The emphasis here is on fun, family dining, in a landmark
location. Casual dress; cocktails. **Parking:** on-site. **Cards:** AX, DC, DS, MC, VI.

FINLEY'S AMERICAN RESTAURANT   **Lunch:** $4-$8   **Dinner:** $6-$15   **Phone:** 517/323-4309
▼▼   **Location:** I-96, exit 93B, 2 mi e. 5615 W Saginaw Hwy 48917. **Hours:** 11 am-10 pm, Fri & Sat-11 pm. Closed:
              11/25, 12/25. **Features:** Everyone is welcome at the casual family restaurant. Baby back ribs and such
American   succulent steak as top sirloin and New York strip are popular specialties on a menu that centers on good
              basic fare. The uniformed staff provides friendly, prompt service. Casual dress; cocktails. **Parking:** on-site.
Cards: AX, DC, DS, MC, VI.

JOHNNY ROCKETS   **Lunch:** $5-$7   **Dinner:** $5-$7   **Phone:** 517/377-9900
▼▼   **Location:** US 127, exit Lake Lansing Rd, just w; in the Eastwood Towne Center. 2950 Towne Center Blvd 48912.
              Hours: 11 am-10 pm, Fri & Sat-11 pm, Sun 11 am-9 pm. Closed major holidays. **Features:** The 1950s
American   retro diner serves hamburgers, hot dogs and other comfort foods in a loud dining room that evokes a
              nostalgic feel. Casual dress. **Parking:** on-site. **Cards:** AX, DS, MC, VI.

MCALISTER'S DELI   **Lunch:** $5-$7   **Dinner:** $5-$7   **Phone:** 517/482-3354
▼▼   **Location:** US 127, exit Lake Lansing Rd, just w; in the Eastwood Towne Center. 2901 Preyde Blvd 48912. **Hours:** 11
              am-9 pm. Closed major holidays. **Features:** A quick break from shopping, the often crowded delicatessen
Deli/Subs   features a large variety of made-to-order sandwiches and salads. Casual dress. **Parking:** on-site.
Sandwiches   **Cards:** AX, DS, MC, VI.

MITCHELL'S FISH MARKET   **Lunch:** $8-$12   **Dinner:** $18-$25   **Phone:** 517/482-3474
▼▼ ▼▼   **Location:** Jct US 127 and Lake Lansing Rd, just w; in Eastwood Towne Center. 2975 Preyde Blvd 48912.
              Hours: 11:30 am-10 pm, Fri & Sat-11 pm, Sun 11:30 am-9 pm. Closed major holidays.
Seafood   **Reservations:** suggested. **Features:** Part of a small but growing chain, the whimsical, nautically themed
              restaurant changes its menu daily to reflect more than a dozen daily specials flown in from around the
world. While the fresh fish and accompanying raw bar are the main focus, the menu also lists a number of steak, pasta and
chicken selections. Casual dress; cocktails. **Parking:** on-site. **Cards:** AX, DC, MC, VI.

P.F. CHANG'S CHINA BISTRO   **Lunch:** $9-$12   **Dinner:** $9-$12   **Phone:** 517/267-3833
▼▼ ▼▼   **Location:** Jct US 127 and Lake Lansing Rd; just w; in Eastwood Towne Center. 2425 Lake Lansing Rd 48912.
              Hours: 11 am-10 pm, Fri & Sat-midnight. Closed major holidays. **Reservations:** accepted.
Chinese   **Features:** Reproduction Xi'an terra cotta warriors stand watch over diners in the elegant dining room,
              where service is decidedly casual. While soothing lettuce wraps are a popular selection, a host of standard
and Asian/American fusion dishes, such as Chef Roy's favorite chicken, integrate fresh vegetables and Chinese accents to
great success. Casual dress; cocktails. **Parking:** on-site. **Cards:** AX, MC, VI.

LAPEER pop. 9,072

──────── WHERE TO STAY ────────

BEST WESTERN LAPEER INN *Book at aaa.com* **Phone:** (810)667-9444

 SAVE

Small-scale Hotel

All Year [ECP] 1P: $72-$77 2P: $72-$77 XP: $5 F12
Location: I-69, exit 155, 2 mi n on SR 24. 770 West St 48446. **Fax:** 810/667-3744. **Facility:** 90 units. 74 one-bedroom standard units, some with whirlpools. 16 one-bedroom suites ($102-$135) with whirlpools. 2 stories (no elevator), interior corridors. **Parking:** on-site. **Terms:** age restrictions may apply. **Amenities:** irons, hair dryers. *Fee:* video library, high-speed Internet. *Some:* safes, honor bars. **Dining:** 11 am-10 pm, Fri & Sat-11 pm, Sun noon-9 pm, cocktails. **Pool(s):** heated outdoor, heated indoor. **Leisure Activities:** sauna, whirlpool, putting green, indoor recreation center, exercise room. *Fee:* game room. **Guest Services:** valet laundry. **Business Services:** meeting rooms. **Cards:** AX, CB, DC, DS, JC, MC, VI. **Special Amenities:** free expanded continental breakfast and free newspaper.

SOME UNITS

FAIRFIELD INN LAPEER *Book at aaa.com* **Phone:** (810)245-7700

SAVE

Small-scale Hotel

All Year 1P: $69-$125 2P: $69-$125
Location: I-69, exit 155, 2 mi n on SR 24, just e. 927 Demille Rd 48446. **Fax:** 810/245-7294. **Facility:** 72 one-bedroom standard units, some with whirlpools. 3 stories, interior corridors. *Bath:* combo or shower only. **Parking:** on-site. **Terms:** age restrictions may apply, [ECP] meal plan available. **Amenities:** dual phone lines, irons. **Pool(s):** small heated indoor. **Leisure Activities:** whirlpool, exercise room. **Guest Services:** valet and coin laundry. **Business Services:** meeting rooms. **Cards:** AX, DC, DS, MC, VI.

SOME UNITS

──────── WHERE TO DINE ────────

E.G. NICK'S **Lunch:** $6-$9 **Dinner:** $10-$16 **Phone:** 810/664-6200

American

Location: 0.5 mi s on SR 24 and 21. 825 S Main St 48446. **Hours:** 11 am-10 pm, Fri & Sat-11 pm, Sun noon-9 pm. **Closed:** 11/25, 12/25. **Features:** Located in a bustling retail area near the interstate, this casual restaurant offers a menu of old favorites and innovative dishes including planked whitefish and their house specialty of basted ribs. Casual dress; cocktails. **Parking:** on-site. **Cards:** AX, CB, DC, DS, MC, VI.

LELAND pop. 2,033

──────── WHERE TO STAY ────────

MANITOU MANOR BED & BREAKFAST **Phone:** 231/256-7712

Bed & Breakfast

5/15-11/1 [BP] 1P: $125-$140 2P: $125-$140 XP: $15 F12
4/1-5/14 & 11/2-3/31 [BP] 1P: $95 2P: $95 XP: $15 F12
Location: 0.8 mi s on SR 22 from jct SR 204. 147 Manitou Tr W 49654 (PO Box 864). **Fax:** 231/256-7941. **Facility:** This B&B is a refurbished farm house. Smoke free premises. 5 one-bedroom standard units. 2 stories (no elevator), interior corridors. *Bath:* shared or private, combo or shower only. **Parking:** on-site. **Terms:** 2 night minimum stay - weekends, 7 day cancellation notice-fee imposed, no pets allowed (owner's pets on premises). **Leisure Activities:** horseshoes. **Guest Services:** TV in common area. **Cards:** DS, MC, VI.

──────── WHERE TO DINE ────────

THE COVE **Lunch:** $5-$8 **Dinner:** $12-$19 **Phone:** 231/256-9834

American

Location: Just w of Main St. 111 River St 49654. **Hours:** Open 5/15-10/15; 11 am-9 pm, Fri & Sat-10 pm; to 10 pm 5/30-9/4. **Reservations:** suggested, in season. **Features:** Window tables and patio seating afford great views of Lake Michigan and the Manitou Islands. Seafood chowder and varied preparations of whitefish, such as macadamia nut whitefish, garlic Parmesan whitefish and campfire whitefish, are menu specialties. Casual dress; cocktails. **Parking:** street. **Cards:** AX, MC, VI.

LEWISTON pop. 990

──────── WHERE TO STAY ────────

GARLAND **Phone:** (989)786-2211

SAVE

Resort
Small-scale Hotel

4/29-10/31 & 12/27-3/6 1P: $89-$269
Location: 4.8 mi s. 4700 N Red Oak Rd 49756. **Fax:** 989/786-2254. **Facility:** Lodge, condo and villa units are available on this property's 3,500 wooded acres near a public airstrip; sleigh rides are offered in winter. 182 units. 56 one-bedroom standard units, some with whirlpools. 1 two-bedroom suite. 125 cottages, some with whirlpools. 1-3 stories, interior/exterior corridors. *Bath:* combo or shower only. **Parking:** on-site and valet, winter plug-ins. **Terms:** open 4/29-10/31 & 12/27-3/6, check-in 4 pm, 2 night minimum stay - weekends, 14 day cancellation notice, [MAP] meal plan available. **Amenities:** voice mail. *Some:* irons, hair dryers. **Dining:** Herman's, see separate listing. **Pool(s):** heated outdoor. **Leisure Activities:** sauna, whirlpools, 3 lighted tennis courts, cross country skiing, ice skating, rental snowmobiles, recreation programs in season, bicycle trails, hiking trails, exercise room, sports court, volleyball. *Fee:* fishing, golf-72 holes, golf instruction, bicycles. **Guest Services:** gift shop, valet laundry, airport transportation-Garland Airport. **Business Services:** conference facilities. **Cards:** AX, DC, DS, MC, VI. **Special Amenities:** free room upgrade and preferred room (each subject to availability with advanced reservations).

SOME UNITS

——— WHERE TO DINE ———

HERMAN'S   **Lunch: $7-$11**   **Dinner: $19-S33**   **Phone: 989/786-2211**

Location: 4.8 mi s; in Garland. CR 489 49756. **Hours:** Open 4/18-11/23 & 12/26-3/15; 5:30 am-11 pm; 6:30 am-10 pm in winter. **Reservations:** required. **Features:** Intimate dining. Enjoy the up-north atmosphere with view from a window seat. Regional Michigan cuisine. Entrees include such delicacies as fresh salmon,

American

pheasant and venison. The steak, if you don't have it overcooked, will melt in your mouth. Dressy casual; cocktails; entertainment. **Parking:** on-site and valet. **Cards:** AX, DC, DS, MC, VI.

LEXINGTON pop. 1,104

——— WHERE TO STAY ———

INN THE GARDEN BED & BREAKFAST   **Phone: 810/359-8966**

	1/1-3/31 [BP]	1P: $85-$130	2P: $85-$130	XP: $10	F6
	6/1-9/30 [BP]	1P: $90-$120	2P: $90-$120	XP: $10	F6
	4/1-5/31 & 10/1-12/31 [BP]	1P: $85-$110	2P: $85-$110	XP: $10	F6

Historic Bed & Breakfast

Location: Center of town. 7156 Huron Ave 48450. Fax: 810/359-2119. **Facility:** Spacious grounds and a small greenhouse provide fresh herbs and produce for the breakfasts at this attractive Victorian-style house. Smoke free premises. 4 units. 3 one-bedroom standard units. 1 two-bedroom suite ($110-$120). 3 stories (no elevator), interior corridors. *Bath:* combo or shower only. **Parking:** on-site. **Terms:** check-in 4 pm, 2 night minimum stay - seasonal & weekends, 7 day cancellation notice, no pets allowed (owner's dog on premises). **Amenities:** video library.   SOME UNITS

LINCOLN PARK —See Detroit p. 262.

LINWOOD

——— WHERE TO DINE ———

LINWOOD CORNERS RESTAURANT   **Lunch: $2-$4**   **Dinner: $6-$11**   **Phone: 989/697-5141**

Location: I-75, exit 173, 2.3 mi e on Linwood Rd, then 0.3 mi n on SR 13. 44 N Huron 48634. **Hours:** 5 am-8 pm. Closed: 12/25; also 12/24 for dinner. **Features:** Home-style comfort foods, such as roast turkey, pork

American

chops, steak and good old apple pie, make up the bulk of the family-oriented menu at the casual restaurant. Casual dress. **Parking:** on-site. **Cards:** DS, MC, VI.

LIVONIA —See Detroit p. 262.

LUDINGTON pop. 8,357

——— WHERE TO STAY ———

FOUR SEASONS LODGING BREAKFAST   **Phone: 231/843-3448**

| | 7/2-8/31 [ECP] | 1P: $85-$175 | 2P: $85-$175 |
| | 5/1-7/1 & 9/1-10/24 [ECP] | 1P: $65-$130 | 2P: $65-$130 |

Motel

Location: Jct US 31, 2.6 mi w on US 10. 717 E Ludington Ave 49431. Fax: 231/843-2635. **Facility:** Smoke free premises. 33 units. 30 one-bedroom standard units. 3 one-bedroom suites. 1 story, interior/exterior corridors. *Bath:* combo or shower only. **Parking:** on-site. **Terms:** open 5/1-10/24, 3 day cancellation notice-fee imposed. **Amenities:** *Some:* hair dryers. **Leisure Activities:** bicycles, exercise room. **Business Services:** meeting rooms. **Cards:** AX, DS, MC, VI. *(See color ad below)*   SOME UNITS

FEE   FEE   FEE

HOLIDAY INN EXPRESS *Book at aaa.com* Phone: 231/845-7004

(AAA) (SAVE)

	6/26-8/31	1P: $112-$349	2P: $112-$349	XP: $10	F17
	11/1-3/31	1P: $62-$189	2P: $62-$189	XP: $10	F17
	9/1-10/31	1P: $72-$179	2P: $72-$179	XP: $10	F17
	4/1-6/25	1P: $62-$119	2P: $62-$119	XP: $10	F17

Small-scale Hotel **Location:** Jct US 31, 1.3 mi w on US 10. Located in a commercial area. 5323 W US 10 49431. **Fax:** 231/843-1677. **Facility:** 102 units. 100 one-bedroom standard units, some with whirlpools. 1 one- and 1 two-bedroom suites with whirlpools, some with kitchens. 2-3 stories, interior corridors. *Bath:* combo or shower only. **Parking:** on-site. **Terms:** cancellation fee imposed, pets ($10 extra charge). **Amenities:** irons, hair dryers. *Some:* CD players. **Pool(s):** heated indoor. **Leisure Activities:** sauna, whirlpool, playground, exercise room, horseshoes, shuffleboard. *Fee:* game room. **Guest Services:** coin laundry. **Business Services:** meeting rooms. **Cards:** AX, CB, DC, DS, JC, MC, VI. *(See color ad card insert & below)*

THE INN AT LUDINGTON Phone: (231)845-7055

| | All Year [BP] | 1P: $100-$125 | 2P: $100-$125 | XP: $20 | F10 |

Location: Jct US 31, 2.7 mi w on US 10. 701 E Ludington Ave 49431. **Facility:** Smoke free premises. 6 one-bedroom standard units. 2 stories (no elevator), interior corridors. *Bath:* combo or shower only. **Parking:** on-site. **Terms:** 7 day cancellation notice-fee imposed, package plans, no pets allowed (owner's pet on premises). **Cards:** AX, DS, MC, VI.

Bed & Breakfast

(ASK) [image icons]

THE LAMPLIGHTER BED & BREAKFAST Phone: (231)843-9792

(AAA) (SAVE)

| | All Year [BP] | 1P: $115-$155 | 2P: $115-$155 |

Location: Jct US 31, 2.8 mi w on US 10. 602 E Ludington Ave 49431. **Fax:** 231/843-1840. **Facility:** This restored turn-of-the-20th-century Victorian home has an ambience of European-style elegance. Smoke free premises. 5 one-bedroom standard units, some with whirlpools. 2 stories (no elevator), interior corridors. *Bath:* shower only. **Parking:** on-site. **Terms:** check-in 4 pm, age restrictions may apply, 7 day cancellation notice, no pets allowed (owner's pet on premises). **Cards:** AX, DS, MC, VI. **Special Amenities:** free full breakfast and free local telephone calls.

Bed & Breakfast

[image icons]

SNYDERS SHORELINE INN LLC Phone: (231)845-1261

| | 6/16-9/6 [CP] | 1P: $119-$289 | 2P: $119-$289 |
| | 5/7-6/15 & 9/7-10/17 [CP] | 1P: $89-$215 | 2P: $89-$215 |

Small-scale Hotel **Location:** On SR 116, 0.3 mi w of US 10. 903 W Ludington Ave 49431 (PO Box 667). **Fax:** 231/843-4441. **Facility:** Smoke free premises. 44 one-bedroom standard units, some with whirlpools. 2 stories (no elevator), interior/exterior corridors. *Bath:* combo or shower only. **Parking:** on-site. **Terms:** open 5/7-10/17, 5 day cancellation notice-fee imposed. **Amenities:** video library, voice mail. *Some:* hair dryers. **Pool(s):** heated outdoor. **Leisure Activities:** whirlpool. **Cards:** AX, DS, MC, VI.

SOME UNITS

[image icons]

SUPER 8 MOTEL   *Book at aaa.com*   Phone: 231/843-2140

	6/20-8/20	1P: $100-$229	2P: $105-$229	XP: $5	F12
	8/21-11/1	1P: $75-$175	2P: $79-$175	XP: $5	F12
	4/1-6/19	1P: $65-$160	2P: $69-$160	XP: $5	F12
	11/2-3/31	1P: $55-$130	2P: $59-$130	XP: $5	F12

Small-scale Hotel **Location:** Jct US 31, 1 mi w on US 10. 5005 W US 10 49431. Fax: 231/843-1753. **Facility:** 64 units. 57 one- and 2 two-bedroom standard units, some with whirlpools. 4 one- and 1 two-bedroom suites ($85-$229). 3 stories (no elevator), interior corridors. *Bath:* combo or shower only. **Parking:** on-site. **Terms:** cancellation fee imposed, [ECP] meal plan available, pets ($5 extra charge, in designated units). **Amenities:** hair dryers. *Some:* video games (fee). **Pool(s):** heated indoor. **Leisure Activities:** sauna, whirlpool, playground, exercise room. *Fee:* game room. **Guest Services:** gift shop, coin laundry. **Business Services:** meeting rooms. **Cards:** AX, CB, DC, DS, JC, MC, VI. *(See color ad below)*   SOME UNITS

FEE

VIKING ARMS INN **Phone:** (231)843-3441

6/11-9/5 [CP]	1P: $75-$120	2P: $75-$160	XP: $10
4/1-6/10 [CP]	1P: $60-$90	2P: $60-$100	XP: $10
9/6-10/31 [CP]	1P: $55-$90	2P: $55-$95	XP: $10
11/1-3/31 [CP]	1P: $45-$60	2P: $45-$60	XP: $10

Motel   **Location:** Jct US 31, 2.2 mi w on US 10. 930 E Ludington Ave 49431. Fax: 231/845-7703. **Facility:** 45 one-bedroom standard units, some with whirlpools. 1 story, interior/exterior corridors. *Bath:* combo or shower only. **Parking:** on-site. **Terms:** age restrictions may apply, 7 day cancellation notice-fee imposed. **Amenities:** video library (fee), hair dryers. **Pool(s):** heated outdoor. **Leisure Activities:** whirlpool. **Business Services:** meeting rooms. **Cards:** MC, VI. **Special Amenities:** free continental breakfast and free local telephone calls. *(See color ad p 346)*

SOME UNITS

🍽️ 📶 VCR DATA PORT 💻 / ⊠ 🛢 📠 /

——— **WHERE TO DINE** ———

P M STEAMERS **Dinner:** $9-$17 **Phone:** 231/843-9555

Steak & Seafood **Location:** Corner of Loomis St and Lewis St; center. 502 W Loomis 49431. **Hours:** Open 4/1-12/31; 5 pm-9 pm, Sat from 4 pm; hours may vary. **Reservations:** suggested. **Features:** Across from the city marina, the casual waterfront restaurant is a comfortable place for family dining. The menu includes a good selection of steaks, seafood, pizza and burgers—as well as mouthwatering desserts. Sunday brunch is popular during summer. Casual dress; cocktails. **Parking:** on-site. **Cards:** AX, MC, VI.

🍸 ⊠

SCOTTY'S **Lunch:** $3-$7 **Dinner:** $9-$20 **Phone:** 231/843-4033

American **Location:** 1.8 mi w of jct US 10 and 31. 5910 E Ludington Ave 49431. **Hours:** 11:30 am-2 & 5-9 pm, Fri & Sat-10 pm; 11:30 am-2 & 5-10 pm, Sun 9 am-1 pm 6/1-9/30. Closed major holidays. **Features:** Popular dishes include the roast prime rib of beef - the specialty of the house along with several seafood dishes such as their "renowned" lake perch or the seafood kabob. Booths available for more intimate dining. Casual dress; cocktails. **Parking:** on-site. **Cards:** AX, MC, VI.

🍸 ⊠

LUNA PIER pop. 1,483

——— **WHERE TO STAY** ———

SUPER 8 MOTEL-LUNA PIER *Book at aaa.com* **Phone:** (734)848-8880

4/1-9/30 [CP]	1P: $54-$69	2P: $69-$78	XP: $6	F12
10/1-3/31 [CP]	1P: $45-$54	2P: $59-$69	XP: $6	F12

Small-scale Hotel **Location:** I-75, exit 6. 4163 Super 8 Dr 48157. Fax: 734/848-6146. **Facility:** 49 one-bedroom standard units, some with whirlpools. 3 stories, interior corridors. *Bath:* combo or shower only. **Parking:** on-site. **Amenities:** hair dryers. **Pool(s):** small heated indoor. **Business Services:** fax (fee). **Cards:** AX, CB, DC, DS, JC, MC, VI.

SOME UNITS

ASK SD 🍽️ 📶 📺 DATA PORT 💻 / ⊠ 🛢 📠 /

——— **WHERE TO DINE** ———

GANDERS FAMILY RESTAURANT **Lunch:** $6-$8 **Dinner:** $7-$13 **Phone:** 734/848-8913

American **Location:** I-75, exit 6, just e. 4219 Luna Pier Rd 48157. **Hours:** 6 am-9 pm, Fri & Sat-10 pm. Closed: 12/25. **Features:** Fresh lake perch, hamburgers, chicken sandwiches and steaks are among home-style menu selections at this friendly restaurant. Pictures and ceramic figures of geese decorate the casual dining room. Diner-style service is friendly and efficient. Casual dress. **Parking:** on-site. **Cards:** AX, DS, MC, VI.

⊠

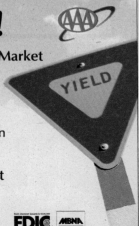

MACKINAC ISLAND pop. 523   (See map and index starting on p. 352)

------ WHERE TO STAY ------

GRAND HOTEL
Phone: (906)847-3331   62

(AAA) (SAVE)   6/11-8/28 [MAP]   1P: $333-$563   2P: $398-$628   XP: $99   F11
5/4-6/10 & 8/29-10/31 [MAP]   1P: $293-$523   2P: $358-$588   XP: $99   F11

Classic Historic Resort Large-Scale Hotel
Location: Overlooking the Straits of Mackinac. Mackinac Island 49757. Fax: 906/847-3259. **Facility:** Those seeking a formal ambience will appreciate this historic 1887 hotel's strict after-six dress code. 385 units. 375 one-bedroom standard units. 6 two-bedroom suites ($1176-$1256). 4 cottages. 6 stories, interior corridors. *Bath:* some shared or private. **Parking:** no self-parking. **Terms:** open 5/4-10/31, 10 day cancellation notice-fee imposed. **Amenities:** video library (fee), safes, honor bars, irons, hair dryers. **Dining:** 2 restaurants, 7:30 am-9:30, noon-2 & 6:30-10 pm, cocktails, entertainment. **Pool(s):** heated outdoor. **Leisure Activities:** sauna, whirlpools, 4 tennis courts, recreation programs in season, jogging, exercise room, volleyball, game room. *Fee:* golf-18 holes, bicycles. **Guest Services:** gift shop, valet laundry. **Business Services:** conference facilities, business center. **Cards:** AX, DC, DS, MC, VI. *(See ad below)*

SOME UNITS

HARBOUR VIEW INN   *Book at aaa.com*
Phone: (906)847-0101   64

(AAA) (SAVE)   5/28-8/28 [ECP]   1P: $145-$235   2P: $145-$235   XP: $20
5/7-5/27 & 8/29-10/31 [ECP]   1P: $85-$235   2P: $85-$235   XP: $20

Small-scale Hotel
Location: 4 blks e. Huron St 49757 (PO Box 1207). Fax: 906/847-3998. **Facility:** Smoke free premises. 65 units. 47 one-bedroom standard units, some with whirlpools. 18 one-bedroom suites ($165-$345). 4 stories (no el-evator), interior corridors. *Bath:* combo or shower only. **Parking:** no self-parking. **Terms:** open 5/7-10/31, 2-3 night minimum stay - weekends, 10 day cancellation notice-fee imposed. **Leisure Activities:** whirlpool. **Business Services:** meeting rooms. **Cards:** AX, CB, DC, DS, MC, VI. **Special Amenities:** free expanded continental breakfast and free local telephone calls. *(See color ad below)*

SOME UNITS

(See map and index starting on p. 352)

THE INN ON MACKINAC
Phone: (906)847-3360 63
♥♥♥ ◆◆ 5/5-10/2 [ECP] 1P: $104-$300 2P: $104-$300 XP: $15 F5
Location: 3 blks e. Main St 49757 (PO Box 476). Fax: 906/847-6110. **Facility:** Smoke free premises. 44 one-
Bed & Breakfast bedroom standard units. 5 stories, interior corridors. *Bath:* combo or shower only. **Parking:** no self-parking.
Amenities: *Some:* hair dryers. **Cards:** MC, VI. **Terms:** open 5/5-10/2, 2 night minimum stay - weekends, cancellation fee imposed, package plans.

ISLAND HOUSE HOTEL
Phone: (906)847-3347 61
◆◆◆ SAVE 6/2-9/6 1P: $180-$300 2P: $185-$309 XP: $20 D13
♥♥♥ ♥♥♥ 5/7-6/1 & 9/7-10/23 1P: $150-$260 2P: $150-$260 XP: $20 D13
Historic **Location:** 3 blks e. 1 Lake Shore Dr 49757 (PO Box 1410). Fax: 906/847-3819. **Facility:** Accommodations vary in
Small-scale Hotel this renovated 1852 historic hotel. 97 units. 94 one-bedroom standard units. 3 two-bedroom suites ($400-
$600) with whirlpools. 4 stories, interior corridors. **Parking:** no self-parking. **Terms:** open 5/7-10/23, 3 day
cancellation notice-fee imposed, [BP] & [MAP] meal plans available. **Amenities:** voice mail, hair dryers.
Some: safes, irons. **Dining:** 2 restaurants, 7:30 am-10:30 & 5:30-10 pm, cocktails, entertainment. **Pool(s):**
heated indoor. **Leisure Activities:** sauna, whirlpool, recreation programs, playground. *Fee:* bicycles. **Business Services:**
meeting rooms. **Cards:** AX, DS, MC, VI. *(See color ad below)*

SOME UNITS

[icons]

(See map and index starting on p. 352)

LAKE VIEW HOTEL AND CONFERENCE CENTER　　　　　　　　　　　　　Phone: (906)847-3384　[66]

(AAA) (SAVE)	5/27-6/10	1P: $139-$251	2P: $139-$251	XP: $25	F17
	5/7-5/26	1P: $99-$200	2P: $99-$200	XP: $25	F17
▽▽▽▽	6/11-8/26	1P: $189	2P: $189	XP: $25	F17
	8/27-10/17	1P: $139	2P: $139	XP: $25	F17

Small-scale Hotel **Location:** Just w. 1 Huron St 49757 (PO Box 190). Fax: 906/847-6283. **Facility:** 85 one-bedroom standard units, some with whirlpools. 4 stories, interior corridors. **Parking:** no self-parking. **Terms:** open 5/7-10/17, 10 day cancellation notice-fee imposed. **Dining:** 7:30 am-10 pm, cocktails. **Pool(s):** heated indoor. **Leisure Activities:** sauna, whirlpool. **Business Services:** conference facilities. **Cards:** DS, MC, VI. *(See color ad below)*

SOME UNITS

(S/D) (¶¶) (Y) (≋) / (✕) (✕K) /

MURRAY HOTEL　　　　　　　　　　　　　　　　　　　　Phone: (906)847-3360　[65]

| ▽▽▽▽ | 5/5-10/9 [ECP] | 1P: $69-$250 | 2P: $69-$250 | XP: $15 | F5 |

Location: Center. Located opposite Arnold Ferry Dock. Main St 49757 (PO Box 476). Fax: 906/847-6110.
Small-scale Hotel **Facility:** Smoke free premises. 69 one-bedroom standard units, some with whirlpools. 4 stories, interior corridors. *Bath:* combo or shower only. **Parking:** no self-parking. **Terms:** open 5/5-10/9, 2 night minimum stay - weekends, 14 day cancellation notice-fee imposed, package plans. **Leisure Activities:** whirlpool. **Cards:** MC, VI.

(ASK) (S/D) (¶+) (✕) (☎)

For nearly 100 years members have counted on AAA for their emergency road service needs, maps, TripTiks and travel information & services.

Insurance

B ut did you know...

Insure With Someone You Trust®

you can also trust AAA to provide you with insurance protection. Most[1] AAA clubs provide a variety of insurance products for all phases of your life, at competitive rates from leading companies in their markets. Policies most often available include coverage for your:

- Automobile
- Home
- Life
- Boat
- RV
- Trip Cancellation
- Travel Delay/Lost Baggage

Call your local AAA office today and ask one of our knowledgeable insurance representatives to help you with your insurance needs.

[1]Due to state regulations and local restrictions, insurance is not available through all AAA clubs.

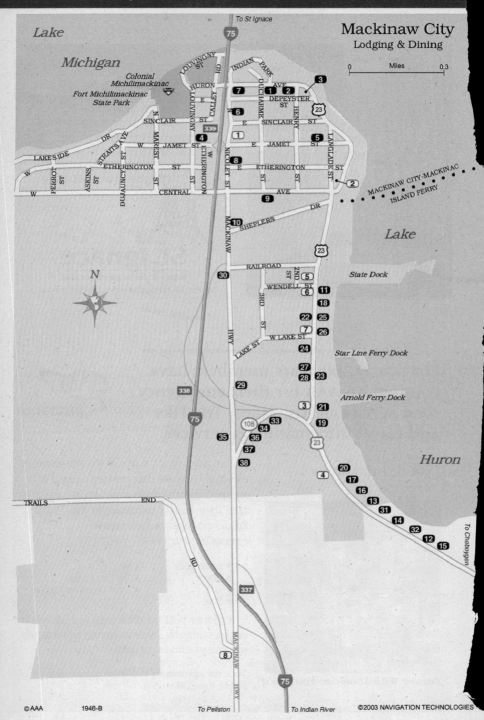

To St Ignace

Mackinaw City
Lodging & Dining

0   Miles   0.3

Lake
Michigan

Colonial
Michilimackinac
Fort Michilimackinac
State Park

Lake

MACKINAW CITY-MACKINAC
ISLAND FERRY

State Dock

Star Line Ferry Dock

Arnold Ferry Dock

Huron

N

To Cheboygan

TRAILS   END

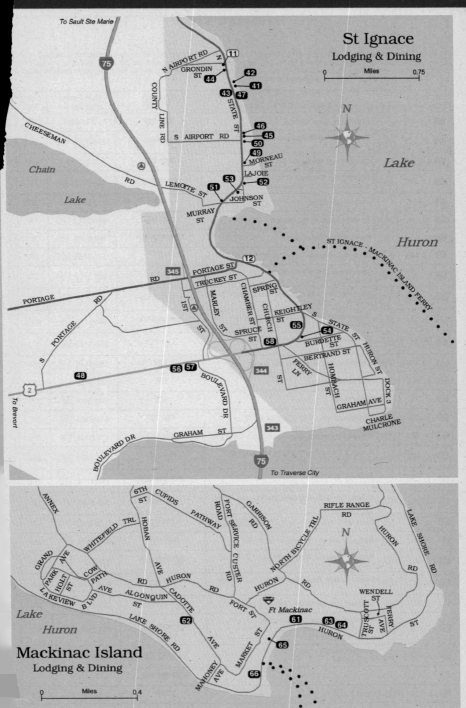

St Ignace
Lodging & Dining

Miles
0   0.75

To Sault Ste Marie

75

N AIRPORT RD
11
GRONDIN
ST
44
42
41
43
47
STATE ST
46
S AIRPORT RD
45
50
49
MORNEAU
LAJOIE
53
52
51
LEMOTTE ST
JOHNSON
ST
MURRAY
ST

CHEESEMAN

Chain
Lake
Lake

COUNTY LINE RD

RD

ST IGNACE - MACKINAC ISLAND FERRY

Lake

Huron

12
345
PORTAGE ST
RD
TRUCKEY ST
SPRING
ST
PORTAGE   RD
MARLEY ST
CHAMBER ST
CHURCH ST
KEIGHTLEY
1ST ST
S   PORTAGE
SPRUCE ST
55
STATE ST
54
BURDETTE
58
ST
BERTRAND ST
56 57
FERRY LN
HURON ST
2
48
BOULEVARD DR
344
ST
HOMBACH ST
DOCK 3
To Brevort
343
GRAHAM   ST
BOULEVARD DR
GRAHAM AVE
CHARLE
MULCRONE
75
To Traverse City

Mackinac Island
Lodging & Dining

Miles
0   0.4

ANNEX
6TH ST
CUPIDS
PATHWAY
FORT SERVICE ROAD
GARRISON RD
RIFLE RANGE RD
LAKE SHORE RD
HURON RD
WHITEFIELD TRL
HOBAN AVE
CUSTER RD
NORTH BICYCLE TRL
GRAND AVE
PARK AVE
COW PATH
RD
HURON AVE
HURON RD
RD
HOLT ST
LAKEVIEW B LVD
ALGONQUIN ST
CADOTTE AVE
FORT ST
WENDELL ST
TRUSCOTT ST
FERRY AVE
62
LAKE SHORE RD
MARKET ST
Ft Mackinac
61
63 64
HURON
Lake
Huron
65
MAHONEY AVE
66

Mackinaw City

This index helps you "spot" where approved accommodations and restaurants are located on the corresponding detailed maps.
Lodging rate ranges are for comparison only and show the property's high season; rates are per night, unless only weekly (W)
rates are available. Restaurant rate range is for dinner, unless only lunch (L) is served. Turn to the listing page for more detailed
rate information and consult display ads for special promotions.

Spotter/Map Page Number	OA	MACKINAW CITY - Lodgings	Diamond Rating	Rate Range High Season	Listing Page
1 / p. 352		Lighthouse View Motel	◆◆	$45-$95	380
2 / p. 352	AAA	Super 8 Motel Bridgeview - see color ad p 367, p 84	◆◆	$49-$179 SAVE	385
3 / p. 352		Budget Host Mackinaw City	◆◆	$72-$128	370
4 / p. 352	AAA	Holiday Inn Express at the Bridge - see color ad p 384, p 378, inside back cover	◆◆◆	$55-$259 SAVE	377
5 / p. 352		Lamplighter Motel	◆	$54-$97	380
6 / p. 352	AAA	Econo Lodge at the Bridge	◆◆	$60-$180 SAVE	374
7 / p. 352	AAA	Parkside Inn-Bridgeside	◆◆◆	$58-$198 SAVE	382
8 / p. 352	AAA	Motel 6-Downtown - see color ad p 384	◆	$47-$169 SAVE	380
9 / p. 352	AAA	Downing's Downtown Motor Inn - see color ad p 374	◆◆	$58-$155 SAVE	374
10 / p. 352	AAA	Baymont Inn & Suites-Mackinaw City - see color ad p 369	◆◆◆	$99-$199 SAVE	369
11 / p. 352	AAA	Best Western-Dockside Waterfront Inn - see color ad starting on p 358, p 368, p 84	◆◆◆	$58-$198 SAVE	369
12 / p. 352	AAA	Clearwater Lakeshore Motel - see color ad p 373	◆◆	$58-$149 SAVE	373
13 / p. 352	AAA	Beachcomber Motel on the Water	◆	$59-$145 SAVE	369
14 / p. 352	AAA	The Beach House	◆	$57-$160 SAVE	369
15 / p. 352	AAA	Chief Motel	◆	$49-$99 SAVE	371
16 / p. 352	AAA	Waterfront Inn - see color ad p 372	◆◆	$59-$124 SAVE	387
17 / p. 352	AAA	Chippewa Motor Lodge - see color ad p 372	◆◆	$59-$124 SAVE	371
18 / p. 352	AAA	Super 8 Motel-Beachfront - see color ad p 365, p 84	◆◆	$48-$178 SAVE	385
19 / p. 352	AAA	Clarion Hotel Beachfront - see color ad starting on p 362, p 84	◆◆◆	$58-$198 SAVE	372
20 / p. 352	AAA	Quality Inn & Suites Beachfront - see color ad p 383	◆◆	$69-$199 SAVE	382
21 / p. 352	AAA	Days Inn - see color ad opposite title page	◆◆	$139-$159 SAVE	374
22 / p. 352	AAA	Rainbow Motel - see color ad p 382	◆◆	$48-$149 SAVE	382
23 / p. 352	AAA	Ramada Limited Waterfront - see color ad p 386	◆◆◆	$99-$189 SAVE	385
24 / p. 352	AAA	Econo Lodge Bayview - see color ad p 366, p 84	◆◆	$38-$168 SAVE	376
25 / p. 352	AAA	Comfort Inn Lakeside - see color ad p 375	◆◆◆	$58-$198 SAVE	374
26 / p. 352	AAA	Hamilton Inn Select-Beachfront - see color ad starting on p 360, inside front cover, p 84, card insert	◆◆	$38-$198 SAVE	377
27 / p. 352	AAA	Comfort Suites - see color ad p 364,, p 84	◆◆◆	$58-$198 SAVE	374
28 / p. 352		Hampton Inn of Mackinaw City	◆◆◆	$70-$300	377
29 / p. 352	AAA	Capri Motel	◆	$49-$89 SAVE	371

Spotter/Map Page Number	OA	MACKINAW CITY - Lodgings (continued)	Diamond Rating	Rate Range High Season	Listing Page
30 / p. 352		Ramada Inn Conference Resort - see color ad p 383	◇◇	$109-$209	382
31 / p. 352	AAA	Northpointe Inn - see color ad p 381	◇◇◇	$99-$129 SAVE	380
32 / p. 352	AAA	Grand View Resort-Beachfront - see color ad p 376	◇◇	$38-$188 SAVE	377
33 / p. 352	AAA	Travelodge-Bayview - see color ad p 387	◇◇	$32-$188 SAVE	387
34 / p. 352	AAA	Best Western Thunderbird Inn - see color ad p 371	◇◇◇	$59-$139 SAVE	370
35 / p. 352	AAA	Kings Inn	◇	$59-$99 SAVE	380
36 / p. 352	AAA	Anchor Budget Inns - see color ad p 357	◇◇	$52-$119 SAVE	357
37 / p. 352	AAA	Budget Inns-Starlite	◇	$49-$149 SAVE	371
38 / p. 352	AAA	Best Western of Mackinaw City - see color ad p 370	◇◇◇	$59-$139 SAVE	370
		MACKINAW CITY - Restaurants			
1 / p. 352	AAA	Chippewa Room at Audie's	◇◇	$11-$30	388
2 / p. 352	AAA	Dixie's Saloon	◇	$11-$18	388
3 / p. 352	AAA	The Embers	◇	$10-$15	388
4 / p. 352	AAA	Mario's Ristorante	◇	$9-$17	389
5 / p. 352	AAA	Anna's Country Buffet - see color ad p 388	◇	$7-$14	388
6 / p. 352	AAA	Admiral's Table	◇	$8-$20	388
7 / p. 352	AAA	Lighthouse Restaurant	◇◇	$11-$34	389
8 / p. 352	AAA	Neath the Birches	◇◇	$11-$34	389
		ST. IGNACE - Lodgings			
41 / p. 352	AAA	Kewadin Casino Lakefront Inn	◇◇	$89-$109 SAVE	434
42 / p. 352		Bay View Motel	◇	$54-$76	427
43 / p. 352	AAA	Days Inn St. Ignace - see color ad p 432, card insert	◇◇	$59-$149 SAVE	432
44 / p. 352		Tradewinds Motel	◇	$55-$79	437
45 / p. 352	AAA	Quality Inn Lakefront - see color ad p 437	◇◇	$94-$164 SAVE	434
46 / p. 352	AAA	K-Royale Motor Inn - see color ad p 436	◇◇	$58-$155 SAVE	434
47 / p. 352	AAA	Days Inn Lakefront & Suites - see color ad p 432, card insert	◇◇◇	$79-$169 SAVE	430
48 / p. 352	AAA	Four Star Motel	◇	$40-$47 SAVE	433
49 / p. 352	AAA	Comfort Inn - see color ad opposite title page	◇◇	$49-$198 SAVE	429
50 / p. 352	AAA	Holiday Inn Express Lakefront - see color ad p 435	◇◇◇	$140-$230 SAVE	433
51 / p. 352	AAA	Budget Host Inn - see color ad p 430	◇◇	$74-$156 SAVE	428
52 / p. 352	AAA	Best Western Harbour Pointe Lakefront - see color ad p 428	◇◇◇	$89-$198 SAVE	427
53 / p. 352	AAA	Wayside Motel	◇	$35-$75 SAVE	437
54 / p. 352		Aurora Borealis Motor Inn - see ad p 427	◇◇	$49-$89	427
55 / p. 352	AAA	Econo Lodge Inn & Suites - see color ad p 434	◇◇	$69-$130 SAVE	432
56 / p. 352	AAA	Super 8 of St. Ignace	◇◇	$78-$119 SAVE	437

Spotter/Map Page Number	OA	ST. IGNACE - Lodgings (continued)	Diamond Rating	Rate Range High Season	Listing Page
57 / p. 352	AAA	Quality Inn St. Ignace	◇◇	$100-$165 SAVE	434
58 / p. 352	AAA	Rodeway Inn	◇◇	$75-$155 SAVE	437
		ST. IGNACE - Restaurants			
11 / p. 352		North Bay Inn	◇	$8-$15	438
12 / p. 352	AAA	The Galley Restaurant & Bar	◇	$9-$16	438
		MACKINAC ISLAND - Lodgings			
61 / p. 352	AAA	Island House Hotel - see color ad p 349	◇◇	$180-$309 SAVE	349
62 / p. 352	AAA	Grand Hotel - see ad p 348	◇◇◇◇	$333-$628 SAVE	348
63 / p. 352		The Inn on Mackinac	◇◇	$104-$300	349
64 / p. 352	AAA	Harbour View Inn - see color ad p 348	◇◇◇	$145-$235 SAVE	348
65 / p. 352		Murray Hotel	◇◇	$69-$250	350
66 / p. 352	AAA	Lake View Hotel and Conference Center - see color ad p 350	◇◇◇	$139-$251 SAVE	350

Get the Complete Picture.

When making travel plans online at **aaa.com**, look for lodgings and attractions with an online photo gallery or online TourBook® ad. The photographs and descriptive text allow you to "virtually" experience the property or attraction prior to making your reservations or buying your tickets.

Properties with a photo gallery or an ad are easily located in the online TourBook or Internet TripTik®/Traveler of aaa.com. Simply begin your search by entering your trip criteria such as destination, and then look for the listings featuring the camera icon.

So, the next time you're making travel plans look to aaa.com for <u>complete</u> travel information.

MACKINAW CITY pop. 859   (See map and index starting on p. 352)

──────── WHERE TO STAY ────────

ANCHOR BUDGET INNS

					Phone: (231)436-5553	36
(AAA) SAVE	6/25-8/17 [CP]	1P: $52-$119	2P: $52-$119		XP: $5	F12
	4/1-6/24 & 8/18-11/15 [CP]	1P: $29-$79	2P: $29-$79		XP: $5	F12

▽▽▽
♦♦
Motel

Location: I-75, exit 338 southbound, 0.3 mi e; exit 337 northbound, just ne. 138 US 31 49701 (PO Box 812). Fax: 231/436-7440. **Facility:** 34 units. 32 one- and 2 two-bedroom standard units, some with whirlpools. 2 stories (no elevator), interior/exterior corridors. **Parking:** on-site. **Terms:** open 4/1-11/15, 3 day cancellation notice-fee imposed, weekly rates available, package plans - seasonal. **Amenities:** *Some:* hair dryers. **Pool(s):** heated indoor. **Leisure Activities:** whirlpool, snowmobiling, playground. *Fee:* game room. **Cards:** AX, CB, DC, DS, MC, VI. **Special Amenities:** free expanded continental breakfast and early check-in/late check-out. *(See color ad below)*

SOME UNITS

🅂 🕆 ⛵ ✕ 🎥 🔒 📺 / ✕ 📷 /

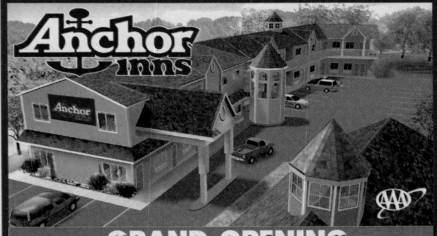

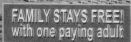

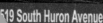 

(See map and index starting on p. 352)

BAYMONT INN & SUITES-MACKINAW CITY   *Book at aaa.com*   Phone: (231)436-7737    ⑩

△△△ SAVE
▽▽▽▽▽

6/24-8/22 [ECP]	1P: $99-$199	2P: $99-$199
8/23-10/23 [ECP]	1P: $79-$109	2P: $79-$109
5/28-6/23 [ECP]	1P: $69-$109	2P: $69-$109
4/23-5/27 [ECP]	1P: $59-$89	2P: $59-$89

Small-scale Hotel **Location:** I-75, exit 338. Located at entrance to Mackinaw Crossings. 109 S Nicolet St 49701 (PO Box 860, MACKINAW). Fax: 231/436-5427. **Facility:** 80 one-bedroom standard units, some with whirlpools. 3 stories, interior corridors. *Bath:* combo or shower only. **Parking:** on-site. **Terms:** open 4/23-10/23, pets ($50 deposit, in smoking units). **Amenities:** video games, voice mail, irons, hair dryers. **Pool(s):** heated indoor. **Leisure Activities:** whirlpool, snowmobiling, exercise room. **Guest Services:** coin laundry. **Business Services:** meeting rooms. **Cards:** AX, DC, DS, MC, VI. **Special Amenities:** free local telephone calls and free newspaper. *(See color ad below)*

SOME UNITS
[S🆔] [🛏] [↕] [🎮] [🏊] [✕] [🎬] [DATA PORT] [💻] / [✕] [🍴] [📷] /
FEE

BEACHCOMBER MOTEL ON THE WATER   Phone: 231/436-8451   ⑬

△△△ SAVE
▽▽▽

6/25-8/22 [CP]	1P: $59-$145	2P: $59-$145	XP: $5	F5
5/1-6/24 & 8/23-10/31 [CP]	1P: $35-$95	2P: $37-$99	XP: $5	F5

Motel **Location:** 1 mi s on US 23. Located on Lake Huron. 1011 S Huron Ave 49701 (PO Box 159). **Facility:** 22 units. 21 one-bedroom standard units, some with whirlpools. 1 cottage. 1-2 stories (no elevator), exterior corridors. *Bath:* combo or shower only. **Parking:** on-site. **Terms:** open 5/1-10/31, 3 day cancellation notice, small pets only ($10 extra charge). **Amenities:** video library (fee). **Leisure Activities:** pool privileges, playground. **Cards:** AX, DS, MC, VI. **Special Amenities:** free continental breakfast and free local telephone calls.

SOME UNITS
[S🆔] [🛏] [↕] / [✕] [VCR] [🍴] [📷] /
FEE

THE BEACH HOUSE   Phone: (231)436-5353   ⑭

△△△ SAVE
▽▽▽

6/25-9/6 [CP]	2P: $57-$160
4/30-6/24 & 9/7-10/18 [CP]	2P: $39-$115

Cottage **Location:** 1.3 mi s. Located on Lake Huron. 11490 W US 23 St 49701 (PO Box 141). Fax: 231/436-4057. **Facility:** 28 units. 3 one-bedroom standard units. 25 cottages ($39-$160). 1 story, exterior corridors. *Bath:* combo or shower only. **Parking:** on-site. **Terms:** open 4/30-10/18, 14 day cancellation notice-fee imposed, small pets only ($20 extra charge). **Pool(s):** heated indoor. **Leisure Activities:** whirlpool, basketball, horseshoes, volleyball. **Cards:** DS, MC, VI.

SOME UNITS
[🛏] [🏊] [✕] [🎬] [🅿] / [🍴] /
FEE

BEST WESTERN-DOCKSIDE WATERFRONT INN   *Book at aaa.com*   Phone: (231)436-5001   ⑪

△△△ SAVE
▽▽▽▽▽

6/25-8/21 [BP]	1P: $58-$198	2P: $58-$198
4/1-6/24, 8/22-11/30 & 3/1-3/31 [BP]	1P: $38-$148	2P: $38-$148

Motel **Location:** I-75, exit 338 northbound, just n to Central Ave, just e to Huron Ave, then just s; exit 338 southbound, 0.8 mi se. Located on Lake Huron. 505 S Huron Ave 49701 (PO Box 722). Fax: 231/436-5933. **Facility:** 112 one-bedroom standard units, some with whirlpools. 4 stories, exterior corridors. **Parking:** on-site. **Terms:** open 4/1-11/30 & 3/1-3/31, 3 day cancellation notice-fee imposed, weekly rates available, package plans. **Amenities:** video library (fee), dual phone lines, voice mail, irons, hair dryers. **Pool(s):** heated indoor. **Leisure Activities:** whirlpool, rental paddleboats, sun deck. **Business Services:** meeting rooms. **Cards:** AX, CB, DC, DS, MC, VI. **Special Amenities:** free full breakfast and free local telephone calls. *(See color ad starting on p 358, p 368 & p 84)*

SOME UNITS
[S🆔] [↕] [🏊] [✕] [🎬] [DATA PORT] [🍴] [💻] / [✕] [VCR] /
FEE

(See map and index starting on p. 352)

BEST WESTERN OF MACKINAW CITY *Book at aaa.com* Phone: (231)436-5544
AAA [SAVE]
Motel

6/25-8/21 [ECP]	1P: $59-$139	2P: $59-$139	XP: $10
4/16-6/24 & 8/22-10/23 [ECP]	1P: $38-$99	2P: $38-$99	XP: $5

Location: I-75, exit 337 northbound, 0.5 mi n; exit 338 southbound, 0.5 mi s. 112 Old US 31 49701 (PO Box 77
Fax: 231/436-7180. **Facility:** 73 one-bedroom standard units, some with whirlpools. 2 stories (no elevato
exterior corridors. **Parking:** on-site. **Terms:** open 4/16-10/23, 3 day cancellation notice. **Amenities:** iro
hair dryers. **Pool(s):** heated indoor. **Leisure Activities:** whirlpool. **Guest Services:** coin laundry. **Cards:** A
CB, DC, DS, MC, VI. **Special Amenities:** free expanded continental breakfast and early check-in/late check-out.
(See color ad below)

SOME UNITS

BEST WESTERN THUNDERBIRD INN *Book at aaa.com* Phone: (231)436-5433 **34**
AAA [SAVE]
Motel

6/25-8/21 [ECP]	1P: $59-$139	2P: $69-$139	XP: $10	F18
4/23-6/24 & 8/22-10/23 [ECP]	1P: $39-$99	2P: $39-$99	XP: $5	F18

Location: I-75, exit 337 northbound, just ne; exit 338 southbound, 0.7 mi se. 146 Old US 31 49701 (PO Box 251).
Fax: 231/436-7212. **Facility:** 50 one-bedroom standard units, some with whirlpools. 2 stories (no elevator),
exterior corridors. **Terms:** open 4/23-10/23, 3 day cancellation notice-fee imposed.
Amenities: irons, hair dryers. **Pool(s):** heated indoor. **Leisure Activities:** sauna, whirlpool, playground.
Guest Services: coin laundry. **Cards:** AX, CB, DC, DS, MC, VI. **Special Amenities:** free expanded continental breakfast and
free room upgrade (subject to availability with advanced reservations). *(See color ad p 371)*

SOME UNITS

BUDGET HOST MACKINAW CITY Phone: (231)436-5543 **3**
Motel

6/18-8/28	1P: $72-$122	2P: $78-$128	XP: $8	F16
8/29-10/17	1P: $44-$94	2P: $48-$98	XP: $8	F16
5/7-6/17	1P: $42-$92	2P: $46-$96	XP: $8	F16

Location: I-75, exit 339, just n of town. Located opposite of the Straits of Mackinac. 517 N Huron Ave 49701.
Facility: 23 one-bedroom standard units. 2 stories (no elevator), exterior corridors. **Parking:** on-site. **Terms:** open 5/7-10/17, 3
day cancellation notice-fee imposed. **Pool(s):** heated outdoor. **Leisure Activities:** playground. **Cards:** AX, DS, MC, VI.

SOME UNITS

(See map and index starting on p. 352)

BUDGET INNS-STARLITE

Phone: (231)436-5959 [37]

Motel

7/2-9/6 [ECP]	2P: $49-$149	XP: $10	F18
9/7-10/31 [CP]	2P: $39-$98	XP: $10	F18
6/16-7/1 [ECP]	2P: $39-$98	XP: $10	F18
4/1-6/15 [CP]	2P: $28-$69	XP: $10	F18

Location: I-75, exit 338 southbound, 0.3 mi e; exit 337 northbound, then just ne. 116 Old US 31 49701 (PO Box 758). **Parking:** on-site. **Terms:** open 4/1-10/31, 3 day cancellation notice-fee imposed, small pets only ($15 extra charge). **Pool(s):** heated outdoor. **Leisure Activities:** whirlpool, playground, basketball. *Fee:* game room. **Cards:** AX, DC, MC, VI. **Special Amenities:** free expanded continental breakfast and free local telephone calls.

SOME UNITS

CAPRI MOTEL

Phone: (231)436-5498 [29]

Motel

6/23-9/8	1P: $49-$59	2P: $59-$89	XP: $5	F16
4/1-6/22 & 9/9-3/31	1P: $29-$59	2P: $39-$59	XP: $5	F16

Location: I-75, exit 338, just s. Located across from the information center. 801 S Nicolet St 49701. Fax: 231/436-7328. **Facility:** 27 one-bedroom standard units. 1 story, exterior corridors. **Parking:** on-site. **Terms:** cancellation fee imposed, [CP] meal plan available, small pets only ($10 extra charge). **Pool(s):** heated outdoor. **Leisure Activities:** snowmobiling, picnic tables and grills, playground, horseshoes, volleyball. **Cards:** AX, DS, MC, VI. **Special Amenities:** free continental breakfast.

SOME UNITS

CHIEF MOTEL

Phone: 231/436-7981 [15]

Motel

6/25-8/22	1P: $49-$99	2P: $56-$99	XP: $5
5/22-6/24 & 8/23-9/11	1P: $32-$59	2P: $38-$65	XP: $5

Location: 1 mi s. 10470 US 23 49701 (PO Box 175). **Facility:** 16 one-bedroom standard units. 1 story, exterior corridors. *Bath:* combo or shower only. **Parking:** on-site. **Terms:** open 5/22-9/11, cancellation fee imposed. **Pool(s):** heated outdoor. **Cards:** MC, VI. **Special Amenities:** free local telephone calls.

SOME UNITS

CHIPPEWA MOTOR LODGE

Phone: 231/436-8661 [17]

Motel

7/1-8/14 [CP]	1P: $59-$124	2P: $59-$124
8/15-10/17 [CP]	1P: $32-$89	2P: $32-$89
5/1-6/30 [CP]	1P: $29-$89	2P: $29-$89

Location: 1 mi se on US 23. Located on Lake Huron. 929 S Huron Ave 49701 (PO Box 518). Fax: 231/436-8661. **Facility:** 39 units. 26 one-bedroom standard units. 13 cabins ($59-$189). 1-3 stories (no elevator), exterior corridors. *Bath:* combo or shower only. **Parking:** on-site. **Terms:** open 5/1-10/17, 3 day cancellation notice. **Pool(s):** heated indoor. **Leisure Activities:** whirlpool, playground, shuffleboard. *Fee:* game room. **Cards:** DS, MC, VI. **Special Amenities:** free continental breakfast and free local telephone calls. *(See color ad p 372)*

SOME UNITS

(See map and index starting on p. 352)

CLARION HOTEL BEACHFRONT *Book at aaa.com* Phone: (231)436-5539 **19**

AAA SAVE 6/25-8/21 [BP] 1P: $58-$198 2P: $58-$198
4/1-6/24 & 8/22-11/30 [BP] 1P: $38-$148 2P: $38-$148
Motel **Location:** I-75, exit 337 northbound, 0.5 mi n to US 23, 0.3 mi e; exit 338 southbound, 0.8 mi se on US 23. Located on Lake Huron. 905 S Huron Ave 49701 (PO Box 508). Fax: 231/436-7107. **Facility:** 112 units. 85 one- and 27 two-bedroom standard units, some with whirlpools. 2-4 stories, exterior corridors. **Parking:** on-site. **Terms:** open 4/1-11/30, 3 day cancellation notice-fee imposed, weekly rates available, package plans. **Amenities:** video library (fee), dual phone lines, voice mail, irons, hair dryers. **Pool(s):** heated indoor. **Leisure Activities:** whirlpool, sun deck, playground. **Guest Services:** tanning facility. **Business Services:** meeting rooms. **Cards:** AX, CB, DC, DS, MC, VI. **Special Amenities:** free full breakfast. *(See color ad starting on p 362 & p 84)*

SOME UNITS

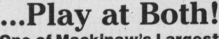

(ee map and index starting on p. 352)

CLEARWATER LAKESHORE MOTEL

AAA SAVE

Motel

7/1-8/15	1P: $58-$149	2P: $58-$149	XP: $10
5/14-6/30 & 8/16-10/23	1P: $38-$129	2P: $38-$129	XP: $6

Phone: (231)436-7800   **12**

F14
F14

Location: On US 23, 1 mi s. Located on Lake Huron. 1247 S Huron Ave 49701 (PO Box 327). **Facility:** 40 units. 36 one-bedroom standard units, some with whirlpools. 2 one- and 2 two-bedroom suites ($110-$325) with efficiencies. 2 stories (no elevator), interior/exterior corridors. **Parking:** on-site. **Terms:** open 5/14-10/23, 3 day cancellation notice-fee imposed, [CP] meal plan available. **Amenities:** hair dryers. *Some:* irons. **Pool(s):** heated indoor. **Leisure Activities:** whirlpool, playground, basketball, horseshoes. **Cards:** AX, DS, MC, VI. **Special Amenities:** free continental breakfast and early check-in/late check-out. *(See color ad below)*

SOME UNITS

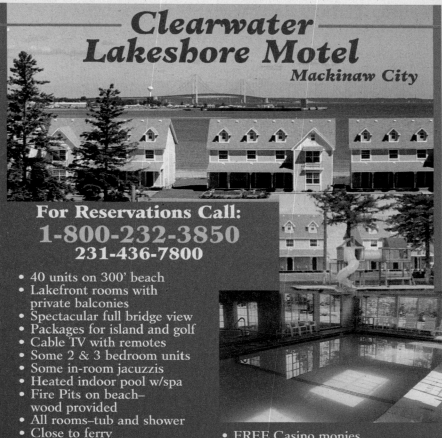

(See map and index starting on p. 352)

COMFORT INN LAKESIDE   Book at aaa.com

Phone: (231)436-5057

AAA SAVE
Motel

| 6/25-8/21 [ECP] | 1P: $58-$198 | 2P: $58-$198 | XP: $10 |
| 5/1-6/24 & 8/22-10/30 [ECP] | 1P: $38-$148 | 2P: $38-$148 | XP: $10 |

Location: I-75, exit 337 northbound, 0.5 mi n to US 23, 0.3 mi e, then just n; exit 338 southbound, 0.8 mi se on US 2 then just n. Located on Lake Huron. 611 S Huron Ave 49701 (PO Box 40). Fax: 231/436-7385. **Facility:** 60 on bedroom standard units, some with whirlpools. 3 stories (no elevator), exterior corridors. **Parking:** on-si **Terms:** open 5/1-10/30, cancellation fee imposed, package plans. **Amenities:** irons, hair dryers. **Pool(s** heated indoor. **Leisure Activities:** whirlpool. **Cards:** AX, CB, DC, DS, MC, VI. **Special Amenities:** free expanded continent breakfast and preferred room (subject to availability with advanced reservations). *(See color ad p 375)*

SOME UNIT

COMFORT SUITES

Phone: (231)436-5929   27

AAA SAVE
Small-scale Hotel

| 6/25-8/21 [BP] | 1P: $58-$198 | 2P: $58-$198 |
| 4/1-6/24 & 8/22-11/30 [BP] | 1P: $38-$148 | 2P: $38-$148 |

Location: I-75, exit 337 northbound, 0.5 mi n to US 23, just e to Huron Ave, then just n; exit 338 southbound, 0.8 mi se on US 23, just n. Located opposite ferry boat docks. 720 S Huron Ave 49701 (PO Box 282). Fax: 231/436-8132. **Facility:** 40 units. 13 one-bedroom standard units, some with whirlpools. 18 one- and 9 two-bedroom suites ($58-$288), some with whirlpools. 3 stories, interior/exterior corridors. **Bath:** combo or shower only. **Parking:** on-site. **Terms:** open 4/1-11/30, 3 day cancellation notice-fee imposed, weekly rates available, package plans. **Amenities:** video library (fee), dual phone lines, voice mail, irons, hair dryers. **Leisure Activities:** pool privileges. **Cards:** AX, CB, DC, DS, MC, VI. **Special Amenities:** free full breakfast and free local telephone calls. *(See color ad p 364 & p 84)*

SOME UNITS

DAYS INN   Book at aaa.com

Phone: (231)436-5557   21

AAA SAVE
Motel

6/30-8/31	1P: $139-$159	2P: $139-$159	XP: $10	F
6/16-6/29	1P: $79-$139	2P: $79-$139	XP: $10	F
5/1-6/15 & 9/1-10/31	1P: $59-$129	2P: $59-$129	XP: $10	F

Location: I-75, exit 337 northbound, 0.5 mi n to US 23, 0.3 mi e; exit 338 southbound, 0.8 mi se on US 23. Located next to the ferry boat docks. 825 S Huron Ave 49701 (PO Box 252). Fax: 231/436-5703. **Facility:** 84 one-bedroom standard units, some with whirlpools. 2 stories (no elevator), exterior corridors. **Parking:** on-site. **Terms:** open 5/1-10/31, cancellation fee imposed, [BP] meal plan available, pets ($15 fee). **Amenities:** voice mail, hair dryers. **Dining:** 7 am-9 pm; hours may vary, cocktails. **Pool(s):** heated indoor. **Leisure Activities:** putting green, playground. **Guest Services:** coin laundry. **Business Services:** meeting rooms. **Cards:** AX, CB, DC, DS, MC, VI. **Special Amenities:** free expanded continental breakfast and free local telephone calls. *(See color ad opposite title page)*

SOME UNITS
FEE   FEE   FEE

DOWNING'S DOWNTOWN MOTOR INN

Phone: (231)436-5528   9

AAA SAVE
Small-scale Hotel

6/15-9/10	1P: $58-$98	2P: $68-$155	XP: $10	F18
9/11-3/31	1P: $48-$95	2P: $58-$110	XP: $10	F18
4/1-6/14	1P: $48	2P: $58	XP: $10	F18

Location: Center. 202 E Central Ave 49701 (PO Box 747). Fax: 231/436-5346. **Facility:** 42 units. 36 one-bedroom standard units, some with whirlpools. 6 one-bedroom suites ($98-$175) with whirlpools. 2 stories (no elevator), interior/exterior corridors. **Parking:** on-site. **Terms:** 3 day cancellation notice-fee imposed. **Pool(s):** heated indoor. **Leisure Activities:** whirlpool, snowmobiling, exercise room. *Fee:* game room. **Cards:** AX, DC, DS, MC. **Special Amenities:** free local telephone calls. *(See color ad below)*

SOME UNITS

ECONO LODGE AT THE BRIDGE   Book at aaa.com

Phone: (231)436-5026   6

AAA SAVE
Motel

| 6/18-9/6 | 1P: $60-$180 | 2P: $60-$180 | XP: $8 |
| 4/1-6/17 & 9/7-3/31 | 1P: $45-$90 | 2P: $45-$90 | XP: $8 |

Location: I-75, exit 339. 412 N Nicolet St 49701 (PO Box 69). Fax: 231/436-4172. **Facility:** 32 one-bedroom standard units. 1-2 stories (no elevator), exterior corridors. **Parking:** on-site. **Cards:** AX, DS, MC, VI **Special Amenities:** free local telephone calls and preferred room (subject to availability with advanced reservations).

SOME UNITS

(See map and index starting on p. 352)

ECONO LODGE BAYVIEW   *Book at aaa.com*   Phone: (231)436-5777

AAA SAVE

Motel

6/25-8/21   1P: $38-$168   2P: $38-$168
4/1-6/24 & 8/22-11/30   1P: $38-$98   2P: $38-$98
Location: I-75, exit 337 northbound, 0.5 mi n to US 23, 0.3 mi e, then just n; exit 338 southbound, 0.8 mi se on US
then just n. Located opposite the ferry boat docks. 712 S Huron Ave 49701 (PO Box 282). Fax: 231/436-7(
Facility: 46 one-bedroom standard units, some with whirlpools. 1-2 stories (no elevator), exterior corrid
Parking: on-site. **Terms:** open 4/1-11/30, 3 day cancellation notice-fee imposed, weekly rates availa
package plans. **Amenities:** video library (fee), dual phone lines, voice mail. **Pool(s):** heated indoor. **Leisure Activities:** sa
whirlpool, playground. **Cards:** AX, CB, DC, DS, MC, VI. **Special Amenities:** free local telephone calls.
(See color ad p 366 & p 84)

SOME UNITS

(…map and index starting on p. 352)

…ND VIEW RESORT-BEACHFRONT

Phone: (231)436-8100

 SAVE   5/1-10/20 [BP]   1P: $38-$188   2P: $38-$188

Motel   **Location:** 1 mi s. Located on Lake Huron. 1143 S Huron Ave 49701 (PO Box 750). Fax: 231/436-8200. **Facility:** 23 units. 22 one-bedroom standard units. 1 one-bedroom suite ($59-$299) with kitchen. 2 stories (no elevator), exterior corridors. **Parking:** on-site. **Terms:** open 5/1-10/20, 3 day cancellation notice-fee imposed, package plans, pets ($10 extra charge, in designated units). **Amenities:** irons, hair dryers. **Pool(s):** heated outdoor. **Leisure Activities:** whirlpool, playground. *Fee:* jet ski. **Cards:** AX, CB, DC, DS, JC, MC, VI. **Special Amenities:** free breakfast and free local telephone calls. *(See color ad p 376)*

SOME UNITS

…MILTON INN SELECT-BEACHFRONT

Phone: (231)436-5493

SAVE   All Year [BP]   1P: $38-$198   2P: $38-$198

Location: I-75, exit 338 northbound, just n to Central Ave, just e to Huron Ave, then just s; exit 338 southbound, 0.8 mi se on US 23, then just n. Located on Lake Huron. 701 S Huron Ave 49701 (PO Box 831). Fax: 231/436-7869. **Facility:** 96 units. 83 one- and 13 two-bedroom standard units, some with whirlpools. 3 stories, interior cor-

…mall-scale Hotel   ridors. **Parking:** on-site. **Terms:** 3 day cancellation notice-fee imposed, weekly rates available, package plans. **Amenities:** video library (fee), dual phone lines, voice mail, irons, hair dryers. *Some:* video games …n laundry. *Fee:* tanning facility. **Business Services:** meeting rooms. **Cards:** AX, CB, DC, DS, MC, VI. **Special Amenities:** …e full breakfast and free local telephone calls.

…ee color ad starting on p 360, inside front cover, p 84 & card insert)

SOME UNITS

…MPTON INN OF MACKINAW CITY   Book at aaa.com

Phone: (231)436-7829

	6/13-9/1 [ECP]	1P: $70-$280	2P: $80-$300	XP: $10	F12
	5/1-6/12 [ECP]	1P: $40-$100	2P: $45-$110	XP: $5	F12
	9/2-10/31 [ECP]	1P: $40-$100	2P: $45-$110	XP: $10	F12

…mall-scale Hotel   **Location:** I-75, exit 337 northbound, 0.5 mi n to US 23, just e to Huron Ave, then just n; exit 338 southbound, 0.8 mi e …US 23. Located opposite the ferry boat docks. 726 S Huron Ave 49701 (PO Box 187). Fax: 231/436-9881. **Facility:** 62 one-bedroom …ndard units. 3 stories, interior corridors. *Bath:* combo or shower only. **Parking:** on-site. **Terms:** open 5/1-10/31, cancellation … imposed. **Amenities:** voice mail, irons, hair dryers. **Pool(s):** heated indoor. **Cards:** AX, DC, DS, JC, MC, VI.

SOME UNITS

…OLIDAY INN EXPRESS AT THE BRIDGE   Book at aaa.com

Phone: (231)436-7100

| | 6/24-8/21 [ECP] | 1P: $55-$259 | 2P: $55-$259 | XP: $6 | F17 |
| | 4/1-6/23 & 8/22-3/31 [ECP] | 1P: $45-$159 | 2P: $45-$159 | XP: $6 | F17 |

…mall-scale Hotel   **Location:** I-75, exit 339. 364 Louvigny 49701. Fax: 231/436-7070. **Facility:** 102 units. 95 one- and 2 two-bedroom standard units, some with whirlpools. 5 one-bedroom suites, some with whirlpools. 4 stories, interior corridors. *Bath:* combo or shower only. **Parking:** on-site. **Terms:** check-in 4 pm, pets ($50 deposit, in designated units). **Amenities:** video library (fee), voice mail, irons, hair dryers. *Some:* dual phone lines. …ol(s): heated indoor. **Leisure Activities:** sauna, whirlpool, snowmobiling, sun deck, exercise room. *Fee:* game room. **Guest …rvices:** coin laundry. **Cards:** AX, CB, DC, DS, JC, MC, VI. **Special Amenities:** free expanded continental breakfast and …e local telephone calls. *(See color ad p 384, p 378 & inside back cover)*

SOME UNITS

Holiday Inn EXPRESS®
"At The Bridge"

2003-2004 National Renovation of the Year Award Winner

- ◆ Kids 17 & Under Stay Free
- ◆ 25" Remote TV with Free HBO/ESPN/CNN
- ◆ Non-smoking Rooms & Suites ◆ Private Balconies
- ◆ Deluxe Jacuzzi & Honeymoon Suites w/ 2 Person Whirlpool, Micro-frige
- ◆ In-room Coffee, Hair Dryers, Irons, Dataports & Voice Mail
- ◆ 24 Hr Desk, Coffee & Tea ◆ Deluxe Fitness Facility
- ◆ Discount Coupons & Casino Packages
- ◆ Elevator ◆ Free Local Calls ◆ Guest Laundry
- ◆ Restaurant Adj, Walk to Shops, Mackinaw Crossings, Laser Show & Outdoor Concerts

1/2 Off Automatic Touch-Free Car Wash for All Guest
(1/2 Block from Hotel)

Enjoy an EXPRESS *Start* Breakfast!

Deluxe Fitness Center

One Block From Hotel

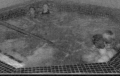

Large Jacuzzi Hot Tub

Indoor Heated Pool

(See map and index starting on p. 352)

KINGS INN

Phone: (231)436-5322

AAA SAVE

6/16-9/7 [CP]	1P: $59-$89	2P: $69-$99
5/1-6/15 & 9/8-10/21 [CP]	1P: $39-$59	2P: $39-$59

Location: I-75, exit 337 northbound, 0.5 mi n; exit 338 southbound, 0.5 mi s. 1020 S Nicolet St 49701 (PO Box Fax: 231/436-5405. **Facility:** 25 one-bedroom standard units, some with whirlpools. 1-2 stories (no eleva
Motel exterior corridors. **Parking:** on-site. **Terms:** open 5/1-10/21, 3 day cancellation notice, small pets only designated units). **Pool(s):** heated outdoor. **Leisure Activities:** playground, volleyball. **Cards:** MC,
Special Amenities: free continental breakfast and free local telephone calls.

SOME UNITS

LAMPLIGHTER MOTEL

Phone: 231/436-5350

6/22-9/1	1P: $54-$97	2P: $54-$97	XP: $5
5/1-6/21 & 9/2-11/1	1P: $28-$74	2P: $28-$74	XP: $5

Motel **Location:** I-75, exit 339, just n of town. Located in a quiet area. 303 Jamet St 49701 (PO Box 719). Fax: 231/436-7022
Facility: Smoke free premises. 10 units. 7 one- and 3 two-bedroom standard units, some with efficiencies
1 story, exterior corridors. **Parking:** on-site. **Terms:** open 5/1-11/1. **Cards:** AX, DC, MC, VI.

SOME UNITS

LIGHTHOUSE VIEW MOTEL

Phone: (231)436-5304

6/25-8/21	1P: $45-$85	2P: $55-$95	XP: $10
8/22-10/31	1P: $35-$55	2P: $45-$65	XP: $10
4/23-6/24	1P: $25-$45	2P: $35-$55	XP: $10

Motel **Location:** I-75, exit 339. Located opposite Straits of Mackinac. 699 N Huron Ave 49701 (PO Box 924).
Fax: 231/436-5304. **Facility:** 24 one-bedroom standard units, some with whirlpools. 2 stories (no elevator), exterior corridors.
Parking: on-site. **Terms:** open 4/23-10/31, 3 day cancellation notice, package plans. **Amenities:** hair dryers. **Pool(s):** heated
indoor. **Leisure Activities:** whirlpool. **Cards:** AX, CB, DC, DS, MC, VI.

SOME UNITS

MOTEL 6-DOWNTOWN   *Book at aaa.com*

Phone: (231)436-8961

AAA SAVE

6/24-8/21	1P: $47-$169	2P: $47-$169	XP: $6
5/1-6/23 & 8/22-10/31	1P: $37-$109	2P: $37-$109	XP: $6

Location: I-75, exit 339; at bridge. 206 N Nicolet St 49701. Fax: 231/436-7317. **Facility:** 53 one-bedroom standar
units, some with whirlpools. 2 stories (no elevator), interior/exterior corridors. **Parking:** on-site, winter plug
Motel ins. **Terms:** open 5/1-10/31, pets (in designated units). **Pool(s):** heated indoor. **Leisure Activities:** whirlpoo
sun deck. **Cards:** AX, CB, DC, DS, MC, VI. **Special Amenities: free local telephone calls and preferre
room (subject to availability with advanced reservations).** *(See color ad p 384)*

SOME UNITS

FEE

NORTHPOINTE INN

Phone: (231)436-9812

AAA SAVE

6/25-8/21	1P: $99-$129	2P: $99-$129	XP: $10
5/7-6/24 & 8/22-10/17	1P: $49-$129	2P: $49-$129	XP: $10

Location: I-75, exit 337 northbound, 0.5 mi n to US 23, then 0.6 mi se; exit 338 southbound, 1.5 mi se on US 23. L
cated on Lake Huron. 1027 S Huron Ave 49701. Fax: 231/436-4010. **Facility:** 98 units. 92 one-bedroom standa
Small-scale Hotel units, some with whirlpools. 6 one-bedroom suites, some with whirlpools. 3 stories, interior corridors. Ba
combo or shower only. **Parking:** on-site. **Terms:** open 5/7-10/17, cancellation fee imposed, [ECP] meal p
available. **Amenities:** hair dryers. **Pool(s):** heated indoor. **Leisure Activities:** whirlpool. **Guest Services:** coin laundry. **Bu
ness Services:** meeting rooms. **Cards:** AX, DS, MC, VI. **Special Amenities: free expanded continental breakfast and fi
local telephone calls.** *(See color ad p 381)*

SOME UNITS

Look For Savings

When you pick up a AAA TourBook® guide, look for establishments that display a bright red AAA logo, SAVE icon, and Diamond rating in their listing. These AAA Official Appointment establishments place a high value on the patronage they receive from AAA members. And, by offering members great room rates*, they are willing to go the extra mile to get your business.

So, when you turn to the AAA TourBook guide to make your travel plans, look for the establishments that will give you the special treatment you deserve.

See TourBook Navigator section, page 14, for complete details.

(See map and index starting on p. 352)

PARKSIDE INN-BRIDGESIDE — *Book at aaa.com* Phone: (231)436-8301

(AAA) (SAVE)

6/25-8/18	1P: $58-$198	2P: $58-$198	XP: $10
5/1-6/24 & 8/19-10/25	1P: $58-$168	2P: $58-$168	XP: $10

Motel

Location: I-75, exit 39. Located opposite of Fort Michilimackinac. 771 N Huron Ave 49701 (PO Box 788) Fax: 231/436-7587. **Facility:** 54 one-bedroom standard units, some with whirlpools. 1-3 stories, exterior corridors. **Parking:** on-site. **Terms:** open 5/1-10/25, 3 day cancellation notice, [ECP] meal plan available. **Amenities:** video library (fee), hair dryers. *Some:* irons. **Pool(s):** heated indoor. **Leisure Activities:** whirlpool, exercise room. *Fee:* game room. **Guest Services:** coin laundry. **Business Services:** meeting rooms. **Cards:** AX, DS, MC, VI. **Special Amenities: free expanded continental breakfast and free local telephone calls.**

SOME UNITS

[icons] FEE

QUALITY INN & SUITES BEACHFRONT — *Book at aaa.com* Phone: (231)436-5051

(AAA) (SAVE)

6/25-8/29 [ECP]	1P: $69-$199	2P: $69-$199	XP: $10
8/30-10/17 [ECP]	1P: $33-$135	2P: $33-$135	XP: $10
4/24-6/24 [ECP]	1P: $31-$129	2P: $31-$129	XP: $10

Motel

Location: 1 mi se on US 23. Located on Lake Huron. 917 S Huron Ave 49701 (PO Box 519). Fax: 231/436-7221. **Facility:** 74 units. 63 one- and 3 two-bedroom standard units, some with whirlpools. 8 one-bedroom suites ($89-$259). 1-4 stories, exterior corridors. *Bath:* combo or shower only. **Parking:** on-site. **Terms:** open 4/24-10/17. **Amenities:** hair dryers. *Some:* irons. **Pool(s):** heated indoor. **Leisure Activities:** sauna, whirlpool, playground, volleyball. **Business Services:** meeting rooms. **Cards:** AX, CB, DC, DS, MC, VI. **Special Amenities: free expanded continental breakfast and free local telephone calls.** *(See color ad p 383)*

SOME UNITS

[icons]

RAINBOW MOTEL Phone: 231/436-5518

(AAA) (SAVE)

6/26-8/15	1P: $48-$139	2P: $54-$149	XP: $10
8/16-10/16	1P: $32-$109	2P: $34-$149	XP: $10
5/7-6/25	1P: $32-$82	2P: $34-$104	XP: $10

Motel

Location: I-75, exit 337 northbound, 0.5 mi n to US 23, 0.3 mi e, then just n; exit 338 southbound, 0.8 mi se on US 23, then just n. 602 S Huron Ave 49701 (PO Box 546). Fax: 231/436-7006. **Facility:** 29 one-bedroom standard units, some with whirlpools. 1 story, exterior corridors. *Bath:* combo or shower only. **Parking:** on-site. **Terms:** open 5/10-10/16, 3 day cancellation notice. **Pool(s):** heated indoor. **Leisure Activities:** whirlpools, putting green, picnic tables & barbecue grill, playground, limited exercise equipment, basketball. **Cards:** AX, CB, DC, DS, JC, MC, VI. **Special Amenities: free local telephone calls and preferred room (subject to availability with advanced reservations).** *(See color ad below)*

SOME UNITS

[icons]

RAMADA INN CONFERENCE RESORT — *Book at aaa.com* Phone: (231)436-5535

6/16-9/6	1P: $109-$209	2P: $109-$209	XP: $10
5/7-6/15 & 9/7-10/30	1P: $79-$179	2P: $79-$179	XP: $10

Large-scale Hotel

Location: I-75, exit 338. 450 S Nicolet 49701 (PO Box 57). Fax: 231/436-5849. **Facility:** 148 one-bedroom standard units, some with whirlpools. 3 stories, interior corridors. **Parking:** on-site, winter plug-ins. **Terms:** open 5/7-10/30, check-in 4 pm, [CP] meal plan available, pets ($50 deposit, $10 extra charge). **Amenities:** voice mail, irons, hair dryers. *Some:* video games. **Pool(s):** heated indoor. **Leisure Activities:** sauna, whirlpool. *Fee:* game room. **Guest Services:** coin laundry. **Business Services:** meeting rooms. **Cards:** AX, DC, DS, MC, VI. *(See color ad p 383)*

SOME UNITS

[icons] FEE

RAMADA LIMITED WATERFRONT *Book at aaa.com* Phone: (231)436-5055 **23**

(AAA) (SAVE)

▽▽▽

6/18-8/28 [ECP]	1P: $99-$189	2P: $99-$189	XP: $10	F18
8/29-10/2 [ECP]	1P: $69-$159	2P: $69-$159	XP: $10	F18
4/23-6/17 [ECP]	1P: $49-$139	2P: $49-$139	XP: $10	F18
10/3-10/24 [ECP]	1P: $49-$119	2P: $49-$119	XP: $10	F18

Small-scale Hotel **Location:** I-75, exit 337 northbound, 0.5 mi n to US 23, just e to Huron Ave, then just n; exit 338 southbound, 0.8 mi se on US 23. Located on Lake Huron. 723 S Huron Ave 49701 (PO Box 547). Fax: 231/436-5921. **Facility:** 42 units. 40 one- and 2 two-bedroom standard units, some with whirlpools. 3 stories, interior corridors. **Parking:** on-site. **Terms:** open 4/23-10/24, cancellation fee imposed. **Amenities:** voice mail, irons, hair dryers. **Pool(s):** heated indoor. **Leisure Activities:** whirlpools. **Guest Services:** coin laundry. **Cards:** AX, CB, DC, DS, MC, VI. **Special Amenities:** free expanded continental breakfast and free local telephone calls. *(See color ad p 386)*

SOME UNITS

[icons] / ☒ ▣ /

SUPER 8 MOTEL-BEACHFRONT Phone: (231)436-7111 **18**

(AAA) (SAVE)

▽▽▽

Motel

| 6/25-8/21 | 1P: $48-$178 | 2P: $48-$178 |
| 4/1-6/24 & 8/22-11/30 | 1P: $38-$128 | 2P: $38-$128 |

Location: I-75, exit 337 northbound, 0.5 mi n to US 23, 0.3 mi e, then just n; exit 338 southbound, 0.8 mi se on US 23, then just n. Located on Lake Huron. 519 S Huron Ave 49701 (PO Box 566). Fax: 231/436-7869. **Facility:** 59 one-bedroom standard units, some with whirlpools. 2 stories (no elevator), exterior corridors. **Parking:** on-site. **Terms:** open 4/1-11/30, 3 day cancellation notice-fee imposed, weekly rates available, package plans. **Pool(s):** heated indoor. **Leisure Activities:** sauna, whirlpool, rental paddleboats, fishing. **Cards:** AX, CB, DC, DS, MC, VI. **Special Amenities:** free local telephone calls and early check-in/late check-out. *(See color ad p 365 & p 84)*

SOME UNITS

[icons] / ☒ /

SUPER 8 MOTEL BRIDGEVIEW Phone: (231)436-5252 **2**

(AAA) (SAVE)

▽▽▽

Small-scale Hotel

| 6/25-8/21 [ECP] | 1P: $49-$179 | 2P: $49-$179 |
| 4/1-6/24 & 8/22-11/30 [ECP] | 1P: $38-$128 | 2P: $38-$128 |

Location: I-75, exit 339 northbound (Nicolet St), just n, then just e. Located opposite Straits of Mackinac. 601 N Huron Ave 49701 (PO Box 98). Fax: 231/436-7836. **Facility:** 65 units. 61 one-bedroom standard units, some with whirlpools. 4 one-bedroom suites ($68-$288). 2-3 stories, interior/exterior corridors. **Parking:** on-site. **Terms:** open 4/1-11/30, 3 day cancellation notice-fee imposed, weekly rates available, package plans, pets ($50 deposit, in designated units). **Amenities:** *Some:* video games. **Pool(s):** heated indoor. **Leisure Activities:** sauna, whirlpool, snowmobiling, exercise room. *Fee:* game room. **Guest Services:** coin laundry. **Cards:** AX, CB, DC, DS, MC, VI. **Special Amenities:** free expanded continental breakfast and free local telephone calls. *(See color ad p 367 & p 84)*

SOME UNITS

[icons] FEE / ☒ ▣ ▣ /

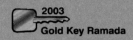

TRAVELODGE-BAYVIEW *Book at aaa.com* Phone: (231)436-7900 **33**

AAA SAVE
5/1-10/31 [BP] 1P: $32-$188 2P: $32-$188

Motel
Location: I-75, exit 337 northbound, 0.5 mi n to US 23, just e; exit 338 southbound, 0.7 mi se on US 23. 900 S Huron Ave 49701 (PO Box 298). Fax: 231/436-7300. **Facility:** 47 one-bedroom standard units; some with whirlpools. 1-2 stories (no elevator), exterior corridors. **Parking:** on-site. **Terms:** open 5/1-10/31, 3 day cancellation notice-fee imposed, package plans, pets (in limited units). **Amenities:** irons, hair dryers. **Pool(s):** heated outdoor, heated indoor. **Leisure Activities:** whirlpool, children's video library, playground, basketball, volleyball. **Cards:** AX, CB, DC, DS, JC, MC, VI. **Special Amenities:** free full breakfast and free local telephone calls. *(See color ad below)*

SOME UNITS

WATERFRONT INN Phone: 231/436-5527 **16**

AAA SAVE
7/1-8/14 [CP]	1P: $59-$124	2P: $59-$124
8/15-10/17 [CP]	1P: $32-$89	2P: $32-$89
5/1-6/30 [CP]	1P: $29-$89	2P: $29-$89

Motel
Location: 1 mi s on US 23. Located on Lake Huron. 1009 S Huron Ave 49701 (PO Box 302). Fax: 231/436-5527. **Facility:** 69 units. 63 one- and 3 two-bedroom standard units. 3 cottages ($59-$189). 1-2 stories (no elevator), exterior corridors. *Bath:* combo or shower only. **Parking:** on-site. **Terms:** open 5/1-10/17, 3 day cancellation notice. **Pool(s):** heated indoor. **Leisure Activities:** whirlpool, playground, shuffleboard. *Fee:* game room. **Cards:** AX, DS, MC, VI.
Special Amenities: free continental breakfast and free local telephone calls. *(See color ad p 372)*

SOME UNITS

—— WHERE TO DINE ——

ADMIRAL'S TABLE   Lunch: $5-$10   Dinner: $8-$20   Phone: 231/436-5687   6
Location: Opposite Mackinac Island Ferry Docks; center. 502 S Huron Ave 49701. **Hours:** Open 5/3-10/20; 7 am-9 pm; to 10 pm 7/1-9/2. **Features:** Visit the warm, friendly restaurant for such favorites as prime rib and Great Lakes whitefish. Servers in sport tops, shorts and sneakers pass through the restaurant, appointed in a nautical theme. The seasonal breakfast buffet is especially popular. Casual dress; cocktails. **Parking:**
Steak & Seafood on-site. **Cards:** AX, DC, DS, MC, VI.

ANNA'S COUNTRY BUFFET   Lunch: $6-$9   Dinner: $7-$14   Phone: 231/436-5195   5
Location: Just se; opposite ferry docks. 416 S Huron Ave 49701. **Hours:** Open 5/1-10/31; 7 am-9:30 pm. **Features:** Although the buffet is popular at breakfast, lunch and dinner, you're welcomed to order from a menu of traditional favorites. The laid-back dining room has a large gift shop in the back section. Casual dress; cocktails. **Parking:** on-site. **Cards:** AX, DC, DS, MC, VI. *(See color ad below)*
American

CHIPPEWA ROOM AT AUDIE'S   Dinner: $11-$30   Phone: 231/436-5744   1
Location: I-75, exit 339; at bridge. 314 Nicolet St 49701. **Hours:** 5 pm-10 pm; hours vary seasonally. Closed: 11/25, 12/25. **Reservations:** suggested. **Features:** American Indian artwork and knickknacks enhance the dining room, where guests can enjoy the leisurely atmosphere. Six tasty preparations of whitefish stand out on the varied menu. The dessert array includes many tempting choices. Opening at 7:30 a.m., this place
American offers a good choice for casual family dining. Casual dress; cocktails. **Parking:** on-site. **Cards:** MC, VI.

DIXIE'S SALOON   Lunch: $6-$8   Dinner: $11-$18   Phone: 231/436-5449   2
Location: Corner of Central St and Huron Ave; center. 401 E Central St 49701. **Hours:** 11 am-10 pm; noon-9 pm 9/4-5/27. Closed: 11/25, 12/25. **Features:** The impressive two-story restaurant—with its massive wood beams, attractive wood decor and warm atmosphere—welcomes all. Booths along the windows on the lower and upper levels provide a view of the water and ferry docks. Choice cuts of steak stand out amid a
American selection of American dishes and snacks. Casual dress; cocktails. **Parking:** street. **Cards:** AX, DS, MC, VI.

THE EMBERS   Lunch: $5-$7   Dinner: $10-$15   Phone: 231/436-5773   3
Location: 0.5 mi s on US 23. 810 S Huron Ave 49701. **Hours:** Open 4/1-10/31; 7 am-10 pm; 8 am-9 pm 4/1-5/29. **Features:** The restaurant's specialty is its smorgasbord, a tempting array of such selections as roast beef, broasted chicken, Cajun whitefish, crab legs and shrimp stir-fry. A daily breakfast buffet also is available. Service is prompt and pleasant. Casual dress; cocktails. **Parking:** on-site. **Cards:** DS, MC, VI.
American

LIGHTHOUSE RESTAURANT   Dinner: $11-$34   Phone: 231/436-5191   (7)

American

Location: I-75, exit 337 northbound, 0.5 mi n to US 23, 0.8 mi e, then just n; exit 338 southbound, 0.8 mi se on US 23, then just n. 618 S Huron Ave 49701. **Hours:** Open 4/1-11/15; 4 pm-10 pm; hours vary off season. **Features:** Tender prime rib, whitefish and all-you-can-eat crab legs are favorite selections at the comfortable restaurant, a hot spot with the tourist crowd. The copper-top bar, wall-mounted brass lamps and lighthouse-motif candles decorate the dining room. Casual dress; cocktails. **Parking:** on-site. **Cards:** AX, CB, DC, DS, MC, VI.

MARIO'S RISTORANTE   Dinner: $9-$17   Phone: 231/436-7818   (4)

Italian

Location: Just s on US 23. 918 S Huron Ave 49701. **Hours:** Open 5/10-10/20; 4 pm-9 pm; to 10 pm in summer. **Features:** Order the Italian sampler to taste a nice selection of manicotti, cannelloni and meat and cheese ravioli, or opt for a delicious pizza. During the summer, seating is nice on the breezy patio. Casual dress; cocktails. **Parking:** on-site. **Cards:** AX, DC, DS, MC, VI.

NEATH THE BIRCHES   Dinner: $11-$34   Phone: 231/436-5401   (8)

Steak & Seafood

Location: I-75, exit 337 northbound; exit 338 (Cheboygan-Alpena) southbound, 1 mi s of blinker on Old US 31 (SR 108). M-108 49701. **Hours:** Open 5/1-10/22; 4 pm-9 pm, Fri & Sat-10 pm. **Features:** In a natural, wooded setting, the restaurant is frequently visited by wild turkeys, raccoons and deer that live nearby. Slow-roasted prime rib, which is served with homemade bread and the salad bar is a succulent choice. Service is warm and friendly. Casual dress; cocktails. **Parking:** on-site. **Cards:** AX, CB, DC, DS, MC, VI.

——— *The following restaurant has not been evaluated by AAA* ———
but is listed for your information only.

DARROW'S FAMILY RESTAURANT   Phone: 231/436-5514

[fyi]   Not evaluated. **Location:** I-75, exit 339, just w. 1106 Louvigny St 49701. **Features:** Old-fashioned, home-style cooking includes such specialties as fresh whitefish, hamburgers and pie.

MADISON HEIGHTS —*See Detroit p. 264.*

MANCELONA pop. 1,408

——— WHERE TO DINE ———

WINDMILL FARMS   Lunch: $4-$7   Dinner: $8-$22   Phone: 231/587-5258

American

Location: 1.5 mi e. 2927 CR 38 49659. **Hours:** Open 4/1-10/31 & 12/1-3/31; 11 am-9 pm, Fri & Sat-10 pm, Sun noon-8 pm; hours may vary off season. Closed: 1/1, 12/24, 12/25; also Mon in winter. **Features:** The family-owned and operated restaurant, decorated with rustic accents, is locally known for its succulent, barbecue baby back ribs and a Sunday special of roast pork. Among wonderful, in-house dessert is the sinful hot fudge caramel cream puff. Casual dress; cocktails. **Parking:** on-site. **Cards:** DS, MC, VI.

MANCHESTER pop. 2,160

——— WHERE TO DINE ———

DAN'S RIVER GRILL   Lunch: $6-$10   Dinner: $10-$17   Phone: 734/428-9500

American

Location: Downtown. 223 E Main St 48158. **Hours:** 11 am-9 pm, Sat-10 pm. Closed major holidays. **Features:** Housed in a former hardware store with exposed brick walls and oak paneling, the eatery featuers several large picture windows overlooking the town stream and former mill. A comedy club on the lower level is popular on weekends. Dressy casual; cocktails. **Parking:** street. **Cards:** AX, CB, DC, DS, MC, VI.

MANISTEE pop. 6,586

——— WHERE TO STAY ———

DAYS INN · *Book at aaa.com*

Small-scale Hotel

6/25-9/5 [CP]	1P: $75-$150	2P: $75-$150	XP: $10 · F16
5/22-6/24 [CP]	1P: $55-$100	2P: $55-$100	XP: $10 · F16
9/6-3/31 [CP]	1P: $55-$90	2P: $55-$90	XP: $10 · F16
4/1-5/21 [CP]	1P: $55-$80	2P: $55-$80	XP: $10 · F16

Phone: (231)723-8385

Location: 1.3 mi s on US 31. 1462 Manistee Hwy 49660. Fax: 231/723-2154. **Facility:** 94 one-bedroom standard units, some with whirlpools. 2 stories (no elevator), interior corridors. **Parking:** on-site, winter plug-ins. **Amenities:** hair dryers. **Pool(s):** heated indoor. **Leisure Activities:** whirlpool, snowmobiling. *Fee:* game room. **Guest Services:** coin laundry. **Business Services:** meeting rooms. **Cards:** AX, DC, DS, MC, VI. *(See color ad card insert)*

SOME UNITS

HILLSIDE MOTEL

Motel

6/16-9/15	1P: $55-$125	2P: $60-$125	XP: $10 · F16
9/16-10/31	1P: $40-$65	2P: $45-$75	XP: $10 · F16
4/15-6/15	1P: $40-$65	2P: $45-$70	XP: $10 · F16

Phone: 231/723-2584

Location: 1.5 mi s. 1675 US 31 S 49660. Fax: 231/723-0578. **Facility:** 20 one-bedroom standard units. 2 stories, exterior corridors. *Bath:* combo or shower only. **Parking:** on-site, winter plug-ins. **Terms:** open 4/15-10/31, cancellation fee imposed, small pets only ($8 extra charge, no cats). **Pool(s):** heated outdoor. **Leisure Activities:** whirlpool, playground. **Cards:** AX, DS, MC, VI.

SOME UNITS

LITTLE RIVER CASINO RESORT

Large-scale Hotel

All Year	1P: $99-$139	2P: $99-$139	XP: $10 · F18

Phone: 231/723-1535

Location: Jct US 31 and SR 22. 2700 Orchard Hwy 49660 (PO Box 417). Fax: 231/398-2593. **Facility:** Located in a rural area, this casino is popular with the locals and the folks who drive here from downstate. 100 one-bedroom standard units. 2 stories, interior corridors. *Bath:* combo or shower only. **Parking:** on-site, winter plug-ins. **Terms:** check-in 4 pm, 2-3 night minimum stay - seasonal. **Amenities:** dual phone lines, voice mail, irons, hair dryers. **Pool(s):** heated indoor. **Leisure Activities:** sauna, whirlpool, snowmobiling, exercise room. **Guest Services:** gift shop. **Business Services:** conference facilities. **Cards:** AX, DS, MC, VI.

SOME UNITS

MANISTEE INN & MARINA

Small-scale Hotel

6/7-9/8 [ECP]	1P: $90-$159	2P: $90-$159	XP: $10 · F12
9/9-12/15 [ECP]	1P: $68-$129	2P: $68-$129	XP: $10 · F12
4/1-6/6 [ECP]	1P: $60-$129	2P: $60-$129	XP: $10 · F12
12/16-3/31 [ECP]	1P: $54-$119	2P: $54-$119	XP: $10 · F12

Phone: 231/723-4000

Location: US 31, just w; downtown. Located in a commercial area. 378 River St 49660. Fax: 231/723-0007. **Facility:** 25 one-bedroom standard units, some with whirlpools. 2 stories, interior corridors. **Parking:** on-site. **Terms:** cancellation fee imposed. **Amenities:** video library (fee), irons, hair dryers. **Leisure Activities:** boat dock. *Fee:* massage. **Guest Services:** coin laundry. *Fee:* tanning facility. **Business Services:** meeting rooms. **Cards:** AX, DC, DS, MC, VI.

SOME UNITS

FEE FEE

MICROTEL INN & SUITES · *Book at aaa.com*

Small-scale Hotel

All Year [CP]	1P: $62-$105	2P: $62-$105	XP: $10 · F16

Phone: (231)398-0008

Location: Jct US 31 and SR 55, just n of town. Located at the outskirts of town. 226 Parkdale Ave 49660. Fax: 231/398-2770. **Facility:** 83 one-bedroom standard units. 3 stories, interior corridors. *Bath:* combo or shower only. **Parking:** on-site. **Cards:** AX, CB, DC, DS, MC, VI.

SOME UNITS

SUPER 8 MOTEL   *Book at aaa.com*   Phone: (231)398-8888
▼▼▼ ▼▼▼   6/28-9/2 [CP]   1P: $70-$120   2P: $75-$130   XP: $5   F17
               9/3-12/31 [CP]   1P: $69-$105   2P: $79-$119   XP: $5   F17
Small-scale Hotel 4/1-6/27 & 1/1-3/31 [CP] 1P: $54-$100 2P: $60-$110   XP: $5   F17
Location: 1 mi n on US 31. 220 Arthur St 49660. **Fax:** 231/398-8888. **Facility:** 67 one-bedroom standard units, some with whirlpools. 2 stories (no elevator), interior corridors. **Bath:** combo or shower only. **Parking:** on-site. **Amenities:** *Some:* hair dryers. **Guest Services:** coin laundry. **Cards:** AX, DS, MC, VI.

SOME UNITS
(ASK) (SD) (&) (DATA PORT) / (✕) (🛏) (🖥) /

──────── WHERE TO DINE ────────

FOUR FORTY WEST   **Lunch:** $4-$7   **Dinner:** $10-$26   Phone: 231/723-7902
▼▼▼   **Location:** Just w. 440 W River St 49660. **Hours:** 11 am-10 pm, Sun from 10 am; to 9 pm Sun-Thurs 1/1-5/30.
American   **Features:** Overlooking the scenic Manistee River, the casual restaurant is open and airy, with lots of
             windows. Menu favorites include varied preparations of local seafood, as well as prime rib, barbecue ribs
DS, MC, VI. and Mike's club sandwich with tasty boneless chicken. Casual dress; cocktails. **Parking:** street. **Cards:** AX,

(✕)

MANISTIQUE pop. 3,583

──────── WHERE TO STAY ────────

BEACHCOMBER MOTEL   Phone: (906)341-2567
(AAA) (SAVE)   5/30-9/1 [BP]   1P: $52-$60   2P: $64-$88   XP: $5   F
               4/1-5/29 & 9/2-3/31 [BP] 1P: $46-$56   2P: $50-$65   XP: $5   F
▼▼▼   **Location:** 1 mi e on US 2. Located opposite Lake Michigan. 795 E Lakeshore Dr 49854 (3944 Brenior Dr, HESPERIA,
Motel   49421). **Fax:** 906/341-2700. **Facility:** 20 one-bedroom standard units. 1 story, exterior corridors. **Parking:** on-
             site. **Leisure Activities:** snowmobiling. **Business Services:** fax. **Cards:** DS, MC, VI. **Special Amenities:**
             free full breakfast and early check-in/late check-out.

SOME UNITS
(SD) (🍴+) / (✕) (🐾) (🖥) (🖨) /

BEST WESTERN-THE BREAKERS MOTEL   Phone: 906/341-2410
▼▼▼ ▼▼▼   Property failed to provide current rates
Motel   **Location:** 2 mi e on US 2. Located opposite Lake Michigan. 1199 E Lakeshore Dr 49854 (PO Box 322).
             Fax: 906/341-2207. **Facility:** 40 one-bedroom standard units, some with whirlpools. 2 stories (no elevator),
hair dryers. **Pool(s):** heated indoor/outdoor. **Leisure Activities:** whirlpool, rental bicycles. **Fee:** game room. **Guest Services:**
coin laundry.

SOME UNITS
(🛏) (🍴+) (🏊) (✕) (📷) (DATA PORT) (☕) / (✕) (🛏) (🖨) /
FEE

BUDGET HOST/MANISTIQUE MOTOR INN   Phone: (906)341-2552
▼▼▼   All Year   1P: $49-$60   2P: $55-$65   XP: $5   F12
Motel   **Location:** On US 2, 3.5 mi e. Located in a semi-rural area. 6031 W US Hwy 2 49854-9108. **Fax:** 906/341-2552.
             Facility: 26 one-bedroom standard units, some with whirlpools. 1 story, exterior corridors. **Bath:** combo or
             shower only. **Parking:** on-site, winter plug-ins. **Terms:** cancellation fee imposed. **Pool(s):** heated outdoor.
Leisure Activities: snowmobiling, playground. **Cards:** AX, CB, DC, DS, MC, VI.

SOME UNITS
(🍴+) (🏊) (📷) / (✕) (🛏) /

COMFORT INN   *Book at aaa.com*   Phone: 906/341-6981
(AAA) (SAVE)   6/11-10/3   1P: $99-$159   2P: $99-$159   XP: $10   F18
               4/1-6/10 & 10/4-3/31 1P: $69-$109   2P: $69-$109   XP: $10   F18
▼▼▼ ▼▼▼   **Location:** 0.5 mi e on US 2. Located opposite Lake Michigan. 726 E Lakeshore Dr 49854. **Fax:** 906/341-6339.
Small-scale Hotel **Facility:** 57 one-bedroom standard units, some with whirlpools. 2 stories (no elevator), interior corridors.
Parking: on-site. **Terms:** [ECP] meal plan available, pets ($10 extra charge). **Amenities:** hair dryers. *Some:* irons. **Leisure Activities:** whirlpool, snowmobiling, rental bicycles, exercise room. **Guest Services:** coin laundry. **Business Services:** meeting rooms. **Cards:** AX, DC, DS, MC, VI. **Special Amenities:** free continental breakfast and early check-in/late check-out.

SOME UNITS
(SD) (🛏) (🍴+) (✕) (DATA PORT) (☕) / (✕) (🛏) (🖨) /
FEE   FEE FEE

ECONO LODGE LAKESHORE   *Book at aaa.com*   Phone: (906)341-6014
▼▼▼ ▼▼▼   7/1-9/15 [ECP]   1P: $89-$119   2P: $89-$119   XP: $10   F18
               6/16-6/30 [ECP]   1P: $69-$109   2P: $69-$109   XP: $10   F18
               9/16-3/31 [ECP]   1P: $69-$99   2P: $69-$99   XP: $10   F18
Motel   4/1-6/15 [ECP]   1P: $59-$99   2P: $59-$99   XP: $10   F18
Location: 1.5 mi e on US 2. Located opposite Lake Michigan. 1101 E Lakeshore Dr 49854 (PO Box 184). **Fax:** 906/341-2979. **Facility:** 32 one-bedroom standard units, some with whirlpools. 1 story, interior/exterior corridors. **Bath:** combo or shower only. **Parking:** on-site, winter plug-ins. **Amenities:** *Some:* irons. **Leisure Activities:** whirlpool, snowmobiling, exercise room. **Cards:** AX, DC, DS, MC, VI.

SOME UNITS
(ASK) (SD) (&) (✕) (📷) (☕) / (✕) (🛏) (🖨) /

HOLIDAY INN EXPRESS   *Book at aaa.com*   Phone: (906)341-3777
(AAA) (SAVE)   6/18-9/28   1P: $99-$149   2P: $99-$149   XP: $10   F
               4/1-6/17 & 9/29-3/31 1P: $69-$99   2P: $69-$99   XP: $10   F
▼▼▼ ▼▼▼   **Location:** 1.4 mi e on US 2. Located opposite Lake Michigan. 955 E Lakeshore Dr 49854. **Fax:** 906/341-7457.
Small-scale Hotel **Facility:** 55 one-bedroom standard units, some with whirlpools. 2 stories (no elevator), interior corridors.
Bath: combo or shower only. **Parking:** on-site. **Terms:** [ECP] meal plan available. **Amenities:** dual phone lines, voice mail, irons, hair dryers. **Leisure Activities:** snowmobiling. **Guest Services:** coin laundry. **Special Amenities:** free continental breakfast and free local telephone calls.
Cards: AX, CB, DC, DS, JC, MC, VI.

SOME UNITS
(SD) (📷) (DATA PORT) / (✕) (🛏) (🖥) /
FEE

KEWADIN CASINO INN

Small-scale Hotel

Phone: 906/341-6911

All Year 1P: $45-$60 2P: $45-$60 XP: $10 F18
Location: 2.5 mi e on US 2. Located in a semi-commercial area. Lakeshore Dr 49854 (Rt 1, Box 1938).
Fax: 906/341-6471. **Facility:** 40 one-bedroom standard units, some with whirlpools. 2 stories (no elevator),
interior corridors. **Parking:** on-site. **Terms:** small pets only ($10 extra charge). **Pool(s):** heated indoor.
Leisure Activities: basketball. *Fee:* game room. **Guest Services:** coin laundry, area transportation-casino
shuttle. **Cards:** AX, DC, DS, MC, VI. **Special Amenities:** free continental breakfast and early check-
in/late check-out.

SOME UNITS

MAPLE CITY

——— WHERE TO DINE ———

LEELANAU COUNTRY INN **Dinner:** $16-$25 Phone: 231/228-5060

American

Location: 4.5 mi n on CR 667, then just w on SR 22. 149 E Harbor Hwy 49664. **Hours:** 5 pm-9 pm; hours may
vary off season. Closed: 11/25, 12/25; also 12/25. **Features:** Opposite Little Traverse Lake, the renovated 1891 inn is a comfortable spot for upscale casual
dining. A combination of seafood, steaks, chicken and pasta makes up the menu. For dessert, try the
chocolate mousse cake with raspberry-chocolate sauce. Casual dress; cocktails. **Parking:** on-site. **Cards:** MC, VI.

MAPLE VALLEY

——— WHERE TO DINE ———

MAPLE VALLEY RESTAURANT & LOUNGE **Dinner:** $8-$22 Phone: 989/389-7005

American

Location: I-75, exit 227 (SR 55), just w. 4995 E West Branch Rd 48656. **Hours:** 4 pm-9 pm, Fri & Sat-10 pm,
Sun noon-8 pm. Closed: 11/25, 12/24, 12/25. **Features:** Inviting up-north type dining room, with wood
chainsaw carvings, deer antler chandeliers, and wildlife mounts and artwork. Although walleye, ribs and
prime rib remain their specialties, they also have lighter fare and pasta dishes. Casual dress; cocktails.
Parking: on-site. **Cards:** DC, DS, MC, VI.

MARENISCO

——— WHERE TO DINE ———

THE FISHERMAN RESORT RESTAURANT **Lunch:** $4-$7 **Dinner:** $8-$15 Phone: 906/842-3366

Steak & Seafood

Location: 2 mi e on US 2, 10 mi n on SR 64; on Lake Gogebic. M-64 49947. **Hours:** 7 am-10 pm, Sun-8 pm.
Closed: 11/25, 12/25; also 4/1-4/30. **Features:** Overlooking a scenic lake, the casual restaurant is a
favorite spot for locals and tourists alike. Steak, ribs, chops, burgers and seafood are among familiar menu
offerings. Turtle pie stands out on the dessert menu. Casual dress; cocktails. **Parking:** on-site.
Cards: MC, VI.

MARINE CITY pop. 4,652

——— WHERE TO STAY ———

THE HEATHER HOUSE

Historic Bed
& Breakfast

Phone: 810/765-3175

6/1-10/31 [BP] 1P: $115-$155 2P: $135-$175 XP: $20 F6
4/1-5/31, 11/1-12/18 & 2/14-3/31 [BP] 1P: $110-$145 2P: $120-$165 XP: $20 F6
Location: I-94, exit 248 (Marine City Hwy), 14 mi e on SR 29. 409 N Main 48039. Fax: 810/765-5639. **Facility:** Overlooking the St. Clair River, this Queen Anne house features two turrets and a wraparound porch that affords
a great view of passing boats. Smoke free premises. 4 one-bedroom standard units, some with whirlpools.
3 stories (no elevator), interior corridors. *Bath:* combo or shower only. **Parking:** on-site. **Terms:** open 4/1-12/18 & 2/14-3/31, 7
day cancellation notice-fee imposed, package plans, no pets allowed (owner's cats on premises). **Amenities:** video library, irons,
hair dryers. **Cards:** AX, DC, MC, VI.

MARQUETTE pop. 19,661

——— WHERE TO STAY ———

BIRCHMONT MOTEL

Motel

Phone: 906/228-7538

6/4-11/1 [CP] 1P: $45-$55 2P: $55-$65
5/1-6/3 [CP] 1P: $39-$50 2P: $45-$60
Location: On US 41 and SR 28, 4.3 mi s. Located opposite Lake Superior. 2090 US 41 S 49855 (92 Woodland Rd,
FAIRFIELD, VT, 05455). Fax: 906/226-0486. **Facility:** 29 one-bedroom standard units. 2 stories (no elevator),
exterior corridors. **Parking:** on-site. **Terms:** open 5/1-11/1, weekly rates available, pets ($6 extra charge).
Pool(s): heated outdoor. **Cards:** AX, DS, MC, VI. **Special Amenities:** free local telephone calls and early
check-in/late check-out.

SOME UNITS

BUDGET HOST-BRENTWOOD MOTOR INN

Motel

Phone: 906/228-7494

All Year [CP] 1P: $42-$50 2P: $48-$55 XP: $3
Location: On US 41 and SR 28, 2.8 mi w. Located in a semi-commercial area. 2603 US 41 W 49855. **Facility:** 41 one-
bedroom standard units. 2 stories (no elevator), exterior corridors. *Bath:* combo or shower only. **Parking:** on-
site, winter plug-ins. **Terms:** weekly rates available. **Amenities:** *Some:* hair dryers. **Cards:** DC, MC, VI.
Special Amenities: free continental breakfast.

SOME UNITS

CEDAR MOTOR INN
▼▼▼
Small-scale Hotel

Phone: (906)228-2280

All Year   1P: $50-$68   2P: $60-$70   XP: $5   F5
Location: On US 41 and SR 28, 2.8 mi w. Located in a semi-commercial area. 2523 US 41 W 49855. **Fax:** 906/228-2280. **Facility:** 44 one-bedroom standard units. 2 stories (no elevator), interior/exterior corridors. *Bath:* combo or shower only. **Parking:** on-site. **Pool(s):** heated indoor. **Leisure Activities:** sauna, whirlpool. **Business Services:** meeting rooms. **Cards:** AX, DC, DS, MC, VI.

SOME UNITS
[♦] [≈] [☆] [DATA PORT] [▣] / [✕] [▮] [▣] /

COMFORT SUITES   *Book at aaa.com*
▼◆◆◆▼
Small-scale Hotel

Phone: (906)228-0028

6/11-10/23   1P: $102-$155   2P: $112-$155   XP: $10   F18
10/24-3/31   1P: $92-$145   2P: $102-$145   XP: $10   F18
4/1-6/10   1P: $89-$145   2P: $99-$145   XP: $10   F18
Location: On US 41 and SR 28, 2.5 mi w. Located in a semi-commercial area. 2463 US 41 W 49855. **Fax:** 906/228-3893. **Facility:** 60 one-bedroom standard units, some with whirlpools. 3 stories, interior corridors. *Bath:* combo or shower only. **Parking:** on-site, winter plug-ins. **Terms:** [ECP] meal plan available. **Amenities:** irons, hair dryers. *Some:* high-speed Internet. **Pool(s):** heated indoor. **Leisure Activities:** sauna, whirlpool, exercise room. **Guest Services:** gift shop, coin laundry. **Business Services:** meeting rooms. **Cards:** AX, CB, DC, DS, JC, MC, VI. *(See color ad below)*

SOME UNITS
[ASK] [S⊙] [♦] [Y] [⌂] [≈] [✕] [☆] [DATA PORT] [▮] [▣] [▣] / [✕] /

DAYS INN   *Book at aaa.com*
▼▼ ▼▼
Small-scale Hotel

Phone: (906)225-1393

6/11-9/11   1P: $70-$118   2P: $80-$128   XP: $6   F18
9/12-3/31   1P: $60-$109   2P: $70-$119   XP: $6   F18
4/1-6/10   1P: $59-$109   2P: $69-$119   XP: $10   F18
Location: On US 41 and SR 28, 2.3 mi w. Located in a semi-commercial area. 2403 US 41 W 49855. **Fax:** 906/225-9845. **Facility:** 65 one-bedroom standard units. 2 stories, interior corridors. **Parking:** on-site, winter plug-ins. **Terms:** [ECP] meal plan available. **Amenities:** irons, hair dryers. **Pool(s):** heated indoor. **Leisure Activities:** sauna, whirlpools. **Guest Services:** gift shop. **Business Services:** meeting rooms. **Cards:** AX, CB, DC, DS, JC, MC, VI. *(See color ad below & card insert)*

SOME UNITS
[ASK] [S⊙] [♦] [≈] [☆] [DATA PORT] / [✕] [▮] [▣] [▣] /

HOLIDAY INN   *Book at aaa.com*
▼▼ ▼▼
Large-scale Hotel

Phone: (906)225-1351

All Year   1P: $115   2P: $120
Location: On US 41 and SR 28, 1.8 mi w. Located in a semi-commercial area. 1951 US 41 W 49855. **Fax:** 906/228-4329. **Facility:** 190 units. 186 one-bedroom standard units. 4 one-bedroom suites. 5 stories, interior corridors. *Bath:* combo or shower only. **Parking:** on-site. **Terms:** pets ($25 fee). **Amenities:** voice mail, irons, hair dryers. **Pool(s):** heated indoor. **Leisure Activities:** sauna, whirlpool, snowmobiling, exercise room. *Fee:* game room. **Guest Services:** valet and coin laundry. **Business Services:** meeting rooms. **Cards:** AX, CB, DC, DS, JC, MC, VI.

SOME UNITS
[ASK] [S⊙] [✦] [⌂] [♦] [Y] [⌂] [≈] [✕] [☆] [DATA PORT] [▣] / [✕] [▮] [▣] /
FEE

IMPERIAL MOTEL
▼▼
Motel

Phone: (906)228-7430

All Year   1P: $45-$55   2P: $59-$79   XP: $5   F12
Location: On US 41 and SR 28, 2.8 mi w. Located in a semi-commercial area. 2493 US 41 W 49855. **Fax:** 906/228-3883. **Facility:** 43 one-bedroom standard units. 2 stories (no elevator), exterior corridors. **Parking:** on-site, winter plug-ins. **Pool(s):** heated indoor. **Leisure Activities:** sauna, basketball. **Business Services:** fax (fee). **Cards:** AX, DC, DS, MC, VI.

SOME UNITS
[ASK] [S⊙] [♦] [≈] [☆] / [✕] [DATA PORT] [▮] /

LANDMARK INN
(AAA) [SAVE]
▼◆▼
Classic
Large-scale Hotel

Phone: (906)228-2580

5/1-10/31   1P: $112-$132   2P: $112-$132
4/1-4/30 & 11/1-3/31   1P: $95-$109   2P: $95-$109
Location: Downtown. 230 N Front St 49855. **Fax:** 906/228-5676. **Facility:** Renovated 1930's hotel. 62 units. 58 one-bedroom standard units, some with whirlpools. 4 one-bedroom suites ($159-$219). 6 stories, interior corridors. *Bath:* combo or shower only. **Parking:** on-site. **Terms:** package plans. **Amenities:** voice mail, hair dryers. **Dining:** Heritage Room, see separate listing. **Leisure Activities:** sauna, whirlpools, exercise room. **Guest Services:** gift shop, valet laundry, airport transportation (fee)-Sawyer International Airport. **Business Services:** conference facilities. **Cards:** AX, DC, DS, MC, VI.

SOME UNITS
[S⊙] [✦] [♦] [Y] [⌂] [✕] [☆] [DATA PORT] [▣] / [✕] [VCR] [▮] [▣] /
FEE   FEE

NORDIC BAY LODGE

Phone: 906/226-7516

AAA SAVE
Motel

All Year   2P: $55-$110
Location: On US 41 and SR 28, 1.8 mi se. Located opposite Lake Superior. 1880 US 41 S 49855. Fax: 906/226-0699. **Facility:** 41 one-bedroom standard units. 2 stories (no elevator), exterior corridors. **Parking:** on-site. **Terms:** package plans, small pets only (in designated units). **Amenities:** *Some:* high-speed Internet, hair dryers. **Dining:** 7-11 am; hours may vary. **Leisure Activities:** sauna, snowmobiling, rental bicycles, hiking trails. **Guest Services:** coin laundry. **Business Services:** meeting rooms. **Cards:** AX, DS, MC, VI.
Special Amenities: free newspaper and early check-in/late check-out.

SOME UNITS

RAMADA INN

Book at aaa.com

Phone: (906)228-6000

All Year   1P: $99-$109   2P: $109-$119   XP: $5   F18
Large-scale Hotel
Location: 0.5 w on US 41 business route. 412 W Washington St 49855. Fax: 906/228-2963. **Facility:** 113 units. 107 one-bedroom standard units. 6 one-bedroom suites, some with whirlpools. 2-7 stories, interior corridors. **Parking:** on-site. **Terms:** [AP] meal plan available. **Amenities:** voice mail, irons, hair dryers. **Pool(s):** heated indoor. **Leisure Activities:** sauna, whirlpool. *Fee:* game room. **Guest Services:** valet and coin laundry. **Business Services:** meeting rooms. **Cards:** AX, CB, DC, DS, MC, VI.

SOME UNITS
FEE   FEE

SUPER 8 MOTEL

Phone: 906/228-8100

All Year   1P: $48-$53   2P: $62-$70   XP: $9   F12
Small-scale Hotel
Location: On US 41 and SR 28, 1 mi w. Located in a semi-commercial area. 1275 US 41 W 49855. Fax: 906/228-8100. **Facility:** 80 one-bedroom standard units. 2 stories (no elevator), interior corridors. **Parking:** on-site, winter plug-ins. **Terms:** [CP] meal plan available. **Pool(s):** heated indoor. **Leisure Activities:** sauna, whirlpool. **Guest Services:** coin laundry. **Business Services:** meeting rooms. **Cards:** AX, DC, MC, VI.

SOME UNITS

TRAVELODGE

Book at aaa.com

Phone: 906/249-1712

AAA SAVE
Small-scale Hotel

All Year [CP]   1P: $63   2P: $69   XP: $6
Location: Jct US 41 S and SR 28 E. Located in a semi-commercial area. 1010 M-28 E 49855. Fax: 906/249-9051. **Facility:** 39 one-bedroom standard units, some with whirlpools. 2 stories (no elevator), interior corridors. *Bath:* combo or shower only. **Parking:** on-site, winter plug-ins. **Terms:** pets ($5 extra charge, in designated units). **Amenities:** hair dryers. **Pool(s):** heated indoor. **Leisure Activities:** whirlpool, snowmobiling. **Business Services:** meeting rooms. **Cards:** AX, CB, DC, MC, VI. **Special Amenities:** free continental breakfast and free newspaper.

SOME UNITS
FEE

WHERE TO DINE

GREAT HUNAN

Chinese
Cards: MC, VI.

Lunch: $5-$7   **Dinner: $8-$13**   **Phone: 906-226-8649**
Location: On US 41 and SR 28, 2.8 mi w. 2680 US 41 W 49855. **Hours:** 11:30 am-9 pm, Fri & Sat-10 pm, Sun noon-8:30 pm. Closed: 11/25. **Features:** If you like seafood, try the seafood combination dish, which blends crab, fresh fish and vegetables in a tasty sauce. Otherwise, you can't go wrong with the excellent selection and great value of traditional choices. Service is friendly and attentive. **Parking:** on-site.

HERITAGE ROOM

American

Lunch: $7-$9   **Dinner: $15-$23**   **Phone: 906/228-2580**
Location: Downtown; in Landmark Inn. 230 N Front St 49855. **Hours:** 6:30 am-2 & 5:30-10 pm; hours may vary. **Reservations:** accepted. **Features:** In the Landmark Inn, the dining room has a large antique gas chandelier from the old courthouse, and it's installed upside-down. On the menu are well-prepared dishes and homemade desserts. Casual dress; cocktails. **Parking:** on-site. **Cards:** AX, DC, DS, MC, VI.

NORTHWOODS SUPPER CLUB

AAA
American

Lunch: $5-$8   **Dinner: $8-$28**   **Phone: 906/228-4343**
Location: 3.5 mi w on US 41 and SR 28, 0.3 mi s at sign. **Hours:** 11 am-10 pm, Fri & Sat-11 pm, Sun 10 am-10 pm. Closed: 12/24-12/26; also Mon. **Features:** Beef is aged in the on-site meat shop, and desserts are prepared in the in-house bakery at the charming, log cabin restaurant. One of the dining rooms looks out at a lovely waterfall in the back. The grounds are appointed with fresh flowers. Cocktails. **Parking:** on-site. **Cards:** AX, DS, MC, VI.

THE OFFICE SUPPER CLUB

American
cocktails. **Parking:** street. **Cards:** AX, DC, DS, MC, VI.

Dinner: $14-$31   **Phone: 906/228-9335**
Location: US 41 business route; center. 154 W Washington St 49855. **Hours:** 4 pm-10 pm. Closed: 12/25. **Reservations:** suggested. **Features:** The cozy, moderately upscale supper club prepares a number of temping starters, excellent traditional dishes and the best in certified Angus beef. Only a few can eat all of the cowboy French-cut rib-eye steak, a 24-ounce treat with mushroom Madeira sauce. Casual dress;

STEER & STEIN

Steak House
Cards: AX, MC, VI.

Lunch: $4-$7   **Dinner: $7-$14**   **Phone: 906/228-7011**
Location: On US 41 and SR 28, 3.5 mi w. US Hwy 41 W 49855. **Hours:** 11 am-2 & 4-9 pm, Fri & Sat-10 pm. Closed: 12/25. **Features:** Grill your own steak on an indoor barbecue pit, or enjoy selections of pasta, chicken and seafood. The decor of the cozy, romantic dining room shows a Southwestern flair. The Snickers and Bailey's Irish creme cheesecakes are decadent desserts. Cocktails. **Parking:** on-site.

THE VIERLING RESTAURANT & MARQUETTE HARBOR BREWERY
Historic   **Lunch:** $4-$7   **Dinner:** $10-$15   **Phone:** 906/228-3533
American
Location: Corner Front and Main sts. 119 S Front St 49855. **Hours:** 11 am-10 pm. Closed major holidays; also Sun. **Features:** An antique bar, stained-glass windows and varied memorabilia decorate the casual 1883 saloon, which is restored to an Old World elegance. A good selection of microbrewed beers complements such dishes as Lake Superior whitefish, ribs and steak. Casual dress; cocktails. **Parking:** street. **Cards:** AX, DS, MC, VI.

------ *The following restaurants have not been evaluated by AAA* ------
but are listed for your information only.

SWEET WATER CAFE
[fyi]   **Phone:** 906/226-7009
Not evaluated. **Location:** Just n. 517 N 3rd 49855. **Features:** Most of the cafe's great tasting food is made from scratch using natural, organic and locally raised food.

UPFRONT & COMPANY
[fyi]   **Phone:** 906/228-5200
Not evaluated. **Location:** Center. 102 E Main St 49855. **Features:** On the downtown restaurant's menu are fresh fish, steak, pasta and pizza.

MARSHALL pop. 7,459

------ **WHERE TO STAY** ------

AMERIHOST INN-MARSHALL
Book at aaa.com   **Phone:** (269)789-7890
Small-scale Hotel

6/1-9/15 [CP]	1P: $84-$149	2P: $89-$149	XP: $5	F18
9/16-3/31 [CP]	1P: $74-$129	2P: $79-$149	XP: $5	F18
4/1-5/31 [CP]	1P: $74-$129	2P: $79-$129	XP: $5	F18

Location: I-69, exit 36, just se. 204 Winston Dr 49068. Fax: 269/789-7891. **Facility:** 61 one-bedroom standard units, some with whirlpools. 2 stories (no elevator), interior corridors. *Bath:* combo or shower only. **Parking:** on-site. **Amenities:** voice mail, safes (fee), irons, hair dryers. **Pool(s):** heated indoor. **Leisure Activities:** sauna, whirlpool, exercise room. **Guest Services:** valet laundry. **Business Services:** meeting rooms. **Cards:** AX, DC, DS, MC, VI.

ARBOR INN OF HISTORIC MARSHALL
Motel   **Phone:** (269)781-7772
All Year   1P: $45-$65   2P: $50-$69   XP: $5   F14
Location: I-69, exit 36, just w. 15435 W Michigan Ave 49068. Fax: 269/781-2660. **Facility:** 48 one-bedroom standard units, some with kitchens. 1 story, exterior corridors. **Parking:** on-site, winter plug-ins. **Terms:** check-in 4 pm, [CP] meal plan available, pets ($5 extra charge, in limited units). **Pool(s):** outdoor. **Cards:** AX, DS, MC, VI. **Special Amenities:** free continental breakfast and free local telephone calls.

HOLIDAY INN EXPRESS
Book at aaa.com   **Phone:** 269/789-9301
Small-scale Hotel
All Year [ECP]   1P: $99-$189   2P: $99-$189   XP: $8   F18
Location: I-94, exit 110. 17252 Sam Hill Dr 49068. Fax: 269/789-9301. **Facility:** 66 units. 65 one-bedroom standard units, some with whirlpools. 1 one-bedroom suite with whirlpool. 3 stories, interior corridors. *Bath:* combo or shower only. **Parking:** on-site. **Amenities:** high-speed Internet (fee), dual phone lines, voice mail, irons, hair dryers. **Pool(s):** small heated indoor. **Leisure Activities:** exercise room. **Guest Services:** valet laundry. **Cards:** AX, CB, DC, DS, JC, MC, VI.

THE NATIONAL HOUSE INN
Historic Bed & Breakfast   **Phone:** (269)781-7374
All Year   1P: $105   2P: $150   XP: $15   F7
Location: Fountain Circle; downtown. 102 S Parkview St 49068. Fax: 269/781-4510. **Facility:** In downtown Marshall, in front of the circle, this faithfully restored inn was once a stop on the stagecoach road to Chicago. Smoke free premises. 15 units. 13 one-bedroom standard units. 2 one-bedroom suites ($150). 2 stories, interior corridors. *Bath:* combo or shower only. **Parking:** on-site. **Terms:** 7 day cancellation notice, [BP] meal plan available. **Guest Services:** gift shop. **Cards:** AX, MC, VI.

ROSE HILL INN B & B
Historic Bed & Breakfast   **Phone:** 269/789-1992
All Year [BP]   1P: $99-$140   2P: $99-$140
Location: Fountain Circle, just n to Mansion St, 0.7 mi w; downtown. 1110 Verona Rd 49068. Fax: 269/781-4723. **Facility:** An elegant 1860 Italianate-style mansion with a large front porch, the B&B is set on three acres of groomed grounds which include a tennis court. Smoke free premises. 6 one-bedroom standard units. 2 stories, interior corridors. *Bath:* combo or shower only. **Parking:** on-site. **Terms:** age restrictions may apply, 14 day cancellation notice-fee imposed, no pets allowed (owner's cat on premises). **Amenities:** hair dryers. **Pool(s):** outdoor. **Leisure Activities:** tennis court. **Cards:** AX, MC, VI.

------ **WHERE TO DINE** ------

MARIA'S FINE PASTRIES AND EATERY
Deli/Subs Sandwiches   **Lunch:** $6-$9   **Phone:** 269/781-3070
Location: Downtown. 130 W Michigan Ave 49068. **Hours:** 11 am-3 pm, Sat from 11:30 am. Closed major holidays; also Sun. **Features:** The limited daily specials, sandwiches and salads are meant to whet the appetite for the enticing cakes, pies and pastries, which are made daily on site. The charming downtown restaurant has exposed brick walls and hardwood floors. Casual dress. **Parking:** street. **Cards:** DS, MC, VI.

SCHULER'S Classic   **Lunch:** $9-$13   **Dinner:** $15-$26   **Phone:** 269/781-0600

American

Location: Just e of US 27 and circle, 1 mi s of I-94. 115 S Eagle St 49068. **Hours:** 11 am-9 pm, Fri & Sat-10 pm, Sun 10 am-9 pm. Closed: 12/25. **Reservations:** suggested. **Features:** Childhood memories of eating freshly baked bread and butter are evoked as you savor the flavor of the homemade bread at this almost 100-year-old establishment. The atmosphere whisks you away to the early 20th-century and allows you to experience lovingly created foods like your great grandmother might have prepared for the family table. Hearty portions of the many German inspired dishes will satisfy even the hungriest of diners, and desserts will tempt even the most strong willed of dieters. Casual dress; cocktails. **Parking:** on-site. **Cards:** AX, DC, DS, MC, VI.

MARYSVILLE pop. 9,684

———— **WHERE TO STAY** ————

DAYS INN OF PORT HURON-MARYSVILLE   *Book at aaa.com*   **Phone:** (810)364-8400

AAA SAVE

Motel

All Year [CP]   1P: $45-$70   2P: $45-$70   XP: $10   F12
Location: I-94, exit 266, 3 mi e on Business Rt I-94. 70 Gratiot Blvd 48040. **Fax:** 810/364-8401. **Facility:** 26 one-bedroom standard units, some with whirlpools. 1 story, exterior corridors. **Parking:** on-site, winter plug-ins. **Terms:** cancellation fee imposed. **Amenities:** video library, hair dryers. **Pool(s):** heated outdoor. **Cards:** AX, DC, DS, MC, VI. **Special Amenities:** free continental breakfast and early check-in/late check-out.
(See color ad card insert)

SOME UNITS

SUPER 8 MOTEL PORT HURON/MARYSVILLE   *Book at aaa.com*   **Phone:** (810)364-7500

AAA SAVE

Small-scale Hotel

All Year [CP]   1P: $60-$175   2P: $60-$175   XP: $5   F12
Location: I-94, exit 266, 1 mi e, 0.3 mi s of Port Huron on I-94 business loop. Located in a secluded area. 1484 Gratiot Blvd 48040. **Fax:** 810/364-4423. **Facility:** 70 one-bedroom standard units, some with whirlpools. 2 stories, interior/exterior corridors. *Bath:* combo or shower only. **Parking:** on-site. **Amenities:** hair dryers. **Pool(s):** heated indoor. **Leisure Activities:** whirlpool, exercise room. *Fee:* game room. **Guest Services:** coin laundry. **Business Services:** meeting rooms. **Cards:** AX, DS, MC, VI. **Special Amenities:** free continental breakfast and free local telephone calls.

SOME UNITS

MEARS

─── **WHERE TO STAY** ───

DUNES WATERFRONT RESORT   Phone: 231/873-5500

W̌W̌W̌W̌ 6/18-9/6   1P: $120-$170   2P: $145-$200   XP: $10   F12
Small-scale Hotel 4/1-6/17 & 9/7-10/30   1P: $80-$140   2P: $100-$160   XP: $10   F12
Location: US 31, exit Hart/Mears, 7 mi w to Silver Lake, follow signs. Overlooking Silver Lake and sand dunes. 1180 N Shore Dr 49436. Fax: 231/873-7653. **Facility:** 72 one-bedroom standard units, some with whirlpools. 4 stories, interior corridors. *Bath:* combo or shower only. **Parking:** on-site. **Terms:** open 4/1-10/30, 2-3 night minimum stay - seasonal weekends, 7 day cancellation notice-fee imposed, package plans - seasonal. **Amenities:** video library (fee), irons, hair dryers. **Pool(s):** heated indoor. **Leisure Activities:** whirlpool, boat dock, exercise room. *Fee:* game room. **Guest Services:** coin laundry. **Business Services:** meeting rooms. **Cards:** DS, MC, VI. *(See color ad below)*

SOME UNITS

🍴➕ 📠 🏊 ✖️ 📺 📁 💻 / ✖️ 📼 🔌/
FEE

SIERRA SANDS AT THE DUNES/SILVER LAKE   Phone: (231)873-1008

Ⓐ Ⓐ Ⓐ SAVE   6/25-8/21   1P: $109-$139   2P: $109-$139   XP: $5   F
W̌W̌ W̌W̌ 4/1-6/24 & 8/22-10/31   1P: $59-$139   2P: $59-$139   XP: $5   F
Motel **Location:** US 31, exit Hart/Mears, 6 mi w, follow signs. 7990 W Hazel Rd 49436. Fax: 231/873-7799. **Facility:** 41 units. 37 one- and 3 two-bedroom standard units. 1 two-bedroom suite ($99-$249) with kitchen. 2 stories (no elevator), exterior corridors. **Parking:** on-site. **Terms:** open 4/1-10/31, 7 day cancellation notice-fee imposed. **Amenities:** video library (fee), hair dryers. *Some:* DVD players, video games, irons. **Pool(s):** heated outdoor. **Leisure Activities:** whirlpool, barbecue grills, picnic area, playground. **Cards:** DS, MC, VI. *(See color ad below)*

SOME UNITS

Ⓢ🐕 🐾 ✖️ 📺 🔌 📁 / ✖️ 📼 📺 💻 /

MENOMINEE pop. 9,131

———— WHERE TO STAY ————

AMERICINN OF MENOMINEE *Book at aaa.com* Phone: (906)863-8699

5/15-3/31	1P: $83-$125	2P: $83-$125	XP: $6 F17
4/1-5/14	1P: $79-$119	2P: $79-$119	XP: $6 F17

Small-scale Hotel **Location:** 0.8 mi n on US 41. Located on the shores of Green Bay. 2330 10th St 49858. Fax: 906/863-8190. **Facility:** 63 units. 59 one-bedroom standard units, some with whirlpools. 4 one-bedroom suites, some with whirlpools. 2 stories (no elevator), interior corridors. *Bath:* combo or shower only. **Parking:** on-site. **Terms:** [CP] meal plan available. **Amenities:** hair dryers. *Some:* irons. **Pool(s):** heated indoor. **Leisure Activities:** whirlpool, boat ramp, playground. **Guest Services:** coin laundry. **Business Services:** meeting rooms. **Cards:** AX, DC, DS, MC, VI. *(See color ad p 311)*

SOME UNITS

[ASK] [SD] [T+] [🏊] [🛁] [✕] [📷] [DATA PORT] [💻] / [✕] [🍴] [🖥] /
FEE

ECONO LODGE ON THE BAY *Book at aaa.com* Phone: (906)863-4431

All Year 1P: $64-$149 2P: $69-$149 XP: $10 F

Small-scale Hotel **Location:** 1 mi n on US 41. Located on the shores of Green Bay. 2516 10th St 49858. Fax: 906/863-3069. **Facility:** 49 units. 48 one-bedroom standard units. 1 one-bedroom suite ($99-$180) with efficiency. 2 stories (no elevator), interior corridors. **Parking:** on-site, winter plug-ins. **Terms:** cancellation fee imposed, small pets only ($25 deposit, $25 extra charge, in designated units). **Amenities:** hair dryers. *Some:* irons. **Leisure Activities:** sauna, exercise room. **Guest Services:** *Fee:* tanning facility. **Business Services:** meeting rooms. **Cards:** AX, DS, MC, VI. **Special Amenities:** free continental breakfast and free local telephone calls.

SOME UNITS

[SD] [🛁] [T+] [📷] [DATA PORT] [💻] / [✕] [🖥] [🍴] /
FEE

———— WHERE TO DINE ————

BERGS' LANDING **Dinner:** $12-$25 Phone: 906/863-8034

American **Location:** From US 41, just e on 10th Ave; in historic district. 450 1st St 49858. **Hours:** 5 pm-9 pm, Fri & Sat-10 pm, Sun-8 pm. Closed major holidays. **Features:** Jack Daniels New York strip stands out on a menu of traditionally prepared steak and seafood choices. The nautically appointed dining room overlooks Green Bay. The atmosphere is lively and upbeat, as is the staff, which provides efficient service. Casual dress; cocktails. **Parking:** on-site. **Cards:** AX, DC, DS, MC, VI.

[Y] [✕]

SCHLOEGELS BAY VIEW **Lunch:** $5-$6 **Dinner:** $6-$9 Phone: 906/863-7888

American **Location:** 1 mi n on US 41. 2720 10th St 49858. **Hours:** 6:30 am-8:30 pm. Closed: 11/25, 12/25. **Features:** Guests can enjoy panoramic views of Green Bay from the quiet dining room, attractively decorated with local art. The menu lists a wide selection of family-style foods. Homemade pies and fresh bread and "pasties" make mouths water. Service is friendly. Casual dress. **Parking:** on-site. **Cards:** MC, VI.

[M] [✕]

MIDLAND pop. 41,685

———— WHERE TO STAY ————

ASHMAN COURT MARRIOTT CONFERENCE HOTEL *Book at aaa.com* Phone: (989)839-0500

All Year 1P: $79-$199 2P: $79-$199

Large-scale Hotel **Location:** Corner of Main and Ashman sts; downtown. 111 W Main St 48640. Fax: 989/837-6000. **Facility:** 121 units. 112 one-bedroom standard units. 9 one-bedroom suites ($99-$199) with whirlpools. 6 stories, interior corridors. *Bath:* combo or shower only. **Parking:** on-site. **Amenities:** dual phone lines, voice mail, irons, hair dryers. **Dining:** The Crossings, see separate listing. **Pool(s):** heated indoor. **Leisure Activities:** whirlpool, jogging, exercise room. *Fee:* bicycles, game room. **Guest Services:** sundries, valet laundry. **Business Services:** conference facilities, business center. **Cards:** AX, CB, DC, DS, JC, MC, VI.

SOME UNITS

[ASK] [✈] [T] [🍴] [🏊] [✕] [📷] [DATA PORT] [💻] / [✕] [🖥] [🍴] /

BEST WESTERN VALLEY PLAZA RESORT *Book at aaa.com* Phone: (989)496-2700

All Year 1P: $83 2P: $83 XP: $10 F18

Large-scale Hotel **Location:** US 10, exit Midland/Bay City Rd. Located in a commercial area. 5221 Bay City Rd 48642. Fax: 989/496-9233. **Facility:** 162 units. 160 one-bedroom standard units. 2 one-bedroom suites ($131-$181) with whirlpools. 2 stories, interior corridors. **Parking:** on-site. **Terms:** check-in 4 pm, [BP] meal plan available, package plans, small pets only. **Amenities:** voice mail, safes (fee), irons, hair dryers. **Pool(s):** heated indoor, wading. **Leisure Activities:** sauna, whirlpool, putting green, ice skating, basketball, horseshoes, volleyball. *Fee:* massage, game room. **Guest Services:** valet laundry. **Business Services:** conference facilities. **Cards:** AX, CB, DC, DS, MC, VI.

SOME UNITS

[ASK] [SD] [✈] [🛁] [T] [Y] [🏊] [🛁] [✕] [DATA PORT] [💻] / [✕] [🖥] [🍴] /
FEE FEE

FAIRVIEW INN Phone: (989)631-0070

All Year 1P: $68-$99 2P: $68-$99

Small-scale Hotel **Location:** Jct US 10 and Eastman Rd. Located in a commercial area. 2200 W Wackerly St 48640. Fax: 989/631-1604. **Facility:** 90 units. 83 one-bedroom standard units. 7 one-bedroom suites. 2 stories (no elevator), interior corridors. **Parking:** on-site, winter plug-ins. **Terms:** [ECP] meal plan available, pets ($25 deposit). **Amenities:** voice mail. *Some:* irons, hair dryers. **Pool(s):** heated indoor. **Leisure Activities:** whirlpool, exercise room. **Guest Services:** coin laundry, airport transportation-Tri-City Airport. **Business Services:** meeting rooms. **Cards:** AX, DC, DS, MC, VI. **Special Amenities:** free continental breakfast and free local telephone calls.

SOME UNITS

[SD] [✈] [🛁] [T+] [🏊] [📷] [DATA PORT] / [✕] [VCR] [🖥] [🍴] /
FEE FEE

HAMPTON INN   *Book at aaa.com*   **Phone:** (989)837-4000
All Year   1P: $82-$129   2P: $82-$129
Location: US 10, exit Eastman Rd, just n. Located opposite Midland Mall. 6701 Eastman Ave 48642.
Small-scale Hotel   Fax: 989/837-7241. **Facility:** 87 units. 78 one-bedroom standard units, some with whirlpools. 9 one-bedroom
suites ($119-$175), some with whirlpools. 3 stories, interior corridors. *Bath:* combo or shower only. **Parking:**
on-site. **Terms:** check-in 4 pm, [ECP] meal plan available. **Amenities:** video games, dual phone lines, voice mail, irons, hair
dryers. **Pool(s):** heated indoor. **Leisure Activities:** whirlpool, exercise room. **Guest Services:** valet and coin laundry. *Fee:* tanning facility. **Business Services:** meeting rooms. **Cards:** AX, CB, DC, DS, JC, MC, VI. *(See color ad below)*

SOME UNITS

[ASK] [SD] [⏱+] [🎨] [🏊] [📷] [💻] / [✕] [🔒] [🖨] /

HOLIDAY INN   *Book at aaa.com*   **Phone:** (989)631-4220
All Year   1P: $85-$199   2P: $85-$199   XP: $10   F18
Location: Jct US 10 and Eastman Rd. 1500 W Wackerly St 48640. Fax: 989/631-3776. **Facility:** 235 units. 219
one-bedroom standard units, some with whirlpools. 16 one-bedroom suites ($166-$199) with whirlpools. 2
stories (no elevator), interior/exterior corridors. **Parking:** on-site, winter plug-ins. **Terms:** check-in 4 pm, [BP]
Large-scale Hotel   & [CP] meal plans available, pets (in smoking units). **Amenities:** video games, voice mail, irons, hair dryers.
Some: dual phone lines. **Dining:** 6 am-11 pm, Fri & Sat-midnight, cocktails. **Pool(s):** heated indoor. **Leisure
Activities:** sauna, whirlpool, indoor recreation area, exercise room, basketball, volleyball. *Fee:* racquetball courts, game room.
Guest Services: valet and coin laundry, airport transportation-MBS International Airport. **Business Services:** conference facili-
ties, business center. **Cards:** AX, CB, DC, DS, JC, MC, VI. **Special Amenities:** free local telephone calls and free newspaper.

SOME UNITS

[SD] [⏱+] [🐾] [🍽] [🍸] [🏊] [✕] [📷] [💻] / [✕] [VCR] [🔒] [🖨] /

PLAZA SUITES HOTEL
Phone: (989)496-0100
Small-scale Hotel
All Year [BP]　　　　　　　　1P: $105　　　　　　2P: $105　　　　　　XP: $10　　　　　F18
Location: US 10, exit Midland/Bay City Rd. Located in a commercial area. 5221 Bay City Rd 48642. Fax: 989/496-2353. **Facility:** 74 units. 66 one-bedroom standard units. 8 one-bedroom suites ($131-$181) with whirlpools. 2 stories (no elevator), interior corridors. **Parking:** on-site. **Terms:** check-in 4 pm, package plans, small pets only. **Amenities:** dual phone lines, voice mail, safes (fee), honor bars, irons, hair dryers. **Leisure Activities:** Fee: massage. **Guest Services:** valet laundry. **Cards:** AX, CB, DC, DS, MC, VI.

SOME UNITS

SLEEP INN OF MIDLAND   *Book at aaa.com*
Phone: 989/837-1010
Small-scale Hotel
All Year [ECP]　　　　　　　1P: $69-$99　　　　　2P: $79-$140
Location: Jct US 10 and Eastman Rd. Located in a commercial area. 2100 W Wackerly 48640. Fax: 989/837-2470. **Facility:** 79 units. 77 one-bedroom standard units, some with whirlpools. 2 one-bedroom suites ($99-$140) with whirlpools. 3 stories, interior corridors. *Bath:* combo or shower only. **Parking:** on-site. **Amenities:** voice mail, irons, hair dryers. **Pool(s):** heated indoor. **Leisure Activities:** sauna. **Guest Services:** coin laundry. **Business Services:** meeting rooms. **Cards:** AX, CB, DS, MC, VI. **Special Amenities:** free expanded continental breakfast and free local telephone calls. *(See ad p 399)*

SOME UNITS

WHERE TO DINE

BAMBOO GARDEN
Lunch: $5-$8　　　　　Dinner: $9-$14　　　　　Phone: 989/832-7967
Chinese
Location: Jct US 10 and Eastman Rd, 1 mi s, then 0.5 mi w. 2600 N Saginaw Rd 48640. **Hours:** 11:30 am-2 & 4-8:30 pm, Fri-9:30 pm, Sat 5 pm-9:30 pm, Sun noon-8 pm. Closed: 1/1, 11/25, 12/25. **Reservations:** suggested, weekends. **Features:** Szechuan and Shanghai cuisine are specialties on a menu that lists entrees from many regions of China. The comfortable, intimate dining room is decorated with attractive Oriental furnishings and appointments. Lunch buffet. Casual dress; cocktails. **Parking:** on-site. **Cards:** DS, MC, VI.

CAFE TANDOORI
Lunch: $5-$7　　　　　Dinner: $8-$15　　　　　Phone: 989/631-0362
Indian
Location: Jct US 10 and Eastman Rd, 1 mi s, then 0.5 mi w. 2600 N Saginaw Rd 48640. **Hours:** 11:30 am-2 & 5-9 pm, Sat noon-3 & 5-9 pm, Sun noon-3 & 5-8 pm. Closed major holidays. **Reservations:** accepted. **Features:** This restaurant offers a selection of traditional Indian dishes and breads, cooked in a Tandoor over - a device dating to the 10th century, made of clay and shaped like a hugh vase. Casual dress; cocktails. **Parking:** on-site. **Cards:** AX, MC, VI.

CHINA PALACE
Lunch: $4-$7　　　　　Dinner: $7-$17　　　　　Phone: 989/832-3177
Chinese
Location: Just n of US 10 business route. 1908 S Saginaw Rd 48640. **Hours:** 11 am-9:30 pm, Fri-10:30 pm, Sat noon-10:30 pm, Sun noon-8:30 pm. Closed major holidays. **Reservations:** suggested. **Features:** In business since the mid-1980s, the restaurant has several dining areas, all of which are decorated in an Oriental motif. Mongolian beef is among the delicious dishes of Mandarin, Szechuan, Hunan and Shanghai cuisine. The atmosphere is family-friendly. Casual dress; cocktails. **Parking:** on-site. **Cards:** AX, DS, MC, VI.

THE CROSSINGS
Lunch: $5-$10　　　　　Dinner: $13-$25　　　　　Phone: 989/837-6030
American
Location: Corner of Main and Ashman sts; downtown; in Ashman Court Marriott Conference Hotel. 111 W Main St 48640. **Hours:** 6:30 am-2 & 5-10 pm, Sat & Sun from 7 am. **Features:** The restaurant is great for couples or businesspeople who seek a relaxed setting in which to enjoy conversation. An extensive lunch buffet is popular on weekdays. The cozy summer terrace overlooks the picturesque waterfront. Service is friendly. Cocktails. **Parking:** on-site. **Cards:** AX, CB, DC, DS, MC, VI.

The following restaurants have not been evaluated by AAA but are listed for your information only.

CORKY'S STEAKHOUSE
Phone: 989/496-0096
[fyi]
Not evaluated. **Location:** US 10, exit Midland Bay City Rd. 5100 Bay City Rd 48642. **Features:** This popular steakhouse has been voted one of the best places to come for steaks and is close to the Interstate exit.

HELLO SUSHI
Phone: 989/633-6070
[fyi]
Not evaluated. **Location:** Center; at Ashman Court. 111 W Main St 48640. **Features:** Located in the lounge of the Ashman Court Marriott Conference Hotel, this is the place to go if you like sushi.

MILAN pop. 4,775

WHERE TO STAY

SLEEP INN & SUITES   *Book at aaa.com*
Phone: (734)439-1400
Small-scale Hotel
4/1-12/31　　　　1P: $59-$169　　　　2P: $59-$169　　　　XP: $6　　　　F18
1/1-3/31　　　　1P: $49-$129　　　　2P: $49-$129　　　　XP: $6　　　　F18
Location: I-23, exit 27, just w. 1230 Dexter St 48160. Fax: 734/439-4181. **Facility:** 63 one-bedroom standard units, some with whirlpools. 3 stories, interior corridors. *Bath:* shower only. **Parking:** on-site. **Terms:** [CP] meal plan available. **Amenities:** dual phone lines, voice mail, safes, hair dryers. **Pool(s):** heated indoor. **Leisure Activities:** exercise room. **Guest Services:** valet and coin laundry. **Business Services:** meeting rooms. **Cards:** AX, CB, DC, DS, JC, MC, VI.

SOME UNITS

MILFORD —*See Detroit p. 266.*

MIO pop. 2,016

──────── **WHERE TO STAY** ────────

HINCHMAN ACRES RESORT   **Phone: (989)826-3267**
⬡⬡ [SAVE]   All Year   1P: $60-$100   2P: $70-$150
▽▽ ▽▽   **Location:** 0.5 mi n on SR 33 and 72. Located on the Au Sable River. 702 N Morenci St 48647 (PO Box 220).
Cottage   Fax: 989/826-2289. **Facility:** 11 cottages. 1 story, exterior corridors. *Bath:* combo or shower only. **Parking:**
on-site. **Terms:** 2-7 night minimum stay - weekdays in summer, 30 day cancellation notice-fee imposed.
Amenities: hair dryers. **Leisure Activities:** rental canoes, rental tubes & rafts, cross country skiing, recre-
ation programs, bike trails, indoor recreation area, hiking trails, playground, basketball, horseshoes, shuffleboard, volleyball. *Fee:* fishing, ski equipment, snowshoes, game room. **Guest Services:** coin laundry. **Cards:** AX, DS, MC, VI.
Special Amenities: free local telephone calls and preferred room (subject to availability with advanced reservations).

MIO MOTEL   **Phone: 989/826-3248**
▽▽ ▽▽   All Year   1P: $50-$60   2P: $50-$65   XP: $10   F12
Motel   **Location:** Just n on SR 33 and 72. 415 N Morenci St 48647. **Facility:** 25 one-bedroom standard units. 2 stories,
exterior corridors. *Bath:* combo or shower only. **Parking:** on-site, winter plug-ins. **Terms:** 3 day cancellation
notice. **Cards:** MC, VI.
SOME UNITS

MONROE pop. 22,076

──────── **WHERE TO STAY** ────────

AMERIHOST INN-MONROE   *Book at aaa.com*   **Phone: (734)384-1600**
⬡⬡ [SAVE]   All Year   1P: $79-$145   2P: $79-$145   XP: $6   F18
▽▽ ▽▽   **Location:** I-75, exit 11 (Laplaisance Rd), just w. Located opposite an outlet mall. 14774 La Plaisance Rd 48161.
Small-scale Hotel   Fax: 734/384-1180. **Facility:** 63 one-bedroom standard units. 2 stories, interior corridors. *Bath:* combo or
shower only. **Parking:** on-site. **Amenities:** voice mail, safes (fee), irons, hair dryers. **Pool(s):** heated indoor.
Leisure Activities: sauna, whirlpool, exercise room. **Guest Services:** valet laundry. **Business Services:**
meeting rooms. **Cards:** AX, CB, DC, DS, JC, MC, VI. **Special Amenities: free expanded continental
breakfast and free newspaper.**
SOME UNITS

BEST WESTERN   *Book at aaa.com*   **Phone: (734)289-2330**
⬡⬡ [SAVE]   All Year [CP]   1P: $60-$100   2P: $65-$100   XP: $5   F16
▽▽ ▽▽   **Location:** I-75, exit 15 (SR 50). 1900 Welcome Way 48162. Fax: 734/289-3683. **Facility:** 120 one-bedroom stan-
Motel   dard units. 2 stories, exterior corridors. *Bath:* combo or shower only. **Parking:** on-site. **Terms:** weekly rates
available. **Amenities:** video games (fee), voice mail. **Pool(s):** heated outdoor. **Cards:** AX, CB, DS, MC, VI.
Special Amenities: free continental breakfast and free local telephone calls.
SOME UNITS

COMFORT INN   *Book at aaa.com*   **Phone: (734)384-1500**
⬡⬡ [SAVE]   6/1-8/31   1P: $80   2P: $80
▽▽ ▽▽   9/1-11/1   1P: $70   2P: $70
4/1-5/31   1P: $60   2P: $60
11/2-3/31   1P: $55   2P: $55
Small-scale Hotel   **Location:** I-75, exit 11 (Laplaisance Rd), just w. Located opposite an outlet mall. 6500 Albain Rd 48161.
Fax: 734/384-1515. **Facility:** 64 one-bedroom standard units, some with whirlpools. 3 stories, interior corridors. *Bath:* combo or shower only. **Parking:** on-site. **Terms:** weekly rates available, [ECP] meal plan available, package plans,
pets ($10 extra charge). **Amenities:** safes (fee), irons, hair dryers. **Pool(s):** heated indoor. **Leisure Activities:** whirlpool, bar-
becue grill, exercise room. **Guest Services:** valet and coin laundry. **Business Services:** meeting rooms, business center.
Cards: AX, DC, DS, MC, VI. **Special Amenities: free continental breakfast and free local telephone calls.**
SOME UNITS
FEE

HAMPTON INN   *Book at aaa.com*   **Phone: (734)289-5700**
▽▽▽▽   6/1-8/31   1P: $79-$125   2P: $89-$125
4/1-5/31 & 9/1-3/31   1P: $69-$125   2P: $69-$125
Small-scale Hotel   **Location:** I-75, exit 15 (SR 50), just e. 1565 N Dixie Hwy 48162. Fax: 734/289-3300. **Facility:** 74 one-bedroom
standard units, some with whirlpools. 3 stories, interior corridors. *Bath:* combo or shower only. **Parking:** on-
site. **Terms:** cancellation fee imposed, [ECP] meal plan available. **Amenities:** video games (fee), dual phone lines, voice mail,
irons, hair dryers. **Pool(s):** heated indoor. **Leisure Activities:** sauna, whirlpool, exercise room. **Guest Services:** valet and coin
laundry. **Business Services:** meeting rooms, business center. **Cards:** AX, DC, DS, JC, MC, VI.
SOME UNITS
FEE

HOLIDAY INN EXPRESS HOTEL & SUITES   *Book at aaa.com*   **Phone: (734)242-6000**
▽▽▽▽   All Year [ECP]   1P: $109-$119   2P: $129-$139   XP: $10   F19
Small-scale Hotel   **Location:** I-75, exit 15 (SR 50), just w. 1225 N Dixie Hwy 48162. Fax: 734/242-0555. **Facility:** 161 units. 158 one-
bedroom standard units, some with whirlpools. 3 two-bedroom suites ($129-$259) with efficiencies. 4 stories,
interior corridors. *Bath:* combo or shower only. **Parking:** on-site. **Amenities:** video games, dual phone lines,
voice mail, irons, hair dryers. **Pool(s):** heated indoor. **Leisure Activities:** whirlpool, exercise room. *Fee:* game room. **Guest
Services:** valet and coin laundry. **Business Services:** meeting rooms, business center. **Cards:** AX, CB, DC, DS, MC, VI.
SOME UNITS

HOMETOWN INN   *Book at aaa.com*   **Phone:** 734/289-1080
AAA **[SAVE]**   All Year [CP]   1P: $60-$85   2P: $60-$85   XP: $5   F16
♦♦ ♦♦   **Location:** I-75, exit 15 (SR 50). 1885 Welcome Way 48162. **Fax:** 734/289-1673. **Facility:** 89 one-bedroom stan-
Motel   dard units, some with whirlpools. 1 story, exterior corridors. **Parking:** on-site. **Terms:** 2 night minimum stay
- 6/1-8/31, weekly rates available. **Guest Services:** coin laundry. **Business Services:** meeting rooms.
Cards: AX, DC, DS, MC, VI.

SOME UNITS

LOTUS BED AND BREAKFAST, LC   **Phone:** 734/735-1077
♦♦ ♦♦   All Year   1P: $110   2P: $110
Historic Bed   **Location:** I-75, exit 11 (Laplaisance Rd), 2.5 mi w to Scott St, just n to 4th St, just w. 324 Washington St 48161.
& Breakfast   **Fax:** 734/735-1077. **Facility:** Many downtown attractions are within walking distance of this restored 1870
Italianate-style mansion. Smoke free premises. 4 units. 2 one-bedroom standard units. 2 one-bedroom
suites. 3 stories (no elevator), interior corridors. **Parking:** on-site. **Terms:** check-in 4 pm, 3 day cancellation
notice-fee imposed, [CP] meal plan available, no pets allowed (owner's cat on premises). **Guest Services:** complimentary
laundry. **Cards:** MC, VI.

SOME UNITS

──────── **WHERE TO DINE** ────────

BOLLES HARBOR CAFE   **Lunch:** $5-$7   **Dinner:** $6-$8   **Phone:** 734/457-2233
♦♦   **Location:** I-75, exit 11 (Laplaisance Rd), 2 mi e. 13986 Laplaisance Rd 48161. **Hours:** 6 am-2 pm, Fri & Sat-8
American   pm. Closed major holidays. **Features:** Family-owned and operated, the cozy, nautically themed shanty
restaurant seems perfectly suited in the midst of a busy marina. Breakfasts feature Dutch baby apple
pancakes and cinnamon-raisin French toast, while lunches and dinners center on sandwiches, burgers and
homemade daily specials. Casual dress. **Parking:** on-site. **Cards:** AX, DS, MC, VI.

DOLCE VITA ITALIAN GRILLE   **Lunch:** $6-$9   **Dinner:** $13-$19   **Phone:** 734/241-6100
♦♦ ♦♦   **Location:** Just s of jct US 24 (Telegraph Rd) and Stewart Rd; in Foodtown Plaza. 391 N Telegraph Rd 48162.
Hours: 11 am-10 pm, Fri-11 pm, Sat noon-11 pm, Sun noon-10 pm. Closed major holidays.
Italian   **Reservations:** accepted. **Features:** Two large, silver figurines greet diners just inside the casually elegant
dining room. Focusing on a mix of Northern and Southern Italian specialties, the menu lists such meat,
fresh seafood and pasta preparations as lamb chops a la menta; salmon bella vista and ravioli Bolognese. Casual dress;
cocktails. **Parking:** on-site. **Cards:** AX, MC, VI.

ERNIE'S EATERY & SPIRITS   **Lunch:** $5-$8   **Dinner:** $10-$14   **Phone:** 734/242-2330
♦♦   **Location:** Just n of W Dunbar Rd. 15425 S Dixie Hwy 48161. **Hours:** 7 am-10 pm, Fri-Sun to 11 pm. Closed
major holidays. **Features:** Located in front of a bowling alley, this comfortable family restaurant serves
American   pizzas, hamburgers and fish specials. The turtle soup is a popular choice, but leave room for homemade
desserts. Casual dress; cocktails. **Parking:** on-site. **Cards:** AX, MC, VI.

JOE'S FRENCH-ITALIAN INN   **Lunch:** $6-$12   **Dinner:** $10-$23   **Phone:** 734/289-2800
♦♦ ♦♦   **Location:** I-75, exit 15 (SR 50), 2 mi e. 2896 N Dixie Hwy 48162. **Hours:** 11 am-9:30 pm, Sat 4
pm-10:30 pm, Sun 4 pm-9:30 pm. Closed: 1/1, 12/25. **Reservations:** suggested. **Features:** Stained glass
American   and an attractive mural help to set an Italian theme in the quiet, casual restaurant. The menu of French
and Italian specialties includes preparations of seafood, prime rib and veal—in addition to a lengthy
selection of pasta dishes. Casual dress; cocktails. **Parking:** on-site. **Cards:** AX, MC, VI.

QUATRO'S   **Lunch:** $5-$7   **Dinner:** $8-$18   **Phone:** 734/242-6788
♦♦ ♦♦   **Location:** Jct US 24 (Telegraph Rd) and Stewart Rd; adjacent to Meijer Shopping Center. 1295 Stewart Rd 48162.
Hours: 11 am-10 pm, Fri & Sat 4 pm-midnight, Sun noon-8 pm. Closed: 1/1, 12/25.
American   **Reservations:** suggested, weekends. **Features:** Prime rib, crab legs and seafood fettuccine stand out
on a menu of varied choices. Decor that reflects the style of a modern tavern gives the dining room a warm,
cozy feel. A popular restaurant with locals, the place delivers consistent friendly service. Casual dress; cocktails. **Parking:**
on-site. **Cards:** AX, MC, VI.

MOUNT CLEMENS — *See Detroit p. 266.*

MOUNT PLEASANT pop. 25,946

──────── **WHERE TO STAY** ────────

BAYMONT INN-MOUNT PLEASANT   *Book at aaa.com*   **Phone:** (989)775-5555
♦♦ ♦♦   5/1-9/30 [ECP]   1P: $74-$119   2P: $74-$119   XP: $5   F
4/1-4/30 [ECP]   1P: $64-$119   2P: $64-$119   XP: $5   F
Small-scale Hotel   10/1-3/31 [ECP]   1P: $59-$109   2P: $59-$109   XP: $5   F
Location: Jct US 27 and SR 20 E, just e. 5858 E Pickard St 48858. **Fax:** 989/775-5566. **Facility:** 102 one-bedroom
standard units, some with whirlpools. 3 stories, interior corridors. **Parking:** on-site, winter plug-ins. **Terms:** package plans.
Amenities: video games (fee), voice mail, irons, hair dryers. **Pool(s):** heated indoor. **Leisure Activities:** whirlpool. **Guest Serv-
ices:** coin laundry. **Cards:** AX, DS, MC, VI.

SOME UNITS

BEST WESTERN INN   *Book at aaa.com*   **Phone:** (989)772-1101
AAA SAVE   All Year   1P: $79-$99   2P: $79-$99
◆◆◆ ◆◆◆   **Location:** Jct US 27 and SR 20 E, just e. 5770 E Pickard Ave 48858. Fax: 989/772-8986. **Facility:** 51 one-bedroom
           standard units. 1 story, interior corridors. **Parking:** on-site, winter plug-ins. **Terms:** [CP] meal plan available.
           Amenities: irons, hair dryers. **Pool(s):** heated indoor. **Leisure Activities:** sauna, whirlpool. **Cards:** AX, CB,
Small-scale Hotel DC, DS, MC, VI. **Special Amenities:** free continental breakfast and free local telephone calls.
                                                                                        SOME UNITS
                                          [SB] [ॐ] [⛱] [🎬] [DATA PORT] [💻] / [✕]

COMFORT INN   *Book at aaa.com*   **Phone:** (989)772-4000
◆◆◆ ◆◆◆   All Year   1P: $71-$116   2P: $71-$116   XP: $10   F16
           Location: 2 mi s on US 27 business route. 2424 S Mission St 48858. Fax: 989/773-6052. **Facility:** 138 units. 126
Small-scale Hotel one-bedroom standard units, some with whirlpools. 12 one-bedroom suites with whirlpools. 2 stories (no el-
           evator), interior corridors. *Bath:* combo or shower only. **Parking:** on-site, winter plug-ins. **Terms:** check-in 4
pm, [ECP] meal plan available. **Amenities:** voice mail, irons, hair dryers. **Pool(s):** heated indoor. **Leisure Activities:** exercise
room. *Fee:* game room. **Guest Services:** valet and coin laundry. **Business Services:** conference facilities. **Cards:** AX, DC, DS,
MC, VI. *(See color ad below)*
                                                                                        SOME UNITS
                              [ASK] [SB] [ॐ] [&] [⬚] [⛱] [🎬] [DATA PORT] [💻] / [✕] [VCR] [🔒] [⊞] /

FAIRFIELD INN BY MARRIOTT   *Book at aaa.com*   **Phone:** (989)775-5000
AAA SAVE   All Year   1P: $62-$105   2P: $62-$105
◆◆◆ ◆◆◆   **Location:** 2 mi s on US 27 business route. 2525 S University Park Dr 48858. Fax: 989/773-1371. **Facility:** 74 one-
           bedroom standard units, some with whirlpools. 3 stories, interior corridors. *Bath:* combo or shower only.
           Parking: on-site. **Terms:** check-in 4 pm. **Amenities:** irons, hair dryers. **Pool(s):** heated indoor. **Leisure Ac-**
Small-scale Hotel **tivities:** whirlpool, hiking trails. **Guest Services:** valet laundry. **Cards:** AX, DC, DS, MC, VI.
           (See color ad below)
                                                                                        SOME UNITS
                                      [SB] [ॐ] [&] [⛱] [🛏] [🎬] [DATA PORT] / [✕] [🔒] [⊞] /
                                                                            FEE

GREEN SUITES   **Phone:** (989)772-1703
◆◆◆ ◆◆◆   All Year   1P: $59-$185   2P: $59-$185   XP: $10   F18
Motel   **Location:** Jct US 27 and SR 20, just e on SR 20, then just n. 1900 Summerton Rd 48858. Fax: 989/772-1721.
           Facility: 42 units. 22 one-bedroom standard units. 20 one-bedroom suites ($79-$585) with kitchens (utensil
           deposit required). 2 stories, exterior corridors. *Bath:* shower only. **Parking:** on-site. **Terms:** check-in 4 pm, 3
day cancellation notice, weekly rates available, package plans. **Amenities:** voice mail, hair dryers. *Some:* irons. **Cards:** AX, CB,
DC, DS, JC, MC, VI.
                                                                                        SOME UNITS
                              [ASK] [SB] [ॐ] [🛏] [DATA PORT] [💻] / [✕] [🔒] [⊞] /
                                                       FEE

HAMPTON INN   *Book at aaa.com*   Phone: (989)772-5500
▼▼◆▼▼
All Year   1P: $75-$119   2P: $75-$119
Small-scale Hotel **Location:** Jct US 27 and SR 20, just w on SR 20. 5205 E Pickard Rd 48858. **Fax:** 989/772-7401. **Facility:** 89 one-bedroom standard units, some with whirlpools. 3 stories, interior corridors. *Bath:* combo or shower only. **Parking:** on-site, winter plug-ins. **Terms:** check-in 4 pm, 2 night minimum stay - seasonal, cancellation fee imposed, [ECP] meal plan available. **Amenities:** video games, voice mail, irons, hair dryers. **Pool(s):** heated indoor. **Leisure Activities:** whirlpool, exercise room. *Fee:* game room. **Guest Services:** valet and coin laundry. **Business Services:** meeting rooms, fax (fee). **Cards:** AX, DC, DS, MC, VI. *(See color ad below)*

SOME UNITS

HOLIDAY INN   *Book at aaa.com*   Phone: (989)772-2905
▼▼◆▼▼
All Year   1P: $89-$159   2P: $89-$159   XP: $10   F16
Resort   **Location:** Jct US 27 and SR 20 E. 5665 E Pickard Ave 48858. **Fax:** 989/772-4952. **Facility:** Featuring extensive
Small-scale Hotel recreational options and an 18-hole golf course, this hotel is a short drive from the casino. 184 one-bedroom standard units, some with whirlpools. 2-3 stories, interior/exterior corridors. *Bath:* combo or shower only. **Parking:** on-site, winter plug-ins. **Terms:** check-in 4 pm, 3 day cancellation notice-fee imposed, package plans, small pets only. **Amenities:** video games (fee), voice mail, irons, hair dryers. **Pool(s):** outdoor, heated indoor. **Leisure Activities:** sauna, whirlpools, fishing, snowmobiling, playground. *Fee:* golf-18 holes, racquetball courts, massage, game room. **Guest Services:** gift shop, valet and coin laundry. *Fee:* tanning facility. **Business Services:** conference facilities. **Cards:** AX, DS, JC, MC, VI.

SOME UNITS

MICROTEL INN   *Book at aaa.com*   Phone: (989)772-7777
▼▼◆▼▼
4/1-11/1 [CP]   1P: $54-$99   2P: $54-$99
11/2-3/31 [CP]   1P: $49-$99   2P: $49-$99
Small-scale Hotel **Location:** Jct US 27 and SR 20. 5500 E Pickard Rd 48858. **Fax:** 989/773-5144. **Facility:** 82 one-bedroom standard units. 3 stories, interior corridors. *Bath:* combo or shower only. **Parking:** on-site. **Cards:** AX, CB, DC, DS, MC, VI.

SOME UNITS

SOARING EAGLE CASINO & RESORT   Phone: (989)775-7777
(AAA) (SAVE)
All Year   1P: $119-$209   2P: $119-$209   XP: $10   F7
▼▼◆▼▼ Resort   **Location:** US 27, 1.5 mi e on SR 20, just s on Leaton Rd. 6800 Soaring Eagle Blvd 48858. **Fax:** 989/775-5686.
Large-scale Hotel **Facility:** American Indian artwork adorns this resort, which offers casual and fine dining, recreational facilities, a casino and luxurious rooms. 512 units. 491 one-bedroom standard units, some with whirlpools. 21 one-bedroom suites ($299-$369) with whirlpools. 7 stories, interior corridors. *Bath:* combo or shower only. **Parking:** on-site and valet. **Terms:** check-in 4 pm, 2 night minimum stay - weekends, 3 day cancellation notice, package plans. **Amenities:** video games (fee), voice mail, irons, hair dryers. *Some:* dual phone lines. **Dining:** 4 restaurants, 7 am-10:30 pm, cocktails, also, The Water Lily, see separate listing, entertainment. **Pool(s):** heated indoor. **Leisure Activities:** whirlpools, steamrooms, recreation programs, playground, exercise room, spa. **Guest Services:** gift shop, valet laundry, airport transportation (fee)-Tri-City Airport, area transportation. **Business Services:** conference facilities. **Cards:** AX, DC, DS, MC, VI. **Special Amenities: free local telephone calls and free newspaper.** *(See color ad p 405)*

SOME UNITS

FEE

SUPER 8 MOTEL   *Book at aaa.com*   Phone: 989/773-8888
▼▼◆▼▼
All Year   1P: $53-$125   2P: $53-$125
Small-scale Hotel **Location:** 1.8 mi s on US 27 business route. 2323 S Mission 48858. **Fax:** 989/772-5371. **Facility:** 142 one-bedroom standard units, some with whirlpools. 3 stories, interior corridors. *Bath:* combo or shower only. **Parking:** on-site, winter plug-ins. **Terms:** cancellation fee imposed, [CP] meal plan available. **Amenities:** video games (fee), hair dryers. **Guest Services:** coin laundry. **Cards:** AX, DC, DS, MC, VI.

SOME UNITS

------ WHERE TO DINE ------

EMBERS

Lunch: $6-$16   Dinner: $18-$29   Phone: 989/773-5007

American

Location: 1.3 mi s on US 27 business route. 1217 S Mission St 48858. **Hours:** 11:30 am-10 pm, Sat from 4 pm, Sun 10 am-7 pm. Closed major holidays; also 12/24. **Features:** A delicious, Chinese red sauce glazes the one-pound pork chop for which the restaurant is known. The intimate dining room sets the tone for a moderately upscale experience. A professional, friendly staff provides efficient service with good follow-up. Casual dress; cocktails. **Parking:** on-site. **Cards:** AX, DC, DS, MC, VI.

LA SENORITA

Lunch: $5-$7   Dinner: $7-$12   Phone: 989/772-1331

Mexican

Location: 2.8 mi s on US 27 business route. 1516 S Mission St 48858. **Hours:** 11 am-10 pm, Fri & Sat-11 pm; 11 am-midnight, Sun noon-10 pm 5/29-9/4. Closed: 11/25, 12/24, 12/25 & Easter. **Features:** Fun-type restaurant for either casual or family dining. The Mexican decor throughout is inviting. Mesquite grill items. Sizzling fajitas. Casual dress; cocktails. **Parking:** on-site. **Cards:** AX, DC, DS, MC, VI.

THE WATER LILY

Dinner: $20-$30   Phone: 989/775-7777

Seafood

Location: From US 27, 1.5 mi e on SR 20, just s on Leaton Rd; in Soaring Eagle Casino & Resort. 6800 Soaring Eagle Dr 48858. **Hours:** 7 am-10:30 & 5-10:30 pm. **Reservations:** suggested. **Features:** For a special occasion or night to remember, visit this casual, yet upscale, spot. Choose from a wide range of dishes— from American to seafood to wild game. Representative of the outstanding fare is the Western elk tenderloin with red onion marmalade, savory plum cornbread stuffing and lingonberry cognac glace. Wine recommendations are well-paired with each dish. Dressy casual; cocktails. **Parking:** on-site. **Cards:** AX, DS, MC, VI.

MUNISING pop. 2,539

------ WHERE TO STAY ------

ALGER FALLS MOTEL

Phone: (906)387-3536

6/27-8/30 & 12/1-3/31	1P: $48-$65	2P: $48-$65	XP: $4 F12
4/1-6/26 & 8/31-11/30	1P: $35-$48	2P: $35-$48	XP: $4 F12

Motel

Location: 2 mi e on SR 28 and 94. E9427 SR 28 49862. Fax: 906/387-5228. **Facility:** 17 units. 16 one-bedroom standard units. 1 cottage ($65-$105). 1 story, exterior corridors. **Parking:** on-site, winter plug-ins. **Terms:** small pets only. **Leisure Activities:** snowmobiling, heated garage for snowmobiles. *Fee:* game room. **Guest Services:** coin laundry. **Cards:** DS, MC, VI. **Special Amenities:** free local telephone calls.

SOME UNITS

BEST WESTERN   *Book at aaa.com*

Phone: (906)387-4864

12/21-3/31	1P: $89-$129	2P: $89-$129
6/16-9/10	1P: $89-$119	2P: $89-$119
9/11-12/20	1P: $59-$99	2P: $69-$109
4/1-6/15	1P: $59-$99	2P: $59-$99

Motel

Location: 3 mi e on SR 28. Located in a semi-rural area. M-28 49862 (PO Box 30, WETMORE, 49895). Fax: 906/387-2038. **Facility:** 80 units. 68 one-bedroom standard units, some with whirlpools. 12 one-bedroom suites. 2 stories (no elevator), interior/exterior corridors. **Parking:** on-site, winter plug-ins. **Terms:** 3 day cancellation notice, [CP] & [ECP] meal plans available, small pets only. **Amenities:** irons, hair dryers. **Dining:** 7 am-10 pm; hours vary off season, cocktails. **Pool(s):** heated indoor. **Leisure Activities:** sauna, whirlpool, snowmobiling, playground. *Fee:* game room. **Guest Services:** gift shop, coin laundry. **Cards:** AX, CB, DC, DS, MC, VI.

SOME UNITS

COMFORT INN   *Book at aaa.com*

Phone: (906)387-5292

All Year [CP]	1P: $75-$110	2P: $75-$110

Small-scale Hotel

Location: 1.5 mi e on SR 28. Located in a semi-commercial area. M-28 E 49862 (PO Box 276). Fax: 906/387-3753. **Facility:** 61 one-bedroom standard units. 2 stories (no elevator), interior corridors. **Parking:** on-site, winter plug-ins. **Terms:** 3 day cancellation notice, small pets only (in smoking units). **Amenities:** hair dryers. *Some:* irons. **Pool(s):** heated indoor. **Leisure Activities:** whirlpool, snowmobiling, exercise room. **Guest Services:** coin laundry. **Business Services:** meeting rooms. **Cards:** AX, CB, DC, DS, JC, MC, VI.

SOME UNITS

DAYS INN   *Book at aaa.com*

Phone: (906)387-2493

All Year	1P: $75-$110	2P: $75-$110

Small-scale Hotel

Location: 0.5 mi e on SR 28. On M-28 49862 (PO Box 403). Fax: 906/387-5214. **Facility:** 66 units. 63 one-bedroom standard units. 3 one-bedroom suites ($125-$150), some with whirlpools. 2 stories (no elevator), interior corridors. **Parking:** on-site. **Terms:** 3 day cancellation notice, pets (in designated units). **Amenities:** hair dryers. **Pool(s):** heated indoor. **Leisure Activities:** sauna, whirlpool, snowmobiling. **Guest Services:** gift shop. **Cards:** AX, CB, DC, DS, JC, MC, VI. *(See color ad card insert)*

SOME UNITS

SUNSET MOTEL

Phone: (906)387-4574

6/16-9/6 & 12/10-3/31	1P: $60-$65	2P: $60-$65	XP: $4 D5
4/1-6/15 & 9/7-12/9	1P: $45-$50	2P: $45-$50	XP: $4 D5

Motel

Location: 1 mi e on E Munising Ave (CR 58). Located on Munising Bay. 1315 Bay St 49862 (PO Box 291). **Facility:** 18 units. 8 one- and 9 two-bedroom standard units, some with efficiencies. 1 cottage. 1-2 stories (no elevator), exterior corridors. *Bath:* combo or shower only. **Parking:** on-site. **Terms:** weekly rates available, pets ($10 extra charge, limit 1, in smoking units, small dogs only). **Leisure Activities:** boat dock, fishing, snowmobiling, playground. **Cards:** DS, MC, VI. **Special Amenities:** early check-in/late check-out and preferred room (subject to availability with advanced reservations).

SOME UNITS

FEE

SUPER 8 MOTEL-MUNISING

			Phone: 906/387-2466
✨✨✨	All Year	1P: $49-$92	2P: $64-$104	XP: $10	F12

Small-scale Hotel
Location: 2.5 mi e on SR 28. Located in a semi-commercial area. M-28 & Fed Hwy 13 49862 (PO Box 359, 49682). Fax: 906/387-2355. **Facility:** 43 one-bedroom standard units, some with whirlpools. 2 stories (no elevator), interior corridors. **Parking:** on-site, winter plug-ins. **Terms:** cancellation fee imposed, [CP] meal plan available. **Leisure Activities:** sauna, whirlpool, snowmobiling. **Cards:** DS, MC, VI.

SOME UNITS
$\boxed{\text{S}_D}$ ⊠ $\boxed{\text{VCR}}$ 🐾 $\boxed{\text{DATA PORT}}$ / ⊠ 🛗 🖥 /

TERRACE MOTEL

			Phone: 906/387-2735
⚹⚹⚹ SAVE	6/25-9/5 & 12/3-3/31	1P: $50	2P: $50-$55
✨	4/1-6/24 & 9/6-12/2	1P: $40	2P: $40-$45

Motel
Location: 0.5 mi e, just off SR 28. Located in a residential area. 420 Prospect 49862. Fax: 906/387-2754. **Facility:** 18 units. 14 one- and 4 two-bedroom standard units. 1 story, exterior corridors. *Bath:* combo or shower only. **Parking:** on-site. **Terms:** 3 day cancellation notice, pets ($3 extra charge). **Leisure Activities:** sauna, snowmobiling, heated garage for snowmobiles, recreation room. **Cards:** DS, MC, VI. **Special Amenities: free newspaper and preferred room (subject to availability with advanced reservations).**

SOME UNITS
$\boxed{\text{S}_D}$ 🛏 ⊠ $\boxed{\text{K}}$ 🐾 / ⊠ /
FEE

------- **WHERE TO DINE** -------

DOGPATCH

	Lunch: $4-$7	**Dinner:** $9-$14	Phone: 906/387-9948
✨			

American
Location: Just off SR 28; center. 820 E Superior St 49862. **Hours:** 7 am-9 pm. Closed: 12/25. **Features:** Established in 1966, the restaurant is a great place to take your kids for a relaxed meal. The menu lists country-style breakfasts, a great selection of sandwiches and charbroiled steaks. The popular seafood buffet with all the fixings is served nightly. Casual dress; cocktails. **Parking:** on-site.

Cards: MC, VI.

🍽 ⊠

MUSKEGON pop. 40,105

------- **WHERE TO STAY** -------

COMFORT INN

	Book at aaa.com			Phone: (231)739-9092
✨✨✨✨	6/1-9/1 [ECP]	1P: $129-$199	2P: $129-$199	XP: $5	F18
	4/1-5/31 & 9/2-3/31 [ECP]	1P: $79-$199	2P: $79-$199	XP: $5	F18

Small-scale Hotel
Location: Jct US 31 and CR B-72, exit Sherman Blvd. Located next to a shopping mall. 1675 E Sherman Blvd 49444. Fax: 231/739-2264. **Facility:** 117 one-bedroom standard units, some with efficiencies and/or whirlpools. 2 stories (no elevator), interior corridors. **Parking:** on-site. **Amenities:** voice mail, irons, hair dryers. *Fee:* video library, safes. **Pool(s):** heated outdoor, heated indoor. **Leisure Activities:** exercise room. *Fee:* game room. **Guest Services:** valet and coin laundry. **Business Services:** meeting rooms, business center. **Cards:** AX, CB, DC, DS, MC, VI.

SOME UNITS
$\boxed{\text{ASK}}$ $\boxed{\text{S}_D}$ 🍴 🍽 🏊 🐾 $\boxed{\text{DATA PORT}}$ 🖥 / ⊠ $\boxed{\text{VCR}}$ 🛗 🖥 /
FEE

HOLIDAY INN-MUSKEGON HARBOR

		Phone: 231/722-0100
✨✨✨	Property failed to provide current rates	

Large-scale Hotel
Location: Center. 939 3rd St 49440. Fax: 231/722-5118. **Facility:** 201 one-bedroom standard units, some with whirlpools. 8 stories, interior corridors. *Bath:* combo or shower only. **Parking:** on-site. **Terms:** check-in 4 pm. **Amenities:** video games, dual phone lines, voice mail, irons, hair dryers. **Pool(s):** heated indoor. **Leisure Activities:** sauna, whirlpool, steamroom, exercise room. **Guest Services:** valet laundry. **Business Services:** conference facilities. *(See ad below)*

SOME UNITS
🔌 🍴 🍽 🎱 🏊 ⊠ 🐾 $\boxed{\text{DATA PORT}}$ 🖥 / ⊠ 🛗 /
FEE

——— WHERE TO DINE ———

FINLEY'S AMERICAN RESTAURANT   **Lunch:** $5-$9   **Dinner:** $8-$16   **Phone:** 231/733-9928
♦♦♦
Location: 3 mi s, just w of US 31 business route. 3055 Henry St 49441. **Hours:** 11 am-10 pm, Fri & Sat-11 pm.
American
Closed: 11/25, 12/25. **Features:** Casual family dining, steak, seafood, chicken and a favorite - baby back ribs. Casual dress; cocktails. **Parking:** on-site. **Cards:** AX, DC, DS, MC, VI.
☒

NINO'S   **Lunch:** $5-$16   **Dinner:** $5-$16   **Phone:** 231/733-2921
♦♦♦
Location: US 31, exit Sherman Blvd, 0.7 mi w. 919 E Sherman Blvd 49444. **Hours:** 6 am-9 pm, Fri & Sat-10 pm,
Italian
Sun 8 am-3 pm. Closed: 1/1, 11/25, 12/25. **Features:** The popular restaurant serves reasonably priced dishes and delicious homemade desserts and pies. Casual dress. **Parking:** on-site. **Cards:** AX, MC, VI.
☒

TONY'S RESTAURANT   **Lunch:** $5-$8   **Dinner:** $9-$18   **Phone:** 231/739-7196
♦♦♦ ♦♦♦
Location: 2.8 mi s, just e of Henry St. 785 W Broadway 49441. **Hours:** 11 am-9 pm, Fri-11 pm, Sat 5 pm-11 pm.
Steak House
Closed major holidays; also Sun. **Reservations:** suggested, weekends. **Features:** Family-owned and operated since 1969. Greek themed dining room with picturesque lighted murals on the walls. Good selection of steak, chops, chicken and seafood as well as unique daily specials not often found in a steakhouse such as Hungarian Goulash on Mondays, or Souviaki (pork kebab) served on Thursdays. Casual dress; cocktails. **Parking:** on-site. **Cards:** AX, CB, DC, DS, MC, VI.
🍽 ☒

——— *The following restaurant has not been evaluated by AAA* ———
but is listed for your information only.

RAFFERTY'S   **Phone:** 231/722-4461
[fyi]
Not evaluated. **Location:** Center. 601 Terrace Point 49441. **Features:** Located downtown on Muskegon lake, the dockside restaurant serves walleye, lake perch and prime rib.

NEWBERRY pop. 2,686

——— WHERE TO STAY ———

BEST WESTERN NEWBERRY   *Book at aaa.com*   **Phone:** (906)293-4000
AAA [SAVE]
All Year [CP]   1P: $54-$91   2P: $62-$99   XP: $8   F12
♦♦♦♦
Location: On SR 28, 1 mi e of SR 123. Located in a semi-rural area. 12956 SR 28 49868. Fax: 906/293-4005.
Small-scale Hotel
Facility: 66 units. 64 one-bedroom standard units, some with whirlpools. 1 one- and 1 two-bedroom suites ($151-$197). 2 stories, interior corridors. *Bath:* combo or shower only. **Parking:** on-site. **Amenities:** safes (fee), irons, hair dryers. **Pool(s):** heated indoor. **Leisure Activities:** sauna, whirlpool, snowmobiling. **Guest Services:** coin laundry. **Business Services:** meeting rooms. **Cards:** AX, CB, DC, DS, JC, MC, VI.
Special Amenities: free continental breakfast.
SOME UNITS
🔊 🛏 📶 🛋 🏊 ☒ 🎦 [DATA PORT] 💻 / ☒ 🔌 📷 /
FEE   FEE

COMFORT INN TAHQUAMENON FALLS   *Book at aaa.com*   **Phone:** 906/293-3218
AAA [SAVE]
All Year   1P: $69-$89   2P: $89-$125   XP: $10   F18
♦♦♦♦
Location: Jct SR 28 and 123. Jct SR 123 & 28 49868 (13954 St Hwy M-28). Fax: 906/293-9375. **Facility:** 54 one-
Small-scale Hotel
bedroom standard units, some with whirlpools. 2 stories (no elevator), interior corridors. *Bath:* combo or shower only. **Parking:** on-site. **Terms:** [ECP] meal plan available. **Amenities:** irons, hair dryers. **Leisure Activities:** sauna, whirlpool, snowmobiling. *Fee:* game room. **Guest Services:** gift shop, coin laundry. **Business Services:** meeting rooms. **Cards:** AX, DC, DS, MC, VI. **Special Amenities:** free continental breakfast and free local telephone calls.
SOME UNITS
🔊 🛏 ☒ 🎦 [DATA PORT] 💻 / ☒ 🔌 📷 /

——— WHERE TO DINE ———

TIMBER CHARLIE'S FOOD "N" SPIRITS   **Lunch:** $4-$7   **Dinner:** $9-$18   **Phone:** 906/293-3363
AAA
Location: On SR 123, north side of town. 110 Newberry Ave 49868. **Hours:** 10:30 am-9 pm, Sun from noon; to
♦♦♦
10 pm in season. Closed: 11/25, 12/25 & Easter; also for dinner 12/24. **Features:** Baby back ribs, Italian
American
and Mexican fare and a tempting variety of sizzling steaks make up the restaurant's varied menu. Knotty pine walls and wildlife art contribute to the rustic atmosphere. Tourists and locals alike frequent the casual eatery. Casual dress; cocktails. **Parking:** street. **Cards:** AX, DS, MC, VI.
☒

NEW BUFFALO pop. 2,200

——— WHERE TO STAY ———

BEST WESTERN PLAZA HOTEL   *Book at aaa.com*   **Phone:** (269)469-4193
AAA [SAVE]
7/1-9/7 [ECP]   1P: $129-$229   XP: $10   F17
♦♦♦♦
9/8-10/31 [ECP]   1P: $99-$219   XP: $10   F17
11/1-3/31 [ECP]   1P: $89-$189   XP: $10   F17
4/1-6/30 [ECP]   1P: $89-$169   XP: $10   F17
Small-scale Hotel
Location: I-94, exit 1 (La Porte Rd), just w. 18800 La Porte Rd 49117. Fax: 269/469-4211. **Facility:** 69 units. 61 one-bedroom standard units, some with whirlpools. 8 one-bedroom suites ($189-$255). 3 stories, interior corridors. *Bath:* combo or shower only. **Parking:** on-site. **Terms:** 2 night minimum stay - weekends in season, cancellation fee imposed. **Amenities:** dual phone lines, voice mail, irons, hair dryers. **Pool(s):** heated indoor. **Leisure Activities:** whirlpool, exercise room. **Guest Services:** valet and coin laundry. **Cards:** AX, CB, DC, MC, VI. **Special Amenities:** free expanded continental breakfast and free newspaper. *(See color ad p 409)*
SOME UNITS
🔊 🛏 🏋 🛋 🏊 🎦 [DATA PORT] 💻 / ☒ 🔌 📷 /

GRAND BEACH MOTEL

Motel

Phone: (269)469-1555

5/15-10/15 [CP] 1P: $40-$55 2P: $50-$75
Location: I-94, exit 1 (La Porte Rd), 1.2 mi w to US 12, then 2.5 mi s. 19189 US 12 49117. **Facility:** 14 units. 13 one-bedroom standard units. 1 two-bedroom suite ($70-$90). 1 story, exterior corridors. *Bath:* combo or shower only. **Parking:** on-site. **Terms:** open 5/15-10/15, 2 night minimum stay - weekends, 3 day cancellation notice. **Pool(s):** heated outdoor. **Cards:** DS, MC, VI. **Special Amenities: free continental breakfast and early check-in/late check-out.**

SOME UNITS

HARBOR GRAND HOTEL *Book at aaa.com*
Small-scale Hotel

Phone: (269)469-7700
XP: $20 F11

All Year 1P: $99-$349 2P: $99-$349
Location: I-94, exit 1 (La Porte Rd), 2 mi w. Overlooking marina. 111 Oselka Dr 49117 (111 W Water St). Fax: 269/469-7386. **Facility:** 55 units. 33 one-bedroom standard units, some with whirlpools. 22 one-bedroom suites. 4 stories, interior corridors. *Bath:* combo or shower only. **Parking:** on-site. **Terms:** check-in 4 pm, 2 night minimum stay - weekends, [CP] meal plan available. **Amenities:** hair dryers. **Pool(s):** heated indoor. **Leisure Activities:** whirlpool, bicycles, exercise room. *Fee:* massage. **Business Services:** meeting rooms. **Cards:** AX, DS, MC, VI.

SOME UNITS

HOLIDAY INN EXPRESS HOTEL & SUITES

			Phone: (269)469-1400
6/11-8/14 [ECP]	1P: $89-$189	2P: $89-$189	XP: $6 F19
4/1-6/10 & 8/15-3/31 [ECP]	1P: $79-$189	2P: $79-$189	XP: $6 F19

Small-scale Hotel **Location:** I-94, exit 1 (La Porte Rd), just w. 11500 Holiday Dr 49117. Fax: 269/469-8463. **Facility:** 80 one-bedroom standard units, some with whirlpools. 3 stories, interior corridors. **Bath:** combo or shower only. **Parking:** on-site, winter plug-ins. **Amenities:** dual phone lines, voice mail, irons, hair dryers. **Pool(s):** heated indoor. **Leisure Activities:** whirlpool. *Fee:* game room. **Guest Services:** valet and coin laundry. **Business Services:** meeting rooms. **Cards:** AX, CB, DC, DS, MC, VI. *(See color ad card insert & p 409)*

SOME UNITS
(ASK) (S/D) (&M) (&) (➜) (🛄) (🕸) (DATA PORT) / (✕) (🛗) (🖥) (🖵) /

——— WHERE TO DINE ———

HANNAH'S RESTAURANT

Lunch: $7-$11	**Dinner:** $9-$26	**Phone:** 269/469-1440

Location: I-94, exit 1 (La Porte Rd), 1 mi w. 115 S Whittaker 49117. **Hours:** 11:30 am-10 pm, Fri & Sat-11 pm. Closed: 12/25. **Reservations:** accepted. **Features:** The wide selection offered in this bustling restaurant includes their prime rib specialty dinner, many sandwiches, fresh sauteed seafood, pasta dishes and even some Southwestern style fajitas. The homemade desserts come in ample portions just made to share. American Casual dress; cocktails. **Parking:** on-site. **Cards:** AX, DS, MC, VI.

(🍽) (✕)

REDAMAK'S

Lunch: $4-$9	**Dinner:** $5-$10	**Phone:** 269/469-4522

Location: Just n of jct SR 39; town center. 616 E Buffalo St 49117. **Hours:** Open 4/1-10/31 & 3/1-3/31; noon-9:30 pm. Closed: Easter. **Features:** A local institution, this casual and informal restaurant is known American for its hamburgers. Casual dress; cocktails. **Parking:** on-site.

(🍽) (✕)

RETRO CAFE' & KITE'S KITCHEN

	Lunch: $6-$9	**Phone:** 269/469-1800

Location: I-94, exit 1 (La Porte Rd), 1 mi w, then 0.5 mi s on SR 12. 801 W Buffalo St 49117. **Hours:** 9 am-3 pm. Closed major holidays; also Mon & Tues 4/1-6/30 & 9/1-3/31. **Features:** The charming, country-style American restaurant combines the coziness of a limited number of tables and the bright, cheerful feel of an interior complete with a wall of sepia family pictures. Inventive creations make a strong showing on the breakfast and lunch menu. Casual dress. **Parking:** on-site. **Cards:** MC, VI.

(✕)

NILES pop. 12,204

——— WHERE TO STAY ———

HOLIDAY INN EXPRESS *Book at aaa.com*

			Phone: (269)684-3900
8/1-11/30 [ECP]	1P: $99-$279	2P: $99-$279	XP: $10 F17
5/11-7/31 [ECP]	1P: $94-$279	2P: $99-$279	XP: $10 F17
4/1-5/10 [ECP]	1P: $84-$94	2P: $94-$99	XP: $10 F17
12/1-3/31 [ECP]	1P: $89-$94	2P: $89-$94	XP: $10 F17

Small-scale Hotel **Location:** I-80/90, exit 77, n on SR 933 at state line (SR 933 becomes M-51), 3.5 mi n. 1265 S 11th St (M-51) 49120. Fax: 269/684-2900. **Facility:** 51 units. 43 one-bedroom standard units, some with efficiencies (no utensils) and/or whirlpools. 8 one-bedroom suites ($109-$279). 3 stories, interior corridors. **Bath:** combo or shower only. **Parking:** on-site, winter plug-ins. **Terms:** cancellation fee imposed. **Amenities:** dual phone lines, voice mail, irons, hair dryers. **Pool(s):** heated indoor. **Leisure Activities:** exercise room. **Guest Services:** valet laundry. **Business Services:** business center. **Cards:** AX, DC, DS, MC, VI.

SOME UNITS
(S/D) (🍴) (&) (➜) (🕸) (DATA PORT) (🖥) / (✕) (🛗) (🖵) /

NORTHVILLE —See Detroit p. 266.

NORTON SHORES pop. 22,527

——— WHERE TO STAY ———

AMERIHOST INN-MUSKEGON *Book at aaa.com*

			Phone: (231)798-0220
6/1-9/15 & 12/31-3/31 [CP]	1P: $99-$169	2P: $104-$169	XP: $5 F
4/1-5/31 & 9/16-12/30 [CP]	1P: $79-$129	2P: $84-$129	XP: $5 F

Location: Just se of jct I-96 and US 31; I-96 (westbound), exit 1A, follow signs to race track; from US 31, exit Sternberg Rd, just e to Harvey Rd, 1 mi n. Located opposite the race track. 4677 Harvey Rd 49441. Fax: 231/798-0221. Small-scale Hotel **Facility:** 61 one-bedroom standard units, some with whirlpools. 2 stories (no elevator), interior corridors. **Bath:** combo or shower only. **Parking:** on-site. **Amenities:** voice mail, safes (fee), irons, hair dryers. **Pool(s):** heated indoor. **Leisure Activities:** sauna, whirlpool, exercise room. **Guest Services:** valet laundry. **Business Services:** meeting rooms. **Cards:** AX, DC, DS, MC, VI. **Special Amenities:** free continental breakfast and free newspaper.

SOME UNITS
(S/D) (&) (➜) (✕) (🕸) (DATA PORT) (🖥) / (✕) (🛗) (🖵) /

HAMPTON INN OF MUSKEGON *Book at aaa.com*

			Phone: (231)799-8333
6/1-9/7	1P: $115-$125	2P: $115-$125	
4/1-5/31 & 9/8-3/31	1P: $84	2P: $84-$89	

Location: Just se of jct I-96 and US 31; I-96 (westbound), exit 1A, follow signs to race track; from US 31, exit Sternberg Rd, just e to Harvey Rd, 0.4 mi n, then just w. 1401 E Ellis Rd 49441. Fax: 231/799-8334. **Facility:** 81 units. 80 one-bedroom standard units, some with whirlpools. 1 one-bedroom suite ($125-$169). 4 stories, interior corridors. **Bath:** combo or shower only. **Parking:** on-site. **Terms:** [ECP] meal plan available. **Amenities:** video games, dual phone lines, voice mail, irons, hair dryers. **Pool(s):** heated indoor. **Leisure Activities:** whirlpool, exercise room. **Guest Services:** valet laundry. **Business Services:** meeting rooms. **Cards:** AX, DC, DS, MC, VI.

SOME UNITS
(ASK) (S/D) (🍴) (&M) (&) (➜) (✕) (🕸) (DATA PORT) (🖥) / (✕) (🛗) (🖵) /
FEE FEE

——— *The following lodging was either not evaluated or did not*
meet AAA rating requirements but is listed for your information only.

FAIRFIELD INN BY MARRIOTT   **Phone:** 866/211-4607
  [fyi]   6/16-9/7   1P: $109-$149
           9/8-3/31   1P: $79-$109
Small-scale Hotel 4/1-6/15   1P: $74-$104
    Too new to rate. **Location:** US 31, exit Sternberg Rd, just e to Harvey Rd, 0.5 mi s. Mt Garfield Rd 49444.
Amenities: 85 units, pool. **Cards:** AX, CB, DC, DS, MC, VI.

——— **WHERE TO DINE** ———

——— *The following restaurants have not been evaluated by AAA* ———
but are listed for your information only.

EGG ROLL HOUSE   **Phone:** 231/798-9888
  [fyi] Not evaluated. **Location:** US 31, exit Sternberg Rd, just w. 1084 E Sternberg Rd 49441. **Features:** The popular
restaurant offers a number of reasonably priced Mandarin dishes at this new location.

HOUSE OF CHAN   **Phone:** 231/733-9624
  [fyi] Not evaluated. **Location:** Just s of US 31 business route. 375 Gin Chan Ave 49444. **Features:** This
well-established restaurant serves a popular Chinese-American buffet for lunch and dinner; they also have
a number of Cantonese dishes on the menu.

SAM'S JOINT   **Phone:** 231/798-7155
  [fyi] Not evaluated. **Location:** US 31, exit Fruitport, 0.5 mi w on Pontalana Rd. 6618 Grand Haven Rd 49441.
Features: Memorabilia spills over from the lounge into the dining areas at this fun spot.

NORWAY

——— **WHERE TO STAY** ———

AMERICINN OF NORWAY *Book at aaa.com*   **Phone:** (906)563-7500
  ▼▼▼▼ 5/30-10/9 [ECP]   1P: $73-$83   2P: $78-$88   XP: $5   F12
        4/1-5/29 & 10/10-3/31 [ECP] 1P: $71-$81   2P: $76-$86   XP: $5   F12
Small-scale Hotel **Location:** 0.7 mi w. W 6002 US Hwy 2 49870. Fax: 906/563-5853. **Facility:** 45 units. 42 one-bedroom standard
units, some with whirlpools. 3 one-bedroom suites ($91-$141), some with whirlpools. 2 stories (no elevator),
interior corridors. **Bath:** combo or shower only. **Parking:** on-site. **Terms:** weekly rates available, pets (in smoking units).
Amenities: *Some:* hair dryers. **Pool(s):** heated indoor. **Leisure Activities:** sauna, whirlpool, snowmobiling. **Guest Services:**
coin laundry. **Business Services:** meeting rooms. **Cards:** AX, DC, DS, MC, VI. *(See color ad p 311)*
SOME UNITS

NOVI —See Detroit p. 267.

OKEMOS

——— **WHERE TO STAY** ———

COMFORT INN-E. LANSING/OKEMOS *Book at aaa.com*   **Phone:** (517)349-8700
  ▼▼▼▼ All Year [ECP]   1P: $89-$99   2P: $89-$99   XP: $8   F18
    Location: I-96, exit 110 (Okemos Rd), just e. Located in University Commerce Park. 2209 University Park
Small-scale Hotel 48864. Fax: 517/349-5638. **Facility:** 159 units. 127 one-bedroom standard units, some with whirlpools. 32
one-bedroom suites ($109-$139) with whirlpools. 2 stories (no elevator), interior corridors. **Parking:** on-site.
Terms: weekly rates available, package plans. **Amenities:** voice mail, irons, hair dryers. *Fee:* video games, safes. **Pool(s):**
heated indoor. **Leisure Activities:** saunas, whirlpool, exercise room. **Guest Services:** valet and coin laundry. **Business Services:** meeting rooms. **Cards:** AX, CB, DC, DS, JC, MC, VI. *(See color ad p 294)*
SOME UNITS

FAIRFIELD INN BY MARRIOTT *Book at aaa.com*   **Phone:** 517/347-1000
  ▼▼▼▼ All Year   1P: $75-$89
    Location: I-96, exit 110 (Okemos Rd), 0.3 mi n. Located in an office park. 2335 Woodlake Dr 48864.
Small-scale Hotel Fax: 517/347-5092. **Facility:** 78 one-bedroom standard units, some with whirlpools. 2 stories, interior corri-
dors. **Bath:** combo or shower only. **Parking:** on-site. **Terms:** cancellation fee imposed, weekly rates available,
[ECP] meal plan available, package plans. **Amenities:** irons, hair dryers. **Pool(s):** heated indoor. **Leisure Activities:** whirlpool,
exercise room. **Guest Services:** valet laundry. **Business Services:** meeting rooms. **Cards:** AX, CB, DC, DS, MC, VI.
SOME UNITS

HAMPTON INN & SUITES *Book at aaa.com*   **Phone:** (517)349-6100
  ▼▼▼▼ 1/1-3/31 [ECP]   1P: $109-$199   2P: $109-$199
        6/1-12/31 [ECP]   1P: $104-$199   2P: $104-$199
Small-scale Hotel 4/1-5/31 [ECP]   1P: $99-$179   2P: $99-$179
  Location: I-96, exit 110 (Okemos Rd), 0.5 mi n. 2200 Hampton Pl 48864. Fax: 517/349-0885. **Facility:** 100 units.
91 one-bedroom standard units, some with whirlpools. 9 one-bedroom suites ($119-$199), some with whirlpools. 3 stories, interior corridors. **Bath:** combo or shower only. **Parking:** on-site. **Amenities:** dual phone lines, voice mail, irons, hair dryers. **Pool(s):**
heated indoor. **Leisure Activities:** whirlpool, exercise room. **Guest Services:** sundries, valet and coin laundry, tanning facility.
Business Services: meeting rooms. **Cards:** AX, CB, DC, DS, JC, MC, VI. *(See color ad p 340)*
SOME UNITS

HOLIDAY INN EXPRESS- E. LANSING/OKEMOS | *Book at aaa.com* | | | **Phone:** (517)347-6690
▼▼▼▼ | All Year | 1P: $75-$129 | 2P: $75-$129 | XP: $10 | F18
Small-scale Hotel | **Location:** I-96, exit 110 (Okemos Rd), 0.3 mi n, then just e. Located in University Commerce Park. 2187 University Park Dr 48864. Fax: 517/347-8163. **Facility:** 90 one-bedroom standard units. 2 stories (no elevator), interior corridors. *Bath:* combo or shower only. **Parking:** on-site. **Terms:** age restrictions may apply, [CP] meal plan available. **Amenities:** video games (fee), voice mail, irons, hair dryers. **Guest Services:** valet laundry. **Business Services:** conference facilities. **Cards:** AX, DC, DS, MC, VI. *(See color ad card insert)*

ASK SO T!→ (&) (&) (&) DATA PORT ▣ / X 🛢 🗔 /　SOME UNITS

——— WHERE TO DINE ———

DUSTY'S CELLAR | **Lunch:** $8-$10 | **Dinner:** $19-$24 | **Phone:** 517/349-5150
▼▼▼ | **Location:** Jct Okemos Rd and Grand River Ave, 1 mi e. 1839 Grand River Ave 48864. **Hours:** 11 am-10 pm, Fri & Sat-11 pm, Sun-9 pm. Closed major holidays. **Reservations:** accepted. **Features:** Trellised grapevines on
American | the ceiling and a large vineyard mural frame the small, intimate dining room, which is entered through a wine store. An extensive selection of wines complements dishes that employ tropical flavors from areas as far-flung as Hawaii, Florida and the Caribbean. Among menu accents are New Zealand lamb chops, diver scallops and Lake Superior whitefish. Dressy casual; cocktails. **Parking:** on-site. **Cards:** AX, DC, DS, MC, VI.

(&M) X

STILLWATER GRILL | | **Dinner:** $14-$25 | **Phone:** 517/349-1500
▼▼▼ | **Location:** I-96, exit 110 (Okemos Rd), 0.5 mi n. 3544 Meridian Crossing Dr 48864. **Hours:** 4 pm-10 pm, Fri-11 pm, Sat 3 pm-11 pm, Sun 3 pm-11 pm. Closed major holidays. **Features:** The huge restaurant became popular
American | almost immediately, which translates to a short wait for seating, even on weeknights. Intimate booths, hand-painted murals and copper accents give the room a stylish air, and the open kitchen prepares a menu that focuses on both steaks and several nightly fresh fish or pasta specials. Casual dress; cocktails. **Parking:** on-site. **Cards:** AX, DC, DS, MC, VI.

(&M) Y X

ONEKAMA pop. 647

——— WHERE TO STAY ———

ALPINE MOTOR LODGE-BUDGET HOST | | | **Phone:** 231/889-4281
AAA (SAVE) | 6/26-9/5 [ECP] | 1P: $63-$98 | 2P: $63-$98 |
▼▼▼▼ | 4/1-6/25 & 9/6-3/31 [ECP] | 1P: $50-$70 | 2P: $50-$70 |
Motel | **Location:** Jct US 31 and 8 Mile Rd. 8127 US 31 49675 (PO Box 366). Fax: 231/889-3689. **Facility:** 25 one-bedroom standard units. 1 story, exterior corridors. **Parking:** on-site. **Terms:** office hours 8 am-11 pm. **Pool(s):** heated outdoor. **Leisure Activities:** miniature golf, snowmobiling, horseshoes. **Cards:** DS, MC, VI.
(See color ad p 390) | **Special Amenities:** free expanded continental breakfast and free local telephone calls.

SO ⊃ X (&) DATA PORT 🛢 🗔 / X /　SOME UNITS

ONSTED pop. 813

——— WHERE TO DINE ———

GOLDEN NUGGET | **Lunch:** $7-$11 | **Dinner:** $9-$15 | **Phone:** 517/467-2190
AAA | **Location:** 0.3 mi e. 7305 US 12 49265. **Hours:** 5 pm-9:30 pm, Fri & Sat-11 pm, Sun noon-9 pm. Closed major
▼▼ ▼▼ | holidays; also Mon & Tues 9/1-3/31. **Features:** Turn-of-the-20th-century decor includes leaded-glass
American | chandeliers, antique furnishings and Tiffany-style lamps. The menu samples a little of a lot of things—ranging from steak, pork chops and sandwiches to broiled fish, pizza and homemade cheesecake. Casual dress; cocktails. **Parking:** on-site. **Cards:** AX, DS, MC, VI.

Y X

ONTONAGON pop. 1,769

——— WHERE TO STAY ———

PETERSON'S CHALET COTTAGES | | | **Phone:** 906/884-4230
AAA (SAVE) | All Year | 1P: $100-$150 | 2P: $100-$150 | XP: $15 | D14
▼▼ ▼▼ | **Location:** 1.5 mi sw on SR 64. Located on the shores of Lake Superior. 287 Lakeshore Rd 49953. Fax: 906/884-2965.
Cottage | **Facility:** 16 units. 2 vacation homes ($310-$325) and 14 cottages, some with whirlpools. 1 story, exterior corridors. *Bath:* combo or shower only. **Parking:** on-site, winter plug-ins. **Terms:** check-in 4 pm, 60 day cancellation notice-fee imposed. **Leisure Activities:** canoeing, paddleboats, fishing, cross country skiing, snowmobiling, bicycles, playground, horseshoes, volleyball. *Fee:* kayaks, snowshoes. **Guest Services:** gift shop.
Cards: AX, DS, MC, VI.

(&) X (&) (&) 🛢 🗔 ▣ / X /　SOME UNITS

OSCODA pop. 992

——— WHERE TO STAY ———

AMERICINN OF OSCODA | *Book at aaa.com* | | | **Phone:** (989)739-1986
AAA (SAVE) | 6/7-9/10 | 1P: $89-$119 | 2P: $89-$119 | XP: $5 | F18
▼▼ ▼▼ | 4/1-6/6 & 9/11-3/31 | 1P: $79-$109 | 2P: $79-$109 | XP: $5 | F18
Small-scale Hotel | **Location:** Just w of US 23, at Smith and 2nd sts. Located on the Au Sable River. 720 E Harbor St 48750. Fax: 989/739-1987. **Facility:** 47 units. 44 one-bedroom standard units, some with whirlpools. 3 one-bedroom suites ($129-$189), some with whirlpools. 2 stories (no elevator), interior corridors. *Bath:* combo or shower only. **Parking:** on-site. **Terms:** [ECP] meal plan available. **Amenities:** hair dryers. **Pool(s):** heated indoor. **Leisure Activities:** sauna, whirlpool, boat dock, fishing. **Guest Services:** coin laundry. **Business Services:** meeting rooms. **Cards:** AX, DC, DS, MC, VI. **Special Amenities:** free expanded continental breakfast and free local telephone calls.
(See color ad p 311)

SO T!→ (&M) (&) ⊃ X (&) DATA PORT ▣ / X 🛢 🗔 /　SOME UNITS

REDWOOD MOTOR LODGE

Phone: 989/739-2021

5/20-9/5	1P: $70-$114	2P: $70-$114	XP: $5	F12
9/6-3/31	1P: $50-$99	2P: $50-$99	XP: $5	F12
4/1-5/19	1P: $50-$80	2P: $50-$80	XP: $5	F12

Small-scale Hotel

Location: On US 23, 2.5 mi s. Located on the main highway along the lake. 3111 US 23 48750. Fax: 989/739-1121. **Facility:** 46 units. 37 one-bedroom standard units. 9 cottages ($120-$170), some with whirlpools. 1-2 stories (no elevator), interior/exterior corridors. *Bath:* combo or shower only. **Parking:** on-site, winter plug-ins. **Terms:** check-in 4 pm, 2 night minimum stay - weekends 6/15-9/3, weekly rates available. **Pool(s):** heated indoor. **Leisure Activities:** sauna, whirlpool, indoor recreational area, playground, horseshoes. *Fee:* game room. **Business Services:** meeting rooms. **Cards:** AX, DC, DS, MC, VI. **Special Amenities:** free local telephone calls.

SOME UNITS

SUPER 8 MOTEL   *Book at aaa.com*

Phone: (989)739-8822

6/7-9/9	1P: $83-$142	2P: $83-$142	XP: $5	F12
9/10-10/2	1P: $60-$129	2P: $60-$129	XP: $5	F12
4/1-6/6 & 10/3-3/31	1P: $55-$129	2P: $55-$129	XP: $5	F12

Small-scale Hotel

Location: On US 23, 1.5 mi s. Located on Lake Huron. 4270 N US 23 48750. Fax: 989/739-0160. **Facility:** 76 one-bedroom standard units, some with whirlpools. 2 stories (no elevator), interior corridors. *Bath:* combo or shower only. **Parking:** on-site. **Terms:** 2 night minimum stay - weekends. **Pool(s):** heated indoor. **Leisure Activities:** sauna, whirlpool, playground. *Fee:* game room. **Guest Services:** coin laundry. **Cards:** AX, DS, MC, VI. **Special Amenities:** free continental breakfast.

SOME UNITS

------ **WHERE TO DINE** ------

WILTSE'S BREW PUB & FAMILY RESTAURANT   **Lunch:** $4-$6   **Dinner:** $7-$14   Phone: 989/739-2231

American

Location: On CR F-41, 1 mi nw of US 23. 5606 F-41 48750. **Hours:** 7 am-9 pm, Fri & Sat-10 pm; 7 am-10 pm, Fri & Sat-11 pm 5/30-9/6. Closed: 11/25, 12/25. **Features:** Craft brewed ale and lager brewed on premise. Good selection of main dishes, from specialties like Paul Bunyan's Mess Burger served with everything but the kitchen sink to the sirloin tips which has been a popular dish for over 18 years. Casual dress; cocktails. **Parking:** on-site. **Cards:** MC, VI.

OWOSSO pop. 15,713

------ **WHERE TO DINE** ------

EDDIE O'FLYNN'S   **Lunch:** $4-$7   **Dinner:** $9-$12   Phone: 989/723-6741

American

Location: On SR 21, 1.8 mi w. 2280 W SR 21 48867. **Hours:** 11 am-10 pm, Fri-11 pm, Sat 4 pm-11 pm, Sun 11 am-5 pm. Closed major holidays; also Sun 9/6-5/30. **Features:** Antique furnishings and knickknacks, including plenty of 1950s memorabilia, decorate the dining room. The broad menu lists ribs, steak, fish, burgers, salad, stir-fry and pitas, plus a variety of tempting desserts. Drop in for breakfast on the weekend. Casual dress; cocktails. **Parking:** on-site. **Cards:** AX, DS, MC, VI.

PARADISE pop. 4,191

------- WHERE TO STAY -------

BEST WESTERN LAKEFRONT INN & SUITES   *Book at aaa.com*   **Phone:** (906)492-3770

(AAA) (SAVE)   6/17-9/6   1P: $138-$165   2P: $138-$165
               10/19-3/31   1P: $110-$130   2P: $110-$130
▽▽▽▽   4/1-6/16 & 9/7-10/18   1P: $100-$120   2P: $100-$120
               Location: On SR 123, just s. Located on the shores of Whitefish Bay. 8112 N SR 123 49768 (PO Box 55).
Small-scale Hotel   Fax: 906/492-3771. **Facility:** 41 one-bedroom standard units. 3 stories, interior corridors. **Parking:** on-site, winter plug-ins. **Terms:** 3 day cancellation notice-fee imposed, [CP] meal plan available. **Amenities:** voice mail, irons, hair dryers. **Pool(s):** heated indoor. **Leisure Activities:** sauna, whirlpool, snowmobiling. **Guest Services:** coin laundry. **Business Services:** meeting rooms. **Cards:** AX, CB, DC, MC, VI. **Special Amenities:** free continental breakfast and free local telephone calls. *(See color ad below)*

SOME UNITS

(S/D) (🍴) (🏊) (🍽) (📹) (DATA PORT) (💻) / (🍽) (📱) (🗄) /

PARADISE INN   **Phone:** 906/492-3940

(AAA) (SAVE)   All Year   1P: $55-$75   2P: $55-$89
▽▽ ▽▽   **Location:** On SR 123; center. SR 123 & Whitefish Point Rd 49768 (PO Box 134). Fax: 906/492-3943. **Facility:** 36 one-bedroom standard units, some with whirlpools. 2 stories (no elevator), interior corridors. **Parking:** on-site, winter plug-ins. **Terms:** cancellation fee imposed, [CP] meal plan available. **Amenities:** video library
Small-scale Hotel (fee). **Leisure Activities:** snowmobiling. **Guest Services:** coin laundry. **Business Services:** meeting rooms. **Cards:** AX, DS, MC, VI. **Special Amenities:** free continental breakfast and free local telephone calls.

SOME UNITS

(S/D) (🍴) / (🍽) (VCR) (📱) (🗄) /
FEE

PAW PAW pop. 3,363

------- WHERE TO STAY -------

QUALITY INN & SUITES   *Book at aaa.com*   **Phone:** (269)655-0303

(AAA) (SAVE)   5/23-9/28 [ECP]   1P: $65-$129
               4/1-5/22 & 9/29-3/31 [ECP]   1P: $59-$109
▽▽▽▽   **Location:** I-94, exit 60, just nw. 153 Ampey Rd 49079 (PO Box 228). Fax: 269/657-1015. **Facility:** 65 units. 52 one-bedroom standard units, some with whirlpools. 13 one-bedroom suites, some with efficiencies. 2 stories, in-
Small-scale Hotel terior corridors. **Bath:** combo or shower only. **Parking:** on-site. **Terms:** small pets only ($10 extra charge, in smoking units). **Amenities:** voice mail, irons, hair dryers. **Pool(s):** heated indoor. **Leisure Activities:** exercise room. **Guest Services:** coin laundry. **Business Services:** meeting rooms. **Cards:** AX, CB, DC, DS, JC, MC, VI. **Special Amenities:** free expanded continental breakfast and free newspaper.

SOME UNITS

(S/D) (🛏) (🍴) (♿) (♿) (🎧) (🏊) (📹) (DATA PORT) (💻) / (🍽) (📱) (🗄) /
FEE

SUPER 8 MOTEL   **Phone:** 269/657-1111

(AAA) (SAVE)   All Year   1P: $70-$150   2P: $70-$150   XP: $5   F14
▽▽▽▽   **Location:** I-94, exit 60. 111 Ampey Rd 49074. Fax: 269/657-4040. **Facility:** 51 one-bedroom standard units, some with whirlpools. 3 stories, interior corridors. **Bath:** combo or shower only. **Parking:** on-site. **Terms:** can-
Small-scale Hotel cellation fee imposed, [ECP] meal plan available. **Amenities:** irons, hair dryers. **Pool(s):** heated indoor. **Leisure Activities:** exercise room. **Guest Services:** valet laundry. **Cards:** AX, CB, DC, DS, MC, VI. **Special Amenities:** free continental breakfast.

SOME UNITS

(S/D) (🍴) (♿) (🏊) (📹) (DATA PORT) (💻) / (🍽) /

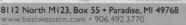

——— WHERE TO DINE ———

LA CANTINA

Italian

Dinner: $14-$18
Location: Downtown. 139 W Michigan Ave 49079. **Hours:** Open 4/1-12/24 & 1/15-3/31; 5 pm-10 pm. Closed major holidays; also Mon. **Reservations:** accepted. **Features:** Raffini wrapped chianti bottles decorate the entry way to this comfortable restaurant which boasts large picture windows overlooking a serene brook and a menu that features a wide variety of traditional Italian dishes. Casual dress; cocktails. **Parking:**
on-site. **Cards:** DS, MC, VI.

Phone: 269/657-7033

PELLSTON pop. 600

——— WHERE TO STAY ———

HOLIDAY INN EXPRESS PELLSTON   *Book at aaa.com*   **Phone:** (231)539-7000
Small-scale Hotel

5/28-9/7   1P: $129-$239   2P: $129-$239
4/1-5/27 & 9/8-3/31 1P: $99-$209   2P: $99-$209
Location: 1.2 mi n. Located opposite the airport. 1600 US 31 N 49769. Fax: 231/539-7010. **Facility:** 52 one-bedroom standard units, some with whirlpools. 2 stories (no elevator), interior corridors. *Bath:* combo or shower only. **Parking:** on-site, winter plug-ins. **Terms:** [CP] meal plan available, pets ($25 extra charge). **Amenities:** video library (fee), dual phone lines, voice mail, irons, hair dryers. **Pool(s):** heated indoor. **Leisure Activities:** whirlpool, snowmobiling, exercise room. **Fee:** game room. **Guest Services:** coin laundry. **Business Services:** meeting rooms. **Cards:** AX, DC, DS, MC, VI. *(See color ad card insert & p 377)*

SOME UNITS

ASK S/D 🛏 🐕 ♿ ⬇ ✕ 🎦 DATA PORT / ✕ VCR 📶 /
FEE   FEE FEE

——— WHERE TO DINE ———

DAM SITE INN
American

Dinner: $11-$26
Location: On US 31, 1.5 mi s of town; near the Dam on the Maple River. US 31 49769. **Hours:** Open 4/19-10/17; 5 pm-9 pm, Sun 3 pm-8 pm; 5 pm-10 pm, Sun 3 pm-9 pm 7/1-8/31. Closed: Mon except 7/1-8/31.
Features: Family-style preparations of chicken, steak and seafood are what the casual restaurant is all about. In business since 1953, the establishment offers views of the dam from many dining room windows.
Service is friendly and efficient. Casual dress; cocktails. **Parking:** on-site. **Cards:** MC, VI.

Phone: 231/539-8851

PETOSKEY pop. 6,080

──── **WHERE TO STAY** ────

APPLE TREE INN
Book at aaa.com   Phone: 231/348-2900

6/13-8/31	1P: $110-$165	2P: $110-$165	XP: $10	F12
9/1-10/31	1P: $84-$165	2P: $84-$165	XP: $10	F12
11/1-3/31	1P: $69-$155	2P: $69-$155	XP: $10	F12
4/1-6/12	1P: $65-$110	2P: $65-$110	XP: $10	F12

Small-scale Hotel **Location:** 1.1 mi s on US 131. 915 Spring St 49770. Fax: 231/348-9748. **Facility:** Smoke free premises. 37 one-bedroom standard units, some with whirlpools. 4 stories, interior corridors. **Parking:** on-site, winter plug-ins. **Terms:** [ECP] meal plan available. **Amenities:** video library (fee). **Pool(s):** heated indoor. **Leisure Activities:** whirlpool. **Guest Services:** valet and coin laundry. **Cards:** AX, DC, DS, MC, VI. **Special Amenities:** free expanded continental breakfast and free local telephone calls. *(See color ad below)*

BAYWINDS INN
Phone: 231/347-4193

6/4-10/24	1P: $105-$165	2P: $105-$165	XP: $5	F17
10/25-3/31	1P: $60-$165	2P: $60-$165	XP: $5	F17
4/1-6/3	1P: $55-$125	2P: $55-$125	XP: $5	F17

Small-scale Hotel **Location:** 1 mi s on US 131. 909 Spring St 49770. Fax: 231/347-5927. **Facility:** 50 one-bedroom standard units, some with whirlpools. 2 stories, interior corridors. **Parking:** on-site, winter plug-ins. **Terms:** cancellation fee imposed, [CP] meal plan available. **Amenities:** hair dryers. *Some:* irons. **Pool(s):** heated indoor. **Leisure Activities:** whirlpool, playground, exercise room. **Cards:** AX, DS, MC, VI. *(See color ad p 417)*

SOME UNITS

BEST WESTERN INN OF PETOSKEY
Book at aaa.com   Phone: (231)347-3925

5/28-9/4 [ECP]	1P: $85-$155	2P: $90-$160	XP: $5	F16
9/5-3/31 [ECP]	1P: $62-$155	2P: $67-$160	XP: $5	F16
4/1-5/27 [ECP]	1P: $62-$110	2P: $67-$115	XP: $5	F16

Motel **Location:** 1.3 mi s on US 131. Located in a commercial area. 1300 Spring St 49770. Fax: 231/347-3341. **Facility:** 85 units. 83 one- and 2 two-bedroom standard units, some with whirlpools. 2 stories (no elevator), interior/exterior corridors. **Parking:** on-site. **Terms:** package plans. **Amenities:** irons, hair dryers. **Pool(s):** heated indoor. **Leisure Activities:** sauna, whirlpool, exercise room. *Fee:* game room. **Business Services:** meeting rooms. **Cards:** AX, DS, MC, VI. **Special Amenities:** free expanded continental breakfast and free newspaper. *(See color ad p 417)*

SOME UNITS

Victorian Charm Near Little Traverse Bay In Picturesque Petoskey

Reservations Call:
1-800-204-1748
231-347-4193
US 131, 909 Spring St., Petoskey, MI 49770
www.baywindsinn.com

ECONO LODGE — *Book at aaa.com*

Phone: (231)348-3324

6/16-9/5	1P: $65-$95	2P: $70-$135	XP: $6	F18
12/10-3/31	1P: $50-$95	2P: $55-$135	XP: $6	F18
4/1-6/15 & 9/6-12/9	1P: $50-$80	2P: $55-$90	XP: $6	F18

Motel

Location: 2 mi s of US 31. Located next to a casino. 1858 US 131 S 49770. **Fax:** 231/348-3521. **Facility:** 59 one-bedroom standard units. 2 stories (no elevator), exterior corridors. **Parking:** on-site, winter plug-ins. **Terms:** package plans. **Pool(s):** small heated indoor. **Leisure Activities:** whirlpool. **Cards:** AX, DC, DS, MC, VI. **Special Amenities:** free continental breakfast and free local telephone calls.

SOME UNITS

HAMPTON INN & SUITES — *Book at aaa.com*

Phone: 231/348-9555

5/25-3/31 [ECP]	1P: $99-$159	2P: $104-$164
4/1-5/24 [ECP]	1P: $69-$109	2P: $74-$114

Small-scale Hotel

Location: 1.2 mi s on US 131. Located in a commercial area. 920 Spring St 49770. **Fax:** 231/348-9666. **Facility:** 77 one-bedroom standard units, some with whirlpools. 4 stories, interior corridors. **Bath:** combo or shower only. **Parking:** on-site. **Terms:** check-in 4 pm, cancellation fee imposed, package plans. **Amenities:** video games, dual phone lines, voice mail, irons, hair dryers. **Pool(s):** heated indoor. **Leisure Activities:** whirlpool, exercise room. **Guest Services:** valet and coin laundry. **Business Services:** meeting rooms, business center. **Cards:** AX, DC, DS, MC, VI.

SOME UNITS

STAFFORD'S PERRY HOTEL

Phone: (231)347-4000

All Year	1P: $85-$240	2P: $85-$240	XP: $15	F14

Historic Small-scale Hotel

Location: Center. Adjoins the Gas Light District. Bay & Lewis sts 49770. **Fax:** 231/347-0636. **Facility:** Historic 1899 hotel. Variety of units. 80 one-bedroom standard units. 3 stories, interior corridors. **Bath:** combo or shower only. **Parking:** on-site. **Terms:** cancellation fee imposed, [CP] & [ECP] meal plans available, package plans - seasonal. **Amenities:** *Some:* dual phone lines, hair dryers. **Leisure Activities:** whirlpool. **Guest Services:** gift shop, valet laundry. **Business Services:** meeting rooms. **Cards:** AX, DS, MC, VI.

SOME UNITS

SUPER 8 MOTEL — *Book at aaa.com*

Phone: (231)439-8000

6/27-3/31	1P: $55-$130	2P: $55-$130		
5/23-6/26	1P: $90-$110	2P: $90-$110		
4/1-5/22	1P: $55-$59	2P: $55-$59	XP: $6	F18
			XP: $6	F18

Small-scale Hotel

Location: US 31, 1 mi w of jct US 131. Located in a semi-commercial area. 2645 Charlevoix Ave 49770. **Fax:** 231/439-8004. **Facility:** 56 one-bedroom standard units, some with efficiencies. 2 stories (no elevator), interior corridors. **Bath:** combo or shower only. **Parking:** on-site. **Terms:** [CP] meal plan available. **Pool(s):** heated indoor. **Leisure Activities:** whirlpool. **Guest Services:** coin laundry. **Business Services:** meeting rooms. **Cards:** AX, DC, DS, MC, VI.

SOME UNITS

——— *The following lodging was either not evaluated or did not* ———
meet AAA rating requirements but is listed for your information only.

VICTORIES CASINO & HOTEL   **Phone:** 231/347-6041
[fyi]   5/28-9/6   1P: $79-$109   2P: $79-$109   XP: $15   F17
             4/1-5/27 & 9/7-3/31   1P: $59-$99   2P: $79-$109   XP: $15   F17
Large-scale Hotel Under major renovation, scheduled to be completed October 2003. **Last rated:** ▼▼ **Location:** 1.5 mi s. 1444
US 131 S 49770. Fax: 231/347-3331. **Facility:** 136 units. 126 one-bedroom standard units. 10 one-bedroom
suites ($79-$119). 5 stories, interior corridors. *Bath:* combo or shower only. **Parking:** on-site, winter plug-ins. **Terms:** check-in 4
pm, 3 day cancellation notice-fee imposed, package plans - seasonal, 18% service charge. **Amenities:** voice mail, irons, hair
dryers. **Pool(s):** heated indoor. **Leisure Activities:** whirlpool, exercise room. **Guest Services:** coin laundry. **Business Services:**
meeting rooms. **Cards:** AX, DS, MC, VI. *(See color ad p 419)*

SOME UNITS
(ASK) (S/D) (†1) (Y) (&) (≈) (DATA PORT) (💻) / (✕) (VCR) (🖥) (📷) /

——— **WHERE TO DINE** ———

CITY PARK GRILL   **Lunch:** $6-$8   **Dinner:** $10-$18   **Phone:** 231/347-0101
▼▼ ▼▼   **Location:** Center. 432 E Lake St 49770. **Hours:** 11:30 am-10 pm. Closed: 11/25, 12/24, 12/25.
          Features: Ernest Hemingway is reputed to have spent a fair amount of time at the massive 100 year old
American mirrored cherry bar that dominates this casual restaurant. The honey-grilled pork chops marinated in
jalapenos, soy sauce and Dijon mustard lead a continental menu that offers a wide range of choices.
Casual dress; cocktails. **Parking:** street. **Cards:** AX, MC, VI.
(✕)

VILLA RISTORANTE ITALIANO   **Dinner:** $18-$30   **Phone:** 231/347-1440
▼▼ ▼▼   **Location:** US 131, just s of jct US 31. 887 Spring St 49770. **Hours:** 4:30 pm-10:30 pm; hours may vary. Closed
          major holidays; also Sun. **Reservations:** suggested, in season. **Features:** Gnocchi and shrimp with
Italian   gorgonzola represent traditional preparations of Italian cuisine. The homemade Italian ice cream is hard to
top as a meal finisher. Casual dress; cocktails. **Parking:** on-site. **Cards:** AX, MC, VI.
(✕)

PLAINWELL pop. 3,933

——— **WHERE TO STAY** ———

COMFORT INN   *Book at aaa.com*   **Phone:** 269/685-9891
(AAA) (SAVE)   All Year   1P: $79-$200   2P: $79-$200   XP: $5   F18
                   Location: US 131, exit 49A, just e. 622 Allegan St 49080. Fax: 269/685-9892. **Facility:** 65 units. 64 one-bedroom
▼▼ ▼▼   standard units, some with whirlpools. 1 one-bedroom suite ($160-$250) with whirlpool. 2 stories (no elevator),
Small-scale Hotel interior corridors. **Parking:** on-site. **Terms:** [CP] meal plan available, pets ($10 extra charge).
                   Amenities: dual phone lines, voice mail, irons, hair dryers. **Pool(s):** outdoor. **Business Services:** meeting
                   rooms. **Cards:** AX, DC, DS, MC, VI. **Special Amenities:** free continental breakfast and free local tele-
phone calls.

SOME UNITS
(S/D) (🐾) (†1+) (≈) (★) (DATA PORT) (💻) / (✕) (🖥) /
      FEE   FEE

——— **WHERE TO DINE** ———

LONDON GRILL-BOMBAY   **Dinner:** $10-$20   **Phone:** 269/685-1877
▼▼ ▼▼   **Location:** US 131, exit 49A, 2 mi e; center. 200 E Bridge 49080. **Hours:** 5 pm-10 pm. Closed major holidays.
          Features: The quintessential British pub, this small, lively space is adorned with British and Colonial Indian
Provincial British memorabilia. A small menu reflects a mix of both British pub favorites and Indian curries. Casual dress;
cocktails. **Parking:** street. **Cards:** AX, DS, MC, VI.
(& M) (✕)

PLYMOUTH —See Detroit p. 269.

PONTIAC —See Detroit p. 270.

PORTAGE pop. 44,897

——— **WHERE TO DINE** ———

EMPIRE CHINESE BUFFET   **Lunch:** $5-$7   **Dinner:** $8-$11   **Phone:** 269/323-7000
▼▼   **Location:** I-94, exit 76 (S Westnedge Ave), 0.5 mi s; in South Town Plaza. 6255 S Westnedge Ave 49002. **Hours:** 11
Chinese   am-10 pm, Fri & Sat-11 pm. Closed major holidays. **Features:** Tucked in a strip mall, the restaurant won't
          disappoint fans of buffets. The selection of typical Chinese and American offerings is ample. Casual dress.
          Parking: on-site. **Cards:** AX, DS, MC, VI.
(✕)

FINLEY'S AMERICAN RESTAURANT   **Lunch:** $5-$8   **Dinner:** $7-$18   **Phone:** 269/323-1104
▼▼   **Location:** I-94, exit 78, 1 mi s. 6301 S Westnedge Ave 49002. **Hours:** 11 am-10 pm, Fri & Sat-11 pm. Closed:
Steak House 11/25, 12/25. **Features:** Casual friendly service marks this family-oriented restaurant. They offer something
          for everyone as the menu covers everything from steak to seafood to sandwiches. Casual dress; cocktails.
          Parking: on-site. **Cards:** AX, DC, DS, MC, VI.
(& M) (✕)

PORT AUSTIN pop. 737

─────── WHERE TO STAY ───────

THE GARFIELD INN
Phone: 989/738-5254

Historic Bed
& Breakfast

All Year [BP]   1P: $100-$130   2P: $100-$130   XP: $25
Location: Just s on SR 53; downtown. 8544 Lake St 48467 (PO Box 366). Fax: 989/738-6384. **Facility:** This 1830s-era inn features French-style architecture and is two blocks from Lake Huron. Designated smoking area. 6 one-bedroom standard units. 3 stories (no elevator), interior corridors. *Bath:* some shared or private, combo or shower only. **Parking:** on-site. **Terms:** cancellation fee imposed. **Dining:** restaurant, see separate listing. **Cards:** AX, DC, DS, MC, VI.

🍽 ✕ 💻

LAKE STREET MANOR BED & BREAKFAST
Phone: 989/738-7720

Historic Bed
& Breakfast

5/28-9/1   1P: $70-$80   2P: $70-$80
5/1-5/27 & 9/2-10/31   1P: $60-$70   2P: $60-$70
Location: Just s of downtown on SR 53. 8569 Lake St 48467. **Facility:** Near downtown and Saginaw Bay, this late-1800's Victorian summer home offers a fenced garden. 5 one-bedroom standard units. 2 stories (no elevator), interior/exterior corridors. *Bath:* some shared or private, combo or shower only. **Parking:** on-site. **Terms:** open 5/1-10/31, 2 night minimum stay - seasonal & weekends, cancellation fee imposed, [ECP] meal plan available, package plans, no pets allowed (owner's dog on premises). **Amenities:** video library. **Leisure Activities:** whirlpool, bicycles. **Cards:** MC, VI.

ASK 📞

LAKE VISTA MOTEL & COTTAGES RESORT
Phone: 989/738-8612

🔺🔺🔺 SAVE

Motel

6/11-9/15   1P: $92-$165   2P: $102-$195   XP: $15
4/10-6/10   1P: $68-$150   2P: $68-$175   XP: $15
9/16-11/30   1P: $68-$150   2P: $68-$150   XP: $15
Location: On SR 25 (Spring St), 0.5 mi w of town. 168 W Spring St 48467 (PO Box 429). Fax: 989/738-8612. **Facility:** 17 units. 10 one-bedroom standard units. 7 two-bedroom suites ($165-$190) with kitchens (no utensils). 1-2 stories (no elevator), exterior corridors. *Bath:* combo or shower only. **Parking:** on-site. **Terms:** open 4/10-11/30, 2 night minimum stay - weekends in motel, 7 day cancellation notice-fee imposed, package plans - seasonal. **Pool(s):** heated outdoor. **Leisure Activities:** fishing, barbecue grills, sandbox, swing set, horseshoes. *Fee:* live bait & tackle. **Guest Services:** gift shop, coin laundry. **Cards:** AX, DS, MC, VI.

SOME UNITS
🚣 ✕ 📞 / 🖥 🖨 💻 /

─────── WHERE TO DINE ───────

THE FARM RESTAURANT
Dinner: $16-$24
Phone: 989/874-5700

🔺🔺🔺

Regional American

Location: SR 53 (Van Dyke Rd), 2 mi w. 699 Port Crescent Rd 48467. **Hours:** Open 5/15-11/1; 5 pm-10 pm, Sun noon-8 pm; weekends only 9/1-11/1. Closed major holidays; also Mon. **Reservations:** accepted. **Features:** Located 8 miles from Port Austin, this converted farmhouse serves as a training kitchen for Livonia's Schoolcraft Culinary Program and uses locally grown ingredients to create innovative dishes. Casual dress; cocktails. **Parking:** on-site. **Cards:** MC, VI.

✕

THE GARFIELD INN Historic
Lunch: $6-$9   **Dinner:** $17-$25   **Phone:** 989/738-5254

🔺🔺

American

Location: Downtown; in The Garfield Inn. 8544 Lake St 48467. **Hours:** Open 4/1-12/31 & 2/15-3/30; 11:30 am-2 & 5-9 pm, Fri & Sat 5:30 pm-9 pm 9/6-3/30, Sun 9 am-1 pm; hours may vary off season. Closed: 11/25, 12/25; also Mon-Thurs 9/6-3/30. **Reservations:** suggested. **Features:** Near the beautiful sandy shores of Lake Huron, the 1930s Victorian Inn is a sophisticated spot for intimate, formal dining. The restaurant garners praise for its innovative preparations. During the summer, request garden seating for a relaxed experience. Casual dress; cocktails. **Parking:** on-site. **Cards:** AX, DS, MC, VI.

🅼 🍸 ✕

PORT HURON pop. 32,338

─────── WHERE TO STAY ───────

AMERIHOST INN-PORT HURON   *Book at aaa.com*
Phone: (810)364-8000

🔺🔺🔺 SAVE

🔺🔺🔺🔺

Small-scale Hotel

All Year [ECP]   1P: $59-$119   2P: $59-$119   XP: $6   F17
Location: I-94, exit 269, just w. Located opposite an outlet mall. 1611 Range Rd 48074. Fax: 810/364-8844. **Facility:** 60 one-bedroom standard units, some with whirlpools. 2 stories, interior corridors. *Bath:* combo or shower only. **Parking:** on-site. **Amenities:** dual phone lines, voice mail, safes (fee), irons, hair dryers. **Pool(s):** heated indoor. **Leisure Activities:** sauna, whirlpool, exercise room. **Guest Services:** valet laundry. **Business Services:** meeting rooms. **Cards:** AX, DC, DS, MC, VI. **Special Amenities:** free expanded continental breakfast and free newspaper.

SOME UNITS
📶 🎥 🚣 ✕ 📷 DATA PORT 💻 / ✕ VCR 🖥 🖨 /

COMFORT INN   *Book at aaa.com*
Phone: (810)982-5500

🔺🔺

Small-scale Hotel

All Year [ECP]   1P: $69-$149   2P: $69-$149   XP: $10   F18
Location: I-94, exit 274 (Water St). 1700 Yeager St 48060. Fax: 810/982-7199. **Facility:** 80 one-bedroom standard units, some with whirlpools. 2 stories, interior corridors. **Parking:** on-site. **Amenities:** hair dryers. *Some:* irons. **Pool(s):** heated indoor. **Leisure Activities:** whirlpool, exercise room. *Fee:* game room. **Guest Services:** valet and coin laundry. **Business Services:** meeting rooms. **Cards:** AX, CB, DC, DS, JC, MC, VI.

SOME UNITS
ASK 📶 🍽 🔕 🚣 ✕ 📷 DATA PORT / ✕ VCR 🖥 🖨 💻 /

FAIRFIELD INN BY MARRIOTT *Book at aaa.com* Phone: (810)982-8500

▼▼▼ 5/29-9/5 [ECP] 1P: $55-$129
4/1-5/28 & 9/6-3/31 [ECP] 1P: $49-$114

Small-scale Hotel **Location:** I-94, exit 274 (Water St). 1635 Yeager St 48060. **Fax:** 810/982-4114. **Facility:** 63 one-bedroom standard units, some with whirlpools. 3 stories, interior corridors. *Bath:* combo or shower only. **Parking:** on-site. **Amenities:** irons, hair dryers. **Pool(s):** small heated indoor. **Leisure Activities:** whirlpool, exercise room. **Guest Services:** valet laundry. **Cards:** AX, DC, DS, MC, VI.

SOME UNITS
FEE FEE

HAMPTON INN *Book at aaa.com* Phone: (810)966-9000

▼▼▼ All Year 1P: $79-$119 2P: $84-$124 XP: $5 F18

Small-scale Hotel **Location:** I-94, exit 274 (Water St). 1655 Yeager St 48060. **Fax:** 810/966-9010. **Facility:** 71 one-bedroom standard units, some with whirlpools. 3 stories, interior corridors. *Bath:* combo or shower only. **Terms:** [ECP] meal plan available. **Amenities:** dual phone lines, voice mail, irons, hair dryers. **Pool(s):** heated indoor. **Leisure Activities:** whirlpool, exercise room. **Guest Services:** valet laundry. **Business Services:** meeting rooms. **Cards:** AX, DC, DS, MC, VI.

SOME UNITS

HOLIDAY INN EXPRESS HOTEL & SUITES *Book at aaa.com* Phone: (810)987-5999

▼▼▼ 12/31-3/31 1P: $89-$199 2P: $89-$199
6/1-9/1 1P: $89-$189 2P: $89-$189
4/1-5/31 & 9/2-12/30 1P: $79-$139 2P: $79-$139

Small-scale Hotel **Location:** Business loop I-69 and 94 E, then e. Located beside Blue Water Bridge. 1720 Hancock St 48060. **Fax:** 810/987-5954. **Facility:** 96 units. 93 one-bedroom standard units, some with whirlpools. 3 one-bedroom suites ($109-$199) with whirlpools. 4 stories, interior corridors. *Bath:* combo or shower only. **Parking:** on-site. **Terms:** 3 night minimum stay - weekends 1/1-1/31 & 7/1-7/31, [ECP] meal plan available. **Amenities:** irons, hair dryers. **Pool(s):** heated indoor. **Leisure Activities:** whirlpool, exercise room. *Fee:* game room. **Guest Services:** valet and coin laundry. **Business Services:** meeting rooms, business center. **Cards:** AX, CB, DC, DS, JC, MC, VI. *(See color ad card insert)*

SOME UNITS

RAMADA LIMITED *Book at aaa.com* Phone: (810)987-1600

▼▼▼ All Year 1P: $59-$99

Small-scale Hotel **Location:** I-94, exit 274 (Water St), just n. 2282 Water St 48060. **Fax:** 810/987-5479. **Facility:** 63 one-bedroom standard units, some with whirlpools. 3 stories, interior corridors. *Bath:* combo or shower only. **Parking:** on-site. **Terms:** 10 day cancellation notice, weekly rates available, [CP] meal plan available. **Amenities:** dual phone lines, voice mail, irons, hair dryers. **Pool(s):** heated indoor. **Leisure Activities:** exercise room. **Guest Services:** valet and coin laundry. **Business Services:** meeting rooms. **Cards:** AX, CB, DC, DS, JC, MC, VI.

SOME UNITS
FEE

THOMAS EDISON INN *Book at aaa.com* Phone: (810)984-8000

▼▼▼ All Year 1P: $89-$140 2P: $89-$140 XP: $10 F

Small-scale Hotel **Location:** 1.5 mi n, just e on Thomas Edison Pkwy, off Pine Grove Ave. Located beside Blue Water Bridge. 500 Thomas Edison Pkwy 48060. **Fax:** 810/984-3230. **Facility:** 149 units. 145 one-bedroom standard units, some with whirlpools. 4 one-bedroom suites ($165-$225) with whirlpools. 3 stories, interior/exterior corridors. **Parking:** on-site, winter plug-ins. **Terms:** cancellation fee imposed, [AP], [BP], [CP] & [MAP] meal plans available. **Amenities:** voice mail, irons, hair dryers. **Pool(s):** heated indoor. **Leisure Activities:** sauna, whirlpool. **Guest Services:** gift shop, valet laundry, area transportation. **Business Services:** conference facilities. **Cards:** AX, DC, DS, MC, VI.

SOME UNITS

------ **WHERE TO DINE** ------

BISTRO 1882 Lunch: $11-$14 Dinner: $16-$25 Phone: 810/966-6900

▼▼▼ **Location:** 2333 Gratiot Ave 48060. **Hours:** 11 am-3 & 5:30-8:30 pm. Closed major holidays. **Reservations:** suggested. **Features:** Tucked away almost under the Blue Water Bridge, this small and intimate dining room offers a modest but creative menu in a classy dining room warmed with exposed brick walls and upscale lighting. Dressy casual; cocktails. **Parking:** on-site. **Cards:** AX, DC, DS, MC, VI.

American

FOGCUTTER Lunch: $8-$10 Dinner: $12-$22 Phone: 810/987-3300

▼▼▼ **Location:** On top of Peoples Bank Bldg; downtown. 511 Fort St 48060. **Hours:** 11 am-9 pm, Fri & Sat-10 pm, Sun 10 am-8 pm; Sunday brunch. Closed: 1/1, 12/25. **Reservations:** suggested. **Features:** Perched atop a downtown office complex, this casual seafood restaurant offers a bounty of seafood items including lake perch, whitefish, and frog legs. Casual dress; cocktails. **Parking:** on-site. **Cards:** AX, DC, DS, MC, VI.

American

QUAY STREET BREWING COMPANY Lunch: $6-$12 Dinner: $6-$12 Phone: 810/982-4100

▼▼▼ **Location:** Adjacent to drawbridge; downtown. 330 Quay St 48060. **Hours:** 11:30 am-9 pm, Fri & Sat-10 pm, Sun noon-8 pm. **Features:** Situated on the riverfront, this microbrewery not only offers a variety of hand crafted brews but also features selections from other Michigan microbreweries. As well as offering traditional bar American foods, the menu offers a few surprises such as house version of Louisiana's famous muffuletta and grilled lamb burgers. Casual dress; cocktails. **Parking:** street. **Cards:** AX, DC, DS, MC, VI.

PORTLAND pop. 3,798

-------- WHERE TO STAY --------

BEST WESTERN AMERICAN HERITAGE INN   *Book at aaa.com*   Phone: (517)647-2200
(AAA) (SAVE)   All Year   1P: $69-$79   2P: $79-$89
Location: I-96, exit 77, just n. 1681 Grand River Ave 48875. Fax: 517/647-2250. **Facility:** 48 one-bedroom standard units, some with whirlpools. 2 stories (no elevator), interior corridors. *Bath:* combo or shower only.
Small-scale Hotel **Parking:** on-site. **Terms:** small pets only. **Amenities:** video library (fee), irons, hair dryers. **Pool(s):** heated indoor. **Leisure Activities:** whirlpool, exercise room. *Fee:* game room. **Guest Services:** coin laundry. **Business Services:** meeting rooms. **Cards:** AX, CB, DC, DS, MC, VI. **Special Amenities:** free continental breakfast and early check-in/late check-out.

SOME UNITS

PORT SANILAC pop. 658

-------- WHERE TO STAY --------

THE RAYMOND HOUSE AND INN   Phone: 810/622-8800
(AAA) (SAVE)   7/1-9/6 [BP]   1P: $95-$110   2P: $95-$110   XP: $15   D18
9/7-3/31 [BP]   1P: $85-$95   2P: $85-$95   XP: $15   D18
5/1-6/30 [BP]   1P: $75-$95   2P: $75-$95   XP: $15   D18
4/1-4/30 [BP]   1P: $65-$85   2P: $65-$85   XP: $15   D18
Historic Bed **Location:** Just s of downtown on SR 25. 111 S Ridge St 48469 (PO Box 439). Fax: 810/622-8485. **Facility:** This el-
& Breakfast egant house, in a sleepy harbor village, is walking distance from the Lake Huron waterfront and the Port Sanilac Lighthouse. Smoke free premises. 7 one-bedroom standard units. 3 stories (no elevator), interior
corridors. *Bath:* some shared or private, shower only. **Parking:** on-site. **Terms:** package plans, no pets allowed (owner's dogs
on premises). **Amenities:** video library. *Some:* irons, hair dryers. **Guest Services:** gift shop. **Cards:** DS, MC, VI.

PRUDENVILLE pop. 1,737

-------- WHERE TO STAY --------

SHEA'S LAKE FRONT LODGE   Phone: 989/366-5910
(AAA) (SAVE)   5/28-9/7 & 12/25-3/31   1P: $59   2P: $63   XP: $4   F18
4/1-5/27 & 9/8-12/24   1P: $42   2P: $45   XP: $4   F18
Location: I-75, exit 227, 8 mi w on SR 55. Located in a semi-residential area. 125 12th St 48651 (PO Box 357).
Facility: This log-structured 1925 lodge is on shaded grounds high above the sandy beach of Houghton
Classic Lake. Inviting public areas and unpretentious units and cottages. 39 units. 34 one-bedroom standard units.
Small-scale Hotel 5 cottages. 2 stories (no elevator), interior/exterior corridors. *Bath:* combo or shower only. **Parking:** on-site.
Terms: 10 day cancellation notice, weekly rates available, [CP] meal plan available, small pets only. **Leisure
Activities:** rental boats, rental paddleboats, boat dock, fishing, snowmobiling, badminton, barbecue pits, playground, basketball,
shuffleboard, volleyball. *Fee:* game room. **Cards:** AX, DC, DS, MC, VI. **Special Amenities:** free continental breakfast.
(See ad p 325)

SOME UNITS

SWISS INN LAKE RESORT   Phone: (989)366-7881
5/1-8/31   1P: $50-$85   2P: $50-$85
1/1-3/31   1P: $45-$85   2P: $45-$85
Motel   9/1-12/31   1P: $45-$65   2P: $45-$65
4/1-4/30   1P: $40-$55   2P: $40-$55
Location: On SR 55, 0.3 mi e of jct SR 18. Located in a commercial area. 472 W Houghton Lake Dr 48651 (PO Box 204). **Facility:** 11 one-
bedroom standard units. 1 story, exterior corridors. *Bath:* shower only. **Parking:** on-site, winter plug-ins. **Terms:** cancellation fee
imposed, weekly rates available. **Amenities:** video library (fee). **Leisure Activities:** rental boats, rental paddleboats, boat dock,
fishing, snowmobiling, horseshoes, shuffleboard, volleyball. **Cards:** AX, DS, MC, VI.

SOME UNITS

-------- WHERE TO DINE --------

BRASS LANTERN   Dinner: $11-$20   Phone: 989/366-8312
Location: Just e on SR 18 and 55. 729 Houghton Lake Dr 48651. **Hours:** 4 pm-9 pm, Fri & Sat-10 pm; to 10
pm, Sun noon-9 pm 5/23-9/4; hours may vary. Closed: 11/25, 12/25 & Easter. **Features:** Barbecue ribs,
American New York strip and roasted salmon stand out on a diverse menu of beef, seafood, chicken and pasta
dishes. The warm, inviting dining room has the ambience of a rustic cabin, with a log interior, fireplace and
brass wall sculptures. Casual dress; cocktails. **Parking:** on-site. **Cards:** DS, MC, VI.

ROCHESTER —See Detroit p. 271.

ROCHESTER HILLS —See Detroit p. 271.

ROCKFORD pop. 4,626

-------- WHERE TO DINE --------

-------- *The following restaurant has not been evaluated by AAA
but is listed for your information only.* --------

SAM'S JOINT   Phone: 616/866-3324
(fyi)   Not evaluated. **Location:** Center. 19 N Main St 49341. **Features:** Memorabilia spills over from the lounge into
the dining areas at this fun spot.

ROGERS CITY pop. 3,322

——— WHERE TO STAY ———

DRIFTWOOD MOTEL
Phone: (989)734-4777

♦♦♦ ♦♦♦

Motel

6/14-9/12	1P: $80-$95	2P: $80-$95
4/1-6/13 & 9/13-10/17	1P: $70-$85	2P: $70-$85
10/18-3/31	1P: $70-$75	2P: $70-$75

Location: 1 mi nw on US 23 business route. Overlooking Lake Huron. 540 W Third St 49779. **Facility:** 44 one-bedroom standard units. 2 stories, exterior corridors. **Parking:** on-site, winter plug-ins. **Amenities:** hair dryers. **Pool(s):** heated indoor. **Leisure Activities:** whirlpool, snowmobiling. **Cards:** AX, DC, DS, MC, VI.

SOME UNITS

⊞ 🏊 🎥 ▣ / ✕ /

——— WHERE TO DINE ———

WATERS EDGE
Lunch: $4-$6   **Dinner: $9-$19**   **Phone: 989/734-4747**

♦♦ ♦♦

American

Location: Adjacent to Driftwood Motel. 530 W Third St 49779. **Hours:** 11 am-9:30 pm; hours may vary. Closed: 1/1, 12/25. **Reservations:** suggested. **Features:** The restaurant delivers such well-prepared food as whitefish, prime rib, chicken and pasta. The nautically themed dining room, affords views of Lake Huron. For dessert, try the Kentucky Derby pie. Casual dress; cocktails. **Parking:** on-site. **Cards:** AX, DC, DS, MC, VI.

🍸 ✕

ROMEO —See Detroit p. 271.

ROMULUS —See Detroit p. 271.

ROSEVILLE —See Detroit p. 275.

ROTHBURY pop. 416

——— WHERE TO DINE ———

——— *The following restaurant has not been evaluated by AAA* ———
but is listed for your information only.

SUNDANCE SALOON & STEAKHOUSE
Phone: 231/894-4444

[fyi]

Not evaluated. **Location:** Located at the Double JJ Resort. Water Rd 49452. **Features:** The casual restaurant overlooks the golf course of an adult-exclusive resort.

ROYAL OAK —See Detroit p. 276.

SAGINAW pop. 61,799

——— WHERE TO STAY ———

BEST WESTERN - SAGINAW   *Book at aaa.com*
Phone: (989)755-0461

♦♦♦ ♦♦♦

Large-scale Hotel

All Year [ECP]	1P: $59-$99	2P: $59-$99	XP: $10	F17

Location: I-75, exit 149B (SR 46). Located in a commercial area. 1408 S Outer Dr 48601. Fax: 989/755-0600. **Facility:** 158 one-bedroom standard units. 4 stories, interior corridors. **Parking:** on-site. **Amenities:** video games, irons, hair dryers. **Pool(s):** heated indoor. **Leisure Activities:** sauna, whirlpool, racquetball court, exercise room. *Fee:* game room. **Guest Services:** valet and coin laundry. **Business Services:** meeting rooms. **Cards:** AX, CB, DC, DS, JC, MC, VI.

SOME UNITS

ASK 🆂Ⓓ ✈ 🛏 🏊 ✕ 🎥 DATAPORT ▣ / ✕ 🖥 /

COMFORT SUITES   *Book at aaa.com*
Phone: (989)797-8000

♦♦♦♦

Small-scale Hotel

All Year	1P: $59-$79	2P: $59-$79	XP: $6	F18

Location: I-675, exit 6, 0.6 mi w on Tittabawassee Rd. Located in a commercial area. 5180 Fashion Square Blvd 48603. Fax: 989/797-8000. **Facility:** 66 one-bedroom standard units. 3 stories, interior corridors. *Bath:* combo or shower only. **Parking:** on-site. **Terms:** [ECP] meal plan available. **Amenities:** irons. *Some:* hair dryers. **Pool(s):** small heated indoor. **Leisure Activities:** whirlpool. **Guest Services:** valet laundry. **Business Services:** meeting rooms. **Cards:** AX, CB, DC, DS, MC, VI.

SOME UNITS

ASK 🆂Ⓓ ⊞ ♿M 🔧 🏊 🛗 🎥 DATAPORT 🖥 🍽 ▣ / ✕ /
FEE

FAIRFIELD INN   *Book at aaa.com*
Phone: (989)797-6100

♦♦♦

Small-scale Hotel

All Year	1P: $59-$79	2P: $59-$79	XP: $6	F18

Location: I-675, exit 6, 0.5 mi w on Tittabawassee Rd. Located in a commercial area. 5200 Fashion Square Blvd 48603. Fax: 989/797-6100. **Facility:** 76 one-bedroom standard units. 3 stories, interior corridors. *Bath:* combo or shower only. **Parking:** on-site, winter plug-ins. **Terms:** [ECP] meal plan available. **Amenities:** voice mail, irons. **Pool(s):** heated indoor. **Leisure Activities:** whirlpool. **Guest Services:** valet laundry. **Business Services:** meeting rooms. **Cards:** AX, CB, DC, DS, MC, VI.

SOME UNITS

🆂Ⓓ ⊞ ♿M 🔧 🏊 🛗 🎥 DATAPORT / ✕ 🖥 🍽 /
FEE

FOUR POINTS BY SHERATON SAGINAW *Book at aaa.com* **Phone:** (989)790-5050
All Year 1P: $69 2P: $69 XP: $10 F17
Location: I-675, exit 6, just w on Tittabawassee Rd. Located in a commercial area. 4960 Towne Centre Rd 48604.
Large-scale Hotel **Fax:** 989/790-1466. **Facility:** 156 one-bedroom standard units. 6 stories, interior corridors. **Parking:** on-site.
Terms: [AP] meal plan available. **Amenities:** video games, high-speed Internet, dual phone lines, voice mail,
irons, hair dryers. *Some:* fax. **Pool(s):** heated indoor/outdoor. **Leisure Activities:** sauna, whirlpool, exercise room. **Guest Services:** gift shop, valet laundry. **Business Services:** conference facilities. **Cards:** AX, CB, DC, DS, MC, VI. *(See color ad p 5)*

SOME UNITS
ASK SD ✈ 🛏 🍴 🍸 🏊 ✖ 🎞 DATA PORT 💻 / ✖ VCR 📶 /
FEE

HAMPTON INN *Book at aaa.com* **Phone:** (989)792-7666
All Year [CP] 1P: $64-$83 2P: $64-$83
Location: Jct I-675 and Tittabawassee Rd. Located in a commercial area. 2222 Tittabawassee Rd 48604.
Small-scale Hotel **Fax:** 989/792-3213. **Facility:** 120 one-bedroom standard units. 2 stories (no elevator), interior corridors.
Parking: on-site, winter plug-ins. **Amenities:** video games, voice mail, irons, hair dryers. **Pool(s):** heated
outdoor. **Guest Services:** valet laundry. **Business Services:** meeting rooms. **Cards:** AX, CB, DC, DS, MC, VI.
(See color ad below)

SOME UNITS
ASK SD 🍴 🏊 📶 🎞 DATA PORT 💻 / ✖ 📶 /
FEE

HOWARD JOHNSON PLAZA, SAGINAW CONVENTION CENTER **Phone:** (989)753-6608
All Year [BP] 1P: $69-$89 2P: $69-$89 XP: $5 F18
Location: I-675, exit 2, just s. Located opposite the Saginaw County Event Center. 400 Johnson St 48607.
Large-scale Hotel **Fax:** 989/753-2387. **Facility:** 177 one-bedroom standard units. 8 stories, interior corridors. *Bath:* combo or
shower only. **Parking:** on-site. **Terms:** [MAP] meal plan available. **Amenities:** video games, voice mail, irons,
hair dryers. **Pool(s):** heated indoor. **Leisure Activities:** whirlpool, exercise room. **Guest Services:** valet laundry. **Business Services:** conference facilities. **Cards:** AX, DC, DS, MC, VI.

SOME UNITS
ASK SD ✈ 🍴 🍸 ♿ 🏊 DATA PORT 💻 / ✖ 📶 /

MONTAGUE INN **Phone:** 989-752-3939
All Year 1P: $70-$195
Location: 1.5 mi s. Located on the shores of Lake Linton. 1581 S Washington Ave 48601. Fax: 989/752-3159.
Country Inn **Facility:** This elegantly restored Georgian mansion is on manicured grounds overlooking Lake Linton and
Ojibway Island. Smoke free premises. 17 units. 15 one-bedroom standard units. 2 one-bedroom suites, some
with whirlpools. 2-3 stories, interior corridors. *Bath:* combo or shower only. **Parking:** on-site. **Terms:** package plans. **Guest Services:** valet laundry. **Business Services:** meeting rooms. **Cards:** AX, DS, MC, VI.

ASK SD 🍴 📶 ✖

MOTEL 6 SAGINAW *Book at aaa.com* **Phone:** (989)754-8414
5/30-10/30 1P: $41-$54 2P: $48-$61 XP: $7 F18
10/31-3/31 1P: $40-$43 2P: $42-$45 XP: $2 F18
4/1-5/29 1P: $40-$42 2P: $42-$44 XP: $2 F18
Motel **Location:** I-75, exit 149B (SR 46). Located in a commercial area. 966 S Outer Dr 48601. Fax: 989/754-8926.
Facility: 79 one-bedroom standard units. 2 stories (no elevator), exterior corridors. **Parking:** on-site. **Terms:** small pets only.
Amenities: video games, voice mail. **Cards:** AX, CB, DC, DS, MC, VI.

SOME UNITS
🛏 📶 🎞 / ✖ DATA PORT 📶 📺 /

——— WHERE TO DINE ———

FORBIDDEN CITY RESTAURANT
Lunch: $4-$6   Dinner: $7-$14   Phone: 989/799-9340
(AAA)
▼▼▼▼ ▼▼▼
Chinese
Location: SR 58, 2 mi n on SR 84; in Town Campus Mall. 4024 Bay Rd 48603. **Hours:** 11 am-9:30 pm, Fri & Sat-10 pm, Sun noon-8:30 pm. Closed major holidays; also for lunch 9/4 & for dinner 12/24. **Reservations:** suggested, weekends. **Features:** A local fixture since 1973, this comfortable restaurant is decorated with red tablecloths, wood accents and Oriental artwork. The focus is on Mandarin-style food, such as almond chicken and Mongolian beef. Try the crab cheese appetizers or the vegetable bean curd soup. Service is professional and friendly. Casual dress; cocktails. **Parking:** on-site. **Cards:** AX, MC, VI.

HUNAN RESTAURANT
Lunch: $5-$6   Dinner: $7-$18   Phone: 989/792-0303
▼▼▼▼ ▼▼▼
Chinese
Location: SR 58, 2.5 mi n on SR 84; opposite Fashion Square Mall. 3109 Bay Plaza 48604. **Hours:** 11:15 am-9:30 pm, Fri & Sat-10 pm, Sun noon-9 pm. Closed major holidays. **Features:** Hunan, Szechuan and Mandarin dishes, such as beef with broccoli and sweet and sour pork, are served in plentiful portions. The quiet dining rooms are decorated with classy, Oriental appointments. Servers are friendly and adept at follow-up. Casual dress; cocktails. **Parking:** on-site. **Cards:** AX, DC, DS, MC, VI.

KABOB AND CURRY HOUSE
Lunch: $5-$7   Dinner: $8-$15   Phone: 989/497-4400
▼▼▼▼ ▼▼▼
Indian
Location: On SR 84, 2 mi n of SR 58. 4070 Bay Rd 48603. **Hours:** noon-3 & 5-9 pm, Sun 11 am-5 pm. Closed major holidays. **Reservations:** accepted. **Features:** As the name impies, this restaurant offers a selection of tradition Indian dishes from vegetarian delights to non-vegetarian dinners such as boti kabob- tender pieces of lamb marinated in yogurt, giner, garlic, and spices and cooked in the char-broiler. Casual dress; cocktails. **Parking:** on-site. **Cards:** AX, MC, VI.

KINGS HOUSE CHINESE RESTAURANT
Lunch: $3-$5   Dinner: $4-$5   ·Phone: 989/790-1072
▼▼▼
Chinese
MC, VI.
Location: SR 58, 1.5 mi n of SR 84. 3649 Bay Rd 48603. **Hours:** 11 am-9 pm. Closed major holidays; also Sun 6/1-8/31. **Features:** Delicious soup and tasty, Cantonese-style chow mein are popular selections at the unpretentious family restaurant. Lots of plants and pictures of the Great Wall enhance the warm, bright dining room. The menu also lists several American choices. Casual dress. **Parking:** on-site. **Cards:** DS,

SULLIVAN'S
Lunch: $5-$8   Dinner: $7-$15   Phone: 989/799-1940
▼▼▼▼
American
DS, MC, VI.
Location: 5 mi w on SR 46. 5235 Gratiot Rd 48603. **Hours:** 7 am-9 pm. Closed: 11/25, 12/25. **Features:** Serving the area since 1946, the restaurant delivers home-cooked daily specials, as well as such dishes as seafood, Swiss steak and chicken. Soups and sandwiches are favorite lighter fare. Wood and brass accents lend to the contemporary feel. Casual dress; cocktails. **Parking:** on-site. **Cards:** AX,

TONY'S
Lunch: $4-$6   Dinner: $6-$9   Phone: 989/249-8669
▼▼▼▼
American
Location: I-675, exit 6, 0.7 mi w on Tittabawassee Rd, then just s. 4880 Fashion Square Blvd 48603. **Hours:** 7 am-10 pm, Thurs-Sat to 11 pm. Closed major holidays. **Features:** The restaurant is well known in the area for its steak sandwiches and WOP salad, as well as huge portions for breakfast, lunch and dinner. Save room for one of the tempting desserts. Casual dress. **Parking:** on-site. **Cards:** MC, VI.

——— *The following restaurant has not been evaluated by AAA* ———
but is listed for your information only.

HELLO SUSHI
Phone: 989/790-0022
[fyi]
Not evaluated. **Location:** I-675, exit 6, 0.5 mi w. 2575 Tittabawassee Rd 48604. **Features:** This is the place to go for sushi in Saginaw, and it's close to the shopping centers.

ST. CLAIR pop. 5,802

——— WHERE TO STAY ———

ST. CLAIR INN
Book at aaa.com
Phone: (810)329-2222
(AAA) [SAVE]
▼▼▼▼ ▼▼▼
Historic
Small-scale Hotel
All Year   1P: $85-$145   2P: $85-$145   XP: $10   F12
Location: 1.3 mi n on SR 29. 500 N Riverside Ave 48079. Fax: 810/329-7664. **Facility:** Modeled after an English inn, this historic hotel was built in the heyday of the Great Lakes excursion ships and features many river-view rooms. 79 units. 74 one-bedroom standard units, some with whirlpools. 4 one-bedroom suites ($240). 1 cottage. 2 stories (no elevator), interior corridors. *Bath:* combo or shower only. **Parking:** on-site. **Terms:** cancellation fee imposed, package plans. **Amenities:** voice mail. *Some:* hair dryers. **Dining:** 7 am-9 pm, Fri & Sat-10 pm, Sun 8 am-9 pm, cocktails. **Leisure Activities:** boat dock, fishing. **Guest Services:** valet laundry. **Business Services:** conference facilities. **Cards:** AX, MC, VI.

SOME UNITS
[🍴] [🚫] [DATA PORT] [▢] / [✕] [VCR] [🔌] /
FEE

——— WHERE TO DINE ———

RIVER CRAB
Lunch: $6-$14   Dinner: $14-$30   Phone: 810/329-2261
(AAA)
▼▼▼▼ ▼▼▼
Seafood
Location: Adjacent to River Crab Blue Water Inn. 1337 N River Rd 48079. **Hours:** 11:30 am-9 pm, Fri & Sat-10:30 pm, Sun 10 am-8:30 pm. Closed: 1/1, 12/25. **Reservations:** suggested. **Features:** Overlooking the St. Clair River, the restaurant is warm and romantic—a perfect spot for couples. The menu lists a lengthy selection of daily fish specials, such as salmon in a flavorful mustard sauce. Casual dress; cocktails. **Parking:** on-site and valet. **Cards:** AX, DC, DS, MC, VI.

ST. IGNACE pop. 2,678   (See map and index starting on p. 352)

───── WHERE TO STAY ─────

AURORA BOREALIS MOTOR INN   Phone: 906/643-7488   **54**
♦♦♦ ♦♦♦
        6/24-8/21   1P: $49-$89   2P: $49-$89   XP: $6
        8/22-11/13   1P: $39-$79   2P: $39-$79   XP: $5
        4/1-6/23   1P: $39-$69   2P: $39-$69   XP: $5
Motel   **Location:** 1 mi e of bridge tollgate on I-75 business route and US 2. 635 W US 2 49781. **Facility:** 56 one-bedroom standard units. 2 stories (no elevator), exterior corridors. **Parking:** on-site. **Terms:** open 4/1-11/13, check-in 3:30 pm. **Cards:** DS, MC, VI. **(See ad below)**
SOME UNITS

BAY VIEW MOTEL   Phone: 906/643-9444   **42**
♦
        6/25-9/7   1P: $54-$64   2P: $58-$76   XP: $5
        4/1-6/24, 9/8-10/30 & 3/16-3/31 1P: $32-$48   2P: $32-$48   XP: $5
Motel   **Location:** 3 mi n of bridge tollgate on I-75 business route. Located on the lake. 1133 N State St 49781. **Facility:** 23 one-bedroom standard units. 1-2 stories (no elevator), exterior corridors. .Bath: combo or shower only.
Parking: on-site. **Terms:** open 4/1-10/30 & 3/16-3/31, pets ($5 extra charge). **Cards:** DS, MC, VI.
SOME UNITS
FEE

BEST WESTERN HARBOUR POINTE LAKEFRONT   Phone: (906)643-6000   **52**
AAA SAVE
        7/2-8/21   1P: $89-$198   2P: $89-$198
♦♦♦ ♦♦♦
        4/16-7/1 & 8/22-10/30 1P: $55-$159   2P: $55-$159
Small-scale Hotel **Location:** 2 mi n of bridge tollgate on I-75 business route. Located on Lake Huron. 797 N State St 49781. Fax: 906/643-6946. **Facility:** 150 units. 140 one- and 10 two-bedroom standard units, some with whirlpools. 3 stories, interior/exterior corridors. **Parking:** on-site. **Terms:** open 4/16-10/30, cancellation fee imposed, [ECP] meal plan available, package plans. **Amenities:** video library (fee), irons. **Pool(s):** heated outdoor, heated indoor. **Leisure Activities:** whirlpools, playground. Fee: game room. **Guest Services:** coin laundry. **Cards:** AX, DC, DS, MC, VI. **Special Amenities:** free continental breakfast and early check-in/late check-out.
(See color ad starting on p 428)
SOME UNITS
FEE

(See map and index starting on p. 352)

BUDGET HOST INN

		Phone: 906/643-9666	🏨51
6/24-8/21 [BP]	1P: $74-$156	2P: $74-$156	XP: $6	F4
4/1-6/23 & 8/22-3/31 [BP]	1P: $58-$135	2P: $58-$135	XP: $6	F4

Small-scale Hotel

Location: 1.8 mi n of bridge tollgate on I-75 business route. Located in a commercial area. 700 N State St 49781. Fax: 906/643-9126. **Facility:** 58 units. 45 one-bedroom standard units, some with whirlpools. 3 one- and 10 two-bedroom suites, some with whirlpools. 2 stories, interior/exterior corridors. **Parking:** on-site, winter plug-ins. **Terms:** pets ($20 deposit). **Amenities:** *Some:* hair dryers. **Pool(s):** heated indoor. **Leisure Activities:** whirlpool, snowmobiling, playground. *Fee:* game room. **Guest Services:** coin laundry. **Business Services:** meeting rooms. **Cards:** AX, CB, DC, DS, MC, VI. **Special Amenities:** free full breakfast and free local telephone calls.
(See color ad p 430)

SOME UNITS

(See map and index starting on p. 352)

COMFORT INN   *Book at aaa.com*   **Phone:** (906)643-7733   **49**

AAA [SAVE]   4/1-10/16 [BP]   1P: $49-$198   2P: $49-$198   XP: $10   F18
             10/17-3/31 [BP]   1P: $49-$138   2P: $49-$138   XP: $10   F18

◆◆◆◆   **Location:** 2 mi n of bridge tollgate on I-75 business route. Located on Lake Huron. 927 N State St 49781.
Small-scale Hotel Fax: 906/643-6420. **Facility:** 100 units. 97 one-bedroom standard units, some with whirlpools. 3 one-
                   bedroom suites. 4 stories, interior corridors. **Parking:** on-site. **Terms:** cancellation fee imposed, package
playground. *Fee:* game room. **Cards:** AX, DS, MC, VI. **Special Amenities:** free full breakfast and free local telephone
calls. *(See color ad opposite title page)*   SOME UNITS

[S/D] [🍴] [≈] [✕] [🎥] [DATA PORT] [🛏] [▣] / [✕] [☕] /

Overlooking Mackinac Island on Lake Huron

Indoor and Outdoor Pools

Family Units & Suites

Best Western

Harbour Pointe Lakefront
1-800-642-3318
www.harbourpointe.com
797 North State, St. Ignace, MI 49781 · 906-643-6000

(See map and index starting on p. 352)

DAYS INN LAKEFRONT & SUITES   *Book at aaa.com*   Phone: 906/643-8008   **47**

6/11-8/28 [ECP]	1P: $79-$169	2P: $79-$169	XP: $6	F12
8/29-10/9 [ECP]	1P: $69-$129	2P: $69-$129	XP: $6	F12
10/10-3/31 [ECP]	1P: $59-$109	2P: $59-$109	XP: $6	F12
4/1-6/10 [ECP]	1P: $59-$99	2P: $59-$99	XP: $6	F12

Small-scale Hotel **Location:** 2.8 mi n of bridge tollgate on I-75 business route. Located on Lake Huron. 1067 N State St 49781. Fax: 906/643-9400. **Facility:** 105 units. 93 one- and 1 two-bedroom standard units, some with whirlpools. 11 one-bedroom suites ($89-$249), some with whirlpools. 2-3 stories, interior corridors. **Parking:** on-site. **Terms:** package plans. **Amenities:** irons, hair dryers. **Pool(s):** heated indoor. **Leisure Activities:** sauna, whirlpools, exercise room, volleyball. *Fee:* game room. **Guest Services:** coin laundry. **Cards:** AX, CB, DC, DS, JC, MC, VI. **Special Amenities:** free expanded continental breakfast and free local telephone calls. *(See color ad p 432 & card insert)*

SOME UNITS

Put Yourself in the Driver's Seat With a Low-Rate Auto Loan from AAA

Loans for new and used cars or to refinance an existing loan.

It's easy to apply!

- Complete the easy application on aaa.com or call 1-800-699-1208.

- Receive a response in 15 minutes during business hours.*

- Upon approval, receive a Blank Check,®* delivered free overnight (a $15 value), that allows you to shop like a cash buyer.

Business hours are Monday through Friday, 9 a.m. to 5:30 p.m. and Saturday, 8 a.m. to noon Pacific Time. Blank Check® is a registered trademark of PeopleFirst Finance, LLC. Individuals with less than excellent credit may be offered higher rates or may qualify for the PeopleFirst Custom Finance Program. Not available in New Hampshire and North Dakota. Check with your local club for more details. Loans provided by PeopleFirst.com. Available at participating AAA clubs only.

DAYS INN ST. IGNACE *Book at aaa.com*   **Phone:** (906)643-7777 [43]

(AAA) (SAVE)   6/11-8/28 [ECP]   1P: $59-$149   2P: $59-$149   XP: $6   F12
              8/29-10/9 [ECP]   1P: $59-$119   2P: $59-$119   XP: $6   F12
▽▽ ▽▽   5/1-6/10 & 10/10-10/23 [ECP]   1P: $49-$89   2P: $49-$89   XP: $6   F12
Motel   **Location:** 2.8 mi n of bridge tollgate on I-75 business route. Located opposite Lake Huron. 1074 N State St 49781. **Fax:** 906/643-9400. **Facility:** 74 one-bedroom standard units, some with whirlpools. 2 stories (no elevator), exterior corridors. **Parking:** on-site. **Terms:** open 5/1-10/23, package plans. **Amenities:** irons, hair dryers. **Pool(s):** heated indoor. **Leisure Activities:** whirlpool. *Fee:* game room. **Guest Services:** coin laundry. **Cards:** AX, CB, DC, DS, JC, MC, VI. *(See color ad below & card insert)*

SOME UNITS

ECONO LODGE INN & SUITES *Book at aaa.com*   **Phone:** (906)643-9688 [55]

(AAA) (SAVE)   6/24-8/31 [CP]   1P: $69-$130   2P: $69-$130   XP: $6   F18
              4/1-6/23 & 9/1-3/31 [CP]   1P: $49-$89   2P: $49-$99   XP: $6   F18
▽▽ ▽▽   **Location:** Just e on I-75 business route and US 2. 680 W US 2 49781. **Fax:** 906/643-6320. **Facility:** 77 units. 70
Motel   one- and 7 two-bedroom standard units, some with whirlpools. 1-2 stories (no elevator), interior/exterior corridors. **Parking:** on-site, winter plug-ins. **Pool(s):** heated indoor. **Leisure Activities:** whirlpool, snowmobiling, playground, shuffleboard. *Fee:* game room. **Business Services:** meeting rooms. **Cards:** AX, CB, DC, DS, MC, VI. **Special Amenities:** free continental breakfast and free local telephone calls. *(See color ad p 434)*

SOME UNITS

Lake Huron Access Excellent Rates

All Queen & King Size Beds
Indoor Pool & Whirlpool Spa
Sundeck · Lake Huron Access · Continental Breakfast
In-Room Heartshaped Whirlpool Spas · Refrigerators
In-Room Fresh Brewed Coffee · Hair Dryer · In-Room Iron
and Ironing Board · Coin Laundry · Gameroom · Kids Stay Free
Free Shuttle to Mackinac Island Ferries and Kewadin Shores Casino
Close to Restaurants & Shopping · Our Best Values & Best Rates

Sunday–Thursday
20% Discount
Off Published Rates
Offered for 3 Day Stays,
Excluding Holiday
and Special Events

DAYS INN ST. IGNACE

Reservations: 800-251-6718
1074 North State Street · St. Ignace, MI 49781 (906) 643-7777 · www.daysinn.com

FOUR STAR MOTEL   Phone: 906/643-9360   **48**
 [AAA] [SAVE] 6/20-9/8   2P: $40-$47   XP: $4
        5/19-6/19 & 9/9-10/5   2P: $36-$42   XP: $4
 ▼▼▼   **Location:** On US 2, 2 mi w. 1064 US 2 W 49781. **Facility:** 20 units. 19 one- and 1 two-bedroom standard units.
 Motel 1-2 stories (no elevator), exterior corridors. *Bath:* combo or shower only. **Parking:** on-site. **Terms:** open 5/19-
        10/5, 3 day cancellation notice. **Leisure Activities:** playground. **Cards:** AX, MC, VI.   [🍴][🅿][📺][🚭]

HOLIDAY INN EXPRESS LAKEFRONT   *Book at aaa.com*   Phone: (906)643-0200   **50**
 [AAA] [SAVE] 6/21-9/15   2P: $140-$230   XP: $10   F16
        9/16-12/31   2P: $88-$140   XP: $10   F16
 ▼▼▼▼   4/1-6/20 & 1/1-3/31   2P: $60-$100   XP: $10   F16
 Small-scale Hotel **Location:** 2.3 mi n of bridge tollgate on I-75 business route. 965 N State St 49781. Fax: 906/643-0133. **Facility:** 85
        one-bedroom standard units, some with whirlpools. 4 stories, interior corridors. *Bath:* combo or shower only.
        Parking: on-site. **Terms:** 2-3 night minimum stay - weekends, 3 day cancellation notice-fee imposed, [ECP]
 meal plan available, package plans - seasonal. **Amenities:** irons, hair dryers. **Pool(s):** heated indoor. **Leisure Activities:** whirlpool, snowmobiling. **Guest Services:** coin laundry. **Cards:** AX, CB, DC, DS, JC, MC, VI. *(See color ad p 435)*
                                                                                        SOME UNITS
        [S🄳][🍴][📶][🏊][📺][DATA PORT] /[🚫]/

KEWADIN CASINO LAKEFRONT INN
Phone: (906)643-8411 **41**

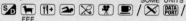

6/27-10/18   1P: $89-$109   2P: $89-$109   XP: $10   F16
4/1-6/26 & 10/19-3/31   1P: $66-$80   2P: $66-$80   XP: $10   F16

Motel

Location: 3 mi n of bridge tollgate on I-75 business route. Located on Lake Huron. 1131 N State St 49781. Fax: 906/643-8924. **Facility:** 85 one-bedroom standard units, some with whirlpools. 2 stories (no elevator), interior/exterior corridors. **Parking:** on-site. **Terms:** [CP] meal plan available. **Amenities:** irons, hair dryers. **Pool(s):** heated indoor. **Leisure Activities:** whirlpool, snowmobiling, indoor recreation area, playground. **Guest Services:** coin laundry. **Business Services:** meeting rooms. **Cards:** AX, DC, DS, MC, VI. **Special Amenities:** free continental breakfast and early check-in/late check-out.

SOME UNITS

K-ROYALE MOTOR INN
Phone: (906)643-7737 **46**

7/3-8/16 [CP]   1P: $58-$155   2P: $62-$155   XP: $7   F18
4/1-7/2 & 8/17-10/30 [CP]   1P: $45-$125   2P: $45-$125   XP: $7   F18

Motel

Location: 2.3 mi n of bridge tollgate on I-75 business route. Located on Lake Huron. 1037 N State St 49781. Fax: 906/643-8556. **Facility:** 95 units. 93 one- and 2 two-bedroom standard units. 3 stories (no elevator), exterior corridors. **Parking:** on-site. **Terms:** open 4/1-10/30. **Pool(s):** indoor. **Leisure Activities:** whirlpool, playground, volleyball. **Fee:** game room. **Guest Services:** gift shop, coin laundry. **Business Services:** meeting rooms. **Cards:** CB, MC, VI. *(See color ad p 436)*

SOME UNITS

QUALITY INN LAKEFRONT   *Book at aaa.com*
Phone: (906)643-7581 **45**

6/28-9/4   1P: $94-$160   2P: $102-$164   XP: $6   F18
4/10-6/27 & 9/5-10/31   1P: $44-$124   2P: $48-$116   XP: $6   F18

Motel

Location: 2.3 mi n of bridge tollgate on I-75 business route. Located on Lake Huron. 1021 N State St 49781. Fax: 906/643-8573. **Facility:** 66 one-bedroom standard units, some with whirlpools. 3 stories, exterior corridors. **Parking:** on-site. **Terms:** open 4/10-10/31, 3 day cancellation notice-fee imposed, [CP] meal plan available. **Amenities:** voice mail, irons, hair dryers. **Pool(s):** heated indoor. **Leisure Activities:** whirlpool, sun deck, playground. **Cards:** AX, CB, DC, DS, JC, MC, VI. *(See color ad p 437)*

SOME UNITS

QUALITY INN ST. IGNACE   *Book at aaa.com*
Phone: (906)643-9700 **57**

6/11-9/12 [ECP]   1P: $100-$155   2P: $110-$165   XP: $10   F18
4/1-6/10 & 9/13-3/31 [ECP]   1P: $60-$85   2P: $70-$95   XP: $10   F18

Small-scale Hotel

Location: Jct I-75 and US 2 W. 913 Boulevard Dr 49781. Fax: 906/643-6762. **Facility:** 57 one-bedroom standard units, some with whirlpools. 2 stories (no elevator), interior corridors. **Parking:** on-site, winter plug-ins. **Terms:** package plans - seasonal, pets ($10 extra charge). **Amenities:** irons, hair dryers. **Pool(s):** heated indoor. **Leisure Activities:** sauna, whirlpool, exercise room, basketball. **Fee:** snowmobiling, bicycles, game room. **Guest Services:** gift shop, coin laundry. **Business Services:** meeting rooms, PC. **Cards:** AX, DC, DS, MC, VI. **Special Amenities:** free expanded continental breakfast and free local telephone calls.

SOME UNITS

FEE

Beachfront Luxury

Specials *include*:*

3 nights stay,
double occupancy,
children stay FREE,
FREE *2 Ferry Tickets,*
FREE *2 mini-Golf games,*
$60 Casino coupon.
* excludes Holidays & Events
Upon Availability

$155 to $230
April - July 3 &
Aug 18 - Oct 26

$229
July 6 - Aug 17

Call before July 2
for other discounts.

AAA, Seniors & Group Tours
Discount Rates

Vacation on the Water, where every room overlooks Lake Huron,
Surround yourself by a private sandy beach and play in the sand,
Enjoy spectacular sunrise and moon rise panoramic views
Overlooking beautiful historic Mackinac Island!

* FREE Continental Breakfast
* Children stay FREE
* FREE Boat Launch
* FREE Shuttle to Mackinac Is. Ferry
* FREE Shuttle to Casino
* Indoor Heated Pool
* Indoor Whirlpool Spa
* Balcony overlooking the Lake
* Outdoor BBQ, Picnic and Play areas
* Indoor Game Room and Sun Deck
* Group Meeting Room

* In room Refrigerators
* In room Remote control Color TV
* Two room Family Suites, sleeps 7
* Guest Laundry
* Standard, Queen & King Beds
* Non-Smoking Rooms are Available
* Direct-Dial Phones in every room
* Close to Restaurants, Shops & Golf
* Close to Mackinac Island Ferry
* Close to Tahquamenon Falls
* Special Saving Packages offered

Treat yourself to a relaxing vacation on the Beach!
Call Today!   **(800) 882-7122 or (906) 643-7737**

Location: 2-1/2 Miles North of the Bridge on I-75 Business Loop
E-mail: cmuscott@portup.com
Royal Motor Inn   1037 N. State Street, St. Ignace, MI 49781

Trust AAA to take you there.

On a 3-, 4- or 7-Night *Disney Cruise Line®* vacation, adults, kids and teens delight to the kind of entertainment only Disney can create – including a visit to Disney's private island, *Castaway Cay*. And when you book your cruise through AAA Travel, you'll enjoy special member benefits and a great rate!

www.aaa.com

Ships' Registry: The Bahamas
As to Disney properties/artwork: ©Disney K7988203 **CST#1022229-50**

RODEWAY INN   *Book at aaa.com*

AAA SAVE

			Phone: (906)643-8511	58
6/1-9/1	1P: $75-$155	2P: $75-$155	XP: $6	F18
4/1-5/31	1P: $65-$125	2P: $65-$125	XP: $6	F18
9/2-11/30	1P: $60-$120	2P: $60-$120	XP: $6	F18
1/1-3/31	1P: $55-$120	2P: $55-$120	XP: $6	F18

Small-scale Hotel **Location:** Jct I-75 business route and US 2, just e. Located in a commercial area. 750 W US 2 49781. Fax: 906/643-6358. **Facility:** 42 one-bedroom standard units, some with whirlpools. 1-2 stories, interior/exterior corridors. **Parking:** on-site, winter plug-ins. **Terms:** open 4/1-11/30 & 1/1-3/31, [CP] meal plan available. **Amenities:** *Some:* hair dryers. **Pool(s):** heated indoor. **Leisure Activities:** whirlpool, snowmobiling. **Cards:** AX, DS, MC, VI. **Special Amenities:** free continental breakfast and free local telephone calls.

SOME UNITS

SUPER 8 OF ST. IGNACE

AAA SAVE

			Phone: 906/643-7616	56
6/20-8/29	1P: $78-$119	2P: $78-$119	XP: $5	F5
8/30-10/23	1P: $62-$88	2P: $68-$88	XP: $5	F5
4/1-6/19 & 10/24-3/31	1P: $58-$78	2P: $62-$88	XP: $5	F5

Small-scale Hotel **Location:** I-75, exit 344B, 0.5 mi w. Located in a commercial area. 923 W US 2 49781. Fax: 906/643-9286. **Facility:** 61 one-bedroom standard units, some with whirlpools. 3 stories, interior corridors. *Bath:* combo or shower only. **Parking:** on-site. **Terms:** [CP] meal plan available. **Amenities:** *Some:* hair dryers. **Pool(s):** heated indoor. **Leisure Activities:** whirlpool, snowmobiling. **Guest Services:** coin laundry. **Cards:** AX, DC, DS, MC, VI. **Special Amenities:** free continental breakfast and free local telephone calls.

SOME UNITS

TRADEWINDS MOTEL

Motel

			Phone: 906/643-9388	44
6/22-9/5	1P: $55-$65	2P: $69-$79	XP: $10	F6
4/1-6/21 & 9/6-10/28	1P: $36-$48	2P: $39-$59	XP: $5	F6

Location: 3 mi n of bridge tollgate on I-75 business route. Located opposite Lake Huron. 1190 N State St 49781. Fax: 906/643-9388. **Facility:** 25 one-bedroom standard units. 1 story, exterior corridors. *Bath:* shower only. **Parking:** on-site. **Terms:** open 4/1-10/28. **Pool(s):** heated outdoor. **Leisure Activities:** playground. **Cards:** DS, MC, VI.

SOME UNITS

WAYSIDE MOTEL

AAA SAVE

Motel

			Phone: 906/643-8944	53
All Year [CP]	1P: $35-$50	2P: $40-$75	XP: $5	F11

Location: 2 mi n of bridge tollgate on I-75 business route. Located in a semi-commercial area. 751 N State St 49781. Fax: 906/643-0207. **Facility:** 19 one-bedroom standard units. 1 story, exterior corridors. *Bath:* combo or shower only. **Parking:** on-site. **Terms:** cancellation fee imposed, small pets only ($5 extra charge). **Leisure Activities:** snowmobiling, basketball. **Cards:** DS, MC, VI. **Special Amenities:** free continental breakfast and free local telephone calls.

SOME UNITS

FEE

—— WHERE TO DINE ——

THE GALLEY RESTAURANT & BAR   **Lunch:** $5-$7   **Dinner:** $9-$16   **Phone:** 906/643-7960 ⑫
    Location: Center. 241 N State St 49781. **Hours:** Open 5/1-10/23; 7 am-10 pm. **Features:** On the shores of
Lake Huron, the restaurant features photographs of freighters, lighthouses and ships as well as wildlife
prints of ducks and loons. Great Lakes whitefish, trout and juicy roast prime rib are well-prepared and
flavorful. Casual dress; cocktails. **Parking:** on-site. **Cards:** DS, MC, VI.

Steak & Seafood

NORTH BAY INN   **Lunch:** $4-$6   **Dinner:** $8-$15   **Phone:** 906/643-8304 ⑪
    Location: 3 mi n of bridge tollgate on I-75 business route. 1192 N State St 49781. **Hours:** Open 5/1-10/30; 7 am-9
pm; to 10 pm 6/16-9/2. **Features:** Plants, flowers and paintings and photographs by local artists enhance
American   the warm, comfortable feel of the dining room, a popular spot for family dining. Charbroiled steaks,
whitefish, pasta and ribs are representative of menu options. Service is friendly. Casual dress; cocktails.
Parking: on-site. **Cards:** MC, VI.

ST. JOSEPH pop. 8,789

—— WHERE TO STAY ——

THE BOULEVARD INN & BISTRO   *Book at aaa.com*   **Phone:** (269)983-6600

| | 4/1-10/31 | 1P: $155-$190 | 2P: $155-$190 | XP: $20 | F18 |
| | 11/1-3/31 | 1P: $135-$170 | 2P: $135-$170 | XP: $20 | F18 |

Small-scale Hotel   **Location:** I-94, exit 23, 5 mi n on Red Arrow Hwy, just w on Broad St, then just s; downtown. 521 Lake Blvd 49085.
Fax: 269/983-0520. **Facility:** 82 one-bedroom suites, some with whirlpools. 3 stories, interior corridors.
Parking: on-site. **Terms:** check-in 4 pm. **Amenities:** dual phone lines, voice mail, irons, hair dryers.
Dining: Bistro On The Boulevard, see separate listing. **Leisure Activities:** exercise room. **Guest Services:**
valet laundry. **Business Services:** meeting rooms, business center. **Cards:** AX, DC, DS, MC, VI.

SOME UNITS

FEE

CLARION HOTEL   *Book at aaa.com*   **Phone:** (269)983-7341

	5/28-10/31	1P: $74-$79	2P: $79-$84	XP: $10	F18
	11/1-3/31	1P: $64-$74	2P: $69-$79		
	4/1-5/27	1P: $64-$74	2P: $69-$79	XP: $10	F18

Small-scale Hotel   **Location:** I-94, exit 27 eastbound, 5 mi nw to Main St; exit 33 westbound, 4.8 mi w on Business Rt I-94, then nw to Main
St. 100 Main St 49085. Fax: 269/983-0650. **Facility:** 149 one-bedroom standard units, some with whirlpools. 7 stories, interior corridors. *Bath:* combo or shower only. **Parking:** on-site. **Amenities:** irons, hair dryers. **Pool(s):** heated indoor. **Leisure Activities:** sauna, whirlpool, exercise room. *Fee:* game room. **Guest Services:** valet and coin laundry. **Business Services:** meeting
rooms, business center. **Cards:** AX, CB, DC, DS, JC, MC, VI. *(See color ad below)*

SOME UNITS

HOLIDAY INN EXPRESS HOTEL & SUITES   *Book at aaa.com*   **Phone:** (269)982-0004

| | 5/1-10/31 [ECP] | 1P: $135-$249 | 2P: $135-$249 | XP: $10 | F18 |
| | 4/1-4/30 & 11/1-3/31 [ECP] | 1P: $92-$199 | 2P: $92-$199 | XP: $10 | F18 |

Small-scale Hotel   **Location:** I-94, exit 23, 3.5 mi n. 3019 Lake Shore Dr 49085. Fax: 269/982-0023. **Facility:** 82 units. 75 one-
bedroom standard units, some with whirlpools. 7 two-bedroom suites ($135-$249), some with whirlpools. 3
stories, interior corridors. *Bath:* combo or shower only. **Parking:** on-site. **Terms:** cancellation fee imposed. **Amenities:** dual
phone lines, voice mail, irons, hair dryers. **Pool(s):** heated indoor. **Leisure Activities:** whirlpool, exercise room. **Guest Services:**
complimentary laundry. **Business Services:** meeting rooms, business center. **Cards:** AX, DC, DS, JC, MC, VI.

SOME UNITS

——— **WHERE TO DINE** ———

BISTRO ON THE BOULEVARD   Lunch: $9-$12   Dinner: $18-$24   Phone: 269/983-3882
▼▼▼▼   **Location:** I-94, exit 23, 5 mi n on Red Arrow Hwy, just w on Broad St, then just s; downtown; in The Boulevard Inn & Bistro. 521 Lake Blvd 49085. **Hours:** 6 am-9:30 pm. Closed: 12/25. **Reservations:** accepted. **Features:** This bistro presents a seasonally changing menu of Mediterranean dishes that incorporate local and international ingredients. The patio, which faces the water, is a popular seating spot. Representative of offerings are Mediterranean-style trout, shrimp pastis and steak frites. Casual dress; cocktails. **Parking:** on-site. **Cards:** AX, DC, DS, MC, VI.

American

Ⓧ

CLEMENTINE'S TOO   Lunch: $6-$14   Dinner: $9-$20   Phone: 269/983-0990
▼▼ ▼▼   **Location:** I-94, exit 27 (SR 63), 2.6 mi n to Napier Ave, 0.3 mi e to Langley Ave, 1 mi n. 1235 Broad St 49085. **Hours:** 11 am-10 pm, Fri & Sat-11 pm, Sun noon-10 pm; to 11 pm, Fri & Sat-midnight, Sun noon-11 pm 5/31-9/6. Closed major holidays. **Features:** This is a relaxed family restaurant located next to the marina and a short walk from downtown. The menu features a lot of salads and lighter entrees with the house specialty being a hot apple dumpling dessert. Casual dress; cocktails. **Parking:** on-site. **Cards:** AX, DS, MC, VI.

American

Ⓜ Ⓨ Ⓧ

MANSION GRILLE BY THE LAKE   Lunch: $6-$9   Dinner: $11-$25   Phone: 269/982-1500
▼▼▼   **Location:** I-94, exit 23, 3.5 mi n. 3029 Lake Shore Dr 49085. **Hours:** 11 am-2 & 5-10 pm, Sat & Sun from 5 pm. Closed major holidays; also 12/24 & Mon. **Reservations:** suggested. **Features:** In a renovated 1892 mansion, the restaurant overlooks Lake Michigan. Dining is relaxed in the dining rooms and on the lovely front porch. The menu delivers large portions of such dishes as shrimp rangoon and broiled lobster with garlic mashed potatoes. Cocktails. **Parking:** on-site. **Cards:** AX, DS, MC, VI.

American

Ⓜ Ⓨ Ⓧ

PUMP HOUSE GRILLE   Lunch: $7-$11   Dinner: $12-$18   Phone: 269/983-0001
▼▼▼   **Location:** Downtown. 214 State St 49085. **Hours:** 11 am-10 pm, Fri & Sat-11 pm. Closed major holidays. **Reservations:** accepted. **Features:** In the downtown area, the casually upscale bistro is known for its signature item: deep-fried dill pickles. Many selections, including baby back ribs and slow-cooked prime rib, are prepared in the on-site smoker. Dressy casual; cocktails. **Parking:** street. **Cards:** AX, DC, DS, MC, VI.

American

Ⓜ Ⓧ

SCHU'S GRILL & BAR   Lunch: $4-$10   Dinner: $7-$15   Phone: 269/983-7248
▼▼▼   **Location:** Between Pleasant and Ship sts; downtown. 501 Pleasant St 49085. **Hours:** 11 am-10 pm, Fri & Sat-11 pm, Sun noon-9 pm. Closed: 12/25. **Features:** Rustic appointments give the casual dining room the ambience of a warm, friendly lodge. Traditional comfort foods, ranging from burgers and steaks to pasta and overstuffed sandwiches, please all members of the family. The local crowd flocks to this place. Casual dress; cocktails. **Parking:** street. **Cards:** AX, DS, MC, VI.

American

Ⓨ Ⓧ

ST. LOUIS pop. 4,494

——— **WHERE TO DINE** ———

THE COUNTRY INN   Lunch: $5-$7   Dinner: $9-$14   Phone: 989/681-2213
▼▼▼   **Location:** On SR 46, 1 mi e of US 127. 1875 W Monroe Rd 48880. **Hours:** 11 am-8:30 pm, Sun-4 pm. Closed major holidays; also Mon. **Reservations:** accepted. **Features:** Country knickknacks decorate the homey dining room, an inviting spot in which families can relax. Sandwiches on fresh baked bread, homemade soup and such entrees as deep-fried cod are well-prepared and wholesome. Service is friendly and prompt. Casual dress. **Parking:** on-site. **Cards:** DS, MC, VI.

American

Ⓧ

SANDUSKY pop. 2,745

——— **WHERE TO STAY** ———

WEST PARK INN   Phone: 810/648-4300
▼▼▼   All Year [BP]   1P: $55-$70   XP: $5
Location: In town on SR 46. 440 W Sanilac 48471. Fax: 810/648-4300. **Facility:** 29 one-bedroom standard units, some with whirlpools. 1-2 stories (no elevator), interior/exterior corridors. *Bath:* combo or shower only. **Parking:** on-site, winter plug-ins. **Amenities:** hair dryers. *Some:* irons. **Leisure Activities:** whirlpool, exercise room. **Guest Services:** valet laundry. **Business Services:** meeting rooms. **Cards:** AX, CB, DC, DS, MC, VI.

Small-scale Hotel

SOME UNITS
🍽 Ⓨ 📺 / Ⓧ 📼 🔌 📞 /

SAUGATUCK pop. 1,065—See also DOUGLAS.

——— **WHERE TO STAY** ———

BEST WESTERN PLAZA HOTEL OF SAUGATUCK   Phone: (269)857-7178
Ⓐ Ⓢ   4/1-10/1   1P: $139-$209   2P: $139-$209   XP: $5   F17
10/2-3/31   1P: $79-$149   2P: $79-$149   XP: $5   F17
▼▼▼▼   **Location:** I-196, exit 41, 1.3 mi sw on CR A2. Located in a semi-commercial area. 3457 Blue Star Hwy 49453. Fax: 269/857-7169. **Facility:** 52 one-bedroom standard units, some with whirlpools. 2 stories (no elevator), interior corridors. **Parking:** on-site. **Terms:** 2 night minimum stay - weekends 7/1-8/31, cancellation fee imposed, [ECP] meal plan available. **Amenities:** irons, hair dryers. **Pool(s):** heated indoor. **Leisure Activities:** whirlpool, exercise room. **Guest Services:** coin laundry. **Business Services:** meeting rooms. **Cards:** AX, DC, DS, MC, VI. *(See color ad p 409)*

Small-scale Hotel

SOME UNITS
🏊 📺 🔌 💻 / Ⓧ 📞 /

CAPTAIN'S QUARTERS

◇ Motel

			Phone: (269)857-2525	
7/1-9/10	1P: $79-$149	2P: $89-$159	XP: $10	F17
9/11-10/31	1P: $70-$110	2P: $80-$120	XP: $10	F17
5/1-6/30	1P: $50-$105	2P: $60-$105	XP: $10	F17

Location: I-196, exit 41, 2 mi s; exit 36, 2 mi n. 3242 Blue Star Hwy (CR A2) 49453. **Facility:** 16 one-bedroom standard units. 1 story, exterior corridors. *Bath:* combo or shower only. **Parking:** on-site. **Terms:** open 5/1-10/31, 2 night minimum stay - weekends, 7 day cancellation notice-fee imposed. **Amenities:** hair dryers. **Cards:** DS, MC, VI.

SOME UNITS
[A$K] [S/D] [📞] [🖥] / [✕] [📠] /

SAUGATUCK'S VICTORIAN INN

AAA [SAVE]
▽▽▽
Bed & Breakfast

			Phone: (269)857-3325
5/1-10/31	1P: $120-$220	2P: $120-$220	
11/1-3/31	1P: $105-$195	2P: $105-$195	
4/1-4/30	1P: $95-$185	2P: $95-$185	

Location: Center of downtown. 447 Butler St 49453. Fax: 269/857-6043. **Facility:** Built in 1905 as the residence of the Koenig Hardware store owners, the inn includes an art gallery on the premises. Smoke free premises. 7 one-bedroom standard units, some with whirlpools. 2 stories (no elevator), interior corridors. *Bath:* combo or shower only. **Parking:** on-site. **Terms:** 2-3 night minimum stay - weekends in season, 7 day cancellation notice, [BP] meal plan available, no pets allowed (owner's pet on premises). **Amenities:** hair dryers. **Cards:** AX, DS, MC, VI.

[🍴+] [✕]

THE TIMBERLINE INN & SUITES   *Book at aaa.com*

AAA [SAVE]
▽▽▽▽
Motel

			Phone: (269)857-2147	
All Year	1P: $50-$140	2P: $60-$160	XP: $10	F7

Location: I-196, between exits 36 and 41, on CR A2. Located in a quiet, country setting. 3353 Blue Star Hwy 49453 (PO Box 666). Fax: 269/857-2147. **Facility:** 28 units. 27 one-bedroom standard units, some with whirlpools. 1 one-bedroom suite ($125-$190) with kitchen. 1 story, exterior corridors. *Bath:* combo or shower only. **Parking:** on-site, winter plug-ins. **Terms:** office hours 10 am-10 pm, 2-3 night minimum stay - seasonal & weekends, 7 day cancellation notice-fee imposed, [CP] meal plan available. **Pool(s):** heated outdoor. **Leisure Activities:** whirlpool, picnic area, playground, horseshoes, volleyball. **Cards:** MC, VI. **Special Amenities:** free continental breakfast and free local telephone calls.

SOME UNITS
[🏊] [✕] [🎦] [🖥] / [✕] [DATA PORT] [📠] [🍳] /
FEE

———— WHERE TO DINE ————

———— The following restaurant has not been evaluated by AAA ————
but is listed for your information only.

PUMPERNICKEL'S EATERY   Phone: 269/857-1196

[fyi]   Not evaluated. **Location:** Center. 202 Butler St 49453. **Features:** This restaurant serves breakfast, a number of items from the grill, as well as sandwiches served on thick sliced bread, flour tortilla or plain bagel.

SAULT STE. MARIE pop. 16,542

———— WHERE TO STAY ————

BEST WESTERN SAULT STE MARIE   *Book at aaa.com*

AAA [SAVE]
▽▽▽▽
Small-scale Hotel

			Phone: (906)632-2170	
All Year	1P: $59-$109	2P: $59-$109	XP: $10	F17

Location: I-75, exit 392, 0.3 mi ne. 4281 I-75 business loop 49783. Fax: 906/632-7877. **Facility:** 96 units. 87 one-bedroom standard units, some with whirlpools. 9 one-bedroom suites ($99-$169), some with efficiencies. 2 stories, interior/exterior corridors. *Bath:* combo or shower only. **Parking:** on-site. **Terms:** [ECP] meal plan available, pets ($15 fee, in designated units). **Amenities:** video library (fee), voice mail, irons, hair dryers. *Some:* DVD players. **Pool(s):** heated indoor. **Leisure Activities:** sauna, snowmobiling. *Fee:* game room. **Guest Services:** coin laundry. **Business Services:** meeting rooms. **Cards:** AX, CB, DC, DS, MC, VI. **Special Amenities:** free expanded continental breakfast and free room upgrade (subject to availability with advanced reservations). *(See color ad below)*

SOME UNITS
[S/D] [🛏] [🍴+] [♿] [🏊] [✕] [✕] [🎦] [DATA PORT] [📠] [🍳] [🖥] / [VCR] /
FEE   FEE

BUDGET HOST CRESTVIEW INN

Motel

Phone: (906)635-5213

	1P: $49-$59	2P: $59-$79	XP: $5	F12
6/15-10/15 [CP]				
4/1-6/14 & 10/16-3/31 [CP]	1P: $39-$49	2P: $49-$69	XP: $5	F12

Location: I-75, exit 392, 2.8 mi ne on I-75 business loop. Located in a semi-commercial area. 1200 Ashmun St 49783. Fax: 906/635-9672. **Facility:** 43 one-bedroom standard units. 1 story, exterior corridors. *Bath:* combo or shower only. **Parking:** on-site, winter plug-ins. **Terms:** pets (in smoking units). **Cards:** AX, DS, MC, VI. **Special Amenities:** free continental breakfast and free local telephone calls. *(See color ad below)*

SOME UNITS

COMFORT INN   *Book at aaa.com*

Small-scale Hotel

Phone: (906)635-1118

| 5/16-10/15 [ECP] | 1P: $69-$99 | 2P: $69-$99 | XP: $5 | F18 |
| 4/1-5/15 & 10/16-3/31 [ECP] | 1P: $49-$79 | 2P: $49-$79 | XP: $5 | F18 |

Location: I-75, exit 392, at business spur. Located in front of Cascade Crossing Strip Mall. 4404 I-75 Business Spur 49783. Fax: 906/635-1119. **Facility:** 86 one-bedroom standard units, some with whirlpools. 2 stories, interior corridors. *Bath:* combo or shower only. **Parking:** on-site. **Terms:** package plans. **Amenities:** safes (fee), irons, hair dryers. **Pool(s):** heated indoor. **Leisure Activities:** whirlpool, snowmobiling, exercise room. **Guest Services:** coin laundry. **Cards:** AX, DS, MC, VI. **Special Amenities:** free local telephone calls and free newspaper. *(See color ad p 442)*

SOME UNITS

DAYS INN   *Book at aaa.com*

Small-scale Hotel

Phone: (906)635-5200

| 5/16-10/15 [ECP] | 1P: $69-$99 | 2P: $69-$99 | XP: $10 | F18 |
| 4/1-5/15 & 10/16-3/31 [ECP] | 1P: $49-$79 | 2P: $49-$79 | XP: $10 | F18 |

Location: I-75, exit 392, 0.8 mi ne on I-75 business loop. Located in a commercial area. 3651 I-75 Business Spur 49783. Fax: 906/635-9750. **Facility:** 84 one-bedroom standard units, some with whirlpools. 2 stories, interior corridors. **Parking:** on-site. **Terms:** package plans. **Amenities:** safes (fee), hair dryers. *Some:* irons. **Pool(s):** heated indoor. **Leisure Activities:** whirlpool, snowmobiling, limited exercise equipment. *Fee:* game room. **Guest Services:** coin laundry. **Cards:** AX, DC, DS, MC, VI. **Special Amenities:** free expanded continental breakfast and free room upgrade (subject to availability with advanced reservations). *(See color ad card insert)*

SOME UNITS

DORAL MOTEL

Motel

Phone: (906)632-6621

| 6/16-10/30 | 1P: $59-$69 | 2P: $59-$69 | XP: $5 | F13 |
| 5/15-6/15 | 1P: $42-$49 | 2P: $42-$49 | XP: $5 | F13 |

Location: On I-75 business loop, just e of town. Located opposite Locks Boat Tour. 518 E Portage Ave 49783. Fax: 906/635-1089. **Facility:** 20 one-bedroom standard units. 2 stories (no elevator), exterior corridors. **Parking:** on-site. **Terms:** open 5/15-10/30, weekly rates available. **Pool(s):** heated outdoor. **Leisure Activities:** sauna, whirlpool. *Fee:* game room. **Cards:** DS, MC, VI. **Special Amenities:** free local telephone calls and early check-in/late check-out.

SOME UNITS

HAMPTON INN   *Book at aaa.com*   Phone: (906)635-3000

	6/1-10/31	1P: $65-$99	2P: $80-$104
◆◆◆	4/1-5/31	1P: $55-$85	2P: $60-$90
Small-scale Hotel	11/1-3/31	1P: $55-$85	2P: $60-$85

Location: I-75, exit 392, 1 mi ne on I-75 business loop. 3295 I-75 business loop 49783. Fax: 906/635-0034. **Facility:** 82 one-bedroom standard units, some with whirlpools. 3 stories, interior corridors. *Bath:* combo or shower only. **Parking:** on-site. **Terms:** cancellation fee imposed. **Amenities:** voice mail, irons, hair dryers. **Pool(s):** heated indoor. **Leisure Activities:** whirlpool, snowmobiling. **Guest Services:** valet laundry. **Cards:** AX, CB, DS, MC, VI.

SOME UNITS

ASK ⓢⒹ 🅣 🕭 🏊 🎥 DATA PORT 🛢 🖵 🖥 / ✕ /

HOLIDAY INN EXPRESS   *Book at aaa.com*   Phone: (906)632-3999

◆◆◆ SAVE	6/16-10/20 [ECP]	1P: $69-$99	2P: $69-$99	XP: $10	F18
◆◆◆	4/1-6/15 & 10/21-3/31 [ECP]	1P: $55-$89	2P: $55-$89	XP: $10	F18

Small-scale Hotel   **Location:** I-75, exit 394. 1171 Riverview Way 49783. Fax: 906/632-9633. **Facility:** 97 one-bedroom standard units, some with whirlpools. 5 stories, interior corridors. *Bath:* combo or shower only. **Parking:** on-site, winter plug-ins. **Terms:** check-in 4 pm, cancellation fee imposed, package plans. **Amenities:** irons, hair dryers. **Pool(s):** heated indoor. **Leisure Activities:** whirlpool, exercise room. *Fee:* game room. **Guest Services:** valet and coin laundry. **Business Services:** meeting rooms. **Cards:** AX, CB, DC, DS, JC, MC, VI. **Special Amenities:** free local telephone calls and free newspaper. *(See color ad card insert)*

SOME UNITS

ⓢⒹ 🅼 🕭 🏊 ✕ 🎥 DATA PORT 🖵 / ✕ 🛢 🖥 /

KEWADIN CASINO HOTEL & CONVENTION CENTER   *Book at aaa.com*   Phone: (906)632-0530

◆◆	7/1-10/20	1P: $89-$133	2P: $89-$133	XP: $10	F18
	4/1-6/30	1P: $70-$119	2P: $70-$119	XP: $10	F18
Large-scale Hotel	10/21-3/30	1P: $63-$113	2P: $63-$113	XP: $10	F18

Location: I-75, exit 392, 2 mi ne on I-75 business loop, 1.5 mi e on Marquette Ave, then just s. 2186 Shunk Rd 49783. Fax: 906/635-4945. **Facility:** 319 units. 299 one-bedroom standard units, some with whirlpools. 20 one-bedroom suites with whirlpools. 2-5 stories, interior corridors. *Bath:* combo or shower only. **Parking:** on-site. **Terms:** package plans - seasonal. **Amenities:** voice mail, irons, hair dryers. *Some:* video games. **Pool(s):** heated indoor. **Leisure Activities:** sauna, whirlpool, steamrooms, snowmobiling, exercise room. *Fee:* game room. **Guest Services:** gift shop, valet laundry. **Business Services:** conference facilities. **Cards:** AX, CB, DC, DS, MC, VI.

SOME UNITS

🎲 ASK ⓢⒹ ✈ 🍴 🍸 🕭 🏊 ✕ 🎥 / ✕ DATA PORT 🛢 🖵 🖥 /

LA FRANCE TERRACE MOTEL
Phone: (906)632-7823

Motel

6/18-9/7	1P: $49-$59	2P: $52-$75	XP: $5 F12
9/8-10/24	1P: $42-$52	2P: $45-$65	XP: $5 F12
5/1-6/17	1P: $39-$49	2P: $42-$62	XP: $5 F12

Location: I-75, exit 392, 2.3 mi ne on I-75 business loop. 1608 Ashmun St 49783. **Facility:** 30 units. 20 one- and 10 two-bedroom standard units. 1 story, exterior corridors. **Parking:** on-site. **Terms:** open 5/1-10/24, pets (dogs only, in designated units). **Pool(s):** heated outdoor. **Leisure Activities:** playground. **Cards:** AX, DS, MC, VI.
Special Amenities: free continental breakfast and free local telephone calls. *(See color ad below)*

SOME UNITS

LAWSON MOTEL
Phone: (906)632-3322

Motel

7/1-9/9	1P: $48-$58	2P: $48-$68	XP: $5 F5
9/10-10/14	1P: $36-$48	2P: $42-$48	XP: $5 F5
4/1-6/30	1P: $36-$46	2P: $42-$48	XP: $5 F5
10/15-3/31	1P: $34-$42	2P: $38-$48	XP: $5 F5

Location: I-75, exit 392, 2 mi ne on I-75 business loop. 2049 Ashmun St 49783. Fax: 906/632-4234. **Facility:** 16 one-bedroom standard units. 2 stories (no elevator), exterior corridors. **Parking:** on-site. **Leisure Activities:** playground. **Guest Services:** airport transportation-Sanderson's Field Airport. **Cards:** AX, DC, DS, MC, VI.
(See color ad below)

SOME UNITS

MID-CITY MOTEL
Phone: (906)632-6832

Motel

6/14-10/16	1P: $48-$54	2P: $54-$58	XP: $5 D16
10/17-3/31	1P: $36-$48	2P: $48-$52	XP: $5 D16
4/1-6/13	1P: $36-$48	2P: $46-$52	XP: $5 D16

Location: Just e of town, on I-75 business loop. 304 E Portage Ave 49783. **Facility:** 26 one-bedroom standard units. 2 stories (no elevator), exterior corridors. *Bath:* combo or shower only. **Parking:** on-site, winter plug-ins. **Terms:** small pets only. **Cards:** AX, CB, DC, DS, JC, MC, VI.

SOME UNITS

RAMADA PLAZA HOTEL OJIBWAY *Book at aaa.com*

Phone: (906)632-4100

5/14-10/15	1P: $85-$155	2P: $85-$155	XP: $10	F18
4/1-5/13 & 10/16-3/31	1P: $69-$125	2P: $69-$125	XP: $10	F18

AAA SAVE

Classic
Large-scale Hotel

Location: Just w of I-75 business loop; center of downtown. 240 W Portage Ave 49783. Fax: 906/632-6050. **Facility:** This historic 1928 hotel has renovated common areas. Some rooms overlook the Soo Locks. 71 units. 65 one-bedroom standard units. 6 one-bedroom suites ($150-$250) with whirlpools. 6 stories, interior corridors. **Parking:** on-site, winter plug-ins. **Terms:** cancellation fee imposed, [AP] & [BP] meal plans available, package plans - seasonal. **Amenities:** voice mail, irons, hair dryers. **Dining:** Freighters, see separate listing. **Pool(s):** heated indoor. **Leisure Activities:** sauna, whirlpool, exercise room. **Guest Services:** valet and coin laundry, area transportation. **Business Services:** meeting rooms, business center. **Cards:** AX, DC, DS, MC, VI. **Special Amenities:** free newspaper and early check-in/late check-out. *(See color ad opposite title page)*

SOME UNITS

ROYAL MOTEL

Phone: (906)632-6323

5/1-10/15	1P: $38-$46	2P: $46-$54	XP: $6	F13

Motel

MC, VI.

Location: I-75, exit 392, 2 mi ne on I-75 business loop. Located in a commercial area. 1707 Ashmun St 49783. **Facility:** 20 one-bedroom standard units. 1 story, exterior corridors. *Bath:* combo or shower only. **Parking:** on-site. **Terms:** open 5/1-10/15, small pets only. **Leisure Activities:** playground, basketball. **Cards:** DC,

SOME UNITS

SKYLINE MOTEL

Phone: 906/632-3393

7/1-9/10	1P: $48-$52	2P: $52-$62	XP: $5	F12
9/11-10/15	1P: $34-$44	2P: $42-$48	XP: $5	F12
4/1-6/30 & 10/16-3/31	1P: $32-$38	2P: $38-$48	XP: $5	F12

Motel

Location: I-75, exit 392, 1.5 mi ne. Located in a commercial area. 2601 I-75 Business Loop 49783. **Facility:** 24 one-bedroom standard units. 2 stories (no elevator), exterior corridors. **Parking:** on-site, winter plug-ins. **Terms:** cancellation fee imposed, weekly rates available. **Leisure Activities:** snowmobiling. **Cards:** AX, DS, MC, VI.

SOME UNITS

SUNSET MOTEL

Phone: 906/632-3906

6/1-10/15	1P: $42-$46	2P: $42-$46	XP: $4	

AAA SAVE

Motel

Location: I-75, exit 386, 0.3 mi e to jct SR 28 and CR H-63. 8929 S Mackinaw Tr 49783. **Facility:** 15 one-bedroom standard units. 1 story, exterior corridors. *Bath:* combo or shower only. **Parking:** on-site. **Terms:** open 6/1-10/15, small pets only. **Leisure Activities:** playground, basketball. **Cards:** DS, MC, VI. **Special Amenities:** free local telephone calls.

SOME UNITS

SUPER 8 MOTEL

Phone: 906/632-8882

6/14-10/17	1P: $63-$68	2P: $68-$78	XP: $5	F17
5/3-6/13	1P: $50-$55	2P: $55-$71	XP: $5	F17
4/1-5/2	1P: $44-$49	2P: $49-$65	XP: $5	F17
10/18-3/31	1P: $45-$50	2P: $50-$60	XP: $5	F17

Small-scale Hotel

Location: I-75, exit 392, 0.5 mi ne. Located in a commercial area. 3826 I-75 Business Loop 49783. Fax: 906/632-3766. **Facility:** 61 one-bedroom standard units, some with whirlpools. 2 stories (no elevator), interior corridors. **Parking:** on-site. **Terms:** [CP] meal plan available, pets ($50 deposit). **Leisure Activities:** snowmobiling. **Guest Services:** coin laundry. **Cards:** AX, CB, DC, DS, MC, VI.

SOME UNITS

FEE

WHERE TO DINE

ABNER'S

Lunch: $4-$6   Dinner: $8-$19   Phone: 906/632-4221

American

Location: I-75, exit 392, 1.3 mi ne. 2865 I-75 Business Spur 49783. **Hours:** 8 am-midnight, Sun-10 pm. Closed: 11/25, 12/25. **Reservations:** accepted. **Features:** The "backwoods buffet", available for breakfast, lunch and dinner, lays out a nice variety of home-style dishes made from scratch. Fireplaces, hardwood floors and country antiques contribute to the warm, homey ambience. Service is friendly. Casual dress; cocktails. **Parking:** on-site. **Cards:** AX, DC, MC, VI.

THE ANTLER'S

Lunch: $5-$8   Dinner: $9-$19   Phone: 906/632-3571

American

Location: 8 blks e at end of I-75 business spur. 804 E Portage Ave 49783. **Hours:** 11 am-10 pm, closing times vary in winter. Closed: 11/25, 12/24, 12/25 & Easter. **Features:** More than 200 mounted animals and a bell-and-whistle sound display lend to the casual ambience of the large, noisy restaurant. A tasty homemade barbecue sauce wakes up the flavor in slow-cooked baby back ribs. Service is friendly and efficient. Casual dress; cocktails. **Parking:** on-site. **Cards:** MC, VI.

CUP OF THE DAY

Lunch: $4-$8   Dinner: $4-$8   Phone: 906/635-7272

American

Location: Center. 406 Ashmun St 49783. **Hours:** 7 am-8 pm. Closed: 1/1, 11/25, 12/25. **Features:** As you might guess from the name, the restaurant specializes in coffee drinks. The menu centers on lighter fare—salad, sandwiches and delicious dessert. A wide variety of juice is available at the raw juice bar. Casual dress. **Parking:** street. **Cards:** DS, MC, VI.

FREIGHTERS

Lunch: $7-$10   Dinner: $15-$25   Phone: 906/632-4211

American

Location: Just w of I-75 business loop; center of downtown; in Ramada Plaza Hotel Ojibway. 240 W Portage 49783. **Hours:** 7 am-9 pm. **Features:** Overlooking the Soo Locks and a little park below, the intimate restaurant is a comfortable spot for casual upscale dining. The specials are always a treat, especially the succulent prime rib offered on Sunday nights. Cocktails. **Parking:** on-site. **Cards:** AX, CB, DC, MC, VI.

GREAT WALL

Chinese

Lunch: $4-$6   Dinner: $7-$14   Phone: 906/635-1188

Location: I-75, exit 392, 0.9 mi ne on I-75 business spur. 3440 I-75 Business Spur 49783. **Hours:** 11 am-9:30, Fri & Sat-10:30 pm, Sun 11:30 am-9:30 pm; hours vary off season. Closed: 11/25, 12/25. **Features:** This restaurant features a popular buffet, which has a great selectin of Hunan, Szechuan, and Cantonese-style dishes. Casual dress; beer & wine only. **Parking:** on-site. **Cards:** AX, DS, MC, VI.

LA SENORITA

Mexican

Lunch: $4-$7   Dinner: $8-$13   Phone: 906/632-1114

Location: Jct I-75 and I-75 business spur, exit 392. 4478 I-75 Business Spur 49783. **Hours:** 11 am-10 pm, Fri & Sat-11 pm, Sun noon-10 pm. Closed major holidays. **Reservations:** accepted. **Features:** This family friendly restaurant offers such traditional favorites as burritos, enchiladas and fajitas, as well as mesquite-grilled entrees served in a festive, lively atmosphere. Vibrant Mexican decorations brighten the dining room. Casual dress; cocktails. **Parking:** on-site. **Cards:** AX, DC, DS, MC, VI.

STUDEBAKERS

American

Lunch: $4-$8   Dinner: $9-$20   Phone: 906/632-4262

Location: I-75, exit 392, 0.8 mi ne. 3583 I-75 Business Spur 49783. **Hours:** 7 am-9 pm, Fri & Sat-10 pm; 7 am-10 pm 6/1-10/15. Closed: 11/25, 12/25. **Reservations:** accepted. **Features:** An interesting collection of old Studebaker pictures—as well as parts and other period collectibles—decorates the restaurant, which is likely to stir feelings of nostalgia. The specialty is whitefish, which is served pan-fried, broiled or deep-fried. Casual dress; cocktails. **Parking:** on-site. **Cards:** AX, MC, VI.

The following restaurant has not been evaluated by AAA but is listed for your information only.

FRANK'S PLACE

[fyi]

Phone: 906/632-7487

Not evaluated. **Location:** Center. 123 W Portage Ave 49783. **Features:** This well-established family restaurant is close to the locks, and serves breakfast all day as well as a number of items on the menu from meatball soup, to sandwiches, to traditional dinners.

SAWYER

——— WHERE TO STAY ———

SUPER 8 MOTEL

Small-scale Hotel

Book at aaa.com

Phone: (269)426-8300

5/1-9/30 [CP]	1P: $59-$89	2P: $64-$104
4/1-4/30 & 10/1-3/31 [CP]	1P: $55-$85	2P: $60-$90

Location: I-94, exit 12 (Sawyer Rd), just e. 12850 Super Dr 49125. Fax: 269/426-6500. **Facility:** 61 one-bedroom standard units, some with whirlpools. 3 stories, interior corridors. *Bath:* combo or shower only. **Parking:** on-site. **Terms:** 5 day cancellation notice, weekly rates available, package plans. **Amenities:** voice mail. *Some:* hair dryers. **Pool(s):** heated indoor. **Business Services:** meeting rooms. **Cards:** AX, DC, DS, MC, VI. **Special Amenities:** free continental breakfast and free local telephone calls.

SOME UNITS

——— WHERE TO DINE ———

HORSEFEATHERS RESTAURANT & MARKET

American

Lunch: $8-$15   Dinner: $12-$18   Phone: 269/426-3237

Location: I-94, exit 12 (Sawyer Rd), 0.3 mi w, then just n. 12857 Three Oaks Rd 49125. **Hours:** 11:30 am-10 pm, Fri-11 pm, Sat noon-11 pm, Sun 11 am-10 pm. Closed major holidays. **Features:** Contemporary American cuisine such as hearty soups, harbor chicken marsala and barbecued ribs are all prominently featured in this attractive and whimsical roadside diner. Casual dress; cocktails. **Parking:** on-site. **Cards:** MC, VI.

SHELBYVILLE

——— WHERE TO DINE ———

BAY POINTE RESTAURANT   Historic

American

Lunch: $7-$10   Dinner: $17-$24   Phone: 269/672-5202

Location: US 131, exit 59, 4 mi e on 124th to dead end, then 2 mi s. 11456 Marsh Rd 49344. **Hours:** 11:30 am-3 & 5-10 pm, Sat from 5 pm, Sun 10:30 am-1:30 pm; Fri & Sat 5 pm-10 pm 1/1-3/3. Closed: 12/25; also Mon. **Features:** The 1902 Dutch Colonial house affords beautiful views of the adjacent lake. Specialties of whitefish, Yankee Springs pork loin and roasted duck stand out on the varied menu. Desserts change often. The dining room is casual, with a slightly elegant flair. Semi-formal attire; cocktails. **Parking:** on-site. **Cards:** AX, DS, MC, VI.

SILVER CITY

——— WHERE TO STAY ———

AMERICINN LODGE & SUITES

Large-scale Hotel

Book at aaa.com

Phone: (906)885-5311

6/16-10/15 & 1/1-3/31	1P: $89-$99	2P: $89-$99	XP: $6	F12
4/1-6/15 & 10/16-12/31	1P: $79-$89	2P: $79-$89	XP: $6	F12

Location: On SR 107, 0.3 mi w of SR 64. Located on the shores of Lake Superior. 120 Lincoln Ave (120 Lincoln Ave, ONTONAGON, 49953). Fax: 906/885-5847. **Facility:** 71 units. 65 one-bedroom standard units, some with whirlpools. 6 one-bedroom suites. 3 stories, interior corridors. *Bath:* combo or shower only. **Parking:** on-site, winter plug-ins. **Terms:** cancellation fee imposed, [CP] & [ECP] meal plans available, pets ($10 extra charge, no cats). **Amenities:** irons, hair dryers. **Pool(s):** heated indoor. **Leisure Activities:** sauna, whirlpool, fishing, snowmobiling, exercise room. **Guest Services:** gift shop, coin laundry. **Business Services:** meeting rooms. **Cards:** AX, DC, DS, MC, VI. *(See color ad p 311)*

SOME UNITS

FEE

MOUNTAIN VIEW LODGES

Phone: 906/885-5256

▼▼▼ All Year   1P: $119-$134   2P: $119-$134   XP: $12   D17

Cottage **Location:** Jct SR 107 and 64, 0.8 mi w. Located on the shores of Lake Superior. 237 SR 107 49953 (237 SR 107, ON-
TONAGON). Fax: 906/885-5947. **Facility:** 11 cottages. 1 story, exterior corridors. **Parking:** on-site.
units). **Leisure Activities:** snowmobiling. **Cards:** AX, DS, MC, VI.   **Terms:** check-in 4 pm, 2 night minimum stay, 14 day cancellation notice-fee imposed, pets (in designated

[icons]

TOMLINSON'S RAINBOW LODGING

Phone: (906)885-5348

Ⓐ SAVE 6/15-10/20 & 12/21-3/31   1P: $69-$139   2P: $69-$139   XP: $5   F12
▼▼▼   4/1-6/14 & 10/21-12/20   1P: $50-$125   2P: $55-$125   XP: $5   F12

Motel **Location:** SR 64, just e of jct SR 107. Located opposite Lake Superior. 2900 SR 64 49953 (2900 SR 64, ONTONAGON).
Fax: 906/885-5272. **Facility:** 17 units. 12 one-bedroom standard units, some with kitchens. 2 one-, 1 two-
and 1 three-bedroom suites ($85-$99), some with efficiencies, kitchens and/or whirlpools. 1 vacation home
($139). 1 story, exterior corridors. *Bath:* combo or shower only. **Parking:** on-site, winter plug-ins. **Terms:** 7
day cancellation notice, weekly rates available, [ECP] meal plan available, small pets only ($5 fee, $50 deposit, no cats). **Leisure
Activities:** sauna, whirlpool, paddleboats, snowmobiling, screen-house gazebo on Lake Superior, playground. *Fee:* miniature
golf. **Guest Services:** coin laundry, tanning facility. **Cards:** AX, DS, MC, VI.

SOME UNITS

[icons] / [icons] /

SOUTHFIELD —*See Detroit p. 277.*

SOUTHGATE —*See Detroit p. 281.*

SOUTH HAVEN pop. 5,021

——— **WHERE TO STAY** ———

CARRIAGE HOUSE AT THE HARBOR BED & BREAKFAST

Phone: 269/639-2161

Ⓐ SAVE All Year   2P: $120-$280

▼▼◆▼ **Location:** 1.2 mi n of downtown on Dyckman Ave, just s on North Shore Dr. Located in a residential area. 118 Woodman
St 49090. Fax: 269/639-2308. **Facility:** Just a block from Lake Michigan, this B&B is decorated with antiques
Bed & Breakfast and others rooms with gas fireplaces or views of the harbor. Smoke free premises. 11 one-bedroom standard
units, some with whirlpools. 3 stories (no elevator), interior corridors. *Bath:* combo or shower only. **Parking:**
on-site. **Terms:** 2 night minimum stay - weekends 5/1-10/31, age restrictions may apply. **Amenities:** video
library, hair dryers. **Business Services:** meeting rooms. **Cards:** AX, MC, VI.

[icons]

GUESTHOUSE INTERNATIONAL LIGHTHOUSE INN   *Book at aaa.com*

Phone: (269)639-9900

Ⓐ SAVE 5/21-9/6 [ECP]   1P: $89-$145   2P: $89-$145   XP: $5   F18
         9/7-11/1 [ECP]   1P: $89-$105   2P: $89-$105   XP: $5   F18
▼▼◆▼   4/1-5/20 [ECP]   1P: $79-$99   2P: $79-$99   XP: $5   F18
         .11/2-3/31 [ECP]   1P: $69-$89   2P: $69-$89   XP: $5   F18

Small-scale Hotel **Location:** I-196, exit 20 (Phoenix Rd), just e. 1555 Phoenix St 49090. Fax: 269/639-8068. **Facility:** 91 units. 90
one-bedroom standard units, some with whirlpools. 1 one-bedroom suite ($119-$205) with whirlpool. 3 sto-
ries, interior corridors. *Bath:* combo or shower only. **Parking:** on-site, winter plug-ins. **Terms:** check-in 4 pm, 3 day cancellation
notice. **Amenities:** irons, hair dryers. *Some:* DVD players. **Pool(s):** heated indoor. **Leisure Activities:** whirlpool, exercise room.
Guest Services: coin laundry. **Business Services:** meeting rooms. **Cards:** AX, DS, MC, VI. **Special Amenities:** free expanded
continental breakfast and free newspaper.

SOME UNITS

[icons] / [icons] /

HAMPTON INN   *Book at aaa.com*

Phone: 269/639-8550

▼▼◆▼ All Year   1P: $79-$179   2P: $79-$179

Small-scale Hotel **Location:** I-196, exit 20 (Phoenix Rd), just e. 04299 Cecilia Dr 49090. Fax: 269/639-8555. **Facility:** 62 units. 60
one-bedroom standard units, some with whirlpools. 2 one-bedroom suites with whirlpools. 3 stories, interior
corridors. *Bath:* combo or shower only. **Parking:** on-site. **Terms:** [ECP] meal plan available. **Amenities:** dual
phone lines, voice mail, irons, hair dryers. **Pool(s):** heated indoor. **Leisure Activities:** whirlpool, exercise room. **Guest Services:**
coin laundry. **Business Services:** meeting rooms. **Cards:** AX, CB, DC, DS, JC, MC, VI.

SOME UNITS

[icons] / [icons] /

HOLIDAY INN EXPRESS HOTEL & SUITES   *Book at aaa.com*

Phone: (269)637-8800

▼▼◆▼ 6/1-9/12 [ECP]   1P: $99-$199   2P: $99-$199   XP: $10   F18
        4/1-5/31 [ECP]   1P: $69-$149   2P: $69-$149   XP: $10   F18
Small-scale Hotel 9/13-11/30 [ECP]   1P: $79-$129   2P: $79-$129   XP: $10   F18
        12/1-3/31 [ECP]   1P: $69-$109   2P: $69-$109   XP: $10   F18

Location: I-196, exit 20 (Phoenix Rd), 0.5 mi e. 1741 Phoenix Rd 49090. Fax: 269/637-8810. **Facility:** 62 units. 61 one-bedroom standard units, some with whirlpools. 1 one-bedroom suite with whirlpool. 3 stories, interior corridors. *Bath:* combo or shower only.
Parking: on-site. **Amenities:** dual phone lines, voice mail, irons, hair dryers. **Pool(s):** heated indoor. **Leisure Activities:** exercise room. **Guest Services:** valet laundry. **Business Services:** meeting rooms. **Cards:** AX, DC, DS, MC, VI.

SOME UNITS

[icons] / [icons] /

INN AT THE PARK BED & BREAKFAST

Phone: 269/639-1776

▼▼◆▼ 7/1-9/6 [BP]   1P: $140-$235   2P: $140-$235
        9/7-10/31 [BP]   1P: $110-$205   2P: $110-$205
        4/1-6/30 [BP]   1P: $80-$205   2P: $80-$205
Bed & Breakfast 11/1-3/31 [BP]   1P: $80-$175   2P: $80-$175

Location: I-196, exit 20 (Phoenix Rd), 0.9 mi w, just n on Broadway, then just w; across the bridge. 233 Dyckman Ave 49090.
Fax: 269/639-2409. **Facility:** Stained glass and sun-filled common areas add to the appeal of this Victorian-style home resembling a country inn. Smoke free premises. 9 one-bedroom standard units, some with whirlpools. 2 stories (no elevator), interior
corridors. *Bath:* combo or shower only. **Parking:** on-site. **Terms:** 2-3 night minimum stay - weekends, age restrictions may apply,
14 day cancellation notice. **Amenities:** video library. **Business Services:** meeting rooms. **Cards:** AX, MC, VI.

[icons]

Free Breakfast Bar

- **Clean Comfortable Rooms**

- **Indoor Pool & Spa** (at most locations)

- **Free Local Phone Calls**

- **Data Port Access**

- **In-room Hair Dryers, Iron & Ironing Boards**

- **Priority Club® Worldwide Program - Free Airline Miles**

Stay Smart®
& SAVE UP TO
20% OFF
PUBLISHED ROOM RATES

Valid only at participating Michigan Holiday Inn Express® Hotels. Present coupon at check-in only. Not valid with any other discounts.

Stay Smart®
& SAVE UP TO
20% OFF
PUBLISHED ROOM RATES

Valid only at participating Michigan Holiday Inn Express® Hotels. Present coupon at check-in only. Not valid with any other discounts.

Stay Smart®
& SAVE UP TO
20% OFF
PUBLISHED ROOM RATES

Valid only at participating Michigan Holiday Inn Express® Hotels. Present coupon at check-in only. Not valid with any other discounts.

Stay Smart®
& SAVE UP TO
20% OFF
PUBLISHED ROOM RATES

Valid only at participating Michigan Holiday Inn Express® Hotels. Present coupon at check-in only. Not valid with any other discounts.

Holiday Inn Express® Hotels are conveniently located throughout Michigan.
Check AAA listings within this book or call 1-800-HOLIDAY to make your reservations.

Allen Park •
3600 Enterprise Dr.
313-323-3500

Coldwater
630 E. Chicago St.
517-279-0900

Canton •
3950 S. Lotz Road
734-721-5500

Houghton Lake
200 Cloverleaf Lane
989-422-STAY (7829)

Indian River
4375 Brudy Rd.
231-238-3000

Lansing / Okemos
2187 University Park Dr.
517-347-6690

Ludington
5323 West US 10
231-845-7004

New Buffalo •
11500 Holiday Dr.
269-469-1400

Pellston
1600 US 31 N
231-539-7000

Port Huron •
1720 Hancock St.
810-987-5999

Sault Ste. Marie
1171 Riverview Way
906-632-3999

Traverse City •
3536 Mt. Hope Rd.
231-938-2600

• Denotes Holiday Inn Express®
Hotel & Suites location

Stay Smart®

Free Breakfast Bar

- **Clean Comfortable Rooms**
- **Indoor Pool & Spa** (at most locations)
- **Free Local Phone Calls**
- **Data Port Access**
- **In-room Hair Dryers, Iron & Ironing Boards**
- **Priority Club® Worldwide Program - Free Airline Miles**

Holiday Inn EXPRESS®

Stay Smart®

Stay Smart®
& SAVE UP TO
20% OFF
PUBLISHED ROOM RATES

Valid only at participating Michigan Holiday Inn Express® Hotels. Present coupon at check-in only. Not valid with any other discounts.

Stay Smart®
& SAVE UP TO
20% OFF
PUBLISHED ROOM RATES

Valid only at participating Michigan Holiday Inn Express® Hotels. Present coupon at check-in only. Not valid with any other discounts.

Stay Smart®
& SAVE UP TO
20% OFF
PUBLISHED ROOM RATES

Valid only at participating Michigan Holiday Inn Express® Hotels. Present coupon at check-in only. Not valid with any other discounts.

Stay Smart®
& SAVE UP TO
20% OFF
PUBLISHED ROOM RATES

Valid only at participating Michigan Holiday Inn Express® Hotels. Present coupon at check-in only. Not valid with any other discounts.

Holiday Inn Express® Hotels are conveniently located throughout Michigan.
Check AAA listings within this book or call 1-800-HOLIDAY to make your reservations.

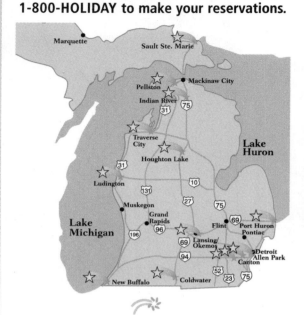

Holiday Inn EXPRESS®

Allen Park •
3600 Enterprise Dr.
313-323-3500

Coldwater
630 E. Chicago St.
517-279-0900

Canton •
3950 S. Lotz Road
734-721-5500

Houghton Lake
200 Cloverleaf Lane
989-422-STAY (7829)

Indian River
4375 Brudy Rd.
231-238-3000

Lansing / Okemos
2187 University Park Dr.
517-347-6690

Ludington
5323 West US 10
231-845-7004

New Buffalo •
11500 Holiday Dr.
269-469-1400

Pellston
1600 US 31 N
231-539-7000

Port Huron •
1720 Hancock St.
810-987-5999

Sault Ste. Marie
1171 Riverview Way
906-632-3999

Traverse City •
3536 Mt. Hope Rd.
231-938-2600

• Denotes Holiday Inn Express®
Hotel & Suites location

Stay Smart®

OLD HARBOR INN

Phone: (269)637-8480

AAA [SAVE]

6/1-8/31	1P: $119-$299	2P: $119-$299	XP: $10 F18
9/1-10/31	1P: $79-$219	2P: $79-$219	XP: $10 F18
4/1-5/31	1P: $79-$209	2P: $79-$209	XP: $10 F18
11/1-3/31	1P: $79-$199	2P: $79-$199	XP: $10 F18

Small-scale Hotel **Location:** I-196, exit 20 (Phoenix Rd), 1 mi w, just n on Center St. Overlooking the marina. 515 Williams St 49090. Fax: 269/637-9496. **Facility:** 44 units. 43 one-bedroom standard units, some with efficiencies and/or whirlpools. 1 two-bedroom suite ($199-$299). 3 stories, interior/exterior corridors. **Parking:** on-site. **Terms:** [CP] meal plan available. **Amenities:** irons. *Some:* hair dryers. **Dining:** 5 pm-10 pm, cocktails. **Pool(s):** small heated indoor. **Leisure Activities:** whirlpool. **Guest Services:** coin laundry. **Business Services:** meeting rooms. **Cards:** AX, DC, DS, MC, VI. **Special Amenities:** free continental breakfast and free local telephone calls.

SOME UNITS

SAND CASTLE INN

Phone: 269/639-1110

All Year [BP]	1P: $125-$275	2P: $125-$275	XP: $20

Bed & Breakfast **Location:** I-196, exit 20 (Phoenix Rd), 0.9 mi w, just n on Broadway, then just w; across the bridge. 203 Dyckman Ave 49090. Fax: 269/637-1050. **Facility:** The inn offers a retreat-like ambience and is within walking distance of the river, the lake and downtown. Smoke free premises. 9 one-bedroom standard units. 3 stories (no elevator), interior/exterior corridors. *Bath:* shower only. **Parking:** on-site. **Terms:** age restrictions may apply, 10 day cancellation notice-fee imposed. **Amenities:** video library, hair dryers. **Cards:** AX, DS, MC, VI.

THE VICTORIA RESORT B&B

Phone: 269/637-6414

5/28-8/31 [ECP]	1P: $90-$185	2P: $90-$185	XP: $20
9/1-10/31 [ECP]	1P: $65-$165	2P: $65-$165	XP: $15
4/1-5/27 & 11/1-3/31 [ECP]	1P: $59-$145	2P: $59-$145	XP: $10

Small-scale Hotel **Location:** I-196, exit 20 (Phoenix Rd), 0.9 mi w, just n on Broadway to Dyckman Ave, just w to Park St, 0.4 mi n, then just e. 241 Oak St 49090. Fax: 269/637-6127. **Facility:** Designated smoking area. 14 units. 7 one-bedroom standard units, some with whirlpools. 5 cottages ($1190-$1295), some with whirlpools. 2 one-bedroom suites with whirlpools. 1-2 stories (no elevator), interior/exterior corridors. **Parking:** on-site. **Terms:** 2 night minimum stay - weekends, 7 day cancellation notice-fee imposed, package plans - seasonal & 11/1-4/30, no pets allowed (owner's pets on premises). **Amenities:** video library, hair dryers. **Pool(s):** outdoor. **Leisure Activities:** tennis court, bicycles, playground, basketball, shuffleboard. **Cards:** MC, VI.

SOME UNITS

──────── **WHERE TO DINE** ────────

CLEMENTINE'S

American

Lunch: $9-$14 **Dinner:** $9-$20 Phone: 269/637-4755

Location: I-196, exit 20 (Phoenix Rd), 2.5 mi w. 500 Phoenix St 49090. **Hours:** 11 am-11 pm, Fri & Sat-midnight, Sun noon-11 pm. Closed major holidays. **Features:** This is a relaxed, family restaurant located right downtown. The menu features alot of salad and lighter entrees with the house specialty being a hot apple dumpling dessert. Casual dress; cocktails. **Parking:** street. **Cards:** AX, DS, MC, VI.

HAWKSHEAD

American

Lunch: $8-$14 **Dinner:** $17-$30 Phone: 269/639-2146

Location: I-196, exit 22, just e on N Shore Dr, 2.5 mi n on 71st St/103rd Ave, then 0.4 mi e. 6959 105th Ave 49090. **Hours:** 11 am-9:30 pm. Closed major holidays. **Reservations:** accepted. **Features:** Located in a converted Tudor house, this relaxing space with large floor to ceiling windows allows a good view of the golf course and landscaped gardens. A creative touch is evident on this continental menu that not only offers steaks and duck but also seafood such as shrimp and locally caught whitefish. Dressy casual; cocktails. **Parking:** on-site. **Cards:** MC, VI.

MAGNOLIA GRILLE AT THE IDLER RIVERBOAT

American

Lunch: $7-$12 **Dinner:** $17-$23 Phone: 269/637-8435

Location: I-196, exit 20 (Phoenix Rd), 1 mi w, just n on Center St; in Old Harbor Village. 515 Williams St #10 49090. **Hours:** Open 5/1-9/11; 11 am-2 & 5-10 pm, Fri & Sat-11 pm, Sun 11 am-3 & 4-9 pm. **Reservations:** suggested, weekends. **Features:** Docked at Nichols Landing on the Black River, the floating riverboat restaurant has many windows that look out at natural settings. Blackened prime rib, Bloody Mary linguine and piquant seafood jambalaya are representative of tasty menu offerings. Casual dress; cocktails. **Parking:** street. **Cards:** AX, DC, DS, MC, VI.

PHOENIX STREET CAFE

Deli/Subs
Sandwiches

Lunch: $5-$7 Phone: 269/637-3600

Location: I-196, exit 20 (Phoenix Rd). 524 Phoenix St 49090. **Hours:** 7 am-3 pm. Closed major holidays. **Features:** Resort posters adorn the walls of this cheerful downtown restaurant, specializing in house made soups and an extensive sandwich menu. Casual dress. **Parking:** on-site and street. **Cards:** AX, MC, VI.

SEAWOLF RESTAURANT

American

Dinner: $21-$35 Phone: 269/637-2007

Location: I-196, exit 2 (North Shore Dr), 1 mi w, then 0.5 mi n. 176 Blue Star Hwy 49090. **Hours:** Open 5/12-12/31; 5 pm-10 pm, Sun-9 pm. Closed major holidays; also Mon-Wed 10/1-12/31. **Reservations:** accepted. **Features:** A short distance from the hotels, the casually refined restaurant has been in business since 1922. Seasonal produce is integrated into such traditional dishes as tangerine martini shrimp, pan-seared chicken breasts stuffed with seafood and grilled lamb chops. Casual dress; wine only. **Parking:** on-site. **Cards:** MC, VI.

THE THREE PELICANS

American

Lunch: $7-$13 **Dinner:** $16-$30 Phone: 269/637-5123

Location: I-196, exit 22 (Phoenix Rd), 0.9 mi w, just n on Broadway, 0.5 mi w on Dyckman Ave, then just s. 38 North Shore Dr 49090. **Hours:** Open 4/25-10/24; 11:30 am-10 pm, Fri & Sat-11 pm, Sun-9 pm; hours and days vary, call to verify. **Reservations:** suggested. **Features:** The atmosphere is nautical inside the cozy restaurant, a favorite spot for boaters and beachgoers. Ribs stand out on a menu of traditional surf and turf choices. Opt for seating on the outdoor deck to watch boats pass by on the peaceful Black River. Casual dress; cocktails. **Parking:** on-site. **Cards:** AX, DC, DS, MC, VI.

SPRING LAKE pop. 2,514

------- WHERE TO STAY -------

GRAND HAVEN WATERFRONT HOLIDAY INN *Book at aaa.com* **Phone:** (616)846-1000

▼▼▼▼ 7/1-9/4 1P: $169-$199 2P: $169-$199 XP: $20 F17
5/21-6/30 1P: $149-$179 2P: $149-$179 XP: $20 F17
4/1-5/20 & 9/5-3/31 1P: $129-$149 2P: $129-$149 XP: $20 F17

Large-scale Hotel **Location:** On SR 104, just e of US 131. Located on the river. 940 W Savidge St 49456. **Fax:** 616/846-0462. **Facility:** 123 one-bedroom standard units, some with whirlpools. 4 stories, interior corridors. *Bath:* combo or shower only. **Parking:** on-site. **Terms:** check-in 4 pm, 2-3 night minimum stay - weekends 6/1-8/31, cancellation fee imposed, [AP] meal plan available, package plans, pets ($25 extra charge, dogs only). **Amenities:** dual phone lines, voice mail, irons, hair dryers. **Pool(s):** heated outdoor, heated indoor. **Leisure Activities:** whirlpool, recreation programs, bicycles, exercise room, horseshoes, volleyball. *Fee:* charter fishing. **Guest Services:** valet and coin laundry. **Business Services:** meeting rooms. **Cards:** AX, CB, DC, DS, JC, MC, VI.

(ASK) (S/D) 🛏 🍴 🍸 📺 🏊 ✕ 🎦 (DATA PORT) 💻 / ✕ 🛗 SOME UNITS FEE

STERLING pop. 533

------- WHERE TO DINE -------

IVA'S CHICKEN DINNERS **Lunch:** $5-$7 **Dinner:** $8-$14 **Phone:** 989/654-3552

(AAA) **Location:** I-75, exit 195, 1.8 mi e on Sterling Rd/State, 0.3 mi s on Saginaw St, follow signs. 201 Chestnut St 48659. **Hours:** 11:30 am-8:30 pm. Closed: Tues 11/16-1/14 & Mon-Wed 1/15-5/15. **Features:** Family-owned since ▼▼ 1938, the restaurant—in a late-19th-century house—features family- and plate-style chicken, steak, chops and seafood. Pictures around the laid-back dining room are of a religious nature. Servers are friendly and

American efficient. Casual dress; cocktails. **Parking:** on-site. **Cards:** MC, VI.

✕

STERLING HEIGHTS —*See Detroit p. 282.*

STEVENSVILLE pop. 1,191

------- WHERE TO STAY -------

BAYMONT INN & SUITES-ST. JOSEPH (STEVENSVILLE) *Book at aaa.com* **Phone:** (269)428-9111

(AAA) (SAVE) 6/1-8/31 1P: $69-$89 2P: $69-$89
4/1-5/31 & 9/1-3/31 1P: $59-$79 2P: $59-$79

▼▼▼ **Location:** I-94, exit 23, just w. 2601 W Marquette Woods Rd 49127. **Fax:** 269/428-6774. **Facility:** 100 units. 98 one-bedroom standard units. 2 one-bedroom suites ($79-$89), some with kitchens. 3 stories, interior corri-

Small-scale Hotel dors. *Bath:* combo or shower only. **Parking:** on-site. **Terms:** [ECP] meal plan available, small pets only. **Amenities:** video games (fee), voice mail, irons, hair dryers. **Guest Services:** valet and coin laundry. **Business Services:** meeting rooms. **Cards:** AX, DC, DS, MC, VI. **Special Amenities:** free local telephone calls and free newspaper.

(S/D) 🛏 🍴 (&M) 🦽 📷 ♿ 🎦 (DATA PORT) 💻 / ✕ 🛗 🖨 / SOME UNITS

HAMPTON INN *Book at aaa.com* **Phone:** (269)429-2700

▼▼▼ 5/1-10/31 [ECP] 1P: $99-$119 2P: $99-$119
4/1-4/30 & 11/1-3/31 [ECP] 1P: $89 2P: $89

Small-scale Hotel **Location:** I-94, exit 23, just se. 5050 Red Arrow Hwy 49127. **Fax:** 269/429-5552. **Facility:** 75 one-bedroom standard units, some with whirlpools. 3 stories, interior corridors. *Bath:* combo or shower only. **Parking:** on-site. **Amenities:** video games, dual phone lines, voice mail, irons, hair dryers. **Pool(s):** heated indoor. **Guest Services:** valet laundry. **Business Services:** meeting rooms, fax (fee). **Cards:** AX, DS, MC, VI.

(ASK) (S/D) 🛏 🍴 (&M) 🦽 📷 ♿ 🎦 (DATA PORT) 💻 / ✕ 🛗 🖨 SOME UNITS FEE

PARK INN INTERNATIONAL *Book at aaa.com* **Phone:** (269)429-3218

(AAA) (SAVE) 5/21-9/5 [BP] 1P: $89-$119 2P: $89-$119 XP: $8 F18
4/1-5/20 & 9/6-3/31 [BP] 1P: $69-$74 2P: $69-$74 XP: $8 F18

▼▼ ▼▼ **Location:** I-94, exit 23, 0.5 mi n. 4290 Red Arrow Hwy 49127. **Fax:** 269/429-8882. **Facility:** 90 units. 81 one-bedroom standard units, some with efficiencies and/or whirlpools. 9 one-bedroom suites ($109-$154), some

Small-scale Hotel with efficiencies and/or whirlpools. 2 stories (no elevator), interior/exterior corridors. *Bath:* combo or shower only. **Parking:** on-site. **Amenities:** high-speed Internet, voice mail, irons, hair dryers. **Dining:** 6 am-9 pm, Fri & Sat-10 pm, Sun 7:30 am-2 pm, cocktails. **Pool(s):** small heated outdoor, heated indoor. **Leisure Activities:** whirlpool, bocci, exercise room, basketball, horseshoes, shuffleboard, volleyball. **Guest Services:** valet and coin laundry. **Business Services:** meeting rooms. **Cards:** AX, CB, DC, DS, JC, MC, VI.

(S/D) 🛏 🍴 🦽 📷 ✕ 🎦 (DATA PORT) 💻 / ✕ 🛗 🖨 / SOME UNITS FEE FEE

------- *The following lodging was either not evaluated or did not* -------
meet AAA rating requirements but is listed for your information only.

CHALET ON THE LAKE **Phone:** 269/465-6365

(fyi) Did not meet all AAA rating requirements for some guest rooms at time of last evaluation on 06/25/2003. **Location:** I-94, exit 23 (John Beers), just w, then 0.8 mi n. 5340 Notre Dame Ave 49127. Facilities, services, and decor

Cottage characterize a mid-range property.

——— **WHERE TO DINE** ———

GRANDE MERE INN
Steak & Seafood
Dinner: $11-$23   **Phone:** 269/429-3591
Location: I-94, exit 23, 1.5 mi s. 5800 Red Arrow Hwy 49127. **Hours:** 4:30 pm-9:30 pm, Fri & Sat-10 pm. Closed major holidays; also Sun & Mon. **Reservations:** suggested. **Features:** The popular restaurant is a local favorite for fresh seafood specialties, including blue gill and lake perch, as well as succulent ribs. Views of Lake Michigan are certain to enhance your experience. Try to save room for dessert; it won't disappoint.
Casual dress; cocktails. **Parking:** on-site. **Cards:** AX, DC, DS, MC, VI.

SCHULER'S
American
Lunch: $8-$11   **Dinner:** $10-$24   **Phone:** 269/429-3273
Location: I-94, exit 23, just sw. 5000 Red Arrow Hwy 49127. **Hours:** 11 am-10 pm, Fri-11 pm, Sat noon-11 pm, Sun noon-9 pm. **Closed:** 12/25. **Features:** Cozy and trendy define the atmosphere in the casual dining room, which is inviting to all members of the family. Attractive artwork hangs on cream-painted barn-siding walls. Representative of menu choices are pork medallions in a sweet sauce. Casual dress; cocktails.
Parking: on-site. **Cards:** AX, DC, DS, MC, VI.

STURGIS pop. 11,285

——— **WHERE TO STAY** ———

GREEN BRIAR MOTOR LODGE
AAA [SAVE]
Motel
Phone: (269)651-2361

	1P:	2P:	XP:	
5/1-10/31	1P: $38-$42	2P: $48-$55	XP: $5	F10
4/1-4/30 & 11/1-3/31	1P: $28-$32	2P: $32-$38	XP: $4	F10

Location: I-90, exit 121 (SR 66), 0.4 mi n. 71381 S Centerville Rd 49091. **Fax:** 269/651-2361. **Facility:** 19 one-bedroom standard units. 1 story, exterior corridors. **Parking:** on-site. **Terms:** weekly rates available, small pets only ($5 extra charge). **Pool(s):** outdoor. **Cards:** AX, DS, MC, VI.

SOME UNITS

HAMPTON INN
AAA [SAVE]
Small-scale Hotel
Book at aaa.com
Phone: (269)651-4210

	1P:	2P:
4/1-4/30 & 11/1-3/31 [ECP]	1P: $89-$129	2P: $94-$134
4/1-4/30 & 11/1-3/31 [ECP]	1P: $79-$129	2P: $84-$134

Location: I-90, exit 121 (SR 66), 0.4 mi n. 71451 S Centerville Rd 49091. **Fax:** 269/651-7085. **Facility:** 60 one-bedroom standard units. 3 stories, interior corridors. *Bath:* combo or shower only. **Parking:** on-site. **Amenities:** voice mail, irons. **Pool(s):** heated indoor. **Leisure Activities:** whirlpool. **Business Services:** fax. **Cards:** AX, CB, DC, DS, MC, VI.

SOME UNITS

SUTTONS BAY pop. 589

——— **WHERE TO STAY** ———

RED LION MOTOR LODGE
Motel
Phone: 231/271-6694

	1P:	2P:	XP:	
6/1-9/1	1P: $90-$110	2P: $95-$115	XP: $10	F18
9/2-3/31	1P: $65-$95	2P: $75-$105	XP: $10	F18
4/1-5/31	1P: $65-$95	2P: $75-$95	XP: $10	F18

Location: 5 mi s on SR 22. Located opposite the bay on main highway. 4290 S West Bay Shore Rd 49682. **Fax:** 231/271-5227. **Facility:** Smoke free premises. 16 units. 14 one- and 2 two-bedroom standard units, some with efficiencies. 1 story, exterior corridors. *Bath:* combo or shower only. **Parking:** on-site, winter plug-ins. **Terms:** pets ($10 extra charge). **Cards:** AX, DS, MC, VI.

SOME UNITS

——— **WHERE TO DINE** ———

BOONE'S PRIME TIME PUB
American
Lunch: $6-$9   **Dinner:** $12-$20   **Phone:** 231/271-6688
Location: On SR 22; center. 102 St. Joseph Ave 49682. **Hours:** 11 am-11 pm, Sun from noon. **Closed:** 11/25, 12/25 & Easter. **Features:** Specialties here include steak, shrimp, fish, chicken, soup and sandwiches. Casual dress; cocktails. **Parking:** street. **Cards:** MC, VI.

CAFE BLISS
Seafood
Dinner: $14-$27   **Phone:** 231/271-5000
Location: On SR 22; center. 420 St. Joseph's Ave 49682. **Hours:** Open 5/31-10/31; 5 pm-10 pm. **Closed:** Mon. **Reservations:** suggested. **Features:** Although this restaurant is specializing in seafood, they are well known for their vegetarian and ethnic cuisine. They use natural, fresh, healthful ingredients. A small number of their house specialties are sold in jars, and make a nice gift. Casual dress; cocktails. **Parking:** street. **Cards:** AX, DS, MC, VI.

EDDIE'S VILLAGE INN
American
Lunch: $4-$8   **Dinner:** $9-$17   **Phone:** 231/271-3300
Location: On SR 22; center. 201 St. Joseph Ave 49682. **Hours:** 7 am-10 pm. **Closed:** 11/25, 12/25. **Features:** Established in 1871 as the Union Hotel, the popular restaurant serves traditional fare, as well as several Mexican dishes and daily specials. Casual dress; cocktails. **Parking:** on-site. **Cards:** MC, VI.

TAWAS CITY pop. 2,005

——— WHERE TO STAY ———

DALE MOTEL
(AAA) (SAVE)
◆◆◆◆
Motel

Phone: 989/362-6153

5/1-10/31	1P: $45-$70	2P: $50-$82	XP: $6 D14
4/1-4/30 & 11/1-3/31	1P: $35-$50	2P: $40-$60	XP: $6 D14

Location: On US 23, 1.6 mi s. Located in a semi-commercial area. 1086 US 23 S 48763. Fax: 989/362-6154. **Facility:** 16 one-bedroom standard units. 1 story, exterior corridors. **Parking:** on-site, winter plug-ins. **Terms:** 5 day cancellation notice-fee imposed, weekly rates available, package plans. **Cards:** AX, DC, MC, VI.

SOME UNITS
📷 🔳 📺 / ✕ /

DAYS INN-TAWAS CITY   *Book at aaa.com*
(AAA) (SAVE)
◆◆◆◆ ◆◆◆◆
Small-scale Hotel

Phone: (989)362-0088

7/1-9/6 [ECP]	1P: $120-$130	2P: $120-$130	XP: $6 F18
4/1-6/30 & 9/7-3/31 [ECP]	1P: $70-$100	2P: $70-$100	XP: $6 F18

Location: 1.5 mi s on US 23. 1020 W Lake St 48763. Fax: 989/362-0088. **Facility:** 41 one-bedroom standard units, some with whirlpools. 2 stories (no elevator), interior corridors. **Parking:** on-site. **Terms:** check-in 4 pm, 3 day cancellation notice, package plans - seasonal. **Amenities:** irons, hair dryers. **Pool(s):** heated indoor. **Leisure Activities:** whirlpool, putting green, playground. **Guest Services:** coin laundry. **Business Services:** meeting rooms. **Cards:** AX, DC, DS, MC, VI. **Special Amenities:** free expanded continental breakfast and free local telephone calls. *(See color ad card insert)*

SOME UNITS
🆂🅳 🏊 ✕ 📷 🖥️ 🔳 📺 📺 / ✕ /

TAWAS MOTEL-RESORT
(AAA) (SAVE)
◆◆◆◆
Motel

Phone: (989)362-3822

5/15-9/20 [CP]	1P: $55-$85	2P: $55-$85
4/1-5/14 & 9/21-3/31 [CP]	1P: $35-$50	2P: $45-$65

Location: On US 23, 1.8 mi s. 1124 US 23 S 48764 (PO Box 248). Fax: 989/362-3822. **Facility:** 19 one-bedroom standard units, some with whirlpools. 1 story, exterior corridors. **Bath:** combo or shower only. **Parking:** on-site, winter plug-ins. **Terms:** package plans, pets (with prior approval). **Pool(s):** heated outdoor. **Leisure Activities:** sauna, whirlpool, playground, basketball, horseshoes, shuffleboard. **Fee:** game room. **Cards:** AX, DS, MC, VI. **Special Amenities:** free local telephone calls and preferred room (subject to availability with advanced reservations).

SOME UNITS
🆂🅳 🛏️ 🏊 ✕ 📷 🔳 / ✕ 🖥️ 📺 📺 /

TAYLOR —*See Detroit p. 283.*

TECUMSEH pop. 8,574

——— WHERE TO STAY ———

TECUMSEH INN MOTEL
◆◆◆◆
Motel

Phone: 517/423-7401

All Year	1P: $49	2P: $55	XP: $5 F16

Location: On SR 50, 1.5 mi w. 1445 W Chicago Blvd 49286. Fax: 517/423-3324. **Facility:** 61 one-bedroom standard units. 2 stories (no elevator), interior corridors. **Parking:** on-site. **Terms:** small pets only ($25 deposit). **Dining:** Fox's Pizza Den, see separate listing. **Guest Services:** complimentary evening beverages, valet laundry. **Cards:** AX, MC, VI.

SOME UNITS
🛏️ 🍴 🍸 📷 🖥️ 📺 / ✕ 📼 🔳 📺 /
FEE

——— WHERE TO DINE ———

EVANS STREET STATION
(AAA)
◆◆◆◆ ◆◆◆◆
American

Lunch: $8-$12   Dinner: $12-$25   Phone: 517/424-5555

Location: Just s of SR 50; 15 mi w of US 23, exit 17 (Dundee); downtown. 110 S Evans St 49286. **Hours:** 11 am-9 pm, Fri-10 pm, Sat 4 pm-10 pm, Sun 10 am-2 pm. Closed major holidays. **Reservations:** accepted. **Features:** Ansel Adams prints adorn the walls of this upscale yet comfortable family owned restaurant. Global influences run rampant through the creative menu, which features a wide range of seafood, pasta and steaks. Dressy casual; cocktails. **Parking:** on-site. **Cards:** AX, DS, MC, VI.

🅼 🍸 ✕

FOX'S PIZZA DEN
◆◆◆◆
Pizza

Dinner: $6-$10   Phone: 517/423-7000

Location: On SR 50, 1.5 mi w; in Tecumseh Inn Motel. 1441 W Chicago Blvd 49286. **Hours:** 4:30 pm-10 pm. Closed major holidays; also Mon. **Features:** This family-style pizzeria delivers a wide assortment of gourmet pizza, stromboli, hoagies and sandwiches. The owner's hobby is airplanes, which is appropriately reflected in the many aviation pictures that adorn the walls. Casual dress; beer & wine only. **Parking:** on-site. **Cards:** AX, MC, VI.

✕

THOMPSONVILLE pop. 457

------ WHERE TO STAY ------

CRYSTAL MOUNTAIN   *Book at aaa.com*   Phone: (231)378-2000

(AAA) (SAVE)
▼▼▼

Resort
Small-scale Hotel

12/1-3/31	1P: $89-$299	2P: $89-$299	XP: $20 F6
4/1-11/30	1P: $79-$289	2P: $79-$289	XP: $20 F6

Location: On SR 115, 2 mi w. 12500 Crystal Mountain Dr 49683. Fax: 231/378-2998. **Facility:** This scenic year-round resort on Michigan's Lower Peninsula features golf as well as downhill and cross-country skiing. 222 units. 83 one-bedroom standard units, some with efficiencies and/or whirlpools. 51 one- and 29 two-bedroom suites ($129-$439), some with kitchens and/or whirlpools. 59 cottages, some with whirlpools. 1-3 stories (no elevator), interior/exterior corridors. **Bath:** combo or shower only. **Parking:** on-site. **Terms:** check-in 6 pm, 14 day cancellation notice-fee imposed, [MAP] meal plan available. **Amenities:** irons, hair dryers. *Some:* voice mail. **Dining:** 2 restaurants, 11 am-10 pm, Fri & Sat-11 pm, also, The Wildflower Restaurant, see separate listing. **Pool(s):** heated outdoor, heated indoor. **Leisure Activities:** whirlpool, cross country skiing, snowmobiling, ice skating, recreation programs, hiking trails, exercise room. *Fee:* golf-36 holes, golf equipment, golf instruction, practice center, family golf clinic & junior golf privileges, 2 tennis courts, downhill skiing, bicycles. **Guest Services:** gift shop, coin laundry, airport transportation (fee)-Cherry Capital Airport. **Business Services:** conference facilities, business center. **Cards:** AX, DC, DS, MC, VI. **Special Amenities:** free local telephone calls.

SOME UNITS

⊹ ｜⑪ ⍖ ⋔ ⌕ ⊸ ⊠ VCR ⁑ ▤ ▤ ▱ / ⊠ DATA PORT /
FEE

------ WHERE TO DINE ------

THE WILDFLOWER RESTAURANT   Lunch: $6-$10   Dinner: $9-$25   Phone: 231/378-2000

▼▼

American

Location: On SR 115, 2 mi w; in Crystal Mountain. 12500 Crystal Mountain Dr 49683. **Hours:** 7-11 am, 11:30-2 & 5-10 pm; hours vary off season. **Reservations:** suggested. **Features:** Relax and enjoy a casual dining experience in the comfortable restaurant. A good selection of menu items includes chicken and pasta dishes, as well as tasty seafood and savory steak, which is cooked to your liking. Service is friendly and prompt. Cocktails. **Parking:** on-site. **Cards:** AX, DC, DS, MC, VI.

⍖ ⊠

THREE RIVERS pop. 7,328

------ WHERE TO STAY ------

HOLIDAY INN EXPRESS HOTEL & SUITES   *Book at aaa.com*   Phone: (269)278-7766

▼▼▼

Small-scale Hotel

All Year	1P: $89-$128	2P: $89-$128	XP: $10 F12

Location: Jct of US 131 and SR 60 (W Broadway St). 1207 W Broadway St 49093. Fax: 269/278-7722. **Facility:** 56 one-bedroom standard units, some with whirlpools. 2 stories, interior corridors. **Bath:** combo or shower only. **Parking:** on-site. **Terms:** [ECP] meal plan available. **Amenities:** voice mail, irons, hair dryers. *Some:* dual phone lines. **Pool(s):** heated indoor. **Leisure Activities:** whirlpool, exercise room. **Guest Services:** valet and coin laundry. **Business Services:** meeting rooms. **Cards:** AX, CB, DC, DS, MC, VI.

SOME UNITS

(ASK) S/D ⌕M ⌕ ⊘ ⊸ ⁑ DATA PORT / ⊠ ▤ ▤ ▱ /

SUPER 8 MOTEL   *Book at aaa.com*   Phone: 269/279-8888

▼▼

Small-scale Hotel

All Year	1P: $54-$84	2P: $59-$89	XP: $5 F12

Location: Jct US 131 and SR 60 (Broadway St). 711 US 131 49093. Fax: 269/273-2658. **Facility:** 56 one-bedroom standard units, some with whirlpools. 3 stories, interior corridors. **Parking:** on-site. **Terms:** [ECP] meal plan available, small pets only ($10 fee). **Amenities:** hair dryers. *Some:* irons. **Pool(s):** heated indoor. **Guest Services:** valet and coin laundry. **Business Services:** meeting rooms. **Cards:** AX, DS, MC, VI.

SOME UNITS

(ASK) S/D ⌕M ⁑ ⌕ ⊸ ⁑ DATA PORT ▤ ▤ / ⊠ /
FEE

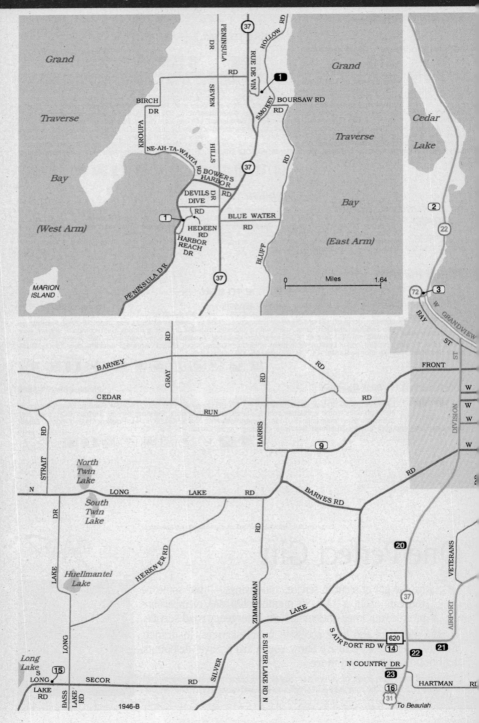

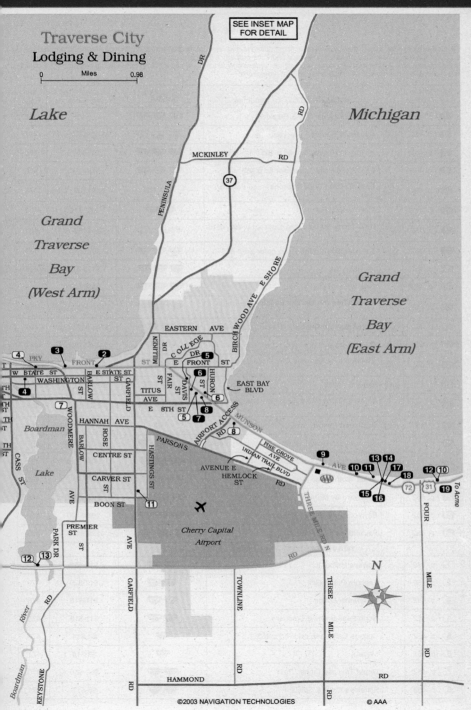

Traverse City

This index helps you "spot" where approved accommodations and restaurants are located on the corresponding detailed maps. Lodging rate ranges are for comparison only and show the property's high season; rates are per night, unless only weekly (W) rates are available. Restaurant rate range is for dinner, unless only lunch (L) is served. Turn to the listing page for more detailed rate information and consult display ads for special promotions.

Spotter/Map Page Number	OA	TRAVERSE CITY - Lodgings	Diamond Rating	Rate Range High Season	Listing Page
1 / p. 452		Chateau Chantal Bed & Breakfast	◈◈◈	$135	458
2 / p. 452	AAA	**Bayshore Resort** - see color ad p 458	◈◈◈	$160-$240 SAVE	458
3 / p. 452		Holiday Inn - see color ad p 465	◈◈◈	$179-$199	466
4 / p. 452		Park Place Hotel - see color ad p 466	◈◈◈	$189-$199	466
5 / p. 452	AAA	**Best Western Four Seasons** - see color ad p 459	◈◈	$99-$169 SAVE	458
6 / p. 452		Pine Crest Motel	◈◈	$75-$160	467
7 / p. 452	AAA	**Days Inn & Suites** - see color ad p 463, card insert	◈◈◈	$89-$169 SAVE	461
8 / p. 452	AAA	**Traverse Bay Lodge** - see color ad p 468	◈◈◈	$139-$229 SAVE	469
9 / p. 452		Hampton Inn	◈◈◈	$135-$199	465
10 / p. 452		Park Shore Resort	◈◈◈	$159-$289	466
11 / p. 452	AAA	**Cherry Tree Inn On The Beach** - see color ad p 460	◈◈◈	$129-$189 SAVE	459
12 / p. 452	AAA	**Waterfront Inn Resort** - see color ad p 469	◈◈	$145-$175 SAVE	469
13 / p. 452	AAA	**Quality Inn**	◈◈	$40-$170 SAVE	467
14 / p. 452	AAA	**AmericInn of Traverse City** - see color ad p 311	◈◈◈	$89-$172 SAVE	457
15 / p. 452	AAA	**Motel 6 - 4065**	◈◈	$76-$120 SAVE	466
16 / p. 452		The Grand Beach Resort Hotel - see color ad p 464	◈◈◈	$129-$400	463
17 / p. 452	AAA	**Driftwood Resort** - see color ad p 462	◈	$75-$175 SAVE	462
18 / p. 452		Sugar Beach Resort Hotel - see color ad p 464	◈◈◈	$129-$450	467
19 / p. 452		Pointes North Inn - see color ad p 467	◈◈◈	$190-$285	467
20 / p. 452	AAA	**Great Wolf Lodge** - see color ad p 465	◈◈◈	$179-$420 SAVE	465
21 / p. 452		Courtyard By Marriott - see ad p 462	◈◈◈	$104-$169	460
22 / p. 452		Baymont Inn & Suites-Traverse City	◈◈◈	$65-$170	458
23 / p. 452		Fairfield Inn by Marriott	◈◈◈	$89-$149	462
		TRAVERSE CITY - Restaurants			
1 / p. 452		Bower's Harbor Inn	◈◈	$18-$28	470
2 / p. 452		Foghorn Pub & Grill	◈◈	$12-$20	470
3 / p. 452		Freshwater Lodge	◈◈	$11-$18	470
4 / p. 452		North Peak Brewing Company	◈◈	$11-$18	471
5 / p. 452		Cottage Cafe - see color ad p 463	◈	$8-$14	470
6 / p. 452		Mabel's	◈	$9-$15	471
7 / p. 452		Grand Traverse Dinner Train	◈◈	$62-$65	470
8 / p. 452		Schelde's Grille & Spirits	◈◈	$8-$17	471

Spotter/Map Page Number	OA	TRAVERSE CITY - Restaurants (continued)	Diamond Rating	Rate Range High Season	Listing Page
⑨ / p. 452		Rancho Grande	▽▽	$9-$15	471
⑩ / p. 452	AAA	Reflections - see color ad p 469	▽▽	$8-$26	471
⑪ / p. 452		La Senorita	▽	$8-$12	471
⑫ / p. 452		Auntie Pasta's Italian Cafe	▽▽	$12-$18	470
⑬ / p. 452		Panda North	▽	$8-$14	471
⑭ / p. 452		La Senorita	▽	$8-$12	470
⑮ / p. 452		Boone's Long Lake Inn	▽▽	$12-$22	470
⑯ / p. 452		Don's Drive Inn	▽	$6-$12	470

Get more for your money.

Exclusively for AAA members!

- **Best available rate for dates of stay.**
- **Over 1 million rooms to fit your budget.**
- **100% satisfaction guarantee.**

AAA Preferred Lodging Partners

Best Western	Hampton Inn	Quality Inn
Clarion	Hampton Inn & Suites	Renaissance Hotels
Comfort Inn	Hilton Garden Inn	Residence Inn
Comfort Suites	Hilton Hotels	Rodeway Inn
Courtyard by Marriott	Homewood Suites	Sheraton Hotels & Resorts
Days Inn	Hyatt Hotels	Sleep Inn
DoubleTree Hotels	La Quinta Inn	SpringHill Suites
Econo Lodge	La Quinta Inn & Suites	St. Regis
Embassy Suites	Luxury Collection	TownePlace Suites
Fairfield Inn	Mainstay Suites	W Hotels
Four Points by Sheraton	Marriott Hotels, Resorts, Suites	Westin Hotels & Resorts

Visit Over 1,100 AAA Offices **Click** aaa.com **Call** 866-AAA-SAVE

Valid AAA Membership required. Not valid with other discounts or promotions. Good at participating locations only. Other restrictions may apply. Offers subject to change without notice.

TRAVERSE CITY pop. 14,532 (See map and index starting on p. 452)

──────── WHERE TO STAY ────────

AMERICINN OF TRAVERSE CITY | *Book at aaa.com* | | **Phone:** (231)938-0288 | **14**
| 6/28-8/31 | 1P: $89-$172 | 2P: $89-$172 | XP: $10 | F12
| 5/1-6/27 | 1P: $75-$172 | 2P: $75-$172 | XP: $10 | F12
| 4/1-4/30 & 9/1-3/31 | 1P: $55-$89 | 2P: $55-$89 | XP: $10 | F12

Location: On US 31, 4.4 mi e. Located in a commercial area. 1614 US 31 N 49686. Fax: 231/938-0262. **Facility:** 48 Small-scale Hotel units. 45 one-bedroom standard units, some with whirlpools. 3 one-bedroom suites, some with whirlpools. 2 stories, interior corridors. *Bath:* combo or shower only. **Parking:** on-site. **Terms:** [ECP] meal plan available. **Pool(s):** heated indoor. **Leisure Activities:** sauna, whirlpool. **Guest Services:** coin laundry. **Business Services:** meeting rooms. **Cards:** AX, CB, DC, DS, MC, VI. **Special Amenities:** free expanded continental breakfast and free local telephone calls. *(See color ad p 311)*

SOME UNITS

(See map and index starting on p. 452)

BAYMONT INN & SUITES-TRAVERSE CITY *Book at aaa.com*   Phone: (231)933-4454   **22**
All Year   1P: $65-$170   2P: $65-$170   XP: $5   F18
Location: 3.5 mi s on SR 37. Located in a commercial area. 2326 N US 31 S 49684. Fax: 231/933-5212.
Small-scale Hotel   **Facility:** 121 one-bedroom standard units, some with whirlpools. 3 stories, interior corridors. *Bath:* combo or shower only. **Parking:** on-site, winter plug-ins. **Terms:** cancellation fee imposed. **Amenities:** video games (fee), dual phone lines, voice mail, irons, hair dryers. **Pool(s):** heated indoor. **Leisure Activities:** whirlpool, playground, exercise room. **Guest Services:** valet and coin laundry. **Business Services:** meeting rooms. **Cards:** AX, DC, DS, MC, VI.

SOME UNITS

ASK ⎙ 🍽 ⬤ 🏊 ✖ 👨 DATA PORT ▮ 🖥 ▭ / ✖ /

BAYSHORE RESORT *Book at aaa.com*   Phone: (231)935-4400   **2**
6/13-9/5 [ECP]   1P: $160-$240   2P: $160-$240   XP: $10   F12
9/6-10/23 [ECP]   1P: $93-$205   2P: $93-$205   XP: $10   F12
4/1-6/12 [ECP]   1P: $93-$190   2P: $93-$190   XP: $10   F12
10/24-3/31 [ECP]   1P: $71-$185   2P: $81-$185   XP: $10   F12
Small-scale Hotel   **Location:** 0.8 mi e on US 31. Located along the bay. 833 E Front St 49686. Fax: 231/935-0262. **Facility:** Smoke free premises. 120 units. 112 one-bedroom standard units, some with whirlpools. 8 one-bedroom suites ($195-$360) with whirlpools. 4 stories, interior corridors. **Parking:** on-site. **Terms:** check-in 4 pm, 2 night minimum stay - seasonal, with Saturday stayover. **Amenities:** high-speed Internet, irons, hair dryers. **Pool(s):** heated indoor. **Leisure Activities:** whirlpool, rental boats, rental paddleboats, exercise room. *Fee:* jet boats, jet skis, game room. **Guest Services:** coin laundry, airport transportation-Cherry Capitol. **Business Services:** meeting rooms. **Cards:** AX, DC, DS, VI. **Special Amenities:** free expanded continental breakfast and free local telephone calls. *(See color ad below)*

SOME UNITS

✈ 🍽 🏊 ✖ ✖ 👨 DATA PORT / ▮ 🖥 /

BEST WESTERN FOUR SEASONS *Book at aaa.com*   Phone: (231)946-8424   **5**
6/13-8/22   1P: $99-$169   2P: $99-$169   XP: $7   F17
4/1-6/12 & 8/23-3/31   1P: $69-$139   2P: $69-$139   XP: $7   F17
Location: 2 mi e on US 31. Located in a semi-commercial area on 5 acres. 305 Munson Ave 49686.
Fax: 231/946-1971. **Facility:** 111 units. 106 one-bedroom standard units, some with whirlpools. 5 one-bedroom suites with whirlpools, some with efficiencies. 1-2 stories (no elevator), interior/exterior corridors.
Motel   **Parking:** on-site, winter plug-ins. **Terms:** cancellation fee imposed, package plans, pets ($10 fee, in designated units). **Amenities:** video library (fee), irons, hair dryers. **Pool(s):** heated outdoor, heated indoor. **Leisure Activities:** whirlpool. *Fee:* game room. **Cards:** AX, CB, DC, DS, JC, MC, VI. **Special Amenities:** free continental breakfast and free local telephone calls. *(See color ad p 459)*

SOME UNITS

🍽 🛏 🍴 🏊 DATA PORT 🖥 / ✖ VCR ▮ ▭ /
FEE

CHATEAU CHANTAL BED & BREAKFAST   Phone: 231/223-4110   **1**
All Year   1P: $135   2P: $135   XP: $25   F3
Location: 12 mi n on SR 37. Located in a rural area. 15900 Rue de Vin 49686. Fax: 231/223-4110. **Facility:** Evening wine tastings are offered at this elegant property set on a high ridge with sweeping views of the vineyards
Bed & Breakfast   and bay. Smoke free premises. 11 units. 2 one-bedroom standard units. 8 one- and 1 two-bedroom suites ($165-$175), some with kitchens and/or whirlpools. 2-3 stories, interior corridors. *Bath:* combo or shower only. **Parking:** on-site.
Terms: 2 night minimum stay - weekends, 7 day cancellation notice-fee imposed. **Amenities:** irons. **Cards:** AX, CB, DC, DS, JC, MC, VI.

✖ DATA PORT

(See map and index starting on p. 452)

CHERRY TREE INN ON THE BEACH

			Phone: 231/938-8888	11
AAA SAVE	6/18-8/21	2P: $129-$189	XP: $10	F17
	8/22-10/24	2P: $83-$189	XP: $10	F17
◇◇◇	4/1-6/17	2P: $69-$92	XP: $10	F17
	10/25-3/31	2P: $69-$89	XP: $10	F17

Small-scale Hotel Location: On US 31, 5.7 mi e. Located on the main road along the bay. 2345 US 31 N 49686. Fax: 231/938-3333. **Facility:** Smoke free premises. 75 units. 51 one-bedroom standard units, some with whirlpools. 24 one-bedroom suites ($109-$299), some with whirlpools. 4-5 stories, interior corridors. *Bath:* combo or shower only. **Parking:** on-site. **Terms:** 2 night minimum stay - weekends in spring & fall, [ECP] meal plan available. **Amenities:** video library (fee), DVD players, video games, CD players, voice mail, safes, irons, hair dryers. *Some:* dual phone lines. **Pool(s):** heated indoor. **Leisure Activities:** whirlpool, putting green, exercise room. *Fee:* jet boat, jet skis, game room. **Guest Services:** coin laundry. **Business Services:** meeting rooms. **Cards:** AX, DC, DS, MC, VI. *(See color ad p 460)*

(See map and index starting on p. 452)

COURTYARD BY MARRIOTT · *Book at aaa.com* · Phone: (231)929-1800 **21**

Small-scale Hotel

6/1-9/1	1P: $104-$169	2P: $104-$169	
9/2-3/31	1P: $69-$114	2P: $69-$114	
5/1-5/31	1P: $75-$105	2P: $75-$105	
4/1-4/30	1P: $69-$99	2P: $69-$99	

Location: 3.2 mi s on US 31, then just w. Located in a commercial area. 3615 S Airport Rd W 49684. **Fax:** 231/929-1808. **Facility:** 83 units. 80 one-bedroom standard units, some with whirlpools. 3 one-bedroom suites with whirlpools. 3 stories, interior corridors. *Bath:* combo or shower only. **Parking:** on-site. **Terms:** cancellation fee imposed, [BP] meal plan available. **Amenities:** video games, dual phone lines, voice mail, irons, hair dryers. **Pool(s):** heated indoor. **Leisure Activities:** whirlpool, exercise room. **Guest Services:** valet and coin laundry. **Business Services:** meeting rooms. **Cards:** AX, CB, DC, DS, MC, VI. *(See ad p 462)*

SOME UNITS

(See map and index starting on p. 452)

DAYS INN & SUITES   *Book at aaa.com*

	6/5-8/24 [ECP]	1P: $89-$169	2P: $89-$169	Phone: (231)941-0208	7
	8/25-10/18 [ECP]	1P: $69-$149	2P: $69-$149	XP: $10	F17
	10/19-3/31 [ECP]	1P: $49-$149	2P: $49-$149	XP: $10	F17
	4/1-6/4 [ECP]	1P: $59-$139	2P: $59-$139	XP: $10	F17
				XP: $10	F17

Small-scale Hotel **Location:** 2 mi e on US 31. 420 Munson Ave 49686. Fax: 231/941-7521. **Facility:** 181 units. 131 one-bedroom standard units, some with whirlpools. 50 one-bedroom suites ($89-$249), some with whirlpools. 2 stories, interior corridors. **Parking:** on-site, winter plug-ins. **Amenities:** voice mail, hair dryers. **Fee:** video games, safes. *Some:* irons. **Pool(s):** heated indoor. **Leisure Activities:** whirlpool, picnic area with grills, playground, exercise room. **Guest Services:** coin laundry, airport transportation-Traverse City Airport. **Business Services:** meeting rooms. **Cards:** AX, CB, DC, DS, JC, MC, VI. **Special Amenities:** free expanded continental breakfast and free newspaper. *(See color ad p 463 & card insert)*

SOME UNITS

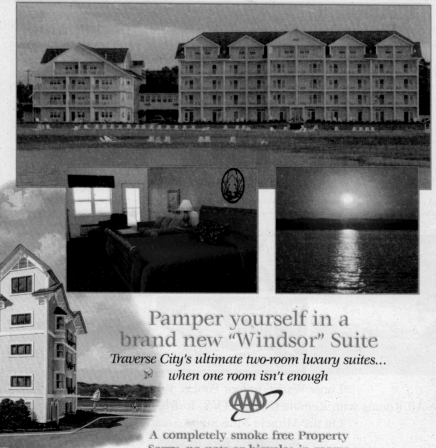

(See map and index starting on p. 452)

DRIFTWOOD RESORT

Phone: 231/938-1600 ⑰

	6/18-9/5	1P: $75-$175	2P: $75-$175	XP: $5	F12
AAA SAVE	9/6-10/31	1P: $45-$95	2P: $45-$95	XP: $5	F12
◇	4/1-6/17 & 11/1-3/31	1P: $35-$85	2P: $45-$95	XP: $5	F12

Motel

Location: On US 31, 4.5 mi e. Located on the bay. 1861 US 31 N 49686. Fax: 231/938-2178. **Facility:** 39 units. 38 one- and 1 two-bedroom standard units, some with kitchens and/or whirlpools. 2 stories (no elevator), interior/exterior corridors. **Parking:** on-site. **Terms:** 3 night minimum stay - 6/25-9/5, cancellation fee imposed, weekly rates available. **Pool(s):** heated indoor. **Leisure Activities:** whirlpool. *Fee:* game room. **Cards:** DS, MC, VI. **Special Amenities:** free local telephone calls and preferred room (subject to availability with advanced reservations). *(See color ad below)*

SOME UNITS

⊓↑ ⊃ ▯ ⊡ ⊒ / DATA PORT /

FAIRFIELD INN BY MARRIOTT   *Book at aaa.com*

Phone: (231)922-7900 ㉓

◇◇◇	7/2-9/1	1P: $89-$149
	6/1-7/1	1P: $79-$129
Small-scale Hotel	4/1-5/31 & 9/2-3/31	1P: $62-$89

Location: 3.6 mi s on SR 37. Located in a quiet area. 3701 N Country Dr 49684. Fax: 231/946-8845. **Facility:** 85 one-bedroom standard units, some with whirlpools. 3 stories, interior corridors. *Bath:* combo or shower only. **Parking:** on-site. **Terms:** cancellation fee imposed, [CP] meal plan available. **Amenities:** irons, hair dryers. **Pool(s):** heated indoor. **Leisure Activities:** whirlpool, snowmobiling, exercise room. **Guest Services:** valet and coin laundry. **Cards:** AX, DC, DS, MC, VI.

SOME UNITS

ASK S▯ ⊓↑ ⬧M ⬧ ⊃ ✕ ⋈ DATA PORT ⊒ / ✕ ▯ ⊡ /

(See map and index starting on p. 452)

THE GRAND BEACH RESORT HOTEL

Book at aaa.com

Phone: (231)938-4455 **16**

Small-scale Hotel

6/25-9/5 [ECP]	1P: $129-$400	2P: $129-$400	XP: $10	F17
4/1-6/24 [ECP]	1P: $59-$269	2P: $59-$269	XP: $10	F17
9/6-10/23 [ECP]	1P: $89-$249	2P: $89-$249	XP: $10	F17
10/24-3/31 [ECP]	1P: $59-$199	2P: $59-$199	XP: $10	F17

Location: On US 31, 4.5 mi e. Located on the main road along the bay. 1683 US 31 N 49686. Fax: 231/938-4435. **Facility:** 97 units. 96 one-bedroom standard units, some with whirlpools. 1 three-bedroom suite with kitchen and whirlpool. 3 stories, interior corridors. **Parking:** on-site. **Terms:** cancellation fee imposed, package plans - seasonal & weekends. **Amenities:** video library (fee), irons, hair dryers. **Pool(s):** heated indoor. **Leisure Activities:** whirlpool, exercise room. *Fee:* paddleboats, game room. **Guest Services:** coin laundry. **Business Services:** meeting rooms. **Cards:** AX, CB, DC, DS, MC, VI. *(See color ad p 464)*

SOME UNITS

Two-Room Suites

Deluxe Suites

Indoor Pool & Spa

Executive Business Zone Rooms with Data Ports

Workout Room

Cottage Cafe Restaurant with Papa's Den Lounge

Days Inn's
Chairman's Award Hotel
Last 13 Years

Welcome to Traverse City!

Experience Quality, Comfort, Convenience and Gracious Hospitality

- Indoor Pool & Spa
- Relaxing Sundeck
- 2 Person Jacuzzi/Fireplace Suites
- Business Zone Rooms with Data Ports
- Complimentary Continental Breakfast
- Movie & Video Game Rentals
- Voice Mail/Fax/Copy Services
- Meeting/Conference Room
- Cottage Cafe with Papa's Den Lounge

DAYS INN & SUITES

420 Munson Avenue · Traverse City, MI 49686 · 1-231-941-0208

For Reservations Call: 1-800-982-3297

www.tcdaysinn.com · e-mail: info@tcdaysinn.com

(See map and index starting on p. 452)

GREAT WOLF LODGE
Phone: (231)941-3600 **20**

1/1-3/31	2P: $179-$420	XP: $15
6/4-8/28	2P: $209-$399	XP: $15
4/1-6/3 & 8/29-12/31	2P: $129-$399	XP: $15

Large-scale Hotel **Location:** 2.3 mi s on US 31 and SR 37. 3575 N US Hwy 31 S 49684. Fax: 231/941-3700. **Facility:** Smoke free premises. 281 units. 251 one- and 30 two-bedroom standard units, some with whirlpools. 4 stories, interior corridors. *Bath:* combo or shower only. **Parking:** on-site. **Terms:** check-in 4 pm, 2-3 night minimum stay - in season, cancellation fee imposed. **Amenities:** video games, voice mail, irons, hair dryers. **Dining:** 2 restaurants, 7 am-10 pm, cocktails. **Pool(s):** heated outdoor, 2 heated indoor, 2 wading. **Leisure Activities:** whirlpools, indoor water park, recreation programs, exercise room, spa. **Fee:** game room. **Guest Services:** gift shop, coin laundry. **Business Services:** meeting rooms. **Cards:** AX, DC, DS, MC, VI. **Special Amenities:** free local telephone calls. *(See color ad below)*

SOME UNITS

🍽 📺 🏊 ⌧ ✕ 🎦 [DATA PORT] 🛏 📷 🖨 / (VCR) /

HAMPTON INN *Book at aaa.com*
Phone: (231)946-8900 **9**

6/25-8/28 [ECP]	1P: $135-$189	2P: $145-$199
8/29-10/24 [ECP]	1P: $95-$149	2P: $105-$159
4/1-6/24 [ECP]	1P: $75-$129	2P: $85-$139
10/25-3/31 [ECP]	1P: $75-$89	2P: $85-$99

Small-scale Hotel **Location:** On US 31 and SR 72, 4.3 mi e. Located opposite the state park beach area. 1000 US 31 N 49686. Fax: 231/946-2817. **Facility:** 127 one-bedroom standard units. 4 stories, interior corridors. **Parking:** on-site. **Terms:** check-in 4 pm, 1-2 night minimum stay - seasonal weekends, cancellation fee imposed, package plans - seasonal. **Amenities:** video games, voice mail, irons, hair dryers. **Pool(s):** heated indoor. **Leisure Activities:** whirlpool. **Guest Services:** valet laundry. **Business Services:** meeting rooms. **Cards:** AX, DC, DS, MC, VI.

SOME UNITS

(ASK) [S/D] ⊁ 🍽 🏊 ♿ 🎦 [DATA PORT] 🖨 / ✕ 🛏 📷 /
FEE FEE

(See map and index starting on p. 452)

HOLIDAY INN — *Book at aaa.com* — Phone: (231)947-3700 — **3**

7/1-9/6	1P: $179-$199	2P: $179-$199	XP: $10	F
9/7-10/31	1P: $139-$159	2P: $139-$159	XP: $10	F
4/1-6/30	1P: $109-$139	2P: $109-$139	XP: $10	F
11/1-3/31	1P: $109-$129	2P: $109-$129	XP: $10	F

Large-scale Hotel

Location: 0.5 mi e on US 31. Located along the bay. 615 E Front St 49686. Fax: 231/947-0361. **Facility:** 179 one-bedroom standard units, some with whirlpools. 4 stories, interior corridors. *Bath:* combo or shower only. **Parking:** on-site. **Terms:** check-in 4 pm, pets ($10 extra charge). **Amenities:** voice mail, irons, hair dryers. **Pool(s):** heated indoor. **Leisure Activities:** sauna, whirlpool, boat dock, fishing, exercise room. *Fee:* sailboats, charter fishing. **Guest Services:** gift shop, valet and coin laundry. **Business Services:** conference facilities. **Cards:** AX, CB, DC, DS, JC, MC, VI. *(See color ad p 465)*

SOME UNITS

MOTEL 6 - 4065 — *Book at aaa.com* — Phone: 231-938-3002 — **15**

			XP: $3	F17
6/11-9/5	1P: $76-$100	2P: $80-$120	XP: $3	F17
4/1-6/10 & 9/6-3/31	1P: $36-$76	2P: $42-$82	XP: $3	F17

Small-scale Hotel

Location: On US 31, 4.3 mi e. Located in a commercial area. 1582 US 31 N 49686. Fax: 231/938-3179. **Facility:** 45 one-bedroom standard units. 2 stories, interior corridors. **Parking:** on-site. **Terms:** 7 day cancellation notice-fee imposed, pets ($6 extra charge, in designated units). **Pool(s):** heated indoor. **Leisure Activities:** whirlpool. **Guest Services:** coin laundry. **Cards:** AX, CB, DC, DS, MC, VI.

SOME UNITS

PARK PLACE HOTEL — *Book at aaa.com* — Phone: (231)946-5000 — **4**

6/1-9/6	1P: $189-$199	2P: $189-$199	XP: $10	F16
9/7-10/31	1P: $139-$149	2P: $139-$149	XP: $10	F16
4/1-5/31 & 11/1-3/31	1P: $119-$129	2P: $119-$129	XP: $10	F16

Large-scale Hotel **Location:** Corner of E State and Park sts; center. 300 E State St 49684. Fax: 231/946-2772. **Facility:** 140 units. 137 one-bedroom standard units. 3 one-bedroom suites ($309). 4-10 stories, interior corridors. **Parking:** on-site, winter plug-ins. **Terms:** check-in 4 pm, 3 day cancellation notice-fee imposed. **Amenities:** video games, high-speed Internet, voice mail, irons, hair dryers. **Pool(s):** heated indoor. **Leisure Activities:** sauna, whirlpool, exercise room. **Guest Services:** gift shop, valet laundry. **Business Services:** conference facilities. **Cards:** AX, DC, DS, MC, VI. *(See color ad below)*

SOME UNITS

PARK SHORE RESORT — *Book at aaa.com* — Phone: 231/947-3800 — **10**

5/28-9/5	1P: $159-$289	2P: $159-$289	XP: $10	F18
9/6-10/30	1P: $89-$209	2P: $89-$209	XP: $10	F18
10/31-3/31	1P: $69-$179	2P: $69-$179	XP: $10	F18
4/1-5/27	1P: $69-$159	2P: $69-$159	XP: $10	F18

Small-scale Hotel

Location: On US 31, 3.2 mi e. Located on the main road along the bay. 1401 US 31 N 49686. Fax: 231/947-9900. **Facility:** 80 units. 74 one-bedroom standard units, some with whirlpools. 6 one-bedroom suites ($159-$289), some with efficiencies and/or whirlpools. 4 stories, interior corridors. *Bath:* combo or shower only. **Parking:** on-site. **Terms:** check-in 4 pm, 2 night minimum stay - weekends, cancellation fee imposed, [ECP] meal plan available. **Amenities:** voice mail, safes (fee), irons, hair dryers. *Some:* dual phone lines. **Pool(s):** heated indoor. **Leisure Activities:** whirlpool, exercise room. *Fee:* paddleboats, sailboats, game room. **Guest Services:** coin laundry. **Business Services:** meeting rooms. **Cards:** AX, DC, DS, MC, VI.

SOME UNITS

(See map and index starting on p. 452)

PINE CREST MOTEL   Phone: 231/947-8900   **6**

	7/1-9/4	1P: $75-$150	2P: $85-$160	XP: $10	D3
Motel	9/5-10/31	1P: $58-$150	2P: $68-$160	XP: $10	D3
	4/1-6/30	1P: $58-$95	2P: $68-$125	XP: $10	D3
	11/1-3/31	1P: $38-$95	2P: $48-$120	XP: $10	D3

Location: 2 mi e on US 31. Located in a commercial area. 360 Munson Ave 49686. Fax: 231/947-8900. **Facility:** 35 one-bedroom standard units, some with whirlpools. 2 stories (no elevator), exterior corridors. **Parking:** on-site, winter plug-ins. **Terms:** 2 night minimum stay - weekends in season, [CP] meal plan available. **Amenities:** video library (fee), irons. *Some:* hair dryers. **Pool(s):** heated outdoor, small heated indoor. **Leisure Activities:** whirlpool. **Cards:** AX, CB, DC, DS, MC, VI.

SOME UNITS

POINTES NORTH INN   Phone: (231)938-9191   **19**

	6/29-9/5	1P: $190-$285	2P: $190-$285
Condominium	4/1-6/28	1P: $100-$210	2P: $100-$210
	9/6-10/31	1P: $100-$185	2P: $100-$185
	11/1-3/31	1P: $70-$185	2P: $70-$185

Location: On US 31, 5 mi e. Located on the bay. 2211 US 31 N 49686. Fax: 231/938-0070. **Facility:** One buiding with an elevator. 51 units. 50 one-bedroom standard units with whirlpools. 1 one-bedroom suite with kitchen and whirlpool. 3 stories (no elevator), exterior corridors. **Parking:** on-site. **Terms:** cancellation fee imposed, [CP] meal plan available. **Amenities:** voice mail, irons, hair dryers. **Pool(s):** heated outdoor. **Leisure Activities:** volleyball. **Cards:** AX, MC, VI. *(See color ad below)*

SOME UNITS

QUALITY INN   *Book at aaa.com*   Phone: (231)929-4423   **13**

All Year [CP]   1P: $40-$170   2P: $40-$170   XP: $10   F
Location: On US 31, 3.3 mi e. Located on the main road along bay. 1492 US 31 N 49686. Fax: 231/929-7842.
Facility: 96 units. 94 one-bedroom standard units, some with whirlpools. 2 one-bedroom suites. 2-3 stories, interior/exterior corridors. *Bath:* combo or shower only. **Parking:** on-site, winter plug-ins. **Terms:** check-in 4
Small-scale Hotel   pm, cancellation fee imposed, weekly rates available, pets ($10 fee, in designated rooms). **Amenities:** video games, safes (fee), irons, hair dryers. **Pool(s):** heated indoor. **Leisure Activities:** whirlpool. **Guest Services:** valet laundry. **Cards:** AX, CB, DC, DS, MC, VI. **Special Amenities: free continental breakfast and free local telephone calls.**

SOME UNITS

FEE

SUGAR BEACH RESORT HOTEL   *Book at aaa.com*   Phone: (231)938-0100   **18**

	6/25-9/5 [ECP]	1P: $129-$450	2P: $129-$450	XP: $10	F17
Small-scale Hotel	4/1-6/24 [ECP]	1P: $59-$269	2P: $59-$269	XP: $10	F17
	9/6-10/23 [ECP]	1P: $89-$249	2P: $89-$249	XP: $10	F17
	10/24-3/31 [ECP]	1P: $59-$199	2P: $59-$199	XP: $10	F17

Location: On US 31, 4.8 mi e. Located on the main road along the bay. 1773 US 31 N 49686. Fax: 231/938-0200. **Facility:** 97 units. 96 one-bedroom standard units, some with whirlpools. 1 three-bedroom suite ($109-$459) with kitchen and whirlpool. 3 stories, interior corridors. *Bath:* combo or shower only. **Parking:** on-site, winter plug-ins. **Terms:** cancellation fee imposed, package plans - seasonal & weekends. **Amenities:** video library (fee), irons, hair dryers. **Pool(s):** heated indoor. **Leisure Activities:** whirlpool, exercise room. *Fee:* paddleboats, game room. **Guest Services:** coin laundry. **Business Services:** meeting rooms. **Cards:** AX, DC, DS, MC, VI. *(See color ad p 464)*

SOME UNITS

(See map and index starting on p. 452)

TRAVERSE BAY LODGE   *Book at aaa.com*   Phone: (231)947-5436   **8**

6/25-8/26	1P: $139-$229	2P: $139-$229	XP: $10	F18
5/28-6/24	1P: $99-$169	2P: $99-$169	XP: $10	F18
8/27-3/31	1P: $89-$149	2P: $89-$149	XP: $10	F18
4/1-5/27	1P: $69-$129	2P: $69-$129	XP: $10	F18

Small-scale Hotel **Location:** 2.3 mi e on US 31. 460 Munson Ave 49686. Fax: 231/947-0859. **Facility:** 61 units. 60 one-bedroom standard units, some with whirlpools. 1 one-bedroom suite with kitchen. 2 stories, interior corridors. *Bath:* combo or shower only. **Parking:** on-site. **Terms:** check-in 4 pm, cancellation fee imposed, [ECP] meal plan available. **Amenities:** hair dryers. **Pool(s):** heated indoor. **Leisure Activities:** whirlpool, exercise room. *Fee:* game room. **Business Services:** meeting rooms. **Cards:** AX, CB, DC, DS, MC, VI. *(See color ad p 468)*

SOME UNITS

WATERFRONT INN RESORT   Phone: (231)938-1100   **12**

6/25-8/21 [ECP]	1P: $145-$165	2P: $155-$175	XP: $10	F18
8/22-10/23 [ECP]	1P: $64-$145	2P: $69-$150	XP: $10	F18
4/1-6/24 [ECP]	1P: $64-$120	2P: $69-$125	XP: $10	F18
10/24-3/31 [ECP]	1P: $64-$114	2P: $69-$119	XP: $10	F18

Small-scale Hotel **Location:** On US 31, 4.8 mi e. Located on the bay. 2061 US 31 N 49686. Fax: 231/938-9711. **Facility:** 127 one-bedroom standard units, some with efficiencies and/or whirlpools. 4 stories, interior corridors. **Parking:** on-site. **Terms:** check-in 4 pm. **Amenities:** voice mail. **Dining:** Reflections, see separate listing. **Pool(s):** heated indoor. **Leisure Activities:** saunas, whirlpool, exercise room. *Fee:* game room. **Guest Services:** airport transportation-Cherry Capital Airport. **Business Services:** conference facilities. **Cards:** AX, CB, DC, DS, MC, VI. **Special Amenities:** free continental breakfast and free newspaper. *(See color ad below)*

SOME UNITS

(See map and index starting on p. 452)

——— The following lodging was either not evaluated or did not ———
meet AAA rating requirements but is listed for your information only.

HAWTHORN SUITES LTD
Phone: 866/429-8467
[fyi]
Under construction, scheduled to open June 2004. **Location:** On US 31, 1.5 mi e; downtown. 135 Munson Ave
Small-scale Hotel
49686. **Planned Amenities:** coffeemakers, microwaves, refrigerators, pool.

——— **WHERE TO DINE** ———

AUNTIE PASTA'S ITALIAN CAFE   **Lunch:** $7-$10   **Dinner:** $12-$18   **Phone:** 231/941-8147   [12]
Location: On the river at Logans Landing. 2030 S Airport Rd 49684. **Hours:** 11 am-10 pm, Fri & Sat-11 pm, Sun
noon-10 pm. Closed: 11/25, 12/25. **Features:** Freshly-baked breads and desserts accompany pasta, veal,
Italian
and Italian dishes, served in a dining room over-looking the Boardman River. Pizza and subs served in
Zio's. Casual dress; cocktails. **Parking:** on-site. **Cards:** AX, DS, MC, VI.

BOONE'S LONG LAKE INN   **Dinner:** $12-$22   **Phone:** 231/946-3991   [15]
Location: 5.5 mi sw, 1.3 mi s on US 31, 4 mi sw on Silver Lake Rd, 1.5 mi w off Secor Rd. 7208 Secor Rd 49684.
Hours: 4 pm-10 pm, Sat-11 pm, Sun noon-10 pm. Closed: 11/25, 12/25; also for dinner 12/24.
Steak & Seafood
Features: Casual dining. The 18-ounce New York strip steak is still the "house specialty", but you may
want to try one of the nightly specials or the fresh seafood which is worth the wait to get seated when they
are busy. Casual dress; cocktails. **Parking:** on-site. **Cards:** AX, MC, VI.

BOWER'S HARBOR INN   Historic   **Dinner:** $18-$28   **Phone:** 231/223-4222   [1]
Location: 0.8 mi n on SR 37, 8.8 mi nw. 13512 Peninsula Dr 49686. **Hours:** 5 pm-10 pm, Fri & Sat-11 pm; 5
pm-9 pm, Fri & Sat-10 pm 11/1-4/15. Closed: 11/25, 12/25; also 12/24 for dinner.
American
Reservations: suggested. **Features:** Casually upscale dining in a restored home on west Bay. The cuisine
is unique, with dishes such as the Fish in a Bag, an "Inn Tradition" served with shrimp, king crab, scallops
and orange roughy, and Horseradish crusted New York strip, the Harbor Duck to the Frenched Rack of Spring Lamb. The
Bowery - located in back, is also a fun place to eat. Casual dress; cocktails. **Parking:** on-site. **Cards:** AX, DS, MC, VI.

COTTAGE CAFE   **Lunch:** $5-$8   **Dinner:** $8-$14   **Phone:** 231/947-9261   [5]
Location: 2 mi ne on US 31. 420 Munson Ave 49684. **Hours:** 7 am-10 pm. Closed: 12/25. **Features:** The
family-style restaurant delivers such familiar fare as pot pies, beef stew, shepherd's pie and local whitefish.
American
Antiques, knickknacks and pictures decorate the dining room, which resembles a cozy cottage. Service is
courteous and efficient. Casual dress. **Parking:** on-site. **Cards:** AX, DS, MC, VI. *(See color ad p 463)*

DON'S DRIVE INN   **Lunch:** $6-$12   **Dinner:** $6-$12   **Phone:** 231/938-1860   [16]
Location: On US 31, 4.8 mi e. 2030 US 31 N 49686. **Hours:** 10:30 am-10 pm; hours vary off season. Closed:
1/1, 11/25, 12/25. **Features:** This 1950s diner still has the great burgers and shakes being served in the
American
atmosphere of that era. Casual dress. **Parking:** on-site. **Cards:** DS, MC, VI.

FOGHORN PUB & GRILL   **Lunch:** $6-$9   **Dinner:** $12-$20   **Phone:** 231/932-8993   [2]
Location: On SR 22, 1 mi n of SR 72. 12930 M-22 49684. **Hours:** 11 am-10 pm, Sun noon-9 pm. Closed:
11/25, 12/25 & Easter. **Features:** Opposite West Grand Traverse Bay, the restaurant and lounge prepares
American
a good selection of finger foods, salads and land and sea dishes. Casual dress; cocktails. **Parking:**
on-site. **Cards:** MC, VI.

FRESHWATER LODGE   **Lunch:** $5-$13   **Dinner:** $11-$18   **Phone:** 231/932-4694   [3]
Location: On SR 22, just n of SR 72. 13890 S West Bayshore Dr 49684. **Hours:** 11 am-11 pm, Fri &
Sat-midnight, Sun 10 am-10 pm. Closed: 11/25, 12/25. **Features:** Opposite the bay, the restaurant nurtures
American
a warm, up-north atmosphere, in part due to its high stone fireplaces and hunting and fishing memorabilia.
Hand-cut lodge steak is marinated in a sweet and savory sauce then flame-broiled to the patron's liking.
Casual dress; cocktails. **Parking:** on-site. **Cards:** AX, DS, MC, VI.

GRAND TRAVERSE DINNER TRAIN   **Lunch:** $47-$50   **Dinner:** $62-$65   **Phone:** 231/933-3768   [7]
Location: Historic station on Boardman Lake; center. 642 Railroad Pl 49686. **Hours:** train departs noon & 6:30
pm; schedules vary with season. **Reservations:** required. **Features:** Get a taste of nostalgia on the
American
charming tour of the scenic Grand Traverse Bay area. All tables are next to windows on the comfortable
Pullman-style dining coaches. The monthly changing menu highlights a limited selection of gourmet
cuisine. Casual dress; cocktails. **Parking:** on-site. **Cards:** DS, MC, VI.

LA SENORITA   **Lunch:** $5-$10   **Dinner:** $8-$12   **Phone:** 231/946-4545   [14]
Location: 3.5 mi s on SR 37. 2455 N US 31 S 49684. **Hours:** 11 am-10 pm, Fri & Sat-11 pm; to 11 pm, Fri &
Sat-midnight, Sun noon-10 pm 5/29-9/4. Closed: 11/25, 12/25 & Easter. **Features:** Casual dining in a warm
Mexican
atmosphere with Mexican knickknacks throughout. Good variety of reasonably priced Mexican dishes,
MC, VI.
snacks and salad. Mesquite cooked items. Casual dress; cocktails. **Parking:** on-site. **Cards:** AX, DS,

(See map and index starting on p. 452)

LA SENORITA **Lunch:** $5-$10 **Dinner:** $8-$12 **Phone:** 231/947-8820 ⑪
♦♦♦ **Location:** 1.3 mi s of jct US 31, SR 37 and 72 (Old Mission Peninsula). 1245 S Garfield 49685. **Hours:** 11 am-10
Mexican pm, Fri & Sat-11 pm; to 11 pm, Fri & Sat-midnight, Sun noon-10 pm 5/29-9/4. Closed: 11/25, 12/25 &
Easter. **Features:** Casual dining. Warm atmosphere with Mexican knickknacks throughout. Good variety of
reasonably priced Mexican dishes, snacks and salad. Mesquite cooked items. Smoking permitted in the
lounge only (on Sundays). Casual dress; cocktails. **Parking:** on-site. **Cards:** AX, DS, MC, VI. 🍸 ✕

MABEL'S **Lunch:** $5-$9 **Dinner:** $9-$15 **Phone:** 231/947-0252 ⑥
♦♦♦ **Location:** 2.4 mi e on US 31. 457 Munson Ave 49686. **Hours:** 7 am-11 pm. Closed: 11/25, 12/25.
American **Features:** The popular family restaurant has a number of reasonably priced menu items and vegetarian
choices, as well as lighter fare and children's dishes. The award-winning Traverse City cherry pie is worth
savoring. Casual dress. **Parking:** on-site. **Cards:** AX, DS, MC, VI.
✕

NORTH PEAK BREWING COMPANY **Lunch:** $6-$13 **Dinner:** $11-$18 **Phone:** 231/941-7325 ④
♦♦♦ ♦♦♦ **Location:** Center. 400 W Front St 49686. **Hours:** 11 am-11 pm, Fri & Sat-midnight, Sun 11 am-10 pm; 11
American am-midnight, Fri & Sat-1 am 5/31-9/6. Closed: 11/25, 12/25. **Features:** Located downtown, beers brewed
on location, serving wood-fired pizza, snacks and steaks. Casual dress; cocktails. **Parking:** on-site.
Cards: AX, DS, MC, VI. 🍸 ✕

PANDA NORTH **Lunch:** $4-$8 **Dinner:** $8-$14 **Phone:** 231/929-9722 ⑬
♦♦♦ **Location:** 3.5 mi s on US 31 and SR 37, 2 mi e. 2038 S Airport Rd 49684. **Hours:** 11 am-9:30 pm, Fri &
Chinese Sat-10:30 pm. Closed: 11/25. **Reservations:** suggested, weekends. **Features:** On the river at Logans
Landing, the restaurant lays out a tempting, all-you-can-eat lunch and dinner buffet. Such selections as
soups and egg rolls complement entrees of sweet and sour chicken, lomein and beef with broccoli.
Servers are pleasant and prompt. Casual dress. **Parking:** on-site. **Cards:** AX, MC, VI. ✕

RANCHO GRANDE **Lunch:** $5-$9 **Dinner:** $9-$15 **Phone:** 231/933-5420 ⑨
♦♦♦ ♦♦♦ **Location:** Jct US 31, SR 37 and W Front St, 1 mi sw; at Oleson's Plaza West. 3860-5 N Long Lake Rd 49684.
Mexican **Hours:** 11 am-9:30 pm, Fri-10 pm, Sat & Sun from noon. Closed major holidays. **Features:** After a warm
welcome, patrons can start with made-from-scratch black bean soup, enjoy an entree, then finish the meal
with one of the tempting desserts. Casual dress; cocktails. **Parking:** on-site. **Cards:** AX, DS, MC, VI.
Ⓜ 🍸 ✕

REFLECTIONS **Dinner:** $8-$26 **Phone:** 231/938-2321 ⑩
ⒶⒶⒶ **Location:** On US 31, 4.8 mi e; in Waterfront Inn Resort. 2061 US 31 N 49686. **Hours:** 5 pm-9:30 pm; hours may
♦♦♦ ♦♦♦ vary. Closed: 9/6, 11/25, 12/25; also Sun off season. **Reservations:** suggested. **Features:** Rooftop dining
American room overlooking the bay. Noted for their fresh fish dishes and juicy steaks. Try the "Smoked Whitefish
Pate" as an appetizer and the "Old Mission Salad" - but be careful - they're filling, and the main dishes are
hearty. Casual dress; cocktails. **Parking:** on-site. **Cards:** AX, DC, DS, MC, VI. *(See color ad p 469)*
🍸 ✕

SCHELDE'S GRILLE & SPIRITS **Lunch:** $5-$7 **Dinner:** $8-$17 **Phone:** 231/946-0981 ⑧
♦♦♦ ♦♦♦ **Location:** 2.8 mi ne on US 31 and SR 72. 714 Munson Ave 49684. **Hours:** 11 am-10 pm, Fri-11 pm, Sat & Sun 8
American am-10 pm. Closed: 11/25, 12/25; also 12/24 for dinner. **Features:** Casual dining. Featured items include
chicken, steak and seafood. The baked crab and artichoke dip appetizer is a great way to start your meal.
The prime rib and the St. Louis Style BBQ ribs are favorites. For a sandwich try their "famous" Reuben.
Casual dress; cocktails. **Parking:** on-site. **Cards:** AX, DS, MC, VI. 🍸 ✕

WINDOWS **Dinner:** $21-$38 **Phone:** 231/941-0100
♦♦♦ ♦♦♦ ♦♦♦ **Location:** Jct SR 72 and 22, 6.5 mi n on SR 22. 7677 West Bayshore Dr 49684. **Hours:** Open 4/1-2/15; 5 pm-9
Continental pm, Fri & Sat-10 pm. Closed: 11/25, 12/25; also Sun & Mon 11/1-5/6. **Reservations:** required.
Features: Located on the banks of West Grand Traverse Bay, this restaurant offers up-scale dining,
featuring American cuisine that draws on French and Cajun influences. They also have an extensive,
award winning wine list. Dressy casual; cocktails. **Parking:** on-site. **Cards:** AX, DC, DS, MC, VI.
✕

———— *The following restaurants have not been evaluated by AAA* ————
but are listed for your information only.

APACHE TROUT GRILL **Phone:** 231/947-7079
[fyi] Not evaluated. **Location:** 2 mi n on SR 22; jct SR 22 and 72. 13671 S West Bayshore Dr 49684. **Features:** On the
bay, the restaurant affords good views of the water from inside and on the seasonal patio. Specialties
include seafood and steaks, as well as a number of mixed-grill items.

DILL'S OLDE TOWNE SALOON **Phone:** 231/947-7534
[fyi] Not evaluated. **Location:** Center. 423 S Union St 49686. **Features:** A favorite local restaurant noted for a
variety of dishes, especially the chicken and pasta selections.

GORDIE HOWE'S TAVERN & EATERY **Phone:** 231/929-4693
[fyi] Not evaluated. **Location:** Just s of jct US 31, SR 37 and 72 (Old Mission Peninsula). 851 S Garfield 49686.
Features: This family restaurant is filled with hockey memorabilia, and serves BBQ ribs, prime rib, burgers,
salads and pizza.

MODE'S BUM STEER **Phone:** 231/947-9832
[fyi] Not evaluated. **Location:** Center. 125 E Front St 49686. **Features:** This small, loud, smoky tavern is one of the
best places in town for steaks and prime rib. Children under 8 not allowed after 5 pm.

(See map and index starting on p. 452)

OMELETTE SHOPPE AND BAKERY   **Phone:** 231/946-0590
[fyi]   Not evaluated. **Location:** Center. 1209 E Front 49686. **Features:** One of two locations in town, noted for their
               award winning breakfast and lunch.

SLEDER'S FAMILY TAVERN   **Phone:** 231/947-9213
[fyi]   Not evaluated. **Location:** Just w of US 31. 717 Randolph 49684. **Features:** Established in 1882, the tavern
               features an array of hearty American favorites.

TRENTON —See Detroit p. 283.

TROUT LAKE

———————— WHERE TO STAY ————————

CASTLEWOOD INN & SUITES   **Phone:** (906)569-3276
▼▼▼ ▼▼▼   12/21-3/31   1P: $69-$79   2P: $89-$99   XP: $10   F18
            6/16-9/1   1P: $69-$79   2P: $79-$99   XP: $10   F18
Motel   4/1-6/15 & 9/2-12/20   1P: $55-$75   2P: $69-$89   XP: $10   F18
            Location: On SR 123, 1.3 mi s. 22321 S Hwy 123 49793 (PO Box 127). **Fax:** 906/569-3261. **Facility:** 41 one-
bedroom standard units, some with whirlpools. 2 stories (no elevator), exterior corridors. **Parking:** on-site. **Terms:** [BP] meal plan
available. **Pool(s):** heated indoor. **Leisure Activities:** sauna, whirlpool, snowmobiling, playground, shuffleboard. *Fee:* game
room. **Cards:** AX, CB, DC, DS, JC, MC, VI.
                                                                                    SOME UNITS

(A$K) (S🌙) (†¶) (➮) (✕) (♣) / (✕) /

TROY —See Detroit p. 284.

UNION PIER

———————— WHERE TO STAY ————————

GARDEN GROVE BED & BREAKFAST   **Phone:** (269)469-6346
▼▼▼▼▼   4/1-10/31   2P: $119-$179
            11/1-3/31   2P: $89-$149
Bed & Breakfast **Location:** I-94, exit 6 (Union Pier Rd), 0.5 mi w. 9549 Union Pier Rd 49129. **Fax:** 269/469-3419. **Facility:** Brightly
painted, well-appointed rooms enhance this 1925 cottage-style home whose large terraces overlook wooded
gardens. Designated smoking area. 4 one-bedroom standard units, some with whirlpools. 2 stories (no elevator), interior corridors. **Parking:** on-site. **Terms:** check-in 4 pm, 2 night minimum stay - in season, 10 day cancellation notice-fee imposed.
Amenities: video library. *Some:* CD players. **Leisure Activities:** whirlpool, bicycles. **Cards:** AX, DS, MC, VI.
                                                                                    SOME UNITS

(A$K) (S🌙) (✕) (VCR) / (🖥) /

RIVERS EDGE BED & BREAKFAST   **Phone:** 269/469-6860
▼▼▼▼▼   All Year [BP]   1P: $99-$175   2P: $110-$185   XP: $25   F10
            Location: I-94, exit 6 (Union Pier Rd), 0.5 mi w to Community Hall Rd, then 1 mi s. Located in a quiet area. 9902 Com-
Bed & Breakfast munity Hall Rd 49129. **Fax:** 269/469-9138. **Facility:** On 30 acres of orchards and woodlands, the B&B is well
suited for outdoor enthusiasts; each guest room has rocking chairs and a gas fireplace. Designated smoking
area. 8 units. 5 one-bedroom standard units with whirlpools. 3 one-bedroom suites ($180-$230) with whirlpools. 2 stories (no elevator), interior/exterior corridors. **Parking:** on-site. **Terms:** check-in 4 pm, 2 night minimum stay - weekends, age restrictions
may apply, 7 day cancellation notice-fee imposed, no pets allowed (owner's dog on premises). **Amenities:** video library. *Some:*
CD players. **Leisure Activities:** canoeing, fishing, cross country skiing, bicycles. **Business Services:** meeting rooms.
Cards: AX, DS, MC, VI.
                                                                                    SOME UNITS

(✕) (✕) (VCR) / (📠) (🖥) (🖨) /

SANDPIPER INN   **Phone:** 269/469-1146
(AAA) (SAVE)   5/1-9/6   1P: $150-$265   2P: $150-$265
            9/7-10/31   1P: $110-$245   2P: $110-$245
▼▼▼▼   4/1-4/30 & 11/1-3/31   1P: $80-$195   2P: $80-$195
Bed & Breakfast **Location:** I-94, exit 6 (Union Pier Rd), 2 mi w, just s. 16136 Lakeview Ave 49129 (PO Box 607). **Fax:** 269/469-8091.
            Facility: Smoke free premises. 9 one-bedroom standard units, some with whirlpools. 3 stories (no elevator),
            interior corridors. **Parking:** on-site. **Terms:** office hours 9 am-7 pm, check-in 4 pm, 2 night minimum stay -
weekends, 14 day cancellation notice-fee imposed. **Amenities:** video library, voice mail. **Leisure Activities:** bicycles. **Cards:** AX,
DS, MC, VI.

(†¶➜) (✕) (VCR)

——————— **The following lodgings were either not evaluated or did not** ———————
         meet AAA rating requirements but are listed for your information only.

PINE GARTH COTTAGES   **Phone:** 269/469-1642
[fyi]   Did not meet all AAA rating requirements for some public areas at time of last evaluation on 06/20/2003.
               Location: I-94, exit 6 (Union Pier Rd), 2 mi w, then 0.4 mi n. 15790 Lakeshore Rd 49129 (PO Box 347). Facilities, serv-
Cottage   ices, and decor characterize a mid-range property.

PINE GARTH INN   Phone: 269/469-1642

[fyi]

Bed & Breakfast

Did not meet all AAA rating requirements for some guest rooms at time of last evaluation on 06/20/2003. **Location:** I-94, exit 6 (Union Pier Rd), 2 mi w, then 0.4 mi n. 15790 Lakeshore Rd 49129 (PO Box 347). Facilities, services, and decor characterize a mid-range property.

SWEETHAVEN RESORT   Phone: 269/469-0332

[fyi]

Cabin

Did not meet all AAA rating requirements for some guest rooms at time of last evaluation on 06/20/2003. **Location:** I-94, exit 6 (Union Pier Rd), just w. Located in rural area. 9517 Union Pier Rd 49129. Facilities, services, and decor characterize a mid-range property.

------ **WHERE TO DINE** ------

MILLER'S COUNTRY HOUSE   Lunch: $7-$9   Dinner: $18-$26   Phone: 269/469-5950

American

Location: I-94, exit 6 (Union Pier Rd), 1 mi w, then 0.3 mi s. 16409 Red Arrow Hwy 49129. **Hours:** 5 pm-11 pm, Sat & Sun from noon. Closed: 11/25, 12/24, 12/25; also Tues 9/2-5/30. **Features:** A comfy roadside establishment featuring a large, airy dining room that looks out over gardens and a small pond. New Zealand rack of lamb and American selections make up the varied menu. Casual dress; cocktails. **Parking:** on-site. **Cards:** AX, DC, DS, MC, VI.

RED ARROW ROADHOUSE   Dinner: $8-$20   Phone: 269/469-3939

American

Location: I-94, exit 6 (Union Pier Rd), 1 mi w, then 0.5 mi n. 15710 Red Arrow Hwy 49129. **Hours:** 5 pm-10 pm, Fri-11 pm, Sat & Sun noon-10 pm. Closed major holidays; also Tues & Wed 10/1-5/1. **Features:** From the outside, the eatery is the quintessential roadhouse of the '40s and '50s, while inside is a comfortable, casual interior of knotty pine and mounted trophy heads. This spot is a popular draw for locals and want-to-be locals. The menu centers on creative interpretations of such classics as broasted chicken dinners, broiled Lake Superior whitefish, crispy Baja fish tacos and a variety of comfort foods. Casual dress; cocktails. **Parking:** on-site. **Cards:** AX, DS, MC, VI.

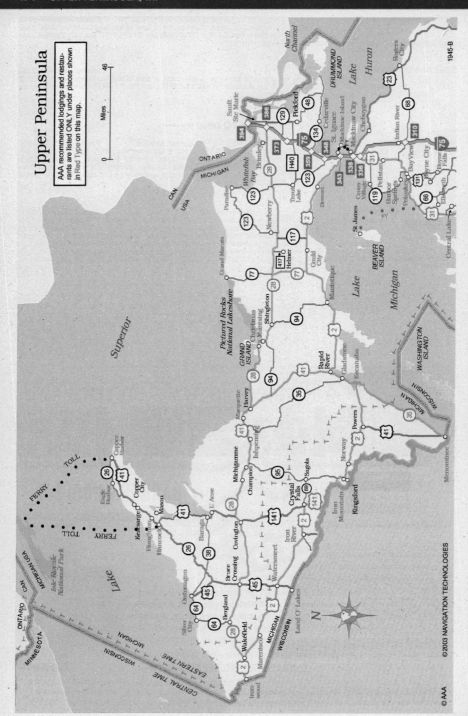

Upper Peninsula

AAA recommended lodgings and restaurants are listed ONLY under places shown
in Red Type on this map.

Miles   46

1945-B

©2003 NAVIGATION TECHNOLOGIES

© AAA

UPPER PENINSULA

To help you more easily locate accommodations in the Upper Peninsula region of Michigan, please see the map on page 474. You can find accommodation listings under the alphabetical header for each city whose name appears on the map in red type.

UTICA —*See Detroit p. 287.*

WALKER pop. 21,842—*See also GRAND RAPIDS.*

———— WHERE TO STAY ————

AMERIHOST INN-GRAND RAPIDS NORTH   *Book at aaa.com*
Phone: (616)791-8500
All Year   1P: $72-$78   2P: $75-$81   XP: $6   F16
Small-scale Hotel
Location: I-96, exit 28 (Walker Ave), just s. Located in a commercial area. 2171 Holton Ct 49544. Fax: 616/791-8630. **Facility:** 60 one-bedroom standard units, some with whirlpools. 2 stories (no elevator), interior corridors. *Bath:* combo or shower only. **Parking:** on-site. **Terms:** [ECP] meal plan available. **Amenities:** voice mail, safes (fee), irons, hair dryers. **Pool(s):** heated indoor. **Leisure Activities:** sauna, whirlpool, exercise room. **Business Services:** meeting rooms. **Cards:** AX, CB, DC, DS, JC, MC, VI. **Special Amenities: free expanded continental breakfast and free newspaper.**

SOME UNITS

BAYMONT INN & SUITES-GRAND RAPIDS NORTH   *Book at aaa.com*
Phone: (616)735-9595
All Year   1P: $79-$99
Small-scale Hotel
Location: I-96, exit 28 (Walker Ave), just s. Located in a commercial area. 2151 Holton Ct NW 49544. Fax: 616/735-9600. **Facility:** 89 one-bedroom standard units, some with whirlpools. 4 stories, interior corridors. *Bath:* combo or shower only. **Parking:** on-site. **Terms:** [ECP] meal plan available. **Amenities:** video games, voice mail, irons, hair dryers. **Pool(s):** heated indoor. **Leisure Activities:** whirlpool, exercise room. **Guest Services:** valet and coin laundry. **Business Services:** meeting rooms. **Cards:** AX, CB, DC, DS, MC, VI.

SOME UNITS

HAMPTON INN- GRAND RAPIDS NORTH   *Book at aaa.com*
Phone: 616/647-1000
All Year   1P: $85   2P: $89
Small-scale Hotel
Location: I-96 and SR 37, exit Alpine Rd, just ne. Located in a commercial area. 500 Center Dr 49544 (500 Center Dr, GRAND RAPIDS). Fax: 616/647-1001. **Facility:** 84 units. 81 one-bedroom standard units, some with whirlpools. 3 one-bedroom suites ($99-$149). 4 stories, interior corridors. *Bath:* combo or shower only. **Parking:** on-site, winter plug-ins. **Terms:** cancellation fee imposed, [ECP] meal plan available. **Amenities:** video games, dual phone lines, voice mail, irons, hair dryers. **Pool(s):** heated indoor. **Leisure Activities:** whirlpool, exercise room. **Guest Services:** valet laundry. **Business Services:** meeting rooms. **Cards:** AX, CB, DC, DS, MC, VI.

SOME UNITS

HOLIDAY INN EXPRESS HOTEL & SUITES   *Book at aaa.com*
Phone: (616)647-4100
All Year   1P: $89-$139   2P: $89-$139
Small-scale Hotel
Location: I-96 and SR 37, exit Alpine Rd, just ne. Located in a semi-commercial area. 358 RiverRidge Dr 49544. Fax: 616/647-4101. **Facility:** 94 one-bedroom standard units, some with whirlpools. 3 stories, interior corridors. *Bath:* combo or shower only. **Parking:** on-site. **Amenities:** video games, high-speed Internet, dual phone lines, voice mail, irons, hair dryers. **Pool(s):** heated indoor. **Leisure Activities:** whirlpool, exercise room. **Fee:** game room. **Guest Services:** valet and coin laundry. **Business Services:** meeting rooms, business center. **Cards:** AX, DC, DS, MC, VI.

SOME UNITS

SPRINGHILL SUITES BY MARRIOTT   *Book at aaa.com*
Phone: 616/785-1600
All Year   1P: $109-$129   2P: $109-$129
Small-scale Hotel
Location: I-96 and SR 37, exit Alpine Rd, just ne. Located in a semi-commercial area. 450 Center Dr 49544. Fax: 616/785-1601. **Facility:** 76 one-bedroom standard units, some with whirlpools. 3 stories, interior corridors. *Bath:* combo or shower only. **Parking:** on-site, winter plug-ins. **Terms:** cancellation fee imposed, [ECP] meal plan available. **Amenities:** video games, voice mail, irons, hair dryers. **Pool(s):** small heated indoor. **Leisure Activities:** whirlpool, exercise room. **Guest Services:** sundries, valet and coin laundry. **Business Services:** meeting rooms, business center. **Cards:** AX, CB, DC, DS, MC, VI.

SOME UNITS

WALLED LAKE —*See Detroit p. 288.*

WALTZ —*See Detroit p. 288.*

WARREN —*See Detroit p. 288.*

WATERFORD —*See Detroit p. 290.*

WATERSMEET

——— WHERE TO STAY ———

DANCING EAGLES RESORT LAC VIEUX DESERT CASINO
Phone: (906)358-4949
All Year   1P: $60-$160   2P: $60-$160   XP: $10   F17

Large-scale Hotel
Location: 1.8 mi n of US 2. N5384 US Hwy 45 49969 (PO Box 99). **Fax:** 906/358-4950. **Facility:** Although the casino is in a rural area, it is recommended that you make reservations for a room ahead of time, as it's very popular with gamblers. 129 units. 124 one-bedroom standard units, some with whirlpools. 5 one-bedroom suites ($85-$140), some with whirlpools. 2 stories, interior corridors. *Bath:* combo or shower only. **Parking:** on-site, winter plug-ins. **Terms:** check-in 4 pm, cancellation fee imposed, [CP] meal plan available, pets ($100 deposit, in smoking units). **Amenities:** voice mail. **Pool(s):** heated indoor. **Leisure Activities:** sauna, whirlpool, snowmobiling, exercise room. *Fee:* golf-9 holes, game room. **Guest Services:** gift shop, coin laundry. **Business Services:** meeting rooms. **Cards:** AX, DC, DS, MC, VI.

SOME UNITS

🎲 ASK 🅂 🐑 🍽 🛜 ➿ 🚫 🚷 💻 / ✕ 🖧 📞 📶 /
FEE

WEST BLOOMFIELD —*See Detroit p. 291.*

WEST BRANCH pop. 1,926

——— WHERE TO STAY ———

QUALITY INN-FOWARDS CONFERENCE CENTER   *Book at aaa.com*   **Phone:** (989)345-3503
AAA SAVE
6/1-10/31   1P: $83-$99   2P: $89-$105   XP: $6   F18
4/1-5/31 & 11/1-3/31   1P: $76-$96   2P: $82-$102   XP: $6   F18

Small-scale Hotel
Location: I-75, exit 212 (Cook Rd). Located next to a factory outlet mall. 2980 Cook Rd 48661 (PO Box 369). **Fax:** 989/345-4194. **Facility:** 80 one-bedroom standard units, some with whirlpools. 2 stories, interior corridors. *Bath:* combo or shower only. **Parking:** on-site, winter plug-ins. **Amenities:** video library (fee), irons, hair dryers. *Some:* dual phone lines. **Dining:** 6 am-11 pm, cocktails. **Pool(s):** heated indoor. **Leisure Activities:** whirlpool. *Fee:* game room. **Guest Services:** gift shop, valet laundry. **Business Services:** conference facilities. **Cards:** AX, CB, DC, DS, JC, MC, VI. **Special Amenities:** free local telephone calls and free newspaper. *(See color ad below)*

SOME UNITS

🅂 🍽 🍽 🛜 ➿ 💻 / ✕ VCR 📞 📶 /
FEE

SUPER 8 MOTEL   *Book at aaa.com*   **Phone:** (989)345-8488
AAA SAVE   5/15-10/15 [CP]   1P: $72-$82   2P: $77-$88   XP: $6   F18
◆◆◆◆   4/1-5/14 & 10/16-3/31 [CP]   1P: $60-$70   2P: $66-$76   XP: $6   F18
          Location: I-75, exit 212 (Cook Rd). Located next to a factory outlet mall. 2596 Austin's Way 48661 (PO Box 338).
          Fax: 989/345-8497. **Facility:** 77 one-bedroom standard units, some with whirlpools. 2 stories (no elevator),
Small-scale Hotel   interior corridors. *Bath:* combo or shower only. **Parking:** on-site, winter plug-ins. **Terms:** small pets only.
          Amenities: video library (fee). **Pool(s):** heated indoor. **Leisure Activities:** whirlpool. *Fee:* game room.
Guest Services: coin laundry. **Cards:** AX, CB, DC, DS, JC, MC, VI. **Special Amenities: free continental breakfast and free
local telephone calls.** *(See ad below)*

SOME UNITS

[S&D] [🐾] [↕] [♿] [🏊] / [✕] [VCR] [DATA PORT] [❚] [📷] [▭] /
                                                              FEE

———— **WHERE TO DINE** ————

COYLES   **Lunch:** $3-$5   **Dinner:** $6-$11   **Phone:** 989/343-9440
AAA   **Location:** I-75, exit 215, 1 mi e on SR 55. 3444 M-55 48661. **Hours:** 8 am-10 pm, Fri & Sat-11 pm. Closed:
◆◆◆   12/25. **Features:** Patrons can pick and choose from the wide assortment of tempting options on the lunch
          and dinner buffets or order from a menu of reasonably priced items. Casual dress; cocktails. **Parking:**
American   on-site. **Cards:** DC, MC, VI.   [✕]

WHITE CLOUD pop. 1,420

———— **WHERE TO STAY** ————

THE SHACK   **Phone:** 231/924-6683
◆◆◆◆   All Year [BP]   1P: $60-$190   2P: $60-$190
          Location: From stoplight; 5.5 mi w to Jugville. Located on Robinson Lake. 2263 W 14th St 49349. Fax: 231/924-5065.
Small-scale Hotel   **Facility:** Smoke free premises. 44 units. 42 one- and 2 two-bedroom standard units, some with whirlpools.
          1-2 stories (no elevator), interior/exterior corridors. *Bath:* combo or shower only. **Parking:** on-site. **Terms:** 20
day cancellation notice-fee imposed. **Amenities:** voice mail, hair dryers. *Some:* irons. **Leisure Activities:** paddleboats, fishing,
cross country skiing, horseshoes, shuffleboard, volleyball. *Fee:* game room. **Business Services:** meeting rooms. **Cards:** DS,
MC, VI.

SOME UNITS

[✕] [✕] [DATA PORT] [▭] / [VCR] [❚] [📷] /

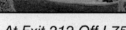

WHITEHALL pop. 2,884

———— WHERE TO STAY ————

BEST WESTERN INN & SUITES OF WHITEHALL *Book at aaa.com* Phone: (231)893-4833
▼▼▼
5/31-9/1 [CP] 1P: $119-$229 2P: $119-$229 XP: $5 F18
4/1-5/30 & 9/2-3/31 [CP] 1P: $69-$109 2P: $69-$109 XP: $5 F18
Small-scale Hotel **Location:** US 31, exit Whitehall, just e. Located in a semi-commercial area. 2822 N Durham Rd 49461. Fax: 231/893-2423. **Facility:** 74 units. 65 one-bedroom standard units, some with whirlpools. 9 one-bedroom suites, some with whirlpools. 3 stories, interior corridors. *Bath:* combo or shower only. **Parking:** on-site, winter plug-ins. **Terms:** cancellation fee imposed. **Amenities:** voice mail, safes (fee), irons, hair dryers. **Pool(s):** heated indoor. **Leisure Activities:** whirlpool. *Fee:* game room. **Guest Services:** valet laundry. **Cards:** AX, CB, DC, DS, JC, MC, VI.

SOME UNITS
ASK SD TI+ & 2 ☞ DATA PORT ☐ / ✕ ☐ ☐ /

LAKE LAND MOTEL Phone: 231/894-5644
AAA SAVE
6/18-9/6 1P: $60-$65 2P: $70-$75 XP: $5
4/1-6/17 & 9/7-10/31 1P: $40-$45 2P: $45-$50 XP: $5
▼ 11/1-3/31 1P: $35-$40 2P: $40-$45 XP: $5
Motel **Location:** On US 31 business route, 0.8 mi w of US 31. Located in a commercial area. 1002 E Colby St 49461. **Facility:** 12 one-bedroom standard units. 1 story, exterior corridors. **Parking:** on-site. **Terms:** 2 night minimum stay - weekends in summer, small pets only ($5 extra charge). **Cards:** AX, DS, MC, VI.
Special Amenities: free local telephone calls and early check-in/late check-out.

SOME UNITS
🐾 TI+ ☐ / ✕ /
FEE

RAMADA INN *Book at aaa.com* Phone: (231)893-3030
AAA SAVE
5/28-8/31 [CP] 1P: $119 2P: $119 XP: $5 F17
4/1-5/27 & 9/1-3/31 [CP] 1P: $69 2P: $69 XP: $5 F17
▼▼▼ **Location:** US 31, exit Whitehall/Montague, just e. 2865 Colby Rd 49461. Fax: 231/893-0030. **Facility:** 66 one-
Small-scale Hotel bedroom standard units, some with whirlpools. 2 stories (no elevator), interior corridors. **Parking:** on-site. **Terms:** cancellation fee imposed, [AP] & [BP] meal plans available. **Amenities:** video library (fee), dual phone lines, voice mail, irons, hair dryers. **Dining:** 6:30 am-1 & 5-9 pm, Sun 8 am-noon, cocktails. **Pool(s):** heated outdoor. **Leisure Activities:** sauna, exercise room. *Fee:* game room. **Guest Services:** coin laundry. **Business Services:** meeting rooms. **Cards:** AX, CB, DC, DS, MC, VI. **Special Amenities:** free continental breakfast and free newspaper.
(See color ad p 409)

SOME UNITS
SD TI 2 ✕ ☞ DATA PORT ☐ / ✕ VCR ☐ ☐ /
FEE

———— WHERE TO DINE ————

PINHEAD'S GUTTERS & GRUB **Lunch:** $5-$10 **Dinner:** $5-$12 Phone: 231/894-4103
▼▼ ▼▼ **Location:** Just w of center. 115 South Lake 49461. **Hours:** 4 pm-10 pm, Fri-11 pm, Sat 11 am-11 pm, Sun
American noon-9 pm. Closed: 1/1, 11/25, 12/25. **Features:** The friendly restaurant is a cozy place in which to enjoy such choices as wood-fired pizza and half-pound burgers while bowling a few frames. The loud and lively atmosphere attracts boaters and vacationers during summer and families during winter. Casual dress; cocktails. **Parking:** on-site. **Cards:** AX, DS, MC, VI.
Ψ

WHITMORE LAKE pop. 6,574

———— WHERE TO STAY ————

BEST WESTERN WHITMORE LAKE *Book at aaa.com* Phone: (734)449-2058
AAA SAVE
All Year [CP] 1P: $75-$79 2P: $75-$79 XP: $6 F12
▼▼▼ **Location:** US 23, exit 53, just e. 9897 Main St 48189. Fax: 734/449-8635. **Facility:** 61 units. 59 one-bedroom standard units. 1 one- and 1 two-bedroom suites ($95-$150), some with kitchens and/or whirlpools. 2 stories, Motel exterior corridors. **Parking:** on-site, winter plug-ins. **Terms:** pets ($25 extra charge, in limited units). **Amenities:** irons, hair dryers. **Pool(s):** heated indoor. **Leisure Activities:** sauna. **Guest Services:** coin laundry. **Business Services:** meeting rooms. **Cards:** AX, DC, DS, MC, VI. **Special Amenities:** free continental breakfast and free local telephone calls.

SOME UNITS
SD 🛏 TI+ 2 ☞ DATA PORT ☐ ☐ / ✕ /
FEE

WILLIAMSTON pop. 3,441

———— WHERE TO STAY ————

ACORN MOTEL Phone: (517)655-6793
AAA SAVE
All Year 1P: $52 2P: $59 XP: $4 F15
▼ **Location:** I-96, exit 117, 1.5 mi n, 0.7 mi e on SR 43. 2346 E Grand River Ave 48895 (PO Box 327). Fax: 517/655-4309. **Facility:** 8 one-bedroom standard units. 1 story, exterior corridors. **Parking:** on-site. Motel **Terms:** 3 day cancellation notice-fee imposed. **Cards:** MC, VI.

SOME UNITS
SD DATA PORT ☐ ☐ ☐ / ✕ /

TOPLIFF'S TARA BED & BREAKFAST Phone: 517/655-8860
▼▼▼ All Year [BP] 1P: $65-$115 2P: $75-$125 XP: $15
Location: I-96, exit 117, just s, 3.5 mi w. 251 Noble Rd 48895. Fax: 847/556-0241. **Facility:** Built in 1905, this rural
Bed & Breakfast farmhouse is in a serene, natural setting; it has been restored and is furnished with period antiques. Smoke free premises. 5 one-bedroom standard units, some with whirlpools. 3 stories (no elevator), interior corridors. *Bath:* some shared or private, combo or shower only. **Parking:** on-site. **Terms:** check-in 4 pm, 10 day cancellation notice-fee imposed, package plans, no pets allowed (owner's pet on premises). **Amenities:** hair dryers. **Pool(s):** outdoor. **Guest Services:** gift shop. **Cards:** DC, JC, VI.

SOME UNITS
2 ✕ ☎ / 🅦 /

------ **WHERE TO DINE** ------

RED CEDAR GRILL
⬥⬥ ⬥⬥
American

Lunch: $7-$10   **Dinner:** $10-$15   **Phone:** 517/655-3766
Location: I-96, exit 117, 1.5 mi n; downtown. 150 E Grand River Ave 48895. **Hours:** 11 am-10 pm, Fri & Sat-11 pm, Sun noon-9 pm. Closed major holidays. **Reservations:** accepted. **Features:** An eclectic mixture of art and mirrors adorns the walls of this casual, open concept restaurant. A large and varied menu features a number of creatively prepared dishes and makes for interesting reading in its own right. Casual dress; cocktails. **Parking:** on-site. **Cards:** AX, DC, DS, MC, VI.

                                                               🔲M 🍸 ✕

WIXOM —*See Detroit p. 291.*

WOODHAVEN —*See Detroit p. 291.*

WYOMING pop. 69,368—*See also GRAND RAPIDS.*

------ **WHERE TO STAY** ------

HAMPTON INN GRAND RAPIDS SOUTH   *Book at aaa.com*   **Phone:** (616)261-5500
⬥⬥⬥⬥
Small-scale Hotel

All Year [ECP]   1P: $89-$129   2P: $89-$129
Location: US 131 and 54th St, exit 78. Located in a commercial area. 755 54th St SW 49509. Fax: 616/261-9120. **Facility:** 139 one-bedroom standard units, some with whirlpools. 4 stories, interior corridors. *Bath:* combo or shower only. **Parking:** on-site. **Terms:** check-in 4 pm. **Amenities:** voice mail, irons, hair dryers. **Pool(s):** heated indoor. **Leisure Activities:** whirlpool, exercise room. *Fee:* game room. **Guest Services:** valet and coin laundry. **Business Services:** meeting rooms. **Cards:** AX, DC, DS, MC, VI.

                                                 SOME UNITS
ASK Ⓢ🄳 🚻➧ 🔲 📷 🛏 ✕ 🐾 DATA/PORT ▭ / ✕ 🛆 /
                                                             FEE

HOWARD JOHNSON PLAZA HOTEL   *Book at aaa.com*   **Phone:** 616/241-6444
🔺🔺🔺 SAVE
⬥⬥ ⬥⬥
Large-scale Hotel

1/2-3/31   1P: $79-$99   2P: $79-$99
4/1-1/1   1P: $79   2P: $79
Location: On SR 11, 0.3 mi e of US 131, exit 28th St. Located in a commercial area. 255 28th St SW 49548. Fax: 616/241-1807. **Facility:** 155 one-bedroom standard units. 5 stories, interior corridors. **Parking:** on-site. **Terms:** check-in 4 pm, cancellation fee imposed. **Amenities:** voice mail, irons, hair dryers. **Dining:** 6:30 am-11 pm, Sun 7 am-4 pm, cocktails. **Pool(s):** heated outdoor, heated indoor. **Leisure Activities:** sauna, whirlpool, putting green, exercise room, shuffleboard. *Fee:* pool tables, game room. **Guest Services:** valet and coin laundry. **Business Services:** meeting rooms. **Cards:** AX, CB, DC, DS, MC, VI.

                                                 SOME UNITS
Ⓢ🄳 🍴 🍸 🛏 ✕ 🐾 DATA/PORT ▭ / ✕ 🛆 🖨 /

RAMADA LIMITED   *Book at aaa.com*   **Phone:** (616)452-1461
⬥⬥ ⬥⬥
Small-scale Hotel

4/1-8/31   1P: $62-$79   2P: $69-$79   XP: $7   F18
9/1-3/31   1P: $59-$69   2P: $65-$69   XP: $7   F18
Location: On SR 11, 0.4 mi e of US 131. Located in a commercial area. 65 28th St SW 49548. Fax: 616/452-5115. **Facility:** 54 one-bedroom standard units, some with whirlpools. 2 stories (no elevator), interior/exterior corridors. **Parking:** on-site. **Terms:** [ECP] meal plan available. **Amenities:** voice mail. *Some:* irons, hair dryers. **Pool(s):** small heated indoor. **Leisure Activities:** exercise room. **Cards:** AX, CB, DC, DS, MC, VI.

                                                 SOME UNITS
ASK Ⓢ🄳 🚻➧ 🛏 🐾 DATA/PORT / ✕ 🛆 /

SUPER 8 MOTEL   *Book at aaa.com*   **Phone:** (616)530-8588
⬥⬥⬥
Motel
MC, VI.

All Year   1P: $47-$57   2P: $54-$59   XP: $5   F12
Location: US 131, exit 79. Located in a commercial area. 727 44th St SW 49509. Fax: 616/530-8588. **Facility:** 62 one-bedroom standard units. 3 stories (no elevator), interior corridors. **Parking:** on-site, winter plug-ins. **Terms:** weekly rates available, small pets only ($10 fee). **Amenities:** safes (fee). **Cards:** AX, DC, DS,

                                                 SOME UNITS
ASK Ⓢ🄳 🐕 🚻➧ 🐾 / ✕ 🛆 🖨 /
                                                 FEE

------ **WHERE TO DINE** ------

------ *The following restaurant has not been evaluated by AAA* ------
but is listed for your information only.

ORIENTAL FOREST
fyi

                                               Phone: 616/538-9988
Not evaluated. **Location:** US 131, exit 78, just w. 5316 Clyde Park SW 49509. **Features:** The popular all-you-can-eat buffet serves Cantonese, Hunan and Szechuan-style Chinese food.

YPSILANTI pop. 22,362

——— WHERE TO STAY ———

PARISH HOUSE INN

♦♦ ♦♦

Historic Bed & Breakfast

Phone: (734)480-4800

All Year 1P: $85-$110 2P: $95-$160 XP: $25
Location: I-94, exit 183, 0.5 mi n; downtown. Located in the historic district. 103 S Huron St 48197. Fax: 734/480-7472. **Facility:** This 1893 Queen Anne-style inn was formerly a parsonage. Smoke free premises. 8 units. 7 one-bedroom standard units. 1 one-bedroom suite. 3 stories (no elevator), interior corridors. *Bath:* combo or shower only. **Parking:** on-site. **Terms:** check-in 4 pm, 7 day cancellation notice. **Amenities:** video library, voice mail. **Business Services:** meeting rooms. **Cards:** AX, DS, MC, VI.

SOME UNITS

YPSILANTI MARRIOTT AT EAGLE CREST

AAA SAVE

♦♦♦ ♦♦♦

Resort
Large-scale Hotel

Book at aaa.com

Phone: (734)487-2000

All Year 1P: $99-$179 2P: $109-$189 XP: $10 F18
Location: I-94, exit 183, just se. 1275 S Huron St 48197. Fax: 734/487-0773. **Facility:** Bordering a river and the rolling terrain of a golf course, this big-city hotel is in a country-club setting. 236 one-bedroom standard units. 8 stories, interior corridors. **Parking:** on-site, winter plug-ins. **Amenities:** high-speed Internet (fee), dual phone lines, voice mail, irons, hair dryers. **Dining:** 6:30 am-2 & 5-11 pm, cocktails. **Pool(s):** heated indoor. **Leisure Activities:** sauna, whirlpool, steamroom, boat dock, fishing, tennis court, cross country skiing, exercise room, volleyball. *Fee:* golf-18 holes, driving range, game room. **Guest Services:** gift shop, valet laundry. **Business Services:** conference facilities, business center. **Cards:** AX, CB, DC, DS, MC, VI. **Special Amenities:** free newspaper. *(See color ad p 193)*

SOME UNITS

——— WHERE TO DINE ———

HAAB'S

AAA

♦♦♦ ♦♦♦

American

Lunch: $6-$11 Dinner: $9-$19 Phone: 734/483-8200
Location: Downtown. 18 W Michigan Ave 48197. **Hours:** 11 am-9 pm, Fri & Sat-10 pm. Closed: 12/25. **Reservations:** suggested, weekends. **Features:** A local landmark since 1934, the longtime favorite is known for its rustic-looking dining room and traditional menu of delicious, well-prepared beef and seafood. Casual dress; cocktails. **Parking:** on-site. **Cards:** AX, DC, DS, MC, VI.

LADY'S GRILL & BAR

♦♦♦ ♦♦♦

American

Lunch: $7-$17 Dinner: $7-$17 Phone: 734/483-2800
Location: In depot town. 36 E Cross St 48198. **Hours:** 11 am-10 pm, Fri & Sat-11 pm, Sun 10 am-9 pm. Closed major holidays. **Features:** In Historic Depot Town, the restaurant once played host to a U.S. president. While not serving statesmen, the cozy bistro serves an assortment of vegetarian and non-vegetarian dishes, including lasagna, black Angus burgers and Traverse City chicken. Casual dress; cocktails. **Parking:** on-site and street. **Cards:** AX, DC, MC, VI.

Wisconsin

ABBOTSFORD pop. 1,956

———— WHERE TO STAY ————

SLEEP INN
Small-scale Hotel

Book at aaa.com
All Year [ECP]
Phone: (715)223-3337
1P: $69-$84   2P: $69-$84   XP: $5   F18
Location: SR 29, exit 132 (SR 13), just se. 300 E Elderberry Rd 54405 (PO Box 590). Fax: 715/223-0508. **Facility:** 60 one-bedroom standard units, some with whirlpools. 3 stories, interior corridors. *Bath:* combo or shower only. **Parking:** on-site, winter plug-ins. **Terms:** check-in 4 pm, pets ($15 extra charge, in designated units). **Amenities:** voice mail. *Some:* irons, hair dryers. **Pool(s):** small heated indoor. **Leisure Activities:** exercise room. *Fee:* game room. **Business Services:** meeting rooms, fax (fee). **Cards:** AX, CB, DC, DS, JC, MC, VI.

———— WHERE TO DINE ————

ABBY CAFE
American

Lunch: $4-$8   **Dinner:** $4-$8   **Phone:** 715/223-3943
Location: On Business Rt 29; downtown. 206 E Spruce 54405. **Hours:** 6 am-10 pm. Closed: 11/25, 12/25. **Features:** Simple, made-from-scratch entrees and homemade desserts are the draw at the popular diner. The country decor is representative of the surrounding farming community. Casual dress. **Parking:** on-site. **Cards:** MC, VI.

ALGOMA pop. 3,357

———— WHERE TO STAY ————

ALGOMA BEACH MOTEL & CONDOS
Small-scale Hotel

Book at aaa.com
Phone: (920)487-2828
5/29-3/31   1P: $79-$259   2P: $79-$259   XP: $15   F15
4/1-5/28   1P: $59-$199   2P: $59-$199   XP: $15   F15
Location: Jct SR 22 and 72; 2' mi n on SR 22. Located on the shores of Lake Michigan. 1500 Lake St 54201. Fax: 920/487-2844. **Facility:** 32 units. 28 one-bedroom standard units, some with efficiencies and/or whirlpools. 4 vacation homes. 1-2 stories (no elevator), interior/exterior corridors. *Bath:* combo or shower only. **Parking:** on-site. **Terms:** 3 day cancellation notice, weekly rates available, [CP] meal plan available, package plans - 11/1-4/30, pets ($15 extra charge, in smoking units). **Amenities:** voice mail. *Some:* irons, hair dryers. **Leisure Activities:** fishing, beachside picnic tables & grills. **Cards:** AX, CB, DC, DS, JC, MC, VI. **Special Amenities:** free continental breakfast and free local telephone calls.

SCENIC SHORE INN

Phone: 920/487-3214

▼▼▼	6/16-9/6	1P: $49	2P: $59	XP: $8	F15
	9/7-10/31	1P: $45	2P: $54	XP: $8	F15
Motel	4/1-6/15	1P: $40	2P: $49	XP: $8	F15
	11/1-3/31	1P: $36	2P: $44	XP: $8	F15

Location: Jct SR 54, 0.8 mi s on SR 42. Located opposite Lake Michigan. 2221 Lake St 54201. **Facility:** 13 one-bedroom standard units. 2 stories (no elevator), exterior corridors. **Parking:** on-site, winter plug-ins. **Terms:** 3 day cancellation notice-fee imposed, small pets only (in smoking units). **Leisure Activities:** Fee: charter fishing. **Cards:** AX, DS, MC, VI.

------- WHERE TO DINE -------

PORTSIDE II RESTAURANT

Lunch: $4-$7 **Dinner: $6-$16** **Phone: 920/487-9704**

Location: 0.3 mi nw on SR 42. 709 N Water St 54201. **Hours:** 4 am-10 pm; 6 am-9 pm 11/1-5/30. Closed: 12/25. **Features:** Right off the main highway, the family restaurant offers a number of sandwiches, dinners and odds and ends. Breakfast is served all day. Casual dress; beer & wine only. **Parking:** on-site. **Cards:** MC, VI.

American

ANTIGO pop. 8,560

------- WHERE TO STAY -------

NORTHWOODS BIRCH INN

Phone: (715)623-0506

▼▼▼	All Year	1P: $60-$71	2P: $66-$77	XP: $5	F17

Location: On US 45 N, 0.3 mi n of jct SR 64 E. 525 Memory Ln 54409. Fax: 715/623-0602. **Facility:** 45 one-bedroom standard units. 2 stories, interior corridors. *Bath:* combo or shower only. **Parking:** on-site. **Terms:** cancellation fee imposed, [CP] meal plan available. **Amenities:** voice mail, irons, hair dryers. **Pool(s):** small heated indoor. **Leisure Activities:** whirlpool. **Cards:** AX, DC, DS, MC, VI.

Small-scale Hotel

SUPER 8 MOTEL-ANTIGO   *Book at aaa.com*

Phone: (715)623-4188

▼▼▼	5/21-9/26 [CP]	1P: $75-$85	2P: $75-$85	XP: $5	F12
	4/1-5/20 & 9/27-3/31 [CP]	1P: $59-$69	2P: $59-$69	XP: $5	F12

Small-scale Hotel **Location:** On US 45 at jct SR 64 E. 535 Century Ave 54409. Fax: 715/623-5787. **Facility:** 52 one-bedroom standard units, some with whirlpools. 2 stories (no elevator), interior corridors. *Bath:* combo or shower only. **Parking:** on-site, winter plug-ins. **Terms:** pets ($15 extra charge, in smoking units). **Amenities:** safes (fee). **Pool(s):** heated indoor. **Leisure Activities:** whirlpool. **Business Services:** meeting rooms. **Cards:** AX, CB, DC, DS, MC, VI.

APPLETON pop. 70,087

------- WHERE TO STAY -------

APPLETON WINGATE INN   *Book at aaa.com*

Phone: (920)993-1200

(AAA) [SAVE]	4/1-7/25	1P: $59-$129	2P: $59-$129	XP: $10	F
▼▼▼▼	8/3-3/31	1P: $23-$59	2P: $23-$59	XP: $10	F

Small-scale Hotel **Location:** US 41, exit 137 (SR 125), just nw. 300 Mall Dr 54913. Fax: 920/993-9090. **Facility:** 80 one-bedroom standard units. 3 stories, interior corridors. *Bath:* combo or shower only. **Parking:** on-site, winter plug-ins. **Terms:** open 4/1-7/25 & 8/3-3/31, [ECP] meal plan available. **Amenities:** high-speed Internet, dual phone lines, voice mail, irons, hair dryers. **Pool(s):** small heated indoor. **Leisure Activities:** whirlpool, exercise room. **Guest Services:** valet laundry. **Business Services:** meeting rooms, business center. **Cards:** AX, CB, DC, DS, JC, MC, VI. **Special Amenities:** free expanded continental breakfast and free local telephone calls.

BEST WESTERN MIDWAY HOTEL   *Book at aaa.com*

Phone: 920/731-4141

(AAA) [SAVE]	All Year [CP]	1P: $89-$109	2P: $89-$109	XP: $10	F18
▼▼ ▼▼					

Location: US 41, exit 137 (SR 125), 0.5 mi e. Located in a commercial area. 3033 W College Ave 54914. Fax: 920/731-6343. **Facility:** 105 one-bedroom standard units, some with whirlpools. 2 stories (no elevator), interior corridors. **Parking:** on-site, winter plug-ins. **Terms:** [ECP] meal plan available, pets ($10 extra charge, in designated units). **Amenities:** voice mail, irons, hair dryers. **Dining:** 6:30 am-10 pm, Sat & Sun from 11 am, cocktails. **Pool(s):** heated indoor. **Leisure Activities:** sauna, whirlpool, domed recreation area, exercise room. **Guest Services:** valet laundry, area transportation-within 4 mi. **Business Services:** meeting rooms. **Cards:** AX, DC, DS, MC, VI. **Special Amenities:** free continental breakfast and free newspaper.

Small-scale Hotel

BUDGETEL INN APPLETON   *Book at aaa.com*

Phone: (920)734-6070

▼▼ ▼▼	4/1-8/15	1P: $49-$79	2P: $54-$84	XP: $5	F18
Motel	8/16-3/31	1P: $49-$69	2P: $54-$74	XP: $5	F18

Location: US 41, exit 137 (SR 125), just e. Located in a commercial area. 3920 W College Ave 54914. Fax: 920/734-0460. **Facility:** 83 one-bedroom standard units. 2 stories (no elevator), interior/exterior corridors. *Bath:* combo or shower only. **Parking:** on-site, winter plug-ins. **Terms:** [CP] meal plan available, small pets only ($25 deposit, in designated units). **Amenities:** video games (fee), voice mail, irons, hair dryers. **Pool(s):** heated outdoor. **Leisure Activities:** 2 tennis courts, volleyball. **Guest Services:** valet and coin laundry. **Business Services:** meeting rooms. **Cards:** AX, CB, DC, DS, MC, VI.

COMFORT SUITES COMFORT DOME   *Book at aaa.com*   **Phone:** (920)730-3800
All Year [CP]   1P: $90-$130   2P: $100-$140   XP: $10   F18
Location: US 41, exit 138 (Wisconsin Ave), just e. Located in a commercial area. 3809 W Wisconsin Ave 54914.
Small-scale Hotel Fax: 920/730-9558. **Facility:** 130 one-bedroom standard units, some with kitchens and/or whirlpools. 2 stories (no elevator), interior corridors. **Fee:** video games, safes. *Some:* high-speed Internet. **Pool(s):** heated indoor. **Leisure Activities:** sauna, whirlpool, exercise room. **Fee:** game room. **Guest Services:** complimentary evening beverages, valet and coin laundry, area transportation. **Business Services:** meeting rooms. **Cards:** AX, CB, DC, DS, JC, MC, VI.
SOME UNITS

COUNTRY INN & SUITES BY CARLSON   *Book at aaa.com*   **Phone:** (920)830-3240
All Year   1P: $69-$200   2P: $69-$200   XP: $10   F18
Location: US 41, exit 137 (W SR 125), just nw. Located in a commercial area. 355 Fox River Dr 54913.
Fax: 920/830-9868. **Facility:** 106 units. 97 one-bedroom standard units, some with whirlpools. 9 one-bedroom suites, some with whirlpools. 3 stories, interior corridors. *Bath:* combo or shower only. **Parking:** on-
Small-scale Hotel site, winter plug-ins. **Terms:** [ECP] meal plan available, small pets only (in smoking units). **Amenities:** video games (fee), voice mail, irons, hair dryers. **Pool(s):** heated indoor. **Leisure Activities:** whirlpool, limited exercise equipment. **Guest Services:** valet and coin laundry, area transportation-mall. **Business Services:** meeting rooms. **Cards:** AX, DC, DS, MC, VI. **Special Amenities:** free expanded continental breakfast and free local telephone calls.
(See color ad starting on p 580 & below)
SOME UNITS

EXEL INN OF APPLETON   *Book at aaa.com*   **Phone:** (920)733-5551
All Year [CP]   1P: $36-$56   2P: $42-$62   XP: $6   F18
Location: US 41, exit 137 (SR 125), just e. Located in a commercial area. 210 Westhill Blvd 54914.
Fax: 920/733-7199. **Facility:** 104 one-bedroom standard units, some with whirlpools. 2 stories (no elevator),
Motel   interior corridors. **Parking:** on-site. **Terms:** weekly rates available, small pets only (in smoking units). **Amenities:** irons. *Some:* hair dryers. **Leisure Activities:** limited exercise equipment. **Guest Services:** coin laundry. **Cards:** AX, CB, DC, DS, MC, VI. **Special Amenities:** free continental breakfast and early check-
in/late check-out.
SOME UNITS
FEE FEE

FAIRFIELD INN BY MARRIOTT   *Book at aaa.com*   **Phone:** (920)954-0202
4/1-10/31 [ECP]   1P: $75-$81   2P: $75-$81   XP: $6   F18
11/1-3/31 [ECP]   1P: $70-$76   2P: $70-$76   XP: $6   F18
Location: US 41, exit 137 (W SR 125), just nw. Located in a commercial area. 132 Mall Dr 54913. Fax: 920/954-0202.
Small-scale Hotel **Facility:** 63 one-bedroom standard units. 3 stories, interior corridors. **Parking:** on-site, winter plug-ins. **Amenities:** irons, hair dryers. **Pool(s):** small heated indoor. **Leisure Activities:** whirlpool. **Guest Services:** valet laundry. **Cards:** AX, DC, DS, MC, VI.
SOME UNITS

HAMPTON INN APPLETON   *Book at aaa.com*   Phone: (920)954-9211

▽▽▽▽▽   9/1-3/31 [ECP]   1P: $84-$99   2P: $94-$109
4/1-5/31 [ECP]   1P: $79-$89   2P: $89-$99
6/1-8/31 [ECP]   1P: $89-$99   2P: $99

Small-scale Hotel   **Location:** US 41, exit 137 (W SR 125), just nw. Located in a commercial area. 350 Fox River Dr 54913. Fax: 920/954-6514. **Facility:** 123 one-bedroom standard units. 4 stories, interior corridors. *Bath:* combo or shower only. **Parking:** on-site. **Terms:** 30 day cancellation notice, package plans - seasonal 9/1-5/31. **Amenities:** video games (fee), voice mail, irons, hair dryers. **Pool(s):** small heated indoor. **Leisure Activities:** whirlpool, limited exercise equipment. **Guest Services:** valet laundry, area transportation. **Business Services:** meeting rooms. **Cards:** AX, CB, DC, DS, MC, VI.

SOME UNITS
[ASK] [S/D] [✦] [†|✦] [🖥] [⟳] [🛫] [🎥] [DATA PORT] [💻] / [⊠] [📶] [🖨] /
FEE FEE

MICROTEL INN & SUITES   *Book at aaa.com*   Phone: (920)997-3121

(AAA) [SAVE]   All Year   1P: $49-$73   2P: $63-$73   XP: $5   F16
▽▽▽▽▽   **Location:** US 41, exit 137 (W SR 125), just nw. Located in a commercial area. 321 Metro Dr 54913. Fax: 920/997-3321. **Facility:** 79 one-bedroom standard units. 3 stories, interior corridors. *Bath:* combo or shower only. **Parking:** on-site, winter plug-ins. **Terms:** [CP] meal plan available, pets ($10 deposit, in smoking units). **Leisure Activities:** whirlpool, limited exercise equipment. **Guest Services:** valet laundry.
Small-scale Hotel   **Business Services:** meeting rooms. **Cards:** AX, DC, DS, MC, VI. **Special Amenities: free continental breakfast and free local telephone calls.**

SOME UNITS
[🛏] [†|✦] [🖥] [🎥] [DATA PORT] / [⊠] [📶] [🖨] [💻] /
FEE

RADISSON PAPER VALLEY HOTEL   *Book at aaa.com*   Phone: (920)733-8000

(AAA) [SAVE]   All Year   1P: $99-$179   2P: $99-$179   XP: $10   F17
▽▽▽▽▽   **Location:** 3 mi e of US 41, exit 137 (SR 125); downtown. 333 W College Ave 54911. Fax: 920/733-9220. **Facility:** 390 one-bedroom standard units, some with whirlpools. 7 stories, interior corridors. *Bath:* combo or shower only. **Parking:** on-site (fee). **Terms:** cancellation fee imposed. **Amenities:** high-speed Internet. *Some:*
Large-scale Hotel   mail, irons, hair dryers. *Some:* high-speed Internet. **Dining:** 2 restaurants, 6 am-11 pm, Sat & Sun from 6:30 am, cocktails, also, Vince Lombardi's Steakhouse, see separate listing. **Pool(s):** heated indoor. **Leisure Ac-**
tivities: sauna, whirlpool, miniature golf, exercise room. *Fee:* game room. **Guest Services:** gift shop, valet laundry. **Business Services:** conference facilities, business center. **Cards:** AX, CB, DC, DS, JC, MC, VI. *(See color ad below & p 583)*

SOME UNITS
[S/D] [✦] [†|] [🍷] [🖥] [⟳] [🛫] [✗] [🎥] [DATA PORT] [💻] / [⊠] [VCR] [📶] [🖨] /
FEE FEE FEE

RESIDENCE INN BY MARRIOTT   *Book at aaa.com*   Phone: (920)954-0570

▽▽▽▽▽   All Year   1P: $109   2P: $109
Location: US 41, exit 137 (W SR 125), just nw on Mall Dr. Located in a commercial area. 310 Metro Dr 54913.
Small-scale Hotel   Fax: 920/954-0570. **Facility:** 66 units. 18 one-bedroom standard units with efficiencies. 36 one- and 12 two-bedroom suites, some with efficiencies or kitchens. 3 stories, interior corridors. *Bath:* combo or shower only. **Parking:** on-site, winter plug-ins. **Terms:** 3 day cancellation notice-fee imposed, [BP] meal plan available, pets ($25 fee, $10 extra charge). **Amenities:** dual phone lines, voice mail, irons, hair dryers. **Pool(s):** small heated indoor. **Leisure Activities:** whirlpool, exercise room, sports court. **Guest Services:** complimentary evening beverages: Mon-Thurs, valet and coin laundry. **Business Services:** meeting rooms. **Cards:** AX, DC, DS, MC, VI.

SOME UNITS
[ASK] [S/D] [🛏] [†|✦] [🖥] [⟳] [🛫] [✗] [🎥] [DATA PORT] [📶] [🖨] [💻] / [⊠] [VCR] /
FEE

SUPER 8 MOTEL *Book at aaa.com*   Phone: (920)731-0880

All Year   1P: $50-$80   2P: $50-$85

Motel

Location: US 41, exit 137 (SR 125), just e. Located in a commercial area. 3624 W College Ave 54914. Fax: 920/731-0880. **Facility:** 81 one-bedroom standard units. 2 stories (no elevator), interior corridors. **Parking:** on-site, winter plug-ins. **Terms:** [CP] meal plan available. **Amenities:** video games (fee). **Leisure Activities:** limited exercise equipment. **Guest Services:** coin laundry. **Cards:** AX, CB, DC, DS, MC, VI.

SOME UNITS
FEE FEE

WOODFIELD SUITES APPLETON *Book at aaa.com*   Phone: (920)734-7777

All Year   1P: $84-$104   2P: $94-$114   XP: $10

Small-scale Hotel

Location: US 41, exit 137 (SR 125), just e. Located in a commercial area. 3730 W College Ave 54914. Fax: 920/734-0049. **Facility:** 98 units. 23 one-bedroom standard units. 75 one-bedroom suites ($94-$114), some with efficiencies and/or whirlpools. 2 stories, interior corridors. **Parking:** on-site, winter plug-ins. **Terms:** [ECP] meal plan available, pets ($50 deposit, $10 extra charge). **Amenities:** video games (fee), voice mail, irons, hair dryers. **Pool(s):** heated indoor. **Leisure Activities:** sauna, whirlpool, steamroom, exercise room. **Guest Services:** sundries, complimentary evening beverages, valet and coin laundry. **Business Services:** meeting rooms. **Cards:** AX, CB, DC, DS, MC, VI.

SOME UNITS
FEE

————— *The following lodging was either not evaluated or did not* —————
meet AAA rating requirements but is listed for your information only.

COPPERLEAF HOTEL   Phone: 920/749-0303

[fyi]   All Year [ECP]   1P: $119-$169   2P: $119-$169   XP: $10   F17

Small-scale Hotel

Too new to rate, opening scheduled for December 2003. **Location:** US 41, exit 137 (SR 125), 3 mi e of US 41 on College Ave; downtown. 300 W College Ave 54911 (PO Box 2016, 54912). Fax: 920/749-2883. **Amenities:** 73 units, coffeemakers, microwaves, refrigerators. **Cards:** AX, DS, MC, VI. **(See color ad p 484)**

————— **WHERE TO DINE** —————

FOX RIVER BREWING COMPANY & RESTAURANT   Lunch: $6-$10   Dinner: $7-$18   Phone: 920/991-0000

American

Location: US 41, exit 138 (Wisconsin Ave), just sw; in Fox River Mall. 4301 W Wisconsin Ave 54915. **Hours:** 11 am-10 pm, Fri & Sat-11 pm. Closed: 11/25, 12/25 & Easter. **Reservations:** accepted. **Features:** Gourmet pizza and Cap'n Crunch chicken are prepared in the wood-stone oven of the open display kitchen. Beers are created in the second-story brewery loft, and burgers, sandwiches and pasta complete the menu. Seating is available in the dining room or on the seasonal patio. Casual dress; cocktails. **Parking:** on-site. **Cards:** AX, MC, VI.

MONGO'S   Lunch: $7   Dinner: $14   Phone: 920/730-8304

Mongolian

Location: Just n of College Ave, via Richmond; center. 231 W Franklin 54911. **Hours:** 11 am-2 & 5-9:30 pm, Sat from 5 pm. Closed major holidays. **Reservations:** suggested. **Features:** Diners can create stir-fry combinations from fresh ingredients and watch capable cooks prepare them at the unusual, downtown restaurant. The atmosphere is accented by ethnic background music, dim lighting and draped tapestries. Casual dress; cocktails. **Parking:** on-site. **Cards:** AX, DC, MC, VI.

PRIME QUARTER STEAK HOUSE   Dinner: $12-$16   Phone: 920/738-1900

Steak House

Location: US 41, exit 137, just ne. 500 Westhill Blvd 54914. **Hours:** 5 pm-10 pm, Sat from 4 pm, Sun 4 pm-9 pm. Closed major holidays. **Reservations:** accepted. **Features:** Here's an opportunity to barbecue: first fix a salad at the fresh salad bar and then step up to one of three large grills to prepare your favorite choice cut of beef just the way you like it. To complete the plate, add a hot baked potato and Texas toast done on the grill. Professional help is standing by if needed, or they will cook for you. Casual dress; cocktails. **Parking:** on-site. **Cards:** AX, CB, DC, DS, MC, VI.

THE SEASONS   Lunch: $7-$11   Dinner: $16-$27   Phone: 920/993-9860

American

Location: US 41, exit 137 (SR 125), then just sw; in Nicolet Square. 213 S Nicolet Rd 54914. **Hours:** 11:30 am-2:30 & 5-10 pm, Sat from 5 pm. Closed major holidays; also Sun. **Reservations:** suggested. **Features:** Fresh ingredients and attractive entree presentations make this American bistro popular with both business and leisure guests. Complemented by an extensive wine list, the menu, which changes seasonally, always features fresh fish. Delicious desserts are made in-house. Patio dining is offered in season, and smoking is permitted only in the lounge. Dressy casual; cocktails. **Parking:** on-site. **Cards:** AX, DC, DS, MC, VI.

TRIM B'S   Lunch: $4-$19   Dinner: $4-$19   Phone: 920/734-9204

American

Location: Just s of College Ave at jct Lawrence St; downtown. 201 S Walnut St 54911. **Hours:** 11 am-10 pm, Fri-11 pm, Sat 4 pm-10 pm, Sun 4 pm-9 pm. Closed: 11/25, 12/25. **Reservations:** accepted, except Fri. **Features:** Seafood dinners—including fresh perch, planked Lake Superior whitefish, shrimp and pike—are popular at the established, centrally located restaurant. A nautical theme characterizes the dining room. Other tempting choices are Wisconsin cheddar cheese soup and chef specials. Steaks and chicken and pasta dishes round out the menu. Casual dress; cocktails. **Parking:** on-site. **Cards:** AX, DS, MC, VI.

VICTORIA'S   Lunch: $5-$12   Dinner: $7-$16   Phone: 920/730-9595

Italian

Location: At jct Walnut St, 2.7 mi e of US 41, exit 137; downtown. 503 W College Ave 54911. **Hours:** 11 am-10 pm, Sun & Mon-9 pm. Closed: 11/25, 12/25 & Easter; also 12/24 after 4 pm. **Features:** Huge servings of fresh, flavorful food are the norm at the centrally located eatery. Among the numerous menu selections are Sicilian and Italian specialties, salads, seafood, made-to-order gourmet pizzas and create-your-own pasta dishes with a variety of sauces and meats. Casual dress; cocktails. **Parking:** street. **Cards:** AX, DC, DS, MC, VI.

VINCE LOMBARDI'S STEAKHOUSE
Steak & Seafood

Dinner: $16-$32   Phone: 920/380-9390

Location: 3 mi e of US 41, exit 137 (SR 125); downtown; in Radisson Paper Valley Hotel. 333 W College Ave 54911. **Hours:** 5 pm-10 pm, Sun-9 pm. **Closed:** 1/1, 7/4; also for dinner 12/24. **Reservations:** suggested. **Features:** This restaurant is a shrine to the former Green Bay Packer coach. The restaurant abounds with memorabilia of both a personal nature and equipment and photographs depicting his many football exploits. The restaurant appeals to those hungry for some of the finest steak in this area and those looking for a glimpse into the life of the legend and the man. The atmosphere is decidedly upscale but with a casual ambience. Casual dress; cocktails. **Parking:** on-site (fee). **Cards:** AX, CB, DC, DS, MC, VI. *(See color ad p 485)*

WISCONSIN MACHINE SHED RESTAURANT
American

Lunch: $4-$9   Dinner: $7-$20   Phone: 920/830-2326

Location: US 41, exit 137 (SR 125), just nw. 220 N Fox River Dr 54913. **Hours:** 6 am-10 pm, Sun 7 am-9 pm. **Closed:** 1/1, 11/25, 12/25. **Features:** Very hearty portions of farm style cooking, specializing in pork and beef. Foods are made from scratch. The restaurant is dedicated to the American farmer and uses real dairy products and locally produced meats. Friendly servers in overalls. Well-stocked gift shop. Casual dress; cocktails. **Parking:** on-site. **Cards:** AX, CB, DC, DS, MC, VI.

ARBOR VITAE

——— WHERE TO DINE ———

MARTY'S PLACE NORTH
American

Dinner: $8-$30   Phone: 715/356-4335

Location: 5.8 mi n on US 51 from jct SR 47. 2721 US 51 N 54568. **Hours:** 4:30 pm-10 pm. **Closed:** 11/25, 12/24, 12/25; also week of Easter. **Reservations:** accepted. **Features:** A warm, "up-north" ambience pervades the cozy dining room, which is decorated with log walls, stone accents and wildlife prints. The restaurant is known locally for specialty dinners of stuffed orange roughy, veal Oscar, roast duck and Oriental steak. Casual dress; cocktails. **Parking:** on-site. **Cards:** AX, DS, MC, VI.

ARCADIA pop. 2,402

——— WHERE TO STAY ———

RKD MOTEL
Motel

Phone: 608/323-3338

| | 1P: $40 | 2P: $50 | XP: $5 | F12 |

Location: On SR 95, 0.6 mi w of jct SR 93. 915 E Main St 54612. Fax: 608/323-7416. **Facility:** 27 one-bedroom standard units. 1 story, exterior corridors. *Bath:* combo or shower only. **Parking:** on-site, winter plug-ins. **Terms:** cancellation fee imposed, weekly rates available, pets ($5 extra charge). **Business Services:** fax. **Cards:** AX, DS, MC, VI.

SOME UNITS
FEE

ASHLAND pop. 8,620

——— WHERE TO STAY ———

AMERICINN OF ASHLAND   *Book at aaa.com*
Small-scale Hotel

Phone: (715)682-9950

6/11-10/9 [ECP]	1P: $89-$139	2P: $89-$139	XP: $6	F17
12/24-3/31 [ECP]	1P: $79-$119	2P: $79-$119	XP: $6	F17
4/1-6/10 & 10/10-12/23 [ECP]	1P: $79-$109	2P: $79-$109	XP: $6	F17

Location: On US 2, 2.1 mi e of jct SR 13 S. 3009 Lakeshore Dr E 54806. Fax: 715/682-9964. **Facility:** 64 units. 62 one-bedroom standard units, some with whirlpools. 2 one-bedroom suites ($109-$149). 2 stories (no elevator), interior corridors. *Bath:* combo or shower only. **Parking:** on-site, winter plug-ins. **Terms:** cancellation fee imposed, pets ($6 fee, $20 deposit). **Amenities:** hair dryers. *Some:* irons. **Pool(s):** heated indoor. **Leisure Activities:** sauna, whirlpool, pool table, kiddie corner with movies, exercise room. **Guest Services:** coin laundry. **Business Services:** meeting rooms, business center. **Cards:** AX, DS, MC, VI. **Special Amenities:** free expanded continental breakfast and free local telephone calls. *(See color ad p 576)*

SOME UNITS
FEE

ANDERSON MOTEL
Motel

Phone: 715/682-4658

6/11-10/10	1P: $49-$99	2P: $59-$99	XP: $10	F10
10/11-3/31	1P: $35-$59	2P: $39-$69	XP: $10	F10
4/1-6/10	1P: $32-$59	2P: $39-$69	XP: $10	F10

Location: 1.8 mi w on US 2. 2200 W Lakeshore Dr 54806. Fax: 715/685-9887. **Facility:** 18 one-bedroom standard units. 1 story, exterior corridors. **Parking:** on-site, winter plug-ins. **Amenities:** *Some:* hair dryers. **Leisure Activities:** snowmobile & waterfront trail. **Cards:** AX, CB, DC, DS, MC, VI. **Special Amenities:** free local telephone calls.

SOME UNITS

BEST WESTERN HOLIDAY HOUSE   *Book at aaa.com*
Small-scale Hotel

Phone: (715)682-5235

5/28-10/10	1P: $71-$124	2P: $76-$129	XP: $5	F12
12/24-3/31	1P: $79-$109	2P: $84-$119	XP: $5	F12
4/1-5/27 & 10/11-12/23	1P: $51-$109	2P: $56-$114	XP: $5	F12

Location: 2.5 mi w. On 30600 US Hwy 2 54806. Fax: 715/682-4730. **Facility:** 65 units. 64 one-bedroom standard units. 1 one-bedroom suite. 2 stories (no elevator), interior/exterior corridors. *Bath:* combo or shower only. **Parking:** on-site, winter plug-ins. **Terms:** [CP] & [ECP] meal plans available. **Amenities:** irons, hair dryers. **Dining:** 5 pm-10 pm, Sun from 10 am; Sunday brunch, cocktails. **Pool(s):** heated indoor. **Leisure Activities:** whirlpool, fishing. *Fee:* game room. **Business Services:** administrative services (fee). **Cards:** AX, CB, DC, DS, JC, MC, VI. **Special Amenities:** free continental breakfast and free local telephone calls.

SOME UNITS

SUPER 8 MOTEL **Book at aaa.com**
All Year 1P: $45-$120 2P: $45-$120 XP: $6 F12
Location: On US 2 at jct 16th Ave. 1610 W Lakeshore Dr 54806. Fax: 715/682-9377. **Facility:** 70 one-bedroom
Small-scale Hotel standard units. 2 stories (no elevator), interior corridors. *Bath:* combo or shower only. **Parking:** on-site, winter plug-ins. **Terms:** [CP] meal plan available, small pets only ($50 deposit, $10 extra charge).
Amenities: *Some:* hair dryers. **Pool(s):** small heated indoor. **Leisure Activities:** whirlpool. **Guest Services:** coin laundry. **Business Services:** meeting rooms, fax (fee). **Cards:** AX, DC, DS, MC, VI.

SOME UNITS

——— WHERE TO DINE ———

THE BREAKWATER CAFE **Lunch:** $4-$6 **Dinner:** $6-$10 **Phone:** 715/682-8388

American **Location:** On US 2, 1.2 mi e of jct SR 13 S. 1808 Lakeshore Dr E 54806. **Hours:** 5 am-10 pm. Closed: 12/25.
Features: The casual, family-friendly restaurant delivers an all-day menu of breakfast choices, plus sandwiches, soups, salads and burgers. The views of Lake Superior are beautiful. Delicious homemade baked goods include caramel rolls and doughnuts. Casual dress. **Parking:** on-site. **Cards:** MC, VI.

ZEIS'S PLATTER RESTAURANT **Dinner:** $10-$25 **Phone:** 715/682-2626

American **Location:** 2 mi w on US 2, follow signs for Prentice Park, just s. 315 Turner Rd 54806. **Hours:** 4:30 pm-10 pm.
Closed: 1/1, 7/4, 12/25. **Reservations:** suggested. **Features:** A charmingly restored turn-of-the-20th-century home welcomes diners. Country Victorian decor sets the stage. Regional cuisine shows interest both for a contemporary, unusual contrast of flavors and a respect for tradition. Squash bisque is drizzled with maple syrup, roasted duck is accompanied with perfumes of citrus and cranberries, and planked fish— fish filet backed on a maple board—echoes of Lake Superior old times and methods. Casual dress; cocktails. **Parking:** on-site. **Cards:** DS, MC, VI.

BAILEYS HARBOR —See Door County p. 500.

BALDWIN pop. 2,667

——— WHERE TO STAY ———

AMERICINN OF BALDWIN **Book at aaa.com**
All Year 1P: $64-$134 2P: $69-$143 XP: $5 F18
Location: I-94, exit 19 (US 63), just ne. 500 Baldwin Plaza Dr 54002. Fax: 715/684-5890. **Facility:** 65 units. 59
Small-scale Hotel one-bedroom standard units, some with whirlpools. 6 one-bedroom suites, some with whirlpools. 2 stories, interior corridors. *Bath:* combo or shower only. **Parking:** on-site, winter plug-ins. **Terms:** weekly rates available, [ECP] meal plan available. **Amenities:** hair dryers. **Pool(s):** heated indoor. **Leisure Activities:** whirlpool. *Fee:* game room. **Guest Services:** coin laundry. **Business Services:** meeting rooms. **Cards:** AX, DC, MC, VI. *(See color ad p 576)*

SOME UNITS

SUPER 8 MOTEL **Book at aaa.com** **Phone:** (715)684-2700
4/1-10/31 [ECP] 1P: $66-$78 2P: $66-$78
11/1-3/31 [ECP] 1P: $63-$73 2P: $63-$73
Small-scale Hotel **Location:** I-94, exit 19 (US 63), just se. 2110 10th Ave 54002. Fax: 715/684-2750. **Facility:** 61 one-bedroom standard units, some with whirlpools. 2 stories, interior corridors. *Bath:* combo or shower only. **Parking:** on-site, winter plug-ins. **Terms:** check-in 4 pm, cancellation fee imposed, pets (with prior approval). **Pool(s):** small heated indoor. **Leisure Activities:** whirlpool. *Fee:* game room. **Guest Services:** coin laundry. **Business Services:** meeting rooms. **Cards:** AX, CB, DC, DS, MC, VI.

SOME UNITS

BARABOO pop. 10,711

——— WHERE TO STAY ———

BEST WESTERN BARABOO INN **Book at aaa.com** **Phone:** (608)356-1100
7/3-9/6 [ECP] 1P: $79-$129 2P: $89-$129 XP: $10 F12
4/1-7/2 & 9/7-3/31 [ECP] 1P: $52-$129 2P: $62-$129 XP: $10 F12
Location: On US 12, 0.3 mi n of SR 33. 725 W Pine St 53913. Fax: 608/356-4585. **Facility:** 84 units. 83 one-bedroom standard units. 1 one-bedroom suite with whirlpool. 3 stories, interior corridors. *Bath:* combo or
Small-scale Hotel shower only. **Parking:** on-site. **Terms:** 2 night minimum stay - seasonal, cancellation fee imposed. **Amenities:** irons, hair dryers. *Some:* dual phone lines. **Dining:** 4 pm-10 pm, cocktails. **Pool(s):** heated indoor. **Leisure Activities:** whirlpool, exercise room. **Guest Services:** valet and coin laundry. **Business Services:** meeting rooms. **Cards:** AX, CB, DC, DS, MC, VI. **Special Amenities:** free expanded continental breakfast and free local telephone calls.

SOME UNITS

HO-CHUNK CASINO & HOTEL **Phone:** 608/356-6210
5/17-3/31 1P: $130-$150 2P: $130-$150 XP: $10 F
4/1-5/16 1P: $89-$99 2P: $89-$99 XP: $10 F
Large-scale Hotel **Location:** I-90/94, exit 92, 2.6 mi e on US 12. S 3214 Hwy 12 53913. Fax: 608/355-1501. **Facility:** 315 units. 313 one-bedroom standard units, some with whirlpools. 2 one-bedroom suites ($89-$270) with whirlpools. 4 stories, interior corridors. *Bath:* combo or shower only. **Parking:** on-site and valet. **Terms:** check-in 4 pm. **Amenities:** dual phone lines, voice mail, safes, hair dryers. *Some:* irons. **Leisure Activities:** exercise room. *Fee:* game room. **Guest Services:** gift shop, coin laundry, area transportation. **Business Services:** conference facilities, fax (fee). **Cards:** AX, DS, MC, VI.

SOME UNITS

PARK PLAZA BARABOO   *Book at aaa.com*

Phone: (608)356-6422

(AAA) (SAVE)

All Year   1P: $79-$159   2P: $79-$159   XP: $10   F17

Location: On US 12, 0.3 mi n of SR 33. 626 W Pine St 53913. Fax: 608/356-0520. **Facility:** 84 units. 72 one-bedroom standard units, some with whirlpools. 8 one- and 4 two-bedroom suites, some with whirlpools. 5 stories, interior corridors. **Parking:** on-site. **Terms:** check-in 4 pm, cancellation fee imposed, [ECP] meal plan available, small pets only (1st floor). **Amenities:** dual phone lines, voice mail, irons, hair dryers. **Dining:** 7 am-10 pm, cocktails. **Pool(s):** heated indoor. **Leisure Activities:** whirlpool, steamroom, exercise room. *Fee:* game room. **Guest Services:** valet and coin laundry. **Business Services:** meeting rooms. **Cards:** AX, DC, DS, MC. **Special Amenities:** free expanded continental breakfast and early check-in/late check-out.

Small-scale Hotel

SOME UNITS

PINEHAVEN BED & BREAKFAST

Phone: (608)356-3489

(AAA) (SAVE)

5/1-11/1 [BP]   2P: $99-$145   XP: $10
4/1-4/30 & 11/2-2/28 [BP]   2P: $79-$125   XP: $10

Location: On SR 33, 4.8 mi e from jct US 12. Located in a quiet, rural area. E13083 Hwy 33 53913. Fax: 608/356-0818. **Facility:** The outstanding feature of this B&B is its scenic location amid rolling hills, a farm pond and mature conifers; a gazebo offers panoramic views. 5 units. 4 one-bedroom standard units. 1 two-bedroom suite with kitchen and whirlpool. 2 stories (no elevator), interior/exterior corridors. **Parking:** on-site. **Terms:** open 4/1-2/28, 2 night minimum stay - seasonal weekends, age restrictions may apply, 7 day cancellation notice-fee imposed. **Amenities:** *Some:* hair dryers. **Leisure Activities:** boating, paddleboats, fishing, hiking trails. **Cards:** MC, VI. **Special Amenities:** free full breakfast and free local telephone calls.

Bed & Breakfast

SOME UNITS

----- **WHERE TO DINE** -----

LOG CABIN FAMILY RESTAURANT AND BAKERY   **Lunch:** $4-$7   **Dinner:** $6-$13   **Phone:** 608/356-8034

Location: 2.5 mi e on SR 33 from jct US 12. 1215 8th St 53913. **Hours:** 6 am-10 pm. Closed: 11/25, 12/25 & Easter; also also 12/24 for dinner. **Features:** This restaurant is made of log construction and is popular with locals and visitors alike. The food tastes great and many of the items are homemade. Breakfast is served all day. Casual dress. **Parking:** on-site. **Cards:** DS, MC, VI.

American

BARRON pop. 3,284

----- **WHERE TO STAY** -----

BARRON MOTEL & RV CAMPGROUND

Phone: 715/637-3154

All Year   1P: $43-$55   2P: $53-$62   XP: $6   F16

Location: On US 8, 1 mi e of jct SR 25 N. 1521 E Division Ave 54812. Fax: 715/637-9254. **Facility:** 11 one-bedroom standard units. 1 story, exterior corridors. **Parking:** on-site, winter plug-ins. **Amenities:** hair dryers. **Cards:** AX, DS, MC, VI.

Motel

SOME UNITS

BAYFIELD pop. 611

----- **WHERE TO STAY** -----

BAYFIELD ON THE LAKE

Phone: 715/779-3621

6/15-10/16   1P: $180-$220   2P: $180-$220   XP: $20   F6
4/1-6/14 & 10/17-3/31   1P: $120-$150   2P: $120-$150   XP: $20   F6

Location: Just s of SR 13. Located on lakefront. 10 S 1st St 54814 (PO Box 70). Fax: 715/779-3181. **Facility:** An attractive house, the property offers large accommodations, many with balconies or patios that showcase the view of the bay. 6 units. 1 one-, 2 two- and 3 three-bedroom suites with kitchens, some with whirlpools. 3 stories (no elevator), interior corridors. **Parking:** on-site, winter plug-ins. **Terms:** check-in 4 pm, 2 night minimum stay - weekends, 10 day cancellation notice-fee imposed, weekly rates available. **Amenities:** irons, hair dryers. *Some:* CD players. **Guest Services:** complimentary laundry. **Cards:** MC, VI.

Condominium

SOME UNITS

COOPER HILL HOUSE

Phone: 715/779-5060

5/14-10/24   1P: $96-$106   2P: $99-$109
4/1-5/13 & 10/25-3/31   1P: $79   2P: $79

Location: On SR 13. 33 S 6th St 54814 (PO Box 1288). Fax: 715/779-3999. **Facility:** This quiet home has an old-fashioned charm; guest rooms are furnished with heirlooms and antiques. Smoke free premises. 4 one-bedroom standard units. 2 stories (no elevator), interior corridors. *Bath:* combo or shower only. **Parking:** on-site. **Terms:** off-site registration, 2 night minimum stay - weekends, age restrictions may apply, 7 day cancellation notice-fee imposed, [ECP] meal plan available. **Cards:** MC, VI.

Historic Bed & Breakfast

OLD RITTENHOUSE INN

Phone: 715/779-5111

All Year   2P: $99-$299   XP: $20   F3

Location: Just w on SR 13. 301 Rittenhouse Ave 54814 (PO Box 584). Fax: 715/779-5887. **Facility:** Two late-1800s Victorian mansions decorated with antiques make up this stately hillside inn; most rooms have fireplaces and some have bay views. Smoke free premises. 25 units. 21 one-bedroom standard units, some with whirlpools. 4 one-bedroom suites ($249-$299) with whirlpools. 3 stories (no elevator), interior corridors. *Bath:* combo or shower only. **Parking:** on-site, winter plug-ins. **Terms:** check-in 3:30 pm, [AP] meal plan available. **Amenities:** *Some:* CD players. **Dining:** dining room, see separate listing. **Guest Services:** area transportation. **Business Services:** meeting rooms. **Cards:** MC, VI.

Historic Country Inn

SOME UNITS

——— WHERE TO DINE ———

OLD RITTENHOUSE INN
▼▼▼
Continental

Lunch: $7-$15   **Dinner:** $45   **Phone:** 715/779-5111
Location: Just w on SR 13; in Old Rittenhouse Inn. 301 Rittenhouse Ave 54814. **Hours:** 7:30 am-9:15 & 5-9 pm, hours may vary off season; also 11 am-2:30 pm 5/15-10/15. **Reservations:** suggested. **Features:** A charming, Victorian-style restaurant in a restored 1890 mansion, this restaurant offers incredible atmosphere for diners who seek romance and fine dining. The decor is classic and elegant, yet not intimidating in the least. The waitstaff is thoroughly knowledgeable about the constantly changing menu. The various courses of the prix fixe menu do not disappoint the palatte. Everything is fresh, well-prepared and a joy to eat. **Casual dress; cocktails. Parking:** on-site. **Cards:** MC, VI.

[X]

BAYSIDE —See Milwaukee p. 588.

BEAVER DAM pop. 15,169

——— WHERE TO STAY ———

AMERICINN LODGE & SUITES
▼▼▼▼
Small-scale Hotel

Book at aaa.com
All Year [ECP]   1P: $75-$120   2P: $75-$120   XP: $6   F12
Phone: (920)356-9000
Location: US 151, exit 134 (CR B/Industrial Dr). 325 Seippel Blvd 53916 (PO Box 718). **Fax:** 920/356-9094. **Facility:** 64 units. 63 one-bedroom standard units, some with whirlpools. 1 one-bedroom suite with whirlpool. 3 stories, interior corridors. *Bath:* combo or shower only. **Parking:** on-site, winter plug-ins. **Terms:** pets ($10 extra charge, in designated units). **Amenities:** dual phone lines, hair dryers. *Some:* irons. **Pool(s):** small heated indoor. **Leisure Activities:** whirlpool, limited exercise equipment. **Guest Services:** valet and coin laundry. **Business Services:** meeting rooms, fax (fee). **Cards:** AX, CB, DC, DS, MC, VI. *(See color ad p 576)*

SOME UNITS
[ASK] [S/D] [🛏] [📶] [⚙] [🚲] [📹] [DATA PORT] [💻] / [X] [VCR] [🔌] [▭] /
FEE   FEE

SUPER 8 MOTEL
▼▼
Small-scale Hotel

Book at aaa.com
All Year   1P: $48-$77   2P: $57-$77   XP: $6   F12
Phone: 920/887-8880
Location: US 151, exit 132 (SR 33), just w. 711 Park Ave 53916 (PO Box 778). **Fax:** 920/887-8880. **Facility:** 50 one-bedroom standard units. 3 stories (no elevator), interior corridors. **Parking:** on-site, winter plug-ins. **Terms:** [CP] meal plan available, pets ($50 deposit). **Guest Services:** valet and coin laundry. **Business Services:** fax. **Cards:** AX, CB, DC, DS, MC, VI.

SOME UNITS
[ASK] [S/D] [🛏] [📶] [🚲] [📹] [DATA PORT] / [X] /
FEE

——— WHERE TO DINE ———

BENVENUTO'S ITALIAN GRILL
▼▼▼
Italian

Lunch: $6-$8   **Dinner:** $7-$15   **Phone:** 920/887-7994
Location: US 151, exit 132 (SR 33), just sw. 831 Park Ave 53916. **Hours:** 11 am-10:30 pm, Fri & Sat-11 pm, Sun-10 pm. **Closed:** 11/25, 12/24, 12/25. **Reservations:** accepted. **Features:** The casual eatery's menu comprises Italian and American fare, including gourmet calzones, pasta, ribs, wood-fired pizzas, meatball sandwiches, steaks, mushroom and mozzarella burgers, walleye pike and popcorn shrimp. **Casual dress; cocktails. Parking:** on-site. **Cards:** AX, DS, MC, VI.

[Y] [X]

THE NILE CLUB
▼▼▼
American

Dinner: $7-$23   **Phone:** 920/885-6611
Location: US 151, exit 132 (SR 33), 4.2 mi e. W 6711 Hwy 33 53916. **Hours:** 5 pm-10 pm, Sun 10 am-2 & 4-9 pm. **Closed:** 12/25; also Mon. **Features:** The distinctive pyramid-shaped building stands out in a landscape of Wisconsin farms. The Egyptian decor and relaxing background music enhance the restaurant's appeal. Supper club fare includes broiled or pan-fried seafood, steak and fowl. **Casual dress; cocktails. Parking:** on-site. **Cards:** AX, MC, VI.

[Y] [X]

BELOIT pop. 35,775

——— WHERE TO STAY ———

COMFORT INN OF BELOIT
▼▼▼
Small-scale Hotel

Book at aaa.com
5/1-11/30   1P: $64-$109   2P: $69-$109   XP: $5   F18
4/1-4/30   1P: $59-$99   2P: $64-$104   XP: $5   F18
12/1-3/31   1P: $54-$84   2P: $59-$89   XP: $5   F18
Phone: (608)362-2666
Location: I-90, exit 185A, just w at jct I-43 and SR 81. 2786 Milwaukee Rd 53511. **Fax:** 608/362-2666. **Facility:** 56 one-bedroom standard units. 2 stories, interior corridors. **Parking:** on-site, winter plug-ins. **Terms:** weekly rates available, [ECP] meal plan available, pets ($10 extra charge). **Amenities:** irons, hair dryers. **Pool(s):** small heated indoor. **Leisure Activities:** whirlpool. **Cards:** AX, DC, DS, JC, MC, VI.

SOME UNITS
[ASK] [S/D] [🛏] [📶] [🚲] [📹] [DATA PORT] [🔌] [▭] [💻] / [X] /
FEE

ECONO LODGE
[AAA] [SAVE]
▼▼▼
Motel

Book at aaa.com
4/1-9/5   1P: $54-$70   2P: $59-$75   XP: $6   F18
9/6-3/31   1P: $45-$59   2P: $45-$59   XP: $6   F18
Phone: (608)364-4000
Location: I-90, exit 185A, 0.3 mi w. 2956 Milwaukee Rd 53511. **Fax:** 608/365-2611. **Facility:** 78 one-bedroom standard units. 1 story, interior/exterior corridors. **Parking:** on-site. **Terms:** pets ($10 fee). **Dining:** 6 am-10 pm. **Guest Services:** coin laundry. **Cards:** AX, DC, DS, MC, VI.

SOME UNITS
[S/D] [🛏] [📶] [Y] [📹] / [X] [💻] /
FEE

FAIRFIELD INN & SUITES   *Book at aaa.com*

Phone: (608)365-2200

5/1-9/1 [CP]	1P: $90-$125	2P: $90-$125
4/1-4/30 [CP]	1P: $69-$99	2P: $69-$99
9/2-3/31 [CP]	1P: $69-$89	2P: $69-$89

Location: I-90, exit 185A, just sw. Located in a commercial area. 2784 Milwaukee Rd 53511. Fax: 608/365-7067.
Small-scale Hotel **Facility:** 94 units. 93 one-bedroom standard units, some with whirlpools. 1 one-bedroom suite ($90-$125). 3 stories, interior corridors. *Bath:* combo or shower only. **Parking:** on-site, winter plug-ins. **Terms:** 2-5 night minimum stay - seasonal & weekends. **Amenities:** video games (fee), voice mail, irons, hair dryers. **Pool(s):** small heated indoor. **Leisure Activities:** whirlpool, exercise room. **Guest Services:** valet and coin laundry. **Business Services:** meeting rooms. **Cards:** AX, DC, DS, MC, VI. **Special Amenities:** free continental breakfast and free local telephone calls.
(See color ad below)

SOME UNITS

HOLIDAY INN EXPRESS   *Book at aaa.com*

Phone: (608)365-6000

			XP: $6
All Year [ECP]	1P: $79-$129	2P: $79-$129	

Location: I-90, exit 185A, just w at jct I-43 and SR 81. 2790 Milwaukee Rd 53511. Fax: 608/365-1974. **Facility:** 73 one-bedroom standard units, some with whirlpools. 2 stories, interior corridors. **Parking:** on-site, winter plug-ins. **Amenities:** dual phone lines, voice mail, irons, hair dryers. **Pool(s):** heated indoor. **Leisure Activities:** whirlpool, exercise room. **Guest Services:** valet and coin laundry. **Business Services:** meeting rooms, fax (fee). **Cards:** AX, CB, DC, DS, JC, MC, VI. **Special Amenities:** free expanded continental breakfast and free local telephone calls.

SOME UNITS

SUPER 8 MOTEL   *Book at aaa.com*

Phone: (608)365-8680

			XP: $5	F12
All Year	1P: $54-$74	2P: $59-$79		

Location: I-90, exit 185A, just w at jct I-43 and SR 81. 3002 Milwaukee Rd 53511. Fax: 608/365-2411. **Facility:** 64 one-bedroom standard units. 2 stories (no elevator), interior corridors. **Parking:** on-site, winter plug-ins.
Small-scale Hotel **Terms:** pets ($10 extra charge, dogs only). **Amenities:** safes (fee). **Guest Services:** coin laundry.
Cards: AX, CB, DC, DS, MC, VI.

SOME UNITS

FEE

------ **WHERE TO DINE** ------

BUTTERFLY CLUB

Dinner: $11-$18

Phone: 608/362-8577

Location: I-90, exit 185B, 1.5 mi e on I-43, exit 2, then 0.5 mi e. 5246 E CR X 53511. **Hours:** 5 pm-9:30 pm, Fri & Sat-10 pm, Sun noon-8 pm. Closed: 1/1, 12/24, 12/25; also Mon. **Reservations:** suggested.
American **Features:** Picturesque rural setting with deck dining in season. Fish fry on Wednesday and Friday. Established in 1924. Offering USDA prime Angus steak, poultry and seafood. Cinnamon rolls accompany all meals. Dressy casual; cocktails. **Parking:** on-site. **Cards:** AX, DC, DS, MC, VI.

GUN CLUB

Dinner: $16-$23

Phone: 608/362-9900

Location: I-90, exit 185A, 2 mi w, then 0.5 mi s. 1122 E Colley Rd 53511. **Hours:** 5 pm-9 pm, Sat 4:30 pm-10 pm, Sun 4 pm-9 pm. Closed major holidays; also Mon. **Reservations:** suggested. **Features:** In operation since 1938, the restaurant is known for its hearty steaks and chops. Casual dress; cocktails. **Parking:** on-site. **Cards:** AX, MC, VI.

BERLIN pop. 5,305

------ **WHERE TO STAY** ------

BEST WESTERN COUNTRYSIDE   *Book at aaa.com*

Phone: (920)361-4411

5/16-10/15 [CP]	1P: $79-$109	2P: $84-$119	XP: $6 F12
1/1-3/31 [CP]	1P: $74-$88	2P: $79-$94	XP: $7 F12
4/1-5/15 & 10/16-12/31 [CP]	1P: $69-$83	2P: $74-$89	XP: $6 F12

Location: On SR 49, at jct CR F. Located in a commercial area. 227 Ripon Rd 54923. Fax: 920/361-1125.
Motel **Facility:** 20 one-bedroom standard units. 2 stories (no elevator), interior corridors. **Parking:** on-site, winter plug-ins. **Terms:** office hours 7 am-11 pm, pets (small dogs only). **Amenities:** irons, hair dryers. **Leisure Activities:** whirlpool, exercise room. **Guest Services:** valet laundry. **Cards:** AX, DC, DS, MC, VI. **Special Amenities:** free continental breakfast and free local telephone calls.

SOME UNITS

——— **WHERE TO DINE** ———

JEFF'S ON THE SQUARE

American

Dinner: $8-S15   **Phone:** 920/361-4847

Location: Center. 116 N Capron St 54923. **Hours:** 4 pm-10 pm, Fri from 11 am. Closed major holidays. **Reservations:** accepted. **Features:** Broasted chicken and fish, seafood, steaks, ribs and pizza are some of the carefully prepared items that keep locals coming back. The rich cheesecake is made in house. The restaurant may be busy at peak times. Casual dress; cocktails. **Parking:** street. **Cards:** MC, VI. 🍸 ⊠

BIRCHWOOD pop. 518

——— **WHERE TO STAY** ———

COBBLESTONE B & B

Phone: 715/354-3494

Bed & Breakfast

All Year [BP]   1P: $69-$89   2P: $79-$99   XP: $20

Location: 0.8 mi e of jct SR 53 and Main St; center. 319 S Main St 54817. **Facility:** Smoke free premises. 5 units. 2 one- and 3 two-bedroom standard units. 2 stories (no elevator), interior corridors. *Bath:* some shared, combo or shower only. **Parking:** on-site and street. **Terms:** 10 day cancellation notice, package plans, no pets allowed (owner's pet on premisex). **Amenities:** video library, hair dryers. **Leisure Activities:** horseshoes. **Cards:** DS, MC, VI.

SOME UNITS

(ASK) (SD) (T+) (⊠) (AK) / (VCR) (🕿) /

BLACK RIVER FALLS pop. 3,618

——— **WHERE TO STAY** ———

BEST WESTERN-ARROWHEAD LODGE & SUITES   *Book at aaa.com*

Phone: (715)284-9471

Small-scale Hotel

5/1-10/31	1P: $62-$90	2P: $62-$96	XP: $6 F17
4/1-4/30 & 11/1-3/31	1P: $58-$75	2P: $58-$81	XP: $6 F17

Location: I-94, exit 116, at jct SR 54. 600 Oasis Rd 54615. **Fax:** 715/284-9664. **Facility:** 143 units. 114 one-bedroom standard units, some with whirlpools. 29 one-bedroom suites ($62-$200), some with whirlpools. 2-3 stories, interior corridors. *Bath:* combo or shower only. **Parking:** on-site, winter plug-ins. **Terms:** [ECP] meal plan available, small pets only. **Amenities:** voice mail, irons, hair dryers. *Some:* dual phone lines. **Dining:** 5 pm-10 pm; closed Sun, cocktails. **Pool(s):** heated indoor. **Leisure Activities:** whirlpool, rental paddleboats, ice skating, access to ATV snowmobile trails, hiking trails, jogging. **Guest Services:** coin laundry. **Business Services:** meeting rooms, administrative services (fee). **Cards:** AX, CB, DC, DS, JC, MC, VI. **Special Amenities: free expanded continental breakfast and free room upgrade (subject to availability with advanced reservations).** *(See color ad below)*

SOME UNITS

(SD) (🐾) (T+) (🍸) (&) (⊘) (≈) (⊠) (★) (DATA PORT) (☕) / (⊠) (VCR) (🔌) (🖨) /

DAYS INN   *Book at aaa.com*

Phone: (715)284-4333

Small-scale Hotel

5/28-9/30 & 12/16-3/31	1P: $69-$89	2P: $81-$89
4/1-5/27 & 10/1-12/15	1P: $60-$79	2P: $69-$89

Location: I-94, exit 116, just w. 919 Hwy 54 E 54615. **Fax:** 715/284-9068. **Facility:** 84 one-bedroom standard units, some with whirlpools. 2 stories (no elevator), interior corridors. *Bath:* combo or shower only. **Parking:** on-site, winter plug-ins. **Terms:** small pets only (in smoking units). **Amenities:** irons, hair dryers. **Pool(s):** heated indoor. **Leisure Activities:** sauna, whirlpool. *Fee:* game room. **Guest Services:** coin laundry. **Business Services:** meeting rooms, administrative services (fee). **Cards:** AX, CB, DC, DS, MC, VI. **Special Amenities: free expanded continental breakfast and free local telephone calls.** *(See color ad card insert)*

SOME UNITS

(SD) (🐾) (T+) (&) (≈) (⊠) (★) (☕) / (⊠) (DATA PORT) (🔌) (🖨) /
FEE   FEE

HOLIDAY INN EXPRESS HOTEL & SUITES *Book at aaa.com* **Phone:** (715)284-0888

5/28-9/5 [ECP]	1P: $94-$124	2P: $94-$124	XP: $6 F19
4/1-5/27 & 9/6-3/31 [ECP]	1P: $74-$104	2P: $74-$104	XP: $6 F19

Small-scale Hotel **Location:** I-94, exit 116. W10170 Hwy 54 E 54615. **Fax:** 715/284-9789. **Facility:** 75 one-bedroom standard units, some with whirlpools. 2 stories (no elevator), interior corridors. *Bath:* combo or shower only. **Parking:** on-site, winter plug-ins. **Amenities:** irons, hair dryers. **Pool(s):** heated indoor, wading. **Leisure Activities:** whirlpool, exercise room. **Guest Services:** coin laundry. **Business Services:** meeting rooms, fax (fee). **Cards:** AX, CB, DC, DS, JC, MC, VI.

SOME UNITS

(ASK) (SD) 🐕 🍴 🏊 📷 (DATA PORT) 💻 / ✖ 🛢 📟 /

——— **WHERE TO DINE** ———

THE RUSTIC MILL SUPPER CLUB **Dinner:** $7-$22 **Phone:** 715/284-4913

American   **Location:** 2.3 mi s. Hwy 54 54615. **Hours:** 5 pm-10 pm. **Closed:** 11/25, 12/25; also Tues. **Reservations:** suggested. **Features:** Cozy setting in a feed and flour mill built in 1866. Vaulted ceiling, knotty pine walls and fireplace enhance the ambience. Some tables have a nice view of a small river and waterfall. Specializes in prime rib and seafood. Homemade soup. Smoking in lounge only. Casual dress; cocktails. **Parking:** on-site. **Cards:** MC, VI.

🍸 ✖

BOSCOBEL pop. 3,047

——— **WHERE TO STAY** ———

SAND'S MOTEL **Phone:** 608/375-4167

All Year	2P: $45-$67	XP: $5 F12

Motel   **Location:** On US 61, 0.5 mi nw. Truck parking on premises. Hwy 61 N 53805 (300 Elm St). **Facility:** 32 one-bedroom standard units. 1 story, interior/exterior corridors. *Bath:* combo or shower only. **Parking:** on-site, winter plug-ins. **Terms:** small pets only. **Amenities:** *Some:* hair dryers. **Cards:** AX, CB, DS, MC, VI.

SOME UNITS

🛬 🐕 📷 / ✖ /

SUPER 8 MOTEL **Phone:** 608/375-8000

6/1-10/31	1P: $61-$81	2P: $66-$86	XP: $5 F14
4/1-5/31 & 11/1-3/31	1P: $56-$81	2P: $61-$86	XP: $5 F14

Small-scale Hotel   **Location:** Just s on US 61. 1700 Elm St 53805. **Fax:** 608/375-9199. **Facility:** 40 one-bedroom standard units, some with whirlpools. 2 stories (no elevator), interior corridors. *Bath:* combo or shower only. **Parking:** on-site, winter plug-ins. **Amenities:** video library (fee). **Pool(s):** heated indoor. **Leisure Activities:** sauna, whirlpool, limited exercise equipment. **Guest Services:** tanning facility. **Business Services:** meeting rooms. **Cards:** AX, DC, DS, MC, VI.

SOME UNITS

(ASK) (SD) 🐕 🏊 ✖ 📷 (DATA PORT) / ✖ (VCR) 🛢 📟 💻

BOULDER JUNCTION

——— **WHERE TO STAY** ———

BOULDER JUNCTION MOTOR LODGE **Phone:** 715/385-2825

All Year	1P: $59-$99	2P: $55-$99	XP: $10 F6

Motel   **Location:** Just w on CR K. 10432 Main St 54512 (PO Box 294). **Facility:** 20 one-bedroom standard units, some with whirlpools. 1 story, interior corridors. **Parking:** on-site, winter plug-ins. **Terms:** 3 day cancellation notice, weekly rates available, package plans - seasonal. **Leisure Activities:** whirlpool, snowmobiling. **Cards:** DC, DS, MC, VI.

SOME UNITS

🍴 🛢 / ✖ /

WHITE BIRCH VILLAGE **Phone:** 715/385-2182

5/22-10/10 Wkly	2P: $600-$1500

Resort Vacation Home   **Location:** On CR K, 8 mi se. Located on White Birch Lake. 8764 Hwy K 54512 (PO Box 284). **Fax:** 715/385-2537. **Facility:** Fireplaces, park-like grounds and a lakefront setting distinguish these one- to four-bedroom vacation homes. 14 vacation homes, some with whirlpools. 1-2 stories (no elevator), exterior corridors. *Bath:* combo or shower only. **Parking:** on-site. **Terms:** open 5/22-10/10, check-out 9 am, 3 night minimum stay, 30 day cancellation notice-fee imposed. **Amenities:** video library. *Some:* irons. **Leisure Activities:** rental boats, canoeing, paddleboats, boat dock, fishing, playground, basketball, horseshoes, shuffleboard, volleyball. *Fee:* game room. **Guest Services:** coin laundry.

SOME UNITS

🐎 ✖ 🛢 📟 💻 / ✖ (K) (W) 🌀 /

——— **WHERE TO DINE** ———

THE GUIDE'S INN **Dinner:** $9-$23 **Phone:** 715/385-2233

American   **Location:** Just s on CR M and K. Hwy M 54512. **Hours:** 5 pm-10 pm; hours may vary. **Closed:** 11/25, 12/24, 12/25 & Easter. **Features:** This restaurant offers Continental cuisine prepared by a chef certified by the American Culinary Association. Fresh ingredients, complimentary fresh French bread and appetizer tray, and a wide menu variety are the hallmarks. Cocktails. **Parking:** on-site. **Cards:** MC, VI.

🍸 ✖

BOWLER pop. 343

------- WHERE TO STAY -------

KONKAPOT LODGE
Phone: 715/787-4747
All Year   1P: $84-$132   2P: $84-$132   XP: $10   F5
▼▼▼▼
Location: On CR A, 4.7 mi e. W12635 CR A 54416. Fax: 715/787-4749. **Facility:** 28 one-bedroom standard units,
Small-scale Hotel some with whirlpools. 2 stories (no elevator), interior corridors. **Parking:** on-site. **Terms:** 3 day cancellation
notice, [ECP] meal plan available. **Amenities:** irons, hair dryers. **Guest Services:** gift shop. **Business Serv-
ices:** meeting rooms. **Cards:** AX, DC, DS, MC, VI.

SOME UNITS
📷 🖥 / ⊗ 🔌 🖥 💻 /

BROOKFIELD —*See Milwaukee p. 589.*

BROWN DEER —*See Milwaukee p. 591.*

BURLINGTON pop. 9,936

------- WHERE TO STAY -------

AMERICINN LODGE & SUITES   *Book at aaa.com*
Phone: (262)534-2125
All Year [ECP]   1P: $65-$109   2P: $75-$139   XP: $6   F18
▼▼▼ ▼▼▼
Location: 3 mi n on SR 36 and 83, at jct CR W. Located in a commercial area. 205 S Browns Lake Rd 53105.
Small-scale Hotel Fax: 262/534-5221. **Facility:** 50 units. 42 one-bedroom standard units, some with whirlpools. 7 one- and 1
two-bedroom suites ($89-$149) with efficiencies. 2 stories (no elevator), interior corridors. *Bath:* combo or
shower only. **Parking:** on-site. **Terms:** cancellation fee imposed. **Amenities:** hair dryers. *Some:* irons. **Pool(s):** small heated indoor. **Leisure Activities:** whirlpool. **Guest Services:** coin laundry. **Business Services:** meeting rooms. **Cards:** AX, CB, DC, DS,
MC, VI. *(See color ad p 576)*

SOME UNITS
(ASK) 🅂 🔌 🍴 🔬 🌀 🏊 📷 🔌 💻 / ⊗ 🖥 🖥 /

RAINBOW MOTEL
Phone: (262)763-2491
(AAA) (SAVE)   4/1-9/15   1P: $50-$66   2P: $58-$74   XP: $8   F12
               9/16-3/31   1P: $48-$58   2P: $58-$66   XP: $8   F12
▼▼
Location: 0.5 mi ne on SR 36 and 83. Located in a commercial area. 733 Milwaukee Ave 53105. Fax: 262/763-2431.
Facility: 45 one-bedroom standard units. 2 stories (no elevator), exterior corridors. **Parking:** on-site, winter
Small-scale Hotel plug-ins. **Terms:** office hours 7 am-midnight, cancellation fee imposed, weekly rates available. **Pool(s):**
heated outdoor. **Leisure Activities:** shuffleboard, volleyball. **Guest Services:** valet laundry. **Cards:** DC,
MC, VI. **Special Amenities:** free local telephone calls and early check-in/late check-out.

SOME UNITS
🅂 🍴 🏊 📷 🔌 🖥 💻 / ⊗ (VCR)
FEE

------- WHERE TO DINE -------

THE COTTONPICKER   **Lunch:** $4-$10   **Dinner:** $12-$25   Phone: 262/534-5151
▼▼ ▼▼
Location: 3 mi n on SR 36 and 83; at jct CR W. 210 S Browns Lake Rd 53105. **Hours:** 11:30 am-10 pm, Fri &
Sat-10:30 pm, Sun 10 am-9 pm. Closed: 11/25, 12/25; also for dinner 12/24. **Reservations:** suggested.
American   **Features:** Window tables in the country-themed dining room overlook a pretty courtyard landscape and
soothing pond. The menu comprises such well-prepared entrees as prime rib, steak Oscar and roast duck.
Don't pass up the sinful chocolate mocha cheesecake. Casual dress; cocktails. **Parking:** on-site. **Cards:** AX, MC, VI.

🍸 ⊗

CABLE

------- WHERE TO STAY -------

CONNORS BED & BREAKFAST
Phone: (715)798-3661
All Year   1P: $85-$105   2P: $85-$105   XP: $15   D7
▼▼▼▼
Location: 1.7 mi n on US 63, then 0.3 mi e on Birch Ln. Located in a quiet, rural area. 14140 Brich Ln 54821.
Bed & Breakfast Fax: 715/798-3663. **Facility:** On 77 acres, this rural B&B offers access to many outdoor activities; accommodations include a cabin that is 110 years old. Smoke free premises. 4 units. 2 one-bedroom standard units,
some with whirlpools. 1 one-bedroom suite. 1 cabin ($105). 2 stories (no elevator), interior corridors. **Parking:** on-site. **Terms:** 7
day cancellation notice-fee imposed, weekly rates available, package plans. **Amenities:** *Some:* hair dryers. **Leisure Activities:** cross country skiing, hiking trails. **Guest Services:** gift shop. **Cards:** AX, MC, VI.

SOME UNITS
⊗ 🖥 💻 / 📷 📺 (VCR) 📻 🖥 /

LAKEWOODS RESORT
Phone: 715/794-2561
(AAA) (SAVE)   All Year   1P: $69-$250   2P: $95-$350   XP: $15   F18
▼▼▼▼
Location: On CR M, 8 mi e. 21540 CR M 54821. Fax: 715/794-2553. **Facility:** Spacious tree-covered grounds
surround these lodge-, cottage- and apartment-style units, some of which offer lake views. 92 units. 84 one-
Resort   bedroom standard units, some with whirlpools. 8 one-bedroom suites, some with kitchens and/or whirlpools.
Small-scale Hotel 1-3 stories, interior/exterior corridors. **Parking:** on-site, winter plug-ins. **Terms:** 2 night minimum stay - weekends, 30 day cancellation notice-fee imposed, weekly rates available, [AP], [BP], [CP], [ECP] & [MAP] meal
plans available, package plans, pets ($50 fee, in designated units). **Amenities:** video library (fee), dual
phone lines, voice mail, irons, hair dryers. *Some:* CD players. **Dining:** 7 am-3:30 & 5-10 pm, cocktails. **Pool(s):** heated outdoor,
heated indoor. **Leisure Activities:** sauna, whirlpool, rental boats, rental canoes, rental paddleboats, fishing, 2 tennis courts,
cross country skiing, ice skating, tobogganing, recreation programs, rental bicycles, hiking trails, jogging, playground, volleyball.
Fee: sailboats, marina, kayaks, pontoons, golf-18 holes, snowmobiling, ski equipment. **Guest Services:** gift shop, coin laundry,
area transportation (fee). **Business Services:** meeting rooms, business center. **Cards:** AX, DC, DS, MC, VI. *(See ad p 525)*

SOME UNITS
🅇 🐾 🍴 🍸 🔬 🌀 🏊 ⊗ 📷 🔌 💻 / ⊗ (VCR) 🖥 🖥 /
FEE FEE

CADOTT pop. 1,345

──────── WHERE TO STAY ────────

COUNTRYSIDE MOTEL
Phone: 715/289-4000
▼▼ ▼▼
All Year   1P: $38-$80   2P: $45-$80   XP: $7   F10
Motel   **Location:** SR 29, exit 91 (SR 27), just s. Located in a rural setting. 545 Lavorata Rd 54727. **Fax:** 715/289-4572. **Facility:** 18 one-bedroom standard units, some with whirlpools. 1 story, interior corridors. **Parking:** on-site, winter plug-ins. **Terms:** office hours 8 am-10 pm. **Leisure Activities:** playground. **Business Services:** fax (fee). **Cards:** AX, DC, DS, MC, VI.

SOME UNITS
🛏 ⓘ⁺ 🎥 ᴅᴀᴛᴀᴘᴏʀᴛ / ✕ /

CALEDONIA

──────── WHERE TO DINE ────────

SEBASTIANS
Dinner: $14-$24   **Phone: 212/681-5465**
▼▼▼
American   **Location:** On SR 32 at jct 5 Mile Rd. 6025 Douglas Ave 53402. **Hours:** 5 pm-9 pm, Fri & Sat-10 pm. Closed major holidays; also Sun & Mon. **Reservations:** suggested. **Features:** The family-owned and operated restaurant offers fine country dining in a casual atmosphere. Fresh fish, choice meats, distinctive sauces and homemade desserts are notable. Great care is given to the presentation of all courses. Dressy casual; cocktails. **Parking:** on-site. **Cards:** AX, DS, MC, VI.

🍽 ✕

CAMERON pop. 1,546

──────── WHERE TO STAY ────────

VIKING MOTEL
Book at aaa.com   **Phone: 715/458-2111**
▼▼
All Year   1P: $50-$55   2P: $55-$66   XP: $6
Motel   **Location:** On US 8 and CR SS. 201 S 1st St 54822 (PO Box 264). **Facility:** 20 one-bedroom standard units. 1 story, exterior corridors. **Parking:** on-site, winter plug-ins. **Terms:** pets (with prior approval). **Cards:** DS, MC, VI.

SOME UNITS
ⒶⓈⓀ Ⓢᴅ 🛏 ⓘ⁺ 💻 / ✕ /

CAMP DOUGLAS pop. 592

──────── WHERE TO STAY ────────

K & K MOTEL
Phone: 608/427-3100
ⒶⒶⒶ 🆂🅰🆅🅴
▼▼
Motel   All Year   1P: $45-$65   2P: $60-$65   XP: $5   F12
Location: I-90/94, exit 55, just s. 219 Hwy 12 & 16 54618. **Fax:** 608/427-3824. **Facility:** 14 one-bedroom standard units. 1 story, exterior corridors. *Bath:* combo or shower only. **Parking:** on-site, winter plug-ins. **Terms:** small pets only ($5-$10 fee). **Amenities:** video library. **Guest Services:** coin laundry. *Fee:* tanning facility. **Business Services:** administrative services. **Cards:** AX, CB, DC, DS, MC, VI. **Special Amenities:** free local telephone calls and early check-in/late check-out.

SOME UNITS
Ⓢᴅ 🛏 ⓘ⁺ Ⓥᴄʀ 🎥 ⊟ 🖥 / ✕ /
FEE

──────── WHERE TO DINE ────────

TARGET BLUFF SUPPER CLUB   **Lunch: $5-$16**   **Dinner: $5-$16**   **Phone: 608/427-6542**
▼▼ ▼▼
German   **Location:** I-90/94, exit 55, just s. 208 SR 12 & 16 54618. **Hours:** 11 am-10 pm. Closed: 11/25, 12/25; also for dinner 12/24. **Reservations:** accepted. **Features:** Unique hand-painted murals of castles and countryside adorn the walls of this Bavarian-themed restaurant. The menu consists of Old World German specialties as well as traditional American favorites. A few seafood dishes are also offered. Casual dress; cocktails. **Parking:** on-site. **Cards:** AX, DC, DS, MC, VI.

🍽 ✕

CARTER

──────── WHERE TO STAY ────────

INDIAN SPRINGS LODGE AND CONFERENCE CENTER
Phone: (715)473-6300
ⒶⒶⒶ 🆂🅰🆅🅴
▼▼▼▼
Small-scale Hotel
5/28-9/9 & 1/1-3/31 [BP]   1P: $75-$85   2P: $75-$85   XP: $15   F17
4/1-5/27 & 9/10-12/31 [BP]   1P: $65-$75   2P: $65-$75   XP: $15   F17
Location: Just n. SR 32 54566 (PO Box 249, WABENO). **Fax:** 715/473-5908. **Facility:** Nice view of surrounding area. 99 units. 97 one-bedroom standard units, some with whirlpools. 2 one-bedroom suites. 2 stories, interior corridors. *Bath:* combo or shower only. **Parking:** on-site, winter plug-ins. **Terms:** check-in 4 pm, 3 day cancellation notice-fee imposed, [AP] meal plan available. **Amenities:** hair dryers. **Dining:** 7 am-9 pm, Fri & Sat-10 pm, cocktails. **Pool(s):** heated indoor. **Leisure Activities:** whirlpool. *Fee:* game room. **Guest Services:** gift shop, coin laundry. **Business Services:** meeting rooms. **Cards:** AX, DS, MC, VI.

SOME UNITS
🎲 Ⓢᴅ 🍴 📺 ⓘ⁺ ♿ 🏊 🎥 / ✕ Ⓥᴄʀ ᴅᴀᴛᴀᴘᴏʀᴛ ⊟ 🖥 💻 /
FEE

CASHTON pop. 1,005

─────── **WHERE TO STAY** ───────

AGES PAST COUNTRY HOUSE **Phone:** 608/654-5950

(AAA) (SAVE)   All Year [BP]   1P: $100-$135   2P: $100-$135   XP: $30   F
▼▼▼▼ **Location:** Just e of center. 1223 Front St 54619. Fax: 608/654-5709. **Facility:** Chandeliers from Belgium and antique furnishings dating to 1600 are featured in this 1898 Victorian home, which was formerly a Catholic rectory. Smoke free premises. 4 one-bedroom standard units. 2 stories (no elevator), interior corridors. **Parking:**
Bed & Breakfast on-site, winter plug-ins. **Terms:** check-in 4 pm, age restrictions may apply, 7 day cancellation notice, [AP] meal plan available. **Amenities:** CD players, irons, hair dryers. **Dining:** Back Door Cafe', see separate listing. **Guest Services:** gift shop, complimentary laundry. **Cards:** AX, DC, DS, MC, VI. **Special Amenities:** free local telephone calls and early check-in/late check-out.

[TI] [X] [VCR] [▐] [DATA PORT]

─────── **WHERE TO DINE** ───────

BACK DOOR CAFE'   **Lunch:** $8-$15   **Dinner:** $15-$25   **Phone:** 608/654-5950
▼▼▼ **Location:** Just e of center; in Ages Past Country House. 1223 Front St 54619. **Hours:** 11 am-2 & 6-9 pm. Closed major holidays; also Sun & Mon. **Reservations:** required. **Features:** Each night the dining room of the
American Ages Past Country House is transformed into a European cafe for guests' relaxation and dining pleasure. A one-time table seating keeps patrons from feeling pressured or hurried. Among delicacies are duck in fig sauce, lamb chops and beef Wellington. The wine list offers a good selection, and servers are happy to help with pairings and suggestions. Dressy casual; cocktails. **Parking:** on-site. **Cards:** AX, DS, MC, VI.

[X]

CEDARBURG —See Milwaukee p. 591.

CHIPPEWA FALLS pop. 12,925

─────── **WHERE TO STAY** ───────

AMERICINN MOTEL & SUITES   *Book at aaa.com*   **Phone:** 715/723-5711
▼▼▼ ▼▼▼ All Year   1P: $74-$94   2P: $74-$94
  Location: 2 mi s on SR 124, access via CR J. 11 W South Ave 54729. Fax: 715/723-5254. **Facility:** 62 units. 61
Small-scale Hotel one-bedroom standard units, some with whirlpools. 1 one-bedroom suite ($114-$134) with whirlpool. 2 stories, interior corridors. *Bath:* combo or shower only. **Parking:** on-site, winter plug-ins. **Terms:** cancellation fee imposed, [CP] meal plan available, small pets only (in designated units). **Amenities:** irons, hair dryers. **Pool(s):** heated indoor. **Leisure Activities:** whirlpool. **Business Services:** fax (fee). **Cards:** AX, CB, DC, DS, MC, VI. *(See color ad p 576)*

SOME UNITS
[SD] [🐾] [ﯦ] [🛗] [🏊] [🚭] [▐] [DATA PORT] [▭] / [X] [VCR] [▐] [▭] /
FEE

COUNTRY INN BY CARLSON   *Book at aaa.com*   **Phone:** (715)720-1414
▼▼▼▼ All Year [ECP]   1P: $63-$115   2P: $70-$123   XP: $8   F17
  Location: Jct SR 124 and CR J. 1021 W Park Ave 54729. Fax: 715/720-1122. **Facility:** 62 one-bedroom standard
Small-scale Hotel units, some with whirlpools. 2 stories (no elevator), interior corridors. *Bath:* combo or shower only. **Parking:** on-site, winter plug-ins. **Terms:** cancellation fee imposed. **Amenities:** voice mail, irons, hair dryers. **Pool(s):** small heated indoor. **Leisure Activities:** whirlpool. **Guest Services:** valet and coin laundry. **Business Services:** fax (fee). **Cards:** AX, DC, DS, MC, VI. *(See color ad starting on p 580)*

SOME UNITS
[ASK] [SD] [ﯦ+] [ﯦ] [🏊] [🚭] [▐] [DATA PORT] [▭] / [X] [▐] /

PARK INN   *Book at aaa.com*   **Phone:** (715)723-2281
(AAA) (SAVE)   All Year [BP]   1P: $79-$119   2P: $89-$119   XP: $10   F18
▼▼▼ ▼▼ **Location:** Jct SR 124 and CR J. 1009 W Park Ave 54729. Fax: 715/723-2283. **Facility:** 67 one-bedroom standard
Small-scale Hotel units, some with kitchens and/or whirlpools. 1 story, interior/exterior corridors. **Parking:** on-site, winter plug-ins. **Terms:** [AP] meal plan available, small pets only ($10 extra charge). **Amenities:** high-speed Internet, irons, hair dryers. **Dining:** 6:30 am-10 pm, cocktails. **Pool(s):** heated indoor. **Leisure Activities:** whirlpool. **Guest Services:** valet laundry, airport transportation-Chippewa Valley Regional Airport. **Business Services:** meeting rooms, fax (fee). **Cards:** AX, DC, DS, MC, VI. **Special Amenities:** free full breakfast and free local telephone calls.

SOME UNITS
[SD] [✈] [🛏] [TI] [Y] [🏊] [🚭] [▐] [DATA PORT] [▭] / [X] [▐] [▭] /
FEE

─────── **WHERE TO DINE** ───────

THE FILL INN STATION   **Lunch:** $5-$12   **Dinner:** $5-$12   **Phone:** 715/723-6551
▼▼▼ **Location:** Corner of Bay and Columbia sts; downtown. 104 W Columbia St 54729. **Hours:** 11 am-10 pm. Closed major holidays; also Sun. **Reservations:** accepted. **Features:** This converted gas station features original
American brick pillars and a monkey wrench on the door. The menu consists of hand-made pizza, sandwiches and salad, prepared to order beef and buffalo burgers and a few Mexican dishes. Casual dress; cocktails. **Parking:** on-site. **Cards:** AX, DS, MC, VI.

[Y] [X]

COLUMBUS pop. 4,479

─────── **WHERE TO STAY** ───────

THE COLUMBUS SUPER 8   *Book at aaa.com*   **Phone:** 920/623-8800
▼▼ ▼▼ All Year [CP]   1P: $54-$79   2P: $59-$84   XP: $5   F12
  Location: US 151, exit 118 (SR 16/60), just ne. 219 Industrial Dr 53925. Fax: 920/623-3304. **Facility:** 50 one-
Small-scale Hotel bedroom standard units, some with whirlpools. 3 stories, interior corridors. **Parking:** on-site, winter plug-ins. **Terms:** pets (with prior approval). **Amenities:** hair dryers. *Some:* dual phone lines. **Pool(s):** heated indoor. **Leisure Activities:** whirlpool. **Guest Services:** coin laundry. **Business Services:** meeting rooms. **Cards:** AX, CB, DC, DS, MC, VI.

SOME UNITS
[ASK] [SD] [🐾] [ﯦ] [🏊] [🚭] [DATA PORT] [▭] / [X] [VCR] [▐] [▭] /
FEE

COUDERAY pop. 96

——— WHERE TO DINE ———

THE HIDEOUT

American

Dinner: $10-$25   **Phone:** 715/945-2746
Location: On CR CC, 6 mi n. 12101 W CR CC 54828. **Hours:** Open 5/13-12/31; 4 pm-9 pm, Sun noon-7 pm. Closed major holidays; also Mon; Tues & Wed 9/1-12/31. **Reservations:** suggested. **Features:** At the 500-acre former estate of Al Capone, the restaurant is a quiet, relaxed spot that's popular with tourists. The menu includes some Italian specialties, as well as seafood, steak & chops. After dining, enjoy a guided tour. Casual dress; cocktails. **Parking:** on-site. **Cards:** MC, VI.

CRANDON pop. 1,961

——— WHERE TO STAY ———

FOUR SEASONS MOTEL   **Phone:** 715/478-3377
Motel

| | All Year | 1P: $38-$45 | 2P: $38-$45 | XP: $5 | F10 |

Location: 0.5 mi w on US 8. Located in a commercial area. 304 W Glen 54520 (PO Box 37). **Fax:** 715/478-3785. **Facility:** 20 one-bedroom standard units. 1 story, interior/exterior corridors. **Parking:** on-site, winter plug-ins. **Terms:** cancellation fee imposed. **Leisure Activities:** snowmobiling. **Business Services:** meeting rooms. **Cards:** CB, DC, MC, VI.

SOME UNITS

CRIVITZ pop. 998

——— WHERE TO STAY ———

SHAFFER PARK RESORT   **Phone:** 715/854-2186
Motel

| | 12/26-3/31 | 1P: $55-$72 | 2P: $55-$72 | XP: $10 | F3 |
| | 4/1-11/29 | 1P: $49-$72 | 2P: $49-$72 | XP: $10 | F3 |

Location: 5 mi w on CR W. Located on the Peshtigo River. N 7217 Shaffer Rd 54114. **Facility:** 28 units. 27 one-bedroom standard units with efficiencies. 1 cottage ($95-$135). 1 story, exterior corridors. *Bath:* shower only. **Parking:** on-site. **Terms:** open 4/1-11/29 & 12/26-3/31, 2-3 night minimum stay - weekends, 14 day cancellation notice, weekly rates available, pets ($5 extra charge, dogs only). **Leisure Activities:** boating, rental paddleboats, boat dock, fishing, tennis court, cross country skiing, snowmobiling, playground, horseshoes, volleyball. **Cards:** MC, VI.

FEE

CUMBERLAND pop. 2,280

——— WHERE TO DINE ———

5 O'CLOCK CLUB   **Dinner:** $10-$20   **Phone:** 715/822-2924
American

Location: 3.5 mi n on US 63 from jct SR 48, then 0.4 mi e. 2639 7th St 54829. **Hours:** Open 4/1-2/28; 5 pm-10 pm; limited hours in winter. Closed major holidays; also Mon. **Reservations:** suggested. **Features:** This is a unique restaurant that offers a wide variety of flavorful foods in a rural and picturesque setting on a lakeshore. The dining room sports a fun nautical theme. The menu offerings range from fresh seafood and steak to pasta and Chinese. A nice selection of homemade desserts are presented tableside on a tray. Casual dress; cocktails. **Parking:** on-site. **Cards:** DS, MC, VI.

DE FOREST pop. 7,368

——— WHERE TO STAY ———

HOLIDAY INN EXPRESS   *Book at aaa.com*   **Phone:** 608/846-8686
Small-scale Hotel

| | 4/1-9/1 [ECP] | 1P: $79-$109 | 2P: $79-$109 |
| | 9/2-3/31 [ECP] | 1P: $74-$99 | 2P: $74-$99 |

Location: I-90/94, exit 126 (CR V), just e. 7184 Morrisonville Rd 53532. **Fax:** 608/846-8687. **Facility:** 72 one-bedroom standard units, some with whirlpools. 3 stories, interior corridors. *Bath:* combo or shower only. **Parking:** on-site, winter plug-ins. **Terms:** pets ($20 deposit). **Amenities:** irons, hair dryers. **Pool(s):** small heated indoor. **Leisure Activities:** whirlpool. **Guest Services:** valet and coin laundry. **Business Services:** meeting rooms. **Cards:** AX, DC, DS, JC, MC, VI.

FEE   SOME UNITS

——— WHERE TO DINE ———

TONY'S   **Lunch:** $4-$7   **Dinner:** $6-$15   **Phone:** 608/846-2755
Italian

Location: I-90/94, exit 126, 0.5 mi e. 637 W North St 53532. **Hours:** 4 pm-8:30 pm, Thurs 11 am-3 & 4-8:40 pm, Fri 11 am-2 & 4-9:30 pm, Sat 4 pm-9 pm, Sun 3 pm-8 pm. Closed major holidays; also Mon. **Reservations:** accepted. **Features:** Stuffed, gourmet white and traditional-style pizzas are prepared at the casual restaurant. Casual dress; cocktails. **Parking:** on-site. **Cards:** AX, DC, MC, VI.

DELAFIELD —See Milwaukee p. 591.

DELAVAN pop. 7,956

———— WHERE TO STAY ————

LAKE LAWN RESORT   *Book at aaa.com*   Phone: (262)728-7950

(AAA) [SAVE]   5/21-9/30 .   1P: $119-$319   2P: $119-$319   XP: $20   F17
▽▽▽▽   4/1-5/20 & 10/1-3/31   1P: $99-$249   2P: $99-$249   XP: $20   F17
        Location: I-43, exit 21 (SR 50), 1 mi e. Located in a rural area. 2400 E Geneva St 53115. Fax: 262/728-2347.
Resort   **Facility:** Water views enhance many guest rooms at this lakefront resort set on spacious, tree-covered
Large-scale Hotel   grounds. 284 units. 274 one-bedroom standard units. 8 one- and 2 three-bedroom suites ($199-$339), some
        with kitchens. 2 stories, interior/exterior corridors. *Bath:* combo or shower only. **Parking:** on-site.
        Terms: check-in 4 pm, 2 night minimum stay - weekends, 5 day cancellation notice, package plans.
Amenities: video games (fee), voice mail, irons. *Some:* hair dryers. **Dining:** 2 restaurants, 7 am-10 pm, cocktails. **Pool(s):** outdoor, heated indoor. **Leisure Activities:** sauna, whirlpool, rental boats, fishing, 3 lighted tennis courts, ice skating, recreation
programs, walking trail, petting zoo, playground, spa. *Fee:* sailboats, marina, waterskiing, cruise boat, jet ski,
pontoon, golf-18 holes, miniature golf, driving range, cross country skiing, carriage rides, horse drawn sleds in winter, bicycles,
horseback riding. **Guest Services:** gift shop, valet laundry, area transportation-dog track. **Business Services:** conference facilities, business center. **Cards:** AX, CB, DC, DS, MC, VI.

SOME UNITS
[S/D] [🍽] [Ⴤ] [🏄] [♿] [⚙] [🏊] [ᕦ] [✕] [☂] [DATA PORT] / [✕] [VCR] [▯] /

SUPER 8 MOTEL-DELAVAN   *Book at aaa.com*   Phone: (262)728-1700

(AAA) [SAVE]   All Year [CP]   1P: $59-$199   2P: $69-$199
▽▽   **Location:** I-43, exit 21 (SR 50), just w. Located in a commercial area. 518 Borg Rd 53115. Fax: 262/728-1700.
        Facility: 69 one-bedroom standard units. 2 stories (no elevator), interior corridors. **Parking:** on-site, winter
        plug-ins. **Amenities:** video library (fee). **Guest Services:** coin laundry. **Business Services:** meeting rooms.
Small-scale Hotel   **Cards:** AX, CB, DC, DS, JC, MC, VI. **Special Amenities:** free continental breakfast and free local tele-
        phone calls.

SOME UNITS
[S/D] [🍽] [⚙] [☂] [DATA PORT] [▭] / [✕] [VCR] [▯] /
FEE

———— WHERE TO DINE ————

MILLIE'S RESTAURANT & SHOPPING VILLAGE   Lunch: $5-$15   Phone: 262/728-2434

▽▽   **Location:** 3.5 mi s on 2nd St (becomes CR O); at jct S Shore Dr. N 2484 CR O 53115. **Hours:** 8 am-4 pm. Closed:
        11/25, 12/25; also Mon-Fri 1/1-2/28, Mon 3/1-6/30 & 9/2-12/31. **Features:** On beautiful landscaped
American   grounds with English gardens, the charming restaurant comprises five dining rooms decorated with
        antiques. The menu outlines Pennsylvania Dutch-style dinners, as well as sandwiches and salads. The
various flavored pancakes are a hit among breakfast dishes that are served all day. Casual dress; cocktails. **Parking:** on-site.

[✕]

DE PERE pop. 20,559

———— WHERE TO STAY ————

KRESS INN   *Book at aaa.com*   Phone: (920)403-5100

▽▽▽   All Year [ECP]   1P: $104-$124
        Location: US 41, exit 163 (Main St), 1 mi e, then just s on 3rd St. Located next to Norbert College. 300 Grant St 54115.
Small-scale Hotel   Fax: 920/403-5198. **Facility:** 46 units. 44 one-bedroom standard units, some with whirlpools. 2 one-bedroom
        suites ($134-$279) with efficiencies (no utensils). 3 stories, interior corridors. *Bath:* shower only. **Parking:**
on-site. **Terms:** small pets only ($25 deposit). **Amenities:** high-speed Internet, dual phone lines, voice mail, irons, hair dryers.
Leisure Activities: limited exercise equipment. **Guest Services:** valet laundry. **Business Services:** meeting rooms. **Cards:** AX,
DC, DS, MC, VI.

SOME UNITS
[ASK] [S/D] [🐾] [🍽] [♿] [⚙] [☂] [DATA PORT] [▯] [🛏] [▭] / [✕] /
FEE

SLEEP INN & SUITES GREEN BAY/DE PERE   *Book at aaa.com*   Phone: (920)338-8800

▽▽▽   All Year   1P: $69-$99   2P: $69-$99   XP: $5   F17
        Location: US 41, exit 161. 1600 Lawrence Dr 54115. Fax: 920/338-8881. **Facility:** 76 one-bedroom standard
Small-scale Hotel   units, some with whirlpools. 3 stories, interior corridors. *Bath:* combo or shower only. **Parking:** on-site.
        Terms: 7 day cancellation notice, [ECP] meal plan available, package plans - seasonal. **Amenities:** dual
phone lines, voice mail, safes (fee), irons, hair dryers. **Pool(s):** heated indoor. **Leisure Activities:** whirlpool, exercise room.
Guest Services: coin laundry. **Business Services:** meeting rooms, business center. **Cards:** AX, CB, DC, DS, JC, MC, VI.

SOME UNITS
[ASK] [S/D] [♿] [⚙] [🏊] [☂] [DATA PORT] [▭] / [✕] [▯] [🛏] /

———— WHERE TO DINE ————

A'S RESTAURANT & MUSIC CAFE   Lunch: $5-$8   Dinner: $9-$15   Phone: 920/336-2277

▽▽▽   **Location:** On east side of bridge; center. 112 N Broadway 54115. **Hours:** 11 am-1:30 & 5-9:30 pm. Closed major
        holidays; also Sun, Mon for lunch. **Reservations:** accepted. **Features:** Greek shrimp, tenderloin Sicilia and
American   chicken saltimboca are among flavorful selections on a menu of charbroiled seafood, chicken and beef
        selections. Musicians perform several nights a week. The dining room has the cozy feel of a French cafe.
Casual dress; cocktails. **Parking:** on-site. **Cards:** AX, DC, MC, VI.

[Ⴤ] [✕]

BLACK & TAN GRILLE   Dinner: $13-$22   Phone: 920/336-4430

▽▽▽   **Location:** US 41, exit 163 (Main St), 1 mi e. 101 Fort Howard Ave 54115. **Hours:** 5 pm-9 pm, Fri & Sat-10 pm,
        Sun-8 pm. Closed: 11/25, 12/25 & Easter. **Reservations:** accepted. **Features:** The contemporary
American   restaurant serves traditional dishes with a twist and prides itself on offering cuisine different from what is
        common in the area. The menu changes seasonally, and Fridays and Saturdays always feature something
special. Dressy casual; cocktails. **Parking:** street. **Cards:** AX, MC, VI.

[Ⴤ] [✕]

DODGEVILLE pop. 4,220

———— WHERE TO STAY ————

BEST WESTERN QUIET HOUSE & SUITES
Book at aaa.com

AAA [SAVE]
▽▽▽▽ ▽

Small-scale Hotel

Phone: 608/93■

	1P: $89-$108	2P: $99-$118	XP: $10
5/16-12/31 [CP]			
4/1-5/15 & 1/1-3/31 [CP]	1P: $69	2P: $79	XP: $10

Location: On US 18, just e of jct SR 23. 1130 N Johns St 53533. **Fax:** 608/935-7724. **Facility:** 39 units. 35 one-bedroom standard units, some with whirlpools. 4 one-bedroom suites, some with whirlpools. 2 stories (no elevator), interior corridors. *Bath:* combo or shower only. **Parking:** on-site, winter plug-ins. **Terms:** package plans - seasonal, pets ($15 extra charge, in designated units). **Amenities:** irons, hair dryers. **Pool(s):** heated indoor/outdoor. **Leisure Activities:** whirlpool, limited exercise equipment. **Business Services:** meeting rooms. **Cards:** AX, CB, DC, DS, MC, VI. **Special Amenities:** free continental breakfast and free newspaper. *(See color ad p 579)*

SOME UNITS

[S⊘] [🛏] [📶] [🛁] [🚫] [🏊] [♨] [DATA PORT] [🔒] [📺] [🍽] / [✕] /
FEE

HOUSE ON THE ROCK INN
▽▽▽▽ ▽

Small-scale Hotel

Phone: 608/935-3711

	1P: $69-$199	
All Year [CP]		

Location: On SR 23, 1 mi n of jct US 18. 3591 SR 23 53533. **Fax:** 608/935-1691. **Facility:** 174 units. 154 one-bedroom standard units. 20 one-bedroom suites. 3-4 stories, interior corridors. *Bath:* combo or shower only. **Parking:** on-site. **Terms:** package plans. **Amenities:** voice mail. *Some:* video games (fee), irons, hair dryers. **Pool(s):** heated outdoor, 2 heated indoor, wading. **Leisure Activities:** whirlpools, exercise room. *Fee:* game room. **Guest Services:** gift shop, coin laundry. **Business Services:** meeting rooms. **Cards:** AX, DS, MC, VI.

SOME UNITS

[Y] [♨M] [♿] [🚫] [🏊] [✕] [♨] [DATA PORT] / [✕] [🔒] [📺] /

PINE RIDGE MOTEL
AAA [SAVE]
▽▽▽

Motel

Phone: 608/935-3386

5/21-10/26	1P: $35-$55	2P: $45-$65	XP: $3	F9
4/1-5/20	1P: $30-$45	2P: $35-$55	XP: $3	F9
10/27-3/31	1P: $25-$35	2P: $30-$41	XP: $3	F9

Location: On CR YZ, 0.5 mi e of jct SR 23. Large vehicle parking on site. 405 CR YZ 53533. **Facility:** 22 one-bedroom standard units. 1 story, exterior corridors. *Bath:* combo or shower only. **Parking:** on-site, winter plug-ins. **Terms:** cancellation fee imposed, small pets only ($5 fee). **Cards:** AX, DS, MC, VI. **Special Amenities:** free local telephone calls and preferred room (subject to availability with advanced reservations).

SOME UNITS

[S⊘] [🛏] [♨] / [✕] [🔒] [📺] /
FEE

SUPER 8 MOTEL OF DODGEVILLE
Book at aaa.com

AAA [SAVE]
▽▽▽▽ ▽

Small-scale Hotel

Phone: (608)935-3888

6/4-9/6	1P: $60-$70	2P: $70-$80	XP: $5	F12
9/7-10/31	1P: $52-$64	2P: $60-$74	XP: $5	F12
4/1-6/3	1P: $46-$60	2P: $56-$70	XP: $5	F12
11/1-3/31	1P: $44-$50	2P: $46-$52	XP: $5	F12

Location: Just n of US 18. 1308 Johns St 53533. **Fax:** 608/935-3888. **Facility:** 43 one-bedroom standard units, some with whirlpools. 2 stories (no elevator), interior corridors. **Parking:** on-site, winter plug-ins. **Terms:** 12 day cancellation notice, [ECP] meal plan available, pets ($50 deposit). **Leisure Activities:** whirlpool, exercise room. **Guest Services:** coin laundry. **Business Services:** meeting rooms. **Cards:** AX, CB, DC, DS, JC, MC, VI.

SOME UNITS

[S⊘] [🛏] [📶] [🚫] [♨] [DATA PORT] / [✕] [VCR] [🔒] [📺] /
FEE   FEE

———— WHERE TO DINE ————

THYM'S RESTAURANT
▽▽▽

American

Dinner: $8-$20   **Phone:** 608/935-3344

Location: On SR 23, 1.5 mi n of jct US 18. 3625 State Hwy 23 N 53533. **Hours:** 5 pm-9 pm. Closed: 12/25. **Reservations:** accepted. **Features:** The family-owned restaurant prepares nightly specials, as well as steaks, seafood and chicken. Friendly service and a relaxed atmosphere make this place enjoyable for a hearty meal. Cocktails. **Parking:** on-site. **Cards:** AX, DS, MC, VI.

[Y] [✕]

DOOR COUNTY

WHERE TO STAY

Phone: 920/839-2617

| 1P: $75 | 2P: $75 | XP: $10 |
| 1P: $65 | 2P: $65 | XP: $10 |

Motel

Location: Just w of SR 57; between Bluff Rd and Howard St. Located in a quiet area. 8076 Guy St 54202 (Box 51). **Facility:** Smoke free premises. 6 one-bedroom standard units. 1 story, exterior corridors. **Parking:** on-site. **Terms:** open 5/1-10/31, 2 night minimum stay - weekends, 7 day cancellation notice, package plans. **Cards:** DC, MC, VI.

SOME UNITS

GORDON LODGE

Phone: 920/839-2331

Resort
Small-scale Hotel

| 6/18-10/16 | 1P: $120-$256 | 2P: $120-$256 | XP: $29 |
| 5/28-6/17 | 1P: $100-$220 | 2P: $100-$220 | XP: $12 |

Location: 0.8 mi n on SR 57, 6.5 mi ne on CR Q. Located on the shores of Lake Michigan. 1420 Pine Dr 54202 (PO Box 189). Fax: 920/839-2450. **Facility:** Fronting on the North Bay of Lake Michigan, the property features cottages and lodge units, several with fireplaces. 40 units. 20 one-bedroom standard units. 20 cottages. 1 story, interior/exterior corridors. **Bath:** combo or shower only. **Parking:** on-site. **Terms:** open 5/28-10/16, check-in 3:30 pm, 2 night minimum stay - weekends, 18 day cancellation notice. **Dining:** 7:30 am-10 & 5:30-8:30 pm, cocktails. **Pool(s):** heated outdoor. **Leisure Activities:** whirlpool, boating, fishing, putting green, 2 lighted tennis courts, badminton, fitness trail, ping pong, rental bicycles, basketball, shuffleboard. **Business Services:** meeting rooms. **Cards:** AX, DS, MC, VI. *(See color ad below)*

SOME UNITS

WHERE TO DINE

THE COMMON HOUSE

Dinner: $10-$29

Phone: 920/839-2708

American

Location: On SR 57, at south end of village. 8041 Hwy 57 54202. **Hours:** Open 5/1-10/31; 5:30 pm-10 pm. **Reservations:** suggested. **Features:** The converted 1890 hardware store delivers an eclectic menu of creatively prepared and thoughtfully presented dishes, such as mouthwatering pork tenderloin, duckling, rack of lamb and poached salmon. An extensive selection of wine complements the food. Casual dress; cocktails. **Parking:** street. **Cards:** DS, MC, VI.

EGG HARBOR pop. 250

WHERE TO STAY

THE ASHBROOKE

Phone: 920/868-3113

Small-scale Hotel

| All Year | 1P: $89-$189 | 2P: $99-$199 | XP: $25 |

Location: Just n on SR 42. 7942 Egg Harbor Rd 54209. Fax: 920/868-9684. **Facility:** Smoke free premises. 36 units. 28 one-bedroom standard units, some with whirlpools. 8 one-bedroom suites with whirlpools. 2 stories (no elevator), interior corridors. **Parking:** on-site. **Terms:** 2 night minimum stay - weekends, age restrictions may apply, 14 day cancellation notice-fee imposed, package plans. **Amenities:** video library, irons, hair dryers. **Pool(s):** heated indoor. **Leisure Activities:** sauna, whirlpool, exercise room. **Cards:** AX, DC, MC, VI.

BAY POINT INN

Phone: 920/868-3297

Condominium

| All Year | 1P: $199-$239 | 2P: $199-$239 | XP: $20 | F6 |

Location: On SR 42, just n. Located on a bluff, overlooking Green Bay. 7933 Hwy 42 54209. Fax: 920/868-2876. **Facility:** The inn, which overlooks Green Bay, features a patio or balcony with each room. Smoke free premises. 10 one-bedroom suites with efficiencies, some with whirlpools. 2 stories (no elevator), exterior corridors. **Parking:** on-site, winter plug-ins. **Terms:** 3 night minimum stay - weekends in summer, 14 day cancellation notice, weekly rates available, [ECP] meal plan available. **Amenities:** video library, CD players, dual phone lines, voice mail, irons, hair dryers. **Pool(s):** heated outdoor. **Leisure Activities:** whirlpool. **Business Services:** meeting rooms. **Cards:** AX, CB, DC, DS, MC, VI.

LANDMARK RESORT   *Book at aaa.com*   Phone: 920/868-3205

AAA SAVE

6/25-10/16	1P: $92-$359
5/28-6/24	1P: $91-$290
4/1-5/27 & 10/17-3/31	1P: $74-$199

Resort
Condominium

Location: 1 mi sw on CR G and Hillside Tr; 1 mi nw of SR 42 from jct Hillside Tr. Located on a buff overlooking Green Bay. 7643 Hillside Rd 54209. Fax: 920/868-2569. **Facility:** Views of the bay enhance some of this resort's one- and two-bedroom condo units. 293 units. 151 one-, 134 two- and 8 three-bedroom suites with kitchens. 2-3 stories, interior corridors. **Parking:** on-site, winter plug-ins. **Terms:** check-in 4 pm, 2 night minimum stay - weekends 7/1-8/31, 14 day cancellation notice-fee imposed, package plans - seasonal. **Amenities:** video library (fee), voice mail, irons, hair dryers. **Dining:** The Landmark, see separate listing. **Pool(s):** 3 heated outdoor, heated indoor. **Leisure Activities:** whirlpools, steamrooms, adjacent to 36-hole golf course, 5 tennis courts (3 lighted), cross country skiing, snowmobiling, ice skating, recreation programs, exercise room, basketball, horseshoes, shuffleboard, volleyball. *Fee:* game room. **Guest Services:** gift shop, coin laundry. **Business Services:** conference facilities. **Cards:** AX, DC, DS, MC, VI. **Special Amenities:** free local telephone calls.

LULL-ABI INN OF EGG HARBOR   Phone: 920/868-3135

		XP: $10
4/19-10/25	2P: $59-$119	

Motel

Location: On SR 42, just n. 7928 SR 42 54209 (PO Box 527). Fax: 920/868-2521. **Facility:** 23 units. 18 one-bedroom standard units. 5 one-bedroom suites. 2 stories (no elevator), exterior corridors. *Bath:* combo or shower only. **Parking:** on-site. **Terms:** open 4/19-10/25, 2 night minimum stay - seasonal weekends, 14 day cancellation notice-fee imposed. **Amenities:** hair dryers. **Leisure Activities:** whirlpool. **Cards:** AX, DS, MC, VI.

SOME UNITS

MARINER MOTEL & COTTAGES   Phone: 920/868-3131

AAA SAVE

6/11-8/23	1P: $63-$137	2P: $63-$137	XP: $9
8/24-10/16	1P: $58-$137	2P: $58-$137	XP: $6
5/11-6/10	1P: $55-$92	2P: $55-$92	XP: $6

Motel

Location: 2 mi s on CR G, w at sign. Overlooking the Green Bay. 7505 Mariner Rd 54209. **Facility:** 26 units. 22 one-bedroom standard units, some with efficiencies. 4 cabins. 1-2 stories (no elevator), exterior corridors. *Bath:* combo or shower only. **Parking:** on-site. **Terms:** open 5/11-10/16, 21 day cancellation notice, 60 day in cottages, weekly rates available. **Pool(s):** heated outdoor. **Leisure Activities:** boating, canoeing, boat dock, fishing, bicycles, hiking trails. **Cards:** DC, MC, VI. **Special Amenities:** free local telephone calls. *(See color ad below)*

SOME UNITS

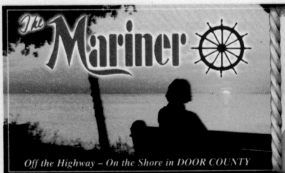

The Mariner

Enjoy a private sunset every night
from your room near the shore!
Surrounded by 60 peaceful acres.

Deluxe rooms & suites
• Cottages • Pool • Private pier
• Boats • Bikes • Walking trails
Golf – 15 minutes to 4 courses

7505 Mariner Rd.
Egg Harbor, WI 54209
920-868-3131

Off the Highway – On the Shore in DOOR COUNTY

The Shallows Resort

Get away to our Secluded Waterfront Resort on Beautiful Horseshoe Bay

Along 375 feet of private shoreline, nestled in a secluded wooded setting, lies the Shallows Resort... the perfect place for your next family getaway. Stay in our charming, private 1- to 3-bedroom cottages, townhouses, or luxury homes, or in our waterfront Shoreside Motel. All guests can enjoy the resort's heated pool, whirlpool, tennis courts, bikes, boats, and grills. Near golf courses, horseback riding, hiking, and shopping.

AAA Approved

7353 Horseshoe Bay Road, Egg Harbor, WI 54209   www.shallows.com   800-257-1560

THE SHALLOWS

Phone: 920/868-3458

AAA (SAVE)
🔻🔻🔻
Resort Motel

6/25-8/28 [CP]	1P: $110-$145	2P: $110-$145	XP: $20
5/28-6/24 & 8/29-10/31 [CP]	1P: $85-$115	2P: $85-$115	XP: $20
4/30-5/27 [CP]	1P: $65-$80	2P: $65-$80	XP: $20

Location: On CR G, 2.5 mi s. Located on the shores of Green Bay. 7353 Horse Shoe Bay Rd, Hwy G 54209 (PO Box 20). Fax: 920/868-2327. **Facility:** Most of the accommodations at this wooded resort offer water views; some units have fireplaces. 34 units. 16 one-bedroom standard units, some with efficiencies. 8 one- and 4 two-bedroom suites ($85-$240) with efficiencies. 3 vacation homes ($150-$350) and 3 cottages ($90-$250). 1-2 stories (no elevator), exterior corridors. *Bath:* combo or shower only. **Parking:** on-site. **Terms:** open 4/30-10/31, 3-4 night minimum stay - seasonal, 30 day cancellation notice-fee imposed. **Amenities:** *Some:* CD players, hair dryers. **Pool(s):** heated outdoor. **Leisure Activities:** whirlpool, boating, canoeing, fishing, tennis court, lakeside evening campfires, bicycles, playground, basketball. Cards: AX, DS, MC, VI. *(See color ad p 501)*

SOME UNITS

🏊 ✕ 🔲 🖥 / ✕ 🅚 VCR ☎ 🖳 /

——— WHERE TO DINE ———

THE LANDMARK

🔻🔻 🔻🔻
American

Lunch: $7-$10   **Dinner:** $12-$25   Phone: 920/868-3205

Location: 1 mi sw on CR G and Hillside Tr; 1 mi nw of SR 42 from jct Hillside Tr; in Landmark Resort. 7643 Hillside Rd 54209. **Hours:** 6:30 am-2 & 5-9:30 pm; hours vary off season. **Reservations:** accepted. **Features:** The restaurant sits on a bluff and offers an outstanding view of Green Bay; bring your camera for some exceptional sunset shots. Casual dress; cocktails. **Parking:** on-site. Cards: AX, DC, DS, MC, VI.

🍸 ✕

TRIO RESTAURANT

🔻🔻🔻
Italian

Dinner: $11-$18   Phone: 920/868-2090

Location: Jct CR E,. on SR 42. 4655 CR E 54209. **Hours:** Open 5/10-10/25; 5 pm-9 pm, Fri & Sat-9:30 pm. **Features:** The monthly changing menu samples a good variety of well-prepared French and Italian country "peasant" foods, all served in hearty portions. The atmosphere has the flavor and energy of an upbeat bistro. Casual dress; beer & wine only. **Parking:** on-site. Cards: AX, DC, DS, MC, VI.

✕

VILLAGE CAFE

🔻
American

Lunch: $6-$8   Phone: 920/868-3342

Location: On SR 42, just n of jct CR E. 7918 Egg Harbor Rd 54209. **Hours:** 7 am-2 pm; hours may vary. **Features:** Known for homemade delights, the restaurant specializes in lighter fare. Gourmet omelets and fresh fruit are popular selections from the breakfast menu. For lunch, diners favor specialty salads, burgers and sandwiches. Casual dress; beer & wine only. **Parking:** on-site. Cards: DS, MC, VI.

✕

ELLISON BAY

——— WHERE TO STAY ———

GRAND VIEW MOTEL

AAA (SAVE)
🔻🔻 🔻🔻
Motel

Phone: 920/854-5150

6/4-10/24 [CP]	1P: $68-$141	2P: $75-$141	XP: $8	D14
5/7-6/3 [CP]	1P: $61-$110	2P: $61-$110	XP: $8	D14

Location: On SR 42, 0.6 mi s. Located high on buff overlooking the coastline and village. 11885 Hwy 42 54210 (PO Box 135). Fax: 920/854-7538. **Facility:** Smoke free premises. 28 one-bedroom standard units, some with whirlpools. 2 stories (no elevator), exterior corridors. **Parking:** on-site. **Terms:** open 5/7-10/24, 2-3 night minimum stay - seasonal, 14 day cancellation notice-fee imposed. **Amenities:** *Some:* irons, hair dryers. **Leisure Activities:** bicycles, hiking trails, jogging, basketball. **Guest Services:** gift shop, valet laundry. Cards: AX, DS, MC, VI. **Special Amenities:** free continental breakfast and free local telephone calls.

SOME UNITS

✕ ✕ 🔲 / 🖥 /

PARKSIDE INN

AAA (SAVE)
🔻🔻 🔻🔻
Motel

Phone: 920/854-9050

6/18-10/17		2P: $89-$99	XP: $8
5/1-6/17 & 10/18-10/31		2P: $69-$79	XP: $8

Location: On SR 42, 0.3 mi s. Located across from the village park on the bay. 11946 Hwy 42 54210. Fax: 920/854-9050. **Facility:** Smoke free premises. 15 one-bedroom standard units. 2 stories (no elevator), exterior corridors. *Bath:* combo or shower only. **Parking:** on-site. **Terms:** open 5/1-10/31, 7 day cancellation notice-fee imposed. Cards: DS, MC, VI. **Special Amenities:** free continental breakfast and free local telephone calls.

🐂 ✕ 🔲 🖥

WAGON TRAIL RESORT, RESTAURANT & CONFERENCE CENTER

AAA (SAVE)
🔻🔻🔻🔻
Resort
Large-scale Hotel

Phone: (920)854-2385

7/2-10/23	1P: $109-$159	2P: $109-$159	XP: $10	F17
5/14-7/1	1P: $89-$139	2P: $89-$139	XP: $10	F17
4/1-5/13 & 10/24-3/31	1P: $59-$89	2P: $59-$89	XP: $10	F17

Location: 3.5 mi se on Mink River Rd; 6 mi ne of Sister Bay. Located in a rural area, opposite the bay. 1041 CR ZZ 54210. Fax: 920/854-5278. **Facility:** The property features lodge and vacation homes within a natural setting on Rowley's Bay. 114 units. 73 one-bedroom standard units, some with whirlpools. 3 two- and 4 three-bedroom suites ($129-$269) with efficiencies. 27 vacation homes ($129-$339) and 7 cabins ($159-$239), some with whirlpools. 1-3 stories, interior/exterior corridors. *Bath:* combo or shower only. **Parking:** on-site, winter plug-ins. **Terms:** 7 night minimum stay - vacation homes in summer, 10 day cancellation notice-fee imposed. **Amenities:** *Some:* irons, hair dryers. **Dining:** Grandma's Swedish Restaurant & Bakery, see separate listing. **Pool(s):** heated indoor. **Leisure Activities:** sauna, whirlpool, rental boats, rental paddleboats, fishing, tennis court, cross country skiing, snowmobiling, rental bicycles, playground, exercise room, basketball, volleyball. *Fee:* marina, game room. **Guest Services:** gift shop, coin laundry. **Business Services:** conference facilities. Cards: DS, MC, VI. **Special Amenities:** free newspaper.

SOME UNITS

$🅳 🍴 ♿ 🅿 🏊 ✕ / ✕ 🅚 🔲 🖥 🖳 /

-------- **WHERE TO DINE** --------

GRANDMA'S SWEDISH RESTAURANT & BAKERY   Lunch: $5-$9   Dinner: $10-$17   Phone: 920/854-2385
▼▼▼ ▼▼▼   **Location:** 3.5 mi se on Mink River Rd; 6 mi ne of Sister Bay; in Wagon Trail Resort, Restaurant & Conference Center.
1041 Hwy ZZ 54210. **Hours:** 7:30 am-9 pm; hours vary with season. **Features:** Overlooking a picturesque
American   lake, the Swedish country dining room is a quaint spot for home-cooking and tempting bakery treats.
Especially popular is the fish boil and Swedish smorgasbord, available three nights a week, June through
October. Casual dress; beer & wine only. **Parking:** on-site. **Cards:** DS, MC, VI.

MINK RIVER BASIN SUPPER CLUB   Dinner: $15-$34   Phone: 920/854-2250
Ⓐ   **Location:** On SR 42; center. 12010 Hwy 42 54210. **Hours:** 5 pm-9:30 pm, Sat & Sun-10 pm; winter hours vary.
Closed: 11/25, 12/25. **Reservations:** accepted. **Features:** The menu samples a wide variety of home-style
▼▼▼ ▼▼   selections, ranging from fresh fish, pasta and duck to prime rib and baby back ribs. Premium wine created
American   from Door County fruit include some nonalcoholic selections. The dessert bar is especially popular. Casual
dress; cocktails. **Parking:** on-site. **Cards:** AX, DC, DS, MC, VI.   Ⓨ

T. ASHWELL'S   Dinner: $19-$39   Phone: 920/854-4306
▼▼▼ ▼▼   **Location:** Jct SR 42, just e. 11976 Mink River Rd 54210. **Hours:** Open 5/16-2/16; 5 pm-10 pm. Closed: Tues.
Reservations: suggested. **Features:** The contemporary restaurant serves traditional dishes with a twist
American   and prides itself on offering cuisine different from what is common in the area. The menu changes
seasonally, and Fridays and Saturdays always feature something special. Dressy casual; cocktails.
Parking: on-site. **Cards:** AX, CB, DC, DS, MC, VI.   Ⓨ ⊠

THE VIKING GRILL   Lunch: $5-$11   Dinner: $10-$17   Phone: 920/854-2998
▼▼   **Location:** On SR 42; center. 12029 Hwy 42 54210. **Hours:** 6 am-8 pm; to 9 pm 6/15-10/15. Closed: 11/25,
12/25 & Easter; also 3/1-3/31. **Features:** Nightly fish boils draw hungry crowds to the family-oriented
American   restaurant from late May through mid-October. Tourists enjoy experiencing the event, which is a big part of
area culture. Other choices center on familiar fare, such as broasted chicken. Casual dress; cocktails.
Parking: on-site. **Cards:** AX, DS, MC, VI.   Ⓨ ⊠

EPHRAIM pop. 353

-------- **WHERE TO STAY** --------

EPHRAIM GUEST HOUSE   Phone: 920/854-2319
▼▼▼ ▼▼   8/18-10/31   2P: $95-$165   XP: $12   F7
6/14-8/17   2P: $150-$160   XP: $12   F7
11/1-3/31   2P: $80-$160   XP: $12   F7
Condominium   4/1-6/13   2P: $80-$105   XP: $12   F7
Location: Just n of Village Hall, then just e. Located in a quiet area. 3042 Cedar St 54211 (PO Box 349). **Facility:** Smoke free premises.
14 units. 7 one-, 6 two- and 1 three-bedroom suites ($95-$225) with kitchens, some with whirlpools. 2 stories (no elevator),
interior/exterior corridors. **Parking:** on-site. **Terms:** 21 day cancellation notice-fee imposed. **Amenities:** video library, irons, hair
dryers. **Leisure Activities:** whirlpool. **Guest Services:** coin laundry. **Cards:** AX, DS, MC, VI.

(ASK) ⓈⒹ ⑪⁺ ⊠ (VCR) 🖥 🖨 🖵

TROLLHAUGEN LODGE, SUITE, MOTEL & LOG CABIN   Phone: 920/854-2713
Ⓐ (SAVE)   8/16-10/17 [CP]   1P: $69-$102   2P: $69-$102   XP: $10   D12
6/25-8/15 [CP]   1P: $89-$92   2P: $89-$92   XP: $10   D12
▼▼▼ ▼▼   10/18-10/31 [CP]   1P: $59-$72   2P: $59-$72   XP: $10   D12
Motel   4/30-6/24 [CP]   1P: $49-$72   2P: $49-$72   XP: $10   D12
Location: 0.6 mi n of Village Hall. 10176 Rt 42 54211 (PO Box 142). **Facility:** Smoke free premises. 14 units. 13
one-bedroom standard units. 1 cabin ($109-$149). 1-2 stories (no elevator), interior/exterior corridors. *Bath:*
shower only. **Parking:** on-site. **Terms:** open 4/30-10/31, 2 night minimum stay - some weekends, 7 day cancellation notice-fee
imposed. **Amenities:** hair dryers. **Leisure Activities:** whirlpool. **Cards:** DS, MC, VI. **Special Amenities: free continental
breakfast and free local telephone calls.**   SOME UNITS

ⓈⒹ ⊠ 🖥 🖨 🖵 / (VCR) /

FISH CREEK

——— WHERE TO STAY ———

HOMESTEAD SUITES
Phone: 920/868-3748

◇◇◇	6/13-8/28 [ECP]	2P: $139-$189	XP: $10	F16
	8/29-10/30 [ECP]	2P: $94-$189	XP: $10	F16
Small-scale Hotel	4/1-6/12 [ECP]	2P: $79-$149	XP: $10	F16
	10/31-3/31 [ECP]	2P: $69-$139	XP: $10	F16

Location: 0.3 mi n on SR 42. Located next to Peninsula State Park. 4006 Main St 54212 (PO Box 730). Fax: 920/868-2874. **Facility:** Smoke free premises. 64 units. 48 one-bedroom standard units, some with whirlpools. 16 two-bedroom suites with kitchens and whirlpools. 2 stories (no elevator), interior/exterior corridors. **Parking:** on-site. **Terms:** 2-3 night minimum stay - weekends, 21 day cancellation notice, package plans. **Amenities:** video library. *Some:* irons. **Pool(s):** 2 heated outdoor, heated indoor. **Leisure Activities:** sauna, whirlpools, exercise room. *Fee:* game room. **Guest Services:** coin laundry. **Business Services:** meeting rooms. **Cards:** DS, MC, VI.

JULIE'S PARK CAFE & MOTEL
Phone: 920/868-2999

◇◇	6/25-8/21	1P: $79-$106	2P: $79-$106	XP: $10
	8/22-10/17	1P: $69-$96	2P: $69-$96	XP: $10
Motel	4/15-6/24	1P: $55-$81	2P: $55-$81	XP: $10
	10/18-11/1	1P: $41-$78	2P: $41-$78	XP: $10

Location: On SR 42, 0.3 mi n. Located at the entrance to Peninsula State Park. 4020 Hwy 42 54212 (PO Box 548). Fax: 920/854-7722. **Facility:** Smoke free premises. 13 units. 12 one- and 1 two-bedroom standard units. 1 story, exterior corridors. *Bath:* combo or shower only. **Parking:** on-site. **Terms:** open 4/15-11/1, 10 day cancellation notice, weekly rates available, small pets only ($15 extra charge, in designated units). **Cards:** DS, MC, VI.

SOME UNITS

SETTLEMENT COURTYARD INN
Phone: 920/868-3524

AAA SAVE	7/2-10/23	1P: $119-$134	2P: $124-$139	XP: $12	F4
	10/24-3/31	1P: $72-$134	2P: $77-$139	XP: $12	F4
◇◇◇	5/14-7/1	1P: $84-$99	2P: $89-$104	XP: $12	F4
	4/1-5/13	1P: $67-$77	2P: $72-$82	XP: $12	F4

Small-scale Hotel **Location:** On SR 42, 1 mi s. Located in a rural area. 9126 Hwy 42 54212 (PO Box 729). Fax: 920/868-3048. **Facility:** 33 units. 29 one- and 1 two-bedroom standard units, some with whirlpools. 1 one- and 2 two-bedroom suites ($119-$229) with whirlpools. 2 stories (no elevator), interior corridors. **Parking:** on-site, winter plug-ins. **Terms:** 2-3 night minimum stay - seasonal & weekends, 10 day cancellation notice, weekly rates available, package plans - seasonal. **Amenities:** *Some:* irons, hair dryers. **Leisure Activities:** cross country skiing, hiking trails, horseshoes. **Cards:** AX, DS, MC, VI. **Special Amenities:** free local telephone calls and early check-in/late check-out. *(See color ad below)*

SOME UNITS

THE WHITE GULL INN
Phone: (920)868-3517

◇◇◇◇	All Year [BP]	1P: $130-$259	2P: $136-$265

Location: Just w of SR 42; center. 4225 Main St 54212 (PO Box 160). Fax: 920/868-2367. **Facility:** This country inn built in 1896 has nicely appointed rooms, most with gas fireplaces; phone for seasonal closures. Smoke Historic free premises. 17 units. 10 one-bedroom standard units, some with whirlpools. 3 one-bedroom suites, some Country Inn with whirlpools. 4 cottages. 1-2 stories (no elevator), interior/exterior corridors. *Bath:* combo or shower only. **Parking:** on-site. **Terms:** 2 night minimum stay - weekends, 14 day cancellation notice, package plans - in winter. **Amenities:** video library, CD players, hair dryers. *Some:* voice mail. **Dining:** dining room, see separate listing. **Business Services:** PC. **Cards:** AX, CB, DC, DS, MC, VI.

SOME UNITS

—————— WHERE TO DINE ——————

THE COOKERY
♦♦♦
American

Lunch: $5-$9   **Dinner:** $9-$13   **Phone:** 920/868-3634
Location: On SR 42; center. 4135 Hwy 42 54212. **Hours:** Open 4/1-10/31; 7 am-9 pm; open some weekends off season. Closed: 11/25; also 11/30-12/25. **Features:** Flavorful foods cooked from scratch include the specialty creamy whitefish chowder. Desserts, cinnamon rolls and other baked goods are made on the premises. The dining room has a cozy, country-style ambience. Service is upbeat and friendly. Casual dress; beer & wine only. **Parking:** street. **Cards:** MC, VI.   ⊠

ENGLISH INN
♦♦♦
Continental
Cards: MC, VI.

Dinner: $18-$50   **Phone:** 920/868-3076
Location: On SR 42, 2 mi n. 3713 Hwy 42 54212. **Hours:** Open 5/3-10/27; 5 pm-9 pm. **Features:** Three attractive dining areas are decorated in an English theme with lots of wood and beautiful stained glass. Baked grouper and prime rib stand out on a menu of veal, pasta, ribs, beef, lamb and seafood. Delicious desserts are made on the premises. Casual dress; cocktails; entertainment. **Parking:** on-site.   ⛉ ⊠

WHITE GULL INN Country Inn
♦♦
American

Lunch: $7-$10   **Dinner:** $17-$21   **Phone:** 920/868-3517
Location: Just w of SR 42; center; in The White Gull Inn. 4225 Main St 54212. **Hours:** 7:30 am-2:30 & 5-8 pm. Closed: 11/25, 12/25. **Reservations:** suggested, for dinner. **Features:** Enjoy traditional fish boils at dinner or hearty breakfasts of cherry-stuffed French toast. The 1896 country inn is appointed with period antiques. Such dishes as crabmeat and wild rice salad are delicious and satisfying. Servers are pleasant. Casual dress; beer & wine only. **Parking:** street. **Cards:** AX, DC, DS, MC, VI.   ⊠

GILLS ROCK

—————— WHERE TO STAY ——————

HARBOR HOUSE INN
♦♦
Bed & Breakfast

	Phone: 920/854-5196

	1P: $69-$185	2P: $69-$185	XP: $20	D18
6/25-10/17 [ECP]	1P: $69-$185	2P: $69-$185	XP: $20	D18
5/28-6/24 & 10/18-10/30 [ECP]	1P: $59-$175	2P: $59-$175	XP: $20	D18
4/30-5/27 [ECP]	1P: $49-$165	2P: $49-$165	XP: $20	D18

Location: On SR 42; center. Located across from Weburg's Wharf. 12666 SR 42 54210. **Facility:** Smoke free premises. 14 units. 12 one-bedroom standard units, some with whirlpools. 2 cottages ($129-$139). 1-2 stories (no elevator), interior/exterior corridors. **Bath:** combo or shower only. **Parking:** on-site. **Terms:** open 4/30-10/30, 21 day cancellation notice-fee imposed, weekly rates available, pets ($20 extra charge). **Leisure Activities:** sauna, whirlpool, rental bicycles. **Cards:** AX, MC, VI.

🐾 ⊠ ⊠ ☎ / VCR 🛏 🖥 /
FEE

MAPLE GROVE MOTEL
♦
Motel

Property failed to provide current rates   **Phone:** 920/854-2587
Location: On SR 42, 0.3 mi e, 1.5 mi w of car ferry. Located in a rural area. 809 SR 42 54210. Fax: 920/854-7817. **Facility:** 6 units. 4 one- and 2 two-bedroom standard units. 1 story, exterior corridors. **Bath:** shower only. **Parking:** on-site. **Terms:** open 5/1-11/1, pets ($5 extra charge).

SOME UNITS
🐾 ☎ 🛏 🖥 / ⊠ /
FEE

"It's making a 'thumping' sound."

SISTER BAY pop. 886

--- WHERE TO STAY ---

BIRCHWOOD LODGE

Phone: (920)854-7195

6/20-8/21	1P: $159-$164	2P: $159-$164	XP: $10	F18
8/22-10/31	1P: $104-$145	2P: $104-$145	XP: $10	F18
4/1-6/19 & 11/1-3/31	1P: $79-$99	2P: $79-$99	XP: $10	F18

Small-scale Hotel

Location: Jct SR 42 and 57, just se. Located in a semi-rural area. 337 Hwy 57 54234 (PO Box 646). Fax: 920/854-9385. **Facility:** Smoke free premises. 46 units. 39 one-bedroom standard units with whirlpools. 6 one- and 1 two-bedroom suites with kitchens, some with whirlpools. 3 stories, interior corridors. *Bath:* combo or shower only. **Parking:** on-site. **Terms:** 14 day cancellation notice-fee imposed. **Amenities:** video library (fee), hair dryers. **Pool(s):** heated outdoor, heated indoor. **Leisure Activities:** sauna, whirlpool, tennis court, snowmobiling, exercise room. *Fee:* game room. **Guest Services:** coin laundry. **Business Services:** meeting rooms. **Cards:** AX, CB, DC, MC, VI. **Special Amenities:** early check-in/late check-out and preferred room (subject to availability with advanced reservations). *(See color ad below)*

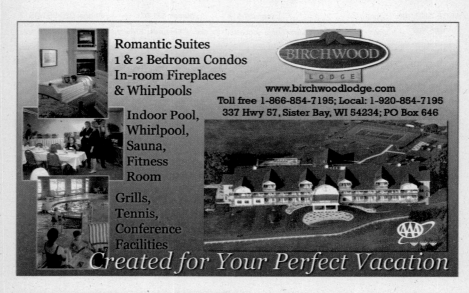

Romantic Suites
1 & 2 Bedroom Condos
In-room Fireplaces
& Whirlpools

BIRCHWOOD LODGE

www.birchwoodlodge.com
Toll free 1-866-854-7195; Local: 1-920-854-7195
337 Hwy 57, Sister Bay, WI 54234; PO Box 646

Indoor Pool,
Whirlpool,
Sauna,
Fitness
Room

Grills,
Tennis,
Conference
Facilities

Created for Your Perfect Vacation

Experience the
Country House Resort

Adult Atmosphere with the Romance & Charm of a Country Inn
and the Amenities of an Elegant Resort on the Shores of Sister Bay

IN the WOODS...ON the WATER...OFF the HIGHWAY

• Twenty-seven scenic wooded acres & 1,100' of shoreline
• 46 rooms & suites, some with whirlpool & fireplace
• All rooms have refrig, coffee, cable TV, VCP, hair dryer
• Private balconies overlooking bay, fountains & gardens
• Heated pool, 14' whirlpool, tennis, nature trails & dock
• Complimentary continental breakfast, bikes & boats
• Family owned/managed, catering to your special occasions
❤Romance Packages; Nov.-April, 2 nights, candlelight dinner
❅Open all year, limited office hours/amenities Nov.-April

715 N. Highland Road, Sister Bay, Door County, WI 54234
1-888-424-1318 • 920-854-4551 • Fax 920-854-9809
email: countryhouse@dcwis.com
Take a virtual tour at: www.country-house.com

THE COUNTRY HOUSE RESORT

Phone: 920/854-4551

6/18-10/17 [ECP]	1P: $113-$186	2P: $113-$186	XP: $22
10/18-3/31 [CP]	1P: $91-$155	2P: $91-$155	XP: $22
5/7-6/17 [ECP]	1P: $91-$155	2P: $91-$155	XP: $22
4/1-5/6 [CP]	1P: $70-$135	2P: $70-$135	XP: $22

Resort Motel   **Location:** 0.5 mi s on SR 42, just w. Located in a quiet, secluded area overlooking the water. 715 N Highland Rd 54234. Fax: 920/854-9809. **Facility:** The resort, on 16 wooded acres, offers a parklike setting, and many rooms feature balconies overlooking the water. 46 units. 37 one-bedroom standard units, some with whirlpools. 4 one- and 5 two-bedroom suites ($137-$325) with whirlpools, some with kitchens. 2 stories (no elevator), exterior corridors. **Parking:** on-site, winter plug-ins. **Terms:** 3 night minimum stay - weekends 6/1-10/31, age restrictions may apply, 14 day cancellation notice-fee imposed, [ECP] meal plan available, package plans - seasonal & midweek. **Amenities:** voice mail, irons, hair dryers. *Some:* DVD players. **Pool(s):** heated outdoor. **Leisure Activities:** whirlpool, boating, fishing, tennis court, bicycles, hiking trails, horseshoes, shuffleboard, volleyball. **Business Services:** meeting rooms. **Cards:** AX, CB, DC, DS, MC, VI. **Special Amenities:** free continental breakfast and free local telephone calls. *(See color ad p 506)*

SOME UNITS

PHEASANT PARK RESORT

Phone: (920)854-7287

6/18-8/21	1P: $175-$259	2P: $175-$259	XP: $12	F6
8/22-3/31	1P: $88-$259	2P: $88-$259	XP: $12	F6
5/14-6/17	1P: $105-$208	2P: $105-$208	XP: $12	F6
4/1-5/13	1P: $88-$162	2P: $88-$162	XP: $12	F6

Condominium   **Location:** Just e on Mill Rd, then just n. Located in a semi-rural area. 130 Park Ln 54234 (PO Box 230). Fax: 920/854-4195. **Facility:** All units have balconies and fireplaces. Smoke free premises. 58 units. 43 one- and 15 two-bedroom suites with kitchens and whirlpools. 3 stories, interior corridors. **Parking:** on-site, winter plug-ins. **Terms:** cancellation fee imposed. **Amenities:** video library (fee), irons, hair dryers. **Pool(s):** heated outdoor, heated indoor. **Leisure Activities:** sauna, whirlpool, 2 tennis courts, snowmobiling, ice skating, playground, exercise room, basketball. *Fee:* bicycles, game room. **Guest Services:** coin laundry. **Business Services:** meeting rooms. **Cards:** DS, MC, VI.

VOYAGER INN

Phone: 920/854-4242

5/27-10/18	1P: $66-$95	2P: $66-$95	XP: $7
5/7-5/26 & 10/19-11/1	1P: $60-$70	2P: $60-$70	XP: $7

Motel   **Location:** Jct SR 42, 0.5 mi se. Located in a quiet area. 232 SR 57 54234. Fax: 920/854-2670. **Facility:** 29 one-bedroom standard units. 2 stories (no elevator), interior/exterior corridors. **Parking:** on-site. **Terms:** open 5/7-11/1, 14 day cancellation notice-fee imposed, package plans - seasonal. **Pool(s):** heated outdoor. **Leisure Activities:** sauna, whirlpool, horseshoes. **Cards:** DC, MC, VI.

SOME UNITS

——— WHERE TO DINE ———

SISTER BAY CAFE

Lunch: $3-$13   **Dinner:** $9-$15   **Phone:** 920/854-2429

Location: On SR 42; downtown. 611 N Bayshore Dr 54234. **Hours:** Open 4/1-10/31; 8 am-3 & 5-8:30 pm; hours vary seasonally. **Features:** The restaurant delivers Norwegian specialties, such as lapskaus, meatballs and salmon. Entrees are attractively presented. The dining room is appointed with well-coordinated Scandinavian decor, including watercolors and flags. Casual dress; beer & wine only. **Parking:** on-site.

American

Cards: MC, VI.

STURGEON BAY pop. 9,437

——— WHERE TO STAY ———

AMERICINN OF STURGEON BAY

Book at aaa.com   **Phone:** 920/743-5898

7/1-10/31	1P: $99-$164	2P: $109-$174	XP: $10	F12
5/1-6/30	1P: $79-$129	2P: $89-$139	XP: $10	F12
4/1-4/30 & 11/1-3/31	1P: $69-$129	2P: $69-$129	XP: $10	F12

Small-scale Hotel   **Location:** On SR 42/57, 0.5 mi s of jct CR C/S. Located in a commercial area. 622 S Ashland Ave 54235. Fax: 920/743-6899. **Facility:** 46 units. 43 one-bedroom standard units, some with whirlpools. 3 one-bedroom suites, some with whirlpools. 2 stories, interior corridors. *Bath:* combo or shower only. **Parking:** on-site, winter plug-ins. **Terms:** 2 night minimum stay - weekends 7/1-10/31, [ECP] meal plan available. **Amenities:** irons, hair dryers. **Pool(s):** heated indoor. **Leisure Activities:** sauna, whirlpool. **Guest Services:** coin laundry. **Business Services:** meeting rooms. **Cards:** AX, DC, DS, MC, VI. *(See color ad p 576)*

SOME UNITS

BEST WESTERN MARITIME INN

Book at aaa.com   **Phone:** (920)743-7231

7/1-10/31 [CP]	1P: $89-$95	2P: $96-$102	XP: $7	F12
5/10-6/30 [CP]	1P: $68-$83	2P: $75-$90	XP: $7	F12
4/1-5/9 & 11/1-3/31 [CP]	1P: $49-$65	2P: $56-$72	XP: $7	F12

Small-scale Hotel   **Location:** 1 mi n on Business Rt SR 42/57. Located in a commercial area. 1001 N 14th Ave 54235. Fax: 920/743-9341. **Facility:** 90 one-bedroom standard units, some with whirlpools. 2 stories (no elevator), interior corridors. **Parking:** on-site, winter plug-ins. **Terms:** 7 day cancellation notice. **Amenities:** irons, hair dryers. **Pool(s):** heated indoor. **Leisure Activities:** whirlpool. *Fee:* game room. **Cards:** AX, CB, DC, DS, JC, MC, VI. **Special Amenities:** free continental breakfast and early check-in/late check-out.

SOME UNITS

CHERRY HILLS LODGE & GOLF RESORT

Phone: 920/743-4222

9/7-11/1	1P: $89-$115	2P: $89-$115	XP: $15
7/1-9/6	1P: $115	2P: $115	XP: $15
4/1-6/30	1P: $89-$97	2P: $89-$97	XP: $15
1/31-3/14	1P: $59	2P: $59	XP: $15

Small-scale Hotel **Location:** 5 mi n on SR 42, 1.5 mi w on CR P. Located in a rural area. 5905 Dunn Rd 54235. Fax: 920/743-4222. **Facility:** Smoke free premises. 31 one-bedroom standard units, some with whirlpools. 2 stories, interior corridors. **Parking:** on-site. **Terms:** open 4/1-11/1 & 1/31-3/14, 14 day cancellation notice-fee imposed, package plans. **Amenities:** hair dryers. **Dining:** The Restaurant at Cherry Hills, see separate listing. **Pool(s):** heated outdoor. **Leisure Activities:** whirlpool, hiking trails. **Fee:** golf-18 holes, driving range. **Business Services:** meeting rooms. **Cards:** AX, DS, MC, VI. **Special Amenities:** early check-in/late check-out.

LEATHEM SMITH LODGE & MARINA

Book at aaa.com　　　　　　Phone: 920/743-5555

7/1-9/6 [ECP]	1P: $105-$210	2P: $105-$210	XP: $15	F9
9/7-10/23 [ECP]	1P: $99-$210	2P: $99-$210	XP: $15	F9
4/1-6/30 [ECP]	1P: $77-$175	2P: $77-$175	XP: $15	F9
10/24-3/31 [ECP]	1P: $72-$149	2P: $72-$149	XP: $15	F9

Resort
Small-scale Hotel **Location:** SR 42/57, exit Utah St, 0.5 mi n of Bay View Bridge, then just w. Located opposite the bay. 1640 Memorial Dr 54235. Fax: 920/743-5355. **Facility:** Across from the marina, the lodge features a variety of room types, and its suites have gas fireplaces. 63 units. 51 one-bedroom standard units, some with whirlpools. 12 one-bedroom suites ($103-$210) with whirlpools. 2 stories (no elevator), interior corridors. **Parking:** on-site, winter plug-ins. **Terms:** 3 day cancellation notice-fee imposed, package plans - 11/1-4/30. **Amenities:** video library (fee). *Some:* irons. **Dining:** 11:30 am-1:30 & 5:30-9 pm; hours may vary seasonally, cocktails. **Pool(s):** heated outdoor. **Leisure Activities:** excursion boat, 2 tennis courts. **Fee:** marina, golf-9 holes. **Guest Services:** gift shop. **Business Services:** meeting rooms. **Cards:** AX, DS, MC, VI. **Special Amenities:** free expanded continental breakfast. *(See color ad below)*

SOME UNITS

SCOFIELD HOUSE BED & BREAKFAST

Phone: 920/743-7727

5/1-11/15	1P: $112-$220	2P: $112-$220	XP: $20
4/1-4/30 & 11/16-3/31	1P: $84-$210	2P: $84-$210	XP: $20

Location: Center. Located in a residential area. 908 Michigan St 54235-0761. Fax: 920/743-7727. **Facility:** This elegantly restored 1902 Victorian home has stained-glass windows and many original furnishings; some rooms feature gas fireplaces and whirlpools. Smoke free premises. 6 one-bedroom standard units, some with whirlpools. 3 stories (no elevator), interior corridors. *Bath:* combo or shower only. **Parking:** on-site. **Terms:** 2 night minimum stay - weekends 5/1-11/15, age restrictions may apply, 14 day cancellation notice-fee imposed, [BP] meal plan available. **Amenities:** video library. *Some:* CD players. **Cards:** MC, VI. **Special Amenities:** free full breakfast and free local telephone calls.

Bed & Breakfast

SOME UNITS

STONE HARBOR RESORT & CONFERENCE CENTER

Property failed to provide current rates　　　Phone: 920/746-0700

Location: Center. 107 N 1st Ave 54235 (PO Box 630). **Facility:** Designated smoking area. 161 units. 117 one-bedroom standard units, some with kitchens and/or whirlpools. 40 one- and 4 two-bedroom suites with kitchens and whirlpools. 2 stories, interior corridors. *Bath:* combo or shower only. **Parking:** on-site, winter plug-ins. **Amenities:** voice mail, irons, hair dryers. **Pool(s):** heated outdoor, heated indoor. **Leisure Activities:** sauna, whirlpool, exercise room. **Guest Services:** gift shop, valet and coin laundry.

Small-scale Hotel

SOME UNITS

SUPER 8 MOTEL

Phone: 920/743-9211

Small-scale Hotel

7/3-11/4	1P: $84-$94	2P: $91-$101	XP: $7	F12
5/6-7/2	1P: $63-$73	2P: $70-$80	XP: $7	F12
4/1-5/5 & 11/5-3/31	1P: $44-$54	2P: $51-$61	XP: $7	F12

Location: 1 mi s on Business Rt SR 42/57. Located in a commercial area. 409 Green Bay Rd 54235. Fax: 920/743-4143. **Facility:** 63 one-bedroom standard units, some with whirlpools. 2 stories (no elevator), interior corridors. **Parking:** on-site, winter plug-ins. **Terms:** 30 day cancellation notice, [CP] meal plan available, pets ($20 deposit). **Pool(s):** heated indoor. **Leisure Activities:** whirlpool. **Cards:** AX, DC, MC, VI.

SOME UNITS

(ASK) SD 🛏 🍴 📶 🏊 DATA PORT / ✕ 🛋 📺 /
FEE

WHITE LACE INN

Phone: 920/743-1105

Bed & Breakfast

5/28-10/23 [BP]	1P: $120-$235	2P: $120-$235	XP: $15
4/1-5/27 & 10/24-3/31 [BP]	1P: $70-$220	2P: $70-$220	XP: $15

Location: Center. Located in a residential area. 16 N 5th Ave 54235. Fax: 920/743-8180. **Facility:** Close to downtown, this B&B has tastefully decorated rooms in four historic homes; breakfast is served in the main house. Smoke free premises. 18 one-bedroom standard units, some with whirlpools. 2 stories (no elevator), interior corridors. *Bath:* combo or shower only. **Parking:** on-site. **Terms:** 2-3 night minimum stay - weekends, age restrictions may apply, 14 day cancellation notice-fee imposed. **Amenities:** video library, irons. *Some:* CD players. **Guest Services:** gift shop. **Cards:** AX, CB, DC, DS, MC, VI. **Special Amenities:** free full breakfast and free local telephone calls.

SOME UNITS

✕ ☎ / 📶 VCR 🛋 /

────── WHERE TO DINE ──────

THE RESTAURANT AT CHERRY HILLS   Lunch: $4-$6   Dinner: $9-$18   Phone: 920/743-4222

American

Location: 5 mi n on SR 42, 1.5 mi w on CR P; in Cherry Hills Lodge & Golf Resort. 5905 Dunn Rd 54235. **Hours:** Open 5/25-10/15; 8 am-1:30 & 5:30-8 pm; hours may vary. Closed: 12/25; also for dinner Mon. **Reservations:** accepted. **Features:** The restaurant specializes in made-to-order continental cuisine, fresh seafood and beef, including delicious whitefish and prime rib. The dining room and breezy outdoor deck look out over the golf course and countryside. Stop by for the great Sunday breakfast buffet and brunch. Casual dress; cocktails. **Parking:** on-site. **Cards:** AX, DC, DS, MC, VI.

✕

**The previous listings were for Door County.
This page resumes the alphabetical listings of cities in Wisconsin.**

EAGLE RIVER pop. 1,443

——— **WHERE TO STAY** ———

CHANTICLEER INN   Phone: 715/479-4486

(AAA) (SAVE)   6/15-9/6   1P: $125-$175   2P: $125-$175   XP: $12   F16
                 4/1-6/14 & 9/7-3/31   1P: $62-$160   2P: $62-$160   XP: $12   F16
▼▼▼▼   **Location:** 2 mi e on SR 70, 0.5 mi n. Located on a chain of lakes. 1458 E Dollar Lake Rd 54521. Fax: 715/479-0004.
Resort   **Facility:** Condos, motel units and one- to three-bedroom villas are offered at this resort on a chain of lakes.
Large-scale Hotel 55 units. 29 one-bedroom standard units, some with efficiencies and/or whirlpools. 10 two- and 8 three-
bedroom suites ($115-$175) with kitchens. 8 cottages ($775-$2200), some with whirlpools. 1-3 stories (no elevator), exterior corridors. **Parking:** on-site, winter plug-ins. **Terms:** 2-3 night minimum stay - weekends, 30
day cancellation notice-fee imposed. **Amenities:** *Some:* hair dryers. **Dining:** 5:30 pm-8:30 pm, Sat & Sun 8 am-10 & 5:30-8:30
pm; to 9:30 pm 6/16-9/14; closed Tues 9/5-6/17, cocktails. **Leisure Activities:** rental boats, rental canoes, boat dock, fishing,
cross country skiing, snowmobiling, hiking trails, jogging, playground, basketball, volleyball. *Fee:* pontoon boat, 2 tennis courts
(1 lighted), game room. **Guest Services:** gift shop, coin laundry. **Business Services:** meeting rooms. **Cards:** DS, MC, VI.

SOME UNITS
[⊓] [Y] [♿] [✕] [▣] / [✕] [VCR] [DATA PORT] [🔌] [🖼] /

DAYS INN   *Book at aaa.com*   Phone: (715)479-5151

(AAA) (SAVE)   7/1-9/15   1P: $75-$92   2P: $80-$97   XP: $6   F18
                 9/16-3/31   1P: $71-$92   2P: $76-$97   XP: $6   F18
▼▼▼▼   4/1-6/30   1P: $71-$81   2P: $76-$86   XP: $6   F18
Small-scale Hotel **Location:** 0.5 mi n on US 45. Located in a commercial area. 844 Railroad St N 54521. Fax: 715/479-8259.
                 Facility: 93 one-bedroom standard units, some with whirlpools. 2 stories (no elevator), interior corridors.
Bath: combo or shower only. **Parking:** on-site, winter plug-ins. **Terms:** pets ($10 fee). **Amenities:** irons, hair
dryers. **Pool(s):** heated indoor. **Leisure Activities:** sauna, whirlpool, snowmobiling. *Fee:* game room. **Guest Services:** coin
laundry. **Business Services:** meeting rooms. **Cards:** AX, CB, DC, DS, MC, VI. **Special Amenities:** free expanded continental
breakfast and free local telephone calls. *(See color ad card insert)*

SOME UNITS
[S/D] [⊓] [ℍ] [⟨⟩] [⟲] [✕] [🐾] [DATA PORT] [▣] / [✕] [🔌] [🖼] /
FEE

TRAVELER'S INN MOTEL   Phone: (715)479-4403

(AAA) (SAVE)   All Year   1P: $40-$80   2P: $45-$80   XP: $5   F19
▼   **Location:** Center of downtown. 309 Wall St 54521 (PO Box 1175). Fax: 715/479-4404. **Facility:** 27 one-bedroom
Motel   standard units, some with efficiencies (utensils extra charge) and/or whirlpools. 2 stories (no elevator),
                 interior/exterior corridors. *Bath:* combo or shower only. **Parking:** on-site, winter plug-ins. **Terms:** [CP] meal
plan available, pets (with prior approval, in smoking units). **Leisure Activities:** snowmobiling. **Cards:** AX, DS,
MC, VI. **Special Amenities:** free continental breakfast and early check-in/late check-out.

SOME UNITS
[S/D] [⊓] [ℍ] / [✕] [🔌] [🖼] [▣] /

——— **WHERE TO DINE** ———

*The following restaurant has not been evaluated by AAA
but is listed for your information only.*

RIVERSTONE   Dinner: $10-$21   Phone: 715/479-8467

(AAA)   Under major renovation. **Location:** 3 mi n on US 45, 0.3 mi e; on the grounds of Pine-Aire Resort Campground.
[fyi]   219 N Railroad St 54521. **Hours:** Open 5/1-10/20; 5 pm-9 pm; to 10 pm 6/1-8/25; also Fri-Sun 8-11 am
American   6/1-8/25; hours vary off season. Closed: Wed. **Features:** Delightful entrees, many local ingredients,
                 delicious hearth breads and homemade dessert. Known for pan fried Blue Gill, Veal Chardonnay and Pork
Filet Normandy. Salad prepared tableside. Mexican dishes Sunday-Tuesday. Glassed, climate-controlled
wine room. Casual dress; cocktails. **Parking:** on-site. **Cards:** AX, DC, MC, VI.

[♿M] [✕]

EAST TROY pop. 3,564

——— **WHERE TO STAY** ———

COUNTRY INN & SUITES   *Book at aaa.com*   Phone: (262)642-2100

(AAA) (SAVE)   All Year [ECP]   1P: $74-$134   2P: $80-$139   XP: $6   F17
▼▼▼   **Location:** I-43, exit 36, at jct SR 120. Located in a commercial, residential area. 2921 O'Leary Ln 53120.
                 Fax: 262/642-9811. **Facility:** 51 units. 36 one-bedroom standard units, some with whirlpools. 15 one-
Small-scale Hotel bedroom suites. 2 stories (no elevator), interior corridors. *Bath:* combo or shower only. **Parking:** on-site,
                 winter plug-ins. **Terms:** 2 night minimum stay - seasonal & weekends, package plans, pets (with prior ap-
proval). **Amenities:** dual phone lines, voice mail, irons, hair dryers. **Pool(s):** small heated indoor. **Leisure
Activities:** whirlpool. **Guest Services:** valet and coin laundry. **Business Services:** meeting rooms. **Cards:** AX, CB, DC, DS,
MC, VI. **Special Amenities:** free expanded continental breakfast and preferred room (subject to availability with advanced reservations). *(See color ad starting on p 580)*

SOME UNITS
[S/D] [⊓] [♿M] [⟨⟩] [⟲] [ℍ] [🐾] [DATA PORT] [▣] / [✕] [🔌] [🖼] /
FEE

——— **WHERE TO DINE** ———

ROMA'S RISTORANTE   Dinner: $6-$20   Phone: 262/642-5353

▼▼ ▼▼   **Location:** I-43, exit 38, just w on CR 20, then just n. N8416 CR ES 53120. **Hours:** 4 pm-9 pm, Fri & Sat-10 pm.
Italian   Closed: 7/4. **Features:** Folks in the mood for a taste of Italian food can try fettuccine, manicotti, cannelloni,
                 lasagna or pizza. Among other choices are veal, ribs, chicken and steak. Casual dress; cocktails. **Parking:**
on-site. **Cards:** AX, DS, MC, VI.

[Y] [✕]

EAU CLAIRE pop. 61,704

------ **WHERE TO STAY** ------

AMERICINN MOTEL & SUITES
Book at aaa.com
Phone: (715)874-4900

All Year   1P: $59-$135   2P: $59-$135   XP: $6   F17

Location: I-94, exit 59, jct US 12. 6200 Texaco Dr 54703. Fax: 715/874-4901. **Facility:** 50 units. 45 one-bedroom standard units, some with whirlpools. 5 one-bedroom suites, some with whirlpools. 2 stories, interior corridors. **Bath:** combo or shower only. **Parking:** on-site, winter plug-ins. **Terms:** 7 day cancellation notice, [ECP] meal plan available, pets ($25 deposit). **Amenities:** hair dryers. **Pool(s):** heated indoor. **Leisure Activities:** sauna, whirlpool. **Guest Services:** coin laundry. **Business Services:** meeting rooms, fax (fee). **Cards:** AX, DC, DS, MC, VI.
Small-scale Hotel
(See color ad p 576)

SOME UNITS
[icons]

ANTLERS MOTEL
Phone: (715)834-5313

All Year [CP]   1P: $42-$50   2P: $52-$62   XP: $5   F12

Location: Jct US 12 and 53. 2245 S Hastings Way 54701. Fax: 715/839-7582. **Facility:** 33 one-bedroom standard units. 1-2 stories, exterior corridors. **Parking:** on-site, winter plug-ins. **Leisure Activities:** playground. **Business Services:** fax (fee). **Cards:** AX, DS, MC, VI. **Special Amenities:** free continental breakfast and free local telephone calls.
Motel

SOME UNITS
[icons]

BEST WESTERN WHITE HOUSE INN
Book at aaa.com
Phone: (715)832-8356

All Year   1P: $59-$125   2P: $65-$135   XP: $10   F16

Location: On US 53, 1.3 mi n of jct US 12. 1828 S Hastings Way 54701. Fax: 715/836-9686. **Facility:** 66 one-bedroom standard units, some with whirlpools. 2 stories (no elevator), interior corridors. **Parking:** on-site, winter plug-ins. **Terms:** weekly rates available, [ECP] meal plan available. **Amenities:** voice mail, irons, hair dryers. **Pool(s):** heated indoor. **Leisure Activities:** sauna, whirlpool. *Fee:* game room. **Guest Services:** valet laundry. **Business Services:** meeting rooms. **Cards:** AX, CB, DC, DS, JC, MC, VI.
Small-scale Hotel

SOME UNITS
[icons]

COMFORT INN
Book at aaa.com
Phone: (715)833-9798

All Year [ECP]   1P: $59-$109   2P: $69-$119   XP: $5   F18

Location: I-94, exit 65, 1.3 mi n on SR 37, just s of jct US 12. 3117 Craig Rd 54701. Fax: 715/833-9798. **Facility:** 56 one-bedroom standard units. 2 stories (no elevator), interior corridors. **Parking:** on-site, winter plug-ins. **Terms:** package plans, pets ($10 extra charge). **Amenities:** *Some:* irons, hair dryers. **Pool(s):** small heated indoor. **Leisure Activities:** whirlpool. **Business Services:** fax (fee). **Cards:** AX, CB, DC, DS, MC, VI.
Small-scale Hotel

SOME UNITS
[icons]

COUNTRY INN & SUITES BY CARLSON
Book at aaa.com
Phone: (715)832-7289

All Year   1P: $77-$102   2P: $85-$102   XP: $8   F

Location: I-94, exit 70, 0.8 mi n on US 53, then just ne on CR AA (Golf Rd). 3614 Gateway Dr 54701. Fax: 715/832-7289. **Facility:** 58 one-bedroom standard units. 3 stories, interior corridors. **Bath:** combo or shower only. **Parking:** on-site, winter plug-ins. **Terms:** [CP] meal plan available, pets ($20 deposit, in smoking units). **Amenities:** irons, hair dryers. **Pool(s):** small heated indoor. **Leisure Activities:** whirlpool. **Guest Services:** valet laundry. **Business Services:** fax (fee). **Cards:** AX, CB, DC, DS, JC, MC, VI. **Special Amenities:** free expanded continental breakfast and free newspaper. *(See color ad starting on p 580)*
Small-scale Hotel

SOME UNITS
[icons]

DAYS INN-WEST
Book at aaa.com
Phone: (715)874-5550

All Year [CP]   1P: $50-$100   2P: $50-$100   XP: $8   F17

Location: I-94, exit 59, jct US 12. 6319 Truax Ln 54703. Fax: 715/874-6101. **Facility:** 71 one-bedroom standard units, some with whirlpools. 2 stories (no elevator), interior corridors. **Bath:** combo or shower only. **Parking:** on-site, winter plug-ins. **Terms:** pets ($25 deposit, in smoking units). **Amenities:** hair dryers. *Some:* irons. **Pool(s):** small heated indoor. **Leisure Activities:** whirlpool, exercise room. **Guest Services:** coin laundry. **Business Services:** fax (fee). **Cards:** AX, CB, DC, DS, JC, MC, VI. *(See color ad card insert)*
Small-scale Hotel

SOME UNITS
[icons]

ECONO LODGE
Book at aaa.com
Phone: 715/833-8818

6/1-9/30 [CP]	1P: $55-$90	2P: $65-$125	XP: $6 F17
4/1-5/31 [CP]	1P: $45-$60	2P: $55-$65	XP: $6 F17
10/1-3/31 [CP]	1P: $40-$60	2P: $45-$65	XP: $6 F17

Location: I-94, exit 68, just n on SR 93, just w on Golf Rd, then just s. 4608 Royal Dr 54701. Fax: 715/833-8970. **Facility:** 36 one-bedroom standard units, some with whirlpools. 1 story, interior corridors. **Parking:** on-site, winter plug-ins. **Terms:** pets (dogs only, with prior approval). **Business Services:** fax (fee). **Cards:** AX, CB, DC, DS, JC, MC, VI.
Small-scale Hotel

SOME UNITS
[icons]

EXEL INN OF EAU CLAIRE
Book at aaa.com
Phone: (715)834-3193

All Year [CP]   1P: $38-$58   2P: $45-$65   XP: $6   F18

Location: I-94, exit 65, 1.3 mi n on SR 37, just w of jct US 12. 2305 Craig Rd 54701. Fax: 715/839-9905. **Facility:** 100 units. 99 one-bedroom standard units, some with whirlpools. 1 one-bedroom suite ($95-$105) with kitchen (no utensils). 2 stories (no elevator), interior corridors. **Parking:** on-site, winter plug-ins. **Terms:** weekly rates available, small pets only. **Amenities:** irons, hair dryers. **Leisure Activities:** limited exercise equipment, game room. **Guest Services:** coin laundry. **Business Services:** fax (fee). **Cards:** AX, CB, DC, DS, MC, VI. **Special Amenities:** free continental breakfast and early check-in/late check-out.
Small-scale Hotel

SOME UNITS
[icons]

HAMPTON INN — *Book at aaa.com*

▼▼▼▼ All Year   1P: $79-$129   2P: $89-$139   **Phone:** (715)833-0003
                                                                                                      XP: $10   F18
Small-scale Hotel   **Location:** I-94, exit 65, 1.3 mi n on SR 37, just s of jct US 12. 2622 Craig Rd 54701. **Fax:** 715/833-0915. **Facility:** 106 one-bedroom standard units. 3 stories, interior corridors. **Parking:** on-site. **Terms:** [CP] meal plan available. **Amenities:** voice mail, irons, hair dryers. *Fee:* video games, high-speed Internet. **Pool(s):** small heated indoor. **Leisure Activities:** whirlpool, limited exercise equipment. **Guest Services:** valet laundry. **Business Services:** meeting rooms, fax (fee). **Cards:** AX, CB, DC, DS, MC, VI.

SOME UNITS
(ASK) (S☒) (┆┆+) (⊘) (🏊) (🐾) (DATA PORT) (▣) / (✕) (📶) (📠)   FEE

HEARTLAND INN — *Book at aaa.com*

▼▼ All Year [ECP]   1P: $75-$85   2P: $75-$85   **Phone:** (715)839-7100
                                                                                                      XP: $5   F18
Small-scale Hotel   **Location:** I-94, exit 70, 0.8 mi n on US 53, just w on CR AA (Golf Rd), then just s. 4075 Commonwealth Ave 54701. **Fax:** 715/839-7050. **Facility:** 86 one-bedroom standard units. 2 stories, interior corridors. **Parking:** on-site, winter plug-ins. **Terms:** pets (in designated units). **Amenities:** hair dryers. *Some:* irons. **Pool(s):** small heated indoor. **Leisure Activities:** sauna. **Guest Services:** valet and coin laundry. **Business Services:** meeting rooms, PC. **Cards:** AX, DC, DS, MC, VI. *(See color ad below)*

SOME UNITS
(ASK) (S☒) (🐾) (┆┆+) (🐾) (🛗) (🐾) (▣) / (✕) (📶) (📠)   FEE

HOLIDAY INN CAMPUS AREA — *Book at aaa.com*

▼▼▼▼ All Year   1P: $75-$125   **Phone:** (715)835-2211
Small-scale Hotel   **Location:** I-94, exit 65, 1.3 mi n on SR 37, just w of jct US 12. 2703 Craig Rd 54701. **Fax:** 715/835-1249. **Facility:** 137 one-bedroom standard units, some with whirlpools. 2 stories (no elevator), interior corridors. *Bath:* combo or shower only. **Parking:** on-site. **Terms:** [AP] meal plan available, pets ($15 extra charge, in smoking units). **Amenities:** irons, hair dryers. **Pool(s):** heated indoor. **Leisure Activities:** whirlpool, limited exercise equipment. *Fee:* game room. **Guest Services:** valet and coin laundry. **Business Services:** meeting rooms. **Cards:** AX, DC, DS, MC, VI.

SOME UNITS
(ASK) (S☒) (🐾) (┆┆) (🍴) (Y) (&M) (🐾) (🏊) (✕) (🐾) (DATA PORT) (▣) / (✕) (📶) (📠) /   FEE

MAPLE MANOR MOTEL

(AAA) (SAVE)   All Year   1P: $30-$47   2P: $37-$49   **Phone:** (715)834-2618
▼   **Location:** I-94, exit 70, 3 mi n on US 53, exit US 12 (Clairemont Ave), just se, follow signs for Storrs Ave. 2507 S Hastings Way 54701. **Fax:** 715/834-1148. **Facility:** 34 one-bedroom standard units. 1 story, exterior corridors.
Motel   **Parking:** on-site, winter plug-ins. **Terms:** weekly rates available, [BP] meal plan available, small pets only. **Dining:** 6:30 am-1:30 & 5-9 pm, Sun-11:30 am, cocktails. **Guest Services:** valet laundry. **Business Services:** fax (fee). **Cards:** AX, DC, DS, MC, VI. **Special Amenities:** free expanded continental breakfast and free local telephone calls.

SOME UNITS
(S☒) (🐾) (🍴) (Y) (🐾) / (✕) (📶) (📠) /

OTTER CREEK INN

▼▼▼▼ All Year [BP]   1P: $70-$150   2P: $100-$190   **Phone:** 715/832-2945
Bed & Breakfast   **Location:** 0.5 mi e of jct US 53, on north side of US 12. 2536 Hillcrest Pkwy 54720. **Fax:** 715/832-4607. **Facility:** On a hillside along Otter Creek, this English Tudor is decorated in a country-Victorian theme and features some rooms with gas fireplaces. Smoke free premises. 6 one-bedroom standard units with whirlpools. 3 stories (no elevator), interior corridors. **Parking:** on-site. **Terms:** check-in 4 pm, age restrictions may apply, 8 day cancellation notice. **Amenities:** video library. **Pool(s):** heated outdoor. **Business Services:** fax (fee). **Cards:** AX, CB, DC, DS, MC, VI.

SOME UNITS
(🐾) (✕) (VCR) / (📶) /

PARK INN & SUITES INTERNATIONAL — *Book at aaa.com*

(AAA) (SAVE)   All Year   1P: $99-$109   2P: $109-$119   **Phone:** (715)838-9989
▼▼▼▼   XP: $10   F18
Small-scale Hotel   **Location:** I-94, exit 65, just n. 3340 Mondovi Rd 54701. **Fax:** 715/832-2542. **Facility:** 85 units. 45 one-bedroom standard units, some with whirlpools. 40 one-bedroom suites, some with whirlpools. 3 stories, interior corridors. *Bath:* combo or shower only. **Parking:** on-site. **Terms:** [ECP] meal plan available, small pets only ($10 extra charge). **Amenities:** voice mail, irons, hair dryers. **Pool(s):** small heated indoor. **Leisure Activities:** whirlpool, limited exercise equipment. *Fee:* game room. **Guest Services:** valet and coin laundry. **Business Services:** meeting rooms, fax. **Cards:** AX, CB, DC, DS, MC, VI. **Special Amenities:** free expanded continental breakfast and free local telephone calls.

SOME UNITS
(S☒) (🐾) (&M) (🐾) (🏊) (✕) (🐾) (DATA PORT) (▣) / (✕) (📶) (📠) /   FEE

THE PLAZA HOTEL & SUITES
Phone: (715)834-3181

All Year   1P: $69-$99   2P: $69-$179

Location: I-94, exit 65, 1.3 mi n on SR 37, just w of jct US 12. 1202 W Clairemont Ave 54701. Fax: 715/834-1630.

Small-scale Hotel **Facility:** 233 units. 228 one-bedroom standard units, some with whirlpools. 5 one-bedroom suites with whirlpools. 2-5 stories, interior corridors. *Bath:* combo or shower only. **Parking:** on-site, winter plug-ins.
Terms: [AP] meal plan available, package plans, small pets only ($15 fee). **Amenities:** voice mail, irons, hair dryers. *Fee:* video games, high-speed Internet. *Some:* dual phone lines. **Pool(s):** heated indoor, wading. **Leisure Activities:** whirlpool, exercise room. *Fee:* game room. **Guest Services:** gift shop, valet and coin laundry. **Business Services:** conference facilities, business center. **Cards:** AX, CB, DC, DS, MC, VI.

SOME UNITS

RAMADA INN CONVENTION CENTER
Book at aaa.com   **Phone:** (715)835-6121

All Year [BP]   1P: $70-$110   2P: $70-$110

Location: S Barstow at Gibson sts; downtown. 205 S Barstow St 54701. Fax: 715/835-3592. **Facility:** 122 one-bedroom standard units, some with whirlpools. 8 stories, interior corridors. **Parking:** on-site. **Terms:** cancellation fee imposed, [AP] meal plan available, pets ($10 fee, in smoking units). **Amenities:** voice mail, irons,
Large-scale Hotel hair dryers. **Dining:** 6:30 am-2 & 5:30-9 pm, cocktails. **Pool(s):** small heated indoor. **Leisure Activities:** limited exercise equipment. **Guest Services:** valet and coin laundry, area transportation. **Business Services:** conference facilities. **Cards:** AX, CB, DC, DS, JC, MC, VI. **Special Amenities:** free newspaper and early check-in/late check-out.

SOME UNITS

——— WHERE TO DINE ———

FANNY HILL DINNER THEATRE AND DINING ROOM
Dinner: $12-$30   **Phone:** 715/836-8184

Location: Jct US 12 and SR 37, 1 mi nw on US 12, 0.3 mi w on Menomonie St, 0.5 mi s on Ferry St, then 1.5 mi w; in Fanny Hill Victorian Inn. 3919 Crescent Ave 54703. **Hours:** 5 pm-9 pm, Fri & Sat-10 pm, Sun 10 am-2 & 5-9 pm. Closed major holidays; also Mon & Tues. **Reservations:** suggested. **Features:** A quaint Victorian
American charm infuses the dining room, which is decorated with enchanting seasonal accents. Many windows afford panoramic river valley views. Grilled pork tenderloin stands out on a menu of creative entrees. Servers exude charm and hospitality. Dressy casual; cocktails. **Parking:** on-site. **Cards:** AX, CB, DC, DS, MC, VI.

MONA LISA'S RESTAURANT
Dinner: $7-$24   **Phone:** 715/839-8969

Location: At 5th Ave; downtown. 428 Water St 54703. **Hours:** 4 pm-11 pm, Fri & Sat-midnight. Closed major holidays; also Sun & Mon. **Features:** In historic downtown, the trendy restaurant prepares creative and contemporary Italian cuisine, which contrasts with the decor: wood floors and lofty high ceilings from a
Italian century ago. Local markets and friends' gardens provide inspiration for the weekly menu. Fish, pasta and meat dishes are interpreted with gaiety and flair. Guests can order from an extensive list of martinis or choose from among a good variety of wines by the glass. Casual dress; cocktails. **Parking:** street. **Cards:** AX, MC, VI.

NORTHWOODS PUB & GRILL
Lunch: $6-$18   Dinner: $6-$18   **Phone:** 715/552-0510

Location: I-94, exit 70 (US 53), just nw; at end of Oakwood Mall. 3560 Oakwood Mall Dr 54701. **Hours:** 11 am-10 pm, Fri & Sat-11 pm, Sun 11 am-8 pm. Closed major holidays. **Features:** Bustling with activity and the happy laughter of friends out for a good time, the local pub proudly features homemade beers and sodas.
American The thematic decor incorporates canoes, wood beams and artifacts reminiscent of Alaska. The menu suggests culinary explorations of elk, deer and buffalo steaks, while trout, walleye and salmon complete the Nordic feast. Well-known American fare is also featured. Casual dress; cocktails. **Parking:** on-site. **Cards:** AX, DS, MC, VI.

PEKING GARDEN
Lunch: $4-$6   Dinner: $6-$10   **Phone:** 715/835-3229

Location: I-94, exit 68, 1.2 mi n on SR 93, just w on Mall Dr; in Hamilton Square Shopping Center. 2823 E Hamilton Sq 54701. **Hours:** 11 am-9:30 pm, Fri & Sat-10:30 pm. Closed major holidays; also Sun. **Reservations:** accepted. **Features:** Smaller restaurant with simple decor and good food. Traditional
Chinese selection of egg foo young, chow mein, beef, pork, chicken dishes and chef's suggestions. Daily buffet from 11 am-2 pm. Good value for the dollar. Casual dress; beer only. **Parking:** on-site.

RANDY'S FAMILY RESTAURANT
Lunch: $5-$10   Dinner: $5-$10   **Phone:** 715/839-8449

Location: I-94, exit 65, 1.3 mi n on SR 37, just s of jct US 12. 1132 W MacArthur 54701. **Hours:** 6 am-10 pm, Fri & Sat-10:30 pm. Closed: 11/25, 12/25 & Easter; also Sun. **Reservations:** accepted. **Features:** Family-operated for more than 40 years, the nice, casual restaurant serves generous portions of
American tasty comfort foods, including an extensive selection of tempting fresh pies. Each meal, including the tasty daily specials, is accompanied by a complimentary cup of warm, homemade vanilla pudding. Breakfast is served all day. Casual dress. **Parking:** on-site. **Cards:** MC, VI.

SWEETWATERS RESTAURANT & BAR
Lunch: $6-$8   Dinner: $8-$22   **Phone:** 715/834-5777

Location: Just w of jct US 12 and SR 37. 1104 W Clairemont Ave 54701. **Hours:** 11 am-9 pm, Fri-10 pm, Sat 4 pm-10 pm. Closed: 12/25. **Reservations:** suggested. **Features:** Nice variety of seafood, steak and pasta is attractively presented. Outdoor seasonal dining. Casual environment, seating conducive to small groups,
American families and couples. Casual dress; cocktails. **Parking:** on-site. **Cards:** AX, DC, DS, MC, VI.

EDGERTON pop. 4,933

——— WHERE TO STAY ———

COMFORT INN
▼▼▼▼
Small-scale Hotel

Book at aaa.com
All Year [ECP] 1P: $49-$175 2P: $49-$175 XP: $8 F18
Location: I-90, exit 163, just e. 11102 Goede Rd 53534. Fax: 608/884-4490. **Facility:** 50 one-bedroom standard units, some with whirlpools. 2 stories (no elevator), interior corridors. *Bath:* combo or shower only. **Parking:** on-site. **Terms:** pets ($10 deposit). **Amenities:** irons, hair dryers. **Pool(s):** small heated indoor. **Leisure Activities:** whirlpool. **Guest Services:** valet and coin laundry. **Business Services:** meeting rooms. **Cards:** AX, CB, DC, DS, JC, MC, VI.

Phone: (608)884-2118

SOME UNITS
(ASK) (S₂) (🛏) (🔌) (♿) (♨) (📷) (DATA PORT) (💻) / (✕) (🔌) (📷) /
FEE

EGG HARBOR —See Door County p. 500.

ELKHART LAKE pop. 1,021

——— WHERE TO STAY ———

THE OSTHOFF RESORT
(AAA) (SAVE)
▼▼▼ ▼▼▼
Resort
Condominium

Book at aaa.com
5/27-9/30 1P: $200-$500 2P: $200-$500
10/1-3/31 1P: $170-$355 2P: $170-$355
4/1-5/26 1P: $160-$335 2P: $160-$335
Location: 0.5 mi w of SR 67 via CR A/J, then 0.4 mi nw. Located in a rural area. 101 Osthoff Ave 53020. Fax: 920/876-3228. **Facility:** All accommodations at this rural, family-oriented resort are contemporary in style and offer balconies and gas fireplaces; some have lake views. Designated smoking area. 145 units. 123 one-, 20 two- and 2 three-bedroom suites with efficiencies, some with whirlpools. 4 stories, interior corridors. *Bath:* combo or shower only. **Parking:** on-site and valet. **Terms:** cancellation fee imposed. **Amenities:** voice mail, irons, hair dryers. *Fee:* video library, high-speed Internet. **Dining:** 7 am-9 pm, Fri & Sat-10 pm, cocktails. **Pool(s):** 2 heated outdoor, heated indoor. **Leisure Activities:** saunas, whirlpools, rental boats, rental canoes, rental paddleboats, fishing, 2 tennis courts, ice skating, recreation programs, bocci, rental bicycles, exercise room, basketball, volleyball. *Fee:* sailboats, waterskiing, massage, game room. **Guest Services:** gift shop, valet and coin laundry. **Business Services:** conference facilities, administrative services (fee), PC. **Cards:** AX, DC, DS, MC, VI. **Special Amenities:** free newspaper. *(See color ad p 577)*

Phone: (920)876-3366

(🍴) (🍸) (🎣) (♿) (♨) (🚲) (✕) (✕) (VCR) (📷) (DATA PORT) (🔌) (📷) (💻)

ELKHORN pop. 7,305

——— WHERE TO STAY ———

AMERICINN
▼▼▼ ▼▼▼
Small-scale Hotel

Book at aaa.com
5/15-10/1 [ECP] 1P: $78-$169 2P: $78-$169 XP: $6 F14
4/1-5/14 & 10/2-3/31 [ECP] 1P: $68-$159 2P: $68-$159 XP: $6 F14
Location: I-43, exit 25, just s. Located in a commercial area. 210 E Commerce Ct 53121. Fax: 262/723-5623. **Facility:** 58 units. 49 one-bedroom standard units, some with whirlpools. 8 one- and 1 two-bedroom suites, some with efficiencies or kitchens. 2 stories, interior corridors. *Bath:* combo or shower only. **Parking:** on-site, winter plug-ins. **Terms:** cancellation fee imposed. **Amenities:** dual phone lines. *Some:* irons, hair dryers. **Pool(s):** small heated indoor. **Leisure Activities:** sauna, whirlpool. **Guest Services:** coin laundry. **Business Services:** meeting rooms. **Cards:** AX, DC, DS, MC, VI. *(See color ad p 576)*

Phone: (262)723-7799

SOME UNITS
(ASK) (&M) (♿) (♨) (🚲) (📷) (DATA PORT) (💻) / (✕) (🔌) (📷) /

ELLISON BAY —See Door County p. 502.

ELM GROVE —See Milwaukee p. 592.

EPHRAIM —See Door County p. 503.

FENNIMORE pop. 2,387

——— WHERE TO STAY ———

FENMORE HILLS MOTEL
▼▼▼ ▼▼▼
Small-scale Hotel

4/1-11/30 1P: $56-$61 2P: $65-$70 XP: $6 F14
12/1-3/31 1P: $53-$58 2P: $62-$67 XP: $6 F14
Location: 2.4 mi w. 5814 Hwy 18 W 53809. **Facility:** 24 one-bedroom standard units, some with whirlpools. 2 stories, interior corridors. **Parking:** on-site, winter plug-ins. **Terms:** package plans, small pets only. **Leisure Activities:** jogging. **Guest Services:** coin laundry. **Business Services:** meeting rooms. **Cards:** DS, MC, VI.

Phone: 608/822-3281

SOME UNITS
(S₂) (🛏) (📷) (🔌) / (✕) (📷) /

FIFIELD

——— WHERE TO DINE ———

NORTHWOODS SUPPER CLUB
▼▼▼
American

Location: Jct SR 13 and 70. N14066 S Flameau Ave 54524. **Hours:** 4:30 pm-9 pm, Sun 4 pm-8 pm. **Closed:** 12/24, 12/25; also Mon. **Reservations:** suggested. **Features:** Generous portions of traditional favorites, such as succulent prime rib, are what the family-oriented restaurant is all about. The Saturday prime rib buffet and Friday night fish fry are popular offerings, as are the wholesome and flavorful homemade soups. Casual dress; cocktails. **Parking:** on-site. **Cards:** AX, CB, DC, DS, MC, VI.

Dinner: $10-$20 **Phone:** 715-762-4447

(🍸) (✕)

FISH CREEK —See Door County p. 504.

FITCHBURG

──────── WHERE TO STAY ────────

QUALITY INN & SUITES *Book at aaa.com*
Phone: 608/274-7200
(AAA) (SAVE) All Year   1P: $79-$129   2P: $79-$129   XP: $10   F17
◇◇◇ **Location:** US 12/18, exit 260 (Fish Hatchery/CR D), then 1.5 mi s at jct CR PD. 2969 Cahill Main 53711.
Fax: 608/274-7720. **Facility:** 75 units. 50 one-bedroom standard units. 25 one-bedroom suites, some with
Small-scale Hotel whirlpools. 4 stories, interior corridors. *Bath:* combo or shower only. **Parking:** on-site. **Terms:** pets ($25 fee,
with prior approval). **Amenities:** high-speed Internet, dual phone lines, voice mail, irons, hair dryers. **Pool(s):**
small heated indoor. **Leisure Activities:** whirlpool, exercise room. *Fee:* game room. **Guest Services:** gift
shop, complimentary evening beverages, valet and coin laundry, area transportation. **Business Services:** meeting rooms, business center. **Cards:** AX, DC, DS, MC, VI. **Special Amenities: free full breakfast.**

SOME UNITS

FOND DU LAC pop. 42,203

──────── WHERE TO STAY ────────

BAYMONT INN & SUITES-FOND DU LAC *Book at aaa.com*
Phone: (920)921-4000
(AAA) (SAVE) 4/1-9/1   1P: $79-$149   2P: $89-$159   XP: $10   F18
9/2-3/31   1P: $69-$149   2P: $79-$159   XP: $10   F18
◇◇◇ **Location:** Sw of jct US 41 and 151. Located in a commercial area. 77 Holiday Ln 54937. Fax: 920/921-4472.
Small-scale Hotel **Facility:** 79 one-bedroom standard units, some with whirlpools. 2 stories (no elevator), interior corridors.
Parking: on-site, winter plug-ins. **Terms:** pets ($10 extra charge). **Amenities:** voice mail, safes (fee), irons,
hair dryers. *Some:* high-speed Internet. **Pool(s):** small heated indoor. **Leisure Activities:** whirlpool, limited
exercise equipment. *Fee:* game room. **Guest Services:** complimentary evening beverages: Sun-Thurs, valet and coin laundry.
Business Services: meeting rooms. **Cards:** AX, DC, DS, MC, VI. **Special Amenities: free local telephone calls and free
newspaper.**

SOME UNITS

COUNTRY INN & SUITES BY CARLSON *Book at aaa.com*
Phone: (920)924-8800
◇◇◇ 6/1-8/31   1P: $90-$299
9/1-3/31   1P: $72-$179
Small-scale Hotel 5/1-5/31   1P: $81-$169
4/1-4/30   1P: $72-$169
Location: I-41, exit 96B, 1 mi sw of jct US 41 and 151. Located in a commercial area. 121 Merwin Way 54937. Fax: 920/322-9166.
Facility: 65 units. 44 one- and 2 two-bedroom standard units, some with whirlpools. 19 one-bedroom suites ($99-$299), some
with whirlpools. 3 stories, interior corridors. *Bath:* combo or shower only. **Parking:** on-site. **Terms:** [ECP] meal
plan available. **Amenities:** high-speed Internet, voice mail, irons, hair dryers. *Some:* dual phone lines. **Pool(s):** small heated indoor. **Leisure Activities:** whirlpool, exercise room. **Guest Services:** valet and coin laundry. **Business Services:** meeting rooms.
Cards: AX, DC, DS, MC, VI. *(See color ad starting on p 580)*

SOME UNITS

ECONO LODGE OF FOND DU LAC *Book at aaa.com*
Phone: (920)923-2020
◇◇ 6/1-8/31   1P: $59-$74   2P: $64-$79   XP: $5   F18
4/1-5/31 & 9/1-3/31   1P: $59-$69   2P: $59-$74   XP: $5   F18
Small-scale Hotel **Location:** On SR 23, 0.3 mi e jct of US 41. Located in a commercial area. 649 W Johnson St 54935.
Fax: 920/929-9352. **Facility:** 48 one-bedroom standard units. 2 stories (no elevator), interior corridors. *Bath:*
combo or shower only. **Parking:** on-site, winter plug-ins (fee). **Terms:** [CP] meal plan available. **Pool(s):** small heated indoor.
Leisure Activities: whirlpool. **Guest Services:** valet laundry. **Cards:** AX, CB, DC, DS, MC, VI.

SOME UNITS

HOLIDAY INN *Book at aaa.com*
Phone: 920/923-1440
◇◇◇ 7/21-8/25   1P: $120-$200   2P: $130-$210   XP: $10   F19
6/1-7/20 & 8/26-3/31   1P: $120-$150   2P: $130-$160   XP: $10   F19
Small-scale Hotel 4/1-5/31   1P: $110-$140   2P: $120-$150   XP: $10   F19
Location: On US 151, just sw of jct US 41. Located in a commercial area. 625 W Rolling Meadows Dr 54937.
Fax: 920/923-1366. **Facility:** 139 one-bedroom standard units. 2 stories (no elevator), interior corridors. *Bath:* combo or shower
only. **Parking:** on-site, winter plug-ins. **Terms:** [AP] meal plan available, pets ($100 deposit). **Amenities:** voice mail, irons, hair
dryers. *Some:* high-speed Internet. **Pool(s):** heated indoor. **Leisure Activities:** sauna, whirlpool, exercise room, shuffleboard.
Guest Services: complimentary evening beverages: Sun-Thurs, valet and coin laundry, area transportation. **Business Services:**
meeting rooms. **Cards:** AX, CB, DC, DS, MC, VI.

SOME UNITS

MICROTEL INN & SUITES
Phone: 920/929-4000
(AAA) (SAVE) All Year   1P: $40-$70   2P: $45-$80   XP: $5   F16
◇◇ **Location:** Jct US 41 and 151. Located in a commercial area. 920 S Military Rd 54935. Fax: 920/929-4001.
Facility: 79 one-bedroom standard units. 3 stories, interior corridors. *Bath:* combo or shower only. **Parking:**
on-site. **Terms:** [CP] meal plan available, pets ($10 extra charge). **Leisure Activities:** whirlpool, limited ex-
Small-scale Hotel ercise equipment. **Guest Services:** valet laundry. **Business Services:** meeting rooms. **Cards:** AX, CB, DC,
DS, JC, MC, VI. **Special Amenities: free continental breakfast and free local telephone calls.**

SOME UNITS

RAMADA PLAZA HOTEL *Book at aaa.com* Phone: (920)923-3000

(AAA) (SAVE)

7/1-8/31	1P: $89-$179	2P: $99-$189	XP: $10	F18
4/1-6/30 & 9/1-3/31	1P: $59-$149	2P: $69-$159	XP: $10	F18

Historic
Large-scale Hotel

Location: Downtown. Located in the business district. 1 N Main St 54935. Fax: 920/923-2561. **Facility:** A renovated 1923 hotel. 132 units. 125 one-bedroom standard units. 7 one-bedroom suites ($99-$269), some with whirlpools. 8 stories, interior corridors. **Parking:** on-site. **Terms:** weekly rates available, package plans - seasonal, pets ($10 extra charge). **Amenities:** voice mail, irons, hair dryers. **Dining:** 6:30 am-1:30 & 5-9 pm, Fri & Sat-9:30 pm, Sun 6:30 am-2 pm, cocktails. **Pool(s):** heated indoor. **Leisure Activities:** sauna, whirlpool. *Fee:* massage. **Guest Services:** valet laundry. **Business Services:** conference facilities, administrative services (fee). **Cards:** AX, CB, DC, DS, MC, VI. **Special Amenities: free expanded continental breakfast and free local telephone calls.**

SOME UNITS

FEE

SUPER 8 MOTEL *Book at aaa.com* Phone: 920/922-1088

4/1-9/30	1P: $51-$56	2P: $56-$61	XP: $5	F12
10/1-3/31	1P: $50	2P: $55	XP: $5	F12

Small-scale Hotel

Location: US 41, exit SR 23, just n on east frontage road (CR VV). Located in a commercial area. 391 N Pioneer Rd. 54935. Fax: 920/922-1088. **Facility:** 47 one-bedroom standard units. 2 stories (no elevator), interior corridors. **Parking:** on-site, winter plug-ins. **Terms:** [CP] meal plan available, pets ($10 fee). **Amenities:** safes (fee), hair dryers. **Guest Services:** coin laundry. **Business Services:** meeting rooms. **Cards:** AX, CB, DC, DS, JC, MC, VI.

SOME UNITS

FEE

------- **WHERE TO DINE** -------

ROLLING MEADOWS FAMILY RESTAURANT **Lunch:** $6-$14 **Dinner:** $6-$14 **Phone:** 920/922-9140

American
cocktails.

Location: Just nw of jct US 41 and 151. 947 S Rolling Meadows Dr 54937. **Hours:** 6 am-9 pm. Closed: 11/25. **Reservations:** accepted. **Features:** The menu covers a broad territory, with an extensive selection of sandwiches, salad and soup; all-day breakfast choices, and steak, seafood and Italian entrees. Desserts are homemade. The Friday night fish fry and weekend prime rib specials are popular. Casual dress; cocktails. **Parking:** on-site. **Cards:** AX, DC, DS, MC, VI.

SCHREINER'S RESTAURANT **Lunch:** $4-$12 **Dinner:** $4-$12 **Phone:** 920/922-0590

American

Location: Jct US 41 and SR 23. 168 N Pioneer Rd 54935. **Hours:** 6:30 am-8:30 pm. Closed: 11/25, 12/25 & Easter. **Features:** This popular restaurant has been serving up homestyle meals of comfort foods since 1938. There is an inhouse bakery that produces fresh desserts daily. Breakfast is served all day. Tours of the kitchen are available upon request. Casual dress; cocktails. **Parking:** on-site. **Cards:** AX, DS, MC, VI.

FONTANA pop. 1,600

------- **WHERE TO STAY** -------

FONTANA VILLAGE INN Phone: 262/275-6700

5/23-9/2	1P: $98-$128	2P: $98-$128	XP: $10	F15
4/1-5/22 & 9/3-11/2	1P: $68-$88	2P: $68-$88	XP: $10	F15
11/3-3/31	1P: $48-$68	2P: $48-$68	XP: $10	F15

Motel

Location: On SR 67. Located in a commercial area. 100 Dewey Ave 53125. Fax: 262/275-8004. **Facility:** 22 onebedroom standard units, some with whirlpools. 2 stories (no elevator), exterior corridors. **Parking:** on-site. **Terms:** office hours 8 am-10 pm, 3 day cancellation notice-fee imposed, [CP] meal plan available. **Amenities:** voice mail, hair dryers. **Guest Services:** coin laundry. **Cards:** AX, MC, VI.

SOME UNITS

FORT ATKINSON pop. 11,621

------- **WHERE TO STAY** -------

BEST WESTERN COURTYARD INN *Book at aaa.com* Phone: 920/563-6444

(AAA) (SAVE)

4/1-12/31		2P: $63-$99	XP: $10	F12
1/1-3/31		2P: $45-$79	XP: $10	F12

Small-scale Hotel

Location: 2 mi s on SR 26 business route. 1225 Janesville Ave 53538. Fax: 920/563-9510. **Facility:** 58 units. 56 one-bedroom standard units, some with whirlpools. 2 one-bedroom suites ($85-$155). 2 stories (no elevator), interior corridors. **Parking:** on-site, winter plug-ins. **Terms:** weekly rates available, [ECP] meal plan available. **Amenities:** safes (fee), irons, hair dryers. **Pool(s):** small heated indoor. **Leisure Activities:** whirlpool, gazebo, exercise room. **Guest Services:** gift shop, valet and coin laundry. **Business Services:** meeting rooms. **Cards:** AX, DC, DS, MC, VI. **Special Amenities: free continental breakfast and free newspaper.**

SOME UNITS

FEE

HOLIDAY INN EXPRESS HOTEL & SUITES *Book at aaa.com* Phone: (920)563-3600

All Year	1P: $89-$159	2P: $89-$159	

Small-scale Hotel

Location: Jct SR 26 Bypass and US 12. 1680 Madison Ave 53538. Fax: 920/563-3030. **Facility:** 78 one-bedroom standard units, some with whirlpools. 3 stories, interior corridors. *Bath:* combo or shower only. **Parking:** on-site, winter plug-ins. **Terms:** [ECP] meal plan available. **Amenities:** dual phone lines, voice mail, irons, hair dryers. **Pool(s):** heated indoor. **Leisure Activities:** whirlpool, exercise room. *Fee:* game room. **Guest Services:** valet and coin laundry. **Business Services:** meeting rooms, fax (fee). **Cards:** AX, CB, DC, DS, JC, MC, VI.

SOME UNITS

——— WHERE TO DINE ———

THE ORIGINAL STOCKADE RESTAURANT & PUB   **Lunch:** $6-$14   **Dinner:** $6-$14   **Phone:** 920/568-9498
American
Location: On US 12, 0.4 mi e of jct SR 26. 855 Lexington Blvd 53538. **Hours:** 11 am-9 pm, Fri & Sat 8 am-11 pm, Sun 8 am-9 pm. Closed major holidays. **Reservations:** accepted. **Features:** The distinctive log fort restaurant is decorated with historical pictures of the area. Among features that cater to children are crayons on the tables and an activity room. Offerings range from sandwiches, burgers and salads to steaks, pork and "Wisconsin-Mex.". Casual dress; cocktails. **Parking:** on-site. **Cards:** AX, DC, DS, MC, VI.

SALAMONE'S   **Dinner:** $5-$10   **Phone:** 920/563-9213
Pizza
Location: On US 12; just nw of downtown. 1245 Madison Ave 53538. **Hours:** 4 pm-11 pm. Closed major holidays; also Tues. **Features:** Delicious deep-dish and thin-crust pizzas are made from fresh ingredients at the family-owned restaurant. Some traditional dishes, including pasta and sausage with marinara sauce, are also listed on the dinner menu. Italian background music and beautiful murals add to the ambience. A brew pub is adjacent. Casual dress; cocktails. **Parking:** on-site. **Cards:** MC, VI.

FRANKLIN —See Milwaukee p. 593.

GENESEE DEPOT —See Milwaukee p. 593.

GERMANTOWN —See Milwaukee p. 593.

GILLS ROCK —See Door County p. 505.

GLENDALE —See Milwaukee p. 594.

GRAFTON —See Milwaukee p. 595.

GREEN BAY pop. 102,313

——— WHERE TO STAY ———

AIRPORT SETTLE INN   *Book at aaa.com*   **Phone:** (920)499-1900
Small-scale Hotel
All Year   1P: $66-$85   2P: $71-$85   XP: $5   F17
Location: US 41, exit 165, 1 mi w on SR 172, just s on CR (EB). Located in a commercial area. 2620 S Packerland Dr 54313. Fax: 920/499-1973. **Facility:** 115 one-bedroom standard units, some with whirlpools. 2 stories (no elevator), interior corridors. **Bath:** combo or shower only. **Parking:** on-site, winter plug-ins. **Terms:** cancellation fee imposed. **Amenities:** irons, hair dryers. **Pool(s):** small heated indoor. **Leisure Activities:** whirlpool, exercise room. *Fee:* game room. **Guest Services:** valet laundry, area transportation. **Business Services:** meeting rooms. **Cards:** AX, CB, DC, DS, MC, VI.
SOME UNITS

AMERICINN   *Book at aaa.com*   **Phone:** (920)434-9790
Small-scale Hotel
All Year   1P: $60-$140   2P: $65-$140   XP: $5   F12
Location: US 41, exit 170, 0.3 mi w. Located in a commercial area. 2032 Velp Ave 54303. Fax: 920/434-8790. **Facility:** 82 units. 73 one-bedroom standard units, some with whirlpools. 9 one-bedroom suites, some with whirlpools. 3 stories, interior corridors. **Bath:** combo or shower only. **Parking:** on-site, winter plug-ins. **Terms:** 30 day cancellation notice, [ECP] meal plan available, pets ($10 extra charge). **Amenities:** hair dryers. *Some:* irons. **Pool(s):** heated indoor. **Leisure Activities:** whirlpool, exercise room. **Guest Services:** coin laundry. **Business Services:** meeting rooms. **Cards:** AX, DC, DS, MC, VI. *(See color ad p 576)*
SOME UNITS
FEE

AMERIHOST INN-GREEN BAY   *Book at aaa.com*   **Phone:** (920)406-8200
Small-scale Hotel
All Year [ECP]   1P: $85-$299   2P: $85-$299   XP: $10   F17
Location: I-43, exit 183 (Mason St). Located in an office park. 2911 Voyager Dr 54311. Fax: 920/406-8130. **Facility:** 60 one-bedroom standard units, some with whirlpools. 2 stories (no elevator), interior corridors. **Bath:** combo or shower only. **Parking:** on-site. **Amenities:** voice mail, safes (fee), irons, hair dryers. **Pool(s):** heated indoor. **Leisure Activities:** sauna, whirlpool, exercise room. **Guest Services:** valet laundry. **Business Services:** meeting rooms. **Cards:** AX, DC, DS, MC, VI. **Special Amenities:** free expanded continental breakfast and free local telephone calls.
SOME UNITS
FEE   FEE

THE ASTOR HOUSE   **Phone:** (920)432-3585
Historic Bed & Breakfast
All Year [ECP]   1P: $89-$115   2P: $120-$159
Location: On SR 57, just s of jct SR 54. Located in a semi-residential area. 637 S Monroe Ave 54301. Fax: 920/436-3145. **Facility:** This restored 1888 home, close to downtown and Lambeau Field, has such modern amenities as gas fireplaces and in-room whirlpools. Smoke free premises. 5 one-bedroom standard units, some with whirlpools. 3 stories (no elevator), interior corridors. **Bath:** combo or shower only. **Parking:** on-site. **Terms:** check-in 4 pm, 30 day cancellation notice. **Amenities:** video library, CD players, irons, hair dryers. *Some:* high-speed Internet. **Cards:** AX, DS, MC, VI. **Special Amenities:** free expanded continental breakfast and free local telephone calls.

BAYMONT INN-GREEN BAY *Book at aaa.com* Phone: (920)494-7887
(AAA) (SAVE) All Year 1P: $62-$109 2P: $70-$120 XP: $10 F18
◆◆ ◆◆ **Location:** US 41, exit 164 (Oneida St), just e. Located in a commercial area. 2840 S Oneida St 54304.
Fax: 920/494-3370. **Facility:** 78 one-bedroom standard units. 2 stories (no elevator), interior corridors.
Small-scale Hotel **Parking:** on-site, winter plug-ins. **Terms:** [ECP] meal plan available, small pets only. **Amenities:** video
games, voice mail, irons, hair dryers. **Guest Services:** valet laundry. **Cards:** AX, DC, DS, MC, VI.
Special Amenities: free local telephone calls and free newspaper.
SOME UNITS

BAY MOTEL Phone: 920/494-3441
(AAA) (SAVE) All Year 1P: $40-$50 2P: $45-$60 XP: $5 F18
◆◆ **Location:** US 41, exit 167 (Lombardi Ave), 0.4 mi e to Marlee, then 0.6 mi n. 1301 S Military Ave 54304.
Fax: 920/494-8260. **Facility:** 53 one-bedroom standard units. 1 story, exterior corridors. *Bath:* combo or
Motel shower only. **Parking:** on-site, winter plug-ins. **Terms:** pets ($5 extra charge). **Dining:** Bay Motel Restaurant,
see separate listing. **Business Services:** meeting rooms, fax (fee). **Cards:** AX, DS, MC, VI.
Special Amenities: free local telephone calls and free newspaper.
SOME UNITS

BEST WESTERN SUITES *Book at aaa.com* Phone: (920)494-8790
(AAA) (SAVE) 6/1-12/31 1P: $75-$129 2P: $85-$139 XP: $10 F17
◆◆ ◆◆ 4/1-5/31 & 1/1-3/31 1P: $62-$72 2P: $72-$82 XP: $10 F17
Location: US 41, exit 164 (Oneida St), just e to Ramada Way, then just n. Located in a commercial area. 2815 Ramada
Small-scale Hotel Way 54304. Fax: 920/494-8749. **Facility:** 78 one-bedroom standard units, some with whirlpools. 2 stories (no
elevator), interior corridors. *Bath:* combo or shower only. **Parking:** on-site, winter plug-ins. **Terms:** [ECP]
meal plan available. **Amenities:** irons, hair dryers. **Pool(s):** heated indoor. **Leisure Activities:** whirlpool.
Fee: game room. **Guest Services:** valet and coin laundry. **Cards:** AX, CB, DC, DS, MC, VI. **Special Amenities: free expanded
continental breakfast and free local telephone calls.**
SOME UNITS

BEST WESTERN WASHINGTON ST INN & CONFERENCE CENTER *Book at aaa.com* Phone: (920)437-8771
(AAA) (SAVE) All Year [ECP] 1P: $69-$109 2P: $79-$119 XP: $10 F18
◆◆ ◆◆ **Location:** On east side of Fox River, just s of Walnut St (SR 29); center of downtown. 321 S Washington St 54301-4214.
Fax: 920/437-3839. **Facility:** 125 units. 115 one-bedroom standard units. 10 one-bedroom suites ($109-
$149) with kitchens, some with whirlpools. 2 stories (no elevator), interior corridors. **Parking:** on-site, winter
Small-scale Hotel plug-ins. **Terms:** cancellation fee imposed, package plans. **Amenities:** voice mail, irons, hair dryers. **Pool(s):**
heated indoor, wading. **Leisure Activities:** saunas, whirlpool, putting green, exercise room. *Fee:* game room.
Guest Services: valet laundry, airport transportation-A Straubel International Airport. **Business Services:** meeting rooms.
Cards: AX, DC, DS, MC, VI. **Special Amenities: free expanded continental breakfast and free local telephone calls.**
SOME UNITS

CANDLEWOOD SUITES Phone: (920)430-7040
◆◆ ◆◆ All Year 1P: $75-$95 2P: $75-$95 XP: $10
Location: US 41, exit 168 (Mason St), 4 mi e. Located in a commercial area. 1125 E Mason St 54301.
Small-scale Hotel Fax: 920/430-7050. **Facility:** 86 units. 74 one-bedroom standard units with efficiencies. 12 one-bedroom
suites with efficiencies. 3 stories, interior corridors. *Bath:* combo or shower only. **Parking:** on-site, winter
plug-ins. **Amenities:** video library, CD players, dual phone lines, voice mail, irons, hair dryers. *Some:* high-speed Internet.
Leisure Activities: exercise room. **Guest Services:** sundries, complimentary laundry. **Cards:** AX, DC, DS, MC, VI.
SOME UNITS

COMFORT INN *Book at aaa.com* Phone: (920)498-2060
◆◆ ◆◆ 9/16-3/31 [ECP] 1P: $55-$140 2P: $61-$140 XP: $6 F17
6/10-9/15 [ECP] 1P: $65-$130 2P: $72-$130 XP: $6 F17
Small-scale Hotel 4/1-6/9 [ECP] 1P: $60-$130 2P: $66-$130 XP: $6 F17
Location: US 41, exit 164 (Oneida St), just e. Located in a commercial area. 2841 Ramada Way 54304.
Fax: 920/498-2060. **Facility:** 60 one-bedroom standard units. 2 stories (no elevator), interior corridors. **Parking:** on-site, winter
plug-ins. **Terms:** 30 day cancellation notice. **Amenities:** irons, hair dryers. **Pool(s):** heated indoor. **Leisure Activities:** whirlpool.
Guest Services: valet laundry. **Cards:** AX, DC, DS, MC, VI.
SOME UNITS

COUNTRY INN & SUITES BY CARLSON *Book at aaa.com* Phone: (920)336-6600
◆◆ ◆◆ 7/27-1/31 [ECP] 1P: $69-$139 2P: $79-$139 XP: $10 F18
4/1-7/26 & 2/1-3/31 [ECP] 1P: $69-$75 2P: $79-$85 XP: $10 F18
Small-scale Hotel **Location:** US 41, exit 164 (Oneida St), just nw. Located next to a bowling alley. 2945 Allied St 54304.
Fax: 920/336-6618. **Facility:** 75 one-bedroom standard units, some with whirlpools. 2 stories, interior corridors. *Bath:* combo or shower only. **Parking:** on-site, winter plug-ins. **Terms:** 10 day cancellation notice-fee imposed, package
plans. **Amenities:** voice mail, irons, hair dryers. *Some:* dual phone lines. **Pool(s):** heated indoor. **Leisure Activities:** whirlpool,
exercise room. *Fee:* game room. **Guest Services:** coin laundry. **Cards:** AX, DC, DS, MC, VI.
(See color ad starting on p 580)
SOME UNITS

DAYS INN-LAMBEAU FIELD   *Book at aaa.com*   Phone: (920)498-8088

7/2-9/5 & 1/1-3/31 [CP]	1P: $79-$99	2P: $79-$99	XP: $5 F
4/1-7/1 & 9/6-12/31 [CP]	1P: $54-$79	2P: $54-$79	XP: $5 F

Location: US 41, exit 167 (Lombardi Ave), 1.4 mi e, just s. 1978 Holmgren Way 54304. Fax: 920/498-8492. **Facility:** 77 one-bedroom standard units. 2 stories (no elevator), interior corridors. **Parking:** on-site, winter plug-ins. **Terms:** pets ($10 extra charge, in smoking units). **Amenities:** hair dryers. **Pool(s):** heated indoor. **Leisure Activities:** whirlpool. **Business Services:** meeting rooms. **Cards:** AX, CB, DC, DS, MC, VI.
Small-scale Hotel
Special Amenities: free continental breakfast and free local newspaper. *(See color ad below & card insert)*

SOME UNITS

EXEL INN OF GREEN BAY   *Book at aaa.com*   Phone: (920)499-3599

All Year [CP]	1P: $40-$60	2P: $46-$66	XP: $6 F18

Location: US 41, exit 164 (Oneida St), just e. Located in a commercial area. 2870 Ramada Way 54304. Fax: 920/498-4055. **Facility:** 104 one-bedroom standard units, some with whirlpools. 2 stories (no elevator), interior corridors. **Parking:** on-site. **Terms:** weekly rates available, small pets only (in smoking units). Small-scale Hotel **Amenities:** irons, hair dryers. **Leisure Activities:** exercise room. **Guest Services:** valet and coin laundry. **Cards:** AX, CB, DC, DS, MC, VI. **Special Amenities:** free continental breakfast and early check-in/late check-out.

SOME UNITS
FEE FEE

EXTENDED STAY AIRPORT   *Book at aaa.com*   Phone: (920)499-3600

6/1-8/31	1P: $50-$70	2P: $55-$75	XP: $5 F17
4/1-5/31 & 9/1-3/31	1P: $45-$60	2P: $50-$65	XP: $5 F17

Small-scale Hotel
Location: US 41, exit 165, 1 mi w on SR 172, just s. Located in a commercial area. 1639 Commanche Ave 54313. Fax: 920/965-6520. **Facility:** 76 one-bedroom standard units with efficiencies. 2 stories, interior corridors. *Bath:* combo or shower only. **Parking:** on-site, winter plug-ins. **Terms:** cancellation fee imposed, weekly rates available. **Amenities:** dual phone lines, voice mail, irons. **Guest Services:** valet and coin laundry. **Business Services:** meeting rooms. **Cards:** AX, CB, DC, DS, MC, VI.

SOME UNITS

FAIRFIELD INN BY MARRIOTT   *Book at aaa.com*   Phone: (920)497-1010

All Year	1P: $60-$115	2P: $65-$120	XP: $5 F18

Location: US 41, exit 164 (Oneida St), just e. 2850 S Oneida St 54304. Fax: 920/497-3098. **Facility:** 62 one-bedroom standard units. 3 stories, interior corridors. *Bath:* combo or shower only. **Parking:** on-site. **Amenities:** high-speed Internet, voice mail, irons, hair dryers. **Pool(s):** small heated indoor. **Leisure Activities:** whirlpool. **Guest Services:** valet laundry. **Cards:** AX, DC, DS, JC, MC, VI. **Special Amenities:** free continental breakfast and free local telephone calls. *(See color ad below)*
Small-scale Hotel

SOME UNITS

HAMPTON INN GREEN BAY

Book at aaa.com

Phone: (920)498-9200

All Year [CP]   1P: $59-$159   2P: $59-$159   XP: $10   F18

Location: US 41, exit 164 (Oneida St), just e. Located in a commercial area. 2840 Ramada Way 54304. Fax: 920/498-3376. **Facility:** 115 one-bedroom standard units. 4 stories, interior corridors. **Parking:** on-site. **Terms:** cancellation fee imposed. **Amenities:** video games, voice mail, irons, hair dryers. **Pool(s):** heated indoor. **Leisure Activities:** whirlpool, exercise room. **Guest Services:** valet laundry. **Business Services:** meeting rooms. **Cards:** AX, CB, DC, DS, JC, MC, VI.

Small-scale Hotel

SOME UNITS

HILTON GARDEN INN

Book at aaa.com

Phone: (920)405-0400

All Year   1P: $80-$150   2P: $80-$150   XP: $10   F18

Location: US 41, exit 167 (Lombardi Ave), 1.6 mi e. 1015 Lombardi Ave 54304. Fax: 920/405-0512. **Facility:** 125 one-bedroom standard units, some with whirlpools. 5 stories, interior corridors. *Bath:* combo or shower only. **Parking:** on-site. **Terms:** cancellation fee imposed, [BP], [CP] & [ECP] meal plans available. **Amenities:** video games, high-speed Internet, dual phone lines, voice mail, irons, hair dryers. **Pool(s):** heated indoor. **Leisure Activities:** whirlpool, exercise room. **Guest Services:** sundries, valet and coin laundry. **Business Services:** meeting rooms, business center. **Cards:** AX, CB, DC, DS, JC, MC, VI.

Small-scale Hotel

SOME UNITS

HOLIDAY INN CITY CENTRE

Book at aaa.com

Phone: (920)437-5900

All Year   1P: $89-$109   2P: $89-$109

Location: Downtown. Located opposite the Port Plaza Mall. 200 Main St 54301. Fax: 920/437-1199. **Facility:** 146 one-bedroom standard units. 7 stories, interior corridors. *Bath:* combo or shower only. **Parking:** on-site. **Terms:** cancellation fee imposed, [AP] meal plan available, pets ($25 deposit). **Amenities:** video games, voice mail, irons, hair dryers. **Pool(s):** heated indoor. **Leisure Activities:** sauna, exercise room. *Fee:* marina. **Guest Services:** valet and coin laundry. **Business Services:** meeting rooms, business center. **Cards:** AX, CB, DC, DS, JC, MC, VI.

Large-scale Hotel

SOME UNITS

HOWARD JOHNSON INN & CONFERENCE CENTER

Book at aaa.com

Phone: (920)499-5121

4/1-9/30   1P: $63-$73   2P: $63-$73   XP: $10   F17
10/1-3/31   1P: $53-$63   2P: $53-$63   XP: $10   F17

Location: SR 172, exit SR 32 (Ashland Ave), just se on US 41 business route. 2580 S Ashland Ave 54304. Fax: 920/499-6777. **Facility:** 146 one-bedroom standard units. 2 stories (no elevator), interior/exterior corridors. *Bath:* combo or shower only. **Parking:** on-site. **Terms:** [AP] meal plan available. **Amenities:** voice mail, irons, hair dryers. **Pool(s):** heated indoor. **Leisure Activities:** whirlpool. *Fee:* miniature golf, game room. **Guest Services:** valet and coin laundry. **Business Services:** conference facilities. **Cards:** AX, DC, DS, MC, VI. *(See color ad p 584)*

Large-scale Hotel

SOME UNITS

MICROTEL INN & SUITES

Book at aaa.com

Phone: (920)338-9000

All Year [CP]   1P: $52-$125   2P: $62-$125   XP: $10   F17

Location: US 41, exit 164 (Oneida St), just sw. Located in a commercial area. 3031 Allied St 54304. Fax: 920/338-9100. **Facility:** 68 one-bedroom standard units, some with whirlpools. 3 stories, interior corridors. **Parking:** on-site, winter plug-ins. **Amenities:** *Some:* irons. **Pool(s):** heated indoor. **Leisure Activities:** whirlpool. **Guest Services:** coin laundry. **Cards:** AX, DC, DS, MC, VI. **Special Amenities:** free continental breakfast and free local telephone calls.

Small-scale Hotel

SOME UNITS

RADISSON HOTEL & CONFERENCE CENTER

Book at aaa.com

Phone: (920)494-7300

All Year   1P: $79-$149   2P: $79-$149   XP: $10   F12

Location: US 41, exit 165, 2 mi w on SR 172. Connected to a casino. 2040 Airport Dr 54313. Fax: 920/494-9599. **Facility:** 409 units. 369 one-bedroom standard units. 40 one-bedroom suites, some with whirlpools. 3-6 stories, interior corridors. *Bath:* combo or shower only. **Parking:** on-site. **Terms:** cancellation fee imposed, [BP] & [ECP] meal plans available. **Amenities:** video games, dual phone lines, voice mail, irons, hair dryers. *Some:* high-speed Internet. **Dining:** 3 restaurants, 6 am-10 pm, cocktails. **Pool(s):** heated indoor, lap. **Leisure Activities:** sauna, whirlpool, exercise room. **Guest Services:** gift shop, valet laundry, airport transportation-Austin Straubel International Airport, area transportation-within 5 mi. **Business Services:** conference facilities, business center. **Cards:** AX, CB, DC, DS, MC, VI. **Special Amenities:** free newspaper and free room upgrade (subject to availability with advanced reservations). *(See color ad p 521 & p 583)*

Large-scale Hotel

SOME UNITS

RAMADA PLAZA GREEN BAY

Book at aaa.com

Phone: (920)499-0631

All Year   1P: $83-$114   2P: $93-$124   XP: $10   F17

Location: US 41, exit 164 (Oneida St), just e to Ramada Way, then 0.3 mi n. Located in a commercial area. 2750 Ramada Way 54304. Fax: 920/499-5476. **Facility:** 148 one-bedroom standard units, some with whirlpools. 5 stories, interior corridors. *Bath:* combo or shower only. **Parking:** on-site. **Terms:** [BP] meal plan available, pets ($15 extra charge). **Amenities:** high-speed Internet, voice mail, irons, hair dryers. *Fee:* video games, safes. **Dining:** 6 am-10 pm, cocktails. **Pool(s):** heated indoor, wading. **Leisure Activities:** sauna, whirlpool, waterslide, indoor water park, exercise room. **Guest Services:** valet laundry, airport transportation-A Straubel International Airport. **Business Services:** meeting rooms, business center. **Cards:** AX, CB, DC, DS, JC, MC, VI. **Special Amenities:** free full breakfast and free newspaper.

Large-scale Hotel

SOME UNITS

RESIDENCE INN BY MARRIOTT   *Book at aaa.com*   **Phone:** 920/435-2222

All Year   1P: $99-$159   2P: $99-$159

Location: SR 172, exit Riverside Dr, 1.1 mi n on SR 57, then just e. Located in a semi-commercial area. 335 W St Joseph St 54301. Fax: 920/435-4068. **Facility:** 96 units. 72 one- and 24 two-bedroom standard units with kitchens. 2 stories (no elevator), exterior corridors. **Parking:** on-site. **Terms:** cancellation fee imposed, [BP] meal plan available, pets ($150 fee, $5 extra charge). **Amenities:** voice mail, irons, hair dryers. **Pool(s):** heated outdoor. **Leisure Activities:** whirlpool, sports court, basketball, volleyball. **Guest Services:** complimentary evening beverages: Mon-Thurs, valet and coin laundry. **Business Services:** meeting rooms. **Cards:** AX, DC, DS, MC, VI.

Small-scale Hotel

SOME UNITS

SUPER 8 MOTEL   *Book at aaa.com*   **Phone:** 920/494-2042

	6/13-10/2 [ECP]	1P: $64-$72	2P: $71-$79
	10/3-3/31 [ECP]	1P: $62-$70	2P: $69-$77
	4/1-6/12 [ECP]	1P: $60-$69	2P: $67-$77

Location: US 41, exit 164 (Oneida St), just e. Located in a commercial area. 2868 S Oneida St 54304. Fax: 920/494-6959. **Facility:** 83 one-bedroom standard units. 2 stories (no elevator), interior corridors. **Parking:** on-site, winter plug-ins. **Terms:** 3 day cancellation notice-fee imposed, pets ($25 deposit). **Amenities:** voice mail, irons. *Some:* high-speed Internet. **Leisure Activities:** sauna, whirlpool. **Guest Services:** valet and coin laundry, airport transportation-A Straubel International Airport. **Business Services:** meeting rooms. **Cards:** AX, CB, DC, DS, MC, VI. **Special Amenities:** free expanded continental breakfast and free local telephone calls.

Small-scale Hotel

SOME UNITS

THE TUNDRA LODGE RESORT & WATERPARK Phone: (920)405-8700
AAA SAVE All Year 1P: $119-$299 2P: $119-$299
▼▼▼▼ **Location:** US 41, exit 167 (Lombardi Ave), 2 mi e. 865 Lombardi Ave 54304. Fax: 920/405-1997. **Facility:** 161 units.
Large-scale Hotel 104 one-bedroom standard units, some with whirlpools. 57 one-bedroom suites. 3 stories, interior corridors.
Bath: combo or shower only. **Parking:** on-site. **Terms:** 3 day cancellation notice-fee imposed.
Amenities: high-speed Internet, voice mail, hair dryers. **Dining:** 3 restaurants, 6:30 am-10 pm, cocktails.
Pool(s): heated indoor, 2 wading. **Leisure Activities:** whirlpools, waterslide, indoor waterpark, exercise
room. *Fee:* game room. **Guest Services:** gift shop, valet and coin laundry, tanning facility. **Business Services:** meeting rooms.
Cards: AX, CB, DC, DS, MC, VI. *(See color ad p 521)*

SOME UNITS

🅂🄳 🅄 🍽 🛎 ⓜ 🔊 🏊 ✕ 📷 🖧 🔌 🔲 🖼 🖥 / ✕ /

WINGATE INN AIRPORT *Book at aaa.com* Phone: (920)617-2000
▼▼▼▼ All Year [BP] 1P: $69-$85 2P: $69-$95 XP: $10 F17
Location: US 41, exit 165, 2 mi w on SR 172. Located opposite casino. 2065 Airport Dr 54313. Fax: 920/617-2001.
Small-scale Hotel **Facility:** 80 units. 76 one-bedroom standard units. 4 one-bedroom suites ($149-$189) with whirlpools. 3 sto-
ries, interior corridors. *Bath:* combo or shower only. **Parking:** on-site. **Terms:** package plans.
Amenities: video games, high-speed Internet, dual phone lines, voice mail, safes, irons, hair dryers. **Leisure Activities:** whirl-
pool, exercise room. **Guest Services:** sundries, valet and coin laundry. **Business Services:** meeting rooms, business center.
Cards: AX, CB, DC, DS, MC, VI.

SOME UNITS

ASK 🅂🄳 🔌 🍽 🔊 📷 🖧 🔲 🖼 🖥 / ✕ /

───── WHERE TO DINE ─────

BAY MOTEL RESTAURANT **Lunch:** $6-$10 **Dinner:** $6-$10 Phone: 920/494-3441
▼▼ **Location:** US 41, exit 167 (Lombardi Ave), 0.4 mi e to Marlee, then 0.6 mi n; in Bay Motel. 1301 S Military Ave 54304.
American **Hours:** 6 am-8 pm. Closed: 11/25, 12/25; also 12/24 & 1/1 for dinner. **Reservations:** accepted.
Features: The casual restaurant is popular for its menu of reasonably priced food and friendly service.
Breakfast is served all day, and the menu includes salads, deluxe burgers and sandwiches, as well as
standard fare. Casual dress. **Parking:** on-site. **Cards:** AX, DC, DS, MC, VI.
✕

BISTRO JOHN PAUL **Dinner:** $17-$22 Phone: 920/432-2897
AAA **Location:** 2 mi e of downtown on US 141/SR 29. 1244 Main St 54302. **Hours:** 5 pm-9 pm. Closed major
▼▼▼▼ holidays; also Sun & Mon. **Reservations:** required. **Features:** Mouthwatering, made-to-order French
American cuisine shows eye-catching presentation and thoughtful preparation. The decor of the late
19th-century restaurant, originally a hardware store, is country French. The tempting menu changes
weekly. Dressy casual; cocktails. **Parking:** on-site. **Cards:** AX, DC, DS, MC, VI.
✕

BRETT FAVRE'S STEAKHOUSE **Dinner:** $13-$26 Phone: 920/499-6874
▼▼▼ **Location:** US 41, exit 167 (Lombard Ave), 1.6 mi e; behind Hilton Garden Inn. 1004 Brett Favre Pass 54304.
American **Hours:** 4 pm-10 pm, Sat from 3 pm, Sun 3 pm-9 pm. Closed: 11/25, 12/25. **Reservations:** accepted.
Features: You'll find this restaurant close to Lambeau Field, where many of the football pictures that
decorate the walls were taken. Here they offer a selection of steaks, prime rib, seafood, pasta, poultry and
a few Southern dishes. Fish fry on Friday nights. Casual dress; cocktails. **Parking:** on-site. **Cards:** AX, DC, MC, VI.
🍽 ✕

EVES SUPPER CLUB **Lunch:** $5-$12 **Dinner:** $10-$50 Phone: 920/435-1571
▼▼▼▼ **Location:** 1 mi n on SR 57 from jct SR 172. 2020 Riverside Dr 54301. **Hours:** 11 am-2 & 5-closing, Sat from 5
American pm. Closed major holidays; also Sun. **Features:** Overlooking the Fox River, the casual restaurant affords
great fourth-floor views. Steak and seafood specialties include tenderloin, ribeye and walnut-crusted baked
salmon. For dessert, try one of the cheesecakes. Service is friendly and efficient. Casual dress; cocktails.
Parking: on-site. **Cards:** AX, DC, DS, MC, VI.
✕

LORELIE **Lunch:** $4-$7 **Dinner:** $7-$15 Phone: 920/432-5921
▼▼ **Location:** 1.8 mi n from jct SR 172. 1412 S Webster Ave 54301. **Hours:** 11:30 am-1:30 & 5-9:30 pm, Fri-10 pm,
German Sat 5 pm-10 pm. Closed major holidays; also Sun. **Reservations:** accepted. **Features:** A limited selection
of German dishes—plus well-seasoned steak—are listed on the family-operated restaurant's menu. The
place is filled with locals, who enjoy catching up with their friends at other tables. The service is friendly
and efficient. Casual dress; cocktails. **Parking:** on-site. **Cards:** MC, VI.
🍽 ✕

LOS BANDITOS **Lunch:** $6-$18 **Dinner:** $6-$18 Phone: 920/432-9462
▼▼▼ **Location:** 2.1 mi e of downtown on US 141/SR 29. 1258 Main St 54302. **Hours:** 11:30 am-11:30 pm, Sun 4
Mexican pm-10 pm. Closed major holidays. **Features:** The downtown restaurant is well known for its Mexican
dishes and friendly service. Casual dress; cocktails. **Parking:** on-site. **Cards:** AX, DC, DS, MC, VI.
🍽 ✕

LOS BANDITOS WEST **Lunch:** $6-$18 **Dinner:** $6-$18 Phone: 920/494-4505
▼▼ **Location:** US 41, exit 168 (Mason St), just w. 2335 W Mason St 54303. **Hours:** 11:30 am-11:30 pm, Sun 4 pm-10
Mexican pm. Closed major holidays. **Features:** Located just west of highway US 41, this eatery is well-known for
their Mexican dishes. Casual dress; cocktails. **Parking:** on-site. **Cards:** AX, DC, DS, MC, VI.
🍽 ✕

MACKINAWS GRILL & SPIRITS **Lunch:** $6-$9 **Dinner:** $9-$20 Phone: 920/406-8000
▼▼▼ **Location:** I-43, exit 183 (Mason St). 2925 Voyager Dr 54311. **Hours:** 11 am-10 pm, Sun 9 am-9 pm. Closed: 1/1,
American 11/25, 12/25. **Features:** The new rustic restaurant presents an extensive menu that lists a little something
for everyone, or so it claims. Bands perform every Friday in the cabin bar. Casual dress; cocktails.
Parking: on-site. **Cards:** AX, DS, MC, VI.
🍽 ✕

PRIME QUARTER STEAKHOUSE
▽▽ ▽▽
American

Dinner: $12-$25   **Phone:** 920/498-8701
Location: US 41, exit 164 (Oneida St), 0.6 mi ne. 2610 S Oneida St 54304. **Hours:** 5 pm-10 pm, Sat 4 pm-10 pm, Sun 4 pm-9 pm. Closed major holidays. **Reservations:** accepted. **Features:** Grill you own U.S.D.A. choice steak over a live hickory charcoal grill. All dinners include unlimited salad bar, baked potato, and Texas style toast. Casual dress; cocktails. **Parking:** on-site. **Cards:** AX, CB, DC, DS, MC, VI.

THE RITE VIEW
▽▽
American

Lunch: $5-$7   **Dinner:** $10-$14   **Phone:** 920/434-8981
Location: US 41, exit 170, 0.4 mi w. 2130 Velp Ave 54303. **Hours:** 11 am-9:30 pm, Sun 11 am-8 pm. Closed: 11/25, 12/25. **Features:** This restaurant isn't fancy, but the food is good, and the service is friendly. Casual dress; cocktails. **Parking:** on-site. **Cards:** DS, MC, VI.

RIVER'S BEND SUPPER CLUB
▽▽ ▽▽
American

Lunch: $3-$10   **Dinner:** $7-$25   **Phone:** 920/434-1383
Location: US 41, exit 170, just w, then just n. 792 N Riverview Dr 54303. **Hours:** 11:30 am-2 & 5-9:30 pm, Fri & Sat-10 pm, Sun 4:30 pm-9 pm. Closed: 7/4, 11/25, 12/25. **Features:** Along Duck Creek, the family-owned restaurant has been in operation since 1974. On the menu is traditional fare, as well as some well-prepared alternatives and pasta dishes. Casual dress; cocktails. **Parking:** on-site. **Cards:** MC, VI.

SAMMY'S PIZZA AND RESTAURANT
▽▽
Italian

Lunch: $9-$15   **Dinner:** $9-$15   **Phone:** 920/499-6644
Location: US 41, exit 164 (Oneida St), 1.9 mi ne. 2161 S Oneida St 54304. **Hours:** 11 am-10:30 pm, Fri-12:30 am. Closed: 11/25, 12/25 & Easter. **Features:** The family business has been serving pizzas in the area since 1958. The menu also lists a large selection of delicious-tasting dishes made from recipes created at home. Casual dress; cocktails. **Parking:** on-site. **Cards:** MC, VI.

TEN-0-ONE
▽▽ ▽▽
American

Lunch: $6-$10   **Dinner:** $7-$21   **Phone:** 920/432-9787
Location: Just e of downtown on US 141/SR 29. 1001 Main St 54302. **Hours:** 11 am-10 pm, Fri-11 pm, Sun 4 pm-10 pm. Closed: 11/25, 12/25 & Easter. **Reservations:** accepted. **Features:** It shouldn't be hard to find this corner restaurant, which is decorated with a bit of Green Bay nostalgia and serves a wide variety of menu offerings from sandwiches, steaks and prime rib to fresh seafood, pasta and Mexican dishes. Casual dress; cocktails. **Parking:** on-site. **Cards:** AX, DC, MC, VI.

TIMBER LODGE STEAKHOUSE
▽▽ ▽▽
American

Lunch: $6-$10   **Dinner:** $14-$20   **Phone:** 920/498-1005
Location: US 41, exit 164 (Oneida St), 1 mi ne. 2476 S Oneida St 54304. **Hours:** 4 pm-10 pm, Fri & Sat 11 am-11 pm, Sun 11 am-9 pm. Closed: 11/25, 12/25. **Features:** Warm, up-north atmosphere with pine wood beams and fireplaces, in a place where they serve "mosquito bites" for appetizers, and lumberjack specials for dinner. Casual dress; cocktails. **Parking:** on-site. **Cards:** AX, DC, DS, MC, VI.

TITLETOWN BREWING COMPANY
▽▽ ▽▽
American

Lunch: $6-$9   **Dinner:** $6-$15   **Phone:** 920/437-2337
Location: On SR 29 at west end of Fox River Bridge, just w of downtown. 200 Dousman St 54303. **Hours:** 11 am-11 pm, Fri & Sat-midnight. Closed: 11/25, 12/25. **Features:** The microbrewery serves hand-crafted ales and root beer as well as delicious dishes and tempting specials. An 85-foot clock tower, hardwood floors and historical artwork decorate the restored 1899 train depot. Casual dress; cocktails. **Parking:** on-site. **Cards:** AX, DC, DS, MC, VI.

THE WELLINGTON RESTAURANT
▽▽ ▽▽ ▽▽
American

Lunch: $8-$10   **Dinner:** $16-$28   **Phone:** 920/499-2000
Location: US 41, exit 164 (Oneida St), 0.5 mi ne, then 0.5 mi w. 1060 Hansen Rd 54304. **Hours:** 11:30 am-2 & 5-9 pm, Sat from 5 pm. Closed major holidays; also Sun. **Reservations:** suggested. **Features:** On the edge of town, the restaurant is known as a great place for steak. Also on the menu is a selection of fresh seafood, pork and poultry. The relaxing ambience is highlighted by an English motif, soft background music and large windows overlooking the lawn. Dressy casual; cocktails. **Parking:** on-site. **Cards:** AX, DC, MC, VI.

The following restaurant has not been evaluated by AAA but is listed for your information only.

MANDARIN GARDEN
fyi

Phone: 920/499-4459
Not evaluated. **Location:** US 41, exit 164 (Oneida St), 1.2 mi ne. 2394 S Oneida St 54304. **Features:** This well established restaurant has been serving a number of reasonably priced Chinese dishes for many years.

GREENFIELD —See Milwaukee p. 595.

GREEN LAKE pop. 1,100

--- WHERE TO STAY ---

BAY VIEW MOTEL & RESORT
▽
Motel

	2P: $88-$98	XP: $10	D12
5/1-10/31			
4/1-4/30 & 11/1-3/31	2P: $40-$48	XP: $10	D12

Phone: 920/294-6504

Location: 0.3 mi se. 439 Lake St 54941. Fax: 920/294-0888. **Facility:** 17 one-bedroom standard units, some with efficiencies. 1 story, exterior corridors. Bath: combo or shower only. **Parking:** on-site, winter plug-ins. **Terms:** office hours 8 am-10 pm, 2 night minimum stay - weekends, 14 day cancellation notice-fee imposed. **Leisure Activities:** rental boats, boat dock, fishing. **Cards:** MC, VI.

SOME UNITS

LAKESIDE MOTEL
Phone: 920/294-3318

Motel

5/1-11/1	1P: $80-$90	2P: $80-$90	XP: $15	F10
4/1-4/30 & 11/2-3/31	1P: $55-$65	2P: $55-$65	XP: $15	F10

Location: Just w of downtown on Business Rt SR 23. 488 South St 54941. **Fax:** 920/294-0687. **Facility:** Designated smoking area. 15 one-bedroom standard units. 1 story, interior/exterior corridors. *Bath:* combo or shower only. **Parking:** on-site, winter plug-ins. **Terms:** 2-3 night minimum stay - seasonal & weekends, 12 day cancellation notice. **Amenities:** *Some:* hair dryers. **Business Services:** fax. **Cards:** MC, VI.

SOME UNITS

———— **WHERE TO DINE** ————

NORTON'S MARINE DINING ROOM **Lunch:** $6-$14 **Dinner:** $20-$36 Phone: 920/294-6577

Steak & Seafood

Location: 0.7 mi w on Business Rt SR 23. 380 S Lawson Dr 54941. **Hours:** 11 am-3 & 5-10 pm; hours may vary off season. Closed: 12/25; also for dinner 12/24. **Features:** Nautical theme, overlooking Green Lake. Patio seating for lunch. Boat docking available. Supper club type fare featuring yellow fin tuna chops and roast duck. Homemade soup, rolls and dessert. Friday night fish fry of fresh lake perch in season. Casual dress; cocktails. **Parking:** on-site. **Cards:** AX, MC, VI.

HARTFORD —See Milwaukee p. 595.

HAYWARD pop. 2,129

———— **WHERE TO STAY** ————

AMERICINN OF HAYWARD *Book at aaa.com*
Phone: (715)634-2700

Small-scale Hotel

5/16-10/10	1P: $75-$95	2P: $81-$139	XP: $6	F12
12/31-3/31	1P: $60-$100	2P: $70-$120	XP: $6	F12
10/11-12/30	1P: $60-$85	2P: $66-$100	XP: $6	F12
4/1-5/15	1P: $60-$80	2P: $66-$100	XP: $6	F12

Location: On US 63, just n of jct SR 77. 15601 US Hwy 63 54843. **Fax:** 715/634-3958. **Facility:** 42 units. 39 one-bedroom standard units, some with whirlpools. 3 one-bedroom suites ($90-$175). 2 stories, interior corridors. *Bath:* combo or shower only. **Parking:** on-site, winter plug-ins. **Terms:** [ECP] meal plan available, pets ($6 extra charge, in smoking units). **Amenities:** video library, hair dryers. *Some:* irons. **Pool(s):** small heated indoor. **Leisure Activities:** sauna, whirlpool. **Guest Services:** valet laundry. **Business Services:** meeting rooms, PC, fax (fee). **Cards:** AX, DS, MC, VI. *(See color ad p 576)*

SOME UNITS

BEST WESTERN NORTHERN PINE INN *Book at aaa.com*
Phone: (715)634-4959

Small-scale Hotel

4/1-10/5 & 12/20-3/31	1P: $59-$79	2P: $69-$119	XP: $5	F12
10/6-12/19	1P: $49-$59	2P: $59-$119	XP: $5	F12

Location: On SR 27 S, 1.7 mi s of jct US 63. 9966 N Hwy 27 54843. **Fax:** 715/634-8999. **Facility:** 39 units. 38 one-bedroom standard units, some with whirlpool. 1 one-bedroom suite with whirlpool. 1-2 stories (no elevator), interior/exterior corridors. *Bath:* combo or shower only. **Parking:** on-site, winter plug-ins. **Terms:** office hours 7 am-10:30 pm, 3 day cancellation notice, [CP] meal plan available, pets ($5 extra charge). **Amenities:** irons, hair dryers. **Pool(s):** small heated indoor. **Leisure Activities:** sauna, whirlpool. *Fee:* game room. **Business Services:** fax. **Cards:** AX, CB, DC, DS, MC, VI. **Special Amenities:** free continental breakfast.

SOME UNITS

CEDAR INN MOTEL
Phone: 715/634-5332

Motel

6/11-9/15 [CP]	1P: $61-$140	2P: $76-$140	XP: $5	F12
4/1-6/10 & 9/16-3/31 [CP]	1P: $51-$140	2P: $66-$140	XP: $5	F12

Location: On SR 77, just e of jct US 63. 15659 SR 77 54843. **Fax:** 715/634-1343. **Facility:** 23 one-bedroom standard units, some with whirlpools. 1 story, interior corridors. **Parking:** on-site, winter plug-ins. **Leisure Activities:** sauna, whirlpool, limited exercise equipment. **Business Services:** fax (fee). **Cards:** AX, DC, MC, VI.

SOME UNITS

COMFORT SUITES *Book at aaa.com*
Phone: 715/634-0700

Small-scale Hotel

6/12-10/17 [CP]	1P: $90-$165	2P: $90-$165	XP: $10	F18
4/1-6/11 & 10/18-3/31 [CP]	1P: $70-$135	2P: $70-$135	XP: $10	F18

Location: On CR B, 0.5 mi s of jct SR 27. 15586 CR B 54843. **Fax:** 715/634-0800. **Facility:** 60 one-bedroom standard units, some with whirlpools. 2 stories, interior corridors. *Bath:* combo or shower only. **Parking:** on-site, winter plug-ins. **Terms:** pets ($10 fee, $25 deposit). **Amenities:** irons, hair dryers. **Pool(s):** heated indoor. **Leisure Activities:** sauna, whirlpool, rental paddleboats, boat dock, fishing, cross country skiing, snowmobiling, exercise room. *Fee:* game room. **Guest Services:** coin laundry. **Business Services:** meeting rooms, administrative services (fee). **Cards:** AX, CB, DC, DS, JC, MC, VI.

SOME UNITS

EDELWEISS MOTEL
Phone: 715/634-4679

Motel

6/16-3/31 [CP]	1P: $49-$59	2P: $55-$65	XP: $5	F15
4/1-6/15 [CP]	1P: $39-$49	2P: $49-$59	XP: $5	F15

Location: On SR 27, 1.8 mi s of jct US 63. Hwy 27 S & Park Rd 54843 (16081 W Park Rd). **Facility:** 8 one-bedroom standard units. 1 story, exterior corridors. **Parking:** on-site, winter plug-ins. **Cards:** AX, DS, MC, VI.

GRAND PINES RESORTS/HOME OF THE ORIGINAL FAMOUS DAVE'S   Phone: 715/462-3564

(AAA) (SAVE)   6/5-9/6   2P: $99
(diamond diamond diamond) 4/1-6/4 & 9/7-3/31   2P: $79

Resort Cottage   **Location:** 8.5 mi e on CR B. 12355 W Richardson Bay Rd 54843. Fax: 715/462-9754. **Facility:** Handcrafted furniture completes the eclectic and North Woods-theme decor of these cabins and motel units. 33 units. 10 one-bedroom standard units with whirlpools. 23 cottages ($165-$325), some with whirlpools. 1-2 stories (no elevator), exterior corridors. *Bath:* combo or shower only. **Parking:** on-site. **Terms:** check-out 8 am, 2 night minimum stay - weekends 6/1/10/31, cancellation fee imposed, weekly rates available, package plans. **Amenities:** irons, hair dryers. *Fee:* video library, high-speed Internet. *Some:* DVD players. **Dining:** The Original Famous Dave's, see separate listing. **Leisure Activities:** rental boats, fishing, pontoon, snowmobile trail. **Guest Services:** gift shop. **Business Services:** meeting rooms. **Cards:** AX, DS, MC, VI. **Special Amenities:** free local telephone calls and early check-in/late check-out.
(See color ad below)

SOME UNITS
(icons) / (icons) /

HAYWARD INN & SUITES   *Book at aaa.com*   Phone: 715/634-4100
(diamond diamond diamond) 4/1-10/10   1P: $94-$135   2P: $94-$135   XP: $6   F
10/11-3/31   1P: $84-$120   2P: $84-$120   XP: $6   F
Small-scale Hotel   **Location:** On SR 27 S, 0.7 mi s of jct US 63. 10290 Hwy 27 S 54843 (PO Box 1010). Fax: 715/634-2403. **Facility:** 66 units. 58 one-bedroom standard units, some with whirlpools. 8 one-bedroom suites ($120-$140) with whirlpools. 2 stories, interior corridors. **Parking:** on-site, winter plug-ins. **Amenities:** voice mail, irons, hair dryers. **Pool(s):** small heated indoor. **Leisure Activities:** whirlpool. *Fee:* game room. **Business Services:** meeting rooms, administrative services (fee). **Cards:** AX, DC, DS, MC, VI.

SOME UNITS
(icons) / (icons) /

LUMBERMAN'S MANSION INN
Phone: 715/634-3012

▼▼▼

Historic Bed & Breakfast

Property failed to provide current rates
Location: Just w of US 63; corner of 4th St and Kansas Ave. 15844 E 4th St 54843 (PO Box 554). Fax: 715/634-5724. **Facility:** Whirlpools are featured in every guest room of this 1887 Queen Anne Victorian, which is within walking distance of downtown. Smoke free premises. 5 units. 3 one-bedroom standard units with whirlpools. 2 one-bedroom suites with whirlpools. 2 stories (no elevator), interior corridors. **Parking:** on-site. **Amenities:** video library. **Guest Services:** complimentary evening beverages. **Business Services:** meeting rooms, administrative services (fee).

⊠ 🅐🅒 🆅🅲🆁 ☎

ROSS' TEAL LAKE LODGE AND TEAL WING GOLF CLUB
Phone: (715)462-3631

▼▼▼ ▼▼▼

Historic Resort Cabin

6/20-8/19	1P: $260-$350	2P: $260-$350
8/20-10/10	1P: $190-$280	2P: $190-$280
4/1-6/19 & 10/11-3/31	1P: $130-$280	2P: $130-$280

Location: On SR 77, 20 mi ne of jct US 63. Located in Chequamegon-Nicolet National Forest. 12425 N Ross Rd 54843. Fax: 715/462-9187. **Facility:** This family-owned lakefront resort is within the Chequamegon-Nicolet National Forest and features a challenging 18-hole golf course. 23 units. 2 one-bedroom standard units. 21 cabins. 1 story, exterior corridors. **Parking:** on-site, winter plug-ins. **Terms:** cancellation fee imposed, weekly rates available, [AP], [BP], [CP], [ECP] & [MAP] meal plans available, package plans, pets ($5 extra charge). **Amenities:** video library. **Pool(s):** heated outdoor. **Leisure Activities:** sauna, rental boats, rental canoes, rental sailboats, boat dock, fishing, tennis court, cross country skiing, bicycles, hiking trails, jogging, horseshoes, shuffleboard. *Fee:* golf-18 holes. **Guest Services:** coin laundry. **Business Services:** meeting rooms. **Cards:** MC, VI.

SOME UNITS

🐄 🍴 🍸 🏊 ⊠ 🅐🅒 ☎ 🗄 📶 / 🆅🅲🆁
FEE   FEE

SUPER 8 MOTEL
Book at aaa.com
Phone: (715)634-2646

▼▼▼

Small-scale Hotel

All Year 1P: $50-$75 2P: $50-$75 XP: $7 F12
Location: On SR 27, 0.3 mi s of jct US 63. 10444 N SR 27 54843. Fax: 715/634-6482. **Facility:** 46 one-bedroom standard units, some with whirlpools. 1-2 stories (no elevator), interior/exterior corridors. **Parking:** on-site, winter plug-ins. **Pool(s):** small heated indoor. **Leisure Activities:** whirlpool. **Cards:** AX, DS, MC, VI.

SOME UNITS

🅐🆂🅺 🆂🅳 🐄 🍴 🏊 / ⊠ 🅳🅰🆃🅰 /
                                                          🅿🅾🆁🆃

——— WHERE TO DINE ———

CHIPPEWA INN
Dinner: $11-$22
Phone: 715/462-3648

🔺🔺🔺
▼▼ ▼▼
German

Location: On CR B, at jct CR A, 15 mi e. 9702 N CR B 54843. **Hours:** 5 pm-10 pm; hours vary seasonally. Closed: Tues. **Reservations:** suggested. **Features:** Set on a quiet, secluded location on the Chequamegon National Forest scenic drive, the restaurant delivers a mixture of American dishes and German specialties. Famous for their relish tray featuring asssorted salad, vegetables and cheese spread. Casual dress; cocktails. **Parking:** on-site. **Cards:** MC, VI.

🍸 ⊠

CLUB 77
Dinner: $12-$30
Phone: 715/462-3712

🔺🔺🔺
▼▼ ▼▼
American

Location: On SR 77, 8 mi e. 10494 N Airport Rd 54843. **Hours:** 5 pm-9 pm. Closed: Mon-Wed 10/1-6/1. **Reservations:** suggested. **Features:** Located just outside of town, this well-known area restaurant features excellent food in a casual and non-pretentious manner. Unlike most restaurants, all diners receive a tray of crudites, a cheese fondue and diced bread for dipping. Very popular with locals and out-of-towners, this is a good choice for a hearty meal. Casual dress; cocktails. **Parking:** on-site. **Cards:** MC, VI.

🍸 ⊠

MAXIMILIAN INN
Dinner: $14-$22
Phone: 715/865-2080

▼▼ ▼▼
American

Location: On SR 27, 0.6 mi s of jct SR 70 W. 15866 W State Rd 27/70 54871. **Hours:** 5 pm-10 pm. Closed: Sun-Wed 11/1-5/15. **Reservations:** suggested, on weekends. **Features:** The varied menu dabbles in both German and American cuisine, with such tempting offerings as fresh fish, barbecue ribs, steaks, seafood and schnitzels. An alpine theme prevails in the casual dining room. Delicious desserts are made from scratch. Cocktails. **Parking:** on-site. **Cards:** DS, MC, VI.

🍸 ⊠

THE ORIGINAL FAMOUS DAVE'S
Lunch: $7-$19
Dinner: $7-$19
Phone: 715/462-3352

▼▼ ▼▼
Barbecue

Location: 8.5 mi e on CR B; in Grand Pines Resorts/Home of The Original Famous Dave's. 12355 W Richardson Bay Rd 54843. **Hours:** 10 am-10 pm, Sun from 8 am. Closed: 11/25, 12/24, 12/25. **Reservations:** suggested, summer. **Features:** The Southern-style barbecue shack, tucked amid the towering pines on Big Round Lake, is known for its flavorful, Texas-style beef brisket, Georgian-chopped pork, country roast chicken and pit barbecue ribs. During the summer, outdoor seating is a favorite. Casual dress; cocktails. **Parking:** on-site. **Cards:** AX, CB, DC, DS, MC, VI.

🍸 ⊠

HAZELHURST

——— WHERE TO DINE ———

JACOBI'S OF HAZELHURST
Dinner: $15-$25
Phone: 715/356-5591

▼▼ ▼▼
Continental

Location: 0.3 mi s on US 51, 0.3 mi w on Oneida St. 9820 Cedar Falls Rd 54531. **Hours:** 5 pm-9 pm, Sat-10 pm. Closed: Mon; Sun-Wed 10/15-5/1. **Features:** This intimate restaurant is easily recognized by its pastel house-like exterior with beautiful seasonal flower landscaping. A complimentary appetizer is served. Soup, bread and dessert are all made in-house. Try the signature garlic-stuffed beef filet. Casual dress; cocktails. **Parking:** on-site. **Cards:** MC, VI.

🍸 ⊠

Everything you need to travel. Including this handy bookmark.

Book in advance and as a AAA/CAA member you'll always save at Choice hotels.* Plus, it's easy to earn nights or flights with our reward programs at any of our over 3,000 locations across the U.S. Just visit your local AAA/CAA office or call 800.228.1AAA to book your next stay.

CHOICE HOTELS
INTERNATIONAL ®

**choicehotels.com
800.228.1AAA**

The Power of Being There. **GO** ®

CHOICE HOTELS INTERNATIONAL

Call us at 800.228.1AAA or visit us on the Web at choicehotels.com for more information and reservations.

AAA TourBookMark

Lodging Listing Symbols

Member Values
(see pg. 14)

- **AAA** Official Appointment
- **SAVE** Offers minimum 10% discount
- **ASK** May offer discount
- **S/D** Offers senior discount
- **fyi** Informational listing only

Member Services

- Airport transportation
- Pets allowed
- Restaurant on premises
- Restaurant off premises (walking distance)
- 24-hour room service
- Cocktail lounge
- Child care

Accessibility Features
(see pg. 18)

- Accessibility features
- Roll-in showers
- Hearing impaired

Leisure Activities

- Full Service Casino
- Pool
- Health Club on premises
- Health Club off premises
- Recreational activities

In-Room Amenities

- Non-smoking rooms
- No air conditioning
- No TV
- No Cable TV
- VCR
- Movies
- Data port/modem line
- No telephones
- Refrigerator
- Microwave
- Coffee maker

Call property for detailed information about fees & restrictions relating to the lodging listing symbols.

CHOICE HOTELS INTERNATIONAL ®1

Your trip across America starts here.

Econo Lodge ®

Rodeway Inn ®

CHOICE HOTELS INTERNATIONAL ®

choicehotels.com
800.228.1AAA

BEST WESTERN JANESVILLE *Book at aaa.com*   Phone: (608)756-4511

AAA (SAVE)
All Year   1P: $69-$199   2P: $69-$199   XP: $10   F18
Location: I-90, exit 171A (SR 26), just e. 3900 Milton Ave 53546. Fax: 608/756-0025. **Facility:** 105 one-bedroom standard units. 2-3 stories, interior corridors. **Parking:** on-site, winter plug-ins. **Terms:** cancellation fee imposed, small pets only ($10 fee). **Amenities:** voice mail, irons, hair dryers. **Dining:** 11 am-10 pm, Sat & Sun from 7 am, cocktails. **Pool(s):** heated indoor. **Leisure Activities:** whirlpool, domed recreation area, exercise
Small-scale Hotel   room. *Fee:* game room. **Guest Services:** valet laundry, area transportation. **Business Services:** meeting rooms. **Cards:** AX, DC, DS, MC, VI. **Special Amenities: free continental breakfast and free newspaper.**
(See color ad below)

SOME UNITS

HAMPTON INN-JANESVILLE *Book at aaa.com*   Phone: (608)754-4900

All Year [ECP]   1P: $79-$129   2P: $79-$129
Location: I-90, exit 171A (SR 26), just ne. 2400 Fulton St 53546. Fax: 608/754-4980. **Facility:** 99 one-bedroom standard units, some with whirlpools. 3 stories, interior corridors. *Bath:* combo or shower only. **Parking:** on-
Small-scale Hotel   site, winter plug-ins. **Amenities:** video games (fee), voice mail, irons, hair dryers. **Pool(s):** small heated indoor. **Leisure Activities:** whirlpool. **Guest Services:** valet laundry. **Business Services:** meeting rooms. **Cards:** AX, DC, DS, MC, VI.

SOME UNITS

HOLIDAY INN EXPRESS & JANESVILLE CONFERENCE CENTER *Book at aaa.com*   Phone: (608)756-3100

All Year [ECP]   1P: $77-$79   2P: $77-$79   XP: $8   F19
Location: I-90, exit 171C (US 14), just e. 3100 Wellington Pl 53546. Fax: 608/756-3111. **Facility:** 142 units. 137
Small-scale Hotel   one-bedroom standard units, some with whirlpools. 5 one-bedroom suites. 5 stories, interior corridors. *Bath:* combo or shower only. **Parking:** on-site. **Amenities:** voice mail, irons, hair dryers. **Pool(s):** heated indoor.
Leisure Activities: whirlpool, exercise room. *Fee:* game room. **Guest Services:** valet and coin laundry, area transportation.
Business Services: meeting rooms. **Cards:** AX, CB, DC, DS, JC, MC, VI.

SOME UNITS

MICROTEL INN *Book at aaa.com*   Phone: (608)752-3121

AAA (SAVE)
All Year [CP]   1P: $46-$66   2P: $46-$76   XP: $5   F16
Location: I-90, exit 171C (US 14), just se. 3121 Wellington Pl 53546. Fax: 608/752-3321. **Facility:** 61 one-bedroom standard units. 2 stories (no elevator), interior corridors. *Bath:* combo or shower only. **Parking:** on-site.
Terms: pets ($10 extra charge). **Guest Services:** valet laundry. **Business Services:** meeting rooms, fax
Small-scale Hotel   (fee). **Cards:** AX, CB, DC, DS, MC, VI. **Special Amenities: free continental breakfast and free local telephone calls.**

SOME UNITS

RAMADA INN *Book at aaa.com*   Phone: (608)756-2341

AAA (SAVE)
All Year   1P: $70-$82   2P: $80-$92   XP: $10   F17
Location: I-90, exit 171A (SR 26), just sw. 3431 Milton Ave 53545. Fax: 608/756-4183. **Facility:** 189 units. 188 one-bedroom standard units, some with whirlpools. 1 one-bedroom suite ($85-$210) with whirlpool. 2 stories (no elevator), interior corridors. **Parking:** on-site, winter plug-ins. **Terms:** [AP] meal plan available, package
Small-scale Hotel   plans. **Amenities:** video games (fee), voice mail, irons, hair dryers. *Some:* CD players. **Dining:** 6 am-2 & 5-9 pm, Sun 7 am-9 pm, cocktails. **Pool(s):** small heated indoor. **Leisure Activities:** sauna, whirlpool, putting green, exercise room. **Guest Services:** valet and coin laundry, area transportation. **Business Services:** meeting rooms.
Cards: AX, CB, DC, DS, JC, MC, VI. **Special Amenities: free local telephone calls and free newspaper.**

SOME UNITS

SELECT INN *Book at aaa.com*   Phone: (608)754-0251

AAA (SAVE)
All Year   1P: $35-$45   2P: $42-$52   XP: $5   F16
Location: I-90, exit 171A (SR 26), just sw. 3520 Milton Ave 53545. Fax: 608/754-0251. **Facility:** 62 units. 61 one-bedroom standard units. 1 one-bedroom suite. 2 stories, interior corridors. *Bath:* combo or shower only.
Parking: on-site. **Terms:** weekly rates available, [CP] meal plan available, small pets only ($25 deposit).
Small-scale Hotel   **Amenities:** safes (fee). *Some:* hair dryers. **Guest Services:** coin laundry. **Business Services:** fax (fee).
Cards: AX, DC, DS, MC, VI. **Special Amenities: free continental breakfast.** *(See color ad p 552)*

SOME UNITS

------ **WHERE TO DINE** ------

PEKING CHINESE RESTAURANT   **Lunch:** $4-$6   **Dinner:** $7-$14   **Phone:** 608-752-9177
Chinese
Location: On SR 26, 0.4 mi s of jct US 14. 2632 Milton Ave 53545. **Hours:** 11:30 am-2 & 4-10 pm. Closed major holidays; also Sun. **Reservations:** accepted. **Features:** Ornate Oriental appointments, such as hanging lamps and sconces, decorate the cozy dining room. Northern Mandarin and Szechuan specialties, as well as chef specials of Szechuan squid and Peking duck, are served in large portions. The luncheon menu offers an exceptionally good value. Family dinners are available in the evening. Casual dress; cocktails. **Parking:** on-site. **Cards:** DS, MC, VI.

ROHERTY'S   **Lunch:** $5-$12   **Dinner:** $9-$17   **Phone:** 608-752-2393
American
Location: On SR 26, 0.6 mi s of jct US 14. 2121 Milton Ave 53545. **Hours:** 11 am-9 pm, Fri & Sat-10 pm. Closed major holidays. **Reservations:** accepted. **Features:** Family-owned and operated since 1903, the restaurant is known for Irish dishes and such American standbys as salads, sandwiches, chicken, steak and seafood. Only USDA choice, corn-fed beef is served. Fish fry, a Wisconsin tradition, is available daily. Servers are friendly and prompt. Smoking is allowed only in the lounge. Casual dress; cocktails. **Parking:** on-site. **Cards:** AX, DS, MC, VI.

JEFFERSON pop. 7,338

------ **WHERE TO STAY** ------

RODEWAY INN   *Book at aaa.com*   **Phone:** (920)674-4404
Motel
All Year   1P: $55-$99   2P: $55-$99   XP: $5   F
Location: On SR 26, 1.2 mi s of jct US 18. Located in a commercial area. 1456 S Ryan Ave 53549. Fax: 920/674-9034. **Facility:** 42 one-bedroom standard units, some with whirlpools. 2 stories (no elevator), interior corridors. *Bath:* combo or shower only. **Parking:** on-site, winter plug-ins. **Terms:** 30 day cancellation notice, weekly rates available, [ECP] meal plan available, pets ($10 extra charge). **Amenities:** high-speed Internet. *Some:* irons, hair dryers. *Fee:* DVD players. **Pool(s):** small heated indoor. **Leisure Activities:** whirlpool, limited exercise equipment. **Guest Services:** coin laundry. **Business Services:** meeting rooms. **Cards:** AX, DC, DS, MC, VI.

JOHNSON CREEK pop. 1,581

------ **WHERE TO STAY** ------

DAYS INN-JOHNSON CREEK   *Book at aaa.com*   **Phone:** (920)699-8000
Small-scale Hotel
All Year   1P: $68-$90   2P: $68-$90   XP: $5   F12
Location: I-94, exit 267 (SR 26), just ne. W4545 Linmar Ln 53038 (PO Box 69). Fax: 920/699-8000. **Facility:** 45 units. 44 one-bedroom standard units, some with whirlpools. 1 one-bedroom suite with whirlpool. 2 stories (no elevator), interior corridors. *Bath:* combo or shower only. **Parking:** on-site, winter plug-ins. **Terms:** [CP] meal plan available, pets ($50 deposit, $5 extra charge). **Amenities:** hair dryers. *Some:* irons. **Pool(s):** small heated indoor. **Leisure Activities:** whirlpool, exercise room. *Fee:* game room. **Guest Services:** coin laundry. **Business Services:** meeting rooms, fax (fee). **Cards:** AX, CB, DC, DS, JC, MC, VI. **Special Amenities:** free continental breakfast and free local telephone calls. *(See color ad card insert)*

KAUKAUNA pop. 12,983

------ **WHERE TO STAY** ------

SETTLE INN   *Book at aaa.com*   **Phone:** (920)766-0088
Small-scale Hotel
1/1-3/31   1P: $55-$72   2P: $65-$82   XP: $5   F17
6/1-9/30   1P: $65-$75   2P: $70-$80   XP: $5   F17
4/1-5/31   1P: $57-$67   2P: $64-$74   XP: $5   F17
10/1-12/31   1P: $55-$65   2P: $60-$70   XP: $5   F17
Location: US 41, exit 148, just e. Located in a commercial area. 1201 Maloney Rd 54130. Fax: 920/766-9428. **Facility:** 46 one-bedroom standard units, some with whirlpools. 2 stories (no elevator), interior corridors. **Parking:** on-site. **Terms:** pets ($3 extra charge). **Amenities:** *Some:* hair dryers. **Pool(s):** heated indoor. **Leisure Activities:** whirlpool. **Guest Services:** coin laundry. **Cards:** AX, DS, MC, VI.

KENOSHA pop. 90,352

------ **WHERE TO STAY** ------

BEST WESTERN EXECUTIVE INN   *Book at aaa.com*   **Phone:** (262)857-7699
Small-scale Hotel
7/1-8/28 [CP]   1P: $94-$186   2P: $94-$186
8/29-3/31 [CP]   1P: $84-$167   2P: $84-$167
4/1-6/30 [CP]   1P: $82-$166   2P: $82-$166
Location: I-94, exit 344 (SR 50), just nw. Located in a commercial area. 7220 122nd Ave 53142. Fax: 262/857-2698. **Facility:** 116 units. 112 one-bedroom standard units. 4 one-bedroom suites, some with whirlpools. 4 stories, interior corridors. **Parking:** on-site. **Terms:** cancellation fee imposed. **Amenities:** video games (fee), voice mail, irons, hair dryers. **Pool(s):** small heated indoor. **Leisure Activities:** whirlpool. *Fee:* game room. **Guest Services:** valet laundry. **Business Services:** meeting rooms. **Cards:** AX, CB, DC, DS, MC, VI. **Special Amenities:** free continental breakfast and free newspaper.

COUNTRY INN & SUITES BY CARLSON   *Book at aaa.com*   Phone: (262)857-3680

(AAA) [SAVE]
▽▽▽▽

6/1-8/31	1P: $80-$120	2P: $87-$127	XP: $7	F18
9/1-3/31	1P: $75-$112	2P: $84-$119	XP: $7	F18
4/1-5/31	1P: $75-$110	2P: $82-$117	XP: $7	F18

Location: I-94, exit 344 (SR 50), just nw. Located in a commercial area. 7011 122nd Ave 53142. Fax: 262/857-3670.
Small-scale Hotel **Facility:** 89 units. 62 one-bedroom standard units, some with whirlpools. 27 one-bedroom suites ($100-$150). 3 stories, interior corridors. *Bath:* combo or shower only. **Parking:** on-site, winter plug-ins. **Terms:** [ECP] meal plan available, small pets only ($10 extra charge, with prior approval, in smoking units). **Amenities:** voice mail, irons, hair dryers. **Pool(s):** heated indoor. **Leisure Activities:** whirlpool, exercise room. *Fee:* game room. **Guest Services:** valet and coin laundry. **Business Services:** meeting rooms. **Cards:** AX, CB, DC, DS, MC, VI. **Special Amenities:** free expanded continental breakfast and free local telephone calls. *(See color ad starting on p 580 & below)*

SOME UNITS

[S▢] [🛏] [🍴] [🗣M] [♿] [🎥] [🏊] [✕] [🐾] [DATA PORT] [💻] / [✕] [🔒] [🖨] /
FEE

HOLIDAY INN EXPRESS-HARBORSIDE   *Book at aaa.com*   Phone: (262)658-3281

▽▽▽▽

5/28-8/29	1P: $89-$165	2P: $99-$175	XP: $10	F19
8/30-3/31	1P: $99-$145	2P: $109-$155	XP: $10	F19
4/1-5/27	1P: $89-$135	2P: $99-$145	XP: $10	F19

Small-scale Hotel **Location:** Just ne of jct SR 32 and 158; downtown. 5125 6th Ave 53140. Fax: 262/658-3420. **Facility:** 111 one-bedroom standard units. 5 stories, interior corridors. **Parking:** on-site. **Terms:** 2 night minimum stay - weekends 5/31-10/31, cancellation fee imposed, [ECP] meal plan available, small pets only ($25 fee). **Amenities:** high-speed Internet (fee), dual phone lines, voice mail, irons, hair dryers. **Pool(s):** wading. **Leisure Activities:** whirlpool. *Fee:* game room. **Guest Services:** complimentary evening beverages: Mon-Fri, valet and coin laundry. **Business Services:** conference facilities, administrative services (fee). **Cards:** AX, CB, DC, DS, JC, MC, VI.

SOME UNITS

[ASK] [S▢] [🛏] [🍴] [🎥] [⚕] [🐾] [DATA PORT] [💻] / [✕] [🔒] [🖨] /
FEE   FEE FEE

QUALITY SUITES   *Book at aaa.com*   Phone: (262)857-3450

(AAA) [SAVE]
▽▽▽▽

7/1-8/28 [BP]	1P: $109-$251	2P: $109-$251	
1/1-3/31 [BP]	1P: $101-$204	2P: $101-$204	
8/29-12/31 [BP]	1P: $98-$201	2P: $98-$201	
4/1-6/30 [BP]	1P: $97-$201	2P: $97-$201	

Small-scale Hotel **Location:** I-94, exit 344 (SR 50), just nw. Located in a commercial area. 7206 122nd Ave 53142. Fax: 262/857-2378. **Facility:** 72 units. 2 one-bedroom standard units. 70 one-bedroom suites, some with whirlpools. 3 stories, interior corridors. *Bath:* combo or shower only. **Parking:** on-site. **Terms:** cancellation fee imposed. **Amenities:** dual phone lines, voice mail, irons, hair dryers. *Fee:* video library, video games. **Pool(s):** small heated indoor. **Leisure Activities:** whirlpool, limited exercise equipment. *Fee:* game room. **Guest Services:** valet and coin laundry. **Business Services:** meeting rooms, business center. **Cards:** AX, CB, DC, DS, MC, VI. **Special Amenities:** free full breakfast and free local telephone calls.

SOME UNITS

[S▢] [✈] [🍴] [♿] [🎥] [🏊] [✕] [VCR] [⚕] [DATA PORT] [🔒] [🖨] [💻] / [✕] /

--------- **WHERE TO DINE** ---------

BOAT HOUSE PUB & EATERY   **Lunch:** $8-$22   **Dinner:** $8-$22   **Phone:** 262/654-9922

▽▽▽ ▽▽▽
American

Location: Just ne of jct SR 32 and 158; downtown. 4917 7th Ave 53140. **Hours:** 11 am-10 pm, Sat & Sun from 8 am. Closed: 12/25 & Easter. **Reservations:** accepted. **Features:** The nautical-themed restaurant affords great views of Lake Michigan, particularly from the seasonal outdoor seating. Although the menu focus is on seafood, other offerings include sandwiches, barbecue chicken and ribs, weekly specials and such homemade soups as fresh clam chowder. Courtesy customer docking is available. Casual dress; cocktails. **Parking:** on-site. **Cards:** AX, DS, MC, VI.

[🍽] [✕]

MANGIA

Italian

Lunch: $8-$15 **Dinner:** $13-$26 **Phone:** 262/652-4285

Location: On SR 32 N, 0.4 mi n of jct SR 50. 5717 Sheridan Rd 53140. **Hours:** 11:30 am-2 & 5-9 pm, Fri-10 pm, Sat 5 pm-10 pm, Sun 4 pm-9 pm. Closed major holidays. **Reservations:** suggested. **Features:** Among outstanding offerings are fresh seafood, wonderful pasta and daily specials. Aromas of rosemary, garlic and a hint of smoke from the wood-burning oven waft through the air. Representative of delectable in-house desserts are tiramisu and creme brulee. Dressy casual; cocktails. **Parking:** on-site (fee). **Cards:** AX, DS, MC, VI.

TASTE OF WISCONSIN

American

Lunch: $6-$12 **Dinner:** $6-$12 **Phone:** 262/857-9110

Location: I-94, exit 344 (SR 50), 0.3 mi w. 7515 125th Ave 53142. **Hours:** 9 am-9 pm. Closed: 12/25; also for dinner 12/24. **Reservations:** accepted. **Features:** Wisconsin's German heritage is reflected in the restaurant's food. Entrees made from fresh ingredients include bratwurst, sausage and split roast chicken. The on-premises bakery provides bread and tempting desserts. Not surprisingly, cheese and a selection of local microbrews are popular, too. Casual dress; cocktails. **Parking:** on-site. **Cards:** AX, DS, MC, VI.

KEWAUNEE pop. 2,806

——— WHERE TO STAY ———

THE HISTORIC KARSTEN INN *Book at aaa.com* **Phone:** (920)388-3800

Small-scale Hotel

5/24-10/31	1P: $79-$149	2P: $79-$149	XP: $10	F12
4/1-5/23 & 11/1-3/31	1P: $59-$89	2P: $59-$89	XP: $10	F12

Location: Center. 122 Ellis St 54216. Fax: 920/388-3808. **Facility:** 23 one-bedroom standard units, some with whirlpools. 3 stories (no elevator), interior corridors. *Bath:* combo or tub only. **Parking:** on-site. **Terms:** 3 day cancellation notice-fee imposed, [ECP] meal plan available, small pets only ($25 fee). **Amenities:** voice mail, irons, hair dryers. **Dining:** Zum Engel, see separate listing. **Business Services:** meeting rooms. **Cards:** AX, DC, DS, MC, VI.

——— WHERE TO DINE ———

PORT O'CALL

American

Lunch: $5-$7 **Dinner:** $11-$20 **Phone:** 920/388-4883

Location: On SR 42; center. 310 Milwaukee St 54216. **Hours:** 11 am-9 pm; hours may vary. Closed: 11/25, 12/25 & Easter. **Features:** Overlooking the harbor, the casual restaurant and lounge affords a good view of the activities on the water. Casual dress; cocktails. **Parking:** on-site. **Cards:** MC, VI.

ZUM ENGEL

German

Lunch: $4-$7 **Dinner:** $10-$19 **Phone:** 920/388-3800

Location: Center; in The Historic Karsten Inn. 122 Ellis St 54216. **Hours:** 11:30 am-1:30 & 5-8 pm, Fri & Sat-9 pm, Sun 10 am-2 pm. Closed: Mon. **Reservations:** accepted. **Features:** In the city's oldest inn, the Victorian-style dining room serves some of the area's best German fare. Friday night ushers in a popular land-and-sea buffet. Casual dress; beer & wine only. **Parking:** on-site. **Cards:** AX, DC, DS, MC, VI.

KIMBERLY pop. 6,146

——— WHERE TO STAY ———

AMERIHOST INN-KIMBERLY *Book at aaa.com* **Phone:** (920)788-4400

Small-scale Hotel

All Year [ECP]	1P: $69-$199	2P: $79-$199	XP: $10	F18

Location: US 41, exit 145 (SR 441), 2.7 mi s to CR CE, then 0.4 mi e. Located in a commercial area. 761 Truman St 54136. Fax: 920/788-4466. **Facility:** 63 one-bedroom standard units, some with whirlpools. 2 stories (no elevator), interior corridors. *Bath:* combo or shower only. **Parking:** on-site. **Amenities:** voice mail, safes (fee), irons, hair dryers. **Pool(s):** heated indoor. **Leisure Activities:** sauna, whirlpool, exercise room. **Guest Services:** valet laundry. **Business Services:** meeting rooms. **Cards:** AX, DC, DS, MC, VI. **Special Amenities:** free expanded continental breakfast and free local telephone calls.

SOME UNITS

HILTON GARDEN INN *Book at aaa.com* **Phone:** (920)730-1900

Small-scale Hotel

All Year	1P: $79-$209	2P: $79-$209	XP: $10	F17

Location: US 41, exit 145 (SR 441), 2.7 mi s to CR CE, then 0.4 mi e. Located in a commercial area. 720 Eisenhower Dr 54136. Fax: 920/734-7565. **Facility:** 125 one-bedroom standard units, some with whirlpools. 5 stories, interior corridors. *Bath:* combo or shower only. **Parking:** on-site. **Amenities:** video games, high-speed Internet, dual phone lines, voice mail, irons, hair dryers. **Dining:** 6:30 am-10 & 5-9 pm, Sat & Sun 7-11 am, cocktails. **Pool(s):** heated indoor. **Leisure Activities:** whirlpool, exercise room. **Guest Services:** sundries, valet and coin laundry. **Business Services:** meeting rooms, business center. **Cards:** AX, CB, DC, DS, JC, MC, VI. **Special Amenities:** free newspaper.

SOME UNITS

KOHLER pop. 1,926

——— WHERE TO STAY ———

THE AMERICAN CLUB

Book at aaa.com

(AAA) (SAVE)
▼▼▼▼▼

Classic Historic Resort Large-Scale Hotel

5/1-10/31	1P: $245-$275	2P: $275-$305	XP: $15 F16
11/1-3/31	1P: $145-$185	2P: $175-$215	XP: $15 F16
4/1-4/30	1P: $142-$182	2P: $172-$212	XP: $15 F16

Phone: (920)457-8000

Location: I-43, exit 126, 0.5 mi w on SR 23, 1 mi s on CR Y and Highland Dr. Located in a residential area. Highland Dr 53044. Fax: 920/457-0299. **Facility:** Built in 1918 to house workers for the Kohler Company, this grand resort offers extensive grounds and year-round recreational activities. 237 units. 216 one-bedroom standard units with whirlpools. 21 one-bedroom suites ($310-$1015) with whirlpools. 3 stories, interior corridors. **Parking:** on-site and valet. **Terms:** check-in 4 pm, 2-3 night minimum stay - weekends in summer, 7 day cancellation notice-fee imposed, package plans, no pets allowed (kennels available). **Amenities:** video games (fee), CD players, dual phone lines, voice mail, safes, honor bars, irons, hair dryers. *Some:* high-speed Internet. **Dining:** 6:30 am-11 pm, cocktails, also, The Immigrant Restaurant & Winery, The Wisconsin Room, The Horse & Plow, Blackwolf Run, see separate listings. **Pool(s):** 2 heated indoor, small heated indoor. **Leisure Activities:** saunas, whirlpools, steamrooms, rental canoes, rental paddleboats, fishing, ice skating, tobogganing, recreation programs, rental bicycles, hiking trails, jogging, spa. *Fee:* charter fishing, golf-72 holes, 12 tennis courts (8 indoor, 12 lighted), cross country skiing, snowmobiling, carriage rides, dog sledding, trap shooting, horseback riding. **Guest Services:** gift shop, valet laundry, airport transportation (fee)-Sheboygan County Municipal Airport, area transportation-within village. **Business Services:** conference facilities, business center. **Cards:** AX, CB, DC, DS, MC, VI. **Special Amenities: free newspaper and free room upgrade (subject to availability with advanced reservations).** *(See color ad p 578)*

SOME UNITS

[icons] FEE ... DATA PORT ... VCR FEE

INN ON WOODLAKE

Book at aaa.com

(AAA) (SAVE)
▼▼▼

Small-scale Hotel

5/1-10/31	1P: $157-$172	2P: $177-$192	XP: $10 F16
11/1-3/31	1P: $95-$125	2P: $115-$125	XP: $10 F16
4/1-4/30	1P: $92-$102	2P: $112-$122	XP: $10 F16

Phone: (920)452-7800

Location: I-43, exit 126, 0.5 mi w on SR 23, 0.5 mi s on CR Y and Highland Dr; in Woodlake Shopping Center. 705 Woodlake Rd 53044. Fax: 920/452-6288. **Facility:** 121 one-bedroom standard units, some with whirlpools. 3 stories, interior corridors. **Bath:** combo or shower only. **Parking:** on-site. **Terms:** check-in 4 pm, 2-3 night minimum stay - weekends in summer, 7 day cancellation notice-fee imposed, package plans, no pets allowed (kennels available). **Amenities:** video games (fee), CD players, dual phone lines, voice mail, irons, hair dryers. **Leisure Activities:** fishing, hiking trails, jogging. *Fee:* some American Club privileges. **Guest Services:** valet and coin laundry, area transportation-health club. **Business Services:** meeting rooms. **Cards:** AX, CB, DC, DS, MC, VI. **Special Amenities: free continental breakfast and free newspaper.** *(See color ad p 578)*

SOME UNITS

[icons] FEE ... DATA PORT ... VCR FEE

——— WHERE TO DINE ———

BLACKWOLF RUN
▼▼▼▼
American

Lunch: $7-$15   **Dinner: $17-$30**   **Phone: 920/457-4446**

Location: I-43, exit 126, 0.5 mi w on SR 23, 1 mi s on CR Y and Highland Dr; in Blackwolf Run Golf Course Club House; at The American Club. 1111 W Riverside Dr 53044. **Hours:** 11 am-10 pm; from 6 am 5/1-10/31; 11 am-3 & 6-10 pm 11/1-4/30. Closed: Sun, Mon 11/1-4/30. **Reservations:** suggested. **Features:** In the clubhouse of the Blackwolf Run PGA Championship Golf Course, the impressive Canadian log cabin structure overlooks the Sheboygan River and golf course. The seasonally changing menu features hearty portions of foods from the heartland. Specialties include Angus beef, wild game, fish, seafood and free-range chicken. Casual dress; cocktails. **Parking:** on-site. **Cards:** AX, CB, DC, DS, JC, MC, VI.

CUCINA
▼▼▼
Italian

Lunch: $7-$15   **Dinner: $14-$20**   **Phone: 920/452-3888**

Location: I-43, exit 126, 0.5 mi w on SR 23, 0.5 mi s on CR Y and Highland Dr; in Woodlake Shopping Center. 725 E Woodlake Rd 53044. **Hours:** 11 am-9:30 pm, Fri & Sat-10 pm. Closed: 1/1, 11/25, 12/25. **Reservations:** suggested. **Features:** Delicious pasta, veal, seafood and gourmet pizza are among the traditional dishes available at this bistro. Fresh ingredients, ample use of garlic, eye-catching dessert presentations and professional service complete the dining experience. Window tables and the seasonal terrace overlook Wood Lake. Casual dress; cocktails. **Parking:** on-site. **Cards:** AX, DC, DS, MC, VI.

THE HORSE & PLOW
▼▼▼
American

Lunch: $9-$12   **Dinner: $10-$19**   **Phone: 920/457-8888**

Location: I-43, exit 126, 0.5 mi w on SR 23, 1 mi s on CR Y and Highland Dr; in The American Club. Highland Dr 53044. **Hours:** 11 am-10 pm. **Features:** Comfortable booths, lovely glass and a caring staff make this a popular spot. The menu offers a wide variety of items such as Wisconsin three cheese soup, Sheboygan sausage, quesadillas, wings, burgers, sandwiches and salads. A very large screen TV keeps sports fans up-to-date on the latest events. Casual dress; cocktails. **Parking:** on-site. **Cards:** AX, CB, DC, DS, JC, MC, VI.

THE IMMIGRANT RESTAURANT & WINERY
▼▼▼ ▼▼▼
Regional American

Dinner: $30-$45   **Phone: 920/457-8888**

Location: I-43, exit 126, 0.5 mi w on SR 23, 1 mi s on CR Y and Highland Dr; in The American Club. Highland Dr 53044. **Hours:** 6 pm-10 pm. Closed: Sun & Mon 11/1-4/30. **Reservations:** suggested. **Features:** What once housed a bowling alley and laundry for immigrant workers now celebrates the heritage of people who helped grow Kohler Co. into a multinational corporation. The menu is contemporary, and adventurous offerings incorporate international influences. Service is formal and detailed while remaining refreshingly unpretentious. For a special treat, consider the seven-course degustation menu paired with specially selected wines. Semi-formal attire; cocktails. **Parking:** on-site and valet. **Cards:** AX, CB, DC, DS, JC, MC, VI.

THE WISCONSIN ROOM
▼▼▼
Regional American

Dinner: $19-$34   **Phone: 920/457-8888**

Location: I-43, exit 126, 0.5 mi w on SR 23, 1 mi s on CR Y and Highland Dr; in The American Club. Highland Dr 53044. **Hours:** 6:30 am-11 & 6-9 pm, Sat 6:30 am-11:30 & 6-10 pm, Sun 7 am-1 & 6-10 pm. **Reservations:** suggested. **Features:** The main dining room features a menu of Wisconsin and regional specialties that incorporate products from the upper Midwest. The wine list is all American. Dressy casual; cocktails. **Parking:** on-site and valet. **Cards:** AX, CB, DC, DS, JC, MC, VI.

LA CROSSE pop. 51,818

──────── WHERE TO STAY ────────

BEST WESTERN-MIDWAY HOTEL   *Book at aaa.com*   **Phone:** (608)781-7000

| | 6/1-10/31 | 1P: $89-$123 | 2P: $99-$133 | XP: $10 | F17 |
| | 4/1-5/31 & 11/1-3/31 | 1P: $86-$119 | 2P: $96-$129 | XP: $10 | F17 |

Location: I-90, exit 3, 1 mi s on US 53. 1835 Rose St 54603. Fax: 608/781-3195. **Facility:** 121 one-bedroom standard units, some with whirlpools. 2 stories (no elevator), interior corridors. **Parking:** on-site, winter plug-ins.
Small-scale Hotel **Terms:** [AP] meal plan available. **Amenities:** video library (fee), dual phone lines, voice mail, irons, hair dryers. *Some:* high-speed Internet. **Dining:** 6:30 am-10 pm, Sat & Sun from 7 am, cocktails, entertainment. **Pool(s):** heated indoor. **Leisure Activities:** sauna, whirlpool, boat dock, miniature golf, domed recreation area, exercise room, volleyball. **Guest Services:** valet laundry, area transportation-Amtrak station. **Business Services:** meeting rooms. **Cards:** AX, DC, DS, MC, VI. *(See color ad below)*

SOME UNITS

🅂⬇ ✈ 🍴 🍸 📷 ⇌ ✕ VCR 👟 DATA PORT 🖥 / ✕ 🔒 📷 /

BROOKSTONE INN   *Book at aaa.com*   **Phone:** (608)781-1400
| | 4/1-10/31 [CP] | 1P: $49-$80 | 2P: $55-$85 |
| | 11/1-3/31 [CP] | 1P: $49-$70 | 2P: $55-$70 |

Location: I-90, exit 3, 1 mi s on US 53. 1830 Rose St 54603. Fax: 608/781-3948. **Facility:** 84 units. 82 one-bedroom standard units, some with whirlpools. 2 one-bedroom suites ($85-$140). 3 stories, interior corridors.
Small-scale Hotel **Parking:** on-site. **Terms:** cancellation fee imposed. **Amenities:** irons, hair dryers. **Pool(s):** small heated indoor. **Leisure Activities:** whirlpool, limited exercise equipment. *Fee:* game room. **Guest Services:** valet laundry. **Business Services:** meeting rooms, fax (fee). **Cards:** AX, CB, DC, DS, MC, VI. **Special Amenities:** free continental breakfast and free local telephone calls. *(See color ad below)*

SOME UNITS

🅂⬇ 🍴 🍸 ⇌ ✕ 👟 DATA PORT 🖥 / ✕ 🔒 📷 /

CHATEAU LA CROSSE   *Book at aaa.com*
AAA **SAVE**   All Year [BP]   1P: $99-$200   2P: $135-$225   XP: $50   Phone: 608/796-1090
Historic Country Inn   **Location:** On SR 16 at jct US 53; downtown; at east end of Mississippi River Bridge. 410 Cass St 54601. Fax: 608/796-0700. **Facility:** This 1854 stone house, known as the Mons Anderson House, features decoratively painted ceilings, ornate wood floors and several antique fireplaces. Smoke free premises. 6 units. 5 one-bedroom standard units, some with whirlpools. 1 two-bedroom suite ($125-$350) with kitchen. 4 stories (no elevator), interior/exterior corridors. *Bath:* combo or shower only. **Parking:** on-site. **Terms:** check-in 4 pm, age restrictions may apply, cancellation fee imposed, weekly rates available, no pets allowed (owner's pet on premises). **Amenities:** video library, hair dryers. **Dining:** 7 am-8 pm; dinner by reservation only, cocktails. **Guest Services:** gift shop, complimentary laundry, area transportation-train and bus depots. **Business Services:** fax. **Cards:** AX, CB, DC, DS, MC, VI.

SOME UNITS

COURTYARD BY MARRIOTT-DOWNTOWN
MISSISSIPPI RIVERFRONT   *Book at aaa.com*   Phone: 608/782-1000
    4/1-10/31   1P: $92-$139   2P: $92-$139
    11/1-3/31   1P: $89-$139   2P: $89-$139
Small-scale Hotel   **Location:** Just w of US 53; downtown. 500 Front St 54601. Fax: 608/796-1827. **Facility:** 78 one-bedroom standard units, some with kitchens and/or whirlpools. 3 stories, interior corridors. *Bath:* combo or shower only. **Parking:** on-site. **Amenities:** dual phone lines, voice mail, irons, hair dryers. **Pool(s):** small heated indoor. **Leisure Activities:** whirlpool, limited exercise equipment. **Guest Services:** valet and coin laundry, area transportation. **Business Services:** meeting rooms. **Cards:** AX, CB, DC, DS, JC, MC, VI.

SOME UNITS

DAYS INN HOTEL & CONFERENCE CENTER   *Book at aaa.com*   Phone: (608)783-1000
AAA **SAVE**   5/1-10/31   1P: $94-$99   2P: $94-$99   XP: $5   F18
    4/1-4/30 & 11/1-3/31   1P: $79-$89   2P: $79-$89   XP: $5   F18
Small-scale Hotel   **Location:** I-90, exit 3, just sw; on French Island. 101 Sky Harbour Dr 54603. Fax: 608/783-2948. **Facility:** 148 units. 144 one-bedroom standard units. 4 one-bedroom suites with whirlpools. 2 stories (no elevator), interior corridors. **Parking:** on-site. **Terms:** [AP] meal plan available, pets ($10 extra charge). **Amenities:** voice mail, hair dryers. *Some:* irons. **Dining:** 6:30 am-1 & 5-9 pm, Sat-10 pm, Sun 6:30 am-9 pm, cocktails. **Pool(s):** heated indoor. **Leisure Activities:** whirlpool, limited exercise equipment. **Guest Services:** valet laundry. **Business Services:** meeting rooms, fax (fee). **Cards:** AX, CB, DC, DS, MC, VI. **Special Amenities:** free local telephone calls and free newspaper.** *(See color ad card insert)*

SOME UNITS

FEE

EXEL INN OF LA CROSSE   *Book at aaa.com*   Phone: (608)781-0400
AAA **SAVE**   All Year [CP]   1P: $37-$57   2P: $43-$63   XP: $6   F18
Small-scale Hotel   **Location:** I-90, exit 3, 0.8 mi s on US 53. 2150 Rose St 54603. Fax: 608/781-1216. **Facility:** 101 one-bedroom standard units, some with whirlpools. 2 stories (no elevator), interior corridors. **Parking:** on-site. **Terms:** weekly rates available, small pets only (in smoking units). **Amenities:** irons. **Leisure Activities:** limited exercise equipment. **Guest Services:** coin laundry. **Business Services:** fax (fee). **Cards:** AX, CB, DC, DS, MC, VI. **Special Amenities:** free continental breakfast and early check-in/late check-out.

SOME UNITS

FEE FEE

GUEST HOUSE MOTEL   Phone: (608)784-8840
AAA **SAVE**   All Year   1P: $55-$65   2P: $60-$75   XP: $6   F12
Small-scale Hotel   **Location:** 0.5 mi s on US 14, 61 and SR 33. 810 S 4th St 54601. Fax: 608/782-5598. **Facility:** 39 one-bedroom standard units. 2 stories (no elevator), interior corridors. *Bath:* combo or shower only. **Parking:** on-site, winter plug-ins. **Terms:** small pets only ($10 deposit). **Amenities:** voice mail. **Dining:** 7-11 am, Sun 7:30-11:30 am. **Pool(s):** small heated outdoor. **Business Services:** fax (fee). **Cards:** AX, DC, MC, VI.

SOME UNITS

FEE

HAMPTON INN   *Book at aaa.com*   Phone: (608)781-5100
    5/1-10/31 [ECP]   1P: $69-$129   2P: $69-$129
Small-scale Hotel   4/1-4/30 & 11/1-3/31 [ECP]   1P: $69-$89   2P: $69-$89
Location: I-90, exit 3, 0.9 mi s on US 53. 2110 Rose St 54603. Fax: 608/781-3574. **Facility:** 101 one-bedroom standard units. 2 stories (no elevator), interior corridors. **Parking:** on-site. **Amenities:** video games (fee), high-speed Internet, voice mail, irons, hair dryers. **Pool(s):** small heated indoor. **Leisure Activities:** whirlpool, limited exercise equipment. **Guest Services:** valet laundry. **Business Services:** meeting rooms, fax (fee). **Cards:** AX, DC, DS, MC, VI.

SOME UNITS

FEE FEE

HOLIDAY INN HOTEL & SUITES *Book at aaa.com* Phone: (608)784-4444

AAA SAVE

WWWW

Small-scale Hotel

6/1-9/30	1P: $109-$129	2P: $109-$129	XP: $10	F17
4/1-5/31 & 10/1-3/31	1P: $99-$109	2P: $99-$109	XP: $10	F17

Location: Downtown. 200 Pearl St 54601. Fax: 608/784-4480. **Facility:** 114 one-bedroom standard units, some with whirlpools. 5 stories, interior corridors. *Bath:* combo or shower only. **Parking:** on-site. **Terms:** check-in 4 pm. **Amenities:** voice mail, irons, hair dryers. *Fee:* video games, high-speed Internet. *Some:* dual phone lines. **Dining:** 6:30 am-10 pm, Sat & Sun from 7 am, cocktails. **Pool(s):** small heated indoor. **Leisure Activities:** whirlpool. **Guest Services:** valet and coin laundry. **Business Services:** meeting rooms, fax (fee). **Cards:** AX, CB, DC, DS, JC, MC, VI. **Special Amenities:** free local telephone calls and free newspaper. *(See color ad below)*

SOME UNITS

THE RADISSON HOTEL LA CROSSE   *Book at aaa.com*   **Phone:** (608)784-6680

⬢⬢ [SAVE]   All Year   1P: $129-$169   2P: $139-$179   XP: $15   F17

▽▽▽▽▽   **Location:** Just w of US 53; downtown. 200 Harborview Plaza 54601. Fax: 608/784-6694. **Facility:** 169 one-bedroom standard units, some with whirlpools. 8 stories, interior corridors. **Parking:** on-site. **Terms:** small pets only. **Amenities:** dual phone lines, voice mail, irons, hair dryers. **Dining:** 2 restaurants, 6:30 am-11 pm, Fri & Sat from 7 am, cocktails. **Pool(s):** heated indoor. **Leisure Activities:** whirlpool, exercise room. *Fee:* game room. **Guest Services:** gift shop, valet laundry. **Business Services:** conference facilities. **Cards:** AX, CB, DC, DS, MC, VI. **Special Amenities: free newspaper and free room upgrade (subject to availability with advanced reservations).** *(See color ad p 536 & p 583)*

Large-scale Hotel

SOME UNITS

✈ 🛏 📶 🍴 📺 🌀 🐾 ✕ 🍽 [DATA PORT] 🖥 / ✕ [VCR] 🔌 📠 /
FEE

SUPER 8 OF LA CROSSE   *Book at aaa.com*   **Phone:** (608)781-8880

⬢⬢ [SAVE]   All Year   1P: $69-$99   2P: $76-$113

▽▽ ▽▽   **Location:** I-90, exit 3, 1.2 mi s on US 53. 1625 Rose St 54603. Fax: 608/781-4366. **Facility:** 82 one-bedroom standard units, some with whirlpools. 2 stories (no elevator), interior corridors. **Parking:** on-site. **Terms:** [CP] meal plan available. **Amenities:** voice mail, hair dryers. **Pool(s):** heated indoor. **Leisure Activities:** whirlpool, exercise room. **Guest Services:** coin laundry. **Cards:** AX, DC, DS, MC, VI. **Special Amenities: free continental breakfast and free local telephone calls.**

Small-scale Hotel

SOME UNITS

[S�W]🐾🍽[DATA PORT]🖥 / ✕ [VCR] 🔌 📠 /

──────── **WHERE TO DINE** ────────

DOC POWELL'S   **Lunch:** $6-$16   **Dinner:** $6-$16   **Phone:** 608/785-7026

▽▽▽▽   **Location:** Just w of US 53; downtown. 200 Main St 54601. **Hours:** 11 am-10 pm. Closed: 7/4, 12/25; also Sun.

American   **Reservations:** accepted. **Features:** Named after a local historic figure, the restaurant is known for its microbrews, diverse menu and homemade bread pudding. Creativity is exhibited in the recipes and food presentations. Casual dress; cocktails. **Parking:** street. **Cards:** AX, DC, DS, MC, VI.   🍽 ✕

EDWARDO'S PIZZA WAGON   **Dinner:** $8-$14   **Phone:** 608/783-8282

▽▽▽▽   **Location:** I-90, exit 3, 0.5 mi s. 1930 Rose St 54601. **Hours:** 4 pm-11 pm. Closed major holidays.

American   **Reservations:** accepted. **Features:** Family-owned and operated since 1955, the restaurant prepares pizzas in a wood-fired oven. Natural ingredients, custom dough and fresh vegetables make the pizza a standout. An extensive beer selection is offered. Casual dress; cocktails. **Parking:** on-site. **Cards:** AX,

MC, VI.   🍽 ✕

THE FREIGHT HOUSE RESTAURANT   Historic   **Dinner:** $9-$30   **Phone:** 608/784-6211

⬢⬢   **Location:** Just w of US 53; downtown. 107 Vine 54601. **Hours:** 5:30 pm-10 pm, Fri & Sat 5 pm-10:30 pm, Sun

▽▽▽▽   5 pm-9:30 pm. Closed: 11/25, 12/24, 12/25 & Easter. **Reservations:** suggested. **Features:** The former railroad freight house, built in the late 1800s, features timbers, three fireplaces and historic pictures. Menu offerings include teriyaki preparations of chicken and steak. Prime rib and Alaskan crab legs are complemented by many wines. Casual dress; cocktails. **Parking:** on-site. **Cards:** AX, DC, DS, MC, VI.

American   🍽 ✕

MR D'S   **Lunch:** $5-$7   **Dinner:** $5-$7   **Phone:** 608/784-6737

▽   **Location:** 0.4 mi e of US 53, jct West Ave and State St; downtown. 1146 State St 54601. **Hours:** 6 am-3 pm, Fri & Sat-7:30 pm. Closed major holidays. **Features:** A local fixture since 1967, the neighborhood cafe delivers lighter fare: creative sandwiches, hearty soup and mouthwatering baked goods, especially its signature fritters. Friendly servers in street clothes show menu familiarity and good follow-up. Casual dress; wine only. **Parking:** on-site. **Cards:** AX, DS, MC, VI.

American   ✕

PICASSO'S CAFE   **Lunch:** $6-$9   **Dinner:** $6-$17   **Phone:** 608/784-4485

▽▽▽▽   **Location:** I-90, exit 3, 3.2 mi s on US 53; in Sampson Gallery. 600 N Third St 54601. **Hours:** 7 am-9 pm, Fri-10 pm, Sat 8 am-10 pm, Sun 8 am-3 pm. Closed: 7/4, 11/25, 12/25. **Reservations:** accepted. **Features:** Voodoo fettuccine, blackened chicken pita, seafood sparkler and the very veggie sandwich are examples of unusual selections on the restaurant's diverse menu. Lots of windows and fun artwork give this cafe a California feel. Desserts are homemade. Casual dress; cocktails. **Parking:** on-site. **Cards:** AX, DS, MC, VI.   ✕

American

PIGGY'S RESTAURANT   **Dinner:** $9-$28   **Phone:** 608/784-4877

▽▽▽▽   **Location:** Just w of US 53; downtown. 328 S Front St 54601. **Hours:** 5 pm-10 pm, Sun 4 pm-9 pm. Closed: 11/25, 12/25; also 5/27, 12/24 for dinner. **Reservations:** suggested. **Features:** Hickory-smoked, American-cut pork chops, baby back ribs, prime steak and seafood are specialties at this restaurant on the Mississippi River. The comprehensive wine list is lengthier than the menu. The antique wood bar is a focal point of the dining room. Casual dress; cocktails. **Parking:** on-site. **Cards:** AX, CB, DC, DS, MC, VI.   ✕

American

LADYSMITH pop. 3,932

──────── **WHERE TO STAY** ────────

AMERICINN LODGE AND SUITES   *Book at aaa.com*   **Phone:** 715-532-7811

▽▽▽▽   All Year   1P: $69-$119   2P: $75-$125   XP: $6   F12

Small-scale Hotel   **Location:** On SR 27, 0.5 mi s of US 8. 700 W 9th St S 54848. Fax: 715/532-7397. **Facility:** Smoke free premises. 41 units. 38 one-bedroom standard units, some with whirlpools. 3 one-bedroom suites ($80-$130), some with whirlpools. 2 stories (no elevator), interior corridors. *Bath:* combo or shower only. **Parking:** on-site. **Amenities:** high-speed Internet, hair dryers. *Some:* irons. **Pool(s):** heated indoor, wading. **Leisure Activities:** sauna, whirlpool. **Guest Services:** gift shop, coin laundry. **Business Services:** meeting rooms. **Cards:** AX, DC, DS, MC, VI. *(See color ad p 576)*

SOME UNITS

[ASK] 📺 🐾 ✕ 🍽 [DATA PORT] 🖥 / 🔌 📠 /

AMERICINN MOTEL *Book at aaa.com* Phone: 715/532-6650

◆◆◆ 9/15-3/31 1P: $62-$103 2P: $68-$109 XP: $6 F12
4/1-9/14 1P: $59-$100 2P: $65-$106 XP: $6 F12

Small-scale Hotel **Location:** On SR 27, 0.5 mi s of US 8. 800 W College Ave 54848. Fax: 715/532-6987. **Facility:** 38 one-bedroom standard units. 2 stories, interior corridors. *Bath:* combo or shower only. **Parking:** on-site, winter plug-ins. **Terms:** [ECP] meal plan available. **Pool(s):** small heated indoor. **Leisure Activities:** sauna, whirlpool. **Business Services:** meeting rooms. **Cards:** AX, DS, MC, VI. *(See color ad p 576)*

SOME UNITS

ASK ⓈD 📶 🏊 🎥 DATA PORT 💻 / ✕ VCR 🔌 📷 /

LAKE DELTON pop. 1,982

──────── **WHERE TO STAY** ────────

LAKE DELTON TRAVELODGE Phone: 608/355-0700

◆◆ Property failed to provide current rates
Location: I-90/94, exit 92 (US 12), just s. E 10892 Fern Dell Rd 53940. Fax: 608/355-0793. **Facility:** 100 one-bedroom standard units. 3 stories, interior corridors. *Bath:* combo or shower only. **Parking:** on-site. **Pool(s):** heated indoor, wading. **Leisure Activities:** whirlpool. *Fee:* game room. **Guest Services:** coin laundry.

Small-scale Hotel

SOME UNITS

🛏 🏃M 🏊 🎥 DATA PORT 💻 / ✕ /

LAKE GENEVA pop. 7,148

──────── **WHERE TO STAY** ────────

BELLA VISTA SUITES HOTEL *Book at aaa.com* Phone: (262)248-2100

AAA SAVE 6/12-9/4 [CP] 1P: $208-$284 2P: $208-$284 XP: $15 F12
4/1-6/11 & 9/5-3/31 [CP] 1P: $142-$200 2P: $142-$200 XP: $15 F12

◆◆◆ **Location:** Just s of SR 50. Located across from Lake Geneva. 335 Wrigley Dr 53147. Fax: 262/248-2125. **Facility:** Smoke free premises. 39 units. 33 one- and 6 two-bedroom suites with whirlpools, some with Small-scale Hotel kitchens. 4 stories, interior corridors. *Bath:* combo or shower only. **Parking:** on-site. **Terms:** check-in 4 pm, 2 night minimum stay - weekends 6/11-9/4, 3 day cancellation notice-fee imposed, package plans. **Amenities:** video library (fee), dual phone lines, voice mail, irons, hair dryers. *Some:* DVD players, CD players. **Dining:** 5:30-10:30 pm; closed Mon, cocktails. **Pool(s):** heated indoor. **Leisure Activities:** whirlpool, exercise room. *Fee:* boat dock, massage. **Guest Services:** valet laundry. **Business Services:** meeting rooms. **Cards:** AX, DC, DS, MC, VI. **Special Amenities:** free continental breakfast and free newspaper.

ⓈD 🍴 🏃M 🏊 ✕ ✕ VCR DATA PORT 🔌 📷 💻

BUDGET HOST DIPLOMAT MOTEL Phone: (262)248-1809

AAA SAVE 5/30-9/15 1P: $68-$88 2P: $78-$98 XP: $10 F12
4/1-5/29 1P: $48-$71 2P: $58-$81 XP: $10 F12
◆◆ ◆◆ 9/16-3/31 1P: $51-$68 2P: $58-$71 XP: $10 F12

Motel **Location:** On CR H, 1 mi s of jct SR 50. Located in a commercial, residential area. 1060 Wells St 53147. Fax: 262/248-7215. **Facility:** 23 one-bedroom standard units. 2 stories (no elevator), exterior corridors. **Parking:** on-site, winter plug-ins. **Terms:** office hours 7 am-11 pm, 2 night minimum stay - seasonal, 7 day cancellation notice. **Pool(s):** heated outdoor. **Cards:** AX, DS, MC, VI. **Special Amenities:** free local telephone calls and early check-in/late check-out.

SOME UNITS

ⓈD 🏊 🎥 🔌 / ✕ 📷 /

THE COVE OF LAKE GENEVA   *Book at aaa.com*   Phone: (262)249-9460

▼▼▼

5/28-8/31	1P: $175-$350	2P: $175-$350
4/23-5/27 & 9/1-3/31	1P: $110-$285	2P: $110-$285
4/1-4/22	1P: $80-$175	2P: $80-$175

Condominium   **Location:** Just s of SR 50. Located across from Lake Geneva. 111 Center St 53147. Fax: 262/249-1532. **Facility:** Gas fireplaces are featured in all of the property's accommodations. 211 units. 149 one-bedroom standard units with efficiencies and whirlpools. 59 one- and 3 two-bedroom suites with whirlpools, some with efficiencies or kitchens. 4 stories, interior corridors. *Bath:* combo or shower only. **Parking:** on-site. **Terms:** 2 night minimum stay - weekends in season, 3 day cancellation notice-fee imposed. **Amenities:** video library (fee), voice mail, irons, hair dryers. *Some:* CD players. **Pool(s):** 2 heated outdoor, heated indoor. **Leisure Activities:** sauna, whirlpools, lighted tennis court, exercise room, basketball. *Fee:* game room. **Guest Services:** gift shop, coin laundry, area transportation (fee). **Business Services:** conference facilities. **Cards:** AX, DC, DS, MC, VI.

SOME UNITS

(ASK) (S/D) (TI) (Y) (&M) (&) (➤) (✕) (VCR) (DATA PORT) (🗄) (🖼) (💻) / (✕) /

GENERAL BOYD'S BED & BREAKFAST   Phone: (262)248-3543

(AAA) (SAVE)   All Year [BP]   2P: $100-$145   XP: $25

▼▼▼   **Location:** Jct CR BB and SR 120, 2.7 mi s of downtown. Located in a rural area. W2915 County Trunk BB 53147. Fax: 262/248-3362. **Facility:** An 1843 Colonial Revival farmhouse on five acres of landscaped grounds, this spacious B&B is accented with a large collection of antiques. Smoke free premises. 4 one-bedroom standard units. 2 stories (no elevator), interior corridors. *Bath:* combo or shower only. **Parking:** on-site. **Terms:** office hours 8 am-8 pm, 2 night minimum stay - seasonal, age restrictions may apply, 5 day cancellation notice-fee imposed, weekly rates available. **Amenities:** hair dryers. *Some:* CD players. **Leisure Activities:** croquet, horseshoes. **Cards:** DS, MC, VI.

Bed & Breakfast

SOME UNITS

(✕) / (VCR) (☎) /

GRAND GENEVA RESORT & SPA   *Book at aaa.com*   Phone: (262)248-8811

(AAA) (SAVE)

6/4-10/16	1P: $249-$319	2P: $249-$319	XP: $10	F18
10/17-3/31	1P: $169-$219	2P: $169-$219	XP: $15	F18
4/1-6/3	1P: $159-$199	2P: $159-$199	XP: $10	F18

▼▼ ▼▼   **Location:** On SR 50, just e of jct US 12. Located in a quiet area. 7036 Grand Geneva Way 53147 (PO Box 130). Resort   Fax: 262/249-4763. **Facility:** This sprawling spa resort features Frank Lloyd Wright-inspired architecture and Large-scale Hotel   has multiple golf courses on its 1,300 acres of rolling countryside. 355 units. 352 one-bedroom standard units, some with whirlpools. 3 one-bedroom suites ($229-$500) with whirlpools. 2 stories, interior corridors. **Parking:** on-site and valet. **Terms:** check-in 4 pm, 3 night minimum stay - with Saturday stayover, 3 day cancellation notice-fee imposed, $10 service charge. **Amenities:** voice mail, irons, hair dryers. *Fee:* video library, video games, high-speed Internet. *Some:* CD players. **Dining:** 3 restaurants, 6:30 am-11 pm, Fri & Sat-midnight, cocktails, also, Ristorante Brissago, see separate listing, entertainment. **Pool(s):** heated outdoor, 2 heated indoor, wading. **Leisure Activities:** saunas, whirlpools, steamrooms, rental paddleboats, access to nearby Moose Mountain indoor/outdoor water park, recreation programs, 3845 ft lighted airport runway, hiking trails, playground, spa, volleyball. *Fee:* golf-36 holes, 6 tennis courts (2 indoor, 6 lighted), downhill & cross country skiing, ice skating, bicycles, horseback riding. **Guest Services:** gift shop, valet laundry, area transportation-within 5 mi. *Fee:* beauty salon. **Business Services:** conference facilities, business center. **Cards:** AX, CB, DC, DS, JC, MC, VI. **Special Amenities:** free newspaper. *(See color ad p 538)*

SOME UNITS

(S/D) (TI) (24i) (Y) (🏋) (∅) (➤) (🚭) (✕) (VCR) (🎦) (DATA PORT) (💻) / (✕) (🗄) /

——— WHERE TO DINE ———

GILBERT'S   Lunch: $9-$16   Dinner: $19-$42   Phone: 262/248-6680

▼▼▼ ▼▼▼   **Location:** Center. 327 Wrigley Dr 53147. **Hours:** 5 pm-9 pm, Fri & Sat-10 pm; also 11 am-2 pm 5/27-8/30. Continental   Closed: 1/1, 12/24, 12/25 & Easter; also Sun & Mon. **Reservations:** accepted. **Features:** Take time to enjoy the carefully prepared and artistically presented dishes created from market-fresh, organically grown produce that is used whenever possible. The comfortable ambiance of this grand, circa-1800 Summer mansion combined with caring service can leave guests feeling coddled. Some tables afford lovely lake views. Dressy casual; cocktails. **Parking:** on-site. **Cards:** AX, CB, DC, DS, MC, VI.

(Y) (✕)

RISTORANTE BRISSAGO   Dinner: $10-$30   Phone: 262/248-8811

▼▼▼   **Location:** On SR 50, just e of jct US 12; in Grand Geneva Resort & Spa. 7036 Grand Geneva Way 53147. **Hours:** 5 pm-10 pm. Closed: Mon. **Reservations:** suggested. **Features:** Careful attention is paid to the preparation Northern   of traditional pastas, wood-roasted pizza and veal dishes in this dining room overlooking the Wisconsin Italian   countryside. Service is professional and attentive. The imported Milano sorbets are wonderful. Dressy casual; cocktails. **Parking:** on-site and valet. **Cards:** AX, DC, DS, MC, VI. *(See color ad p 538)* (Y) (✕)

SCUTTLEBUTTS   Lunch: $6-$13   Dinner: $7-$16   Phone: 262/248-1111

▼▼ ▼▼   **Location:** Just s of SR 50; lakeside. 831 Wrigley 53147. **Hours:** 7 am-9 pm, Fri & Sat-10 pm; hours may vary in winter. **Features:** The casual restaurant features a selection of flavorful gourmet burgers, sandwiches and American   salads, as well as a handful of Swedish specialties. Large windows in the dining room look out over Lake Geneva. Key lime pie and specialty ice cream desserts are wonderful. Casual dress; cocktails. **Parking:** street. **Cards:** MC, VI.

(Y) (✕)

LAKE MILLS pop. 4,843

─── WHERE TO DINE ───

PINE KNOLL SUPPER CLUB   **Lunch:** $4-$8   **Dinner:** $10-$20   **Phone:** 920/648-2303
~~~ ~~~   **Location:** I-94, exit 259, 3 mi n. N7755 Hwy 89 53551. **Hours:** 4:30 pm-9 pm, Fri 11 am-2 & 4:30-9:30 pm, Sun
American   10 am-8 pm. Closed: 1/1, 7/4, 12/24, 12/25; also Mon. **Reservations:** suggested. **Features:** Supper club
                   fare highlights such selections as breaded or broiled seafood, hand-cut steaks and succulent ribs. Rolling
                   farmland characterizes the rural setting. Dining rooms blend contemporary and Early American influences.
Sunday brunch is popular. Casual dress; cocktails. **Parking:** on-site. **Cards:** CB, DC, DS, MC, VI.   ⓨ ⓧ

LANCASTER pop. 4,070

─── WHERE TO STAY ───

BEST WESTERN WELCOME INN   *Book at aaa.com*   **Phone:** (608)723-4162
~~~   4/1-10/31 [CP]   1P: $58-$68   2P: $68-$78   XP: $7   F12
                11/1-3/31 [CP]   1P: $56-$68   2P: $64-$76   XP: $7   F12
Small-scale Hotel   **Location:** Just w of downtown square. 420 W Maple St 53813. Fax: 608/723-4843. **Facility:** 22 one-bedroom stan-
                dard units. 2 stories (no elevator), interior corridors. **Parking:** on-site. **Amenities:** irons, hair dryers. **Guest**
Services: coin laundry. **Cards:** AX, CB, DC, DS, MC, VI.

SOME UNITS
ASK Sⓓ 📷 DATA🗖 📖 / ⓧ 🛢 /

MAPLE HARRIS GUEST HOUSE   **Phone:** 608/723-4717
~~~ ~~~   All Year   1P: $55   2P: $79   XP: $20   F6
                Location: Just w of downtown square. Located in a residential area. 445 W Maple St 53813. **Facility:** Smoke free
Bed & Breakfast premises. 6 one-bedroom standard units. 2 stories (no elevator), interior/exterior corridors. *Bath:* combo or shower only. **Parking:** street. **Terms:** check-in 4 pm, 14 day cancellation notice,
weekly rates available, [BP] meal plan available. **Amenities:** *Some:* irons. **Guest Services:** TV in common area. **Cards:** DC,
MC, VI.

SOME UNITS
ⓧ 🎵 DATA🗖 / 🛢 🖼 📖 /

LAND O'LAKES

─── WHERE TO STAY ───

SUNRISE LODGE   **Phone:** (715)547-3684
~~~~   All Year   1P: $79-$95   2P: $165-$180   XP: $79   D16
Cottage   **Location:** 2 mi s on US 45, 2.8 mi e on CR E, then 1 mi n. Located on the west shore of Lac Vieux Desert. 5894 W
                Shore Dr 54540. Fax: 715/547-6110. **Facility:** The lodge offers cottages and detached houses. 24 units. 5 va-
                cation homes and 19 cottages. 1-2 stories (no elevator), exterior corridors. *Bath:* combo or shower only.
Parking: on-site, winter plug-ins. **Terms:** 21 day cancellation notice-fee imposed, weekly rates available, [AP], [BP], [CP] &
[MAP] meal plans available, package plans. **Amenities:** video library, hair dryers. **Leisure Activities:** rental canoes, rental canoes,
boat dock, fishing, miniature golf, tennis court, cross country skiing, snowmobiling, recreation programs in season, bicycles, playground, basketball, horseshoes, shuffleboard, volleyball. *Fee:* game room. **Guest Services:** gift shop. **Business Services:**
meeting rooms. **Cards:** DC, MC, VI.

➜ 🐾 🍽 ⓧ ⓥⓒⓡ ✆ 🛢 🖼 📖

LA POINTE

─── WHERE TO STAY ───

MADELINE ISLAND MOTEL   **Phone:** 715/747-3000
AAA SAVE   7/1-9/1   1P: $90   2P: $95   XP: $10   F18
                5/1-6/30 & 9/2-12/1   1P: $60   2P: $80   XP: $10   F18
~~~   **Location:** Just e of ferry boat landing. 261 Colonel Woods Ave 54850 (PO Box 51). Fax: 715/747-3003. **Facility:** 11
Motel   one-bedroom standard units. 2 stories, exterior corridors. *Bath:* combo or shower only. **Parking:** on-site.
                Terms: open 5/1-12/1, 3 day cancellation notice-fee imposed, weekly rates available, [CP] meal plan avail-
                able. **Leisure Activities:** rental canoes, badminton, board games, rental bicycles, hiking trails, horseshoes,
volleyball. *Fee:* miniature golf. **Guest Services:** airport transportation-La Pointe Airport, area transportation-marina. **Cards:** DC,
DS, MC, VI. **Special Amenities:** free continental breakfast and free local telephone calls.

SOME UNITS
➜ 🍴 ⓧ ✆ 🛢 🖼 / ⓧ /

LODI pop. 2,882

─── WHERE TO STAY ───

VICTORIAN TREASURE INN   **Phone:** (608)592-5199
AAA SAVE   All Year [BP]   1P: $119-$219   2P: $129-$239   XP: $20
                Location: Just w of jct SR 60 and 113. 115 Prairie St 53555. Fax: 608/592-7147. **Facility:** Leaded, stained-glass
~~~ ~~~   windows, hardwood floors and decoratively trimmed pocket doors accent these two 19th-century Victorian
Bed & Breakfast homes. Smoke free premises. 7 units. 2 one-bedroom standard units, some with whirlpools. 5 one-bedroom
                suites with whirlpools. 2 stories (no elevator), interior/exterior corridors. **Parking:** on-site. **Terms:** 2 night
                minimum stay - weekends, age restrictions may apply, 14 day cancellation notice-fee imposed.
Amenities: CD players, irons, hair dryers. **Leisure Activities:** *Fee:* massage. **Guest Services:** gift shop. **Cards:** AX, DS,
MC, VI. **Special Amenities:** free full breakfast and free local telephone calls.

SOME UNITS
Sⓓ 🍴 ⓧ / 🎵 ⓥⓒⓡ 🛢 🖼 📖 /

LOMIRA pop. 2,233

——— WHERE TO STAY ———

AMERIHOST INN & SUITES   *Book at aaa.com*   Phone: (920)269-7477
AAA SAVE   All Year [ECP]   1P: $74-$80   2P: $74-$80   XP: $6   F18
▽▽▽▽   **Location:** US 41, exit 85 (SR 67), just nw. 645 E Ave 53048. Fax: 920/269-7738. **Facility:** 60 one-bedroom stan-
            dard units, some with whirlpools. 2 stories (no elevator), interior corridors. *Bath:* combo or shower only.
Small-scale Hotel   **Parking:** on-site. **Amenities:** voice mail, safes (fee), irons, hair dryers. **Pool(s):** small heated indoor. **Leisure**
            Activities: whirlpool, seasonal patio, limited exercise equipment. **Business Services:** meeting rooms.
            Cards: AX, CB, DC, DS, MC, VI. **Special Amenities: free expanded continental breakfast and free**
newspaper.   SOME UNITS

[icons]

LUCK pop. 1,210

——— WHERE TO STAY ———

LUCK COUNTRY INN   Phone: 715/472-2000
AAA SAVE   5/23-11/30   1P: $61-$77   2P: $61-$77   XP: $9   F16
▽▽ ▽▽   12/1-3/31   1P: $55-$77   2P: $55-$77   XP: $9   F16
            4/1-5/22   1P: $50-$77   2P: $50-$77   XP: $9   F16
Small-scale Hotel   **Location:** Jct SR 35 and 48. 10 Robertson Rd 54853 (PO Box 242). Fax: 715/472-2171. **Facility:** 38 units. 37 one-
            bedroom standard units. 1 one-bedroom suite ($83-$94) with kitchen. 2 stories, interior corridors. *Bath:*
            combo or shower only. **Parking:** on-site, winter plug-ins. **Terms:** cancellation fee imposed. **Dining:** 6 am-9
pm; Sun-Thurs to 8 pm in winter, wine/beer only. **Pool(s):** small heated indoor. **Leisure Activities:** sauna, whirlpool. **Guest Serv-**
ices: gift shop. **Business Services:** meeting rooms, administrative services (fee). **Cards:** AX, DC, MC, VI.
                                                                                              SOME UNITS

[icons]

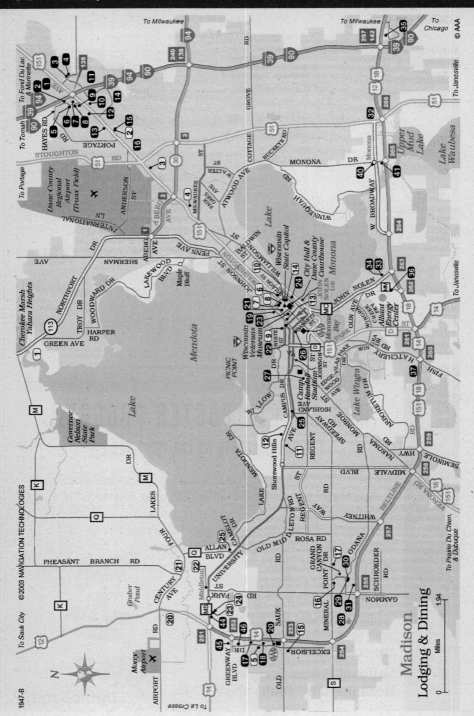

Madison
Lodging & Dining

© AAA

Madison and Vicinity

This index helps you "spot" where approved accommodations and restaurants are located on the corresponding detailed maps. Lodging rate ranges are for comparison only and show the property's high season; rates are per night, unless only weekly (W) rates are available. Restaurant rate range is for dinner, unless only lunch (L) is served. Turn to the listing page for more detailed rate information and consult display ads for special promotions.

Spotter/Map Page Number	OA	MADISON - Lodgings	Diamond Rating	Rate Range High Season	Listing Page
1 / p. 542		Woodfield Suites-Madison	◇◇◇	$89-$129	553
2 / p. 542		Fairfield Inn By Marriott	◇◇	$57	548
3 / p. 542		GrandStay Residential Suites	◇◇◇	$89	549
4 / p. 542	AAA	Staybridge Suites - see color ad p 552	◇◇◇	$119 SAVE	553
5 / p. 542		Hampton Inn-East	◇◇◇	$79-$119	549
6 / p. 542	AAA	Red Roof Inn-Madison	◇◇	$45-$75 SAVE	551
7 / p. 542	AAA	Select Inn - see color ad p 552	◇◇	$39-$75 SAVE	552
8 / p. 542		Residence Inn	◇◇◇	$89-$129	551
9 / p. 542		Comfort Inn Madison	◇◇◇	$69-$189	547
10 / p. 542	AAA	Best Western East Towne Suites - see color ad p 545	◇◇◇	$69-$99 SAVE	545
11 / p. 542		Courtyard by Marriott-Madison East	◇◇◇	$109-$129	547
12 / p. 542	AAA	Econo Lodge of Madison	◇◇	$45-$79 SAVE	548
13 / p. 542	AAA	Crowne Plaza Hotel and Resort - see color ad p 547	◇◇◇	$99-$209 SAVE	548
14 / p. 542	AAA	Microtel Inn & Suites	◇◇	$46-$59 SAVE	551
15 / p. 542	AAA	Exel Inn of Madison	◇◇	$40-$76 SAVE	548
16 / p. 542	AAA	Holiday Inn Madison East - see color ad p 550	◇◇◇	$79-$149 SAVE	550
17 / p. 542		Comfort Suites	◇◇◇	$89-$250	547
18 / p. 542		Holiday Inn Hotel & Suites	◇◇◇	$137-$198	549
19 / p. 542	AAA	Mansion Hill Inn	◇◇◇◇	$150-$310 SAVE	550
20 / p. 542		Baymont Inn & Suites-Madison West	◇◇◇	$59-$109	545
21 / p. 542	AAA	The Madison Concourse Hotel & Governor's Club - see color ad p 546	◇◇◇	$109-$169 SAVE	550
22 / p. 542		Canterbury Inn	◇◇◇	$110-$375	546
23 / p. 542	AAA	Best Western Inn On The Park	◇◇	$99-$129 SAVE	545
24 / p. 542		Hilton Madison Monona Terrace	◇◇◇	$119-$229	549
25 / p. 542	AAA	Best Western InnTowner & the Highland Club	◇◇◇	$79-$219 SAVE	545
26 / p. 542	AAA	Howard Johnson Plaza Hotel - see color ad p 584	◇◇◇	$105-$150 SAVE	550
28 / p. 542		Residence Inn By Marriott-Madison West	◇◇◇	$119-$169	551
29 / p. 542		Hampton Inn West	◇◇◇	$74-$109	549
30 / p. 542	AAA	Radisson Inn Madison - see color ad p 583	◇◇◇	$79-$129 SAVE	551
31 / p. 542		Best Western West Towne Suites	◇◇	$49-$109	546
32 / p. 542	AAA	Days Inn-Madison - see color ad card insert, p 548	◇◇	$68-$83 SAVE	548

Spotter/Map Page Number	OA	MADISON - Lodgings (continued)	Diamond Rating	Rate Range High Season	Listing Page
33 / p. 542		Sheraton Madison Hotel	◆◆◆	$119-$139	552
34 / p. 542	AAA	Holiday Inn Express-Madison	◆◆◆	$79-$115 SAVE	549
35 / p. 542	AAA	Wingate Inn	◆◆◆	$79-$109 SAVE	553
36 / p. 542	AAA	Clarion Suites Central - see color ad p 546	◆◆◆	$89-$184 SAVE	547
37 / p. 542	AAA	Super 8 Motel - see color ad p 553	◆◆	$49-$99 SAVE	553
		MADISON - Restaurants			
1 / p. 542		The Mariner's Inn	◆◆	$14-$40	554
2 / p. 542	AAA	Imperial Garden-East	◆◆	$8-$13	554
3 / p. 542		Prime Quarter Steak House	◆	$15	555
4 / p. 542		Ella's Kosher Style Deli & Ice Cream Parlor	◆	$7-$8	554
5 / p. 542		George's Chop House	◆◆	$9-$15	554
6 / p. 542		Bellini	◆◆	$14-$22	554
7 / p. 542		The Blue Marlin	◆◆◆	$22-$30	554
8 / p. 542		L'Etoile	◆◆◆	$23-$36	554
9 / p. 542	AAA	Nadia's Restaurant	◆◆◆	$17-$26	555
10 / p. 542	AAA	Cafe Continental	◆◆	$10-$30	554
11 / p. 542		Smoky's Club	◆◆	$10-$25	555
12 / p. 542		Sa-Bai Thong	◆◆	$6-$15	555
13 / p. 542		White Horse Inn	◆◆	$12-$23	555
14 / p. 542		Johnny Delmonico's	◆◆◆	$9-$31	554
15 / p. 542		Biaggi's	◆◆	$9-$16	554
16 / p. 542		Timber Lodge Steakhouse	◆◆	$12-$20	555
17 / p. 542		Otto's Restaurant and Bar	◆◆◆	$18-$25	555
		MONONA - Lodgings			
40 / p. 542	AAA	AmericInn of Madison South/Monona - see color ad p 576	◆◆◆	$79-$159 SAVE	604
41 / p. 542	AAA	Country Inn & Suites By Carlson - see color ad starting on p 580	◆◆◆	$79-$95 SAVE	605
		MIDDLETON - Lodgings			
44 / p. 542	AAA	Staybridge Suites by Holiday Inn - see color ad p 552	◆◆◆	$119 SAVE	560
45 / p. 542		Fairfield Inn Madison West/Middleton	◆◆◆	$59-$109	560
46 / p. 542	AAA	Marriott Madison West - see color ad p 551	◆◆◆	$98-$179 SAVE	560
		MIDDLETON - Restaurants			
20 / p. 542		Fitzgerald's of Middleton	◆◆	$10-$20	561
21 / p. 542		Stamm House at Pheasant Branch	◆◆	$10-$18	561
22 / p. 542		Tortillas	◆◆	$7-$19	561
23 / p. 542		Louisianne's Etc	◆◆◆	$12-$30	561
24 / p. 542		Hubbard Avenue Diner	◆	$5-$10	561
25 / p. 542	AAA	Imperial Garden West	◆◆◆	$7-$14	561

MADISON pop. 208,054 (See map and index starting on p. 542)

──────── WHERE TO STAY ────────

BAYMONT INN & SUITES-MADISON WEST *Book at aaa.com* Phone: (608)831-7711 **20**
All Year 1P: $59-$99 2P: $69-$109 XP: $10 F
Small-scale Hotel **Location:** US 12 and 14, exit 253 (Old Sauk Rd), just nw. 8102 Excelsior Dr 53717. Fax: 608/831-1942. **Facility:** 129 one-bedroom standard units, some with kitchens and/or whirlpools. 2 stories (no elevator), interior corridors. *Bath:* combo or shower only. **Parking:** on-site, winter plug-ins. **Terms:** 14 day cancellation notice, [ECP] meal plan available. **Amenities:** video games (fee), high-speed Internet, voice mail, irons, hair dryers. **Pool(s):** heated indoor. **Leisure Activities:** sauna, whirlpool, exercise room. **Guest Services:** complimentary evening beverages: Mon, Wed, Fri & Sat, valet and coin laundry, area transportation. **Business Services:** meeting rooms. **Cards:** AX, CB, DC, DS, MC, VI.

SOME UNITS
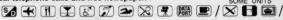

BEST WESTERN EAST TOWNE SUITES *Book at aaa.com* Phone: (608)244-2020 **10**
All Year [BP] 1P: $69-$86 2P: $77-$99 XP: $8 F14
Location: I-90/94, exit 135A, just sw on US 151. 4801 Annamark Dr 53704. Fax: 608/244-3434. **Facility:** 123 units. 119 one-bedroom standard units, some with whirlpools. 4 stories. 4 stories, interior corridors. **Parking:** on-site. **Terms:** cancellation fee imposed, pets ($20 deposit). **Amenities:** irons, hair dryers. Small-scale Hotel **Pool(s):** small heated indoor. **Leisure Activities:** whirlpool, limited exercise equipment. **Guest Services:** valet laundry. **Business Services:** meeting rooms. **Cards:** AX, CB, DC, DS, MC, VI. **Special Amenities:** free full breakfast and free local telephone calls. *(See color ad below)*

SOME UNITS

FEE   FEE

BEST WESTERN INN ON THE PARK *Book at aaa.com* Phone: (608)257-8811 **23**
4/1-11/6 & 2/17-3/31 1P: $99-$129 2P: $99-$129 XP: $10 F18
11/7-2/16 1P: $69-$99 2P: $69-$99 XP: $10 F18
Location: Downtown. Located opposite the Wisconsin State Capitol. 22 S Carroll 53703. Fax: 608/257-5995. **Facility:** 213 units. 177 one-bedroom standard units. 36 one-bedroom suites ($129-$179). 9 stories, interior Small-scale Hotel corridors. **Parking:** valet. **Amenities:** high-speed Internet, dual phone lines, voice mail, irons, hair dryers. **Dining:** 7 am-2 & 5-9 pm, cocktails. **Pool(s):** heated indoor. **Leisure Activities:** sauna, whirlpool, exercise room. **Guest Services:** gift shop, valet laundry, area transportation-University of Wisconsin. **Business Services:** meeting rooms. **Cards:** AX, CB, DC, DS, MC, VI. **Special Amenities:** free newspaper and free room upgrade (subject to availability with advanced reservations).

SOME UNITS

BEST WESTERN INNTOWNER & THE HIGHLAND CLUB *Book at aaa.com* Phone: (608)233-8778 **25**
All Year 1P: $79-$209 2P: $89-$219 XP: $10 F12
Location: 2.3 mi nw. 2424 University Ave 53726. Fax: 608/233-1325. **Facility:** 176 units. 171 one-bedroom standard units. 5 one-bedroom suites ($149-$279), some with whirlpools. 4 stories, interior corridors. *Bath:* Small-scale Hotel combo or shower only. **Parking:** on-site. **Terms:** package plans - seasonal. **Amenities:** video games (fee), voice mail, irons, hair dryers. *Some:* CD players, high-speed Internet. **Dining:** 6:30 am-2 & 5-10 pm, Sun-9 pm, cocktails. **Pool(s):** small heated indoor. **Leisure Activities:** whirlpool, exercise room. *Fee:* game room. **Guest Services:** valet laundry, area transportation-within 2 mi. **Business Services:** meeting rooms, fax (fee). **Cards:** AX, CB, DC, DS, MC, VI. **Special Amenities:** free local telephone calls and free newspaper.

SOME UNITS

(See map and index starting on p. 542)

BEST WESTERN WEST TOWNE SUITES   *Book at aaa.com*   Phone: (608)833-4200   **31**
All Year [BP]   1P: $49-$99   2P: $59-$109   XP: $10   F16
Location: US 12 and 14, exit 255 (Gammon Rd), just e on Odana Rd, then just sw. 650 Grand Canyon Dr 53719.
Small-scale Hotel   Fax: 608/833-5614. **Facility:** 101 units. 76 one-bedroom standard units, some with efficiencies and/or whirl-
pools. 25 one-bedroom suites ($59-$149), some with efficiencies. 2 stories, interior corridors. **Parking:** on-
site, winter plug-ins. **Terms:** weekly rates available, pets ($25 deposit, with prior approval). **Amenities:** safes (fee), irons, hair
dryers. **Leisure Activities:** exercise room. **Guest Services:** valet and coin laundry. **Business Services:** meeting rooms.
Cards: AX, CB, DC, DS, MC, VI.

SOME UNITS
(ASK) (SD) (icons) FEE / (icons)

CANTERBURY INN   **Phone:** (608)258-8899   **22**
All Year   1P: $110-$355   2P: $130-$375   XP: $20   F6
Location: Just w of State St; downtown. Located above a book store. 315 W Gorham St 53703. Fax: 608/283-2541.
Bed & Breakfast   **Facility:** This well-appointed B&B features hand-painted murals and guest rooms themed after characters
from classic literature. Smoke free premises. 6 one-bedroom standard units, some with whirlpools. 2 stories,
interior corridors. **Parking:** valet. **Terms:** check-in 4 pm, 14 day cancellation notice-fee imposed, [ECP] meal plan available.
Amenities: CD players, voice mail, irons, hair dryers. **Guest Services:** valet laundry. **Cards:** AX, CB, DC, DS, MC, VI.

SOME UNITS
(ASK) (SD) (icons) (VCR) (icons) / (icons) /

(See map and index starting on p. 542)

CLARION SUITES CENTRAL *Book at aaa.com* Phone: (608)284-1234 36
(AAA) (SAVE) All Year 1P: $89-$184 XP: $5 F
▽▽▽▽ Location: US 12 and 18, exit 262 (Rimrock Rd), just nw. Located next to Alliant Energy Center. 2110 Rimrock Rd 53713.
Fax: 608/284-9401. **Facility:** 140 units. 98 one-bedroom standard units. 42 one-bedroom suites with efficien-
Small-scale Hotel cies. 8 stories, interior corridors. *Bath:* combo or shower only. **Parking:** on-site. **Terms:** [BP] meal plan available, pets ($25 extra charge, with prior approval). **Amenities:** video games (fee), voice mail, irons, hair
dryers. **Pool(s):** heated indoor. **Leisure Activities:** whirlpool, exercise room. **Guest Services:** complimentary evening beverages: Mon-Thurs, valet and coin laundry, area transportation-downtown. **Business Services:** meeting rooms,
business center. **Cards:** AX, DC, DS, MC, VI. **Special Amenities: free expanded continental breakfast and free local telephone calls.** *(See color ad p 546)*

[icons] FEE

COMFORT INN MADISON *Book at aaa.com* Phone: (608)244-6265 9
▽▽▽▽ All Year [ECP] 1P: $69-$129 2P: $69-$189 XP: $10 F18
Location: I-90/94, exit 135A, just w on US 151. 4822 E Washington Ave 53704. Fax: 608/244-1293. **Facility:** 152
Small-scale Hotel units. 150 one-bedroom standard units, some with whirlpools. 2 one-bedroom suites ($99-$189) with whirlpools. 2-6 stories, interior corridors. *Bath:* combo or shower only. **Parking:** on-site. **Amenities:** video games
(fee), voice mail, irons, hair dryers. **Pool(s):** small heated indoor. **Leisure Activities:** whirlpool, exercise room. **Guest Services:**
valet and coin laundry, area transportation. **Business Services:** conference facilities. **Cards:** AX, CB, DC, DS, MC, VI.

SOME UNITS
[icons]

COMFORT SUITES *Book at aaa.com* Phone: (608)836-3033 17
▽▽▽ All Year 1P: $89-$250 2P: $89-$250 XP: $10 F18
Location: US 12 and 14, exit 252 (Greenway Blvd), just sw. 1253 John Q Hammons Dr 53717. Fax: 608/836-0949.
Small-scale Hotel **Facility:** 95 one-bedroom standard units, some with whirlpools. 3 stories, interior corridors. *Bath:* combo or
shower only. **Parking:** on-site. **Terms:** [ECP] meal plan available. **Amenities:** high-speed Internet, voice
mail, safes (fee), irons, hair dryers. **Pool(s):** heated indoor. **Leisure Activities:** whirlpool, exercise room. *Fee:* game room. **Guest
Services:** complimentary evening beverages: Mon-Sat, valet and coin laundry, area transportation. **Business Services:** meeting
rooms. **Cards:** AX, DC, DS, MC, VI.

SOME UNITS
[icons]

COURTYARD BY MARRIOTT-MADISON EAST *Book at aaa.com* Phone: (608)661-8100 11
▽▽▽ 6/6-9/4 1P: $109-$129
9/5-3/31 1P: $94-$129
4/1-6/5 1P: $89-$119
Small-scale Hotel Location: I-90/94, exit 135C (High Crossing Blvd). 2502 Crossroads Dr 53718. Fax: 608/661-8101. **Facility:** 127
units. 121 one-bedroom standard units, some with whirlpools. 6 one-bedroom suites ($149-$169). 4 stories, interior corridors.
Bath: combo or shower only. **Parking:** on-site. **Terms:** cancellation fee imposed, [BP] meal plan available. **Amenities:** video
games (fee), high-speed Internet, dual phone lines, voice mail, irons, hair dryers. **Pool(s):** small heated indoor. **Leisure Activities:** whirlpool, exercise room. **Guest Services:** valet and coin laundry. **Business Services:** meeting rooms, business center.
Cards: AX, DS, MC, VI.

SOME UNITS
[icons]

(See map and index starting on p. 542)

CROWNE PLAZA HOTEL AND RESORT *Book at aaa.com* Phone: (608)244-4703 🔢 13
AAA SAVE All Year 1P: $99-$199 2P: $99-$209 XP: $10 F17
AAAA Location: I-90/94, exit 135A, 0.4 mi w on US 151. 4402 E Washington Ave 53704. Fax: 608/244-7829. **Facility:** 226 one-bedroom standard units, some with whirlpools. 6 stories, interior corridors. **Parking:** on-site.
Large-scale Hotel **Terms:** check-in 4 pm, cancellation fee imposed. **Amenities:** voice mail, irons, hair dryers. *Fee:* video games, high-speed Internet. *Some:* fax. Dining: 6 am-11 pm, cocktails. **Pool(s):** heated indoor. **Leisure Activities:** whirlpool, limited exercise equipment. **Guest Services:** gift shop, valet and coin laundry. **Business Services:** conference facilities, business center. **Cards:** AX, CB, DC, DS, JC, MC, VI. **Special Amenities:** early check-in/late check-out and free room upgrade (subject to availability with advanced reservations). *(See color ad p 547)*

SOME UNITS

🅂🄳 ✈ 🐾 🍽 🍸 🅿 🐕 🎤 📶 💻 / ✕ 🗄 /

DAYS INN-MADISON *Book at aaa.com* Phone: 608/223-1800 🔢 32
AAA SAVE All Year [ECP] 1P: $68-$83 2P: $68-$83 XP: $10 F
AAAA Location: US 12 and 18, exit 266 (US 51), just ne. 4402 E Broadway Service Rd 53716. Fax: 608/223-1374. **Facility:** 65 one-bedroom standard units, some with whirlpools. 3 stories, interior corridors. *Bath:* combo or shower only. **Parking:** on-site, winter plug-ins. **Terms:** pets ($50 deposit). **Amenities:** voice mail, irons, hair dryers.
Small-scale Hotel **Pool(s):** small heated indoor. **Leisure Activities:** whirlpool, exercise room. **Business Services:** meeting rooms. **Cards:** AX, DC, MC, VI. *(See color ad card insert & below)*

SOME UNITS

🅂🄳 🐾 🅿 🐕 🎤 📶 / ✕ 🗄 📠 💻
FEE

ECONO LODGE OF MADISON *Book at aaa.com* Phone: (608)241-4171 🔢 12
AAA SAVE All Year 1P: $45-$75 2P: $49-$79 XP: $4 F17
AAAA Location: I-90/94, exit 135A, just w on US 151. 4726 E Washington Ave 53704. Fax: 608/241-1715. **Facility:** 98 one-bedroom standard units. 2 stories (no elevator), interior corridors. *Bath:* combo or shower only. **Parking:** on-site, winter plug-ins. **Terms:** weekly rates available, [ECP] meal plan available, pets ($10 extra charge, in
Small-scale Hotel designated units). **Amenities:** safes (fee). *Some:* video games, fax, hair dryers. **Guest Services:** coin laundry. **Business Services:** meeting rooms. **Cards:** AX, DC, DS, MC, VI. **Special Amenities:** free expanded continental breakfast.

SOME UNITS

🅂🄳 🐾 🅿 🐕 🐕 🎤 / ✕ 📹 📶 🗄 📠 💻 /
FEE FEE

EXEL INN OF MADISON *Book at aaa.com* Phone: (608)241-3861 🔢 15
AAA SAVE All Year [CP] 1P: $40-$70 2P: $46-$76 XP: $6 F18
AAAA Location: I-90/94, exit 135A, 0.5 mi w on US 151. 4202 E Towne Blvd 53704. Fax: 608/241-9752. **Facility:** 100 one-bedroom standard units, some with whirlpools. 2 stories, interior corridors. *Bath:* combo or shower only. **Parking:** on-site. **Terms:** weekly rates available, small pets only. **Amenities:** irons, hair dryers. **Leisure Activities:** limited exercise equipment. **Guest Services:** coin laundry. **Business Services:** fax (fee). **Cards:** AX, CB, DC, DS, MC, VI.
Small-scale Hotel **Special Amenities:** free continental breakfast and early check-in/late check-out.

SOME UNITS

🅂🄳 🐾 🅿 🎤 📶 💻 / ✕ 🗄 📠
FEE FEE

FAIRFIELD INN BY MARRIOTT *Book at aaa.com* Phone: 608/249-5300 🔢 2
AAAA All Year 1P: $57
Motel Location: I-90/94, exit 135A, just sw on US 151. 4765 Hayes Rd 53704. Fax: 608/240-9335. **Facility:** 135 one-bedroom standard units. 3 stories, interior/exterior corridors. *Bath:* combo or shower only. **Parking:** on-site, winter plug-ins. **Terms:** [ECP] meal plan available. **Amenities:** irons, hair dryers. **Pool(s):** small heated outdoor. **Guest Services:** valet laundry. **Cards:** AX, DC, DS, MC, VI.

SOME UNITS

ASK 🅂🄳 🅿 🐾 🐕 🐕 🎤 📶 💻 / ✕ /
FEE

(See map and index starting on p. 542)

GRANDSTAY RESIDENTIAL SUITES

Book at aaa.com — Phone: (608)241-2500 **3**

▽▽▽▽ — All Year — 1P: $89 — 2P: $89

Small-scale Hotel — **Location:** US 51, exit 98A, just e, then 0.5 mi s. 5317 High Crossing Blvd 53718. **Fax:** 608/241-0900. **Facility:** 53 units. 8 one-bedroom standard units with kitchens. 41 one- and 4 two-bedroom suites ($139) with kitchens. 3 stories, interior corridors. *Bath:* combo or shower only. **Parking:** on-site. **Terms:** weekly rates available, [CP] meal plan available. **Amenities:** video games (fee), high-speed Internet, voice mail, irons, hair dryers. **Pool(s):** small heated indoor. **Leisure Activities:** whirlpool, putting green, exercise room, basketball. **Guest Services:** valet and coin laundry. **Business Services:** meeting rooms. **Cards:** AX, DC, DS, JC, MC, VI.

SOME UNITS

`(ASK)` `(S/D)` `(🛏)` `(&M)` `(&)` `(≈)` `(✕)` `(♥)` `(DATA PORT)` `(🖪)` `(🖵)` `(💻)` / `(✕)` /

HAMPTON INN-EAST

Book at aaa.com — Phone: (608)244-9400 **5**

▽▽▽▽ — 6/1-10/31 [ECP] — 1P: $79-$119 — 2P: $79-$119
11/1-3/31 [ECP] — 1P: $79-$109 — 2P: $79-$109
4/1-5/31 [ECP] — 1P: $74-$99 — 2P: $74-$99

Small-scale Hotel — **Location:** I-90/94, exit 135A, just w on US 151. 4820 Hayes Rd 53704. **Fax:** 608/244-7177. **Facility:** 116 one-bedroom standard units. 4 stories, interior corridors. *Bath:* combo or shower only. **Parking:** on-site, winter plug-ins. **Amenities:** video games (fee), voice mail, irons, hair dryers. **Pool(s):** small heated indoor. **Leisure Activities:** whirlpool, limited exercise equipment. **Guest Services:** valet laundry. **Business Services:** meeting rooms. **Cards:** AX, CB, DC, DS, MC, VI.

SOME UNITS

`(ASK)` `(S/D)` `(†)` `(&M)` `(&)` `(∅)` `(≈)` `(♥)` `(DATA PORT)` `(💻)` / `(✕)` `(🖪)` `(🖵)` /
FEE FEE

HAMPTON INN WEST

Book at aaa.com — Phone: (608)833-3511 **29**

▽▽▽▽ — 4/1-11/1 & 3/1-3/31 — 1P: $74-$99 — 2P: $84-$109
11/2-2/28 — 1P: $69-$94 — 2P: $79-$104

Small-scale Hotel — **Location:** US 12 and 14, exit 255 (Gammon Rd), just n, then 0.5 mi e on Odana Rd. 516 Grand Canyon Dr 53719. **Fax:** 608/833-7140. **Facility:** 122 one-bedroom standard units. 5 stories, interior corridors. *Bath:* combo or shower only. **Parking:** on-site. **Terms:** [CP] meal plan available. **Amenities:** video games (fee), dual phone lines, voice mail, irons, hair dryers. **Pool(s):** small heated indoor. **Leisure Activities:** whirlpool, limited exercise equipment. **Guest Services:** valet laundry. **Business Services:** meeting rooms. **Cards:** AX, CB, DC, DS, MC, VI.

SOME UNITS

`(ASK)` `(S/D)` `(†)` `(&M)` `(&)` `(≈)` `(♥)` `(DATA PORT)` `(💻)` / `(✕)` `(🖪)` `(🖵)` /
FEE FEE

HILTON MADISON MONONA TERRACE

Phone: (608)255-5100 **24**

▽▽▽▽ — All Year — 1P: $119-$129 — 2P: $219-$229 — XP: $10 — F18

Large-scale Hotel — **Location:** 2 blks e of Capitol Square; downtown. 9 E Wilson St 53703. **Fax:** 608/251-4550. **Facility:** 240 units. 237 one-bedroom standard units. 3 one-bedroom suites with whirlpools. 13 stories, interior corridors. *Bath:* combo or shower only. **Parking:** on-site (fee) and valet. **Terms:** 3 day cancellation notice-fee imposed. **Amenities:** video games (fee), dual phone lines, voice mail, irons, hair dryers. **Pool(s):** small heated indoor. **Leisure Activities:** whirlpool, exercise room. **Guest Services:** gift shop, valet laundry. **Business Services:** meeting rooms, administrative services (fee). **Cards:** AX, CB, DC, DS, MC, VI.

SOME UNITS

`(ASK)` `(✈)` `(†)` `(24†)` `(Y)` `(&)` `(∅)` `(≈)` `(♥)` `(DATA PORT)` `(💻)` / `(✕)` `(🖪)` /
FEE

HOLIDAY INN EXPRESS-MADISON

Book at aaa.com — Phone: (608)255-7400 **34**

`(AAA)` `(SAVE)`
▽▽▽▽ — All Year [ECP] — 1P: $79-$109 — 2P: $85-$115 — XP: $6 — F18

Small-scale Hotel — **Location:** US 12 and 18, exit 263 (John Nolen Dr), just ne. 722 John Nolen Dr 53713. **Fax:** 608/255-3152. **Facility:** 92 one-bedroom standard units, some with whirlpools. 4 stories, interior corridors. *Bath:* combo or shower only. **Parking:** on-site. **Terms:** weekly rates available, [CP] meal plan available, small pets only (in smoking units). **Amenities:** irons, hair dryers. *Some:* high-speed Internet. **Pool(s):** small heated indoor. **Leisure Activities:** whirlpool, limited exercise equipment. **Guest Services:** complimentary evening beverages, valet laundry. **Business Services:** business center. **Cards:** AX, CB, DC, DS, MC, VI. **Special Amenities:** free expanded continental breakfast and free local telephone calls.

SOME UNITS

`(S/D)` `(🛏)` `(†)` `(&)` `(∅)` `(≈)` `(♥)` `(DATA PORT)` `(💻)` / `(✕)` `(🖪)` `(🖵)` /

HOLIDAY INN HOTEL & SUITES

Book at aaa.com — Phone: (608)826-0500 **18**

▽▽▽▽ — 6/1-10/31 — 1P: $137-$188 — 2P: $147-$198 — XP: $10 — F16
4/1-5/31 & 11/1-3/31 — 1P: $127-$178 — 2P: $137-$188 — XP: $10 — F16

Small-scale Hotel — **Location:** US 12 and 14, exit 253 (Old Sank Rd), 0.5 mi nw. 1109 Fourier Dr 53717. **Fax:** 608/826-0550. **Facility:** 158 units. 157 one-bedroom standard units, some with whirlpools. 1 one-bedroom suite ($165-$250). 4 stories, interior corridors. *Bath:* combo or shower only. **Parking:** on-site. **Terms:** [AP] meal plan available. **Amenities:** high-speed Internet, dual phone lines, voice mail, irons, hair dryers. *Fee:* video games, safes. **Pool(s):** heated indoor, wading. **Leisure Activities:** whirlpool, waterslide, exercise room. *Fee:* game room. **Guest Services:** gift shop, complimentary evening beverages, valet and coin laundry, area transportation. **Business Services:** meeting rooms, business center. **Cards:** AX, CB, DC, DS, JC, MC, VI.

SOME UNITS

`(ASK)` `(S/D)` `(✈)` `(†)` `(Y)` `(&M)` `(&)` `(∅)` `(≈)` `(✕)` `(♥)` `(DATA PORT)` `(🖪)` `(🖵)` `(💻)` / `(✕)` `(VCR)` /

(See map and index starting on p. 542)

HOLIDAY INN MADISON EAST   *Book at aaa.com*   **Phone:** (608)244-2481   🔟
⬥⬥⬥ (SAVE)   All Year   1P: $79-$139   2P: $79-$149   XP: $10   F17
▼▼▼   **Location:** I-90/94, exit 135A, 1 mi w on US 151. 3841 E Washington Ave 53704. **Fax:** 608/244-0383. **Facility:** 197 one-bedroom standard units. 2 stories, interior corridors. *Bath:* combo or shower only. **Parking:** on-site.
Terms: cancellation fee imposed, small pets only (in designated units). **Amenities:** video games (fee), voice
Small-scale Hotel   mail, irons, hair dryers. **Dining:** 6:30 am-2 & 5-10 pm, cocktails. **Pool(s):** heated indoor. **Leisure Activi-
ties:** whirlpool, limited exercise equipment. *Fee:* game room. **Guest Services:** valet laundry. **Business Serv-
ices:** meeting rooms. **Cards:** AX, CB, DC, DS, JC, MC, VI. **Special Amenities:** early check-in/late check-out.
(See color ad below)

SOME UNITS

🆚 ✈ 🛏 🍽 🍸 ♿ 📷 🏊 ✕ 🎦 🖧 💻 / ✕ 📠 🖳 /

HOWARD JOHNSON PLAZA HOTEL   *Book at aaa.com*   **Phone:** (608)251-5511   26
⬥⬥⬥ (SAVE)   All Year   1P: $105-$150   2P: $105-$150   XP: $10   F18
▼▼▼   **Location:** 0.5 mi sw of Capitol Square. Located adjacent to University of Wisconsin Campus. 525 W Johnson St 53703.
Fax: 608/251-4824. **Facility:** 163 units. 159 one-bedroom standard units. 4 one-bedroom suites. 7 stories,
interior corridors. *Bath:* combo or shower only. **Parking:** on-site. **Terms:** check-in 4 pm. **Amenities:** video
Small-scale Hotel   games (fee), voice mail, irons, hair dryers. **Dining:** 6 am-1:30 & 5-10 pm, cocktails. **Pool(s):** heated indoor.
Leisure Activities: whirlpool, exercise room. **Guest Services:** valet laundry, area transportation-campus
area. **Business Services:** meeting rooms, fax (fee). **Cards:** AX, CB, DC, DS, JC, MC, VI. **Special Amenities:** free newspaper
and early check-in/late check-out. *(See color ad p 584)*

SOME UNITS

🆚 ✈ 🍽 🍸 ♿ 📷 🏊 ✕ 🎦 🖧 💻 / ✕ 📼 🖳 /
FEE

THE MADISON CONCOURSE HOTEL & GOVERNOR'S CLUB   *Book at aaa.com*   **Phone:** (608)257-6000   21
⬥⬥⬥ (SAVE)   All Year   1P: $109-$159   2P: $119-$169   XP: $10   F16
▼▼▼   **Location:** Just n of Capitol Square; downtown. 1 W Dayton St 53703. **Fax:** 608/257-5280. **Facility:** 356 one-
bedroom standard units, some with whirlpools. 13 stories, interior corridors. *Bath:* combo or shower only.
Parking: on-site and valet. **Terms:** cancellation fee imposed. **Amenities:** voice mail, irons, hair dryers. *Fee:*
Large-scale Hotel   video games, high-speed Internet. *Some:* CD players, dual phone lines. **Dining:** 6:30 am-2 & 5-10 pm, cocktails. **Pool(s):** small heated indoor. **Leisure Activities:** sauna, whirlpool, exercise room. *Fee:* massage,
game room. **Guest Services:** gift shop, valet laundry, area transportation-University vicinity, beauty salon. **Business Services:**
conference facilities, business center. **Cards:** AX, CB, DC, DS, MC, VI. *(See color ad p 546)*

SOME UNITS

🆚 ✈ 🍽 🍸 ♿ 📷 🏊 ✕ 🎦 🖧 💻 / ✕ 📼 🖳 /
FEE FEE

MANSION HILL INN   **Phone:** (608)255-3999   19
⬥⬥⬥ (SAVE)   All Year   1P: $150-$280   2P: $170-$310   XP: $20
▼▼▼ ▼▼▼   **Location:** Just n of Capitol Square; downtown. 424 N Pinckney St 53703. **Fax:** 608/255-2217. **Facility:** This 1858
stone mansion, which is furnished with antiques, features some rooms with four-poster beds. Smoke free
Historic Bed   premises. 11 units. 10 one-bedroom standard units, some with whirlpools. 1 one-bedroom suite with whirl-
& Breakfast   pool. 3 stories (no elevator), interior corridors. *Bath:* combo or shower only. **Parking:** valet. **Terms:** check-in
4 pm, age restrictions may apply, 3 day cancellation notice, [CP] meal plan available. **Amenities:** honor bars,
irons, hair dryers. **Guest Services:** complimentary evening beverages, valet laundry. **Cards:** AX, MC, VI.
Special Amenities: free continental breakfast and free newspaper.

🖧 ✕ 📼 🎦 🖧

(See map and index starting on p. 542)

MICROTEL INN & SUITES · *Book at aaa.com* · Phone: (608)242-9000 · **14**
F16
AAA SAVE · All Year [CP] · 1P: $46-$59 · 2P: $51-$59 · XP: $5
Location: I-90/94, exit 135A, just s, then 0.5 mi e. 2139 E Springs Dr 53704. Fax: 608/242-8700. **Facility:** 100 one-bedroom standard units, some with whirlpools. 3 stories, interior corridors. **Parking:** on-site, winter plug-ins.
Small-scale Hotel · **Terms:** weekly rates available, pets ($10 extra charge). **Amenities:** *Some:* irons. **Cards:** AX, CB, DC, DS, MC, VI. **Special Amenities:** free continental breakfast and free newspaper.
SOME UNITS

RADISSON INN MADISON · *Book at aaa.com* · Phone: (608)833-0100 · **30**
F18
AAA SAVE · All Year · 1P: $79-$129 · 2P: $79-$129 · XP: $10
Location: US 12 and 14, exit 255 (Gammon Rd), 0.5 mi e on Odana. Located in a commercial area. 517 Grand Canyon Rd 53719. Fax: 608/833-6543. **Facility:** 153 units. 147 one-bedroom standard units. 6 one-bedroom suites ($139-$169), some with whirlpools. 2 stories, interior corridors. **Parking:** on-site. **Terms:** [AP] meal plan
Small-scale Hotel · available. **Amenities:** high-speed Internet, dual phone lines, voice mail, safes (fee), irons, hair dryers. **Dining:** 6:30 am-2 & 5-10 pm, cocktails. **Pool(s):** heated indoor. **Leisure Activities:** whirlpool, exercise room. **Guest Services:** valet laundry. **Business Services:** meeting rooms, business center. **Cards:** AX, CB, DC, DS, JC, MC, VI. **Special Amenities:** free newspaper and free room upgrade (subject to availability with advanced reservations).
(See color ad p 583)
SOME UNITS

RED ROOF INN-MADISON · *Book at aaa.com* · Phone: (608)241-1787 · **6**
F18
AAA SAVE · 6/13-8/14 · 1P: $45-$70 · 2P: $50-$75 · XP: $5
4/1-6/12 & 8/15-3/31 · 1P: $40-$60 · 2P: $40-$60
Location: I-90/94, exit 135A, just sw on US 151. 4830 Hayes Rd 53704. Fax: 608/241-7034. **Facility:** 108 one-bedroom standard units. 2 stories, exterior corridors. *Bath:* combo or shower only. **Parking:** on-site.
Motel · **Terms:** small pets only. **Amenities:** video games (fee), voice mail. **Cards:** AX, CB, DC, DS, MC, VI. **Special Amenities:** free local telephone calls and free newspaper.
SOME UNITS

RESIDENCE INN · *Book at aaa.com* · Phone: (608)244-5047 · **8**
All Year · 1P: $89-$129 · 2P: $89-$129
Location: I-90/94, exit 135A, just sw on US 151. 4862 Hayes Rd 53704. Fax: 608/244-5047. **Facility:** 66 units. 54
Small-scale Hotel · one- and 12 two-bedroom suites with kitchens. 3 stories, interior corridors. *Bath:* combo or shower only. **Parking:** on-site. **Terms:** 7 day cancellation notice, pets ($25 deposit, $10 extra charge). **Amenities:** voice mail, irons, hair dryers. **Pool(s):** small heated indoor. **Leisure Activities:** whirlpool, exercise room, sports court. **Guest Services:** valet and coin laundry. **Business Services:** meeting rooms. **Cards:** AX, DC, DS, MC, VI.
SOME UNITS

RESIDENCE INN BY MARRIOTT-MADISON WEST · *Book at aaa.com* · Phone: (608)833-8333 · **28**
All Year · 1P: $119-$169
Location: US 12 and 14, exit 254 (Mineral Point Rd), 0.4 mi e, then just s. 501 D'Onofrio Dr 53719. Fax: 608/833-2693.
Condominium · **Facility:** Designed for the extended-stay traveler or families, many of these apartment-style units feature fireplaces. 80 one-bedroom standard units with kitchens. 2 stories, exterior corridors. **Terms:** weekly rates available, [BP] meal plan available, pets ($150 fee, $5 extra charge). **Amenities:** voice mail, irons, hair dryers. **Pool(s):** heated outdoor. **Leisure Activities:** whirlpool, exercise room, sports court. **Guest Services:** valet and coin laundry. **Business Services:** meeting rooms. **Cards:** AX, DC, DS, MC, VI.
SOME UNITS

(See map and index starting on p. 542)

SELECT INN   *Book at aaa.com*   Phone: (608)249-1815   **7**

All Year   1P: $39-$70   2P: $46-$75   XP: $5   F16
Location: I-90/94, exit 135A, just sw on US 151. 4845 Hayes Rd 53704. Fax: 608/249-1815. **Facility:** 97 units. 96 one-bedroom standard units, some with kitchens. 1 one-bedroom suite with kitchen. 3 stories (no elevator), interior corridors. *Bath:* combo or shower only. **Parking:** on-site. **Terms:** weekly rates available, [CP] meal plan available, small pets only ($25 deposit, $5 extra charge). **Amenities:** safes. *Some:* hair dryers. **Leisure Activities:** whirlpool. **Business Services:** meeting rooms. **Cards:** AX, DC, DS, MC, VI. **Special Amenities:** free continental breakfast. *(See color ad below)*
Small-scale Hotel

SOME UNITS
(icons) FEE

SHERATON MADISON HOTEL   *Book at aaa.com*   Phone: (608)251-2300   **33**
All Year   1P: $119-$139   2P: $119-$139
Location: US 12 and 18, exit 263 (John Nolen Dr), just n. 706 John Nolen Dr 53713. Fax: 608/251-1189. **Facility:** 237 units. 235 one-bedroom standard units. 2 one-bedroom suites. 8 stories, interior corridors. **Parking:** on-site. **Terms:** [AP] meal plan available, package plans - weekends. **Amenities:** video games (fee), dual phone lines, voice mail, irons, hair dryers. *Some:* fax. **Pool(s):** heated indoor. **Leisure Activities:** sauna, whirlpool, exercise room. *Fee:* game room. **Guest Services:** gift shop, valet laundry, area transportation. **Business Services:** conference facilities, business center. **Cards:** AX, CB, DC, DS, JC, MC, VI.
Large-scale Hotel

SOME UNITS
(icons)

(See map and index starting on p. 542)

STAYBRIDGE SUITES   *Book at aaa.com*   Phone: (608)241-2300   **4**

(AAA) (SAVE)
▼▼▼▼
Small-scale Hotel

All Year [ECP]   1P: $119   2P: $119
Location: US 151, exit 98A, just e, then 0.5 mi s on High Crossing Blvd. 3301 City View Dr 53718. Fax: 608/241-8845.
Facility: 90 units. 47 one-bedroom standard units with kitchens. 34 one- and 9 two-bedroom suites ($129-$179) with kitchens. 3 stories, interior corridors. *Bath:* combo or shower only. **Parking:** on-site. **Terms:** pets ($75 fee). **Amenities:** dual phone lines, voice mail, irons, hair dryers. *Fee:* video library, high-speed Internet. **Pool(s):** small heated indoor. **Leisure Activities:** whirlpool, patio with gas grill, library, exercise room. **Guest Services:** sundries, complimentary evening beverages: Tues-Thurs, area transportation. **Business Services:** meeting rooms, business center. **Cards:** AX, CB, DC, DS, MC, VI. **Special Amenities: free expanded continental breakfast and free local telephone calls.** *(See color ad p 552)*

SOME UNITS

(icons) FEE /⊠/

SUPER 8 MOTEL   *Book at aaa.com*   Phone: (608)258-8882   **37**

(AAA) (SAVE)
▼▼▼
Small-scale Hotel

All Year [ECP]   1P: $49-$99   2P: $49-$99
Location: US 12 and 18, exit 260B, just w on north frontage road. 1602 W Beltline Hwy 53713. Fax: 608/258-9575. **Facility:** 88 units. 87 one-bedroom standard units. 1 one-bedroom suite ($99-$129) with whirlpool. 3 stories, interior corridors. *Bath:* combo or shower only. **Parking:** on-site, winter plug-ins. **Terms:** check-in 4 pm, 2 night minimum stay - weekends, pets ($10 fee, in 2nd floor smoking units). **Amenities:** irons. **Pool(s):** heated indoor. **Leisure Activities:** whirlpool, limited exercise equipment. **Guest Services:** coin laundry. **Business Services:** business center. **Cards:** AX, CB, DC, DS, JC, MC, VI. **Special Amenities: free expanded continental breakfast and free local telephone calls.** *(See color ad below)*

SOME UNITS

(icons) FEE /⊠ 🖥📺/

WINGATE INN   *Book at aaa.com*   Phone: (608)224-1500   **35**

(AAA) (SAVE)
▼▼▼
Small-scale Hotel

4/1-10/6 & 3/1-3/31 [BP]   1P: $79-$109   2P: $79-$109   XP: $10   F17
10/7-2/28 [BP]   1P: $69-$99   2P: $69-$99   XP: $10   F17
Location: I-90, exit 142B, just e on US 12 and 18, then w on south frontage road. 3510 Mill Pond Rd 53718. Fax: 608/224-0586. **Facility:** 100 one-bedroom standard units, some with whirlpools. 4 stories, interior corridors. *Bath:* combo or shower only. **Parking:** on-site. **Terms:** cancellation fee imposed, package plans. **Amenities:** video games (fee), high-speed Internet, dual phone lines, voice mail, safes, irons, hair dryers. **Pool(s):** heated indoor. **Leisure Activities:** whirlpool, exercise room. **Guest Services:** valet and coin laundry. **Business Services:** meeting rooms, business center. **Cards:** AX, DC, DS, MC, VI. **Special Amenities: free full breakfast and free local telephone calls.**

SOME UNITS

(icons) /⊠ VCR/ FEE

WOODFIELD SUITES-MADISON   *Book at aaa.com*   Phone: (608)245-0123   **1**

▼▼▼
Small-scale Hotel

All Year   1P: $89-$109   2P: $109-$129
Location: US 151, exit 98B (American Pkwy), just sw. 5217 E Terrace Dr 53718. Fax: 608/245-1644. **Facility:** 120 units. 60 one-bedroom standard units. 60 one-bedroom suites, some with efficiencies and/or whirlpools. 4 stories, interior corridors. *Bath:* combo or shower only. **Parking:** on-site. **Terms:** [ECP] meal plan available, pets ($10 deposit). **Amenities:** video games (fee), dual phone lines, voice mail, irons, hair dryers. **Pool(s):** heated indoor. **Leisure Activities:** whirlpool, limited exercise equipment. **Guest Services:** complimentary evening beverages, valet and coin laundry, area transportation. **Business Services:** meeting rooms. **Cards:** AX, CB, DC, DS, MC, VI.

SOME UNITS

(icons) FEE /⊠ VCR/

(See map and index starting on p. 542)

———— WHERE TO DINE ————

BELLINI
Italian
Dinner: $14-$22   **Phone: 608/250-0097**   6
Location: Just e of Capitol Square; downtown. 401 E Washington Ave 53703. **Hours:** 5 pm-9 pm, Fri & Sat-10 pm. Closed major holidays; also Sun. **Reservations:** suggested. **Features:** Creative Italian-American dishes are served in the beautifully restored landmark church, which features original stained-glass windows and woodwork. The menu includes mouthwatering pastas and pizzas, as well as the delicious dessert specialty: cheesecake wrap. Casual dress; cocktails. **Parking:** street. **Cards:** AX, CB, DS, MC, VI.

BIAGGI'S
Italian
Lunch: $5-$9   **Dinner:** $9-$16   **Phone:** 608/664-0024   15
Location: US 12 and 14, exit 254 (Mineral Point Rd), just e, 0.5 mi n. 601 Junction Rd 53717. **Hours:** 11 am-10 pm, Fri & Sat-11 pm, Sun-9 pm. Closed major holidays. **Reservations:** accepted. **Features:** Diners looking for great Italian food at affordable prices need look no further. The restaurant's made-to-order pastas, pizzas and entrees won't bust the budget. On the menu are daily specials, as well as such classics as lasagna and fettuccine Alfredo. The casually elegant atmosphere makes this a great choice for business or romantic dining. Casual dress; cocktails. **Parking:** on-site. **Cards:** AX, DS, MC, VI.

THE BLUE MARLIN
Seafood
Lunch: $8-$10   **Dinner:** $22-$30   **Phone:** 608/255-2255   7
Location: Just n of Capitol Square; downtown. 101 N Hamilton St 53703. **Hours:** 11:30 am-2:30 & 5:30-10 pm. Closed: 7/4, 12/25; also Mon. **Reservations:** suggested. **Features:** Grilled seafood dishes center on fresh tuna, swordfish, salmon and live Maine lobster. Dressy casual; cocktails. **Parking:** on-site (fee) and street. **Cards:** AX, DC, DS, MC, VI.

CAFE CONTINENTAL
Italian
Lunch: $9-$12   **Dinner:** $10-$30   **Phone:** 608/251-4880   10
Location: Just e of Capitol Square; downtown. 108 King St 53703. **Hours:** 11 am-10 pm, Sun 9 am-9 pm. Closed: 11/25, 12/24, 12/25. **Reservations:** suggested. **Features:** A zinc bar is the centerpiece of the trendy Parisian-themed dining room, marked by hanging lamps, high ceilings and soft lighting. The menu centers on creatively prepared pasta, gourmet pizza and Continental cuisine. In-house desserts are rich. Casual dress; cocktails. **Parking:** street. **Cards:** AX, MC, VI.

ELLA'S KOSHER STYLE DELI & ICE CREAM PARLOR   **Lunch:** $3-$8 **Dinner:** $7-$8 **Phone:** 608/241-5291   4
Ethnic
Location: I-90/94, exit 135A, 3 mi w on US 151. 2902 E Washington Ave 53704. **Hours:** 10 am-11 pm, Fri & Sat-midnight; to 10 pm, Fri & Sat-11 pm in winter. Closed: 11/25, 12/25. **Features:** The extensive menu primarily centers on kosher sandwiches and salad. Antique and motorized toys, which decorate the charming restaurant, please adults and children alike. Noteworthy on the dessert menu is the delicious, old-fashioned frozen custard. Casual dress. **Parking:** on-site. **Cards:** MC, VI.

GEORGE'S CHOP HOUSE
American
Lunch: $6-$8   **Dinner:** $9-$15   **Phone:** 608/826-0555   5
Location: US 12 and 14, exit 253 (Old Sauk Rd), 0.5 mi w; adjacent to Holiday Inn Hotel & Suites. 1109 Fourier Dr 53717. **Hours:** 6:30 am-10 pm, Fri-Sun 7 am-11 pm. Closed major holidays. **Reservations:** accepted. **Features:** This hybrid steakhouse exerts a subtle Tuscan influence in both its attractive decor and food. In addition to eight 21-day-aged steaks, this place serves such Italian favorites as calamari fritte, salmone alla griglia and lasagna Bolognese. Casual dress; cocktails. **Parking:** on-site. **Cards:** AX, DC, DS, MC, VI.

IMPERIAL GARDEN-EAST
Chinese
Lunch: $6-$8   **Dinner:** $8-$13   **Phone:** 608/249-0466   2
Location: I-90/94, exit 135A, 0.5 mi w on US 151. 4214 E Washington Ave 53704. **Hours:** 11:30 am-2 & 4-9:30 pm, Fri-10:30 pm, Sat 11:30 am-10:30 pm, Sun 11:30 am-9 pm. Closed: 11/25, 12/24, 12/25. **Reservations:** suggested, weekends. **Features:** Traditional specialties—such as cashew chicken, Mongolian beef and the happy family platter—are filling and flavorful. Also featured is a sushi bar. An attractive tiger carving is among beautiful Asian appointments in the moderately upscale dining room. Lighting is subtle. Dressy casual; cocktails. **Parking:** on-site. **Cards:** AX, DS, MC, VI.

JOHNNY DELMONICO'S
Steak & Seafood
Dinner: $9-$31   **Phone:** 608/257-8325   14
Location: Corner of Doty St; downtown. 130 S Pinckney St 53703. **Hours:** 5 pm-9 pm, Fri & Sat-10 pm. Closed: 1/1, 12/25. **Reservations:** suggested. **Features:** Near the State Capitol, the stylish and trendy dining room specializes in premium aged steaks, fresh fish and seafood. Menu options include oysters on the half shell, free-range chicken, French-style pork chops, roasted lamb shank and sirloin burgers. Seating is comfortable, and the service is refined. Casual dress; cocktails. **Parking:** on-site. **Cards:** AX, MC, VI.

L'ETOILE
Regional American
Dinner: $23-$36   **Phone:** 608/251-0500   8
Location: On Capitol Square; downtown. 25 N Pinckney St 53703. **Hours:** 6 pm-8:45 pm, Fri 5:30 pm-9:45 pm, Sat 5 pm-9:45 pm. Closed major holidays; also Sun. **Reservations:** suggested. **Features:** This restaurant is known for using locally grown, fresh ingredients. The chef and proprietor takes pride in selecting Wisconsin grown vegetables, seasonings, dairy products and meats for the seasonally changing menu. Great attention is given to food presentation. There is a team approach to service. Dressy casual; cocktails. **Parking:** street. **Cards:** DC, DS, MC, VI.

THE MARINER'S INN
Steak & Seafood
Dinner: $14-$40   **Phone:** 608/246-3120   1
Location: 6 mi n on SR 113, just w on CR M, then left on Westport Rd 0.3 mi, follow signs. 5339 Lighthouse Bay Dr 53704. **Hours:** 5 pm-9:30 pm, Fri & Sat 4:30 pm-10 pm, Sun 4:30 pm-9 pm. Closed major holidays; also 12/24 & Super Bowl Sun. **Reservations:** accepted. **Features:** Located on the north shore of Lake Mendota, the restaurant offers a straight forward seafood menu along with a few beef selections. You can enjoy a view of a picturesque marina and the lake from most tables. Casual dress; cocktails. **Parking:** on-site. **Cards:** MC, VI.

(See map and index starting on p. 542)

NADIA'S RESTAURANT **Dinner:** $17-$26 **Phone:** 608/257-1740 ⑨
AAA **Location:** 0.4 mi w of Capitol Square; downtown. 508 State 53703. **Hours:** 5 pm-11 pm, Sun-10 pm. Closed: 7/4,
▽▽▽▽ 12/25. **Reservations:** suggested. **Features:** In the bustling State Street area, the restaurant offers such
traditional French Provencal cuisine as roasted lamb and chicken amaretto. Dressy casual; cocktails.
French **Parking:** street. **Cards:** AX, DS, MC, VI. ⴲ ╳

OTTO'S RESTAURANT AND BAR **Dinner:** $18-$25 **Phone:** 608/274-4044 ⑰
▽▽▽▽ **Location:** US 12 and 14, exit 254 (Mineral Point Rd), 1 mi e. 6405 Mineral Point Rd 53705. **Hours:** 5 pm-10 pm.
Closed major holidays; also Sun. **Reservations:** suggested. **Features:** Set in a beautifully restored 1870s
Mediterranean stone farmhouse, this restaurant offers fine Mediterranean cuisine and certified angus steaks. The upscale
lounge, seasonal patio dining and live jazz are some highlights of this restaurant, but the real stars are the
beautifully adorned entrees, including grilled salmon in grape leaves, oven roasted sea bass, and grilled loin lamb chops.
Dressy casual; cocktails. **Parking:** on-site. **Cards:** AX, DS, MC, VI.

PRIME QUARTER STEAK HOUSE **Dinner:** $15 **Phone:** 608/244-3520 ③
▽▽▽ **Location:** On US 151, just w of jct US 51. 3520 E Washington Ave 53704. **Hours:** 5 pm-10 pm, Sat from 4 pm,
Sun 4 pm-9 pm. Closed major holidays. **Reservations:** suggested. **Features:** Choose from a fine selection
Steak House of USDA choice steak, tuna or salmon. Enjoy a beverage and socialize as you grill-your-own steak on an
open charcoal pit. All entrees are the same price and include all-you-can-eat baked potatoes, Texas toast
and salad bar. Casual dress; cocktails. **Parking:** on-site. **Cards:** AX, DS, MC, VI. ⴲ ╳

QUIVEY'S GROVE STONE HOUSE, STABLE GRILL Historic **Dinner:** $12-$23 **Phone:** 608/273-4900
▽▽▽ ▽▽▽ **Location:** US 18 and 151, exit PD, just w, then 0.6 mi s. 6261 Nesbitt Rd 53719. **Hours:** 5 pm-9 pm, Fri & Sat-10
pm. Closed major holidays; also Sun. **Reservations:** suggested. **Features:** The converted 1855 rural
American mansion and rustic stable are appointed with period furnishings. The menu includes such dishes as baked
trout, roast duck, roast pork and the chicken/mushroom-filled popover. The five-acre estate is in the historic
district. Casual dress; cocktails. **Parking:** on-site. **Cards:** AX, DS, MC, VI. ⴲ ╳

SA-BAI THONG **Lunch:** $6-$8 **Dinner:** $6-$15 **Phone:** 608/828-9565 ⑫
▽▽▽ ▽▽▽ **Location:** US 12 and 14, exit 255 (Gammon Rd), 0.3 mi e. 6802 Odana Rd 53719. **Hours:** 11 am-2:30 & 4:30-9
pm, Fri-10 pm, Sat 11 am-10 pm, Sun 5 pm-9 pm. Closed major holidays. **Reservations:** suggested.
Thai **Features:** The eatery is a hot destination for an adventure in tastes of the East. Delicious dishes, made
from fresh ingredients and with homemade sauces, are created using old family recipes. Casual dress;
cocktails. **Parking:** on-site. **Cards:** AX, DS, MC, VI. ╳

SMOKY'S CLUB **Dinner:** $10-$25 **Phone:** 608/233-2120 ⑪
▽▽▽ ▽▽▽ **Location:** On University Ave, 0.5 mi e of jct Midvale Blvd. 3005 University Ave 53705. **Hours:** 5 pm-10 pm. Closed
major holidays; also Sun & Tues. **Reservations:** accepted. **Features:** The popular, established restaurant
Steak House attracts much of its clientele from the university. Complementary bread baskets and relishes on ice, along
with homemade soups and succulent, sizzling steaks served with fries or hash browns, satisfy the heartiest
appetites. Smoking is allowed only in the lounge. Casual dress; cocktails. **Parking:** on-site. **Cards:** AX, DS, MC, VI. ⴲ ╳

TIMBER LODGE STEAKHOUSE **Lunch:** $6-$12 **Dinner:** $12-$20 **Phone:** 608/827-6444 ⑯
▽▽▽ ▽▽▽ **Location:** US 12 and 18, exit Gammon Rd, then 1 mi e. 6613 Mineral Point Rd 53705. **Hours:** 11 am-3 & 4-10 pm,
Fri & Sat 11 am-11 pm, Sun 11 am-9 pm. Closed: 11/25, 12/24, 12/25. **Features:** The steak house isn't
Steak House just for meat and potato lovers. In addition to top-quality aged and hand-cut steaks, the menu lists tasty
seafood and chicken entrees. A favorite is prairie chicken—barbecue chicken wrapped in bacon and
topped with two cheeses. Casual dress; cocktails. **Parking:** on-site. **Cards:** AX, DS, MC, VI. ⓜ ⴲ ╳

WHITE HORSE INN **Dinner:** $12-$23 **Phone:** 608/255-9933 ⑬
▽▽▽ ▽▽▽ **Location:** Just off Capitol Square; next to Civic Center. 202 N Henry 53703. **Hours:** 5 pm-10 pm, Fri & Sat-11 pm,
Sun 10 am-2 & 5-9 pm. **Reservations:** suggested. **Features:** A good selection of wine complements such
American dishes as grilled stuffed pork tenderloin, White Horse shrimp and scallops and Caesar planked Atlantic
salmon. The dining room has the ambience of an American bistro—quiet, upscale and dignified. Casual
dress; cocktails. **Parking:** on-site. **Cards:** AX, DC, MC, VI. ⴲ ╳

MANITOWISH WATERS

—— **WHERE TO DINE** ——

BLUE BAYOU INN **Dinner:** $15-$25 **Phone:** 715/543-2537
AAA **Location:** At Spider Lake Bridge, 3 mi s of CR W on US 51. 288 US Hwy 51 54545. **Hours:** Open 5/1-10/31; 5
▽▽▽▽ pm-9 pm; hours may vary. Closed: Sun. **Reservations:** accepted. **Features:** The lakefront restaurant
delivers authentic Louisiana Cajun-Creole cuisine, with such choices as seafood gumbo, jambalaya and
Regional shrimp Creole with steamed rice and vegetables. A nice selection of beer and wine is available. Servers
American are knowledgeable. Smoking in lounge only. Casual dress; cocktails. **Parking:** on-site. **Cards:** DS, MC, VI.
ⴲ ╳

MICHAEL'S **Lunch:** $4-$7 **Phone:** 715/543-2550
▽▽ **Location:** On US 51, 5 mi s. 397 S US 51 54545. **Hours:** 7 am-4 pm; to 9:30 pm in summer. Closed: 11/25,
12/24, 12/25. **Features:** Homemade baked goods, flavorful soup and hearty chili are tasty, basically
American prepared favorites at the quaint country cafe. Breakfast selections are served well into the afternoon.
DS, MC, VI. During the summer, the soda fountain brings in a good crowd. Casual dress. **Parking:** on-site. **Cards:** AX,
╳

MANITOWOC pop. 34,053

———— WHERE TO STAY ————

COMFORT INN   *Book at aaa.com*   **Phone:** (920)683-0220
▽▽▽ ▽▽▽
7/16-8/31	1P: $89-$99	2P: $93-$99
6/1-7/15	1P: $79-$95	2P: $85-$99
4/1-5/31	1P: $59-$69	2P: $61-$71
9/1-3/31	1P: $49-$59	2P: $54-$64

Small-scale Hotel

Location: I-43, exit 149, just e. Located in a commercial area. 2200 S 44th St 54220. **Fax:** 920/683-0220. **Facility:** 47 one-bedroom standard units. 2 stories (no elevator), interior corridors. **Parking:** on-site, winter plug-ins. **Terms:** [ECP] meal plan available. **Amenities:** irons, hair dryers. **Leisure Activities:** whirlpool. **Guest Services:** valet laundry. **Cards:** AX, DC, DS, MC, VI.

SOME UNITS
(ASK) (S/D) 🐾 🍴⁺ 🎦 📠 💻 / ✕ 🛄 🖥 /

HOLIDAY INN   *Book at aaa.com*   **Phone:** (920)682-6000
▽▽▽ ▽▽▽
6/2-10/31	1P: $99-$110	2P: $105-$115
4/1-6/1 & 11/1-3/31	1P: $85-$95	2P: $95-$105

Large-scale Hotel   **Location:** I-43, exit 149, just e. Located in a commercial area. 4601 Calumet Ave 54220. **Fax:** 920/682-6140. **Facility:** 204 units. 198 one-bedroom standard units. 6 one-bedroom suites ($135-$155). 3 stories, interior corridors. *Bath:* combo or shower only. **Parking:** on-site. **Terms:** cancellation fee imposed, [AP] meal plan available, pets ($150 deposit). **Amenities:** video games, dual phone lines, voice mail, irons, hair dryers. *Some:* high-speed Internet. **Pool(s):** heated indoor. **Leisure Activities:** sauna, whirlpool, playground, exercise room. *Fee:* game room. **Guest Services:** gift shop, valet laundry. **Business Services:** conference facilities, business center. **Cards:** AX, CB, DC, DS, JC, MC, VI.

SOME UNITS
(ASK) (S/D) 🔌 🐾 🛏 🍴 🍸 ♿ 🏊 ✕ 🎦 📠 💻 / ✕ 🛄 🖥 /
       FEE   FEE FEE

———— WHERE TO DINE ————

FOUR SEASONS   **Lunch:** $4-$9   **Dinner:** $4-$9   **Phone:** 920/683-1444
▽▽
American
Location: I-43, exit 149, 0.9 mi e. 3950 Calumet Ave 54220. **Hours:** 5:30 am-11 pm. **Features:** The casual restaurant features an extensive menu of simple recipes and offers a coffee-shop ambience that is comfortable for families and popular with the locals. Breakfast is served all day. Dessert and bread are made on the premises. Casual dress; wine only. **Parking:** on-site. **Cards:** MC, VI.   ✕

———— *The following restaurant has not been evaluated by AAA* ————
but is listed for your information only.

LUIGI'S   **Phone:** 920/684-4200
(fyi)
Not evaluated. **Location:** I-43, exit 149, 1 mi w on US 151. 6124 Calumet Ave 54220. **Features:** This eatery is well-known for its traditional, pan and Chicago style pizza.

MARINETTE pop. 11,749

———— WHERE TO STAY ————

BEST WESTERN RIVERFRONT INN   *Book at aaa.com*   **Phone:** (715)732-1000
(AAA) (SAVE)
6/1-10/31	1P: $84-$94	2P: $84-$94	XP: $10	F17
11/1-3/31	1P: $79-$89	2P: $79-$89	XP: $10	F17
4/1-5/31	1P: $69-$79	2P: $69-$79	XP: $10	F17

▽▽▽ ▽▽▽
Location: Just w of US 41; downtown. 1821 Riverside Ave 54143. **Fax:** 715/732-0800. **Facility:** 120 one-bedroom
Large-scale Hotel   standard units, some with whirlpools. 6 stories, interior corridors. **Parking:** on-site. **Amenities:** video games, high-speed Internet (fee), voice mail, irons, hair dryers. **Dining:** 6 am-10 pm, cocktails. **Pool(s):** heated indoor. **Leisure Activities:** whirlpool, limited exercise equipment. **Guest Services:** valet and coin laundry. **Business Services:** conference facilities. **Cards:** AX, CB, DC, DS, JC, MC, VI. **Special Amenities:** free local telephone calls and free newspaper.

SOME UNITS
(S/D) 🍴 🍸 🐾 🎦 📠 💻 / ✕ 🛄 🖥 /

COMFORT INN OF MARINETTE   *Book at aaa.com*   **Phone:** 715/732-2321
(AAA) (SAVE)
5/1-10/31	1P: $65-$90	2P: $71-$100	XP: $6	F
4/1-4/30 & 11/1-3/31	1P: $54-$80	2P: $60-$86	XP: $6	F

▽▽▽ ▽▽▽
Location: 2 mi s on US 41. Located in a commercial area. 2180 Roosevelt Rd 54143. **Fax:** 715/732-3663.
Facility: 48 one-bedroom standard units, some with whirlpools. 2 stories (no elevator), interior corridors.
Small-scale Hotel   *Bath:* combo or shower only. **Parking:** on-site, winter plug-ins. **Terms:** cancellation fee imposed, [ECP] meal plan available. **Amenities:** irons, hair dryers. *Some:* high-speed Internet. **Leisure Activities:** whirlpool, exercise room. **Business Services:** meeting rooms. **Cards:** AX, DC, DS, MC, VI. **Special Amenities:** free continental breakfast.

SOME UNITS
(S/D) 🍴⁺ ♿ 🎦 📠 💻 / ✕ (VCR) 🛄 🖥 /
                                                           FEE

———— WHERE TO DINE ————

MEMORIES RESTAURANT   **Lunch:** $3-$6   **Dinner:** $3-$6   **Phone:** 715/735-3348
▽▽
American
Location: 0.5 mi s of US 41; downtown. 1378 Main St 54143. **Hours:** 5:30 am-7 pm, Sun from 6:30 am. Closed: 12/25. **Features:** Step back into the 1950s at this casual downtown restaurant known for its homestyle sandwiches and chargrilled burgers. Soup, chili, bread and old-fashioned dessert are made in-house. Breakfast is served all day. Casual dress. **Parking:** on-site. **Cards:** MC, VI.   ✕

MARSHFIELD pop. 18,800

———— WHERE TO STAY ————

AMERIHOST INN AND SUITES-MARSHFIELD   *Book at aaa.com*

(AAA) (SAVE)
▼▼▼

Small-scale Hotel

All Year [ECP]   1P: $68-$88   2P: $68-$88   XP: $6   F18

Phone: (715)384-5240

Location: On SR 97, 1.2 mi n of SR 13. 2107 N Central Ave 54449. Fax: 715/384-4812. **Facility:** 60 one-bedroom standard units, some with whirlpools. 2 stories, interior corridors. *Bath:* combo or shower only. **Parking:** on-site. **Terms:** cancellation fee imposed. **Amenities:** voice mail, safes (fee), irons, hair dryers. **Pool(s):** heated indoor. **Leisure Activities:** whirlpool, exercise room. **Guest Services:** valet laundry. **Business Services:** meeting rooms, fax (fee). **Cards:** AX, DC, DS, MC, VI. **Special Amenities:** free expanded continental breakfast and free local telephone calls.

SOME UNITS

COMFORT INN   *Book at aaa.com*

▼▼▼

Small-scale Hotel

All Year [ECP]   1P: $59   2P: $59   XP: $5   F18

Phone: 715/387-8691

Location: On SR 97, 0.6 mi n of jct SR 13. Located in a commercial area. 114 E Upham St 54449. Fax: 715/387-3001. **Facility:** 46 one-bedroom standard units, some with whirlpools. 2 stories (no elevator), interior corridors. **Parking:** on-site, winter plug-ins. **Terms:** [ECP] meal plan available. **Amenities:** video library (fee), irons, hair dryers. **Pool(s):** heated indoor. **Leisure Activities:** whirlpool. **Cards:** AX, DC, DS, MC, VI.

SOME UNITS   FEE

PARK MOTEL

(AAA) (SAVE)
▼▼▼

Motel

All Year   1P: $35-$39   2P: $42-$46   XP: $5   F12

Phone: (715)387-1741

Location: 1 mi s on SR 13. Located next to Wildwood Park and Zoo. 1806 S Roddis Ave 54449. Fax: 715/387-0290. **Facility:** 20 one-bedroom standard units. 1 story, exterior corridors. *Bath:* combo or shower only. **Parking:** on-site, winter plug-ins. **Terms:** office hours 6 am-midnight, 3 day cancellation notice-fee imposed, weekly rates available, small pets only ($10 fee, with prior approval). **Cards:** AX, DS, MC, VI. **Special Amenities:** free local telephone calls and free room upgrade (subject to availability with advanced reservations).

SOME UNITS   FEE

SUPER 8   *Book at aaa.com*

▼▼▼

Small-scale Hotel

6/1-9/30   1P: $57-$62   2P: $62-$67   XP: $5   F12
4/1-5/31 & 10/1-3/31   1P: $54-$59   2P: $59-$64   XP: $5   F12

Phone: 715/387-2233

Location: On SR 97, 0.8 mi n of jct SR 13. Located in a commercial area. 1651 N Central Ave 54449. Fax: 715/384-8366. **Facility:** 104 one-bedroom standard units, some with whirlpools. 2 stories (no elevator), interior corridors. **Parking:** on-site, winter plug-ins. **Terms:** [CP] meal plan available. **Amenities:** hair dryers. **Pool(s):** heated indoor. **Leisure Activities:** whirlpool. *Fee:* game room. **Business Services:** meeting rooms. **Cards:** AX, DC, DS, MC, VI.

SOME UNITS   FEE

———— WHERE TO DINE ————

ROYAL TOKYO

▼▼▼

Japanese

Dinner: $15-$25

Phone: 715/486-8868

Location: Just e of Central Ave; adjacent to railroad tracks; downtown. 112 E 1st St 54449. **Hours:** 4:30 pm-9:30 pm. Closed: 11/25, 12/25. **Reservations:** accepted. **Features:** Skilled teppanyaki chefs put on quite a show as they prepare your food before your eyes on heated steel grills. Visitors tend to socialize at the large tables in this professionally restored train depot. Miso soup, a variety of sushis and entrees of beef, seafood & chicken highlight the menu. Dressy casual; cocktails. **Parking:** on-site. **Cards:** AX, DC, MC, VI.

MAUSTON pop. 3,740

———— WHERE TO STAY ————

BEST WESTERN PARK OASIS INN   *Book at aaa.com*

(AAA) (SAVE)
▼▼▼

Small-scale Hotel

5/1-9/30   1P: $85-$150   2P: $90-$160   XP: $5   F17
4/1-4/30 & 10/1-3/31   1P: $70-$145   2P: $75-$150   XP: $5   F17

Phone: (608)847-6255

Location: I-90/94, exit 69, just se. W5641 Hwy 82 E 53948. Fax: 608/847-7311. **Facility:** 53 units. 51 one-bedroom standard units, some with whirlpools. 2 one-bedroom suites ($115-$170), some with kitchens. 3 stories, interior corridors. **Parking:** on-site, winter plug-ins. **Terms:** [AP] meal plan available. **Amenities:** safes, irons, hair dryers. **Dining:** 5 am-10 pm, cocktails. **Pool(s):** small heated outdoor, small heated indoor. **Leisure Activities:** sauna, whirlpool, horseshoes. *Fee:* miniature golf, game room. **Guest Services:** gift shop, valet and coin laundry. **Business Services:** meeting rooms. **Cards:** AX, CB, DC, DS, MC, VI. **Special Amenities:** free local telephone calls and free newspaper.

SOME UNITS

COUNTRY INN BY CARLSON   *Book at aaa.com*

(AAA) (SAVE)
▼▼▼

Small-scale Hotel

4/25-9/30 [ECP]   1P: $81-$89   2P: $89-$97   XP: $8   F18
4/1-4/24 & 10/1-3/31 [ECP]   1P: $66-$74   2P: $74-$82   XP: $8   F18

Phone: (608)847-5959

Location: I-90/94, exit 69, just ne. 1001 SR 82 53948. Fax: 608/847-4160. **Facility:** 62 one-bedroom standard units, some with whirlpools. 2 stories (no elevator), interior corridors. **Parking:** on-site, winter plug-ins. **Terms:** small pets only ($5 extra charge). **Amenities:** irons, hair dryers. **Pool(s):** small heated indoor. **Leisure Activities:** whirlpool. *Fee:* game room. **Guest Services:** coin laundry. **Business Services:** meeting rooms, administrative services (fee). **Cards:** AX, DC, DS, MC, VI. **Special Amenities:** free expanded continental breakfast and free newspaper. *(See color ad starting on p 580)*

SOME UNITS   FEE

SUPER 8 MOTEL   *Book at aaa.com*   **Phone:** 608/847-2300
▼▼ ▼▼   6/1-9/30   1P: $58-$71   2P: $69-$89   XP: $5   F17
             10/1-3/31   1P: $56-$72   2P: $60-$76   XP: $5   F17
Motel   4/1-5/31   1P: $53-$70   2P: $58-$74   XP: $6   F17
          Location: I-90/94, exit 69, just ne. 1001A Hwy 82 E 53948. **Fax:** 608/847-6769. **Facility:** 49 units. 47 one-bedroom
standard units. 2 one-bedroom suites with whirlpools. 2 stories (no elevator), interior corridors. **Parking:** on-site, winter plug-ins.
Terms: 7 day cancellation notice, pets ($5 extra charge). **Amenities:** dual phone lines, hair dryers. **Pool(s):** small heated indoor.
Leisure Activities: whirlpool. **Guest Services:** coin laundry. **Cards:** AX, DC, DS, MC, VI.
                                                                                      SOME UNITS
                                                           🛏️ 🍽️ 🏊 🎥 📠 📶 🖥️ 🖨️ 🖥️ / ✕ /
                                                           FEE

MAYVILLE pop. 4,902

─────── **WHERE TO STAY** ───────

THE MAYVILLE INN   **Phone:** 920/387-1234
▼▼▼▼   All Year   1P: $60-$99   2P: $60-$99   XP: $10   F12
          Location: 1.3 mi w on SR 28. Located adjacent to a large park. 701 S Mountin Dr 53050 (PO Box 86).
Small-scale Hotel **Fax:** 920/387-1234. **Facility:** 29 one-bedroom standard units, some with whirlpools. 2 stories, interior corri-
          dors. **Parking:** on-site, winter plug-ins. **Terms:** office hours 6 am-10 pm, [CP] meal plan available. **Guest**
Services: valet laundry. **Business Services:** meeting rooms. **Cards:** AX, DS, MC, VI.
                                                                                      SOME UNITS
                                                                    🍽️ 📶 📶 / ✕ 🖥️ /
                                                                    FEE

MAZOMANIE pop. 1,485

─────── **WHERE TO DINE** ───────

THE OLD FEED MILL   **Lunch:** $5-$7   **Dinner:** $11-$21   **Phone:** 608/795-4909
▼▼ ▼▼   **Location:** 0.3 mi n of US 14. 114 Cramer Dr 53560. **Hours:** 11 am-2 & 4:30-8 pm, Fri & Sat-9 pm, Sun 10
          am-2:30 & 4:30-8 pm. Closed: 12/25; also Mon. **Reservations:** accepted. **Features:** Country cooking is
American   dished up at a wonderfully restored 1857 flour feed mill furnished with antiques. Each day, the restaurant
          grinds its own flour for use in breads and pastries. Pot roast and pot pie are mouthwatering choices, as is
scrumptious bread pudding from the dessert menu. Casual dress; cocktails. **Parking:** on-site. **Cards:** AX, DS, MC, VI. ✕

MEDFORD pop. 4,350

─────── **WHERE TO STAY** ───────

AMERICINN OF MEDFORD   *Book at aaa.com*   **Phone:** 715-748-2330
▼▼ ▼▼   All Year [ECP]   1P: $69-$97   2P: $75-$103   XP: $6   F12
          Location: On SR 13, 0.5 mi s of jct SR 64. 435 S 8th St 54451. **Fax:** 715/748-5543. **Facility:** 38 units. 37 one-
Small-scale Hotel bedroom standard units. 1 one-bedroom suite. 2 stories (no elevator), interior corridors. *Bath:* combo or
          shower only. **Parking:** on-site. **Terms:** cancellation fee imposed. **Pool(s):** heated indoor. **Leisure Activi-**
ties: sauna, whirlpool. **Business Services:** meeting rooms. **Cards:** AX, DC, DS, MC, VI. *(See color ad p 576)*
                                                                                      SOME UNITS
                                                  🍽️ ♿ 🏊 🎥 📶 🖥️ / ✕ 🖥️ /

MALIBU INN MOTEL   **Phone:** 715-748-3995
▼▼ ▼▼   All Year   1P: $59   2P: $67   XP: $8   F10
          Location: On SR 13, 0.6 mi n of jct SR 64. 854 N 8th St 54451. **Fax:** 715/748-3995. **Facility:** 26 units. 24 one-
Motel   bedroom standard units. 2 one-bedroom suites ($85-$135). 1 story, interior corridors. **Parking:** on-site, winter
          plug-ins. **Terms:** [CP] meal plan available. **Pool(s):** small heated indoor. **Leisure Activities:** sauna, whirl-
pool. **Business Services:** fax (fee). **Cards:** AX, DS, MC, VI.
                                                                                      SOME UNITS
                                                           🍽️ 🏊 📶 / ✕ 🖥️ 🖥️ /

─────── **WHERE TO DINE** ───────

MEDFORD CAFE   **Lunch:** $5-$8   **Dinner:** $5-$8   **Phone:** 715-748-2233
▼▼   **Location:** On SR 13, 0.5 mi s of jct SR 64. 403 S 8th St 54451. **Hours:** 6 am-9 pm. Closed: 11/25, 12/25.
          Reservations: accepted. **Features:** This restaurant features a homey and contemporary decor that is in a
American   country and patriotic theme. The menu consists of a traditional selection of sandwiches and burgers, as
          well as a variety of country dinners. Casual dress. **Parking:** on-site. **Cards:** AX, DS, MC, VI.   ✕

MENOMONIE pop. 14,937

─────── **WHERE TO STAY** ───────

AMERIHOST INN & SUITES MENOMONIE   *Book at aaa.com*   **Phone:** (715)233-1500
(AAA) (SAVE)   All Year   1P: $69-$129   2P: $69-$129
          Location: I-94, exit 45 (CR B), just sw. 1721 Plaza Dr NE 54751. **Fax:** 715/233-6198. **Facility:** 62 one-bedroom
▼▼▼▼   standard units, some with whirlpools. 3 stories, interior corridors. *Bath:* combo or shower only. **Parking:** on-
          site. **Amenities:** high-speed Internet, dual phone lines, voice mail, safes, irons, hair dryers. **Pool(s):** heated
Small-scale Hotel indoor. **Leisure Activities:** whirlpool, limited exercise equipment. **Guest Services:** valet and coin laundry.
          Business Services: meeting rooms. **Cards:** AX, CB, DC, DS, JC, MC, VI. **Special Amenities:** free ex-
panded continental breakfast and free local telephone calls.
                                                                                      SOME UNITS
                                          📶 🍽️ ♿ ♿ 🏊 🎥 📶 🖥️ / ✕ 📼 🖥️ 🖥️ /

COUNTRY INN & SUITES   *Book at aaa.com*   Phone: (715)235-5664
AAA SAVE

7/1-9/30	1P: $89-$99	2P: $89-$99	XP: $10 F18
4/1-6/30 & 10/1-3/31	1P: $79-$89	2P: $79-$89	XP: $10 F18

Location: I-94, exit 41 (SR 25), just se. 320 Oak Ave 54751. Fax: 715/233-3241. **Facility:** 68 units. 57 one-bedroom standard units, some with whirlpools. 11 one-bedroom suites. 3 stories, interior corridors. *Bath:* combo or shower only. **Parking:** on-site, winter plug-ins. **Terms:** pets ($25 fee). **Amenities:** high-speed Internet, dual phone lines, voice mail, irons, hair dryers. **Pool(s):** small heated indoor. **Leisure Activities:** exercise room. **Guest Services:** coin laundry. **Business Services:** meeting rooms, administrative services (fee). **Cards:** AX, DC, DS, MC, VI. **Special Amenities:** free continental breakfast and free local telephone calls.
(See color ad starting on p 580)

MENOMONIE MOTEL 6 #4109   *Book at aaa.com*   Phone: 715/235-6901

All Year	1P: $38-$52	2P: $44-$58	XP: $3 F17

Location: I-94, exit 41 (SR 25), just se. 2100 Stout St 54751 (603 Grandview Hts). Fax: 715/235-8664. **Facility:** 63 one-bedroom standard units. 3 stories, interior corridors. *Bath:* combo or shower only. **Parking:** on-site. **Terms:** weekly rates available, package plans. **Amenities:** high-speed Internet (fee). **Guest Services:** coin laundry. **Business Services:** administrative services (fee). **Cards:** AX, DC, DS, MC, VI.

SUPER 8 MOTEL-MENOMONIE   *Book at aaa.com*   Phone: (715)235-8889

5/28-9/5 [CP]	1P: $60-$90	2P: $60-$90	XP: $6 F12
9/6-12/31 [CP]	1P: $50-$70	2P: $50-$70	XP: $6 F12
4/1-5/27 & 1/1-3/31 [CP]	1P: $49-$69	2P: $49-$69	XP: $6 F12

Location: I-94, exit 41 (SR 25), just s. 1622 N Broadway 54751. Fax: 715/235-9127. **Facility:** 81 one-bedroom standard units. 3 stories, interior corridors. **Parking:** on-site, winter plug-ins. **Terms:** pets ($15 fee). **Amenities:** safes (fee). **Pool(s):** heated indoor. **Leisure Activities:** whirlpool. **Guest Services:** coin laundry. **Business Services:** meeting rooms, administrative services (fee). **Cards:** AX, CB, DC, DS, MC, VI.

MEQUON *—See Milwaukee p. 596.*

MERRILL pop. 10,146

——— **WHERE TO STAY** ———

AMERICINN LODGE & SUITES OF MERRILL   *Book at aaa.com*   Phone: (715)536-7979

All Year	1P: $79-$139	2P: $79-$139	XP: $5 F12

Location: US 51, exit 208, 0.5 mi w on SR 64. 3300 E Main St 54452. Fax: 715/536-7975. **Facility:** 45 one-bedroom standard units, some with whirlpools. 2 stories, interior corridors. *Bath:* combo or shower only. **Parking:** on-site. **Terms:** weekly rates available, small pets only ($10 fee). **Amenities:** high-speed Internet (fee), irons, hair dryers. **Pool(s):** heated indoor. **Leisure Activities:** sauna, whirlpool. **Business Services:** meeting rooms. **Cards:** AX, CB, DC, DS, MC, VI. *(See color ad p 576)*

PINE RIDGE INN   *Book at aaa.com*   Phone: (715)536-9526
AAA SAVE

6/1-9/30	1P: $45-$58	2P: $49-$85	XP: $5 F12
1/1-3/31	1P: $40-$54	2P: $42-$59	XP: $5 F12
10/1-12/31	1P: $40-$54	2P: $42-$58	XP: $5 F12
4/1-5/31	1P: $40-$52	2P: $45-$54	XP: $5 F12

Location: I-39, exit 208, just w. 200 S Pine Ridge 54452. Fax: 715/536-4520. **Facility:** 40 one-bedroom standard units, some with kitchens. 2 stories (no elevator), interior corridors. **Parking:** on-site, winter plug-ins. **Terms:** cancellation fee imposed, weekly rates available, [CP] & [ECP] meal plans available, pets ($5 extra charge, with prior approval). **Pool(s):** heated indoor. **Leisure Activities:** whirlpool. **Business Services:** fax (fee). **Cards:** AX, DS, MC, VI. **Special Amenities:** free continental breakfast and free local telephone calls.

SUPER 8 MOTEL   *Book at aaa.com*   Phone: 715/536-6880
AAA SAVE

All Year	1P: $60-$110	2P: $67-$121	XP: $7 F13

Location: I-39, exit 208, 0.5 mi w on SR 64. 3209 E Main St 54452. Fax: 715/539-2602. **Facility:** 57 units. 56 one-bedroom standard units, some with whirlpools. 1 one-bedroom suite. 2 stories (no elevator), interior corridors. *Bath:* combo or shower only. **Parking:** on-site, winter plug-ins. **Terms:** [ECP] meal plan available, pets ($5 fee). **Amenities:** *Some:* irons, hair dryers. **Pool(s):** small heated indoor. **Leisure Activities:** sauna, whirlpool. *Fee:* game room. **Guest Services:** valet and coin laundry. **Business Services:** meeting rooms, fax. **Cards:** AX, CB, DC, DS, MC, VI. **Special Amenities:** free expanded continental breakfast and free local telephone calls.

MIDDLETON pop. 15,770   (See map and index starting on p. 542)

──────── WHERE TO STAY ────────

FAIRFIELD INN MADISON WEST/MIDDLETON   *Book at aaa.com*   **Phone:** 608/831-1400   **45**
▼▼▼▼   4/1-10/31   1P: $59-$99   2P: $69-$109
         11/1-3/31   1P: $59-$89   2P: $59-$89
Small-scale Hotel   **Location:** US 12 and 14, exit 252 (Greenway Blvd), just w. 8212 Greenway Blvd 53562. **Fax:** 608/831-1435. **Facility:** 104 one-bedroom standard units. 3 stories, interior corridors. *Bath:* combo or shower only. **Parking:** on-site, winter plug-ins. **Terms:** cancellation fee imposed, [CP] meal plan available. **Amenities:** video games (fee), dual phone lines, irons, hair dryers. **Pool(s):** small heated indoor. **Leisure Activities:** whirlpool. **Guest Services:** valet laundry. **Business Services:** meeting rooms. **Cards:** AX, CB, DC, DS, MC, VI.

SOME UNITS

MARRIOTT MADISON WEST   *Book at aaa.com*   **Phone:** (608)831-2000   **46**
(AAA) (SAVE)   All Year   1P: $98-$179
▼▼▼▼   **Location:** US 12 and 14, exit 252 (Greenway Blvd), then just w. 1313 John Q Hammons Dr 53562. **Fax:** 608/831-2040. **Facility:** 292 units. 256 one-bedroom standard units. 36 one-bedroom suites, some with whirlpools. 10 stories, interior corridors. **Parking:** on-site. **Terms:** check-in 4 pm. **Amenities:** high-speed Internet (fee), dual phone lines, voice mail, irons, hair dryers. **Dining:** 6 am-9 pm, cocktails, nightclub. **Pool(s):** heated indoor.
Large-scale Hotel   **Leisure Activities:** sauna, whirlpool, sun deck, exercise room. **Guest Services:** gift shop, valet and coin laundry, area transportation. **Business Services:** conference facilities, business center. **Cards:** AX, CB, DC, DS, JC, MC, VI. **Special Amenities:** free newspaper. *(See color ad p 551)*

SOME UNITS
FEE

STAYBRIDGE SUITES BY HOLIDAY INN   *Book at aaa.com*   **Phone:** (608)664-5888   **44**
(AAA) (SAVE)   All Year [ECP]   1P: $119   2P: $119
▼▼▼▼   **Location:** US 12 and 14, exit University Ave, just nw. 7790 Elmwood Ave 53562. **Fax:** 608/664-5877. **Facility:** 91 units. 34 one-bedroom standard units with kitchens. 46 one- and 11 two-bedroom suites ($129-$189) with kitchens. 3 stories, interior corridors. *Bath:* combo or shower only. **Parking:** on-site. **Terms:** pets ($150 fee).
Small-scale Hotel   **Amenities:** dual phone lines, voice mail, irons, hair dryers. *Fee:* video games, high-speed Internet. **Pool(s):** small heated indoor. **Leisure Activities:** whirlpool, sun deck, board games, barbecue grills, library, exercise room. **Guest Services:** gift shop, complimentary evening beverages: Tues-Thurs, valet and coin laundry, area transportation. **Business Services:** meeting rooms, business center. **Cards:** AX, CB, DC, DS, MC, VI. **Special Amenities:** free expanded continental breakfast and free local telephone calls. *(See color ad p 552)*

SOME UNITS
FEE

(See map and index starting on p. 542)

─────── *The following lodging was either not evaluated or did not* ───────
meet AAA rating requirements but is listed for your information only.

HILTON GARDEN INN MADISON WEST/MIDDLETON   **Phone:** 608/831-2220
[fyi]   Under construction, scheduled to open October 2004. **Location:** US 12 and 14, exit 252 (Greenway Blvd), just left,
Small-scale Hotel   then right. 1801 Deming Way 53562. **Planned Amenities:** coffeemakers, microwaves, refrigerators, pool.

─────── **WHERE TO DINE** ───────

FITZGERALD'S OF MIDDLETON   **Lunch:** $5-$10   **Dinner:** $10-$20   **Phone:** 608/831-7107   [20]
▼▼ ▼▼   **Location:** On US 12, just n of jct US 14. 3112 W Beltline Hwy 53562. **Hours:** 11 am-2 & 5-9:30 pm, Fri 11 am-2
American   & 4:30-10:30 pm, Sat 5 pm-10:30 pm, Sun 10 am-2 & 4:30-9:30 pm. Closed major holidays.
Reservations: accepted. **Features:** The classic Wisconsin supper club prepares great steaks and
seafood. Locals flock here on Fridays for the fish fry. If these aren't good enough reasons to visit, factor in
friendly service and an inviting atmosphere. Casual dress; cocktails. **Parking:** on-site. **Cards:** AX, DS, MC, VI.   🍸✕

HUBBARD AVENUE DINER   **Lunch:** $5-$10   **Dinner:** $5-$10   **Phone:** 608/831-6800   [24]
▼▼   **Location:** US 12 and 14, exit University Ave, just e to Aurora St, just s to Hubbard Ave. 7445 Hubbard Ave 53562.
American   **Hours:** 7 am-9 pm, Fri-10 pm, Sat 7:30 am-10 pm, Sun 7:30 am-9 pm. Closed major holidays.
Features: The classic American diner features an award-winning 1940s design. It's hard to resist the
scrumptious, baked-from-scratch desserts when you spot them in the display case upon entering the
restaurant. The burgers, sandwiches and classic meatloaf and mashed potatoes are just as mouthwatering; it's hard to go
wrong with anything on this menu. Casual dress; beer & wine only. **Parking:** on-site. **Cards:** MC, VI.   ✕

IMPERIAL GARDEN WEST   **Lunch:** $5-$9   **Dinner:** $7-$14   **Phone:** 608/238-6445   [25]
ⒶⒶⒶ   **Location:** US 12 and 14, exit 251, 1.7 mi e on University Ave. 2039 Allen Blvd 53562. **Hours:** 11:30 am-2 & 4-9:30
▼▼▼   pm, Fri-10:30 pm, Sat 4 pm-10:30 pm, Sun 4 pm-9 pm. Closed: 7/4, 11/25, 12/24, 12/25.
Chinese   **Reservations:** accepted. **Features:** This restaurant has a large menu selection of traditional pork, beef,
chicken, lamb, duck and seafood dishes. There are also some vegetarian entrees including rice and
noodles. This restaurant is well-established and locally popular. Dressy casual; cocktails. **Parking:** on-site.
Cards: AX, DC, DS, MC, VI.   🍸✕

LOUISIANNE'S ETC   **Dinner:** $12-$30   **Phone:** 608/831-1929   [23]
▼▼▼   **Location:** Se of jct US 12 and University Ave, via Parmenter. 7464 Hubbard Ave 53562. **Hours:** 5 pm-10 pm,
Cajun   Mon-9 pm. Closed major holidays; also Sun. **Reservations:** suggested. **Features:** The piquant Creole
flavors of New Orleans infuse colorfully presented dishes of seafood, beef and chicken. Original stone
walls and soft lighting give the dining room an almost cavernous feel. The sounds of live jazz resonate off
the walls. Casual dress; cocktails. **Parking:** street. **Cards:** AX, DS, MC, VI.   🍸✕

MORELS   **Dinner:** $15-$22   **Phone:** 608/836-7151
▼▼ ▼▼   **Location:** 4.1 mi sw on Airport Rd at jct US 12. 4635 Chalet St 53562. **Hours:** 5 pm-9 pm, Fri & Sat-9:30 pm,
American   Sun 4:30 pm-9 pm. Closed: Mon. **Reservations:** suggested. **Features:** The chef's creative, seasonally
changing menu takes advantage of the freshest vegetables, fruits and locally produced meats, including
pheasant, elk and duckling. A good variety of fresh fish entrees, as well as USDA prime beef, pork and
some chicken selections, satisfy those looking for something more tame. Desserts are made in house. Wildlife artwork adorns
the walls of the rural dining room. Casual dress; cocktails. **Parking:** on-site. **Cards:** AX, MC, VI.   🍸✕

STAMM HOUSE AT PHEASANT BRANCH   **Dinner:** $10-$18   **Phone:** 608/831-5835   [21]
▼▼ ▼▼   **Location:** US 14, 1 mi e. 6625 Century Ave 53562. **Hours:** 5 pm-10 pm. Closed major holidays.
American   **Reservations:** accepted. **Features:** The restored 1847 stone tavern has housed everything from a post
office to runaway slaves on the Underground Railroad. Today it is home to one of the area's best-loved
restaurants. The most popular menu item is chicken and dumplings, served in a good-size helping. Entrees
are served with a delicious side of green bean salad and fresh dinner rolls. Casual dress; cocktails. **Parking:** on-site.
Cards: MC, VI.   🍸✕

TORTILLAS   **Lunch:** $7-$19   **Dinner:** $7-$19   **Phone:** 608/836-0017   [22]
▼▼ ▼▼   **Location:** Just se of jct US 12. 6913 University Ave 53562. **Hours:** 11 am-10 pm, Fri & Sat-11 pm, Sun-9 pm.
Southwest   Closed major holidays. **Features:** Southwestern and New Mexican fare is served amid rustic decor and
Mexican   vibrant Southwest rugs. Guests can't go wrong with anything on the menu, but the green chile burger,
green chile stew, Sante Fe sirloin and Roswell rack of lamb are the best of the best. The prickly pear
margarita is a good choice for wetting the whistle. Casual dress; cocktails. **Parking:** on-site. **Cards:** AX,
DS, MC, VI.   🍸✕

Destination Milwaukee
pop. 596,974

Milwaukee is naturally a great spot for water sports: Not only is the city right on Lake Michigan, it's also divided in half by the Milwaukee River.

*T*hose who would rather stay dry can hit the mall, cheer on the area's sports teams and attend a performance by the opera or ballet.

Milwaukee D.C.D.

Milwaukee City Hall
Built in 1895, city hall boasts a 350-foot bell tower that can be seen for miles. (See listing page 153)

Greater Milwaukee CVB

Skylight Opera Theater, Milwaukee.
Colorful costumes play a major role in the productions held at this theater. (See mention page 157)

*P*laces included in this AAA Destination City:

Indian Summer Fest, Milwaukee.
American Indian tribes showcase their culture with elaborate costumes and demonstrations. (See mention page 158)

Dining, Milwaukee.
Catch a cool breeze and a hot bite at one of the many restaurants lining the Milwaukee River.

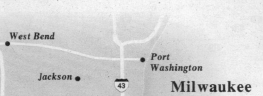

West Bend

Port Washington

Jackson

43

Milwaukee

Cedarburg   Grafton

Germantown

41

Mequon

Brown Deer   Bayside

Glendale

45

Whitefish Bay

Pewaukee

Wauwatosa

Brookfield
Elm Grove

See Downtown map page 564

Waukesha

New
Berlin   Greenfield

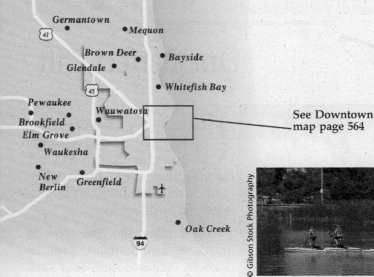

Oak Creek

94

Veterans Park, Milwaukee.
Paddling on hydrobikes is the perfect way to get around on one of the more than 15,000 inland lakes Wisconsin has to offer. (See mention page 156)

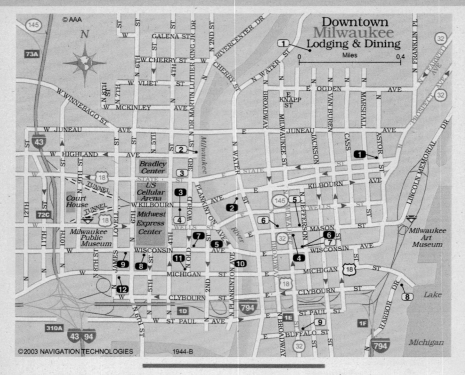

One Perfect Gift

Give the gift of security, service, and savings–buy someone you care about a AAA gift membership. AAA memberships provide your loved ones more than emergency road service.

AAA members also have access to travel services, insurance, financial services, exclusive Show Your Card & Save® discounts, bail bond services, and more.

Give them more than a gift. Give them AAA. And let them discover how AAA can simplify their lives. Call or stop by your nearest AAA office today. And make AAA the one for you.

Downtown Milwaukee

This index helps you "spot" where approved accommodations and restaurants are located on the corresponding detailed maps. Lodging rate ranges are for comparison only and show the property's high season; rates are per night, unless only weekly (W) rates are available. Restaurant rate range is for dinner, unless only lunch (L) is served. Turn to the listing page for more detailed rate information and consult display ads for special promotions.

Spotter/Map Page Number	OA	DOWNTOWN MILWAUKEE - Lodgings	Diamond Rating	Rate Range High Season	Listing Page
1 / p. 564	AAA	Park East Hotel	♦♦♦	$89-$250 SAVE	572
2 / p. 564	AAA	Wyndham Milwaukee Center - see color ad p 572	♦♦♦	$118 SAVE	573
3 / p. 564	AAA	Hyatt Regency Milwaukee - see color ad p 571	♦♦♦	$99-$175 SAVE	571
4 / p. 564		Hotel Metro-Milwaukee	♦♦♦	$189-$259	571
5 / p. 564	AAA	Howard Johnson Inn & Suites - see color ad p 584	♦♦♦	$89-$159 SAVE	571
6 / p. 564	AAA	The Pfister Hotel - see color ad p 572	♦♦♦♦	$169-$295 SAVE	572
7 / p. 564	AAA	Best Western Inn Towne Hotel	♦♦♦	$99-$119 SAVE	570
8 / p. 564	AAA	Hilton Milwaukee City Center - see color ad p 570	♦♦♦	$99-$239 SAVE	570
9 / p. 564	AAA	Holiday Inn Milwaukee City Centre	♦♦♦	$99-$149 SAVE	571
10 / p. 564		Residence Inn-Downtown Milwaukee	♦♦♦	$129-$154	573
11 / p. 564		Courtyard Milwaukee Downtown	♦♦♦	$79-$132	570
12 / p. 564		Ramada Inn City Centre	♦♦	$102-$111	573
		DOWNTOWN MILWAUKEE - Restaurants			
1 / p. 564		Sanford Restaurant	♦♦♦♦	$45-$75	574
2 / p. 564		Third Street Pier	♦♦♦	$20-$47	574
3 / p. 564	AAA	Mader's German Restaurant	♦♦	$18-$24	573
4 / p. 564		Polaris	♦♦♦	$17-$35	574
5 / p. 564		Watts Tea Shop	♦♦	$6-$12(L)	574
6 / p. 564		Karl Ratzsch's Restaurant	♦♦	$15-$28	573
7 / p. 564	AAA	Celia - see color ad p 572	♦♦♦♦	$16-$28	573
8 / p. 564		Piece's Of Eight	♦♦	$16-$25	573
9 / p. 564		Coquette Cafe	♦♦	$8-$17	573

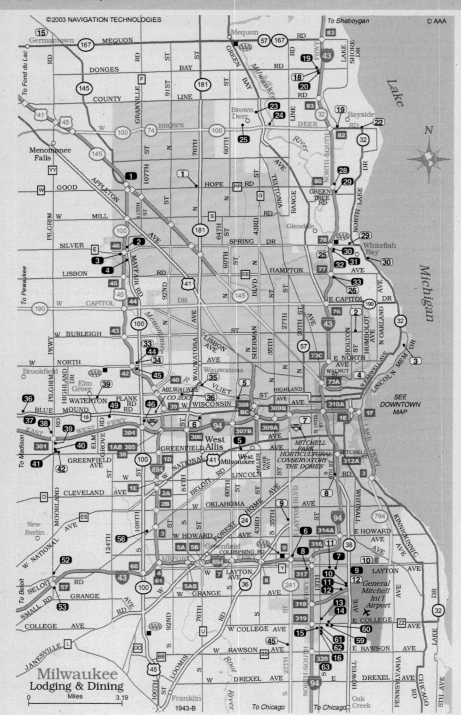

©2003 NAVIGATION TECHNOLOGIES

© AAA

Milwaukee
Lodging & Dining

0 _____ 3.19
Miles

1943-B

✈ Airport Accommodations

Spotter/Map Page Number	OA	GENERAL MITCHELL INTERNATIONAL	Diamond Rating	Rate Range High Season	Listing Page
12 / p. 566	AAA	AmeriSuites-Milwaukee Airport, 0.5 mi w of terminal	▽▽▽	$84-$114 SAVE	575
11 / p. 566	AAA	Clarion Hotel Airport, 0.5 mi w of terminal	▽▽▽	$84-$169 SAVE	579
13 / p. 566	AAA	Country Inns & Suites By Carlson, 2.3 mi s of terminal	▽▽▽	$82-$117 SAVE	579
16 / p. 566	AAA	Econo Lodge Airport, 2.9 mi s of terminal	▽▽	$39-$199 SAVE	579
9 / p. 566		Four Points by Sheraton Milwaukee Airport, 0.5 mi w of terminal	▽▽▽	$79-$99	582
14 / p. 566	AAA	Hampton Inn-Milwaukee Airport, 2.7 mi s of terminal	▽▽▽	$69-$129 SAVE	582
7 / p. 566	AAA	Holiday Inn Hotel and Suites, 1.3 mi w of terminal	▽▽▽	$140-$180 SAVE	584
6 / p. 566	AAA	Hospitality Inn, 3.5 mi nw of terminal	▽▽▽	$100-$250 SAVE	584
8 / p. 566		Howard Johnson Milwaukee Airport Inn, 2.8 mi nw from terminal	▽▽	$119-$149	586
15 / p. 566	AAA	Radisson Hotel Milwaukee Airport, 2.8 mi s of terminal	▽▽▽	$99-$159 SAVE	586
10 / p. 566	AAA	Super 8 Motel-Milwaukee Airport, 0.5 mi w of terminal	▽▽	$69-$199 SAVE	586
62 / p. 566		Comfort Suites Milwaukee Airport, 2.9 mi s of terminal	▽▽▽	$119-$249	597
60 / p. 566	AAA	Exel Inn of Milwaukee South, 2.8 mi s of terminal	▽▽	$47-$69 SAVE	598

Milwaukee and Vicinity

This index helps you "spot" where approved accommodations and restaurants are located on the corresponding detailed maps. Lodging rate ranges are for comparison only and show the property's high season; rates are per night, unless only weekly (W) rates are available. Restaurant rate range is for dinner, unless only lunch (L) is served. Turn to the listing page for more detailed rate information and consult display ads for special promotions.

Spotter/Map Page Number	OA	MILWAUKEE - Lodgings	Diamond Rating	Rate Range High Season	Listing Page
1 / p. 566	AAA	Hilton Garden Inn Milwaukee Park Place	▽▽▽	$169 SAVE	584
2 / p. 566		Hampton Inn-Milwaukee NW	▽▽▽	$79-$99	582
3 / p. 566	AAA	AmeriSuites Milwaukee/West - see color ad p 575, p 570	▽▽▽	$79-$119 SAVE	575
4 / p. 566	AAA	Baymont Inn & Suites Milwaukee NW - see color ad p 597	▽▽	$79-$99 SAVE	575
5 / p. 566	AAA	Best Western Woodsview Inn	▽▽	$62-$92 SAVE	578
6 / p. 566	AAA	Hospitality Inn	▽▽▽	$100-$250 SAVE	584
7 / p. 566	AAA	Holiday Inn Hotel and Suites - see color ad p 583	▽▽▽	$140-$180 SAVE	584
8 / p. 566		Howard Johnson Milwaukee Airport Inn - see color ad p 584	▽▽	$119-$149	586
9 / p. 566		Four Points by Sheraton Milwaukee Airport - see color ad p 5	▽▽▽	$79-$99	582
10 / p. 566	AAA	Super 8 Motel-Milwaukee Airport	▽▽	$69-$199 SAVE	586
11 / p. 566	AAA	Clarion Hotel Airport	▽▽▽	$84-$169 SAVE	579
12 / p. 566	AAA	AmeriSuites-Milwaukee Airport - see color ad p 575, p 570	▽▽▽	$84-$114 SAVE	575
13 / p. 566	AAA	Country Inns & Suites By Carlson - see color ad starting on p 580	▽▽▽	$82-$117 SAVE	579
14 / p. 566	AAA	Hampton Inn-Milwaukee Airport - see color ad p 582	▽▽▽	$69-$129 SAVE	582

Spotter/Map Page Number	OA	MILWAUKEE - Lodgings (continued)	Diamond Rating	Rate Range High Season	Listing Page
15 / p. 566	AAA	**Radisson Hotel Milwaukee Airport** - see color ad p 586, p 583	◆◆◆	$99-$159 SAVE	586
16 / p. 566	AAA	**Econo Lodge Airport**	◆◆	$39-$199 SAVE	579
		MILWAUKEE - Restaurants			
1 / p. 566		Yen Ching Restaurant	◆◆	$8-$13	588
2 / p. 566		West Bank Cafe	◆	$5-$17	588
3 / p. 566		Bartolotta's Lake Park Bistro	◆◆	$10-$35	587
4 / p. 566		Au Bon Appetit Restaurant & Catering	◆◆	$8-$14	587
5 / p. 566		Saz's State House	◆◆	$7-$22	588
6 / p. 566		Heinemann's Restaurant	◆◆	$5-$7	587
7 / p. 566		Dream Dance	◆◆◆◆	$27-$38	587
8 / p. 566		Old Town Serbian Gourmet House	◆◆	$12-$18	587
9 / p. 566		Paul's Omega Family Restaurant	◆	$8-$17	587
10 / p. 566		The Packing House	◆◆	$10-$23	587
11 / p. 566		Prime Quarter Steak House	◆◆	$12-$16	587
12 / p. 566		Jalapeno Loco	◆◆	$5-$18	587
		MEQUON - Lodgings			
19 / p. 566		The Chalet Motel of Mequon	◆◆	$79-$159	596
20 / p. 566	AAA	**Best Western Quiet House & Suites** - see color ad p 579	◆◆◆	$95-$105 SAVE	596
		MEQUON - Restaurants			
18 / p. 566		The Centennial	◆◆	$5-$13	596
19 / p. 566		Heinemann's Restaurant	◆	$5-$9	596
		BROWN DEER - Lodgings			
23 / p. 566		Holiday Inn Express	◆◆◆	$109-$139	591
24 / p. 566		Four Points by Sheraton Milwaukee North - see color ad p 5	◆◆◆	$245	591
25 / p. 566		Courtyard by Marriott Milwaukee North Brown Deer	◆◆◆	$169-$199	591
		GLENDALE - Lodgings			
28 / p. 566		Residence Inn by Marriott	◆◆◆	$109-$299	594
29 / p. 566	AAA	**Manchester East Hotel & Suites** - see color ad p 585	◆◆◆	$109-$119 SAVE	594
30 / p. 566	AAA	**Exel Inn of Milwaukee Northeast**	◆◆	$50-$91 SAVE	594
31 / p. 566		Woodfield Suites Milwaukee-Glendale	◆◆◆	$129-$199	594
32 / p. 566		Baymont Inn Milwaukee-Glendale - see color ad p 597	◆◆◆	$64-$94	594
33 / p. 566	AAA	**Hilton Milwaukee River**	◆◆◆	$79-$102 SAVE	594
		GLENDALE - Restaurants			
25 / p. 566		The Bavarian Inn	◆	$9-$18	595
26 / p. 566		Anchorage Restaurant	◆◆◆	$16-$24	595
		BROOKFIELD - Lodgings			
36 / p. 566		TownePlace Suites by Marriott	◆◆◆	$59-$99	590
37 / p. 566		Courtyard by Marriott/Brookfield	◆◆◆	$59-$129	589
38 / p. 566		Sheraton Milwaukee Brookfield	◆◆◆	$79-$149	590

Spotter/Map Page Number	OA	BROOKFIELD - Lodgings (continued)	Diamond Rating	Rate Range High Season	Listing Page
39 / p. 566	AAA	Best Western Midway Hotel	◆◆◆	$79-$149 (SAVE)	589
40 / p. 566		Embassy Suites Hotel-Milwaukee West	◆◆◆	$89-$189	589
41 / p. 566		Country Inn & Suites Milwaukee West - see color ad starting on p 580	◆◆◆	$79-$129	589
		WAUWATOSA - Lodgings			
44 / p. 566	AAA	Radisson Hotel Milwaukee West - see color ad p 583	◆◆◆	$159-$164 (SAVE)	601
45 / p. 566	AAA	Holiday Inn Express-Mayfair - see color ad p 582	◆◆◆	$104-$159 (SAVE)	601
46 / p. 566	AAA	Exel Inn of Milwaukee West	◆◆	$47-$84 (SAVE)	600
		WAUWATOSA - Restaurants			
33 / p. 566	AAA	Heinemann's Restaurant	◆◆	$5-$8	601
34 / p. 566		RJ's an American Bar & Grille	◆◆	$15-$25	601
35 / p. 566		Ristorante Bartolotta	◆◆◆	$16-$29	601
36 / p. 566		Eddie Martini's	◆◆◆	$18-$34	601
		ELM GROVE - Lodgings			
49 / p. 566	AAA	Sleepy Hollow Inn - see color ad p 588	◆	$47-$80 (SAVE)	592
		ELM GROVE - Restaurant			
39 / p. 566		Elm Grove Inn	◆◆◆	$18-$25	593
		NEW BERLIN - Lodgings			
52 / p. 566		Holiday Inn Express Hotel and Suites-New Berlin	◆◆◆	$99-$124	596
53 / p. 566	AAA	Baymont Inn & Suites Milwaukee-New Berlin - see color ad p 597	◆◆◆	$69-$89 (SAVE)	596
		NEW BERLIN - Restaurant			
42 / p. 566		Charcoal Grill & Rotisserie	◆◆	$12-$20	597
		GREENFIELD - Lodgings			
56 / p. 566		Golden Key Motel	◆	$45-$75	595
		OAK CREEK - Lodgings			
59 / p. 566		MainStay Suites Oak Creek	◆◆◆	$69-$199	598
60 / p. 566	AAA	Exel Inn of Milwaukee South	◆◆	$47-$69 (SAVE)	598
61 / p. 566	AAA	Red Roof Inn-Milwaukee	◆	$47-$71 (SAVE)	598
62 / p. 566		Comfort Suites Milwaukee Airport	◆◆◆	$119-$249	597
63 / p. 566	AAA	Baymont Inn & Suites Milwaukee-Airport - see color ad p 597	◆◆	$79-$99 (SAVE)	597
		GERMANTOWN - Restaurant			
15 / p. 566		Jerry's Old Town	◆◆	$14-$26	594
		BAYSIDE - Restaurant			
22 / p. 566		Pandl's in Bayside	◆◆◆	$12-$30	588
		WHITEFISH BAY - Restaurants			
29 / p. 566		Heinemann's Restaurant	◆◆	$5-$8	602
30 / p. 566		Jack Pandl's Whitefish Bay Inn	◆◆	$17-$24	602
		FRANKLIN - Restaurant			
45 / p. 566		Judy's Family Restaurant	◆◆	$8-$16	593

DOWNTOWN MILWAUKEE (See map and index starting on p. 564)

──────── WHERE TO STAY ────────

BEST WESTERN INN TOWNE HOTEL   *Book at aaa.com*   Phone: (414)224-8400   **7**

(AAA) (SAVE)

▽▽◇▽▽

12/31-3/31	1P: $99-$119	2P: $99-$119	XP: $10	F17
6/1-9/1	1P: $89-$109	2P: $89-$109	XP: $10	F17
4/1-5/31 & 9/2-12/30	1P: $59-$79	2P: $59-$79	XP: $10	F17

Location: Corner of Wisconsin Ave and N Old World 3rd St. 710 N Old World 3rd St 53203. Fax: 414/224-8696. **Facility:** 97 one-bedroom standard units. 12 stories, interior corridors. *Bath:* combo or shower only. **Parking:** on-site (fee). **Terms:** [AP] meal plan available, package plans - seasonal, small pets only. **Amenities:** voice mail, irons, hair dryers. *Some:* dual phone lines. **Dining:** 7 am-10 pm. **Leisure Activities:** exercise room. **Guest Services:** valet laundry. **Business Services:** meeting rooms. **Cards:** AX, CB, DC, DS, JC, MC, VI. **Special Amenities:** free local telephone calls and free newspaper.

Large-scale Hotel

SOME UNITS

[S D] [🛏] [📞] [🍽] [🛎] [♿] [🐾] [DATA PORT] [💻] / [✕] [VCR] [🔌] [📷] /   FEE

COURTYARD MILWAUKEE DOWNTOWN   *Book at aaa.com*   Phone: (414)291-4122   **11**

▽▽◇▽▽

All Year   1P: $79-$132   2P: $79-$132

Location: I-794, exit 1A (Plankinton Ave), just n, then just w. 300 W Michigan St 53203. Fax: 414/291-4188. **Facility:** 169 units. 151 one-bedroom standard units, some with whirlpools. 18 one-bedroom suites. 6 stories, interior corridors. *Bath:* combo or shower only. **Parking:** on-site (fee). **Terms:** [BP] meal plan available. **Amenities:** high-speed Internet, dual phone lines, voice mail, irons, hair dryers. **Pool(s):** heated indoor. **Leisure Activities:** whirlpool, exercise room. **Guest Services:** sundries, valet laundry. **Business Services:** meeting rooms, business center. **Cards:** AX, CB, DC, DS, MC, VI.

Small-scale Hotel

SOME UNITS

[🍽] [♿] [📞] [📷] [DATA PORT] [💻] / [✕] [🔌] [📷] /

HILTON MILWAUKEE CITY CENTER   *Book at aaa.com*   Phone: (414)271-7250   **8**

(AAA) (SAVE)

▽▽◇▽▽

All Year   1P: $99-$239   2P: $99-$239   XP: $20   F18

Location: Corner of W Wisconsin Ave and 5th St. 509 W Wisconsin Ave 53203. Fax: 414/271-1039. **Facility:** 730 units. 706 one-bedroom standard units. 11 one- and 13 two-bedroom suites, some with whirlpools. 24 stories, interior corridors. *Bath:* combo or shower only. **Parking:** on-site (fee). **Amenities:** video games (fee), dual phone lines, voice mail, irons, hair dryers. *Some:* CD players. **Dining:** 3 restaurants, 6:30 am-midnight, cocktails. **Pool(s):** heated indoor, wading. **Leisure Activities:** whirlpool, waterslide, indoor water park, exercise room. *Fee:* game room. **Guest Services:** gift shop, valet laundry. **Business Services:** conference facilities, business center. **Cards:** AX, CB, DC, DS, JC, MC, VI. *(See color ad below)*

Large-scale Hotel

SOME UNITS

[🍽] [🍷] [♿M] [🛎] [🌊] [📷] [DATA PORT] [💻] / [✕] [VCR] [🔌] /

(See map and index starting on p. 564)

HOLIDAY INN MILWAUKEE CITY CENTRE Book at aaa.com Phone: 414/273-2950 **9**
(AAA) (SAVE) All Year 1P: $99-$139 2P: $104-$149 XP: $10 F18
▼▼▼▼ **Location:** Corner of W Wisconsin Ave and 6th St. 611 W Wisconsin Ave 53203. Fax: 414/273-7662. **Facility:** 247
units. 246 one-bedroom standard units. 1 one-bedroom suite. 10 stories, interior corridors. **Parking:** on-site
Large-scale Hotel (fee) and valet. **Terms:** cancellation fee imposed, [AP], [BP] & [CP] meal plans available. **Amenities:** video
games (fee), dual phone lines, voice mail, irons, hair dryers. **Dining:** 6 am-2 & 5-10 pm, cocktails. **Pool(s):**
heated outdoor. **Leisure Activities:** exercise room. **Guest Services:** valet laundry. **Business Services:** conference facilities, business center. **Cards:** AX, DC, DS, JC, MC, VI. **Special Amenities:** free local telephone calls and free
newspaper.

SOME UNITS
🍴 🍸 📠 🏊 📹 📠 🖥 / ⊠ 🔒 📷 /

HOTEL METRO-MILWAUKEE Book at aaa.com Phone: (414)272-1937 **4**
▼▼▼ 5/28-9/2 1P: $189-$259 2P: $189-$259 XP: $25 F18
4/1-5/27 & 9/3-3/31 1P: $169-$239 2P: $169-$239 XP: $25 F18
Small-scale Hotel **Location:** Corner of Mason and Milwaukee sts. 411 E Mason St 53202. Fax: 414/223-1158. **Facility:** 65 units. 16
one-bedroom standard units. 47 one- and 2 two-bedroom suites, some with whirlpools. 6 stories, interior corridors. Bath: combo or shower only. **Parking:** on-site (fee) and valet. **Terms:** 2 night minimum stay - seasonal. **Amenities:** video
library (fee), CD players, dual phone lines, voice mail, safes, honor bars, irons, hair dryers. **Leisure Activities:** bicycles. **Guest
Services:** valet laundry. **Business Services:** meeting rooms, fax. **Cards:** AX, CB, DC, DS, JC, MC, VI.

SOME UNITS
🐾 🍴 24 🍸 ♿ ♿ 📠 📹 VCR 📹 📠 / ⊠ /
FEE

HOWARD JOHNSON INN & SUITES Book at aaa.com Phone: (414)271-4656 **5**
(AAA) (SAVE) 4/1-9/6 [ECP] 1P: $89-$159 2P: $89-$159 XP: $10 F18
9/7-3/31 [ECP] 1P: $69-$139 2P: $69-$139 XP: $10 F18
▼▼▼▼ **Location:** I-794, exit 10, 0.3 mi n on Plankinton, just w. 176 W Wisconsin Ave 53203. Fax: 414/329-4656.
Facility: 142 one-bedroom standard units, some with whirlpools. 10 stories, interior corridors. Bath: combo
Large-scale Hotel or shower only. **Parking:** on-site (fee). **Terms:** check-in 4 pm. **Amenities:** dual phone lines, voice mail, irons,
hair dryers. Some: safes (fee). **Leisure Activities:** exercise room. **Guest Services:** sundries, valet and coin
laundry. **Business Services:** meeting rooms. **Cards:** AX, DC, DS, MC, VI. **Special Amenities:** free expanded continental
breakfast and free newspaper. (See color ad p 584)

SOME UNITS
S/D 🍴 ♿ ♿ 📠 📠 🖥 / ⊠ 🔒 📷 /

HYATT REGENCY MILWAUKEE Book at aaa.com Phone: (414)276-1234 **3**
(AAA) (SAVE) 4/1-11/15 1P: $99-$175 2P: $99-$175 XP: $25 F18
11/16-3/31 1P: $89-$149 2P: $89-$149 XP: $25 F18
▼▼▼▼ **Location:** At N 3rd St. Walkway to Midwest Express Center and Grand Ave Mall. 333 W Kilbourn Ave 53203.
Fax: 414/276-6338. **Facility:** 484 units. 465 one-bedroom standard units. 19 one-bedroom suites. 18 stories,
Large-scale Hotel interior corridors. Bath: combo or shower only. **Parking:** on-site (fee). **Terms:** cancellation fee imposed.
Amenities: voice mail, irons, hair dryers. Some: CD players, dual phone lines, fax, safes. **Dining:** 2 restau-
rants, 7 am-midnight, cocktails, also, Polaris, see separate listing. **Leisure Activities:** exercise room. **Guest Services:** gift shop,
valet laundry. **Business Services:** conference facilities, business center. **Cards:** AX, CB, DC, DS, JC, MC, VI.
(See color ad below)

SOME UNITS
🍴 🍸 ♿ ♿ 📠 📠 / ⊠ VCR 🔒 📷 🖥 /
FEE FEE FEE

(See map and index starting on p. 564)

PARK EAST HOTEL   *Book at aaa.com*   **Phone:** (414)276-8800   **①**
◇◇◇ SAVE   All Year   1P: $89-$250   2P: $89-$250   XP: $10   **F**
▽▽▽▽   **Location:** Between Marshall and Astor sts. 916 E State St 53202. Fax: 414/765-1919. **Facility:** 159 units. 155 one-
bedroom standard units, some with whirlpools. 4 one-bedroom suites, some with kitchens. 5 stories, interior
corridors. *Bath:* combo or shower only. **Parking:** on-site. **Terms:** cancellation fee imposed, [ECP] meal plan
Small-scale Hotel   available. **Amenities:** video games (fee), voice mail, irons, hair dryers. **Dining:** 6:30-9:30 am, 11:30-2 & 5-10
pm, Sun 7-10 am, cocktails. **Leisure Activities:** exercise room. **Guest Services:** valet and coin laundry, area
transportation-downtown. **Business Services:** meeting rooms, business center. **Cards:** AX, CB, DC, DS, JC, MC, VI.
Special Amenities: free expanded continental breakfast and free newspaper.

SOME UNITS

FEE   FEE

THE PFISTER HOTEL   *Book at aaa.com*   **Phone:** 414/273-8222   **⑥**
◇◇◇ SAVE   5/1-10/31   1P: $169-$295   2P: $169-$295
▽▽▽▽ ◇◇◇◇   11/1-3/31   1P: $159-$295   2P: $159-$295
▽▽▽▽   4/1-4/30   1P: $169-$249   2P: $189-$269
Location: Corner of E Wisconsin Ave and Mason St. 424 E Wisconsin Ave 53202. Fax: 414/273-5025. **Facility:** Built
Large-scale Hotel   in 1893 by Milwaukee industrialist Guido Pfister, this landmark hotel is now home to an impressive collection
of Victorian art. 307 units. 236 one-bedroom standard units. 63 one- and 8 two-bedroom suites, some with
whirlpools. 8-23 stories, interior corridors. **Parking:** on-site (fee) and valet. **Terms:** cancellation fee imposed, weekly rates available. **Amenities:** video games (fee), voice mail, safes, honor bars, irons, hair dryers. **Dining:** 3 restaurants, 6 am-10 pm, cocktails, also, Celia, see separate listing, entertainment. **Pool(s):** heated indoor. **Leisure Activities:** exercise room. *Fee:* massage.
Guest Services: gift shop, valet laundry. **Business Services:** conference facilities, PC. **Cards:** AX, DC, DS, MC, VI.
(See color ad below)

SOME UNITS

(See map and index starting on p. 564)

RAMADA INN CITY CENTRE *Book at aaa.com*   Phone: 414/272-8410   **12**

6/25-9/6	1P: $102	2P: $111	XP: $9	F18
4/1-6/24	1P: $91	2P: $100	XP: $9	F18
9/7-12/31	1P: $86	2P: $95	XP: $9	F18
1/1-3/31	1P: $85	2P: $94	XP: $9	F18

Small-scale Hotel

Location: I-794, exit 1A (Plankinton Rd), just n, then 0.4 mi w. 633 W Michigan St 53203. Fax: 414/272-4651. **Facility:** 155 one-bedroom standard units. 7 stories, interior corridors. **Parking:** on-site. **Amenities:** voice mail, irons, hair dryers. **Pool(s):** heated outdoor. **Leisure Activities:** limited exercise equipment. **Guest Services:** valet laundry. **Business Services:** meeting rooms, fax (fee). **Cards:** AX, CB, DC, DS, JC, MC, VI.

SOME UNITS

RESIDENCE INN-DOWNTOWN MILWAUKEE *Book at aaa.com*   Phone: (414)224-7890   **10**

5/1-8/31 [ECP]	1P: $129-$154
9/1-8/31 [ECP]	1P: $79-$144
4/1-4/30 [ECP]	1P: $99-$139

Small-scale Hotel   **Location:** I-794, exit 1A (Plankinton Ave), just n at jct Wisconsin Ave. Located on the Riverwalk. 648 N Plankinton Ave 53203. Fax: 414/224-7923. **Facility:** 131 units. 84 one-bedroom standard units with kitchens. 36 one- and 11 two-bedroom suites with kitchens. 8 stories, interior corridors. *Bath:* combo or shower only. **Parking:** on-site (fee). **Terms:** cancellation fee imposed. **Amenities:** high-speed Internet (fee), dual phone lines, voice mail, irons, hair dryers. **Leisure Activities:** exercise room. **Guest Services:** complimentary evening beverages: Mon-Thurs, valet laundry. **Business Services:** meeting rooms. **Cards:** AX, CB, DC, DS, JC, MC, VI.

SOME UNITS

WYNDHAM MILWAUKEE CENTER   *Book at aaa.com*   Phone: (414)276-8686   **2**

4/1-10/2	1P: $118	2P: $118	XP: $10	F17
3/1-3/31	1P: $105	2P: $105	XP: $10	F17
10/3-2/28	1P: $101	2P: $101	XP: $10	F17

Large-scale Hotel   **Location:** At Water St. 139 E Kilbourn Ave 53202. Fax: 414/276-8007. **Facility:** 220 one-bedroom standard units. 10 stories, interior corridors. *Bath:* combo or shower only. **Parking:** on-site (fee). **Terms:** cancellation fee imposed. **Amenities:** high-speed Internet, dual phone lines, voice mail, irons, hair dryers. *Fee:* video games, safes. **Dining:** 6:30 am-11 pm, cocktails. **Leisure Activities:** saunas, whirlpool, steamrooms, sun deck, exercise room. **Guest Services:** gift shop, valet laundry. **Business Services:** conference facilities, fax. **Cards:** AX, DC, DS, MC, VI. **Special Amenities:** free newspaper. *(See color ad p 572)*

SOME UNITS

——— WHERE TO DINE ———

CELIA   Lunch: $10-$15   Dinner: $16-$28   Phone: 414/390-3832   **7**

Continental

Location: Corner of E Wisconsin Ave and Mason St; in The Pfister Hotel. 424 E Wisconsin Ave 53202. **Hours:** 11:30 am-2 & 5-10 pm, Sat from 5 pm. Closed: Sun. **Reservations:** suggested. **Features:** Bright, elegant, sumptuous and contemporary are the words that best describe this newest addition to Milwaukee's fine dining scene. The atmosphere is upscale casual with a very relaxed yet luxurious feel, and the service staff is attentive and friendly. The ever changing menu features food and stylings from a global marketplace, while balancing creativity and eye appeal with a Midwestern sensibility for value. Rounding out the experience is an award winning wine list to suit all tastes. Dressy casual; cocktails. **Parking:** on-site (fee) and valet. **Cards:** AX, CB, DC, DS, JC, MC, VI. *(See color ad p 572)*

COQUETTE CAFE   Lunch: $6-$10   Dinner: $8-$17   Phone: 414/291-2655   **9**

French

Location: Just s of St Paul St; in Historic Third Ward; center. 316 N Milwaukee St 53202. **Hours:** 11 am-10 pm, Fri-11 pm, Sat 5 pm-11 pm. Closed major holidays; also Sun. **Reservations:** suggested. **Features:** In a historic building, the lively French-style cafe offers a menu of fine bistro cuisine. Among choices are mussels, cassoulet, pork chops, roast chicken and thin-crust, French-style pizzas. Casual dress; cocktails. **Parking:** on-site and street. **Cards:** AX, CB, DC, DS, JC, MC, VI.

KARL RATZSCH'S RESTAURANT Historic   Dinner: $15-$28   Phone: 414/276-2720   **6**

German

Location: Jct E Mason and N Milwaukee sts. 320 E Mason St 53202. **Hours:** 4:30 pm-9:30 pm, Sat-10 pm. Closed major holidays; also Sun. **Reservations:** suggested. **Features:** This German themed restaurant offers a charming Old World atmosphere and has been family-owned and operated since 1904. Menu selections are homemade. The kassler rippchen is a wonderful dinner choice consisting of pork chops, sauerkraut and potato dumplings. The potato soup makes for a great start to your dining experience with a tasty blend of seasonings and large chunks of potato in a creamy base. Casual dress; cocktails. **Parking:** on-site and valet. **Cards:** AX, DC, DS, MC, VI.

MADER'S GERMAN RESTAURANT Historic   Lunch: $8-$11   Dinner: $18-$24   Phone: 414/271-3377   **3**

German

Location: Jct W State and N 3rd sts. 1037 N Old World 3rd St 53203. **Hours:** 11:30 am-9 pm, Fri & Sat-10 pm, Sun from 10:30 am. Closed: for dinner 12/24. **Reservations:** suggested. **Features:** This family-owned and operated restaurant has been a local favorite since 1902. All meals are prepared in German tradition with a Continental flair. The setting is that of Germany with the many medieval pieces of weaponry, steins, wood carvings and glassware throughout. Noted for their unique dishes of oxtail soup, sauerbraten and homemade apple or cherry strudel. For the beer lover, there are over 200 imported and domestic beers. Also, a wine list boasting over 100 vintage wines. Casual dress; cocktails. **Parking:** on-site and valet. **Cards:** AX, DC, DS, MC, VI.

PIECE'S OF EIGHT   Lunch: $7-$14   Dinner: $16-$25   Phone: 414/271-0597   **8**

American

Location: I-794, exit Van Buren St, then e on Michigan St to lakeside. 550 N Harbor Dr 53202. **Hours:** 11 am-3 & 4:30-10 pm, Fri & Sat-11 pm, Sun 9 am-2 & 4-10 pm. **Reservations:** suggested. **Features:** On the historic downtown cargo pier, the restaurant affords excellent views of Lake Michigan and Milwaukee's skyline. On the menu are traditional preparations of chicken, beef, freshwater and saltwater fish and pasta. Servers are knowledgeable. Casual dress; cocktails. **Cards:** AX, DC, DS, MC, VI.

(See map and index starting on p. 564)

POLARIS   **Dinner:** $17-$35   **Phone:** 414/276-1234   (4)
▼▼▼▼ **Location:** At N 3rd St; in Hyatt Regency Milwaukee. 333 W Kilbourn Ave 53203. **Hours:** 5 pm-10:30 pm, Sun also
10 am-2:30 pm. **Reservations:** suggested. **Features:** Diners can appreciate beautiful views of the city
American skyline from many perspectives at the top-floor revolving restaurant. Dressy casual; cocktails. **Parking:**
on-site (fee). **Cards:** AX, CB, DC, DS, JC, MC, VI.

SANFORD RESTAURANT   **Dinner:** $45-$75   **Phone:** 414/276-9608   (1)
▼▼▼ ▼▼▼ **Location:** Southeast corner of N Jackson and Pleasant sts. 1547 N Jackson St 53202. **Hours:** 5:30 pm-9 pm,
Fri-10 pm, Sat 5 pm-10 pm. Closed major holidays; also Sun. **Reservations:** suggested. **Features:** In a
American small residential building, the cozy, intimate dining room is home to a wonderful adventure. The competent,
smartly attired wait staff employs a seamless team approach to service, making guests feel special and at
ease. The ever-changing menu offers three-, four-, five- and seven-course options. Cuisine is as varied as the market and
often includes game dishes. Presentations are creative and eye-appealing, and everything is prepared to order. Dressy casual;
cocktails. **Parking:** valet and street. **Cards:** AX, DC, DS, MC, VI.

THIRD STREET PIER   **Dinner:** $20-$47   **Phone:** 414/272-0330   (2)
▼▼▼ **Location:** Just s of jct Juneau Ave; in Riverfront Plaza Building. 1110 N Old World 3rd St 53203. **Hours:** 5 pm-10
pm, Sun 4 pm-9 pm. Closed major holidays; also 12/24. **Reservations:** suggested. **Features:** On the
Steak & Seafood Milwaukee River, the restaurant benefits from a wonderful location. Diners can watch boats cruising the
river while enjoying dinner in an elegant setting. In addition to steak and seafood specialties, weekly
specials are offered. Start off with hearty seafood chowder followed by tender filet mignon. Finish the meal with a slice of
apple strudel. Live jazz adds to the ambience Friday and Saturday. Dressy casual; cocktails. **Parking:** valet. **Cards:** AX, DC,
DS, MC, VI.

WATTS TEA SHOP   Historic   **Lunch:** $6-$12   **Phone:** 414/291-5120   (5)
▼▼▼ ▼▼▼ **Location:** E Mason and N Jefferson sts. 761 N Jefferson St 53202. **Hours:** 9 am-4 pm. Closed major holidays;
also Sun. **Reservations:** suggested. **Features:** This family-owned and operated restaurant is a local
American favorite. It was established in 1926 and is located on the second floor of the George Watts & Son
Incorporated building. It is known for its homemade bread, soup, salad, sandwiches and dessert. Afternoon
tea is from 2:30-4 pm daily. Casual dress. **Parking:** valet. **Cards:** AX, DS, MC, VI.

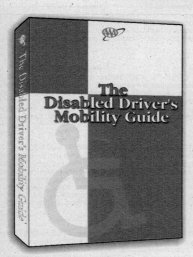

MILWAUKEE pop. 596,974 (See map and index starting on p. 566)

──────── WHERE TO STAY ────────

AMERISUITES-MILWAUKEE AIRPORT *Book at aaa.com*   Phone: (414)744-3600   🔲**12**
(AAA) (SAVE)   All Year   1P: $84-$104   2P: $94-$114   XP: $10   F14
▼▼▼   **Location:** I-94, exit 318 (Airport), 1.1 mi e, just n on Howell Ave (SR 38), then just w. 200 W Grange Ave 53207.
Fax: 414/744-4188. **Facility:** 99 one-bedroom standard units. 4 stories, interior corridors. **Parking:** on-site.
Small-scale Hotel   **Terms:** cancellation fee imposed, [BP] meal plan available. **Amenities:** video games (fee), high-speed Internet, voice mail, irons, hair dryers. **Leisure Activities:** exercise room. **Guest Services:** sundries, valet and coin laundry. **Business Services:** meeting rooms, business center. **Cards:** AX, CB, DC, DS, JC, MC, VI.
Special Amenities: free full breakfast and free local telephone calls. *(See color ad below & p 570)*

SOME UNITS

AMERISUITES MILWAUKEE/WEST *Book at aaa.com*   Phone: (414)462-3500   🔲**3**
(AAA) (SAVE)   All Year   1P: $79-$109   2P: $89-$119   XP: $10   F14
▼▼▼   **Location:** US 45, exit 46 (Silver Spring Dr), just w. 11777 W Silver Spring Dr 53225. Fax: 414/462-8166. **Facility:** 123 one-bedroom standard units. 4 stories, interior corridors. **Parking:** on-site. **Terms:** [BP] meal plan available.
Amenities: video games (fee), high-speed Internet, dual phone lines, voice mail, irons, hair dryers. **Leisure**
Small-scale Hotel   **Activities:** exercise room. **Guest Services:** sundries, valet and coin laundry. **Business Services:** meeting rooms, fax. **Cards:** AX, CB, DC, DS, JC, MC, VI. **Special Amenities:** free full breakfast and free local
telephone calls. *(See color ad below & p 570)*

SOME UNITS

BAYMONT INN & SUITES MILWAUKEE NW *Book at aaa.com*   Phone: (414)535-1300   🔲**4**
(AAA) (SAVE)   All Year   1P: $79-$99
▼▼▼   **Location:** US 45, exit 46 (Silver Spring Rd), just se. 5442 N Lovers Lane Rd 53225. Fax: 414/535-1724. **Facility:** 117 units. 115 one-bedroom standard units. 2 one-bedroom suites ($89-$119). 3 stories, interior corridors.
Parking: on-site. **Terms:** [ECP] meal plan available, small pets only ($50 deposit). **Amenities:** video games
Small-scale Hotel   (fee), voice mail, irons, hair dryers. **Leisure Activities:** limited exercise equipment. **Guest Services:** valet and coin laundry. **Business Services:** meeting rooms, fax (fee). **Cards:** AX, CB, DC, DS, MC, VI.
Special Amenities: free local telephone calls and free newspaper. *(See color ad p 597)*

SOME UNITS

FEE

Quiet Nights, Rest Assured.

AmericInn® provides travelers a quiet night's stay and allows you relax and unwind in private. You can talk above a whisper without waking your neighbors. And you'll sleep without being disturbed by your neighbors. Now that's something worth thinking about!

◆ Large indoor recreation area with pool, sauna and whirlpool

◆ Welcoming lobby with a large fireplace & cozy conversation areas

◆ Complimentary enhanced continental breakfast

◆ Private one and two-room whirlpool & fireplace suites

◆ Children 12 and under stay free with an adult

AmericInn's are independently owned and operated.
Amenities may vary slightly between locations.

Reservations: 800-634-3444 www.americinn.com

The Osthoff Resort

Your Place On The Lake™

All-suite accommodations, four seasons of recreation, fine American and Continental cuisine, spa services, breathtaking beachfront scenery, children's activity program, and Old World charm combine with all the services and amenities of a premier AAA Four Diamond resort destination.

To make reservations, call 800.876.3399 or visit www.osthoff.com

OSTHOFF RESORT

Elkhart Lake, WI • www.osthoff.com • 920.876.3366

(See map and index starting on p. 566)

BEST WESTERN WOODSVIEW INN *Book at aaa.com*   **Phone:** (414)671-6400   **5**

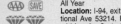

All Year   1P: $62-$92   2P: $62-$92
Location: I-94, exit 308B, 0.5 mi s on Miller Pkwy, just w on SR 59. Located adjacent to Veterans Hospital. 5501 W National Ave 53214. **Fax:** 414/671-1029. **Facility:** 62 one-bedroom standard units, some with kitchens and/or whirlpools. 3 stories, interior corridors. *Bath:* combo or shower only. **Parking:** on-site. **Terms:** [ECP] meal
Small-scale Hotel plan available. **Amenities:** voice mail, safes (fee), irons, hair dryers. *Some:* dual phone lines. **Dining:** 11 am-11 pm; closed Sun. **Pool(s):** heated indoor. **Leisure Activities:** whirlpool, game room. **Guest Services:** valet laundry. **Business Services:** meeting rooms. **Cards:** AX, CB, DC, DS, JC, MC, VI. **Special Amenities:** free continental breakfast and free local telephone calls.

SOME UNITS

(See map and index starting on p. 566)

CLARION HOTEL AIRPORT   *Book at aaa.com*   Phone: (414)481-2400   ⑪
All Year   1P: $84-$169   2P: $84-$169   XP: $10   F
Location: I-94, exit 318 (Airport), 1.1 mi e at jct SR 38. 5311 S Howell Ave 53207. Fax: 414/481-4471. **Facility:** 180 units. 156 one-bedroom standard units. 23 one- and 1 two-bedroom suites, some with whirlpools. 3 stories, interior corridors. *Bath:* combo or shower only. **Parking:** on-site. **Terms:** [CP] meal plan available.
Small-scale Hotel   **Amenities:** video games (fee), dual phone lines, voice mail, irons, hair dryers. *Some:* high-speed Internet (fee). **Dining:** 6:30 am-10 pm, Sun 9 am-9 pm, cocktails. **Pool(s):** heated indoor. **Leisure Activities:** limited exercise equipment. **Guest Services:** valet and coin laundry. **Business Services:** conference facilities, business center. **Cards:** AX, CB, DC, DS, JC, MC, VI. **Special Amenities:** free continental breakfast and free local telephone calls.

SOME UNITS

🆎 ✈ 🍴 📺 ♿Ⓜ ♿ 🍷 🚲 🐕 DATA PORT 💻 / ✕ 🧳 📷 /

COUNTRY INNS & SUITES BY CARLSON   *Book at aaa.com*   Phone: (414)762-6018   ⑬
All Year   1P: $82-$112   2P: $89-$117   XP: $7   F18
Location: I-94, exit 319, just e on College Ave (CR ZZ). 6200 S 13th St 53221. Fax: 414/762-8806. **Facility:** 81 units. 53 one-bedroom standard units, some with whirlpools. 28 one-bedroom suites ($95-$150). 3 stories, interior corridors. *Bath:* combo or shower only. **Parking:** on-site. **Terms:** [ECP] meal plan available. **Amenities:** dual
Small-scale Hotel   phone lines, voice mail, irons, hair dryers. **Pool(s):** small heated indoor. **Leisure Activities:** whirlpool, exercise room. *Fee:* game room. **Guest Services:** valet and coin laundry. **Business Services:** meeting rooms, fax (fee). **Cards:** AX, CB, DC, DS, MC, VI. **Special Amenities:** free expanded continental breakfast and free local telephone calls. *(See color ad starting on p 580)*

SOME UNITS

🆎 ✈ 🍴 ♿ 🏊 ✕ 🐕 DATA PORT 💻 / ✕ 🧳 📷 /

ECONO LODGE AIRPORT   *Book at aaa.com*   Phone: (414)764-2510   ⑯
All Year [CP]   1P: $39-$199   2P: $49-$199   XP: $5   F17
Location: I-94, exit 319, just e on College Ave (CR ZZ), then just s. Located in a commercial area. 6541 S 13th St 53221. Fax: 414/764-2510. **Facility:** 106 one-bedroom standard units. 2 stories (no elevator), interior corridors.
Motel   *Bath:* shower only. **Parking:** on-site, winter plug-ins. **Amenities:** video library (fee). **Cards:** AX, CB, DC, DS, JC, MC, VI. **Special Amenities:** free continental breakfast and free local telephone calls.

SOME UNITS

🆎 🍴 ♿ 🐕 DATA PORT / ✕ VCR 🧳 📷 💻 /
FEE FEE FEE

Country Hospitality.

Wherever your travels take you, a cozy
lobby fireplace, comfortable guest rooms and a
friendly staff are always waiting for you.

Wisconsin

Appleton	Mauston (Wisconsin Dells)	Prairie du Chien
Chippewa Falls	Menomonie	River Falls
East Troy	Milwaukee-Airport	Shawano
Eau Claire	Milwaukee-West	Sparta
Fond du Lac	Platteville	Stevens Point
Germantown	Port Washington (Milwaukee)	Turtle Lake
Green Bay		Waunakee (Madison)
Kenosha		Wausau (Schofield)
Madison (Monona)		West Bend

COUNTRY INNS & SUITES BY CARLSON

A Cozy Stay At A
Comfortable Price

800-456-4000
www.countryinns.com/wiaaa

(See map and index starting on p. 566)

FOUR POINTS BY SHERATON MILWAUKEE AIRPORT   *Book at aaa.com*   **Phone:** (414)481-8000   **9**
All Year   1P: $79-$99   2P: $79-$99   XP: $10   F17
Location: I-94, exit 318 (Airport), 1.1 mi e to Howell Ave (SR 38), 0.7 mi n. Located in a commercial area. 4747 S Howell
Large-scale Hotel   Ave 53207. Fax: 414/481-8065. **Facility:** 508 units. 504 one-bedroom standard units, some with whirlpools. 4
one-bedroom suites. 6 stories, interior corridors. *Bath:* combo or shower only. **Parking:** on-site.
Amenities: video games (fee), voice mail, irons, hair dryers. *Some:* dual phone lines. **Pool(s):** heated outdoor, small heated indoor. **Leisure Activities:** exercise room. **Guest Services:** gift shop, valet and coin laundry. **Business Services:** conference facilities, business center. **Cards:** AX, CB, DC, DS, JC, MC, VI. *(See color ad p 5)*

SOME UNITS

(ASK) (SD) (free) (restaurant) (bar) (accessible) (no smoking) (pool) (recreation) (DATA PORT) (microwave) (refrigerator) / (X) /

HAMPTON INN-MILWAUKEE AIRPORT   *Book at aaa.com*   **Phone:** (414)762-4240   **14**
(AAA) (SAVE)   All Year [ECP]   1P: $69-$129   2P: $69-$129
Location: I-94, exit 319, just e on College Ave (CR ZZ). Located in a commercial area. 1200 W College Ave 53221.
Fax: 414/762-9810. **Facility:** 105 one-bedroom standard units. 3 stories, interior corridors. *Bath:* combo or
shower only. **Parking:** on-site. **Terms:** package plans. **Amenities:** video games (fee), high-speed Internet,
Small-scale Hotel   dual phone lines, voice mail, irons, hair dryers. **Pool(s):** small heated indoor. **Leisure Activities:** whirlpool,
limited exercise equipment. **Guest Services:** valet laundry. **Business Services:** meeting rooms. **Cards:** AX,
CB, DC, DS, JC, MC, VI. **Special Amenities:** free expanded continental breakfast and early check-in/late check-out.
(See color ad below)

SOME UNITS

(SD) (free) (restaurant) (&M) (accessible) (no smoking) (pool) (recreation) (DATA PORT) (microwave) / (X) /

HAMPTON INN-MILWAUKEE NW   *Book at aaa.com*   **Phone:** (414)466-8881   **2**
All Year [BP]   1P: $79-$99   2P: $79-$99
Location: US 45, exit 46 (Silver Spring Dr), just ne. 5601 N Lovers Lane Rd 53225. Fax: 414/466-3840. **Facility:** 108
one-bedroom standard units. 4 stories, interior corridors. *Bath:* combo or shower only. **Parking:** on-site.
Small-scale Hotel   **Amenities:** video games (fee), voice mail, irons, hair dryers. **Pool(s):** small heated indoor. **Leisure Activi-
ties:** whirlpool, limited exercise equipment. **Guest Services:** valet laundry. **Business Services:** meeting rooms, fax (fee).
Cards: AX, DC, DS, MC, VI.

SOME UNITS

(ASK) (SD) (restaurant) (&) (&M) (accessible) (no smoking) (pool) (recreation) (DATA PORT) (microwave) / (X) (refrigerator) (microwave) /
                                                                                  FEE   FEE

The One That Does It All

For years, people have turned to AAA for their emergency road service needs. But AAA is more than just towing. Access to AAA's travel services can give you the world. Its financial services can help you pay for it. And AAA insurance can give you the peace of mind to enjoy the ride. Plus, AAA gives you exclusive Show Your Card & Save® offers, bail bond benefits, and much more.

Discover the ways AAA can simplify your life. Call or stop by your nearest AAA office today to find out about the specific products and services they offer.

(See map and index starting on p. 566)

HILTON GARDEN INN MILWAUKEE PARK PLACE

AAA **SAVE**
Small-scale Hotel

Book at aaa.com

			Phone: (414)359-9823	**1**
1/1-3/31	1P: $169	2P: $169	XP: $20	F17
4/1-12/31	1P: $79-$159	2P: $79-$159	XP: $20	F17

Location: US 45, exit 43B (Good Hope Rd), just e, then 0.5 mi n at jct SR 100 and 145 (107th St). 11600 W Park Pl 53224. Fax: 414/359-9824. **Facility:** 126 units. 124 one-bedroom standard units. 2 one-bedroom suites ($99-$179). 3 stories, interior corridors. *Bath:* combo or shower only. **Parking:** on-site. **Amenities:** video games (fee), high-speed Internet, dual phone lines, voice mail, irons, hair dryers. **Dining:** 6 am-2 & 5-10 pm, Sat & Sun 7 am-noon & 5-10 pm, cocktails. **Pool(s):** heated indoor. **Leisure Activities:** sauna, whirlpool, sun deck, exercise room, game room. **Guest Services:** valet and coin laundry. **Business Services:** conference facilities, business center. **Cards:** AX, DC, DS, MC, VI. **Special Amenities:** free newspaper.

SOME UNITS

HOLIDAY INN HOTEL AND SUITES

AAA **SAVE**
Small-scale Hotel

Book at aaa.com

| | | | Phone: (414)482-4444 | **7** |
| All Year | 1P: $140-$180 | 2P: $140-$180 | | |

Location: I-94, exit 317, 1.3 mi e. Located in a commercial, residential area. 545 W Layton Ave 53207. Fax: 414/482-1111. **Facility:** 130 units. 118 one-bedroom standard units, some with whirlpools. 12 one-bedroom suites with kitchens. 3 stories, interior corridors. *Bath:* combo or shower only. **Parking:** on-site. **Terms:** [BP] meal plan available. **Amenities:** video games (fee), dual phone lines, voice mail, irons, hair dryers. **Dining:** 6 am-10 & 4-11 pm, cocktails. **Pool(s):** heated indoor. **Leisure Activities:** whirlpool, sun deck with grill, limited exercise equipment. *Fee:* game room. **Guest Services:** gift shop, valet and coin laundry. **Business Services:** meeting rooms, business center. **Cards:** AX, DC, DS, MC, VI. **Special Amenities:** free local telephone calls and free newspaper. *(See color ad p 583)*

SOME UNITS

HOSPITALITY INN

AAA **SAVE**
Small-scale Hotel

Book at aaa.com

| | | | Phone: (414)282-8800 | **6** |
| All Year [ECP] | 1P: $100-$250 | 2P: $100-$250 | | |

Location: I-894, exit 9 (SR 241), just n. 4400 S 27th St 53221. Fax: 414/282-7713. **Facility:** 192 units. 121 one-bedroom standard units, some with whirlpools. 71 one-bedroom suites, some with whirlpools. 3-5 stories, interior/exterior corridors. *Bath:* combo or shower only. **Parking:** on-site. **Terms:** 2 night minimum stay - some weekends, weekly rates available, [BP], [CP], [ECP] & [MAP] meal plans available. **Amenities:** voice mail, irons, hair dryers. *Some:* dual phone lines. **Dining:** 6 am-10 pm, wine/beer only. **Pool(s):** 2 small heated indoor. **Leisure Activities:** sauna, whirlpool, limited exercise equipment. *Fee:* game room. **Guest Services:** valet and coin laundry. **Business Services:** meeting rooms, fax (fee). **Cards:** AX, DC, DS, MC, VI. **Special Amenities:** free expanded continental breakfast and free newspaper.

SOME UNITS

When You Really Need to Speak Their Language... Let the IDP Speak for You

When traveling overseas, carry an **International Driving Permit...** even if you're not planning to drive. Should you need to communicate with foreign authorities, this recognizable form of identification can help you get on your way more quickly. Valid in over 150 countries, the permit contains information translated into ten languages.

Before you travel the world, travel to any AAA office for your International Driving Permit. Bring your valid U.S. driver's license, $10, and two passport-size photos (also available at AAA offices).

Travel With Someone You Trust®

(See map and index starting on p. 566)

HOWARD JOHNSON MILWAUKEE AIRPORT INN — *Book at aaa.com* — Phone: (414)282-7000 — **8**

▼▼▼▼ 5/16-9/1 — 1P: $119-$149 — 2P: $119-$149
4/1-5/15 & 9/2-3/31 — 1P: $99 — 2P: $99
Small-scale Hotel **Location:** I-94, exit 317. Located in a commercial area. 1716 W Layton Ave 53221. Fax: 414/282-1552. **Facility:** 96 one-bedroom standard units, some with whirlpools. 2 stories (no elevator), interior corridors. *Bath:* combo or shower only. **Parking:** on-site. **Amenities:** *Some:* irons, hair dryers. **Pool(s):** heated outdoor. **Guest Services:** coin laundry. **Business Services:** meeting rooms. **Cards:** AX, DS, MC, VI. *(See color ad p 584)*

SOME UNITS

(ASK) (SD) (+K) (⊟) (Y) (⊷) (≋) (☂) (DATA PORT) / (X) (⊟) (▤) (⊟) /

RADISSON HOTEL MILWAUKEE AIRPORT — *Book at aaa.com* — Phone: (414)764-1500 — **15**

(AAA) (SAVE) 6/1-8/31 — 1P: $99-$159 — 2P: $99-$159 — XP: $10 — F17
4/1-5/31 & 9/1-3/31 — 1P: $79-$139 — 2P: $79-$139 — XP: $10 — F17
▼▼▼▼ **Location:** I-94, exit 319, just e on College Ave (CR ZZ). Located in a commercial area. 6331 S 13th St 53221.
Fax: 414/764-6531. **Facility:** 159 one-bedroom standard units. 3 stories, interior corridors. *Bath:* combo or
Small-scale Hotel shower only. **Parking:** on-site, winter plug-ins. **Terms:** weekly rates available. **Amenities:** video games (fee), dual phone lines, voice mail, irons, hair dryers. **Dining:** 6 am-2 & 5-10 pm, cocktails. **Pool(s):** heated indoor. **Leisure Activities:** sun deck, exercise room. *Fee:* game room. **Guest Services:** valet and coin laundry, area transportation-upon availability. **Business Services:** conference facilities, PC. **Cards:** AX, CB, DC, DS, JC, MC, VI. **Special Amenities: free newspaper.** *(See color ad below & p 583)*

SOME UNITS

(SD) (+K) (⊟) (Y) (☒) (⊘) (≋) (X) (☂) (DATA PORT) (⊟) / (X) (VCR) (⊟) /

SUPER 8 MOTEL-MILWAUKEE AIRPORT — *Book at aaa.com* — Phone: (414)481-8488 — **10**

(AAA) (SAVE) All Year [CP] — 1P: $69-$199 — 2P: $79-$199
▼▼▼ **Location:** I-94, exit 318 (Airport), 1.1 mi e, just n on Howell Ave (SR 38). 5253 S Howell Ave 53207.
Fax: 414/481-8086. **Facility:** 116 one-bedroom standard units. 3 stories, interior corridors. **Parking:** on-site,
winter plug-ins. **Leisure Activities:** whirlpool. **Guest Services:** coin laundry. **Business Services:** meeting
Small-scale Hotel rooms, fax (fee). **Cards:** AX, CB, DC, DS, JC, MC, VI. **Special Amenities: free continental breakfast and
free local telephone calls.**

SOME UNITS

(SD) (+K) (⊟) (⊘) (☂) (⊟) / (X) (VCR) (DATA PORT) (⊟) (▤) /

(See map and index starting on p. 566)

——— WHERE TO DINE ———

AU BON APPETIT RESTAURANT & CATERING
Dinner: $8-$14   **Phone:** 414/278-1233   ④
Location: Just e of jct Van Buren Ave, at jct Humboldt Ave. 1016 E Brady St 53202. **Hours:** 5 pm-9 pm, Fri & Sat-10 pm. Closed major holidays; also Sun & Mon. **Reservations:** suggested. **Features:** This family-owned and operated restaurant offers Mediterranean food with a Lebanese and French flair Lebanese   prepared by the owner/chef. It is a small, intimate restaurant with cozy seating and gracious owners who welcome you immediately upon entering with a friendly hello and a warm bon appetit as you begin to eat. The Royal coucous with chicken is a wonderful entree of choice with a variety of herbs and spices making for a tasty dinner treat. Basque chicken is a specialty of the house. Casual dress; beer & wine only. **Parking:** street. **Cards:** MC, VI.

BARTOLOTTA'S LAKE PARK BISTRO
Lunch: $8-$15   **Dinner:** $10-$35   **Phone:** 414/962-6300   ③
Location: I-43, exit 74 (Locust St), 2 mi e to Lake Dr, then just s; in Lake Park. 3133 E Newberry Blvd 53211. **Hours:** 11:30 am-2 & 5:30-9 pm, Fri-10 pm, Sat 5 pm-10 pm, Sun 10:30 am-2 & 5-8 pm. Closed major French   holidays. **Reservations:** suggested. **Features:** A fabulous view of Lake Michigan is offered as you dine at this elegant restaurant in Lake Park. The exterior setting is striking and a welcomed site. The interior is stylishly decorated and gives one a bistro feel. Menu offerings are varied and capture the essence of French cooking with wonderful herbs and sauces. Specialties include the grilled Atlantic salmon, filet medallions a'poivre and the praline parfait is a fabulous dessert choice with the creative presentation and wonderful flavor. Dressy casual; cocktails. **Parking:** on-site. **Cards:** AX, DC, DS, MC, VI.

DREAM DANCE
Dinner: $27-$38   **Phone:** 414/847-7883   ⑦
Location: Located in Potawatomi Bingo Casino. 1721 W Canal St 53233. **Hours:** 5 pm-9 pm, Fri & Sat-10 pm. Closed: Sun & Mon. **Reservations:** suggested. **Features:** Inside the Potawatomi Bingo Casino, the refined oasis—away from the noise and smoke of the casino floor—features a ceiling stretched with wood beams, American   walls of bark, antler lamps and white tablecloths. Concentrating on contemporary American food, the menu lists specially raised venison, veal chop, rack of lamb and several seafood dishes, including butter-poached lobster. Diners are asked to select their steak knives from a wood box the attentive servers deliver. Dressy casual; cocktails. **Parking:** on-site and valet. **Cards:** AX, DS, MC, VI.

HEINEMANN'S RESTAURANT
Lunch: $4-$7   **Dinner:** $5-$7   **Phone:** 414/258-6800   ⑥
Location: Just s of jct US 18 (W Bluemound Rd). 317 N 76th St 53213. **Hours:** 7 am-8 pm, Sun-2:30 pm. Closed major holidays; also for dinner 12/24. **Features:** A local favorite established in 1923, this restaurant is American   known for its made-from-scratch menu items. Only natural ingredients are used in the homemade bread, sauces and soup. There are no preservatives, which is something of which they pride themselves. The setting is country cozy and the service staff is friendly and welcoming. Casual dress; beer & wine only. **Parking:** on-site. **Cards:** MC, VI.

JALAPENO LOCO
Lunch: $5-$18   **Dinner:** $5-$18   **Phone:** 414/483-8300   ⑫
Location: Jct Layton Ave, 0.5 mi s. 5067 S Howell Ave 53207. **Hours:** 11 am-10 pm, Fri & Sat-11 pm. Closed major holidays. **Features:** No need to fly south—an authentic taste of Mexico is available right here. Mexican   Chimichangas, burritos, fajitas, quesadillas, flautas and more are served in a warm and friendly atmosphere. Casual dress; cocktails. **Parking:** on-site. **Cards:** MC, VI.

OLD TOWN SERBIAN GOURMET HOUSE
Lunch: $5-$9   **Dinner:** $12-$18   **Phone:** 414/672-0206   ⑧
Location: I-94, exit 312B (W Lincoln Ave), just w. 522 W Lincoln Ave 53207. **Hours:** 11:30 am-2:30 & 5-10 pm. Closed major holidays; also Mon. **Reservations:** suggested. **Features:** Flavorful foods and unusual recipes are the draw at the family-operated restaurant, a local fixture for more than 30 years. Old World Ethnic   decor and ethnic background music set the mood. Among selections of Serbian/European cuisine are preparations of chicken, beef, lamb, fish and veal. Locals favor such hearty, made-from-scratch entrees as moussaka, goulash and Burak beef. Casual dress; cocktails. **Parking:** on-site. **Cards:** AX, DC, DS, MC, VI.

THE PACKING HOUSE
Lunch: $6-$10   **Dinner:** $10-$23   **Phone:** 414/483-5054   ⑩
Location: 0.5 mi e of Howell Ave (SR 38). 900 E Layton Ave 53207. **Hours:** 11:30 am-2 & 5-10 pm, Fri 11:30 am-2 & 4-11 pm, Sat 5-11 pm, Sun 10 am-1:30 & 4-9 pm. Closed: for dinner 12/24. Steak & Seafood   **Reservations:** suggested. **Features:** Choose from a variety of cuts and preparations, including garlic-stuffed fillet, beef Wellington and filet Oscar. Seafood—such as Canadian walleye and king crab legs—also is offered. Rounding out the menu are a few vegetarian dishes, prime rib, chops, ribs and poultry. Dressy casual; cocktails. **Parking:** on-site. **Cards:** AX, DC, DS, MC, VI.

PAUL'S OMEGA FAMILY RESTAURANT
Lunch: $6-$13   **Dinner:** $8-$17   **Phone:** 414/645-6595   ⑨
Location: I-894, exit 9, 0.9 mi n SR 241. 3473 S 27th St 53215. **Hours:** 24 hours. **Features:** The lengthy menu dabbles in many varieties of food, ranging from barbecue and seafood dishes to traditional Italian and Greek   Greek cuisine. Breakfast items are served all day. Plates are piled high with tasty offerings. Baked goods are homemade. Casual dress; cocktails. **Parking:** on-site. **Cards:** DS, MC, VI.

PRIME QUARTER STEAK HOUSE
Dinner: $12-$16   **Phone:** 414/769-1300   ⑪
Location: Just w of jct S 13th St. 909 W Layton Ave 53221. **Hours:** 5 pm-10 pm, Sat from 4 pm, Sun 4 pm-9 pm. Closed major holidays. **Reservations:** accepted. **Features:** Here's an opportunity to barbecue: first fix a salad at the fresh salad bar and then step up to one of three large grills to prepare your favorite choice Steak House   cut of beef just the way you like it. To complete the plate, add a hot baked potato and Texas toast done on the grill. Professional help is standing by if needed, or they will cook for you. Casual dress; cocktails. **Parking:** on-site. **Cards:** AX, CB, DC, DS, MC, VI.

(See map and index starting on p. 566)

SAZ'S STATE HOUSE   Lunch: $7-$14   Dinner: $7-$22   Phone: 414/453-2410   ⑤
Location: Jct of Hawley Rd overpass. 5539 W State St 53208. **Hours:** 11 am-9:30 pm, Fri & Sat-11 pm, Sun 10:30 am-2 & 3-9 pm, Mon 11 am-9 pm. Closed: 12/25; also for dinner 12/24. **Reservations:** accepted.
American   **Features:** The popular, bustling restaurant has been serving tasty food since 1976. Fall-off-the-bone pork and beef barbecue with Saz's own award-winning sauces is the big draw. The recipe for delicious cottage fries has been perfected over many years. Casual dress; cocktails. **Parking:** on-site. **Cards:** AX, DS, MC, VI.

WEST BANK CAFE   Dinner: $5-$17   Phone: 414/562-5555   ②
Location: Jct N Fratney St. 732 E Burleigh St 53212. **Hours:** 5:30 pm-9:30 pm, Fri & Sat-10 pm. Closed major holidays. **Features:** In a residential neighborhood, the restaurant is simple and unpretentious. The menu is Vietnamese   anything but ordinary, with thick curries that are slightly sweet and catfish cooked in a Vietnamese clay pot.
DC, DS, MC, VI.   Vegetarian and European entrees also are offered. Casual dress; cocktails. **Parking:** on-site. **Cards:** AX,

YEN CHING RESTAURANT   Lunch: $5-$6   Dinner: $8-$13   Phone: 414/353-6677   ①
Location: Just w of SR 181 (76th St). 7630 W Good Hope Rd 53223. **Hours:** 11:30 am-2 & 4:30-9:30 pm, Fri-10 pm, Sat 4:30 pm-10 pm, Sun 11:30 am-2:30 & 4:30-9 pm. Closed: 7/4, 11/25. **Features:** Sweet and sour Chinese   pork and almond chicken are among examples of Mandarin cuisine on the restaurant's extensive menu. The decor is Oriental, with carved, red-stained wood throughout. Servers exhibit strong knowledge of the menu and preparation style. Casual dress; cocktails. **Parking:** on-site. **Cards:** AX, DS, MC, VI.

The Milwaukee Vicinity

BAYSIDE pop. 4,518   (See map and index starting on p. 566)

—— WHERE TO DINE ——

PANDL'S IN BAYSIDE   Lunch: $6-$15   Dinner: $12-$30   Phone: 414/352-7300   ㉒
Location: I-43, exit 82A, 1.1 mi e on SR 100/32 (Brown Deer Rd) at jct Lake Dr. 8825 N Lake Dr 53217.
Hours: 11:30 am-10 pm, Fri & Sat-11 pm, Sun 10 am-2 & 4:30-9 pm. Closed major holidays.
American   **Reservations:** suggested. **Features:** The casual restaurant has the atmosphere of a country club. Many windows in the open dining room afford views of a seasonally changing wooded landscape. Fresh fish is the house specialty, but flavorful preparations of steak and lamb also line the varied menu. Dressy casual; cocktails. **Parking:** on-site. **Cards:** AX, DC, DS, MC, VI.

BROOKFIELD pop. 38,649 (See map and index starting on p. 566)

———— WHERE TO STAY ————

BAYMONT INN & SUITES MILWAUKEE-BROOKFIELD *Book at aaa.com*   **Phone:** (262)782-9100
(AAA) (SAVE)
▼▼▼
Small-scale Hotel

5/21-9/5	1P: $79-$99	2P: $79-$99
9/6-3/31	1P: $59-$79	2P: $59-$79
4/1-5/20	1P: $59-$74	2P: $59-$74

Location: I-94, exit 297, just e on US 18. 20391 W Bluemound Rd 53045. Fax: 262/782-8560. **Facility:** 97 units. 94 one-bedroom standard units. 3 one-bedroom suites ($99-$139). 3 stories, interior corridors. **Parking:** on-site, winter plug-ins. **Terms:** [ECP] meal plan available, small pets only. **Amenities:** voice mail, irons, hair dryers. *Fee:* video games, high-speed Internet. **Leisure Activities:** exercise room. **Guest Services:** valet and coin laundry. **Business Services:** meeting rooms. **Cards:** AX, CB, DC, DS, MC, VI. **Special Amenities:** free local telephone calls and free newspaper. *(See color ad p 597)*

SOME UNITS

BEST WESTERN MIDWAY HOTEL *Book at aaa.com*   **Phone:** (262)786-9540   **39**
(AAA) (SAVE)
▼▼▼
Small-scale Hotel

All Year [ECP]   1P: $79-$139   2P: $89-$149   XP: $10   F17

Location: I-94, exit 301A, just s. Located in a commercial area. 1005 S Moorland Rd 53005. Fax: 262/786-4561. **Facility:** 125 units. 108 one-bedroom standard units. 17 one-bedroom suites ($139-$169). 6 stories, interior corridors. **Parking:** on-site. **Amenities:** video library (fee), voice mail, irons, hair dryers. *Some:* high-speed Internet, fax, honor bars. **Dining:** 6:30 am-9 pm; Sunday brunch, cocktails. **Pool(s):** heated indoor. **Leisure Activities:** sauna, whirlpool, domed recreation area, limited exercise equipment. *Fee:* game room. **Guest Services:** valet laundry, area transportation-within 10 mi. **Business Services:** meeting rooms. **Cards:** AX, DC, DS, MC, VI. **Special Amenities:** free local telephone calls and preferred room (subject to availability with advanced reservations).

SOME UNITS

FEE   FEE

COUNTRY INN & SUITES MILWAUKEE WEST *Book at aaa.com*   **Phone:** (262)782-1400   **41**
▼▼▼
Large-scale Hotel

4/1-10/29	1P: $79-$129	2P: $79-$129	XP: $10 F19
10/30-3/31	1P: $69-$119	2P: $69-$119	XP: $10 F19

Location: I-94, exit 301A, just se. Located in a commercial area. 1250 S Moorland Rd 53005. Fax: 262/782-1408. **Facility:** 150 one-bedroom standard units, some with whirlpools. 3 stories, interior corridors. *Bath:* combo or shower only. **Parking:** on-site. **Terms:** [ECP] meal plan available. **Amenities:** dual phone lines, voice mail, irons, hair dryers. *Some:* high-speed Internet (fee). **Pool(s):** small heated indoor. **Leisure Activities:** whirlpool, exercise room. *Fee:* game room. **Guest Services:** sundries, valet and coin laundry. **Business Services:** conference facilities, business center. **Cards:** AX, CB, DC, DS, MC, VI. *(See color ad starting on p 580)*

SOME UNITS

COURTYARD BY MARRIOTT/BROOKFIELD *Book at aaa.com*   **Phone:** 262/821-1800   **37**
▼▼▼
Small-scale Hotel

All Year   1P: $59-$129

Location: I-94, exit 297 eastbound, 2.2 mi e on US 18; exit 301B westbound, 1.5 mi n on Moorland Rd, then 0.3 mi w on US 18. 16865 W Bluemound Rd 53005. Fax: 262/821-1548. **Facility:** 148 units. 138 one-bedroom standard units. 10 one-bedroom suites ($129-$159). 3 stories, interior corridors. *Bath:* combo or shower only. **Parking:** on-site. **Terms:** [BP] meal plan available. **Amenities:** high-speed Internet, voice mail, irons, hair dryers. **Pool(s):** small heated indoor. **Leisure Activities:** whirlpool, exercise room. **Guest Services:** valet and coin laundry. **Business Services:** meeting rooms. **Cards:** AX, CB, DC, DS, JC, MC, VI.

SOME UNITS

EMBASSY SUITES HOTEL-MILWAUKEE WEST *Book at aaa.com*   **Phone:** (262)782-2900   **40**
▼▼▼
Small-scale Hotel

All Year [BP]   1P: $89-$179   2P: $99-$189   XP: $20   F18

Location: I-94, exit 301 (A and B), just s. 1200 S Moorland Rd 53008-1463 (PO Box 1463). Fax: 262/796-9159. **Facility:** 203 units. 199 one- and 4 two-bedroom suites, some with whirlpools. 5 stories, interior corridors. **Parking:** on-site. **Terms:** check-in 4 pm, cancellation fee imposed, [AP] meal plan available. **Amenities:** video games (fee), irons, hair dryers. **Pool(s):** heated indoor. **Leisure Activities:** sauna, whirlpool, steamroom, exercise room. **Guest Services:** gift shop, complimentary evening beverages, valet and coin laundry, area transportation. **Business Services:** conference facilities, business center. **Cards:** AX, CB, DC, DS, JC, MC, VI.

SOME UNITS

HAMPTON INN-BROOKFIELD *Book at aaa.com*   **Phone:** (262)796-1500
▼▼▼
Small-scale Hotel

All Year   1P: $79-$139   2P: $89-$149   XP: $10   F17

Location: I-94, exit 297, just e on US 18. 575 N Barker Rd 53045. Fax: 262/796-0977. **Facility:** 120 one-bedroom standard units. 4 stories, interior corridors. *Bath:* combo or shower only. **Parking:** on-site. **Terms:** [CP] meal plan available. **Amenities:** video games (fee), high-speed Internet, dual phone lines, voice mail, irons, hair dryers. **Pool(s):** small heated indoor. **Leisure Activities:** whirlpool, exercise room. **Guest Services:** valet laundry. **Business Services:** meeting rooms. **Cards:** AX, DC, DS, MC, VI.

SOME UNITS

HOMESTEAD STUDIO SUITES HOTEL-MILWAUKEE/BROOKFIELD *Book at aaa.com*   **Phone:** (262)782-9300
▼▼▼
Small-scale Hotel

All Year   1P: $49-$64   2P: $54-$69   XP: $5   F17

Location: I-94, exit 297, 1.1 mi e on US 18, just e. 325 N Brookfield Rd 53045. Fax: 262/782-9451. **Facility:** 137 one-bedroom standard units with efficiencies. 3 stories, interior corridors. *Bath:* combo or shower only. **Parking:** on-site. **Terms:** office hours 6:30 am-11 pm, pets ($75 fee). **Amenities:** voice mail, irons. **Guest Services:** sundries, valet and coin laundry. **Business Services:** meeting rooms. **Cards:** AX, CB, DC, DS, JC, MC, VI.

SOME UNITS

FEE   FEE

(See map and index starting on p. 566)

SHERATON MILWAUKEE BROOKFIELD *Book at aaa.com* Phone: (262)364-1100 **38**
All Year   1P: $79-$149   2P: $79-$149   XP: $10   F17
Location: I-94, exit 301B, just n. Located in a commercial area. 375 S Moorland Rd 53005. Fax: 262/786-5210.
Large-scale Hotel **Facility:** 389 units. 382 one-bedroom standard units. 7 one-bedroom suites. 6 stories, interior corridors. *Bath:* combo or shower only. **Parking:** on-site. **Terms:** 3 day cancellation notice-fee imposed. **Amenities:** dual phone lines, voice mail, irons, hair dryers. *Some:* high-speed Internet (fee), fax. **Pool(s):** heated outdoor, heated indoor. **Leisure Activities:** sauna, whirlpool, exercise room. **Guest Services:** valet and coin laundry. **Business Services:** conference facilities, business center. **Cards:** AX, CB, DC, DS, JC, MC, VI.

SOME UNITS
(ASK) (S⌀) (✕) (🍴) (⛍) (⌨) (🏊) (✕) (🐾) (DATA PORT) (▭) / (✕) (▐) (📷) /

TOWNEPLACE SUITES BY MARRIOTT *Book at aaa.com* Phone: 262/784-8450 **36**
All Year   1P: $59-$99
Location: I-94, exit 297 eastbound, 2.1 mi e on US 18; exit 301B westbound, 1.5 mi n on Moorland Rd, then 0.4 mi w
Small-scale Hotel on US 18. 600 N Calhoun Rd 53005. Fax: 262/784-8503. **Facility:** 112 units. 92 one-bedroom standard units with kitchens. 20 two-bedroom suites ($79-$119) with kitchens. 2-3 stories, interior corridors. *Bath:* combo or shower only. **Parking:** on-site. **Terms:** cancellation fee imposed, pets ($25-$75 fee). **Amenities:** dual phone lines, voice mail, irons, hair dryers. **Pool(s):** small heated outdoor. **Leisure Activities:** exercise room. **Guest Services:** valet and coin laundry. **Cards:** AX, CB, DC, DS, JC, MC, VI.

SOME UNITS
(ASK) (S⌀) (🐾) (🛏) (🏊) (DATA PORT) (▐) (🖭) (▭) / (✕) (VCR) /
FEE

WYNDHAM GARDEN HOTEL-BROOKFIELD *Book at aaa.com* Phone: (262)792-1212
(AAA) (SAVE) All Year   1P: $59-$99   2P: $59-$109   XP: $10   F17
Location: I-94, exit 297, 1.5 mi e on US 18. 18155 W Bluemound Rd 53045. Fax: 262/792-1201. **Facility:** 178 units. 169 one-bedroom standard units. 9 one-bedroom suites ($69-$109). 3 stories, interior corridors. *Bath:* combo or shower only. **Parking:** on-site. **Terms:** cancellation fee imposed. **Amenities:** voice mail, irons, hair dryers.
Small-scale Hotel *Fee:* video games, high-speed Internet. *Some:* CD players. **Dining:** 6:30 am-10 pm, cocktails. **Pool(s):** small heated indoor. **Leisure Activities:** whirlpool, complete locker room facilities, exercise room. **Guest Services:** valet laundry, airport transportation-within 5 mi, area transportation. **Business Services:** meeting rooms. **Cards:** AX, CB, DC, DS, MC, VI.

SOME UNITS
(S⌀) (✕) (🍴) (🏊) (⛍) (⌨) (📶) (🐾) (✕) (🐾) (DATA PORT) (▭) / (✕) /

━━━━━━ **WHERE TO DINE** ━━━━━━

HEINEMANN'S RESTAURANT Lunch: $4-$8   Dinner: $4-$8   Phone: 262/792-1500
(AAA) **Location:** I-94, exit 297, 1.5 mi e on US 18. 18000-A W Bluemound Rd 53045. **Hours:** 7 am-8 pm, Fri-9 pm, Sun from 7:30 am. Closed major holidays. **Reservations:** accepted. **Features:** The established, family-oriented restaurant delivers fresh, flavorful items, such as soups, sandwiches and salads. All courses are made from scratch without additives or preservatives. Noteworthy are the aromatic baked goods and tantalizing
American desserts. Casual dress; beer & wine only. **Parking:** on-site. **Cards:** DS, MC, VI.   (✕)

JAKE'S RESTAURANT Dinner: $18-$29   Phone: 262/781-7995
Location: Just n off SR 190, 1.7 mi e of jct SR 164. 21445 Gumina Rd 53072. **Hours:** 5 pm-9 pm, Fri-10 pm, Sat 4:30 pm-10 pm, Sun 5 pm-8 pm. Closed major holidays; also 12/24 & Super Bowl Sun.
American **Reservations:** accepted, except Saturday. **Features:** On a small hilltop in a rural area, the restaurant has been a local favorite since the 1970s. Although the exterior and interior design is rustic in appearance, tables are set in an intimate style and a large fireplace central to the dining room offers a romantic charm. The menu is varied with poultry, steak, pork chops, prime rib and seafood choices, as well as a few seasonal selections. Casual dress; cocktails. **Parking:** on-site. **Cards:** AX, CB, DC, MC, VI.   (⛍) (🍷) (✕)

KOPP'S FROZEN CUSTARD Lunch: $3-$5   Dinner: $3-$5   Phone: 262/789-1359
Location: I-94, exit 297, 1.1 mi e on US 18. 18880 W Bluemound Rd 53045. **Hours:** 11 am-10 pm. Closed major holidays. **Features:** Don't leave Milwaukee without trying frozen custard. Kopp's is just one of many outlets offering this dairy treat. Watch for street sign postings of daily flavors in addition to chocolate and vanilla.
American Casual dress. **Parking:** on-site.   (✕)

TASTE OF INDIA Lunch: $7   Dinner: $9-$15   Phone: 262/796-8200
Location: I-94, exit 297, 1.6 mi e on US 18; in Brookmound Plaza. **Hours:** 11:30 am 3 & 5-10 pm, Fri & Sat-10:30 pm. **Reservations:** accepted. **Features:** This clean, bright and open restaurant is located at the
Indian back of a small strip mall kitty-corner to the Wyndham Garden Hotel. It features a small buffet lunch service and an expanded a la carte menu at dinner with a sampling of vegetarian, meat and seafood dishes. There is an excellent selection of Indian breads available as well. Casual dress; beer & wine only. **Parking:** on-site. **Cards:** AX, DC, DS, MC, VI.   (✕)

BROWN DEER pop. 12,170   (See map and index starting on p. 566)

———— **WHERE TO STAY** ————

COURTYARD BY MARRIOTT MILWAUKEE NORTH BROWN DEER   *Book at aaa.com* Phone: (414)355-7500   **25**
4/1-8/31   1P: $169-$199   2P: $169-$199
9/1-3/31   1P: $159-$189   2P: $159-$189
Small-scale Hotel   **Location:** On SR 100, 0.7 mi w of jct SR 57. 5200 W Brown Deer Rd 53223. Fax: 414/355-8900. **Facility:** 122 units. 118 one-bedroom standard units, some with whirlpools. 4 one-bedroom suites ($189-$219). 4 stories, interior corridors. **Parking:** on-site. **Amenities:** video games (fee), dual phone lines, voice mail, irons, hair dryers. **Pool(s):** small heated indoor. **Leisure Activities:** whirlpool, exercise room. **Guest Services:** valet and coin laundry. **Business Services:** meeting rooms. **Cards:** AX, CB, DC, DS, JC, MC, VI.

SOME UNITS
(ASK) (S☐) (¶¶) (占M) (⚷) (🌀) (🏊) (💺) (DATA PORT) (💻) / (✕) (🔌) (🖼) /

FOUR POINTS BY SHERATON MILWAUKEE NORTH   *Book at aaa.com*   Phone: (414)355-8585   **24**
5/1-9/30   1P: $245   2P: $245   XP: $10   F17
4/1-4/30 & 10/1-3/31   1P: $159   2P: $159   XP: $10   F17
Small-scale Hotel   **Location:** I-43, exit 82 (Brown Deer Rd), 2 mi w. 8900 N Kildeer Ct 53209. Fax: 414/355-3566. **Facility:** 149 units. 127 one-bedroom standard units. 22 one-bedroom suites. 6 stories, interior corridors. *Bath:* combo or shower only. **Parking:** on-site. **Terms:** cancellation fee imposed, package plans - seasonal & weekends. **Amenities:** video games (fee), dual phone lines, voice mail, irons, hair dryers. *Some:* high-speed Internet (fee). **Pool(s):** heated outdoor, heated indoor. **Leisure Activities:** sauna, whirlpool, limited exercise equipment. **Guest Services:** valet laundry, area transportation. **Business Services:** conference facilities, business center. **Cards:** AX, CB, DC, DS, JC, MC, VI. *(See color ad p 5)*

SOME UNITS
(ASK) (S☐) (✈) (¶¶) (24↻) (⚷) (⚷) (🏊) (💺) (DATA PORT) (💻) / (✕) (🔌) (🖼) /

HOLIDAY INN EXPRESS   *Book at aaa.com*   Phone: 414/355-1300   **23**
5/31-8/31   1P: $109-$139   2P: $109-$139   XP: $10   F18
4/1-5/30 & 9/1-3/31   1P: $99-$129   2P: $99-$129   XP: $10   F18
Small-scale Hotel   **Location:** Just nw of jct SR 100 and 57. 4443 W Schroeder Dr 53223. Fax: 414/355-7368. **Facility:** 78 units. 77 one-bedroom standard units, some with whirlpools. 1 one-bedroom suite with whirlpool. 3 stories, interior corridors. *Bath:* combo or shower only. **Parking:** on-site, winter plug-ins. **Amenities:** high-speed Internet, dual phone lines, voice mail, irons, hair dryers. *Some:* fax. **Pool(s):** small heated indoor. **Leisure Activities:** whirlpool, exercise room. **Guest Services:** valet laundry. **Business Services:** meeting rooms, business center. **Cards:** AX, CB, DC, DS, MC, VI.

SOME UNITS
(ASK) (S☐) (¶¶) (占M) (⚷) (🌀) (🏊) (💺) (DATA PORT) (💻) / (✕) (🔌) (🖼) /

CEDARBURG pop. 10,908

———— **WHERE TO STAY** ————

THE WASHINGTON HOUSE INN
All Year   2P: $92-$232   XP: $20   Phone: (262)375-3550
Historic Bed   **Location:** Downtown. Located in a boutique shopping area. W62 N573 Washington Ave 53012. Fax: 262/375-9422.
& Breakfast   **Facility:** The inn, furnished with period antiques, collectibles and reproductions, offers some fireplace rooms. 34 units. 32 one-bedroom standard units, some with whirlpools. 2 one-bedroom suites ($202-$232) with whirlpools. 3 stories, interior corridors. **Parking:** on-site. **Amenities:** video library (fee), hair dryers. **Leisure Activities:** sauna. **Guest Services:** complimentary evening beverages. **Business Services:** meeting rooms. **Cards:** AX, CB, DC, MC, VI.

SOME UNITS
(ASK) (S☐) (¶¶) (➕) (VCR) (💺) (DATA PORT) / (✕) (💻) /

———— **WHERE TO DINE** ————

CREAM & CREPE CAFE   Historic   **Lunch:** $4-$9   **Dinner:** $4-$9   Phone: 262/377-0900
Location: At Cedar Creek Settlement; downtown. N70 W6340 Bridge Rd 53012. **Hours:** 10 am-8 pm, Sun 11
American   am-5 pm, Mon 10 am-5 pm. Closed major holidays. **Reservations:** accepted. **Features:** Soups, sandwiches, entrees and dessert crepes are served in a rustic old mill. Casual dress; beer & wine only. **Parking:** on-site. **Cards:** AX, DS, MC, VI.

(✕)

KLUG'S CREEKSIDE INN   **Lunch:** $7-$11   **Dinner:** $8-$18   Phone: 262/377-0660
Location: Downtown. N58 W6194 Columbia Rd 53012. **Hours:** 11 am-2 & 4-9 pm, Fri & Sat-9:30 pm, Sun 10
American   am-2 & 4-8 pm. Closed major holidays; also Mon. **Reservations:** suggested. **Features:** Antiques and local art decorate the owner-operated restaurant. The menu blends American favorites, such as prime rib and barbecue ribs, with German entrees. The strawberry Schaum torte is particularly tasty. Service is friendly and attentive. Casual dress; cocktails. **Parking:** on-site. **Cards:** AX, CB, DC, MC, VI.

(🍷) (✕)

DELAFIELD pop. 6,472

———— **WHERE TO STAY** ————

BAYMONT INN & SUITES MILWAUKEE-DELAFIELD   *Book at aaa.com*   Phone: (262)646-8500
(AAA) (SAVE)   All Year   1P: $64-$79   2P: $64-$79
Location: I-94, exit 287, just s on SR 83, then just e. 2801 Hillside Dr 53018. Fax: 262/646-7660. **Facility:** 96 units.
93 one-bedroom standard units. 3 one-bedroom suites ($104-$129). 3 stories, interior corridors. *Bath:* combo
or shower only. **Parking:** on-site, winter plug-ins. **Terms:** [ECP] meal plan available, small pets only (in
Small-scale Hotel   smoking units). **Amenities:** video games (fee), voice mail, irons, hair dryers. *Some:* dual phone lines.
Pool(s): small heated indoor. **Leisure Activities:** whirlpool, exercise room. **Guest Services:** valet and coin
laundry. **Business Services:** meeting rooms. **Cards:** AX, CB, DC, DS, MC, VI. **Special Amenities:** free local telephone calls
and free newspaper. *(See color ad p 597)*

SOME UNITS
(S☐) (🐾) (¶¶) (占M) (⚷) (🌀) (🏊) (💺) (DATA PORT) (💻) / (✕) (🔌) (🖼) /

HOLIDAY INN EXPRESS   *Book at aaa.com*   Phone: 262/646-7077

All Year [ECP]   1P: $109-$129   2P: $109-$129

Location: I-94, exit 287, just n, then just e. 3030 Golf Rd 53018. Fax: 262/646-7088. **Facility:** 84 one-bedroom standard units. 3 stories, interior corridors. *Bath:* combo or shower only. **Parking:** on-site, winter plug-ins. **Terms:** cancellation fee imposed. **Amenities:** video games (fee), voice mail, irons, hair dryers. **Pool(s):** heated indoor. **Leisure Activities:** whirlpool. *Fee:* game room. **Guest Services:** valet laundry. **Business Services:** meeting rooms. **Cards:** AX, DC, DS, MC, VI. **Special Amenities:** free expanded continental breakfast and free local telephone calls. *(See color ad below)*

Small-scale Hotel

SOME UNITS

FEE

——— WHERE TO DINE ———

FISHBONE'S   **Dinner:** $16-$30   Phone: 262/646-4696

Cajun

Location: I-94, exit 287, just n, then just w. 1704 Milwaukee St 53018. **Hours:** 4 pm-11 pm, Fri & Sat 3 pm-midnight, Sun 4 pm-10 pm. Closed major holidays; also Mon, Sun 10/1-2/1. **Features:** This is the place to be for real Cajun in a great atmosphere of upbeat, bright colors and artwork. Menu options include tempting jambalaya, Cajun pasta dishes and desserts such as bourbon pecan pie. Diners may have to remind themselves they're along the banks of Lake Nagawicka in Wisconsin and not on Bourbon Street in Louisiana. Casual dress; cocktails. **Parking:** on-site. **Cards:** AX, MC, VI.

SAXE'S CASUAL FINE DINING   **Lunch:** $5-$9   **Dinner:** $9-$19   Phone: 262/968-4600

American

Location: I-94, exit 287, 2.7 mi s on SR 83, then 0.4 mi w on US 18. W 325 S 1767 Mickle Rd 53018. **Hours:** 11 am-10 pm, Sun from 9:30 am. Closed: 1/1, 7/4, 12/25; also Mon. **Features:** Baked ribs coated in barbecue sauce as well as fresh fish specials are among traditional American menu selections. Art deco lighting and attractive art decorate the Southwestern dining room. The menu of tempting desserts changes frequently. Casual dress; cocktails. **Parking:** on-site. **Cards:** AX, DC, DS, MC, VI.

SEVEN SEAS ON NAGAWICKA LAKE   **Dinner:** $14-$25   Phone: 262/367-3903

Steak & Seafood

Location: I-94, exit 287, 1.2 mi n on SR 83, 0.7 mi w. 1807 Nagawicka Rd 53029. **Hours:** 5 pm-10 pm, Sun 10:30 am-2 & 4-9 pm. Closed: 1/1, 12/24, 12/25; also Tues 10/15-4/30. **Reservations:** accepted, except Fri. **Features:** Relax in the lovely, lakefront setting to enjoy creative preparations of seafood, beef and poultry. Such entrees as roast goose with cherry compote or broiled Atlantic salmon with dill-hollandaise sauce are complemented by an extensive list of wines. Dressy casual; cocktails. **Parking:** on-site. **Cards:** AX, DC, DS, MC, VI.

WATERSTREET BREWERY LAKE COUNTRY   **Lunch:** $6-$16   **Dinner:** $10-$24   Phone: 262/646-7878

American

Location: I-94, exit 287, just nw. 3191 Golf Rd 53018. **Hours:** 11 am-11 pm, Fri & Sat-midnight. Closed: 11/25, 12/25. **Reservations:** accepted. **Features:** Served here are a variety of salads, sandwiches, pasta and some seafood and steak preparations. Try homemade pot pie or daily soup specials. Several beers, including seasonal specialties, are brewed on the premises. The dining room reflects a Western flair. Casual dress; cocktails. **Parking:** on-site. **Cards:** AX, DS, MC, VI.

ELM GROVE pop. 6,249   (See map and index starting on p. 566)

——— WHERE TO STAY ———

SLEEPY HOLLOW INN   Phone: (262)782-8333   49

Motel

6/1-9/4   1P: $47-$80   2P: $56-$80   XP: $5   F18
4/1-5/31 & 9/5-3/31   1P: $47-$60   2P: $50-$60   XP: $5   F18

Location: I-94, exit 304, just n on SR 100, 1 mi w on US 18. 12600 W Bluemound Rd 53122. Fax: 262/782-8304. **Facility:** 31 units. 28 one- and 3 two-bedroom standard units. 1 story, exterior corridors. *Bath:* combo or shower only. **Parking:** on-site, winter plug-ins. **Terms:** 2 night minimum stay - weekends in summer, [CP] meal plan available. **Pool(s):** outdoor. **Leisure Activities:** playground, volleyball. **Cards:** AX, DS, MC, VI. **Special Amenities:** free continental breakfast and free local telephone calls. *(See color ad p 588)*

SOME UNITS

FEE

(See map and index starting on p. 566)

———— WHERE TO DINE ————

ELM GROVE INN   **Lunch:** $9-$14   **Dinner:** $18-$25   **Phone:** 262/782-7090   39
▼▼▼   **Location:** Center. 13275 Watertown Plank Rd 53122. **Hours:** 11:30 am-2 & 5-9:30 pm, Sat from 5 pm. Closed
                major holidays; also Sun. **Reservations:** suggested. **Features:** Once a stagecoach stop, the
Continental   mid-19th-century inn now operates as a casually upscale restaurant that is popular with businesspeople at
                lunch and those looking for a special night out at dinner. Service is attentive and knowledgeable. Among
decadent desserts are assorted souffles and cognac. Dressy casual; cocktails. **Parking:** on-site. **Cards:** AX, DS, MC, VI.

FRANKLIN pop. 29,494   (See map and index starting on p. 566)

———— WHERE TO DINE ————

JUDY'S FAMILY RESTAURANT   **Lunch:** $8-$16   **Dinner:** $8-$16   **Phone:** 414/761-3665   45
▼▼▼   **Location:** Just n of jct Rawson Ave. 6840 S 27th St 53154. **Hours:** 24 hours. **Features:** Bright, contemporary,
                comfortable surroundings coupled with prompt, efficient, friendly service and generous portions of good
American   food make Judy's a destination for anyone who wants super value. The menu offers great variety including
                dishes such as full breakfasts, seafood, steak, roast turkey, stir-frys, pasta, sandwiches, salads, homemade
desserts and more, including a children's menu. Casual dress; cocktails. **Parking:** on-site. **Cards:** DS, MC, VI.

GENESEE DEPOT

———— WHERE TO DINE ————

THE UNION HOUSE   Historic   **Dinner:** $16-$30   **Phone:** 262/968-4281
▼▼▼   **Location:** On SR 83; downtown. S42 W31320 Hwy 83 53127. **Hours:** 4:30 pm-9 pm, Fri & Sat-10 pm. Closed
                major holidays; also Sun & Mon. **Reservations:** suggested. **Features:** In a quaint and historic inn, the
American   restaurant offers a specialty of beef Wellington, as well as fresh fish, poultry and creative preparations of
                game. The Friday fish fry is as much an event as it is a dinner. Servers show good menu knowledge.
Casual dress; cocktails. **Parking:** on-site. **Cards:** AX, CB, DC, DS, MC, VI.

GERMANTOWN pop. 13,700   (See map and index starting on p. 566)

———— WHERE TO STAY ————

AMERICINN LODGE & SUITES OF GERMANTOWN   *Book at aaa.com*   **Phone:** (262)502-9750
(AAA) SAVE   All Year [ECP]   1P: $74-$149   2P: $74-$149   F12
▼▼▼   **Location:** US 41 and 45, exit Lannon/Mequon rds, then just e on SR 167 to Maple Rd. W190 N10862 Commerce Cir
Small-scale Hotel 53022. Fax: 262/502-9751. **Facility:** 47 units. 43 one-bedroom standard units, some with whirlpools. 4 one-
                bedroom suites, some with whirlpools. 2 stories, interior corridors. *Bath:* combo or shower only. **Parking:** on-
                site. **Amenities:** hair dryers. *Some:* irons. **Pool(s):** small heated indoor. **Leisure Activities:** whirlpool. **Guest
                Services:** valet and coin laundry. **Business Services:** meeting rooms. **Cards:** AX, DC, DS, MC, VI.
Special Amenities: free expanded continental breakfast and free local telephone calls. *(See color ad p 576)*

SOME UNITS

COUNTRY INN & SUITES BY CARLSON   *Book at aaa.com*   **Phone:** (262)251-7700
(AAA) SAVE   All Year   1P: $82-$84   XP: $6   F18
▼▼▼   **Location:** US 41 and 45, exit Lannon/Mequon rds, then just e on SR 167. W188 N11020 Maple Rd 53022.
Small-scale Hotel Fax: 262/251-7919. **Facility:** 62 one-bedroom standard units, some with whirlpools. 2 stories, interior corri-
                dors. *Bath:* combo or shower only. **Parking:** on-site. **Terms:** cancellation fee imposed, [ECP] meal plan avail-
                able. **Amenities:** irons, hair dryers. *Some:* high-speed Internet. **Pool(s):** heated indoor. **Leisure
                Activities:** whirlpool, limited exercise equipment. **Guest Services:** gift shop, valet and coin laundry. **Busi-
ness Services:** meeting rooms. **Cards:** AX, DC, DS, MC, VI. **Special Amenities: free expanded continental breakfast and
free local telephone calls.** *(See color ad starting on p 580)*

SOME UNITS

HOLIDAY INN EXPRESS MILWAUKEE NW-GERMANTOWN   *Book at aaa.com*   **Phone:** (262)255-1100
(AAA) SAVE   All Year [ECP]   1P: $69-$109   2P: $69-$109
▼▼▼   **Location:** US 41 and 45, exit CR Q (County Line Rd), then just w. W 177 N9675 Riversbend Ln 53022.
Small-scale Hotel Fax: 262/255-1086. **Facility:** 74 one-bedroom standard units. 2 stories, interior corridors. *Bath:* combo or
                shower only. **Parking:** on-site. **Amenities:** video games (fee), irons, hair dryers. **Pool(s):** small heated in-
                door. **Leisure Activities:** whirlpool, limited exercise equipment. **Guest Services:** game room. **Guest Services:** valet
                laundry. **Business Services:** meeting rooms. **Cards:** AX, CB, DC, DS, JC, MC, VI. **Special Amenities: free
expanded continental breakfast and free newspaper.** *(See color ad p 585)*

SOME UNITS

SUPER 8 MOTEL-GERMANTOWN/MILWAUKEE   *Book at aaa.com*   **Phone:** (262)255-0880
(AAA) SAVE   6/1-8/31 [ECP]   1P: $62-$79   2P: $69-$89   XP: $6   F12
▼▼▼   4/1-5/31 & 9/1-3/31 [ECP]   1P: $62-$68   2P: $72-$78   XP: $6   F12
Small-scale Hotel **Location:** US 41 and 45, exit CR Q (County Line Rd), then just w. N96 W17490 County Line Rd 53022.
                Fax: 262/255-7741. **Facility:** 100 one-bedroom standard units. 2 stories (no elevator), interior corridors.
                Bath: combo or shower only. **Parking:** on-site. **Terms:** pets ($50 deposit). **Amenities:** *Some:* irons. **Pool(s):**
                small heated indoor. **Leisure Activities:** whirlpool. *Fee:* game room. **Guest Services:** coin laundry.
Cards: AX, CB, DC, DS, MC, VI. **Special Amenities: free expanded continental breakfast and free local telephone calls.**
(See color ad p 586)

SOME UNITS

FEE

(See map and index starting on p. 566)

——— **WHERE TO DINE** ———

JERRY'S OLD TOWN   **Dinner:** $14-$26   **Phone:** 262/251-4455   ⑮
♦♦♦ ◆◆   **Location:** 0.4 mi n on SR 145 from jct SR 167, just nw on Fond Du Lac Ave, then just w. N 116 W 15841 Main St
            53022. **Hours:** 4 pm-10 pm, Fri & Sat-10:30 pm, Sun-9 pm. Closed major holidays.
Barbecue   **Reservations:** suggested. **Features:** Patrons go hog wild over the delicious homemade food and eclectic
            swine decor of the laid-back restaurant, which was founded in 1878. Servings of such dishes as tender
barbecue ribs, corn-fed steer steak, blackened seafood and Cajun chicken satisfy all appetites. The huge "pig slop" ice cream
dessert is worth a squeal for delight. Casual dress; cocktails. **Parking:** on-site. **Cards:** AX, MC, VI.
                                                                                              🍸 ✕

GLENDALE pop. 13,367   (See map and index starting on p. 566)

——— **WHERE TO STAY** ———

BAYMONT INN MILWAUKEE-GLENDALE   *Book at aaa.com*   **Phone:** (414)964-8484   ㉜
♦♦♦ ◆◆   6/1-8/31   1P: $64-$89   2P: $69-$94   XP: $5   F18
            4/1-5/31 & 9/1-3/31 1P: $64-$79   2P: $69-$84   XP: $5   F18
Small-scale Hotel **Location:** I-43, exit 78A (Silver Spring Dr), 0.4 mi se. 5110 N Port Washington Rd 53217. Fax: 414/964-2110.
winter plug-ins. **Facility:** 103 one-bedroom standard units, some with kitchens. 3 stories, interior corridors. **Parking:** on-site,
winter plug-ins. **Terms:** [ECP] meal plan available, pets ($50 deposit). **Amenities:** video games (fee), voice mail, irons, hair
dryers. **Business Services:** fax (fee). **Cards:** AX, CB, DC, DS, MC, VI. *(See color ad p 597)*
                                              (ASK) (S🄳) 🛏 🐾 📷 (DATA PORT) 💻 / ✕ 📱 📧 /   SOME UNITS
                                                                    FEE

EXEL INN OF MILWAUKEE NORTHEAST   *Book at aaa.com*   **Phone:** (414)961-7272   ㉚
(AAA) (SAVE)   All Year [CP]   1P: $50-$80   2P: $61-$91   XP: $6   F18
♦♦♦ ◆◆   **Location:** I-43, exit 78A (Silver Spring Dr), just se. 5485 N Port Washington Rd 53217. Fax: 414/961-1721.
            Facility: 124 one-bedroom standard units, some with whirlpools. 3 stories, interior corridors. **Parking:** on-
            site, winter plug-ins. **Terms:** weekly rates available, small pets only. **Amenities:** irons, hair dryers. **Leisure**
Small-scale Hotel **Activities:** exercise room. **Guest Services:** coin laundry. **Cards:** AX, CB, DC, DS, MC, VI.
            Special Amenities: free continental breakfast and early check-in/late check-out.
                                              (S🄳) 🛏 🛏 📷 (DATA PORT) 💻 / ✕ 📱 📧 /   SOME UNITS
                                                                                              FEE   FEE

HILTON MILWAUKEE RIVER   *Book at aaa.com*   **Phone:** (414)962-6040   ㉝
(AAA) (SAVE)   All Year   1P: $79-$102   2P: $79-$102   XP: $15   F18
♦♦♦ ◆◆   **Location:** I-43, exit 77A northbound, just e on Hampton Ave; exit 78A southbound, just e on Silver Springs Dr, then just
            s. 4700 N Port Washington Rd 53212. Fax: 414/962-6166. **Facility:** 163 one-bedroom standard units. 5 stories,
            interior corridors. *Bath:* combo or shower only. **Parking:** on-site. **Terms:** 3 day cancellation notice, [BP] meal
Small-scale Hotel plan available. **Amenities:** high-speed Internet, dual phone lines, voice mail, irons, hair dryers. **Dining:** An-
            chorage Restaurant, see separate listing. **Pool(s):** small heated indoor. **Leisure Activities:** exercise room.
Guest Services: valet laundry. **Business Services:** meeting rooms. **Cards:** AX, CB, DC, DS, JC, MC, VI. **Special Amenities:**
free expanded continental breakfast and free newspaper.
                                      (S🄳) 🍴 🍸 🏋M 🐾 📷 (DATA PORT) 💻 / ✕ 📱 /   SOME UNITS

MANCHESTER EAST HOTEL & SUITES   *Book at aaa.com*   **Phone:** (414)351-6960   ㉙
(AAA) (SAVE)   5/30-8/28   1P: $109-$119   2P: $109-$119   XP: $10   F17
♦♦♦ ◆◆   4/1-5/29 & 8/29-3/31 1P: $99-$109   2P: $99-$109   XP: $10   F17
            Location: I-43, exit 80 (Good Hope Rd), just e. 7065 N Port Washington Rd 53217. Fax: 414/351-5194. **Facility:** 133
            units. 125 one-bedroom standard units, some with whirlpools. 8 one-bedroom suites ($119-$129). 3 stories,
Small-scale Hotel interior corridors. **Parking:** on-site. **Terms:** package plans - seasonal. **Amenities:** voice mail, irons, hair
            dryers. *Some:* high-speed Internet. **Dining:** 6:30-9:30 am, 11:30-2 & 5-8:30 pm, Fri-9:30 pm, Sat 7:30-10:30
am, 11:30-2 & 5-9:30 pm, Sun 7:30-10:30 am, cocktails. **Pool(s):** heated indoor. **Leisure Activities:** sauna, whirlpool, atrium
recreation area, exercise room. **Guest Services:** valet laundry, airport transportation-Milwaukee County Airport. **Business Services:** conference facilities, business center. **Cards:** AX, CB, DC, DS, MC, VI. **Special Amenities: free full breakfast and free
local telephone calls.** *(See color ad p 585)*
                              (S🄳) ✈ 🍴 🍸 🏊 🐾 ✕ 📷 (DATA PORT) 📱 📧 💻 / ✕ (VCR) /   SOME UNITS

RESIDENCE INN BY MARRIOTT   *Book at aaa.com*   **Phone:** (414)352-0070   ㉘
♦♦♦ ◆◆   6/1-9/30 [BP]   1P: $109-$299   2P: $109-$299
            4/1-5/31 & 10/1-3/31 [BP] 1P: $89-$199   2P: $89-$199
Small-scale Hotel **Location:** I-43, exit 80 (Good Hope Rd), just e. 7275 N Port Washington Rd 53217. Fax: 414/352-3743. **Facility:** 96
            units. 90 one-bedroom standard units with kitchens. 6 one-bedroom suites with kitchens. 2 stories, exterior
corridors. *Bath:* combo or shower only. **Parking:** on-site. **Terms:** check-in 4 pm, cancellation fee imposed, pets ($175 fee, $6
extra charge). **Amenities:** voice mail, irons, hair dryers. **Pool(s):** heated outdoor. **Leisure Activities:** whirlpool, limited exercise
equipment, sports court. **Guest Services:** valet and coin laundry, area transportation. **Business Services:** meeting rooms.
Cards: AX, CB, DC, DS, JC, MC, VI.
                              (ASK) (S🄳) ✈ 🐾 🍴 🏋 📷 🐾 ✕ 📷 (DATA PORT) 📱 📧 💻 / ✕ /   SOME UNITS
                                                        FEE

WOODFIELD SUITES MILWAUKEE-GLENDALE   *Book at aaa.com*   **Phone:** (414)962-6767   ㉛
♦♦♦ ◆◆   6/1-9/14   1P: $129-$189   2P: $139-$199   XP: $10   F18
            4/1-5/31 & 9/15-3/31 1P: $99-$139   2P: $109-$149   XP: $10   F18
Small-scale Hotel **Location:** I-43, exit 78A (Silver Spring Dr), just se. 5423 N Port Washington Rd 53217. Fax: 414/962-8811.
            Facility: 109 units. 30 one-bedroom standard units. 79 one-bedroom suites, some with efficiencies and/or
whirlpools. 4 stories, interior corridors. *Bath:* combo or shower only. **Parking:** on-site. **Terms:** [ECP] meal plan available, pets
($50 deposit). **Amenities:** video games (fee), voice mail, irons, hair dryers. **Pool(s):** heated indoor. **Leisure Activities:** whirl-
pool, exercise room. *Fee:* game room. **Guest Services:** complimentary evening beverages, valet and coin laundry. **Business
Services:** meeting rooms. **Cards:** AX, CB, DC, DS, MC, VI.
                              (ASK) (S🄳) 🛏 🍴 🏋M 🐾 🐾 ✕ (VCR) 📷 (DATA PORT) 📱 📧 💻 / ✕ /   SOME UNITS
                                                        FEE

(See map and index starting on p. 566)

——— **WHERE TO DINE** ———

ANCHORAGE RESTAURANT   **Lunch:** $8-$16   **Dinner:** $16-$24   **Phone:** 414/962-4710   26
▽▽▽▽   **Location:** I-43, exit 77A northbound, just e on Hampton Ave; exit 78A southbound, just e on Silver Springs Dr, then
just s; in Hilton Milwaukee River. 4700 N Port Washington Rd 53212. **Hours:** 6:30 am-2:30 & 4:30-10 pm, Sat 7
Seafood   am-2:30 & 4:30-10 pm, Sun 7 am-1 & 4:30-10 pm. Closed: 1/1, 11/25, 12/25. **Reservations:** suggested.
Features: Great Lakes fresh fish and seafood from the Gulf of Mexico and the Pacific and Atlantic Oceans
is offered along with traditional flavorful soups and sauces. Try red snapper soup for some "zing." Tables overlook the
Milwaukee River. Casual dress; cocktails. **Parking:** on-site. **Cards:** AX, DC, DS, JC, MC, VI.   🍽 ✕

THE BAVARIAN INN   **Lunch:** $7   **Dinner:** $9-$18   **Phone:** 414/964-0300   25
▽▽▽   **Location:** I-43, exit 78A (Silver Spring Dr), just s, then 0.4 mi w of Port Washington Rd. 700 W Lexington Blvd 53217.
Hours: 11:30 am-2 & 5-9 pm, Fri-10 pm, Sat 5 pm-9 pm, Sun 10:30 am-2 pm. Closed: 12/24, 12/25; also
German   Mon. **Reservations:** accepted. **Features:** Ethnic decor and a festive atmosphere add to the charm of the
relaxed restaurant, a favorite for great German food. Menu choices include bratwurst, potato pancakes,
pork chops, spaetzle and potato salad. The daily luncheon buffet and Sunday brunch are popular. Guests can enjoy the
traditional Friday fish fry while soaking up live entertainment. Casual dress; cocktails. **Parking:** on-site. **Cards:** AX, DC, DS,
MC, VI.   🍽 ✕

GRAFTON pop. 10,312

——— **WHERE TO STAY** ———

BAYMONT INN & SUITES MILWAUKEE-GRAFTON   *Book at aaa.com*   **Phone:** (262)387-1180
🔺🔺🔺 SAVE   All Year   1P: $69-$109
▽▽▽ ▽▽▽   **Location:** I-43, exit 92 (SR 60), just w, then just s. Located in a quiet area. 1415 Port Washington Rd 53024.
Fax: 262/387-1168. **Facility:** 67 units. 62 one-bedroom standard units, some with whirlpools. 5 one-bedroom
Small-scale Hotel   suites. 4 stories, interior corridors. *Bath:* combo or shower only. **Parking:** on-site, winter plug-ins.
Amenities: video games (fee), dual phone lines, voice mail, irons, hair dryers. **Pool(s):** heated indoor.
Leisure Activities: exercise room. **Guest Services:** coin laundry. **Business Services:** meeting rooms.
Cards: AX, DS, MC, VI. **Special Amenities:** free local telephone calls and free newspaper.   SOME UNITS
🔲 ⌨ 🏊 🎦 📠 💻 / ✕ 🛏 🖥 /

GREENFIELD pop. 35,476   (See map and index starting on p. 566)

——— **WHERE TO STAY** ———

GOLDEN KEY MOTEL   **Phone:** 414/543-5300   56
▽▽▽   6/1-8/31   1P: $45-$55   2P: $50-$75   XP: $5
4/1-5/31   1P: $42-$50   2P: $45-$65   XP: $5
Motel   9/1-3/31   1P: $40-$45   2P: $45-$55   XP: $5
Location: I-894, exit 3, 0.5 mi w on Beloit Rd (CR T), just n on SR 100. 3600 S 108th St 53228. Fax: 414/543-5300.
Facility: 23 one-bedroom standard units. 2 stories, interior/exterior corridors. **Parking:** on-site. **Terms:** weekly rates available.
Amenities: voice mail, hair dryers. *Some:* DVD players. **Pool(s):** small heated outdoor. **Business Services:** fax (fee).
Cards: AX, DS, MC, VI.   SOME UNITS
ASK 🔲 🍴 🏊 🎦 📠 🛏 / ✕ VCR /

HARTFORD pop. 10,905

——— **WHERE TO STAY** ———

AMERICINN MOTEL & SUITES   *Book at aaa.com*   **Phone:** (262)673-2200
▽▽▽   All Year   1P: $70-$130   2P: $70-$130   XP: $6   F12
Location: On SR 60, 1 mi e of center. 1527 E Sumner St 53027. Fax: 262/673-4741. **Facility:** 46 units. 43 one-
Small-scale Hotel   bedroom standard units, some with whirlpools. 3 one-bedroom suites. 2 stories (no el-
evator), interior corridors. *Bath:* combo or shower only. **Parking:** on-site, winter plug-ins. **Terms:** [ECP] meal
plan available. **Amenities:** irons, hair dryers. **Pool(s):** heated indoor. **Leisure Activities:** whirlpool. **Guest Services:** coin
laundry. **Business Services:** meeting rooms, fax (fee). **Cards:** AX, DC, DS, MC, VI. *(See color ad p 576)*   SOME UNITS
ASK 🔲 🍴 🔳 ⌨ 🖊 🏊 🎦 📠 💻 / ✕ 🛏 🖥 /

SUPER 8 MOTEL-HARTFORD   *Book at aaa.com*   **Phone:** 262/673-7431
▽▽▽ ▽▽▽   7/25-8/10 [ECP]   1P: $85-$125   2P: $100-$150   XP: $15   F12
4/1-7/24 & 8/11-12/31 [ECP]   1P: $55-$85   2P: $65-$100   XP: $7   F12
Small-scale Hotel   1/1-3/31 [ECP]   1P: $43   2P: $50   XP: $15   F12
Location: On SR 60, 1.1 mi e of center. 1539 E Sumner St 53027. Fax: 262/673-3080. **Facility:** 32 one-bedroom
standard units, some with whirlpools. 2 stories (no elevator), interior corridors. **Parking:** on-site, winter plug-ins. **Terms:** cancel-
lation fee imposed, pets ($10 extra charge). **Leisure Activities:** whirlpool. **Business Services:** meeting rooms. **Cards:** AX, DS,
MC, VI.   SOME UNITS
ASK 🔲 🐕 🍴 🎦 / ✕ 🛏 🖥 /
FEE

JACKSON pop. 4,938

──── WHERE TO STAY ────

HAWTHORN INN AND SUITES OF JACKSON   **Phone:** (262)677-1133

6/19-9/9 [BP]	1P: $79-$119	2P: $79-$119	XP: $10	F17
9/10-3/31 [BP]	1P: $74-$119	2P: $74-$119	XP: $10	F17
4/1-6/18 [BP]	1P: $74-$89	2P: $74-$89	XP: $10	F17

Small-scale Hotel **Location:** Nw of jct US 45 and SR 60. Located next to a business park. W227 N16890 Tillie Lake Ct 53037. **Fax:** 262/677-1144. **Facility:** 54 units. 50 one-bedroom standard units, some with whirlpools. 4 one-bedroom suites ($110-$150). 2 stories (no elevator), interior corridors. *Bath:* combo or shower only. **Parking:** on-site. **Terms:** cancellation fee imposed, pets ($50 deposit). **Amenities:** high-speed Internet, dual phone lines, voice mail, irons, hair dryers. **Pool(s):** small heated indoor. **Leisure Activities:** whirlpool. *Fee:* game room. **Guest Services:** sundries, valet and coin laundry. **Business Services:** meeting rooms. **Cards:** AX, DS, MC, VI.

SOME UNITS

MEQUON pop. 21,823   (See map and index starting on p. 566)

──── WHERE TO STAY ────

BEST WESTERN QUIET HOUSE & SUITES   *Book at aaa.com*   **Phone:** 262/241-3677   **20**

All Year [ECP]	1P: $95-$105	2P: $95-$105	XP: $10	F12

Location: I-43, exit 85 (Mequon Rd), just w on SR 167, then 1 mi s. 10330 N Port Washington Rd 53092. **Fax:** 262/241-3707. **Facility:** 54 units. 51 one-bedroom standard units, some with whirlpools. 3 one-bedroom suites. 2 stories (no elevator), interior corridors. **Parking:** on-site. **Terms:** package plans - seasonal, pets ($15 extra charge). **Amenities:** voice mail, irons, hair dryers. **Pool(s):** heated indoor/outdoor. **Leisure Activities:** whirlpool, exercise room. **Guest Services:** valet laundry. **Cards:** AX, CB, DC, DS, MC, VI. **Special Amenities: free expanded continental breakfast and free newspaper.** *(See color ad p 579)*

SOME UNITS

THE CHALET MOTEL OF MEQUON   **Phone:** 262/241-4510   **19**

6/25-8/21	1P: $79-$149	2P: $89-$159	XP: $10	F18
4/1-6/24 & 8/22-3/31	1P: $59-$119	2P: $69-$129	XP: $10	F18

Motel **Location:** I-43, exit 85 (Mequon Rd), just w on SR 167, then 1 mi s. 10401 N Port Washington Rd 53092. **Fax:** 262/241-5542. **Facility:** 53 one-bedroom standard units. 2 stories (no elevator), exterior corridors. *Bath:* combo or shower only. **Parking:** on-site. **Terms:** 2-3 night minimum stay - seasonal weekends, cancellation fee imposed, weekly rates available, pets ($10 extra charge, in smoking units). **Amenities:** voice mail. *Some:* irons, hair dryers. **Guest Services:** complimentary laundry. **Cards:** AX, DC, DS, MC, VI.

SOME UNITS

──── WHERE TO DINE ────

THE CENTENNIAL   **Lunch:** $5-$7   **Dinner:** $5-$13   **Phone:** 262/241-4353   **18**

Location: I-43, exit 85, just w on SR 167, then 1 mi s. 10352 N Port Washington Rd 53092. **Hours:** 11:30 am-10 pm, Fri & Sat-10:30 pm. Closed: for dinner 12/31. **Features:** This restaurant prides itself on its food, and it shows. Flashes of creativity are evident in the extensive variety of sandwiches, homemade soups and entrees made with quality ingredients. A 100-year-old decorative wood bar is the centerpiece of the dining room, which has the atmosphere of a casual pub. Casual dress; cocktails. **Parking:** on-site. **Cards:** MC, VI.

American

HEINEMANN'S RESTAURANT   **Lunch:** $5-$9   **Dinner:** $5-$9   **Phone:** 414/352-2244   **19**

Location: I-43, exit 82A, just e. 333 W Brown Deer Rd 53217. **Hours:** 7 am-8 pm, Sun from 7:30 am. Closed major holidays; also for dinner 12/24. **Features:** The well-established, family-oriented restaurant delivers fresh, flavorful items, such as soup, sandwiches and salad, made from scratch without additives or preservatives. Highly noteworthy are the aromatic baked goods and tantalizing desserts. Casual dress; beer & wine only. **Parking:** on-site. **Cards:** MC, VI.

American

NEW BERLIN pop. 38,220   (See map and index starting on p. 566)

──── WHERE TO STAY ────

BAYMONT INN & SUITES MILWAUKEE-NEW BERLIN   *Book at aaa.com*   **Phone:** (262)717-0900   **53**

4/1-9/30	1P: $69-$89	2P: $69-$89
10/1-3/31	1P: $49-$69	2P: $49-$69

Location: I-43, exit 57 (Moorland Rd), just se. 15300 W Rock Ridge Rd 53151. **Fax:** 262/717-0905. **Facility:** 88 one-bedroom standard units, some with whirlpools. 4 stories, interior corridors. *Bath:* combo or shower only.

Small-scale Hotel **Parking:** on-site. **Terms:** [ECP] meal plan available. **Amenities:** video games (fee), voice mail, irons, hair dryers. **Pool(s):** small heated indoor. **Leisure Activities:** whirlpool, exercise room. **Guest Services:** valet and coin laundry. **Business Services:** meeting rooms. **Cards:** AX, CB, DC, DS, MC, VI. **Special Amenities: free local telephone calls and free newspaper.** *(See color ad p 597)*

SOME UNITS

HOLIDAY INN EXPRESS HOTEL AND SUITES-NEW BERLIN   *Book at aaa.com*   **Phone:** (262)787-0700   **52**

All Year	1P: $99-$124	2P: $99-$124

Location: I-43, exit 57 (Moorland Rd), just ne. Located in a commercial area. 15451 W Beloit Rd 53151. **Fax:** 262/787-0738. **Facility:** 101 one-bedroom standard units. 4 stories, interior corridors. *Bath:* combo or

Small-scale Hotel shower only. **Parking:** on-site. **Terms:** cancellation fee imposed, [ECP] meal plan available. **Amenities:** video games (fee), dual phone lines, voice mail, irons, hair dryers. **Pool(s):** heated indoor. **Leisure Activities:** whirlpool, exercise room. **Guest Services:** valet and coin laundry. **Business Services:** meeting rooms. **Cards:** AX, CB, DC, DS, JC, MC, VI.

SOME UNITS

(See map and index starting on p. 566)

──────── WHERE TO DINE ────────

CHARCOAL GRILL & ROTISSERIE   Lunch: $8-$15   Dinner: $12-$20   Phone: 262/432-3000   42
◆◆◆ ◆◆◆   **Location:** I-94, exit 301A, 0.5 mi s on Moorland Rd, then just e. 15375 W Greenfield Ave 53151. **Hours:** 11 am-11
American   pm. Closed major holidays. **Features:** Pheasant Wellington, venison schnitzel, seared elk medallions,
          bison steak, fresh fish and Wisconsin prairie wild rice are among fresh items served at the distinctive
allowed only in the lounge. Casual dress; cocktails. **Parking:** on-site. **Cards:** AX, DC, DS, MC, VI.   🍽 ✕

OAK CREEK pop. 28,456   (See map and index starting on p. 566)

──────── WHERE TO STAY ────────

BAYMONT INN & SUITES MILWAUKEE-AIRPORT   *Book at aaa.com*   Phone: (414)762-2266   63
 ⒶⒶⒶ SAVE   4/1-10/31   1P: $79-$99   2P: $79-$99
          11/1-3/31   1P: $54-$74   2P: $54-$74
◆◆◆ ◆◆◆   **Location:** I-94, exit 320, just se on Rawson Ave (CR BB). Located in a commercial area. 7141 S 13th St 53154.
Small-scale Hotel   Fax: 414/762-0513. **Facility:** 98 units. 96 one-bedroom standard units. 2 one-bedroom suites ($89-$129). 3
stories, interior corridors. **Parking:** on-site, winter plug-ins. **Terms:** [ECP] meal plan available, small pets
only. **Amenities:** video games (fee), voice mail, irons, hair dryers. **Leisure Activities:** exercise room. **Guest**
Services: valet and coin laundry. **Cards:** AX, CB, DC, DS, MC, VI. **Special Amenities:** free local telephone calls and free
newspaper. *(See color ad below)*
                                                                                          SOME UNITS
          🆂🅳 🐾 🍴 📷 🔌 💻 / ✕ 🔋 📠 /

COMFORT SUITES MILWAUKEE AIRPORT   *Book at aaa.com*   Phone: (414)570-1111   62
◆◆◆ ◆◆◆   6/1-8/31   1P: $119-$249   XP: $10   F17
          4/1-5/31 & 9/1-3/31   1P: $89-$249   XP: $10   F17
Small-scale Hotel   **Location:** I-94, exit 319, just e on College Ave (CR 22), then just s. 6362 S 13th St 53154. Fax: 414/570-3333.
          Facility: 138 units. 136 one-bedroom standard units, some with whirlpools. 2 two-bedroom suites with whirl-
pools. 3 stories, interior corridors. *Bath:* combo or shower only. **Parking:** on-site. **Terms:** cancellation fee imposed.
Amenities: dual phone lines, voice mail, irons, hair dryers. *Fee:* video games, safes. *Some:* high-speed Internet. **Pool(s):** heated
indoor. **Leisure Activities:** whirlpool, limited exercise equipment. *Fee:* game room. **Guest Services:** complimentary evening
beverages, valet and coin laundry, area transportation. **Business Services:** meeting rooms. **Cards:** AX, DC, DS, MC, VI.
                                                                                          SOME UNITS
          A$K 🆂🅳 ✈ 🐾 🍴 🅼 📷 🔌 ➿ ✕ 📷 🔌 🔋 📠 💻 / ✕ VCR /

(See map and index starting on p. 566)

EXEL INN OF MILWAUKEE SOUTH *Book at aaa.com*   **Phone:** (414)764-1776   60
(AAA) (SAVE)   6/1-9/30 [CP]   1P: $47-$69   2P: $47-$69   XP: $6   F18
    4/1-5/31 & 10/1-3/31 [CP]   1P: $35-$47   2P: $41-$53   XP: $6   F18
    Location: I-94, exit 319, just e. 1201 W College Ave 53154. Fax: 414/762-8009. **Facility:** 109 one-bedroom standard units, some with whirlpools. 2 stories (no elevator), interior corridors. **Parking:** on-site. **Terms:** weekly
Small-scale Hotel   rates available, small pets only (in smoking units). **Amenities:** irons. **Leisure Activities:** exercise room.
Guest Services: coin laundry. **Cards:** AX, CB, DC, DS, MC, VI. **Special Amenities:** free continental breakfast and early check-in/late check-out.

MAINSTAY SUITES OAK CREEK *Book at aaa.com*   **Phone:** (414)571-8800   59
    All Year   1P: $69-$199   2P: $69-$199   XP: $10   F18
    Location: I-94, exit 319, just e. 1001 W College Ave 53154. Fax: 414/571-8820. **Facility:** 76 units. 37 one-bedroom standard units with efficiencies. 37 one- and 2 two-bedroom suites with efficiencies. 3 stories, interior corridors. *Bath:* combo or shower only. **Parking:** on-site. **Terms:** weekly rates available, [ECP] meal plan
available, pets ($15 extra charge). **Amenities:** dual phone lines, voice mail, irons, hair dryers. **Leisure Activities:** limited exercise equipment. **Guest Services:** valet and coin laundry. **Business Services:** business center. **Cards:** AX, CB, DC, DS,
MC, VI.

RED ROOF INN-MILWAUKEE *Book at aaa.com*   **Phone:** (414)764-3500   61
(AAA) (SAVE)   5/30-8/28   1P: $47-$66   2P: $52-$71   XP: $5   F18
    8/29-9/25   1P: $40-$55   2P: $45-$60   XP: $5   F18
    4/1-5/29   1P: $36-$54   2P: $41-$59   XP: $5   F18
Motel   9/26-3/31   1P: $36-$50   2P: $41-$55   XP: $5   F18
    Location: I-94, exit 319, just e on College Ave (CR 22). Located in a commercial area. 6360 S 13th St 53154.
Fax: 414/764-5138. **Facility:** 108 one-bedroom standard units. 2 stories (no elevator), exterior corridors.
Parking: on-site. **Terms:** small pets only. **Amenities:** video games (fee), voice mail. **Cards:** AX, CB, DC, DS, MC, VI.
Special Amenities: free local telephone calls and free newspaper.

OCONOMOWOC pop. 12,382

———— **WHERE TO STAY** ————

OLYMPIA RESORT & CONFERENCE CENTER *Book at aaa.com*   **Phone:** (262)369-4999
(AAA) (SAVE)   All Year   1P: $145-$165   2P: $145-$165   XP: $15   F16
    Location: I-94, exit 282 (SR 267), 1 mi n. 1350 Royale Mile Rd 53066. Fax: 262/369-4998. **Facility:** 256 units. 241 one-bedroom standard units, some with whirlpools. 15 one-bedroom suites ($225-$500), some with whirlpools. 4 stories, interior corridors. **Parking:** on-site. **Terms:** cancellation fee imposed, package plans - weekends. **Amenities:** voice mail, irons, hair dryers. **Dining:** 2 restaurants, 6:30 am-10 pm, Sat & Sun 8 am-5:30
Resort   pm, cocktails. **Pool(s):** heated outdoor, heated indoor. **Leisure Activities:** saunas, whirlpools, steamrooms,
Large-scale Hotel   spa. *Fee:* game room. **Guest Services:** gift shop, valet and coin laundry. **Business Services:** conference
facilities, business center. **Cards:** AX, CB, DC, DS, MC, VI. **Special Amenities:** free newspaper and free room upgrade (subject to availability with advanced reservations).

OKAUCHEE

———— **WHERE TO DINE** ————

GOLDEN MAST INN   **Dinner:** $19-$30   **Phone:** 262/567-7047
    Location: SR 16, exit 178 (Sawyer), 1 mi n, follow signs. W349 N5293 Lacy's Ln 53069. **Hours:** 5 pm-10 pm, Sun
    11 am-2 & 4-9 pm. Closed: Mon. **Reservations:** accepted. **Features:** From entering this grand
German   Bavarian-style restaurant with high ceilings and liberal use of wood, rock and glass, to the last bite of apple
    strudel; you'll experience authentic German cuisine and a setting to match. The menu offers seafood and
steak, but the key elements are the veal dumpling soup, Wiener Schnitzel, beef rouladen, kassler ripchen, and other German
touches. Plus, the view of Okauchee Lake from the dining room is delightful. Dressy casual; cocktails. **Parking:** on-site.
Cards: AX, MC, VI.

PEWAUKEE pop. 11,783

———— **WHERE TO STAY** ————

COMFORT SUITES *Book at aaa.com*   **Phone:** (262)506-2000
    All Year   1P: $79-$129   2P: $89-$139   XP: $10   F18
    Location: I-94, exit 294 (CR J), just nw. N24121 Tower Pl 53072 (PO Box 430). Fax: 262/523-5848. **Facility:** 94
Small-scale Hotel   units. 84 one-bedroom standard units, some with whirlpools. 10 one-bedroom suites, some with efficiencies
    (no utensils) and/or whirlpools. 3 stories, interior corridors. *Bath:* combo or shower only. **Parking:** on-site,
winter plug-ins. **Terms:** check-in 4 pm, [ECP] meal plan available. **Amenities:** video games (fee), voice mail, irons, hair dryers.
Some: dual phone lines. **Pool(s):** heated indoor. **Leisure Activities:** whirlpool, exercise room. **Guest Services:** gift shop, valet
and coin laundry. **Business Services:** meeting rooms. **Cards:** AX, CB, DC, DS, MC, VI.

THE RADISSON HOTEL PEWAUKEE   *Book at aaa.com*   Phone: (262)506-6300
▼▼▽▽▽   All Year   1P: $109-$149   2P: $109-$149   XP: $10   F18
    Location: I-94, exit 294 (CR J), just nw. N 14 W 24140 Tower Pl 53072. Fax: 262/523-1299. **Facility:** 119 units. 112
Small-scale Hotel   one-bedroom standard units, some with whirlpools. 5 one- and 2 two-bedroom suites ($139-$499), some with
    kitchens and/or whirlpools. 3 stories, interior corridors. *Bath:* combo or shower only. **Parking:** on-site.
Terms: [BP] meal plan available. **Amenities:** video games (fee), dual phone lines, voice mail, irons, hair dryers. *Some:* CD
players, safes. **Dining:** Thunder Bay Grille, see separate listing. **Pool(s):** heated indoor. **Leisure Activities:** whirlpool, exercise
room. **Guest Services:** gift shop, valet laundry. **Business Services:** conference facilities, business center. **Cards:** AX, CB, DC,
DS, MC, VI. *(See color ad p 583)*

SOME UNITS
(ASK) (S⊅) (¶¶) (⬭) (&) (≋) (✲) (DATA PORT) (⬛) / (✕) (VCR) (🛢) (🖾) /

──────── **WHERE TO DINE** ────────

THUNDER BAY GRILLE   **Lunch:** $6-$10   **Dinner:** $7-$15   Phone: 262/523-4244
▽▽▽   **Location:** I-94, exit 294 (CR J), just nw; in The Radisson Hotel Pewaukee. N 14W 24130 Tower Pl 53072. **Hours:** 11
    am-10 pm, Fri & Sat-11 pm, Sun 10 am-9 pm. Closed major holidays. **Features:** Log chairs, antlers on the
American   walls and canoes in the rafters contribute to the folksy northwoods atmosphere at this casual restaurant.
    The large variety of foods includes homemade soup, hand-cut steaks, fresh fish, pasta, slow-roasted prime
rib and hardwood-smoked ribs. Casual dress; cocktails. **Parking:** on-site. **Cards:** AX, DC, DS, MC, VI.
(&M) (⬭) (✕)

WISCONSIN MACHINE SHED RESTAURANT   **Lunch:** $6-$11   **Dinner:** $8-$20   Phone: 262/523-1322
▽▽▽   **Location:** I-94, exit 294 (CR J), just nw. N14 W24145 Tower Pl 53072. **Hours:** 6 am-10 pm, Sun 7 am-9 pm.
    Closed: 1/1, 11/25, 12/25. **Reservations:** accepted. **Features:** Antiques and farm implements decorate the
American   decidedly rustic dining room. Tried-and-true comfort foods—such as pot roast, ham and roast pork—please
    every member of the family. The Friday night fish fry draws a hungry crowd. Servers in overalls are friendly
and prompt. Casual dress; cocktails. **Parking:** on-site. **Cards:** AX, DC, DS, MC, VI.
(⬭) (✕)

PORT WASHINGTON pop. 10,467

──────── **WHERE TO STAY** ────────

BEST WESTERN HARBORSIDE   *Book at aaa.com*   Phone: (262)284-9461
(AAA) (SAVE)   5/28-9/4   1P: $79-$169   XP: $10   F
    4/1-5/27 & 9/5-3/31   1P: $69-$159   XP: $10   F
▼▼▽▽   **Location:** On SR 43, waterfront of Lake Michigan; downtown. Located between shops and harbor. 135 E Grand Ave
Small-scale Hotel   53074. Fax: 262/284-3169. **Facility:** 96 units. 92 one-bedroom standard units, some with whirlpools. 4 one-
    bedroom suites ($99-$179) with whirlpools. 5 stories, interior corridors. **Parking:** on-site, winter plug-ins.
    Terms: [BP] meal plan available, package plans - seasonal, pets (in smoking units). **Amenities:** video games
(fee), voice mail, irons, hair dryers. *Some:* dual phone lines. **Dining:** 6:30-9:30 am, Sat & Sun-10:30 am; closed Mon. **Pool(s):**
heated indoor. **Leisure Activities:** sauna, whirlpool, fishing, limited exercise equipment. *Fee:* game room. **Guest Services:** valet
and coin laundry. **Business Services:** meeting rooms. **Cards:** AX, CB, DC, DS, MC, VI. **Special Amenities:** free local telephone calls and free newspaper. *(See color ad below)*

SOME UNITS
(S⊅) (🐾) (¶¶) (⬭) (&) (≋) (✕) (✲) (DATA PORT) (⬛) / (✕) (🛢) (🖾) /

COUNTRY INN & SUITES BY CARLSON   *Book at aaa.com*   Phone: (262)284-2100
▼▽▽▽   All Year   1P: $77-$92   2P: $77-$92   XP: $6   F18
    Location: I-43, exit 100 (SR 32 S), just ne. 350 E Seven Hills Rd 53074. Fax: 262/284-6740. **Facility:** 85 units. 58
Small-scale Hotel   one-bedroom standard units, some with whirlpools. 27 one-bedroom suites ($102-$182), some with whirl-
    pools. 3 stories, interior corridors. *Bath:* combo or shower only. **Parking:** on-site. **Terms:** [ECP] meal plan
available. **Amenities:** high-speed Internet, dual phone lines, voice mail, irons, hair dryers. **Pool(s):** small heated indoor. **Leisure
Activities:** whirlpool, exercise room. *Fee:* game room. **Guest Services:** complimentary evening beverages: Sun-Thurs, coin
laundry. **Business Services:** conference facilities. **Cards:** AX, DC, DS, MC, VI. *(See color ad starting on p 580)*

SOME UNITS
(ASK) (S⊅) (⬭) (&) (≋) (✕) (✲) (DATA PORT) (⬛) / (✕) (🛢) (🖾) /

─────── **WHERE TO DINE** ───────

BEANIES

Mexican

Lunch: $5-$11   **Dinner:** $5-$11   **Phone:** 262/284-7200
Location: On SR 32; downtown. 102 E Grand Ave 53074. **Hours:** 11 am-9 pm, Fri & Sat-10 pm, Sun noon-8 pm. **Closed:** 12/24, 12/25 & Easter. **Features:** Just off the waterfront, the tiny restaurant hits the spot for those seeking tasty food at a reasonable price. In addition to Mexican favorites, subs and burgers make up the menu. Complimentary chips and salsa accompany every meal. Casual dress; beer & wine only. **Parking:** on-site. **Cards:** MC, VI.

SMITH BROS 'FISH SHANTY' RESTAURANT

Seafood

Lunch: $5-$13   **Dinner:** $5-$18   **Phone:** 262/284-5592
Location: I-43, exit 96, 2 mi e on SR 33, 1.5 mi e on SR 32 at waterfront. 100 N Franklin St 53074. **Hours:** 11 am-10 pm, Fri & Sat-11 pm; 11 am-9 pm, Fri & Sat-10 pm 9/2-5/27. **Closed:** 11/25, 12/25; also for dinner 12/24. **Reservations:** suggested. **Features:** Enjoy a nice view of the harbor from the relaxed dining room. A menu of mostly American fare shows a heavy concentration on seafood, particularly Great Lakes fish. The summer patio is comfortable and breezy. Servers are knowledgeable and efficient. Casual dress; cocktails. **Parking:** on-site. **Cards:** AX, DC, DS, MC, VI.

WAUKESHA pop. 64,825

─────── **WHERE TO STAY** ───────

BEST WESTERN WAUKESHA GRAND   *Book at aaa.com*   **Phone:** (262)524-9300

Small-scale Hotel

All Year [ECP]   1P: $69-$89   2P: $75-$95   XP: $6   F18
Location: I-94, exit 293, just s on CR T. 2840 N Grandview Blvd 53072. Fax: 262/524-9305. **Facility:** 97 one-bedroom standard units, some with whirlpools. 3 stories, interior corridors. *Bath:* combo or shower only. **Parking:** on-site. **Terms:** weekly rates available, small pets only. **Amenities:** irons, hair dryers. **Pool(s):** small heated indoor. **Leisure Activities:** whirlpool, exercise room. **Guest Services:** coin laundry. **Business Services:** business center. **Cards:** AX, CB, DC, DS, MC, VI. **Special Amenities:** free expanded continental breakfast and free newspaper.

RAMADA LIMITED   *Book at aaa.com*   **Phone:** (262)547-7770

Small-scale Hotel

All Year [ECP]   1P: $50-$145   2P: $55-$145   XP: $10   F16
Location: I-94, exit 297, 1 mi w on US 18. 2111 E Moreland Blvd 53186. Fax: 262/547-0688. **Facility:** 92 one-bedroom standard units, some with whirlpools. 2 stories (no elevator), interior corridors. **Parking:** on-site, winter plug-ins. **Terms:** cancellation fee imposed, pets ($10 extra charge). **Amenities:** voice mail, irons, hair dryers. **Pool(s):** small heated indoor. **Leisure Activities:** sauna, whirlpool, limited exercise equipment. **Guest Services:** valet and coin laundry. **Business Services:** meeting rooms. **Cards:** AX, CB, DC, DS, JC, MC, VI. **Special Amenities:** free expanded continental breakfast and free local telephone calls.

SELECT INN   **Phone:** (262)786-6015

Small-scale Hotel

6/1-9/30   1P: $60-$75   2P: $65-$80   XP: $5   F16
4/1-5/31 & 10/1-3/31   1P: $44-$54   2P: $49-$59   XP: $5   F16
Location: I-94, exit 297, just w on CR JJ (Bluemound Rd). 2510 Plaza Ct 53186. Fax: 262/786-5784. **Facility:** 99 one-bedroom standard units. 3 stories (no elevator), interior corridors. *Bath:* combo or shower only. **Parking:** on-site. **Terms:** weekly rates available, [ECP] meal plan available, small pets only ($25 deposit, $5 extra charge). **Amenities:** safes (fee). *Some:* hair dryers. **Guest Services:** coin laundry. **Business Services:** meeting rooms. **Cards:** AX, DC, DS, MC, VI. **Special Amenities:** free expanded continental breakfast. *(See color ad p 552)*

─────── **WHERE TO DINE** ───────

WEISSGERBER'S GASTHAUS

German

Lunch: $8-$12   **Dinner:** $17-$25   **Phone:** 262/544-4460
Location: I-94, exit 293, just s on CR T. 2720 N Grandview Blvd 53188. **Hours:** 11:30 am-2 & 5-10 pm, Sat from 5 pm. Closed major holidays; also Sun. **Reservations:** suggested. **Features:** Enjoy an authentic Bavarian experience complete with Old World decor, servers in ethnic period uniforms and genuine cuisine. The menu features a special Bavarian bean soup, sausage lover's selections and a few American favorites. The tortes and pies are made in-house. Dressy casual; cocktails. **Parking:** on-site. **Cards:** AX, DC, DS, MC, VI.

WAUWATOSA pop. 47,271   (See map and index starting on p. 566)

─────── **WHERE TO STAY** ───────

EXEL INN OF MILWAUKEE WEST   *Book at aaa.com*   **Phone:** (414)257-0140

Small-scale Hotel

All Year [CP]   1P: $47-$79   2P: $53-$84   XP: $6   F18
Location: I-94, exit 304B, just n on SR 100. 115 N Mayfair Rd 53226. Fax: 414/475-7875. **Facility:** 122 one-bedroom standard units, some with whirlpools. 2 stories (no elevator), interior corridors. **Parking:** on-site. **Terms:** weekly rates available, small pets only (in smoking units). **Amenities:** irons, hair dryers. **Leisure Activities:** limited exercise equipment. **Guest Services:** coin laundry. **Cards:** AX, CB, DC, DS, MC, VI. **Special Amenities:** free continental breakfast and early check-in/late check-out.

(See map and index starting on p. 566)

HOLIDAY INN EXPRESS-MAYFAIR   *Book at aaa.com*   Phone: (414)778-0333   **45**

AAA [SAVE]   6/16-8/31 [ECP]   1P: $104-$159   2P: $104-$159
WWWW   4/1-6/15 & 9/1-3/31 [ECP]   1P: $99-$149   2P: $99-$149
            Location: US 45, exit 42A, just n on SR 100, then just w. 11111 W North Ave 53226. Fax: 414/778-0331. **Facility:** 122
Small-scale Hotel units. 114 one-bedroom standard units, some with whirlpools. 8 one-bedroom suites ($129-$159). 3 stories,
            interior corridors. *Bath:* combo or shower only. **Parking:** on-site. **Terms:** 14 day cancellation notice.
            Amenities: voice mail, irons, hair dryers. **Guest Services:** valet laundry. **Business Services:** meeting
rooms. **Cards:** AX, CB, DC, DS, JC, MC, VI. **Special Amenities: free expanded continental breakfast and free local telephone calls.** *(See color ad p 582)*

SOME UNITS

[icons]

RADISSON HOTEL MILWAUKEE WEST   *Book at aaa.com*   Phone: (414)257-3400   **44**

AAA [SAVE]   1/2-3/31   1P: $159-$164   2P: $159-$164   XP: $10   F18
WWWW   4/1-1/1   1P: $154-$159   2P: $154-$159   XP: $10   F18
            Location: US 45, exit 42A, just n on SR 100 at jct North Ave. Located across from shopping center. 2303 N Mayfair Rd
Small-scale Hotel 53226. Fax: 414/257-0900. **Facility:** 151 units. 149 one-bedroom standard units. 2 one-bedroom suites
            ($235-$295). 8 stories, interior corridors. *Bath:* combo or shower only. **Parking:** on-site. **Amenities:** voice
            mail, irons, hair dryers. **Dining:** RJ's an American Bar & Grille, see separate listing. **Pool(s):** heated indoor.
Leisure Activities: sauna, exercise room. **Guest Services:** valet laundry, area transportation-within 5 mi. **Business Services:**
conference facilities. **Cards:** AX, CB, DC, DS, JC, MC, VI. **Special Amenities: early check-in/late check-out and free room
upgrade (subject to availability with advanced reservations).** *(See color ad p 583)*

SOME UNITS

[icons]

─────── **WHERE TO DINE** ───────

EDDIE MARTINI'S   **Lunch:** $9-$17   **Dinner:** $18-$34   Phone: 414/771-6680   **36**
WWWW   **Location:** US 45, exit 40, 0.7 mi e. 8612 W Watertown Plank Rd 53226. **Hours:** 11:30 am-2 & 5-10 pm, Fri-11
Traditional   pm, Sat 5 pm-11 pm, Sun 4 pm-8 pm. Closed major holidays. **Reservations:** suggested. **Features:** The
American   casually elegant 1940s-style supper club is locally known for excellent food and professional service.
             Steak, chops and seafood are prepared with high-quality ingredients. Signature items include the ocean
DS, MC, VI.   martini appetizer and bread pudding dessert. Dressy casual; cocktails. **Parking:** on-site. **Cards:** AX, DC,

[icons]

HEINEMANN'S RESTAURANT   **Lunch:** $5-$8   **Dinner:** $5-$8   Phone: 414/774-5200   **33**
AAA   **Location:** US 45, exit 42A, just e, then 0.5 mi n on SR 100. 2717 N Mayfair Rd 53226. **Hours:** 7 am-8 pm, Fri-9
WWW WW   pm, Sun 7:30 am-8 pm. Closed major holidays. **Features:** This well-established, family-oriented restaurant
American   delivers fresh, flavorful items, such as soup, sandwiches and salad, made from scratch without additives or
             perservatives. Highly noteworthy are the aromatic baked goods and tantalizing desserts. Casual dress.
             Parking: on-site. **Cards:** MC, VI.

[icon]

RISTORANTE BARTOLOTTA   **Dinner:** $16-$29   Phone: 414/771-7910   **35**
WWWW   **Location:** Just w of jct Wauwatosa Ave; downtown. 7616 W State St 53213. **Hours:** 5:30 pm-9:30 pm, Fri & Sat 5
Northern   pm-10 pm, Sun 5 pm-8 pm. Closed major holidays. **Reservations:** suggested. **Features:** The bustling
Italian   trattoria captures the essence of rustic, peasant-style cooking. Roasted chicken and veal are cooked in a
             large, wood-burning oven. Duck, lamb and fresh seafood are included in other creative offerings, as well as
             varied pasta dishes. Service is upscale and attentive. The strictly Italian wine list remains true to its roots.
In season, a few outdoor tables are available. Dressy casual; cocktails. **Parking:** valet and street. **Cards:** AX, CB, DC, DS,
MC, VI.

[icon]

RJ'S AN AMERICAN BAR & GRILLE   **Lunch:** $8-$14   **Dinner:** $15-$25   Phone: 414/257-3400   **34**
WWW WW   **Location:** US 45, exit 42A, just n on SR 100 at jct North Ave; in Radisson Hotel Milwaukee West. 2303 N Mayfair Rd
American   53226. **Hours:** 6 am-2 & 5-10 pm, Sat & Sun from 7 am. **Reservations:** suggested. **Features:** Convenient
             to the Mayfair Shopping Mall, the contemporary hotel restaurant has an Art Deco motif. The menu offers
casual; cocktails. **Parking:** on-site. **Cards:** AX, CB, DC, DS, JC, MC, VI.

[icons]

WEST BEND pop. 28,152

─────── **WHERE TO STAY** ───────

COUNTRY INN & SUITES BY CARLSON   *Book at aaa.com*   Phone: (262)334-9400
WWW WW   5/1-9/30 [CP]   1P: $89-$155   2P: $95-$161   XP: $6   F18
            1/1-3/31 [CP]   1P: $89-$151   2P: $95-$157   XP: $6   F18
            4/1-4/30 & 10/1-12/31 [CP] 1P: $87-$149   2P: $93-$155   XP: $6   F18
Small-scale Hotel **Location:** US 45, exit Paradise Rd, just se. Located in a commercial area. 2000 Gateway Ct 53095.
Fax: 262/334-9504. **Facility:** 58 units. 46 one-bedroom standard units, some with whirlpools. 12 one-bedroom suites, some with
whirlpools. 3 stories, interior corridors. **Parking:** on-site, winter plug-ins. **Terms:** cancellation fee imposed, [ECP] meal plan available. **Amenities:** voice mail, irons, hair dryers. **Pool(s):** small heated indoor. **Leisure Activities:** whirlpool. **Guest Services:**
valet laundry. **Business Services:** meeting rooms. **Cards:** AX, DC, DS, MC, VI. *(See color ad starting on p 580)*

SOME UNITS

[icons]

─────── **WHERE TO DINE** ───────

OMICRON FAMILY RESTAURANT   **Lunch:** $6-$11   **Dinner:** $6-$11   Phone: 262/335-0777
WWW   **Location:** US 45, exit Paradise Rd, 0.4 mi e, 0.3 mi n. 1505 S Main St 53095. **Hours:** 6 am-10 pm, Fri & Sat-11
American   pm. Closed: 12/24, 12/25. **Features:** Reasonably priced selections of primarily comfort foods mingle with
             an array of all-day breakfast items and some Greek fare on the diverse menu. The atmosphere is
             family-friendly and unpretentious. Several beers and wines are listed. Casual dress; beer & wine only.
Parking: on-site. **Cards:** MC, VI.

WHITEFISH BAY pop. 14,163 (See map and index starting on p. 566)

——— WHERE TO DINE ———

HEINEMANN'S RESTAURANT   **Lunch:** $5-$8   **Dinner:** $5-$8   **Phone:** 414/964-6060   ㉙

♦♦♦ ♦♦♦

American

Location: I-43, exit 78, 0.5 mi e. 412 E Silver Spring Dr 53217. **Hours:** 7 am-8 pm, Sat-4 pm, Sun 7:30 am-3 pm. Closed major holidays. **Features:** A local favorite since 1960, this restaurant is known for its made-from-scratch menu items. Only natural ingredients are used in the homemade bread, sauces and soup and there are no preservatives. The setting is cozy and the service staff is friendly and welcoming. Casual dress; beer & wine only. **Parking:** street. **Cards:** MC, VI.

[✕]

JACK PANDL'S WHITEFISH BAY INN   **Lunch:** $7-$13   **Dinner:** $17-$24   **Phone:** 414/964-3800   ㉚

♦♦♦ ♦♦♦

American

Location: On SR 32, 0.6 mi s of jct Silver Spring Dr. 1319 E Henry Clay St 53217. **Hours:** 11:30 am-2:30 & 5-9 pm, Fri & Sat-10 pm, Sun 10:30 am-2:30 & 4-8 pm. Closed major holidays. **Reservations:** suggested. **Features:** This designated county landmark has been operated by the same family since 1915. Fresh de-boned whitefish is the house specialty, but the German pancakes are also notable. Dressy casual; cocktails. **Parking:** on-site. **Cards:** AX, DC, DS, MC, VI.

[Y] [✕]

This ends listings for the Milwaukee Vicinity.
The following page resumes the alphabetical listings of
cities in Wisconsin.

MINERAL POINT pop. 2,617

------- WHERE TO STAY -------

COMFORT INN
◈◈◈
Small-scale Hotel

Book at aaa.com
5/21-10/21 [ECP]   1P: $60-$150   2P: $60-$150   XP: $8   F18
4/1-5/20 & 10/22-3/31 [ECP]   1P: $50-$140   2P: $50-$140   XP: $8   F18

Phone: (608)987-4747

Location: On US 151, 0.6 mi n of jct SR 23 and 39. 1345 Business Park Rd 53565. Fax: 608/987-4545. **Facility:** 50 one-bedroom standard units, some with whirlpools. 2 stories (no elevator), interior corridors. *Bath:* combo or shower only. **Parking:** on-site, winter plug-ins. **Terms:** pets ($25 deposit). **Amenities:** safes, irons, hair dryers. **Pool(s):** heated indoor. **Leisure Activities:** whirlpool. **Guest Services:** coin laundry. **Business Services:** meeting rooms. **Cards:** AX, CB, DC, DS, JC, MC, VI.

SOME UNITS
(ASK) (S/D) [dog] (TI+) (&) (≈) (※) (DATA PORT) (▭) / (✕) (📧) (💼) /
FEE

REDWOOD MOTEL
AAA SAVE
◈◈◈
Motel

4/1-10/31   1P: $45-$49   2P: $54-$59   XP: $5   F5
11/1-3/31   1P: $39-$45   2P: $45-$51   XP: $5   F5

Phone: (608)987-2317

Location: On US 151, just n of jct SR 23 and 39. 625 Dodge St 53565. Fax: 608/987-2317. **Facility:** 26 one-bedroom standard units. 2 stories (no elevator), interior corridors. **Parking:** on-site, winter plug-ins. **Terms:** weekly rates available, [CP] & [ECP] meal plans available, package plans - in winter, small pets only ($10 fee, in smoking units). **Leisure Activities:** shuffleboard. **Cards:** AX, CB, DC, DS, JC, MC.

SOME UNITS
(S/D) [dog] (TI+) (DATA PORT) / (✕) /
FEE

------- WHERE TO DINE -------

BREWERY CREEK
◈◈◈
American

Lunch: $7-$9   **Dinner:** $8-$15   **Phone:** 608/987-3298

Location: Downtown. 23 Commerce St 53565. **Hours:** 11:30 am-8 pm 6/1-10/31; Thurs-Sat 11/1-5/31. **Features:** With its walls of limestone, original oak ceiling joints and pine plank flooring, the quaint establishment exudes English charm. In fact, many furnishings were imported from England pubs. The menu combines staple pub items, such as burgers, with pastas, steaks and daily chef's specials. Patrons can sip a tasty microbrew or a homemade root beer. Casual dress; beer & wine only. **Parking:** street. **Cards:** AX, DS, MC, VI.

(✕)

MINOCQUA

------- WHERE TO STAY -------

AMERICINN OF MINOCQUA
AAA SAVE
◈◈◈
Small-scale Hotel

Book at aaa.com
6/11-10/16   1P: $99-$159   2P: $99-$159   XP: $6   F17
1/1-3/31   1P: $79-$139   2P: $79-$139   XP: $6   F17
4/1-6/10 & 10/17-12/31   1P: $69-$99   2P: $69-$99   XP: $6   F17

Phone: (715)356-3730

Location: On US 51; center. Located across from Torpy Park. 700 Hwy 51 54548 (PO Box 115). Fax: 715/356-6958. **Facility:** 66 units. 60 one-bedroom standard units, some with whirlpools. 6 one-bedroom suites ($89-$159) with whirlpools. 2 stories (no elevator), interior corridors. *Bath:* combo or shower only. **Parking:** on-site, winter plug-ins. **Terms:** cancellation fee imposed, [ECP] meal plan available, pets ($50 fee). **Amenities:** hair dryers. *Some:* irons. **Pool(s):** heated indoor. **Leisure Activities:** sauna, whirlpool. **Guest Services:** coin laundry. **Business Services:** meeting rooms. **Cards:** AX, DS, MC, VI. **Special Amenities:** free expanded continental breakfast and free local telephone calls.
(See color ad p 576)

SOME UNITS
(S/D) [dog] (TI+) (&) (≈) (※) (DATA PORT) (▭) / (✕) (📧) (💼) /
FEE

COMFORT INN-MINOCQUA
◈◈◈
Small-scale Hotel

Book at aaa.com
All Year [ECP]   1P: $49-$99   2P: $49-$99   XP: $6   F18

Phone: (715)358-2588

Location: On US 51 at jct SR 70 W. Located in a commercial area. 8729 US 51 N 54548. Fax: 715/356-1402. **Facility:** 51 one-bedroom standard units, some with whirlpools. 2 stories (no elevator), interior corridors. **Parking:** on-site, winter plug-ins. **Terms:** pets ($10 extra charge, in designated units). **Amenities:** safes (fee), irons, hair dryers. **Pool(s):** small heated indoor. **Leisure Activities:** whirlpool, limited exercise equipment. **Business Services:** meeting rooms. **Cards:** AX, CB, DC, DS, MC, VI.

SOME UNITS
(ASK) (S/D) [dog] (TI+) (≈) (※) (DATA PORT) (▭) / (✕) (VCR) (📧) (💼) /
FEE

LAKEVIEW MOTOR LODGE
AAA SAVE
◈◈◈
Motel

6/7-9/5   1P: $86-$116   2P: $86-$116   XP: $8   F12
10/10-3/31   1P: $41-$116   2P: $41-$116   XP: $8   F12
9/6-10/9   1P: $68-$93   2P: $68-$93   XP: $8   F12
4/1-6/6   1P: $41-$93   2P: $41-$93   XP: $8   F12

Phone: (715)356-5208

Location: North end of US 51 bridge; downtown. Located on Lake Minocqua. 311 E Park Ave 54548 (PO Box 575). Fax: 715/356-1412. **Facility:** 41 one-bedroom standard units, some with whirlpools. 2 stories (no elevator), interior/exterior corridors. *Bath:* combo or shower only. **Parking:** on-site, winter plug-ins. **Terms:** 2 night minimum stay - weekends 7/1-8/31, [ECP] meal plan available, pets ($8 extra charge). **Amenities:** hair dryers. **Leisure Activities:** sauna, whirlpool, boat dock, fishing, playground. **Cards:** AX, DS, MC, VI. **Special Amenities:** free expanded continental breakfast and free local telephone calls.

SOME UNITS
(S/D) [dog] (TI+) (✕) (※) (DATA PORT) (▭) / (✕) (📧) (💼) /
FEE

THE POINTE WATERFRONT RESORT HOTEL

Phone: (715)356-4431

AAA SAVE	9/6-3/31	2P: $59-$239
▽▽▽▽	6/18-9/5	2P: $114-$219
	4/1-5/13	2P: $59-$189
	5/14-6/17	2P: $74-$179

Condominium **Location:** On US 51, just s of downtown. Overlooking Lake Minocqua. 8269 S Hwy 51 54548 (PO Box 880). **Fax:** 715/356-7821. **Facility:** Located high on a bluff overlooking Lake Minocqua. Smoke free premises. 69 units. 12 one-bedroom standard units with efficiencies, some with whirlpools. 48 one- and 9 two-bedroom suites with kitchens, some with whirlpools. 3 stories (no elevator), interior/exterior corridors. **Parking:** on-site, winter plug-ins. **Terms:** check-in 4 pm, 2-7 night minimum stay - seasonal & weekends, cancellation fee imposed, [ECP] meal plan available. **Amenities:** video library (fee), irons, hair dryers. **Pool(s):** heated indoor. **Leisure Activities:** sauna, whirlpool, boat dock, fishing, snowmobiling, gas grill, picnic areas, playground, exercise room, basketball. *Fee:* game room. **Guest Services:** gift shop, coin laundry. **Business Services:** meeting rooms. **Cards:** AX, MC, VI.

SOME UNITS

SUPER 8 MOTEL

Phone: 715/356-9541

AAA SAVE	6/15-9/14	1P: $70-$80	2P: $80-$90	XP: $10	F12
	4/1-6/14 & 9/15-3/31	1P: $55-$65	2P: $65-$75	XP: $10	F12

▽ Motel **Location:** On US 51 at jct SR 70 W. Located in a commercial area. 8730 Hwy 51 N 54548 (PO Box 325). **Fax:** 715/358-2152. **Facility:** 33 one-bedroom standard units, some with whirlpools. 1 story, interior/exterior corridors. **Parking:** on-site, winter plug-ins. **Terms:** check-in 4 pm, 2 night minimum stay - weekends 7/1-8/31, pets ($10 extra charge, in smoking units). **Leisure Activities:** snowmobiling. **Cards:** AX, CB, DC, DS, MC, VI. **Special Amenities:** free local telephone calls and free newspaper.

SOME UNITS

THE WATERS OF MINOCQUA

Phone: (715)358-4000

▽▽▽	6/11-9/5	1P: $99-$239
	4/1-6/10 & 9/6-3/31	1P: $79-$219

Large-scale Hotel **Location:** On US 51, 1 mi s. 8116 S Hwy 51 54548 (PO Box 1053). **Fax:** 715/358-4010. **Facility:** 106 units. 100 one-bedroom standard units, some with whirlpools. 6 one-bedroom suites. 3 stories, interior corridors. *Bath:* combo or shower only. **Parking:** on-site, winter plug-ins. **Terms:** [MAP] meal plan available. **Amenities:** high-speed Internet, dual phone lines, voice mail, hair dryers. **Pool(s):** heated indoor, heated indoor/outdoor, wading. **Leisure Activities:** whirlpool, cross country skiing, snowmobiling, exercise room. *Fee:* game room. **Guest Services:** gift shop, coin laundry. **Business Services:** meeting rooms. **Cards:** AX, DC, DS, MC, VI.

——— WHERE TO DINE ———

LITTLE SWISS VILLAGE

Lunch: $4-$10 Phone: 715/356-3675

▽▽ American **Location:** 3 mi s on US 51, 2.5 mi w. 7650 Blue Lake Rd 54548. **Hours:** Open 5/9-10/5; 8 am-3 pm; hours vary off season. Closed: Mon & Tues 9/13-10/3. **Reservations:** accepted. **Features:** Windowside tables in the quaint dining room overlook a whimsical chipmunk village called Chesterville, in addition to the beautifully landscaped grounds and nearby lake. Tasty choices include Swiss and German pancakes, waffles and omelets. Casual dress. **Parking:** on-site. **Cards:** DS, MC, VI.

MAMA'S SUPPER CLUB

Dinner: $6-$17 Phone: 715/356-5070

▽▽ ▽▽ Italian **Location:** 3 mi w of town. 10486 Hwy 70 54548. **Hours:** 5 pm-10 pm. Closed: 11/25, 12/24, 12/25; also 3/30. **Reservations:** accepted. **Features:** Overlooking a small lake, the dining room is charming and casual. The menu centers on traditional Italian preparations, such as Sicilian veal and a wide variety of pasta. You'll also find American dishes, including a succulent tenderloin steak. Casual dress; cocktails. **Parking:** on-site. **Cards:** AX, CB, DC, DS, MC, VI.

NORWOOD PINES SUPPER CLUB

Dinner: $10-$25 Phone: 715/356-3666

▽▽ ▽▽ American **Location:** On SR 70, 2 mi w of jct US 51. 10171 Hwy 70 W 54548. **Hours:** 5 pm-10 pm. Closed: 12/24, 12/25; also Sun. **Reservations:** accepted. **Features:** This restaurant offers an authentic Northwoods Supper Club experience complete with a traditional menu, friendly service and warm decor. Supper clubs are a tradition in rural Wisconsin. As you enter the restaurant, the scent of the pine trees permeates the air. Casual dress; cocktails. **Parking:** on-site. **Cards:** CB, DC, DS, MC, VI.

——— *The following restaurant has not been evaluated by AAA* ———
but is listed for your information only.

MINOCQUA BREWING COMPANY

Phone: 715/358-3040

fyi Not evaluated. **Location:** 238 Lake Shore Dr 54548. **Features:** Located on the water's edge in the downtown area, this restaurant is in a restored 1927 lodge building.

MONONA pop. 8,018 (See map and index starting on p. 542)

——— WHERE TO STAY ———

AMERICINN OF MADISON SOUTH/MONONA

Book at aaa.com Phone: (608)222-8601 40

AAA SAVE	All Year [ECP]	1P: $79-$159	2P: $79-$159

▽▽▽▽ Small-scale Hotel **Location:** US 12 and 18, exit 265 (Monona Dr), just nw. 101 W Broadway 53716-3901. **Fax:** 608/222-4070. **Facility:** 62 units. 59 one-bedroom standard units, some with whirlpools. 3 one-bedroom suites, some with whirlpools. 3 stories, interior corridors. *Bath:* combo or shower only. **Parking:** on-site, winter plug-ins. **Terms:** package plans, pets ($5 extra charge). **Amenities:** dual phone lines, voice mail, hair dryers. *Some:* CD players. **Pool(s):** small heated indoor. **Leisure Activities:** sauna, whirlpool, game room. **Guest Services:** valet and coin laundry. **Business Services:** meeting rooms. **Cards:** AX, DC, DS, MC, VI. **Special Amenities:** free local telephone calls and free newspaper. *(See color ad p 576)*

SOME UNITS

(See map and index starting on p. 542)

COUNTRY INN & SUITES BY CARLSON   *Book at aaa.com*   Phone: (608)221-0055   **41**
AAA SAVE   All Year   1P: $79-$89   2P: $85-$95   XP: $6   F18
WWW   **Location:** US 12 and 18, exit 265 (Monona Dr), just nw. 400 River Pl 53716. Fax: 608/221-9809. **Facility:** 87 units. 68 one-bedroom standard units, some with whirlpools. 19 one-bedroom suites ($100-$150). 3 stories, interior corridors. *Bath:* combo or shower only. **Parking:** on-site. **Terms:** [ECP] meal plan available.
Small-scale Hotel   **Amenities:** voice mail, irons, hair dryers. **Pool(s):** small heated indoor. **Leisure Activities:** whirlpool, exercise room. *Fee:* game room. **Guest Services:** valet and coin laundry. **Business Services:** meeting rooms.
Cards: AX, CB, DC, DS, MC, VI. **Special Amenities:** free expanded continental breakfast and free local telephone calls.
(See color ad starting on p 580)

SOME UNITS

MONROE pop. 10,843

──────── WHERE TO STAY ────────

AMERICINN OF MONROE   *Book at aaa.com*   Phone: 608-328-3444
WWWW   5/1-9/30   1P: $74-$114   2P: $82-$122   XP: $8   F12
    4/1-4/30 & 3/1-3/31   1P: $69-$109   2P: $77-$117   XP: $8   F12
Small-scale Hotel   10/1-2/28   1P: $64-$104   2P: $72-$112   XP: $8   F12
    Location: On SR 69 S, 0.4 mi s from jct SR 81/11. 424 4th Ave 53566. Fax: 608/328-3454. **Facility:** 54 one-bedroom standard units, some with whirlpools. 2 stories (no elevator), interior corridors. *Bath:* combo or shower only. **Parking:** on-site, winter plug-ins. **Terms:** [CP] meal plan available. **Amenities:** hair dryers. **Pool(s):** small heated indoor. **Leisure Activities:** whirlpool. *Fee:* game room. **Guest Services:** coin laundry. **Business Services:** meeting rooms. **Cards:** AX, DS, MC, VI.
(See color ad p 576)

SOME UNITS

GASTHAUS MOTEL   Phone: (608)328-8395
AAA SAVE   All Year   1P: $35-$44   2P: $42-$52   XP: $5   F12
WWW   **Location:** 1.5 mi s on SR 69. 685 30th St 53566. Fax: 608/328-8383. **Facility:** 18 one-bedroom standard units. 1 story, exterior corridors. **Parking:** on-site, winter plug-ins. **Amenities:** voice mail. **Leisure Activities:**
Motel   Fee: bicycles. **Cards:** AX, DS, MC, VI. **Special Amenities:** early check-in/late check-out and free room upgrade (subject to availability with advanced reservations).

SOME UNITS
FEE

SUPER 8 MOTEL   Phone: (608)325-1500
WWW   All Year [ECP]   1P: $48-$78   2P: $54-$84   XP: $5   F12
Small-scale Hotel   **Location:** On SR 69 S, 0.5 mi s of jct SR 81/11. 500 6th St 53566. Fax: 608/325-1500. **Facility:** 42 one-bedroom standard units, some with whirlpools. 2 stories (no elevator), interior corridors. **Parking:** on-site, winter plug-ins. **Amenities:** video library (fee). *Some:* high-speed Internet. **Leisure Activities:** whirlpool. **Cards:** AX, CB, DC, DS, MC, VI.

SOME UNITS
FEE

──────── WHERE TO DINE ────────

PEPPERCORN CAFE   Lunch: $6-$8   Dinner: $9-$17   Phone: 608/329-2233
WW   **Location:** Just s of jct SR 69 N/11/81. 180 18th Ave N 53566. **Hours:** 11:30 am-1:30 & 5-9 pm, Fri & Sat-10 pm.
Continental   Closed major holidays; also Sun & Mon. **Reservations:** suggested. **Features:** All entrees—including barbecue ribs, daily fresh fish specials and the signature peppercorn steak—are made to order in the lively restaurant. Beverages include fine cocktails, locally brewed beers and Italian sodas. Desserts are a real treat. Try white chocolate mousse with Godiva chocolate sauce or raisin bread pudding with caramel. Casual dress; cocktails. **Parking:** on-site. **Cards:** AX, DC, DS, MC, VI.

MONTELLO pop. 1,397

──────── WHERE TO DINE ────────

TIMBERS SUPPER CLUB   Dinner: $8-$18   Phone: 920/293-4589
WWWW   **Location:** 8 mi n on SR 22; between Wautoma and Montello, 2.7 mi n of jct CR J. SR 22 54960. **Hours:** Open
American   4/1-12/31 & 2/15-3/31; 4:30 pm-10 pm. Closed: 11/25, 12/24, 12/25; also Tues & Wed.
    Reservations: accepted. **Features:** Prime rib and barbecue ribs are served daily in the popular, family-owned and operated restaurant. The modest dining room is in a tree grove in the beautiful Wisconsin countryside. Daily specials, homemade soups, broiled or fried seafood, some pork and poultry entrees and lighter selections complete the menu. Casual dress; cocktails. **Parking:** on-site. **Cards:** MC, VI.

MOSINEE pop. 4,063

──────── WHERE TO STAY ────────

AMERIHOST INN-MOSINEE   *Book at aaa.com*   Phone: (715)693-9000
AAA SAVE   All Year   1P: $73-$79   2P: $73-$79   XP: $6   F16
WWW   **Location:** I-39, exit 179 (SR 153), just sw. Located in a quiet area. 400 Orbiting Dr 54455. Fax: 715/693-9006. **Facility:** 53 one-bedroom standard units, some with whirlpools. 2 stories (no elevator), interior corridors. *Bath:* combo or shower only. **Parking:** on-site, winter plug-ins. **Terms:** 3 day cancellation notice, [ECP] meal
Small-scale Hotel   plan available. **Amenities:** irons, hair dryers. *Fee:* high-speed Internet, safes. **Pool(s):** small heated indoor. **Leisure Activities:** whirlpool, limited exercise equipment. **Guest Services:** valet laundry. **Business Services:** meeting rooms, fax (fee). **Cards:** AX, CB, DC, DS, JC, MC, VI. **Special Amenities:** free expanded continental breakfast and free newspaper.

SOME UNITS

COMFORT INN
♦♦♦♦

Small-scale Hotel

Book at aaa.com
All Year [ECP]

Phone: **715/355-4449**

| | 1P: $59-$79 | 2P: $59-$79 | XP: $6 | F17 |

Location: I-39, exit 185 (US Business Rt 51), just se. Located in a commercial area. 1510 County Hwy XX 54455. Fax: 715/359-0603. **Facility:** 60 one-bedroom standard units, some with whirlpools. 2 stories (no elevator), interior corridors. **Parking:** on-site, winter plug-ins. **Terms:** small pets only ($30 fee, in designated units, with prior approval). **Amenities:** irons, hair dryers. **Pool(s):** small heated indoor. **Leisure Activities:** whirlpool. **Guest Services:** valet laundry. **Business Services:** meeting rooms. **Cards:** AX, CB, DC, DS, JC, MC, VI.

SOME UNITS
ASK SD [icons] DATA PORT / X [icons] /
FEE

RODEWAY INN
♦♦♦♦

Small-scale Hotel

Book at aaa.com
All Year [ECP]

Phone: **715/355-3030**

| | 1P: $55-$75 | 2P: $55-$75 | XP: $6 | F17 |

Location: I-39, exit 185 (US Business Rt 51), just se. Located in a commercial area. 904 Industrial Park Ave 54455. Fax: 715/355-4770. **Facility:** 39 one-bedroom standard units, some with whirlpools. 2 stories (no elevator), interior corridors. **Parking:** on-site. **Amenities:** video library (fee). **Pool(s):** small heated indoor. **Leisure Activities:** whirlpool, limited exercise equipment. **Guest Services:** valet laundry. **Business Services:** meeting rooms. **Cards:** AX, CB, DC, DS, JC, MC, VI.

SOME UNITS
ASK SD [icons] DATA PORT / X VCR [icons] /
FEE

STONEY CREEK INN
♦♦♦♦

Small-scale Hotel

All Year

Phone: **(715)355-6858**

| | 1P: $74-$175 | 2P: $84-$175 | XP: $10 | F18 |

Location: I-39, exit 185 (US Business Rt 51), just e. Located in a commercial area. 1100 Imperial Ave 54455. Fax: 715/355-0913. **Facility:** 107 one-bedroom standard units, some with whirlpools. 3 stories, interior corridors. **Bath:** combo or shower only. **Parking:** on-site, winter plug-ins. **Terms:** cancellation fee imposed, [ECP] meal plan available. **Amenities:** voice mail, hair dryers. *Some:* irons. **Pool(s):** heated indoor. **Leisure Activities:** sauna, whirlpool, snowmobiling, exercise room. *Fee:* game room. **Guest Services:** gift shop, valet and coin laundry, area transportation. **Business Services:** conference facilities, fax (fee). **Cards:** AX, CB, DC, DS, MC, VI.

SOME UNITS
ASK SD [icons] DATA PORT / X VCR [icons] /
FEE

The following lodging was either not evaluated or did not meet AAA rating requirements but is listed for your information only.

THE LODGE AT CEDAR CREEK
[fyi]

Small-scale Hotel

Phone: **715/241-6300**

Under construction, scheduled to open June 2004. **Location:** I-39, exit 185 (US Business Rt 51). 805 Creske Ave 54455 (PO Box 247). Fax: 715/241-6306. **Planned Amenities:** restaurant, coffeemakers, microwaves, refrigerators, pool. *(See color ad p 639)*

NEENAH pop. 24,507

--------- WHERE TO STAY ---------

DAYS INN OF FOX CITIES
♦♦♦♦

Motel

Book at aaa.com
All Year [CP]

Phone: **(920)720-9020**

| | 1P: $49-$95 | 2P: $56-$100 | XP: $5 | F12 |

Location: US 41, exit 131 (Winneconne Ave), just e, then just n. Located in a commercial area. 495 S Greenbay Rd 54956. Fax: 920/720-9020. **Facility:** 51 one-bedroom standard units, some with whirlpools. 2 stories, interior corridors. **Parking:** on-site, winter plug-ins. **Terms:** cancellation fee imposed, small pets only ($10 extra charge, with prior approval). **Amenities:** hair dryers. **Pool(s):** small heated indoor. **Leisure Activities:** whirlpool. **Cards:** AX, DC, DS, MC, VI.

SOME UNITS
ASK SD [icons] / X [icons] /
FEE

HOLIDAY INN NEENAH RIVERWALK
♦♦♦

Small-scale Hotel

Book at aaa.com
1/1-3/31
4/1-12/31

Phone: **(920)725-8441**

| | 1P: $89-$126 | 2P: $89-$126 | XP: $10 | F19 |
| | 1P: $89-$123 | 2P: $89-$123 | XP: $10 | F19 |

Location: US 41, exit 132 (Main St), 2 mi e; downtown. Located in a commercial area. 123 E Wisconsin Ave 54956 (PO Box 795, 54957-0795). Fax: 920/725-4387. **Facility:** 107 one-bedroom standard units. 7 stories, interior corridors. **Parking:** on-site. **Terms:** [AP], [BP] & [CP] meal plans available, package plans - weekends, pets ($75 deposit, in designated units). **Amenities:** video games (fee), high-speed Internet, voice mail, irons, hair dryers. **Pool(s):** heated indoor. **Leisure Activities:** whirlpool, exercise room. **Guest Services:** valet laundry. **Business Services:** meeting rooms. **Cards:** AX, CB, DC, DS, MC, VI.

SOME UNITS
ASK [icons] DATA PORT / X VCR [icons] /
FEE   FEE

--------- WHERE TO DINE ---------

CALIBAN'S
♦♦♦

American

Lunch: $6-$15   Dinner: $7-$17   Phone: **920/725-0573**

Location: Corner of Church St; downtown. 134 W Wisconsin Ave 54956. **Hours:** 11 am-2 & 4:30-9:30 pm, Fri & Sat-10 pm. Closed major holidays; also Sun. **Reservations:** accepted. **Features:** Hardwood floors and a high, pressed-tin ceiling distinguish the city's oldest building. The menu lays out a nice selection of homemade sandwiches and soups, as well as thin-crust pizzas and build-your-own fettuccine choices. An extensive selection of beers is offered. Casual dress; cocktails. **Parking:** street. **Cards:** DS, MC, VI.

[icons]

NEW BERLIN —*See Milwaukee p. 596.*

NEW LISBON pop. 1,436

────── **WHERE TO STAY** ──────

EDGE O' THE WOOD MOTEL   Phone: 608/562-3705
(AAA) (SAVE)   6/1-8/31   1P: $45-$70   2P: $55-$80   XP: $7   F5
               9/1-12/31   1P: $32-$60   2P: $39-$79   XP: $7   F5
▽▽ ▽▽   4/1-5/31 & 1/1-3/31 1P: $29-$45   2P: $35-$55   XP: $7   F5
Motel   **Location:** I-90/94, exit 61 (SR 80), just e. W 7396 Frontage Rd 53950. Fax: 608/562-3912. **Facility:** 21 one-
               bedroom standard units. 1 story, exterior corridors. **Parking:** on-site, winter plug-ins. **Terms:** cancellation fee
               imposed, weekly rates available, package plans - weekly & monthly, small pets only. **Pool(s):** heated outdoor.
Leisure Activities: picnic area with grill, playground, basketball. **Guest Services:** coin laundry. **Cards:** DS, MC, VI.

SOME UNITS

TRAVELODGE OF NEW LISBON   Phone: (608)562-5141
(AAA) (SAVE)   5/23-10/16 [CP]   1P: $55-$90   2P: $70-$110   XP: $8   F17
               4/1-5/22 & 10/17-3/31 [CP] 1P: $48-$90 2P: $55-$100 XP: $8   F17
▽▽ ▽▽   **Location:** I-90/94, exit 61 (SR 80), just ne. 1700 E Bridge St 53950. Fax: 608/562-6205. **Facility:** 61 one-bedroom
Small-scale Hotel standard units, some with whirlpools. 3 stories, interior corridors. *Bath:* combo or shower only. **Parking:** on-
               site, winter plug-ins. **Terms:** pets ($50 deposit). **Amenities:** video library, voice mail, safes (fee), hair dryers.
               Some: dual phone lines. **Pool(s):** small heated indoor. **Leisure Activities:** whirlpool. *Fee:* game room. **Busi-
ness Services:** meeting rooms. **Cards:** AX, CB, DC, DS, JC, MC, VI. **Special Amenities:** free continental breakfast and free
newspaper.

SOME UNITS

NEW LONDON pop. 7,085

────── **WHERE TO STAY** ──────

AMERICINN LODGE & SUITES OF NEW LONDON   *Book at aaa.com*   Phone: (920)982-5700
               All Year [ECP]   1P: $59-$89   2P: $69-$99   XP: $8   F17
▽▽▽▽   **Location:** US 45, exit US 54, just n. Located in a commercial area. 1404 N Shawano St 54961. Fax: 920/982-5769.
Small-scale Hotel **Facility:** 49 units. 43 one-bedroom standard units, some with whirlpools. 6 one-bedroom suites ($99-$169),
               some with kitchens and/or whirlpools. 2 stories, interior corridors. *Bath:* combo or shower only. **Parking:** on-
site, winter plug-ins. **Terms:** small pets only ($10 extra charge). **Amenities:** irons, hair dryers. *Some:* high-speed Internet.
Pool(s): heated indoor. **Leisure Activities:** whirlpool, exercise room. **Guest Services:** coin laundry. **Business Services:**
meeting rooms. **Cards:** AX, DS, MC, VI. *(See color ad p 576)*

SOME UNITS

RIDGEMARK INNS   Phone: 920/982-7907
(AAA) (SAVE)   All Year   2P: $42-$115   XP: $5   F12
▽▽ ▽▽   **Location:** US 45, exit US 54, just n. Located in a commercial area. 1409 N Shawano St 54961. Fax: 920/982-7907.
               Facility: 42 one-bedroom standard units, some with whirlpools. 2 stories (no elevator), interior corridors.
Small-scale Hotel **Parking:** on-site, winter plug-ins. **Terms:** [ECP] meal plan available, pets ($8 extra charge).
               Amenities: *Some:* hair dryers. **Pool(s):** small heated indoor. **Leisure Activities:** whirlpool. **Guest Services:**
               coin laundry. **Business Services:** meeting rooms. **Cards:** AX, DS, MC, VI. **Special Amenities:** free conti-
nental breakfast and free local telephone calls.

SOME UNITS

────── **WHERE TO DINE** ──────

HALF NELSON'S RESTAURANT   **Lunch:** $7-$23   **Dinner:** $7-$23   Phone: 920/982-1600
▽▽ ▽▽   **Location:** US 45, exit US 54, just n. 1601 N Shawano St 54961. **Hours:** 11 am-9 pm, Fri & Sat-10 pm. Closed:
American   11/25, 12/25. **Features:** The dining room is filled with sports photographs and memorabilia. On the menu is
               a selection of pasta, ribs, steak and Mexican dishes, as well as perch and walleye for those who enjoy
               fish. Booth and table seating are available. Casual dress; cocktails. **Parking:** on-site. **Cards:** AX, DS,
MC, VI.

NEW RICHMOND pop. 6,310

────── **WHERE TO STAY** ──────

AMERICINN MOTEL   *Book at aaa.com*   Phone: 715/246-3993
▽▽ ▽▽   9/1-3/31   1P: $85-$134   2P: $85-$134   XP: $6   F16
               4/1-8/31   1P: $69-$134   2P: $69-$134   XP: $6   F16
Small-scale Hotel **Location:** Just s on SR 65. 1020 S Knowles Ave 54017. Fax: 715/246-3207. **Facility:** 45 one-bedroom standard
               units, some with whirlpools. 2 stories (no elevator), interior corridors. *Bath:* combo or shower only. **Parking:**
on-site, winter plug-ins. **Terms:** [CP] & [ECP] meal plans available, pets ($25 deposit). **Amenities:** irons, hair dryers. **Pool(s):**
heated indoor. **Leisure Activities:** sauna, whirlpool. **Business Services:** administrative services (fee). **Cards:** AX, CB, DC, DS,
JC, MC, VI. *(See color ad p 576)*

SOME UNITS

SUPER 8 MOTEL   *Book at aaa.com*   **Phone:** (715)246-7829
▿▿▿   All Year   1P: $54-$79   2P: $59-$89   XP: $8
    Location: Just s on SR 65. 1561 Dorset Ln 54017. Fax: 715/246-9754. **Facility:** 34 units. 33 one-bedroom stan-
Small-scale Hotel   dard units, some with whirlpools. 1 one-bedroom suite. 2 stories (no elevator), interior corridors. **Parking:**
    on-site, winter plug-ins. **Terms:** [ECP] meal plan available, pets ($15 extra charge). **Amenities:** dual phone
lines. **Business Services:** administrative services. **Cards:** AX, DC, DS, MC, VI.

SOME UNITS

OAK CREEK —*See Milwaukee p. 597.*

OCONOMOWOC —*See Milwaukee p. 598.*

OKAUCHEE —*See Milwaukee p. 598.*

ONALASKA pop. 14,839

———— **WHERE TO STAY** ————

BAYMONT INN & SUITES LACROSSE-ONALASKA   *Book at aaa.com*   **Phone:** (608)783-7191
AAA [SAVE]   All Year [ECP]   1P: $74-$109
▿▿▿▿   **Location:** I-90, exit 5, just ne. 3300 Kinney Coulee Rd N 54650. Fax: 608/783-1557. **Facility:** 67 one-bedroom
    standard units, some with whirlpools. 3 stories, interior corridors. *Bath:* combo or shower only. **Parking:** on-
Small-scale Hotel   site, winter plug-ins. **Terms:** pets ($5 fee). **Amenities:** voice mail, irons, hair dryers. *Some:* dual phone lines.
    Pool(s): heated indoor. **Leisure Activities:** whirlpool, exercise room. **Guest Services:** valet and coin
    laundry. **Business Services:** meeting rooms. **Cards:** AX, DC, DS, MC, VI. **Special Amenities:** free local
telephone calls and free newspaper.

SOME UNITS

COMFORT INN   *Book at aaa.com*   **Phone:** (608)781-7500
▿▿▿   6/1-10/15 [CP]   1P: $69-$114   2P: $74-$119   XP: $5   F18
    4/1-5/31 & 10/16-3/31 [CP]   1P: $64-$84   2P: $69-$89   XP: $5   F18
Small-scale Hotel   **Location:** I-90, exit 4, just e on SR 157, then e on CR SS. 1223 Crossing Meadows Dr 54650. Fax: 608/781-7500.
    Facility: 69 one-bedroom standard units. 2 stories (no elevator), interior corridors. **Parking:** on-site, winter
plug-ins. **Amenities:** irons, hair dryers. **Pool(s):** small heated indoor. **Leisure Activities:** whirlpool. **Guest Services:** valet
laundry. **Business Services:** meeting rooms. **Cards:** AX, CB, DC, DS, JC, MC, VI.

SOME UNITS

HAMPTON INN OF ONALASKA   *Book at aaa.com*   **Phone:** (608)779-5000
▿▿▿   5/3-11/6   1P: $84-$149   2P: $89-$149
    4/1-5/2 & 11/7-3/31   1P: $79-$109   2P: $89-$109
Small-scale Hotel   **Location:** I-90, exit 5, 0.4 mi e on SR 16, just w on CR OS, then just s on Market Dr. 308 Hampton Ct 54650.
    Fax: 608/779-9199. **Facility:** 107 one-bedroom standard units, some with whirlpools. 3 stories, interior corri-
dors. *Bath:* combo or shower only. **Parking:** on-site. **Terms:** [CP] meal plan available. **Amenities:** video games (fee), voice mail,
irons, hair dryers. **Pool(s):** heated indoor. **Leisure Activities:** whirlpool, limited exercise equipment. **Guest Services:** valet and
coin laundry. **Business Services:** meeting rooms, fax (fee). **Cards:** AX, DC, DS, MC, VI.

SOME UNITS

HOLIDAY INN EXPRESS   *Book at aaa.com*   **Phone:** (608)783-6555
▿▿▿   All Year [ECP]   1P: $89-$109   2P: $99-$129
    Location: I-90, exit 5, 1 mi e. 9409 Hwy 16 54650. Fax: 608/783-6554. **Facility:** 75 one-bedroom standard units,
Small-scale Hotel   some with whirlpools. 3 stories, interior corridors. *Bath:* combo or shower only. **Parking:** on-site, winter plug-
    ins. **Terms:** cancellation fee imposed. **Amenities:** irons, hair dryers. **Pool(s):** heated indoor. **Leisure Activi-
ties:** whirlpool, exercise room. **Guest Services:** valet and coin laundry. **Business Services:** meeting rooms. **Cards:** AX; DC,
DS, MC, VI.

SOME UNITS

MICROTEL INN   *Book at aaa.com*   **Phone:** (608)783-0833
AAA [SAVE]   6/1-10/31 [CP]   1P: $52-$57   2P: $57-$62   XP: $5   F16
▿▿▿   4/1-5/31 & 11/1-3/31 [CP]   1P: $44-$49   2P: $49-$52   XP: $5   F16
    Location: I-90, exit 5, just ne. 3240 N Kinney Coulee Rd 54650. Fax: 608/783-0988. **Facility:** 63 one-bedroom
Small-scale Hotel   standard units. 3 stories, interior corridors. *Bath:* combo or shower only. **Parking:** on-site. **Terms:** cancella-
    tion fee imposed, pets ($5 extra charge). **Guest Services:** valet laundry. **Cards:** AX, DS, MC, VI.
    Special Amenities: free continental breakfast and free local telephone calls.

SOME UNITS

———— **WHERE TO DINE** ————

SEVEN BRIDGES RESTAURANT   **Dinner:** $8-$29   **Phone:** 608/783-6103
▿▿▿   **Location:** I-90, exit 3, 2 mi n on SR 35. 910 2nd Ave N 54650. **Hours:** 5 pm-9 pm, Fri & Sat-10 pm. Closed
    major holidays. **Reservations:** accepted. **Features:** This restaurant offers nice views of the Black River
Steak & Seafood   and Lake Onalaska, especially at sunset. The walls are adorned with wildlife prints, and pictures of the
    local history. Casual dress; cocktails. **Parking:** on-site. **Cards:** AX, CB, DC, DS, MC, VI.

TRADITIONS RESTAURANT
Dinner: $18-$25
Phone: 608/783-0200

American

Location: I-90, exit 3, 1 mi n on SR 35. 201 Main St 54650. **Hours:** 5:30 pm-10 pm. Closed major holidays; also Sun & Mon. **Reservations:** suggested. **Features:** In historic downtown, the upscale, fine-dining restaurant is in a restored bank and lets patrons dine in the vault for a more intimate experience. The palate-tempting, monthly changing menu reflects the tastes of the season. Dressy casual; cocktails. **Parking:** on-site. **Cards:** AX, DS, MC, VI.

OSCEOLA pop. 2,421

─────── WHERE TO STAY ───────

RIVER VALLEY INN
Phone: (715)294-4060

Small-scale Hotel

All Year   1P: $65-$120   2P: $65-$120   XP: $7   F16
Location: Just n on SR 35. 1030 Cascade St 54020 (PO Box 726). Fax: 715/294-4038. **Facility:** 32 units. 29 one-bedroom standard units, some with whirlpools. 3 one-bedroom suites ($90-$120). 2 stories (no elevator), interior corridors. **Parking:** on-site, winter plug-ins. **Terms:** [ECP] meal plan available, package plans, pets ($5 extra charge). **Amenities:** Some: irons. **Pool(s):** small heated indoor. **Leisure Activities:** whirlpool. Fee: video games in pool area, books and board games. **Guest Services:** valet and coin laundry. **Business Services:** meeting rooms. **Cards:** AX, DC, DS, MC, VI. **Special Amenities: free expanded continental breakfast and free local telephone calls.**

OSHKOSH pop. 62,916

─────── WHERE TO STAY ───────

AMERICINN OF OSHKOSH
Book at aaa.com
Phone: (920)232-0300

Small-scale Hotel

All Year [ECP]   1P: $69-$89   2P: $69-$89   XP: $6   F14
Location: US 41, exit 116 (SR 44), 0.5 mi e. 1495 W South Park Ave 54902. Fax: 920/232-0669. **Facility:** 65 one-bedroom standard units, some with whirlpools. 2 stories (no elevator), interior corridors. *Bath:* combo or shower only. **Parking:** on-site, winter plug-ins. **Amenities:** hair dryers. **Pool(s):** heated indoor. **Leisure Activities:** sauna, whirlpool. **Guest Services:** valet and coin laundry. **Business Services:** meeting rooms. **Cards:** AX, DC, DS, MC, VI. *(See color ad p 576)*

BAYMONT INN OSHKOSH
Book at aaa.com
Phone: (920)233-4190

Small-scale Hotel

All Year   1P: $59-$79   2P: $59-$79
Location: US 41, exit 119, at jct SR 21. Located in a commercial area. 1950 Omro Rd 54902. Fax: 920/233-8197. **Facility:** 97 one-bedroom standard units. 2 stories (no elevator), interior corridors. **Parking:** on-site, winter plug-ins. **Terms:** [ECP] meal plan available, small pets only. **Amenities:** video games (fee), voice mail, irons, hair dryers. **Guest Services:** valet laundry. **Business Services:** meeting rooms. **Cards:** AX, CB, DC, DS, MC, VI. **Special Amenities: free local telephone calls and free newspaper.** *(See color ad p 597)*

FAIRFIELD INN BY MARRIOTT
Book at aaa.com
Phone: (920)233-8504

Small-scale Hotel

5/30-10/2 [ECP]   1P: $70-$150   2P: $70-$150
4/1-5/29 [ECP]   1P: $65-$80   2P: $65-$80
10/3-3/31 [ECP]   1P: $60-$70   2P: $60-$70
Location: US 41, exit 117 (9th Ave), 0.8 mi s on east frontage road. Located in a commercial area. 1800 S Koeller Rd 54902. Fax: 920/233-8504. **Facility:** 57 one-bedroom standard units. 3 stories, interior corridors. **Parking:** on-site, winter plug-ins. **Amenities:** irons, hair dryers. **Pool(s):** small heated indoor. **Leisure Activities:** whirlpool. **Guest Services:** valet laundry. **Cards:** AX, DC, DS, MC, VI.

HAWTHORN INN & SUITES
Book at aaa.com
Phone: (920)303-1133

Small-scale Hotel

All Year [BP]   1P: $89-$249   2P: $99-$299
Location: US 41, exit 116 (SR 44), just w, then just s. 3105 S Washburn St 54904. Fax: 920/303-2103. **Facility:** 77 units. 68 one-bedroom standard units, some with whirlpools. 9 one-bedroom suites ($159-$399) with efficiencies. 3 stories, interior corridors. *Bath:* combo or shower only. **Parking:** on-site, winter plug-ins. **Terms:** pets ($50 deposit). **Amenities:** high-speed Internet (fee), dual phone lines, voice mail, irons, hair dryers. **Pool(s):** heated indoor, wading. **Leisure Activities:** whirlpool, exercise room. **Guest Services:** sundries, valet and coin laundry. **Cards:** AX, CB, DC, MC, VI.

HILTON GARDEN INN OSHKOSH
Book at aaa.com
Phone: (920)966-1300

Small-scale Hotel

All Year   1P: $79-$249   2P: $79-$249   XP: $10   F18
Location: US 41, exit 116 (SR 44), 0.5 mi e. Located next to the airport. 1355 W 20th Ave 54902. Fax: 920/966-1305. **Facility:** 126 units. 124 one-bedroom standard units. 2 one-bedroom suites with whirlpools. 3 stories, interior corridors. *Bath:* combo or shower only. **Parking:** on-site, winter plug-ins. **Terms:** cancellation fee imposed, [BP] meal plan available. **Amenities:** video games (fee), high-speed Internet, dual phone lines, voice mail, irons, hair dryers. *Some:* DVD players. **Pool(s):** heated indoor. **Leisure Activities:** whirlpool, exercise room. Fee: game room. **Guest Services:** sundries, valet and coin laundry, area transportation. **Business Services:** conference facilities, business center. **Cards:** AX, CB, DC, DS, JC, MC, VI.

HOLIDAY INN EXPRESS HOTEL & SUITES   *Book at aaa.com*   Phone: (920)303-1300

▼▼▼▼

Small-scale Hotel

5/1-8/31	1P: $109-$209	2P: $119-$229	XP: $10	F18
1/1-3/31	1P: $95-$125	2P: $105-$135	XP: $5	F18
4/1-4/30 & 9/1-12/31	1P: $75-$110	2P: $99-$125	XP: $5	F18

Location: US 41, exit 119, 0.4 mi sw of jct SR 21. Located in a commercial area. 2251 Westowne Ave 54904. Fax: 920/303-9330. **Facility:** 68 units. 66 one-bedroom standard units, some with whirlpools. 2 two-bedroom suites ($125-$250) with whirlpools. 3 stories, interior corridors. *Bath:* combo or shower only. **Parking:** on-site. **Terms:** [ECP] meal plan available. **Amenities:** voice mail, irons, hair dryers. *Some:* high-speed Internet. **Pool(s):** heated indoor. **Leisure Activities:** whirlpool, exercise room. *Fee:* game room. **Guest Services:** complimentary evening beverages: Mon-Thurs, valet and coin laundry, area transportation. **Business Services:** meeting rooms. **Cards:** AX, CB, DC, DS, MC, VI.

SOME UNITS

(ASK) (SD) [icons] / (X) /

OSHKOSH TRAVELODGE   *Book at aaa.com*   Phone: (920)233-4300

(AAA) (SAVE)

▼▼▼

Motel

6/1-10/31 [CP]	1P: $42-$53	2P: $53-$59
11/1-3/31 [CP]	1P: $42-$46	2P: $46-$53
4/1-5/31 [CP]	1P: $42-$46	2P: $42-$53

Location: US 41, exit 117, just sw. Located in a commercial area. 1015 S Washburn St 54904. Fax: 920/233-4488. **Facility:** 93 one-bedroom standard units. 2 stories (no elevator), exterior corridors. *Bath:* shower only. **Parking:** on-site. **Terms:** weekly rates available, package plans, small pets only ($25 deposit, with prior approval). **Amenities:** hair dryers. **Pool(s):** small heated outdoor. **Guest Services:** coin laundry. **Cards:** AX, CB, DC, DS, MC, VI. **Special Amenities:** free continental breakfast and free local telephone calls.

SOME UNITS

(SD) [icons] / (X) (VCR) (DATA PORT) [icons] /
FEE

PARK PLAZA HOTEL & CONVENTION CENTER   *Book at aaa.com*   Phone: (920)231-5000

(AAA) (SAVE)

▼▼▼ ▼▼▼ ▼▼▼

Small-scale Hotel

6/1-9/30	1P: $79-$129	2P: $79-$129	XP: $10	F16
4/1-5/31 & 10/1-3/31	1P: $69-$99	2P: $69-$99	XP: $10	F16

Location: On shore of Fox River; downtown. 1 N Main St 54901. Fax: 920/231-6706. **Facility:** 179 one-bedroom standard units. 8 stories, interior corridors. **Parking:** on-site. **Terms:** weekly rates available. **Dining:** 6:30 am-2 & 5-10 pm, cocktails. **Pool(s):** heated indoor. **Leisure Activities:** whirlpool, boat dock, limited exercise equipment. *Fee:* game room. **Guest Services:** valet laundry. **Business Services:** conference facilities, business center. **Cards:** AX, DC, DS, MC, VI. **Special Amenities:** free expanded continental breakfast and free local telephone calls.

SOME UNITS

(SD) [icons] / (X) (VCR) [icons] /
FEE FEE FEE

——— WHERE TO DINE ———

FRATELLO'S RESTAURANT & FOX RIVER BREWING COMPANY   Lunch: $6-$12   Dinner: $7-$20   Phone: 920/232-2337

▼▼ ▼▼

American

Location: US 41, exit 119 (Omro Rd), 1 mi e on SR 21. 1501 Arboretum Dr 54901. **Hours:** 11 am-10 pm, Fri & Sat-11 pm, Sun-9 pm. Closed: 12/25. **Reservations:** accepted. **Features:** Nine microbrews are crafted on the premises of this restaurant on the Fox River. Seasonal boat docking and patio dining are available. Menu selections include gourmet pizza, pasta, burgers and a few steak and seafood entrees. Casual dress; cocktails. **Parking:** on-site. **Cards:** AX, MC, VI.

(LM) (Y) (X)

FRIAR TUCK'S   Lunch: $6-$8   Dinner: $6-$8   Phone: 920/231-9555

▼▼

American

Location: US 41, exit 116 (SR 44), 0.4 mi e. 1651 W South Park Ave 54903. **Hours:** 11 am-10 pm, Fri & Sat-11 pm. Closed major holidays. **Features:** "Ye hearty" sandwiches are prepared on a choice of many fresh breads baked in house. Daily homemade soup also are popular. All appetizers are prepared in the deep "friar." Servers are dressed in brown monks' garb. Casual dress; cocktails. **Parking:** on-site. **Cards:** AX, MC, VI.

(Y) (X)

LARA'S TORTILLA FLATS   Lunch: $4-$8   Dinner: $6-$14   Phone: 920/233-4440

▼▼ ▼▼

Northern Mexican

Location: Center. 715 N Main St 54901. **Hours:** 11 am-10 pm. Closed major holidays; also Sun. **Reservations:** accepted. **Features:** Delicious food is made from scratch with fresh ingredients and served with complimentary chips and a choice of salsa. Notable are the daily specials and traditional desserts, such as cookies and caramel, cinnamon chips and ice cream flower. The service staff is attentive. Casual dress; cocktails. **Parking:** on-site. **Cards:** AX, DC, DS, MC, VI.

(Y) (X)

OSSEO pop. 1,669

——— WHERE TO STAY ———

SUPER 8 MOTEL   Phone: 715/597-5000

(AAA) (SAVE)

▼▼ ▼▼

Motel

All Year	1P: $59-$150	2P: $64-$155	XP: $5	F12

Location: I-94, exit 88 (US 10), just se. 50663 Oak Grove Rd 54758. Fax: 715/597-5555. **Facility:** 53 units. 50 one- and 3 two-bedroom standard units, some with whirlpools. 3 stories, interior corridors. *Bath:* combo or shower only. **Parking:** on-site, winter plug-ins. **Terms:** check-in 4 pm. **Pool(s):** heated indoor. **Leisure Activities:** sauna, whirlpool. **Guest Services:** coin laundry. **Business Services:** meeting rooms, administrative services (fee). **Cards:** AX, CB, DC, DS, MC, VI. **Special Amenities:** free continental breakfast and free local telephone calls.

SOME UNITS

[icons] / (X) [icons] /

——— WHERE TO DINE ———

NORSKE NOOK RESTAURANT & BAKERY   Lunch: $3-$11   Dinner: $3-$11   Phone: 715/597-3069

(AAA)

▼▼ ▼▼

Norwegian

Location: I-94, exit 88 (US 10), 0.8 mi w. 207 W 7th St 54758. **Hours:** 5:30 am-10 pm, Sun from 8 am. **Features:** This quaint yet renown restaurant serves homemade Norwegian dishes in addition to sandwiches and breakfast. On-premise bakery produces fresh bread and an excellent selection of pies. Menus change seasonally and includes lefse specialties. Two locations downtown. Casual dress. **Parking:** street. **Cards:** DS, MC, VI.

(X)

PEPIN pop. 878

──── WHERE TO STAY ────

LAKE PEPIN INN
Motel

Phone: 715/442-5400
All Year   1P: $60-$70   2P: $60-$70   XP: $10   D
Location: On SR 35; center. 311 3rd St 54759 (PO Box 301). **Facility:** 7 one-bedroom standard units, some with whirlpools. 1 story, exterior corridors. **Parking:** on-site, winter plug-ins. **Terms:** check-in 4 pm, 3 day cancellation notice-fee imposed. **Guest Services:** gift shop. **Cards:** DS, MC, VI.

──── WHERE TO DINE ────

HARBOR VIEW CAFE
American

Lunch: $10-$20   **Dinner:** $10-$20   **Phone:** 715/442-3893
Location: Just w of SR 35 on Lake Pepin; center. 100 1st St 54759. **Hours:** Open 4/1-11/13 & 3/12-3/31; 11 am-2:30 & 5-9 pm, Sun noon-7:30 pm. Closed: Easter; also Tues & Wed, Mon 3/15-9/6, Thurs 10/14-11/13. **Features:** Creative cuisine made with fresh ingredients and a garlic influence make this restaurant unique in the area. The ambience is highlighted by the historic feel and location on the Mississippi River. Casual dress; cocktails. **Parking:** street.

PEWAUKEE —See Milwaukee p. 598.

PHILLIPS pop. 1,675

──── WHERE TO STAY ────

SUPER 8 MOTEL   *Book at aaa.com*
Small-scale Hotel

Phone: (715)339-2898
All Year   1P: $45-$60   2P: $50-$65   XP: $5   F12
Location: 0.6 mi s on SR 13. Located in a semi-rural area. 726 S Lake Ave 54555. Fax: 715/339-2887. **Facility:** 32 one-bedroom standard units. 2 stories (no elevator), interior corridors. **Parking:** on-site, winter plug-ins. **Terms:** [CP] meal plan available, pets (in smoking units). **Leisure Activities:** whirlpool, snowmobiling. **Cards:** AX, DC, DS, MC, VI.

SOME UNITS

──── WHERE TO DINE ────

BONNIE'S DINER
American

Lunch: $3-$6   **Phone:** 715/339-3404
Location: On SR 13; downtown. 126 S Lake Ave 54555. **Hours:** 5 am-2 pm. Closed: 1/1, 11/25, 12/25. **Features:** The simple, coffee shop-type restaurant is known for its tasty homemade food. Service is friendly, as are the locals who frequent the diner. Breakfast is served all day. Try one of the great pies. Casual dress. **Parking:** on-site.

PLATTEVILLE pop. 9,989

──── WHERE TO STAY ────

COUNTRY INN BY CARLSON   *Book at aaa.com*
Small-scale Hotel

Phone: (608)348-7373
All Year   1P: $65-$114   2P: $71-$120   XP: $6   F18
Location: Jct US 151 and SR 80/81. 630 S Water St 53818. Fax: 608/348-4600. **Facility:** 49 units. 48 one-bedroom standard units, some with whirlpools. 1 one-bedroom suite with whirlpool. 2 stories (no elevator), interior corridors. **Parking:** on-site. **Terms:** [ECP] meal plan available. **Amenities:** irons, hair dryers. **Pool(s):** small heated indoor. **Leisure Activities:** whirlpool. **Guest Services:** coin laundry. **Business Services:** meeting rooms. **Cards:** AX, DC, DS, MC, VI. *(See color ad starting on p 580)*

SOME UNITS

MOUND VIEW INN
Small-scale Hotel

Phone: (608)348-9518
4/1-10/31   1P: $45-$59   2P: $55-$70   XP: $5   F12
11/1-3/31   1P: $40-$50   2P: $50-$65   XP: $5   F12
Location: On US 151, 2 mi n of jct SR 80/81 N. 1755 E Hwy 151 53818. Fax: 608/348-7207. **Facility:** 32 one-bedroom standard units, some with whirlpools. 2 stories, interior corridors. **Parking:** on-site, winter plug-ins. **Terms:** cancellation fee imposed, pets ($20 deposit). **Leisure Activities:** whirlpool, limited exercise equipment. **Fee:** miniature golf. **Guest Services:** valet laundry. **Cards:** AX, DC, MC, VI.

SOME UNITS
FEE

SUPER 8 MOTEL   *Book at aaa.com*
Small-scale Hotel

Phone: (608)348-8800
All Year   1P: $47-$69   2P: $58-$90   XP: $6   F12
Location: Jct US 151 and SR 80. 100 Hwy 80/81 S 53818 (PO Box 413). Fax: 608/348-7233. **Facility:** 72 one-bedroom standard units, some with whirlpools. 2 stories, interior corridors. **Parking:** on-site, winter plug-ins. **Terms:** pets ($10 fee). **Amenities:** *Some:* irons, hair dryers. **Leisure Activities:** whirlpool, steamroom, gazebo. **Guest Services:** valet and coin laundry. **Cards:** AX, DC, DS, MC, VI. **Special Amenities:** free continental breakfast and free local telephone calls.

SOME UNITS
FEE

——— WHERE TO DINE ———

ARTHUR HOUSE
American

Dinner: $8-$16   **Phone:** 608-348-7899

Location: N on SR 80 to Arthur; located on left side of SR 80 in Arthur. 9315 Hwy 80 N 53818. **Hours:** 4:30 pm-9 pm, Fri & Sat-10 pm, Sun 10 am-2 pm. Closed: 12/24, 12/25; also Mon & Tues. **Reservations:** suggested. **Features:** The family-owned restaurant features nightly specials and a children's menu. Prime rib, roast duckling, pond-raised catfish and roast pork loin are among menu options. Nationally known comedy acts provide weekend entertainment. Casual dress; cocktails. **Parking:** on-site. **Cards:** MC, VI.

THE TIMBERS RESTAURANT AND LOUNGE
American

Lunch: $6-$9   **Dinner:** $9-$20   **Phone:** 608-348-2406

Location: On US 151 at jct of SR 80/81. 670 Ellen St 53818. **Hours:** 11 am-1:30 & 5-9 pm, Fri 11 am-1:30 & 3-10 pm, Sat 5 pm-10 pm, Sun 10:30 am-1:30 & 4-8 pm. Closed: 12/24, 12/25. **Reservations:** suggested. **Features:** This restaurant is known for its unique organ/grand piano shows that occur two times nightly. The dining rooms are airy and flowing, and perimeter windows look into the surrounding trees. The lunch menu is casual, while the dinner menu features such entrees as fresh fish, beef, veal, pork and a few vegetarian and pasta dishes. Dressy casual; cocktails. **Parking:** on-site. **Cards:** AX, DS, MC, VI.

PLEASANT PRAIRIE pop. 16,136

——— WHERE TO STAY ———

BAYMONT INN KENOSHA-PLEASANT PRAIRIE   *Book at aaa.com*
(AAA) (SAVE)
Small-scale Hotel

Phone: (262)857-7911

All Year   1P: $53-$89   2P: $58-$98

Location: I-94, exit 344 (SR 50), just e. 7540 118th Ave 53158. Fax: 262/857-2370. **Facility:** 92 one-bedroom standard units. 2 stories (no elevator), interior corridors. **Parking:** on-site, winter plug-ins. **Terms:** [ECP] meal plan available, small pets only (in smoking units). **Amenities:** video games (fee), voice mail, irons, hair dryers. **Guest Services:** valet laundry. **Cards:** AX, CB, DC, DS, MC, VI. **Special Amenities:** free local telephone calls and free newspaper.** *(See color ad p 597)*

SOME UNITS

HAWTHORN SUITES LTD HOTEL   *Book at aaa.com*
(AAA) (SAVE)
Small-scale Hotel

Phone: (262)942-6000

All Year [BP]   1P: $89-$159   2P: $89-$159

Location: I-94, exit 344 (SR 50), 1.5 mi e, then 0.3 mi s. 7887 94th Ave 53158. Fax: 262/942-6100. **Facility:** 81 one-bedroom standard units, some with efficiencies. 3 stories, interior corridors. *Bath:* combo or shower only. **Parking:** on-site. **Terms:** 2 night minimum stay - weekends, cancellation fee imposed, package plans, pets ($50-$100 fee, with prior approval). **Amenities:** video library (fee), dual phone lines, voice mail, irons, hair dryers. **Pool(s):** heated indoor. **Leisure Activities:** whirlpool, limited exercise equipment. **Guest Services:** complimentary evening beverages: Mon-Thurs, valet and coin laundry. **Business Services:** meeting rooms, administrative services (fee). **Cards:** AX, CB, DC, DS, MC, VI.

SOME UNITS
FEE

RADISSON HOTEL & CONFERENCE CENTER KENOSHA   *Book at aaa.com*
Large-scale Hotel

Phone: (262)857-3377

All Year   1P: $109-$119   2P: $109-$119   XP: $10   F

Location: I-94, exit 347 (SR 165), just s on east frontage road. 11800 108th St 53158. Fax: 262/857-3383. **Facility:** 120 units. 102 one-bedroom standard units, some with whirlpools. 18 one-bedroom suites ($149-$169). 6 stories, interior corridors. *Bath:* combo or shower only. **Parking:** on-site. **Amenities:** video games (fee), dual phone lines, voice mail, irons, hair dryers. **Pool(s):** small heated indoor. **Leisure Activities:** whirlpool, exercise room. **Guest Services:** valet laundry, area transportation. **Business Services:** conference facilities, PC. **Cards:** AX, DC, DS, MC, VI. *(See color ad p 583)*

SOME UNITS

PLOVER pop. 10,520

——— WHERE TO STAY ———

AMERICINN-PLOVER/STEVENS POINT   *Book at aaa.com*
(AAA) (SAVE)
Small-scale Hotel

Phone: (715)342-1244

All Year   1P: $69-$105   2P: $69-$105   XP: $5   F12

Location: I-39, exit 153 (CR B), just w. 1501 American Dr 54467. Fax: 715/342-1325. **Facility:** 65 one-bedroom standard units, some with whirlpools. 2 stories (no elevator), interior corridors. *Bath:* combo or shower only. **Parking:** on-site, winter plug-ins. **Terms:** [ECP] meal plan available. **Amenities:** voice mail, hair dryers. *Some:* irons. **Pool(s):** heated indoor. **Leisure Activities:** sauna, whirlpool, exercise room. **Business Services:** meeting rooms. **Cards:** AX, DS, MC, VI. **Special Amenities:** free local telephone calls and free newspaper.** *(See color ad p 576)*

SOME UNITS

——— WHERE TO DINE ———

SKY CLUB
American

Dinner: $9-$23   **Phone:** 715-341-4000

Location: On US 51 business route. 2202 Post Rd 54467. **Hours:** 4 pm-10 pm, Fri & Sat-10:30 pm, Sun 10 am-10 pm. Closed major holidays; also 12/24; also Mon. **Reservations:** accepted. **Features:** This well-established restaurant has been an area fixture since 1961. The restaurant is known for home-style cooking, and guests don't leave hungry! An extensive salad bar is set up at all times. Bread, soup, salad dressings and cheesecakes are made in-house. USDA choice steaks are served sizzling, and there's a good selection of fresh seafood. Casual dress; cocktails. **Parking:** on-site. **Cards:** AX, DC, DS, MC, VI.

PLYMOUTH pop. 7,781

──────── WHERE TO STAY ────────

AMERICINN OF PLYMOUTH   *Book at aaa.com*   Phone: 920/892-2669
◆◆◆ ◆◆◆   All Year   1P: $80-$90   2P: $80-$90
           Location: On Business Rt 23, 1 mi w of jct SR 57. 1708 Eastern Ave 53073. Fax: 920/892-7878. Facility: 38 units.
Small-scale Hotel   37 one-bedroom standard units. 1 one-bedroom suite. 2 stories (no elevator), interior corridors. Bath: combo
           or shower only. Parking: on-site, winter plug-ins. Terms: 2-5 night minimum stay - seasonal, [ECP] meal plan
available. Amenities: hair dryers. Pool(s): small heated indoor. Leisure Activities: sauna, whirlpool. Guest Services: valet
laundry. Business Services: meeting rooms. Cards: AX, DC, DS, MC, VI. *(See color ad p 576)*
                                                                                              SOME UNITS
                                    (ASK) (SD) (TI+) (&) (⚫) (✦) (▣) / (✕) (⬛) (▥) /

──────── *The following lodging was either not evaluated or did not* ────────
meet AAA rating requirements but is listed for your information only.

BAYMONT INN & SUITES PLYMOUTH   Phone: 920/893-6781
  (fyi)   Under construction, scheduled to open May 2004. Location: On SR 57. 678 Walton Dr 53073.
Small-scale Hotel   Fax: 920/893-0986.

PORTAGE pop. 9,728

──────── WHERE TO STAY ────────

BEST WESTERN RESORT & CONFERENCE CENTER   *Book at aaa.com*   Phone: (608)742-2200
◆◆◆ ◆◆◆   All Year   1P: $58-$95   2P: $58-$95
           Location: I-39, exit 92, then s 0.5 mi w. 2701 S CR CX 53901. Fax: 608/742-2200. Facility: 100 units. 95 one-
Small-scale Hotel   bedroom standard units, some with whirlpools. 5 one-bedroom suites ($75-$195) with whirlpools. 5 stories,
           interior corridors. Parking: on-site. Terms: [CP] meal plan available. Amenities: irons, hair dryers. Pool(s):
small heated indoor. Leisure Activities: sauna, whirlpool, limited exercise equipment. Fee: game room. Guest Services: coin
laundry. Business Services: meeting rooms. Cards: AX, DC, DS, MC, VI.
                                                                                              SOME UNITS
                              (ASK) (SD) (TI+) (Y) (⚫) (✕) (✦) (DATA PORT) (▣) / (✕) (⬛) (▥) /

BREESE WAY BED AND BREAKFAST   Phone: (608)742-5281
◆◆◆◆   All Year [BP]   1P: $75-$85   2P: $75-$85
           Location: I-39, exit 92, 2.2 mi s. 816 MacFarlane Rd 53901. Facility: Said to have been built by Wisconsin's first
Bed & Breakfast   secretary of state, this 1880 Italianate Victorian home offers well-appointed rooms. Smoke free premises. 4
           one-bedroom standard units. 2 stories (no elevator), interior corridors. Bath: combo or shower only. Parking:
on-site. Terms: check-in 4 pm, age restrictions may apply, 5 day cancellation notice. Amenities: video library, hair dryers. Guest
Services: complimentary evening beverages, valet laundry.
                                                                                              SOME UNITS
                                            (✕) (☎) / (W) (VCR) (DATA PORT) /

COMFORT SUITES   *Book at aaa.com*   Phone: (608)745-4717
◆◆◆ ◆◆◆   All Year [ECP]   1P: $79-$119   2P: $79-$119   XP: $8   F18
           Location: I-90/94, exit 108A (SR 78). N5780 Kinney Rd 53901. Fax: 608/745-1231. Facility: 83 units. 72 one-
Small-scale Hotel   bedroom standard units, some with whirlpools. 11 one-bedroom suites, some with whirlpools. 3 stories, inte-
           rior corridors. Bath: combo or shower only. Parking: on-site. Terms: check-in 4 pm, 14 day cancellation
notice. Amenities: dual phone lines. Pool(s): heated indoor. Leisure Activities: whirlpools, limited exercise equipment. Fee:
game room. Guest Services: coin laundry. Business Services: meeting rooms. Cards: AX, DC, DS, MC, VI.
                                                                                              SOME UNITS
                         (ASK) (SD) (TI+) (&M) (&) (⚫) (✕) (✦) (DATA PORT) (⬛) (▥) (▣) / (✕) /

SUPER 8 MOTEL-PORTAGE   *Book at aaa.com*   Phone: (608)742-8330
◆◆◆ ◆◆◆   5/28-9/5 [CP]   1P: $59-$89   2P: $59-$89   XP: $5   F12
           9/6-12/31 [CP]   1P: $51-$71   2P: $51-$71   XP: $5   F12
Small-scale Hotel   4/1-5/27 & 1/1-3/31 [CP]   1P: $49-$59   2P: $49-$59   XP: $5   F12
           Location: I-39, exit 92, just s. 3000 New Pinery 53901. Fax: 608/745-0167. Facility: 61 one-bedroom standard
units. 2 stories (no elevator), interior corridors. Parking: on-site, winter plug-ins. Terms: pets ($10 fee). Amenities: safes (fee).
Guest Services: coin laundry. Business Services: meeting rooms. Cards: AX, CB, DC, DS, MC, VI.
                                                                                              SOME UNITS
                              (ASK) (SD) (TI+) (⊘) (✦) (DATA PORT) / (✕) (⬛) (▥) /
                                        FEE

──────── WHERE TO DINE ────────

BLANKENHAUS   Dinner: $7-$17   Phone: 608/742-7555
◆◆ ◆◆   Location: 1 mi se on US 51. 1223 E Wisconsin Ave 53901. Hours: 4 pm-10 pm, Sun from 10:30 am. Closed:
           1/1, 11/25, 12/25; also Mon & for dinner 12/24. Reservations: suggested. Features: Well-coordinated
American   Bavarian decor distinguishes the big, mom-and-pop-type restaurant, a local favorite for traditional surf and
           turf fare. Steak and barbecue ribs, in addition to the Friday fish fry, are popular choices. Service is friendly
and attentive. Casual dress; cocktails. Parking: on-site. Cards: AX, DS, MC, VI.
                                                                                              (Y) (✕)

PORT WASHINGTON —*See Milwaukee p. 599.*

PRAIRIE DU CHIEN pop. 6,018

——— **WHERE TO STAY** ———

AMERICINN LODGE & SUITES   *Book at aaa.com*   **Phone:** (608)326-7878
4/1-11/1   1P: $99-$165   2P: $99-$165   XP: $6   F
11/2-3/31   1P: $90-$155   2P: $90-$155   XP: $6   F
Small-scale Hotel   **Location:** On US 18 W, at east end of Mississippi River Bridge. 130 S Main St 53821. **Fax:** 608/326-7879. **Facility:** 44 units. 40 one-bedroom standard units, some with whirlpools. 4 one-bedroom suites, some with whirlpools. 2 stories, interior corridors. *Bath:* combo or shower only. **Parking:** on-site. **Amenities:** video library, dual phone lines, irons, hair dryers. **Pool(s):** small heated indoor. **Leisure Activities:** whirlpool, limited exercise equipment. **Guest Services:** coin laundry. **Business Services:** meeting rooms. **Cards:** AX, DC, DS, MC, VI. *(See color ad p 576)*

SOME UNITS

BEST WESTERN QUIET HOUSE & SUITES   *Book at aaa.com*   **Phone:** 608/326-4777
5/16-10/31 [CP]   1P: $89-$119   2P: $99-$129   XP: $10   F12
4/1-5/15 & 11/1-3/31 [CP]   1P: $89-$99   2P: $99-$109   XP: $10   F12
Small-scale Hotel   **Location:** On US 18, 1.9 mi e of jct SR 27 N. US 18 and SR 35 53821. **Fax:** 608/326-4787. **Facility:** 42 units. 40 one-bedroom standard units, some with whirlpools. 2 one-bedroom suites, some with whirlpools. 2 stories, interior/exterior corridors. **Parking:** on-site, winter plug-ins. **Terms:** package plans - seasonal, pets ($15 extra charge). **Amenities:** irons, hair dryers. **Pool(s):** small heated indoor. **Leisure Activities:** whirlpool, limited exercise equipment. **Business Services:** meeting rooms. **Cards:** AX, CB, DC, DS, MC, VI. **Special Amenities:** free continental breakfast and free newspaper. *(See color ad p 579)*

SOME UNITS

FEE

BRIDGEPORT INN   **Phone:** 608/326-6082
4/1-10/31   1P: $81-$121   2P: $89-$129   XP: $8   F13
11/1-3/31   1P: $79-$120   2P: $87-$125   XP: $8   F13
Small-scale Hotel   **Location:** On US 18, 2.2 mi e of jct SR 27 N. Hwy 18, 35 & 60 S 53821 (PO Box 436). **Fax:** 608/326-2800. **Facility:** 50 one-bedroom standard units, some with whirlpools. 2 stories, interior corridors. **Parking:** on-site, winter plug-ins. **Terms:** [CP] meal plan available, package plans, pets ($15 extra charge). **Amenities:** hair dryers. *Some:* DVD players. **Pool(s):** small heated indoor. **Leisure Activities:** whirlpool, exercise room. **Guest Services:** valet laundry. **Business Services:** meeting rooms. **Cards:** AX, DC, DS, MC, VI. *(See color ad below)*

SOME UNITS

FEE

BRISBOIS MOTOR INN   **Phone:** (608)326-8404
All Year [CP]   1P: $49-$84   2P: $59-$89   XP: $7   F
Motel   **Location:** On SR 35 N, 0.5 mi n of jct US 18/SR 35 S and 27 N. 533 N Marquette Rd 53821 (PO Box 37). **Fax:** 608/326-0001. **Facility:** 46 units. 45 one-bedroom standard units. 1 one-bedroom suite with kitchen. 2 stories, interior/exterior corridors. *Bath:* combo or shower only. **Parking:** on-site, winter plug-ins. **Terms:** weekly rates available, pets ($7 extra charge). **Amenities:** *Some:* hair dryers. **Pool(s):** small heated outdoor. **Leisure Activities:** playground. **Business Services:** meeting rooms. **Cards:** AX, DC, DS, MC, VI. **Special Amenities:** free continental breakfast and free local telephone calls. *(See color ad p 615)*

SOME UNITS

FEE

COUNTRY INN & SUITES BY CARLSON   *Book at aaa.com*   Phone: (608)326-5700

(AAA) (SAVE)	4/1-10/31 [CP]	1P: $129-$179	2P: $129-$179	XP: $6	F18
▼▼▼▼▼	11/1-3/31 [CP]	1P: $89-$139	2P: $89-$139	XP: $6	F18

Small-scale Hotel   **Location:** On SR 35, 2 mi n of jct US 18/SR 35 S and 27 N. 1801 Cabela's Ln 53821. Fax: 608/326-5725. **Facility:** 64 units. 56 one-bedroom standard units, some with whirlpools. 8 one-bedroom suites ($99-$179). 3 stories, interior corridors. *Bath:* combo or shower only. **Parking:** on-site. **Amenities:** voice mail, irons, hair dryers. **Dining:** 7 am-9 pm, Fri & Sat-10 pm. **Pool(s):** heated indoor, wading. **Leisure Activities:** whirlpool, water-slide, exercise room. *Fee:* game room. **Guest Services:** valet and coin laundry. **Business Services:** meeting rooms. **Cards:** AX, CB, DC, DS, MC, VI. **Special Amenities:** free continental breakfast and free local telephone calls.
(See color ad starting on p 580 & below)

SOME UNITS

DELTA MOTEL   Phone: (608)326-4951

(AAA) (SAVE)	5/15-11/1 [CP]	1P: $37-$55	2P: $47-$79	XP: $10	F12
▼▼▼	11/2-3/31 [CP]	1P: $35-$45	2P: $45-$69	XP: $10	F12
Motel	4/1-5/14 [CP]	1P: $35-$45	2P: $43-$59	XP: $10	F12

Location: On US 18, 1.6 mi e of jct SR N. 1733 1/2 S Marquette Rd 53821. Fax: 608/326-6370. **Facility:** 16 one-bedroom standard units. 1 story, exterior corridors. **Parking:** on-site, winter plug-ins. **Terms:** 2 night minimum stay - most weekends in season. **Guest Services:** area transportation-Riverboat Casino. **Cards:** DS, MC, VI.
Special Amenities: free continental breakfast and free local telephone calls.

HOLIDAY MOTEL   Phone: 608/326-2448

▼▼▼	5/26-11/1	1P: $35-$55	2P: $45-$125	XP: $5	F
Motel	4/1-5/25 & 11/2-3/31	1P: $25-$45	2P: $30-$110	XP: $5	F

Location: On US 18, 1 mi e of jct SR 27 N. 1010 S Marquette Rd 53821. Fax: 608/326-8958. **Facility:** 18 one-bedroom standard units, some with whirlpools. 2 stories, exterior corridors. *Bath:* combo or shower only. **Parking:** on-site, winter plug-ins. **Terms:** cancellation fee imposed, weekly rates available, [CP] meal plan available. **Amenities:** *Some:* hair dryers. **Cards:** AX, CB, DC, DS, JC, MC, VI.

SOME UNITS

SUPER 8 MOTEL   Phone: 608/326-8777
(AAA) (SAVE)   All Year   1P: $65-$75   2P: $69-$79   XP: $10   F12
▼▼▼▼   **Location:** On US 18, 1.9 mi e of jct SR 27 N. 1930 S Marquette Rd 53821. **Fax:** 608/326-2935. **Facility:** 30 one-
bedroom standard units. 2 stories, interior/exterior corridors. **Parking:** on-site, winter plug-ins. **Terms:** small
pets only ($15 extra charge). **Cards:** AX, CB, DC, DS, MC, VI. **Special Amenities:** free local telephone
Small-scale Hotel calls and free newspaper.

SOME UNITS

WINDSOR PLACE INN   Phone: 608/326-7799
(AAA) (SAVE)   5/16-10/31   1P: $79-$109   2P: $89-$119   XP: $10   F12
▼▼▼▼   4/1-5/15 & 11/1-3/31   1P: $79-$89   2P: $89-$99   XP: $10   F12
Location: On US 18, 1.9 mi e of jct SR 27 N. 1936 S Marquette Rd 53821. **Fax:** 608/326-1010. **Facility:** Smoke free
premises. 34 one-bedroom standard units. 2 stories, interior corridors. **Parking:** on-site, winter plug-ins.
Small-scale Hotel **Terms:** package plans - seasonal. **Pool(s):** small heated indoor. **Leisure Activities:** whirlpool, limited exercise equipment. **Business Services:** fax. **Cards:** AX, CB, DC, DS, MC, VI. **Special Amenities:** free local
telephone calls and free newspaper.

SOME UNITS

——— **WHERE TO DINE** ———

FORT MULLIGAN'S GRILL PUB   **Lunch:** $4-$7   **Dinner:** $8-$15   Phone: 608/326-0639
▼   **Location:** Just n of US 18 W; downtown. 214 W Blackhawk 53821. **Hours:** 11 am-9 pm. Closed: 11/25, 12/24,
12/25 & Easter. **Reservations:** accepted. **Features:** Homemade appetizers, sandwiches, salads, pasta,
American   steaks, seafood and fajitas are served at the downtown eatery. Cocktails. **Parking:** on-site. **Cards:** DS,
MC, VI.

PRAIRIE DU SAC pop. 3,231

——— **WHERE TO DINE** ———

BLUE SPOON CREAMERY CAFE   **Lunch:** $7-$10   **Dinner:** $7-$10   Phone: 608/643-0837
▼   **Location:** Downtown. 550 Water St 53578. **Hours:** 6 am-8 pm, Sat from 7 am. Closed major holidays; also
Sun. **Features:** The cozy cafe is adorned with granite tables, wood floors and lots of country charm.
American   Guests can enjoy wonderful homemade soups and delicious sandwiches made from carved-to-order
delicatessen meats and freshly baked breads. For a sweet treat, indulge in smooth, freshly churned
custard or homemade cheesecake. Seasonal dining on the patio lends to panoramic views overlooking the Wisconsin River.
Casual dress; beer & wine only. **Parking:** on-site. **Cards:** AX, MC, VI.

PRESCOTT pop. 3,764

——— **WHERE TO DINE** ———

STEAMBOAT INN   **Dinner:** $13-$19   Phone: 651/480-8222
▼▼ ▼▼   **Location:** On US 10 at east end of St. Croix River Bridge; downtown. 307 Lake St N 54021. **Hours:** 4:30 pm-9 pm,
American   Sun from 10 am; hours may vary 10/1-3/31. Closed: 12/24, 12/25; also Mon & Tues during off season.
Reservations: accepted. **Features:** The well-established restaurant is on the shore of the St. Croix River
at the Minnesota border. Large windows in the dining room and the seasonal outdoor seating area offer
close-up views. A dock caters to those who arrive by boat. The menu has a selection of surf and turf specialties, along with
the traditional Wisconsin Friday night fish fry and Saturday night prime rib. Casual dress; cocktails. **Parking:** on-site.
Cards: AX, DC, DS, MC, VI.

PRESQUE ISLE

——— **WHERE TO DINE** ———

——— *The following restaurant has not been evaluated by AAA* ———
but is listed for your information only.

THE OUTPOST CAFE   Phone: 715/686-2193
(fyi)   Not evaluated. **Location:** Center. 8279 Main St 54557. **Features:** Located in town, this family restaurant with
it's northwoods decor has a number of tables with a view of the countryside.

RACINE pop. 81,855

——— **WHERE TO STAY** ———

COMFORT INN RACINE   *Book at aaa.com*   Phone: (262)886-6055
(AAA) (SAVE)   All Year [ECP]   1P: $59-$199   2P: $69-$199   XP: $6   F17
▼▼ ▼▼   **Location:** I-94, exit 333, 4.1 mi e on SR 20. Located in a commercial area. 1154 Prairie Dr 53406. **Fax:** 262/886-6117.
Facility: 80 one-bedroom standard units. 2 stories (no elevator); interior corridors. **Parking:** on-site, winter
plug-ins. **Amenities:** voice mail, irons, hair dryers. **Leisure Activities:** whirlpool, limited exercise equipment.
Small-scale Hotel **Guest Services:** valet and coin laundry. **Business Services:** meeting rooms. **Cards:** AX, CB, DC, DS, JC,
MC, VI. **Special Amenities:** free expanded continental breakfast and free local telephone calls.

SOME UNITS

FEE FEE

FAIRFIELD INN BY MARRIOTT   *Book at aaa.com*   Phone: 262/886-5000

Property failed to provide current rates

Small-scale Hotel   **Location:** I-94, exit 333, 4.5 mi e on SR 20. Located in a commercial area. 6421 Washington Ave 53406. **Fax:** 262/886-5000. **Facility:** 63 one-bedroom standard units. 3 stories, interior corridors. **Parking:** on-site, winter plug-ins. **Amenities:** irons. **Pool(s):** small heated indoor. **Leisure Activities:** whirlpool. **Guest Services:** valet laundry.

KNIGHTS INN   *Book at aaa.com*   Phone: 262/886-6667

Motel

All Year   1P: $50-$70   2P: $50-$70   XP: $6   F12

Location: I-94, exit 333, 4 mi e on SR 20. Located in a commercial area. 1149 Oakes Rd 53406. **Fax:** 262/886-6667. **Facility:** 104 one-bedroom standard units, some with whirlpools. 1 story, exterior corridors. **Parking:** on-site, winter plug-ins. **Terms:** weekly rates available, [CP] meal plan available. **Guest Services:** valet and coin laundry. **Business Services:** meeting rooms. **Cards:** AX, DC, DS, MC, VI. **Special Amenities:** free continental breakfast and free local telephone calls.

MICROTEL INN & SUITES   *Book at aaa.com*   Phone: (262)554-8855

Small-scale Hotel

6/15-9/15 [CP]   1P: $55-$63   2P: $65-$73   XP: $5   F18
4/1-6/14 & 9/16-3/31 [CP]   1P: $52-$60   2P: $62-$70   XP: $5   F18

Location: On SR 11, 0.5 mi e of jct SR 31. 5419 Durand Ave 53406. **Fax:** 262/554-5005. **Facility:** 79 one-bedroom standard units. 2 stories, interior corridors. *Bath:* combo or shower only. **Parking:** on-site, winter plug-ins. **Terms:** 14 day cancellation notice, pets ($10 extra charge). **Leisure Activities:** whirlpool, limited exercise equipment. **Guest Services:** valet laundry. **Business Services:** meeting rooms, fax (fee). **Cards:** AX, CB, DC, DS, JC, MC, VI. **Special Amenities: free continental breakfast and free local telephone calls.**

RACINE MARRIOTT HOTEL   *Book at aaa.com*   Phone: (262)886-6100

Large-scale Hotel

All Year   1P: $150   2P: $150

Location: I-94, exit 333, 4 mi e on SR 20. Located in a commercial area. 7111 Washington Ave 53406. **Fax:** 262/886-1048. **Facility:** 222 one-bedroom standard units. 5 stories, interior corridors. **Parking:** on-site. **Terms:** small pets only. **Amenities:** voice mail, irons, hair dryers. **Pool(s):** heated indoor. **Leisure Activities:** whirlpool, limited exercise equipment. **Guest Services:** valet laundry. **Business Services:** meeting rooms, business center. **Cards:** AX, DC, DS, MC, VI.

RADISSON INN HARBOUR WALK   *Book at aaa.com*   Phone: (262)632-7777

Small-scale Hotel

5/24-10/31   1P: $129-$229   2P: $129-$229   XP: $10   F18
4/1-5/23 & 11/1-3/31   1P: $119-$199   2P: $119-$199   XP: $10   F18

Location: Just e of Lake Ave; center. Located harborside. 223 Gaslight Cir 53403. **Fax:** 262/632-7334. **Facility:** 121 units. 117 one-bedroom standard units, some with kitchens and/or whirlpools. 4 one-bedroom suites with kitchens. 3 stories, interior corridors. *Bath:* combo or shower only. **Parking:** on-site (fee). **Terms:** [AP] meal plan available. **Amenities:** dual phone lines, voice mail, irons, hair dryers. **Pool(s):** small heated indoor. **Leisure Activities:** whirlpool, limited exercise equipment. **Guest Services:** valet and coin laundry, area transportation. **Business Services:** meeting rooms, business center. **Cards:** AX, CB, DC, DS, JC, MC, VI. *(See color ad p 583)*

SUPER 8-RACINE   *Book at aaa.com*   Phone: (262)884-0486

Small-scale Hotel

6/1-8/31   1P: $55-$70   2P: $60-$70   XP: $5   F17
4/1-5/31 & 9/1-3/31   1P: $50-$55   2P: $55-$60   XP: $5   F17

Location: I-94, exit 333, 4 mi e on SR 20. Located in a commercial area. 7141 Kinzie Ave 53406. **Fax:** 262/884-0486. **Facility:** 61 one-bedroom standard units. 3 stories, interior corridors. *Bath:* combo or shower only. **Parking:** on-site, winter plug-ins. **Terms:** [ECP] meal plan available. **Amenities:** hair dryers. **Guest Services:** valet laundry. **Cards:** AX, DC, DS, MC, VI.

——— WHERE TO DINE ———

CORNER HOUSE   Dinner: $9-$24   Phone: 262/637-1295

American

Location: On SR 20, 0.3 mi w of jct SR 32. 1521 Washington Ave 53403. **Hours:** 5 pm-10 pm, Fri & Sat-11 pm, Sun 4 pm-9 pm. **Closed:** 7/4, 9/6; also 12/24 & Super Bowl Sun. **Reservations:** suggested, weekends. **Features:** Specializing in succulent prime rib servings from petit to large, the restaurant has been owned and operated by the same family since 1945. The Friday night fish fry is popular. Most meals are geared toward hearty appetites, but an extensive lighter fare menu is also available. A complete list of foreign and domestic wines is offered. Casual dress; cocktails. **Parking:** on-site. **Cards:** AX, CB, DC, DS, MC, VI.

THE SUMMIT   Lunch: $6-$10   Dinner: $9-$18   Phone: 262/886-9866

American

Location: I-94, exit 333, 4.4 mi e on SR 20. 6825 Washington Ave 53406. **Hours:** 11:30 am-2 & 5-9 pm, Fri 11:30 am-2 & 4:30-10 pm, Sat 5 pm-10 pm, Sun 10 am-1:30 & 4-8 pm. **Closed:** 7/4; also 12/24 for dinner. **Reservations:** suggested. **Features:** The casual restaurant is a local favorite for traditionally prepared seafood, pasta, steak, chicken and veal. Daily specials and homemade desserts don't disappoint. Stop by on Friday night for the all-you-can-eat fish fry. Dressy casual; cocktails. **Parking:** on-site. **Cards:** AX, CB, DC, DS, MC, VI.

REEDSBURG pop. 7,827

——— WHERE TO STAY ———

COPPER SPRINGS MOTEL
Phone: 608/524-4312

AAA SAVE

Motel

5/28-3/31	1P: $42-$58	2P: $48-$68	XP: $10
4/1-5/27	1P: $39-$48	2P: $44-$48	XP: $10

Location: 2 mi e on SR 23 and 33. E7278 Hwy 23 & 33 53959. Fax: 608/524-9767. **Facility:** Smoke free premises. 16 one-bedroom standard units. 1 story, exterior corridors. *Bath:* combo or shower only. **Parking:** on-site, winter plug-ins. **Terms:** 5 day cancellation notice, weekly rates available, pets (in designated units). **Leisure Activities:** picnic area, horseshoes. **Business Services:** fax (fee). **Cards:** DC, MC, VI.
Special Amenities: free local telephone calls and free newspaper.

SOME UNITS

VIKING SUPER 8
Phone: 608/524-2888

Small-scale Hotel

5/28-8/29	1P: $69-$79	2P: $74-$84	XP: $5 F12
4/1-5/27 & 8/30-3/31	1P: $64-$74	2P: $69-$79	XP: $5 F12

Location: 0.8 mi e on SR 23 and 33. 1470 E Main St 53959 (PO Box 350). Fax: 608/524-9658. **Facility:** 50 one-bedroom standard units, some with whirlpools. 3 stories (no elevator), interior corridors. **Parking:** on-site, winter plug-ins. **Terms:** [ECP] meal plan available. **Pool(s):** small heated indoor. **Leisure Activities:** whirlpool. **Guest Services:** *Fee:* tanning facility. **Business Services:** fax (fee). **Cards:** AX, CB, DC, DS, MC, VI.

SOME UNITS

VOYAGEUR INN & CONFERENCE CENTER
Phone: 608/524-6431

AAA SAVE

Small-scale Hotel

7/1-8/31	1P: $59-$99	2P: $67-$107	XP: $8 F16
4/1-6/30 & 9/1-3/31	1P: $49-$69	2P: $54-$94	XP: $8 F16

Location: 1 mi ne on CR H. 200 Viking Dr 53959 (PO Box 608). Fax: 608/524-0036. **Facility:** 72 one-bedroom standard units, some with whirlpools. 3 stories, interior corridors. **Parking:** on-site, winter plug-ins. **Amenities:** *Some:* hair dryers. **Dining:** Marty's Steakhouse, see separate listing. **Pool(s):** heated indoor. **Leisure Activities:** saunas, whirlpool, exercise room. *Fee:* game room. **Guest Services:** gift shop, complimentary evening beverages. **Business Services:** meeting rooms. **Cards:** AX, DC, DS, MC, VI.

SOME UNITS

——— WHERE TO DINE ———

MARTY'S STEAKHOUSE
Lunch: $4-$6   **Dinner:** $6-$20   Phone: 608/524-6431

American

Location: 1 mi ne on CR H; in Voyageur Inn & Conference Center. 200 Viking Dr 53959. **Hours:** 6:30 am-2 & 5-9 pm, Fri-10 pm, Sat 7 am-11:30 & 5-9 pm, Sun 7 am-2 & 5-9 pm. **Reservations:** accepted. **Features:** Soft music plays in the background in the relaxing dining room. The Friday night seafood buffet is popular, as are the weekly luncheon buffets which offer the guest a good value. Casual dress; cocktails. **Parking:** on-site. **Cards:** AX, DC, DS, MC, VI.

RHINELANDER pop. 7,735

——— WHERE TO STAY ———

AMERICINN OF RHINELANDER   *Book at aaa.com*
Phone: 715/369-9600

Small-scale Hotel

10/1-3/31	1P: $74-$99	2P: $74-$99	XP: $8 F
6/1-9/30	1P: $64-$89	2P: $64-$89	XP: $8 F
4/1-5/31	1P: $59-$84	2P: $59-$84	XP: $8 F

Location: On Business Rt US 8, 0.3 mi e of jct SR 47. Located in a commercial area. 648 W Kemp St 54501. Fax: 715/369-9613. **Facility:** 51 units. 50 one-bedroom standard units, some with whirlpools. 1 one-bedroom suite with whirlpool. 2 stories, interior corridors. *Bath:* combo or shower only. **Parking:** on-site, winter plug-ins. **Terms:** cancellation fee imposed, [ECP] meal plan available, pets (in smoking units). **Amenities:** irons, hair dryers. **Pool(s):** heated indoor. **Leisure Activities:** sauna, whirlpool, putting green, snowmobiling, exercise room. **Guest Services:** coin laundry. **Business Services:** meeting rooms. **Cards:** AX, DC, DS, MC, VI. *(See color ad p 576)*

SOME UNITS

BEST WESTERN CLARIDGE MOTOR INN   *Book at aaa.com*
Phone: (715)362-7100

Large-scale Hotel

All Year	1P: $79-$150	2P: $84-$160	XP: $5 F17

Location: On SR 17; center. 70 N Stevens St 54501. Fax: 715/362-3883. **Facility:** 80 units. 77 one-bedroom standard units. 3 one-bedroom suites with kitchens. 2-4 stories, interior corridors. **Parking:** on-site, winter plug-ins. **Terms:** pets ($10 fee, $25 deposit, in designated units). **Amenities:** voice mail, irons, hair dryers. **Dining:** 6:30 am-2 & 5-10 pm, Sat from 7 am, Sun 7 am-1:30 pm, cocktails. **Pool(s):** heated indoor. **Leisure Activities:** whirlpool, pool table, indoor recreational area, exercise room. *Fee:* game room. **Guest Services:** valet and coin laundry. **Business Services:** meeting rooms. **Cards:** AX, CB, DC, DS, MC, VI. **Special Amenities:** early check-in/late check-out.

SOME UNITS   FEE   FEE

COMFORT INN   *Book at aaa.com*
Phone: (715)369-1100

Small-scale Hotel

9/11-11/1 [ECP]	1P: $71-$101	2P: $77-$107	XP: $6 F18
4/1-9/10 [ECP]	1P: $70-$100	2P: $76-$106	XP: $6 F18
11/2-3/31 [ECP]	1P: $60-$94	2P: $65-$90	XP: $6 F18

Location: On Business Rt US 8, 2.6 mi e of jct SR 47. Located in a commercial area. 1490 Lincoln St 54501. Fax: 715/369-1123. **Facility:** 51 one-bedroom standard units, some with whirlpools. 2 stories (no elevator), interior corridors. **Parking:** on-site, winter plug-ins. **Terms:** pets ($25 deposit, $5 extra charge). **Amenities:** irons, hair dryers. **Pool(s):** heated indoor. **Leisure Activities:** sauna, whirlpool, snowmobiling. **Business Services:** meeting rooms. **Cards:** AX, DC, DS, JC, MC, VI.

SOME UNITS   FEE

HOLIDAY ACRES RESORT   *Book at aaa.com*   Phone: (715)369-1500

6/1-8/31 & 12/26-3/31	2P: $94-$289	XP: $12	F12
9/1-12/25	· 2P: $89-$269	XP: $12	F12
4/1-5/31	2P: $69-$209	XP: $12	F12

Resort
Large-scale Hotel   **Location:** 4.5 mi e on Business Rt US 8, 2.3 mi n on W Lake George Rd. Located on Lake Thompson. 4060 S Shore Dr 54501 (PO Box 460). Fax: 715/369-3665. **Facility:** On a lake, the resort offers lodge rooms and cottages. 59 units. 28 one-bedroom standard units, some with whirlpools. 2 vacation homes ($400-$4200) and 29 cottages ($589-$1599). 1-2 stories (no elevator), interior/exterior corridors. **Parking:** on-site, winter plug-ins. **Terms:** check-in 4 pm, 2 night minimum stay - seasonal weekends, 15 day cancellation notice-fee imposed, weekly rates available, pets ($9 extra charge). **Amenities:** *Some:* voice mail, hair dryers. **Dining:** Three Coins Dining Room, see separate listing. **Pool(s):** heated indoor. **Leisure Activities:** sauna, rental boats, rental canoes, windsurfing, boat dock, fishing, putting green, 2 tennis courts (1 lighted), cross country skiing, snowmobiling, rental bicycles, hiking trails, playground, basketball, horseshoes, shuffleboard, volleyball. *Fee:* sailboats, waterskiing, horseback riding, game room. **Guest Services:** gift shop. **Business Services:** meeting rooms. **Cards:** AX, CB, DC, DS, MC, VI.

SOME UNITS

HOLIDAY INN EXPRESS   *Book at aaa.com*   Phone: (715)369-3600

6/18-9/6 [ECP]	1P: $79-$119	2P: $79-$119	XP: $10	F17
12/24-3/31 [ECP]	1P: $69-$119	2P: $69-$119	XP: $10	F17
9/7-12/23 [ECP]	1P: $69-$109	2P: $69-$109	XP: $10	F17
4/1-6/17 [ECP]	1P: $69-$89	2P: $69-$89	XP: $10	F17

Small-scale Hotel   **Location:** On Business Rt US 8, just e of jct SR 47. Located in a commercial area. 668 W Kemp St 54501 (PO Box 675). Fax: 715/369-3601. **Facility:** 100 one-bedroom standard units, some with whirlpools. 2 stories (no elevator), interior corridors. *Bath:* combo or shower only. **Parking:** on-site, winter plug-ins. **Terms:** cancellation fee imposed, pets ($50 fee, in smoking units). **Amenities:** voice mail, irons, hair dryers. **Pool(s):** heated indoor. **Leisure Activities:** sauna, whirlpool, snowmobiling, exercise room. *Fee:* game room. **Guest Services:** valet and coin laundry. **Business Services:** meeting rooms, business center. **Cards:** AX, CB, DC, DS, JC, MC, VI. **Special Amenities:** free expanded continental breakfast and free local telephone calls.

SOME UNITS

──── **WHERE TO DINE** ────

AL-GEN DINNER CLUB   Dinner: $6-$16   Phone: 715/362-2230

Steak House   **Location:** 2.4 mi e on Business Rt US 8, just n. 3428 Faust Lake Rd 54501. **Hours:** 5 pm-10 pm. Closed: 12/24, 12/25; also Mon. **Reservations:** suggested, Sat. **Features:** Constructed in 1932 using straightened hayrack wires, this log restaurant has a warm interior highlighted with rock fireplaces and wildlife prints. Barbecue ribs and walleye fillets are popular. Casual dress; cocktails. **Parking:** on-site. **Cards:** AX, DS, MC, VI.

THE RHINELANDER CAFE   Lunch: $4-$10   Dinner: S6-$25   Phone: 715/362-2918

American   **Location:** Just w of SR 17; center. 33 N Brown 54501. **Hours:** 7 am-11 pm. Closed: 11/25, 12/25; also for dinner 12/24. **Reservations:** suggested. **Features:** The downtown restaurant and supper club has been owned and operated by same family since 1911. Often packed, the establishment delivers friendly service, a warm atmosphere and good, sometimes creative, food, including a number of Greek specialties. Casual dress; cocktails. **Parking:** on-site. **Cards:** AX, DC, DS, MC, VI.

THREE COINS DINING ROOM   Dinner: $8-$18   Phone: 715/369-1500

Steak & Seafood   **Location:** 4.5 mi e on Business Rt US 8, 2.3 mi n on W Lake George Rd; in Holiday Acres Resort. 4060 S Shore Dr 54501. **Hours:** Open 5/1-3/15; 5 pm-9:30 pm, Sun 8:30 am-1 & 5-9:30 pm; hours vary off season. **Reservations:** accepted. **Features:** Soothing music plays in the background of the attractive rustic dining room, which boasts high ceilings and wood accents. Windows overlook landscaped grounds where wildlife roam. Broiled walleye is excellent. Fresh bread is served in a clay flowerpot. Casual dress; cocktails. **Parking:** on-site. **Cards:** AX, CB, DC, DS, MC, VI.

WOLFF'S LOG CABIN   Lunch: $6-$16   Dinner: $6-$16   Phone: 715/362-2686

American   **Location:** On Business Rt US 8, just e of jct SR 47. 721 W Kemp St 54501. **Hours:** 6:30 am-9:30 pm. Closed: 11/25, 12/25. **Features:** A wide selection of reasonably priced items makes up the menu at the modern restaurant. Casual dress; cocktails. **Parking:** on-site. **Cards:** AX, DS, MC, VI.

RICE LAKE pop. 8,320

──── **WHERE TO STAY** ────

AMERICINN MOTEL   *Book at aaa.com*   Phone: 715/234-9060

All Year	1P: $59-$115	2P: $65-$130	XP: $6	F12

Small-scale Hotel   **Location:** US 53, exit 140, 0.7 mi e on CR 0. 2906 Pioneer Ave S 54868. Fax: 715/736-9060. **Facility:** 43 units. 42 one-bedroom standard units, some with whirlpools. 1 one-bedroom suite with whirlpool. 2 stories (no elevator), interior corridors. *Bath:* combo or shower only. **Parking:** on-site, winter plug-ins. **Terms:** cancellation fee imposed, [ECP] meal plan available. **Amenities:** irons, hair dryers. **Pool(s):** small heated indoor. **Leisure Activities:** whirlpool. *Fee:* game room. **Guest Services:** valet and coin laundry. **Business Services:** meeting rooms. **Cards:** AX, DC, DS, MC, VI. *(See color ad p 576)*

SOME UNITS

CURRIER'S LAKEVIEW RESORT MOTEL   Phone: 715/234-7474

5/17-10/1 [CP]	1P: $52-$77	2P: $62-$87	XP: $6 F18
4/1-5/16 & 10/2-3/31 [CP]	1P: $42-$56	2P: $52-$66	XP: $6 F18

Location: Jct CR O, 1.5 mi n on CR SS, 1 mi e, then n on CR C. 2010 E Sawyer St 54868 (2010-21 1/4 St).
Fax: 715/736-1501. **Facility:** 19 units. 18 one-bedroom standard units, some with kitchens. 1 two-bedroom
suite ($110-$149) with kitchen. 2 stories (no elevator), interior/exterior corridors. *Bath:* combo or shower only.
Motel   **Parking:** on-site, winter plug-ins. **Terms:** 2 night minimum stay - weekends in summer, weekly rates available. **Leisure Activities:** rental boats, canoeing, paddleboats, boat dock, fishing, playground. *Fee:* pontoon boats, small boat
launch. **Guest Services:** gift shop. **Business Services:** fax (fee). **Cards:** AX, DS, MC, VI.

SOME UNITS

MICROTEL INN & SUITES   *Book at aaa.com*   Phone: 715/736-2010

All Year [CP]	1P: $45-$65	2P: $45-$65	XP: $5 F16

Location: US 53, exit 140 (CR O), just ne. 2771 Decker Dr 54868. Fax: 715/736-2012. **Facility:** 57 one-bedroom
standard units. 3 stories, interior corridors. *Bath:* combo or shower only. **Parking:** on-site, winter plug-ins.
Motel   **Terms:** weekly rates available, pets ($10 fee). **Amenities:** high-speed Internet (fee), voice mail. **Leisure Ac-
tivities:** limited exercise equipment. **Business Services:** meeting rooms, fax (fee). **Cards:** AX, DC, DS, MC, VI.

SOME UNITS

--------- WHERE TO DINE ---------

LEHMAN'S SUPPER CLUB   **Lunch:** $3-$11   **Dinner:** $5-$23   Phone: 715/234-2428

Location: Just s on CR SS of jct CR O. 2911 S Main St 54868. **Hours:** 11 am-10 pm, Fri & Sat-10:30 pm,
Sun-9:30 pm. Closed: 11/25, 12/25; also Mon. **Reservations:** suggested, weekends. **Features:** Located on
the southeast side of town, this restaurant features a large dining room and an ample sized lounge.
Emphasizing steak, seafood, chicken and barbecue ribs at dinner, the food is well prepared and fresh.
American   Casual dress; cocktails. **Parking:** on-site. **Cards:** AX, CB, DC, DS, MC, VI.

NORSKE NOOK RESTAURANT & BAKERY   **Lunch:** $6-$8   **Dinner:** $6-$8   Phone: 715/234-1733

Location: US 53, exit 140 (CR O), 0.7 mi e on CR O. 2900 Pioneer Ave 54868. **Hours:** 5:30 am-8 pm, Fri & Sat-10
pm, Sun 8 am-8 pm; to 10 pm in summer. Closed major holidays. **Features:** Norwegian specialties,
sandwiches, breakfast dishes and freshly baked breads and pies are the attraction at the relaxed
restaurant. Casual dress. **Parking:** on-site. **Cards:** DS, MC, VI.
Norwegian

RICHLAND CENTER pop. 5,114

--------- WHERE TO STAY ---------

RAMADA INN & WHITE HOUSE SUPPER CLUB   *Book at aaa.com*   Phone: (608)647-8869

All Year	1P: $70-$105	2P: $75-$110	XP: $5 F12

Location: 0.5 mi e on US 14. 1450 Veterans Dr 53581. Fax: 608/647-7154. **Facility:** 43 units. 40 one-bedroom
standard units, some with whirlpools. 3 one-bedroom suites, some with whirlpools. 2 stories, interior corridors. *Bath:* combo or shower only. **Parking:** on-site, winter plug-ins. **Terms:** [CP] meal plan available.
Small-scale Hotel   **Amenities:** voice mail, irons, hair dryers. *Some:* safes. **Dining:** White House Supper Club, see separate
listing. **Pool(s):** heated indoor. **Leisure Activities:** whirlpool, exercise room. **Guest Services:** valet and coin.
laundry, beauty salon. **Business Services:** conference facilities. **Cards:** AX, DS, MC, VI. **Special Amenities:** free continental
breakfast and free local telephone calls.

SOME UNITS

SUPER 8 MOTEL-RICHLAND CENTER   *Book at aaa.com*   Phone: (608)647-8988

All Year	1P: $65-$80	2P: $75-$90	XP: $5 F12

Location: 0.9 mi e on US 14. 100 Foundry Dr 53581. Fax: 608/647-8988. **Facility:** 45 units. 43 one-bedroom standard units, some with whirlpools. 2 one-bedroom suites ($100-$140) with whirlpools. 2 stories (no elevator),
Small-scale Hotel   interior corridors. **Parking:** on-site. **Terms:** small pets only ($50 deposit). **Amenities:** hair dryers. **Pool(s):**
small heated indoor. **Leisure Activities:** whirlpool, exercise room. *Fee:* game room. **Business Services:** meeting rooms.
Cards: AX, CB, DC, DS, JC, MC, VI.

SOME UNITS

--------- WHERE TO DINE ---------

WHITE HOUSE SUPPER CLUB   **Lunch:** $5-$8   **Dinner:** $6-$23   Phone: 608/647-8869

Location: 0.5 mi e on US 14; in Ramada Inn & White House Supper Club. 1450 Veterans Dr 53581. **Hours:** 11
am-2 & 5-9 pm, Fri 4:30 pm-9:30 pm, Sat 5 pm-9:30 pm, Sun 8:30 am-1 & 4:30-9 pm. Closed major
holidays. **Reservations:** accepted. **Features:** This traditional Wisconsin supper club features steak,
Steak & Seafood   seafood and sandwiches. Lunchtime features a daily "no wait" special. There is a drive-thru for those who
want take-out. Casual dress; cocktails. **Parking:** on-site. **Cards:** AX, DS, MC, VI.

RIPON pop. 6,828

──────── WHERE TO STAY ────────

AMERICINN OF RIPON   *Book at aaa.com*   Phone: (920)748-7578

All Year   1P: $69-$165   2P: $77-$165   XP: $8   F17

Location: 1.8 mi w on SR 23. 1219 W Fond du Lac St 54971. Fax: 920/748-7897. **Facility:** 42 units. 41 one-bedroom standard units, some with whirlpools. 1 one-bedroom suite with whirlpool. 2 stories (no elevator), interior corridors. **Bath:** combo or shower only. **Parking:** on-site, winter plug-ins. **Terms:** cancellation fee imposed, [ECP] meal plan available. **Amenities:** irons. *Some:* hair dryers. **Pool(s):** small heated indoor. **Leisure Activities:** sauna, whirlpool. **Guest Services:** valet laundry, tanning facility. **Business Services:** meeting rooms. **Cards:** AX, DC, MC, VI.

Small-scale Hotel

(See color ad p 576)

SOME UNITS

BEST WESTERN WELCOME INN   *Book at aaa.com*   Phone: (920)748-2821

5/1-9/30   2P: $66-$94   XP: $8   F12

4/1-4/30 & 10/1-3/31   2P: $56-$82   XP: $8   F12

Location: Jct SR 23 and 49. Located in a commercial, residential area. 240 E Fond Du Lac St 54971. Fax: 920/748-2821. **Facility:** 38 one-bedroom standard units, some with whirlpools. 2 stories (no elevator), interior corridors. **Parking:** on-site, winter plug-ins. **Terms:** office hours 6 am-11 pm. **Amenities:** irons, hair dryers. **Guest Services:** valet laundry. **Business Services:** meeting rooms. **Cards:** AX, CB, DC, DS, JC, MC, VI. **Special Amenities:** free continental breakfast and free local telephone calls.

Small-scale Hotel

SOME UNITS

RIVER FALLS pop. 12,560

──────── WHERE TO STAY ────────

COUNTRY INN BY CARLSON   *Book at aaa.com*   Phone: (715)425-9500

5/15-9/30 [ECP]   1P: $80-$150   2P: $80-$150   XP: $6   F18

4/1-5/14 & 10/1-3/31 [ECP]   1P: $75-$115   2P: $75-$115   XP: $6   F18

Location: Just n of jct SR 65 and 35. 1525 Commerce Ct 54022. Fax: 715/425-9200. **Facility:** 46 one-bedroom standard units, some with whirlpools. 2 stories, interior corridors. **Parking:** on-site. **Amenities:** voice mail, irons, hair dryers. **Pool(s):** small heated indoor. **Leisure Activities:** whirlpool. **Guest Services:** coin laundry. **Business Services:** meeting rooms. **Cards:** AX, DC, DS, MC, VI. *(See color ad starting on p 580)*

Small-scale Hotel

SOME UNITS

SUPER 8 MOTEL   *Book at aaa.com*   Phone: (715)425-8388

All Year   1P: $72-$82   2P: $82-$92

Location: On SR 65, 0.5 mi w jct SR 35. 1207 St. Croix St 54022. Fax: 715/425-7103. **Facility:** 48 one-bedroom standard units, some with whirlpools. 2 stories, interior corridors. **Parking:** on-site, winter plug-ins. **Terms:** cancellation fee imposed. **Amenities:** irons, hair dryers. **Pool(s):** small heated indoor. **Leisure Activities:** whirlpool. **Guest Services:** coin laundry. **Business Services:** meeting rooms, administrative services (fee). **Cards:** AX, DC, DS, MC, VI.

Small-scale Hotel

SOME UNITS

ROME pop. 1,700

──────── WHERE TO STAY ────────

SHERMALOT MOTEL   Phone: 715-325-2626

4/1-12/1   1P: $70-$120   2P: $70-$120

Location: 1.5 mi s on SR 13. 1148 W Queens Way 54457. Fax: 715/325-2795. **Facility:** 23 one-bedroom standard units, some with whirlpools. 2 stories (no elevator), exterior corridors. **Parking:** on-site. **Terms:** open 4/1-12/1, 7 day cancellation notice-fee imposed, weekly rates available. **Leisure Activities:** boat ramp, fishing.

Motel

Cards: DS, MC, VI.

SOME UNITS

ST. CROIX FALLS pop. 2,033

──────── WHERE TO STAY ────────

HOLIDAY INN EXPRESS HOTEL & SUITES   *Book at aaa.com*   Phone: (715)483-5775

5/26-10/31   1P: $85-$115   2P: $85-$115   XP: $10   F17

11/1-3/31   1P: $65-$95   2P: $65-$95   XP: $10   F17

4/1-5/25   1P: $65-$85   2P: $65-$95   XP: $10   F17

Location: On US 8, 1.3 mi e of jct SR 35 S. 2190 E US Hwy 8 54024 (PO Box 888). Fax: 715/483-5316. **Facility:** 80 one-bedroom standard units, some with whirlpools. 4 stories, interior corridors. **Bath:** combo or shower only. **Parking:** on-site, winter plug-ins. **Terms:** cancellation fee imposed, package plans, small pets only ($50 deposit, $15 extra charge). **Amenities:** video games (fee), dual phone lines, voice mail, irons, hair dryers. **Dining:** 6:30 am-10 am. **Pool(s):** heated indoor. **Leisure Activities:** whirlpool, exercise room. *Fee:* game room. **Guest Services:** gift shop. **Business Services:** meeting rooms. **Cards:** AX, CB, DC, DS, JC, MC, VI. **Special Amenities:** free expanded continental breakfast and free local telephone calls.

Small-scale Hotel

SOME UNITS

ST. GERMAIN

——— WHERE TO STAY ———

NORTH WOODS REST MOTEL
◇
Motel
Cards: MC, VI.

All Year   1P: $40   2P: $49   **Phone:** 715/479-8770
Location: On SR 70, 0.8 mi e. Located in a semi-commercial area. 8083 Hwy 70 E 54558. **Facility:** 10 one-bedroom standard units. 1 story, exterior corridors. *Bath:* combo or shower only. **Parking:** on-site, winter plug-ins. **Terms:** 3 day cancellation notice, small pets only ($5 fee). **Leisure Activities:** snowmobiling.

SOME UNITS
🛏 📶 📹 🖥 / 📱 /
FEE

——— WHERE TO DINE ———

GOLDEN PINES
◆◆◆
◇◇ ◇◇
American

Dinner: $8-$19   **Phone:** 715/479-7178
Location: On SR 70, 1 mi e. 8000 Hwy 70 E 54558. **Hours:** 4 pm-10 pm; winter hours may vary. Closed: 11/25, 12/25; also Sun. **Reservations:** suggested. **Features:** In a massive log building with open beams, this charming restaurant is warm and inviting. The menu, with most dishes freshly prepared, include prime rib, roast duck, Wiener schnitzel, chops and seafood. Dessert selections include varieties of pies. Casual dress; cocktails. **Parking:** on-site. **Cards:** AX, DS, MC, VI.

Ⓨ

SAUK CITY pop. 3,109

——— WHERE TO STAY ———

CEDARBERRY INN
◆◆◆ SAVE
◇◇◇◇
Small-scale Hotel

All Year   1P: $59-$108   2P: $65-$114   XP: $6   F17
Location: On US 12, 0.5 mi w. 855 Phillips Blvd 53583 (PO Box 634). **Fax:** 608/643-6459. **Facility:** 44 units. 42 one-bedroom standard units, some with whirlpools. 2 one-bedroom suites ($124-$135). 2 stories, interior corridors. **Parking:** on-site, winter plug-ins. **Amenities:** voice mail, irons, hair dryers. **Pool(s):** heated indoor. **Leisure Activities:** sauna, whirlpool. *Fee:* game room. **Guest Services:** sundries, coin laundry. **Business Services:** meeting rooms. **Cards:** AX, DC, DS, MC, VI. **Special Amenities: free continental breakfast and free local telephone calls.**

SOME UNITS
🅂🄳 🏊 ✕ 📹 DATA PORT 🖥 / ✕ 🛁 📺 /

——— WHERE TO DINE ———

GREEN ACRES
◇◇ ◇◇
American

Dinner: $14-$20   **Phone:** 608/643-2305
Location: Jct US 12 and CR 78. 7437 Hwy 78 53583. **Hours:** 4 pm-10 pm. Closed major holidays. **Reservations:** accepted, except Fri. **Features:** This is the place to be for great certified Angus steaks and a popular Friday fish fry. The wine list features varieties from the local Wollersheim Winery. Dressy casual; cocktails. **Parking:** on-site. **Cards:** AX, MC, VI.

Ⓨ ✕

SCHOFIELD pop. 2,117

——— WHERE TO STAY ———

COUNTRY INN & SUITES BY CARLSON   *Book at aaa.com*
◇◇◇◇
Small-scale Hotel

All Year   1P: $68-$78   2P: $78-$88   **Phone:** (715)359-1881
                                                                                                                                 F
Location: On Business Rt US 51, 1 mi n of jct SR 29. Located in a commercial area. 1520 Metro Dr 54476. **Fax:** 715/359-8420. **Facility:** 50 units. 39 one-bedroom standard units. 10 one- and 1 two-bedroom suites, some with kitchens. 2 stories, interior corridors. *Bath:* combo or shower only. **Parking:** on-site, winter plug-ins. **Terms:** [ECP] meal plan available. **Amenities:** dual phone lines, voice mail, irons, hair dryers. **Pool(s):** heated indoor. **Leisure Activities:** whirlpool, limited exercise equipment. **Guest Services:** valet and coin laundry. **Business Services:** meeting rooms. **Cards:** AX, DC, DS, MC, VI. *(See color ad starting on p 580)*

SOME UNITS
ASK 🅂🄳 📶 🚹M 📹 🏊 📹 DATA PORT 🖥 / ✕ 🛁 📺 /

SHAWANO pop. 8,298

——— WHERE TO STAY ———

BEST WESTERN VILLAGE HAUS MOTOR LODGE   *Book at aaa.com*
◆◆◆ SAVE
◇◇◇◇
Small-scale Hotel

6/1-9/5 [BP]   1P: $72-$110   2P: $72-$110   XP: $10   F12
4/1-5/31 & 9/6-3/31 [BP] 1P: $62-$110   2P: $62-$110   XP: $10   F12   **Phone:** (715)526-9595
Location: 2 mi e on SR 29 business route, just n on CR HHH. Located in a semi-commercial area. 201 N Airport Dr 54166. **Fax:** 715/526-9826. **Facility:** 89 one-bedroom standard units. 2 stories (no elevator), interior corridors. *Bath:* combo or shower only. **Parking:** on-site, winter plug-ins. **Terms:** package plans. **Amenities:** irons, hair dryers. *Some:* dual phone lines. **Dining:** 6 am-9 pm, Fri & Sat-10 pm, Sun 7 am-9 pm, cocktails. **Pool(s):** heated indoor. **Leisure Activities:** whirlpool. *Fee:* game room. **Guest Services:** valet laundry. **Business Services:** meeting rooms. **Cards:** AX, DC, DS, JC, MC, VI. **Special Amenities: free full breakfast and free newspaper.**

SOME UNITS
🅂🄳 🍴 Ⓨ 📹 🏊 📹 DATA PORT 🖥 / ✕ 📺VCR 🛁 📺 /
FEE

COUNTRY INN & SUITES BY CARLSON   *Book at aaa.com*   Phone: (715)526-2044

(AAA) [SAVE]   6/2-10/1   1P: $80-$90   2P: $90-$100   XP: $6   F17
▼▼▼▼ ▼▼   4/1-6/1 & 10/2-3/31   1P: $75-$80   2P: $85-$90   XP: $6   F17
Location: 2 mi e on SR 29 business route at jct CR HHH. Located in a semi-commercial area. 104 Airport Rd 54166.
Fax: 715/524-3886. **Facility:** 38 units. 34 one-bedroom standard units, some with whirlpools. 4 one-bedroom
Small-scale Hotel suites ($120-$130), some with whirlpools. 2 stories (no elevator), interior corridors. **Parking:** on-site.
Terms: cancellation fee imposed, [ECP] meal plan available. **Amenities:** voice mail, irons, hair dryers.
Pool(s): heated indoor. **Leisure Activities:** whirlpool, exercise room. **Guest Services:** coin laundry. **Business Services:**
meeting rooms. **Cards:** AX, CB, DC, DS, MC, VI. **Special Amenities:** free expanded continental breakfast and free local
telephone calls. *(See color ad starting on p 580)*

SOME UNITS
[S✓/D] [🍴+] [🏊] [📺] [DATA PORT] [🛁] [📷] [💻] / [✕] /

SUPER 8 MOTEL-SHAWANO   *Book at aaa.com*   Phone: (715)526-6688
▼▼▼▼ ▼▼   5/21-9/5 [CP]   1P: $70-$95   2P: $70-$95   XP: $5   F12
4/1-5/20 & 9/6-3/31 [CP] 1P: $55-$75   2P: $55-$75   XP: $5   F12
Small-scale Hotel **Location:** 1.2 mi e on SR 29 business route. Located in a commercial area. 211 Waukechon St 54166.
Fax: 715/526-6290. **Facility:** 55 one-bedroom standard units, some with whirlpools. 2 stories (no elevator),
interior corridors. **Parking:** on-site, winter plug-ins. **Terms:** pets (with prior approval). **Leisure Activities:** sauna, whirlpool. **Guest
Services:** coin laundry. **Business Services:** meeting rooms. **Cards:** AX, CB, DC, DS, MC, VI.

SOME UNITS
[ASK] [S✓/D] [🐾] [🍴+] [🌙] [📺] / [✕] [VCR FEE] [🛁] [📷] [💻] /

─────── **The following lodging was either not evaluated or did not** ───────
meet AAA rating requirements but is listed for your information only.

COMFORT INN & SUITES, SHAWANO   Phone: 715/524-9090
[fyi]   All Year [ECP]   1P: $55-$149   2P: $59-$169   XP: $8   F18
Too new to rate, opening scheduled for February 2004. Location: SR 29, exit SR 22, then w. W7393 River Bend
Small-scale Hotel Rd 54166. Fax: 715/524-9094. **Amenities:** 65 units, pets, coffeemakers, microwaves, refrigerators, pool.
Cards: AX, CB, DC, DS, MC, VI.

─────── **WHERE TO DINE** ───────

ANELLO'S TORCH LITE   **Dinner:** $7-$25   Phone: 715/526-5680
▼▼ ▼▼   **Location:** 1.8 mi e on SR 29 business route. 1276 E Green Bay St 54166. **Hours:** 4 pm-10 pm, Fri & Sat-11 pm.
Closed: 11/25; also 12/24. **Reservations:** accepted. **Features:** This well-established restaurant offers and
extensive menu selection of both American and Italian dishes. There are traditional steak, chicken,
American   seafood and barbecue ribs. House specialities include delicious lasagna, manicotti and beef-roll sausage.
Casual dress; cocktails. **Parking:** on-site. **Cards:** AX, DS, MC, VI.

[🍸] [✕]

MAIN STREET DINER   **Lunch:** $5-$7   **Dinner:** $6-$8   Phone: 715/524-4916
▼▼   **Location:** Center. 123 N Main St 54166. **Hours:** 4 am-8 pm, Sat 4 am-2 pm, Sun 7 am-2 pm. Closed major
holidays. **Features:** This downtown restaurant is decorated with country knick knacks, and serves ample
American   portions of home-style cooked dishes which make it popular with the locals. Casual dress. **Parking:**
on-site. **Cards:** MC, VI.

[✕]

SHEBOYGAN pop. 50,792

─────── **WHERE TO STAY** ───────

AMERICINN OF SHEBOYGAN   *Book at aaa.com*   Phone: (920)208-8130
(AAA) [SAVE]   6/1-9/30 [ECP]   1P: $90-$300   2P: $90-$300   XP: $9   F18
10/1-3/31 [ECP]   1P: $78-$170   2P: $78-$170   XP: $9   F18
▼▼▼▼ ▼▼   4/1-5/31 [ECP]   1P: $76-$155   2P: $76-$155   XP: $9   F18
Small-scale Hotel **Location:** I-43, exit 123, just e. Located in a commercial area. 3664 S Taylor Dr 53081. Fax: 920/208-8138.
Facility: 61 one-bedroom standard units, some with whirlpools. 3 stories, interior corridors. *Bath:* combo or
shower only. **Parking:** on-site, winter plug-ins. **Terms:** cancellation fee imposed, pets ($7 fee, $50 deposit).
Amenities: hair dryers. **Pool(s):** heated indoor. **Leisure Activities:** whirlpool. **Guest Services:** valet and coin laundry. **Business
Services:** meeting rooms. **Cards:** AX, DC, DS, MC, VI. **Special Amenities:** free expanded continental breakfast and free
local telephone calls. *(See color ad p 576)*

SOME UNITS
[S✓/D] [🐾 FEE] [&] [🏊] [🍴+] [📺] [DATA PORT] [💻] / [✕] [VCR FEE] [🛁] [📷] /

BAYMONT INN SHEBOYGAN *Book at aaa.com* **Phone:** (920)457-2321

AAA SAVE

6/1-9/30	1P: $89-$109	2P: $89-$109
4/1-5/31 & 10/1-3/31	1P: $69-$89	2P: $69-$89

Location: I-43, exit 126, 1 mi e on SR 23. Located in a commercial area. 2932 Kohler Memorial Dr 53081. Fax: 920/457-0827. **Facility:** 96 units. 95 one-bedroom standard units. 1 one-bedroom suite ($99-$119) with kitchen. 2 stories (no elevator), interior corridors. *Bath:* combo or shower only. **Parking:** on-site, winter plug-ins. **Terms:** [ECP] meal plan available, small pets only (with prior approval). **Amenities:** video games (fee), voice mail, irons, hair dryers. **Business Services:** fax (fee). **Cards:** AX, CB, DC, DS, MC, VI. **Special Amenities:** free local telephone calls and free newspaper. *(See color ad p 597)*

SOME UNITS

COMFORT INN-SHEBOYGAN *Book at aaa.com* **Phone:** (920)457-7724

All Year [ECP]	1P: $55-$95	2P: $55-$95	XP: $18

Location: I-43, exit 128, 0.3 mi e on Business Rt 42. Located in a commercial area. 4332 N 40th St 53083. Fax: 920/452-2597. **Facility:** 59 one-bedroom standard units, some with whirlpools. 2 stories (no elevator), interior corridors. **Parking:** on-site, winter plug-ins. **Terms:** pets ($10 extra charge). **Amenities:** safes (fee), irons, hair dryers. **Pool(s):** small heated indoor. **Leisure Activities:** whirlpool. **Guest Services:** valet laundry. **Business Services:** meeting rooms. **Cards:** AX, CB, DC, DS, MC, VI.

SOME UNITS

HARBOR WINDS HOTEL *Book at aaa.com* **Phone:** (920)452-9000

6/2-10/1 & 1/1-3/31	1P: $79-$150	2P: $79-$150	XP: $10	F18
4/1-6/1 & 10/2-12/31	1P: $79	2P: $79	XP: $10	F18

Location: On riverfront boardwalk, s of downtown. 905 S 8th St 53081. Fax: 920/452-0093. **Facility:** 28 one-bedroom standard units. 2 stories, interior corridors. *Bath:* combo or shower only. **Parking:** on-site. **Terms:** 3 day cancellation notice, [ECP] meal plan available. **Amenities:** dual phone lines, voice mail, irons, hair dryers. **Guest Services:** valet laundry. **Business Services:** business center. **Cards:** AX, DC, DS, MC, VI.

SOME UNITS

HOLIDAY INN EXPRESS *Book at aaa.com* **Phone:** (920)451-8700

6/1-10/1	1P: $112-$300	2P: $112-$300	XP: $10	F18
4/1-5/31 & 10/2-3/31	1P: $89-$150	2P: $89-$150	XP: $10	F18

Location: I-43, exit 123, just se. 3823 Germaine Ave 53081. Fax: 920/451-8700. **Facility:** 63 units. 61 one-bedroom standard units, some with whirlpools. 2 one-bedroom suites, some with whirlpools. 2 stories, interior corridors. *Bath:* combo or shower only. **Parking:** on-site, winter plug-ins. **Terms:** 3 day cancellation notice, [ECP] meal plan available. **Amenities:** dual phone lines, voice mail, irons, hair dryers. **Pool(s):** small heated indoor. **Leisure Activities:** limited exercise equipment. **Guest Services:** complimentary evening beverages: Mon-Thurs, valet laundry. **Business Services:** meeting rooms. **Cards:** AX, CB, DC, DS, JC, MC, VI.

SOME UNITS

SLEEP INN & SUITES *Book at aaa.com* **Phone:** (920)694-0099

AAA SAVE

All Year [ECP]	1P: $69-$145	2P: $69-$145	XP: $5	F18

Location: I-43, exit 120, just e. 3912 Motel Rd 53081. Fax: 920/694-0098. **Facility:** 60 one-bedroom standard units, some with whirlpools. 3 stories, interior corridors. *Bath:* combo or shower only. **Parking:** on-site. **Amenities:** high-speed Internet, dual phone lines, safes (fee), irons, hair dryers. **Pool(s):** heated indoor, wading. **Leisure Activities:** whirlpool, waterslide, limited exercise equipment. **Guest Services:** valet and coin laundry. **Business Services:** meeting rooms. **Cards:** AX, DC, DS, MC, VI. **Special Amenities:** free expanded continental breakfast and free local telephone calls.

SOME UNITS

SUPER 8 MOTEL *Book at aaa.com* **Phone:** (920)458-8080

All Year	1P: $54-$69	2P: $59-$74	XP: $5	F12

Location: I-43, exit 126, just ne. 3402 Wilgus Rd 53081. Fax: 920/458-8013. **Facility:** 60 one-bedroom standard units. 2 stories (no elevator), interior corridors. **Parking:** on-site, winter plug-ins. **Terms:** pets ($10 extra charge, small dogs only). **Amenities:** safes (fee). **Guest Services:** coin laundry. **Business Services:** meeting rooms. **Cards:** AX, CB, DC, DS, MC, VI.

SOME UNITS

The following lodging was either not evaluated or did not meet AAA rating requirements but is listed for your information only.

BLUE HARBOR RESORT AND CONFERENCE CENTER

fyi

Under construction, scheduled to open June 2004. **Location:** I-43, exit SR 23 E, s on 8th St, follow over drawbridge and circle the rotary to E Water St. 725 Blue Harbor Dr 53081. Fax: 920/452-2909. **Planned Amenities:** coffeemakers, microwaves, refrigerators, pool. *(See color ad p 623)*

Small-scale Hotel

WHERE TO DINE

CITY STREETS-RIVERSIDE **Lunch:** $6-$10 **Dinner:** $9-$20 **Phone:** 920/457-9050

Location: E of 8th on Virginia; in Riverfront District. 712 Riverfront Dr 53081. **Hours:** 11 am-2 & 5-9 pm, Fri & Sat 5 pm-10 pm. **Closed:** 1/1, 12/24, 12/25; also Sun. **Reservations:** suggested, weekends. **Features:** Within walking distance of Lake Michigan and lakeshore specialty shops, the restaurant is popular for its fresh seafood. The area's nautical theme is maintained in the dining room decor. Good choices include locally caught broiled whitefish and salmon. Steaks, grilled pork loin and other American dishes are also offered. Casual dress; cocktails. **Parking:** on-site. **Cards:** AX, DC, MC, VI.

RUPP'S LODGE DOWNTOWN | **Lunch:** $6-$8 | **Dinner:** $9-$22 | **Phone:** 920/459-8155

American

Location: Downtown. 925 N 8th St 53081. **Hours:** 11 am-2 & 4-9 pm, Fri-10 pm, Sat & Sun 3 pm-9 pm. Closed major holidays. **Reservations:** accepted. **Features:** The family-owned restaurant delivers basic American fare—steaks, sandwiches and specials—with some selections of local fresh fish. The large salad bar is included with meals. Tables are nicely spaced throughout the supper club-style dining room. Casual dress; cocktails. **Parking:** street. **Cards:** AX, DC, DS, MC, VI.

TRATTORIA STEFANO | **Dinner:** $12-$29 | **Phone:** 920/452-8455

Italian

Location: Downtown. 522 S 8th St 53081. **Hours:** 5 pm-9 pm, Fri & Sat-10 pm. Closed major holidays; also Sun. **Reservations:** suggested. **Features:** The informal and lively restaurant, with simple wood tables and a trendy decor, complements its fine Italian dishes with good selection of Italian wines. Casual dress; cocktails. **Parking:** on-site. **Cards:** AX, DC, JC, MC, VI.

SHEBOYGAN FALLS pop. 6,772

——— WHERE TO STAY ———

ROCHESTER INN | | | **Phone:** 920/467-3123

Historic Bed & Breakfast

All Year | 1P: $99-$169 | 2P: $99-$169 | XP: $25 | F10

Location: Just e of downtown via CR PP. 504 Water St 53085. Fax: 920/467-9729. **Facility:** This 1848 Greek Revival B&B features two-level suites, four-poster beds, wet bars and large, jetted tubs. Smoke free premises. 6 units. 1 one-bedroom standard unit with whirlpool. 5 one-bedroom suites ($129-$169), some with whirlpools. 3 stories (no elevator), interior corridors. **Parking:** on-site. **Terms:** age restrictions may apply, 14 day cancellation notice-fee imposed, [BP] & [CP] meal plans available. **Amenities:** irons, hair dryers. *Some:* honor bars. **Guest Services:** valet laundry. **Cards:** AX, MC, VI.

SOME UNITS

SHELL LAKE pop. 1,309

——— WHERE TO STAY ———

——— *The following lodging was either not evaluated or did not* ———
meet AAA rating requirements but is listed for your information only.

AMERICINN OF SHELL LAKE | | **Phone:** 715/468-4494

fyi

Small-scale Hotel

Property failed to provide current rates
Too new to rate, opening scheduled for November 2003. **Location:** US 53, exit County Hwy B. 331 Hwy 63 S 54871. Fax: 715/468-4910. **Amenities:** 41 units, pets, coffeemakers, microwaves, refrigerators, pool. *(See color ad p 576)*

Camper
Sweet Camper

***Travel With Someone
You Trust®***

*I*f camping is where your heart is, then **AAA's CampBook® guides** are for you. With information about campgrounds throughout North America, **CampBooks** provide campers valuable details on camping facilities. From rate information to site descriptions to recreational activities, these guides give campers all the information they need before hitting the trail.

To get your **CampBook guide**, click on **aaa.com** or visit your nearest AAA office.

SIREN pop. 988

——— WHERE TO STAY ———

BEST WESTERN NORTHWOODS LODGE

Book at aaa.com 　　　　　　　　　　　　　Phone: (715)349-7800

(AAA) (SAVE)
▽▽▽▽

Small-scale Hotel

All Year [ECP]　　　1P: $80-$300　　　2P: $80-$300　　　XP: $10　　　F17
Location: On SR 35 at jct SR 70 W and CR B E. 23986 SR 35 S 54872 (PO Box 49). Fax: 715/349-7855. **Facility:** 38 one-bedroom standard units. 2 stories, interior corridors. *Bath:* combo or shower only. **Parking:** on-site, winter plug-ins. **Amenities:** irons, hair dryers. **Pool(s):** heated indoor. **Leisure Activities:** sauna, whirlpool, board games. **Guest Services:** gift shop, coin laundry. **Business Services:** meeting rooms. **Cards:** AX, CB, DC, DS, JC, MC, VI. **Special Amenities:** free expanded continental breakfast and free local telephone calls.

SOME UNITS

THE LODGE AT CROOKED LAKE

Phone: (715)349-2500

(AAA) (SAVE)
▽▽▽

Small-scale Hotel

6/1-10/31 [ECP]　　　1P: $79-$109　　　2P: $79-$109　　　XP: $10　　　F18
4/1-5/31 & 11/1-3/31 [ECP]　　1P: $69-$99　　　2P: $69-$99　　　XP: $10　　　F18
Location: On SR 35, 0.5 mi n of jct SR 70. 24271 SR 35 N 54872 (PO Box 606). Fax: 715/349-2554. **Facility:** 60 one-bedroom standard units, some with whirlpools. 2 stories, interior corridors. *Bath:* combo or shower only. **Parking:** on-site, winter plug-ins. **Terms:** weekly rates available, small pets only ($50 deposit, $10 extra charge). **Amenities:** voice mail. *Some:* CD players. **Dining:** 11 am-10 pm, cocktails. **Pool(s):** heated indoor. **Leisure Activities:** sauna, whirlpool, fishing, cross country skiing, snowmobiling, bicycles, hiking trails, limited exercise equipment. *Fee:* golf-18 holes. **Guest Services:** gift shop, valet laundry, airport transportation-Burnett County Airport, area transportation-Siren Glen Golf Course. **Business Services:** conference facilities, PC, fax (fee). **Cards:** AX, CB, DS, MC, VI. **Special Amenities:** free expanded continental breakfast and free local telephone calls. *(See color ad below)*

SOME UNITS

PINE WOOD MOTEL

Phone: 715/349-5225

(AAA) (SAVE)
▽

Motel

All Year　　　1P: $29-$50　　　2P: $39-$55　　　XP: $5　　　D18
Location: On SR 35, 0.3 mi s of jct SR 70 W and CR B E. 23862 Hwy 35 S 54872. Fax: 715/349-8196. **Facility:** 14 one-bedroom standard units. 1 story, exterior corridors. *Bath:* combo or shower only. **Parking:** on-site, winter plug-ins. **Terms:** cancellation fee imposed, small pets only ($25 deposit, $5 fee). **Cards:** MC, VI.

SOME UNITS

SISTER BAY —*See Door County p. 506.*

SPARTA pop. 8,648

———— **WHERE TO STAY** ————

BEST NIGHTS INN   **Phone:** 608/269-3066

AAA SAVE

	5/15-11/28 [CP]	1P: $39-$99	2P: $49-$139	XP: $10	F12
	11/29-3/31 [CP]	1P: $31-$71	2P: $41-$81	XP: $6	F12
	4/1-5/14 [CP]	1P: $29-$69	2P: $39-$79	XP: $5	F12

Motel

Location: I-90, exit 25 (SR 27), 0.5 mi s. 303 W Wisconsin St 54656. Fax: 608/269-3175. **Facility:** 28 one-bedroom standard units. 1 story, exterior corridors. *Bath:* combo or shower only. **Parking:** on-site, winter plug-ins. **Terms:** cancellation fee imposed, weekly rates available, pets (with prior approval). **Amenities:** *Some:* hair dryers. **Pool(s):** small heated outdoor. **Leisure Activities:** playground. **Cards:** AX, DS, MC, VI.

SOME UNITS

BEST WESTERN SPARTA TRAIL LODGE   *Book at aaa.com*   **Phone:** (608)269-2664

| | 6/1-10/31 | 1P: $94-$114 | | | |
| | 4/1-5/31 & 11/1-3/31 | 1P: $74-$94 | | | |

Small-scale Hotel

Location: I-90, exit 28 (US 16), just w. 4445 Theatre Rd 54656. Fax: 608/269-2994. **Facility:** 80 one-bedroom standard units, some with whirlpools. 3 stories, interior corridors. *Bath:* combo or shower only. **Parking:** on-site. **Terms:** 2 night minimum stay - 6/1-8/31, 30 day cancellation notice, [CP] meal plan available. **Amenities:** voice mail, safes (fee), irons, hair dryers. **Pool(s):** heated indoor, wading. **Leisure Activities:** whirlpool, waterslide, exercise room. *Fee:* game room. **Guest Services:** gift shop, valet and coin laundry. **Business Services:** meeting rooms. **Cards:** AX, DS, MC, VI.

SOME UNITS

COUNTRY INN BY CARLSON   *Book at aaa.com*   **Phone:** (608)269-3110

AAA SAVE

| | 6/1-3/31 [ECP] | 1P: $72-$110 | 2P: $80-$130 | XP: $8 | F18 |
| | 4/1-5/31 [ECP] | 1P: $67-$105 | 2P: $75-$125 | XP: $8 | F18 |

Small-scale Hotel

Location: I-90, exit 25 (SR 27), just n. 737 Avon Rd 54656. Fax: 608/269-6726. **Facility:** 61 one-bedroom standard units. 2 stories (no elevator), interior corridors. **Parking:** on-site, winter plug-ins. **Terms:** small pets only ($5 extra charge). **Amenities:** irons, hair dryers. **Pool(s):** small heated indoor. **Leisure Activities:** whirlpool. **Guest Services:** gift shop, coin laundry. **Cards:** AX, CB, DC, DS, MC, VI. **Special Amenities:** free expanded continental breakfast and free local telephone calls. *(See color ad starting on p 580)*

FEE   SOME UNITS

SUPER 8 SPARTA   *Book at aaa.com*   **Phone:** 608/269-8489

| | 10/1-3/31 | 1P: $72-$82 | 2P: $77-$87 | XP: $5 | |
| | 4/1-9/30 | 1P: $70-$80 | 2P: $75-$85 | XP: $5 | |

Small-scale Hotel

Location: I-90, exit 25 (SR 27), just n. 716 Avon Rd 54656. Fax: 608/269-8449. **Facility:** 49 one-bedroom standard units. 2 stories (no elevator), interior corridors. **Parking:** on-site, winter plug-ins. **Terms:** [CP] meal plan available, small pets only ($5 extra charge). **Amenities:** hair dryers. **Pool(s):** small heated indoor. **Leisure Activities:** whirlpool. **Guest Services:** coin laundry. **Cards:** AX, DC, DS, MC, VI.

FEE

SPOONER pop. 2,653

———— **WHERE TO STAY** ————

BEST WESTERN AMERICAN HERITAGE INN   *Book at aaa.com*   **Phone:** (715)635-9770

AAA SAVE

| | 5/28-9/7 | 1P: $72-$92 | 2P: $84-$99 | XP: $6 | F18 |
| | 4/1-5/27 & 9/8-3/31 | 1P: $69-$80 | 2P: $79-$89 | XP: $6 | F18 |

Small-scale Hotel

Location: On SR 70 at jct US 63, 1 mi w of US 53. 101 Maple St 54801. Fax: 715/635-9774. **Facility:** 45 units. 44 one-bedroom standard units. 1 one-bedroom suite with whirlpool. 2 stories (no elevator), interior corridors. **Parking:** on-site. **Terms:** small pets only (in smoking units). **Amenities:** irons, hair dryers. **Pool(s):** heated indoor. **Leisure Activities:** sauna, whirlpool, snowmobiling, bicycles, hiking trails. *Fee:* game room. **Business Services:** meeting rooms. **Cards:** AX, CB, DC, DS, MC, VI. **Special Amenities:** free continental breakfast and early check-in/late check-out.

SOME UNITS

COUNTRY HOUSE MOTEL & RV PARK   **Phone:** 715/635-8721

AAA SAVE

	6/1-10/15	1P: $50-$80	2P: $60-$109	XP: $6	F12
	10/16-3/31	1P: $50-$74	2P: $60-$80	XP: $6	F12
	4/1-5/31	1P: $49-$73	2P: $59-$79	XP: $6	F12

Motel

Location: On US 63, 0.5 mi s of jct SR 70. 717 S River St 54801-9692. **Facility:** 23 one-bedroom standard units. 1-2 stories, interior/exterior corridors. *Bath:* combo or shower only. **Parking:** on-site, winter plug-ins. **Terms:** pets ($4-$5 extra charge, with prior approval). **Amenities:** video library. **Pool(s):** small heated indoor. **Leisure Activities:** whirlpool. *Fee:* video games. **Business Services:** meeting rooms. **Cards:** AX, DS, MC, VI. **Special Amenities:** free local telephone calls and preferred room (subject to availability with advanced reservations).

FEE   SOME UNITS   FEE

———— **WHERE TO DINE** ————

FOXXY'S BAR AND GRILLE   **Dinner:** $15-$25   **Phone:** 715/635-2399

American

Location: Jct River and Elm sts, 1 mi w on Elm St. N5295 Rocky Ridge Rd 54801. **Hours:** 4 pm-9 pm. Closed major holidays. **Reservations:** accepted. **Features:** A short drive from local hotels, the popular, sometimes boisterous restaurant is well known for its extensive menu. Casual dress; cocktails. **Parking:** on-site. **Cards:** AX, DS, MC, VI.

SPRING GREEN pop. 1,444

―――― WHERE TO STAY ――――

HILL STREET
△▽△▽ △▽△▽
Bed & Breakfast

Phone: 608/588-7751

All Year [BP] 1P: $80-$90 2P: $80-$90 XP: $20
Location: Just nw of downtown. 353 W Hill St 53588. **Facility:** Smoke free premises. 7 one-bedroom standard units. 2 stories (no elevator), interior corridors. *Bath:* some shared or private, combo or shower only. **Parking:** on-site. **Terms:** check-in 4 pm, 2 night minimum stay - seasonal weekends, age restrictions may apply, 14 day cancellation notice-fee imposed, no pets allowed (owner's cats on premises). **Guest Services:** TV in common area. **Cards:** MC, VI.

⊠ 🅦 🆉

THE HOUSE ON THE ROCK RESORT
△▽△▽ △▽△▽ △▽△▽
Resort
Small-scale Hotel

Phone: 608/588-7000

4/1-1/3 1P: $95-$205 2P: $95-$205
Location: 2.5 mi s on SR 23, 0.8 mi e on CR C. 400 Springs Dr 53588. Fax: 608/588-2269. **Facility:** All units at this picturesque resort near the Wisconsin River have views of a golf course and surrounding wooded hills. 80 one-bedroom suites with whirlpools. 4 stories, interior corridors. *Bath:* combo or shower only. **Parking:** on-site. **Terms:** open 4/1-1/3. **Amenities:** dual phone lines, voice mail, irons, hair dryers. **Pool(s):** heated outdoor, 2 heated indoor. **Leisure Activities:** saunas, whirlpool, steamrooms, 2 lighted tennis courts, racquetball court, hiking trails, jogging, exercise room, volleyball. *Fee:* golf-27 holes. **Guest Services:** gift shop. **Business Services:** conference facilities. **Cards:** AX, DS, MC, VI.

SOME UNITS
ASK 🆂🅳 🍴 ⊠ 📶 🏊 ✕ 🎥 DATA PORT 🖥 🗄 🖂 / ⊠ /

ROUND BARN LODGE
△▽△▽ △▽△▽
Small-scale Hotel

Phone: 608/588-2568

5/1-10/31 1P: $80-$100 2P: $80-$100 XP: $5 F6
4/1-4/30 1P: $45-$85 2P: $55-$85 XP: $5 F6
11/1-3/31 1P: $45-$85 2P: $45-$85 XP: $5 F6
Location: On US 14, just w of jct SR 23 N. Hwy 14 53588 (PO Box 297). Fax: 608/588-2100. **Facility:** 44 one-bedroom standard units, some with whirlpools. 2 stories (no elevator), interior corridors. **Parking:** on-site, winter plug-ins. **Dining:** dining room, see separate listing. **Pool(s):** outdoor, heated indoor. **Leisure Activities:** sauna, whirlpool. **Business Services:** meeting rooms. **Cards:** AX, DS, MC, VI.

SOME UNITS
🍴 🏊 ✕ / ⊠ DATA PORT 🖥 🗄 🖂 /

SPRING VALLEY INN
△▽△▽ △▽△▽
Small-scale Hotel

Phone: 608/588-7828

5/1-10/31 1P: $85-$100 2P: $85-$115 XP: $5 F12
4/1-4/30 & 11/1-3/31 1P: $55-$85 2P: $55-$90 XP: $5 F12
Location: On US 14 at jct CR C, 3 mi e. 6279 CR C 53588. Fax: 608/588-2821. **Facility:** 35 one-bedroom standard units. 1 story, interior corridors. **Parking:** on-site. **Pool(s):** heated indoor. **Leisure Activities:** sauna, whirlpool, steamroom, cross country skiing, snowmobiling, hiking trails, exercise room. *Fee:* massage, game room. **Guest Services:** gift shop. **Business Services:** meeting rooms. **Cards:** DC, MC, VI.

SOME UNITS
🍴 🍸 🏊 ✕ 🎥 DATA PORT / ⊠ /

USONIAN INN
△▽
Motel

Phone: 608/588-2323

6/12-9/5 [CP] 1P: $49-$75 2P: $55-$75 XP: $5 F19
9/6-10/31 [CP] 1P: $44-$75 2P: $49-$75 XP: $5 F19
5/1-6/11 [CP] 1P: $44-$59 2P: $49-$59 XP: $5 F19
Location: On US 14 at jct SR 23 S. E 5116 Hwy 14 53588 (PO Box 777). **Facility:** Smoke free premises. 11 one-bedroom standard units. 1 story, exterior corridors. *Bath:* shower only. **Parking:** on-site. **Terms:** open 5/1-10/31. **Cards:** DS, MC, VI.

SOME UNITS
⊠ / 🖥 🗄 🖂 /

―――― WHERE TO DINE ――――

THE POST HOUSE-DUTCH KITCHEN
△▽△▽ △▽△▽
American

Lunch: $5-$8 Dinner: $9-$17 Phone: 608/588-2595

Location: Downtown. 127 E Jefferson 53588. **Hours:** 11 am-9 pm, Fri & Sat-10 pm, Sun 9 am-8 pm. Closed major holidays; also Mon 11/1-5/1. **Reservations:** suggested. **Features:** Originally constructed in 1857, this centrally located restaurant is known for its home-style comfort foods. The restaurant houses a unique lounge and garden area designed in the Frank Lloyd Wright tradition. Casual dress; cocktails. **Parking:** street. **Cards:** MC, VI.

🍸 ✕

THE ROUND BARN
△▽△▽ △▽△▽
American

Lunch: $4-$7 Dinner: $10-$17 Phone: 608/588-2568

Location: On US 14, just w of jct SR 23 N; in Round Barn Lodge. US 14 53588. **Hours:** 7 am-2 & 5-9 pm. Closed: Mon & Tues 12/1-3/31. **Reservations:** accepted. **Features:** Once home to 40 cattle, the skillfully converted 1914 round barn now is a cozy place in which diners can sample steak, barbecue ribs, chicken and seafood specialties. The family-oriented restaurant offers several children's selections, as well as a few vegetarian dishes. Casual dress; cocktails. **Parking:** on-site. **Cards:** AX, DC, DS, MC, VI.

🍸 ✕

SPRING GREEN GENERAL STORE
△▽
American

Lunch: $4-$9 Phone: 608/588-7070

Location: Just w of SR 23. 137 S Albany St 53588. **Hours:** 9 am-6 pm, Sat from 8 am, Sun 8 am-4 pm. Closed major holidays. **Features:** The trendy cafe prepares weekend breakfasts and an extensive selection of vegetarian offerings from scratch. Casual dress; beer only. **Parking:** street. **Cards:** AX, DS, MC, VI.

⊠

STANLEY pop. 1,898

─────── WHERE TO STAY ───────

SUPER 8 MOTEL ▼▼ ▼▼
Small-scale Hotel

Book at aaa.com

Phone: 715/644-3332

All Year [CP]   1P: $50-$60   2P: $55-$65   XP: $5   F13
Location: SR 29, exit 101 (CR H), just n. 555 S Broadway 54768 (PO Box 85). Fax: 715/644-2120. **Facility:** 36 one-bedroom standard units, some with whirlpools. 2 stories, interior corridors. **Parking:** on-site, winter plug-ins. **Leisure Activities:** whirlpool. **Business Services:** meeting rooms. **Cards:** AX, CB, DC, DS, JC, MC, VI.

SOME UNITS

STEVENS POINT pop. 24,551

─────── WHERE TO STAY ───────

A VICTORIAN SWAN ON WATER BED & BREAKFAST ▼▼ ▼▼
Bed & Breakfast

Phone: (715)345-0595

All Year   1P: $70-$140   XP: $15
Location: On US 10, 0.7 mi w of jct US 51 business route, then 0.4 mi s. Located in a residential area. 1716 Water St 54481. Fax: 715/345-0569. **Facility:** Smoke free premises. 4 one-bedroom standard units, some with whirlpools. 2 stories (no elevator), interior corridors. *Bath:* combo or shower only. **Parking:** on-site. **Terms:** office hours 8 am-10 pm, age restrictions may apply, 7 day cancellation notice-fee imposed, [BP] meal plan available. **Amenities:** hair dryers. **Business Services:** fax (fee). **Cards:** AX, DS, MC, VI.

BAYMONT INN & SUITES STEVENS POINT AAA SAVE ▼▼ ▼▼
Small-scale Hotel
(See color ad p 597)

Book at aaa.com

Phone: (715)344-1900

All Year   1P: $54-$74   2P: $54-$74
Location: I-39, exit 158B (US 10), just w. Located in a commercial area. 4917 Main St 54481. Fax: 715/344-1254. **Facility:** 71 units. 69 one-bedroom standard units. 2 one-bedroom suites. 3 stories, interior corridors. **Parking:** on-site, winter plug-ins. **Terms:** 18 day cancellation notice, [ECP] meal plan available, small pets only ($50 deposit). **Amenities:** video games (fee), voice mail, irons, hair dryers. **Pool(s):** small heated indoor. **Leisure Activities:** whirlpool, exercise room. **Guest Services:** coin laundry. **Business Services:** meeting rooms. **Cards:** AX, CB, DC, DS, MC, VI. **Special Amenities:** free local telephone calls and free newspaper.

SOME UNITS
FEE

COMFORT SUITES STEVENS POINT ▼▼▼▼
Small-scale Hotel

Book at aaa.com

Phone: (715)341-6000

9/1-3/31   1P: $82-$149   2P: $82-$149
4/1-8/31   1P: $74-$149   2P: $74-$149
Location: I-39, exit 161, on US 51 business route, 0.6 mi s. Located in a commercial area. 300 Division St N 54481. Fax: 715/341-8908. **Facility:** 105 one-bedroom standard units, some with whirlpools. 3 stories, interior corridors. **Parking:** on-site, winter plug-ins. **Terms:** [ECP] meal plan available. **Amenities:** video games (fee), dual phone lines, irons, hair dryers. **Pool(s):** heated indoor. **Leisure Activities:** whirlpool, limited exercise equipment. **Guest Services:** valet and coin laundry. **Business Services:** meeting rooms. **Cards:** AX, CB, DC, DS, JC, MC, VI.

SOME UNITS

COUNTRY INN & SUITES BY CARLSON AAA SAVE ▼▼ ▼▼
Small-scale Hotel

Book at aaa.com

Phone: (715)345-7000

6/1-8/31   1P: $64-$139   2P: $64-$139
4/1-5/31 & 9/1-3/31   1P: $64-$99   2P: $64-$99
Location: I-39, exit 161, on US 51 business route, 0.6 mi s. Located in a commercial area. 301 Division St N 54481. Fax: 715/345-7008. **Facility:** 75 units. 56 one-bedroom standard units, some with whirlpools. 19 one-bedroom suites. 3 stories, interior corridors. *Bath:* combo or shower only. **Parking:** on-site, winter plug-ins. **Terms:** [ECP] meal plan available, pets ($25 extra charge, in designated units). **Amenities:** voice mail, irons, hair dryers. *Some:* high-speed Internet, dual phone lines. **Pool(s):** small heated indoor. **Leisure Activities:** whirlpool, exercise room. **Guest Services:** coin laundry. **Cards:** AX, DC, DS, MC, VI. **Special Amenities:** free expanded continental breakfast and free local telephone calls. *(See color ad starting on p 580)*

SOME UNITS
FEE   FEE

FAIRFIELD INN BY MARRIOTT ▼▼ ▼▼
Small-scale Hotel

Book at aaa.com

Phone: (715)342-9300

All Year [ECP]   1P: $49-$89   2P: $49-$89   XP: $5   F18
Location: I-39, exit 158 (US 10) at jct US 51. Located in a commercial area. 5317 Hwy 10 E 54481. Fax: 715/342-9300. **Facility:** 62 one-bedroom standard units. 3 stories, interior corridors. *Bath:* combo or shower only. **Parking:** on-site, winter plug-ins. **Amenities:** irons, hair dryers. **Pool(s):** small heated indoor. **Leisure Activities:** whirlpool. **Cards:** AX, DC, DS, MC, VI.

SOME UNITS

HAWTHORN INN & SUITES AAA SAVE ▼▼▼▼
Small-scale Hotel

Book at aaa.com

Phone: (715)341-8100

All Year   1P: $69-$79   2P: $69-$79
Location: I-39, exit 168 (US 10), 1 mi e. 1101 Amber Ave 54481. Fax: 715/341-8120. **Facility:** 66 one-bedroom standard units. 3 stories, interior corridors. *Bath:* combo or shower only. **Parking:** on-site. **Terms:** 5 day cancellation notice, [ECP] meal plan available. **Amenities:** voice mail, irons, hair dryers. **Pool(s):** heated indoor. **Leisure Activities:** whirlpool, exercise room. *Fee:* game room. **Guest Services:** complimentary evening beverages: Wed, valet and coin laundry. **Business Services:** meeting rooms, PC. **Cards:** AX, CB, DC, DS, MC, VI. **Special Amenities:** free expanded continental breakfast and free room upgrade (subject to availability with advanced reservations).

SOME UNITS

POINT MOTEL

◆ (Motel)

Book at aaa.com

5/1-8/31	1P: $35-$40	2P: $42-$48	XP: $4	F10
4/1-4/30 & 9/1-3/31	1P: $33-$35	2P: $38-$42	XP: $4	F10

Phone: (715)344-8312

Location: I-39, exit 161 (US 51 business route), just 0.7 mi s. Located in a commercial area. 209 Division St 54481. Fax: 715/344-8313. **Facility:** 44 one-bedroom standard units. 1-2 stories (no elevator), exterior corridors. *Bath:* combo or shower only. **Parking:** on-site, winter plug-ins. **Terms:** office hours 7 am-11:30 pm, small pets only ($5 extra charge). **Amenities:** *Some:* DVD players (fee). **Business Services:** meeting rooms. **Cards:** CB, DC, MC, VI.

SOME UNITS
ASK SD ⛏ 🍴 🎦 DATA PORT 💻 / ✕ VCR 🔒 📷 /
FEE   FEE

─────── WHERE TO DINE ───────

THE RESTAURANT

◆◆◆ American

Dinner: $14-$25   Phone: 715-346-6010

Location: I-39, exit 161 (US 51 business route), just se; in Sentry Headquarters. 1800 N Point Dr 54481. **Hours:** 5 pm-9 pm, Fri & Sat-10 pm. Closed major holidays; also Sun. **Reservations:** suggested. **Features:** The dining room has large windows that overlook a "northwoods" backyard with a wildlife feeding station. The chef makes use of organic and local ingredients, and is happy to accommodate dietary requests. The menu changes seasonally, and the entrees are nicely presented. Scrumptious desserts are prepared in-house. Lunch is served in the more casual Pagliace Taverna from 11 am Mon-Fri. Dressy casual; cocktails. **Parking:** on-site. **Cards:** AX, MC, VI.

🍴 ✕

STOUGHTON pop. 12,354

─────── WHERE TO STAY ───────

CHOSE FAMILY INN

◆◆◆ SAVE ◆◆ Small-scale Hotel

4/1-10/31 [CP]	1P: $66-$72	2P: $72-$78	XP: $6	F14
11/1-3/31 [CP]	1P: $55-$65	2P: $59-$69	XP: $6	F14

Phone: (608)873-0330

Location: On US 51 business route, just w of jct SR 138 S. 1124 W Main St 53589. Fax: 608/873-8904. **Facility:** 53 one-bedroom standard units. 2 stories (no elevator), interior corridors. *Bath:* combo or shower only. **Parking:** on-site, winter plug-ins. **Terms:** cancellation fee imposed, weekly rates available. **Pool(s):** small heated indoor. **Leisure Activities:** whirlpool. **Guest Services:** valet and coin laundry. **Cards:** AX, DC, DS, MC, VI. **Special Amenities:** free continental breakfast and free local telephone calls.

SOME UNITS
SD 🍴 ⛑ 🏊 🛶 🏋 🎦 DATA PORT 💻 / ✕ VCR 🔒 📷 /
FEE FEE FEE

COMFORT INN

◆◆◆◆ Small-scale Hotel

Book at aaa.com

4/1-10/31 [ECP]	1P: $72-$150	2P: $75-$150	XP: $8	F18
11/1-3/31 [ECP]	1P: $72-$140	2P: $75-$140	XP: $8	F18

Phone: (608)877-9000

Location: On US 51 business route, 0.7 mi nw of jct SR 138 S. Truck parking on premises. 660 Nygaard St 53589 (6641 N Kennedy Rd, MILTON, 53563). Fax: 608/877-9799. **Facility:** 50 one-bedroom standard units, some with whirlpools. 2 stories (no elevator), interior corridors. *Bath:* combo or shower only. **Parking:** on-site, winter plug-ins. **Terms:** cancellation fee imposed, package plans. **Amenities:** hair dryers. *Some:* dual phone lines, irons. **Pool(s):** heated indoor. **Leisure Activities:** whirlpool, limited exercise equipment. **Guest Services:** valet and coin laundry. **Business Services:** meeting rooms. **Cards:** AX, CB, DC, DS, MC, VI.

SOME UNITS
ASK SD ⛑ 🏊 🛶 🎦 DATA PORT 💻 / ✕ VCR 🔒 📷 /
FEE

NAESET-ROE BED & BREAKFAST

◆◆◆◆ Historic Bed & Breakfast

All Year [BP]   1P: $75-$165   2P: $85-$175   XP: $25

Phone: 608/877-4150

Location: Just n of US 51 business route; downtown. 126 E Washington St 53589. **Facility:** The restored 1878 Italianate home is furnished with period pieces; guest rooms are well-appointed and some feature whirlpools. Smoke free premises. 4 one-bedroom standard units, some with whirlpools. 2 stories, interior corridors. *Bath:* combo or tub only. **Parking:** on-site. **Terms:** check-in 4 pm, 2 night minimum stay - 7/1-10/31, age restrictions may apply, 7 day cancellation notice-fee imposed, package plans. **Amenities:** hair dryers. *Some:* CD players. **Cards:** DS, MC, VI.

SOME UNITS
✕ ☎ / 📺 VCR

STURGEON BAY —See Door County p. 507.

STURTEVANT pop. 5,287

─────── WHERE TO STAY ───────

BEST WESTERN GRANDVIEW INN

◆◆◆ SAVE ◆◆ Small-scale Hotel

Book at aaa.com

All Year [CP]   1P: $44-$104   2P: $49-$109   XP: $10   F17

Phone: (262)886-0385

Location: I-94, exit 333 (SR 20), just s on west frontage road. 910 S Sylvania Ave 53177. Fax: 262/886-4310. **Facility:** 50 one-bedroom standard units, some with whirlpools. 3 stories (no elevator), interior corridors. **Parking:** on-site. **Amenities:** irons, hair dryers. **Pool(s):** small heated indoor. **Leisure Activities:** whirlpool. *Fee:* game room. **Business Services:** meeting rooms, fax. **Cards:** AX, CB, DC, DS, MC, VI. **Special Amenities:** free continental breakfast.

SOME UNITS
SD 🍴 🛶 🐾 DATA PORT 🔒 💻 / ✕

HOLIDAY INN EXPRESS-RACINE

◆◆◆ SAVE ◆◆ Small-scale Hotel

Book at aaa.com

All Year [ECP]   1P: $69-$99   2P: $69-$99   XP: $6   F18

Phone: (262)884-0200

Location: I-94, exit 333 (SR 20), just se. 13339 Hospitality Ct 53177. Fax: 262/884-0701. **Facility:** 107 one-bedroom standard units, some with whirlpools. 3 stories, interior corridors. *Bath:* combo or shower only. **Parking:** on-site. **Terms:** weekly rates available, [CP] meal plan available, small pets only (in smoking units). **Amenities:** irons, hair dryers. **Pool(s):** small heated indoor. **Leisure Activities:** whirlpool, limited exercise equipment. **Guest Services:** valet and coin laundry. **Business Services:** meeting rooms, business center. **Cards:** AX, CB, DC, DS, MC, VI. **Special Amenities:** free expanded continental breakfast and free local telephone calls.

SOME UNITS
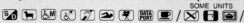
SD 🐾 ⛏ 🏋 ⛑ 🏊 🛶 🎦 DATA PORT 💻 / ✕ 🔒 📷 /

RAMADA LIMITED OF RACINE   *Book at aaa.com*   Phone: 262/884-6840

AAA SAVE | 6/1-8/31 | 1P: $79 | 2P: $89 | XP: $5 | F12
 | 4/1-5/31 & 9/1-3/31 | 1P: $59 | 2P: $59 | XP: $5 | F12

Location: I-94, exit 333 (SR 20), just se. 13340 Hospitality Ct 53177. **Fax:** 262/884-6847. **Facility:** 48 one-bedroom standard units, some with whirlpools. 2 stories (no elevator), interior corridors. **Parking:** on-site, winter plug-ins. **Terms:** [CP] meal plan available. **Amenities:** voice mail, irons, hair dryers. *Fee:* video library, high-speed Internet. **Pool(s):** small heated indoor. **Leisure Activities:** limited exercise equipment. **Guest Services:** valet and coin laundry. **Business Services:** meeting rooms. **Cards:** AX, DC, DS, JC, MC, VI. **Special Amenities:** free continental breakfast and free newspaper.

Small-scale Hotel

SOME UNITS

[icons] SD (11+) 🏊 📺 DATA PORT 🛢 💻 / ✕ VCR 📱 / FEE

SUN PRAIRIE pop. 20,369

──── WHERE TO STAY ────

AMERIHOST INN-SUN PRAIRIE   *Book at aaa.com*   Phone: (608)834-9889

AAA SAVE | 6/1-10/31 [ECP] | 1P: $59-$89 | 2P: $69-$94 | XP: $5 | F12
 | 4/1-5/31 & 11/1-3/31 [ECP] | 1P: $49-$69 | 2P: $54-$79 | XP: $5 | F12

Location: US 151, exit 103 (CR N), just n. 105 Business Park Dr 53590. **Fax:** 608/834-9779. **Facility:** 62 one-bedroom standard units, some with whirlpools. 2 stories, interior corridors. *Bath:* combo or shower only. **Parking:** on-site, winter plug-ins. **Terms:** cancellation fee imposed. **Amenities:** voice mail, safes (fee), irons, hair dryers. **Pool(s):** heated indoor. **Leisure Activities:** whirlpool, exercise room. **Guest Services:** valet laundry. **Business Services:** meeting rooms. **Cards:** AX, CB, DC, DS, JC, MC, VI. **Special Amenities:** free expanded continental breakfast and free local telephone calls.

Small-scale Hotel

SOME UNITS

[icons] SD 💺 🏊 📺 DATA PORT 💻 / ✕ VCR 🛢 📱 /

McGOVERN'S MOTEL & SUITES   Phone: 608/837-7321

AAA SAVE | All Year | 1P: $46-$75 | 2P: $56-$80 | XP: $3

Motel

Location: On US 151, exit 101, 1.2 mi ne. 820 W Main St 53590. **Fax:** 608/825-3800. **Facility:** 54 one-bedroom standard units, some with whirlpools. 2 stories, interior/exterior corridors. *Bath:* combo or shower only. **Parking:** on-site, winter plug-ins. **Terms:** [CP] meal plan available, small pets only ($5 extra charge). **Dining:** 11 am-10 pm, cocktails. **Guest Services:** complimentary laundry. **Business Services:** meeting rooms. **Cards:** AX, DC, DS, MC, VI. **Special Amenities:** free continental breakfast and free newspaper.

SOME UNITS

[icons] SD 🐕 11 / ✕ 🛢 📱 💻 / FEE

SUPERIOR pop. 27,368

──── WHERE TO STAY ────

BARKERS ISLAND INN   Phone: (715)392-7152

AAA SAVE | All Year | 1P: $67-$210 | 2P: $67-$210 | XP: $5 | F18

Location: Just ne of US 2/53; on Barkers Island. Located adjacent to the marina. 300 Marina Dr 54880. **Fax:** 715/392-1180. **Facility:** 112 units. 110 one-bedroom standard units, some with whirlpools. 2 one-bedroom suites with whirlpools. 2 stories (no elevator), interior corridors. **Parking:** on-site. **Terms:** pets ($50 deposit, $10 extra charge). **Amenities:** voice mail. *Some:* hair dryers. **Dining:** 6:30 am-9 pm, Fri & Sat-10 pm, Sun-8:30 pm; hours may vary seasonally. **Pool(s):** heated indoor. **Leisure Activities:** sauna, whirlpool. *Fee:* game room. **Guest Services:** valet and coin laundry. **Business Services:** conference facilities, fax (fee). **Cards:** AX, CB, DC, DS, MC, VI. *(See color ad below)*

Small-scale Hotel

SOME UNITS

[icons] SD 🐕 11 🍷 🏊 ✕ 📺 DATA PORT / ✕ 🛢 📱 💻 / FEE

BEST WESTERN BAY WALK INN

Book at aaa.com

Small-scale Hotel

5/28-9/18 [ECP]	1P: $75-$119	2P: $79-$119	XP: $4	F16
9/19-10/23 [ECP]	1P: $55-$109	2P: $59-$109	XP: $4	F16
4/1-5/27 [ECP]	1P: $55-$85	2P: $59-$89	XP: $4	F16
10/24-3/31 [ECP]	1P: $55-$75	2P: $59-$79	XP: $4	F16

Phone: (715)392-7600

Location: Just e of US 2 on Belknap St. 1405 Susquehanna Ave 54880. Fax: 715/392-7680. **Facility:** 50 one-bedroom standard units, some with whirlpools. 2 stories, interior corridors. **Parking:** on-site, winter plug-ins. **Terms:** small pets only. **Amenities:** video library (fee), irons, hair dryers. **Pool(s):** heated indoor. **Leisure Activities:** sauna, whirlpool. **Fee:** game room. **Guest Services:** valet and coin laundry. **Business Services:** meeting rooms. **Cards:** AX, CB, DC, DS, MC, VI.

SOME UNITS

BEST WESTERN BRIDGEVIEW MOTOR INN

Book at aaa.com

Small-scale Hotel

6/11-10/23 [ECP]	1P: $69-$135	2P: $69-$135	XP: $5	F
5/21-6/10 [ECP]	1P: $49-$115	2P: $49-$115	XP: $5	F
4/1-5/20 & 10/24-3/31 [ECP]	1P: $49-$99	2P: $49-$99	XP: $5	F

Phone: (715)392-8174

Location: 0.8 mi n at south end of Blatnik Bridge. 415 Hammond Ave 54880. Fax: 715/392-8487. **Facility:** 96 units. 85 one-bedroom standard units. 11 one-bedroom suites, some with whirlpools. 2 stories, interior corridors. **Parking:** on-site, winter plug-ins. **Terms:** small pets only. **Amenities:** video games (fee), irons, hair dryers. **Pool(s):** heated indoor. **Leisure Activities:** sauna, whirlpool. **Fee:** game room. **Guest Services:** complimentary evening beverages: Mon-Thurs, coin laundry. **Business Services:** meeting rooms. **Cards:** AX, CB, DC, DS, MC, VI. **Special Amenities:** free expanded continental breakfast and free local telephone calls. *(See color ad below)*

SOME UNITS

DAYS INN-SUPERIOR/BAYFRONT

Book at aaa.com

Small-scale Hotel

6/1-9/5	1P: $69-$109	2P: $79-$119	XP: $10	F18
9/6-10/31	1P: $59-$99	2P: $69-$109	XP: $10	F18
4/1-5/31 & 11/1-3/31	1P: $49-$79	2P: $59-$89	XP: $10	F18

Phone: (715)392-4783

Location: Just n of jct US 2/53. 110 Harborview Pkwy 54880. Fax: 715/392-4787. **Facility:** 111 one-bedroom standard units. 2 stories (no elevator), interior/exterior corridors. *Bath:* combo or shower only. **Parking:** on-site, winter plug-ins. **Terms:** weekly rates available. **Amenities:** hair dryers. **Pool(s):** heated indoor. **Leisure Activities:** sauna, whirlpool. **Fee:** game room. **Guest Services:** coin laundry. **Cards:** AX, CB, DC, DS, MC, VI. *(See color ad card insert)*

SOME UNITS

HOLIDAY INN EXPRESS

Book at aaa.com

Small-scale Hotel

6/18-9/6 [ECP]	1P: $89-$189	2P: $89-$189	XP: $10	F
4/1-6/17 & 9/7-3/31 [ECP]	1P: $79-$169	2P: $79-$169	XP: $10	F

Phone: (715)392-3444

Location: Just n of jct US 2/53. 303 2nd Ave E 54880. Fax: 715/395-7911. **Facility:** 84 one-bedroom standard units, some with whirlpools. 3 stories, interior corridors. *Bath:* combo or shower only. **Parking:** on-site, winter plug-ins. **Terms:** cancellation fee imposed. **Amenities:** high-speed Internet, dual phone lines, voice mail, irons, hair dryers. **Pool(s):** small heated indoor. **Leisure Activities:** whirlpool, limited exercise equipment. **Guest Services:** valet and coin laundry. **Business Services:** meeting rooms, business center. **Cards:** AX, CB, DC, DS, JC, MC, VI.

SOME UNITS

STOCKADE MOTEL

Motel

Phone: 715/398-3585

Property failed to provide current rates

Location: On US 2/53, 2.8 mi se. 1610 E 2nd St 54880. **Facility:** 17 one-bedroom standard units. 1 story, exterior corridors. *Bath:* combo or shower only. **Parking:** on-site, winter plug-ins. **Terms:** office hours 8 am-midnight, small pets only ($10 deposit).

SOME UNITS

SUPER 8 MOTEL OF SUPERIOR

Small-scale Hotel

6/18-9/11 [CP]	1P: $69-$105	2P: $69-$105	XP: $5	F12
9/12-3/31 [CP]	1P: $56-$91	2P: $56-$91	XP: $5	F12
4/1-6/17 [CP]	1P: $54-$89	2P: $54-$89	XP: $5	F12

Phone: (715)398-7686

Location: 6 mi se on US 2/53. 4901 E 2nd St 54880. **Facility:** 40 one-bedroom standard units. 2 stories (no elevator), interior corridors. **Parking:** on-site, winter plug-ins. **Cards:** AX, CB, DC, DS, MC, VI.

SOME UNITS

SUPERIOR INN

Phone: (715)394-7706

AAA SAVE

Small-scale Hotel

6/17-10/21		1P: $65-$69	2P: $105-$120	XP: $4	F18
4/1-6/16		1P: $55-$69	2P: $90-$95	XP: $4	F18
10/22-3/31		1P: $49-$69	2P: $85-$95	XP: $4	F18

Location: 0.8 mi n at south end of Blatnik Bridge. 525 Hammond Ave 54880. Fax: 715/394-7708. **Facility:** 69 units. 68 one-bedroom standard units. 1 one-bedroom suite ($100-$160) with whirlpool. 2 stories, interior corridors. **Parking:** on-site, winter plug-ins. **Terms:** [CP] meal plan available. **Amenities:** voice mail, hair dryers. **Pool(s):** small heated indoor. **Leisure Activities:** sauna, whirlpool. **Business Services:** fax (fee). **Cards:** AX, DS, MC, VI.

SOME UNITS

WHERE TO DINE

THE SHACK SMOKEHOUSE & GRILLE

American

cocktails.

Lunch: $7-$19   **Dinner:** $7-$19   Phone: 715/392-9836
Location: 1.5 mi w. 3301 Belknap St 54880. **Hours:** 11 am-9 pm, Sun-8 pm. Closed: 12/25. **Reservations:** accepted. **Features:** Steak, seafood, chicken, prime rib and the house specialty smokehouse barbecue ribs—in addition to lunch choices of lighter fare—make up a diverse menu at the established restaurant. Service is friendly and unpretentious, and portion sizes are ample. Casual dress; **Parking:** on-site. **Cards:** DC, DS, MC, VI.

THORP pop. 1,536

WHERE TO STAY

AMERICINN LODGE & SUITES   *Book at aaa.com*

AAA SAVE

Small-scale Hotel

Phone: (715)669-5959

1/1-3/31		1P: $67-$131	2P: $87-$131	XP: $8	F12
4/1-12/31		1P: $66-$130	2P: $76-$130	XP: $8	F12

Location: US 29, exit 108 (SR 73), just nw. 203 1/2 W Hill St 54771. Fax: 715/669-5907. **Facility:** 42 one-bedroom standard units, some with whirlpools. 2 stories (no elevator), interior corridors. *Bath:* combo or shower only. **Parking:** on-site. **Terms:** [ECP] meal plan available, pets ($10 fee). **Amenities:** hair dryers. *Some:* irons. **Pool(s):** heated indoor. **Leisure Activities:** sauna, whirlpool. **Guest Services:** coin laundry. **Business Services:** meeting rooms, fax (fee). **Cards:** AX, DS, MC, VI. **Special Amenities:** free expanded continental breakfast and free newspaper. *(See color ad p 576)*

SOME UNITS

TOMAH pop. 8,419

WHERE TO STAY

COMFORT INN-TOMAH   *Book at aaa.com*

Small-scale Hotel

Phone: (608)372-6600

6/17-9/30 [CP]		1P: $69-$109	2P: $74-$114	XP: $5	F18
4/1-5/31 & 10/1-3/31 [CP]		1P: $59-$84	2P: $64-$89	XP: $5	F18

Location: I-94, exit 143 (SR 21), just w. 305 Wittig Rd 54660. Fax: 608/372-6600. **Facility:** 52 one-bedroom standard units. 2 stories (no elevator), interior corridors. **Parking:** on-site, winter plug-ins. **Terms:** pets (in smoking units). **Amenities:** irons, hair dryers. **Pool(s):** small heated indoor. **Leisure Activities:** whirlpool. **Business Services:** fax (fee). **Cards:** AX, CB, DC, DS, JC, MC, VI.

SOME UNITS

CRANBERRY COUNTRY LODGE
Phone: (608)374-2801

5/28-9/7	1P: $79-$189
4/1-5/27 & 9/8-3/31	1P: $59-$189

Small-scale Hotel **Location:** I-94, exit 143 (SR 21), just w. 319 Wittig Rd 54660. Fax: 608/374-2805. **Facility:** 93 units. 54 one-bedroom standard units, some with whirlpools. 39 one-bedroom suites, some with whirlpools. 3 stories, interior corridors. *Bath:* combo or shower only. **Parking:** on-site, winter plug-ins. **Terms:** package plans - seasonal. **Amenities:** voice mail, irons, hair dryers. **Pool(s):** 2 small heated indoor, wading. **Leisure Activities:** whirlpool, waterslide, exercise room. *Fee:* game room. **Guest Services:** gift shop, coin laundry. **Business Services:** conference facilities, business center. **Cards:** AX, DC, DS, MC, VI.

SOME UNITS

ECONO LODGE   *Book at aaa.com*
Phone: (608)372-9100

5/16-10/31	1P: $65-$145	2P: $70-$145	XP: $5	F18
4/1-5/15 & 11/1-3/31	1P: $36-$140	2P: $41-$140	XP: $5	F18

Small-scale Hotel **Location:** I-94, exit 143 (SR 21), just w. 2005 N Superior Ave 54660 (PO Box 169). Fax: 608/372-6003. **Facility:** 77 one-bedroom standard units, some with whirlpools. 2 stories (no elevator), interior/exterior corridors. **Parking:** on-site, winter plug-ins. **Terms:** [CP] meal plan available, pets ($10 extra charge). **Amenities:** video library (fee), hair dryers. **Pool(s):** small heated indoor. **Leisure Activities:** whirlpool. **Guest Services:** coin laundry. **Cards:** AX, CB, DC, DS, JC, MC, VI.

SOME UNITS
FEE

HOLIDAY INN   *Book at aaa.com*
Phone: (608)372-3211

5/28-9/26	1P: $99-$115	2P: $99-$115	XP: $6	F18
4/1-5/27 & 9/27-3/31	1P: $89-$99	2P: $89-$99	XP: $6	F18

Small-scale Hotel **Location:** I-94, exit 143 (SR 21), just e. 1017 E McCoy Blvd 54660 (PO Box 845). Fax: 608/372-3243. **Facility:** 100 one-bedroom standard units. 2 stories (no elevator), interior corridors. **Parking:** on-site, winter plug-ins. **Amenities:** video games (fee), dual phone lines, voice mail, irons, hair dryers. **Pool(s):** heated indoor. **Leisure Activities:** sauna, whirlpool, exercise room. *Fee:* game room. **Guest Services:** valet and coin laundry. **Business Services:** meeting rooms, business center. **Cards:** AX, DC, DS, MC, VI.

SOME UNITS

LARK INN
Phone: (608)372-5981

4/1-10/31 [ECP]	1P: $61-$84	2P: $68-$91	XP: $7	D12
11/1-3/31 [ECP]	1P: $52-$73	2P: $59-$80	XP: $7	D12

Motel **Location:** I-94, exit 143 (SR 21), 1.5 mi s on US 12; 1-90, exit 41, 2 mi n on US 12. 229 N Superior Ave 54660. Fax: 608/372-3009. **Facility:** 25 units. 22 one-bedroom standard units. 2 one- and 1 two-bedroom suites with kitchens. 2 stories, interior/exterior corridors. *Bath:* combo or shower only. **Parking:** on-site, winter plug-ins. **Terms:** pets ($6 extra charge). **Amenities:** dual phone lines, voice mail. *Fee:* video library, high-speed Internet. *Some:* irons, hair dryers. **Leisure Activities:** gazebo. **Guest Services:** gift shop, coin laundry. **Business Services:** meeting rooms. **Cards:** AX, CB, DC, DS, MC, VI. *(See color ad p 633)*

SOME UNITS
FEE

SUPER 8 MOTEL-TOMAH   *Book at aaa.com*
Phone: (608)372-3901

5/21-9/30 [CP]	1P: $58-$78	2P: $58-$78	XP: $5	F12
4/1-5/20 & 10/1-3/31 [CP]	1P: $48-$68	2P: $48-$68	XP: $5	F12

Small-scale Hotel **Location:** I-94, exit 143 (SR 21), just e. 1008 E McCoy Blvd 54660. Fax: 608/372-5792. **Facility:** 65 one-bedroom standard units, some with whirlpools. 2 stories (no elevator), interior corridors. *Bath:* combo or shower only. **Parking:** on-site, winter plug-ins. **Terms:** pets ($10 extra charge). **Amenities:** safes. **Guest Services:** coin laundry. **Business Services:** meeting rooms. **Cards:** AX, CB, DC, DS, MC, VI.

SOME UNITS
FEE

------- WHERE TO DINE -------

BURNSTAD'S EUROPEAN CAFE
Lunch: $5-$7   **Dinner:** $8-$14   **Phone:** 608/372-4040

American **Location:** I-90, exit 43 (SR 21), 1 mi n on US 12 and 16; in Burnstad's European Village. 701 E Clifton St 54660. **Hours:** 8 am-9 pm, Sun-8 pm. Closed: 1/1, 11/25, 12/25; also 12/24 for dinner. **Reservations:** accepted. **Features:** This casual restaurant is adjacent to a quaint gift shop. The menu offers steak, seafood, pork and chicken dishes such as Canadian walleye, Rosemary pork loin and cranberry bog chicken. Light appetite menu and some Italian entrees are available. The bread and desserts are made from scratch in-house. Casual dress; cocktails. **Parking:** on-site. **Cards:** AX, DC, DS, MC, VI.

TOMAHAWK pop. 3,770

------- WHERE TO STAY -------

BEST WESTERN LAKE AIRE MOTEL   *Book at aaa.com*
Phone: (715)453-5189

4/1-9/30 & 1/1-3/15 [CP]	1P: $64-$150	2P: $64-$150	XP: $10	F12
10/1-12/31 & 3/16-3/31 [CP]	1P: $60-$135	2P: $60-$135	XP: $10	F12

Motel **Location:** 0.6 mi n of jct US 8. Located on Lake Nokomis. N 11925 Business Hwy 51 54487. Fax: 715/453-1428. **Facility:** 25 units. 24 one-bedroom standard units, some with efficiencies and/or whirlpools. 1 cottage. 2 stories (no elevator), exterior corridors. **Parking:** on-site, winter plug-ins. **Terms:** 2 night minimum stay - weekends. **Amenities:** irons, hair dryers. **Leisure Activities:** boat dock, fishing, sun deck, grill, horseshoes, volleyball. **Business Services:** fax (fee). **Cards:** AX, CB, DC, DS, MC, VI. **Special Amenities:** free continental breakfast and early check-in/late check-out.

SOME UNITS

COMFORT INN AAA SAVE ▽▽▽▽ *Small-scale Hotel*

Book at aaa.com

Phone: (715)453-8900

5/1-7/31	1P: $75-$115	2P: $75-$115	XP: $5	F18
8/1-3/31	1P: $63-$90	2P: $63-$90	XP: $5	F18
4/1-4/30	1P: $70	2P: $70	XP: $5	F18

Location: US 51, exit 229. 1738 E Comfort Dr 54487. Fax: 715/453-5030. **Facility:** 46 units. 44 one-bedroom standard units. 2 one-bedroom suites. 2 stories, interior corridors. *Bath:* combo or shower only. **Parking:** on-site. **Terms:** check-in 4 pm, [ECP] meal plan available, small pets only ($15 fee). **Amenities:** high-speed Internet, voice mail, irons, hair dryers. **Pool(s):** heated indoor. **Leisure Activities:** exercise room. *Fee:* game room. **Guest Services:** complimentary evening beverages, coin laundry. **Business Services:** meeting rooms. **Cards:** AX, CB, DC, DS, JC, MC, VI. **Special Amenities:** free expanded continental breakfast and free local telephone calls.

SOME UNITS

SUPER 8 MOTEL-TOMAHAWK ▽▽ ▽▽ *Small-scale Hotel*

Book at aaa.com

Phone: 715/453-5210

6/1-9/30	1P: $56-$89	2P: $56-$89	XP: $6	F12
10/1-3/31	1P: $53-$86	2P: $53-$86	XP: $6	F12
4/1-5/31	1P: $53-$80	2P: $53-$80	XP: $6	F12

Location: On US 51 business route, 0.6 mi n of downtown. 108 W Mohawk Dr 54487. Fax: 715/453-9700. **Facility:** 56 units. 54 one-bedroom standard units, some with whirlpools. 2 one-bedroom suites ($83). 3 stories, interior corridors. *Bath:* combo or shower only. **Parking:** on-site, winter plug-ins. **Terms:** [CP] meal plan available, pets ($25 deposit). **Amenities:** hair dryers. **Pool(s):** heated indoor. **Leisure Activities:** sauna, whirlpool. **Guest Services:** coin laundry. **Business Services:** meeting rooms, fax (fee). **Cards:** AX, CB, DC, DS, JC, MC, VI.

SOME UNITS

TREMPEALEAU pop. 1,319

——— **WHERE TO STAY** ———

PLEASANT KNOLL MOTEL ▽▽ ▽▽ *Motel*

Phone: 608/534-6615

All Year	1P: $51-$69	2P: $51-$69	XP: $5	F12

Location: Center. 11451 Main St 54661. **Facility:** 16 one-bedroom standard units, some with kitchens (no utensils). 1-2 stories, exterior corridors. *Bath:* combo or shower only. **Parking:** on-site. **Terms:** 2 night minimum stay - weekends, cancellation fee imposed. **Amenities:** dual phone lines. *Some:* hair dryers. **Leisure Activities:** whirlpool. **Guest Services:** area transportation. **Cards:** AX, DS, MC, VI.

SOME UNITS

TURTLE LAKE pop. 1,065

——— **WHERE TO STAY** ———

COUNTRY INN & SUITES BY CARLSON ▽▽▽▽ *Small-scale Hotel*

Book at aaa.com

Phone: (715)986-2070

5/23-10/17 [CP]	1P: $74-$105	2P: $74-$105	XP: $5	F18
4/1-5/22 & 10/18-3/31 [CP]	1P: $63-$88	2P: $63-$88	XP: $5	F18

Location: On US 8, 0.4 mi e of jct US 63 S. 636 Hwy 8 & 63 54889. Fax: 715/986-2824. **Facility:** 46 one-bedroom standard units. 2 stories, interior corridors. *Bath:* combo or shower only. **Parking:** on-site, winter plug-ins. **Amenities:** voice mail, irons, hair dryers. **Pool(s):** small heated indoor. **Leisure Activities:** whirlpool. **Guest Services:** coin laundry. **Business Services:** meeting rooms, fax (fee). **Cards:** AX, DC, DS, MC, VI. *(See color ad starting on p 580)*

SOME UNITS

ST. CROIX CASINO HOTEL ▽▽ ▽▽ *Small-scale Hotel*

Phone: 715/986-4000

5/26-9/7 [ECP]	1P: $55-$67	2P: $61-$73	XP: $4	F11
4/1-5/25 & 9/8-3/31 [ECP]	1P: $50-$62	2P: $55-$67	XP: $4	F11

Location: On US 8, 0.4 mi e jct US 63 S. 631 Hwy 8 54889 (777 Hwy 8/63). Fax: 715/986-4040. **Facility:** 162 units. 154 one-bedroom standard units. 8 one-bedroom suites ($95-$165) with whirlpools. 3 stories, interior corridors. *Bath:* combo or shower only. **Parking:** on-site. **Amenities:** video games, hair dryers. **Pool(s):** heated indoor. **Leisure Activities:** sauna, whirlpool, limited exercise equipment. **Guest Services:** area transportation. **Business Services:** meeting rooms. **Cards:** AX, DS, MC, VI.

SOME UNITS

TWO RIVERS pop. 12,639

——— **WHERE TO STAY** ———

LIGHTHOUSE INN ON THE LAKE ▽▽ ▽▽ *Small-scale Hotel*

Phone: (920)793-4524

6/1-10/31	1P: $85-$100	2P: $95-$110	XP: $10	F18
4/1-5/31 & 11/1-3/31	1P: $75-$90	2P: $85-$100	XP: $10	F18

Location: 0.3 mi s on SR 42. Located on the shore of Lake Michigan. 1515 Memorial Dr 54241. Fax: 920/793-4524. **Facility:** 67 one-bedroom standard units. 2 stories (no elevator), interior corridors. **Parking:** on-site, winter plug-ins. **Terms:** [AP] meal plan available, package plans. **Amenities:** dual phone lines. *Some:* hair dryers. **Dining:** Waters Edge Restaurant, see separate listing. **Pool(s):** heated indoor. **Leisure Activities:** sauna, whirlpool, fishing, exercise room. **Guest Services:** coin laundry. **Business Services:** conference facilities. **Cards:** AX, CB, DC, DS, MC, VI.

SOME UNITS

RED FOREST BED & BREAKFAST
All Year [BP]   1P: $92   2P: $97   **Phone: (920)793-1794**
XP: $15
Bed & Breakfast   **Location:** Just n of SR 42 on Washington St. Located in a residential area. 1421 25th St 54241. **Fax:** 920/793-3056. **Facility:** This shingle-style 1907 home close to downtown and historical attractions features stained glass, a country dining room and heirloom antiques. Smoke free premises. 4 one-bedroom standard units. 2 stories (no elevator), interior corridors. *Bath:* combo or shower only. **Parking:** on-site. **Terms:** age restrictions may apply, 7 day cancellation notice. **Amenities:** CD players. **Guest Services:** TV in common area. **Cards:** DS, MC, VI.

SOME UNITS

——— **WHERE TO DINE** ———

WATERS EDGE RESTAURANT   **Lunch:** $5-$10   **Dinner:** $8-$22   **Phone:** 920/793-4524
American   **Location:** 0.3 mi s on SR 42; in Lighthouse Inn on the Lake. 1515 Memorial Dr 54241. **Hours:** 6:30 am-10 pm; to 9 pm off season, Sun from 7:30 am. **Reservations:** accepted. **Features:** The views of Lake Michigan are wonderful from this casual restaurant with a nautical theme. The well-seasoned staff is familiar to regular CB, DC, MC, VI.   guests. Bread and soup are made daily in-house. Casual dress; cocktails. **Parking:** on-site. **Cards:** AX,

VERONA pop. 7,052

——— **WHERE TO STAY** ———

SUPER 8 MOTEL-VERONA/MADISON   *Book at aaa.com*
  6/1-10/31 [CP]   1P: $64-$69   2P: $70-$75   **Phone: (608)848-7829**
XP: $6   F18
  4/1-5/31 & 11/1-3/31 [CP]   1P: $60-$65   2P: $66-$71   XP: $6   F18
Small-scale Hotel   **Location:** US 18 and 151, exit 94 southbound; exit 89 northbound, just n. 131 Horizon Dr 53593. **Fax:** 608/848-7833. **Facility:** 43 units. 42 one-bedroom standard units, some with whirlpools. 1 one-bedroom suite ($90-$106). 2 stories, interior corridors. **Parking:** on-site, winter plug-ins. **Terms:** small pets only ($10 fee). **Amenities:** voice mail, safes. *Some:* hair dryers. **Pool(s):** small heated indoor. **Leisure Activities:** whirlpool, exercise room. *Fee:* game room. **Business Services:** meeting rooms. **Cards:** AX, DC, DS, MC, VI.

SOME UNITS
FEE

VIROQUA pop. 4,335

——— **WHERE TO STAY** ———

HICKORY HILL MOTEL
  4/1-11/1   1P: $40-$55   2P: $50-$65   **Phone: (608)637-3104**
XP: $5   F15
  11/2-3/31   1P: $40-$45   2P: $40-$45   XP: $5   F15
Motel   **Location:** 1.8 mi se on SR 14, 27 and 82. Located in a rural area. US 14 S 3955 54665 (PO Box 126). **Fax:** 608/637-8792. **Facility:** 25 one-bedroom standard units, some with efficiencies (no utensils). 1 story, exterior corridors. *Bath:* combo or shower only. **Parking:** on-site, winter plug-ins. **Terms:** weekly rates available, [ECP] meal plan available. **Amenities:** hair dryers. **Pool(s):** small heated outdoor. **Business Services:** fax. **Cards:** AX, DC, MC, VI.

SOME UNITS

VIROQUA SUPER 8
All Year   1P: $58-$150   2P: $63-$150   **Phone: 608/637-3100**
XP: $5   F12
  Location: 1 mi n of center on SR 14, 16 and 27. 1325 N Main St 54665. **Fax:** 608/637-7026. **Facility:** 50 units. 49 one-bedroom standard units, some with whirlpools. 1 two-bedroom suite. 2 stories, interior corridors. *Bath:* combo or shower only. **Parking:** on-site, winter plug-ins. **Terms:** check-in 4 pm, package plans - weekends. Small-scale Hotel   **Pool(s):** small heated indoor. **Leisure Activities:** whirlpool. **Guest Services:** coin laundry. **Business Services:** meeting rooms. **Cards:** AX, CB, DC, MC, VI. **Special Amenities:** free continental breakfast and free local telephone calls.

SOME UNITS

WASHBURN pop. 2,280

——— **WHERE TO DINE** ———

STEAK PIT   **Dinner:** $8-$25
  Phone: 715/373-5492
  Location: Just e of SR 13. 125 Harborview Dr 54891. **Hours:** 5 pm-10 pm, Sun 4 pm-9 pm. **Closed:** 11/25, 12/24, 12/25. **Reservations:** suggested. **Features:** Set alongside Lake Superior with views of the marina. This restaurant is an older style steakhouse that offers a good variety of meat and freshwater fish. Service Steak & Seafood   is unpretentious and friendly and the food is well-prepared. Casual dress; cocktails. **Parking:** on-site. **Cards:** MC, VI.

WATERFORD pop. 4,048

——— **WHERE TO STAY** ———

BAYMONT INNS & SUITES-WATERFORD   *Book at aaa.com*
All Year [ECP]   1P: $66-$98   2P: $66-$98   **Phone: (262)534-4100**
XP: $10   F18
  Location: On SR 36, 1 mi s of jct SR 164. Located next to a residential area. 750 Fox Ln 53185. **Fax:** 262/534-4101. **Facility:** 52 units. 50 one-bedroom standard units, some with whirlpools. 2 one-bedroom suites ($109-$149). 3 stories, interior corridors. *Bath:* combo or shower only. **Parking:** on-site. **Terms:** pets ($50 deposit). Small-scale Hotel   **Amenities:** voice mail, irons, hair dryers. *Some:* DVD players, high-speed Internet. **Pool(s):** small heated indoor. **Leisure Activities:** whirlpool, exercise room. **Guest Services:** valet and coin laundry. **Business Services:** meeting rooms, business center. **Cards:** AX, DC, DS, MC, VI. **Special Amenities:** free expanded continental breakfast.

SOME UNITS
FEE

WATERTOWN pop. 21,598

———— WHERE TO STAY ————

ECONO LODGE ▼▼ ▼▼ *Book at aaa.com* **Phone:** (920)261-9010

5/2-10/31	1P: $64-$74	2P: $69-$79	XP: $5 F18
4/1-5/1 & 11/1-3/31	1P: $54-$64	2P: $59-$69	XP: $5 F18

Small-scale Hotel **Location:** On US 16 and SR 19. 700 E Main St 53094. Fax: 920/261-9204. **Facility:** 38 one-bedroom standard units, some with whirlpools. 2 stories (no elevator), interior corridors. **Parking:** on-site. **Terms:** cancellation fee imposed, [CP] meal plan available, pets ($10 fee; $25 deposit). **Business Services:** meeting rooms. **Cards:** AX, DC, MC, VI.

(ASK) (S⊕) 🐾 (†↑) 📷 (DATA PORT) / ✕ 🛢 🖳 / SOME UNITS FEE

HOLIDAY INN EXPRESS ▼▼▼▼ *Book at aaa.com* **Phone:** (920)262-1910

6/1-8/31	1P: $89-$109	2P: $89-$109	XP: $6 F19
9/1-10/31	1P: $79-$109	2P: $79-$109	XP: $6 F19
4/1-5/31 & 11/1-3/31	1P: $79-$99	2P: $79-$99	XP: $6 F19

Small-scale Hotel **Location:** On SR 26, 1.5 mi s of jct SR 19. 101 Aviation Way 53094 (PO Box 481). Fax: 920/262-0557. **Facility:** 79 one-bedroom standard units, some with whirlpools. 2 stories (no elevator), interior corridors. *Bath:* combo or shower only. **Parking:** on-site, winter plug-ins. **Terms:** [ECP] meal plan available, pets ($50 deposit). **Amenities:** voice mail, irons, hair dryers. *Some:* dual phone lines. **Pool(s):** small heated indoor. **Leisure Activities:** sauna, whirlpool, exercise room. **Guest Services:** valet and coin laundry. **Business Services:** meeting rooms, fax (fee). **Cards:** AX, CB, DC, DS, JC, MC, VI.

(ASK) (S⊕) 🐾 (†↑) (♿) 🛌 ✕ 📷 (DATA PORT) / ✕ 🛢 🖳 / SOME UNITS FEE

SUPER 8 MOTEL ▼▼ ▼▼ *Book at aaa.com* **Phone:** (920)261-1188

All Year	1P: $63-$78	2P: $68-$83	XP: $5 F12

Small-scale Hotel **Location:** On SR 26, 1.5 mi s of jct SR 19. 1730 S Church St 53094 (PO Box 503). Fax: 920/261-1188. **Facility:** 45 units. 44 one-bedroom standard units, some with whirlpools. 1 one-bedroom suite with whirlpool. 2 stories (no elevator), interior corridors. *Bath:* combo or shower only. **Parking:** on-site, winter plug-ins. **Terms:** [CP] meal plan available, pets ($50 deposit). **Pool(s):** small heated indoor. **Leisure Activities:** whirlpool. *Fee:* game room. **Business Services:** meeting rooms, fax. **Cards:** AX, CB, DC, DS, JC, MC, VI.

(ASK) (S⊕) 🐾 (†↑) 🛌 📷 (DATA PORT) / ✕ 🛢 🖳 / SOME UNITS FEE

———— WHERE TO DINE ————

THE UPPER KRUST ▼ American **Lunch:** $5-$7   **Dinner:** $5-$7   **Phone:** 920/206-9202
Location: Just se of jct SR 26 and 19. 210 S Water St 53094. **Hours:** 10 am-7 pm, Fri-8 pm, Sat 11 am-6 pm, Sun 11 am-4 pm. Closed major holidays. **Reservations:** accepted. **Features:** In The Market in the Old Mill District, the popular restaurant has charming country decor. Homemade pies are the big draw, but don't overlook the scrumptious soups, salads and sandwiches made daily from fresh ingredients. Casual dress. **Parking:** on-site. **Cards:** AX, DS, MC, VI.

✕

WAUKESHA —See Milwaukee p. 600.

WAUNAKEE pop. 8,995

———— WHERE TO STAY ————

COUNTRY INN & SUITES BY CARLSON (AAA) (SAVE) ▼▼▼▼ *Book at aaa.com* **Phone:** (608)849-6900

All Year	1P: $78-$89	2P: $78-$89	XP: $8 F18

Small-scale Hotel **Location:** 0.8 mi e on SR 19 and 113. 904 E Main St 53597. Fax: 608/849-5994. **Facility:** 38 units. 37 one-bedroom standard units, some with whirlpools. 1 one-bedroom suite with whirlpool. 2 stories (no elevator), interior corridors. **Parking:** on-site, winter plug-ins. **Terms:** cancellation fee imposed, [ECP] meal plan available. **Amenities:** voice mail, irons, hair dryers. **Pool(s):** small heated indoor. **Leisure Activities:** whirlpool. **Guest Services:** coin laundry. **Business Services:** meeting rooms. **Cards:** AX, DC, DS, JC, MC, VI. **Special Amenities:** free expanded continental breakfast and free local telephone calls. *(See color ad starting on p 580)*

(S⊕) (†↑) 🛌 (DATA PORT) 🖳 / ✕ 🛢 🖳 / SOME UNITS

WAUPACA pop. 5,676

———— WHERE TO STAY ————

BAYMONT INN & SUITES (AAA) (SAVE) ▼▼▼▼ *Book at aaa.com* **Phone:** (715)258-9212

5/28-9/25 [ECP]	1P: $82-$139	2P: $149	XP: $10 F17
4/1-5/27 & 9/26-3/31 [ECP]	1P: $75-$119	2P: $129	XP: $10 F17

Small-scale Hotel **Location:** Jct US 10 and SR 54. Located in a commercial area. 110 Grand Seasons Dr 54981 (PO Box 529). Fax: 715/258-0475. **Facility:** 88 units. 84 one-bedroom standard units, some with whirlpools. 4 one-bedroom suites ($109-$249) with whirlpools. 3 stories, interior corridors. *Bath:* combo or shower only. **Parking:** on-site, winter plug-ins. **Terms:** package plans - seasonal, small pets only ($50 deposit). **Amenities:** video games (fee), voice mail, safes, irons, hair dryers. *Some:* dual phone lines. **Pool(s):** heated indoor. **Leisure Activities:** sauna, whirlpool. *Fee:* massage, game room. **Guest Services:** complimentary evening beverages, valet and coin laundry. **Business Services:** conference facilities. **Cards:** AX, CB, DC, DS, MC, VI. **Special Amenities:** free local telephone calls and free newspaper.

SOME UNITS
(S⊕) 🐾 (†↑) 🍽 (♿) 🌀 🛌 🐾 ✕ 📷 (DATA PORT) 🖳 / ✕ 🛢 🖳 / FEE

──────── *The following lodging was either not evaluated or did not* ────────
meet AAA rating requirements but is listed for your information only.

COMFORT SUITES AT FOXFIRE   **Phone:** 715/942-0500
[fyi]   All Year [ECP]   1P: $55-$149   2P: $59-$169   XP: $8   F18
                         Too new to rate, opening scheduled for April 2004. **Location:** SR 54, exit Foxfire Dr. 199 Foxfire Dr 54981.
Small-scale Hotel **Fax:** 715/942-0501. **Amenities:** 70 units, pets, restaurant, coffeemakers, microwaves, refrigerators, pool,
                   golf. **Cards:** AX, CB, DC, DS, MC, VI.

WAUPUN pop. 10,718

──────── **WHERE TO STAY** ────────

INN TOWN MOTEL   **Phone:** 920/324-4211
▼▼▼   All Year   1P: $38-$42   2P: $48-$52   F10
Motel   **Location:** US 151, exit 146 (SR 49), 1.3 mi w. Located in a residential area. 27 S State St 53963. **Facility:** 16 one-
                 bedroom standard units, some with kitchens. 1 story, exterior corridors. **Parking:** on-site, winter plug-ins.
MC, VI.   **Terms:** office hours 8 am-11 pm, small pets only ($6 extra charge, in designated units). **Cards:** AX, DS,

SOME UNITS
🐾📺🛏🖥/✕ VCR 🖥/
FEE

WAUSAU pop. 38,426

──────── **WHERE TO STAY** ────────

BAYMONT INN-WAUSAU   *Book at aaa.com*   **Phone:** (715)842-0421
AAA SAVE   All Year   1P: $54-$89   2P: $59-$94   XP: $5   F18
▼▼▼ ▼▼▼   **Location:** I-39, exit 192, just e. Located in a commercial area. 1910 Stewart Ave 54401. **Fax:** 715/845-5096.
                 Facility: 95 one-bedroom standard units. 2 stories (no elevator), interior corridors. **Parking:** on-site, winter
                 plug-ins. **Terms:** [ECP] meal plan available, small pets only (in smoking units, with prior approval).
Small-scale Hotel **Amenities:** video games (fee), voice mail, irons, hair dryers. **Pool(s):** small heated indoor. **Leisure Activi-**
                 ties: whirlpool. **Guest Services:** valet laundry. **Cards:** AX, CB, DC, DS, MC, VI. **Special Amenities:** free
local telephone calls and free newspaper. *(See color ad p 597)*

SOME UNITS
S/D 🐾 🕹 🏊 📺 DATA PORT 🖥 / ✕ 🛏 🖥 /

COURTYARD BY MARRIOTT   *Book at aaa.com*   **Phone:** (715)849-2124
▼▼▼ ▼▼▼   All Year   1P: $75-$150
                 Location: I-39, exit 191 (Sherman St), just se. Located in a quiet area. 1000 S 22nd Ave 54401. **Fax:** 715/849-2227.
Small-scale Hotel **Facility:** 84 units. 81 one-bedroom standard units, some with whirlpools. 3 one-bedroom suites ($95-$200).
                 3 stories, interior corridors. *Bath:* combo or shower only. **Parking:** on-site, winter plug-ins. **Terms:** cancella-
tion fee imposed, [BP] meal plan available, package plans - seasonal. **Amenities:** video games (fee), high-speed Internet, dual
phone lines, voice mail, irons, hair dryers. **Pool(s):** small heated indoor. **Leisure Activities:** whirlpool, exercise room. **Guest**
Services: valet and coin laundry. **Business Services:** meeting rooms. **Cards:** AX, DC, DS, JC, MC, VI.

SOME UNITS
ASK S/D 🍴 &M 🔑 🏊 📺 DATA PORT 🖥 / ✕ VCR 🛏 🖥 /

DAYS INN-WAUSAU   *Book at aaa.com*   **Phone:** (715)355-5501
AAA SAVE   All Year   1P: $64-$130   2P: $69-$130
▼▼▼ ▼▼▼   **Location:** I-39, exit 188, just e. Located in a commercial area. 4700 Rib Mountain Dr 54401. **Fax:** 715/355-0710.
                 Parking: on-site, winter plug-ins. **Terms:** pets ($10 fee). **Amenities:** video library, high-speed Internet, dual
Small-scale Hotel phone lines, voice mail, safes (fee), hair dryers. *Some:* DVD players, irons. **Pool(s):** small heated indoor.
                 Leisure Activities: whirlpool. *Fee:* game room. **Guest Services:** valet laundry. **Business Services:** meeting
rooms. **Cards:** AX, DC, DS, MC, VI. **Special Amenities:** free continental breakfast and free local telephone calls.
(See color ad card insert)

SOME UNITS
S/D ✈ 🐾 🍴+ 🏊 📺 DATA PORT 🖥 / ✕ VCR 🛏 🖥 /
FEE

EXEL INN OF WAUSAU   **Phone:** (715)842-0641
AAA SAVE   All Year [CP]   1P: $39-$59   2P: $45-$65   XP: $6   F18
▼▼▼ ▼▼▼   **Location:** I-39, exit 192, just e. Located in a commercial area. 116 S 17th Ave 54401. **Fax:** 715/848-1356.
                 Facility: 122 one-bedroom standard units, some with efficiencies and/or whirlpools. 2 stories (no elevator),
Motel   interior corridors. **Parking:** on-site, winter plug-ins. **Terms:** weekly rates available, small pets only (in desig-
                 nated units). **Amenities:** irons, hair dryers. **Leisure Activities:** exercise room. **Guest Services:** valet and
                 coin laundry. **Cards:** AX, CB, DC, DS, MC, VI. **Special Amenities:** free continental breakfast and early
check-in/late check-out.

SOME UNITS
S/D 🐾 DATA PORT 🖥 / ✕ 🛏 🖥 /

HAMPTON INN   *Book at aaa.com*   **Phone:** (715)848-9700
AAA SAVE   6/1-3/31   1P: $74-$84   2P: $79-$89
▼▼▼ ▼▼▼   4/1-5/31   1P: $69-$84   2P: $74-$89
                 Location: I-39, exit 191 (Sherman St), just n. Located in a commercial area. 615 S 24th Ave 54401.
                 Fax: 715/848-7299. **Facility:** 89 one-bedroom standard units, some with whirlpools. 3 stories, interior corri-
Small-scale Hotel dors. *Bath:* combo or shower only. **Parking:** on-site. **Terms:** [ECP] meal plan available. **Amenities:** video
                 games (fee), dual phone lines, voice mail, irons, hair dryers. *Some:* DVD players. **Pool(s):** small heated in-
door. **Leisure Activities:** whirlpool, limited exercise equipment. **Guest Services:** valet and coin laundry. **Business Services:**
meeting rooms, business center. **Cards:** AX, DC, DS, MC, VI. **Special Amenities:** free expanded continental breakfast and
free local telephone calls.

SOME UNITS
S/D 🍴+ 🔑 🕹 🏊 📺 DATA PORT 🖥 / ✕ VCR 🛏 /

PLAZA HOTEL & SUITES
All Year
Phone: (715)845-4341
1P: $75-$169   2P: $75-$169   XP: $10   F18
Small-scale Hotel
Location: I-39, exit 193, just e. Located in a commercial area. 201 N 17th Ave 54401. Fax: 715/845-4990. **Facility:** 230 units. 219 one-bedroom standard units, some with whirlpools. 11 one-bedroom suites ($99-$169) with whirlpools. 6 stories, interior corridors. **Parking:** on-site, winter plug-ins. **Terms:** cancellation fee imposed, pets ($25 extra charge). **Amenities:** video games (fee), dual phone lines, voice mail, irons, hair dryers. **Pool(s):** heated indoor, wading. **Leisure Activities:** saunas, whirlpools, exercise room. **Fee:** game room. **Guest Services:** gift shop, valet and coin laundry. **Business Services:** conference facilities. **Cards:** AX, CB, DC, DS, MC, VI.

SOME UNITS

(ASK) (S/D) [×] [🛏] [🍴] [🍽] [♨] [🚤] [✕] [📹] [DATA PORT] [🔌] [🖥] [💻] / [✕] /
FEE

RIB MOUNTAIN INN
Phone: 715/848-2802
| | | | |
12/20-1/6 [BP]   1P: $109-$449   2P: $109-$449   XP: $20   F6
1/7-3/31 [BP]   1P: $99-$409   2P: $99-$409   XP: $20   F6
11/20-12/19 [BP]   1P: $89-$309   2P: $89-$309   XP: $15   F6
Small-scale Hotel   4/1-11/19 [BP]   1P: $69-$209   2P: $69-$209   XP: $10   F6
Location: I-39, exit 190 (CR NN), 1 mi w. Located in a residential area. 2900 Rib Mountain Way 54401. Fax: 715/848-1908. **Facility:** 24 units. 18 one-bedroom standard units, some with kitchens and/or whirlpools. 3 two- and 3 three-bedroom suites ($149-$249) with kitchens, some with whirlpools. 2-3 stories, interior/exterior corridors. **Parking:** on-site. **Terms:** office hours 6 am-10 pm, 3 day cancellation notice-fee imposed, pets ($10 extra charge). **Amenities:** video library, voice mail, irons, hair dryers. **Leisure Activities:** sauna, whirlpool, cross country skiing, snowmobiling, hiking trails. **Fee:** downhill skiing. **Guest Services:** coin laundry. **Business Services:** fax. **Cards:** AX, DC, DS, MC, VI.

(ASK) (S/D) [🛏] [✕] [VCR] [✕] [DATA PORT] [🔌] [🖥] [💻]
FEE

ROSENBERRY INN
Phone: 715/842-5733
All Year   1P: $72-$102   2P: $72-$102   XP: $17
Historic Bed & Breakfast
Location: Just n on SR 52, then just w. Located in a residential area. 511 Franklin St 54403. Fax: 715/843-5659. **Facility:** This B&B consists of two historic homes located across the street from one another. Smoke free premises. 8 one-bedroom standard units, some with whirlpools. 2 stories (no elevator), interior/exterior corridors. **Bath:** combo or shower only. **Parking:** on-site. **Terms:** office hours 9 am-10 pm, 10 day cancellation notice. **Amenities:** video library. **Business Services:** fax. **Cards:** MC, VI.

SOME UNITS

[✕] [📶] [🔌] [💻] / [📺] [VCR] [🖥] /

SUPER 8 MOTEL   *Book at aaa.com*
Phone: (715)848-2888
6/19-3/31   1P: $51-$74   2P: $58-$79
4/1-6/18   1P: $39-$54   2P: $45-$58
Small-scale Hotel
Location: I-39, exit 192, just e. Located in a commercial area. 2006 Stewart Ave W 54401. Fax: 715/842-9578. **Facility:** 88 one-bedroom standard units. 2 stories (no elevator), interior corridors. **Bath:** combo or shower only. **Parking:** on-site, winter plug-ins. **Terms:** [CP] meal plan available, small pets only ($5 extra charge). **Pool(s):** small heated indoor. **Leisure Activities:** whirlpool. **Cards:** AX, DC, DS, MC, VI. **Special Amenities:** free continental breakfast and free local telephone calls.

SOME UNITS

(S/D) [🛏] [🍴] [♨] [🔌] [🚤] [📹] [DATA PORT] [✕] [🔌] [💻] /
FEE

Northern Wisconsin's Largest INDOOR Waterpark Resort!

Lodge at Cedar Creek
Grand Opening June 2004

- Beautiful New 140 All-Suite Resort
- Restaurant, Bar, Arcade & Gifts
- Year Round Fun - Skiing, Snowmobiling, Golf, & Cedar Creek Mall
- Weddings, Meetings, Corporate Outing
- Huge Indoor Waterpark - 50,000 sq ft of Family Fun

- Wave Lazy River, Activity Pools with log walk & basketball, 2 whirlpools & more
- Kiddie Water Play Areas & Water-Dumping Treehouse
- Cannonball, Tube & Plunge Waterslides
- Day Pass Waterpark Visitors Welcome

Call Now for Reservations! Lodge at Cedar Creek + I-39 at Wausau, WI
Toll Free: 888-36-LODGE + www.lodgeatcedarcreek.com + 715-241-6300

—————— WHERE TO DINE ——————

CARMELO'S
▼▼ ▼▼
Italian

Dinner: $9-$17   Phone: 715/845-5570
Location: I-39, exit 190, 0.9 mi w. 3607 N Mountain Rd 54401. **Hours:** 5 pm-10 pm, Sun & Mon-9 pm. Closed major holidays. **Reservations:** accepted. **Features:** Convenient to a ski area and golf course, the lively restaurant offers food that is homemade and tasty. Servers are friendly and reliable. Casual dress; cocktails. **Parking:** on-site. **Cards:** AX, DS, MC, VI.

HEREFORD & HOPS
▼▼ ▼▼
American

Lunch: $6-$16   Dinner: $6-$16   Phone: 715/849-3700
Location: I-39, exit 191 (US 51), just se. 2305 Sherman St 54401. **Hours:** 11 am-10 pm, Sun-9 pm. **Reservations:** accepted. **Features:** Diners can grill their own steak, create their own pizza or build their own sandwich while enjoying specialty beers that are brewed on the premises. The friendly staff helps guests become pros at the grills. Casual dress; cocktails. **Parking:** on-site. **Cards:** AX, DC, DS, MC, VI.

MICHAEL'S
▼▼ ▼▼
American
DS, MC, VI.

Dinner: $10-$20   Phone: 715/842-9856
Location: I-39, exit 190 (CR NN), 0.5 mi se. 2901 Rib Mountain Dr 54401. **Hours:** 5 pm-10 pm. Closed major holidays; also Sun. **Reservations:** accepted. **Features:** Fresh seafood, veal specialties and gourmet pizza highlight the menu. Friday night fish fry is popular. The chef is happy to accommodate special requests. Desserts are presented tableside on a tray. Casual dress; cocktails. **Parking:** on-site. **Cards:** AX, CB, DC,

MINO'S CUCINA ITALIANA
▼▼ ▼▼
Italian

Dinner: $11-$30   Phone: 715/675-5939
Location: On CR W, 1.3 mi n of jct SR 52 E, on east side of Wisconsin River. 900 Golf Club Rd 54403. **Hours:** 5 pm-10 pm. Closed major holidays; also Sun. **Reservations:** accepted. **Features:** Patrons can choose from classic dishes or the chef's creations. Seafood, pasta and pizza are popular. The tiramisu, which is made in house, is delicious. Casual dress; cocktails. **Parking:** on-site. **Cards:** AX, DS, MC, VI.

PS 2510 RESTAURANT
▼▼ ▼▼
American

Lunch: $11-$14   Dinner: $11-$20   Phone: 715/845-2510
Location: I-39, exit 192, 0.3 mi w on SR 52. 2510 Stewart Ave 54401. **Hours:** 11 am-10 pm, Sun-9 pm. Closed: 11/25, 12/25. **Features:** This well-established restaurant is locally popular. The menu is vast and varied, and there is a deli and bakery attached. While reservations are not accepted, call-ahead seating is available. Casual dress; cocktails. **Parking:** on-site. **Cards:** AX, DC, DS, MC, VI.

WAUTOMA pop. 1,998

—————— WHERE TO STAY ——————

AMERICINN
▼▼ ▼▼
Small-scale Hotel

Book at aaa.com   Phone: 920/787-5050

6/3-9/2	1P: $109-$169	2P: $117-$177	XP: $8 F17
11/29-3/31	1P: $69-$139	2P: $77-$147	XP: $8 F17
9/3-11/28	1P: $79-$129	2P: $87-$137	XP: $8 F17
4/1-6/2	1P: $69-$119	2P: $77-$127	XP: $8 F17

Location: On SR 21 and 73, 1.2 mi e. W7696 SR 21/73 54982 (PO Box 644). **Fax:** 920/787-5911. **Facility:** 50 units. 34 one-bedroom standard units. 16 one-bedroom suites, some with efficiencies (no utensils) and/or whirlpools. 2 stories (no elevator), interior corridors. *Bath:* combo or shower only. **Parking:** on-site. **Terms:** [ECP] meal plan available, package plans, pets ($25 deposit). **Amenities:** hair dryers. **Pool(s):** heated indoor. **Leisure Activities:** whirlpool. **Guest Services:** coin laundry. **Business Services:** meeting rooms. **Cards:** AX, DS, MC, VI. **(See color ad p 576)**

SOME UNITS
ASK SD ... FEE

SUPER 8 MOTEL-WAUTOMA
▼▼ ▼▼
Small-scale Hotel

Book at aaa.com   Phone: (920)787-4811

5/31-9/25 [CP]	1P: $61-$74	2P: $66-$79	XP: $5 F12
4/1-5/30 & 9/26-3/31 [CP]	1P: $58-$71	2P: $63-$76	XP: $5 F12

Location: On SR 21 and 73, 1.5 mi e. W7607 SR 21 and 73 54982 (PO Box 578). **Fax:** 920/787-4305. **Facility:** 51 units. 50 one-bedroom standard units. 1 one-bedroom suite. 2 stories (no elevator), interior corridors. **Parking:** on-site, winter plug-ins. **Terms:** pets ($25 deposit). **Pool(s):** heated indoor. **Leisure Activities:** sauna, whirlpool. **Guest Services:** coin laundry. **Business Services:** meeting rooms. **Cards:** AX, CB, DC, DS, MC, VI.

SOME UNITS
ASK SD ... FEE

WAUWATOSA —*See Milwaukee p. 600.*

WEST BEND —*See Milwaukee p. 601.*

WESTBY pop. 2,045

—————— WHERE TO DINE ——————

OLD TOWNE INN
AAA
▼▼ ▼▼
American

Dinner: $7-$15   Phone: 608/634-3991
Location: 0.5 mi s on US 14. 101 E Old Town Rd 54667. **Hours:** 5 pm-9 pm, Fri & Sat-10 pm. Closed major holidays; also 12/24 & Mon. **Reservations:** suggested. **Features:** Enjoy casual, quiet dining in the contemporary country restaurant. Steak and seafood make up the bulk of a menu of tried-and-true favorites. Succulent prime rib is the special on Wednesday and on weekends. Sample Mexican fare on Tuesdays. Casual dress; cocktails. **Parking:** on-site. **Cards:** MC, VI.

WESTFIELD pop. 1,217

─────── WHERE TO STAY ───────

WESTFIELD PIONEER MOTOR INN
Phone: 608/296-2135

▼▼▼ ▼▼▼
| | 5/1-9/30 [CP] | 1P: $61-$66 | 2P: $66-$71 | XP: $5 | F12 |
| | 4/1-4/30 & 10/1-3/31 [CP] | 1P: $54-$59 | 2P: $59-$64 | XP: $5 | F12 |

Small-scale Hotel   **Location:** I-39, exit 113 (CR J and E), just nw. Located in a commercial area. 242 N Pioneer Rd 53964 (PO Box 97). Fax: 608/296-3933. **Facility:** 30 one-bedroom standard units, some with whirlpools. 2 stories (no elevator), interior corridors. **Parking:** on-site, winter plug-ins. **Amenities:** hair dryers. *Some:* dual phone lines. **Business Services:** meeting rooms. **Cards:** AX, DS, MC, VI.

SOME UNITS
[S🅓] [📶] [🎥] [💻] / [⊠] [VCR] [DATA PORT] [🔌] [🍽] /
FEE

WEST SALEM pop. 4,540

─────── WHERE TO STAY ───────

AMERICINN   *Book at aaa.com*
Phone: (608)786-3340

▼▼▼
| | All Year | | 2P: $89-$149 | XP: $6 | F12 |

Small-scale Hotel   **Location:** I-90, exit 12, just sw on CR C. 125 Buol Rd 54669. Fax: 608/786-3340. **Facility:** 50 units. 48 one-bedroom standard units, some with whirlpools. 2 one-bedroom suites ($119-$149) with whirlpools. 2 stories (no elevator), interior corridors. *Bath:* combo or shower only. **Parking:** on-site, winter plug-ins. **Terms:** [CP] & [ECP] meal plans available. **Amenities:** hair dryers. *Some:* irons. **Pool(s):** heated indoor. **Leisure Activities:** sauna, whirlpool. **Guest Services:** valet and coin laundry. **Business Services:** meeting rooms. **Cards:** AX, CB, DC, DS, MC, VI.
(See color ad p 576)

SOME UNITS
[A$K] [S🅓] [🐾] [♿] [🛥] [DATA PORT] [💻] / [⊠] [🔌] [🍽] /

WHITEFISH BAY —*See Milwaukee p. 602.*

WHITEWATER pop. 13,437

─────── WHERE TO STAY ───────

AMERIHOST INN & SUITES   *Book at aaa.com*
Phone: (262)472-9400

▼▼▼
| | 4/1-9/30 [ECP] | 1P: $74 | 2P: $74-$79 | XP: $10 | F18 |
| | 10/1-3/31 [ECP] | 1P: $74 | 2P: $74 | XP: $10 | F18 |

Small-scale Hotel   **Location:** On US 12, 0.5 mi w of jct SR 59 W. 1355 W Main St 53190. Fax: 262/472-9404. **Facility:** 61 one-bedroom standard units, some with whirlpools. 2 stories (no elevator), interior corridors. *Bath:* combo or shower only. **Parking:** on-site. **Terms:** package plans, pets ($10 fee, $10 deposit). **Amenities:** voice mail, safes (fee), irons, hair dryers. **Pool(s):** small heated indoor. **Leisure Activities:** sauna, whirlpool, exercise room. **Guest Services:** valet laundry. **Business Services:** meeting rooms. **Cards:** AX, CB, DC, DS, MC, VI.

SOME UNITS
[A$K] [S🅓] [🐾] [📶] [♿M] [🛥] [🎥] [DATA PORT] [💻] / [⊠] [🔌] [🍽] /
FEE

SUPER 8 MOTEL
Phone: 262/473-8818

▼▼▼ ▼▼
	4/1-9/30 [CP]	1P: $79-$109	2P: $89-$114	XP: $5	F12
	10/1-11/30 [CP]	1P: $69-$99	2P: $79-$109	XP: $5	F12
	12/1-3/31 [CP]	1P: $59-$89	2P: $69-$99	XP: $5	F12

Small-scale Hotel   **Location:** On US 12, just e of jct SR 59 E. 917 E Milwaukee St 53190. Fax: 262/473-0688. **Facility:** 50 one-bedroom standard units, some with whirlpools. 2 stories, interior corridors. **Parking:** on-site, winter plug-ins. **Terms:** cancellation fee imposed, pets ($10 deposit). **Amenities:** safes (fee), hair dryers. **Leisure Activities:** whirlpool. **Business Services:** meeting rooms. **Cards:** AX, DS, MC, VI.

SOME UNITS
[A$K] [S🅓] [🐾] [📶] [♿M] [🎥] [DATA PORT] / [⊠] [VCR] [🔌] [🍽] /
FEE   FEE

─────── WHERE TO DINE ───────

RANDY'S FUN HUNTERS BREWERY & RESTAURANT   **Lunch:** $6-$10   **Dinner:** $11-$18   **Phone:** 262/473-8000

▼▼▼   **Location:** On US 12, just e of jct SR 59 E. 841 E Milwaukee St 53190. **Hours:** 11 am-10 pm, Fri-10:30 pm, Sun 10:30 am-9 pm. Closed: 11/25, 12/25; also for dinner 12/24 & Mon. **Reservations:** suggested, except Fri.
American   **Features:** Visitors can watch the brewing operation from the bar area of this laid-back restaurant. On the varied menu are such entrees as barbecue baby back ribs, sandwiches, burgers and salads. Tasty beverages include microbrewed beers and homemade root beer and cream soda. Historic area photographs adorn the walls. Casual dress; cocktails. **Parking:** on-site. **Cards:** DS, MC, VI.
[📺] [⊠]

WILTON pop. 519

─────── WHERE TO DINE ───────

GINA'S PIES ARE SQUARE   **Lunch:** $4-$6   **Dinner:** $4-$6   **Phone:** 608/435-6541

▼▼   **Location:** SR 71, just s. 400 Main St 54670. **Hours:** 10 am-7 pm, Fri & Sat-8 pm; Sun-Thurs 10 am-3 pm 11/1-3/31. Closed major holidays. **Features:** Nestled along the Elroy-Sparta bike trail, the restaurant is legendary among bikers for its delicious square pies. Using a variety of wonderful, seasonal fruits, Gina
American   bakes about 30 pies a day to keep up with demand. The menu also features tasty homemade sandwiches and pizzas that are so tempting it's almost hard to save room for dessert. Casual dress; beer & wine only. **Parking:** street. **Cards:** AX, DS, MC, VI.
[⊠]

WINDSOR pop. 2,533

——— WHERE TO STAY ———

DAYS INN *Book at aaa.com*   Phone: 608/846-7473
(AAA) (SAVE)   All Year   1P: $49-$59   2P: $55-$65   XP: $6   F17
▽▽▽▽   **Location:** I-90/94, exit 131 (SR 19). 6311 Rostad Cir 53598. Fax: 608/846-1571. **Facility:** 54 units. 53 one-bedroom standard units, some with whirlpools. 1 one-bedroom suite ($96-$120). 3 stories, interior corridors. *Bath:* combo or shower only. **Parking:** on-site, winter plug-ins. **Terms:** [ECP] meal plan available, small pets
Small-scale Hotel   only ($50 deposit, $10 extra charge, with prior approval). **Amenities:** voice mail, hair dryers. *Some:* irons. **Pool(s):** small heated indoor. **Leisure Activities:** sauna, whirlpool, exercise room. **Guest Services:** coin laundry. **Business Services:** meeting rooms, fax. **Cards:** AX, CB, DC, DS, JC, MC, VI. *(See color ad card insert)*

SOME UNITS
[icons] FEE

SUPER 8 MOTEL-WINDSOR/NORTH MADISON *Book at aaa.com*   Phone: (608)846-3971
▽▽▽   All Year   1P: $49-$100   2P: $49-$100   XP: $5   F16
Small-scale Hotel   **Location:** I-90/94, exit 131 (SR 19). 4506 Lake Cir 53598. Fax: 608/846-9061. **Facility:** 55 one-bedroom standard units. 2 stories (no elevator), interior corridors. **Parking:** on-site, winter plug-ins. **Terms:** [ECP] meal plan available, small pets only ($20 deposit, $10 extra charge). **Amenities:** *Some:* irons, hair dryers. **Guest Services:** coin laundry. **Cards:** AX, DS, MC, VI.

SOME UNITS
[icons] FEE

WISCONSIN DELLS pop. 2,418

——— WHERE TO STAY ———

ALAKAI HOTEL & SUITES   Phone: (608)253-3803
▽▽▽▽   6/18-9/6   1P: $98-$125   2P: $110-$145   XP: $10   D
           5/28-6/17   1P: $68-$88   2P: $78-$98   XP: $10   D
Small-scale Hotel   4/1-5/27 & 9/7-3/31   1P: $58-$78   2P: $68-$88   XP: $10   D
           Location: I-90/94, exit 92 (US 12), just w. 1030 Wisconsin Dells Pkwy S 53965 (PO Box 766). Fax: 608/254-4679.
Facility: 87 units. 83 one-bedroom standard units. 4 one-bedroom suites. 3 stories, interior corridors. **Parking:** on-site. **Terms:** 2 night minimum stay - weekends, 3 day cancellation notice-fee imposed. **Amenities:** *Some:* hair dryers. **Pool(s):** small heated outdoor, heated indoor, wading. **Leisure Activities:** sauna, whirlpool. *Fee:* game room. **Guest Services:** coin laundry. **Cards:** AX, DC, MC, VI.

SOME UNITS
[icons]

AMERICINN LODGE & SUITES *Book at aaa.com*   Phone: 608/254-1700
(AAA) (SAVE)   6/1-8/31   1P: $109-$229   2P: $109-$229   XP: $8   F12
▽▽▽▽   4/1-5/31 & 9/1-3/31   1P: $74-$189   2P: $74-$189   XP: $8   F12
           Location: I-90/94, exit 87 (SR 13), just e. 550 State Hwy 13 53965. Fax: 608/254-1701. **Facility:** Smoke free premises. 78 units. 77 one-bedroom standard units, some with whirlpools. 1 one-bedroom suite. 3 stories, interior
Small-scale Hotel   corridors. *Bath:* combo or shower only. **Parking:** on-site. **Terms:** 3 day cancellation notice-fee imposed.
           Amenities: high-speed Internet (fee), voice mail, irons, hair dryers. **Pool(s):** heated indoor, wading. **Leisure Activities:** sauna, whirlpool, exercise room. **Guest Services:** coin laundry. **Business Services:** meeting rooms. **Cards:** AX, DC, DS, MC, VI. **Special Amenities:** free expanded continental breakfast and free local telephone calls.
(See color ad p 576)

SOME UNITS
[icons]

BAKER'S SUNSET BAY RESORT   Phone: 608/254-8406
(AAA) (SAVE)   7/3-9/1   1P: $122-$225   2P: $122-$225
▽▽▽   6/13-7/2   1P: $82-$170   2P: $82-$170
           4/1-6/12 & 9/2-3/31   1P: $54-$130   2P: $54-$130
           Location: I-90/94, exit 92 (US 12), 0.5 mi w, right on E Adams St, right on Canyon Rd, then 0.8 mi on left. 921 Canyon
Small-scale Hotel   Rd 53965. Fax: 608/253-2062. **Facility:** 74 units. 51 one-bedroom standard units, some with efficiencies. 19 one- and 4 two-bedroom suites, some with efficiencies, kitchens and/or whirlpools. 1-3 stories, interior/exterior corridors. *Bath:* combo or shower only. **Parking:** on-site. **Terms:** 1-3 night minimum stay - seasonal, 7 day cancellation notice-fee imposed, weekly rates available, package plans - seasonal, pets (with prior approval during off season). **Amenities:** hair dryers. **Pool(s):** heated outdoor, small heated indoor, wading. **Leisure Activities:** sauna, whirlpool, waterslide, boating, fishing, bonfires, yard games, charcoal grills, playground, horseshoes, volleyball. *Fee:* rowboats. **Guest Services:** coin laundry. **Business Services:** meeting rooms. **Cards:** DS, MC, VI. **Special Amenities:** free continental breakfast and early check-in/late check-out.

SOME UNITS
[icons]

BEST WESTERN AMBASSADOR INN AND SUITES *Book at aaa.com*   Phone: 608/254-4477
(AAA) (SAVE)   All Year   1P: $48-$178   2P: $48-$178   XP: $6   F17
▽▽▽   **Location:** I-90/94, exit 87 (SR 13), just e. 610 Frontage Rd S 53965. Fax: 608/253-6662. **Facility:** 181 units. 167 one-bedroom standard units, some with whirlpools. 12 one- and 2 two-bedroom suites ($68-$268), some with kitchens. 3 stories, interior corridors. **Parking:** on-site, winter plug-ins. **Terms:** check-in 4 pm, 3 day cancel-
Small-scale Hotel   lation notice-fee imposed. **Amenities:** irons, hair dryers. **Pool(s):** heated outdoor, heated indoor, wading.
           Leisure Activities: sauna, whirlpools, playground. *Fee:* game room. **Guest Services:** gift shop, coin laundry.
Business Services: meeting rooms. **Cards:** AX, DC, DS, MC, VI. *(See color ad p 643)*

SOME UNITS
[icons] FEE

BLACK HAWK MOTEL

Phone: 608/254-7770

AAA SAVE ♦♦♦ ♦♦♦

Motel

7/16-8/28	1P: $55-$140	2P: $55-$140	XP: $5
6/18-7/15	1P: $45-$135	2P: $45-$135	XP: $5
4/1-6/17	1P: $35-$120	2P: $40-$120	XP: $5
8/29-10/24	1P: $35-$95	2P: $35-$95	XP: $5

Location: I-90/94, exit 87 (SR 13), 2 mi e on SR 13, 16 and 23. 720 Race St 53965 (PO Box 15A). Fax: 608/253-7333. **Facility:** 75 units. 68 one- and 7 two-bedroom standard units, some with kitchens and/or whirlpools. 1-2 stories (no elevator), exterior corridors. **Parking:** on-site. **Terms:** open 4/1-10/24, 3 day cancellation notice-fee imposed, small pets only ($5 deposit). **Amenities:** video library (fee). *Some:* hair dryers. **Pool(s):** heated outdoor, heated indoor, wading. **Leisure Activities:** saunas, whirlpools, waterslide, playground. *Fee:* game room. **Guest Services:** coin laundry, area transportation-bus/train depot. **Cards:** AX, DS, MC, VI. **Special Amenities:** early check-in/late check-out and preferred room (subject to availability with advanced reservations).** *(See color ad p 643)*

SOME UNITS

(S/D) 🐕 FEE 📶 🏊 ⊠ 🖥 📠 / ⊠ VCR FEE 📠

BRIDGE VIEW MOTEL

Phone: 608/254-6114

♦♦♦

Motel

6/20-8/21	1P: $55-$75	2P: $69-$99	XP: $10
8/22-9/18	1P: $45-$65	2P: $69-$89	XP: $10
5/1-6/19 & 9/19-10/31	1P: $35-$45	2P: $49-$69	XP: $10

Location: Just n of SR 13 (Broadway); center. 1020 River Rd 53965. Fax: 608/254-6114. **Facility:** 17 one-bedroom standard units, some with efficiencies. 2 stories, exterior corridors. *Bath:* combo or shower only. **Parking:** on-site. **Terms:** open 5/1-10/31, 2 night minimum stay - weekends, 3 day cancellation notice-fee imposed, package plans - seasonal, pets ($10 extra charge, with prior approval). **Amenities:** hair dryers. **Pool(s):** heated outdoor. **Leisure Activities:** waterslide, playground. **Cards:** DC, MC, VI.

SOME UNITS

(ASK) (S/D) 🐕 FEE 🏊 🖥 / ⊠ 📠 FEE

CHIPPEWA MOTEL

Phone: 608/253-3982

♦♦♦ ♦♦♦

Motel

Property failed to provide current rates

Location: 0.5 mi e on SR 13. 1114 E Broadway 53965. Fax: 608/254-2577. **Facility:** 50 units. 42 one-bedroom standard units, some with whirlpools. 8 one-bedroom suites. 2 stories, interior/exterior corridors. **Parking:** on-site. **Pool(s):** heated outdoor, heated indoor, wading. **Leisure Activities:** sauna, whirlpool, playground. **Guest Services:** coin laundry, area transportation.

SOME UNITS

🍴 🏊 ⊠ 📹 / ⊠ 🖥 📠 /

CHULA VISTA THEME RESORT *Book at aaa.com*

Phone: 608/254-8366

AAA SAVE

6/25-9/5	2P: $149-$309	XP: $8
4/1-6/24 & 9/6-10/30	2P: $119-$309	XP: $8
10/31-3/31	2P: $89-$229	XP: $8

Resort
Large-scale Hotel

Location: From Wisconsin River Bridge, 3 mi n. 4031 N River Rd 53965 (PO Box 30). Fax: 608/254-7653. **Facility:** On the Upper Dells of the Wisconsin River, this family-oriented resort offers several restaurants and a variety of unit types. 291 units. 264 one-bedroom standard units, some with whirlpools. 27 one-bedroom suites. 2-7 stories, interior/exterior corridors. *Bath:* combo or shower only. **Parking:** on-site. **Terms:** check-in 4 pm, 2 night minimum stay - with Saturday stayover 6/1-8/31, 3 day cancellation notice-fee imposed. **Amenities:** video games (fee), voice mail, irons, hair dryers. **Dining:** 4 restaurants, 7 am-10 pm, cocktails. **Pool(s):** 3 heated outdoor, 3 heated indoor. **Leisure Activities:** sauna, whirlpools, waterslide, childrens' activity pool, recreation programs, bonfires, hayrides, entertainment, hiking trails, playground, exercise room, spa, basketball, volleyball. *Fee:* miniature golf, game room. **Guest Services:** gift shop, coin laundry. **Business Services:** meeting rooms, business center. **Cards:** AX, CB, DC, MC, VI. *(See color ad p 644)*

SOME UNITS

COMFORT INN *Book at aaa.com*

Phone: (608)253-3711

AAA SAVE

5/28-9/5	1P: $100-$159	2P: $100-$159	XP: $10 F
4/1-5/27 & 9/6-3/31	1P: $50-$109	2P: $50-$109	XP: $10 F

Small-scale Hotel

Location: I-90/94, exit 87 (SR 13), just e. 703 N Frontage Rd 53965 (PO Box 330). Fax: 608/254-2164. **Facility:** 75 one-bedroom standard units, some with whirlpools. 3 stories, interior corridors. *Bath:* combo or shower only. **Parking:** on-site, winter plug-ins. **Terms:** check-in 4 pm, 2 night minimum stay - weekends in season. **Amenities:** irons, hair dryers. **Pool(s):** small heated indoor. **Leisure Activities:** whirlpool, sun deck in season. **Cards:** AX, CB, DC, DS, JC, MC, VI. **Special Amenities:** free continental breakfast and free local telephone calls. *(See color ad below)*

SOME UNITS

DAY'S END MOTEL *Book at aaa.com*

Phone: (608)254-8171

AAA SAVE

6/18-9/5	1P: $55-$124	2P: $55-$124	XP: $6
5/28-6/17	1P: $41-$98	2P: $41-$98	XP: $6
4/1-5/27 & 9/6-3/31	1P: $34-$88	2P: $34-$88	XP: $6

Motel

Location: I-90/94, exit 85 (US 12), 0.8 mi nw. N 604 Hwy 12-16 53965. **Facility:** 28 units. 27 one-bedroom standard units, some with whirlpools. 1 one-bedroom suite ($98-$192) with whirlpool. 1 story, exterior corridors. *Bath:* combo or shower only. **Parking:** on-site, winter plug-ins. **Terms:** 2 night minimum stay - weekends in season, 3 day cancellation notice-fee imposed, pets ($7 extra charge, with prior approval). **Pool(s):** heated outdoor. **Leisure Activities:** waterslide, miniature golf, playground. **Cards:** AX, DC, DS, MC, VI. **Special Amenities:** early check-in/late check-out and preferred room (subject to availability with advanced reservations). Affiliated with Best Value Inn Brand Membership. *(See ad p 646)*

SOME UNITS
FEE   FEE FEE

DAYS INN OF WISCONSIN DELLS *Book at aaa.com* Phone: (608)254-6444

(AAA) (SAVE)
◆◆◆◆ ◆◆

	6/25-8/25	1P: $85-$130	2P: $85-$130	XP: $10	F12
	5/28-6/24	1P: $52-$90	2P: $52-$90	XP: $10	F12
	4/1-5/27 & 8/26-3/31	1P: $40-$79	2P: $40-$79	XP: $10	F12

Location: I-90/94, exit 87 (SR 13), 1 mi n at jct US 12 and SR 16. 944 Hwy 12 N 53965 (PO Box 381).
Small-scale Hotel Fax: 608/254-6444. **Facility:** 100 units. 99 one-bedroom standard units. 1 one-bedroom suite ($64-$179) with kitchen. 2 stories (no elevator), interior corridors. **Parking:** on-site, winter plug-ins. **Terms:** 2 night minimum stay - weekends in season, cancellation fee imposed, package plans. **Amenities:** hair dryers. **Pool(s):** heated outdoor, heated indoor. **Leisure Activities:** sauna, whirlpool. **Guest Services:** *Fee:* tanning facility. **Business Services:** meeting rooms. **Cards:** AX, CB, DC, DS, JC, MC, VI. **Special Amenities: free continental breakfast and free room upgrade (subject to availability with advanced reservations).** *(See color ad card insert & below)*

SOME UNITS
(S/D) (T↓) (➤) (🎦) / (☒) (🔌) (📠) /
FEE FEE

THE GABLES MOTEL Phone: 608/253-3831

(AAA) (SAVE)
◆◆◆◆ ◆◆

	6/21-8/18	1P: $69-$99	2P: $69-$99	XP: $5
	8/19-9/22	1P: $45-$69	2P: $45-$69	XP: $5
	4/1-6/20	1P: $35-$69	2P: $35-$69	XP: $5
	9/23-3/31	1P: $35-$45	2P: $35-$50	XP: $5

Motel **Location:** Just n of Broadway, US 16, SR 13 and 23; downtown. 822 Oak St 53965. **Facility:** 30 one-bedroom standard units. 2 stories, exterior corridors. **Parking:** on-site, winter plug-ins. **Pool(s):** heated outdoor. **Cards:** AX, DC, MC, VI. *(See color ad on p 647)*

SOME UNITS
(T↓) (➤) (🎦) / (☒) (🔌) (📠) /
FEE FEE

GREAT WOLF LODGE
Phone: (608)253-2222

AAA SAVE
◇◇◇◇◇
Large-scale Hotel

All Year 1P: $279-$379
Location: I-90/94, exit 92 (US 12). 1400 Great Wolf Dr 53965 (PO Box 50). Fax: 608/253-2224. **Facility:** Designated smoking area. 309 units. 296 one-bedroom standard units, some with whirlpools. 13 one-bedroom suites. 3-4 stories, interior corridors. *Bath:* combo or shower only. **Parking:** on-site. **Terms:** check-in 4 pm, cancellation fee imposed. **Amenities:** voice mail, irons, hair dryers. *Fee:* video games, high-speed Internet. **Dining:** 2 restaurants, 7 am-11 pm, cocktails. **Pool(s):** heated outdoor, heated indoor, wading. **Leisure Activities:** whirlpools, waterslide, extensive indoor/outdoor water park facilities with lazy river, exercise room, spa. *Fee:* game room. **Guest Services:** gift shop, valet and coin laundry, area transportation-train depot. **Business Services:** conference facilities. **Cards:** AX, DC, DS, MC, VI. **Special Amenities:** free local telephone calls. *(See color ad below)*

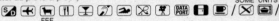

HOWARD JOHNSON HOTEL AND ANTIQUA BAY WATERPARK
Book at aaa.com
Phone: (608)254-8306

AAA SAVE
◇◇◇◇◇
Small-scale Hotel

7/1-9/5	1P: $109-$140	2P: $109-$140	XP: $10	F18
4/1-6/30 & 9/6-3/31	1P: $89-$120	2P: $89-$120	XP: $10	F18

Location: I-90/94, exit 87 (SR 13), just e. 655 Frontage Rd 53965 (PO Box 236). Fax: 608/253-2829. **Facility:** 228 one-bedroom standard units. 2 stories, interior corridors. **Parking:** on-site, winter plug-ins. **Terms:** check-in 4 pm, 3 day cancellation notice, pets ($10 extra charge, with prior approval). **Amenities:** voice mail, irons, hair dryers. **Dining:** 7 am-10 pm, cocktails. **Pool(s):** 3 heated outdoor, 2 heated indoor, wading. **Leisure Activities:** sauna, whirlpools, waterslide, domed recreation area, exercise room. *Fee:* game room. **Guest Services:** gift shop, valet and coin laundry. **Business Services:** meeting rooms. **Cards:** AX, CB, DC, DS, JC, MC, VI. **Special Amenities:** free full breakfast and free local telephone calls. *(See color ad p 648 & p 584)*

SOME UNITS

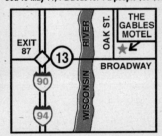

INDIAN TRAIL MOTEL

AAA SAVE

Motel

Phone: 608/253-2641

	6/20-9/4	1P: $45-$150	2P: $45-$150	XP: $10	F13
	5/21-6/19	1P: $40-$110	2P: $40-$110	XP: $10	F13
	9/5-10/18	1P: $35-$99	2P: $35-$99	XP: $10	F13
	5/1-5/20	1P: $35-$95	2P: $35-$95	XP: $10	F13

Location: 0.5 mi e on SR 13, 16 and 23. 1013 Broadway 53965. **Fax:** 608/253-3521. **Facility:** 46 units. 45 one-bedroom standard units, some with whirlpools. 1 vacation home. 1 story, exterior corridors. *Bath:* combo or shower only. **Parking:** on-site. **Terms:** open 5/1-10/18, 2 night minimum stay - weekends 7/1-8/31, 3 day cancellation notice-fee imposed. **Amenities:** *Some:* irons, hair dryers. **Pool(s):** heated outdoor, heated indoor. **Leisure Activities:** sauna, whirlpool, playground. **Fee:** game room. **Guest Services:** coin laundry. **Cards:** AX, DC, MC, VI. **Special Amenities:** free local telephone calls and early check-in/late check-out. *(See color ad below)*

SOME UNITS

KALAHARI

	7/1-8/31	1P: $169-$299	2P: $169-$299	XP: $15	F
	12/21-3/31	1P: $149-$299	2P: $149-$299	XP: $15	F
	4/1-6/30 & 9/1-12/20	1P: $109-$259	2P: $109-$259	XP: $15	F

Phone: 608/254-5466

Location: I-90/94, exit 92 (US 12). 1305 Kalahari Dr 53965 (PO Box 590). Fax: 608/254-4460. **Facility:** This African-themed resort offers expansive indoor and outdoor waterpark facilities with waterslides, a wave pool and several food-court outlets. 378 units. 251 one-bedroom standard units, some with whirlpools. 15 one- and 112 two-bedroom suites ($199-$1200), some with whirlpools. 4 stories, interior corridors. *Bath:* combo or shower only. **Parking:** on-site. **Terms:** check-in 4 pm, 3 day cancellation notice-fee imposed. **Amenities:** voice mail, irons, hair dryers. *Some:* DVD players, CD players, safes. **Dining:** 3 restaurants, 7 am-10 pm, cocktails. **Pool(s):** 3 heated outdoor, 4 heated indoor, 4 wading. **Leisure Activities:** whirlpools, waterslide, waterpark, recreation programs, 10-screen cinema, playground, exercise room, spa, basketball, horseshoes, volleyball. *Fee:* game room. **Guest Services:** gift shop, coin laundry, area transportation-bus & train depot, local attractions. **Business Services:** conference facilities, business center. **Cards:** AX, DS, MC, VI. **Special Amenities:** free newspaper and early check-in/late check-out. *(See color ad below)*

SOME UNITS

LUNA INN & SUITES

AAA SAVE

▼▼ ▼▼

Motel

			Phone: (608)253-2661	
6/15-9/1	1P: $69-$98	2P: $69-$119	XP: $10	F12
5/28-6/14	1P: $59-$89	2P: $59-$99	XP: $10	F12
4/15-5/27	1P: $39-$59	2P: $46-$69	XP: $10	F12
9/2-10/31	1P: $39-$59	2P: $42-$69	XP: $10	F12

Location: I-90/94, exit 92 (US 12), 2.8 mi n. 1111 Wisconsin Dells Pkwy 53965. **Fax:** 608/253-2661. **Facility:** 72 units. 67 one-bedroom standard units, some with whirlpools. 5 one-bedroom suites ($79-$199). 2 stories (no elevator), interior/exterior corridors. **Parking:** on-site. **Terms:** open 4/15-10/31, 2-3 night minimum stay - seasonal & weekends, 3 day cancellation notice-fee imposed. **Amenities:** hair dryers. **Pool(s):** heated outdoor, heated indoor. **Leisure Activities:** whirlpool, waterslide, playground. **Fee:** game room. **Guest Services:** coin laundry. **Cards:** DS, MC. **Special Amenities:** free local telephone calls.

SOME UNITS

⬛️🆂🅳 🕙🕺 🏊 ⌧ 🎥 🗄 / ⌧ 🖼 /

RAINTREE RESORT   *Book at aaa.com*

AAA SAVE

▼▼▼▼▼

Large-scale Hotel

			Phone: (608)253-4386	
7/1-8/31	1P: $110-$135	2P: $135-$170	XP: $10	F10
4/1-6/30 & 9/1-3/31	1P: $95-$110	2P: $110-$145	XP: $10	F10

Location: I-90/94, exit 89 (SR 23), 0.5 mi e, then 1.5 mi n on US 12. 1435 Wisconsin Dells Pkwy 53965. **Fax:** 608/254-4647. **Facility:** 158 units. 142 one-bedroom standard units, some with whirlpools. 16 one-bedroom suites ($155-$275). 3-4 stories, interior corridors. **Bath:** combo or shower only. **Parking:** on-site. **Terms:** check-in 3:30 pm, cancellation fee imposed. **Amenities:** video games (fee), voice mail, irons, hair dryers. **Dining:** 8 am-10 pm, from 3 pm off season, cocktails. **Pool(s):** small heated indoor, heated indoor/outdoor, 2 wading. **Leisure Activities:** whirlpools, waterslide, small indoor/outdoor water park with multiple children activity areas, recreation programs, exercise room. **Fee:** game room. **Guest Services:** gift shop, coin laundry. **Business Services:** meeting rooms, fax (fee). **Cards:** AX, MC, VI. **Special Amenities:** early check-in/late check-out and free room upgrade (subject to availability with advanced reservations).

SOME UNITS

🆂🅳 🕙 🍸 🛗🅼 🐕 🍳 🏊 ⌧ 🎥 📠 🗄 🖼 📺 / ⌧🎥 /

RAMADA LIMITED   *Book at aaa.com*

AAA SAVE

▼▼ ▼▼

Small-scale Hotel

			Phone: (608)254-2218	
7/2-8/21	1P: $89-$131	2P: $89-$131	XP: $10	F18
5/28-7/1	1P: $79-$109	2P: $79-$109	XP: $10	F18
8/22-3/31	1P: $59-$84	2P: $59-$84	XP: $10	F18
4/1-5/27	1P: $59-$79	2P: $59-$79	XP: $10	F18

Location: I-90/94, exit 92 (US 12), 0.3 mi n. 1073 Wisconsin Dells Pkwy 53965 (PO Box 118). **Fax:** 608/254-2696. **Facility:** 73 units. 71 one-bedroom standard units. 2 one-bedroom suites ($77-$196) with whirlpools. 2 stories, interior corridors. **Parking:** on-site, winter plug-ins. **Terms:** check-in 4 pm, 2-3 night minimum stay - weekends in summer, 3 day cancellation notice-fee imposed, package plans. **Amenities:** dual phone lines, voice mail, irons, hair dryers. **Pool(s):** small heated indoor. **Leisure Activities:** sauna, whirlpool. **Fee:** game room. **Guest Services:** coin laundry. **Business Services:** meeting rooms. **Cards:** AX, CB, DC, DS, JC, MC, VI. **Special Amenities:** free expanded continental breakfast and free room upgrade (subject to availability with advanced reservations). *(See color ad p 646)*

SOME UNITS

🆂🅳 🏊 ⌧ 🎥 📠 🖼 / ⌧ 🗄 🖼 /

RODEWAY INN   *Book at aaa.com*

▼▼ ▼▼

Small-scale Hotel

			Phone: (608)254-6492	
All Year	1P: $60-$130	2P: $65-$150	XP: $6	F

Location: I-90/94, exit 89 (SR 23 N), 0.4 mi e. 350 W Munroe Ave 53965. **Fax:** 608/254-4542. **Facility:** 62 one-bedroom standard units, some with whirlpools. 2 stories, interior corridors. **Bath:** combo or shower only. **Parking:** on-site, winter plug-ins. **Terms:** [CP] meal plan available, pets ($10 extra charge). **Amenities:** Some: irons, hair dryers. **Pool(s):** small heated indoor. **Leisure Activities:** whirlpool. **Guest Services:** coin laundry. **Business Services:** meeting rooms. **Cards:** AX, DC, DS, JC, MC, VI.

SOME UNITS

🆂🅺 🆂🅳 🕙 🛗🅼 🐕 🏊 🎥 📠 / ⌧ 🗄 🖼 /
FEE

SKYLINE HOTEL & SUITES *Book at aaa.com*

Phone: (608)253-4841

(AAA) (SAVE)
◆◆◆◆ ◆◆◆◆
Small-scale Hotel

All Year   1P: $49-$129   2P: $49-$129   XP: $5   F16

Location: I-90/94, exit 92 (US 12), 3.2 mi n. 1970 Wisconsin Dells Pkwy 53965. Fax: 608/254-6009. **Facility:** 87 units. 85 one-bedroom standard units, some with whirlpools. 2 two-bedroom suites ($169-$325), some with whirlpools. 3 stories, interior/exterior corridors. **Parking:** on-site, winter plug-ins. **Terms:** office hours 8 am-10 pm, 3 day cancellation notice-fee imposed. **Pool(s):** heated outdoor, 2 heated indoor, 2 wading. **Leisure Activities:** saunas, whirlpools, waterslide, picnic area, playground. *Fee:* game room. **Guest Services:** coin laundry, area transportation. *Fee:* tanning facility. **Business Services:** meeting rooms. **Cards:** AX, DS, MC, VI. **Special Amenities:** free expanded continental breakfast and free local telephone calls. *(See color ad below)*

SOME UNITS

[S/D] [♦↑] [➰] [✕] [♣] [DATA PORT] [▦] [▣] [▤] / [✕] /

SUPER 8 MOTEL *Book at aaa.com*

Phone: 608/254-6464

◆◆◆◆ ◆◆◆◆
Small-scale Hotel

7/2-9/5	1P: $68-$155	2P: $78-$165	XP: $10	F12
5/29-7/1	1P: $61-$135	2P: $71-$145	XP: $10	F12
9/6-3/31	1P: $50-$125	2P: $56-$125	XP: $10	F12
4/1-5/28	1P: $50-$115	2P: $56-$125	XP: $10	F12

Location: I-90/94, exit 87 (SR 13), just e. 800 CR H 53965 (PO Box 467). Fax: 608/254-2692. **Facility:** 125 one-bedroom standard units. 3 stories, interior corridors. **Parking:** on-site, winter plug-ins. **Terms:** [CP] meal plan available. **Amenities:** safes (fee), hair dryers. **Pool(s):** small heated indoor. **Leisure Activities:** sauna, whirlpool. *Fee:* game room. **Guest Services:** coin laundry. **Cards:** AX, CB, DC, DS, MC, VI.

SOME UNITS

[🐾] [♦↑] [📷] [➰] [✕] [DATA PORT] [▣] / [✕] /

TREASURE ISLAND WATER PARK RESORT

Phone: 608/254-8560

◆◆◆◆
Resort
Large-scale Hotel

All Year   1P: $89-$275   2P: $89-$275   XP: $15

Location: I-90/94, exit 87 (SR 13), 1 mi e, then 1 mi n on US 12. 1701 Wisconsin Dells Pkwy 53965 (PO Box 267). Fax: 608/253-9960. **Facility:** This nautically-themed family resort offers an extensive variety of both indoor and outdoor waterparks as well as additional recreational activities. 331 units. 239 one-bedroom standard units. 92 one-bedroom suites with whirlpools. 1-3 stories, interior corridors. *Bath:* combo or shower only. **Parking:** on-site. **Terms:** check-in 4 pm, 3 day cancellation notice-fee imposed. **Amenities:** voice mail, irons, hair dryers. **Pool(s):** 2 heated outdoor, 2 heated indoor, 2 wading. **Leisure Activities:** whirlpools, waterslide, lifeguard on duty, miniature golf, exercise room. *Fee:* game room. **Guest Services:** gift shop, coin laundry. **Cards:** AX, DS, MC, VI.

SOME UNITS

[ASK] [♦] [&] [➰] [✕] [♣] [DATA PORT] [▦] [▣] [▤] / [✕] /

WINTERGREEN RESORT & CONFERENCE CENTER

Phone: 608/254-2285

(AAA) (SAVE)
◆◆◆◆
Small-scale Hotel

All Year   1P: $65-$184   2P: $65-$184

Location: I-90/94, exit 92 (US 12), just n. Located next to casino. 60 Gasser Rd 53965 (PO Box 296). Fax: 608/253-6235. **Facility:** 109 units. 99 one-bedroom standard units, some with whirlpools. 9 one- and 1 three-bedroom suites ($99-$389), some with whirlpools. 3 stories, interior corridors. *Bath:* combo or shower only. **Parking:** on-site. **Terms:** check-in 4 pm, 3 day cancellation notice-fee imposed. **Amenities:** high-speed Internet, voice mail, hair dryers. **Dining:** 7 am-9 pm; Sun-Thurs to 7 pm in winter, cocktails. **Pool(s):** outdoor, heated indoor, 3 wading. **Leisure Activities:** sauna, whirlpools, waterslide, mini water park with pools, waterfalls, children's recreation area, playground, exercise room. *Fee:* game room. **Guest Services:** gift shop, coin laundry. **Business Services:** meeting rooms. **Cards:** AX, DS, MC, VI.

SOME UNITS

[♦] [Y] [📷] [➰] [✕] [♣] [DATA PORT] [▦] [▣] [▤] / [✕] /

──────── *The following lodging was either not evaluated or did not* ────────
meet AAA rating requirements but is listed for your information only.

WILDERNESS HOTEL & GOLF RESORT　　　　　　　　　　　　　Phone: 608/253-8729
[fyi]　　Not evaluated. **Location:** I-90/94, exit 92 (US 12), 0.8 mi n. 511 E Adam St 53965. Facilities, services, and decor characterize a mid-range property.

──────── **WHERE TO DINE** ────────

THE CHEESE FACTORY RESTAURANT　　　Lunch: $5-$9　　　Dinner: $10-$13　　　Phone: 608/253-6065
▼▼▼ ▼▼▼　**Location:** I-90/94, exit 92, 1.3 mi n on US 12. 521 Wisconsin Dells Pkwy S 53965. **Hours:** 9 am-9 pm. Closed:
　　　　　11/25, 12/25; also Tues; Mon-Wed in winter. **Features:** Fresh, flavorful ingredients, unusual international
Vegetarian　recipes and pleasant service are staples at the restored cheese factory. An authentic soda fountain,
　　　　　jukebox and waiters in bow ties add to the nostalgic mood. Homemade desserts are wonderful. Casual
dress. **Parking:** on-site. **Cards:** AX, DS, MC, VI.　　　　　　　　　　　　　　　　　　　　　　[X]

THE DEL-BAR　　　　　　　　　　　Dinner: $17-$38　　　　　　　　　　　Phone: 608/253-1861
▼▼▼ ▼▼▼　**Location:** I-90/94, exit 92, 2.5 mi n on US 12 and SR 23. 800 Wisconsin Dells Pkwy 53940. **Hours:** 4:30 pm-9:30
　　　　　pm, Fri & Sat-10 pm. Closed: 11/25, 12/24, 12/25. **Reservations:** suggested. **Features:** Owned and
American　operated by same family since 1943. Excellent aged steak and fresh seafood. Also featuring Wisconsin
　　　　　duck. Terrace dining in season. Warm atmosphere with soft lighting and soothing player piano background
music. Dressy casual; cocktails. **Parking:** on-site. **Cards:** AX, CB, DC, DS, MC, VI.　　　　　[Y] [X]

FAMILY CHEF RESTAURANT　　　　　Lunch: $5-$12　　　Dinner: $5-$12　　　Phone: 608/254-7969
(AAA)　　**Location:** 0.5 mi e of downtown on SR 16/13/23. 1101 Broadway 53965. **Hours:** Open 4/1-11/6 & 1/15-3/31; 7
▼　　　　am to 10 pm 7/1-8/31. **Features:** This notably clean and well-established restaurant caters to
　　　　　families with its extensive menu selection and casual atmosphere. Comfort foods abound, and fresh
American　strawberry pie is the prize of the day. Casual dress; wine only. **Parking:** on-site. **Cards:** MC, VI.　[X]

FAMOUS DAVE'S　　　　　　　Lunch: $5-$7　　　Dinner: $7-$18　　　Phone: 608/253-6683
▼▼ ▼▼▼　**Location:** Downtown. 435 Broadway 53965. **Hours:** 11 am-8 pm; to 10 pm 6/1-9/1. Closed: 11/25, 12/25.
　　　　　Features: The casual restaurant's claim to fame is its award winning barbecue. Pork sandwiches, rib
Barbecue　platters, burgers, chicken, salads and traditional side dishes are available for dining in or taking out. The
　　　　　lunch menu offers an exceptional value, with large portions at good prices. Casual dress; beer & wine only.
Parking: street. **Cards:** AX, DC, DS, MC, VI.　　　　　　　　　　　　　　　　　　　　　　　[X]

FIELD'S AT THE WILDERNESS　　　　　Dinner: $25-$35　　　　　　　　　Phone: 608/253-1400
(AAA)　　**Location:** I-90/94, exit 92 (US 12), 0.7 mi n. 511 E Adams St 53965. **Hours:** 4:30 pm-10 pm. Closed major
　　　　　holidays. **Reservations:** suggested. **Features:** Inspired by the architecture of Frank Lloyd Wright, the
▼▼▼ ▼　demurely elegant restaurant features a number of stone hearth fireplaces, waterfalls and an exhibition
　　　　　kitchen. The a la carte menu lists contemporary yet creative preparations of steak, chops and fresh
Steak House　seafood, as well as pizzas cooked in a wood-burning oven. Casual dress; cocktails. **Parking:** on-site.
　　　　　Cards: AX, DC, DS, MC, VI.　　　　　　　　　　　　　　　　　　　　　[&M] [Y] [X]

PEDRO'S MEXICAN RESTAURANTE　　　Lunch: $5-$8　　　Dinner: $5-$17　　　Phone: 608/253-7233
▼▼▼ ▼▼▼　**Location:** Just w of downtown on SR 23, 16 and 13. 951 Stand Rock Rd 53965. **Hours:** 11 am-9:30 pm, Fri &
　　　　　Sat-10:30 pm; 11 am-11 pm 5/20-9/20. Closed: 12/24, 12/25. **Reservations:** accepted. **Features:** Sizzling
Mexican　fajitas are a big hit at this restaurant, which delivers favorites from burritos and tacos to enchiladas and
　　　　　nachos. Complimentary fresh chips and salsa accompany all meals. Stucco walls, tile flooring and colorful
decorations add to the South of the Border atmosphere. Casual dress; cocktails. **Parking:** on-site. **Cards:** AX, DS, MC, VI.　[Y] [X]

WALLY'S HOUSE OF EMBERS　　　　　Dinner: $10-$25　　　　　　　　　Phone: 608/253-6411
▼▼▼ ▼▼▼　**Location:** I-90/94, exit 192 (US 12), 2.5 mi n. 935 Wisconsin Dells Pkwy 53940. **Hours:** 4:30 pm-10:30 pm, Sat-11
　　　　　pm. Closed: 11/25, 12/24, 12/25. **Reservations:** suggested. **Features:** Casual dining in family owned
American　restaurant since 1959. Famous for hickory smoked barbecue ribs. Also featuring Austrian veal and fresh
　　　　　fish. Private dining rooms are available. Dressy casual; cocktails. **Parking:** on-site. **Cards:** AX, DC,
MC, VI.　　　　　　　　　　　　　　　　　　　　　　　　　　　　　　　　　　[Y] [X]

WISCONSIN RAPIDS pop. 18,435

──────── **WHERE TO STAY** ────────

AMERICINN MOTEL & SUITES　　*Book at aaa.com*　　　　　　　　Phone: (715)424-3444
▼▼▼ ▼▼▼　All Year　　　　1P: $79-$139　　　2P: $84-$144　　　XP: $6　　　　F18
　　　　　Location: 1.4 mi s on SR 13. Located in a commercial area. 3010 8th St S 54494. Fax: 715/424-3433. **Facility:** 65
Small-scale Hotel　units. 60 one-bedroom standard units, some with whirlpools. 5 one-bedroom suites, some with whirlpools. 2
　　　　　stories (no elevator), interior corridors. *Bath:* combo or shower only. **Parking:** on-site, winter plug-ins.
Terms: [CP] meal plan available. **Amenities:** dual phone lines, hair dryers. *Some:* irons. **Pool(s):** heated indoor. **Leisure Activities:** Fee: game room. **Guest Services:** valet and coin laundry. **Business Services:** meeting rooms. **Cards:** AX, DS, MC, VI.
(See color ad p 576)

SOME UNITS
[icons] [📶] [🛏] [🔧] [❄] [DATA PORT] [🖥] / [X] [🛁] [▭] /

BEST WESTERN RAPIDS MOTOR INN   *Book at aaa.com*   Phone: (715)423-3211
(AAA) [SAVE]
1/1-3/31 [CP]   1P: $66-$76   2P: $66-$76   XP: $10   F12
▽▽▽ ▽▽   5/17-10/20 [CP]   1P: $64-$74   2P: $64-$74   XP: $7   F12
4/1-5/16 & 10/21-12/31 [CP] 1P: $62-$72   2P: $62-$72   XP: $7   F12
Location: 0.5 mi s on SR 13 of jct SR 54. Located in a commercial area. 911 Huntington Ave 54494.
Small-scale Hotel Fax: 715/423-2875. **Facility:** 43 one-bedroom standard units. 2 stories (no elevator), interior corridors.
Parking: on-site. **Terms:** office hours 6 am-11 pm, check-in 4 pm, pets (with prior approval).
Amenities: irons, hair dryers. **Leisure Activities:** whirlpool. **Guest Services:** valet laundry. **Cards:** AX, DC, DS, JC, MC, VI.
Special Amenities: free continental breakfast and early check-in/late check-out.

SOME UNITS
🅢🄳 🐾 🕩 📠 💻 / ✖ 📦 /

HOTEL MEAD   *Book at aaa.com*   Phone: (715)423-1500
(AAA) [SAVE]
All Year   1P: $109-$214   2P: $119-$224   XP: $10   F18
▽▽▽ ▽▽   **Location:** Just e of downtown. Located in a residential area. 451 E Grand Ave 54494. Fax: 715/422-7064.
Facility: 157 one-bedroom standard units, some with whirlpools. 5 stories, interior corridors. *Bath:* combo or
shower only. **Parking:** on-site. **Terms:** check-in 4 pm, 2-3 night minimum stay - seasonal, package plans -
Large-scale Hotel seasonal, pets (with prior approval). **Amenities:** dual phone lines, voice mail, irons, hair dryers.
Dining: Cafe' Mulino, The Grand Avenue Grill, see separate listings. **Pool(s):** heated indoor. **Leisure Activi-**
ties: sauna, whirlpool, exercise room. *Fee:* bicycles, game room. **Guest Services:** valet laundry. **Business Services:** conference facilities, business center. **Cards:** AX, CB, DC, DS, MC, VI. **Special Amenities:** early check-in/late check-out.

SOME UNITS
🅢🄳 🐾 🍴 🍸 📷 ⬇ 🏊 ✖ 📹 📠 💻 / ✖ 📼 📦 📧 /
FEE

QUALITY INN   *Book at aaa.com*   Phone: (715)423-5506
▽▽▽ ▽▽▽
All Year   1P: $65-$72   2P: $72-$82   XP: $6   F18
Location: 1.5 mi s on SR 13. Located in a commercial area. 3120 8th St S 54494. Fax: 715/423-7150. **Facility:** 36
one-bedroom standard units. 2 stories (no elevator), interior corridors. **Parking:** on-site, winter plug-ins.
Small-scale Hotel **Terms:** [ECP] meal plan available. **Amenities:** voice mail. **Pool(s):** heated indoor. **Leisure Activities:** whirl-
pool. **Guest Services:** valet laundry. **Business Services:** meeting rooms. **Cards:** AX, DC, DS, MC, VI.

SOME UNITS
[ASK] 🅢🄳 🕩 ⬇ 📹 📠 💻 / ✖ /

SUPER 8 MOTEL   *Book at aaa.com*   Phone: (715)423-8080
▽▽▽ ▽▽▽
All Year   1P: $48-$63   2P: $53-$68   XP: $5   F12
Location: 1.9 mi s on SR 13 of jct SR 54 W. Located in a commercial area. 3410 8th St S 54494. Fax: 715/423-3595.
Small-scale Hotel **Facility:** 48 one-bedroom standard units. 2 stories (no elevator), interior corridors. **Parking:** on-site, winter
plug-ins. **Terms:** small pets only ($10 extra charge, with prior approval). **Amenities:** safes (fee). **Guest Serv-**
ices: coin laundry. **Cards:** AX, CB, DC, DS, MC, VI.

SOME UNITS
[ASK] 🅢🄳 🐾 🕩 📷 📹 📠 💻 / ✖ 📼 📦 📧 /
FEE

——— WHERE TO DINE ———

CAFE' MULINO
▼▼ ▼▼
Italian

Lunch: $6-$9   **Dinner:** $8-$17   **Phone:** 715/422-7000
Location: Just e of downtown; in Hotel Mead. 451 E Grand Ave 54494. **Hours:** 11:30 am-10:30 pm, Sun 10 am-10 pm. **Closed:** 12/25. **Reservations:** suggested. **Features:** The lively, trattoria-style restaurant delivers regional specialties and traditional Italian cuisine, including pizza cooked in a wood-burning oven. Generous portions are an excellent value. The friendly, casual atmosphere is welcoming to families. Casual dress; cocktails. **Parking:** on-site. **Cards:** AX, CB, DC, DS, MC, VI.

FOUR STARS FAMILY RESTAURANT PANCAKE HOUSE
▼
American

Lunch: $5-$8   **Dinner:** $5-$8   **Phone:** 715/424-4554
Location: 1.5 mi s on SR 13 of jct SR 54. 2911 8th St 54494. **Hours:** 5 am-10 pm. **Reservations:** accepted. **Features:** The popular restaurant's menu selections are vast and varied. Burgers, sandwiches, pitas, salads, pasta and Mexican specialties are featured. All-day breakfast selections include crepes, waffles, omelets and Swedish pancakes. Casual dress; wine only. **Parking:** on-site. **Cards:** AX, MC, VI.

THE GRAND AVENUE GRILL
▼▼ ▼▼
American

Lunch: $5-$10   **Dinner:** $12-$25   **Phone:** 715/422-7000
Location: Just e of downtown; in Hotel Mead. 451 E Grand Ave 54494. **Hours:** 6:30-11 am, 11:30-1:30 & 5-9 pm, Fri & Sat-10 pm, Sun 6:30 am-2 pm. **Closed:** 12/25; also for lunch Sat & Mon. **Reservations:** suggested. **Features:** This traditional grill room offers time-tested favorites in a warm, relaxing atmosphere. Choice steak and seafood highlight the menu. Roast duck, smoked pork chop and Wisconsin venison stew are complements. The chef offers several new specials weekly. Desserts are made in-house and presented tableside on a tray. Service is attentive and capable. The white cloth covered tables, soft lighting and background music make for a comfortable dining experience. Dressy casual; cocktails. **Parking:** on-site. **Cards:** AX, CB, DC, DS, MC, VI.

WITTENBERG pop. 1,177

——— WHERE TO STAY ———

COMFORT INN & WILDERNESS CONFERENCE CENTER
▼▼ ▼▼
Small-scale Hotel

Book at aaa.com   **Phone:** 715/253-3755
All Year [CP]   1P: $49-$129   2P: $57-$137   XP: $5   F
Location: US 29, exit 198, just se. W17267 Red Oak Ln 54499. Fax: 715/253-3759. **Facility:** 64 one-bedroom standard units, some with whirlpools. 3 stories, interior corridors. *Bath:* combo or shower only. **Parking:** on-site. **Terms:** pets ($20 extra charge, must remain caged). **Amenities:** safes, irons, hair dryers. **Pool(s):** heated indoor. **Leisure Activities:** whirlpool, exercise room. **Guest Services:** coin laundry. **Business Services:** meeting rooms. **Cards:** AX, DS, MC, VI.

SOME UNITS

WOODRUFF

——— WHERE TO DINE ———

PLANTATION SUPPER CLUB
AAA
▼▼ ▼▼
American

Dinner: $7-$20   **Phone:** 715/356-9000
Location: 1.5 mi n on US 51, jct SR 70. **Hours:** Open 4/1-2/14; 5 pm-10 pm; hours may vary. **Closed:** Mon. **Reservations:** accepted. **Features:** This traditional northern Wisconsin supper club is well-established, and was first constructed in 1938. The current owners have operated it since 1970. The service is friendly and attentive. The homemade onion rings and giant lobster tail are popular, as is the Friday night fish fry. Smoking in lounge. Casual dress; cocktails. **Parking:** on-site. **Cards:** AX, DC, DS, MC, VI.

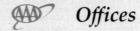

Offices

NATIONAL OFFICE: 1000 AAA DRIVE, HEATHROW, FLORIDA 32746-5063, (407) 444-7000

MICHIGAN

ALLEN PARK—AAA MICHIGAN, 15220 SOUTHFIELD RD, 48101. MON-FRI 8:30-6. (313) 386-7000, *(800) 222-8852.*✛▲

ALPENA—AAA MICHIGAN, 2539 US 23 S, 49707. MON-FRI 8:30-6. (989) 354-2151, *(800) 322-3014.*✛▲

ANN ARBOR—AAA MICHIGAN, 1200 S MAIN ST, 48104. MON-FRI 8:30-6. (734) 930-2250, *(800) 447-5490.*✛▲

ANN ARBOR—AAA MICHIGAN, 2650 CARPENTER RD, 48108. MON-FRI 8:30-6, SAT 8:30-12:30. (734) 973-2800, *(800) 833-4613.*✛▲

BATTLE CREEK—AAA MICHIGAN, 778 W COLUMBIA AVE, 49015. MON-FRI 8:30-6. (616) 962-2500, *(800) 435-0320.*✛▲

BAY CITY—AAA MICHIGAN, 1111 S EUCLID AVE, 48706. MON-FRI 8:30-6. (989) 686-2940, *(800) 322-4517.*✛▲

BIRMINGHAM—AAA MICHIGAN, 34802 WOODWARD AVE, 48009. MON-FRI 8:30-6. (248) 433-8200, *(800) 222-4419.*✛▲

BRIGHTON—AAA MICHIGAN, 8350 W GRAND RIVER AVE, 48116. MON-FRI 8:30-6. (810) 229-7100, *(800) 222-8801.*✛▲

CANTON—AAA MICHIGAN, 2017 N CANTON CENTER RD, 48187. MON-FRI 8:30-6. (734) 844-0146, *(800) 844-0424.*✛▲

CENTER LINE—AAA MICHIGAN, 26522 VAN DYKE, 48015. MON-FRI 8:30-6, SAT 8:30-12:30. (586) 754-2200.✛▲

DEARBORN—AAA MICHIGAN, 1 AUTO CLUB DR, 48126. MON-FRI 8-5:30. (313) 336-1234, *(800) 222-6424.* [Administrative office only]

DEARBORN—AAA MICHIGAN, 18800 HUBBARD DR #100, 48126. MON-FRI 8:30-6, SAT 8:30-12:30. (313) 336-0990.✛▲

DETROIT—AAA MICHIGAN, 7800 W OUTER DR #120, 48235. MON-FRI 8:30-6. (313) 255-9310, *(800) 222-4416.*✛▲

DETROIT—AAA MICHIGAN, 719 GRISWOLD AVE STE 170, 48226. MON-FRI 8:30-6. (313) 237-5500, *(800) 934-8209.*✛▲

DETROIT—AAA MICHIGAN, 9189 CADIEUX, 48224. MON-FRI 8:30-6, SAT 8:30-12:30. (313) 417-2393.✛▲

FARMINGTON HILLS—AAA MICHIGAN, 38751 W 12 MILE RD, 48331. MON-FRI 8:30-6, SAT 8:30-12:30. (248) 994-4330, *(800) 224-1178.*✛▲

FLINT—AAA MICHIGAN, G-5009 W BRISTOL RD, 48507. MON-FRI 8:30-6, SAT 8:30-12:30. (810) 230-8890, *(800) 552-5970.*✛▲

GRAND RAPIDS—AAA MICHIGAN, 4650 PLAINFIELD NE, 49525. MON-FRI 8:30-6. (616) 364-6111, *(800) 442-8304.*✛▲

GRANDVILLE—AAA MICHIGAN, 6305 KENOWA SW, 49418. MON-FRI 8:30-6. (616) 457-8222, *(800) 258-6464.*✛▲

GROSSE POINTE WOODS—AAA MICHIGAN, 19299 MACK AVE, 48236. MON-FRI 8:30-6. (313) 343-6000.✛▲

HOLLAND—AAA MICHIGAN, 587 E 8TH ST, 49423. MON-FRI 8:30-6. (616) 392-5171, *(888) 544-9204.*✛▲

JACKSON—AAA MICHIGAN, 1200 SOUTH WEST AVE, 49203. MON-FRI 8:30-6. (517) 787-7300, *(800) 842-8999.*✛▲

KALAMAZOO—AAA MICHIGAN, 2015 CROSSTOWN PKY W, 49008. MON-FRI 8:30-6, SAT 8:30-12:30. (616) 381-7100, *(800) 851-9692.*✛▲

KENTWOOD—AAA MICHIGAN, 2560 E PARIS AVE SE, 49546. MON-FRI 8:30-6, SAT 8:30-12:30. (616) 957-4455, *(800) 222-3103.*✛▲

LANSING—AAA MICHIGAN, 2829 E GRAND RIVER AVE, 48912. MON-FRI 8:30-6, SAT 8:30-12:30. (517) 487-6171, *(800) 222-9905.*✛▲

LIVONIA—AAA MICHIGAN, 37383 SIX MILE RD, 48152. MON-FRI 8:30-6. (734) 462-7000, *(800) 851-9691.*✛▲

MACOMB—AAA MICHIGAN, 21851 HALL RD, 48044. MON-FRI 8:30-6, SAT 8:30-12:30. (810) 469-4050, *(800) 551-4311.*✛▲

MARQUETTE—AAA MICHIGAN, WESTWOOD MALL, 49855. MON-FRI 8:30-6. (906) 225-6750, *(800) 526-4241.*✛▲

MIDLAND—AAA MICHIGAN, 1900 S SAGINAW RD, 48640. MON-FRI 8:30-6. (989) 832-6500, *(800) 322-4271.*●▲

MOUNT PLEASANT—AAA MICHIGAN, 913 E PICKARD SUITE L, 48858. MON-FRI 8:30-6. (989) 772-6001, *(800) 888-8850.*●▲

MUSKEGON—AAA MICHIGAN, 3575 HENRY ST, 49441. MON-FRI 8:30-6. (231) 739-9363, *(800) 851-9689.*✛▲

PETOSKEY—AAA MICHIGAN, 1321 SPRINGS ST, 49770. MON-FRI 8:30-6. (231) 347-8284, *(800) 294-6503.*✛▲

PORT HURON—AAA MICHIGAN, 933 LAPEER, 48060. MON-FRI 8:30-6. (810) 987-4800, *(800) 462-9968.*✛▲

ROSEVILLE—AAA MICHIGAN, 25195 KELLY RD, 48066. MON-FRI 8:30-6. (586) 774-7000.✛▲

ROYAL OAK—AAA MICHIGAN, 27844 WOODWARD AVE, 48067. MON-FRI 8:30-6. (248) 399-7100, *(866) 676-8757.*✛▲

SAGINAW—AAA MICHIGAN, 3785 BAY RD, 48603. MON-FRI 8:30-6. (989) 790-3240, *(800) 322-1120.*✛▲

SOUTH LYON—AAA MICHIGAN, 582 N LAFAYETTE, 48178. MON-FRI 8:30-6. (248) 437-1729, *(800) 783-1729.*■▲

SOUTHGATE—AAA MICHIGAN, 15150 FORT ST, 48195. MON-FRI 8:30-6. (734) 284-0800, *(800) 222-6612.*✛▲

ST JOSEPH—AAA MICHIGAN, 2090 NILES RD SUITE 200, 49085. MON-FRI 8:30-5:30. (616) 982-0033.▲

TRAVERSE CITY—AAA MICHIGAN, 940 N US 31 N, 49686. MON-FRI 8:30-6, SAT 8:30-12:30. (231) 947-8045, *(800) 442-1742.*✛▲

TROY—AAA MICHIGAN, 25 E LONG LAKE RD, 48085. MON-FRI 8:30-6, SAT 8:30-12:30. (248) 879-2030, *(877) 349-1514.*✛▲

UTICA—AAA MICHIGAN, 45700 MOUND RD, 48317. MON-FRI 8:30-6. (586) 739-1400, *(800) 851-9690.*✛▲

WATERFORD—AAA MICHIGAN, 5140 HIGHLAND RD, 48327. MON-FRI 8:30-6. (248) 618-3440, *(800) 222-2661.*✛▲

WISCONSIN

APPLETON—AAA WISCONSIN, 3215 W COLLEGE AVE, 54914. MON-FRI 8:30-5:30, SAT 9-1. (920) 738-4200, *(800) 236-1300.*✛▲

BELOIT—AAA WISCONSIN, 2787 MILWAUKEE RD #4, 53511. MON-FRI 8:30-5:30, SAT 9-1. (608) 364-2740, *(800) 236-1300.*■

CEDARBURG—AAA WISCONSIN, W62 N208 WASHINGTON AVE, 53012. MON-FRI 8:30-5:30, SAT 9-1. (262) 376-8700.■

DELAFIELD—AAA WISCONSIN, 2566 SUN VALLEY DR D1, 53018. SATURDAY BY APPOINTMENT MON-FRI 8:30-5:30. (262) 646-6111.■

EAU CLAIRE—AAA WISCONSIN, 3436 OAKWOOD HILLS PKY, 54701. MON-FRI 8:30-5:30, SAT 9-1. (715) 836-8640, *(800) 236-1300.*✛▲

FOND DU LAC—AAA WISCONSIN, 504A N ROLLING MEADOWS DR, 54937. MON-FRI 8:30-5:30, SAT 9-1. (920) 923-4805.■

GREEN BAY—AAA WISCONSIN, 2285 S ONEIDA ST #1, 54304. MON-FRI 8:30-5:30, SAT 9-1. (920) 498-6120, *(800) 236-1300.*✛▲

GREEN BAY—AAA WISCONSIN, 2420 UNIVERSITY AVE, 54302. MON-FRI 8:30-5:30. (920) 406-2090.■

JANESVILLE—AAA WISCONSIN, 2900 DEERFIELD DR STE 9C, 53546. MON-FRI 8:30-5:30, SAT 9-1. (608) 755-3960.■▲

KENOSHA—AAA WISCONSIN, 10320 75TH ST SUITE D, 53142. MON-FRI 8:30-5:30. (262) 697-7280.■▲

MADISON—AAA WISCONSIN, 8401 EXCELSIOR DR, 53717. MON-FRI 8:30-5:30, SAT 9-1. (608) 836-6555, *(800) 236-1300.*+▲

MADISON—AAA WISCONSIN, 1701 THIERER RD, 53704. MON-FRI 8:30-5:30, SAT 9-1. (608) 242-6000.■

MADISON—AAA WISCONSIN, 12635 W NORTH AVE, 53005. MON-FRI 9-6, SAT 9-1. (262) 796-8960, *(800) 236-1300.*+▲

MADISON—AAA WISCONSIN, 664 W WASHINGTON AVE, 53703. MON-FRI 8:30-5:30, SAT 9-1. (608) 251-0333, *(800) 236-1300.*+▲

MADISON—AAA WISCONSIN, 1853 NORTHPORT DR, 53704. MON-FRI 8:30-5:30. (608) 246-5186.■

MENOMONEE FALLS—AAA WISCONSIN, W176 N9352 RIVER CREST DR, 53051. MON-FRI 8-5:30. (262) 257-7555.■

MILWAUKEE—AAA WISCONSIN, 4433 S 27TH ST, 53221. MON-FRI 9-6, SAT 9-1. (414) 423-2180, *(800) 236-1300.*+▲

MILWAUKEE—AAA WISCONSIN, 200 W SILVER SPRING DR, 53217. MON-FRI 9-6, SAT 9-1. (414) 963-3060, *(800) 236-1300.*+▲

MILWAUKEE—AAA WISCONSIN, 8333 W APPLETON AVE, 53218. SATURDAY BY APPOINTMENT MON-FRI 8:30-5:30. (414) 535-4040.■

OAK CREEK—AAA WISCONSIN, 2333 W RYAN RD, 53154. MON-FRI 8:30-5:30. (414) 281-4200.■

ONALASKA—AAA WISCONSIN, 1220 CROSSING MEADOWS DR, 54650. MON-FRI 8:30-5:30, SAT 9-1. (608) 783-7412, *(800) 236-1300.*+▲

OSHKOSH—AAA WISCONSIN, 1496 WEST SOUTH PARK AVE, 54902. MON-FRI 8:30-5:30. (866) 823-7665.■

RACINE—AAA WISCONSIN, 5630 WASHINGTON AVE #7, 53406. MON-FRI 8:30-5:30, SAT 9-1. (262) 636-8720, *(800) 236-1300.*+▲

SHEBOYGAN—AAA WISCONSIN, 3104 S BUSINESS DR, 53081. MON-FRI 8:30-5:30. (920) 208-8900.■

WAUKESHA—AAA WISCONSIN, 2020 E MORELAND BLVD, 53186. MON-FRI 9-6, SAT 9-1. (262) 548-1000, *(800) 236-1300.*+▲

WAUSAU—AAA WISCONSIN, 4518 RIB MOUNTAIN DR, 54401. MON-FRI 8:30-5:30. (715) 241-7222.■▲

WEST ALLIS—AAA WISCONSIN, 2255 S 108TH ST, 53227. MON-FRI 8:30-5:30. (414) 327-8880.■

WEST BEND—AAA WISCONSIN, 910 GATEWAY CT, 53095. SATURDAY BY APPOINTMENT MON-FRI 8:30-5:30. (262) 338-0100.■

Dreams Become Reality With AAA Travel

EXPLORE THE MOUNTAINS, THE DESERTS, AND THE CITIES - ANYWHERE, ANYTIME - WITH AAA, THE MOST TRUSTED NAME IN TRAVEL®.

LET AAA TRAVEL TAKE CARE OF ALL YOUR TRAVEL NEEDS. TO RECEIVE EXCLUSIVE AAA MEMBER BENEFITS, CALL OR VISIT YOUR NEAREST AAA TRAVEL OFFICE, OR CLICK ON www.aaa.com TODAY.

Travel With Someone You Trust.®
www.aaa.com

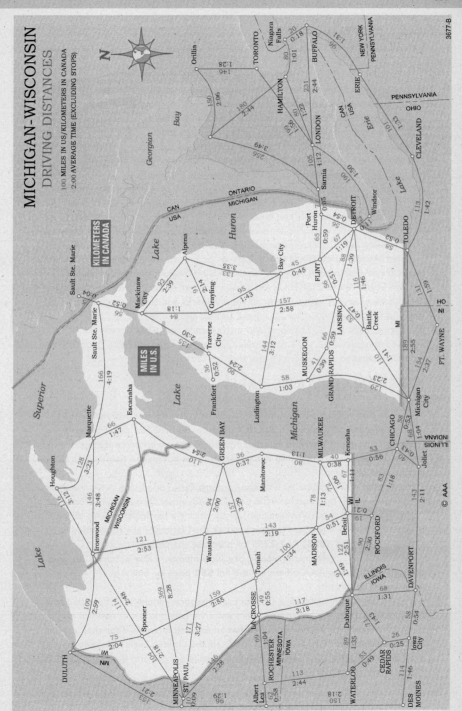

MICHIGAN-WISCONSIN
DRIVING DISTANCES

100 MILES IN US/KILOMETERS IN CANADA
2:00 AVERAGE TIME (EXCLUDING STOPS)

KILOMETERS IN CANADA

MILES IN U.S.

© AAA

3677-B

GOLDEN PASSPORTS

Golden Passports, available in three types, offer benefits and significant savings to individuals who plan to visit federal recreation sites.

The *Golden Eagle Passport*, available for a **$65** annual fee, is valid for entrance only to all federal recreation areas that have an entrance fee. Sites include those operated by the National Forest Service, National Park Service, Bureau of Land Management and the U.S. Fish and Wildlife Service. The passport admits all occupants of a private vehicle at locations where entrance is on a per vehicle basis. At locations where a per person fee is charged, the pass covers the pass holder, spouse, parents and children.

Citizens or permanent residents of the United States who are 62 and older can obtain *Golden Age Passports* for a one-time **$10** fee. Proof of age is required.

Golden Access Passports are free to citizens or permanent residents of the United States (regardless of age) who are medically blind or permanently disabled.

Both *Golden Age* and *Golden Access passports* cover entrance fees for the holder and accompanying private party to all national parks and sites managed by the U.S. Fish and Wildlife Service, the U.S. Forest Service and the Bureau of Land Management, plus half off camping and other fees. When a per person fee is imposed, the pass covers the pass holder, spouse and children. Apply in person at a federally operated area where an entrance fee is charged.

NATIONAL PARKS PASS

The *National Parks Pass*, valid for 1 year from its first use in a park, allows unlimited admissions to all U.S. national parks. The **$50** pass covers all occupants of a private vehicle at parks where the entrance fee is per vehicle. At parks with individual entry fees, the pass covers the pass holder, spouse, parents and children.

As a result of a partnership with the National Park Foundation, AAA members may purchase the pass for **$48**, either through AAA's internet site (www.aaa.com) or by visiting a participating AAA office. Members may also phone the National Park Foundation at **(888) 467-2757** or purchase the pass online at www.nationalparks.org. Non-members may purchase the pass through participating AAA offices for the full **$50** price or online at www.nationalparks.org.

For an upgrade fee of **$15**, a Golden Eagle hologram sticker can be added to a *National Parks Pass*. The hologram covers entrance fees not just at national parks, but at any federal recreation area that has an admission fee. Valid for the duration of the *National Parks Pass* to which it is affixed, the Golden Eagle hologram is available at National Park Service, Fish and Wildlife Service and Bureau of Land Management fee stations.

Border Information

FOR CANADIAN RESIDENTS ENTERING THE UNITED STATES

PASSPORTS to enter the United States or return to Canada are not required for native-born citizens of either country. However, **a Canadian passport remains the best internationally accepted evidence of Canadian citizenship and its use is strongly suggested.** Proof of citizenship must be carried; a certified birth certificate, accompanied by a photo ID will usually suffice. Proof of residence also may be required. Unmarried parents who share custody of children should carry copies of the legal custody documents.

UNITED STATES CUSTOMS permits you to bring, free of duty, for personal use and not intended for sale: clothing, personal effects and equipment appropriate to the trip. Personal effects may include 200 cigarettes *or* 50 cigars *or* 4.4 pounds (2 kgs) of smoking tobacco *or* proportionate amounts of each, and 1 litre of alcoholic beverage. **Cuban cigars are denied entry.**

If you are planning to be in the United States **at least 72 hours,** you may bring gifts up to a fair retail value of $100 (U.S.), provided you have not claimed this exemption within the preceding 6 months. Family members may not combine their gift exemptions. Perfume containing alcohol and valued at more than $5 retail, tobacco products (except for 100 cigars) and alcoholic beverages are excluded from the gift provision.

RADIO COMMUNICATION EQUIPMENT: You may use your Family Radio Service (FRS) radio and cellular phone in the United States without any restrictions.

RETURNING TO CANADA

CANADIAN CUSTOMS allows you to bring, free of duty and taxes, goods valued up to $200 (Canadian) any number of times per year, provided you have been in the United States **48 hours or more.** All goods must accompany you; a written declaration may be required.

You may claim a $50 (Canadian) exemption on goods, excluding alcoholic beverages and tobacco products, if you are returning after an absence of **24 hours or more** and are not using any other exemption. If more than $50 worth of goods are brought back, the regular rate of duty and taxes will be levied on the entire value. This exemption may apply any number of times in a year.

If you are returning after **7 days or more** in the United States (not counting the day of departure from Canada), you may claim an exemption on goods valued up to $750 (Canadian). Goods, other than alcohol and tobacco products, are not required to accompany you; a written declaration may be required.

Permitted within the $200 and $750 exemptions are up to 50 cigars, 200 cigarettes, 200 tobacco sticks and 7 ounces (200 gm) of tobacco and up to 40 ounces (1.14 L) of liquor *or* 1.6 quarts (1.5 L) of wine *or* 9 quarts (8.5 L) of beer and/or ale (or its equivalent of 24 twelve-ounce bottles or cans). You must meet the minimum age requirement of the province entered to claim alcohol or tobacco products. Northwest Territories and Nunavut do not allow you to bring in more than the duty-free allowance of alcohol.

There is nothing to prevent you from importing any quantity of goods, even if you do not qualify for any kind of personal exemption, provided the goods you are importing are not restricted and you pay the full rate of duty and taxes

Special Tariff: When you exceed your $200 or $750 exemptions, a special rate of 7 percent combined duty and taxes is levied on the next $300 value in goods (except tobacco and alcohol) in excess of maximum exemptible amounts, provided the goods are of U.S. origin. Regular duties apply on any amount over that. For detailed information concerning specific duty rates, consult Canadian Customs before leaving on your trip.

All exemptions are individual and may not be combined with those of another person. You may be asked to verify the length of your visit; dated receipts normally constitute proof.

GIFTS to the value of $60 (Canadian) may be sent from abroad, free of duty or taxes. These may not include alcoholic beverages, tobacco products or advertising matter. Gifts valued at over $60 (Canadian) are subject to duty and taxes on the amount in excess of $60. Gifts sent from abroad do not count against your personal exemption, but gifts brought back must be included as part of your exemption.

SAVE *Attraction Admission Discount Index*

RECREATION-WINTER ACTIVITIES

RESTORED VILLAGES & SETTLEMENTS

ROCKS

RUINS

SCENIC DRIVES

SCHOOL BUILDINGS

SCHOOLS

SCHOOLS-ACADEMIES

SCHOOLS-COLLEGES & UNIVERSITIES

VISITOR CENTERS — VISITOR INFORMATION

VISITOR INFORMATION

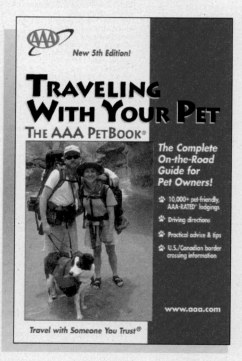

Bed & Breakfast Lodgings Index

Some bed and breakfasts listed below might have historical significance. Those properties are also referenced in the Historical index. The indication that continental [CP] or full breakfast [BP] is included in the room rate reflects whether a property is a Bed-and-Breakfast facility.

Historical Lodgings & Restaurants Index

Some of the following historical lodgings can also be considered as bed-and-breakfast operations. The indication that continental [CP] or full breakfast [BP] is included in the room rate reflects whether a property is a Bed-and-Breakfast facility.

MICHIGAN

ACCOMMODATIONS

RESTAURANTS

WISCONSIN

ACCOMMODATIONS

RESTAURANTS

Resorts Index

Many establishments are located in resort areas; however, the following places have extensive on-premises recreational facilities:

MICHIGAN

ACCOMMODATIONS

WISCONSIN

ACCOMMODATIONS

67

Comprehensive City Index

Here is an alphabetical list of all cities appearing in this TourBook® guide. Cities are presented by state/province. Page numbers under the POI column indicate where points of interest text begins. Page numbers under the L&R column indicate where lodging and restaurant listings begin.

Comprehensive City Index (cont'd)

Drive
See
Stay
Play

DO IT ALL WITH AAA!

Vacation planning, travel and destination information, AAA's famous maps and TripTiks®, TourBook® guides, air, cruise, tour, rail, and hotel reservations, attraction tickets and more! It's all part of the service for AAA members!
Choose whatever method fits you best — online, in person,
or by phone — to enjoy helpful services like these:

- Online TourBook® guide featuring hotel information AAA Diamond ratings.
- Internet TripTik®/Traveler itinerary planner rated No. 1 by the *Wall Street Journal.*
- Travel accessories such as luggage, travel guides, car games for the kids, and more.

- Ready-to-go, 2- to 5-day AAA Drive Trips vacation* for major U.S. and Canadian travel destinations.
- Flights, cruises and tours and expert advice from AAA Travel professionals.
- AAA Travel money options including no fee Travelers Cheques.
- AAA Credit Cards featuring a 5% gas rebate.

With AAA's expert travel information and pricing power behind you, you'll enjoy better quality and value than you'll find anywhere else. And, with AAA's extensive range of products and services, you'll enjoy complete, hassle-free vacation planning from a single source you know and trust.

Before your next vacation, visit www.aaa.com or your nearest AAA office.
Discover the many ways AAA can help you drive more, see more,
stay more and play more!

TRAVEL WITH SOMEONE YOU TRUST®
www.aaa.com
*PRODUCTS AND SERVICES AVAILABLE THROUGH PARTICIPATING AAA AND CAA CLUBS.

LOOK FOR THE RED

*N*ext time you pore over a AAA TourBook® guide in search of a lodging establishment, take note of the vibrant red AAA logo, SAVE icon, and Diamond rating just under a select group of property names! These Official Appointment properties place a high value on the business they receive from dedicated AAA travelers and offer members great room rates*.

* See TourBook Navigator section, page 14, for complete details.

We'll help you get your beauty sleep.

(Not that you don't look great just the way you are.)

Ahhh, the rejuvenating powers of a good night's sleep. Quiet rooms. Comfortable beds. Unstuffy atmosphere. Not to mention room service, a swimming pool, fitness center, restaurant, lounge, and in-room amenities that include everything from a dataport to a hair dryer.* And with us, Kids Eat & Stay Free.** So both you and your wallet can rest easy.

RELAX, it's
Holiday
Inn

For reservations call 1-800-734-4275, your AAA professional or visit *holiday-inn.com/aaa.*